THE NEW ATLANTIC ORDER

This magisterial new history elucidates a momentous transformation process that changed the world: the struggle to create, for the first time, a modern Atlantic order in the long twentieth century (1860–2020). Placing it in a broader historical and global context, Patrick O. Cohrs reinterprets the Paris Peace Conference of 1919 as the original attempt to supersede the Eurocentric "world order" of the age of imperialism and found a more legitimate peace system – a system that could not yet be global but had to be essentially transatlantic. Yet he also sheds new light on why, despite remarkable learning processes, it proved impossible to forge a durable Atlantic peace after the First World War, which became the long twentieth century's cathartic catastrophe. In a wider perspective, this ground-breaking study shows what decisive impact this epochal struggle has had not only for modern conceptions of peace, collective security and an integrative, rule-based international order but also for formative ideas of self-determination, liberal-democratic government and the West.

PATRICK O. COHRS is Professor of International History at the University of Florence. He was Associate Professor of History at Yale University, a Fellow at Harvard University, and Alistair Horne Fellow at St Antony's College, Oxford. He is the author of the acclaimed *The Unfinished Peace after World War I* (Cambridge, 2006).

THE NEW ATLANTIC ORDER

The Transformation of International Politics
1860–1933

PATRICK O. COHRS

CAMBRIDGE
UNIVERSITY PRESS

CAMBRIDGE
UNIVERSITY PRESS

University Printing House, Cambridge CB2 8BS, United Kingdom

One Liberty Plaza, 20th Floor, New York, NY 10006, USA

477 Williamstown Road, Port Melbourne, VIC 3207, Australia

314–321, 3rd Floor, Plot 3, Splendor Forum, Jasola District Centre, New Delhi – 110025, India

103 Penang Road, #05-06/07, Visioncrest Commercial, Singapore 238467

Cambridge University Press is part of the University of Cambridge.

It furthers the University's mission by disseminating knowledge in the pursuit of education, learning, and research at the highest international levels of excellence.

www.cambridge.org
Information on this title: www.cambridge.org/9781107117976
DOI: 10.1017/9781316338988

First published 2022

Printed in the United Kingdom by TJ Books Limited, Padstow Cornwall

A catalogue record for this publication is available from the British Library.

Library of Congress Cataloging-in-Publication Data
Names: Cohrs, Patrick O., author.
Title: The new Atlantic order : the transformation of international politics, 1860-1933 / Patrick O. Cohrs, Università degli Studi, Florence.
Other titles: Transformation of international politics, 1860-1933
Description: Cambridge, United Kingdom ; New York : Cambridge University Press, 2022. | Includes bibliographical references and index.
Identifiers: LCCN 2021058063 (print) | LCCN 2021058064 (ebook) | ISBN 9781107117976 (hardback) | ISBN 9781107542204 (paperback) | ISBN 9781316338988 (epub)
Subjects: LCSH: Europe–Politics and government–1918-1945. | World politics–1919-1932. | World War, 1914-1918–Peace. | Treaty of Versailles (1919 June 28) | Europe, Western–Defenses. | Security, International. | BISAC: HISTORY / United States / 20th Century
Classification: LCC D727 .C575 2022 (print) | LCC D727 (ebook) | DDC 940.5/1–dc23/eng/ 20211130
LC record available at https://lccn.loc.gov/2021058063
LC ebook record available at https://lccn.loc.gov/2021058064

ISBN 978-1-107-11797-6 Hardback

For

Erica

My Mother and My Father
in Memoriam

Paul W. Schroeder
in Memoriam

and My Uncle and Friend Heini Witte-Löffler

CONTENTS

ACKNOWLEDGEMENTS

This book was conceived and written on both sides of the Atlantic, chiefly in Berlin, Oxford, New Haven and Florence. It has taken me a long time to complete it. And I thus have all the more reason to acknowledge first of all, and with immense gratitude, the support and goodwill of my friends – particularly Peter Lagerquist, Florian Rommel, Levin von Trott, Verena Rossbacher, Ken Weisbrode, Oula Silvennoinen, Katharina Montag, Sarah Bulli, Gerd Gauglitz and Andrzej Waśkiewicz – during all the years when I was pushing a rather massive boulder up a rather steep hill.

I especially want to take this opportunity to thank Mauro Campus not only for his most magnanimous friendship and brilliant companionship in exploring the heights and depths of international history but also for the key role he played in clearing the path that eventually led me to Florence. I also thank him, Novella and Livia for making me feel so warmly welcome in Santo Spirito. And I wish to express how grateful I am to Michael Jonas not only for being such a generous friend and endlessly inspiring fellow scholar but also for joining forces with Bernd Wegner and giving me the deeply appreciated opportunity to advance my work – and return to my *Vaterstadt* Hamburg – as visiting professor at Helmut-Schmidt-University in 2017–18. I also thank him, Julia, Paul, Oskar, Sofia und Max for their warm-hearted hospitality in Eimsbüttel. I am grateful to the formidable painter Klaus Hahn for his part in providing an ideal environment for finishing this book. And Susana I thank, with fondest love, for making possible a radiant new dawn.

When I think about the scholars whose work I have found most inspiring in the course of my long voyage towards *The New Atlantic Order* it would be hard to overstate how much I have benefited from the friendship and long-standing dialogue with Paul W. Schroeder, whose pioneering scholarship has indeed transformed the historical study of modern international politics. I shall always remain profoundly indebted to him. On the same grounds I am indebted to Jürgen Osterhammel, whose truly global outlook and ground-breaking insights into the transformation of the world in the long nineteenth century have in many ways incited me to think anew about how the Atlantic and global order were remade in what I call the long twentieth century.

I also once again thank Charles Maier for his unflagging support and ever stimulating exchanges over many years. His path-breaking work on the modern state, the ascendance of modern forms of empire and the *Pax Americana* have been most valuable and thought-provoking throughout. And I especially thank Paul Kennedy not only for having been the friendliest and wisest colleague I have had at and beyond Yale but also for his benign comments on my manuscript, particularly when it was threatened by imperial overstretch. I have gained much from his sense of perspective and mastery – always rising, never falling – of the changing field of international history. I would also like to take this opportunity to express, after many years, how grateful I am to my two favourite teachers – Karl Söffker, who encouraged me to think harder about the problems and iniquities that arose in the age of global imperialism; and Klaus Rommel, who gave me free rein to deepen my love for the English language.

For their benevolent interest, comments and criticism over the years I thank John Darwin, Peter Ghosh, Andrew Hurrell, Rosemary Foot, Samuel Wells, Sherrill Wells, Akira Iriye, John Ikenberry, Zachary Wasserman, Kiran Patel, Bernd Wegner, Jörn Leonhard, Jenifer Van Vleck, Ryan Irwin, Fredrik Logevall, Volker Berghahn, Bruno Cabanes, Mark Lawrence, Talbot Imlay, Kathleen Burk, Francesca Trivellato, Dani Botsman, Alan Mikhail, Adam Tooze, Jost Dülffer, Andrew Preston, Lorena De Vita, Steffen Rimner, Beatrice de Graaf, Haakon Ikonomou, Piotr Kulas and particularly, *in memoriam*, Zara Steiner and Ernest May.

I thank Alistair Horne and St Antony's College for giving me the opportunity to come back to Oxford and lay the groundwork for this book as Alistair Horne Fellow in 2006–07. I am grateful to Ian Shapiro and Yale's McMillan Center for International and Area Studies as well as to Jim Levinsohn and the Jackson Institute for Global Affairs, and to Paul Kennedy and International Security Studies at Yale for providing funding for much of the essential research that yielded this book. I thank the sponsors of the Asakawa Fellowship for enabling me to broaden my horizon and spend a memorable summer of research and exploration at Waseda University in Tokyo in 2016. And I thank the Institute for

Advanced Study at the Central European University for offering me a very congenial and stimulating research and writing environment in 2016–17 – during what sadly proved to be the CEU's final year as lighthouse of liberal scholarship and education in Budapest. Last but not least, I thank Emily Plater for her excellent editorial support, Denise Bannerman for her impeccably precise copy-editing, Felix Altmann for his most valuable help with the index and particularly Stephanie Taylor and Niranjana Harikrishnan for overseeing the production process with so much skill and constructive spirit. And I especially wish to underscore how immensely grateful I am to my editor Michael Watson for his steadfast support and remarkable patience from the moment I first approached him with the idea of writing about the transformation of the Atlantic order to the final stages of the publication process of this rather long book.

Grateful acknowledgement is also made to the following archives for permission to use and quote material from their holdings: Bodleian Library, Oxford; King's College Library, Cambridge; British Library, London; University of Birmingham Library; Library of Congress, Washington, DC; Houghton Research Library and Baker Library, Harvard University, Cambridge, Massachusetts; Sterling Library, Yale University, New Haven, Connecticut; Firestone Library, Princeton University, Princeton, New Jersey; Hoover Presidential Library, West Branch, Iowa; Butler Library, Columbia University, New York; and Pierpont Morgan Library, New York. And I gratefully acknowledge that Philip's, a division of Octopus Publishing Group, has granted permission to use a map of the world, ca.1990, from the *Philip's Atlas of World History* (2007), and that Oxford University Press has granted permission to use maps of Europe in 1914 and 1919 from Zara Steiner's opus *The Lights That Failed* (2005).

My sister Dörthe and my brother-in-law Caleb I thank, with love, for all the warmth and light they have been giving me and for cheering me on particularly when times were unexpectedly tough. I wish I had words to convey – once again – how grateful I am to Gabi and especially to my uncle and friend Heini Witte-Löffler for their invaluable support and generosity, which did not even cease when they concluded that I was mad to devote so much time to writing a book. And I thank Gretchen, with love, for her kindness and magnanimity.

To Erica I will always owe more than I could ever acknowledge here. Ever since I first embarked on this book project, and for many years during which I became all too preoccupied with it, she has been the most magnanimous, patient and encouraging spouse, companion and friend any scholar could wish to have. I thank her with all my heart, and deepest love.

ABBREVIATIONS

AA	*Auswärtiges Amt, Berlin*
ADAP	*Akten zur deutschen auswärtigen Politik*
AN	Archives Nationales, Paris
AR	*Akten der Reichskanzlei*
BDFA	British Documents on Foreign Affairs, eds K. Bourne, D.C. Watt, 2/1: *The Paris Peace Conference of 1919*
BN	Bibliothèque Nationale Paris
BOLDH	*Bulletin officiel de la ligue des droits de l'homme*
CAB	Cabinet Office Papers, British National Archive, London
CAEAN	*Commission des affaires étrangères de l'Assemblée nationale*
CAES	*Commission des affaires étrangères du Sénat*
CID	Committee of Imperial Defence
DBFP	*Documents on British Foreign Policy*
DDF	*Documents diplomatiques français*
DDS	*Documents Diplomatiques Suisses*
Final Covenant	Final Covenant of the League of Nations, 1919, Avalon Project, Yale University
FO	British Foreign Office
FO 371	Foreign Office Political Files, British National Archive, London
FRBNY	Federal Reserve Bank of New York
Friede von Brest-Litovsk	*Der Friede von Brest-Litovsk*, ed. W. Hahlweg (Düsseldorf, 1971)
FRUS	*Papers Relating to the Foreign Relations of the United States*
GP	*Die Große Politik der europäischen Kabinette 1871–1914*, eds. J. Lepsius et al., 40 vols (Berlin 1922–27)
Hansard	Hansard, Parliamentary Debates: House of Commons
HC	House of Commons
House, *Intimate Papers*	*The Intimate Papers of Colonel House*, ed. C. Seymour, 4 vols (Boston, 1926–28)
IMCC	Inter-Allied Military Commission of Control
JOC	*Journal Officiel, Chambre des Députés*
JOS	*Journal Officiel, Sénat*

MAE	Archives du Ministère des Affaires Étrangères, Paris
MF	Archives du Ministère des Finances, Archives Nationales, Paris
NA Maryland	US National Archives, Maryland
NA RG 59	Record Group 59 (Department of State, General Files), US National Archives, Maryland
NA London	British National Archive, London
PA	Politisches Archiv des Auswärtigen Amts, Berlin
Pariser Völkerbundsakte	*Die Pariser Völkerbundsakte vom 14. 2. 1919 und die Gegenvorschläge der deutschen Regierung zur Errichtung eines Völkerbundes* (Berlin, 1919)
PWW	*The Papers of Woodrow* Wilson, ed. A.S. Link, 69 vols (Princeton, NJ, 1966 ff.)
Quellen	*Quellen zur Geschichte des Parlamentarismus und der politischen Parteien* (Düsseldorf, 1959 ff.)
SB	*Stenographische Berichte über die Verhandlungen des Reichstags*
SB Nationalversammlung	*Stenographische Berichte über die Verhandlungen der Verfassunggebenden Deutschen Nationalversammlung (1919)*
Smuts Papers	*Selections from the Smuts Papers*, eds. W. Hancock, J.van der Poel, 7 vols (Cambridge, 1966–73)
UF	*Ursachen und Folgen* (Berlin, 1959 ff.)

MAPS

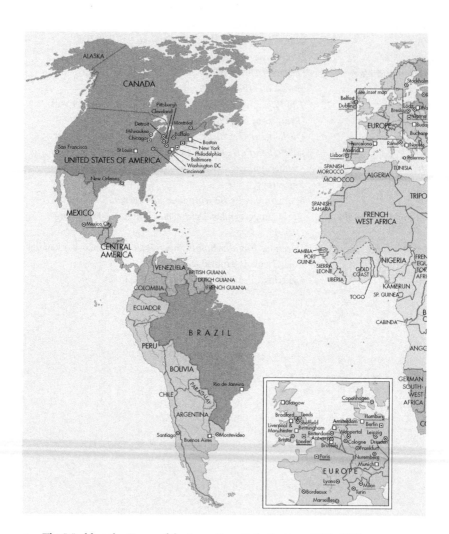

1. The World at the Dawn of the Long Twentieth Century, 1860–1900

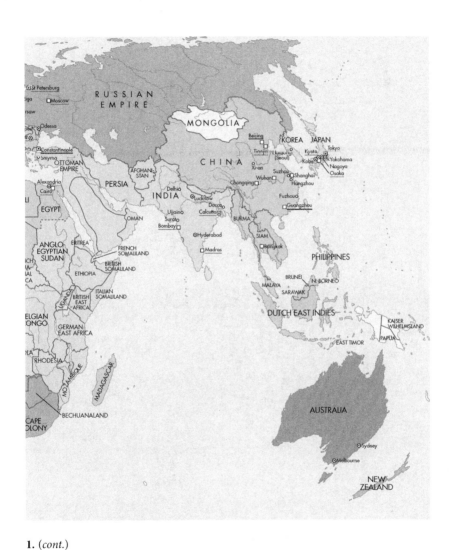

1. (*cont.*)

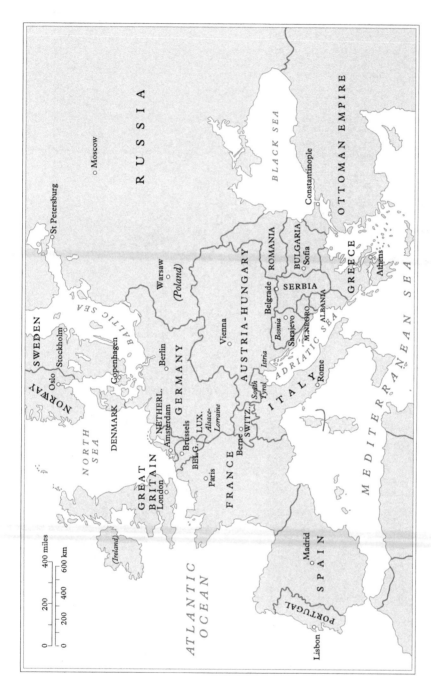

2. Europe in 1914

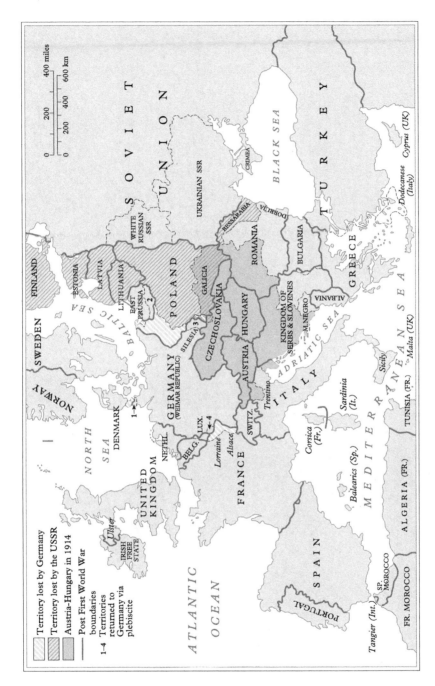

Legend:

- Territory lost by Germany
- Territory lost by the USSR
- Austria-Hungary in 1914
- Post First World War boundaries
- 1-4 Territories returned to Germany via plebiscite

0   200   400 miles
0 200 400 600 km

NORWAY

SWEDEN

FINLAND

ESTONIA

LATVIA

LITHUANIA

EAST PRUSSIA

S O V I E T   U N I O N

WHITE RUSSIAN SSR

UKRAINIAN SSR

CRIMEA

BLACK SEA

POLAND

SILESIA 3

GALICIA

CZECHOSLOVAKIA

AUSTRIA HUNGARY

ROMANIA

BESSARABIA

DOBRUJA

BULGARIA

KINGDOM OF SERBS & SLOVENES

M.NEGRO

ALBANIA

GREECE

TURKEY

Cyprus (UK)

Dodecanese (Italy)

Malta (UK)

Sicily

ITALY

Trentino

ADRIATIC SEA

SWITZ.

Sardinia (It.)

Corsica (Fr.)

Balearics (Sp.)

M E D I T E R R A N E A N   S E A

TUNISIA (FR.)

ALGERIA (FR.)

SPAIN

PORTUGAL

SP. MOROCCO

FR. MOROCCO

Tangier (Int.)

FRANCE

Alsace

Lorraine

LUX.

BELG.

NETH.

GERMANY (WEIMAR REPUBLIC)

1–2

4

DENMARK

BALTIC SEA

NORTH SEA

UNITED KINGDOM

Ulster

IRISH FREE STATE

ATLANTIC OCEAN

3. Europe in 1919

INTRODUCTION

This book seeks to shed new light on a fundamental question – the question of why no durable international order could be created after the First World War – for Europe and for the wider world. And it argues that this requires reappraising a no less fundamental question: why it proved so extremely difficult, and ultimately impossible, to lay the groundwork for a *legitimate* peace in the aftermath of a war that became the formative catastrophe of the "long" twentieth century, which began around 1860 and has reached its end around 2020. As the following analysis aims to show, to provide new and hopefully more illuminating answers to these questions it is crucial to explore as comprehensively as possible how the protagonists of post–First World War peacemaking dealt with the most profound and indeed pivotal challenge that arose during the war and became acute in its aftermath – and which has not been fully understood. It was the challenge to supersede the still Eurocentric world "order" of the age of imperialism – or rather: the war-prone "disorder" to which it had degenerated by 1914 – and to lay foundations for something unprecedented: a new international system that could no longer be European-dominated, and could not yet be global, but had to be essentially *transatlantic*. In short, the core theme of this book is that at the heart of the search for a new global order after the First World War, which reached a first highpoint but did not end in 1919, lay the first and in crucial respects unsuccessful attempt to found a new Atlantic order. Yet what ensued had far-reaching global implications. In many ways, it indeed turned into a struggle over the terms and rules of an Atlantic *world order* for the long twentieth century.

Unquestionably, the Great War propelled momentous changes in the modern international order. But it is critical to understand that it began to transform the relations between Europe and the United States. It not only led to the demise of Europe's Eastern Empires and the collapse of the European state-system of the pre-war era but also altered the international role of the United States dramatically. The American republic, which had already become a world power before 1914, emerged not just as the newly predominant economic and creditor power but also as a pivotal political power, whose intervention ultimately decided the outcome of the war. While it had not yet risen to the position of a clearly pre-eminent hegemon, it was called upon to play a decisive part in setting the terms and rules of the postwar international system. It was a part for which its leading politicians and the wider electorate were insufficiently prepared, and for which the doctrines and traditions that had informed America's pre-war relations with Europe and the rest of the world offered very little guidance. Crucially, the American president Wilson himself had to learn to fulfil this novel role and, essentially, to act as a "first among equals" – or more precisely as *one* of the principal decision-makers – in the process of founding a new order.

The war thus created a novel transatlantic configuration. It led to an unprecedented, though as yet unregulated interconnectedness and, essentially, an asymmetrical interdependence between the United States and Europe. In short, as will be shown, the postwar consolidation of Europe depended in cardinal respects on American cooperation, engagement and systemic leadership in political, financial and economic affairs; but the security and future development of the United States were distinctly less dependent at this stage on what occurred in Europe, though by no means unaffected by it.

Nonetheless, what the Great War made imperative were efforts to forge a new system of international politics that allowed American and European protagonists to come to grips with this new interdependence and to address not only the most pressing but also the more profound and structural problems that it had left in its wake – above all, as will be shown, the problem of how to integrate Germany into the postwar order. It had to be a system that provided a new, more effective security architecture as well as mechanisms and rules that fostered a peaceful settlement of international disputes – disputes that would inevitably arise, particularly in conjunction with the German problem and with the daunting challenge of reorganising Eastern Europe and reconciling, as far as possible, conflicting claims invoking the newly prominent principle of national "self-determination". Here, the question arose how far a novel international organisation, the League of Nations, could furnish such an architecture, and such mechanisms and rules. Yet new transatlantic approaches also had to be found to deal with the immense financial and economic consequences of the war – consequences that would be further complicated by the escalating reparations dispute that came to overshadow the peace conference and its aftermath, and that could not be mastered without the cooperation or at least acquiescence of the newly dominant American power.

As my study seeks to underscore, it was thus no longer possible to re-establish after 1918, in one form or another, the world order, or "disorder", of the pre-war era. Yet, as Wilson would have to acknowledge, nor had the time come for an aspirational American president to propose and compel others, particularly the leaders of the principal European victors Britain and France, to accept a novel kind of "American peace". Crucially, however, neither Europe nor the wider world could be stabilised through a peace settlement imposed by the victors on the basis of more traditional concepts of a "right of the victor" and one-sidedly dominated by their aims and interests. Rather, under the conditions the Great War had created, and after not only but especially Wilson had raised expectations of a peace based on *general* premises of "international justice" and "fair dealing", foundations for a durable and legitimate postwar order could only be laid through what was especially difficult to initiate at this juncture: something approaching as far as possible an accommodating and integrative peace process.[1] Essential was a process in which, at the core, not only the victors but also the vanquished could negotiate on behalf of their claims, interests and *different ideas of what was "just"*, and that thus opened up the possibility of yielding agreements that were, broadly speaking, mutually acceptable.

What had to be negotiated were not only complex compromises about concrete territorial, security, economic and financial issues but also, at a deeper level, agreements about the principles, ground-rules and political foundations of the new order. For without such a process and such essentially *reciprocal* agreements, no modern peace and no modern international order can be consolidated in the longer run. And without them no legitimate Atlantic peace system could be established after 1918.

Departing from older notions of a "peace by the right of the victor" and paving the way for a wider, balanced accommodation of aims, needs and interests was not merely a question of honouring abstract principles of "reciprocal justice". It was a cardinal precondition for stabilising Europe – and for avoiding erosive double standards and legitimacy deficits in the making of the new order. In the specific constellation the Great War created, only those who led the victorious powers could initiate such a process. It would be newly important to give due weight to the claims and interests of those who represented smaller states and of those who fought for the aspirations of national movements in Eastern Europe. Eventually, the question arose whether the western powers should also negotiate a *modus vivendi* with the Bolshevik leaders. Above all, however, it was critical to initiate a "legitimate" peace process between the western powers and Germany.[2]

---

[1] Wilson message to Congress, 2 December 1918, *PWW*, LIII, p. 276, 277–9.

[2] As will be seen, the Great War and its aftermath also marked a formative stage in a much wider *global* struggle, particularly between the interests and claims of the remaining imperial powers and anti-imperial nationalists in the "colonised world" who, partly seizing on Lenin's and Wilson's proclamations, demanded recognition of their "self-determination" claims. But here the prevailing power structures and the vested interests and adapted strategies of those who sought not only to maintain but even to expand the British and French imperial systems – and those who insisted on maintaining informal US imperial prerogatives – impeded any substantive, let alone transformative changes at this juncture. See Manela (2007); Pedersen (2015).

Yet in a period that was marked by nationalisms that had been radicalised during the war as well as by turbulent democratisation processes, the main American and European decision-makers had to meet one further critical requirement: they had to learn to forge agreements, and rules, that each could legitimise in the specific and often conflict-ridden domestic force-fields in which they operated – and this meant: for which they could gain the requisite parliamentary and ultimately electoral support. This was immensely difficult after a war whose – increasingly and then predominantly *transatlantic* – political and ideological battles had left behind profound divisions, especially but not only between the coalitions that had fought against each other. And it became even more challenging at a juncture of international history that witnessed the emergence of a newly dynamic transnational constellation: a constellation in which the disputes over the thorniest issues of peacemaking not only raged in a plethora of national contexts but also across national and continental boundaries and indeed under the scrutiny and pressure of an unprecedentedly interconnected "global public" or public sphere; and in which an unprecedentedly wide spectrum of opinion-makers and pressure-groups, from more or less enlightened internationalist activists to virulent nationalists, clamoured to influence the peace negotiations as well as "world opinion".[3]

Moreover, the catastrophe of the Great War, the ideological conflict it sparked and, notably, the wartime rhetoric of Wilson and other political leaders had also given rise to enormous expectations of what the peace was to generate in terms of security, compensations for the war's sacrifices and, where this applied, the fulfilment of – or respect for – claims to national "self-determination". Yet more often than not these expanded expectations of peace tended to clash; and more often than not they also exceeded the realm of the possible and were thus bound to produce dangerous disappointments – not only among the vanquished but also among the victors, and not only in Europe but also on a global scale. By examining and reappraising all of these dimensions, my analysis seeks to clarify why it proved impossible in 1919 to embark on a peacemaking process that fulfilled essential criteria of legitimacy – and why it thus was not possible, either, to lay foundations for an integrative and durable Atlantic order.

I.   The Overarching Theme

*Peacemaking after the First World War and the Transformation
of the Transatlantic Order in the Long Twentieth Century*

Pursuing a wider, overarching theme this book thus seeks to open up new perspectives on a longer-term and indeed seminal transformation process that

---

[3] See most recently Huber and Osterhammel (2020).

still has to be elucidated: the transformation of the transatlantic political, economic and cultural-intellectual order in what will be called here the long twentieth century. It dawned in the 1860s and seems to approach its dusk roughly 100 years after the Paris Peace Conference – in crucial respects it became an Atlantic century. My study posits that the peacemaking efforts of 1919 marked an important, though ambivalent, stage *but not a real turning-point* in this process. At the core, it was a process through which the prevalent international system was fundamentally recast, not just in terms of the distribution of power and influence but also, and more profoundly, with a view to the prevalent rules, norms, principles and practices of international politics. In short, a qualitatively different, modern international system eventually supplanted the still essentially Eurocentric, and war-prone "order" that had taken shape in the first decades of the long twentieth century – when, from *circa* 1860, the modern states began to emerge that would eventually face each other in the Great War and when developments set in that would culminate in the global competition of the era of high imperialism – and that ultimately would make the catastrophe of 1914 not inevitable, but extremely difficult to avoid.[4]

The new system that came to replace this "order" could only be consolidated after a Second World War, and under the conditions of the Cold War. Yet it developed – in the second half of the long twentieth century – into a remarkably durable and legitimate Atlantic order whose basic foundations had been laid by the mid-1950s and in which the United States came to assume a pivotal hegemonic role. This process went hand in hand with the transformation of the world economic system where the United States came to replace Britain as the pre-eminent power. In this sense, the First World War was not, as George F. Kennan famously put it, the *original* "great seminal catastrophe" of the twentieth century.[5] Nor was its higher meaning that it became the initial cataclysm of a "short" twentieth century that then, as Hobsbawm argued through the prism of the Cold War, came to be dominated by the antagonism between globalising US or western liberal capitalism and Soviet-led global communism.[6] Rather, it should be reinter-

---

[4] For different interpretations and approaches to periodisation, which generally situate the beginning of the Atlantic or American Century later, in the 1890s, see Nolan (2012); Ellwood (2012), pp. 22 ff.; Winkler (2019), pp. 121 ff., 173 ff. For a more expansive interpretation see Weisbrode (2015), pp. 1–3. My conception of the long twentieth century is thus also intended to point beyond, and challenge, Eric Hobsbawm's in many respects still very compelling interpretation of a "long nineteenth century" that began with the eighteenth century's "dual revolution"– the "more political French" and the "(British) industrial" revolution – and ended with the First World War. See Hobsbawm (1962), esp. p. 2; Hobsbawm (1975); Hobsbawm (1987); Bayly (2004) and Osterhammel (2009).

[5] Kennan (1979), pp. 3–4.

[6] Hobsbawm (1994), pp. 1–17, 21 ff.

preted, and understood, as the crucible of the long twentieth century, both in an Atlantic and in a global perspective.

The ultimately frustrated bid to build an Atlantic peace system in the aftermath of the Great War thus has to be illuminated in a wider context – not the context of what has been called the twentieth century's "Thirty Years' War", where allegedly one catastrophic war inevitably led to an even more total Second World War, but rather the context of a "fifty-year" process of successive bids to remake the international order. It has to be interpreted as the initial and formative stage of a process that was never linear but in many ways dialectical, a process in which over time, in response to successive and profound systemic crises – two world wars and one world economic crisis – a new and ultimately more sustainable international system was created. And it has to be understood as a process in which those who forged this system effectively built on, yet also drew lessons from what had been tried in 1919 – and ultimately went beyond the limits of the Paris Peace Conference.

What would eventually be superseded but could not yet be fundamentally transformed after 1918 was the inherently unstable international system that had evolved in the decades before 1914. It was a system that – despite transnational efforts of socialists and liberal "internationalists" to promote fundamental reforms – was dominated by two modes of international politics that were not only intricately intertwined but also decidedly conflict-prone: a European mode of highly competitive balance-of-power politics; and a global mode of ever less restrained imperialist rivalry. At the same time, it was a system that had been transformed by the dynamics of a hierarchical – economic, political, and cultural – globalisation process that the imperialist rivalries between expanding power states had spawned. What escalated across the globe was an essentially limitless competition in which not only the principal European powers but also Japan and the United States participated, the latter as a distinctive imperialist power in East Asia and the Pacific and as the self-proclaimed policing power of the western hemisphere. Their competitive behaviour was premised on the dominant assumption that in an all-embracing struggle, which often came to be interpreted in social Darwinist terms, not only a great power's standing and prosperity but its very survival depended on succeeding as a world power and on pursuing world politics.

What came to prevail in Europe – markedly influenced by this global competition – was the pursuit of high-stakes, "zero-sum" balance-of-power politics, which spurred the emergence of increasingly rigid alliances and alignments that in the end came to divide Europe's more or less highly industrialised and militarised great powers into two antagonistic coalitions. By the time Britain and France concluded the *Entente Cordiale*, in 1904, these changes had largely corroded the European peace system of the earlier nineteenth century, the Vienna system of 1815, in which the rules and practices of the European concert had long maintained a legitimate equilibrium between the great powers, protected the integrity of smaller states like Belgium, and indeed fostered global stability.[7] The nineteenth century's European order thus turned into a system in which in the end no rules, norms, understandings and mechanisms existed any longer that could have prevented the escalation of a regional – Balkan – crisis into an all-out war between the great powers in 1914.

What finally supplanted the unsustainable "old order" that broke down in 1914 and the ill-founded, then reformed but ultimately failing order that emerged after 1918 was an international system that took shape after 1945 and differed from all previous systems of order in modern history. It indeed furnished new ways and mechanisms to cope with the challenges of twentieth-century international relations and the short- and long-term consequences of the era of the two world wars. At the core, it was a distinctive transatlantic system of international politics that was built around a nucleus formed by the United States and the states of western Europe, including (western) Germany, yet eventually extended towards Eastern Europe. It was a reconfigured transcontinental system of sovereign states in which the United States would play decisive part, coming to act not as a novel, more or less benevolent empire but rather as an overall benign hegemon. This system came to be based on an unprecedented – and overall remarkably legitimate and durable – architecture of international agreements, mechanisms and transnational networks, notably the European Recovery Program, the North Atlantic Alliance and the more wide-ranging cooperative links and relations that emerged through and around them. And it was a system that came to be based on distinctive norms, rules and practices, above all those of transatlantic collective security and European supranational integration.

Yet the Euro-Atlantic processes that gave rise to this system also had a formative significance beyond the transatlantic sphere – indeed a universal significance. For they provided a key impetus to the emergence of norms and rules that have remained integral to what one may call the modern world order to this day, however imperfectly they have often been observed, and however forcefully they have been challenged, particularly since the beginning of the twenty-first century: norms and rules designed to protect the sovereignty and integrity of (nation-)states under international law, for the peaceful settlement of international disputes and, crucially, of collective security. What emerged concurrently were new ground-rules for an eventually overall liberal world economic system and a rule-based architecture of international finance that came to be based on the institutions of the Bretton Woods system. The latter provided an essential framework for a remarkable, though far from universal, period of postwar recovery and revitalisation before facing demise

---

[7] See Schroeder (1994), pp. vii–xiii; Schroeder (2004), pp. 158–91.

in the 1970s and massive reform needs ever since, which have become more acute than ever in the era of "total globalisation".

At the same time, transatlantic processes had a crucial influence on the conceptualisation and actual "construction" of both regional and global international institutions and mechanisms, from the League of Nations to the United Nations, from the aforementioned European Recovery Program and the institutional underpinnings of European integration to, eventually, the Conference on Security and Cooperation in Europe. And they likewise propelled remarkable advances in the codification not only of international rights and obligations of states but also of international guarantees for human rights – first, collective rights such as the rights of minorities, then – after 1945 – explicitly *individual* human rights. This way they, finally, played a crucial role in creating a systemic framework and unprecedented development prospects for the evolution of what may be called a transatlantic international society in an increasingly interdependent north Atlantic world, which again had a wider, global significance – and manifold global repercussions. Ultimately, the reconfiguration of the transatlantic order thus also had a formative impact on how the *global* order was reconfigured in the long twentieth century.

The following study seeks to highlight that pursuits of peace and order in the aftermath of the Great War gave some essential impulses to but could only mark a beginning, and in many ways an ambivalent and fraught beginning, of this longer and indeed epochal transformation process. In some ways these pursuits, and the ideas that informed them, prefigured those that gave rise to what became the *Pax Atlantica*, rather than *Pax Americana*, of the era after the Second World War – indeed they did so to a much greater extent than has been acknowledged. Yet it will also have to be elucidated why in other, crucial respects they were so strikingly different, and more limited.

II. The Interpretative Context

A Century of Controversies – and a New Consensus?

The quality and consequences of the efforts to make peace and establish a new order after the Great War became the subject of immense controversy even before the Paris Peace Conference came to a close. And they have remained at the centre of scholarly and public debates to this day – roughly 100 years later. In different ways, and against different historical backgrounds, these debates have all revolved around the question of what kind of peace, and what kind of order, could be established in the aftermath of the epochal cataclysm that ended the long and European-dominated nineteenth century. Yet directly or indirectly, they have also always revolved around the underlying question of what kind of peace, and what kind of order, *should* have been founded. And, ultimately, they have centred on the question why the original peace system that emerged in 1919, the treaty system of Versailles, proved so distinctly more unstable and short-lived than the last major peace settlement that preceded it, that forged at the Congress of Vienna in 1814–15, or – in a different, global constellation – the order that emerged after 1945, and under the conditions of the Cold War. This analysis seeks to challenge some of the most influential interpretations that have dominated this long-standing debate and, in different ways, influenced our understanding of what was and what could be achieved in the aftermath of the Great War.

For a long time, scholarly as well as more popular studies of attempts to remake world order after the First World War have mainly concentrated on the Paris Peace Conference and the Treaty of Versailles. And they have been particularly interested in assessing whether the settlement of 1919 was either too harsh or too lenient; whether the so-called Versailles system was bound to collapse within a generation; and how far it even prepared the ground for the Second World War.[8] But more recently there has also been a growing interest in examining the global implications of the post-1918 reordering processes.[9] And there have been efforts to capture their significance for the longer-term history of twentieth-century international relations.[10] The debates

---

[8] On the peace of Versailles see Boemeke, Feldman and Glaser (1998); Sharp (I/2008); Macmillan (2002); Steiner (2005), pp. 15–70; and the important recent contributions of Leonhard (2018); de Sédouy (2017); Conze (I/2018); Smith (2018); Payk (2018) and Schwabe (2019). Of course, there have also been numerous different appraisals of American and European contributions to post–First World War peacemaking. But the prospects of establishing a transatlantic international order in 1919 have never been systematically examined. To cite but a few notable examples: for studies of Wilson and American diplomacy see Knock (1992); Walworth (1986); Ambrosius (1991); Kennedy (2009); Manela (2007); on different European perspectives see the contributions to Boemeke, Feldman and Glaser (1998); Macmillan (2002); on British perspectives see Fry (2011); Goldstein (1991); Egerton (1978); on French perspectives see Stevenson (1982) and the important study by Jackson (2013); the most thorough study of Wilson's impact on Germany in this period remains Schwabe (1985), the most substantive analysis of German policies remains Krüger (1985).

[9] See esp. Steiner (2005); Cohrs (2006); Boyce (2009); Mulligan (2014); and the in many ways thought-provoking contribution of Tooze (2014) and, most recently, Leonhard (2018). See also Graebner and Bennet (2011). For studies of the long-term legacy of Versailles see Kennedy and Hitchcock (2000); Sharp (2010); Graebner and Bennett (2011); for general syntheses, and "realist" interpretations, see Marks (2002); Keylor (2011).

[10] For studies of the long-term relevance and legacy of Versailles see Kennedy and Hitchcock (2000); Sharp (2010); Graebner and Bennett (2011) and Conze (I/2018), pp. 491 ff. For a recent study re-examining the significance of Wilson and the Paris peace for the rise of "liberal internationalism" see Ikenberry (2020), esp. pp, 1–25, 100–40.

and interpretative perspectives are still evolving. But most recent studies have overall presented a more favourable assessment of the post–First World War peace settlements, particularly the Treaty of Versailles. Essentially, they have concluded that despite their deficiencies and contradictions they represented the best outcome that could be attained under very unfavourable conditions. And they have – rightly – underscored that the peace of Versailles did not inevitably lead to another world war.[11]

Interpretations of the processes and outcomes of 1919 have had a long history of their own. There were early – partisan – endeavours to defend the treaty and peace of Versailles as both just and either appropriately severe or comparatively lenient.[12] But there were even earlier and highly influential critiques that have had a long-term impact not only on scholarly but also on more general perceptions of Versailles in and beyond the twentieth century. In many ways most consequential was the harsh denunciation of what he termed a "Carthaginian peace" that the economist John Maynard Keynes, who had resigned from the British peace delegation in protest, presented in his famous and unsettling tract on *The Economic Consequences of the Peace*. Keynes, who pursued a distinct transatlantic perspective, argued that Wilson had failed to withstand the power-political machinations of the principal European leaders, and the victorious powers had consequently imposed on Germany a settlement that was dictated by erroneous preoccupations such as "frontiers and nationalities", the "balance of power" and Germany's "future enfeeblement". In his view, they had thus utterly failed to make peace on solid, rational premises –premises that would buttress Europe's postwar reconstruction and took into account the essential realities of international – and at the core transatlantic – interdependence, particularly in the financial and economic spheres. Above all, Keynes criticised that the Versailles Treaty's economic terms and reparations clauses placed excessive burdens on Germany and thus threatened to erode the "central support" of Europe's economic and political system. He warned that the peace of 1919 would thus precipitate economic turmoil on and beyond the European continent and ultimately provoke another "war of vengeance".[13]

---

[11] See notably Boemeke, Feldman and Glaser (1998); Macmillan (2002); and the more recent and nuanced appraisals in Steiner (2005), pp. 67–70, Sharp (2010), pp. 211–19; Leonhard (2018), pp. 1254–80; Schwabe (2019), pp. 8–9; For different interpretations see Conze (I/2018) and Cohrs (2006), pp. 20–67.

[12] An important and substantial defence is Tardieu (1921). For Lloyd George's "truth" about the peace treaties see Lloyd George (1938).

[13] Keynes (1919), pp. 9–10, 35 ff. See Skidelsky (1983), pp. 384–8; Markwell (2006). Keynes' appraisal was eventually followed by a number of studies that have emphasised the centrality of the underlying financial and economic interests and forces that influenced the remaking of world order after 1914. See above all Trachtenberg (1980), Soutou (1989), and Krüger (1973); Leonhard (2014), pp. 784–96, and Tooze (2014), pp. 8–16, 288–304.

Keynes' critique was not only eagerly seized upon by contemporary German commentators keen to prove that the treaty and its justification, the stipulation of German war guilt in Article 231, had forced an unjust and draconian peace on Germany. It also prompted a wave of revisionist appraisals and prepared the ground for growing official and public unease with the results of Versailles in Britain and in the United States.[14]

During and after the Second World War the controversies over the peace of Versailles entered a new stage and a new dimension. At their core was hence the question of whether a clear causal link could be established between the outcomes of 1919 and the rise of fascism and, above all, National Socialist "totalitarianism" in the 1930s – and thus, ultimately, between Versailles and the outbreak of a second and even more total and horrendous global war. Long after the end of that war Kennan noted – with some impact on wider public perceptions – that the in his view misguided and unduly punitive peace of Versailles thwarted the necessary process of postwar accommodation and reconciliation with Germany and thus sowed the seeds of the catastrophe of the Second World War. Less severe critics have contended that the peace of 1919 had merely constituted a "truce" in the twentieth century's "Thirty Years' War".[15]

In the academic debate, however, different interpretations came to prevail. Arguably most influential since 1945 in the sphere of more traditional diplomatic history have been "realist" assessments of Versailles and, in a wider context, the requirements of stabilising and pacifying post–First World War Europe. Essentially, "realist" scholars have asserted that the main problem was that no stable and secure balance-of-power system could be established after 1918 that effectively contained the threat posed by German revisionism. And in seeking to explain why this was so they commonly, though not always, have highlighted the illusory nature and destabilising impact of Wilson's "internationalist" aspirations and the assumptions that informed them. Central to "realist" critiques has been the argument that mainly because of Wilson's ideological pursuit of abstract liberal principles and an inevitably ineffective organisation, the League of Nations, the victors of the Great War failed to meet the underlying requirement of postwar security in Europe, namely to impose, and *enforce*, a robust victors' peace – and a new system that placed effective checks on German power and inevitable German revisionism.[16] Most recently, this argument has been reformulated in an

---

[14] See Fry (1998), pp. 587 ff.; Boemeke, Feldman and Glaser (1998), pp. 6–10.

[15] Kennan (1996), p. 21. See also Kissinger (1994), pp. 218–65. For useful overviews, see Bell (III/2007), pp. 15–54; Sharp (2010), pp. 1–5.

[16] Drawing on the ground-breaking analyses of E.H. Carr, Hans Morgenthau put forward the original and probably most influential "realist" critique of Versailles after 1945. See Morgenthau (1952), pp. 4–27; Carr (1937); Carr (1939). For recent "realist" interpretations, see Macmillan (2002); Keylor (2011), pp. 73–9 and Marks (2013). For more

interpretation that re-accentuates the thesis of the "failure" and "fiasco" of Wilsonianism and suggests that the American president's misguided aspirations played a decisive part in thwarting the formation of a "transatlantic democratic alliance" of the victors that French policymakers desired – an alliance sufficiently strong "both to accommodate and control a unified Germany" that remained on the other side of a new "frontier of freedom".[17]

There has also been what could be called a liberal – or internationalist – critique of post–First World War peacemaking. It had considerable impact early on when voiced by liberal and progressive commentators who grew disillusioned with the "realities" of the peace conference. But it became rather marginalised in subsequent debates, particularly after 1945. This critique has centred on the claim that Wilson compromised what he had proclaimed and the leaders of the most powerful states, and empires, after the war failed to make more far-reaching advances towards – or even prevented – what would have been imperative: a peace of conciliation combined with a more radical transformation of the international order. In the liberal-progressive assessment, they thus missed the seminal opportunity to create a more authoritative League of Nations that established binding inter- and transnational rules of conflict resolution, enshrined and promoted genuinely universal "self-determination", and significantly curbed power politics as well as national, and imperial, sovereignty.[18]

New Transnational and Internationalist Perspectives

These concerns and interpretative perspectives have been given new prominence by recent studies that broadly speaking pursue transnational approaches to international history.[19] Of particular interest here are works that have situated the Great War and postwar pacification efforts in a wider context and examined their significance for the evolution of an "international society" in modern global history – or, more precisely, its transformation from an originally hierarchical European, and then Eurocentric international society of states in long nineteenth century towards a new kind of universal international

nuanced analyses of the German problem at Versailles, see Steiner (2005), p. 67–70; and Sharp (I/2008), pp. 109–38, 199–207.

[17] See Tooze (2014), pp. 16, 276, 271–7.

[18] For a typical and influential example of the liberal-progressive critique in the United States, see the editorial "Peace at Any Price", New Republic, 19 (24 May 1919), pp. 100–2. For the background, see Thompson (1987); Fry (1998).

[19] For a useful overview of transnational approaches to international history, see Iriye (2013); Saunier (2013); "AHR Conversation: On Transnational History", American Historical Review 111, no. 5 (December 2006), pp. 1441–64.

society, or in Akira Iriye's words a "global community", in the twentieth century.[20]

Further, while many studies have shown how the First World War led to a radicalisation of nationalism in and beyond Europe, there has been a growing interest in the war's catalytic effect on the rise of novel forms of liberal and socialist or even revolutionary internationalism (as well as other kinds, for example feminist internationalism) not only in Europe and the United States but on a global scale. In the context of this study internationalism will be defined as a view of the world characterised by the recognition, or indeed consciousness, that there are interests, problems and concerns that transcend national, or imperial, boundaries and that the most effective way of safeguarding these wider, shared interests and to address these problems – notably problems of war and peace as well as economic development – is to engage in transnational cooperation.[21] While very different ideas and ideological conceptions evolved about the premises and nature of such cooperation, what they have in common is the notion that it is inherently valuable and beneficial. Such outlooks have a long history that can be traced back to antiquity. But they gained a new quality as the transformative processes of the long twentieth century gave rise to an unprecedented degree not only of globalisation but also of international and ever more global *interdependence*. Especially significant for this analysis is the emergence of ideas and conceptions that propelled aspirations to create institutions and mechanisms beyond the level of the nation-state (or empire) in order to establish and foster *common rules*, above all rules for the resolution of international conflicts and the preservation of peace yet also to advance and regulate economic development.

Numerous studies have highlighted the growing influence of liberal and socialist internationalist conceptions particularly on American and British debates about international order before, during and after the Great War – and their eventual competition with more radical ideas and ideologies that came to culminate in the Bolsheviks' revolutionary internationalism. And they have not only highlighted the consequential confrontation between Lenin's vision and Wilson's alleged "liberal internationalism". They have also accentuated and at times exaggerated the relevance of non-governmental actors – individual activists as well as associations and pressure-groups – that sought to

---

[20] Ground-breaking here have been the works of Hedley Bull and Akira Iriye. See Bull (I/ 1984), pp. 119–25; Bull (II/1984), pp. 217–18; Bull (1995); Iriye (2002), esp. pp. 9–10; Clavin and Sluga (2016). But it should also be noted that many recent transnational studies have obscured the relevance of the Great War for long-term developments between 1870 and 1945. See Rosenberg (2012).

[21] This definition builds on Iriye (2002), pp. 9–11, and Clavin and Sluga (2016), pp. 3 ff. See also Jackson (2013), pp. 2–3; Sluga (2013). The transformation of transnational relations and nationalism in the nineteenth century is illuminated in Osterhammel (2009).

promote different internationalist responses to the war on both sides of the Atlantic, and that not only operated in national contexts but also began to create transnational networks to this end. These notably included pacifists and socialists yet also liberal activists who sought to strengthen international law and, above all, promote arbitration. As has rightly been stressed, these forces essentially drew on internationalist conceptions they had already begun to develop, and to champion, before the war, which holds true both for those who were active in Socialist International and for the liberals who played a key role in preparing the ground for the path-breaking Hague Conventions of 1899 and 1907.[22]

Overall, works highlighting transnational and internationalist aspects have tended to paint an ambivalent picture of the fulcrum period of the First World War. The creation of the League of Nations has been interpreted as the most important and conspicuous manifestation of a new community of nations after a war that had raised the awareness of global interdependence and the need for new forms of organised collaboration in its aftermath.[23] But they have also highlighted how limited the advances towards a truly "internationalist" League were, and how internationalists' hopes that the new institution would be endowed with effective supranational authority and usher in a new era of international law would be massively disappointed by the actual peacemaking process of 1919. This study takes into account such interpretations and approaches, and it will engage with them in many ways. But it also seeks to contribute to bridging a growing and detrimental divide that has opened up between transnational history and the history of international politics. As will be shown, it is essential to analyse the new *interplay* between the policies and pursuits of the leading decision-makers and representatives of states, and the national as well as transnational pursuits of those non-governmental actors whose aim was to transform more traditional diplomacy and world politics.

A New Consensus?

Incorporating transnational perspectives, the most notable among the most recent works on peacemaking after the First World War have also emphasised the global repercussions of what unfolded at and after the Paris Peace Conference. And they have – rightly – underscored not only how daunting the task was that the peacemakers confronted but also how limited their freedom of action became after a war that had not only proved unimaginably destructive but also created daunting domestic pressures and, in particular,

---

[22] See notably Knock (1992); Egerton (1978); and the important new study of Jackson (2013); Sluga (2013); Guieu (2008); Mulligan (2014).
[23] See Iriye (2002), pp. 20–21.

massive expectations.[24] In the light of this, one weighty new synthesis speaks of the "overstrained peace between 1919 and 1923".[25] Another goes so far as to argue that the peacemakers were simply "overwhelmed" and what they negotiated could only disappoint most of the hopes that had been raised, not only those of the vanquished and various claimants of self-determination but also those of the victors, making Paris ultimately a "place of illusions" that were then shattered.[26] Yet what seems to remain the dominant view is that under the adverse conditions the Great War left behind the notable settlement of Versailles represented, for all its weaknesses, an "enormous achievement" and precisely the kind of compromise that was achievable in the summer of 1919.[27] A similar verdict is reached by a recent work that interprets the peacemaking efforts of 1919 as the "venture" of forging a "democratic peace". It argues that Wilson's ideals of a "democratic peace of accommodation and justice" proved irreconcilable with the "power interests" of all the states that had participated in the war. Yet it too emphasises that the inevitable compromise peace of Paris had the potential to gain credibility – and was by no means bound to fail.[28]

While broadening its scope, and adding important nuances, these studies thus essentially confirm what had earlier been posited as the "new consensus", namely that the Versailles settlement furnished the best possible underpinnings for peace and order that could be established in the constellation of 1919.[29] This interpretation had earlier been re-accentuated in what remains the most authoritative study that examines the Paris Peace Conference as part of a longer history of attempts to re-create a more pacific *European* international system between 1918 and 1933, Zara Steiner's *The Lights That Failed*. Its main argument is that while the victor's peace of 1919 was in some respects a "flawed treaty", particularly insofar as it could not "solve the problem of both punishing and conciliating" Germany, it was also a remarkable accomplishment. Indeed, particularly Steiner's work has sought to show that, far from setting the stage for another world war, what the victors decided actually opened up prospects for creating a legitimate postwar order and, particularly through the League of Nations, a "more just international regime". In her assessment, its consolidation thus required some revisions but no fundamental qualitative changes.[30]

[24] This is a core theme of Leonhard (2018). See also Conze (I/2018), pp. 9 ff.
[25] Leonhard (2018), pp. 1260–1.
[26] Conze (I/2018), pp. 32, 9–38, 491 ff.
[27] Leonhard (2018), pp. 1049, 1265; Sharp (2010), pp. 211–19.
[28] Schwabe (2019), pp. 8–9.
[29] See Boemeke, Feldman and Glaser (1998), p. 3; Macmillan (2002); Sharp (2010), pp. 211–19.
[30] See Steiner (2005), pp. 15 ff., 68–70. See also Steiner (2001).

III.   Core Themes

*The Underlying Challenges of Peacemaking in 1919 – and the Need
for a New Atlantic Concert*

This book offers a different interpretation. Its core argument is that it is
more important to understand why it was ultimately not possible in 1919 to
make more substantive advances towards founding a peace order that could
be sustained and gain legitimacy over time. It is more important to explain
why the peace of Versailles became an unstable victors' peace that not only
remained essentially incomplete but even aggravated international instability after the Great War. And it is vital to recognise that what accounted for
the essential *limits* and *deficiencies* of the most complex peacemaking
process in modern history – and for the limits of what it yielded, the
"system of Versailles" – were, at the core, the dynamics, constraints and
ultimate failure of the first bid to establish a new Atlantic order of democratic states. As will be shown, for all the constraints they faced, this bid,
and the struggles it provoked, ultimately came to be decisively shaped by
the – conflicting – priorities and pursuits of the political leaders of the
principal victors, not only those of Wilson but also those of Lloyd George
and Clemenceau.

The following analysis is based on the premise that roughly a century after
the events that changed the course of the long twentieth century the time has
come to go beyond the entrenched frontlines of the interpretative battles that
have been waged over the peace of Versailles. To this end, one should begin by
emphasising that the very idea that a peace conference that was held in the
immediate aftermath of a catastrophe on the scale of the Great War could
somehow create a stable peace, let alone establish a stable international order
that needed no further changes, is misleading. Rather, what had to be
achieved, and what could be achieved in a best-case scenario, was to negotiate
basic peace terms that as far as possible considered and balanced the concerns,
interests and needs of *all* the relevant parties. Yet even more essential were
efforts to establish first underpinnings of a new international system and a
foundational framework of rules, norms, and mechanisms in which necessarily
more drawn-out and complex processes of conflict resolution and consolidation could be pursued – processes through which *over time* a more sustainable postwar order could be created. Even to begin making progress in this
direction was a daunting challenge after 1918.

The negotiations that commenced in January 1919 had manifold global
dimensions and ramifications, in the short term and in the longer term. They
marked a critical juncture at which not only but especially Wilson's rhetorical
championing of a new order *for the world* and a universal League of Nations
raised immense expectations *around the world* – expectations that his own
hierarchical pursuits could not fulfil and that, in a wider perspective, came to

collide with realities of power and configurations of influence that made transformative advances towards a new *global* order elusive. The aftermath of the Great War actually witnessed a reassertion of the prerogatives of "advanced" imperial powers, notably of Britain and France, which now justified their imperial systems in new ways and shaped the League's de facto neo-imperial mandate system. But it nonetheless marked an important stage in the longer and conflict-ridden process in which the legitimacy of imperialism and colonial rule in the extra-European world was corroded and, eventually, decolonisation struggles could be successful.[31]

The processes that began or gained decisive momentum in 1919 also had both direct and indirect repercussions for the reconfiguration of regional order, or the creation of new disorder, beyond Europe. This of course especially applied to the making of the modern Middle East. Here, Anglo-French strategic bargains established, under the guise of the League, the core of the system of mandate states that they in fact controlled and made part of their imperial spheres of influence. But the initial Treaty of Sèvres, dominated by British, French and Greek interests, created a new, and profoundly unstable, status quo in this region after the demise of the Ottoman Empire. The settlement imposed on Turkey would be challenged by Atatürk's nationalist revolution and resistance and, following his victory over Greek and Allied forces, significantly revised by the Lausanne agreements of 1923. The Paris Peace Conference also had major repercussions in East Asia, particularly because it frustrated the hopes of the leaders of the Chinese republic to gain recognition for their claims to "self-determination" and sovereignty – and instead brought the de facto expansion of the Japanese sphere of imperial influence. Here, only the Washington Conference of 1921–22 advanced more concerted attempts to establish a new, though as yet equally unstable status quo in the Far East and the Pacific, including the – still qualified – recognition of Chinese sovereignty.[32] But this study will argue that, essentially, peacemaking after the Great War was dominated by what can be interpreted as the remarkable yet also in key respects inadequate and ill-conceived efforts of the principal victors not just to reorder Europe but to establish a novel transatlantic peace system.

In view of the complexity of the problems and multitude of expectations they faced, the accomplishments of the pivotal peacemakers of 1919 were indeed impressive in many ways. It is not too far-fetched to say that the fact that they managed to forge a peace settlement at all represented a considerable achievement under the circumstances. And it can certainly be maintained that the outcomes of their labours did not inevitably lead to the World Economic

---

[31] See notably Pedersen (2015); Manela (2007). For a concise analysis see Sharp (I/2008), 169–75.

[32] See Macmillan (2002), pp. 306–44, 347–455; for the Middle East, see e.g. Fromkin (2001); for China and East Asia, see Manela (2007); Cohen (2000), pp. 303 ff.; Zachman (2018).

Crisis, the pathologies of the 1930s and the Second World War. Notably, for all the inconsistencies that characterised their efforts they managed to agree on the essentials of a new international organisation, the League, and to hammer out a new covenant of international law and procedures for the peaceful settlement of international conflicts. Though producing contestable results, they began to address innumerable territorial and national questions, having to deal with a constellation in which different claims for national self-determination clashed with one another as well as with conflicting strategic and geopolitical considerations. They began to tackle the daunting challenges of establishing a new security system for Europe – and the world – combining the League's collective security provisions and, originally, more specific Anglo-American guarantees to come to France's aid in case of a future German attack. And, though with less success, they began to grapple with the inextricably intertwined and politically charged issues of war debts, reparations and postwar reconstruction.

Ultimately, however, the crux was that the pursuits and politics of peacemaking that came to prevail in 1919 could not foster a more substantive, integrative and legitimate peace process, and that they did not "solve" but in fact exacerbated the main systemic problems that had to be addressed after the Great War. This is what has to be elucidated, which in turn requires, first of all, a clearer understanding of the underlying challenges. The key problem the protagonists of 1919 could not settle was undoubtedly the German question. Yet what was the German question? It is here interpreted not as the question of how postwar Germany could be most effectively contained but rather of how to accommodate and integrate the defeated power in the postwar order on terms *and through processes* that did not threaten the security and development prospects of its neighbours in the west and in the east but were actually conducive to a new international equilibrium.

This interpretation rests on three premises. The first premise is that, unlike the twentieth century's Second World War the Great War did not end either with the "total defeat" or the "unconditional surrender" of one side. This was essentially the result of the timing and modalities of the armistice that Wilson had mediated. The second premise is that following the armistice, the victors did not have the power – and none of the key decision-makers, including Clemenceau, actually deemed it possible or desirable – to turn back the clock of history, break up Bismarck's Empire, and create some kind of looser nineteenth-century-style German confederation. Whatever its final form and size, the German state was thus set to remain a central factor in the future of Europe, and so was the German power potential: demographic, industrial, financial and economic as well as political and strategic. How to come to terms with this problem became the critical task for those who led the victorious western powers. But they could not hope to meet it in ways that were conducive to Europe's overall stabilisation and pacification without finding ways to master the underlying systemic task they confronted after a war that had so fundamentally transformed the relations between Europe and the United States: namely to lay the basis for a functioning *transatlantic* international system – a new financial and economic architecture but above all a new system of international politics and security.

Yet what kind of system and what kind of "system-building" were required? Essentially, this study seeks to show that following the cataclysm of the Great War it was impossible to found a durable peace by following French maxims and somehow creating a new transatlantic balance-of-power system for the twentieth century of the victors that was then imposed on the vanquished and maintained by coercion: a system that would depend on a – de facto elusive – consensus among the victors to enforce not only power-political and economic containment of Germany but also, and crucially, its longer-term exclusion or ostracisation from the postwar order.[33] In fact, attempting to establish and enforce such a system was bound to have a profoundly destabilising effect and aggravate political and economic insecurity, above all by providing grist to the mills of those in Germany who argued that the outcome of the war, and a peace imposed by the victors, would have to be revised by all available means and, if necessary, by force.

But the conditions and the specific constellation of power and influence the war had left behind did not permit a more far-reaching or even a radical transformation of the international system either. There was to be no new international order along liberal-progressive lines, reinforced by transnational processes of democratisation and constructed around a powerful new international institution, the League, that introduced and maintained universal standards of international law and placed peace-enforcing constraints on state and imperial sovereignty. Only very limited and uneven advances in this direction could be made in the European and transatlantic context. And substantial progress towards such an order was even more elusive on a global scale at this historical juncture.

Instead, what the catastrophe of the First World War made imperative were serious endeavours to establish, for the first time, a different, more regionally specific and more effective international system, essentially a novel Atlantic concert of democratic states that could potentially serve as the nucleus of a new world order. The wider challenge was to create an effective system of "collective security" in which smaller states were accorded a new status of equality under a

---

[33] For French perspectives see Clemenceau speech, 29 December 1918, *Journal Officiel (Chambre)*, 1918, 3732–3; Tardieu memorandum, 20 January 1919, Tardieu MSS 49, MAE. Wilson emerged as the most powerful contemporary critic calling for concerted efforts to overcome balance-of-power politics. See notably his "Peace without Victory" address, 22 January 1917, *PWW*, XL, pp. 536–7. Yet there were also compelling arguments on behalf of a re-adjusted balance-of-power approach to peace. See notably Crowe's memorandum, 7 December 1918, FO 371/3451.

covenant of international law and new, more tangible guarantees for their sovereignty and integrity, but in which the more powerful states could also effectively meet pivotal responsibilities in settling conflicts and maintaining peace and international order. Yet the crucial challenge was to establish *the nucleus* of a twentieth-century concert system that was essentially *integrative*, i.e. set up to include not only the victors and satisfy their essential security concerns but also to foster – sooner rather than later – a stabilising *and restraining* integration of the vanquished, above all the fledgling German republic.

Critical, then, were advances towards a system that not only the victors but also the vanquished could deem legitimate and that would bind all the main powers to common rules and obligations. Particularly essential would be commitments to *mutual* security guarantees and to the peaceful settlement of international conflicts. But no less critical were advances towards a system that furthered rather than hindered the consolidation of Germany's as yet frail and challenged democratic order – and that strengthened the hand of those decision-makers in and beyond the new "Weimar Coalition" governments who were prepared to make commitments of this kind and sought a peaceful accommodation with the western powers.

First conceptual guidelines for a novel Atlantic concert, which was essentially conceived as a system *of* states and to regulate the relations *between* states, appeared most prominently in British peace designs.[34] Yet they can also be discerned in what Wilson came to envisage when he spoke of the need to create, through the League of Nations, a new "international concert which must thereafter hold the world at peace", though in his case the underlying impulse, and rhetorical impetus, remained universalist.[35] Particularly, leading British policymakers like Robert Cecil but de facto also the American president reckoned that the envisaged organisation could provide an essential framework, or platform, for a new, modernised concert system. But these conceptions clashed with the imperatives of French postwar planning, which came to centre on the idea of an exclusive Atlantic alliance – and of turning the League into a means to fortify such an alliance – whose main purpose would be to contain Germany for the foreseeable future. In the eyes of pivotal French actors like Clemenceau and his adviser André Tardieu, this was to create conditions of security that *later* might permit the accommodation of a reduced German state in a postwar order dominated by the western victors.[36]

---

[34] Robert Cecil had a decisive influence on British conceptual planning here. See the "Cecil Plan", 14 December 1918, in Miller (1928), II, pp. 61–4. See also Lloyd George statements, Imperial War Cabinet, 24 December 1918, CAB 23/42.

[35] Wilson address, 22 January 1917, *PWW*, XL, pp. 536–7. See also Wilson's statements, 8 December 1918, Grayson diary, 8 December 1918, *PWW*, LIII, p. 339.

[36] See notably Clemenceau speech, 29 December 1918, *Journal Officiel (Chambre)*, 1918, 3732–3; Tardieu (I/1921), pp. 202–32.

In order to elucidate why it became so critical to found a *novel*, essentially transatlantic concert after the Great War – and why at the same time it proved so hard – it is essential to widen the scope of inquiry. One not only has to reassess the momentous consequences of the war itself, especially for the relations between Europe and the United States, but also to pursue a *longue durée* approach and re-examine the onerous *longer-term* challenges the protagonists of 1919 had to grapple with, challenges that arose from the transformation of the European and global order in the first decades of the long twentieth century. What has to be illuminated are the highly consequential changes that occurred in this period – in the overall system, in the international, domestic and transnational conditions of international politics and, crucially, in the prevalent assumptions, mentalities and political culture that shaped it. What has to be re-appraised are the developments that eventually, in the age of unlimited imperialism, gave rise to ever more polarising power-political rivalries between the European imperialist powers and to an ever more unlimited global "struggle for the survival of the fittest world power" that also came to involve a rising and distinctive American imperialist power. And what has to be highlighted is that these transformative changes not only made an eventual Great War ever harder to avoid but also cast long shadows on the postwar world.

In a wider perspective, the Great War and its pre-history thus created a profound systemic need for the construction of a qualitatively different international system that provided new, more effective instruments to manage and regulate relations between states that, albeit in different ways and to different degrees, had overall expanded their authority and war-making capacities enormously before the war, and had then expanded them further, to unprecedented levels, during the war itself. Almost as critical, though not as crucial as Keynes and later observers have claimed, was the necessity to establish new underpinnings of an economic peace and, as it were, a financial peace after the Great War.[37] Put differently, the challenge was to lay the Atlantic groundwork for a new world economic system, and a new financial order, in order to cope with the war's immense repercussions in these spheres. This would be complicated by the massive war-debt problem that the costly conflict had left behind. And it formed the essential backdrop to what became one of the most intricate and frustrating problems on the peacemaking agenda, the reparations problem. As will be shown, all of these problems were de facto intricately interlinked and required essentially transatlantic "solutions"; it was impossible to work out sustainable agreements without the support of the world's newly pre-

---

[37] See Keynes (1919); Trachtenberg (1980); Tooze (2014), pp. 8–16. For an overview, see Glaser (1998).

eminent and in many ways indispensable financial and economic power – the United States.

The Wider Struggle over the Shape of a New Atlantic Order – and Its Consequences

If it meets its task at all, then, this study will make clear why it was not (yet) possible to lay the basis for a sounder Atlantic economic peace and, above all, a functioning Atlantic concert in the aftermath of the Great War – and why instead only a frail and incomplete peace regime of the victors could be established, which then became known as the "system of Versailles". To this end, it is necessary to broaden the scope of inquiry once more and to show that the negotiations and altercations of 1919 marked a first culmination, but not the end, of a much wider and indeed formative struggle whose significance has not been fully recognised – a struggle that escalated during the Great War and gained new momentum after the armistice of November 1918. What has to be re-appraised is the unprecedentedly fierce and far-reaching political and ideological "war within the war" that the cataclysm of 1914 generated and that turned into a contest not only about the higher purpose and stakes of the war itself but also about the shape of the future world order. As will be shown, this contest, which involved key decision-makers of the principal powers yet also an expanding array of other official and non-official actors, essentially became a *transatlantic* struggle. At the core, it became a political fight over the underpinnings and fundamental principles of a new Atlantic order that also had massive global consequences.

The momentous competition reached a first critical stage in the autumn of 1916 and early 1917 – when Wilson's initiative for a negotiated "peace without victory" collided with the war aims and strategies of all the European belligerents. It then widened into an ever more, all-encompassing struggle after the United States' intervention and the Bolshevik revolution had not only altered the course of the war but also recast the international, transnational and domestic constellations in which peace would eventually have to be negotiated. As my analysis seeks to show, this struggle was of fundamental significance for the wider history of international politics in and beyond the twentieth century and had far-reaching global implications. It proved crucial for recasting ideas and ideological precepts of what were to be the ground-rules and norms of modern international politics – in short, the *political* in international politics. And it generated *not novel or original* but newly comprehensive conceptions and visions of what constituted a legitimate peace and a "modern" inter-national order. Most consequential among these were more far-reaching ideas and conceptions of security, war-prevention and peace preservation that would crystallise in different schemes for a "League of Nations", "collective security" and a new "international concert" – as well as different, more far-reaching notions of a novel economic order that would foster not only postwar reconstruction but also bring financial and economic compensations for the immense sacrifices of the war.

Yet what also gained new prevalence were more aspirational notions of a peace, and order, that would be based on the premise that a durable "deeper" peace required fundamental political reforms within states and societies – essentially the expansion of democratic government in western states and the spread of democracy and "self-government" across Europe. *Eventually*, democratisation was also to unfold on a worldwide scale, but the global visions that western promoters of a democratic peace advanced at this stage remained distinctly hierarchical. Wilson's self-proclaimed mission to make the world "safe for democracy" had a decisive impact here.[38] And, importantly, aspirations to extend self-government and political participation came to overlap with newly influential, yet very disparate conceptions of – national – self-determination, which were not only championed by key figures like Lenin and, eventually, Wilson but also adopted and propagated by the vanguards of national movements in and beyond Europe. But it should not be overlooked that the transatlantic "war within the war" also spurred the emergence of fundamentally different, competing conceptions. They not only comprised, at one end of the spectrum, more radical socialist and notably Bolshevik visions of a new communist order of Soviet republics but also, at the other end of the spectrum, radicalised imperialist conceptions like those advanced by the proponents of a German "victorious peace" who envisaged imposing a Greater German imperial hegemony on Europe. And, on the side of the *Entente* Powers, they included French conceptions of a new, ideologically fortified balance-of-power system to ban the German threat.

The transatlantic struggle that gained momentum during the war was also pivotal for another development that would not only have critical implications for the peacemaking process of 1919 but also major long-term repercussions in the twentieth century. It contributed decisively to a newly virulent "ideologisation" and emphatic moralisation of international politics, which began with the battle between the western "ideas of 1776 and 1789" and the German "ideas of 1914" and then escalated further. This came to create ideological antagonisms in the transatlantic sphere that were far more intense, and divisions that were far deeper, than those that had existed before 1914. And eventually, in the spring of 1919, it gave rise to an – essentially unresolvable – moral and ideological conflict between the western victors and the defeated power Germany, not only over the question of who was responsible for the catastrophe of the Great War but also over the question of what would constitute a veritably "just peace" in its aftermath. This conflict would

---

[38] See Wilson address to Congress, 2 April 1917, *PWW*, XLI, p. 525.

decisively limit the political room for manoeuvre to negotiate a more balanced peace of accommodation between the victors and the vanquished. Finally, the escalating political-cum-ideological struggle was also highly consequential in another respect that would prove vital in this context. It played a critical part in raising such high, in some cases confluent but more often conflicting, expectations about the kind of peace that could and should be made after the catastrophic war. These escalated too, all the way to quasi-millennial expectations that somehow it would be possible to make a novel "peace to end all wars" after what had come ever closer to being a "total war". Eventually, such hopes would be especially encouraged by, and projected onto, the visionary American president. But to a greater or lesser extent they were destined to be frustrated, which in turn created enormous long-term problems.

Incipient Learning Processes, Hierarchical Reordering and Frail Foundations for a New Order. The Actors, the Novel Playing Field and the Crucial Outcomes of 1919

Those who sought to build a new order after 1918 thus had to operate not only under very challenging and unsettled conditions but also a playing-field of international politics that had been significantly altered by the war itself and, crucially, by the transatlantic struggle it had sparked. It was a playing-field marked by a not entirely new but unprecedentedly complex interplay of international, transnational and domestic forces and constraints that made it exceedingly difficult to settle the cardinal issues that had arisen. Even if they had wanted to do so, the peacemakers of 1919 could not act in the manner of their predecessors at the Congress of Vienna who had been essentially aloof from pressing domestic concerns and did not yet have to cope with powerful transnational pressures. Those who would leave their imprint on the peace represented (more or less) democratic states and, at the domestic level, had to grapple with the influence exerted by pressure-groups, political parties, and newly relevant mass media. They had to legitimise their decisions vis-à-vis mass electorates to which they were accountable, yet above all in their respective parliaments. And they faced prevalent expectations and tides of public and electoral opinion that were not conducive to compromise and moderation after four years of escalating wartime nationalism and propaganda on all sides.

Beyond this, the playing-field of peacemaking was characterised by an unparalleled multiplicity and diversity of actors who pursued competing agendas, interests and claims and who strove – on the ground or from afar – to influence the way in which peace was made. This multiplicity came to comprise not only those who represented the victorious great powers – and the vanquished – but also the representatives of smaller states like Belgium, and notably, the leaders of various national(ist) causes in Central and Eastern Europe yet also in other parts of the world who saw an unprecedented opportunity to gain recognition for their claims to self-determination – and sovereign nation-states. It also included a plethora of internationalist and pacifist activists and non-governmental pressure-groups that had long been relatively peripheral and hoped their time to exert their influence on behalf of a liberal-progressive peace had come. But it also of course comprised powerful national interest-groups that were decidedly anti-internationalist and pursued particular national imperatives such as maximal reparations. And, last but not least, it featured actors with a radical agenda of a different kind, Bolshevik leaders and other radical socialists who saw an historical opportunity to push for revolutionary changes across and beyond Europe.

Despite or rather because of this complexity, however, the parameters and outcomes of the Paris Peace Conference would essentially be determined by those who represented the principal victors of the Great War – and who therefore commanded, to a greater or smaller extent, the power and influence of the most powerful states. And in view of the new international and domestic legitimacy requirements that had to be met it was by no means accidental that the most consequential negotiations at Versailles would be pursued, not by diplomats or experts but by the elected leaders of the more or less democratic victorious powers. The "Big Three" would also make the key decisions in what became a distinctly hierarchical peacemaking process dominated by the victors – rather than a novel, more integrative transnational process, as Wilson had originally envisaged.

A central thesis of this book is that it would be misleading to speak of a fundamental clash between a more progressive and egalitarian Wilsonian "internationalism" on the one hand and, on the other, the more or less unreformed power-political strategies pursued by British and French leaders to safeguard vital national and imperial interests. Rather, what shaped the Versailles process and its outcome was the struggle to find some kind of middle ground between three distinctly hierarchical visions of and approaches to postwar order – which essentially were visions of and approaches to a new Atlantic order – that collided yet also converged.

Each of the principal peacemakers – and the advisers on whom they came to rely – had drawn different lessons from the Great War and its pre-history. Each operated on different basic assumptions. Each advocated different answers to the challenges he confronted. Wilson strove first and foremost for an implementation of his – long very vague, and evolving – vision of a fundamental yet evolutionary transformation of the international system: the creation of a hierarchical but essentially integrative new order of democratic states and, as its essential "superstructure", a League of Nations whose members committed themselves to newly constitutive principles of collective security, self-determination and the concerted settlement of international conflicts. Lloyd George and those who shaped British policies sought to promote a less ambitious evolutionary reform of the international system. They were intent on imposing a peace settlement that protected Britain and its imperial system against future German challenges by disarming the vanquished power and placing definite checks on its world-power aspirations. But their underlying aim was to forge a hegemonic partnership with the United States and to create a reconfigured Atlantic concert of great powers within the new institutional framework of the League. This was to become the key instrument for the management of postwar international relations, not least by integrating a chastised republican Germany.

By contrast, Clemenceau and those who shaped French policies had developed ambitious strategies to create a settlement, and order, that predominantly rested on what they regarded as by no means obsolete power-political or *realpolitical* premises. Yet they too pursued a new Atlantic orientation. Their clear priority was to protect France's longer-term security against what they regarded as the inherent threat of renewed German aggression – not only by curtailing German power but also, and crucially, by committing the United States – and Britain – to an unprecedented Atlantic security community of the victors whose core purpose was to contain the defeated power for the foreseeable future.

All of the key peacemakers of Versailles had begun to develop – and to reorientate – their approaches to peace and international order during the war. Crucially, however, they also had to embark on arduous learning processes when faced with the actual problems and intricacies of peacemaking and of establishing a new order in its aftermath. In different ways, they all had to find ways to come to terms with new problems and realities that they only began to comprehend – and to reach beyond often deeply internalised pre-war *and* wartime modes of thinking, viewing the world and approaching international politics that no longer were adequate in the face of the transformative changes the catastrophe of the Great War had wrought. Wilson not only had to learn to transcend his proclivity to respond to these changes by advancing grand but ultimately unduly simplifying and unrealistic ideological visions of a new Americanist world order. He also had to learn that he had neither the political power and financial leverage nor the requisite authority and prestige to impose this vision unilaterally and to compel his main European and Japanese counterparts in Paris to adopt his terms and rules. In fact, he had to learn how to negotiate complex strategic bargains and compromises – above all with the leading statesmen of the *Entente* Powers who had at least as strong a democratic mandate as he had. At this *caesura* of modern international politics, the United States had not yet acquired the decisive political and economic pre-eminence it would have gained by 1945. But even if Wilson had commanded such power he could not have founded a durable international order by acting as a unilateral "prophet" and arbiter of peace.

For their part, the British and French protagonists of peacemaking – and not only they – had to learn how to come to terms with the new "reality" of American power and influence – not only financial but also political – and their unprecedented degree of dependence on the United States. They had to cope with the fact that for the first time in modern international history they were no longer in a position to construct a new order for Europe "among Europeans", as their predecessors had done since 1648, and without the essential yet also very incalculable involvement of an outside power. And they had to find new ways not only of safeguarding what they considered the vital political, economic and security interests of the imperial powers they represented but also of justifying their peace aims, and agendas of imperialist expansion, particularly in view of the enormous though soon waning resonance that Wilson's aspirations had across Europe – and beyond. Above all, however, they had to learn how to forge mutually acceptable agreements about the terms and rules of postwar order with an American leader who had up until then pursued an irritatingly high-handed course and proposed schemes and remedies they considered impractical in crucial respects. And they had to come to terms with a fundamentally disconcerting question – the question of how far Wilson would not only be willing to make tangible long-term commitments to fostering Europe's security and stabilisation but also able to legitimise such unprecedented responsibilities domestically.

It should be recognised, however, that those who were charged with trying to negotiate an acceptable peace on behalf of the nascent Weimar Republic had to undergo even more daunting learning and reorientation processes. Under conditions of powerlessness and domestic turmoil following the November revolution of 1918, figures like the new foreign minister Ulrich von Brockdorff-Rantzau, Matthias Erzberger and the Social Democratic leaders Friedrich Ebert and Philipp Scheidemann had to find ways to initiate nothing less than a fundamental recasting of German foreign policy – in the shadow of defeat and the wider shadow cast by burdensome traditions of Bismarckian and Wilhelmine power politics. With relatively little to build on in terms of useful examples and precedents, they had to learn to develop approaches to peacemaking that amounted to more than a partly genuine yet also tactically motivated appeal to Wilsonian principles.

But the basic terms and rules of the peace negotiations and the eventual settlement were set by those who determined the policies of the victors. And what this study seeks to highlight is that because their approaches to peace and order remained in crucial respects irreconcilable, because of the different legitimation requirements they faced domestically, and because of the scale of the unprecedented challenges they confronted the principal victors could only forge very *tenuous* compromises on the most salient issues – how to safeguard postwar security, how to approach the intertwined problems of reparations and Europe's financial and economic reconstruction, how to meet the overwhelming challenge of reorganising Eastern Europe, and, above all, how to address the German question. More fundamentally, they could not really reach a more substantial agreement on what was to constitute the essential underpinnings and ground-rules of a new Atlantic order. And this came to preclude advances towards what would have been crucial yet also much harder – though not impossible – at this juncture: actual, substantive negotiations with the representatives of the defeated power that led to more broadly conceived compromise agreements.

That the victors found it so difficult to agree on the essentials of an Atlantic peace amongst themselves thus had a critical bearing on why in the end the peacemaking process turned into an – unresolvable – conflict of principle between them and those who sought to represent the interests of the defeated power, essentially a confrontation between different ideological visions of peace and competing moral claims. And it also contributed decisively to the fact that ultimately a more severe victor's peace would be forced on the vanquished and that this would be done in a more humiliating manner than notably Wilson and Lloyd George had earlier envisaged.

The confrontational strategy Brockdorff-Rantzau came to pursue to reinforce German claims for a "Wilsonian peace of justice" played a significant part in the final escalation process. But the decisive parameters for the final confrontation and its outcome were decreed by the key decision-makers of the western powers. And that no progress towards a qualitatively different and potentially more legitimate *peace of accommodation* could be made was also, on a deeper level, due to certain common and distinctly hierarchical rationales and assumptions they had developed about how the peace negotiations and the wider ordering process after the Great War were to proceed. In essence, it was due the fact that while they could not find common ground in many other respects they did come to agree on one central premise, namely that it was their essential prerogative, as leaders of the victorious *and* most civilised powers, to impose a "stern but just" victors' peace and to establish a refashioned international system in which Germany would not (yet) be included but rather put on probation.[39]

This had far-reaching consequences. The new Atlantic order that took shape in 1919 would not only be founded on decidedly weak foundations but also essentially as a *truncated* system of the victors that would not be regarded as legitimate by the vanquished – and that would also come to be viewed as profoundly deficient and unsound in Britain and the United States (not only by liberals, socialists and left-leaning progressives). In many ways, what unfolded in the spring and summer of 1919 marked only the complex and in many ways problematic *beginning* of a longer pacification and

[39] On the broader historical significance of this, see Meier (2010), pp. 36–44.

reordering process that would be required in the aftermath of the unprecedented catastrophe of the Great War. But it also created very adverse conditions
for such a process. Crucially, while it had been decided that the League would
be founded as an organisation of the victors no mechanism had (yet) been
established, and no rules and understandings had been developed for what was
most imperative: longer-term processes of negotiation and accommodation
between the victors and the vanquished that could transform the original
"Versailles system" into a more durable and legitimate Atlantic order, which
also included Germany.

The main task the victors thus confronted was to find ways not only to
consolidate *but to reform* the deficient system of Versailles *after* the Paris
Peace Conference. But any progress in this direction would require substantial
reorientations on all sides – and consistent commitments of the pivotal
powers. Ultimately, then, it is very important to understand that not only
the insufficient Atlantic "order" of 1919 but also the prospect of developing it
into a more durable and peace-enforcing international system would be dealt a
cardinal blow by Wilson's defeat in the "treaty fight" with the Republican
majority in the American Senate and the subsequent retreat of the United
States both from the Treaty of Versailles and the League of Nations. Yet it is as
important to understand that this did not mark the end but merely the
beginning of a new stage in the struggle to forge an Atlantic peace order for
the twentieth century.

IV.   The Architecture of the Book

The structure or "architecture" of this study is conceived to illuminate the
preconditions, dynamics and consequences of this seminal struggle. It comprises four parts and an epilogue that are intended to capture the essential
stages and driving forces, yet also the problems and limits of what remained a
momentous, but incomplete transformation process – and to place this process in the wider context of international history in the long twentieth century.

Part I

The first part examines the wider background and essential preconditions. It
re-appraises not just the immediate causes of the Great War but also the
longer-term transformative changes in the spheres of international, national
and imperialist politics in the formative decades of the long twentieth century
that led to the dissolution of the nineteenth century's Vienna system and in the
end made it so difficult to prevent the escalation of a catastrophe like that of
1914. Particular attention will be paid to the interplay of the intensifying
power-political rivalries between the European imperial states and globalising
imperialist competition. It will be evaluated how the international role of the

United States *began* to change, how the American republic became a peculiar imperialist power among other imperialist powers in an evolving Atlantic-global "order" of empires – and at the same time maintained an essential aloofness from wider international commitments. Yet it will also be examined how both nationally and transnationally operating "internationalists" of various stripes on both sides of the Atlantic sought – in vain – to counteract the prevalent and in their eyes war-prone tendencies of "high international politics" in this period; and it will be shown that they nonetheless advanced ideas and conceptions that would prove formative after 1914.

Part II

The second part begins with an analysis of the catalytic as well as transformative changes that the First World War itself brought about, focusing on the profound impact it had on the relations between Europe and the United States. It then seeks to offer a comprehensive analysis of the transatlantic competition over the terms of peace and the rules of the postwar order that gained momentum during the war, particularly between 1916 and 1918. Further, it explores why it was not possible to end the Great War earlier than in 1918 and why, in particular, it proved impossible to end it through what Wilson proclaimed in 1917: a negotiated "peace without victory". Finally, it re-appraises how the Great War actually came to an end and how an armistice was concluded that set crucial parameters and raised crucial conflicting expectations. And it re-evaluates not only the immediate problems but also the novel and complex systemic challenges that those who sought to make a "peace to end all wars" confronted at the end of 1918.

Part III

The third part focuses on a systematic analysis of how those who became the protagonists of post–First World War peacemaking, the political leaders of the United States, Britain and France and the most influential policymakers and experts who advised them, approached their tasks. It seeks to bring out that these actors built on ideas and conceptions they had developed during the war yet also reorientated their approaches to peace and postwar order significantly after the armistice. And it seeks to show that Wilson and the leading British and French politicians came to Paris with very different underlying aims yet also with what can be seen as distinctive conceptions for a new Atlantic order. At the same time, it will re-evaluate the cardinal international and domestic pressures and constraints they confronted and examine the – waning – influence that non-governmental actors could exert on the peace preparations at this decisive stage. Finally, it will also examine how and under what inauspicious conditions those who sought to negotiate on behalf of the vanquished, the fledgling Republic of Weimar, sought to attain a "Wilsonian peace of justice" and lead postwar Germany into a reconfigured Atlantic order of democratic states.

Part IV

The fourth part then focuses on and seeks to substantiate an "Atlantic interpretation" of the actual peacemaking process of 1919, analysing it as the first actual attempt not only to make a "modern" peace but also to create a new, essentially transatlantic international system. It will re-examine the anatomy and dynamics of this process – as well as the unprecedentedly complex international, transnational and domestic conditions under which it took place. And it will seek to cast fresh light on the question of why, ultimately, it remained contradictory and incomplete in crucial respects, why it came to have essential legitimacy deficits – and why it could not (yet) yield outcomes, and ground-rules, that were conducive to the consolidation of an Atlantic peace order that had the potential to endure.

Epilogue

The epilogue first offers a re-appraisal of the achievements of 1919 but also of the limits and problematic consequences of the first attempt to create an essentially Euro-Atlantic peace order. It then illuminates the far-reaching consequences of Wilson's failure to gain the indispensable backing of a majority in the US Senate for the complex compromises that constituted the peace of Versailles, and for the League of Nations. Yet it also seeks to highlight that the peace struggles of 1919 and the subsequent "treaty fight" by no means marked the end of the search for a more sustainable and legitimate transatlantic peace system after the First World War. It will sketch how this search was resumed on different premises in the mid-1920s and led to the formation of a different kind of transatlantic order, which would be founded on the settlements of London and Locarno (negotiated in 1924/1925), ushered in a period of remarkable Euro-Atlantic stabilisation – yet eventually disintegrated under the impact of the World Economic Crisis. It will conclude with some reflections on two broader questions: how far the ideas, processes and outcomes of the era after the First World War prefigured to a greater extent than has been acknowledged those that led to a more substantive transformation process after 1945: the construction of the *Pax Atlantica* after 1945; and how far what was attempted and eventually failed in the aftermath of the Great War could provide essential lessons – not just for the formative decades after the Second World War but also for the twenty-first century.

V. On My Approach

Towards an Integrative International History

To shed new light on the incipient transformation of the Atlantic international order at the dawn of the long twentieth century my study combines two approaches: a systematic, in crucial respects comparative approach; and – central to my analysis – a systemic approach. More precisely, it seeks to provide an essentially comparative re-appraisal of how and why the approaches of those official and non-governmental actors who had a formative influence on the international policies of the United States and the different key European powers indeed changed under the impact of the Great War – and of how the international, domestic and transnational force-fields on which they acted were transformed. Yet it places this re-appraisal in the framework of an overarching systemic analysis that aims to cast new light on the incipient transformation of the international system in the era of the First World War: from the war-prone "order" of the era of high imperialism towards a new, at the core, transatlantic international system.

By pursuing this combined approach, my study seeks to underscore that that recent tendencies to separate and in many cases establish a dichotomy between "diplomatic history" and "transnational history" have not been conducive to understanding and explaining core problems of modern international history.[40] It proposes that what could be more conducive to this end is the pursuit of what, for lack of a better term, might be called an integrative – and hopefully more comprehensive – international history.

In essence, fundamental changes and continuities in the history of international politics will be illuminated by analysing essential interconnections and interdependencies between four spheres of inquiry: (1) the – crucial – framework or superstructure of the international system; (2) the changing but still vital sphere of "high" international politics, which includes state and governmental policymaking, strategic decision-making processes and inter-governmental relations; (3) the more "transnationally exposed" but still distinctive sphere of domestic politics, or more precisely the sphere of intra-state or, where this applies, intra-imperial politics; and (4) – and finally – the widening scope of what can perhaps best be described as transnational politics or "politics beyond the state and government", which already had gained momentum before 1914 but acquired a new intensity during and after the war. As noted, this encompasses the widening range of activities of different non-governmental actors – of individual activists and opinion-makers as well as parties and pressure-groups that operated in different domestic contexts

---

[40] This tendency manifests itself e.g. in Rosenberg (2012), yet it can also be detected in many other recent contributions to modern transnational history.

yet also increasingly across national, and imperial, boundaries – and that in various ways not only sought to influence the policies of particular states and empires but also, in many cases, to transform the ways in which international relations were conceived and conducted.

The International System, Expanding State Capacities and the Transformation of International Politics

One crucial aim of this study is thus to re-appraise the changing configuration and character of the international system in the era of the Great War – and to re-assess why the prevalent European and world system that had evolved in the first half of the long twentieth century, and collapsed after 1916, had to be so fundamentally remade in the war's aftermath. At one level the evolving, then fundamentally reconfigured "order" of this period can be characterised as a distinctly hierarchical system of states, which was originally dominated by imperial states that operated within a dynamically changing geopolitical and "geo-economic" constellation. It was a constellation in which the distribution – rather than "balance" – of power and influence among the system's principal actors came to be dramatically recast as a consequence of the war. Yet my study posits that at a more fundamental level it is more illuminating – particularly in the context of twentieth-century international history – to work with broader conception of the international system, to define it as a *system of international politics*: as the constituent rules, norms, understandings and assumptions that govern a common and at the same time inherently competitive practice or pursuit – here: the practice of international politics.[41]

Seeking to advance a more comprehensive understanding of what international politics came to comprise, and how profoundly it changed, in the long twentieth century, this study will chiefly examine the policies that were devised and the politics that came to be practised to regulate or at least manage relations between states, which were and remained the pivotal actors. Yet it will also explore how far novel, or not so novel, transnational concepts and practices of, broadly speaking, "new diplomacy" began to change or even

---

[41] This builds on the conceptual categories that Paul W. Schroeder has advanced in his re-interpretation of the nineteenth century's international system. See Schroeder (1994), pp. vii–xiii See also Schroeder (2004), pp. 245–84. In my interpretation, an international system – like other systems – has to be understood as a distinctive *and complex* structure or set of relations with its own prevalent rules and inner workings. Influenced and even to a significant degree shaped, but never entirely controlled by human agency, it creates challenges, dynamics and constraints of its own – for those actors who have leading roles in it yet also for those who are weaker actors within it. It can be conducive to international stability, security, economic development prospects and peace. But it can also generate practices and conditions that heighten insecurity, provoke conflicts that are ever harder to contain and, ultimately, lead to the erosion of international order and to war.

supplant more traditional forms of diplomacy and inter-state politics in this fulcrum phase. And it will show that, in addition to obvious military and strategic considerations, financial and economic factors – from issues of inter-state indebtedness and the thorny question of postwar reparations all the way to the contest over who would set the rules of the world economy – came to play a newly vital role in the politics of war and of peacemaking. But it seeks to explain why these factors were ultimately *not* decisive.[42]

Above all, however, the following analysis is guided by the interest to ascertain how far, under the impact of the First World War and during the reordering process that followed it, the *fundamentals* of international politics came to be altered – how far not only underlying concepts, principles and norms but also the rules and processes of international politics were indeed transformed in a period of tremendous upheaval, complexity, ideologisation and crisis-ridden democratisation. No less, it is to be examined in precisely what ways the scope and "purview" of international politics was actually reconfigured, and essentially expanded – not only in terms of who participated and had a significant role in it but also in terms of what it was supposed or expected to achieve. All of this will be appraised with a focus on the changing relations between the United States and Europe, but also in a global perspective.[43]

Challenges of Learning and the Requirements of a Legitimate Order

My study seeks to confirm that in order to understand what spurred and what constrained or even impeded advances towards a more durable – Atlantic – peace

---

[42] In the age of globalising imperialist competition, financial and economic considerations, and power, undoubtedly came to acquire an even more pivotal significance in world politics than before; and they would be an even more critical factor during the Great War and for the eventual politics of peacemaking. Yet, as will be shown, they mattered less in 1919 than e.g. Keynes stipulated or later observers have claimed. See Keynes (1919) and notably Trachtenberg (1980), Soutou (1989) and Tooze (2014). The standard *longue durée* analysis of economic change and changes in the geopolitical order is and remains Kennedy (1988).

[43] To understand the nature of international politics – ancient and modern – and to grasp what constitutes *the political* in the history of international relations, and how far it came to be altered or remained fundamentally the same across the centuries, it remains vital to engage with the classics, above all Thucydides' *Peloponnesian War* (2009), Machiavelli's *Discourses* (1998) and *The Prince* (1998), Gentz's *Fragments from the Most Recent History of the Political Equilibrium in Europe* (1806); Weber's *Politics as Vocation* (1994), Schmitt's *Concept of the Political* (2007) and *Nomos of the Earth* (2006) and Morgenthau's *Politics among Nations* (1948) as well as the modern classics, especially Schroeder's *Transformation of European Politics* (1994), Meier's *Athens* (2000) and *The Greek Discovery of Politics* (1990), Ikenberry's *After Victory* (2001) and Osterhammel's *Transformation of the World* (2014).

order in the era of the Great War it is imperative to analyse changes in the prevalent ideas and assumptions: the ideas and assumptions that informed the approaches of leading American and European policy- and decision-makers to the practice and legitimation of modern international politics. Of critical significance, however, was the extent to which those who became the key actors had the capacity to embark on learning processes, both individually and collectively. Essentially, it has to be evaluated how far they learned not only to conceptualise but also to foster new and commonly acceptable principles and ground-rules of modern international politics that allowed them to meet unprecedented postwar challenges – and ultimately to create a more resilient and legitimate international system – after those that had prevailed before 1914 had proved unsustainable and indeed produced catastrophic consequences.[44]

Yet what were the essential requirements of a stable and a legitimate peace order in the aftermath of the First World War? It is actually not easy to define a clear set of criteria for what qualifies as a "durable" peace or a "legitimate" order – and, more profoundly, what is meant by "stability" and "legitimacy" in the sphere of international history. But it should nonetheless be attempted. It is vital to recognise, however, that while there are timeless, fundamentally unchanging elements it is also necessary to explore what can be characterised as conducive to stability and as legitimate at a particular stage of history – to gauge, for example, what distinguished core prerequisites in this respect at the time of the Vienna Congress from those prevailing in the era of the Paris Peace Conference. On these premises, this study posits that it was elusive to stabilise Europe or the world after the Great War by creating and enforcing a more effective and somehow more legitimate "balance-of-power" system on new ideological foundations, which uncompromisingly prioritised the power interests of one side – here: the victors – over those of others, notably but not only the vanquished. Rather, what the consolidation of a legitimate and thus more durable order after 1918 required was, ultimately, progress towards a concert of states and peoples that fostered a new, modern international equilibrium: an equilibrium not primarily of power but of rights, security, satisfied interests and development prospects, yet also of responsibilities and obligations within the international system.[45]

---

[44] On learning processes in international politics see also Cohrs (2006), pp. 13–14. For a theoretical approach see Jervis (2017), pp. 217–59. A comprehensive historical analysis, of course, also has to apply this approach to opinion-makers, pressure-groups and other non-governmental actors and to show what learning processes they underwent.

[45] For path-breaking interpretations of the 'political equilibrium' in nineteenth-century European politics see Schroeder (1994) and Schroeder (2004), pp. 223–41. For "realist" approaches that stress the centrality of the balance-of-power paradigm in the analysis of international order see Waltz (1979); Mearsheimer (2001), pp. 42–51.

But, as noted, making any significant progress towards a more legitimate equilibrium of this kind was inconceivable without finding ways to work out legitimate political processes. More precisely, it required reordering processes in which all relevant actors – and not just one arbiter or a combination of victorious great powers – participated and through which *reciprocal* agreements could be negotiated – essentially, complex compromises that, as far as possible, could gain acceptance on all sides and *balanced* each side's vital interests and concerns. And in the wake of the Great War, working towards such an equilibrium was particularly critical in the relations between the victors and the vanquished. This was a tall order indeed. But a further and ever more crucial challenge had emerged in the epoch of the First World War, which indeed set it apart from that of the Congress of Vienna. It was the challenge posed by the newly vital interdependence of international and domestic legitimacy requirements – in an era in which momentous, yet also crisis-ridden and very uneven democratisation processes coincided with a war-induced mobilisation of nationalism and ideological polarisation. In short, political decision-makers had to negotiate – under very adverse conditions – settlements, and rules, that not only balanced the core requirements of security and other vital interests of different states in the international sphere but also allowed each of the protagonists to gain vital domestic backing for what had been negotiated – in their respective parliaments, in the sphere of public opinion and, ultimately, among those who (now) had a say as voters.

At a deeper level, then, this study is especially interested in illuminating how far the massive, in so many ways utterly disruptive catastrophe of the Great War indeed engendered substantive learning and reorientations in the expanding sphere of modern international politics. In other words, it investigates to what extent the war also became a crucible of learning. Yet it also seeks to show why, ultimately, it did not spur something akin to *metanoia*, a real collective "turning around of the mind". To be explored, then, is the underlying question of how far key actors and the wider array of those who sought to shape international politics and, eventually, peacemaking not only had the *capacity* but also *enough time* to learn in order to respond to the consequences of the war in an effective manner. Put differently, it is to be examined how far these actors actually *could* embark on what might be called "constructive" learning processes during and after a war that created such a multiplicity of far-reaching challenges, changes and "new realities" in a relatively short span of time and, particularly from 1916, at an ever accelerating pace.

As will be shown, it was no coincidence that the more significant processes of this kind did not occur during the war itself or immediately after it, under the pressures of the Paris Peace Conference, but at a later stage, in the formative decade of the 1920s. Yet in an analysis that seeks to highlight the *limits* of what could be achieved after the First World War, two further questions have to be probed more thoroughly as well. The first is: To what extent did the war in fact reinforce and to what extent did it actually begin to transform the distinctive yet also in many ways remarkably similar predispositions, worldviews and assumptions about international politics, justice, global hierarchy, democracy and other essential aspects that had come to prevail in the political cultures on both sides of the Atlantic before 1914? And the second is: Which "older" dispositions and worldviews did the war harden, yet also which new ideas and assumptions did it bring to the fore that actually *impeded* or even *prevented* more fundamental learning processes? A different and more succinct way of asking this latter question is: How far did the protagonists of this transformative era become trapped in processes of stunted or even "pathological learning"? How far did what they had learned in the pre-war era and during the war in fact 'interfere with further learning'? And how far did their limited learning make them ultimately less capable of dealing creatively with the challenges that had accumulated by the end of the war – and of building a better new order?[46]

In this context, too, a particular focus will be on the problematic consequences of the ideologisation tendencies the Great War provoked precisely because it shook up so much. As will be shown, however violently they clashed, the radicalisation of older imperialist and nationalist ideologies and the promulgation of novel or newly powerful ideological visions of a "new order", whether Wilsonian or Leninist, had one thing in common: they stood in the way of more genuine and far-reaching learning. Finally, it of course has to be recognised that not only political leaders, key advisers and influential opinion-makers faced tremendous challenges of learning in this period. To effect a genuine transformation and prepare the ground for a "deeper peace" and a more sustainable international order, much broader collective learning and reorientation processes – and indeed changes in mentality – were required in *all* the states and societies that had gone through decades of accelerating change in the era of high imperialism and eventually fought against each other in the Great War.

The Intensified Interdependence of International and Domestic Politics

One further salient trend that the Great War intensified was the intensified, and increasingly complex, interconnectedness and interdependence of international and domestic politics on both sides of the Atlantic: the politics of war and no less the politics of peace. It would not be helpful to revive the concept

---

[46] Essentially, though on a much vaster, global, scale the protagonists of the era of the Great War thus faced challenges of learning that were similar to those the Athenians confronted, and ultimately failed to meet, during the Peloponnesian War. See Meier (2000), p. 516, and Thucydides' magisterial political and moral history of *The Peloponnesian War* (2009), esp. pp. 3–13, 36–48, 90–106, 142–54, 196–9, 301–7.

of "the primacy of domestic politics". Interdependence is a more accurate term here. What has to be captured is, on the one hand, something that was both qualitatively changing and ever more critical: the impact of domestic-political concerns and constraints on international relations; the domestic force-fields under which international politics had to be pursued, and the ever more complex legitimation requirements that its practitioners had to meet. Domestic considerations – elite and public expectations heightened by the mobilisation processes of the war and the need to ensure support on the home front – had a significant impact on processes of international politics and, in particular, peacemaking. But, on the other hand, inter- and transnational developments also had a tremendous influence on domestic politics. This applied to the globalised military-political, economic and ideological competition of the pre-war era just as much as to the escalating political and ideological struggles that the war itself and then the peace negotiations generated. Processes in the international sphere could indeed have a transformative effect. They tested – or undermined – the stability of governments and entire political systems as well as systems of finance and political economy in ways and to a degree not witnessed before.

As will be illuminated, the Great War had a momentous and in some cases dramatic impact on the political systems of all the major belligerents (and of smaller states as well, of course). It put to the test the resilience and capacities of the more liberal systems of the *Entente* Powers – and eventually raised novel challenges for the American polity, including what many – including Wilson – saw as a highly undesirable prospect, namely that the United States would have to become a European-style "security state". With more drastic consequences, it placed enormous stresses on the political regimes of the Central Powers – and Russia. Giving rise to the twofold challenges of Wilson's progressive crusade and Lenin's call for a revolutionary transformation, the war ultimately precipitated the collapse of the old order in all three Eastern Empires – and, in Germany and Austria, it precipitated both revolutionary turmoil and conflict-ridden efforts to establish a new, republican order in the shadow of defeat. Finally, domestic pressures and constraints had a newly important, albeit not decisive, influence on the peacemaking process itself; and in turn that process and its outcome had multifaceted, yet overall profoundly destabilising, domestic-political repercussions on both sides of the Atlantic.

The Transnational Dimensions of International Politics – and Its Key Actors

Yet there was a further trend that gained decisive momentum between 1914 and 1919: the spheres of "classic" international or inter-state politics, domestic and transnational politics became more closely interconnected as well. Put differently, what had already gained ground before the war now seemed to alter the playing-field of international politics more permanently.

At one level, as noted, debates and ideological and political controversies about the stakes of the war and the shape of the postwar order not only took place within different states and "national" public spheres but acquired more distinctive transnational dimensions; this could potentially be conducive to the emergence of a new transnational consciousness, e.g. about the need for a "League of Nations", but against the backdrop of a war that escalated beyond all previously known proportions and in an atmosphere of political and nationalist-ideological warfare on all sides, it was more likely, at this juncture, to amplify antagonistic tendencies both between and within the societies of the belligerents.

At the same time, one can say that the sphere of international politics and of those who sought to exert an influence on it essentially *expanded*; those who occupied leading positions in governments and state or imperial hierarchies and who made policies and decisions on their behalf increasingly had to deal and wrestle with the growing influence of non-governmental actors. Their aspirations, the ideas they spawned and the impulses they gave have to be considered. But the *immediate* impact they had should not be overrated. They contributed to important changes both in the normative and in the political *environment* of international politics. But, as this study will show, the salient processes that reshaped international order in the aftermath of the First World War took place in the sphere of inter-state and inter-governmental relations.

What thus remains integral to an integrated international history is a comprehensive analysis of the changing nature and scope of "high" international politics – and the policymaking and political as well as economic decision-making of those actors who shaped the policies of states and to a greater or lesser degree commanded the levers of state power. Precisely because the international, transnational and domestic force-fields in which they had to act changed so dramatically the significance of these actors, and particularly the centrality of the political leaders of states, has to be re-accentuated. The role they played was arguably even more pivotal than before the war. It was most pivotal when it came to the task of not only developing peace designs but also translating them into a sustainable postwar system. Crucially, they were the only actors who could negotiate and legitimise – or could at least seek to negotiate and legitimise – the inevitable complex compromise agreements that had to be made after the Great War.

Further, a comprehensive analysis can bring out that official decision-makers and policymakers also advanced the most influential conceptions and strategies – those that would have a decisive bearing on how peace would be made and order remade after the war. In some cases, they adopted or adapted ideas proposed by non-governmental activists. But they came to develop their own conceptions, and they mainly drew on the conceptual planning of key advisers and – to a lesser extent – on the advice of influential ministers and officials in governmental bureaucracies. And, as will be shown, political key figures also had the most significant *transnational* influence when it came to changing the parameters of international politics – and the ways in which salient questions of peace and international order were debated. This was due not only to the quality or appeal of what they proposed but also of course to the power they represented. Wilson provides the most striking example here. He became the first governmental leader who actually sought to pursue a new transnational strategy to promote his aims, endeavouring to become the figurehead of a transnational coalition of progressive forces on behalf of a "new world order". The influence of Lenin furnishes the most important counter-example, though it was less formidable than some observers argued at the time or in retrospect.

In the end, my study thus seeks to show that while a balanced analysis of the systemic and structural changes of the international order, the different domestic orders and transnational constellations goes a long way towards explaining why it proved impossible to forge a more durable peace after the Great War, it is still vital to provide something else as well: an in-depth reappraisal of the *subjective* outlooks, worldviews and approaches of the most influential decision-makers – central actors like Wilson, Lloyd George and Clemenceau – and of the policymakers who influenced them most. It is and remains imperative to understand not just their war and peace aims but also the evolving *conceptions* of peace and postwar order. It is and remains critical to gauge on what basis they judged what was, and what was not, legitimate; how they perceived and defined the cardinal challenges they faced and the core interests they sought to defend; how they perceived and interpreted the changing configuration of the international system and their international and domestic room for manoeuvre; how they perceived and interpreted the motives and policies of their allies and enemies; how they came to view and interpret historical precedents and developments that had a bearing on the present – notably, the longer pre-history of the Great War; and how they came to view the meaning and historical impact of the war itself. And it is and remains essential to analyse what *subjective* lessons they drew from the war and its pre-history, how far they actually underwent substantial learning processes, came to adopt different approaches to international politics and, more fundamentally, also altered their underlying assumptions.

The incipient transformation of the transatlantic order in the era of the Great War will thus be analysed from multiple perspectives – American, European, and global. But the focus will be on those who had the most formative impact on this process.

PART I

Inevitable Descent into the Abyss?

The Wider Pre-History of the Great War
The Involution of International Politics at the Dawn
of the Long Twentieth Century

To comprehend why it was so crucial to create a novel, at the core Atlantic international order of the world after the formative war of the long twentieth century – the cataclysm of 1914–23 – and why at the same time founding such an order proved such an immensely arduous task, it is imperative to widen the focus and look at the bigger picture of modern international history. What has to be examined, and reappraised, are not only the deeper origins and indeed the deeper causes of the Great War but also the onerous legacy bequeathed by the unprecedentedly dynamic and far-reaching transformation of the international system that began when the long twentieth century – and the long Atlantic century – dawned, i.e. roughly in 1860.[1] For it was this transformation process that finally led to the disintegration of what constituted the core of the nineteenth century's European and global order, the Vienna system of 1814–15.

The Vienna system had transformed the foundations of European peace and proved remarkably effective until and beyond the European revolutions of 1848, also in placing checks on great-power competition beyond Europe. But in the aftermath of the Crimean War, and more palpably from the 1860s, it would come to be superseded by a qualitatively different system of (more or less) modern, industrialised and unprecedentedly centralised nation-states in and beyond Europe, yet principally in the newly vital Euro-Atlantic sphere. Essentially, what thus took shape was an order – or "disorder" – that was shaped and dominated by those states that would eventually confront each other in the First World War. And it was within this system that eventually, against the backdrop of the first genuine globalisation processes, an unprecedentedly dynamic, all-embracing, and war-prone international competition gained momentum, which culminated in the era of "high imperialism".

---

[1] For alternative interpretative approaches see Weisbrode (2015), pp. 1–3; Nolan (2012); Ellwood (2012), pp. 22ff.; Winkler (2019), pp. 121 ff., 173 ff.;

What is to be illuminated in the following, then, are the most salient *longue durée* changes in international, domestic and transnational politics during the crucial period between the 1860s and 1914. And to be probed in particular are the changes in the prevalent ideas, assumptions, mentalities and political cultures that took place in this period, altered the nature and rules of inter-national politics and, in the end, made a Great War of one kind or another not unavoidable but indeed very likely – or rather: ever harder to avoid. More precisely, the focus will be not only on the impact of the first modern state-formation and globalisation processes that took place in this period but also on the eventual globalisation of European power-politics. And it will be on the wider significance of the parallel "rise" of the United States to the position of a world power that came to participate in the global imperialist competition on its own terms, but in crucial respects continued to remain aloof and disen-gaged from the as yet Eurocentric international system that persisted prior to 1914. At a deeper level, the analysis will illuminate the ever more pervasive effect of both offensive and defensive nationalist ideologies. But chiefly it will gauge the corrosive impact of the ever more hard-headed notions of *Realpolitik* that now came to predominate. And it will highlight the profound influence exerted by transnationally radicalised ideas and ideological maxims from the realm of social and civilisational Darwinism – ideas and maxims that intensified what eventually turned indeed into an ever more unrelenting "struggle for the survival of the fittest world power".

Yet it is important to understand as well that the pre–First World War era also witnessed the emergence of limited but nonetheless significant counter-vailing forces – different kinds of essentially progressive internationalist aspir-ations to contain power politics, work towards a different, more pacific international order and, notably, to promote arbitration and strengthen inter-national law. In particular, political internationalists played a critical role in the pre-history of the seminal Hague conventions of 1899 and 1907. More generally, as will be shown, many of the most important advances in this direction were made in an essentially transatlantic context; and they gave rise to first visions of an alternative transatlantic and global peace system. They would not have any tangible effect on the sphere of "high politics" and the developments that precipitated the Great War. But they in *some* respects generated new or revived older ideas about mechanisms and norms of inter-national order – including notions of a "peace league", self-determination and peace-building through arbitration and democratisation – that would acquire a critical significance thereafter, not only in the struggle over the terms of peace and an essentially *Atlantic* postwar order that ensued during the war but also at the subsequent Paris Peace Conference.

Above all, however, what has to be shown is that in the sphere of inter-national politics the formative first decades of the long twentieth century – and particularly the phase between the 1880s and 1914 – were overall a period of *regression.* Indeed, they can even be called a period of *involution* in terms of the development of mechanisms, rules, norms and practices that were conducive to the management of conflicts and the preservation of a deeper, sustainable peace. Put differently, they stand out as a period in which the ideas and forces that shaped international politics clearly *lagged ever more behind* the dynamic developments that unfolded in the spheres of state formation, state modernisation, and global imperialist competition.

The most obvious result of these regressive tendencies was that, while the United States remained unengaged in critical respects, the crucial and erstwhile essentially integrative European concert system came to be supplanted by an inherently unstable and highly conflict-prone balance-of-power system. And the latter then reinforced an antagonising polarisation process between two *eventually* very rigidified alliance blocs. The crucial consequence of this process was that when the "fateful" crisis of July 1914 escalated the key decision-makers no longer had either a mechanism akin to the European concert to prevent a general war or the mind-sets and imaginations to do what was required to preserve peace.

Over time, the regressive transformation of international politics that occurred at the dawn of the long twentieth century thus not only created essential preconditions for the precarious constellation of 1914. It also had more long-term repercussions. Essentially, those who would be called upon to remake order in the aftermath of the Great War would have very little to build on. And they would face the underlying challenge of having to construct a qualitatively different, "modern" international system while at the same time having to deal with – and while still being in many ways influenced by – the catastrophic legacy of the imperialist age. All of this will now be illuminated as systematically as possible.

1

Peace Through Equilibrium
The Nineteenth Century's Vienna System – and Its Disintegration

It has long been the dominant view that the Congress of Vienna established a balance of power on which the order of nineteenth-century Europe rested – and that it was the abandonment of its principles that ultimately caused the First World War. In this interpretation, European leaders eventually failed to keep the continental balance sufficiently flexible to prevent great-power conflicts from spinning out of control.[1] But as has been convincingly shown more recently, the remarkable and indeed unprecedented effectiveness and durability of the Vienna system of 1815 did not stem from the successful restoration of a viable European balance of power but rather from an indeed *revolutionary* achievement: successful efforts to create a new international equilibrium in Europe and a novel *integrative* system of international politics whose key mechanism was a new Concert of Europe.[2]

I.   The Nature of the Vienna System

In a *longue durée* perspective, the protagonists of the Congress of Vienna established nothing less than the first functioning and lasting peace regime in modern times since the Peace of Westphalia of 1648 – after almost two decades of war in the wake of the French Revolution, which had eventually escalated under the impact of Napoleon's aspiration to conquer and place all of Europe under one imperial regime. Conceived not only to prevent a recurrence of such aspirations but in fact to ban the truly revolutionary threat of great-power *war* from Europe, the Vienna system inaugurated not restorative but indeed forward-looking and "realistically" progressive principles of international politics. Pivotal among these were principles of "collective security", peaceful conflict resolution, and a concerted management and regulation of European affairs. The Congress of Vienna also established more effective guarantees for the independence and rights not just of the great powers but of all European states.

---

[1] See Kissinger (1994), pp. 226–7; Mearsheimer (2001), pp. 42–3; Bridge and Bullen (2004), pp. 1–19.

[2] This has been shown convincingly by Schroeder (1994), especially pp. 443–582. See also Krüger and Schroeder (2001).

In the longer history of international politics, the advances of Vienna were indeed *revolutionary*.[3] They transformed the European order. And by restraining global imperial competition among the European powers for a long time, they also had a significant impact on the emergence of relatively stable "spheres of order" in the world of the nineteenth century. They thus also, and notably, created essential conditions for the largely unchallenged development and expansion of the United States.[4]

Those who played pivotal roles at Vienna, the Austrian statesman Prince Klemens von Metternich and the British foreign secretary Viscount Robert Castlereagh, managed to negotiate an overall remarkably enlightened agreement with the messianic Russian Tsar Alexander I. More importantly, they had indeed undergone crucial learning processes, drawing lessons not only from the decades of ever-escalating war but also from the deficiencies of mechanistic eighteenth-century balance-of-power politics that had allowed the French Revolution to precipitate an all-European conflict. It was on the basis of these learning processes that they came to create an unprecedented *inclusive* instrument and framework for peacekeeping and settling European conflicts – a concert of the great powers.

This concert was originally established through the Quadruple Alliance of the victorious powers, forged in November 1815 with the initial key aim of containing France. Significantly, however, it was soon extended to include the vanquished power – the defeated French Empire, hence once again a monarchy ruled by the Bourbon Charles X. It was thus transformed into an *inclusive* Concert of Europe that at the same time functioned as a *common* European system of "collective security" in which all participating powers committed not only to mutual security guarantees but also to upholding general peace and security in Europe. Above all, however, the concert mechanism was established to permit a cooperative and consultative management of European inter-state relations and to reinforce rules and restraints of the Vienna system. Originally, the protagonists of Vienna envisaged a loose institutionalisation of the concert; and representatives of the powers would for some time indeed meet in periodic congresses to regulate European affairs. The first such congress was then held in Aix-la-Chapelle in 1818. Later, however, the members of the concert would convene or consult on a more ad-hoc basis whenparticular problems and conflicts needed to be addressed. But the general idea that a permanent concert should be maintained and cultivated as the crucial instrument of Europe's peace regime remained the key premise of European international politics until the mid-nineteenth century.[5]

---

[3] Schroeder (1994), pp. 579–81.
[4] See Osterhammel (2009), pp. 679–82.
[5] See Schroeder (1994), pp. 575–93; Jarrett (2014), pp. 149–207, 353–79.

The powers that really played the crucial role in founding this novel European international system were the two undisputed hegemonic powers after the defeat of Napoleon – Britain, arguably the system's pivotal *primus inter pares*, and Russia. Acting as overall "benevolent hegemons" within the new European pentarchy, these powers first cooperated with one small and comparatively vulnerable "middle power", Prussia, and one central power, Austria, that was even more vulnerable both in terms of external threats and the centrifugal pressures of liberalism and nationalism – and thus all the more interested in preserving the equilibrium of 1815.[6] Soon, however, they also came to cooperate with the state that, despite its defeat, remained a genuine European great power – France. Thus, a hallmark of the Vienna system, which indeed set it apart from the "Versailles system" of 1919, was that it quickly evolved into an integrative postwar order rather than a system imposed by the victors that could only be maintained by a forceful containment of the vanquished. This unquestionably buttressed its overall stability and legitimacy.

The systemic architecture of Vienna was originally fortified by the Holy Alliance that Austria and Prussia had concluded with Russia in September 1815. It would provide a superstructure for a remarkably long period of European peace. At a deeper level, the peacemakers of Vienna laid foundations, *not* for a new and better "balance of power" – which was in fact elusive in 1815 and would have caused renewed instability and war – but rather for an unprecedented "political equilibrium" between the European powers – an equilibrium of rights, protections, satisfactions and responsibilities. This equilibrium was underpinned by mutually accepted premises of an evolving *ius Europaeum*, a treaty-based codex of European international law that came to be enshrined in the Congress Act of June 1815 and the second Peace of Paris, concluded in November of the same year. They thus indeed managed to make significant progress towards establishing a general system of law and clearly defined rules in European politics.

In many ways the Vienna system was thus a distinctly hierarchical great-power system, forged by their political leaders and designed to allow them to direct European politics. Yet it also established unprecedented guarantees and assurances of the "rights" and claims of smaller powers like the Netherlands and the re-established Kingdom of Poland or "Congress Poland", though the latter faced continuing threats of Russian interference. The novel "political equilibrium" was based on the smaller powers' "tacit acceptance" of a "general great-power hegemony" as long as this guaranteed their "independence" and "rights".[7] And following the Belgian revolution of 1830, the powers of the European concert came to agree on one further particular mainstay of

---

[6] See Schroeder (1992), esp. pp. 694 ff.; Schroeder (1989), pp. 144 ff.; Jervis (1992).
[7] Schroeder (1994), p. 578.

Europe's nineteenth-century order that would be upheld until the summer of 1914, namely that the integrity and neutrality of the independent Belgian state that was created following the division of the United Netherlands would be guaranteed by all the European powers. For both political and strategic reasons, the British foreign secretary Palmerston and his successors would place a particular emphasis on the sanctity of this guarantee.

Significantly, a similar European approach had already been pursued in 1814–15 to settle one of the most intricate and weighty problems that arose after the defeat of Napoleon and would hence remain one of the key challenges of European politics, namely the German question. More precisely, at this point it was the question of what structure and place in the European system those states, cities and principalities were to have that had formerly been part of the Holy Roman Empire of the German Nation – and later been subsumed under Napoleon's emancipatory and colonial regime in and beyond the Rhenish Federation. The solution the peacemakers of Vienna found can be seen as an in some ways ingenious compromise that was not sustainable in the longer run – because it failed to open up future avenues of accommodation for the rising forces of liberalism and nationalism – but for a considerable period ensured order and peaceful stability in the centre of Europe. What they negotiated was intended to avoid, on the one hand, the creation of too loose and weak a political structure for the German states – and thus a power vacuum that could provoke the ambitions of neighbouring powers. On the other hand, the aim was to avoid establishing a unified German state that would have been unwieldy at first but had the potential to upset the European equilibrium in the longer run – while of course also being incompatible with core Prussian and Austrian interests at this time.

The aspirations of a nascent German nationalist movement in which national-liberal forces dominated yet also aggressive ethnic forms of nationalism came to the fore, were thus pointedly blocked; but they would have been too weak and the dynastic states' interest in self-preservation would have been too strong to permit such an outcome in 1815 anyway. Instead, the Congress of Vienna finally established a loose German Confederation that essentially did not go much beyond a permanent defensive league of all German states and free cities – leaving hopes for a customs union as unfulfilled as aspirations for a constitutional framework of political rights. Within the Confederation, which indeed proved acceptable for its neighbours and conducive to European peace, the rivaling powers Prussia and Austria effectively agreed to an "informal dualism" in which they acted as regional hegemons, one in the north, the other in the south.[8]

---

[8] Schroeder (1994), pp. 547, 538–48; Doering-Manteuffel (2010), pp. 1–18.

In the interpretation of one of the key thinkers who helped to lay the conceptual groundwork for the Vienna system, Friedrich von Gentz, it represented the best possible "realistic", actually effective peace system that European statecraft could produce – and as such a renewal and elaboration of the Westphalian system of 1648.[9] Significantly, Gentz, who acted as Metternich's assistant at the Congress of Vienna, concluded that the principal achievement of the peacemakers had been to lay the groundwork, not for an ambitious – and illusory – "supra-state" league or constitutional order that would not be accepted by Europe's sovereign states but rather for something that, for all its limitations, could actually be expected to preserve peace and foster a viable international order: an "inter-linked political system" that was built on "simple main pillars" and had the potential to "protect the future existence of all states *through mutual guarantees*" and thus also to "promote the inner welfare of each substantially". In Gentz's judgement, it was thus certain to be instrumental in consolidating "the peace of the world".[10]

Fundamentally, the age of the Vienna system indeed witnessed the emergence of what could more properly be called *international* politics, i.e. politics between states and their representatives, which was no longer shaped or *decisively* affected by dynastic concerns but rather pursued on the basis of understandings of *raison d'état*. What was perceived to lie in the interest of a particular state became a pre-eminent factor in international relations. In the formative era of a more or less well-functioning Vienna system between 1815 and the 1840s, maintaining an international concert and its common rules had been core elements of the principal powers' understanding of what constituted the "reason of state" – of what lay in their overriding interest and prevailed over more particular interests, aims and ambitions. Thus, one could say that in this phase *raison d'état* and *"raison de système international"* were not only congruent but actually mutually reinforcing.

The system that had been forged at Vienna thus indeed came to contribute significantly to "the peace of the world". From 1815 and in most respects till the dawn of the long twentieth century, it largely "shielded" the Europeans from the global sphere – while Britain long remained the only real, and expanding, world power. And at the same time, and more importantly, it largely shielded the rest of the world – including the United States – from European expansionism and imperialist competition. The system's precepts and rules essentially restrained the European powers and kept them from turning towards imperialist expansionism outside Europe. It thus indeed contributed to a period of "deglobalisation" prior to the subsequent globalisation processes of the age of imperialism, and the emergence of distinctive

---

[9] Gentz (1806), pp. 337–8; Gentz (1815), p. 346.
[10] Gentz (1815), p. 346. My emphasis.

"spheres of order" in the world. Different sets of rules and norms applied in each sphere.

While there were no strict hierarchy or clearly demarcated dividing-lines between the European system and extra-European "anarchy", the path towards a global states-system in which comparable rules and standards applied was indeed extremely stony. In short, such a system never even came close to gaining contours before 1914.[11] Yet, as should be emphasised, not just Britain's maritime supremacy and provision of a "naval umbrella" but also the rules and restraints of the Vienna system set the exceptionally favourable international conditions that were so vital for the flourishing and expansion of the American republic. These European advances, rather than the unilaterally asserted Monroe Doctrine of 1823, in fact protected the fledgling republic against great-power interference during its most vulnerable state-formation period. And, crucially, they created the environment in which the United States could pursue its expansionist "Manifest Destiny" at the expense of native Americans and its Mexican neighbour, establish an 'Empire of Liberty' on the north American continent, claim preponderance in the American hemisphere and ultimately emerge as a world power.[12]

II. Inherent Limitations of the Vienna System, the Challenges of the European Revolutions of 1848 and the Emergence of Alternative Visions of International Order

Originally, the Vienna system was also strengthened by the Holy Alliance that Metternich and Prussia's leaders had concluded with Alexander I on 26 September 1815 and that was supposed to bind European sovereigns to deal with each other and "their peoples" on the premises of the moral-religious principles of the Christian Gospel, thus banishing war and violence from the European continent. Metternich viewed this alliance and Castlereagh had welcomed it as a means to restrain Alexander's even more aspirational ideological mission to become the patron of Europe. Yet the Austrian chancellor turned what had been envisaged as a *fraternal* union of rulers and people into a *paternal* union of monarchs over their peoples. And following Metternich's guiding impetus, the core doctrine of the Holy Alliance indeed became a doctrine of intervention in the internal affairs of European states (whether they belonged to it nor not) and the alliance itself an instrument of interference and repression, serving to uphold monarchical "order" and absolutist principles against liberal challenges and other "subversive" tendencies.[13] The Holy Alliance – and with it the Vienna system as a whole – thus became

---

[11] Osterhammel (2014), pp. 469–503
[12] See Chapter 3.
[13] See Schroeder (2012), pp. 170–95.

closely linked with, and overall burdened by, the emergence of an in effect regressive system of "order" in continental Europe, the so-called Metternich system.

In some important respects, the Vienna system was undoubtedly not only distinctly hierarchical but also backward- rather than forward-looking. That it became bound up with Metternich's conservative and de facto repressive maxims – and a Holy Alliance regime which sought to suppress all liberal and nationalist aspirations that had emerged in the different European states – would indeed become one of its crucial limitations. In Metternich's judgement, Europe's peace-enforcing equilibrium and the supranational order of the European concert could only be preserved if all the different national, liberal and emancipatory forces that, in his view, threatened them profoundly were reined in. As foreign minister and then as Austrian chancellor, Metternich came to pursue an increasingly rigid policy of political and cultural repression to guard the order of Vienna against what he saw as a radical movement that in fact comprised very contradictory forces, from liberal and progressive to national to romantic, religious and indeed reactionary groupings. In 1823, he put his stamp on the Carlsbad Decrees, which came to symbolise the "Metternich system" and introduced not only preventive censorship of the press and state supervision of universities but also coordinated measures against "subversive" activities in all of the German states, led by Austrian and Prussian officials. Metternich's reactionary policies were particularly problematic because they came to be directed not just against specific "subversive" or revolutionary forces but against the entire liberal constitutional movement that had emerged in and beyond the states of the German Confederation. In a wider context, the Holy Alliance thus alienated the rising liberal-bourgeois – and capitalist – classes whose nationally-orientated claims and interests the Vienna system would have to accommodate if it was to evolve and provide peace and stability in the longer term. The more the significance and power of these classes grew, the more the question arose whether the "Metternich system could be adapted – or whether its protagonists would fight a losing battle in trying to stem the prevalent tides of the time.

It was thus no coincidence that the first really existential challenge the Vienna system and the European concert confronted arose from the European revolutions of 1848. These revolutions had predominantly domestic or inner-state origins. They were triggered not only by economic and social factors, which notably accounted for the widespread peasant protests, but also by political and cultural-ideological discontent that had built up under what both liberal and more radical democratic revolutionaries denounced as the oppressive yoke of the Holy Alliance. What mattered most for the future of the European international order was that soon all the forces and movements that were dissatisfied with "the Vienna system", and in fact mainly sought to overcome the strictures of the "Metternich system", came to the fore. These included not only nationalist liberals but also those who championed – utopian – ideas of a democratic revolution, romantic nationalism and, above all, indeed, those who pursued essentially power-political aims and cloaked them in various ideological guises – liberal, pseudo-liberal and eventually neo-absolutist and reactionary.[14]

Not only leading liberals but also and particularly the more radical revolutionaries of 1848, who sought to found *democratic* nation-states, came to invoke the American example – or what Metternich had earlier called the American republic's "evil doctrines" and "pernicious examples".[15] Yet the Polk administration in Washington, whose means were very limited anyway, pointedly refrained from interfering in inner-European affairs – thereby reasserting a core precept of the Monroe Doctrine – and did not aid the European revolutionaries in any substantial way. President Polk merely held up the example of the American republic and in general terms encouraged those who, in his words, were "imitating our example", had "resolved to be free" and were "struggling to establish free institutions".[16] In the main, the Revolutions of 1848 thus remained a continental European turmoil; and those who formed the avant-gardes of the different "national" revolutionary movements mainly built on their own homegrown liberal conceptions or more radical ideas.

As in 1830, the outbreak of the revolution in 1848 raised the spectre – from the perspectives of the European monarchies – that a revolutionary France could undermine the order of 1815 through "wars of liberation". For the initial revolutionary act had occurred once again in Paris where, in February 1848, not only the "citizen king" Louis-Philippe was forced to resign in favour of Louis Bonaparte but also, in reaction to the protest of the masses, the first republic since 1799 was proclaimed. The head of the Second Republic's provisional government, Alphonse de Lamartine, who had earlier asserted that every "nation" had a right to exercise "self-determination", now championed this as a founding principle of a new European order. He thus declared that the treaties of 1815 were no longer valid. But he also stressed that he accepted the territorial status quo established in Vienna. And, significantly, the provisional government in Paris subsequently made no efforts to ignite a wider European revolution.[17]

The revolutionary tides nonetheless swept across Europe – through Switzerland, the Italian and the German states, including Prussia, through all

---

[14] See Schroeder (1994), pp. 799–802; Sperber (2005). For the global context, see Osterhammel (2014), pp. 534–7.

[15] Metternich note, 1824, in Perkins (1927), p. 167. For the wider context, see Kloppenberg (2016).

[16] Polk, Fourth Annual Message to Congress, 5 December 1848, Miller Center, University of Virginia.

[17] Lamartine (1849); Furet (1988).

parts of the Habsburg Empire, all the way to the Balkans and even to the Ottoman Empire. But despite the efforts of Giuseppe Mazzini and other avant-gardists of the Young Europe movement, who called for an all-European national-democratic renewal, there would be no trans-European nationalist revolution in 1848. Rather, what erupted was a multiplicity of parallel upris-ings. Monarchical regimes were swiftly ousted and replaced by liberal-national ministries, but these then also collapsed very soon because of inner divisions or because they were simply too overwhelmed by the challenges they con-fronted. With the temporary exception of the French Second Republic, they were thus also too weak to withstand the eventual efforts of the conservative or "reactionary" forces to reassert their authority once the storm had blown over. And these would also be the forces that then came to shape continental European politics from 1849 – and ultimately destroy the Vienna system.

As has rightly been stressed, the Vienna system, with its constituent restraints and prevalent rules for a peaceful settlement of conflicts, had in fact allowed the Revolutions of 1848 to occur and proceed without a violent reaction from those rulers and dominant oligarchies whose power they chal-lenged. The regimes of the "old order" for the most part did not use force against their own populations. More importantly, the still prevailing rules and norms of the European concert prevented the revolutionary upheavals from sparking a general European war.[18] Of critical importance here were the moderating policies that the liberal foreign secretary Palmerston pursued on behalf of Britain, which remained the Vienna system's pivotal power and at the same time were largely unaffected by the revolutionary turmoil, only witnessing the Chartists' peaceful campaign to enfranchise workers. Palmerston openly sympathised with some of the aims of the more moderate liberal revolutionaries on the continent, notably their calls for "self-determin-ation" and constitutional monarchies. But he did not actually favour liberal interventionism in support of such aspirations. For his part, and crucially, the leader of the most powerful and autocratic member of the Holy Alliance, Nicholas I, refrained from what both German and Polish revolutionaries feared most, namely the use of Russian military force in a counter-revolutionary intervention, above all to crush the Polish uprising in the Prussian-held Grand Duchy of Posen. To a remarkable extent, even the Tsar remained bound by the restraints of the Vienna system.

Initially, the Revolutions of 1848 seemed to present an epochal opportunity to realise a vision of an alternative international order that was to have a major influence on the conceptions of modern peace and order which would be developed under the impact of the First World War. And that was the vision of a novel European peace effected through a fraternal union of democratic

---

[18] Schroeder (1994), pp. 799–800.

nation-states, which no thinker advanced more forcefully than the Genovese avant-gardist and proselytiser Giuseppe Mazzini. After the *caesura* of 1914, Wilson would emerge as the most powerful actor who – without fully realising it – reinvigorated Mazzinian maxims, albeit in a progressive Americanist guise. An outspoken anti-monarchist, Mazzini had developed his ideas in opposition to the Habsburg Empire and the Holy Alliance. At the heart of his remarkably optimistic vision lay the notion that Europe could find a better way to lasting peace and "good order" if it could be transformed into something akin to an international society or family of democratically constituted nation-states in which an elevated sense of solidarity prevailed over narrow self-interest. Mazzini thus assumed that while fighting collectively for their cause, different national movements would also aid the like-minded aspirations of other nationalities for a state of their own – which, in his conception, were essentially in harmony and all part of the higher cause of all humanity. More civilised nations would then aid less civilised nations.[19]

Having earlier founded the Young Italy movement to get rid of the Habsburgian yoke and establish an Italian nation-state, Mazzini went on to proselytise his creed and coordinate the activities of different national-revolutionary groupings in Europe, asserting that if they could join forces they would have the power to topple the order of the Holy Alliance. To this end, he played a leading part in founding the Young Europe Association in Berne in 1834. Eventually, he would take part in the revolutionary uprisings in 1848. In some important ways, the processes and outcomes of 1848 and 1849 prefigured those that then took place in a transatlantic and global context between 1916 and 1919. Yet they would also manifest that a new European order could not be built in the way Mazzini had envisaged. And they would throw into relief some of the most fundamental challenges that any attempt to create a modern international order had to confront in an era of competing nationalisms – in Europe and other parts of the world. As noted, the different revolutionary processes not only unfolded, and mostly failed, in a distinctly disconnected manner; there were indeed no significant efforts to create links across national boundaries. The various national revolutionary "self-determination" agendas – and the liberal or democratic nationalist ideologies that informed them – also often stood in open conflict with one another, especially in central and eastern Europe.

In fact, not only liberals but also more radical democrats – and early socialists – thought in hierarchical categories – in terms of a hierarchy of political and civilisational achievement and indeed a concomitant hierarchy of

---

[19] Mazzini's schemes for a "United States of Europe" reflected but also went beyond earlier Jeffersonian thinking about a new order of "sister republics" and Kant's maxims for a peace system of republican states. See Mazzini (1847), (1849) and (1850), in Recchia and Urbinati (2009), pp. 57–61, 117–35.

national aspirations. They thus found reasons to view their aims as superior to those of others. Some even went so far as to call for a cleansing "European civil war", not only against the forces of the *ancien régime* but also against "retrograde peoples", as the only way to build a forward-looking new order.[20] Most ominous here were the conflicts that soon escalated between those who aspired to create a "Greater Germany" – which was to include Prussia, the smaller states of the German Confederation and (at least) the German-speaking parts of the Austrian Empire – and the claims of Danish nationalists and the Polish, Czech, Hungarian and other national movements within the Habsburg Empire. The revolutionary upheaval of the mid-nineteenth century thus brought the realities of a far from harmonious "Europe of nations" to the forefront of international and domestic politics. The incendiary conflicts between different nationalist agendas and claims for "self-determination" and statehood would not be resolved and would resurface even more violently during the Great War – particularly in central and eastern Europe.

Yet the watershed year 1848 also brought to the fore another even more radical vision of an alternative European and world order of the future. This vision, which would become particularly influential during the First World War and reverberate through the long twentieth century, was presented to the world in the *Communist Manifesto* that Karl Marx and Friedrich Engels published in February 1848. It was based on a nearly all-encompassing conception of the "laws" of historical and social development that, aided by Engels, Marx had developed and forcefully expounded since the 1830s. At its core stood the premise that historical development was determined by changes in the political economy – and notably in the prevalent "modes of production" – which then had a defining impact on society and what was merely the political "superstructure" – the sphere of political order, state organisation and international relations. Marx posited not only – and famously – that, philosophically, "material life" with all its "contradictions" shaped human "consciousness". He also argued that once the political economy changed the 'superstructure' – the structure of states and the international order – in and beyond Europe would be transformed as well. And pouring scorn over all Mazzinian visions of a liberal "People's International League" and Cobden's sermons about the pacifying blessings of free trade, he came to put forward his own "scientific" vision of a new world order.

In their *Communist Manifesto* – which originally received nothing like the attention it would eventually command as a founding document of a global communist movement – Marx and Engels famously argued that the history of all previous society was the "history of class struggles".[21] Yet their focus,

---

[20] See Winkler (I/2000), p. 128.
[21] Marx and Engels, Communist Manifesto (2008), pp. 1–10.

too, was on developments in Europe and the United States. Indeed, they concentrated on what they identified as the defining struggle of the age, which was unfolding in the most advanced bourgeois-capitalist countries or more precisely *an emerging Euro-Atlantic order* in which the dominant bourgeois-capitalist classes competed – globally – over the largest share in an emerging "world market". Marx posited that what dominated the mid-nineteenth century – which he called the "epoch of the bourgeoisie" – simplified everything because what now culminated was the "great struggle" between "capital and labour", between "the bourgeois" and the rapidly growing masses of "the proletarians" within the different industrialising states. As he saw it, this development had been anticipated in the heartland of industrial capitalism, Britain, and was accelerated by the rise of the capitalist American republic.

Interestingly, anticipating some of the core problems of globalisation, though not predicting its political consequences, both Marx and Engels argued that the global spread of bourgeois capitalism and capitalist competition under the influence of "free trade" ideology was to be welcomed – because it would speed up the dialectical process that would ultimately bring the triumph of the proletarian revolution. For in their eyes, it brought together all the "economic laws" that with their "most astounding contradictions" would act upon each other "on a large scale", eventually "upon the territory of the whole earth". And this in turn was bound to provoke the "struggle" that would eventuate the "emancipation of the proletariat".[22] On the eve of the Revolutions of 1848, Marx had become convinced that this struggle would soon "come to a deci-sion". And he declared that only the "victory of the proletariat over the bourgeoisie" could emancipate all of humanity and allow it to advance towards a genuinely pacific world order. It would mark "the victory over national and industrial conflicts today which create hostility among different peoples" and "signal" the liberation of all "oppressed nations", thus also opening up the only path towards what later socialists would call genuine "self-determination". At the same time, he warned that all the bourgeois parties' invocations of a "(u)nion and brotherhood of nations" were "empty phrases", designed to cement the dominance of capitalist interests and the oppression of workers.[23]

Consequently, Marx, Engels and other revolutionary socialists came to criticise not only what they regarded as Mazzini's deceptive dreams of a union of liberal-bourgeois "democracies". They also positioned themselves against the aspirations of the liberal German revolutionaries of 1848 – while assuming

---

[22] Engels, 'The Free Trade Congress at Brussels', *Northern Star* 520, 9 October 1847; Marx and Engels, *Communist Manifesto* (2008), pp. 35–6.

[23] Marx and Engels, *Communist Manifesto* (2008), pp. 34–5; Marx speech to Fraternal Democrats, London, late 1847, Mazower (2012), p. 53.

that ultimately nothing could stop the inexorable dialectical process that would usher in a communist world order.

Yet the time for a victory of the proletariat had not yet come. In order to strengthen its ability to prevail in the epochal struggle, Marx and Engels subsequently supported the creation of the First International in September 1864. It came into existence under the name "International Workingmen's Association", which had in fact been founded by the English Labour movement pioneers William Randal Cremer and George Odger. The First International came to champion the "right of every people to dispose of itself".[24] But its core mission became the promotion of an "intertwining" of national and international working-class activism so as to ensure that "the workers of different countries" would form a "bond of brotherhood" on the day of the "new revolution", and be empowered to establish a novel transnational order on socialist premises. It should be noted that Cremer and Odger also conceived this order essentially as a Euro-Atlantic system; in their thinking too, revolutionary processes would necessarily peak in the most advanced countries first – before transforming the entire world.[25]

The spectre of a communist revolution was merely a distant threat in 1848. And it was certainly still perceived as peripheral both by the stalwarts of the old order and the protagonists of the liberal-bourgeois revolution. Instead, what resurfaced now and quickly grew into a far more pressing challenge was a different question, which arguably had even more far-reaching implications for the future of Europe, transatlantic relations and the world: *the German question*. In part, the aspirations of the German March revolutionaries, who then constituted a German National Assembly in Frankfurt's *Paulskirche*, were frustrated because of persistent differences between the most important factions that emerged. A dominant faction of more moderate liberals, like the Assembly's president Heinrich von Gagern, favoured an evolutionary process in which political power would be delegated to a new German parliament but the new German state would essentially be established as a constitutional monarchy. By contrast, a minority of more radical democrats, led by Gustav von Struve and Friedrich Hecker, agitated for a clear break with the past and hoped to turn Germany into a federal republic after the example of the United States.

Yet the deeper reason for the failure of the German revolution was that the liberals around Gagern who eventually dominated the National Assembly were politically overwhelmed by a twofold challenge: that of creating a liberal constitution *and* forming a unified nation-state at the same time. In a wider European perspective, the real crux was that it proved impossible to find not

---

[24] See Benner (2018), pp. 156–7.

[25] Collins (1965), p. 37; Marx to Engels, 11 September 1867, Marx and Engels (1987), vol. 42, p. 424.

only a convincing political structure but also appropriate geographical limits for the envisaged German nation-state. What thus emerged was a problem that would hence loom over European international politics and eventually also become a key American concern: how far would it be possible to create a German nation-state that did not upset European peace and stability and that could be integrated into a functioning international system.

The "Greater German solution" that a majority of the *Paulskirche* delegates and notably radicals like Struve favoured would not only have dissolved the Habsburg Empire but also created a power of roughly 70 million in the heart of Europe that, as critics already argued at the time, would have been unacceptable to the other European states. It would also have been incompatible with any European equilibrium, and serious attempts to realise the vision of a republican *Großdeutschland* would likely have caused a general European war.[26] All of this in fact prefigured concerns that, under very different circumstances, would resurface at the end of 1918. Yet even Gagern and liberals who came to advocate a "*kleindeutsche*" solution – a smaller German state founded as a constitutional monarchy led by Prussia and comprising all other German states except for Austria – would see their hopes frustrated. For in the end the Prussian king Frederick William IV refused to accept the crown of a "German Emperor" whose legitimacy depended on a democratic National Assembly. And even a liberal *Kleindeutschland* would have posed major challenges for the by now extremely strained Vienna system.

By contrast, the French revolution of 1848 did not end in failure. The Second Republic survived, even if it was short-lived. Yet even Louis Bonaparte's *coup d'état* of 1852 was not reactionary but established a Second Empire whose hallmarks became a specific French *mélange* of *caesarism* and liberalisation that overall served the interests of France's growing bourgeois-capitalist classes.[27] In his fervent aspiration to shake up the "old" European order and make France once again the continent's premier power, Napoleon III became a prototype of the new generation of power-political practitioners who would put their stamp on European politics in the aftermath of 1848 – and eventually undermine what was left of the Vienna system. As noted, some of the core rules, understandings and restraints of the Vienna system still proved vital for preventing an escalation of the European revolutions of 1848 into a trans-European conflagration. But under the unsettling impact of the revolutionary upheavals, the formerly strong web of the Vienna system began to fray noticeably – though it did not yet come undone entirely.

[26] Winkler (I/2000), pp. 129–30.
[27] Furet (1988), vol. II, pp. 217–398; Osterhammel (2014), pp. 543–5.

III. The Disintegration of the European Concert and the Rise of Unenlightened *Realpolitik*

Rather, it was the eventual frustration of nearly all the revolutionary movements and the resurgence of conservative rulers and oligarchies, after they had weathered out the storm, that proved decisive for the eventual dissolution of the Vienna system and, crucially, the disintegration of the European concert. For these developments not only marked the dawn of an era in which reactionary, neo-absolutist policies and *caesarism* came to prevail – and in which then, notably in France, Prussia, the states of the Northern German Confederation and later in the Habsburg Empire, the ground for a constitutional compromise between old elites and new bourgeois-capitalist classes was prepared. They also set the stage for a new age of hard-headed *Realpolitik* in the sphere of international relations – a period in which the practices, understandings and *raison de système* of the Vienna order came to be undermined and superseded, particularly in continental Europe, by a new dominant mode of hard-headed power politics. This mode was based on a narrow, even reductionist, conception of *Realpolitik* and an equally narrow conception of *raison d'état*. Both conceptions centred on a maxim that the forceful representative of conservative Prussian interests at the German Confederation's federal diet in Frankfurt, Otto von Bismarck, coined in December 1850 – namely that "the only healthy basis for a great state [was] state egoism and not romanticism".[28]

The wider origins of what came to be known as *Realpolitik* – or more precisely of an understanding of politics that was shaped not by ideal-typical or moral concepts but by supposedly "realistic" insights into fallible, imperfect human nature, the requirements of statecraft and the fundamental role of power in interactions between states – can be traced to ancient Greece. Most famously, they found expression in the maxims that Thucydides ascribed to the representatives of the Athenian Empire in a centrepiece of *The Peloponnesian War*, the "Melian Dialogue". The core maxim advanced in this dialogue, which would exert a lasting influence on the thinking and practice of international politics, is that in relations between (city-)states, as in relations between human beings, "questions of justice only arise when there is equal power to compel" and that "in terms of practicality the dominant exact what they can and the weak concede what they must". The more fundamental premise introduced here is that relations between necessarily unequal states, or human beings, were essentially *power* relations in which one sought to dominate the other – and in which "just" or mutually acceptable agreements, or peace settlements, were only conceivable if there was, in modern parlance, some kind of "balance of power" that compelled both parties to conclude them.[29]

---

[28] See Winkler (I/2000), p. 126.
[29] Thucydides (2009), Book V, 89, p. 302.

In early modern European history, broader and more profound conceptions
of what characterised "realistic" politics among states informed and under-
girded the statecraft that established the first modern European state-system,
the Westphalian system of 1648. The pivotal precept here was that after the
experiences of the Thirty Years' War, European states had an overriding
common interest in containing the danger of an uncontrollable war among
them – and that this required a common system of rules to preserve peace and
mutual guarantees to safeguard the fundamental sovereignty of the states
within it. As noted, a renewal and further development of enlightened
Realpolitik was precisely what enabled the protagonists of 1814–15 to establish
the transformative peace order of Vienna.

It was at this point that Friedrich von Gentz emerged as a key thinker who
formulated maxims of an essentially anti-utopian understanding of what could
be characterised as "higher realism" in international politics. Though Gentz did
not explicitly speak of *Realpolitik*, he developed a conception in which the
creation not of a mere balance of power but rather of a "political equilibrium"
between independent states constituted the core principle of "realistic"
European statecraft. His conception, which would influence both British and
continental thinking in the heydays of the Vienna system but then came to be
seen as antiquated, rested on a broader interpretation of *raison d'état*. It
commanded statesmen to subscribe to a *general* system of principles, rules
and guarantees for the maintenance of inter-state peace – and for the reciprocal
protection of their independence.

In his Burkean treatises on "perpetual peace" and Europe's political equilibrium, published in 1800 and 1806, Gentz advanced his ideas in a critical engagement with the "idealistic" normative conceptions that Rousseau and Kant had
proposed to advance towards "perpetual peace". Like them, he was convinced that
relations between states were not entirely in a "state of nature" or anarchy; but in
contrast to them, he argued that it was impossible to establish between "independent peoples" either a common "executive power" or "judicial power" that overrode
state sovereignty or some kind of "universal treaty system" *above* the level of
states. Crucially, Gentz argued that no international "constitution of the peoples"
could be authoritative enough to prevent the interference of a "more powerful
state" in the affairs of a "less powerful".[30] "Realistic" statecraft thus had to
recognise that relations between the more and the less powerful could only be
ordered well if the former came to accept common restraints and to place the
maintenance of a peace-preserving international system above their particular
power interests. This was what in Gentz's view lay at the heart of the Westphalian
system and what also underpinned the Vienna system's political equilibrium.[31]

[30] Gentz (1800), pp. 320–6; Gentz (1806), pp. 334–7.
[31] Gentz (1806), pp. 337–8; Gentz (1815), p. 346.

Significantly, however, the actual term *Realpolitik* was introduced on the threshold of the long twentieth century – *and defined in a much more parochial manner* – by the national-liberal German publicist August Ludwig von Rochau, who became a co-founder of the German *Nationalverein* ("National Association"). Originally, Rochau's widely noted *Basic Premises of Realpolitik* (1853) intended to establish *Realpolitik* as an evocative concept for a more "realistic" orientation of German national-liberal policy after the fiasco of 1848. But it soon turned into a global catchword for the markedly more restricted, "egoistical" and as it were power-centred conception of politics – and "reason of state" – which hence came to dominate. Rochau posited that what fundamentally ruled "the life of a state" was the "law of force", just as the "law of gravity" ruled the physical world. In his view, the question of who or what should rule a state – whether "law" or "virtue", a single individual or a people – was a matter of "philosophical speculation". "(P)ractical politics" revolved around one "simple fact" – namely that "power alone is what can rule". To "rule" thus meant to "exercise power" and only the actor who "has power" could exercise it. This, according to Rochau, was the "basic truth of all politics".[32] Though he never defined precisely what "power" meant, Rochau's notion of *Realpolitik* was to have considerable impact, first on German aspirations for a nation-state, later in Europe and the United States, and eventually in the sphere of world politics.[33]

In the world of "practical" political action, however, not a liberal but a conservative revolutionary would soon put his stamp on the definition of *Realpolitik* and infuse it with real life. In his quest to unify Germany "from above" and then to stabilise it as Europe's central power, Bismarck indeed came to pursue a quintessentially *realpolitical* approach. He became the master practitioner of a radical version of *Realpolitik* that, re-accentuating a profoundly egoistical conception of *raison d'état*, raised "power" to the level of "an idea, an end in itself, an ideology".[34] And, crucially, such doctrines did not remain confined to Germany. They spread transnationally and came to reshape international relations in this phase – first in Europe, then around the world.

In contrast to the makers of the Vienna system, not only Bismarck but also Napoleon III and others who recast European politics from the 1850s clearly focused on how they could use or *revise* the international system in order to assert what they regarded as vital national interests, rather than strengthening the rules and norms of the European concert.[35] The systemic shift their actions caused ushered in a period in which war once again came to be seen as an effective means of international politics. What followed were

---

[32] Rochau (1859), pp. 1–2, 7–8.
[33] Rochau (1859), pp. 54.
[34] Gall (1980), p. 523. For new perspectives, see Lappenküper and Urbach (2016).
[35] See Schroeder (1987).

nearly two decades of intermittent warfare in Europe between 1854 and 1870 –
from the Crimean War to the epochal wars that played such a critical part in
the unification processes of Italy and Germany. These conflicts, and the
deeper-level political changes that had provoked them, would undermine the
Vienna system in key respects. Crucially, they would destroy the Concert of
Europe as the basic mechanism of European peace and of world order – thus
setting the stage for the transformative processes that eventually made another
great war in Europe ever more likely.

The conflict that most obviously marked the *caesura* when the basic bonds
that still held together the powers of a withering European concert and Holy
Alliance were severed, was the Crimean War. It was also the last general
European war in which the United States had no part and which would end
with a peace agreement negotiated exclusively between the European powers.
Characteristically, what triggered the conflict was Napoleon III's aspiration to
break up the Holy Alliance and revise the Vienna system in order to re-establish
France as a first-tier great power on a par with Britain and Russia. In his
calculation, weakening the Tsarist Empire's authority in Europe would hasten
France's re-ascension, and this he sought to achieve by inflicting a humiliating
defeat on it in the Near East. The French emperor demanded that the Ottoman
government hand over control over the Holy Places in and around Jerusalem to
France, rightly anticipating that Nicholas I would regard this as a "revolutionary"
challenge. The Tsar indeed reacted by insisting that the Ottoman Empire
acknowledge his right to act as patron of all of its Christian subjects, and he then
ordered Russian troops to occupy the Ottoman provinces Moldavia and
Wallachia to put pressure on Constantinople. This created a conflict scenario
that soon exposed deep fissures between the European powers.

Following some attempts to settle differences through negotiations within
the concert, the Whig government in London eventually decided to underscore its determination to safeguard the integrity of the Ottoman Empire and
combined with France to dispatch naval forces, which passed through the
Dardanelles in September 1853. The main impetus for this assertive course
had been given by Palmerston, who sought to dampen Russia's imperialist
aspirations in the Near East and simply no longer believed that disputes with
the Tsarist Empire could still be addressed through concert diplomacy.
Encouraged by this Anglo-French signal of support, the Ottoman Empire
declared war on Russia in March 1854, and the wider war that subsequently
escalated between Russia and an alliance of Britain, France and Turkey turned
into a struggle not only over spheres of influence in the critical geostrategic
region that had long been under Ottoman rule, but also between two colliding
sets of world-imperialist interests – those of Britain and Russia. The war that
then centred on battles on the Crimean peninsula ended with a costly victory
of the Allied powers over the Russian Empire and a peace, the peace of Paris of
1856, which from a Russian perspective was perceived as a humiliation.

In concrete terms, supported by Napoleon III, the British government insisted on a settlement designed to bolster the integrity of the Ottoman Empire against future Russian challenges. This was to be achieved by neutralising the Black Sea, extending specific Anglo-French guarantees to the Ottoman government and even admitting it to a diluted European concert.

Yet the outcome of the Crimean War had a significance far beyond these specific terms. It had destructive consequences for the European international system as a whole. The Holy Alliance had collapsed after two of its members, Austria and Prussia, had rejected the Russian plea to observe armed neutrality. More importantly, the period in which the European concert system still basically functioned had come to an end. The Tsarist Empire would no longer act as a decisive power of "order" in continental Europe but turn its attention to revising the newly established status quo in the Near East in order to project its power, finally, through the Turkish Straits into the Mediterranean Sea. And, more significantly, British governments would hence turn away from the leadership role they had played in the concert and concentrate on the consolidation of Britain's global imperial system in what became an era of seemingly splendid aloofness from European affairs.[36]

This created the constellation in which those actors whose underlying aim was to reshape the European state-system in pursuit of their specific aims – by all necessary means, including war – could seize their opportunity. Napoleon III would continue his quest to turn France into continental Europe's predominant power. And, most consequentially, Bismarck, who became Prussian prime minister in 1862 and would shape European politics in the following decades, could push ahead with an ambitious *Realpolitik* of "blood and iron" on behalf of Prussia's conservative monarchy and effect the most significant revision of the European political map since 1815, which would have global repercussions. Significantly, it was through a series of wars – first against Denmark in 1864, then against Austria in 1866 and finally against Napoleon III's Empire in 1870 – that Bismarck was able to rally the forces of liberal nationalism behind his "patriotic cause", instigate his "revolution from above" and ultimately forge a "smaller" German imperial nation-state under Prussian leadership. He thus initiated arguably the most consequential among the state-formation processes that came to reconfigure the international order at the outset of the long twentieth century.[37]

---

[36] See Schroeder (1972); Bridge and Bullen (2004), pp. 114–34.
[37] See most recently Haardt (2020), pp. 7–278.

2

Transformation and Corrosion

The Turn Towards Power Politics and Global Imperialist Competition in the Formative Decades of the Long Twentieth Century

From the 1860s, not only the European system of states but also the global "order" came to be reconfigured and indeed transformed. In continental Europe, the creation of unified, though as yet unconsolidated Italian and German nation-states profoundly altered the international system of 1815. Yet the founding of the Italian kingdom and above all the Bismarck *Reich* was neither inherently incompatible with Europe's peace and equilibrium nor bound to engender processes and conflicts that would eventually escalate in a great war. Europe's future depended on the extent to which key actors, not just in Berlin but also in other European capitals, would be willing and in a position to (re-)create a more effective and indeed a more modern international system – essentially, an adapted European concert system – that allowed them to cope with the new pressures of European politics and competition that the changes of this dynamic period had created.[1]

At the same time, the outcome of the American Civil War, which confirmed that there would indeed be a *United* States, *one* American state – despite the profound divisions that the immensely bloody conflict had left behind – created the preconditions for its rise to the status of a world power – a power whose intervention would then ultimately decide the outcome of the Great War. Parallel, the Meiji Restoration set Japan on the path of becoming the only "non-western" member of a hence globalising club of great powers, which was confirmed by the Japanese victory over the Russian Empire in 1905.

I. A Transformed International Constellation

What thus started to emerge, at the core, was a still very unconsolidated and undeveloped system, or rather constellation, of powerful states which would come to dominate international politics in the era of high imperialism and eventually become the key belligerents in the Great War – and the Second World War. And what thus commenced in a wider context was the long

---

[1] For different interpretations see Hildebrand (1995), pp. 14–33; Bridge and Bullen (2004), pp. 146–74.

twentieth century. More precisely, it dawned when the essential conditions were created for three very powerful, dynamic and mutually reinforcing processes that would then reshape the European, Euro-Atlantic and global order and for the first time create the contours of a novel Euro-Atlantic order: first, the emergence of modern states; second, the onset of what has been called the first true modern globalisation process, driven forward by systemic dynamics in the economic, political and social spheres; and third – and closely bound up with this – a two-level process of ever more *all-embracing* competition between modernising power states. More precisely, what thus began was the era in which European power-political rivalries acquired decisive global dimensions in an immensely dynamic process of imperialist competition. Yet it should not be overlooked that two newly rising extra-European powers now also claimed a place at the top of the world hierarchy – the United States and Japan. Both not only came to engage in this competition – each in its own way – but also to seek to alter its modes and rules.

Significantly, albeit to varying degrees, all of the new-style states that consolidated since the 1860s expanded not only their economic and war-making capabilities but also the remit of their state capacities to levels not witnessed before. And all likewise extended their capacities to build or extend empires or, in the American case, to pursue mostly informal, economically driven forms of imperialism, notably in Latin America and, crucially, in Japan and China. All of the most powerful states of this period thus were or were turning into empires. This indeed also held true for an American republic that, after having created an "empire of liberty" on the north American continent through aggressive expansion and colonisation, had emerged as a first informal, then also formal imperial power both in the western hemisphere and along its new "Pacific Frontier". Whether older or newly unified, what made these states "modern" and different from their predecessors was not only that they were or rapidly became industrial states but also that they acquired immensely extended and far more centralised state machineries, more "rationally efficient" modern bureaucracies and eventually greater military forces and mobilisation capabilities than any state had possessed in the past. Not least because of its distinct geopolitical position the United States underwent a somewhat different transformation. Though some American "world politicians" began to clamour for an expansion of the US navy, it had turned into a still distinctly less militarised industrial power and a distinctly less centralised and "strong" state by 1914. But it had by then acquired a tremendous power and mobilisation *potential*.[2]

---

[2] See Osterhammel (2014), pp. 572–633, esp. pp. 629–33, the classic Kennedy (1988), pp. 191 ff, and Maier (2012).

What propelled these highly dynamic processes of state modernisation were in part economic forces and domestic-political developments – such as the impact of industrialisation and of nationalist and nation-state ideologies. Crucially, however, they were shaped and accelerated – more than in any previous historical period – by growing inter-state and inter-imperial rivalry and competition. Indeed, at the highest level of the global hierarchy, what ensued between those imperial states that were already great powers and those that struggled to join their ranks can best be described as a mutually reinforcing process of state-level modernisation and ever-increasing competition that eventually for the first time became truly global. This process then intensified significantly from the 1880s. Because of the pressures and threats they perceived on account of the ever more far-reaching international competition political leaders and state bureaucracies felt compelled to push forward measures to build stronger, more effective states that would allow them to mobilise their demographic and economic resources in order to keep up with or preferably surpass other states – which were essentially regarded as competitors. Yet the further they pushed ahead such measures, the more they in turn intensified a competitive process that came to have regional and global dimensions – and became *unlimited*.

These developments were to some extent influenced and intensified by the actions of state leaders and governments themselves; but to a marked degree they were also driven forward by others – capitalist elites and other private actors who pursued their own interests and sought to benefit from the opportunities the imperialist age created. Overall, however, what clearly became prevalent among the leading decision-makers and wider elites of these states were distinctly expanded conceptions of *raison d'état* or, put differently, expanded notions of what a state had to do to assert its sovereignty and independence, protect its interests and security, and ensure its development in an ever more competitive and insecure international environment. And from the 1880s, the central axiom became that in order to remain a great power and an *agent* in international politics all states had to become world powers and be recognised as global players.

II. A Confluence of Globalisation Processes – and the Involution of Global "Order" in the Era of Imperialism

Neither the formation of modern states nor the – overall very destabilising – transformation of the international system in this period can be understood without placing both in a wider context and recognising the more fundamental developments that changed both the inner-state and the geopolitical – as well as "geo-economic" – environment in which the powers came to operate and interact – in Europe and on a global scale. These developments came to alter the distribution of power and influence among the international system's principal actors quite dramatically.[3] Particularly important here was the unprecedented dynamism of the industrial revolution, which brought with it uneven yet overall rapid growth of national and imperial economies, and the tremendous demographic changes that this and concomitant developments in the spheres of economic and technological progress, social organisation, sanitation and medical care brought with them. This obviously had profound consequences for the modernisation of states, the capacity and pressure to become industrial military powers with modern mass armies, and the dynamics of relations both between such powers and between them and "weaker" states or objects of their imperial and colonial ambitions.

Yet if one widens the focus and re-assesses these developments and dynamics from a global bird's-eye perspective, it becomes clear that two overarching processes came to have a decisive influence. The first has often been called the first genuine globalisation but in fact can more appropriately be described as a confluence of different globalisation processes. At their core lay undoubtedly the distinctly *hierarchical* and *uneven* globalisation of the international economy – of capital flows, and trade and economic competition and exchange in an era that has rightly been called the "age of capital" and can be regarded as the real take-off phase of modern, globally expanding capitalism – and its transnational principles and practices of investment, competition and profit maximisation.[4] Even more consequential, however, was a second development that was closely bound up with economic globalisation and really gained decisive momentum from the 1880s: the globalisation of formal and informal imperialism – and the global expansion of not only financial and economic but also *power-political* rivalries between imperialist "world powers".

Overall, economic globalisation did not just create an unprecedented degree of economic – and political – interdependence between the principal powers and economies as well as between them and less advanced states and economies. It also led, on a global scale, to unprecedented degrees of commercial interpenetration and domination of stronger over weaker or less advanced economies – with corporations, investors and traders from more advanced economies, and eventually the governments of more developed powers, competing to expand not only their shares in the "world market" but also their spheres of political influence. But the effects of these processes reached far beyond the sphere of finance and economics. What they brought with them can best be described as greatly expanded – and indeed profoundly hierarchical – processes of exchange, transfer and influence-exertion that were transnational, trans-imperial and indeed transcontinental. These occurred not just in the economic but also in the political, social and cultural spheres, and they

[3] See Kennedy (1988), pp. 194–201.
[4] See Hobsbawm (1975), pp. 29–81; Hobsbawm (1987), pp. 34–83.

involved the transfer and exchange not just of capital and goods but also of people – and ideas – not least, as noted, ideas about what it took to be, or become, a competitive "modern" state. All of this occurred on global scale, and it created dynamics *and competitive pressures* that were greater than what human societies had ever experienced before.

The expanding British world system had both prefigured and propelled such trends, particularly since Britain had turned towards "free trade" following Peel's repeal of the Corn Laws in 1846. By 1900, however, only a by then increasingly challenged British financial-cum-economic hegemon maintained an overall commitment to "free trade". All other European powers had established some kind of "neo-mercantilistic" economic organisation and sought to protect key industries and agricultural interests through tariff barriers. And though successive administrations in Washington championed an American version of unrestricted trade on the premises of Hay's "Open Door" notes of 1898, the American Congress still insisted on expanding the far-reaching protectionist tariff regime it had established since the civil war. Even in Britain, the campaign Colonial Secretary Joseph Chamberlain pursued in 1903 for a protective "imperial preference" tariff system received considerable, though not yet decisive, support in the House of Commons and within the Empire.[5]

Despite such tendencies, the web of interconnections and interdependencies that was created during this period became especially dense, and multilayered, in the relations between the economies – and the financial and economic elites – of those powers that now emerged as the most dynamic, advanced and powerful. And by 1900, these clearly were a challenged but still dominant British Empire, the dynamically growing German Empire and the even more dynamically expanding United States. This was an era whose hallmarks were, at one level, both the competition for commercial spheres of influence and the eventual "competitive collaboration" between European, American and Japanese protagonists in the economic "development", and exploitation, of China. It was the era of competitive Anglo-German cooperation in the construction of the Baghdad Railway. And it was, in part, an era marked by the ever intensifying connections and exchanges between leading commercial cities like London, Hamburg and New York – the age of the City of London, which still was the hub of global finance, a rising Wall Street and Albert Ballin's prospering Hapag-Lloyd Hamburg-America Line. Yet all of this was but one segment of a much wider picture.

As is well known, what gained prominence on the eve of the First World War – not just in British or American liberal circles – was the seemingly realistic-optimistic notion that the liberal opinion-maker Norman Angell

---

[5] See Steiner and Neilson (2003), pp. 15–16; Hopkins (2018), pp. 337 ff., 373–82.

advanced in 1910. It was the notion that the interdependent interests that economic exchange and competition generated would, over time, tame and overcome older forms of antagonistic power politics and that, crucially, the fact that they had become so interdependent and derived so many benefits from this, and from economic globalisation, would make a major war between the most advanced industrial states inconceivable. Because such a war, Angell agued, was bound to destroy all mutually beneficial links that had been created – and undermine the world economy as a whole – and thus was certain to inflict more harm on all of them than any of the gains that could be expected from prevailing in a military conflict.[6] Angell's analysis was eminently rational; but he underestimated the underlying – and indeed war-prone – more profound *political* forces and dynamics that made international competition in the age of imperialism so eminently war-*prone*.

While undoubtedly creating a denser web of interconnections and interdependencies than had ever existed before, pre-1914 economic globalisation was in fact highly uneven, benefiting some far more than others. More importantly, it could not have any profoundly pacifying effect *by itself*; in many respects, it was even bound to exacerbate, rather than civilise, imperial competition and political tensions. For economic power and competition were and remained also, and essentially, a function of political – and military – rivalry. They became part and parcel both of the intensifying power-political competition in Europe and the conflicts between imperial world states and those that sought to attain such a status. Essentially, political leaders and wider elites on all sides sought to stay ahead in the global economic struggle with the aim of harnessing economic power in order to strengthen their states' power bases and military capabilities. Thus, the formative decades of the long twentieth century were a period in which world politics *also* became increasingly world economic politics – and in which a state's world power status not only but also depended on how far it succeeded in keeping up in the "struggle for the world market", more precisely the struggle for access to raw materials, resources, and export markets.[7] Hence, the prevalent assumption became that powers had to succeed in the world-economic competition in order to prevail in the ongoing world-political stand-off – and, crucially, to build up the capacities to safeguard their security interests and to be prepared for a possible war.

Crucially, pre-1914 economic globalisation, and competition, thus proceeded in lockstep with another process that came to affect the entire world and proved even more consequential in spurring peace-corroding structural changes: namely, the globalisation of both formal and informal imperialist competition. In turn, this spurred a seminal and profoundly destabilising

---

[6] Angell (1910), pp. ix–xiii, 381–2.
[7] See Osterhammel (2014), pp. 392–402; Cain and Hopkins (2001).

change in the sphere of international politics, which raised its overall stakes immensely and generated massive pressures *and* expectations. In short, most decision-makers and wider elites on all sides – and not just in Europe – came to espouse the underlying assumption that in a contest for the "survival of the fittest", which most actors came to view in social *and civilisational* Darwinist terms, the only way to survive as a *great* power was to do everything possible to do become a *world* power – a world imperial state.

In the famous inaugural lecture he gave in Freiburg in May 1895, the political economist, sociologist and liberal "realist" Max Weber pointedly captured underlying attitudes that came to prevail. Weber urged his audience to realise that even in an era when economic development "beyond national frontiers" had begun to lead to the emergence of an "all-embracing economic community of nations" under the "semblance of peace", the economic – and political – "struggle" between the different "nationalities" in fact not only continued unabated but intensified on a global scale. Using a language suffused with social Darwinist notions, he advanced two axioms: that there simply could be no real "*peace*" in the human "economic *struggle* for existence"; and that relations between states were also essentially power relations. And he impressed on his listeners that what they had to bequeath to their children was not "peace" and "human happiness" but "the *eternal struggle* to preserve and raise the quality of our national species". In this struggle, their only option was to fight for the maximal "elbow-room" in the world.[8]

While some states were far more successful than others in the new era of escalating imperialist competition, all of them thus made immense efforts to modernise and to enhance their capacities to mobilise both economic power and populations. And consequently, despite numerous efforts to mitigate them, both European and global rivalries overall became ever fiercer. Crucially, what state leaders and those who had a real influence on state policies did not manage, or managed only in very limited ways, was either to adapt older or develop new mechanisms, rules and practices that would have allowed them to cope with the dangerous dynamics and potentially very destructive consequences of this competition. In short, they did not find ways to *regulate* it, and even less to *restrain* it, in a peace-enforcing manner.

In Europe, the principal decision-makers made no serious efforts to revive and adapt the practices and rules of the Concert of Europe to this end – but rather allowed them to erode. And in a global perspective they and those who sought to direct the rising American and Japanese powers were as yet far from making any concerted efforts to establish what would have been essential: some kind of global system of rules and restraints that enabled them to preserve a more than superficial peace. And one of the most salient

---

[8] Weber inaugural lecture, May 1895, in Weber (1994), pp. 14–16.

characteristics of this era was that such a system could only have been created around a Euro-Atlantic core. As will be seen, the efforts of liberal and socialist internationalists to push for reforms in this direction, notably through the Hague Peace Conventions, never had a decisive impact on the decisive sphere of "high politics". On the contrary, the understandings and practices of *Realpolitik* as well as an ideologically charged imperialist world politics that actually came to prevail tended to intensify rather than restrain the competition process that ensued between the great powers; and they did eventually raise the spectre of a general war between them. Overall, they made the decades after 1880 one of the most notable periods of *regression* and *involution* in the history of modern international relations.

Put differently, one of the most fundamental problems of the first third of the long twentieth century was that "progress" in the sphere of international politics – and what constituted its dominant norms, rules and assumptions – clearly lagged behind the dynamic developments on the level of states and empires, in the globalising world economy and, crucially, the sphere of escalating inter-state rivalry. What evolved between the 1860s and the 1910s has often been misleadingly characterised as the global "order" of the imperialist age.[9] In fact, it not only became an ever more profoundly hierarchical system in which certain "civilised" great powers accorded themselves and each other key prerogatives vis-à-vis all others: "less civilised" empires, smaller states and of course the territories and peoples that became objects of their colonial aspirations. It also turned into an in essential respects anarchical, conflict-ridden and profoundly disorderly or rather *un-ordered* system – a "non-order" in which conditions were created, and an overall political and mental culture came to dominate, that eventually made the escalation of one of the many systemic crises into an all-out war ever more likely.

III. Mutually Reinforcing Processes. The Interconnected Modes of European and Global Imperialist Competition in the Age of *Weltpolitik*

A closer examination of the overarching systemic changes in this period reveals that in fact *two* interconnected and indeed interdependent processes came to shape and reshape international relations – and, at the same time, both domestic and transnational politics. And it was the confluence of these processes that in the end produced the precarious situation of 1914. These processes began in the 1880s but then indisputably intensified in the 1890s. As already sketched above, it was now that, essentially, two mutually reinforcing modes of hyper-competitive imperialist politics came to prevail. What dominated in Europe was indeed an increasingly immoderate game of

---

[9] For a nuanced analysis see Osterhammel (2009), pp. 682–92.

balance-of-power politics between industrialised and industrialising great powers – a contest in which the stakes of security and sheer "survival" were getting ever higher. What gained momentum in the global arena – and was markedly affected by the rivalries between the European imperial powers – was the ever more accelerating, rapacious and unlimited "game" of all-out imperialist competition.[10]

From the early 1870s and then more obviously after 1880, the relations between the European powers were indeed fundamentally recast. This shift cannot really be explained by concluding that the unification of Germany inevitably upset the earlier European "balance of power" – though the creation of the Bismarck state undoubtedly created serious problems both for the "iron chancellor" himself and for all other European actors, especially the leaders of the French Third Republic. Rather, a more general systemic transformation began – in which Bismarck played a crucial part: the earlier system of the European concert now finally came to be supplanted by a qualitatively differ- ent mode of hard-headed European power and balance-of-power politics, informed by a comparatively myopic understanding of "reason of state" and the primacy or even cult of both national and imperialist *sacro egoismo*.

Somewhat ironically, Bismarck, the statesman who left his *realpolitical* imprint on this era, managed for roughly one decade to moderate European tensions and balance out structural conflicts that his own "blood and iron" pursuit of German unification had been instrumental in creating – notably in the troubled relations between Germany and France. For in his understanding, the "*Staatsraison*" of what he called the "saturated" German power at the heart of Europe now demanded stability, conflict management and the deflection of tensions from the core to the south-east European and colonial "periphery". But even Bismarck could only temporarily restrain the forces and tendencies that were to propel polarisation in Europe and escalating world-political competition; and he left a legacy that proved unsustainable for his successors.

Essentially, the German chancellor endeavoured to ensure the Wilhelmine Empire's security by maintaining a "functioning" balance of power that also was to preserve European peace. And he did so chiefly by forging and then adapting an increasingly complex and in central respects deliberately contra- dictory system of formal alliances and secret alignments whose main purpose was to keep a revanchist French neighbour isolated and to maintain a close understanding between the three Eastern Empires. After the collapse of the League of the Three Emperors in the 1880s, Bismarck's manoeuvres culmin- ated in the creation of a complex and profoundly strained balancing system. While the German Empire entered into a firmer Dual Alliance with the Habsburg Empire, the *Reich* chancellor took pains to "maintain a thread to

---

[10] See Schroeder (I/2004), pp. 171–78.

St Petersburg" and, through the so-called Reinsurance Treaty of June 1887, secretly guaranteed the Tsarist Empire support for ambitions that collided with Austrian interests in the Balkans. Further, Bismarck had also sought to prevent a German turn to extra-European imperialist and colonial ambitions because in his view such ambitions ran counter to what he saw as the primary task: keeping Germany dominant and secure as the power holding Europe's balance of power. This was an orientation he could no longer maintain in the 1880s, when the German Empire joined the ranks of the colonial powers, and which his successors were neither willing nor able to pursue in the new era of escalating world-political competition.[11]

With a view to understanding how markedly the parameters and understandings of European international politics changed in the decades prior to 1914 it is essential to note at the outset that in the "Bismarck era" there were numerous instances when Europe's great powers found ways to settle conflicts peacefully.[12] This notably applied to those arising from the "Eastern question" which both in its Balkan and Ottoman dimensions was to remain a crucial problem of European diplomacy from the Crimean War all the way to the Great War. Here, they confronted some of the critical long-term problems that would become incendiary in the decade before 1914, above all conflicting Austrian and Russian interests in the Balkans, more assertive nationalist aspirations in this intricately multinational region, and the profound geopolitical challenges posed by the decline of the Ottoman Empire.

On a wider canvas, what collided at this point were Russian ambitions to reassert its world-power status by finally gaining guaranteed access to the Mediterranean and Britain's overriding interest to check such aspirations and protect anew the integrity of the Ottoman Empire in order to safeguard its sprawling imperial world system. It is thus all the more noteworthy that there were some attempts to resuscitate understandings and practices of the European concert, particularly to address the "Eastern question". In the wake of yet another Russo-Turkish war, such efforts reached an – ephemeral – high point at the Congress of Berlin in 1878. Here, with Bismarck casting himself in the role of Europe's "honest broker", the assembled representatives of the major European powers negotiated a new status quo and treaty regime for the Balkans, which included guarantees for Bulgaria and the other Balkan states whose borders had been confirmed or redrawn in accordance with great-power interests. Significantly, the Congress of Berlin prevented not only the escalation of a Russo-British war but also the disintegration of the union between the three "conservative" Eastern Empires – though only for a short time. And, more generally, while dissatisfying Bulgarian nationalists and

---

[11] See Canis (2004); Gall (1980), pp. 683–789.
[12] Dülffer et al. (1997).

Russian Pan-Slavists the compromises of Berlin constituted the last major European settlement before 1914 that seemed acceptable to all the interested powers.[13]

But the processes and outcomes of Berlin did not change the overall systemic dynamics. They did not mark the beginning of advances towards a renewed Concert of Europe. Rather, clashes of interest and lines of conflict such as those between Germany and France and Austria-Hungary and Russia soon deepened again and – while both Disraeli and his liberal successor Gladstone returned to policies of pronounced aloofness from European politics – inner-European polarisation processes set in that would prove very hard to reverse. What began in 1879 with the hardening of the German–Austrian Dual Alliance and the parallel straining of relations and eventual alienation rupture between Germany and the Tsarist Empire marked the first stage of this momentous development, which finally eroded the last vestiges of what was still referred to as the European concert and then, in the fundamentally altered world-political environment of the years after 1890, would lead to the formation two antagonistic systems of alliances and alignments. In a wider context, this polarisation was *also* a result of Bismarck's balance-of-power policies, whose rationales fundamentally clashed with what would have been required to rebuild a functioning concert system And, more obviously, it would be exacerbated by the abrasive pursuit of *Weltpolitik* to which Bismarck's successors felt entitled and compelled.

Yet it must not be overlooked that the deterioration of Europe's nineteenth-century international system was also a consequence of hegemonic neglect. More precisely, what contributed to the further degeneration of the concert and impeded any serious attempts to revitalise it was that those who directed the policies of what had been the Vienna system's pivotal power – Britain – had successively retreated from this essential role, first in the 1850s and even more obviously since the Gladstone government had adopted a policy of neutrality during the Franco-Prussian War. Essentially, British decision-makers no longer made a consistent commitment to maintaining overall European peace. Nor, crucially, would they ever take the lead in efforts to reinvigorate the concert and develop its rules and practices further to deal with the intertwined European and global conflicts of the new era. Instead, in the age of Disraeli, Gladstone and Salisbury British governments and wider elites became mainly concerned with the consolidation and defence of Britain's globally expanding "second" empire. At the same time, political decisions came to be strikingly dominated by financial and economic interests. Even more than before, these came to lie at the heart of what key decision-makers defined as essential "British interests" at a time when Britain reached the

---

[13] See Dülffer et al. (1997), pp. 221–48; Hildebrand (1995), pp. 34–64.

height of its predominance as the world's premier financial, industrial and trading power and the "free trade" paradigm had come to prevail. At the same time, what now prevailed was the convenient but erroneous Cobdenite maxim that the global expansion of a free trade regime would not only bring more prosperity to an ever larger number of states and peoples but also exert an ever greater civilising and pacifying influence.[14]

In this period of not so "splendid isolation", Britain long remained the only real world power and by far the strongest naval power. But while it dominated the economic and financial system and ensured a certain measure of global "order" through the preponderance of the Royal Navy, its leading decision-makers and wider elites had to a large extent withdrawn from constructive hegemonic engagement in the crucial political sphere, notably in Europe yet also on a global scale. Essentially, while it seems justified to speak of an approximation of a "Pax Britannica" as long as Britain had still acted as the key underwriter the Vienna system, after 1860 there was no longer anything that could justly be called a "British peace order" in a deeper sense, an order in which it acted as benign hegemon, fostering generally accepted rules and principles.[15]

In his epochal Midlothian campaign of 1878–80, Gladstone would use powerful liberal-moralistic language to call for a renewed European concert system that established and enforced civilised standards of international conduct. From the pulpits of the opposition he famously called for British leadership not only in preserving the "blessings of peace" and acknowledging "the equal rights of all nations" but also in the "cultivation and maintenance of the Concert of Europe", which he essentially envisaged as an instrument of liberal interventionism. In his view, a redefined concert of the great powers had to push for urgently needed reforms in the Ottoman Empire after the "Bulgarian atrocities" and promote "self-determination" in the Balkans. But after he had again become prime minister in 1880, Gladstone would never actually spend much political capital to reinvigorate the European concert. He would maintain a course of aloofness and non-engagement that, eventually, the conservative premier Salisbury would pursue as well. While it would have had more authority and leverage than any other power to do so, a British world power that thus focused on the "avoidance of needless and entangling engagements" effectively did very little to counter the rise of competitive *Realpolitik* and power-political rivalries that now escalated.[16]

What altered the entire playing-field of European politics drastically was the indeed unprecedentedly dynamic and far-reaching process of imperialist

---

[14] See Howe (2007), pp. 26–7.

[15] For different interpretations see Kennedy (1988), pp. 151–8, Osterhammel (2014), pp. 450–61; Kennedy (1980).

[16] Gladstone, 'Third Midlothian speech', 27 November 1879, in: Gladstone (1879), pp. 115 ff.

competition that accelerated from the 1880s. The period of "high" or "new imperialism" brought successive waves of European and then also American and eventually Japanese expansionism. By 1880, the European powers controlled or claimed two-thirds of the earth's land surface. During the next twenty years, following not just a "scramble for Africa" and for colonies and spheres of influence in Asia and the Pacific, the "civilised" powers placed virtually the rest of the "colonisable" world under some form of colonial rule or imperial domination. By 1900, most of humanity thus lived under some form of imperial rule. It has been argued, rightly, that the "accommodation" of extra-European and, broadly speaking, global interests often provided a kind of safety-valve – that European tensions were temporarily neutralised by transferring them to the "global sphere". But what really has to be emphasised if one widens the focus and looks at the bigger picture is what a profoundly *unsettling* and *destabilising* impact the global rivalries of this era came to have – on a global scale, and on the European situation in particular. What ensued was a different, indeed excessive "game" without any clear bounds – a game whose rules and stakes were thus distinct from those of European politics, and in which, on their own terms, the rising world powers Japan and, notably, the United States came to participate as well.

Undoubtedly, the powers and societies that came to engage in this game did so from very different starting positions, which in turn influenced the ways in which they acted. In 1895, Weber had impressed on his audience that the politically irresponsible German bourgeoisie had to face up to the "great political power questions" and realise that "the unification of Germany" was "an adolescent prank" that the "nation" committed 'in her old days' and should have refrained from *if it was to be the end-point and not the starting-point for a German world-power policy*".[17] Yet the post-Bismarckian Empire's actual pursuits of *Weltpolitik* and a "place in the sun" for the late-coming world imperial power – which were pushed forward under Chancellor Bernhard von Bülow and marred by the often erratic interference of Emperor William II – proved indeed unsettling for the increasingly strained international "order" of high imperialism.[18]

In a world that was soon all but parcelled up, German world-political ambitions and the soon dominating "strategy" of Admiral Tirpitz to build a German navy that would rival the British in order to gain critical leverage and thereby allow Germany to pursue global aims "on a par" with British world power were bound to challenge the – actually dynamically changing – global "status quo" that had emerged by the 1890s. This was not only exacerbated by

[17] Weber lecture, May 1895, in Weber (2002), p. 44.
[18] Bülow speech, *Reichstag*, 6 December 1897, *Stenographische Berichte*, IX LP, 5th Session, Vol. I (Berlin, 1898), p. 60. For new perspectives see Grimmer-Solem (2019), pp. 163–212.

the fact that German world-political aspirations were often pursued in a distinctly assertive and unilateral fashion. What also proved particularly challenging was that, because they faced growing domestic pressure to present gains reflecting Germany's new world-power status, Wilheminian decision-makers found it extremely difficult to define clearly the nature and scope of their ambitions. Nor did they think very clearly about the international repercussions of their diffuse and unlimited undertakings. All of this contributed to manoeuvring the German Empire, not into the desired position of strength in which it could afford to pursue a "policy of the free hand" but rather into a position of international isolation, of being "circled out" of the global great-power system.

But in many ways the iron-gloved standard-bearers of Wilhelmine Germany only pursued particularly assertive and maladroit strategies in the same global "great game" in which *all* the leading powers – including the United States – were engaged during this transformative period. Of the major powers, only Germany's Austro-Hungarian allies could never be serious contenders on the global stage and would turn their attention even more than before to extending their influence in the Balkans. While mainly pursuing the priority of forging a European alliance system to counter its dominant German neighbour, the Third Republic struggled to remain in the first ranks of competitive and dynamic world powers – yet still aggressively expanded its imperial sphere of influence in north Africa and south-east Asia. And the Tsarist Empire struggled to remake itself into a competitive world power whose strategic priorities now lay on extending its imperial purview in central and East Asia and on asserting its paternalist influence in the Balkans. After the humiliating defeat in the war against Japan in 1904–05 it would embark on an unprecedented agenda of economic, administrative and military reforms. By contrast, those who shaped the policies of the still dominant and by far the most extensive empire increasingly came to focus on developing more elaborate strategies of imperial defence and appeasement to protect what by then had evolved into a highly complex and far-flung world system whose vulnerability would soon be underscored by the Boer War. But by the end of the 1890s, the most pressing threats British policymakers perceived came, not from the German Empire but from French aspirations in Africa, Russia's ambitions in central Asia challenge and, above all, the looming Russian threat to the vital nexus of the British world system: the eastern Mediterranean, even more crucial since the opening of the Suez Canal.

Fundamentally, however, the overall game of imperialist world politics and the political culture it generated were the same for all the players that were involved. And all leading decision-makers, yet notably the makers of British, German and American "world policies", came to think in terms of a global balance of forces. What thus accelerated was an essentially limitless economic *and* power-political competition – not merely over shares in the world market, opportunities of economic expansion and access to vital resources but also, and increasingly, over formal political and territorial control and imperial spheres of influence. And the potentially peace-enforcing effects of growing financial-cum-economic interdependence between the great powers in this core period of globalisation were indeed clearly outweighed by the fact that world-*economic* competition became a function of a new kind of world-*political* rivalry.[19] The rivalry that ensued from the 1880s was therefore not only more greed-driven and exploitative vis-à-vis those who were colonised or dominated. It not only led to the promulgation of more far-reaching great-power prerogatives and of high imperialist claims that overrode all sovereignty and self-determination claims of states and peoples that were classified as "less civilised and advanced". It also had powerful effects both on *international* politics within Europe and in the Atlantic sphere. And it had a particularly dramatic impact on *domestic* politics on both sides of the Atlantic

IV.   The Impact of Global Competition. Changing Domestic Force-Fields and Systems of Political Order

Indeed, it is hard to understate how profoundly the new globalising competition of the era of high imperialism affected the domestic-political forcefields of all the states that had entered it, and how massive a strain it placed on their different systems of government (though this strain was greater on some than on others and provoked very different elite responses). And it is even more important to emphasise what a crucial part this competition played in setting the systemic stage and creating the crucial *mental* and *ideological* preconditions for the eventual outbreak of a major war. It has to be stressed too, however, that conversely both inner-European and global imperialist rivalries were also profoundly influenced by the fact that inner-state pressures and constraints now had a more tangible bearing on international relations and the decision-making processes of the different governments than in earlier phases of modern history, notably the "golden age" of the Vienna system.

Overall, foreshadowing core problems of the crisis era of the Great War, such pressures and constraints *intensified* these rivalries. They made it harder for decision-makers on all sides to pursue markedly different orientations, let alone to opt out of the global competition. Yet it would be misleading to conclude that this period was characterised by a "primacy of domestic polit-ics". It is more illuminating to speak of a dynamic interdependence and – as noted – of a dynamic and indeed escalatory process of mutual reinforcement. International competition prompted domestic-political responses such as attempts to improve a state's and a society's capacities to act as a world power; and these responses in turn sharpened inter-state and inter-imperial

---

[19] See Angell (1910).

competition – as long as no real progress could be made towards an effective international regime to regulate it.

In the first decades of the long twentieth century, not only the global but also the domestic environment of European and American international politics changed significantly. Even though these changes were much more far-reaching in some countries – notably Britain, France, Germany and the United States – than others – notably the Russian Empire – they created new challenges – challenges that indeed prefigured those that would have to be confronted from 1914. Essentially, foreign policy could ever less be pursued as the "aloof" statecraft of detached, often aristocratic policy- and decision-makers who in some cases were principally accountable to their monarch and generally shielded from many domestic pressures. Domestic factors and concerns thus undoubtedly had a greater impact on international relations than before, and while some fostered inter-state cooperation, most of them tended to increase competitive polarisation and thinking in nationalist and friend–enemy categories. On balance, they thus placed major constraints on political leaders, particularly limiting the room to manoeuvre of those who sought to restrain or "civilise" international power politics through cooperative agreements, concerted action or efforts to strengthen international law.

In a period of uneven but overall unmistakable democratisation and the political emancipation not only of the bourgeois but also of the working classes (except in Russia) "public opinion" and publicised opinion – especially that manifesting itself through a more powerful elite and mass press – exerted a variegated but undeniable influence here. As importantly, more organised and powerful parties emerged – from right-wing nationalist to different shades of liberal and, crucially, increasingly vocal social democratic and socialist parties – that sought not only to influence domestic politics but also the different states' international policies in accordance with their programmatic visions and the interests they represented.[20]

Finally, this also became an era in which pressure and interest groups had a newly prominent impact on state policies, especially those lobbying on behalf of a particular national or imperialist cause. In Germany, the *Kolonialverein*, founded in 1882 and later renamed the German Colonial Association, pushed for a German overseas empire while the *Flottenverein* or "Navy League", founded in 1898, campaigned for Tirpitz's naval expansion programme; and, most influentially, the Pan-German Association, established in 1891, would agitate for an expansive yet undefined "world-power" agenda. In Britain, the changing and more threatening geopolitical constellation contributed to the rise of powerful pressure-groups such as the British Navy League, set up in 1895 to campaign for an expansion of the Royal Navy and its subsequent

---

[20] See Hobsbawm (1987), pp. 84–111; Osterhammel (2014), pp. 598–601.

off-shoot, the Imperial Maritime League (1908); and the Imperial Federation League, formed in 1884, sought to strengthen the future unity of the Empire by promoting reforms whose aim was to turn it into a more coherent imperial federation; from 1895, this cause was taken up by its successor organisation, the British Empire League.

In France, pressure-groups like the *comité de l'Afrique française* (founded in 1895) and others pushed for further colonial expansion and a French version of a "*politique mondial*". They formed what became an influential elite colonial lobby whose efforts were supported and amplified by the *parti colonial* that brought together imperialists from various French parties both in the *Assemblée Nationale* and in the *Sénat*. In Russia, by contrast, the efforts of pressure-groups, imperialist politicians and publicists in the Tsarist regime mainly concentrated on the promotion of Pan-Slavic ideology, seeking to assert Russia's leading role in fostering the unity and protecting the development of the Slavic-speaking peoples – notably in the Balkans. Yet there were also those who came to agitate for modernisation and efforts to make the Russian Empire fit for world-political competition.[21]

Domestic-political considerations, publicised and public opinion, and pressure-groups also had a significant impact on US foreign policies, of course. And because of the way the American republic had been constituted and evolved, all of these factors had already affected its international conduct from much earlier on – like in Britain. Fledgling US pressure-groups with what could broadly be described as an international agenda focused on the expansion of the American navy and on the promotion of US "tutelage" imperialism, especially in the Philippines, and economic expansion. Those who sought to champion the former cause in the era of Mahan and Theodore Roosevelt would form the influential US Navy League in 1902; and soon an even more influential "Big Navy Party" with adherents from the ranks of the Democrats as well as Republicans and Progressives would emerge in the American Congress. Yet it must of course also be stressed that during the same period very determined and powerful *anti*-imperialist and *anti*-militarist or pacifist parties and pressure-groups came to the fore as well, both in Europe and in the United States. As will be seen, they too stepped up their activities – and came to establish important transnational links across the Atlantic.

More broadly, the imperial states of the era of globalising imperialist competition came to pursue a variety of "special paths" to consolidate, adapt and modernise their systems of government and political orders – or to resist modernisation. These processes were propelled by specific internal factors and were informed by different, specific pre-histories in each case; but to a significant degree they had gained momentum in response to the pressures and opportunities of globalisation and international rivalry. On the eve of the

---

[21] For an overview see Kennedy (1988), pp. 202–41; Keiger (1983), pp. 4–24; Lieven (1983).

Great War, a peculiar constellation had been created. On one side stood the comparatively liberal powers Britain and France, or more precisely: a British world power that had begun an evolutionary reform of the Westminster system of parliamentary government and to reform and rationalise its imperial world system, with some policymakers even proposing a Greater Britain, the move towards a federal super state formed by the "mother country" and the "white" Dominions; and a French Third Republic, born of the defeat of 1870 and still the only republic among the European great powers, which had endeavoured to forge effective institutions to counter German predominance and to extend rather than reform France's "liberal" empire. They had eventually aligned with a Russian Empire in which the Tsarist regime's modernisation attempts eventually gave way to even more authoritarian rule and a strong reaction against western-style political liberalism.[22]

On the other side stood a German Empire where, after the unification of 1871, a form of constitutional monarchy had taken shape in which there was a rather high degree of parliamentary representation and political parties played an increasingly significant role – notably, the Social Democrats under their leader August Bebel – but in which neither the Emperor nor the government were ultimately accountable to the *Reichstag* in crucial respects. This particularly applied to cardinal questions of foreign and military policy. Instead of developing towards an effective "modern" system of government that Weber demanded – a system in which the German bourgeoisie took responsibility – the Wilhelminian state thus remained a 'semi-authoritarian', pre-democratic *Machtstaat*, a "power state" in which an 'erratic, impulsive monarch' was allowed to exert disproportionate influence. Similar conditions prevailed in Austria-Hungary, with the added challenges posed by a complex multinational empire.[23]

By contrast, long shielded from geopolitical pressures the United States, reunified and reconstituted after the crucible of the Civil War, had only just begun after 1900 to pursue more ambitious Progressive programmes of political reform. What Theodore Roosevelt embarked upon and what Wilson then pursued on his own terms through the New Freedom agenda intended not only to modernise the American state but also to strengthen the authority of the federal government, and notably the president, at a time when the American republic emerged as an exceptional world power. But this was indeed only the beginning of a drawn-out process in which the balance of power and authority between the president and a powerful Congress were recalibrated within the American system of checks and balances – in particular with a view to international affairs. There was still a long way to go towards the

---

[22] See Bell (I/2007), pp. 92 ff.; Searle (2004); Mayeur and Rebérioux (1984).
[23] See Wehler (2007), pp. 335 ff., 445 ff., 1000 ff.; Nipperdey (1993), pp. 471 ff.

modern "imperial presidency", and the United States was still far from having a powerful central government and state in the European sense. More importantly, the American political system, and the political culture that underlay it, were as yet hardly poised to cope with the demands that a leading role in world affairs brought with it.[24]

As will be shown, the period between the 1860s and 1914 witnessed the rise of new, *per se* transnational forms of internationalism. Above all, however, decision-makers, opinion-makers and wider elites in all of the most powerful states came to use nationalism to mobilise their populations and pursue vital interests. Like imperialist doctrines and "civilising mission" ideologies, this too was intensified by the growing international competition – and sharpened it further. And those who sought to defend the interests of smaller states against great-power encroachments as well as those who tried to assert claims of colonised populations or the interests of weakened empires that had fallen under foreign domination – like the Chinese – developed their own defensive nationalist ideologies as well. Nationalisms and nationalist ideologies took different forms, from somewhat more "liberal" varieties of civic nationalism that prevailed in France or Britain to the more clearly ethnocentric and language-based nationalism that became dominant in state- and nation-building processes in Germany, in Central and Eastern Europe and notably in Russia.[25]

In France, what came to the fore following the humiliating defeat of 1871 was a defensive nationalism connected with the preoccupation to prevent decline, decadence and the dissolution of *la grande nation* – and to prevent it from falling behind in the struggle with the newly founded German nation-state and other competitors. This animated a nationalist agenda not only constructed around the aim of avenging the humiliation at the origin of the Third Republic and reclaiming Alsace-Lorraine, but devised more generally to turn France into a modern, competitive, unified nation-state that could re-assert its great power status. All of this forms part of the wider background to the anti-German *Entente* policies of the influential foreign minister Théophile Delcassé and the even more confrontational course of the most important premier and president of the pre-war period, Raymond Poincaré. Following the Dreyfus affair also, a different, anti-republican and proto-fascist version of nationalism gained ground, which was particularly propagated by Charles Maurras and the *Action Française* from 1899.[26]

---

[24] See Chapter 3.

[25] On the intellectual origins of nineteenth-century nationalism see Benner (2013), pp. 36–55; on nationalisms in the period of high imperialism see Darwin (2013), pp. 341 ff.

[26] Ernest Renan, *Qu'est-ce qu'une nation?* (Paris, 1882).

In Germany, not only right-wing but also more moderate, liberal varieties of nationalism – of the kind the *Nationalverein* championed – as well as more radical forms of democratic or even socialist nationalism had prepared the ideological ground on which Bismarck then "created" a nation-state in which Germany's national "*Lebenskraft*" ("vital power") and potential could find fulfilment. After 1871, such thinking came to underlie the ideology of a strong *Reich* that the historian Heinrich von Treitschke and others propagated and according to which the not only ethnically but also culturally and religiously defined "German nation" was now called upon to unfold its potential and assert its interests in Europe – and eventually in the world.[27]

One more general trend was unquestionably the "ethnicisation" of nationalist thinking. Racial or racist categories were accentuated, for example in the ideological notion of a struggle between "Teutonic" and "Slavic" peoples. But an even more widespread trend, which went beyond thinking in racial categories and was especially prominent on both sides of the Atlantic, was the preoccupation with hierarchies of civilisation and development. What ultimately became predominant was the notion that the perpetual struggle between different "nations" had reached a new stage, turning into an inescapable and unlimited competition between different civilisations for global prevalence in which their very survival was at stake. In turn, this generated more deeply entrenched forms of "civilisational nationalism" – which then became suffused with "civilisational Darwinism". Ideologies of civilisational nationalism and Darwinism became especially prevalent in American state- and nation-building processes. They came to revolve around the notion of a distinctive, indeed both exceptional *and* exemplary US constitution and political culture. Here, the crucial ideological conception of white Anglo-Saxon protestantism's instrumental role in the universally significant rise of the American republic was partly based on ethnic premises. But it essentially derived from ideas of civilisational achievement underpinned by a particular Christian denomination. Similar tendencies could be observed in Victorian and Edwardian Britain – and in the predominantly protestant German *Reich*.[28]

In a broader context, what began to transform international relations since 1848 and then more powerfully and on a more global scale from the 1860s has rightly been called a "dialectic of nationalization and internationalization": nation-states did not pursue their "inner potential" alone; nationalist ideologies and programmatic doctrines spread transnationally. Most consequential, however, was the overarching trend that different offensive-assertive and defensive nationalisms "reacted to one another" and tended to radicalise one another in ways that in turn heightened international antagonisms.[29] All of this had important antecedents in the era of the French revolution, when

---

[27] See Wehler (2007), pp. 1066 ff.
[28] See Hawkins (1997), pp. 61–150, 151–215; Osterhammel (2014), pp. 826 ff.
[29] Osterhammel (2014), p. 631.

French aspirations provoked the emergence of nationalist counter-programmes, notably in the German-speaking world. But it now became a global phenomenon. Unavoidably, this eventually posed particularly acute challenges for all multi-national empires. In Europe, it chiefly challenged the Austro-Hungarian Empire whose rulers would again have to deal with restive Czech, Slovak and other minority nationalities that demanded, at the very least, greater autonomy – and in the end independent states.

V.   "Survival of the Fittest World Power". Prevalent Assumptions and Ideologies

Ultimately, however, what proved more decisive for creating the precarious pre-1914 constellation than competing nationalisms or any other particular economic, domestic or cultural development was the underlying dynamism of the intensifying *political* rivalry between the imperial states in the age of global imperialism. And what mattered most was the prevailing *political culture* and the *mind-sets* and *mentalities* that this rivalry created. Indeed, it was in response to the new opportunities, pressures, and constraints this competition created that essential changes occurred at a deeper level, the level of the understandings and worldviews that shaped the different powers' approaches to international politics – and indeed the main actors' conceptions of the international system.

These deeper-level changes came to hollow out what remained of the international system of the earlier nineteenth century. In essence, what rapidly spread transnationally and came to dominate international relations, first in Europe, then on a global scale, were more radical, unmitigated and ideologically charged doctrines of reason of state, power politics and *Realpolitik*. While they were doubtless also influenced by different national traditions, and took more or less extreme forms, they came to centre on two basic assumptions: the assumption that relations between nations and imperial states were, at the core, an eternal, inexorable *and now global* power struggle; and the assumption that a state's vital interests in this struggle – relating to its security, its political and economic survival and development – had to be pursued by all possible means. In the decades after 1880, these assumptions and this kind of "ends-justify-the-means" thinking virtually came to dominate and overpower all other, alternative conceptions of international politics and a possible international order – though they never marginalised them entirely.

Max Weber indeed encapsulated the newly predominant mode of thought when he declared that beneath all appearances of peace international relations were shaped by an eternal "power struggle", which now had acquired global dimensions. In Weber's interpretation, what constituted the "ultimate and decisive interests" in this essentially irreducible fight were the political and economic "power interests" of the competing nation-states. And the "ultimate criterion" for their international conduct could only be a "reason of state" conception whose premise was that they had to do whatever served these interests in what he saw as the new, ever more all-encompassing and global "form" of the perennial human fight for survival.[30]

What Weber asserted points to one other underlying and profoundly unsettling tendency of the first half of the long twentieth century, a period in which especially the elites of the "most advanced" powers became obsessed with measuring global hierarchy, the "rise and fall" of nations and empires, and all forms of political, economic, social, cultural and scientific "progress". First in Britain, Germany and the United States, then across Europe and eventually around the world, thinking about international politics became coarsened by what has often been called social Darwinism but, as noted, should rather be described as pseudoscientific *civilisational* Darwinism. It centred on the notion that what nations and states were engaged in was essentially a struggle for the survival of the "fittest" civilisation – *and, ultimately, for the survival of the fittest imperial power.* This struggle indeed came to be conceived as an inexorable competition in which one either had to prove stronger and more adaptable than one's competitor and prevail or else fall behind, be relegated from the top tier of the international hierarchy or even go under and be dominated by those that represented a more powerful civilisation.

Echoing Weber, one of the seminal figures of this period, the conservative British premier Salisbury, exemplified this mode of thought in his famous "Dying Nations" speech, delivered in May 1898. Just after Dewey's naval victory in the Bay of Manila, which decided the Spanish-American War, Salisbury declared that one "may roughly divide the nations of the world as the living and the dying". On one side stood "great countries of enormous power growing in power every year, growing in wealth, growing in dominion, growing in the perfection of their organisation" and propelling scientific advance. Among these, which represented "the more enlightened portion of the world", he ranked highest the British Empire, Germany, and the United States, relegating France and Italy to second-tier positions. On the other side stood the weak and decaying nations, or empires, beset by "misgovernment" and corruption: the Ottoman Empire, China, Spain, and Portugal. In Salisbury's pessimistic appraisal, which reflected basic civilisational Darwinist precepts, the underlying process that was reshaping the world was one in which "weak States are becoming weaker and the strong States are becoming stronger", the "living nations" would "gradually encroach on the territory of the dying", and "the seeds and causes of conflict among civilised nations" would "speedily appear" in their fight over "the privilege" of "curing or cutting up these unfortunate patients".[31]

---

[30] Weber lecture, May 1895, in Weber (1994), pp. 16–17
[31] Salisbury speech, Albert Hall, 4 May 1898, *Times*, 5 May 1898.

Thinking of this kind rapidly spread across national and imperial borders and indeed became pervasive; it had a tremendous impact on political cultures and elite mentalities not just in Britain. Not all but a clear majority of decision-makers and wider elites came to espouse the underlying assumption that to survive as a great power required to do everything possible to persevere as a *world* power. And this indeed increasingly came to mean that one had to do everything not just to raise one's civilisational profile but also to pursue effective power politics, maximise one's war-making potential and project one's power globally. By contrast, the idea of concentrating one's energies on efforts to create a more cooperative international system and to defuse this struggle came to be seen by many as illusory or even hazardous. Such notions gained prominence not just at the level of elites but also in the publics of the more "civilised" states and those that sought to join their ranks.

The all-embracing strife that thus ensued prefigured those of the era of the world wars and the Cold War. And yet it should be noted that not all leading decision-makers in this phase came to pursue radical modes of Darwinistic *Realpolitik*. Not even the protagonists of Wilhelminian *Weltpolitik* or French or Russian imperial policies did this. And notably those who directed Britain's international policies often opted for more subtle power-political methods and liberal justifications to safeguard the increasingly threatened interests of the British global imperial system against more assertive European and non-European competitors. In the United States, strong traditions of defining maxims of US international conduct in opposition to European power politics prevented more narrowly interpreted "reason of state" doctrines from shaping American foreign policy. But, as will be seen, the doctrines that US adminis-trations actually advanced to assert national interests – Theodore Roosevelt's expanded Monroe Doctrine and the "Open Door" doctrine – were in fact no less imperialistic and "civilisational Darwinist" than those of their European competitors.

On such premises, elites in *all* states that were or aspired to become imperial world states developed "*raison d'empire*" doctrines and notions of imperial "civilising missions" to legitimise their pursuits. While German policy- and opinion-makers struggled to define a coherent mission, British and French imperialists were more successful in endowing their endeavours with a mission ideology whose core tenet was the spread of the blessings of liberal civilisation. For their part, US elites, while rejecting the language of empire and overt imperialism, developed their own version of a neo-imperial "manifest destiny" and civilisational mission as policing and tutelage power, notably in the western hemisphere and, after 1898, in the Philippines. As will be seen, doctrines of civilisational superiority would soon also underpin aspirations to establish a new code of international law *between those powers that were recognised as civilised*, which led to the Hague Conventions of 1899 and 1907. The most powerful and "advanced" states could subsequently seize on the legal standards they had codified to make even clearer, legally-grounded distinctions between themselves – and their self-accorded prerogatives – and all those who were categorised as less "civilised" or even barbaric and for whom different rules applied. Thus the hierarchical differences between those at the top and those on lower planes of the pyramid of global "order" became even more pronounced.[32]

This obviously stood in fundamental opposition to ideas and practices that would have been needed to advance towards a global system of "equal" rules and norms, which placed effective checks on ever more limitless imperialism. And while some attempts were made after 1900 to lay the groundwork for a more "rational" imperialist world system – around a novel transatlantic core – the dominating assumptions and dynamics of this period simply did not permit any real progress towards a more sustainable order that could be regarded as "legitimate" by more than a small circle of "top tier" powers.

VI. The Crucial Consequences of Globalising Imperial Competition

The dynamic competition between the great powers and those who aspired to join their club had a massive global impact that can hardly be overstated. The decades between 1860 and 1900 indeed saw the emergence, for the first time in world history, of a "hierarchy of physical, economic and cultural power" – a set of institutions, practices and beliefs that underpinned an "imperial world" of "territorial empires", of "informal empires of trade", "unequal treaties and extra-territorial privilege"; concepts of international law disregarded sovereignty unless they applied to states that met certain "standards of civilization" as defined in Europe – and the United States.[33] Indeed, those who could not keep up in the state-formation and state-building competition of this period – those who did not manage to modernise already existing states or form sufficiently strong new states – fell rapidly behind. The critical step was and remained to ascend to the first tier of the global "order" – to join the "club" of world powers – which outside the Euro-Atlantic sphere only Japan managed to do.

Not only smaller or more backward states in Europe – and Latin America – to do but also less adaptable empires like the Ottoman Empire were relegated to a lower level of the international hierarchy, subject to great-power pressures and high-handed behaviour. And while the sovereignty of smaller European states was still formally respected, the practice was often significantly curtailed by those great powers that accorded themselves the prerogative to interfere in their internal affairs. The most important "backward" empire outside the Euro-Atlantic sphere, the Chinese Empire, fell under different regimes of formal and informal, economically-driven imperialist predominance – being first

---

[32] See Chapter 4.
[33] Darwin (2008), pp. 298–9.

divided into different European and Japanese spheres of influence and eventually subject to an "Open Door" regime of "imperialist development", and exploitation, that McKinley's secretary of state John Hay had first proposed in 1899. Other older states or stateless peoples in Asia and Africa of course came to be turned into formal colonies and ruled directly by the competing world empires.

By 1900, a significant movement of – transnationally organised – socialist and progressive anti-imperialists castigated not only to the immorality and inequities of imperialism but also warned that ever-accelerating imperialist competition increasingly raised the danger of violent conflicts and, ultimately, wars of immense destructiveness. But prominent liberal and progressive imperialists in Europe and notably in the United States, assumed that some form of imperial rule and oversight would continue for a long time to come. And while some called for steps to relinquish imperial control and empower imperial subjects to govern themselves, others essentially sought to make imperialism and hierarchical imperialist "development" and processes merely more effective. Essentially, they aimed to replace confrontational competition between the different powers for territories, market shares and spheres of influence with what could be called a common regime of competitive, yet principally economic imperialism. Hay's aspiration to promote an "Open Door" scheme that was to guarantee equal access and commercial opportunities for all powers that had a stake in China can be seen as a prime example of this approach.

The common interest in enforcing their control would soon lead to the first notable instance of a joint "policing action" of the imperialist powers. In 1901 British, German, French, Russian and other European troops joined forces with Japanese troops and American marines to put down the essentially nationalist and anti-imperialist Boxer Rebellion that had threatened both the weak Qing Dynasty and their vested interests. Subsequently, common "imperialist development" projects, such as the funding and oversight of railroad construction through transnational consortiums, were brought underway, which notably involved collaboration between American and Japanese banks and financiers. In propagandistic theory, this was not only supposed to create more lucrative opportunities for all involved but also provide "trickledown" developmental benefits to those whose core sovereignty claims continued to be disregarded. Imperialist domination and exploitation undoubtedly also benefited local elites, not only in China. Overall, however, it was carried out at the expense of the populations that had become subjected to imperial "oversight" or colonial rule. And, crucially, it was pursued with a high-handed disregard for any claims such populations had to decide over their own affairs.[34]

---

[34] See Zimmermann (2002), pp. 443–8, Spence (1999), pp. 229–36, and for the wider background Darwin (2008), pp. 295–364; Osterhammel (2014), pp. 392–468.

On the eve of the Great War, most of the world had come to be divided up and was dominated by different forms of empire. And it seemed as though empires or more precisely imperial states – rather than nation-states – had become the dominant and most powerful form of state organisation and the decisive actors in the world. But the international "order" or rather "disorder" of the era of high imperialism was essentially *unsustainable* in key respects – because of the scale of the hierarchical inequities on which it was based and because of its inherent potential for limitless conflict. It is very likely that it would have corroded or collapsed even if no Great War had broken out – which then, as will be seen, clearly hastened its disintegration. In the short and medium term, many of these – including the German, the Russian and the Austro-Hungarian empires – would collapse as a result of the war, while some imperial systems – the French yet above all the British – proved remarkably resilient in coping with its unprecedented challenges.

But a longer-term analysis can underscore how relatively short-lived these excessive forms of European, American and Japanese imperialism were. And it can accentuate, too, that the very period in which imperialist exploits were most far-reaching, imperialist competition fiercest, and the degree of confidence that the leading empires would continue to rule the world was at an all-time high was also the time when the seeds for their demise were sown – which in larger historical perspective occurred relatively swiftly.

More precisely, it was the period in which the conditions were created – including the rise of anti-imperialist nationalism and socialism in the colonised world, among those who were exposed to "high imperialism" and had received an "imperial education" – that would eventually accelerate this process in the era of decolonisation after the Second World War. Then, American and Soviet Cold-War "super-empires" would emerge. But the over-arching long-term trend clearly tended towards an international system of states, even if the sovereignty and independence of smaller and less powerful states – especially but not only in the so-called third world – would continue to be challenged and often compromised by more powerful states, above all by the United States and the Soviet Union, which in their own distinctive ways would indeed behave like "new empires".[35] In the shorter and medium term, however, what mattered more was that the spiralling global competition between the imperialist powers – and all the mental and ideological changes it entailed – had very definite repercussions for the relations between the European states. Above all, it gave a decisive impetus to the polarisation processes that eventually precipitated the crisis of 1914.

[35] For the wider debate see Osterhammel (2014), pp. 392–6; Westad (2007), pp. 8–72; Münkler (2005), pp. 217–45.

3

The "Ascent" of an Exceptionalist World Power
The American Special Path and Ephemeral Aspirations
for an Atlantic Order of Empires

It was in the most intense phase of global imperialist competition – and of first attempts to make it more "rational" – that a development reached a formative stage that was to have crucial consequences for the transformation of international order in the long twentieth century. After an extended period of largely unhampered development within a highly favourable geopolitical setting, and after undergoing its own economic and industrial revolution, the United States emerged as a distinctive world power.

I. The Dynamic Ascent of an Unprepared World Power

By the 1890s, the American republic had dynamically grown into a state that had the demographic, resource, and cultural-political *potential* to become a, if not *the* leading power in the international system. But it was in many ways strikingly unprepared for such a role. It was against this background that a first generation of political actors began to advance different, still strikingly indefinite and indeed conflicting ideas and visions of how the American republic was to act as a novel world power, how it was to change its interactions with other states and societies, and what it could and should contribute to international order and peace. What ensued after the *caesura* of 1898 can be seen as a formative stage in a controversial debate and indeed a major political struggle within the United States about these salient questions, which took place at a time when in the perception of most key actors the exceptional republic was in the process of becoming not only the most dynamic but also the most advanced power in the world.

There was an elite group of assertive "world politicians" who argued that the time had come for the United States to assume its "duty as a great nation in the world" and the role of a hegemonic policing power not just in the western hemisphere but also in other parts of the world – and to bring its civilising influence to bear on European power politics as well. The key figure of this group of Americanist imperialists was Theodore Roosevelt.[1] Arguably more

[1] Roosevelt to Wolcott, 19 September 1900, Roosevelt (1951–54), II, p. 1400.

90

influential, however, were proponents of a different orientation, a more distinctive Americanist "special path" in international relations – those who like Hay, Roosevelt's influential secretary of state Elihu Root and the Republican president William Taft would seek to "Americanise" imperialist world politics while avoiding any more substantive *political* commitments in the international sphere. They sought to achieve this, and both to pacify international relations and assert vital US interests, by mainly relying on financial and economic means and expanding a supposedly peace-enforcing order of the "Open Door". Yet they also came to focus on the promotion of arbitration and, more broadly, a juridification of international relations both through specific bilateral treaties and the promotion of a novel regime of international law – among "civilised" states – that was to supersede European-style power politics.

What also grew significantly in this transition period, however, was a broader movement of mostly non-governmental "Americanist internationalists" who aspired to instigate more ambitious progressive international reforms. At its helm stood a variegated vanguard of reformist progressives, pacifists and "juridical internationalists". Partly building on domestic reform programmes whose aim was to overcome the inequities of the Gilded Age and create a more effective and democratic American state, the protagonists of this movement essentially sought to pacify the world, and notably Europe, by promoting two processes. At one level, they endeavoured to foster the spread of American-style progressive democracy. On another, leading activists like Benjamin Trueblood, Jane Addams and Nicholas Murray Butler sought to transcend militarist power politics by lobbying not just for disarmament but also for a more comprehensive *and compulsory* regime of international arbitration. Most of these activists thought that such reform measures had to be pursued through a process of transnational exchange and cooperation, notably with like-minded European reformers, in which both sides could learn from one another and bolster their respective efforts. And their activities indeed contributed to the emergence of a broader, essentially transatlantic reform movement.

Yet it has to be stressed that not only their endeavours but all the different attempts in this period to bolster some kind of new American engagement in the world confronted potent counterforces both in US politics and in publicised opinion, which in turn reflected strong currents in the wider American public. Not only traditionalists but also many progressives in the American Congress as well as in the wider force-field of US politics desired to maintain, or reassert, long-term traditions that can be subsumed under the heading of "exceptionalist isolationism". For different reasons – though generally to preserve what they believed was an exceptional American republic – they thus continued to reject any substantial moves towards international commitments and entanglements beyond the western hemisphere, especially in the United States' relations with Europe.

Significantly, it was in the wider context of these debates – and against the backdrop of the United States' growing relevance in the capitalist world economy – that, also around 1900, the contours of a novel international system for the twentieth century became apparent. What emerged, first in the minds of some policymakers, thinkers and activists, were the outlines of a no longer Eurocentric but essentially *Atlantic* world order. But very different visions came to the fore. At the highest levels of political power, general conceptions of a distinctly hierarchical Atlantic system of advanced imperial states were put forward by influential British and American decision-makers, notably Roosevelt and Salisbury's colonial secretary Joseph Chamberlain. Chamberlain came to propose an Anglo-American alliance as the pivot of a reformed imperialist order.[2] Roosevelt would go further and came to envisage an essentially informal "league" of the strongest and most civilised powers.[3] Within it, the United States and the British Empire were to act as the key "policing powers" of a reorganised hierarchical world system and take the lead in regulating the global "balance of power", managing conflicts and fostering the spread of higher standards of civilisation, government, economic organisation and international law.

But both Chamberlain's and Roosevelt's conceptions would be no more than ephemeral visions. Prior to the watershed of the Great War, the United States remained outside and in key respects aloof from the still European-dominated international system, which precisely at this stage fissured into two antagonistic blocs of alliances and alignments. Structurally, this was due to the fact there was still a crucial asymmetry, which had contributed to engendering US traditions of isolationism and unilateralism in the first place. At the core, there was a fundamental discrepancy between American and European ideas about what the preservation of national security required. This still created a vast gulf between an American republic ensconced in its "hemispheric fortress" and European states that had to interact with highly armed neighbours. On the American side it still encouraged prevalent notions of exceptionalist aloofness and aversions to wider international commitments; and it still reinforced the sense that there was no need, and it was in fact dangerous for the future of the republic, to become a "European" power, a "strong state" that engaged in European-style power politics to protect national security and its expanding global interests.

Yet what also gained first contours in this period were visions of a *progressive* "new order" or what could be described as a novel transatlantic international society in which conflicts would be settled through arbitration rather than power struggles or wars, international law replaced old-style diplomacy,

[2] Chamberlain speech, Birmingham, 13 May 1898, in Garvin (1932–69), III, pp. 301–2.
[3] See Roosevelt address "International Peace", 5 May 1910, Hagedorn (1923–26), XIII, p. 415.

and world peace was fostered, at a deeper level, through democratisation processes and concomitant social reforms within the different states. A wide array of not only American but also European activists developed ideas of this kind and sought to promote them – from US Progressives and like-minded British "new Liberal" and Labour reformers to French, German and other European liberals as well as centrist social democrats. These aspirations gained considerable momentum in the two decades before 1914. And one of the most notable achievements of the liberal-bourgeois part of the new transatlantic peace movement would be to prepare the ground for the Hague conventions of 1899 and 1907 and what became the nucleus of a – distinctly limited – regime of international arbitration.

II.   An Exceptionalist Republic and Expansionist Empire of Liberty. How the United States Became a Potential World Power within a Eurocentric World System

To understand why the United States was so ill-equipped around 1900 to become a "progressive hegemon" that played a constructive role in reforming and pacifying the long twentieth century's international order it is imperative to explore more systematically how its political leaders, wider elites and public had acted in the western hemisphere and vis-à-vis Europe and the wider world up until this point. And it is necessary to re-assess America's longer-term "ascent" as an exceptionalist-expansionist "Empire of Liberty" within a nineteenth-century international system that was actually shaped by the European powers. This also helps to illuminate why the Great War came to mark such a watershed for America's relations with Europe and the rest of the world – *and still did not (yet) lead to a substantive change of some of the most fundamental reigning assumptions that governed US international policies.*

The United States' dynamic growth and its "rise" to the status of an economic and eventually also naval and political world power was undoubtedly one of the most momentous developments in international politics during the first decades of the long twentieth century. In the aftermath of the Spanish-American War of 1898, the American imperial republic not only emerged as the self-styled hegemon and "policing power" of the western hemisphere on the premises of an amended Monroe Doctrine. It also expanded its involvement in the global "game" of imperialist competition, notably in the Pacific and East Asia. Here, the annexation of the Philippines and an increasingly assertive pursuit of the "Open Door" policy in China only constituted a new phase in a much longer history of earlier informal American imperialism in this region. This had been pursued ever since the Tyler administration had imposed the far-reaching unequal Treaty of Wanghia on the Qing Dynasty in 1844, which was even more extensive than the Nanjing Treaty that the British Empire had imposed after the First Opium War, in 1842, and that established the "port treaty" system – and on which the American treaty was modelled – and would subsequently manifest itself in Commodore Perry's forcible "opening" of Japan – to US commerce and interpenetration – that would be formalised in the no less imposed and unequal US–Japanese "peace treaty" of 1854.

Essential preconditions for the American ascent were created in two stages. First steps were taken in the era of the Monroe Doctrine, i.e. from the 1820s onwards, yet not so much by American governments that capitalised on the United States' geographic remoteness from external threats, as those who forged a stylised US self-perception would later claim, but rather – as noted – by European actors who created an exceptionally conducive international environment for the fledgling, then expansive republic: British strategists who provided the security umbrella of the British Royal Navy on the premise of common Anglo-American interests and, less well-understood, those who maintained the Vienna international system, which shielded the United States from unwanted European interference. The second stage was characterised by an increasing degree of largely unilateral American agency as an informal, then also formal imperial power and began in the 1860s, propelled by the modernisation and economic growth that followed the preservation of the "union" through the northern victory in the extremely costly American civil war. This was a crucial phase in which the United States extended both its "frontier" beyond the north American continent to the realm of economic and political influence and predominance, mainly in the western hemisphere and the Pacific, emerging as a novel kind of empire and successively expanding the remit of the Monroe Doctrine to fit its expansionist aspirations.[4]

In 1823, President James Monroe had famously asserted as the first salient "principle" of what gradually became a US foreign policy the indeed far-reaching maxim that "the American continents, by the free and independent condition which they have assumed and maintain" were "henceforth not to be considered as subjects for future colonization by any European powers". And, laying down a second basic principle of future US conduct, Monroe declared that the United States, while having always been "anxious and interested spectators" of European affairs, would never take part "in the wars of the European powers" or "in matters relating to themselves"; it would never "interfere in the internal concerns of any of its powers". This second maxim was premised on the notion that the "political system of the [European] powers" was "essentially different" from that of the American republic. These core precepts of what became known as the Monroe Doctrine had in fact been chiefly formulated by Monroe's powerful secretary of state, John Quincy Adams, who indeed was the doctrine's main architect – and a fervent champion of the expansion of an American "Empire of Liberty".

---

[4] See Del Pero (2017), pp. 77–158; Hopkins (2018), pp. 43–94, 239–86.

Like other leading figures of his time, Adams regarded the American polity as the beacon of a superior, more progressive republican order – an exceptional yet also *in the longer run* exemplary "shining republic on a hill" that as it were had a civilisational claim to extend its sovereign domain across the north American continent.[5] Thus, the Monroe Doctrine was also significant insofar as it for the first time clearly manifested US aspirations to establish and oversee an "American peace" – yet first a geographically delimited peace system in the western hemisphere – that was qualitatively different from the nineteenth century's Eurocentric international system. On the other hand, successive US administrations indeed clung to the doctrine's non-entanglement policy, notably – as we have seen – during the European revolutions of 1848–49 when US leaders and publicists encouraged the European revolutionaries to emulate the American example but offered them no support beyond high-minded declarations.

In practical terms, however, it was not only British maritime supremacy in the Atlantic that "enforced" the Monroe Doctrine's first principle and safe-guarded the further evolution of the American republic but also the pacifying influence of the Concert of Europe. As has been argued very convincingly, between the American revolution and the Great War, the United States by and large behaved like a "rent-collecting" state, a "free rider" that depended on and benefited from the willingness of British and European actors to assume responsibilities in the international system yet whose own elites did not consider it necessary or wise to make any meaningful international commitments themselves.[6] While the Monroe Doctrine was held up as a paradigm for self-government and non-entanglement, those who governed and represented the American people continued to reject any wider responsibilities in international politics and made no important contributions to the rules and practices governing international politics at a time of growing globalising competition. This was to have long-term consequences.

Further, in the realm of practical politics – when it came to dealing with "others", European states and less "advanced" peoples, and when vital political and economic interests were at stake – US conduct was far from exemplary and congruent with professed ideals. The nineteenth-century expansion of the "Empire of Liberty" across the north American continent, and the various, often brutal ways in which native peoples were pushed aside or literally all but eliminated, have rightly been interpreted as an aggressive form of imperial colonialism. Yet also in their dealings with Mexico and other states in the western hemisphere, US administrations acted in a markedly unilateral and

---

[5] President Monroe's Seventh Annual Message, 2 December 1823, in LaFeber (1965), pp. 111–14; Adams speech, 4 July 1821, ibid., pp. 44–6. On the Monroe Doctrine see the classic May (1975); Sexton (2011), pp. 49–62.

[6] See Schroeder (2012), pp. 170 ff.

bellicistic manner. This notably occurred during the war with Mexico in 1846–48 when following its annexation of Texas, the Polk administration took pains to present its subsequent actions as a "just war" waged in defence against an "invasion" of Mexican troops that had "shed American blood on American soil".[7]

With a view to the evolution of the modern international system, Lincoln's salient achievement of preserving the unity of the American republic, which was eventually secured through Grant's extremely costly unconditional victory over the Confederate side, indeed had highly significant longer-term consequences for Europe and the wider world. And these consequences in many ways only became palpable in the era of the First World War. Its significance did not so much lie in the fact that it ensured that "government of the people, by the people, for the people" would "not perish from the earth". For such a form of government would presumably also have survived in a smaller "northern union" and although the revolutionary movements of 1848–49 had been largely frustrated, republican and democratic aspirations had by no means been extinguished in Europe or other parts of the world either. What mattered more was that the northern victory allowed the painfully re-United States to transform itself into a global power as *one* distinct federal nation-state, a state that could then bring its power to bear on the long twentieth century's dynamically changing international order and eventually influence the outcomes of both of the world wars that erupted in this century decisively.[8]

Hard on the heels of the period of post-civil war "reconstruction" the second industrial revolution of the Gilded Age led the United States as an integrated economic power from marked recession to the height of world economic power within a time span of only twenty-five years between the mid-1870s and 1900.[9] By then, it had emerged as the most dynamic of the three leading economic powers, even outpacing the German Empire and surpassing the long-dominant Britain. It is worth emphasising, though, that the City of London continued to be the hub and apex of global capital flows and the world financial order while the United States – as the banking crisis of 1907 highlighted – did not yet have an internationally orientated banking system and strong financial institutions at the federal level. It was still far from having acquired the requisite capacities to act as a global financial hegemon. Major reforms that *began* to alter this state of affairs were only initiated on the eve of the First World War, when the Federal Reserve Act of 1913, chiefly designed by Paul Warburg, established a fledgling Federal Reserve System in which the Federal Reserve Bank of New York acted as the lender of last resort.

---

[7] See Sexton (2011), pp. 97–124; Kagan (2006); Cumings (2009).

[8] Lincoln, Gettysburg address, 19 November 1863, in Basler (1953–55), VII, p. 23.

[9] See LaFeber (1994), pp. 157 ff.; Brands (2010).

Significantly, by then the US Treasury had accumulated almost one-third of all available gold reserves in the world.[10]

In the political sphere, the "capitalist revolution" and turbulences of the Gilded Age, with its excesses and tendencies towards monopoly-formation in key sectors like the steel industry and the newly important oil industry, also gave rise not only to anti-trust legislation but also a second "democratic" and indeed "state" revolution in US history. Both have to be placed in a wider international context. They were pursued under the banner of progressivism and indeed gradually transformed the United States into a state that had more in common with its most advanced European counterparts. Progressive reform efforts were notably pushed forward by Roosevelt and then expanded through Woodrow Wilson's New Freedom agenda. Essentially, all of these efforts centred on measures to extend the capacity and authority of the federal government. And they indeed initiated a momentous process that then unfolded in the era of the world wars: the emergence of the modern American state. Yet it should be noted that the American republic of the progressive era was still far from becoming a robust European-style state, let alone a "military state"; and to preserve the US polity as a limited liberal state would be one of Wilson's key concerns.[11]

III. US "Progressive" Imperialism – Civilising Missions and the Significance of the "Open Door"

It was against the backdrop of these transformative economic and political developments that the interest in adopting more assertive and unequivocally imperialist policies finally gained the upper hand. Following the watershed of the war with Spain, the United States also came to pursue a *formal* version of imperialism. Yet this was to remain an interlude, it never changed the predominant US penchant for *informal* domination outside the north American continent. Albeit against vocal domestic opposition – which rallied in the Anti-Imperialist League, founded in Boston in 1898 – the McKinley administration pushed the United States into the ranks of formal imperial powers, not only in the Caribbean, where it de facto took over the former Spanish colonies Cuba and Puerto Rico, but also – through the annexation of the Philippines – in the Pacific.

McKinley and those who supported his course thus followed what Alfred Thayer Mahan, who had by then become a highly influential strategic thinker, called "the dominant note in the world politics of today" – "the extension of national authority over alien communities".[12] They asserted that it was in the national interest to keep the Philippines as a strategic base for US trade in Asia

---

[10] See Kennedy (1988), pp. 201–2, 242–6.
[11] See Brands (2010), pp. 3–120, 541–56; Link (1983).
[12] Mahan (1902). See Ninkovich (2001), pp. 200–46; Mayers (2007), pp. 190–218.

and a vital naval presence in the Pacific. Like many other "progressive" imperialists, Woodrow Wilson, then a professor at Princeton University, went to great lengths to justify US annexationist policies, marshalling hierarchical civilisational arguments on which he would also rely during and after the Great War. Wilson had initially criticised the annexation of the Philippines. But by 1903 he had revised his position. He now subscribed to the notion of a progressive American "civilising mission" – the mission of acting as a "tutelage power" that "with God's help" led the Filipino people, who had been "degraded by corrupt and selfish governors", on "the way to liberty", a path of development and progress that *at some point* was to enable them to exercise self-government.[13]

But the crucial American interests on the "Pacific frontier" clearly lay further east, in China. Thus it was here that Hay asserted what became the most influential doctrine governing American external policies in the first half of the long twentieth century: the aforementioned doctrine of the "Open Door". At the same time, Hay's first "Open Door notes", transmitted in September 1899, marked the first American attempt to recast the rules of global imperialist competition on American terms while politically retaining a "free hand". As noted, ever since the 1840s US policymakers, financiers and business leaders had pushed forward an American version of informal imperialism in east Asia – an imperialism driven by the impetus to expand mainly commercial yet also ideological and religious interests. In forcing an unequal treaty granting extensive trade and missionary privileges on the embattled Qing Dynasty in 1844 – through its informal agent, the Massachusetts businessman Caleb Cushing – the Tyler administration had followed the example of the Treaty of Nanjing that Britain had forced on China in the aftermath of the brutal First Opium War. The Americans had thus joined the British-led "port treaty system" of imperialist domination and exploitation.[14] Less than a decade later followed Commodore Perry's mission to force Japan to open up to US commerce and enter the "modern" economic order.

These concrete pursuits of economic imperialism went hand in hand with the rise of an influential conception that found its key proponent in Lincoln's future secretary of state William Seward. It was based on the premise that an expansion of American commercial-cum-political civilisation was destined have a deeply pacifying effect on the world. Aspiring to follow in the footsteps of John Quincy Adams, Seward came to propound a more expansive interpretation of the Monroe Doctrine. He outlined the vision of a future "union of the nations", by which he meant a world federation built on American-style laws and rules of commercial reciprocity that also furthered peace through an

---

[13] Wilson address, 5 November 1903, *PWW*, XV, p. 41; Wilson address, 26 December 1901, *PWW*, XII, pp. 222–3.
[14] See Spence (2012), pp. 160–3; Del Pero (2017), pp. 159–95.

increasing intermingling of different "races".[15] But Seward was hardly an internationalist; rather, he was an Americanist with an uncommonly broad and confident outlook. In his conception, which revived Alexander Hamilton's maxims of the *Federalist Papers*, America's Anglo-Saxon protestant elites would ultimately oversee the making of a novel global peace regime whose "chief fountain" was to be expanding commerce. Seward proclaimed that a "true" American empire had to draw others into its system by acting as a benign economic leviathan, whose power and attractiveness would grow the more "commerce widens the circle of national influence".[16]

Seward's maxims indeed anticipated the "new" American imperialism around 1900 in some crucial respects. But Hay and other leading US policy-makers of this period basically sought to extend America's "pacifying" pre-eminence *without* taking any decisive steps to forge a new political order, let alone a "union" of nations.[17] And the influence the United States actually came to exert in the western hemisphere, Japan and China was overall far more self-interested and destructive than benign. The concrete aim of Hay's "Open Door" policy was to prevail on the interested European great powers and Japan to agree to an imperialist regime of open access and equal opportunity in China. He thus sought to thwart the aspirations of America's competitors to divide the ailing Chinese Empire into "closed" spheres of influence, which threatened fundamental US interests. Hay feared that the European powers and Japan would use the anti-imperialist Boxer Rebellion, which escalated in the spring of 1900, as a pretext to implement their designs. In a second set of notes, issued in July 1900, he thus explicitly avowed that the United States would "safe guard for the world the principle of equal and impartial trade with all parts of the Chinese Empire" and called on the other powers to preserve its "administrative and territorial integrity".[18]

It is highly characteristic of the prevalent American attitudes in this initial phase of world-political awakening that Hay – who preferred a closer alliance with Britain but realised that this was politically impossible – had asserted his "Open Door" policy unilaterally; he never tried to negotiate common standards with the other powers (not to mention Chinese representatives). Counting on a commonality of Anglo-American interests, he eventually managed to obtain the – conditional – adherence of the other great powers. Yet the premises of the "Open Door" would soon be challenged, on one level by Russia

---

[15] Seward speech, 14 March 1853, in Baker (1853–84), IV, p. 128; Seward letter, 15 March 1844, in Baker (1854–55), p. 230. For an incisive analysis see Hendrickson (2009), pp. 285–9.

[16] Seward speech, Senate, 21 January 1851, in Baker (1854–55), pp. 276–7; Seward speech, 15 March 1844, in Baker (1853–84), III, 498–9.

[17] Seward speech, 3 December 1856, Seward Papers. See Sexton (2011), pp. 128–31.

[18] See Hay to White, "Open Door Note", 6 September 1899, *FRUS 1899*, pp. 129–30.

and Japan, on another by inner-Chinese resistance. In the summer of 1900, the McKinley administration then underscored its determination to have a dominant voice in the future of China by dispatching 2,500 US marines and for the first time participating in a multi-imperial "police force", which then crushed the Boxer uprising and for the time being re-established the "order" of the "Open Door" and imperialist prerogatives.

In the following two decades, successive US administrations – Republican, Progressive and Democrat – and those who represented the interests of American high finance and big corporations – whole-heartedly espoused the "Open Door" doctrine. And in different ways they all propagated its universally beneficial and pacifying effects. Echoing Seward, its most ardent champions even argued that it had the potential to supersede "archaic" European-style imperialism and militaristic power politics with a more rational international regime – a regime that fostered unhampered trade and economic development and, more broadly, the spread of dynamic US-style "liberal" capitalism.[19] The aim to internationalise "Open Door" precepts hence became integral to all future aspirations to globalise an "American peace". The global extension of an "open" commercial regime was supposed to serve not only US interests but also the cause of universal peace because it allegedly fostered universal prosperity and intertwined economic interests in mutually beneficial ways. In practice, however, measures to push for liberalising international trade and access to older and emerging markets mainly benefited the power that was poised to dominate the global economy. The American champions of the "Open Door" thus followed in the footsteps of those who had earlier initiated Britain's turn to "free trade" when it occupied the dominant position in the nineteenth century's world economic system. But in contrast to Britain the United States remained a protectionist power at the same time, with successive Congressional majorities voting in favour of high tariffs to shield domestic industries. Here, too, it thus pursued classic "wanting the best of all worlds" policies. And all administrations that sought to limit such marked double standards confronted powerful Congressional opposition. In 1913, Wilson finally prevailed on Congress to enact the first downward revision of the US tariff since the 1860s. But this remained an exception to the general trend, which would continue after the Great War.

Yet this was not the only rationale for a new American role and mission as a distinctive world power to which an increasing number of decision- and opinion-makers aspired. They came to advance competing ideas and visions for what as yet remained an inchoate and general world-political agenda. These not only included calls for a distinctive progressive "civilising mission" in and beyond the western hemisphere, whose purpose was to foster

---

[19] See Eckes and Zeiler (2003), pp. 9–37, and the classic Williams (II/1972).

self-government and economic modernisation, but also the conception that the American republic was to act as a "policing power" not only in the western hemisphere but also globally. This latter aspiration was emphasised by an influential minority of politicians and strategists – which included Mahan and Wilson's future key antagonist Henry Cabot Lodge – who campaigned for a "large policy": a more ambitious, globally-orientated and distinctly imperialist foreign policy. Yet it was McKinley's successor Roosevelt who became the most powerful advocate of an American version of *Weltpolitik*.[20]

IV.   To Fight for a "Righteous Peace". Theodore Roosevelt and the Aspiration to Make the United States into a Hegemonic Policing Power

An Americanist to the core, Roosevelt not only aspired to prepare the United States for the role of a progressive hegemon in the global order. In the longer run, he indeed sought to recast world politics. Acting on the assumption that its trajectory of civilisational achievement placed the United States at the top of the global hierarchy, he sought to prepare the American state and society for the assumption of world-political responsibilities both by pursuing progressive domestic reforms and by developing a new global vision of America's mission. He argued that Americans to learn not only how to deal with the European rules of power politics but also how to modernise and improve them. And he sought to redefine the responsibilities – and prerogatives – of the strong and most advanced powers both in the maintenance of "global order" and in relations with "weaker" and less advanced states, peoples and "races". Yet he would pursue a more ambitious and indeed "revolutionary" push for global leadership than US political culture, and the American public, could accommodate at this stage.

Roosevelt's first foreign-policy priority as president was to assert the United States' – imperial – hegemony as the unchallenged policing power in the western hemisphere. When in 1902 the dispute between Venezuela and its international creditors raised the concern that a military intervention of the interested European powers, notably Germany, in the heavily indebted country could set a dangerous precedent he acted decisively to expand US prerogatives. In what quickly became known as the "corollary" to the original Monroe Doctrine, which he put forward in his annual message to Congress in December 1904, Roosevelt declared that, as a "civilized nation", the United States would claim the exclusive "right" to intervene in the internal affairs of other states in the western hemisphere if there was – in the judgement of American decision-makers – a need to take action in "flagrant cases" of "chronic wrong-doing or impotence" of governmental authority. Roosevelt

[20] See Nichols (2011), pp. 22–67; Zimmerman (2002).

justified America's new prerogatives as "the exercise of an international police power" on behalf of all "civilised" nations.[21]

Essentially, however, this power would be used to ensure that weak debtor states would fulfil their obligations. Under Roosevelt, the United States indeed came to act as the pre-eminent "police power" in "its" hemisphere, keeping the interference of European powers at bay while in practice using its predominance to enforce its financial and strategic interests. In 1905, marking the beginning of numerous US "policing" actions, he invoked the "corollary" to legitimise intervention in the Dominican Republic, using force and seizing control of its customs and tax revenues to compel the bankrupt government to settle its debts. Once the Roosevelt administration had ensured that the Panama Canal would be built under US control, which then was accomplished between 1904 and 1914, it would also police this hence strategically vital link between the Atlantic and the Pacific.

Of more long-term consequence was Roosevelt's wider aspiration to learn from *and go beyond* the policies of the European powers and lead the United States towards its rightful place in the global system. In the wake of the Spanish-American War, he asserted that if they wished to "retain their self-respect", and the respect of the world, the American people could no longer "refrain from doing their duty as a great nation in the world".[22] Fundamentally, like those who supported his course – among them Mahan and Cabot Lodge – Roosevelt essentially came to view international politics as dominated by a club of great powers and the struggle to preserve a global "balance of power". And he came to envisage America's role as that of the most progressive power that fulfilled the duty of policing the world to this end and spreading the blessings of a more civilised order. By 1910, Roosevelt noted that, owing to its "strength and geographical situation" the American republic had to face up to the responsibility of maintaining "more and more the balance of power of the whole world".[23] In his judgement, it had to do so for the sake of safeguarding US security and economic interests yet also, more broadly, to safeguard the advance of civilisation. What thus had to be ensured was that the most advanced powers – above all the United States and Britain – would oversee the hierarchical global system and confront any powers or forces that threatened to destabilise it.

As Roosevelt saw it, America's new world-political "duty" also made it imperative to prepare the American state, and its people, to fight "righteous"

---

[21] Theodore Roosevelt, "Fourth Annual Message to Congress", 6 December 1904, in Roosevelt (1925), p. 299.

[22] Roosevelt to Wolcott, 19 September 1900, in Morison et al. (1951–54), II, p. 1400.

[23] See Beale (1956), p. 447.

wars for the cause of a "peace of justice".[24] On a deeper level, he was convinced that a just peace could only be secured by being prepared to prevail over any "tyrannous" regimes whose actions embodied "evil" and "barbarism". In an article on "Expansion and Peace", published in 1899, in which he lambasted the European powers for failing to stop the recent Ottoman massacre of Armenians, Roosevelt emphasised that peace was "a great good" but could not be achieved by what the growing pacifist movement advocated, which he characterised as the "selfish and cowardly shrinking from warring against the existence of evil". He never ceased to believe that "(e)very expansion of civilization makes for peace" as "every expansion of a great civilized power means a victory for law, order, and righteousness".[25]

Roosevelt thus also considered it crucial to understand European-style balance-of-power politics and to enlighten the American public, and Congress, about the need to become a credible great power on the world stage. In his view, this required strengthening not only the US federal government but also and notably America's military power.[26] Influenced by Mahan's theses about the decisive influence of sea power on world-historical development, Roosevelt had long campaigned for an expansion of US naval power, arguing that in the interest of national security and to become a respected global power the American republic had to acquire a large modern battle fleet. And with the support of a growing Big Navy Party in Congress his administration would indeed embark on the first stage of a momentous naval expansion programme. In 1880, the US fleet was still smaller than that of France and far behind the dominant British Navy; by 1913 it was among the top three naval powers and poised to become the world's new naval hegemon.[27]

As president, Roosevelt then also took actual steps to demonstrate his determination to assume world-political responsibilities. He not only offered his services as broker of the peace agreement following the Russo-Japanese war, which was concluded in Portsmouth in 1905. Soon thereafter, he also broke with the Monroe Doctrine maxim of non-interference in European affairs when agreeing to mediate in a conflict that had escalated because of a Franco-German dispute over spheres of influence in Morocco. Seeking to "keep matters on an even keel in Europe", the American president would indeed contribute to preparing the ground for the Algeciras conference of 1906, which *temporarily* lessened tensions between France and Germany.

---

[24] Theodore Roosevelt, "Fourth Annual Message to Congress", 6 December 1904, in Roosevelt (1925), pp. 298–9.

[25] Theodore Roosevelt, "Expansion and Peace", in Hagedorn (1923–26), XIII, pp. 332–40, 334–5, 338–40, 333; Harbaugh (1961), p. 513, Laderman (2019), pp. 48 ff.

[26] Roosevelt address, Oxford, 7 June 1910, in Hagedorn (1923), p. 231; Widenor (1980), pp. 222–3.

[27] Mahan (1897), p. 27; Mahan (1902), p. 34. See Kennedy (1988), pp. 202–3.

While Roosevelt did not see the danger of an all-out war, he was keen prevent a further deterioration of relations between increasingly antagonistic blocs within the European system. And he was especially concerned about what he saw as the Wilhelmine Empire's assertive challenges to the European *and* global "balance of power".[28] But the – limited – intervention to resolve the Morocco crisis remained an isolated instance of Rooseveltian activism. More generally, his bid to play a leading part in world politics and to bring America's civilising influence to bear on the European situation remained an interlude. Roosevelt and like-minded US world-politicians had not yet initiated a qualitative shift in US foreign policy.

And yet Roosevelt's ambitions reached even further. He continued to argue that the United States should lead efforts to reform the global order of the imperialist age and to "civilise" the practices and rules of international politics. And it was with these aims in mind that he came to propose, also in 1905, the creation of an exclusive "league" of the most powerful and "civilised" states – essentially the United States and the European great powers (and potentially Japan) – whose core mission would be to stabilise and "police" the international order.[29] Roosevelt's scheme was the most ambitious among the conceptions for a new – essentially Atlantic – great-power system that were developed in the years before 1914. Intent on protecting US sovereignty and core prerogatives under the expanded Monroe Doctrine, he did not envisage an elaborate international institution that would have curtailed the great powers' room to manoeuvre. Rather, his ambition was to create a mechanism through which the leading states could settle conflicts peacefully and form an "international police force" that was supposed to maintain and enforce international order – also by intervening in the affairs of less "civilised" states if this was deemed necessary to safeguard peace and civilisation.[30] Theodore Roosevelt thus put forward a markedly imperialist vision of an international league, which he would advocate again during the Great War – and which only in some respects prefigured Franklin Roosevelt's hegemonic rather than imperial conception of a new global order overseen by "Four Policemen".

V.   Towards an Anglo-American World Order – and an Atlantic League of Empires? British and American Visions

In a wider context, the years around 1900 were a time when not only Roosevelt's but also other, mainly British and American conceptions of a

---

[28] See Roosevelt to Whitelaw Reid, 28 April 1906, in Bishop (1920), I, pp. 468–75; Holmes (2006), pp. 191–201.

[29] Steiner and Neilson (2003), p. 42.

[30] Ibid.; Roosevelt address, 5 May 1910, in Hagedorn (1923–26), p. 415; Widenor (1980), pp. 222–3.

new Atlantic order of imperialist powers came to the fore. What originally had given rise to such visions was the significant Anglo-American rapprochement that, following decades of intermittent tensions since the US civil war, took place in the aftermath of two watershed conflicts – the Spanish-American War and the Boer War. Accordingly, the underlying assumption was that the new order had to emerge around the pivot of a new partnership between the Anglo-American powers.

On the British side, some leading decision-makers had begun to develop a new, transatlantic strategy to protect Britain's global interests ever since 1898 – when, in their perception, the United States had entered world politics while at the same time the far-flung British world system seemed increasingly threatened by its Russian, French and German competitors. The Boer War, which exposed discomforting vulnerabilities, propelled this reorientation further. British "Atlanticists" deemed it advisable to foster not just a *rapprochement* but a kind of informal Anglo-American partnership at the apex of a changing imperialist world order. They were aware of the limits that the traditions of US foreign policy placed on anything approaching a more fully-fledged Anglo-American alliance. But they saw prospects for establishing a cooperative relationship based on compatible interests yet also an underlying civilisational kinship. In their assessment, forging a closer understanding with the United States could thus aid Britain significantly in managing the international system and in protecting the interests of a more vulnerable British imperial system. Notably the future liberal foreign secretary Edward Grey favoured the idea of cultivating an Anglo-Saxon partnership whose deeper roots were "ties of language, origin and race".[31]

Yet the most influential proponent of a new transatlantic orientation was Salisbury's ambitious colonial secretary Joseph Chamberlain, who during the Spanish-American War had come forward as champion of a de facto alliance with the United States. Salisbury himself clung to a more traditional policy. On the one hand, he highlighted Britain's ability to defend its empire self-reliantly and to "maintain against all comers that which we possess". On the other, he was the only leading statesman who at this stage still argued that the only way to save Europe from a disastrous war was to reinvigorate the "Concert ... of Europe" and to put it on a firmer institutional footing as a "federation ... of Europe".[32] Having long nourished a profound disdain for American political culture and capitalist greed, Salisbury thus favoured a renewal of Britain's long-neglected European commitments and clearly rejected a strategic

---

[31] Salisbury speech, Albert Hall, 4 May 1898, *TheTimes*, 5 May 1898. See Roberts (1999), pp. 46–9, 691–2.

[32] Salisbury speech, House of Lords, 19 March 1897, Hansard, House of Lords, 4th series, vol. 47, cls, 1011–14.

compact with the rising American "strong State".[33] By contrast, Chamberlain rejoiced in Commodore Dewey's epochal naval victory in Manila Bay in May 1898 and congratulated the McKinley administration for America's arrival on the world stage. Like other British liberals, he regarded the United States as the most congenial potential partner for Britain, not just in upholding the "Open Door" and preventing the dismemberment of China but also in forging and stabilising something akin to a new "liberal imperial world order".

In May 1898, Chamberlain thus declared that Britain had both a duty and an interest to "establish and maintain bonds of amity with our kinsmen across the Atlantic" and to cultivate common interests, including that in "the cause of humanity and the peaceful development of the world". He argued that "the closer, the more cordial, the fuller and the more definite, these arrangements" would be "with the consent of both people" the better it would be "for both and for the world". Chamberlain thus anticipated Kipling's exhortation that the Americans should join the British in taking up the "white man's burden". The colonial secretary stressed that what he desired initially was merely a "cordial and intimate connection" between the two powers. For he was aware that even such a "connection" would require a departure from long-standing US diplomatic traditions and major efforts to gain the requisite Congressional and popular approval. Yet what he envisaged in the longer term was something far more ambitious, namely that "the Stars and Strips and the Union Jack should wave together over an Anglo-Saxon alliance".[34]

In the autumn of 1899, Chamberlain then put forward an even more ambitious – and unrealistic – scheme, arguing that if "the union between England and America" was "a powerful factor in the cause of peace" then "a new Triple Alliance between the Teutonic race and the two great branches of the Anglo-Saxon race will be a still more potent influence in the future of the world".[35] With a view to their more ambitious aims, Chamberlain's schemes remained essentially stillborn. Grey was not the only British politician who at this stage not only opposed any kind of alliance with Wilhelmine Germany but also stressed that while an Anglo-American partnership with the United States was eminently desirable alliance, proposals were neither realistic nor conducive to forging cordial ties with the United States. And in Washington there was neither the necessary political will nor the requisite room to manoeuvre to contemplate a "diplomatic revolution" of this kind. But influential policymakers on both sides would espouse Chamberlain's general idea of an *informal* Anglo-American cooperation and joint stewardship in the management of world affairs.

---

[33] Salisbury speech, Albert Hall, 4 May 1898, *TheTimes*, 5 May 1898. See Roberts (1999), pp. 46–9, 691–2.

[34] Chamberlain speech, Birmingham, 13 May 1898, in Garvin (1932–69), III, pp. 301–2. See Perkins (1968), pp. 58–61.

[35] Chamberlain speech, Leicester, November 1899, in Gelber (1938), p. 70.

By this time, wider aspirations for a new Anglo-American alignment had indeed found prominent proponents. Particularly English liberals had long sought to draw on the American example to reform Britain and to transform the Empire into a stronger, American-style federation. Eventually, some would even call for a novel Anglo-American commonwealth bringing together the "Anglo-Saxon" peoples as the world's most advanced civilisations. Since the 1860s, John Stuart Mill had exerted a formative influence on British liberal thought in this respect. On the eve of the American civil war, Mill had argued that the United States represented a "more perfect mode of federation" in which above all common "political institutions" buttressed "a feeling of identity of political interest". Mill had pointed to this example as worth studying to advance efforts to extend representative government in Britain. And he had also contemplated the possibility of turning the British Empire and the European state-system into a federation or confederation.[36] Subsequently, the American republic served as a template for liberal reformers and proponents of a new federal imperial order in Victorian Britain. An influential advocate of such reformist visions, the Regius Professor of Modern History at Cambridge, J.R. Seeley, argued that the United States could indeed serve as the prototype for how Britain and its dependencies should be reconfigured into a Greater British federation. And he even posited that in view of the technological and civilisational advances since the eighteenth century, what Burke had deemed impossible, namely the creation of an Anglo-American federation across the Atlantic, might be within reach.

Seeley advanced his theses amidst a rising groundswell of "Americomania" in the 1880s and 1890s, decades in which the "rise" of the United States too was debated in terms of civilisational Darwinism – and Darwin himself agreed with Gladstone that his theory of evolution was borne out by America's ascent and the parallel decline of eastern civilisations.[37] In 1902, the influential editor of the *Pall Mall Gazette*, William Stead, made the case for a union of the English-speaking peoples on essentially American premises. Prophesying that the "Americanization of the World" would be the dominant "Trend of the Twentieth Century", Stead warned that Britain would only be able to retain its "place as the first of world-Powers" if it took steps to "throw in [its] lot with the Americans" and succeeded in "merging the British Empire in the English-speaking United States of the World".[38] Neither Seeley's nor Stead's "grand visions" would ever inspire concrete policies. But they resonated not only among liberals and illuminated some of the most forward-looking British thinking at this juncture.

---

[36] See Mill, 'Considerations on Representative Government', in Mill (1991), pp. 435–46.
[37] See Dicey, "Americomania in English Politics", *The Nation*, 21 January 1886, p. xlii; Desmond and Moore (1992), p. 626; Bell (I/2007), pp. 231–59; Searle (2004), pp. 26–9.
[38] Stead (1902), p. 1, 13.

By contrast, American liberals and progressives of this era, who were indeed influenced by English and Scottish liberal thought, focused mainly on national priorities, namely progressive reforms that "perfected" US democracy. Yet they too argued that European states and societies could benefit from "Americanisation", by which they mainly meant the spread of American-style democracy and political culture. The leading progressive thinker Herbert Croly, who in 1914 would be one of the co-founders of the influential *New Republic*, not only sought to promote the "realization" of the American "ideal" of genuine "democracy" but also to encourage those European "political forces" that struggled for democratic reforms and "international peace". But like other American progressives he remained an exceptionalist, maintaining that the United States was the only nation in which "complete democracy" could be built whereas, because of their different historical trajectories, a meaningful democratisation of European states – and other parts of the world – would take a long time.[39] The vanguard of Progressive thinkers in the United States cultivated connections with like-minded British and other European reformers. Yet ambitious ideas of an Anglo-American or wider transatlantic "federation" were not on their agenda. Nor, of course, were they on the agenda of American governments.

But here, at the level of official policymaking, it was the much less aspirational notion of a closer Anglo-American collaboration, also in the management of global affairs, that indeed found some powerful proponents, particularly among the small but increasingly influential group of American "world politicians", strategists and financiers who sought to alter the course of US foreign policy around 1900. Yet they would envisage such collaboration on American, i.e. distinctly unofficial, terms not as a preliminary step on the path towards a fully-fledged Anglo-American alliance. Nonetheless, what they advocated constituted a significant reorientation. In 1895, the Cleveland administration had still quarrelled with Britain over the Venezuelan boundary dispute, invoking the Monroe Doctrine in order to urge a defiant Salisbury to accept arbitration to settle the dispute over the demarcation of the border between Venezuela and British Guiana; and it had interpreted Salisbury's defiant refusal as a direct challenge to the Monroe Doctrine, even threatening to go to war to enforce it. From 1898, McKinley and his Anglophile secretary of state Hay had come to base US international policies on different assumptions. Like their British counterparts, they affirmed the premise that a war between the two English-speaking powers would and should be unthinkable.

What thus came to prevail – and was echoed but also contested in the wider US political spectrum – amounted to a general understanding that both states were broadly united by common civilisational, cultural, religious and

---

[39] Croly (1909), pp. 1–2, 297–8. See also Croly (1914).

socio-ethnic ties; that they had common or at least compatible interests in the world, notably in the realm of commerce, less in the realm of security; and that they were also bound by a common purpose as the world's most civilised powers. When he was still ambassador in London, Hay had formulated the underlying "Anglo-Americanist" creed by declaring that the two nations were "bound by a tie which we did not forge and which we cannot break" – that they were essentially "joint ministers of the same sacred mission of liberty and progress".[40]

This new Anglo-American orientation also came to be adopted not only by Roosevelt but also by those Republican politicians and strategists who aspired to pursue a "large policy". While most of them had earlier viewed British imperial policies with suspicion, they now favoured a relatively close cooperation with Britain, which they too came to regard as the most congenial partner America could have in international affairs. They thus also sought an informal Anglo-American partnership – while deeming any steps towards a more formalised compact both unnecessary and impossible to legitimise domestically. As Mahan put it in 1902, they concluded that the British Empire was "in external matters" the United States' "natural though not [its] formal ally".[41] Most significantly, Roosevelt, who had earlier talked about annexing Canada, changed his attitude after 1898 and came to emphasise that "the English-speaking peoples" were now "closer together" than ever since 1776 and "that every effort should be made to keep them close together".[42] And subsequently he came to view a fundamental Anglo-American concord as integral to his vision to establish a transatlantic league of "civilised" powers to ensure "the proper policing of the world".[43]

Yet neither the first aspirations for a new Anglo-American concord nor Roosevelt's call for a "league" of policing powers would lead to actual advances towards a reconfigured Atlantic regime before 1914. Nor would they initiate, more broadly, a stabilising reform of the imperialist order that may have prevented the escalation of the Great War. Notably Roosevelt's ideas found no substantive resonance on either side of the Atlantic. In a wider context, the necessary preconditions for a major systemic change of this kind simply did not exist (yet). The asymmetry in terms of security and *perceptions* security and vital interests between the United States on the one hand and Britain and the continental European powers on the other was still too pronounced. Most of the key European decision-makers, who by then were in engaged in an ever more existential high-stakes competition, clearly held that they could only safeguard the security and vital interests of the states they represented through

---

[40] Cited after Campbell (1957), p. 125. See Perkins (1968); Burk (2009), pp. 411–36.
[41] Mahan (1902), p. 34; Zimmermann (2002), pp. 450–1.
[42] Morison (1951–54), II, p. 890.
[43] Roosevelt address, Oxford, 7 June 1910, in Hagedorn (1923), p. 231.

military preparedness and more specific power-political alliances – rather than through some kind of general league. By contrast, Roosevelt's successors in the White House and a majority of American policymakers perceived no threats to national security and saw no vital interests that would have warranted a departure from non-entanglement traditions and the assumption of global commitments within a league; and they reckoned that there was no prospect of legitimising such a departure in the US Congress and in the court of American public opinion. And, significantly, when he entered the White House in 1913 the Democrat Woodrow Wilson clearly focused on domestic reform priorities and distanced himself clearly both from ambitious global policing conceptions and the notion of some kind of special Anglo-American compact.

In core respects, then, in terms of what really had a decisive bearing on global questions of war and peace, the United States was not yet world power in the decades before 1914. It had made no tangible international commit-ments, particularly in the realm of security; it did not engage in diplomacy, international crisis management and conflict resolution in any consistent way. In this sense, it remained on the margins and essentially outside what still remained an essentially Eurocentric system of great powers. Nor was there yet anything approaching a coherent American "world policy" or anything resem-bling a new consensus – among key decision-makers, the executive and Congress, or in the wider American public – about what kind of international role the American republic should play.[44] At the same time, and crucially, what still prevailed among leading US decision- and opinion-makers can be described as a "wanting- the-best-of-all-worlds" mentality. This mentality was informed by a marked and indeed growing confidence that in view of the United States' dynamically expanding economic-cum-political power it would be possible to exert a dominant influence and assert vital commercial and political interests in Europe and the wider world without having to assume actual international responsibilities. And avoiding entanglements in the dan-gerous web of European international rivalries was and remained a critical concern.

But there was one area in which influential policymakers like the Republican secretary of state Root did come to play a leading role in the international arena, and successive American administrations were actually prepared to enter into some, albeit carefully *circumscribed*, commitments. In short, they came to focus on the promotion of international arbitration and, more broadly, a "juridification" of international relations and the expansion of international law. In concrete terms, they prioritised the conclusion of bilateral arbitration treaties – first with Britain and France. And they supported efforts of Trueblood and other non-governmental activists to create an effective

---

[44] Wilson press conference, 28 April 1913, *PWW*, XVII, p. 300.

international arbitration regime. Reflecting the outlook of those who championed this cause, Root argued that clearly defined rules and procedures of arbitration could exert a significant pacifying influence by allowing a rational and "lawful" settlement of international disputes. Yet like other key figures, he insisted that in order to be effective arbitration initially had to be limited to questions amenable to a judicial settlement, i.e. it had to exclude those involving the vital political, security and sovereignty interests of states. In the longer run, however, Root indeed envisaged nothing less than a systemic transformation: a superseding of "old-style" international politics – or as he put it the "substitution of judicial action for diplomatic action" – to create a more lasting "universal peace".[45]

[45] Root address, 15 April 1907, in Bacon and Scott (1916), pp. 128–35, 142, 144.

4

Counterforces – and First Visions of a Novel Transatlantic Peace

Internationalist Aspirations to Overcome Imperialist Power Politics before the Great War

To contain imperialist power politics and pacify international relations through advances in the sphere of international law – and above all arbitration – had by this time also become one of the essential aims of a newly relevant transnational peace movement that had grown rapidly on both sides of the Atlantic since the 1880s. Indeed, the era of globalising power politics and war-prone militarism thus also produced a vigorous countervailing force. This diverse movement, which included pacifists, anti-militarists, progressive reformers and juridical Sinternationalists, contributed significantly to the development of a new "political internationalism" in and beyond the transatlantic sphere – and yet never had a decisive impact on the international politics of this period.

I.   The Emergence of European and American Counterforces

More precisely, what grew was a multiplicity of networks that were formed that linked official but also, and particularly, non-governmental actors from Europe and the United States. Thus a heterogeneous but essentially transatlantic movement gained contours; and what its protagonists advanced can also be seen as first visions of a progressive Atlantic international community. The overriding objective they shared was to avert what they saw as an ever graver danger: that the imperialist and power-political competition between industrial great powers would escalate into a disastrous major war of unprecedented destructiveness. They thus campaigned for advances towards a more sustainable peace. And they sought to achieve such advances not only by championing disarmament and measures to demilitarise different states and societies but also, and crucially, by promoting progressive reforms – both of the international system and within the different states. The longer-term aspiration of the most influential activists was indeed to pave the way for a novel regime of international law and a modern system of rules and mechanisms that furthered a peaceful settlement of international conflicts.[1]

---

[1] See Osterhammel (2014), pp. 505–10; Joll (1992); Sluga (2013); Clavin and Sluga (2016), pp. 3 ff.

From the late 1880s, the Euro-Atlantic peace movement indeed acquired the character of a "transnational lobby". In 1889, the first Universal Peace Congress convened in Paris; by 1913, twenty-three such congresses had been held, the twenty-fourth due to take place in Vienna in September 1914. And by the turn of the century, more than 400 different peace associations had formed in Europe and the United States and cooperated across the Atlantic. Spearheading this lobby was a growing but heterogeneous and ultimately politically marginal combination of peace activists and progressive reformers who indeed saw themselves as counterforces to what they perceived as the most dangerous tendencies of their age, notably the intensification of militarism, imperialist rivalries and "anarchic" power politics and, on a deeper level, the dominance of "materialist" power-political thinking and both social Darwinist and nationalist ideologies.

The particular aims and underlying assumptions of the different peace activists varied considerably. There were those, by then a minority, who on humanist grounds or on religious – Christian, and especially Quaker – premises rejected all forms of war and violence and clung to the vision of a universal peace. Yet the most influential voices within the movement were those who considered the defensive use of force legitimate, were less confident that they could usher in universal peace and thus concentrated on what they regarded as more realistic efforts to reduce the risk of war and pacify international relations. Most activists also sought to fight for the cause of a more peaceful world "from within", i.e. inside the different states. They lobbied for anti-war and anti-militarist ideas. They tried – largely unsuccessfully – to put pressure on the different governments to espouse the cause of general disarmament; they developed and promoted various forms of peace education; and they tried to alert the "consciousness" of what they hoped would be attentive publics to the potential horror of future wars fought under the conditions of the industrial age.[2] Many leading internationalists argued that real progress towards a "pacifist peace" and genuine "peace-building" was inconceivable without far-reaching transnational efforts to spur not only democratisation but also decisive political and social reforms that addressed the deeper causes of violence and war in an era marked by international *and* class struggle.

Yet the cause that proved relatively most successful was the fight for a new system of international arbitration and "rational" rules and instruments for a peaceful accommodation of international disputes. As we have seen, such rules had too often been cast aside in the rougher international system that had taken shape since the dawn of the long twentieth century. But "political internationalism" did not only manifest itself in the liberal-progressive peace

---

[2] Angell (1913), pp. 15–19, 131–51, 342–9; Brock (1968); Nichols (2011); Cooper (II/1991); Benz (1987).

movement. An even more extensive and potentially more powerful movement that took up the struggle for a more pacific and fraternal world – and social – order constituted itself in the Second International, also established in 1889. Yet although the American Socialist Party came to join it – as well as delegates from Latin America and Japan – the Second International remained a predominantly European organisation, mainly bringing together leading representatives of Europe's rapidly growing social democratic parties and trade unions.

It is worth noting, then, that like conceptions of a new imperialist order that were advanced at this stage, most alternative visions – whether liberal or socialist – had a global reach but indeed focused on refashioning the relations between the "civilised" states of the newly crucial Euro-Atlantic sphere. And particularly the ideas of liberal internationalists actually accentuated the hierarchical divisions between what they envisaged as a community of advanced nations in the "civilised world" – whose relations were to be modernised under covenants of international law – and the "less civilised world" where these new rules would not apply or could even be used to extend the dominance of the most powerful states, which could now claim to act as tutelage powers. Only some social democrats and notably more radical socialists – most influentially Lenin – developed an ideology underpinning a more unequivocally global anti-imperialist agenda. Only they insisted uncompromisingly that the entire system of capitalist-driven imperialism and colonialism had to be overcome – through a revolutionary process led by the vanguard of an emancipated proletariat. And only they made the call for the "self-determination" of all peoples, including those living under colonial rule, an integral part of their political-ideological agitation.[3]

II. The Blossoming of a Transatlantic Movement. The Visions and Aspirations of Pacifists and Progressive Reformers

The efforts of pacifists and progressive internationalists gained considerable force in the two decades before 1914. But they would be largely frustrated. Ultimately, they did not have any tangible impact on the prevalent "game" of power-political competition between the great powers, which actually intensified at the same time. And they could not foster changes in the sphere of international politics and inner-state order that were far-reaching enough to permit significant advances towards a progressive Atlantic "order". But it is nonetheless important to re-examine these aspirations because they brought to the fore alternative ideas and approaches that would be seized upon, and

---

[3] See notably Lenin's critique of the Suttgart Congress of the Second International, 1907, Riddell (1984), pp. 36–7, 41–2; Luxemburg, "Friedensutopien", May 1911, in Luxemburg (2018), pp. 18–22, 23–7.

developed further, in reaction to the Great War. And in important respects they also prefigured the conceptions of some of the key actors who would seek to reorder Europe and the world in the war's aftermath.

By 1900, a wide array of pacifist associations had come into existence. In Britain, they included the Society for the Promotion of Permanent and Universal Peace, originally founded in London in 1816; and the Workingmen's Peace Committee that William Randal Cremer had established in 1870 and which chiefly advocated international arbitration. On the European continent, the French lawyer Émile Arnaud, widely credited with having invented the term "pacifism", gave important impulses to a burgeoning trans-European movement on behalf of the pacifist cause. Arnaud aspired to bolster peace by creating a "United States of Europe". In 1861, he had founded the "*Ligue Internationale de la Paix et de la Liberté*". Subsequently, he joined forces with British and Scandinavian yet also German and Austrian pacifists in organising annual peace congresses in different European cities.[4] Parallel, the Austrian pacifists Alfred Hermann Fried and, above all, Bertha von Suttner became the charismatic leading figures of a sizeable pacifist movement in the German and Habsburg Empires, anchored in the German Peace Society, which expanded considerably from the 1890s and also collaborated with pacifists in other European countries and the United States. By 1914, the predominantly bourgeois *Peace Society* had roughly 10,000 members. Neither Suttner nor Fried advocated a complete renunciation of war or unilateral disarmament. Rather, they concentrated on combating imperialist power politics and what Fried called a prevalent "military conception of peace", and they promoted a "pacifist conception of peace" that sought to address the underlying causes of modern wars. In their view, this required a fundamental "transformation" of how states and peoples interacted, not only through the overall renunciation of violence and general disarmament but also through efforts to pacify international rela-tions through mediation and arbitration.[5]

In the United States, what had become a very dynamic American peace movement comprised a wide range of actors. They included more or less radical pacifists who lobbied for universal disarmament; progressive activists who sought to promote international *and* domestic reforms; and juridical internationalists who focused on the promotion of arbitration, cooperated in various ways and came to join forces with like-minded activists in other countries, especially in Europe. Among its leading figures were activists like Trueblood and Edwin Ginn, the social reformer and later founder of the Woman's Peace Party, Jane Addams, the philosopher and psychologist William James, and the internationalist-minded president of Columbia

---

[4] See Arnaud (1895); Arnaud (1901); Cooper (II/1991).
[5] Fried (1905); Suttner (1889); Benz (1987).

University, Nicholas Murray Butler, who gained a reputation as an advocate of peace education and champion of the "judicial settlement" of international conflicts.[6]

The early roots of this movement can be traced back to the activities of predominantly protestant Christian associations, which eventually joined forces in the Church Peace Union. The American Peace Society, founded in New York in 1828, became only the most important among dozens of other organisations seeking to promote the cause of peace that had come into existence by 1900. Its ranks and range of activities grew from 1898 and one year later Trueblood, its most renowned chairman, took its mission in a new direction. He not only stepped up campaigns for arbitration but also proposed a far more ambitious scheme to found a *Federation of the World*. In 1910, Edward Ginn would establish the World Peace Foundation. Its mission was to be to pacify the world by proposing "practical means to promote peace", fostering the spread of commerce, democracy and the rule of law and "educat[ing] the people of all nations to a full knowledge of the waste and destructiveness of war".[7] Those who sought to foster peace and international law then found another potent benefactor in the industrialist Andrew Carnegie who, also in 1910, set up the Carnegie Endowment for International Peace.

Especially in the United States, yet also in Europe, many of the leading pacifists were at the same time reform activists who saw the struggle for political and social justice at the national level and the struggle for peace and a new international community as two elements of the same progressive quest. Indeed, what linked US Progressives, English new Liberals and leading Labour figures like Ramsay MacDonald, French radicals like Léon Bourgeois and leading German progressives, liberals and social democrats was the conviction that not only substantial political reforms – essentially advances towards more democratic political systems – but also progressive social reforms were indispensable to supersede what they saw as the "armed peace" of the imperialist period and build a more sustainable peace in the longer term. At the same time, many progressive reformers were convinced that practices and outlooks that had been developed to advance reforms within states could also be applied to make the international order more cooperative and peaceful. On these premises, what ensued in the Euro-Atlantic sphere around 1900 was not only a newly vibrant transnational exchange of ideas, which indeed

---

[6] See William James, "The Moral Equivalent of War" address, 1906, in James (1971); Addams (1907); Butler (1912). See Nichols (2011), pp. 68–112.

[7] Trueblood (1899); Tryon (1911), pp. 358–371; Brock (1968); World Peace Foundation declaration, Annual Meeting, 12 July 1910, MSS, World Peace Foundation Papers; Rotberg (2007).

spurred mutual learning processes, but also a new kind of transnational politics, which led to numerous efforts to advance common reform agendas.[8]

A core aim of American progressives was to strengthen American democracy, not only by extending suffrage to women (while falling deplorably short of ending the political discrimination of the black population) but also, and crucially, by reforming the American state in an effort to fight political corruption, regulate big business, and remedy the unequal distribution of wealth that had accelerated in the Gilded Age of laissez-faire capitalism. Thus, they finally sought to fulfil what Croly called America's "promise": the "realization" of the American "ideal" of genuine "democracy".[9] They advanced ideas that would be taken up in Roosevelt's and Wilson's progressive reform agendas. Yet like their European counterparts, they regarded their quest as part of a wider international struggle to spread "genuine" self-government. While Jane Addams and a minority of Progressives developed a genuinely internationalist outlook, many others shared Croly's exceptionalist conviction that "complete democracy" could only be realised in the United States. But in 1909 even he predicted – prematurely – that the United States and Europe were "tending towards a condition" of overall progress on the path of democratisation, which could lead to a "closer and more fruitful association" in the future.[10]

European liberals and radicals had long regarded the American democratic experiment as the model of the future they were striving to emulate. But they had also become aware of the iniquities and political corruption that tarnished US democratic politics in the Gilded Age. Like their American counterparts, those who sought to promote democratisation processes in Europe not only hoped to overcome the iniquities and class struggles of the previous decades but also regarded their endeavours as crucial efforts to lay the domestic-political groundwork for international peace. Following in Mazzini's footsteps and anticipating later "democratic peace" theories, they shared the belief that building "fuller" democracies, in which decisions about war and peace no longer lay in the hands of a few insufficiently accountable decision-makers, would also transform relations between states – and end the reign of war-prone power politics.

Yet a new vanguard of progressive reformers on both sides of the Atlantic had concluded that in an age of unregulated capitalism and global competition "formal" democratisation would not be sufficient to foster a "deeper" peace. In their view, the pursuit of substantive social reforms was no less imperative. Their priorities notably included improved labour and wage standards, the extension of health insurance and old-age pension systems, and progressive income taxations to further both fiscal and social justice. At the same time,

[8] For the wider context see Rodgers (2000), pp. 33–75; Dawley (2003), pp. 1–20.
[9] Croly (1909), pp. 1–2, 297–8; Croly (1914).
[10] Croly (1909), pp. 266–7, 297–8.

these reformers saw their initiatives on behalf of social justice as incubatory endeavours, which could provide lessons for the wider transnational struggle to realise the ideals of a "new peace". They argued that precisely because the different states and societies faced so many common challenges – created by capitalist and power-political competition – it was essential to develop not only a new global "consciousness" but also, animated by it, new forms of transnational cooperation and consultation. At a more fundamental level, they placed their hopes in a conscious effort to replace the "materialist" precepts of laissez-faire capitalism and power politics with a new internationalist and cooperative set of values.

This aspiration is encapsulated in the writings and activities of Jane Addams, who emerged as one of the most vocal progressive internationalists before 1914 and, in 1931, would be awarded the Nobel Peace Prize. Proposing more "active" *Newer Ideals of Peace* in 1907, Addams highlighted what she saw as the essential nexus of progressive social reforms at the national level and the requirements of international peace. She held that just as under capitalist conditions workers from very different backgrounds were compelled to join forces by forming trade unions, different peoples were compelled to find analogous ways to ensure peaceful cooperation in a world dominated by capitalist interests. And she expressed her conviction that reforms of the international order that were animated by a new "world consciousness" and awareness of the common challenges facing humanity could replace imperialist politics with a novel cooperative internationalism. The – overly optimistic – premise of her vision was that the "newer social forces" of progressive reform were so "vigorous" that they would create a "newer dynamic peace" that would "extinguish" the possibility of war "at its very source" – essentially by "readjusting moral values" and replacing "military ideals of patriotism" with those of a "rising concern for human welfare".[11] Addams' ideas came to be widely debated in and beyond progressive circles on both sides of the Atlantic. But her version of a "new internationalism" undoubtedly had a less tangible impact than the more modest and "realistic" blueprints other reformist activists championed.

III. The Struggle for an Authoritative Regime of International Arbitration

In many ways, the internationalists who created the most significant network and were most successful in actually exerting some, albeit still very *limited* influence on international politics in the decades preceding the Great War were the advocates of international arbitration. Both the European and the

---

[11] Addams (1907), pp. 3–5, 7–8, 24; Dawley (2003), pp. 16–17.

American standard-bearers of this cause indeed pursued a more limited agenda than either "new internationalists" like Addams or those who had earlier advanced ambitious designs to abolish war. But they still pursued ambitious aims.

The idea to establish codified rules of arbitration and for the pacific settlement of international disputes had a very long pre-history, especially in European thinking about international relations, and eventually also became prominent in American internationalist thought. Basic ideas about setting disputes between different "states" [or *poleis*] through an arbitrator or mediator can already be found in Thucydides' *Peloponnesian War* and the annals of the Roman republic. Yet more elaborate and formative conceptions were developed much later, in the seventeenth century, above all by Hugo Grotius. In his seminal work on *De Jure Belli ac Pacis* (1625), Grotius wrote about "Arbitration" as a commendable way to avoid wars and settle controversies between states. He recommended not only that such controversies "might be settled by disinterested parties" who acted as arbitrators but also that steps should be taken "for compelling the disputants to accept peace in accordance with just laws". The German jurist and scholar Samuel von Pufendorf then further elaborated conceptions of arbitration in his work on *The Law of Nature and Nations*. And in 1693, in his treatise on *The Present and Future Peace* of Europe, the Quaker William Penn went so far as to propose an actual international court of arbitration.[12] During the following two centuries, states time and again resorted to different forms of arbitration and mediation procedures, relying on a third-party arbitrator rather than an international court to resolve bilateral disputes in certain cases. Overall, however, the most existential conflicts, those involving core questions of war, peace and national interest, were hardly ever settled this way. Yet only from the mid-nineteenth century were significant efforts made to take a further decisive step – namely to establish a *general* and *binding* arbitration regime among "civilised" states.[13]

The first notable organisation promoting arbitration was the London Peace Society, founded by the Quaker scientist and philanthropist William Allen. The subsequent emergence of a veritable pro-arbitration movement, which began in the 1840s, was initially also mainly driven by English and American activists. In 1843, the clergyman Henry Richard and the American consul Elihu Burritt convened the first of what became a series of International Peace Congresses in London in 1843. Setting the agenda for the coming decades, the delegates assembled in London resolved to puruse two cardinal objectives: the establishment of an effective regime of international law for the civilised

---

[12] Thucydides (2009); Grotius (2005), II, chapter 23; VIII, pp. 277–8; Pufendorf (1711); Penn (1726), II, pp. 838–48; Fraser (1926), pp. 182–3.

[13] See Mazower (2012), pp. 68–78.

world; and the creation of a permanent international *institution* to safeguard peace and enforce the turn to arbitration and away from what they regarded as outmoded European concert diplomacy.

By 1900, efforts to promote arbitration and a renovation of international law had become the cause of an influential and well-connected transnational elite of international lawyers on both sides of the Atlantic. It remained the cause of a distinct minority, but its protagonists were not only increasingly well-organised but also found ways to gain the support of some political leaders. Here, too, the transatlantic connection and especially the backing of successive US govern- ments – notably that of Roosevelt – proved critical. The advocates of arbitration thus created the most significant network and arguably became the most effective "internationalist" movement of the pre-1914 era – however marginal it remained overall. In part, this was due to the fact that its standard-bearers came to concentrate on a clear set of priorities, above all the demand that all "arbitrable" inter-state disputes should henceforth be settled through a qualified mediating arbitrator or arbitrating body. In a wider perspective, however, they intended to promote more far-reaching reforms – a pacifying modernisation of the inter- national order that was to be spurred above all by the advancement of inter- national law and what could be called a "juridification" of international politics. Essentially, they argued that in the international sphere legal rules and processes would successively supersede diplomatic or political rules and processes.

All of its proponents agreed that arbitration was to be extended as a more civilised and overall pacifying alternative to what they regarded as essentially war-prone secret diplomacy and power politics. But from the outset there were fundamental arguments between leading figures within the movement that were still unresolved when the Great War broke out. Those who exerted most influence considered it crucial to make arbitration workable by restricting its remit to questions that could be seen as "judiciable" – and thus to exclude essentially "political" questions involving security and "national honour". In effect, they thereby conceded that most of the critical issues that could decide over war or peace would still have to be addressed through political processes. More aspirational arbitrationists, however, sought to go further and extend arbitration eventually to *all* relevant international questions. Further, there was disagreement over the crucial question of how arbitration was to be effectively enforced – and whether it could or should be enforced at all. Some argued that this had to be left to state governments. But others insisted that an effective arbitration regime necessarily required an authoritative supranational institution whose decisions had to bind individual states and thus limited their sovereignty in crucial respects. They thus championed the creation of a permanent international court or tribunal.[14]

---

[14] See Dülffer (1981); Joll (1992); Mazower (2012), pp. 65–93.

British and American activists played crucial roles in paving the way for actual advances towards an authoritative – and essentially transatlantic – arbitration regime that were made around the turn of the century. In Britain, it was once again Cremer who became the most influential transatlantic campaigner for international arbitration and who eventually managed to gain the support of Roosevelt. Turning the Workingmen's Peace Committee into the International Arbitration League, Cremer came to campaign for the establishment of an international arbitration tribunal, which was to settle dispute among nations in the manner that Boards of Arbitration had long been used to settle labour disputes.[15] Parallel, a new generation of US peace activists led by Trueblood stepped up efforts to commit not just the American government but also the leaders of other civilised powers to an effective system of arbitration. This cause was then taken up by Nicholas Murray Butler, a leading juridical internationalist who from 1907 would chair the Lake Mohonk Conferences on International Arbitration. Butler argued that the promotion of "true internationalism" required that what had been accomplished "intranationally"– namely to resolve conflicts through mediators or arbitrators under a covenant of law – should also be achieved "internationally", or more precisely in the "civilized world". Crucially, he called for the creation of a "truly" independent permanent international court of arbitration.[16] What Butler envisaged was broadly supported by all the pacifist and internationalist organisations that operated in the United States by this time – not only the American Peace Society but also the American Association for International Conciliation, the World Peace Foundation and the Church Peace Union. And it would soon receive the powerful support of Carnegie's Endowment for International Peace.[17]

But the promotion of arbitration was by no means a purely Anglo-American endeavour. On the European continent, the leading pacifist Émile Arnaud, the Swiss jurist Johann Kaspar Bluntschli and notably the Radical premier Léon Bourgeois emerged as influential advocates of more comprehensive concepts to pacify international relations through *compulsory* arbitration. The advocacy of non-violent methods to resolve international conflicts was integral to Arnaud's liberal humanist approach to pacifism. And on behalf of the "*Ligue Internationale de la Paix et de la Liberté*" he proposed "permanent

---

[15] Evans (1909), p. 51; Ceadel (2000), pp. 86–7.

[16] Butler address, 22 May 1907, in Butler (1912), pp. 4–5, 12–14.

[17] Such aspirations also reinforced the idea that Britain and the United States should set an example to other powers by adopting arbitration procedures to settle bilateral disputes. This idea had gained traction ever since both powers had resorted to arbitration in the famous "Alabama" case, the dispute over damages caused by British-built Confederate warships during the civil war. Subsequently, Gladstone had supported the conclusion of a general arbitration accords, but in 1897 the US Senate blocked the so-called Olney-Pauncefote Treaty.

treaties of arbitration between peoples".[18] In the 1890s, Bourgeois became a torchbearer of international arbitration in and beyond France – and he would eventually continue this mission at the Paris Peace Conference. In his view, arbitration was the most effective and equitable "method" for the "peaceful resolution of international conflicts" that could not be settled by diplomatic means. Bourgeois demanded the establishment of a permanent court of arbitration and the "extension of the domain of international juridical institutions". His overriding aim was to establish a international regime of *compulsory* arbitration – a regime that actually made it mandatory for all "civilised states" to resort to arbitration to settle most conflicts.[19]

In Germany, Bluntschli was the most distinctive legal scholar who sought to advance the cause of international arbitration. In his seminal work on *Modern International Law of Civilised States* Bluntschli had observed in 1878 that it was a "barbarian" aspect of "today's world order" that because of a lack of an established "court of international law", states still tended to choose the path of "self-help", which in the most extreme case meant war to decide serious disputes between them. And he had expressed the hope that future "international-law congresses" would establish the principle of making arbitration procedures mandatory "at least for certain controversial questions".[20] Not only the practitioners and apologists of *Realpolitik* in Germany but also their counterparts in other states regarded such schemes as illusory – and opposed them on the grounds that they threatened core elements of state sovereignty. Yet both in Germany and Austria the call for mandatory arbitration came to be adopted by the rapidly growing pacifist movement that had formed around the *German Peace Society*. Both Suttner and Fried championed efforts to create binding international arbitration agreements, viewing them as integral to the transformative "pacifist conception of peace" that they desired to promote.[21]

IV.   The Significance of the Hague Conventions – and Their Limits

Ironically, the greatest success of this confluence of national and transnational efforts to promote peace and international reforms came precisely at a time of sharpening European polarisation – when the Russian Tsar Nicholas II, whose empire was plagued by structural financial problems and falling behind in the intensifying imperialist competition and European arms race, was induced to explore alternative options and to call for a conference to discuss the limitation of armaments. This then expanded into a seminal gathering that contemporaries hailed as a watershed in the history of the "laws of war" – and of

---

[18]   Arnaud (1895); Arnaud (1901).
[19]   Bourgeois speech, The Hague, 1907, in Bourgeois (1910), pp. 46, 48–9, 58–63.
[20]   Bluntschli (I/1878), pp. 33–4.
[21]   Fried (1905); Suttner (1889).

international arbitration: the First Hague Peace Conference of 1899. Reflecting the Euro-Atlantic dominance in the international hierarchy of the period, twenty of the twenty-six delegations that attended the conference represented European countries; among the others were notably American yet also Japanese and Chinese representatives. But the gathering at The Hague was not an authoritative peace conference in which top-level representatives of governments participated; nor did it have either a mandate to effect a more substantive reform of the international state system.

While predictably failing to yield any tangible progress in the sphere of arms limitation, let alone disarmament, the first Hague Convention of July 1899 not only codified a new set of "laws of warfare" to be observed by "civilised" states. It also established an unprecedented codex of standards and procedures of arbitration for the pacific settlement of international disputes. This included provisions for the mediation of friendly or neutral powers in conflicts between two or more states; the establishment of an International Commission of Inquiry in cases that could not be settled by diplomatic means – and involved neither the 'honour' nor the 'vital interests' of the disputants; and – significantly – the creation of a Permanent Court of Arbitration, which became operative in 1902.

The first Hague Convention thus brought significant innovations in international law. But it did not and *could* not set up an authoritative system of arbitration – a system that actually introduced effective mechanisms (the court's original remit was very limited) and that, crucially, obliged the great powers to pursue arbitration. Essentially, the outcomes of 1899 would thus have no tangible impact at the level of "high politics". Particularly the leading European decision-makers would largely ignore the Hague stipulations when what they regarded as vital concerns commanded other policies. And their prevailing outlooks would not be noticeably affected by "the spirit of The Hague".[22] It was only in the United States that the cause of – limited – arbitration gained more substantive political support. Roosevelt never considered arbitration procedures to be the key to ensuring a "righteous peace". But he welcomed the results of the first Hague Conference and positioned himself as one of the most powerful proponents of *limited* arbitration – which neither impinged on US sovereignty nor on the expanded Monroe Doctrine – as one method (among others) to stabilise relations among "civilised" great powers.[23]

---

[22] The Hague Convention of 1899, in Bevans (1968), I; Dülffer (1981); Abbenhuis (2018); Clark (2007), pp. 61 ff. Significantly, the outcome of The Hague indeed widened the gulf between the rules of conduct among "civilised" powers and their prerogatives to use military and other means to enforce their interests vis-à-vis "less civilised" states and peoples. See Mazower (2012), pp. 77–81.

[23] See Roosevelt to Grey, 3 October 1914, Grey (1925), pp. 139–40.

Responding to the lobbying efforts of Cremer's Inter-Parliamentary Union, Roosevelt actually became the main instigator for a second international conference at The Hague, which was attended by a far greater array of delegates from a total of forty-four states. It resulted in a further convention, finalised in October 1907, which emphatically underscored that all signatories accepted the principle of compulsory arbitration. But the conference had not yielded any meaningful progress where it really mattered, namely in actually committing governments to this principle, notably those of the great powers. Further, the proceedings also confirmed essential limitations of arbitration in the wider context of war prevention. For most delegates adhered to the rationale that in order to be effective at a time when national sovereignty arbitration had to be *limited* – essentially to disputes that were legal rather than "political" in character. This rationale was criticised by more aspirational internationalists who pushed for a faster extension of compulsory arbitration. But what proved decisive was that the "reduced" conception was espoused not only by influential lawyers like John Westlake, who became the British representative on the newly established Permanent Court of Arbitration at The Hague.[24] It was also favoured by most of the statesmen who favoured arbitration.

When submitting the Hague Conventions of 1907 to the Senate, secretary of state Elihu Root echoed the sentiments of most other promoters of arbitration at this time when he declared that they presented "the greatest advance ever made at any single time toward the reasonable and peaceful regulation of international conduct". In his judgement, they had given an "enormous impetus" to a process in which "old-style" diplomacy and international politics would be superseded by international law and legal practices.[25] Nonetheless, he favoured an essentially evolutionary approach. Mindful of reservations in his own country, he deemed it unrealistic and counterproductive to engage in ambitious supranational institution-building – to establish a "parliament of man" that had the authority to "control the conduct of nations by legislation or an international police force with power to enforce national conformity to rules of right conduct".[26] Instead, he endeavoured to find a more "practical and efficient way towards making peace permanent".[27] And, with Roosevelt's backing, Root indeed took the lead in negotiating a series of bilateral arbitration treaties. Between 1908 and 1909 the Roosevelt administration concluded twenty-five such treaties, among them agreements with Britain, France and Germany, all of which reinforced the more limited variant of arbitration,

---

[24] Westlake (1896), pp. 1–20.
[25] Root address, 15 April 1907, in Bacon and Scott (1916), pp. 128, 129–35, 142–4.
[26] Root Nobel lecture, 8 September 1914 (not delivered), in Bacon and Scott (1916), pp. 153–74.
[27] Ibid.

providing that all "justiciable" disputes – except for those involving national "honour" or independence – were to be submitted to a tribunal of the newly established yet still weak Permanent Court of Arbitration.

Roosevelt's successor Taft desired to advance the cause of arbitration significantly further. He proposed more comprehensive arbitration treaties, which – crucially – were now to be extended to cover matters of "national honour" and "vital national interests". He hoped that these could form the basis of a "world model" for the settlement of international disputes that notably the European powers would emulate. To set a precedent, he sought to negotiate agreements of this kind with Britain and France, which were then signed in August 1911. As Taft had argued on behalf of the American Society for the Judicial Settlement of International Disputes in December 1910, if a "positive agreement' could be achieved with these powers to abide by 'the adjudication of an international arbitral court in every issue which can not be settled by negotiation, no matter what it involves, whether honor, territory, or money", the United States would have taken "a long step forward" by demonstrating to the world that it was possible to establish "the same system of due process of law that exists between individuals under a government".[28] But the Senate predictably blocked the ratification of the treaties. Leading senators insisted on amendments, underscoring that vital questions involving American security and commerce had to remain exempt from arbitration. And the president would never seek a ratification of the treaties because he deemed the Senate's reservations unacceptable. Nonetheless, Taft continued his advocacy of arbitration and the more ambitious idea of establishing a mechanism that could counteract what he saw as a highly dangerous development: the division of Europe and the world into "armed camps". To this end he proposed that the court at The Hague should be transformed into a really powerful "arbitral court, supported by the authority and the prestige of all the powerful nations of the earth". Eventually, this would become a key element of the campaign for a "League to Enforce Peace" that Taft would pursue during the Great War.[29]

A vanguard of American international lawyers, which included Root, had even grander aspirations. Through the American Society of International Law, founded in 1905, they rallied behind the objective of pacifying international affairs by eventually superseding "diplomatic action" with "judicial action". And they declared that only such a sea-change would permit real progress towards a lasting "universal peace".[30] To bring it about, they championed the

---

[28] Taft address, 17 December 1910, Taft (1910); Taft statements, 1911 and 1915, in World Peace Foundation (1919), I, pp. 36–7.

[29] Taft address, 30 December 1911, in Peace, March 1912, p. 7; Taft (1914), pp. 112–16. See Wertheim (2011), pp. 797–836.

[30] Root address, 15 April 1907, in Bacon and Scott (1916), pp. 128, 142–4.

idea of creating a truly authoritative international court, modelled on the US
Supreme Court, where independent judges and legal experts were to establish
a non-partisan covenant of international law. States would then be obliged to
submit international disputes to this court. The fundamental conviction that
Root and other proponents of the world court idea shared was that it would
offer a superior way of settling political and economic conflicts that could lead
to war by "reducing clashes of interest and equity to matters of legal
principle".[31] But this remained essentially a vision cherished by only a small
elite of American jurists. It attracted the sympathies of some juridical internationalists elsewhere, notably in Britain and France. But it never gained
significant political support either in the United States, where the Senate
rejected any far-reaching legal constraints on US sovereignty, or in other
countries, where the idea that political leaders rather than a body of unelected
judges had to deal with vital questions of war and peace clearly remained
prevalent.

V.   Towards an Atlantic *société des nations* – or a United States of Europe? Internationalist Visions of the Order of the Future

Because they intended to promote "realistic" step-by-step reforms, the most
influential liberal internationalists of the era of the Hague peace conferences
were remarkably reluctant to put forward more ambitious grand designs of a
new international order and, notably, blueprints for new international institutions. And yet it was one the leading figures of the Hague movement, Léon
Bourgeois, who in 1908 explicitly sketched the vision of a modern "*société des
nations*" or "league of nations", which initially was to include all the signatories of the Hague Conventions. In a lecture he gave at the *École des Sciences
Politiques* in Paris in June 1908, Bourgeois argued that as modern capitalism
had created a de facto 'universal economic community' and an 'international
life' characterised by a high degree of interdependent interests, yet also the
rough rules of "the market" and "competition", it was now imperative to create
another international "community of a superior order" – a "veritable society"
that established a state of "real and deep peace".[32]

Yet at this point Bourgeois still held that it would not be possible to forge a
political union of states and an international parliament in which the gravest
political questions would be settled on the basis of "science" and "law",
because states would simply not accept a "superior set of rules". Thus, he
advocated different priorities, namely to build on the "revolutionary" advances
of The Hague and extend the as yet "incomplete" regime of international

[31] Mazower (2012), pp. 92, 90–3; Kuehl (1969).
[32] Bourgeois speech, 5 June 1908, in Bourgeois (1910), pp. 272–3.

arbitration into a "a juridical *société des nations*" open to all civilised states that accepted the Hague Conventions. In fact, however, what Bourgeois envisaged was an essentially transatlantic league led by the representatives of the major European powers and the United States who, in their work for peace, would be aided by the "force" of enlightened public "opinion".[33] But prior to the catastrophe of the Great War, there was no prospect of making any significant advances towards such a league.

By contrast, only very few, overall more conservative politicians and thinkers in this period argued that a more traditional yet long-neglected instrument of peacekeeping should be reactivated and fortified for an era of world-political competition: the Concert of Europe. As noted, only the British premier Salisbury forcefully advocated an institutionalisation of the concert as an essentially *political* "federation ... of Europe", reasoning that it was the only competent authority to "create law for Europe" and permit the "federated" action. He thus demanded that the concert should be placed on a stronger organisational footing. Salisbury was convinced that it was the only effective instrument to preserve peace and overcome the growing inner-European divisions, and he envisaged no role for the United States within it.[34] Drawing on Castlereagh's ideas, he thus advanced a markedly Eurocentric conception that anticipated core elements of what his son Robert Cecil would eventually turn into the blueprint for an essentially *Atlantic* concert during the Great War, which in turn would have a formative influence in 1919. Prior to the catastrophe of 1914, however, Salisbury's recommendations essentially fell on deaf ears.

Yet the pre-war years also witnessed the re-emergence of more ambitious visions of a more integrated European system or even a "United States of Europe". Ideas of this kind had been put forward time and again since the late 1850s yet now gained wider resonance in liberal-bourgeois and also, as will be seen, in social democratic circles. They never had a significant impact on actual state policies in this phase; but they prefigured ideas that later would indeed have a critical bearing on European international politics – after 1918 and then more powerfully after 1945. In the early phase of Britain's turn to "free trade" in the 1860s, the English political philosopher Herbert Spencer had concluded that there were underlying evolutionary trends towards a European federation and more far-reaching forms of European integration. Analysing what he saw as tendencies such as that of European states to "form alliances" and exercise a restraining influence on one another, the "system, now becoming customary, of settling international disputes by congresses", "the breaking down of commercial barriers" and the "increasing facilities of communication", Spencer interpreted them as "the beginnings of a European

---

[33] Ibid., pp. 272–3, 278–81.
[34] Salisbury speech, House of Lords, 19 March 1897, Hansard, House of Lords, 4th series, vol. 47, cls, 1011–14.

federation – a still larger integration than any now established".[35] In 1878, Bluntschli would present an ambitious scheme for the "Organisation of a European club of states", essentially calling for a European confederation that was to be established on the basis of a common European constitution.[36]

It is noteworthy though that, in contrast to what Bluntschli envisaged, most later conceptions for a more unified Europe were not primarily developed to address the problem of inner-European divisions but rather because of a growing awareness that the European states were no longer unchallenged in global politics and had to face an unprecedented external challenge: that posed by the rise of an increasingly formidable American competitor and the prospect of an overbearing American hegemony in the future. In the eyes of some politicians and intellec-tuals, this essentially called for efforts to construct a "modern" Pan-European political structure. Such notions would re-emerge, on different premises, after the Great War. Before 1914, they especially gained contours in Germany and Austria. As early as 1859, the radical-democratic German politician Julius Fröbel had predicted that America's emergence as an autonomous power would fundamentally change "the relations of the political equilibrium" in Europe and the world. He argued that the United States was bound to become the "opposite pole of a new and more universal order". And he recommended that those states that constituted "occidental Europe" – the west European states and the German and Austro-Hungarian empires – should form a joint political organisation that would allow them to withstand the threat posed by the future predominance of the United States and Russia.[37] In the early twentieth century, some liberal thinkers returned to such ideas, and eventually they too advanced conceptions for a "United States of Europe". Yet at the core of their schemes lay the idea of a European economic community that was essentially conceived as a commercial and customs union designed to counter the ever more dominant commercial-political power of the United States. This notably characterised the blueprint for a European economic community (dominated by the German and Austro-Hungarian empires) that the Austrian economist Julius Wolf proposed and, from 1904, disseminated through the "Central European Economic Association".[38]

For his part, the thundering German philosopher Friedrich Nietzsche had earlier unfurled a vision of a reinvigorated Europe of the future that was decidedly at odds with both progressive democratic ideas and notions of a dawning *Atlantic* order. Nietzsche not only rejected "universalism", "liberalism", "democracy" and socialist ideas but also deemed "Americanism" profoundly inimical to the intellectual and political renewal he desired for Europe – while in fact never really trying to understand American culture,

---

[35] Spencer (1862), pp. 317, 346.
[36] Bluntschli (II/1878), pp. 81–4.
[37] Fröbel (1859), pp. 1–2; Fröbel (1878), pp. 450 ff.
[38] Wolf (1903); Luxemburg (1913), pp. 32–3.

politica and ideas. He apodictically asserted that "the public" and "parliamentar-ianism" were the "organisations most unsuitable" for meeting "the tasks of the coming centuries".[39] Instead, he envisaged the formation of a cosmopolitan humanist elite of "good Europeans" who were to rule over the continent's "mediocre" peoples, struggle to overcome both nihilism and "narrow-minded" nationalist ideologies. Eventually, they were to establish a peaceful trans-European confederation. Only by taking such gigantic strides, Nietzsche argued, intriguingly anticipating some future architects of the European Union, would the "good Europeans" be able to meet what he considered the essential challenge of the long twentieth century: the requirements of a rapidly expanding "world market". Yet, reflecting inflated self-perceptions shared by far too many European thinkers and statesmen at this time, he was clearly mistaken in postulating that it would be possible to forge a novel European *avantgarde*, and league, that would have the power to contain America's "pernicious" influence and to assume "the direction and control of the entire culture of the earth".[40]

More influential, however, would be a conception that the industrialist Walther Rathenau presented in 1913 – which both prefigured core rationales of the twentieth century's European integration process and highlighted the problem of Germany's "semi-hegemony" in Europe. Rathenau argued that there was only one way to solve the predicament of Europe's "central power" and to secure peace: it had to take the lead in founding an "economic customs union" in Central Europe, which the west European states would then join "sooner or later". Thus a unified economic "unit" would be created that was "equal" or even "superior" to the United States – with which it could then peacefully compete. Yet Rathenau developed an even more aspirational vision, believing that economic unification would also be instrumental in overcoming nationalist hatred and power-political rivalries in Europe. He predicted – very prematurely – that if "Europe's economy merged(d)" then "Europe's politics" would merge as well, which would not bring "world peace" or "complete disarmament" but lead to a decisive "alleviation of conflicts" and a "solidar-ity-based civilisation".[41] Less than a year later, the outbreak of the war would dash Rathenau's hopes. And in the midst of a highly charged war-aims debate he would eventually put forward a recalibrated *Mitteleuropa* conception, which was more obviously designed to "unify" Europe under the aegis of a dominant German Empire – against Britain, the United States and Russia.

---

[39] Nietzsche (1999), p. 584; Stephan (2019), pp. 124–32.
[40] Nietzsche (2012), I, pp. 309–11; II, pp. 592–3; Nietzsche (2011), pp. 381–5; Elbe (2016), pp. 1–16, 65–122.
[41] Rathenau article, *Neue Freie Presse*, 25 December 1913, in Rathenau (1928), V, pp. 264 ff. See Gall (2009), pp. 176–8.

The Hague Conventions and all further attempts to develop arbitration, judicial means to pacify international relations and first schemes for some kind of organisation of states in their aftermath were undoubtedly significant steps in the history of modern international law and conceptions of modern international order. But they were far from marking a systemic turning-point in the history of international politics or, crucially, on the path towards the actual construction of a more sustainable peace order – either in the Euro-Atlantic sphere or in a global context. There was one fundamental problem, namely that the progressive internationalist endeavours of this period never really affected the sphere of "high politics" and the overriding dynamics of great-power politics that eventually led into the abyss of 1914. And the same applied to progressive efforts to foster "peace building" through democratisation and political and social reforms, which even in the best-case scenario would have required time and favourable conditions to have a significant impact – conditions that simply did not exist in this period.

At a deeper level, the ideas that progressives advocated did not alter the thinking of the leading policymakers – notably of those European actors who would make the key decisions in the pre-history of the Great War – in any significant way. While some paid homage to the civilising force of arbitration, the overwhelming majority was not prepared to address critical political conflicts and clashes of interests this way and rejected any tangible legal constraints that would have limited their freedom of action to safeguard the security and what they considered the vital national interests of the states they represented. Yet it would be wrong to conclude that the efforts of political internationalists of this formative period bore no fruits at all. As will be shown, they provided significant impulses for visions of a different, more peace-enforcing international system that gained contours during the Great War – and would then influence the peacemaking processes of 1919.

VI.   The Second International – the Struggle between Reformist Social Democrats and Radical Socialists and Their Competing Visions of the Future

But the most influential and organised force in the struggle to combat militarist imperialism and work towards a more pacific international order in the decades before 1914 was not the elite group of liberal internationalists. Rather, it was the transnational movement formed by the rapidly growing socialist parties and a burgeoning labour movement, whose leading figures in 1889 gathered in Paris to found the Second International. They created a far more extensive organisational structure to unify their efforts than the First International had ever had and in 1900 established an executive body, the Socialist Bureau, to guide and coordinate the movement's work. Yet although its activities involved representatives from the American Socialist Party and like-minded parties in Latin America and, eventually, Japan, it essentially remained a Eurocentric organisation. They were united not only in their opposition to prevalent militarism, power politics and the great powers' imperialist and colonial exploits but also in the conviction that at the root of all this lay the dynamic rise of globalising capitalism. And they joined forces to persuade working classes and wider publics – as early as 1891 – that the policies of the "ruling classes" and the underlying forces of capitalist competition threatened to bring on "the catastrophe of [a] world war". Their countervailing internationalist policies found expression in a series of joint manifestoes and resolutions that emerged from the hence regularly held congresses of the Second International.[42]

Very soon, however, the Second International's activities were hampered by fundamental and at times violent disputes over the final direction of their aspirations and the tactics and strategies the movement should adopt. These reflected the famous "*Richtungskämpfe*" or "directional struggles" that also raged within the different socialist parties – between a majority of more moderate social democrats who espoused a reformist, evolutionary approach and a very determined minority of more radical socialists. Their more uncompromising revolutionary Marxist course was shaped by charismatic figures like Lenin and Rosa Luxemburg, who argued that it was imperative not to compromise the core socialist aim of preparing the ground for a proletarian revolution that actually destroyed the entire capitalist system and replaced it with a completely new – and truly pacific – communist order.

Yet what actually prevailed within the Second International before 1914 were the outlooks of the more centrist social democratic internationalists. Vilified by their opponents as "opportunists", they championed a "reformist conception" of politics both at the national and at the international level. In many ways, this can be seen as an extension of the reformist approach that the leading social democratic thinker Eduard Bernstein had developed. Bernstein argued that a gradual transition from capitalism to socialism could be achieved through cumulative legislative and democratic reforms.[43] Nonetheless, even moderate socialists fought for far more substantial reforms of the social and international order than liberal internationalists of this period. A resolution passed at the Second International's congress in Paris in 1900 protested against the so-called peace conferences of European and American bourgeois liberals "such as that in The Hague" and denounced them as a "fraud" that

---

[42] Brussels Congress resolution 1891, Riddell (1984), p. 21. See Joll (1966), pp. 30–55; Koenen (2017), pp. 422–52.

[43] Bernstein (1899).

created only a "delusion" of progress towards peace as long as capitalist society was not thoroughly reformed.[44]

The network of socialist parties thus put forward a more aspirational agenda to ban the danger of a major war and achieve a "deeper peace". They called for an ambitious international compact for the peaceful settlement of inter-state disputes, chiefly through "the serious use of arbitration". But they also inisisted that more far-reaching reforms were needed to get to the root of what militarised international relations, spurred imperialism and heightened the danger of war. In short, they argued that what had to be superseded was the dominance of capitalism and the intensifying capitalist competition between the leading powers – including the most dynamic American power – which had also led to the ever-expanding subjugation of less advanced peoples to colonial rule and imperialist domination. The core assumption was that wars were "part of the very nature of capitalism" and would "cease only" when the "capitalist system", which operated at the expense of the working classes of all countries, was "abolished".[45] The majority within the Second International sought to realise this vision by pursuing step-by-step efforts on two levels. Within states they focused on strengthening social democratic influence in parliaments, democratic reforms, and efforts to make the working classes and wider publics more conscious of the dangers of war-prone capitalism through public agitation and education. In the international sphere, they concentrated on expanding the cooperation of different socialist parties and trade unions and developing a more cohesive transnational platform. Essentially, influential proponents of a more "evolutionary" orientation like the charismatic party leaders August Bebel, Jean Jaurès and, later, Ramsay MacDonald, sought to counter those who campaigned for a violent revolution. They maintained that a reformist approach could not only avert the danger of a major war but also lead to transformative changes.

On these premises, the Second International's manifesto of 1900 had called on "workers' parties in every country" not only to "combat militarism and colonialism" but also to "respond to the world political alliance of the bour- geoisies and the governments to perpetuate war with an alliance of proletar- ians of all countries for perpetual peace".[46] The overriding aim was to establish a new international system, which the Stuttgart resolution of 1907 character- ised as a "*brotherhood*" of socialist nations. Crucially, it insisted that such a fraternal system could only come into existence if it was underpinned by "an economic order on a socialist basis" that eliminated the stranglehold of capitalist competition and brought about "the solidarity of all peoples". This order would be fortified by the natural solidarity among the working classes,

[44] Paris resolution, 1900, Riddell (1984), p. 22.
[45] Stuttgart resolution, 1907, Riddell (1984), pp. 33–5.
[46] Paris Congress resolution, 1900, Riddell (1984), p. 22.

who Jaurès stylised as the "masses of men who collectively love peace and hate war".[47] Affirming such doctrines, the Second International's landmark Basel Congress of 1912 called on the proletarians of all countries to wage "war on war" as "the heralds of a 'proletarian world of peace and fraternity of peoples'" – to raise "protest in the parliaments" and "unite in great mass demonstrations". Beyond this, the Basel manifesto sought to impress on the workers of the world that they could make any major war impossible by declaring a general strike when the capitalist classes wanted to go to war.[48]

Significantly, the debates about how to build a new, emancipatory order that took place among socialist and social democratic parties from the 1890s also gave salient impulses in another respect: they made the "right to national self-determination" a crucial "political-juridical" *and* ideological concept in international politics, which would have major repercussions in the era of the First World War and beyond. As noted, the First International had in 1865 proclaimed its support for the "right of every people to dispose of itself". Subsequently, socialist conceptions of "self-determination" evolved against the backdrop of nationality conflicts in Russia and the Austro-Hungarian Empire and debates about "the colonial question". Seeking to foster a peaceful accommodation of different national groups within a reformed Austro-Hungarian Empire, the leading Austro-Marxists Otto Bauer and Karl Renner after 1900 propounded a conception that defined self-determination as an individual and collective right to "preserve one's own cultural identity". And they emphasised the right to "national-cultural autonomy" rather than outright independence.[49] Yet the Second International had earlier, in 1896, espoused the more far-reaching demand for a universal application of the principle of "national self-determination". And it had declared that all peoples that were subject to colonial rule and exploitation should have the right to seek independence and self-government. By 1907, however, the majority within the organisation had retreated from this position and adopted its own version of a hierarchical-civilisational conception, now linking self-determination to the level of development of "native" populations and their capacity for self-rule.[50]

In a wider context, leading social democrats also began to develop as yet rather abstract and Eurocentric conceptions of a reformed international order. In 1910, Philipp Scheidemann put forward first ideas for a "league of nations", which at first glance appeared similar to what Bourgeois and liberal progressives advocated but in fact went significantly further. For they were

---

[47] Stuttgart congress resolution, 1907, Riddell (1984), p. 34.
[48] Basel Manifesto (1912), pp. 23–7.
[49] See Benner (2018), pp. 156–7; Bauer (1907); Renner (1918); Fisch (2010), pp. 88–9, 133–6.
[50] Majority draft resolution on colonialism, Stuttgart Congress, 1907, Riddell (1984), p. 7–8, 4–5.

indissolubly bound up with the wider social democratic agenda of superseding capitalism and transforming capitalist-imperialist powers into social democratic republics. In the German *Reichstag*, Scheidemann argued that the establishment of an inclusive "league of nations" on a "socialist basis", which defused international conflicts and safeguarded the independence and "self-determination" of its members, was imperative to "prevent the disaster which a war in Europe would mean for the whole of the civilised world". In keeping with social democratic internationalism, Scheidemann presented his vision in universal terms, but what he had in mind was essentially a European league.[51]

In 1911, other prominent social democrats, Georg Ledebour and particularly the party's leading Marxist, Karl Kautsky, went one step further, and further than liberals, in calling for the foundation of a federal "United States of Europe". In his influential review *Neue Zeit*, Kautsky proclaimed that the only real "guarantee for a lasting continuation of peace" was "the unification of the states of the European civilisation", the creation of a European union with "a common trade policy, a federal parliament, a federal government and a federal army". In his vision, a union of this kind would have such a "preponderance of power" that it could either induce the United States and other powers to join it or compel them to disband their armies and navies, thus paving the way for universal disarmament and ushering in an "era of perpetual peace".[52] Overall, however, social democratic ideas for an international "league" or "union" remained comparatively undeveloped.

But such conceptions and the entire evolutionary orientation espoused by reformist social democrats were severely criticised by those who after 1900 emerged as the leading minds within a vanguard of revolutionary Marxist socialists, the strong-minded theorist Rosa Luxemburg and, above all, the exiled leader of the Russian Social Democratic Workers' Party's Bolshevik wing, Vladimir Ilich Lenin. Both Lenin and Luxemburg maintained that what social democratic reformers advocated betrayed Marxist principles and the cardinal objective, which in their view could only be achieved by revolutionary means: a complete triumph of socialism. Lenin argued particularly forcefully that to ensure this triumph all socialist parties had to act as the "vanguard of the proletariat", infusing it with a socialist class consciousness and guiding it in a struggle that had to result in nothing less than the overthrow of the capitalist system. In his analysis, only a revolution of this kind would pave the way for a novel world order of socialist republics.[53]

Like Luxemburg, Lenin based his aims and strategies unequivocally on Marx's materialist conception of history, which he sought to develop further.

---

[51] Scheidemann *Reichstag* speech, 9 December 1910, in Scheidemann (1929), I, p. 151.
[52] Kautsky, "Die Vereinigten Staaten von Europa", *Neue Zeit*, 29 (1910–11), vol. 2, pp. 1205–6.
[53] Lenin (1902); Luxemburg (1899).

He thus postulated that imperialism and the power-political rivalries it entailed marked the final stage in the history of capitalism – a stage in which capitalist competition would inexorably be driven to extremes and thus not only lead to a major war but also create the preconditions for a "social revolution" for which the socialist parties had to prepare the proletariat.[54] And both he and Luxemburg saw the rising American giant as a pivotal power in this process. Lenin described the United States as the most dynamic among the "young capitalist powers" that engaged in the imperialist division of the world.[55] Luxemburg characterised America's development into "an enormous economic area and political power" as one of the most momentous results of "a century of capitalist development" whose expansion would further intensify the imperialist competition between the capitalist powers.[56]

Lenin thus also argued that war was "a necessary product of capitalism", an inherent consequence of the militarism and imperialist competition it generated.[57] And Luxemburg concluded that war could not be eliminated through piecemeal reforms but only "together with the class state" and the entire system of the "the capitalist world market" and capitalist-driven imperialism. Consequently, she also castigated the efforts of the self-styled "bourgeois peace lovers" that had led to the Hague Conventions as "deplorable half-measures" which created the dangerous "illusion" that "world peace" and "disarmament" could be realised "in the framework of the current social order".[58] Lenin was even more ferocious in criticising the self-defeating peace designs of the majority within the Second International, urging it to return to "the revolutionary standpoint in Marxism" and fight for a socialist "new world order".

In developing his own revolutionary agenda, Lenin also began to formulate conceptions of "self-determination" that would have a much wider impact in Europe, the United States and the "colonised world" than those of the reformist social democrats. He in fact endowed "national self-determination" with the meaning that turned it into a crucial international precept of the long twentieth century. Essentially, Lenin came to define self-determination as the supreme "right" of every people to have an independent state and, where this applied, to separate from "foreign-national communities" and empires in which one people dominated others. In 1903, Lenin insisted that the "right of self-determination" of all peoples within the Russian Empire should become a key demand of the Russian Socialist Party. Subsequently, he posited it as a

---

[54] See Lenin pamphlet, 1907, Riddell (1984), pp. 36–42; Lenin (1916), especially pp. 93–123; Luxemburg, 'Friedensutopien', May 1911, in Luxemburg (2018), pp. 23–4.

[55] Lenin (1916), pp. 100, 150.

[56] Luxemburg, 'Friedensutopien', May 1911, in Luxemburg (2018), p. 30.

[57] Lenin's critique of the Stuttgart Congress of the Second International, 1907, Riddell (1984), pp. 36–7, 41–2. See also Lenin (1916), pp. 93–163.

[58] Luxemburg, 'Friedensutopien', May 1911, in Luxemburg (2018), pp. 18–22, 23–4, 27.

universal right that also, and especially, had to be granted to those peoples who were the subjects of colonialism and imperial domination outside Russia and Europe. Yet, drawing on the foundations that Marx and Engels had laid, Lenin regarded the struggle for national self-determination only as a first, intermediate step in the revolutionary process that was to do away with the capitalist-imperialist "old order". As he saw it, true self-determination could only be attained once a new world of Soviet republics had been created in which – through workers' councils and led by a vanguard of socialist parties – the working class determined its own fate in a spirit of transnational class solidarity.[59] Lenin had thus developed a powerful self-determination agenda long before Wilson would advance his less radical and more hierarchical vision of how the blessings of self-government were to be spread in a progressive Americanist "new world order".

The future Bolshevik leader was also more uncompromising than other radical socialists in pushing for a hard-headed dialectical policy that could be summarised under the heading of "to socialism through war". By 1907, he declared that the "essential thing" was to "utilise the crisis created by war to hasten the overthrow of the bourgeoisie" and the capitalist world system – and that the proletariat thus could not "renounce the participation in revolutionary wars".[60] But the majority within Second International adhered to a different position, which was confirmed at the landmark Basel Congress of 1912. It passed a resolution calling on the workers of all countries to wage "war on war" by going on general strike as soon as the ruling capitalists sought to incite them to go to take up arms against each other.[61] Up until the crisis of 1914, Jaurès remained a particularly stalwart proponent of this maxim, and he clung to the belief that the power and solidarity of the working classes would prevent the escalation of any major war. In the midst of the July crisis, the French Socialist Party confirmed its adherence to the Second International's resolution. But after Jaurès' assassination by a fanatical nationalist, the socialists' parliamentary representatives then voted, like the Social Democratic Party in Germany, to support not only essential war credits but also the declaration of a state of emergency.[62]

Because it lacked effective means to counter the efforts of the governments of the eventual belligerents to mobilise the working classes' national-patriotic sentiments, the Second International ultimately proved incapable of becoming the decisive bulwark against the war-prone tendencies of the age. And its

---

[59] Lenin (1960); Lenin (1914), pp. 208–10; Fisch (2010), pp. 136–9. On Marx and Engels see Benner (2018), pp. 156–7.

[60] Riddell (1984), pp. 36–7, 41–2.

[61] Basel Manifesto, *Extraordinary International Socialist Congress at Basel, November 24–25* (Berlin, 1912), pp. 23 ff. See Imlay (2018), pp. 18–19.

[62] See Becker and Krumeich (2008), pp. 21–37, 78–9.

aspirations to prevent a "great war" and create a more lasting internationalist peace were brutally disappointed in 1914. But, as will be shown, formative social democratic ideas and conceptions of peace and international order would be developed further during the war – particularly in Europe – and have a significant bearing on the eventual struggle for a "peace to end all wars". By contrast, Lenin's expectations that a war between the capitalist powers would create a revolutionary constellation were not entirely disappointed. But ultimately the Great War would not set in motion a communist world revolution but a different transatlantic transformation process with global consequences.

5

The Unavoidable War?

Long and Short Roads to the Catastrophe of 1914

It has rightly been emphasised that the period between 1870 and 1914 should not merely be seen or interpreted as the pre-history of the First World War – as a crisis-ridden period of modern history in which all the salient developments in and beyond Europe inexorably led up to its preordained end, the catastrophe of 1914.[1] Indeed, it is important to understand that all the longer-term structural and systemic changes that affected the European international system, transatlantic relations and the politics of global imperialism in the critical first third of the long twentieth century did not *inevitably* lead to the eventual escalation of an all-out war of unprecedented magnitude. This also and particularly holds true for one crucial nexus – the nexus between the increasingly more antagonistic relations between two emerging European alliance blocs, smaller states – notably in the Balkans, and most notably Serbia – and the ailing Ottoman Empire.

I.   Long and Short Roads to the Abyss

It would undoubtedly be wrong to over-determine the causes of the Great War – to build a gigantic pyramid of compelling long- and short-term causes that in retrospect make it seem as though the war was bound to break out sooner or later. Nor should one draw a straight and linear line between global imperialist competition – and the mind-sets and practices it generated – and the eventual descent into the abyss. Neither the "larger impersonal forces" of capitalist globalisation and global imperialist competition, neither the newly prevalent tendencies of social and civilisational Darwinism and chauvinistic nationalist ideologies nor the rise of militarism and increasingly militarised power politics and brinkmanship that marked this period made the war's outbreak *unavoidable*.

And even the most significant systemic change in the sphere of European international politics, the final break-up of the last vestiges of a coherent European international system and the emergence of two opposing blocs of alliances and alignments did not inexorably lead into the abyss of 1914. Nor

---

[1] See Clark (2012), pp. xxiv–xxix; Afflerbach and Stevenson (2007), pp. 1–17.

did the recurrent crises and conflicts that erupted in this period and involved these alliance blocs either directly or indirectly – in the extra-European sphere of imperialist competition, as in Morocco, or, crucially, in the notoriously unstable "periphery" of the Balkans – necessarily lead to the one fateful crisis that then could no longer be contained.

But it is even more important to underscore that all of these processes and developments – and above all the formation of the two antagonistic blocs and dominance of confrontational balance-of-power thinking – created a constellation in which eventually a general war – whose scale and magnitude the protagonists of European politics could only begin to anticipate – became far from improbable but rather increasingly *likely*. Or, more precisely, it became *ever harder to prevent*. What ultimately proved decisive was that, at a deeper level, fundamental changes in the mind-sets, mentalities and basic understandings of the – multiple – actors of European international politics had occurred in the decades before 1914, especially since the early 1890s – changes in the overall political culture that, for all the differences, they shared and that informed their approaches to war and peace, to diplomacy and its domestic legitimation. In short, what now occurred was the culmination of a turn towards a systemic culture of *inherently war-prone* high-stakes power-political rivalry and "zero-sum" balance-of-power politics that had already begun in the 1880s, but now intensified and in the end spun out of control. This not only created new and ever deeper divisions in Europe and eventually prompted a dynamically accelerating polarisation process; it also effectively destroyed the last remnants of the older European state system that had once been regulated by the Concert of Europe.[2]

On one level, this undoubtedly was an inner-European process. Yet it could gain its specific ominous dynamism because it unfolded against the essential backdrop of, and was in essential aspects driven by, *global imperialist rivalries* and *globalising power politics*. It was this process that created a highly precarious constellation in which regional crises that would earlier have been considered peripheral and manageable – such as those that erupted in the Balkans after 1900 – could *acquire* the potential to escalate into a general antagonism between the European great powers. Rapidly becoming ever more polarised, the European situation on the eve of the Great War can thus indeed be likened both to a tinderbox and a time-bomb scenario. This tinderbox was

---

[2] See Schroeder (I/2004), esp. pp. 190–1. For notable contributions to the complex and still politicised debate about what led to the Great War and who bears the chief responsibility for its outbreak see Clark (2012); Mombauer (2013); Otte (2014) and most recently Schmidt (2021). Remarkably, all of these contributions neglect the wider origins of the war and the structural, *longue durée* developments that created essential preconditions for the catastrophe; and they all either downplay or fail to grasp the essential global and transatlantic dimensions of the war's pre-history.

not bound to be set ablaze, and this time-bomb was not bound to explode. But – and this is what matters – they became ever more *prone* to set Europe and the world on fire sooner or later unless fundamental *political* reforms of the international system could be enacted. Yet although the efforts of the European and American champions of arbitration were remarkable, more comprehensive reforms of this kind had not been seriously attempted up until 1914. As a consequence, there were no reliable international mechanisms and no effective rules and norms to which decision-makers could have had recourse to settle conflicts and preserve the general peace when they needed them most.

In a broader context, the developments that immediately preceded the Great War not only revealed the distinctly limited reach of the pacifist and, notably, the arbitration movement. They also threw into stark relief to what extent the United States, and particularly the administrations in Washington, still stood on the side-lines of "high politics" when it came to critical issues of international crisis management and conflict resolution. Roosevelt's very limited intervention as intermediary during the first Morocco crisis would remain an isolated episode. Focusing on financial diplomacy in East Asia, Taft never tried to translate his advocacy of arbitration into concrete initiatives to mediate between Europe's increasingly antagonistic blocs. And when Wilson became president in 1913, he was still far from aspiring to make the United States into the decisive "neutral" mediating nation that led Europe and the world towards a new progressive order. Wilson clearly concentrated on the implementation of his progressive domestic reform programme, the New Freedom agenda, and saw no reason to intercede in European affairs and, eventually, the crisis of 1914. Nor had he yet developed any coherent concep-tions to effect what he in April 1913 called "reasonable" advances in "the promotion of peace". Employing a myopically optimistic rhetoric, the new president merely predicted that a "great deal" could be accomplished in this sphere as the cause of peace was favoured by the underlying "temper" of the opinion of the world.[3]

Wilson thus backed the missionary aspiration of his first secretary of state, William Jennings Bryan, to promote an alternative to European power politics and pacify international relations through so-called cooling-off treaties. Bryan, who had been an eminent figure in the American peace movement, considered it the duty of the American republic to become the "foremost advocate of world-wide peace" as "the leading exponent of Christianity".[4] As secretary of state, he thus quickly seized the initiative to lead efforts to settle all inter-national disputes without recourse to war. And in 1913 and 1914 he indeed

---

[3] Wilson press conference, 28 April 1913, *PWW*, XVII, p. 300.
[4] Bryan to Wilson to House, 1 December 1914, *PWW*, XXXI, p. 379.

managed to negotiate a series of bilateral "cooling-off" agreements with thirty nations, including Britain and France – yet not with the German and Austro-Hungarian Empires. The "Bryan Peace Treaties" were supposed to prevent wars by requiring all signatories to submit disputes to an international commission and observe a cooling-off period until it presented its findings. Yet they did not compel the signatories to act on these findings; and crucially, they did not have any enforcement provisions. As a response to the escalation of Europe's systemic crisis, Bryan's treaties would prove singularly ineffectual – and his pursuits would be overshadowed by the outbreak of the Great War.[5]

II.   The Impact of World-Political Rivalries on Europe – and the Creation of a Profoundly War-Prone Constellation

While it would thus be misleading to establish too direct a causal connection between the intensifying world-political competition after 1880 and the July crisis of 1914, it is essential to understand that this competition and the longer-term systemic changes it both reflected and accelerated did not merely contribute to the rise of tensions in the background. It actually had a formative impact on the process that progressively *eroded* international order in the decades before 1914. For it dramatically altered the shape of the European international system, turning what had once been an inclusive European concert and then devolved into the complex and increasingly volatile balance-of-power "order" of the Bismarck era into a profoundly polarised "system" in which two hostile alliance blocs eventually confronted each other. It was thus highly significant in creating the systemic – and particularly the mental and ideological – conditions that made a major war ever harder to avoid.

Crucially, the dynamics of the struggle between old and aspiring "world powers" had ever more immediate repercussions on inner-European politics, thwarting any attempts to reconstitute, even temporarily, some kind of functioning system for concerted crisis management – and instead raising the stakes of the European power-political "game" still further. Above all, however, they contributed significantly to the creation and fateful "rigidification" of the two European alliance "blocs". And all of this would then decisively narrow the room to manoeuvre decision-makers had when the July crisis escalated.

This overarching and inherently war-prone development entered a new and decisive phase following the conclusion of the Anglo-French *Entente Cordiale* in 1904 and the Anglo-Russian Convention in 1907. And it cannot be stressed often enough that these formative changes took place in a wider and dynamically changing force-field which reached far beyond Europe and the Balkans.

---

[5] See Coletta (1964–69), II, pp. 239–59; Knock (1992), pp. 21–2.

For all of the leading European actors had to deal with the transformative world-political changes the era of globalising imperialism had wrought: the challenges arising from this intense competition, the perceived need to remain among the first tier of *world* powers to remain secure as a great power; the epochal Russian fiasco in the war against Japan that prompted major modern- isation and recuperation efforts of an inherently fragile Tsarist regime; the challenges arising from the ongoing struggle to extend as far as possible imperial spheres of dominance and influence over the remaining "unclaimed" states and territories; and finally – closer to the epicentre of European con- flicts – the challenges arising from the demise of Ottoman rule in the Balkans. All of these developments indeed redirected tensions that had long been deflected to the "periphery" of global imperialist competition – or addressed by making arrangements at the expense of weaker parties – right back to the European continent. At the same time, they spurred an overall tightening of the opposing alliance systems.

Essentially, these developments magnified pressures and constraints for all of the European great powers. But they particularly reduced the room to manoeuvre of those who sought to pursue *Weltpolitik* on behalf of Europe's central power. Bülow and other leading German decision-makers had long believed that they retained a free hand to forge alliances if the need arose, because they espoused the erroneous assumption that the "British whale" and the "Russian bear" would always remain divided by their imperial conflicts. In fact, however, they soon had to confront a scenario in which the German Empire found itself isolated and indeed "circled out" following the two blows of the Anglo-French *Entente* and the Anglo-Russian Convention. This led some, notably Bülow, William II himself and, later, the new head of the Foreign Office, Alfred von Kiderlen-Wächter, to strive all the more to assert "rightful" German claims – notably with a view to Morocco. But they would have to recognise that peremptory German demands and hard-line approaches only stiffened the resistance of the *Entente* Powers and brought them closer together. Nor did efforts to lure Russia away from France by means of repeated alliance offers lead anywhere. And for their part more moderate German decision-makers like Bülow's successor Bethmann Hollweg would have to acknowledge that attempts to escape encirclement through pragmatic attempts to foster collaboration and *détente* with Britain or the Tsarist Empire had only superficial effects.[6]

Yet it is important to note that although some German actors tended to pursue the most blatantly oscillating and disruptive policies in this phase, their French and Russian counterparts now also acted in more one-sided and confrontational ways; and so did their Austrian allies, who increasingly feared

---

[6] See Canis (2011), pp. 48–66, 193 ff.

existential threats to the future of the Habsburg Empire. At the same time, the political leaders of the erstwhile hegemon of the European Concert – which still had comparatively most strategic leverage – at first wavered but then also adopted a new, more one-sided and confrontational orientation. After a period of meandering, the decisive impetus was given by the new liberal foreign secretary Edward Grey.

Under Grey, Britain eventually came to act as a decidedly partisan power, placing *Entente* considerations over general systemic concerns. And the maxim that now came to dominate in the Foreign Office was that in order to protect the security and development of Britain and its imperial system, a pronounced policy of containment had to be adopted to counter what Grey, Eyre Crowe and other "hawks" came to identify, in distinctly ideological terms, as the gravest threat: German aspirations to dominate Europe and challenge Britain's salutary pre-eminence in the world.[7] Crucially, the logic of thinking in terms of antagonistic blocs and friend–enemy relations thus came to prevail *on all sides* – and ultimately marginalised all attempts to collaborate across the new divides in attempts to arrive at mutually acceptable settlements of crises and conflicts. And the impera-tives of power-political rivalries and global dynamics of polarisation now clearly came to overpower the efforts of all the pacifists and internationalists of different stripes to contain or even reverse these war-prone trends.

Contrary to what has often been claimed, the ever more unrestrained global imperialist competition also had *very direct* repercussions for the ever more precarious European "game" of balance-of-power politics. In a wider perspective, the domestic and international pressures of the global "great game" contributed decisively to two highly destabilising general trends: the penchant for *brinkman-ship* once conflicts arose; and the penchant for assertive zero-sum bargaining over spheres of influences. Further, they contributed significantly to a radicalisa-tion of notions of military preparedness that emphasised the need for a rapid mobilisation of forces, resources and populations. All of these notions hardened into core assumptions that came to dominate approaches to international politics on all sides. Finally, the world-political dimension was critical not just for the intensification of militarist thinking but also the almost uninterrupted escalation of arms races between the ever more antagonistic great powers.

This notably applied to the Anglo-German naval race. By 1912, both sides acknowledged that Britain had essentially "won" this race against its German challenger for the foreseeable future. But the political damage this stand-off had caused was immense – particularly because it contributed not only to the hardening anti-British attitudes in Germany but also to the anti-German reorientation of Britain's *Entente* policies and the spread of anti-German

---

[7] Grey memorandum, August 1912, in Lowe and Dockrill (1972), III, pp. 458–9. See Steiner and Neilson (2003), pp. 42–8.

jingoist nationalism in the British public. Even more significant for the crisis constellation of 1914, however, was the intensified race for the expansion of land forces that set in after Russia's defeat against Japan. This epochal defeat prompted major Russian efforts to resurge as a military power that then led to the unprecedentedly far-reaching German army bill of 1913, which in turn provoked renewed armament efforts in France and Britain.

Yet global imperialist competition also had an even more immediate effect. For, crucially, not inner-European rivalries but imperial rivalries in the extra-European sphere propelled the processes that led to the emergence of the *Entente* bloc between 1904 and 1907, which decisively expanded the Franco-Russian alliance of 1890, and the fortification of the alliance of the Central Powers, which centred on the German–Austrian Dual Alliance that had originally been forged in 1879. It was due to world-political preoccupations that British elites had entered into comparatively loose alignments with two powers that it sought to "appease" as global competitors, France and Russia. Very soon, however, key British policymakers – above all a dominant "containment" faction in the Foreign Office that rallied behind Grey – came to push for a firmer system of quasi-alliances whose key purpose was not only to check German expansionism but also to isolate it in the "great game" of global imperialism.

But the first steps on the path towards inner-European polarisation and division had been taken much earlier – first by Bismarck, then by his successors, yet also by French and Russian decision-makers – in the period of Britain's not so "splendid isolation". As noted, those who tried to take over the reins of German foreign policy after Bismarck's resignation, notably the *eminence grise* at the German Foreign Office, Friedrich von Holstein, and later Chancellor Bülow, sought to chart some kind of world-political "new course" but in effect deepened the Empire's international isolation and European divisions. In the east, they deliberately sought to rid themselves of the self-imposed restraints that Bismarck's system had depended on by not renewing the Reinsurance Treaty with Russia in 1890. In the west, the notion that one ought to come to a world-political understanding with Britain was supported by Bülow and others who influenced the often erratic decision-making during William II's reign; but it was never seriously pursued. Attempts to forge an alliance foundered time and again on the rock of irreconcilable interests or perceptions of interests.[8]

Following the shocks of the *Entente Cordiale* and Britain's subsequent convention with Russia, German options became distinctly limited. In fact, all later attempts to soften these alignments and manoeuvre Britain away from them, which Bethmann Hollweg came to pursue with particular vigour, would remain futile. And so would, in a wider sense, all attempts to end Germany's encirclement in Europe and its being "circled out" in the imperial-colonial

---

[8] See Kennedy (1980), pp. 223 ff., 441 ff.

sphere. Thus, while Germany had negotiated a Triple Alliance that also included Italy, it was the pact with the Austro-Hungarian Empire that became the centrepiece of its alliance system in Europe. And this led German decision-makers to support rather than restrain their Austrian ally in the Balkans – even though they reckoned from early on that this alliance was distinctly insufficient to safeguard German security and its future as a world power.[9]

On behalf of the power that remained Germany's structural enemy in Europe, France, the Ribot government had initiated a major structural shift in negotiating the Franco-Russian Military Convention in 1892, which was then followed by a fully-fledged secret alliance of 1894, which provided the hitherto isolated French republic with an essential strategic ally against an otherwise superior German Empire. It was because of these underlying power-political and security concerns that its political leaders remained steadfastly committed to the alliance, even though they found it difficult to justify close bonds with the autocratic Tsar Alexander III. Crucially, French policymakers thus not only went to considerable lengths to cultivate their new partner but also encouraged Russian aspirations in the Balkans rather than restraining them. For its part, Russia had been driven into to the alliance by the renewal of the Triple Alliance and the fear that Britain might associate itself with this combination to contain Russia's ambitions to expand its imperial sphere of influence and finally gain unfettered access to the Mediterranean. Further, there was a marked Russian interest to impede Austrian expansion in the Balkans. The Franco-Russian *entente* thus essentially sprang from consider-ations of European balance-of-power politics that were nonetheless intermin-gled with global-imperial concerns. Its conclusion indeed marked a 'turning-point' in the pre-history of the Great War. It did not become the "fateful alliance" that made an eventual conflict with the German Empire unavoid-able.[10] But it became a central element of the constellation that eventually led to a hardening of two alliance blocs that were increasingly dominated by the central aim to counter the threat posed by the adversarial combination – and through which ultimately preparedness for war rather than peace preservation became the core axiom of international politics.[11]

All the main continental European powers thus realigned themselves in structurally antagonistic "defensive" alliances. And eventually – in the wake of the disconcerting Boer War and against a backdrop of growing imperialist tensions – British decision-makers also felt compelled to abandon the long-standing posture of aloofness, which Salisbury had still vigorously defended in 1898. Essentially, after decades of very limited engagement in maintaining a functioning European peace system Salisbury's successors no longer saw an

[9] See Canis (2011), pp. 191 ff., 215 ff.
[10] Thus Kennan (1984).
[11] See Clark (2012), pp. 127–31; Weitsman (2004), pp. 117–18; Keiger (1983), pp. 4–24.

alternative to entering into bilateral agreements with France and Russia to protect Britain's far-flung world system. It thus became clear that in the eyes of Balfour and those who followed him, Britain's most vital global interests could not be safeguarded by pursuing a novel *transatlantic* strategy – essentially, a shared Anglo-American hegemony. Even though they regarded a *rapprochement* with the United States as eminently desirable, they understood that because of towering domestic obstacles the fledgling American world power could not be a fully-fledged hegemonic alliance partner. Nor were they prepared to rely on the Hague Conventions and advances in international law – or to invest in efforts to renew the European concert. Instead, they opted for a more traditional policy of limited strategic alignments – and appeasement. First came the alliance with the rising Pacific power Japan, forged in 1902. Then, most momentously, Britain concluded the *Entente Cordiale* with its main rival in Africa in 1904 and, in 1907, the Military Convention with its long-time imperial rival in central Asia and the eastern Mediterranean.

It is worth stressing again that British decision-makers originally negotiated the agreements with France and Russia not in order to rein in Germany but to manage the most pressing challenges to the British imperial world system.[12] Crucially, however, these agreements soon changed their character. They hardened into instruments of containment and deterrence that were directed against what now came to be perceived as the greatest danger, that arising from the Wilhelmine Empire's abrasive-assertive pursuits of *Weltpolitik* and, in particular, Admiral Tirpitz's naval expansion programme. Leading Foreign Office strategists and notably the new foreign secretary Grey came to interpret and ideologically magnify these pursuits as outgrowths of an ambitious German agenda to attain a dangerous dictatorial predominance against which it was their duty to defend the British Empire – on behalf of all who cherished "political liberty" in the world.[13]

In fact, the "strategy" Tirpitz advocated, which then led to an unparalleled expansion of the German navy that not only the Kaiser but also a soon highly influential naval movement backed, was not intended to attain global mastery or to threaten Britain and its empire. Rather, its aim was to bolster Germany's world-political aspirations by somehow putting it "on a par" with the British global power. But what Tirpitz unleashed unavoidably posed a substantial challenge not only to Britain's imperial interests but also to its national security – as all German naval power had to be projected through the Channel and thus right through the heart of the British world system. But while the years before 1914 would see repeated efforts to further Anglo-German *détente*, British policymakers essentially refused to "appease" and

---

[12] See Steiner and Neilson (2003), pp. 32–51, 86–99.
[13] Crowe memorandum, 1 January 1907, Gooch and Temperley (1926–38), III, pp. 397–420.

come to some kind of world-political accommodation with a German Empire whose elites displayed, in their eyes, an assertive yet also erratic mode of conduct. By the time of Haldane's famous mission in 1912 it had become clear to both sides that Britain was actually winning the naval arms race and that Tirpitz's strategy had proved highly counterproductive, reinforcing Germany's isolation and exclusion from the world-political game.[14]

What came to dominate British foreign policy once Grey had assumed its reins were the rationales and worldviews of a "containment faction" within the Foreign Office. And its core axiom became that placing a check on the German Empire's aggressive *Weltpolitik* was the challenge that had to be met in the interest of national and imperial security. It was now that the most outspoken advocate of a determined policy of containment, the German-born Eyre Crowe, who in 1912 became undersecretary of state for foreign affairs, could exert a formative influence. In 1907, Crowe famously asserted that as the leading world power Britain was bound by the imperatives of balance-of-power politics to resist any power that challenged its hegemony and aspired to form a hostile coalition against it. And he outlined what became the dominant *ideological* interpretation of Wilhelmine world-political ambitions in and beyond the Foreign Office, which anticipated core elements of British Great War ideology and propaganda. Crowe asserted that the underlying aim of *Weltpolitik* was to establish – by "bullying and blackmail" – nothing less than a "German hegemony, at first in Europe and eventually in the world". He warned that, based on the "evil" of Prussian militarism and authoritarianism, this hegemony would inescapably turn into a "political dictatorship" that would destroy "the liberties of Europe" and fundamentally threaten Britain's existence as a world power. Its mission therefore was to preserve a benign hegemony that, he claimed, was accepted by all other powers because of the championing of "political liberty" and free trade that lay at its core.[15]

Grey was impressed by Crowe's analysis and adopted a very similar outlook. Consequently, he came to view the agreements with France and Russia increasingly as instruments to rein in Germany's alleged dictatorial-hegemonic ambitions. The main tactical aim in this contest became to isolate the German Empire both in Europe and in the sphere of global imperialist competition. In pursuit of this priority he and other British policymakers no longer used Britain's quasi-alliances as instruments to restrain their partners but rather supported their more assertive policies vis-à-vis Germany – and Austria-Hungary – in the interest of strengthening mutual bonds. Like German assertiveness, if in a different way, this contributed both to the

[14] See Kennedy (1980), pp. 416–23.
[15] Crowe memorandum, 1 January 1907, Gooch and Temperley (1926–38), III, pp. 397–420.

rising Anglo-German antagonism and to a further polarisation of the relations between the two increasingly hostile blocs in Europe.

It would doubtless be not only too simplistic but actually wrong to argue that the increasing rigidity of the different European alliances at this juncture was the key factor accounting for the escalation of an all-out war in 1914. What mattered most was that, till the very end, none of the British governments of this period ever reached a real consensus on the crucial question of whether Britain was rigidly committed to go to war if France was attacked by Germany; and there was even less of a commitment vis-à-vis the Tsarist Empire. Nor was the German Empire steadfastly committed to Austria-Hungary, as became apparent during the Balkan wars of 1912 and 1913. To a certain extent, it was even the "fluidity" of these alliances that contributed to bringing on the war, because it created uncertainties and raised dangerous hopes – notably the German hope that Britain would ultimately stay neutral should a war break out between the Central Powers and the Franco-Russian alliance.

Of greater consequence, however, was that now "long-term changes" in the prevalent conceptions of what purposes alliances served became apparent, and these changes had a distinctly war-prone effect. On both sides, the idea that an alliance was primarily a mechanism to manage and restrain inter-state relations had "receded far into the background". Consequently, the different European powers no longer dared to moderate or rein in their partners "for fear of undermining the alliances as indispensable weapons of security". And this indeed made these alliances ultimately useless as instruments of peace. Instead, they became key mechanisms to wage industrial war.[16] But an even more fundamental problem was that the alliance politics that came to prevail in the years before 1914 stood in the way of any serious attempts to initiate more fundamental reforms of the international system – steps towards a more modern and inclusive system in which *all* of the European powers participated and sought to resolve conflicts by peaceful means. Such steps and such reforms rapidly became inconceivable after 1904.

III.   Imperialist *and* Balkan Crises – and the Fateful Shortcomings of European Crisis Management

Instead, the logic of thinking in terms of antagonistic blocs and friend–enemy relations came to prevail on both sides. Such thinking of course seriously limited all attempts to collaborate across the new divides and find mutually acceptable ways to settle conflicts. In the imperial-colonial sphere, this became manifest during the two Moroccan crises of 1905 and 1911. And, crucially, it

---

[16] Schroeder (II/2004), pp. 215–16.

manifested itself in what now turned even more than before into Europe's neuralgic crisis region, the Balkans. Because of the now dominating balance-of-power and alliance concerns *all* the major powers became entangled in these conflicts, which arose in the power vacuum the retreating Ottoman Empire left behind, were fuelled by the expansionist nationalist aspirations of unstable Balkan states, notably Serbia and Bulgaria – and, most ominously, drove a multi-national Austro-Hungarian Empire, whose existential interests came to be affected, into an antagonism with the Russian Empire, which pursued its own expansionist interests yet was also under pressure to act as the "protector of all Slavs". The critical question that thus came to hang over European politics like a Sword of Damocles was how long it would be possible to "localise" tensions and crises – and to prevent them from provoking a greater war. All of this has to be re-examined in greater depth because it is vital to understand precisely which deficiencies of European thinking and approaches to international politics – deficiencies that critical observers on both sides of the Atlantic pointed out at the time – led into the abyss of the Great War and then spawned the incipient transformation of the Atlantic and global order.

Initially, though, it should be stressed that even during the high tide of polarisation and imperialist competition after 1890 some actors in the fractured European system showed remarkable capacities to de-escalate conflicts that were often exacerbated by domestic pressure-groups and increasingly aggressive nationalist publicised opinion. This would be done time and again during the successive crises and wars that erupted in the Balkans – from the Bosnian annexation crisis of 1908 to the first and second Balkan wars of 1912 and 1913. But in some ways the successes of such efforts only accentuated a dangerous tendency. In many quarters, notably in Britain, they reinforced the assumption that it would be possible to muddle through, sort out whatever crisis erupted next and thus keep averting the disaster of a general war, which in turn encouraged a false sense of security against a backdrop of worsening *structural insecurity*. In effect, such short-term crisis management stood in the way of working towards what the Hague internationalists, socialists and other activists demanded – namely more far-reaching *structural changes* – the construction of a modern European peace system.

Yet there was a second, even more detrimental trend. Not only the potential for ever more and increasingly polarising conflicts was growing but also the assertiveness and militancy of key decision-makers within both "blocs". More precisely, what grew not only among military but also political leaders was the readiness to pursue increasingly confrontational and militarised strategies to safeguard national and imperial security and other perceived vital interests. This was not merely a German phenomenon, though in Berlin a particularly precar-ious struggle ensued between the most authoritative military leader Helmuth von Moltke, who came to push for a "defensive" preventive war at the earliest opportunity, and a still preponderant chancellor Bethmann Hollweg who sought to preserve peace. On the side of the *Entente*, the advocates of more assertive approaches also gained dominance, notably in France where President Raymond Poincaré emerged as the most uncompromising hard-liner vis-à-vis Germany and in Russia where foreign minister Sergei Sazonov became the most influential proponent of a forceful interventionist policy, especially in the Balkans. At the same time, though most of the main actors did not fully realise this, not only the international but also the domestic room to manoeuvre they had to "resolve" crises and avert war became dangerously constrained. Parallel the risks of brinkmanship increased immensely.

As described earlier, in the extra-European sphere it had long been customary to use high-handed methods to accommodate competing imperialist interests at the expense of those who were objects of colonial rule or domination. But now, in the dawning era of antagonistic alliances, the rules of this "game" changed too. The behaviour of all interested powers became affected by the polarisation within the European system, and considerations of accommodation and "imperialist reciprocity" came to give way to the imperatives of alliance politics and antagonistic containment. This was thrown into relief during the two telltale crises of the new era, the two Moroccan crises. British policymakers had negotiated the *Entente* with France in part to consolidate Britain's exclusive control over the strategically vital Egyptian "protectorate" and the Suez Canal, striking a deal under which they gained French support in return for backing Delcassé's plan to incorporate Morocco into France's imperial sphere of influence. Seeking to capitalise on this agreement, Delcassé in January 1905 pushed ahead with his scheme, pointedly refraining from offering the German Empire any economic guarantees or compensation. In a feat of his by then habitual "gesture politics" William II used a visit to Tangier in March 1905 to assert German commercial interests and insist on the inviolability of Morocco's independence. Subsequently, after Chancellor Bülow had gone so far as to threaten war, his government insisted on resolving the Franco-German dispute through an international conference. And it had prevailed on Theodore Roosevelt to act as mediator who then helped to ensure France's participation in the conference, which opened in Algeciras in January 1906. Yet while the assembled powers confirmed the "quasi-independence" of Morocco the conference yielded no substantive agreement that all sides could tolerate. Rather, it revealed Berlin's rapidly growing isolation and the deepening divisions between the *Entente* Powers and the "circled-out" German Empire. This confrontational constellation thwarted Roosevelt's strictly informal attempts to mediate an agreement that defused tensions between France and Germany.[17]

---

[17] See Roosevelt to Reid, 28 April 1906, in Bishop (1920), I, pp. 468–75; Holmes (2006), pp. 191–201; Clark (2012), pp. 155–7; Canis (2011), pp. 117–90.

At Algeciras, not only Russia's representatives had been under strict orders to back all French proposals energetically. Crucially, Britain's plenipotentiaries had also demonstratively supported their French *Entente* partner. Grey joined Delcassé in opposing a compensatory port for Germany in west Africa and criticised German demands as egregious. And it was at this point that Crowe castigated German bullying and aspirations for world domination.[18] Conversely, the "humiliation" of Algeciras reinforced the inclination of Bülow and other influential policymakers in Berlin hence to push all the more aggressively for what they regarded as legitimate German claims and adopt even more hostile attitudes towards France and what they viewed as British designs to deny Germany its rightful place in the world of empires. Thus, hostile perceptions and assumptions on both sides reinforced each other and deepened distrust.

In an atmosphere of heightened pressure and growing suspicion, Franco-German confrontations reached a new high point in the summer of 1911 when in a further act of symbolic assertiveness the newly influential imperial state secretary for foreign affairs in Berlin, Alfred von Kiderlen-Wächter, authorised the "Panther leap of Agadir" – the dispatch of a German warship to the Moroccan coast in protest against France's unilateral bid to make all of Morocco a French protectorate. The ensuing second Moroccan crisis provoked two important – and somewhat contradictory – developments. On the one hand, the more belligerent actors on both sides allowed the conflict to escalate to a point where the threat of a general war for the first time appeared on the horizon. On the other, the key players then actually managed to settle the crisis peacefully. The new French premier Joseph Caillaux sought a businesslike accommodation and managed to negotiate a compensatory deal with Kiderlen-Wächter, which was finalised in August 1911. Yet both had underestimated how strong the opposition to a Franco-German compromise had by then become on both sides of the Rhine. This foreshadowed problems besetting Franco-German relations after the Great War. In Paris, not only hawkish Quai d'Orsay officials but also the nationalist press and profoundly anti-German military leadership agitated against an agreement that "betrayed" vital French interests. And in Berlin, ultra-nationalist politicians and publicists agitated against any concessions to France.

It was thus all the more remarkable that both governments did manage to reach a "classic" imperialist *do ut des* agreement in November 1911. Berlin recognised Morocco as an exclusive French protectorate; and in return Germany was assured that its business interests in Morocco would be respected and that it would be compensated with provinces that had been

---

[18] Crowe memorandum, 1 January 1907, Gooch and Temperley (1926–38), III, pp. 406 ff.; Hardinge minute, 10 November 1909, ibid., VI, pp. 311–12; Grey (1925), II, p. 29.

part of French Congo. But the political fall-out was ominous. In short, an agreement of this kind could no longer gain any substantive domestic support on either side. In Germany, a storm of protest erupted amid allegations in the nationalist press that the German Empire's "rightful expectations" had been bitterly disappointed. In France Caillaux's premiership was discredited because of his willingness to strike a compromise with *l'ennemi outre-Rhin*. And his successor Poincaré proclaimed that whenever France offered concessions to the Teutonic empire the Germans abused them. This was to shape his future hard-line policy vis-à-vis France's eastern neighbour.[19]

But the repercussions of the Morocco crisis reached even further. For Grey and those who argued for a more robust containment of the Wilhelmine Empire in Britain interpreted Kiderlen-Wächter's manoeuvres as a further example of dangerous German behaviour. And even the leading radical Liberal David Lloyd George, who had earlier favoured *détente* and pragmatic cooperation with Germany, now signalled that he backed a more confrontational course. In his famous Mansion House speech of 21 July 1911, Asquith's chancellor of the exchequer issued a stern warning. He stressed that it was imperative for Britain to maintain her pre-eminent "place and her prestige among the Great Powers of the world" and to prevent continental powers like France from "overwhelming disaster" or even "national extinction".[20] Lloyd George's warning-call was part of a deliberate strategy he had developed with Grey and Asquith to bypass a strong faction of "radical doves" in the liberal Cabinet who favoured Anglo-German appeasement and to shift to a more assertive policy of containment vis-à-vis the German Empire.

But Grey's course was in fact marked by an underlying ambiguity that was to prove significant in 1914. Behind closed doors, he urged the General Staff, only established in 1906, to coordinate with France's military leadership common mobilisation plans *that were not sanctioned by parliament*, thus unofficially taking steps towards an actual Anglo-French military alliance. But, chiefly to placate continued liberal – and Labour – criticism of his policies, he publicly declared that the Franco-British military plans were merely contingency measures with no binding force. In private, however, Grey underscored that the military conventions did commit Britain to "cooperation with France" as long as the latter's actions were "non-provocative". And yet he would still insist that there was actually no *written* guarantee that Britain would come to France's aid in case of a German aggression. This was still how things stood when the July crisis escalated. But the main shortcoming of Grey's policy was not that it remained ambiguous but rather that he did not make any further serious attempts to use Britain's leverage to

[19] See Clark (2012), pp. 204-14.
[20] Lloyd George, Mansion House speech, 21 July 1911, *The Times*, 22 July 1911, p. 7; Keiger (2016), pp. 285-300.

reclaim the essential role it had earlier played in Europe, namely that of a hegemon buttressing a *common* European concert system that comprised all the relevant powers. Instead, his actions exacerbated the divisions between the two opposing blocs at the very moment when renewed conflicts in the Balkans unsettled European politics more profoudly than ever before.

As noted, the European powers had to deal with the repercussions of the "Eastern question" – the corrosion of the Ottoman Empire, the rise of nation-alisms and consequent turbulences in the Balkans – for many decades. And this had long affected the Habsburg and Tsarist Empires most; but it had also had important indirect repercussions for all other great powers. As long as their nineteenth-century system had not been entirely undermined, the leading powers had found ways to negotiate *general* agreements that to some extent considered the claims of local nationalities but above all accommodated their interests – even though this could no longer be done without accumulat-ing multiple grievances. The last significant accommodation had been achieved at the Congress of Berlin in 1878. Yet Bismarck's actions as "honest broker" and the compromises that were struck established a very short-lived new status quo. South-eastern Europe remained an intrinsically volatile crisis zone in which the Ottoman Empire's weakening grip eventually provoked conflicting nationalist-expansionist aspirations of local powers, notably Serbia and Bulgaria. This provoked a succession of crises and wars that affected not only the clashing interests of the Habsburg and the Tsarist Empires but also, and crucially, those of all the other European empires that had entered into alliances with either Vienna or St Petersburg.

Essentially, the "perhipheral" conflicts of the Balkan region thus came to be irretrievably bound up with concerns and strategic considerations prevailing at the systemic level of European balance-of-power politics. Time and again these conflicts were partially contained. But they were never really settled, and the structural minefield they created remained essentially unaltered. What made the situation even more hazardous was the fact that the empires that had most at stake also faced ever graver internal challenges. Most immediately, this applied to the Austro-Hungarian Empire, which urgently needed to reinforce its cohesion and legitimacy as a multinational empire against centripetal nationalist tendencies. Efforts to address this problem by granting increasing autonomy notably to the empire's "southern Slav" minorities could only provide temporary remedies here.[21] Yet it was the nationalism of its south-eastern neighbours, above all Serbia, that posed the gravest challenge. For their part, those who competed to direct Russia's policies vis-à-vis the Balkans and the Ottoman Empire under Nicholas II faced both domestic and external nationalist pressures to assert its authority as the patron and protector of all

---

[21] See Canis (2016), pp. 335–64; Judson (2016), pp. 333 ff.

Balkan Slavs. But they at the same time represented an inherently expansionist power that also instrumentalised Pan-Slav ideology to extend its sphere of influence; and the manner in which key figures like the foreign minister Aleksandr Izvolsky and his belligerent successor Sazonov asserted Russian claims clearly had a destabilising impact on this critical region.[22]

What first heightened tensions, however, was the decision of the Austro-Hungarian foreign minister Alois von Ährental, in July 1908, to annex the provinces of Bosnia and Herzegovina after the Young Turk rebellion had weakened Ottoman authority further. Although Ährental had struck a deal with his Russian counterpart Izvolsky, under which St Petersburg accepted the annexation in return for Austrian support on the vital issue of "opening" the Straits for Russian warships, strong nationalist opposition at home subsequently forced the Russian government to back Serbian claims for parts of the contested provinces. With the firm backing of the German Empire, the Austrian government then threatened to invade Serbia unless the Pašić government in Belgrade withdrew its demands. While Izvolvsky backed down in the spring of 1909 and conceded the annexation the outcome of the crisis proved a Pyrrhic victory for the Habsburg Empire, because it took the distrust and hostility that had already marred its relations with Russia, and Serbia, to a new level.[23]

Soon thereafter, Italy's war of conquest against the Ottoman Empire in north Africa, which ended with its annexation of Libya in 1912, triggered a succession of even more precarious conflicts, sparking the two Balkan wars of 1912 and 1913 that soon threatened to involve both of the European great-power blocs. The Balkan wars broke out after Serbia and Bulgaria, having joined forces in the "Balkan League", strove to seize the remaining Ottoman provinces in southeastern Europe, Macedonia and what then became the independent state of Albania. Yet before long, they would fight each other over the spoils of the war. Their actions indeed destroyed whatever was left of the "order" of geopolitical balances that was supposed to maintain a modicum of peace in the Balkans. And it was in this explosive constellation that the increasingly antagonistic European powers became enmeshed. It thus indeed prefigured the escalatory dynamics of 1914. In September 1912, both Russia and Austria-Hungary mobilised their troops along their common Galician border after the new Russian foreign minister Sazonov had announced a "trial mobilisation".

More broadly, political decision-makers and strategists in all of the pivotal European capitals now became used to a robust, indeed militarised approach to diplomacy – and strategies in which military mobilisation and the imperative of prevailing in a possible general war threatened to override

[22] Jelavich (2004), pp. 210 ff., 235 ff.
[23] See Clark (2012), pp. 83–7; Glenny (1999), pp. 281–93.

considerations of de-escalation and crisis management. Although Nicholas II agreed to meet with Francis-Joseph in March 1913 in an effort to reduce bilateral tensions, the Tsar was under immense pressure from nationalist politicians and publicists who demanded that he should act forcefully to protect Russia's client states, above all Serbia. When Sazonov oriented Russian policy accordingly, this galvanised Serbian nationalism and encouraged the expansionist agenda of the Serbian prime minister Nikola Pašić. In turn, Russia's assertiveness had been encouraged by its French ally. From Paris, President Poincaré, who now dominated French foreign policy, signalled not only unequivocal support for Sazonov's hard-line approach but also underscored that in his view all Balkan conflicts now immediately brought into play France's vital interests and that in order to counter Austria-Hungary and its German ally he would be prepared to back Russia all the way.[24]

Yet the first and second Balkan wars also revealed what in retrospect has to be regarded as a deceptive capacity of *some* European decision-makers, notably in London and Berlin, to stem the tides of confrontation – at least in the short term. What became even more obvious, however, was that there were no longer even rudiments of a functioning European great-power system that could be relied upon to negotiate, not last-minute fixes but rather more sustainable agreements that actually resolved the disputes at hand. Distinctly *limited* pragmatic collaboration efforts of British and German policymakers paved the way for the London peace conference of May 1913, which produced a peace treaty that confirmed Albania's recognition as an independent state. But this success was ephemeral. Soon the second Balkan war broke out, in which the Serbian government, not feeling bound by the London agreements, sought to defeat Bulgaria and gain control over Macedonia and Albania. Significantly, Austrian diplomats had by then concluded that in view of Pašić's aggressive policies it had become pointless to pursue regular diplomatic procedures vis-à-vis Serbia. Based on an agreement with the other European powers Vienna thus in the autumn of 1913 confronted Belgrade with an ultimatum, demanding the evacuation of all the Albanian territory its troops had occupied within eight days; and Pašić yielded.

In the short term, the Austrian policy of a "hard hand" thus seemed to have paid off. In a wider context, however, the Balkan wars had thrown into relief how isolated the Austro-Hungarian Empire, which received only lukewarm German support, was by now. And they highlighted very inauspicious trends. Both Austrian and Russian leaders were now inclined to pursue military rather than diplomatic strategies. And following Poincaré's lead, the French government actively encouraged Russia's aggressive moves. He and like-minded Quai d'Orsay officials by then espoused the basic rationales of a "Balkan inception"

---

[24] See Keiger (1983), pp. 88 ff.

scenario. They reckoned that a Russian intervention on behalf of Serbia would provide the best trigger for a general mobilisation of Russian forces for a greater two-front war in Europe, which would allow France – and Britain – to prevail in the west.[25] More fundamentally, the crisis also revealed that because of overriding alliance priorities all of the *Entente* Powers – including Britain – had departed from an long-standing axiom of European international politics, namely that the continued existence and vitality of the Austro-Hungarian Empire was not just essential for stabilising the Balkan region but a constitutive element of any stable European "equilibrium".

On the other side of the growing divide, those who struggled to develop a coherent German strategy in the face of these conflicts and tensions remained deeply divided. Whereas Bethmann Hollweg had tried to pursue pragmatic crisis management to contain the conflict, Moltke, and those who like him had come to see an eventual general war as unavoidable, urged the emperor and the imperial government to seize on the Balkan calamities to wage a "defensive" pre-emptive war against the *Entente*. Yet Bethmann's approach still prevailed. For their part, Ährental and other Austrian decision-makers concluded that the resolution of the crisis had proved the effectiveness of a hard-fisted "ultimatum policy" – and that Pašić and Serb nationalists could not be treated like representatives of a "civilised" power". All of this would set precedents for 1914.[26] The crisis-ridden years 1912 and 1913 thus brought to the fore a growing readiness in all capitals, except for London, to pursue assertive, militarised "strategies" – and to view conflicts in the Balkans as a possible prelude to an all-out war, which for different reasons, ranging from fatalism to visions of a successful pre-emptive strike, more and more actors had come to view as inescapable.

IV.   World-Political Competition and Very Limited Prospects for Détente

In retrospect, it is thus all the more worth highlighting that the Balkan imbroglios also prompted some notable – essentially Anglo-German and, less significantly, Russo-German – moves towards détente. But it is as important to stress that these initiatives remained cursory and superficial; they could not halt, let alone reverse, the underlying systemic polarisation and disintegration processes.[27] In an attempt to reduce tensions between the two empires, William II and his cousin Nicholas had met at Baltic Port in the summer of 1912, accompanied by key figures of their governments, including Bethmann Hollweg and the equally conciliatory Russian prime minister Vladimir

[25] See Clark (2012), pp. 301–13, 349 ff.
[26] See Canis (2016), pp. 393–424.
[27] Kießling (2002); Clark (2012), pp. 314–34.

Kokovtsov. Each side assured the other of its fundamentally defensive intentions. Bethmann underscored that his government had no wish to support Austrian adventurism in the Balkans. In return, Kokovtsov stressed the limited aims of Russian policy vis-à-vis the Austro-Hungarian Empire and vowed that his government would refrain from exploiting the ongoing Ottoman difficulties. While these encounters marked the highpoint of Russo-German détente before 1914, the basis for further progress remained very narrow. No substantial agreements were made. No substantive changes within or between the antagonistic alliances that separated the two powers occurred. Crucially, there was no prospect of widening such furtive attempts into a wider, *multilateral* process of détente and communication or even cooperation across Europe's new dividing lines. And only such a process could have prepared the ground for what was really needed to bolster European peace: a structural transformation of Europe's by then war-prone system and systemic culture.

Impulses in this direction could not be given either by the more significant efforts Bethmann Hollweg made in this phase to initiate a process of détente in what constituted the in many ways pivotal relationship in the European system, that between Germany and Britain. The not so enigmatic chancellor was the most important actor in the German Empire's inchoate decision-making structures who realised how isolated Europe's central power had become. Such considerations motivated his initiative to explore new paths to break out of a potential encirclement constellation. His underlying aim was not merely to soften the Anglo-French *Entente* but to foster a more cooperative Anglo-German relationship as a first step towards reconstituting a system of consultation and collaboration among the European great powers. This was to prove an elusive quest. But an analysis of its frustration can illuminate some of the decisive dynamics and deficiencies that eventually led into the abyss of 1914 – dynamics and deficiencies that were *systemic* insofar as they not only concerned one power, Germany, but rather all the key players.[28]

For a long time retrospective assessments of the origins of the Great War have been shaped by the influential interpretation that what really proved decisive in pushing the European powers over the brink was aggressive German behaviour that, fundamentally, stemmed from an underlying continuity of German aspirations in the post-Bismarck era to attain not only predominance in Europe but also "mastery of the world" ("*Weltherrschaft*"). And it has been claimed that this continuity reached from Wilhelmine *Weltpolitik* under Bülow all the way to the excessive war-aims programmes concocted *after* the war's outbreak.[29] But this interpretation is misleading.

---

[28] See Canis (2011), pp. 457–554; Clark (2012), pp. 314–49.
[29] See Fischer (1975). On the controversies Fischer's work has provoked see Mombauer (2002).

There was neither a coherent programme for world domination nor even a coherent government structure where any kind of consensus to this effect could have been reached. Rather, there were competing orientations; and there was a struggle between very different approaches to the pivotal question of how the German Empire was to cope with the security challenges arising from its "middle position" and sustain its future as a "world power". For all the offensive strategies that some actors contemplated, under growing domestic pressure, the underlying thrust of oscillating German policies was – subjectively – *defensive*.

The main preoccupation of those who actually influenced policymaking in Berlin centred on sustaining German independence and development prospects as a great power, *not* on far-reaching programmes of domination. And the threat that came to preoccupy policymakers and military strategists more than any other was that posed by Russia's resurgence after the humiliating defeat against Japan. They feared that the more time the Tsarist Empire had to proceed with the modernisation of its armed forces, the greater the danger would be that it would become an overpowering antagonist. Upon his return from the visit to Russia in the summer of 1912 Bethmann noted how profoundly impressed he was with its revitalisation. Lacking any real understanding of American developments, the German chancellor concluded that Russia's youth was "saturated with futurity" while that in the United States appeared "not to be adding any new element to the common patrimony of humanity".[30]

Yet it was Helmuth von Moltke who became most worried about the consequences of Russia's resurgence. Ever since he had succeeded Schlieffen as chief of the German General Staff in January 1906 Moltke warned time and again that this development threatened to recast the overall balance of forces inexorably against Germany and its Austro-Hungarian ally. In his assessment, this meant that Germany's geopolitical situation was rapidly deteriorating – to a point where the "masterplan" for how it was to prevail in a possible general war – the famous Schlieffen Plan – would be rendered impracticable. For he expected Russia soon to be in a position to marshal such a strong force that the Central Powers could no longer win a two-front war, however decisive the intended initial "lightning strike" against France would be. By this time, Moltke had come to base his strategic recommendations on two rigid assumptions. The first – revealing a highly pessimistic outlook – was that a war between the two hostile alliance blocs would soon be inevitable. The second was that time was on the side of Germany's opponents. On the basis of these assumptions, the chief of the General Staff emerged as the most influential

---

[30] Jules Cambon to Poincaré, 28 July 1912, AMAE, PA-AP, 43, J. Cambon 56, fo. 45.

proponent of a preventive war strategy in Berlin.[31] Such thinking undoubtedly carried the seeds of war and raised the danger that eventually, if yet another crisis erupted, there would be decisive pressure to "solve" the German encirclement problem through war.

But it is important to stress that Moltke by no means set the course of German policy or had a decisive influence on the civilian politicians who did – above all Bethmann Hollweg. And throughout this crisis period, the latter indeed persisted with his attempts to pursue a different strategy – a strategy geared to seeking a new understanding with Britain and thus *averting* the danger of a general two-front war. Yet the structural and political constraints under which he had to operate became ever more immense. This had already been demonstrated by the failure of the famous Haldane mission in February 1912. That Asquith's secretary of state for war had travelled to Berlin for informal talks was as a direct consequence of Bethmann's efforts not only to negotiate an agreement limiting further naval expansion but also to lay foundations for a broader Anglo-German accommodation. He hoped that this would also allow both powers to cooperate in settling conflicts affecting their wider interests – as would then happen during the Balkan wars. To this end, he operated through an informal intermediary, the Hamburgian shipping magnate Albert Ballin, who was horrified by the scenario of a future war between the two trading powers. Yet Haldane's subsequent informal foray to explore the possibility of a bilateral agreement on naval and colonial issues would not yield any results. This was not so much due to a lack of German willingness to offer more substantial concessions in curbing naval growth. The real crux was that the British government saw no reason to make the critical strategic concession Bethmann desired, namely to pledge that Britain would remain neutral in the event of a war between Germany and another continental power that was not caused by German aggression. The prevalent view in London, on which particularly Grey insisted, was that such a pledge was irreconcilable with Britain's *Entente* commitments and, fundamentally, there was no reason to offer Germany anything in return for a concession that one no longer required. For he had – rightly – concluded that by this time Britain was already prevailing in the Anglo-German naval race.[32]

In the aftermath of this failed attempt to place Anglo-German relations on a more constructive footing the German chancellor had to struggle to maintain his détente course midst the adverse realities of progressive polarisation between the blocs and never-ending crises in the Balkans. By December 1912, he felt compelled to go before the *Reichstag* and issue a stern public warning to the *Entente* Powers, declaring that while Germany had used its

---

[31] Moltke memorandum, 2 December 1911, PA-AP, Deutschland, No. 121 geh, vol 1; Fischer (1969), p. 233; Herwig (2003), pp. 164–6; Mombauer (2001), pp. 145 ff., 211, 281.

[32] See Kennedy (1980), pp. 449–51; Kießling (2002).

influence to "localise" the Balkan war the German Empire would take a "firm and determined" stand at the side of its Austro-Hungarian allies if they were "attacked from a third side" and threatened in their "existence". And he underscored that the Germans would then also "fight for the defence of our own position in Europe and for the protection of our own future and security".[33] Reacting strongly to Bethmann's speech, Grey summoned the German ambassador Count Lichnowsky to impress upon him that in the event of a war between Germany and the Franco-Russian alliance, Britain would most likely intervene on the side of the latter.

In turn, William II summoned what became infamous as the "war council" of 8 December 1912, which included Moltke, Tirpitz and other military leaders – but not Bethmann. Those who participated agreed that Austria had to act firmly against Serbia, and Germany had to support its ally should Russia attack it to defend its Serbian client state. The German emperor indeed endorsed Moltke's position that as a war between the opposing blocs was "unavoidable", it ought to be waged "the sooner the better".[34] Yet this did not mean that William II from now on supported a "preventive war" agenda. In fact, he soon sought to reduce tensions, particularly vis-à-vis Russia. More importantly, there was no newly hardened consensus among German military and political leaders; they did not all rally behind a comprehensive plan to place not only the army and navy but also the German economy – and population – on a war footing. No actual preparations to this end were made.[35]

But Moltke's insistence nonetheless had consequences. It was largely due to his pressure that the *Reichstag* had earlier passed the massive army bill for 1913, which prompted another turn of the spiral in the burdensome and war-prone European arms race. Yet Chancellor Bethmann, who despite his curtailed influence remained the most authoritative political actor, persisted with his policy of de-escalation. As noted, he would subsequently redouble his efforts to cooperate with Britain in settling the Balkan crisis and to pave the way for détente with Russia and even with France in the longer term.[36] And his approach for the time being prevailed both over Moltke's demands and the call for decisive action made by the Chief of the Austrian General Staff, Franz Conrad von Hötzendorf.[37] Nonetheless, it should be stressed that Moltke-style "preventive war" thinking would eventually have a powerful impact on the attitudes of all leading German decision-makers, including Bethmann, when the crisis of 1914 escalated.

---

[33] *TheTimes*, 3 December 1912, p. 6.
[34] See Fischer (1969), p. 233; Röhl (1994), pp. 162–3.
[35] See Clark (2012), pp. 329–30.
[36] *TheTimes*, 3 December 1912, p. 6.
[37] Bethmann to Eisendecker, 23 March 1913, in Jarausch (1969), pp. 48 ff.

V. The Inexorable Escalation of the July Crisis

To understand why *and* how the European powers went to war in 1914 – and, more precisely, why and how the crisis caused by the assassination of the heir to the Habsburg throne would escalate into the greatest war the world had seen up to that point, it is doubtless necessary to analyse the rapid succession of decisions, actions and reactions that made the July crisis perhaps one of the most intricate and complex crises in history. Arguably, however, it is even more essential to place this crisis in its proper wider context – to step back from the intricacies, calculations and misperceptions of 1914 and focus on what actually proved decisive for leading Europe into the abyss. What comes into view this way are the longer-term changes in the structural underpinnings, the prevalent ground-rules of international politics, the collective mentalities and, finally, the core characteristics of a political culture that, for all their differences, all protagonists of the July crisis shared. And what becomes clear is that these protagonists did *not* act and wander into a war that none of them wanted as though they were "sleepwalkers".[38]

While it is true that none of them desired or anticipated a conflict of the colossal magnitude of the Great War, by the summer of 1914 most key actors had for different reasons concluded that some kind of major war could or should no longer be avoided – and that what now mattered was to put into effect plans that ensured a swift and decisive victory over the hostile coalition. And while the larger historical forces and developments they had to confront were indeed extremely challenging, it is important to point out that the European decision-makers still had agency and some freedom of action. Their actions, non-actions and decisions – and the perceptions, calculations and underlying assumptions on which they were based – did matter in what had become an extremely complicated high-stakes game. And although European power politics had indeed become ever more unpredictable in a dynamically changing global setting, these actors could potentially still make the difference between war and peace, between crisis management and escalation – as they had done so many times before. Yet by last days of July 1914, their room to manoeuvre to avoid war and preserve even a semblance of peace was rapidly diminishing.[39]

It is thus undoubtedly essential to highlight the *immense complexity* that by then characterised the relations between the great powers. This complexity was compounded by their conflict-ridden and in some cases opaque decision-making structures and domestic politics. This multi-level and multifaceted complexity indeed became a salient factor in its own right. For it made it ever harder to prevent a scenario in which one of the countless crises the powers

[38] Thus Clark's influential but misleading thesis. See Clark (2012), pp. 562, 555–62.
[39] See Otte (2014), esp. pp. 370 ff.

had to deal with would spin out of control. All of this made the European constellation extremely *war-prone*. And what now culminated on *all sides* was the ominous trend that most European decision-makers no longer focused on what was required for the maintenance of peace but rather on fortifying their respective alliances for the purpose of winning a sooner rather than later "inescapable" war. Such considerations now came to shape the perceptions and priorities of the main actors. Most of them now came to think in terms of balance-of-power calculations and war stratagems, and this in turn created ever sharper ideological divisions between "friends" and "enemies". As a result, the two formerly fluid alliance blocs were now rapidly rigidifying. Crucially, no leading actor was still prepared to imagine or push for structural changes – attempts to overcome the divisions and reconstitute the defunct European concert system.[40]

What thus came to dominate tactical and strategic thinking were war scenarios and mobilisation plans. While the German fixation on the Schlieffen Plan exemplified this shift most conspicuously, it was a *general* phenomenon – even if less pronounced in Britain than among the continental powers. And while Moltke's campaign for a "preventive war" was the most radical manifestation of – pessimist – bellicism, it was not exceptional in this critical phase. Not least because of the efforts of juridical internationalists, the notion that offensive war carried an opprobrium had gained ground since the mid-nineteenth century. And in 1914 and thereafter the governments of all belligerents would go to great lengths to stress that they were fighting a defensive war. But in the crisis situation of 1914, the crucial concern eventually became to act in time and do whatever was required to *win* the war. To this end, the military leaders and leading strategists of all the other major powers had long developed more or less offensively orientated war plans. But now the leading civilian policy- and decision-makers either also adopted their outlooks – or they lacked the will or authority to steer European politics in a different direction. At a deeper level, militarised thinking and maxims of "war preparedness", mobilising one's population and maximising one's war-making potential had come to dominate everywhere on the European continent – and also spread in Britain.[41]

Essentially, then, by the time the July crisis escalated, those decision-makers who might still have been in a position to prevent the worst no longer had either the instruments or the imaginations to do so. They no longer pursued policies that would have enabled them, in the first instance, to contain a virulent crisis before it blew up into an all-out conflict. More fundamentally, they no longer had the capacity to preserve peace. Arguably, it actually

---

[40] See Schroeder (I/2004), pp. 165 ff., 190–1; Joll, (1992), pp. 42–108; Clark (2012), pp. 367 ff.
[41] See Herwig (2003), pp. 160–1.

distracts from capturing more essential dimensions of the Great War's origins if one focuses too narrowly on Russian and French mobilisation plans, Moltke's insistence on pre-emptive war or even Bethmann Hollweg's fatalistic notion that if Russia's mobilisation left no other choice the German Empire would have to fight a "defensive" war. Nor should one dwell too much on the question of whether a less ambiguous British commitment to intervene on the side of France – and Russia – in the event of an unprovoked German attack would have provided a crucial element of deterrence and induced German leaders to step back from the brink of war. The real problem lay deeper.

What mattered most was that political leaders *on all sides* had allowed the earlier *inclusive* European states-system to deteriorate into a polarising balance-of-power system that produced *endemic insecurity* (rather than security through "mutual deterrence") and that no longer furnished them with the wherewithal to settle the conflicts they confronted in the age of global imperialism. At the same time, the risks of failing to settle conflicts magnified in view of the newly prevalent assumptions and the intensifying arms race and ideological mobilisation. Put differently, what really proved fatal was that by 1914 the European concert had been completely destroyed – and that despite all the well-intended efforts of The Hague and of socialist internationalists, not even elementary foundations of a new, modern *general* system of order and *concerted* conflict resolution had been put in its place. In short, it was precisely the confluence of *longer-term* processes of involution and corrosion that had taken place during the first third of the long twentieth century which now had catastrophic consequences.

More profoundly, then, the real crux of 1914 was that by this time those political decision-makers who could potentially have averted a major catastrophe had come to espouse practices and outlooks that made effective actions to preserve peace unthinkable. In other words, they had abandoned attempts to create mechanisms and they had "un-learned" approaches that would have allowed them to do what was necessary to build a more substantive peace. Above all, they had abandoned the fundamental maxim that conflicts that affected *all* the major powers, and the international system as a whole, had to be settled by peaceful means and through agreements that indeed accommodated the interests and legitimation requirements of *all* the members of the system. When the by then highly likely "big crisis" escalated, such understandings had long been undermined, and there was no prospect of "reviving" them, under immense pressure, at the eleventh hour. Thus, Grey's proposal in late July 1914 – *on the brink of the abyss* – to defuse the Austro-Serbian and Austro-Russian confrontations through some form of concerted mediation of the remaining European great powers was bound to fail. The escalation of the crisis of course also threw into stark relief just how limited the influence was that pacifist movements, liberal internationalists and the parties of the Second International could exert on those who led the European powers.

Long-term developments and deeper systemic changes thus eventually created the immensely war-prone constellation in which a terrorist act such as the assassination of the heir to the Habsburg throne in Sarajevo on 28 June 1914 could trigger an all-encompassing European crisis – and a spiral of escalation that in early August precipitated the long twentieth century's seminal catastrophe.[42] What ensued, after a short deceptive lull, was an immensely rapid succession of escalatory actions and reactions that was not inherently unstoppable but could no longer be mastered under the conditions and with the assumptions and mentalities that shaped European politics by the summer of 1914.

Once it had been concluded that Serbian state agencies had been complicit in the assassination, the Austro-Hungarian foreign minister Leopold von Berchtold quickly resorted to a hard-fisted policy vis-à-vis Belgrade, seeking to apply the lessons of the previous Balkan war. With the encouragement of Hötzendorf, who had long recommended a preventive war against Serbia, Berchtold posed an ultimatum to the Serbian government. While not accusing it of being directly implicated in the assassination plot, he declared that it had abetted a "subversive movement" that had committed terrorist acts in the past. And he issued a catalogue of ten demands, calling above all for measures to suppress anti-Austrian propaganda and arrest those who were involved in the assassination. Essentially, Berchtold reckoned that this ultimatum would likely be rejected by the Pašić government and therefore justify an Austrian intervention. And, ordering a partial mobilisation against Serbia, he soon put Austria-Hungary on a war footing. More profoundly, like a majority in the Austrian government the foreign minister felt an existential need to demonstrate resolve in order to salvage the Habsburg Empire's status and integrity as a European great power. And he was of course aware that German support for its ally would be crucial in the face of the expected Russian reaction on Serbia's behalf and thus informed Berlin of his plans, appealing for German solidarity.

For his part, Sazonov accused the Austrian government of pursuing an aggressive policy that was "setting fire to Europe" and pushed for a firm Russian reaction to defend the "dignity and integrity of the Serb people", Russia's "brothers in blood". And with the backing of the chief of the Russian general staff, General Yanushkevich, he prepared plans for a partial Russian mobilisation on 24 July. Both Sazonov and Yanushkevich – mistakenly – saw the German Empire as the real power behind Austria's confrontational moves, suspecting it of pursuing by "aggressive methods" a course whose aim was to attain predominance over Europe. They thus assumed that the Austrian ultimatum had been presented with German

---

[42] See Hamilton and Herwig (2004); Clark (2012), pp. 367–554; Becker and Krummeich (2014); Otte (2014).

connivance – and feared that if the ultimatum was successful, it would turn Serbia into a de facto protectorate of the Central Powers. Based on these assumptions, they insisted that Russia had to take a firm stand if it did not want to risk losing all authority as a leading European great power.[43]

Prevailing over the more reluctant premier Viviani, Poincaré now too acted in exactly the same confrontational manner he had displayed during previous Balkan crises, pursuing a pronounced course of firm support for Russia. By the end of July he no longer placed any hopes in any British mediation attempts – and, crucially, he signalled that France would do nothing to restrain its Russian ally unless Germany made decisive moves to do the same vis-à-vis Austria. Essentially, the French president was convinced by then that it would be impossible to avoid a European war and he thus shifted back to his earlier "Balkan inception" maxims. What he considered crucial at this point was as rapid a Russian mobilisation as possible, and his concerns centred on the question whether the British government would indeed be prepared to intervene in support of its allies – while Ambassador Cambon reported from London that the Asquith Cabinet's attitude remained highly ambiguous.[44]

Following important deliberations on 24 and 25 July, the Russian council of ministers, in which the Tsar participated, decided to authorise preparations for a partial mobilisation of troops along Russia's entire European border, which for logistical reasons was a mere prelude to a general mobilisation. And when Poincaré was informed about these decisions he did nothing to oppose them. The Tsarist government's subsequent decision to go ahead and mobilise Russian forces on 30 July, in reaction to the Austrian declaration of war on Serbia on 28 July, then indeed marked the turning-point that transformed the local conflict into an all-European war. It pushed all sides into a "spiral of mobilisation schedules" in which military imperatives now quickly came to override political considerations and any prospects for last-minute diplomatic negotiations to avert war were decisively curtailed. It was the moment when the authority of military leaders prevailed over that of leading politicians – as was the case in Berlin – or when military and civilian leaders proceeded more or less in lockstep – as was the case in Paris – all following the dominant maxim that only a timely mobilisation would permit each side to execute its far-reaching war plans. Only in London did political decision-makers still retain undisputed authority, and only here a substantial debate took place within the deeply divided Asquith Cabinet about the critical question of whether Britain's commitments, or interests, commanded an intervention in an all-out European war.

---

[43] See Clark (2012), pp. 471–87; Lieven (1983).
[44] See Schmidt (2009), pp. 55 ff., 177 ff., 289 ff.

Nowhere was the weakness of the political leadership more pronounced than in Germany. The imperial government's early decision to respond to Berchtold's plea for help with a "blank cheque" of unconditional support on 5 July would undermine all subsequent efforts to restrain Austria and urge a rapid settlement of the dispute with Serbia. Building on his experiences during previous Balkan crises, Bethmann Hollweg sought to promote – yet again – a localisation and diplomatic de-escalation of the conflict, and again contemplated Anglo-German cooperation to this end. Yet he too eventually assumed a pre-emptively defensive position. He reasoned that if the Tsarist Empire intervened on Serbia's side the general war that then was bound to break out would be one forced upon Germany and Austria-Hungary by aggressive Russian policies, which the *Entente* Powers had encouraged – and the German government would have no choice but to fight it to defend itself.[45]

In fact, as things stood, the Russian mobilisation decree was bound to prompt precisely what Moltke had envisaged for years: a swifter counter-mobilisation of German troops and the implementation of the Schlieffen Plan. In turn, these German moves led to the decision in Paris to mobilise all available troops, which reflected a nearly complete consensus between the government and the chief of the French General Staff, Joseph Joffre. The one remaining uncertainty pertained to the reaction of the British government to these rapid developments. To the very end, German decision-makers indeed clung to the hope that Britain might stay neutral or at any rate out of the conflict. But it is highly doubtful that a clearer commitment of the Asquith government to Britain's *Entente* partners and a more unequivocal signal that it would intervene on their side in the case of an "unprovoked" German aggression would have had a decisive deterring effect – or even prevented the outbreak of the Great War. For the key actors in Berlin by this time reacted to Russian moves and were bound, or trapped, by their rigid mobilisation plans.

In London, the pivotal British actor during the July crisis pursued a "meandering path". Grey had soon realised the gravity of the crisis the assassination in Sarajevo had caused. He had sought to restrain Russia and to enlist French support to this end. And he then endeavoured to broker a diplomatic settlement of the escalating dispute between Austria and Russia. Yet he ultimately gave priority to the preservation of the *Entente* and, eventually, came to concentrate on finding a justification for a British intervention in a war he deemed imperative to prevent a German victory and subsequent predominance over continental Europe. Having secured the backing of the Asquith Cabinet, Grey on 24 July proposed that an improvised concert of the

---

[45] Bethmann to Schoen, 27 July 1914; Bethmann to Lichnowsky, 27 July 1914, in Geiss (1963), II, pp. 103 ff.

four great powers that were less immediately involved in the dispute – Britain, France, Germany and Italy – should intervene as mediators and pave the way for a mutually satisfactory settlement between Austria-Hungary and Russia. As in 1913, Grey's strategy hinged on a targeted collaboration with the German government – and the hope that each power could exert a restraining influence on its respective ally. Yet his dominant concern remained not to weaken the cohesion of the *Entente*. Bethmann soon signalled support for Grey's initiative. But the attitude that now dominated in Berlin was one of profound scepticism. While Italy was ruled out as a serious actor in this ad hoc "concert", the combined power of Britain and France threatened to override German influence and made a "fair" consideration of Austrian interests vis-à-vis Serbia seem unlikely. Nonetheless, the German chancellor at first tried to keep the option of mediation open.

But the fundamental problem that both Bethmann and Grey faced in trying to pursue such eleventh-hour crisis management was one that even a more skilful policymaker could not have solved. And that problem was, essentially, that it was no longer *possible* to reconstitute, under extreme pressure, something akin to the old European concert, i.e. an effective multilateral mechanism to resolve conflicts between the great powers. It now became painfully clear that the divisions between the opposing blocs, and the distrust between them, had become far too deep to stop, let alone reverse, the spiral of mobilisation and counter-mobilisation that was set in motion in St Petersburg less than a week after Grey had initiated his mediation initiative. Following the Austrian ultimatum to Serbia, Crowe sought to impress on the foreign secretary that Britain could no longer restrain France and Russia. And, reasserting his ideological view of the European situation, he declared that the Asquith government had to recognise that Britain's interests were "tied up" with those of France and Russia in a "struggle" not over the "possession" of Serbia but rather "between Germany aiming at a political dictatorship in Europe and the Powers who desire to retain individual freedom". This anticipated future British propaganda.[46]

For some days Grey resisted Crowe's views and retained the hope that Bethmann would be able to restrain both Germany's military masters and Austrian hard-liners. And he still had one profound concern, namely that neither the Cabinet nor British "public opinion" would be prepared to intervene in a general European war over the "Serbian quarrel". Nor, crucially, was a majority as yet prepared to go to war because of obligations, or interests, that arose from Britain's alignments with France and Russia. Even Grey himself was still not fully committed to drawing this final consequence. Therefore it

---

[46] Crowe minute, 24 July 1914, Gooch and Temperley (1926–38), XI, no. 101. See Steiner and Neilson (2003), pp. 234–6.

was indeed the German invasion of Belgium and breach of Belgian neutrality – in a politically short-sighted persistence on executing the Schlieffen Plan – that provided Grey and those in the Asquith Cabinet, and the British public, who by then regarded an intervention as imperative, with a moral cause and the crucial ideological justification for intervening in the European conflict. Hitherto strong pacifist and anti-interventionist counter-currents were now pushed to the margins by a clearly dominant interventionist mood.

The crucial decisions were taken during the Cabinet meeting of 2 August when Lloyd George and others who still had not seen a compelling reason for entering the conflict relented and a clear majority agreed that a "strong" German violation of Belgium's neutrality – the protection of which had been a core element of Britain's European policy since 1832 – would constitute a cause for war. More fundamentally, the dominant view was now that in the interest of safeguarding national security and the future of the empire, Britain could not tolerate the threat of a hostile power gaining control over northern France and the lowlands and thus the southern coast of the Channel, Britain's "home waters". This lay behind the Asquith government's "mild" ultimatum to Berlin on 3 August 1914. And – after the German government had failed to give the required assurances that it would withdraw its troops from Belgian soil and henceforth respect Belgian neutrality – it led to the British declaration of war the following day. This finally turned the conflict that had escalated on the European continent into a great and soon global war not only in military but also in political and ideological terms. It was to become a war that would transform Europe and the world. And it was to become the cathartic catastrophe that would eventually both create the need and provide a decisive impetus for the first serious attempt in the modern era to construct a modern – Atlantic – international system.

PART II

The Greatest War – and No Peace without Victory

The Impact of the First World War, Competing Visions of Peace and the Struggle over the Shape of a New – Atlantic – World Order

It is hard to overstate just how massive the changes were that the Great War wrought – in Europe, on a global scale and, in particular for the relations between the European peoples and states and the United States. Yet, as is to be shown in the following, it is crucial to examine these changes more closely and to bring out how far the war had essentially a *catalytic* impact, intensifying trends that had already gained ground before 1914, and where it had a truly *transformative* effect, fundamentally altering the pre-war status quo – and ideas about modern international order. Once this has been clarified, the focus has to shift to an in-depth analysis of the intense – and ever more essentially transatlantic – political and ideological "war within the war" in which, between 1914 and 1918, competing visions of peace and postwar order emerged, collided and influenced one another in manifold ways.

A transatlantic focus can also serve to provide a more persuasive answer to a far from settled question whose examination reveals a lot both about the nature of the war itself and about how it altered the parameters of international politics. This question is, in short, why the First World War could not be ended earlier – and in one way or another through a negotiated "peace without victory", as Wilson aspired to do in 1916 and 1917. Then, of course, it has to be re-assessed how the *Great* War actually was brought to an end in 1918 (while many smaller conflicts continued, notably in eastern Europe). It also has to be examined what kind of basis the Wilson-induced armistice of November 1918 created for a viable peacemaking process – and which immense *and conflicting* expectations it raised both among the victors and the vanquished. Finally, what has to be re-appraised, both in a transatlantic and a global perspective, are not only the urgent problems but also the novel and complex *systemic* challenges that the Great War left behind, especially for those who set out to forge a "peace to end all wars" at the Paris Peace Conference.

6

Tectonic Changes
The Global Consequences of the War and the
Transformation of the Transatlantic Constellation

The Great War, which started as a power struggle between the Central Powers and the *Entente*, came to exceed all previous wars in terms of its scale and intensity, the extent of the mobilisation it came to require and, ultimately, the destruction and casualties it caused. Indeed, the war essentially escalated into a high-stakes struggle of increasingly radical mobilisation, not just of state and military machineries and war economies but also in the political and social spheres, the spheres of ideas and propaganda, and indeed the spheres of individual and social psychology.[1] And it soon became clear that, as the elder Moltke had predicted as early as 1890, this greatest war would and could not be a short conflict with a decisive outcome. Not only because of the advances in military technology but also and above all because of the unprecedented mobilisation requirements that a general industrial war between similarly armed states created, it would prove impossible to bring it to a swift conclusion – either through a decisive victory of one side over the other that allowed it to impose its terms or through a negotiated compromise settlement.

The Great War indeed caused tectonic changes in the international order. It was essentially a war between empires and imperial states into which smaller states and imperial subject populations were drawn on both sides – and then, eventually, the United States. Ultimately, however, the First World War shattered not just Europe's pre-war system of great powers but also shook up the entire global "order" of competing imperial states, such as it had emerged in the formative decades since 1860. It thus initiated a process that would reach another, even more destructive and transformative climax during the Second World War.[2]

Thus, the Great War indeed became the crucible of the long twentieth century rather than the "original catastrophe" of the short twentieth century as which it has long been interpreted.[3] It also profoundly affected the dominant role that European powers and their rivalries had played in the global

---

[1] The most important recent works on the war are Winter (2014), vols. I–III, Stevenson (2012) and Leonhard (2014).

[2] For the broader context see Overy (2021), pp. 2–29.

[3] See the influential if very different interpretations of Kennan (1979), pp. 3–4, and Hobsbawm (1994), pp. 21 ff.

sphere, or more precisely that of extra-European colonialism and imperial domination. It eliminated some powers, notably Germany, as world-political players (for the foreseeable future) while extending the influence of others, notably Britain. Yet it also gave rise to newly potent challenges to pre-war forms of imperialism, particularly those posed by anti-imperialist nationalists and their clamouring for "self-determination".

The war thus *began* to transform the global order. Above all, however, and with many global implications, it marked a critical *caesura* in the relations between Europe and the United States. On the one hand, the costs, sacrifices and losses the war caused, which surpassed all that could have been imagined or expected before its escalation, marked a traumatic watershed experience for European states and societies. On the part of those who would end up among the vanquished – the Central Powers and, in its own way, Russia, it not only led to the destruction of empires but also to widening revolutionary upheavals – starting with the October revolution of 1917 – eventually leaving previous power relations, hierarchies and norms in disarray. Yet the war also created immense reform pressures for those states – the western *Entente* Powers and their allies – that eventually won a costly victory and whose political systems had by and large survived the conflict intact. Overall, the war left all belligerents profoundly exhausted and when it ended, in the west, in November 1918, many observers spoke not just of a seminal European catastrophe but of overall European decline. And what prevailed was a sense of profound crisis that raised the underlying question of whether transformative or even revolutionary changes were needed to cope with the war's consequences and pave the way for a durable peace – both within states and in the international order.

On the other hand, the war had a comparatively less profound impact on American society and politics, even once the United States, following a prolonged period of relative aloofness and official "neutrality", entered the conflict. Here, it caused far fewer casualties and far less political upheaval. But it came to have far-reaching consequences for America's relations with Europe and, more broadly, its role in the world. For the European cataclysm not only turned the United States – not only the leading economic and creditor power in the world. It also became the power that eventually played a decisive part in deciding the outcome of what came to be seen by some as a redemptive war, not so much because of its military engagement but primarily as the key supplier and financier of the *Entente*'s war effort against the Central Powers.

Crucially, the war thus catapulted the American republic into a position for which neither its traditions nor its political culture, neither the ideas nor traditions that had hitherto shaped its self-understanding, self-perception and international conduct had prepared it – namely the position of a hegemonic power in the international system. And it raised the question of how far those who shaped America's international policies, above all wartime president Woodrow Wilson, would be in a position to assume unprecedented hegemonic responsibilities, especially in pacifying Europe but more broadly in founding no less than a new international order in the war's aftermath. Essentially, then, the Great War not merely multiplied and intensified con-nections between the United States and Europe; it indeed began to transform them. It created a new and complex configuration of transatlantic *interdependence*. And it thus brought one question to the forefront of international politics: How far would it be possible to establish for the first time underpinnings for a functioning transatlantic peace order? At a deeper level, the tectonic changes the war engendered required immense reorientations and considerable learning processes on both sides of the Atlantic – reorientations and learning processes that would only begin during the war itself.

I. Unprecedented Mobilisation Needs, Costs and Casualties

The longer the war lasted, the more it escalated beyond all that had been imagined before, and the costlier it became for all sides, the more it escalated on the shifting battlefronts in the east and became – on the western front – an inconceivably blood-letting "war of position" in which the gigantic exertions of both sides by and large cancelled each other out and led to a stalemate, the more the Great War turned not just into a logistical but also political challenge of gigantic proportions. And this meant that the governments and propagandists of all the different belligerents had to focus on one thing above all: they had to expand what turned into unparalleled efforts to mobilise not only soldiers who fought in the mass armies that now confronted each other but entire populations to sustain ever more all-encompassing industrial war efforts.

All in all, roughly 65 million soldiers were sent into battle – 11 million in the German Empire; 8 million in the Austro-Hungarian Empire; 9 million in Britain and its empire; 8.5 million in France and its empire; and 12 million in Russia. By comparison the United States would mobilise a smaller number, 4 million soldiers, but did so in a much shorter time. Behind these figures of course stood countless millions – men and women – who played their part on the home fronts. In the end, the Great War thus indeed came close to becoming the first "total war" in history.[4] And to an extent never witnessed before, it led not only to a "totalisation" of warfare but also to a both qualitative and quantitative surge of violence, exerted on an industrial scale. This became most obvious in the gruesome "materiel battles" of attrition on the western front, yet also characterised the more shifting battlegrounds in Eastern Europe – and took a heavy toll on the belligerent societies, with consequences that reached far beyond the end

---

[4] See Berghahn (2006), pp. 39–47; Chickering and Förster (2006); Leonhard (2014), pp. 83 ff.

of the hostilities. In 1917, the charismatic French wartime premier Georges Clemenceau pointed to a vital dimension of the conflict when he stressed that at its core it represented a profound moral crisis in which ultimately the side that maintained its moral resolve longer than the opposing side, and thus won the "moral war", would prevail.[5]

The longer the war went on, the more enormous not only the moral but also the political, economic and social mobilisation demands became that it placed on the belligerent societies and states. It thus also greatly accelerated the expansion of the modern state that had been going on since the dawn of the long twentieth century. The warring states extended their powers as administrative states, as organisers of more state-directed war economies; as providers of welfare; and as instruments of not only military mobilisation but also of political and psychological mobilisation on the home fronts. The war's developments and pressures thus indeed proved formative for expanded conceptions, and expectations, of what a modern state was, demanded, could do and was supposed to provide. To organise massive and profoundly costly and straining war efforts, the different warring states found different, more or less effective ways of extending their control and authority over wartime societies and economies to a hitherto hardly imaginable extent. This was reflected in the dramatic increase of state expenditure on armaments and the wider war effort.

In Germany, economic mobilisation measures and the organisation of a German war economy came to be directed by Walther Rathenau as head of the newly created War Raw Material Department; and the new challenges led him to envision a mixed economy, a blend of liberal and state-directed economic order, as the model of the future. In 1916, the attempt to gear up for a "total war" through the so-called Hindenburg Programme took German mobilisation efforts to a new level. Overall, the proportion of German national income spent on armaments and related infrastructure and war costs rose from one-fifth before 1914 to almost 50 per cent by its end. Almost exactly the same increase could be witnessed in Britain, where state-directed measures of industrial and general mobilisation for a sustained war effort began to transform the essentially liberal political and economic order of the Edwardian era and prepared the ground for the emergence of a stronger, more interventionist state – and indeed of the modern British welfare state. In France, even more rigidly state-controlled mobilisation programmes by 1918 consumed roughly 40 per cent of its national income.[6]

By contrast, the American government and state apparatus never had to prepare for an "all-out" war effort of existential dimensions (and would not

---

[5] Cited after Winock (2007), p. 431.
[6] See Maier (2012), p. 297.

have been prepared for it at this stage), and when the United States intervened the Wilson administration could afford to pursue mobilisation strategies that did not (yet) require the build-up of an American-style security state. But the impact of the war on the longer-term development of the modern American state should not be underestimated either. Overall, the war's developments thus indeed proved formative for expanded conceptions, and expectations, of what a modern state was, could do and was supposed to provide.[7]

The First World War also proved unprecedentedly costly in material terms, of which the devastations wrought upon the provinces of Belgium and northern France that were the actual sites of trench warfare – and upon the Alpine, East European and extra-European battlegrounds – were only the most visible part. And the ways in which different governments sought meet these costs and raise the necessary means to wage industrial war would have far-reaching political consequences. Pursuing the key priority of ensuring a victory in the war, none of the belligerent governments as yet thought much about these longer-term implications of the tremendous financial obligations they incurred. The Central Powers essentially had to finance their exertions through domestic war bonds, i.e. by borrowing from their own people, on the assumption that following a victory those who had bought bonds would be amply repaid. While similar methods were also used on the side of the *Entente*, here inter-allied and international loans came to have a crucial significance. Initially, Britain was the main financier, then – as will be shown – American loans came to play a decisive part in bankrolling the *Entente*'s war effort.[8]

But even more significant and atrocious were the immaterial costs. The Great War took a hitherto unparalleled human toll. According to the most thorough estimates, it caused approximately 9 million combat deaths and 6 million civilian deaths.[9] Casualties on such an unprecedented scale were not only a military but also a demographic catastrophe, which had massive social, economic, cultural and political repercussions and indeed just as profound psychological ramifications. The war struck some societies harder than others but took a heavy toll on all the major European belligerents. Britain and its empire lost 700,000 soldiers, France and its empire 1.3 million, Russia about 1.8 million, while on the side of the Central Powers more than 2 million German soldiers and 1.1 million soldiers who had fought for the Habsburg Empire died. At the same time, nearly half of all European soldiers fighting the war were wounded, suffered from diseases, the effects of poison gas, and shell shock. In marked contrast to this, "only" 125,000 American soldiers became

---

[7] See Winter (2014), Volume II.
[8] See Ullmann (2014), Leonhard (2014), pp. 784–95.
[9] See Overmans (2004), pp. 663–66.

casualties of the war, of whom roughly 53,000 died in combat; and "only" 5 per cent of the total of American combatants were wounded.[10] In this respect, too, the American experience of the Great War was very different from the European. What occurred "over there" in Europe was not a seminal catastrophe for American society comparable to that of the civil war.

For all of these reasons, the war thus also placed massive pressures on the political systems of the belligerent states. Yet here too it created far greater strains for the political orders of the European states than for the order of the American republic. In Europe, the war and the unprecedented efforts it required tested not only the effectiveness and adaptability but also the legitimacy of the different states' modes of government and political order. Everywhere, the war spurred demands for more political participation. But the tangible political consequences it had differed widely. The wartime governments of the *Entente* Powers had to confront major waves of labour unrest and strikes, which especially affected Britain; and in France a mutiny that involved almost half of the fighting forces erupted at the height of the crisis of 1917. More generally, both *Entente* governments faced magnified demands for political reforms, notably an extension of the franchise. Overall, however, the more democratic political orders of Britain and France proved remarkably resilient. In the United States, the intervention in the war also came to be seen as a test for American democracy; and it increased demands for reforms, for finally building a "true" or more perfect and inclusive American republic – both from progressives who supported the intervention and those who opposed it. More fundamentally, however, the war's developments reinforced the sense that a – progressively improved – American-style democratic government was indeed the model of the future, also for Europe and – ultimately – for the world.[11]

By contrast, the Great War came to undermine the political orders of the Central Powers and the Russian Empire and eventually fomented revolutions. The German Empire's semi-authoritarian government structure would soon manifest its limits, one symptom of which was that by 1917 military leaders, the heads of the Supreme Command, acquired quasi-dictatorial authority, while the so-called majority parties of the *Reichstag* – the Liberals, the Centre Party and the Social Democrats – would step up calls for major reforms – essentially moves to a parliamentary monarchy. Yet their efforts would only begin to bear fruit when the war was practically lost, in October 1918, and decisive steps towards what became the first German republic would only be taken under the impact of defeat. Crucially, all of this would occur in an altered Euro-Atlantic force-field in which Wilson's war-rhetorical

[10] See Nolan (2012), p. 65.
[11] See Croly (1909) and (1914); Kennedy (1980); Link (1954); Link and McCormick (1983); Kloppenberg (1988).

insinuations of a "peace of justice and law and fair dealing" with a democratising Germany came to play a critical, though highly ambivalent role.[12] Even more dramatic were the war's consequences for the Austro-Hungarian monarchy, which – utterly exhausted and no longer capable of containing the centrifugal aspirations of its national minorities – disintegrated irremediably in the autumn of 1918.

No less drastic of course had been the war's impact on Russia where, after the interlude of the reformist Kerensky government, the Tsarist regime would be swept away by the Bolshevik revolution – whose political repercussions were potentially tremendous, also beyond Russia, but initially very difficult to fathom.[13] Essentially, then, all over Central and Eastern Europe the question arose of what new political orders would replace the old once the war had finally ended. As will be seen, the prospects for revolutionary changes along Bolshevik lines would actually be distinctly limited outside Russia. Yet, while opening up new possibilities, the war had not created either favourable conditions for what Wilson, other American progressives and many reformers east of the Rhine sought to push forward in their different ways: democratisation processes and the establishment of viable democratic orders.

II. The Widening of the European into a Global but Essentially Euro-Atlantic War

The Great War started and escalated as a European war, and as long as it lasted continental Europe remained its epicentre. But in many ways it indeed widened into the first global war.[14] The conflict soon expanded into the extra-European colonial sphere, notably in Africa, where British imperial forces prevailed within a short time, occupying hitherto German colonies. Particularly Britain yet also France drew on the manpower and resources their extra-European empires provided. In the British case, this above all concerned the Dominions – and India.[15] Yet the war also became global because, for various reasons, ever more states would be drawn into it. By 1917, all of the world's most powerful states and the most populous dependencies had entered the conflict in one way or another. Of particular import here was doubtless the decisions of those who led the Ottoman Empire. Under the influence of Enver Pasha, the Ottoman government had on 2 August 1914 concluded a secret alliance with the German Empire but then at first stayed neutral and

---

[12] Wilson, "Fourteen Points", 8 January 1918, *PWW*, XLV, pp. 538–9.
[13] See Carr (1950–53), I, pp. 70 ff., 105 ff.
[14] See Stevenson (2012); Winter (2014), volume I, part III; Leonhard (2014).
[15] See Darwin (2009), pp. 305–58; Bouvier, Girault and Thobie (1986); Gerwarth and Manela (2015).

even tried to obtain Anglo-French guarantees against the power it still dreaded most, Russia. When these would not be given, Ottoman decision-makers provoked an allied declaration of war in October 1914, and the Sultan then declared a "holy war" against them. This not only extended the war to the empire's Arab provinces but also hastened its eventual demise, setting the scene for what would turn into a neo-imperial "reorganisation" of the Middle East – and prolonged instability in this part of the world.

The war also had significant repercussions in East Asia. Here, the Japanese foreign minister Kato decided to seize an historical opportunity while the European powers were absorbed by the conflict on their own continent. Following his lead, the government in Tokyo moved ahead to expand the Japanese sphere of influence in China, or more precisely the beleaguered Chinese republic that had been established in 1912, after the overthrow of the hollowed-out Qing Dynasty. By the autumn of 1914, Japanese forces had occupied the hitherto German-controlled province of Shandong – as well as the German-held islands in the north Pacific. And in January 1915, Japan presented the Chinese government with its draconian "Twenty-one Demands", which not only required the latter to cede control over Shandong – and Manchuria – but also to grant Japan a de facto decisive influence on China's political and financial affairs. While rejecting this final demand, the Chinese president, Yuan Shikai, felt compelled to accede to the others in a series of Sino-Japanese "agreements" signed in May 1915. Yet the Chinese government – and notably the nationalist-republican leader Sun Yat-Sen – did not lose sight of the cardinal aim of regaining sovereignty. And in order to improve its negotiating position in this struggle, China eventually entered the war on the side of the Allied powers in August 1917.[16]

Yet what became crucial and produced repercussions on a far wider scale was that in the spring of 1917 the United States was drawn into the war and it hence openly expanded into what, in financial, political and ideological terms, it had already become since 1916: a transatlantic conflict. That the American republic actually entered the conflict was by no means inevitable. It was not due to an underlying Anglo-American political and civilisational kinship or to sinister manoeuvres of American financiers or arms dealers, as would later be alleged. And it indeed occurred against the will of the American president. Ever since his "Appeal to the American People" of 19 August 1914 Wilson had committed the United States to a policy of neutrality, insisting that it "must be neutral in fact, as well as in name" – "impartial in thought, as well as action".[17]

---

[16] See Stevenson (2012), pp. 108–9.

[17] Wilson appeal, 18 August 1914, *PWW*, XXX, pp. 393–4; Wilson, *Message to Congress*, 63rd Congress, 2nd Session, Senate Document no. 566 (Washington, 1914), pp. 3–4.

Under the slogan "too proud to fight", these maxims would inform his conduct until the transformational crisis of early 1917. And his administration would focus on defending American "neutral rights". In Wilson's interpretation, these rights were violated, and American shipping and vital commercial and political interests were increasingly affected, by the naval blockade that Britain imposed against the German Empire and its allies – and, more generally, by what the American president criticised as aggressive British "navalism". But more consequential would be the way in which the German Supreme Command came to pursue its counter-strategy of employing the new U-boat weapon in the Atlantic.[18]

What proved decisive and eventually left Wilson no choice but to seek a declaration of war in April 1917 was one of the most consequential miscalculations in the annals of modern "grand strategy", namely the decision of Germany's military leaders to resume, on 1 February 1917, a policy of unrestricted submarine warfare (which had been scaled back after the sinking of the *Lusitania* in April 1915) even though this was bound to affect American shipping and cost further American lives. That the German secretary of state for foreign affairs Zimmermann had earlier offered an alliance to Mexico in the event that the United States entered the war would further galvanise American public opinion when the contents of his "telegram" were made public in March; but it was merely an additional blunder.[19]

The American intervention as "associated power" on the side of the *Entente* did not immediately turn the scales of the war. In military terms Britain and France would still bear the brunt of the western war effort for a long time. At the time it declared war against the Central Powers the United States had a standing army of only 127,500 men, and the American Expeditionary Force under Pershing would only play an important, yet never a decisive role on the western front from October 1917, and the greater part of American troops only arrived in the spring of 1918. But in a wider context the entry of the US indeed determined the war's outcome of the war because it essentially made it unwinnable for the Central Powers and ensured that the now clearly superior capacity of the western powers in terms of troop strength and war production would sooner or later prevail – with the United States more than compensating for the *Entente* Powers' loss of their Russian ally in the wake of the Bolshevik revolution.

---

[18] Wilson Prolegomenon, ca. 25 November 1916, *PWW*, XL, pp. 67–8.

[19] See Tucker (2007), pp. 53–71, 88–144. British and French efforts to influence US public opinion in favour of intervention proved far more effective than parallel German attempts to ensure US neutrality, particularly by mobilising German-Americans. See Kennedy (1980), pp. 45–92.

III.   The Systemic Impact of the War. The Destruction of the Pre-War Eurocentric International System and Transformation of the Transatlantic Constellation

What thus indeed became the first global war also came to have a massive impact on the international system – the global "order", or rather "disorder", that had emerged in the first decades of the long twentieth century. When one assesses its repercussions from a bird's-eye perspective and in a wider historical context it becomes clear that the war not only accelerated or acted as a catalyst for trends that had already gained momentum before 1914. In crucial but not in all respects it actually had *transformative* consequences. It brought about momentous, indeed tectonic changes in the overall configuration and the distribution of power, influence, status and possibilities within it, which not only affected the relations between the European states that fought or were drawn into the conflict but also those between them and the extra-European world and, especially, the relations between Europe and the United States. The war not only shook up the global hierarchy. It indeed altered the constellation of relations between the more powerful states and peoples – those that also claimed to be the most "civilised" and have the authority to set the rules of "world order" – and less powerful states as well as those who as yet lived under different forms imperialist domination. These changes would not only have a profound effect on the eventual peace negotiations. They also had a formative long-term influence on the future of the long twentieth century's international system.

The Great War thus indeed became something akin to a systemic earthquake. But there are some important distinctions to be made. In short, the war triggered a fundamental crisis of the global system of the era of high imperialism, but it by no means brought about its complete disintegration. Rather, it caused two decisive transformative shifts and one less than transformative change. It essentially destroyed Europe's ever more polarised "balance-of-power" system of the pre-war period; and it fundamentally recast the relations between overall weakened European belligerents and an ascending American power; yet it only undermined some, but by no means all, elements and structural underpinnings of the imperialist "order" outside Europe and the north Atlantic sphere. It thus is essential to grasp that the war made it imperative not just to reorder Europe but also to establish some kind of new Atlantic architecture of order to come to terms with the tectonic changes. Fundamentally, it also created new pressures and indeed a longer-term systemic need for a new, essentially post-imperial architecture of the global order.

But, as will be illuminated further below, what the war actually left behind outside Europe and the north Atlantic sphere were still distinctly hierarchical and unequal structures of power and influence in which the remaining world imperial powers – Britain and France, the East Asian imperial power Japan *and the United States* – could assert and even extend their dominance in new ways.

That the cataclysm of 1914–18 led to a breakdown not only of the pre-war European states-system but also, and crucially, the conflict-prone European "balance system" of competitive power politics should be beyond dispute. By the beginning of 1917, the divisions between Europe's warring imperial great powers had become enormously deep, but the five key powers and the basic configuration of the pre-war system were still more or less intact. If some way had been found to end the war at this stage – as Wilson attempted – it might have been conceivable to make a peace on the basis of a readjusted but not *fundamentally* altered European *status quo ante* – with some American involvement and, possibly, the establishment of a more "conservative" League of Nations.

Following the transformative changes that occurred between the spring of 1917 and November 1918 – which comprised not only the intervention of the United States and the collapse of the Tsarist Empire in the wake of the Bolshevik revolution but also, at the end, the disintegration of the Habsburg Empire and the demise of the Wilhelmine Empire – any attempt to (re-) establish a European order along these lines had become impossible. The basic preconditions for it no longer existed. And, as will be shown, at a deeper level the modes and maxims of European power politics that had prevailed before 1914 had come to be delegitimised to a significant degree, though not in all quarters. A return to some kind of *status quo ante* was made even more inconceivable by the fact that, parallel, the war had opened up a Pandora's Box of invigorated, and competing, nationalist aspirations that were pursued by those who had been minority nationalities within the Eastern Empires. Vying for the support of the *Entente* Powers, and eventually seeking particularly Wilson's backing, the leading figures of these newly potent Central and East European national movements – above all those who championed the Polish and the Czech and Slovak causes – would all invoke the newly prominent principle of national self-determination to further their claims for independent states of their own.

While the war unquestionably also affected the still European-dominated "world order" of the pre-war era, its global impact was indeed far more ambivalent. Overall, it diminished the relative weight of Europe in the world – notably in East Asia. And if one adopts a *longue-durée* perspective, it seems fair to say that it sowed some decisive seeds for the eventual dissolution of all European overseas empires and "classic" imperial power systems.[20] Crucially, however, what the war engendered was only the beginning of a *longer-term*

---

[20] See Gerwarth and Manela (2015).

transformation process. It did *not* yet decisively alter the prevalent hierarchies and distribution of power and influence outside the Euro-Atlantic sphere.

As a result of the war, Germany would lose its overseas empire, and the Ottoman Empire would first lose its Arab provinces and ultimately crumble. But the conflict was far from corroding colonial rule as such. Nor did it (as yet) create conditions that would undermine all the varieties of formal and informal imperialist domination that not only Europeans but also Americans – and the Japanese – had come to practise. Colonialism and imperialist domination would be challenged in new ways – and the legitimacy of imperialism would be questioned in new ways, notably by the avant-gardes of fledgling anti-colonial and anti-imperialist nationalist movements, particularly but not only in China, Korea, India and Egypt. Emboldened by the war's repercussions these avant-gardes saw new political opportunities to advance their struggle not just for greater autonomy but for "self-determination" and independent statehood. And here the war itself and, as will be shown, especially the ideological struggle that it fomented and, at the core, not only Lenin's but also Wilson's eventual rhetoric of universal "self-determination", had a catalytic effect.[21]

But the trajectory and outcome of the Great War essentially left those imperial powers that eventually were among its victors in a significantly more powerful position, and with decidedly more means, to maintain their empires – or even to expand their imperial prerogatives in a novel manner. Overall, Britain's imperial world system proved both remarkably effective and adaptable during the war, and so did by and large France's overseas empire. And crucially, as will be shown, those who led them – and first and foremost those who determined British imperial policies – would adapt older and develop new strategies not only to consolidate existing structures but also to *extend* imperial spheres of influence, chiefly at the expense of the Ottoman Empire in the Middle East. Critical here was the development of "modernised" rationales for the defence and legitimation of imperialist prerogatives. Essentially, this was pursued by adapting liberal imperialist ideas and conceptualising an "imperialist internationalism" that was to allow the most "advanced" imperial powers to retain control of their empires and to renew their claims to act as tutelage powers that oversaw the advances of "less civilised" peoples towards self-determination.[22]

For their part, Japanese leaders not only relied on military power and older sphere-of-influence doctrines but also used their own language of tutelage and notions of a self-accorded mission as Asian patron of progress and development in order to buttress their imperialist claims in China – and to contain Korean nationalism. At the same time, the *Entente* Powers were not

---

[21] See Manela (2007).
[22] See Chapters 11 and 12.

prepared to renounce their privileges and still had the means to uphold them. And while generally coming to back those who struggled for a sovereign Chinese republic, at least rhetorically, Wilson ultimately did not take any meaningful steps to this end – or indeed to relinquish America's "Open Door" prerogatives.[23]

Finally, it should be highlighted in this context that also beyond China no clear American departure from earlier ideas and practices of formal and informal imperialism occurred during Wilson's wartime presidency. Nor did Wilson relinquish core premises of what had become an expanded Monroe Doctrine. Although the president supported a policy that was to prepare the Philippines for independence in the near future, it became clear in 1916 that there was no majority in the American Congress for a commitment to this end. Under a thin veil of progressive proclamations pre-war maxims of paternalistic tutelage and control still retained the upper hand.

Neo imperialist approaches, tutelage assumptions and hierarchical patterns also persisted in the United States' relations with Latin American countries. In late 1914, Wilson had espoused the idea of a Pan-American pact that essentially was to enshrine a "(m)utual guarantee of political independence under republican forms of government and mutual guarantees of territorial integrity". Subsequently, he had proclaimed that the United States no longer had any "claim of guardianship" but instead sought "a full and honourable association as of partners" – "upon a footing of genuine equality and unquestioned independence" – that had "none of the spirit of empire in it".[24]

Wilson's initiative was motivated by the aspiration to turn the United States into an exemplary hegemon in the western hemisphere and to forge a pan-American system that could then serve as a model for war-torn Europe and, indeed, the rest of the world.[25] But after protracted negotiations this endeavour would ultimately fail in the spring of 1916. And what essentially undermined it was the Wilson administration's intervention in the Mexican revolution and civil war, which in 1916 culminated in the – futile – dispatch of an intervention army of 12,000 men under General Pershing to defeat the revolutionary leader Pancho Villa.[26] In short, Wilson by no means initiated a real qualitative departure from the premises of Roosevelt's earlier "corollary" to the Monroe Doctrine. While invoking the mission to promote democracy and independence in the American hemisphere, he too ultimately still

---

[23] See Xu (2014).

[24] House diary, 16 December 1914, *PWW*, XXXI, pp. 469–70; "Draft of a Pan-American Treaty", 16 December 1914, later sent to the governments of Brazil, Argentina and Chile, *ibid.*, pp. 471–3; Wilson, annual message to Congress, 7 December 1915, *PWW*, XXXV, pp. 295–6.

[25] See Knock (1992), pp. 39–44.

[26] See Smith (2012), pp. 52–4, 62–4.

accorded the United States the prerogative to act as an interventionist "hemi-spheric policeman".[27]

In contrast to this, the Great War indeed *transformed* the relations and power configuration between Europe and the United States. Indeed, nowhere was the systemic shift the war caused more pronounced than here. It created a novel transatlantic constellation, which has often been alluded to but not been properly understood. For at the very time when it weakened and exhausted all European belligerents, the war Great War *initiated* a transformation of the United States' role in the international system, with major implications for the further course of international history in the remainder of the long twentieth century. Essentially, it catapulted the American republic, which had already begun to act as a unilateral world power before 1914 but essentially refrained from assuming any major international commitments, into a position where its political leaders and the wider public confronted challenges for which they were decidedly ill-prepared. At the core, they faced the challenge of acting not as *the* but as *a* hegemon in the international system. The war indeed made the United States not only the world's newly dominant economic and financial power but also a power that suddenly had the potential to play a pivotal part in resetting the terms and rules of international politics and recasting inter-national order in its aftermath. But it by no means had turned America into a new "superpower" whose messianic president could eventually decree the essentials of an Americanist "new world order". Rather, by the end of 1918, the United States had become one among several pre-eminent powers, and ultimately Wilson and other American protagonists would especially have to find ways to come to terms with the political leaders of the other main victors of the war, the battered but still powerful imperial states Britain and France.

While clearly moving its centre of gravity westwards, from Europe to the United States, the Great War thus only marked the *beginning* of a world-historical change in the distribution of power, influence and possibilities within the international system. And in a broader perspective it is even more important to understand that the war gave rise to an unprecedented inter-connectedness, and indeed a newly complex *interdependence*, between the United States and Europe, which would have far-reaching consequences. As will be shown, this occurred not just in the financial and economic and eventually in the military sphere, but also in the sphere of international and transnational politics – and in the realm of ideas and ideologies. Political actors and wider publics on both sides of the Atlantic, and on both sides of the trenches, had to come to grips with this new interdependence and the new dynamics it generated.

[27] See Wilson remarks to Mexican editors, 7 June 1918, *PWW*, XLVIII, p. 258.

In retrospect, it is possible to see quite clearly that all of these epochal changes were already well underway by the autumn of 1916. But the decisive systemic "turning-point" came in the wake of America's entry into the war in 1917. At one level, the former net debtor, above all of Britain, became the world's most significant creditor power, above all as financier of British and French war efforts. The more "total" the war became, the more it forced all European belligerents to find new means to cover spiralling expenses. And while the Central Powers became isolated from the world market and cut off from international capital, this gave rise to unprecedented patterns of indebtedness among the Allied powers. In the spring of 1917, British loans still accounted for more than 80 per cent of all inter-allied war credits, most of which were extended to France and eventually amounted to a total of $1.7 billion in current prices. But then a decisive shift occurred in the relations between the *Entente* powers and the United States. In the early stages, as long as the latter remained officially neutral, the New York banking house of J.P. Morgan had become not only the chief agent of *Entente* purchases of weapons, munitions and other equipment in the United States but also, and crucially, the key supplier of private capital, providing approximately $2.3 billion to Britain and France. In the autumn of 1916, a critical juncture was reached that would also have far-reaching long-term repercussions for international politics. It was the moment when, as has rightly been stressed, Britain reached a decisive financial impasse in the war and "financial hegemony passed irrevocably across the Atlantic", namely from Britain to the United States.[28]

The war thus indeed accelerated a momentous transition process: the United States became the world's new financial hegemon, eclipsing Britain which had occupied this position ever since the early eighteenth century and had fortified it after 1815.[29] This was also reflected in another process that now gained momentum: the shifting of the world's financial centre of gravity from the City of London to Wall Street. Though London would recover some of its formerly predominant influence in the 1920s, the main American banks, led by J.P. Morgan, would not only step in and become the most important provider of capital in Latin America but also position themselves to play the same role in Europe. During the war they confined their activities to the *Entente*, but eventually their engagement would significantly affect the financial and political stabilisation of Weimar Germany and the dynamics of postwar debt and reparations politics.

Politically, however, the newly decisive financial and creditor power was hardly prepared for its new role. As noted, it had only very recently begun to establish a "modern" banking system through the Federal Reserve Act of

[28] See Skidelsky (1983), p. 335.
[29] See Kennedy (1988), p. 268.

December 1913. And the head of the Federal Reserve Bank of New York, Benjamin Strong, still had to assert his authority as the nation's new chief agent of financial and monetary policy in the manner of his European counterparts.[30]

By 1916, Britain had not only depleted its gold reserves but also greatly increased its dependence on private US loans to meet its wartime needs and obligations. It was thus no coincidence that Britain's worst financial crisis of the war was brought on by the decision of the newly established US Federal Reserve Board in November 1916 to reduce lending to foreign borrowers and to warn private lenders not to make loans on the security of Allied Treasury bills. By this time, the financial situation of France had become even more precarious. Indeed, British and French decision-makers now had to grapple not only with the financial but also with the political repercussions of their new dependence on the United States. In a wider context, however, both American and *Entente* leaders had to deal with the implications of what was in fact a new pattern of transatlantic *inter*dependence between creditor and debtor powers. Already in October 1916 John Maynard Keynes, then a young Treasury official, had warned that if things went on as they had, Wilson would by the summer of 1917 "be in a position, if he wishes, to dictate his own terms to us". Keynes had thus recommended that Britain's policy towards the United States "should be so directed as not only to avoid any form of reprisal or active irritation but also to conciliate and please".[31]

But Wilson would by no means be in a position to dictate his peace agenda to Britain or France – or indeed to keep the United States out of the war. Following its intervention, the American government then indeed stepped in as the *Entente*'s official lender of last resort, granting a critically important initial $1 billion loan to Britain in the spring of 1917. Yet both *Entente* governments would remain heavily dependent on US capital. The extent of their dependence was revealed in July 1917 when the British War Cabinet sought to impress on the American ambassador that if the US Congress did not extend its loans and continue to vouch for J.P. Morgan's private credits, a financial collapse would be triggered that would destroy the entire financial substructure of the alliance within days.[32]

Subsequently, the American government would indeed extend further essential loans to Britain and France, which were based on the underlying interest in ensuring their continued ability to fight the war and the assumption that both would be able to repay their obligations in its aftermath. The US Congress passed four Liberty Loan Acts authorising a total of $10 billion (of which $8 billion had been allocated by the end of 1918). And the *Entente*

---

[30] Wilson speech, 23 December 1913, *PWW*, XXIX, pp. 63–6.

[31] Keynes memoranda, 10 and 24 October 1916, Keynes (1978), XVI, pp. 197–201; Keynes memorandum, 10 October 1916, ibid., p. 198; Skidelsky (1983), pp. 333–6.

[32] See Kennedy (1980), p. 319.

Powers incurred the most sizeable obligations, in Britain's case roughly $3.7 billion, in France's $2 billion.[33] Parallel, American decision-makers indeed began to think about how they could seize on America's new clout as creditor to political ends. In 1917, Wilson's Treasury secretary William McAdoo proposed using financial levers to force Britain to curb its naval expansion plans. And Wilson himself would later contemplate – in very vague terms – a similar approach to compel British and French leaders to fall in line with his progressive peacemaking agenda and plans for a League of Nations.[34] But, as will be shown, neither he nor any other American policymaker actually developed effective strategies to this end. And, more fundamentally, the complex *inter*dependence between the United States and the *Entente* Powers that the war created simply did not permit a straightforward conversion of financial power into decisive political influence.

Nonetheless, by the end of the war the United States' new financial preponderance had become unequivocal. And at the same time the war had also accelerated its ascent as the pre-eminent power in the global economy. While the conflict had temporarily severed trade relations with the German Empire, which by 1914 had become the most important trading partner and market for American goods, it greatly increased US exports to Britain, France and the other states aligned against the Central Powers. Fundamentally, this also increased transatlantic *interdependence* and American dependence on access to European markets – even though influential American experts like Wilson's later economic adviser Herbert Hoover stressed that the US economy could rely on its domestic market far more than any European state. And, crucially, it spurred the Wilson administration's interest in pushing for "Open Door" premises of unrestricted access – for American commerce – in any post-war settlement.[35]

In financial and economic terms, the United States would thus clearly emerge as the real winner of the war, and this would indeed have important consequences for the eventual peacemaking process. But, as will be shown, it would not prove decisive. It did not put those who directed American policies, above all Wilson, in a commanding position to set the rules of the postwar international order. Though weakened by the war and in important respects dependent on US goodwill, particularly Britain and France remained highly influential. In many ways, they still were pivotal powers too. And even after its eventual defeat Germany remained – in a longer-term perspective – a

---

[33] See Moulton and Pasvolsky (1932), p. 426; Artaud (1978); Burk (1985).

[34] McAdoo to American Ambassador, London, 30 June 1917, RG 39; State Department instructions to US representatives in Paris and London, 19 November 1918, State Department 600.001.591/606a.

[35] Hoover to Wilson, 20 December 1918, O'Brien (1978), pp. 22–3; Hoover, address, 15 October 1928, Hoover Papers, *Commerce*, 1928.

potentially very powerful actor as well; and so did Russia, even after the Bolshevik revolution had brought down the old regime and the country became engulfed in a civil war.

Thus, what the Great War actually created by the end of 1918 was not a compelling scenario for a novel American hegemony but rather a situation of profound systemic instability and, indeed, a complex transatlantic multipolarity. It was a constellation in which the durability of whatever peace was made depended, above all, on the capacity of the most influential American *and* European decision-makers to conceptualise and negotiate mutually acceptable terms and rules for something unprecedented: a modern Atlantic order. All in all, then, the First World War brought about immense and immensely challenging shifts in the international system and power relations. And these shifts also formed the backdrop of a far-ranging and highly consequential political-cum-ideological struggle that escalated from 1914 *and has to be interpreted anew.*

7

The Political and Ideological "War within the War"

The Transatlantic Competition Over the Shape
of the Postwar Order

The long twentieth century's formative cataclysm indeed sparked an unprecedentedly fierce and far-reaching political and ideological "war within the war" – a competition not only about the higher purpose and stakes of the war itself but also about the nature and contours of the future international order. And it is no coincidence that this essentially became a *transatlantic* struggle, which would have crucial repercussions and set essential parameters for the peace conference of 1919. In a wider context, it had a formative impact on ideas and ideological visions of what constituted modern international order and of what was to lie at the core of modern international politics. Yet it also brought to the fore fundamentally conflicting, if not irreconcilable visions of peace, order and politics.

What escalated first, and very soon after the war's outbreak, can best be described as a by and large *inner-European* competition between increasingly expansive war-vindication, war-aim and mobilisation agendas, which were advanced by the *Entente*'s and by the Central Powers' political and military leaders and armies of increasingly zealous public intellectuals, opinionmakers and propagandists. On this competition, which soon acquired a "no-holds-barred" character, Wilson and other American actors at first only had a relatively marginal influence. From 1916, however, and then especially following the United States' entry into the war it turned into a much wider, more fundamental and all-embracing political and ideological struggle in which the American president would come to play a decisive role. And it was in the context of this high-stakes struggle that different, for the most part *not* novel or original but newly comprehensive conceptions of peace and the principles, mechanisms and "membership criteria" of a new, at the core Euro-Atlantic international system were developed.

The inner-European war within the war had commenced straightaway in August 1914. Crucially, however, it then turned into a wider struggle that reached a first critical stage in the autumn of 1916 and early 1917 when Wilson's initiative for a negotiated "peace without victory" challenged and collided with the war aims and strategies of *all* European belligerents. It then entered a new stage, and metamorphosed into a more transformative ideological competition, after the United States' intervention and the Bolshevik revolution had not only altered the course of the war but also recast the international, transnational and domestic constellations in which peace would be negotiated. And it reached a decisive stage once the western powers had won the military conflict with decisive American support. This struggle was to have momentous longer-term consequences for the history of international politics that can still be felt in the twenty-first century. It escalated in a global context, and it spurred the first actually global struggle and "debate" about how the world after the war was to be ordered. But it had the most crucial bearing on how key American and European actors would eventually approach the reordering of Europe and the unprecedented challenge of making an Atlantic peace for the long twentieth century.

Unsurprisingly, the war-aims agendas of the opposing European belligerents clashed violently, and to a greater or lesser degree all of these agendas became radicalised. Because the stakes were so high, and got higher the longer it lasted, the increasingly "total" war became highly politicised. It soon was no longer a merely military or strategic conflict, fought over specific national interests, but rather a moral and civilisational-cultural struggle of unparalleled proportions. And as such it gave rise to a development that had very serious long-term repercussions far beyond the era of the Great War, namely a more far-reaching "ideologisation" and "moralisation" of international politics than had ever been witnessed before. All sides used all the modern means of communication and propaganda they had at their disposal to place their own war efforts and war aims on a higher moral and ideological plain and to denigrate and devalue what their enemies pursued. Though in different ways, all sides indeed emphasised moral and ideological categories to justify sacrifices and unparalleled mobilisation efforts to their own populations. Arguably, however, moral justifications also became so pre-eminent precisely because it proved so difficult for all governments to find persuasive reasons for continuing to fight a war that was taking such an inconceivably high toll.

The ideologisation and moralisation the Great War sparked would be taken to a new level, first through Wilson's engagement on behalf of a "peace without victory", then through his crusade to "make the world safe for democracy" and overcome the authoritarianism and militarism of the Central Powers. And it would be further radicalised once Lenin and Trotsky not only agitated for a "new diplomacy" but also seized on their revolutionary successes to call on the working classes to transform the conflict – finally – into a proletarian war against capitalist-imperialist interests. Eventually, the political and ideological struggle at the heart of the Great War thus *also* became a competition between two novel alternative visions that would anticipate the global Soviet-American rivalry of the Cold War: Wilsonian aspirations to establish a liberal-progressive "new world order" and Lenin's vision to sweep away the capitalist-imperialist system and build a "new order" of Soviet republics. But during the decisive stages of the Great War it was at the core a different transatlantic struggle – an ever fiercer battle between Wilsonianism and the aspirations of mainly American and British liberals and progressives on the one hand and, on the other, different, notably French and German visions of postwar order that essentially rested on power-political and imperialist or neo-imperialist premises.[1]

The transatlantic war within the war thus also produced new and unprecedentedly deep political and ideological cleavages – not only between the antagonistic coalitions but also, and importantly, between competing political groups and forces inside the different belligerent states and neutral powers. In this sense, the Great War created not only new international but also newly pronounced transnational *and* inner-state divisions. At the same time, the war's ideological competition was indeed instrumental for generating conflicting and at the same time profoundly unrealistic, even millennial expectations. And one of the most pervasive yet also most unrealistic expectations it raised was that, following an all but total war, it would be possible to conceive *and actually create* a "total peace" – a "peace to end all wars". The longer the war lasted, the more such expectations would be encouraged by and projected onto Wilson, both empowering the aspirational American president and burdening him with an impossible task.

I. The Ideological-Political Struggle at the Heart of the Great War – and Its Transatlantic Escalation

Soon after the outbreak of the war the governments and official propagandists of the warring powers on both sides began to advance increasingly expansive ideas, aims and agendas that were intended to vindicate their respective war efforts and to ensure the ever more vital mobilisation of their populations and the immense sacrifices they were required to make both on the frontlines and on the home fronts. This became more vital the longer the conflict lasted. But such efforts also went far beyond the sphere of intergovernmental competition. Indeed, on both sides of the trenches official war-aims programmes were surpassed by a wide array of even more radical demands and designs that an unprecedented range of parties, pressure-groups, activists, intellectuals and opinion-makers put forward. While in France, Germany, Austria-Hungary and Russia veritable war-aims movements were formed, what emerged in Britain and eventually in the United States can more appropriately be described as "peace-aims movements".

---

[1] The political-ideological radicalisation of the war made it almost impossible for states that initially had remained neutral not to take sides in the end. This applied to smaller states, like the Scandinavian countries, yet above all to the United States. See Tucker (2007); Jonas (2019). On the fundamental political-philosophical issues raised by modern war see Arendt (2009), pp. 1–10; Arendt (2018), pp. 77–80.

From the outset, both the British and the French governments and those who aided their propaganda efforts declared that the *Entente* Powers were engaged in a defensive war. At the same time, they quickly turned the war into an essentially moral-ideological conflict in which fundamental issues were at stake – a war that had to be fought in defence of liberty and western civilisation against the threat posed by what they portrayed as Prusso-German autocracy, militarism and designs for global domination. In Britain, the Asquith government set the tone by stressing the existential need to protect not only Britain, the Empire and the liberal values and civilisational standards it allegedly represented but also the freedom of Europe against the menace of "Prussian military despotism".[2] Starting with Viviani's *union sacreé* premiership, successive French wartime governments and both official and unofficial French propaganda were even more fervent in proclaiming that they were engaged in a struggle to defend the French republic's – and western – "liberty, justice, and reason", democracy and civilisation against Prusso-German militarism and ambitions to oppress Europe.[3] Not least for mobilisation purposes Lloyd George and Clemenceau would cling to these rationales and paint the conflict in even starker ideological colours. All of this would be magnified by the newly established British Ministry of Information, where from early 1918 the press baron Beaverbrook directed official propaganda, its French equivalent and the press organs and opinion-makers that went to extreme lengths to ensure that their countrymen would fight on to final victory.[4]

Significantly, the *Entente* governments' accentuation of the defensive and morally superior character of their war efforts went hand in hand with the claim that the German Empire's military and political leaders bore the sole and "overwhelming responsibility" for the outbreak of the war.[5] Further, they castigated not only the German breach of pre-war international standards of "civilised conduct", especially through the violation of Belgian neutrality, but also subsequent German "atrocities" against Belgium's civilian population and more general transgressions of "the rules of war" codified at The Hague.[6] They thereby introduced moral categories of "guilt" and "transgression" on which their later claims for "reparation" would be based. As charismatic wartime leader, Lloyd George would use particularly moralistic rhetoric and proclaim,

---

[2] Asquith speeches, Commons, 4 and 6 August 1914, Asquith speech, Hansard, *Commons*, vol. 65, cols. 1925–7 and ff.; Asquith, "A Free Future for the World", Guild Hall, 9 November 1916 (London, 1916).

[3] Viviani speech, 4 August 1914; Viviani speech, 22 December 1914, *Journal Officiel (Chambre)*, 1914, 3110–13, 3124–5.

[4] See Taylor (1980), pp. 875–98.

[5] This Poincaré had declared as early as on 4 August 1914. See Poincaré, *Messages* (1919), pp. 6–8.

[6] Asquith speech, Commons, 4 August 1914, Hansard, *Commons*, vol. 65, cols. 1925–7; Imperial War Cabinet Meeting 32, 15 August 1918, CAB 23/7.

in August 1918, that the western powers had to impose peace terms tantamount to a "penalty" for the German "offence" of violating Belgium's neutrality and, more fundamentally, of starting the war in pursuit of aggressive militaristic objectives.[7]

For their part, the German chancellor Bethmann Hollweg and the official and unofficial war propagandists in Germany took pains to stress from the outset that it was in fact the German Empire that was fighting to defend itself against French and Russian aggression. For a long time, the German government even refrained from presenting any official German war aims so as not to undermine the official "defensive war" propaganda – and it of course refuted all "enemy accusations" of German "war guilt".[8] To provide a legitimising mission for the German war effort a phalanx of German professors and intellectuals had soon begun to propagate what has become known as the – inchoate – "ideas of 1914". Essentially defined against the "western" ideas of 1789 – and eventually also against those of 1776 – these ideas revolved around the notion that the German Empire had to prevail in the war in order to not only to secure Germany's future as a great power but also to preserve "German culture" and forms of "order" – a "people's community" and "justice" that could only be guaranteed by a strong state and had to be defended against the onslaught of western civilisation, liberal individualism and democracy. At the same time, they claimed, Germany had to repulse the brutal onslaught of the backward, inferior Slavic-Russian colossus in the east.[9]

The "ideas of 1914" culminated in the aspiration to endow the German war effort with a special world-historical mission that was generally anti-western and eventually also distinctly anti-American; and from 1916 they came to clash fundamentally with Wilson's ideological crusades. Johann Plenge, the economist who coined the phrase "ideas of 1914", asserted that since 1789 the world had not seen a revolution like "the German revolution of 1914"; the "ideas of German organisation" were destined to prevail over the destructive liberalising forces of the west.[10] While France was predictably portrayed as Germany's vindictive arch enemy, much of the German ideological war effort came to concentrate on what most opinion-makers saw as the most dangerous enemy – the British world power, which allegedly sought to subjugate Germany by all means, including a brutal blockade. In 1915, the economist Werner Sombart advanced the influential notion that the conflict was

[7] Imperial War Cabinet Meeting 32, 15 August 1918, CAB 23/7.
[8] Bethmann Hollweg speech, Reichstag, 4 August 1914, *Reichstagsprotokolle*, August 1914. See Jarausch (1973).
[9] See Winkler (I/2000), pp. 337–43.
[10] Plenge (1915), pp. 173–4; Plenge (1916), p. 82. See Winkler (I/2000), pp. 337–40.

essentially a war between English "traders" and German "heroes", between despicable English "commercialism" and heroic German "militarism".[11]

Following the American declaration of war, this mode of ideological warfare would be extended to the United States, which came to be portrayed as the liberal-capitalist power whose leaders – while using high-flying rhetoric – were intent on defeating Germany in order to assert its global dominance as a new kind of imperial world power. In his infamous *Reflections of a Nonpolitical Man* of 1918 Thomas Mann would eventually seek to offer a more profound – and profoundly strained – defence of German culture against the encroachments of liberal-democratic civilisation and "politics" that Britain, France and the United States represented. He denounced western leaders like Wilson who intended to "*impose*" on Germany their ideas of "human rights, liberty, equality, cosmopolitanism" with "weapons in hand".[12] Politically more consequential, however, would be the propagandistic efforts of the German "Fatherland Party", founded in 1917, to defend a "German freedom" guaranteed by a strong state against the pernicious influence of French war-mongers, English "hypocrites" and, notably, the crusading American president.[13]

The increasingly messianic rhetoric with which Wilson responded to the Great War unquestionably had a decisive impact on the way in which the ideological-moral struggle at the heart of the conflict came to be transformed into a broader, more universal competition with repercussions far beyond Europe and the United States in the watershed year 1917. Yet he had begun to influence this struggle very significantly long before the American republic actually entered the war. While insisting on American "neutrality" in action and in thought, Wilson endeavoured to build a distinctive exceptionalist-exemplarist platform, based on the notion that while all European belligerents had compromised themselves through the catastrophe the United States had finally ascended to the position of a civilisationally superior vanguard power. In his view, it was called on to push both for democratisation processes and steps towards a progressive international order built around what he initially called an "association of nations".[14]

After narrowly winning re-election in November 1916 on the pledge of keeping the country out of the war, Wilson became more assertive, proclaiming that the time had come for the American republic to pursue a new mission in the world – namely to act as an "impartial" umpire that ended the war by mediating a negotiated "peace without victory".

---

[11] Sombart (1915). For the wider "battle" see Hoeres (2004).

[12] Mann (1918), pp. 1, 581.

[13] See "Gründungsaufruf der Deutschen Vaterlandspartei", 2 September 1917, in Mommsen (1960), pp. 420 f.; Winkler (I/2000), I, pp. 352–3.

[14] Wilson remarks, autumn of 1914, in Root (1926), p. 244; Baker memorandum of conversations with Stockton Axson, 8, 10, 11 February 1925, Baker Papers; Baker (1927–39), V, pp. 73–5; Wilson remarks, 20 April 1915, *PWW*, XXXIII, pp. 38–9.

He originally argued – in vain – that only a settlement that stopped the "systematised" mass slaughter in Europe before one side had inflicted a humiliating defeat on the other could usher in what was really needed: a "modern" peace that superseded Europe's entire anachronistic "old order" of competitive alliances and power-political machinations, which he at this stage blamed for the outbreak and escalation of the war.[15] This reflected the views and demands of a vocal minority of progressive US internationalists. Significantly, then, the political-ideological maxims Wilson advanced as long as the United States still remained "neutral" challenged the war-aims agendas and war-vindication strategies of *all* European belligerents – whether they were more democratic or autocratic – in fundamental ways.

Once an intervention in the war had become politically unavoidable, the American president altered the thrust of his agenda markedly. He now came to define the United States' war effort as a crusade not only on behalf of a progressive international order – and American-style "Open Door" capitalism – but also, and more emphatically, on behalf of liberal democracy – and thus into a crusade that was mainly directed against the military and autocratic masters of the German Empire. Accordingly, Wilson characterised the war as a conflict between civilised liberal democracy and military autocracy. And he sought to rally American and world opinion behind the expansive missionary war aim to make Europe and the world "safe for democracy". Wilson explicitly emphasised that in the new order he envisaged, all states that embraced democratic government were to have an "equal" place – and that this also applied to the Central Powers. But he now also stressed that the world could only be made "safe" for democratisation by first defeating German designs for "imperial domination".[16]

This crusading ideology was to have a far-reaching, though highly ambivalent impact – not only on the intensifying struggles between reformers and the forces of the "old order" in the Wilhelmine Empire.[17] In setting his war agenda Wilson had partly been influenced by the ideas of interventionist progressives in the United States, notably those of the young journalist Walter Lippmann. Writing in the new progressive flagship journal, *The New Republic*, Lippmann had urged the president to enter the war on the side of the *Entente* in order to turn it into a moral campaign – a campaign for the cause of "liberalism" and

---

[15] Wilson Prolegomenon, ca. 25 November 1916, *PWW*, XL, pp. 67–70; Wilson Senate address, 22 January 1917, *PWW*, XL, pp. 536–9.

[16] Wilson address to Congress, 2 April 1917, *PWW*, XLI, p. 525–7; Wilson "Fourteen Points" address, 8 January 1918, *PWW*, XLV, pp. 538–9.

[17] From 1917, the impact of Wilson's ideological agenda was heightened by the newly established American Committee on Public Information, headed by the publicist George Creel. It operated as the official American propaganda machinery and became increasingly effective in disseminating Wilson's "vision" at home and abroad. See Creel (1920).

"democracy" and to prevent the "triumph" of "reaction", which Germany's emperor and military leaders represented. Yet he had also sketched a wider (re-)integrationist objective, stressing that America's aim should be not to "destroy" Germany but rather to discredit the forces of militarism and autocracy and then to "force and lure her back to the [western] civilization to which she belongs".[18]

The programmatic agenda that Wilson unfurled and Lippmann and others had helped to develop thus had one overarching theme. It was intended to prepare the ground for the creation of an *essentially inclusive* progressive international order that could also integrate the states and peoples against which the United States now fought alongside the *Entente* Powers. In practice, Wilson's rhetoric not only sharpened, – as it was meant to do, inner-German divisions between the adherents of an expansive *Siegfrieden* and the social democratic and liberal proponents of democratic reforms and a "peace of understanding" in the *Reichstag* that in 1917 sponsored the widely noted "Peace Resolution". It also complicated the task of the reformers, because they now had to defend themselves against the accusation that they were merely doing the bidding of Germany's American enemy. In a more general perspective, the Wilsonian crusade effectively deepened the political-ideological trenches the war had opened up considerably further, accentuating the schism between those who claimed to represent higher values of civilisation and democracy – chiefly the United States, Britain and France – and those who found it increasingly difficult to define a powerful war mission on behalf of German or Austro-Hungarian "freedom" and culture.

It is worth noting in this context that particularly under Wilson's influence the war's ideological battles thus in effect prompted new, more ideologically charged endeavours to demarcate what constituted "the West" and principles of "western civilisation" – no longer, as before 1914, in a hierarchical contrast to "lesser", non-western civilisations but now in opposition to what the Central Powers were supposed to represent. While facing the difficulty of justifying the alliance with Tsarist Russia, those who claimed to speak on behalf of "the West" posited as "essentially western" different notions of liberal order, liberty, democracy, lawfulness and "civilised behaviour" in international affairs. And they contrasted these notions ever more sharply with the Central Powers' non-western militarism, "despotism" and violations of civilised standards of warfare and international politics. Yet what also ensued was in fact a competition between *different* conceptions of "the West" in which Wilson and American progressives challenged British and French claims and asserted that

---

[18] Lippmann, "America's Part in the War", *New Republic* (10 February 1917), pp. 33–4; Lippmann, "The Defense of the Atlantic World", *New Republic* (17 February 1917), p. 60.

they now had come to represent the most advanced occidental power in a new "western" and indeed Atlantic hierarchy.

The challenges that these divisive developments created were compounded by a more general and arguably even more profound problem. In short, while the crisis of the Great War also generated more or less far-reaching forms of internationalism and both liberal and socialist internationalist responses – which have to be examined more closely – it also led to a radicalisation of nationalisms. More precisely, not only the exigencies of the war itself and the ever growing need to mobilise populations but also and especially the expanding ideological and propaganda battles spawned more aggressive forms of both offensive and defensive nationalism – first among the European belligerents, then also in the United States. At the same time, the war of course also sharpened the nationalist agendas of those who now sought to assert their claims for nation-states in Eastern Europe – and of a new vanguard of anti-imperialist nationalists outside Europe.

What now became more aggressive obviously had longer roots and, as we have seen, particularly drew on the nationalist ideologies that had flowered since the onset of the long twentieth century's first globalisation process.[19] But here too the Great War acted as a catalyst, and the more radical currents of nationalism it generated were far from abating after the cataclysm had ended in the west. They continued to generate friction and violence. And, crucially, they now turned into vindictive nationalism on the part of the eventual victors and nationalisms of resentment and revenge on the part of the vanquished. Here, this provided fertile ground for demagogues and propagandists who claimed that they knew how to turn the humiliation of defeat into a glorious future victory. Finding ways to manage and contain radicalised nationalisms thus had to be a critical part of any realistic attempt to build a more durable order after the Great War.

II. Towards More Comprehensive Conceptions of Peace, International Politics and Order

Yet the war and the political-ideological war within it also had momentous effects that went beyond the creation of ever deeper divisions between the two antagonistic camps and the radicalisation of nationalisms and war aims. It was in fact instrumental in spurring significant changes and reorientation processes in the sphere of ideas about peace, international order and the parameters of international politics. Inevitably, the unprecedentedly dynamic struggle generated competing and ideologically charged visions. But this should not obscure that the Great War also became a germination period for different, not entirely

---

[19] See Chapters 2 and 4.

new but newly comprehensive conceptions of modern peace and a modern order, which essentially emerged in the crucial transatlantic struggle.

The most aspirational of these conceptions approximated notions of a "total peace" – a peace that would "end all wars" and vindicate the war's sacrifices; and an order that was to be more durable and legitimate because it was built on new, more comprehensive foundations – and provided new or expanded political, economic and social benefits. But ideas of how this was to be accomplished and, more profoundly, of what was just and legitimate differed widely. More than has previously been acknowledged the transatlantic war of ideas and ideologies thus also transformed and indeed greatly *expanded* the requirements of peacemaking – and the requirements a peace settlement had to meet if it was to endure. They not only related to security and material compensations for the sacrifices and devastations of the war, but also to demands for "justice", substantive political reforms and, where this applied, statehood and self-determination. Further, as will be shown, these requirements were to an unprecedented degree influenced by something else the war and the ideological struggle had raised: massively heightened *expectations* of what the peace settlement and the new order were to bring. And more often than not these expectations came to conflict – with disastrous consequences.

Despite the use of universalist rhetoric, which stimulated worldwide demands for change that would mostly be disappointed, the most powerful and influential of the visions that gained shape during the Great War – among them Wilson's yet also those of key British, French and, eventually, more "progressive" German decision-makers – were essentially conceptions for a new Atlantic order. But the war also brought to the fore very different and as yet very Eurocentric notions of how Europe and the wider world were supposed to be reordered after the war, ranging from one radical imperialist extreme – schemes for a German imperial hegemony over Europe – to another radical revolutionary extreme – Lenin's vision of creating a new communist order of European soviet republics as the decisive first step of a global revolutionary process.

At a deeper level, the First World War indeed became a transformative crisis also insofar as it did not just undermine the pre-war international "order". It also shook up formerly dominant ideas and assumptions about international politics, security, conflict resolution and, of course, the political consequences of modern industrial warfare. It is worth emphasising that, though to varying degrees, the war led decision-makers, strategists, opinion-makers and wider elites *on all sides* to think differently about cardinal questions of peace and global order (while also changing wider collective attitudes in the states and societies that were involved in the struggle, which are much harder to gauge). And it did engender significant learning and reorientation processes – even though these took very different forms, and some reached much further, or deeper, than others.

The catastrophe provoked some genuine and substantive attempts on both sides of the Atlantic to comprehend which underlying *systemic* trends, particularly in the overall political culture and mental world of high imperialism, had led into the abyss of 1914 and then fed the radicalisation of the war. And it led to some remarkable efforts to draw harder political lessons from all of this. But the crucible of the war also became a hotbed for many varieties of stunted or "pathological" learning. It witnessed many instances in which both political leaders and non-governmental actors mainly approached the novel challenges the war posed by drawing on what they learned or what ideas and ideological conceptions they had developed before 1914. And what became even more consequential was that all too often the more or less novel paths these actors sought to pursue, under the pressures of a conflict that unleashed a torrent of "new realities", were half-baked or did not reach far enough; and that the consequences they drew in fact made it much harder for them, and for the societies they represented, to embark on *more far-reaching* and *deeper* learning processes. In the end, both the main decision-makers and the societies of the warring powers were thus much less prepared to think and to do what was really required to build a better, more sustainable postwar order. This manifested itself on both sides of the trenches. It applied to British imperial strategists and French renovators of power politics just as much as to those who sought to develop some kind of blueprint for a *Pax Germanica*.

The effects that such constraining developments produced will be examined in greater depth, and with attention to nuances, in the concrete *and dynamically changing* context of the war's political and ideological battles. But one cardinal development can be highlighted already. In short, especially the ever more dominant tendency of Wilson, Lenin and many other key actors, including the imperialists who championed a "Greater Germany", to resort to grand ideological constructions of what fighting and winning the war was supposed to achieve limited *on all sides* the capacity to persevere in harder processes of learning – of drilling, as it were, the thick planks of political learning. And this in the end made all sides, but particularly those actors who like Wilson maintained *fundamentally* ideological outlooks, distinctly less capable of conceiving and negotiating a peace and a system of order that actually had the potential to address the massive problems and consequences the war had generated in a truly effective manner.[20]

Moreover, for the depth and immensity of the changes it generated the Great War indeed remained "too short" to leave enough time for more substantive processes that could already have made a decisive difference at

[20] See Meier (2000), p. 516.

the Paris Peace Conference. While it was far more destructive and revolutionary than the revolutionary and Napoleonic wars one hundred years earlier, the
First World War was thus far from engendering one prevalent form of
collective learning, let alone a kind of transnational *metanoia* or "turning
around of the mind" that could potentially lead to a substantive agreement
and common understanding about what was required to make a peace that
prevented a repetition of the catastrophe.[21] Rather, it caused very distinctive
and in critical respects conflicting changes in individual and collective mentalities and outlooks among those who sought to influence the shaping of the
postwar order.

On the part of some influential actors, the depth and scale of the catastrophe
indeed prompted remarkable though often rather abstract efforts to draw
more than superficial consequences and pursue qualitatively different
approaches. By and large, these were informed by the realisation that the
competitive balance-of-power politics and alliances of the pre-war era had to
be superseded and that qualitative, indeed transformative changes in the ways
in which the international system was organised and peace preserved were
needed to avoid the escalation of another, even more destructive "modern
war" in the future. Most significant among the not new but newly influential
ideas that these efforts spawned were different essentially liberal conceptions
of a "modern", rules-based international system – to be established around a
transatlantic core – whose key mechanism was to be a novel international
institution. These conceptions – some more aspirational-progressive, some
more evolutionary – would crystallise in an array of schemes for an "association of nations" and "collective security" that not only Wilson and key League
proponents in the British government like Robert Cecil but also numerous
activists and pressure-groups on both sides of the Atlantic put forward. And,
significantly, most of these conceptions would be based on the premise that
major reforms at the international level would not suffice to build a more
durable peace – that it also required far-reaching changes within existing
states, above all their democratisation.

What thus took shape, with momentous global repercussions, were visions
of a new *Atlantic* system of self-governing states and, eventually, a league of
precisely democratic nation-states. For by 1918 those who championed such
visions had adopted the call for a postwar order based on the principle of
national "self-determination". And most of them had come to argue that if
all peoples or nations that had a "rightful" claim were accorded a state, and if
all states, older as well as newly-created ones, were democratised, their
sovereigns – the peoples – would also behave more peacefully in relations
with one another and settle their disputes in a non-violent, lawful manner,

[21] Cf. Schroeder (1994), pp. v–vii.

just as they were supposed to settle disputes within states. Those who developed such liberal-progressive conceptions thus sought to establish high, far-reaching requirements of order. At the same time, they raised very high expectations not just in Europe and the United States but around the world. Moreover, they often presented their designs in *prima facie* global-universalist terms and in a universalist-egalitarian language. Yet they in fact still thought and operated on the basis of distinctive civilisational-hierarchical assumptions; and their designs essentially centred on Europe and the Atlantic sphere.

Wilson would emerge as the most powerful champion not just of a League of Nations but of a wider liberal-progressive vision of a novel *Atlantic* order that was to "end all wars". Yet the war also brought a surge of efforts undertaken by non-governmental advocates of a League and wider international reform schemes, who sought to advance and lobby for even more ambitious ideas of a "new order". A very diverse array of actors and groups took up this cause and, as will be shown, pursued their own, partly converging, often conflicting agendas. They included leading figures of the British Union of Democratic Control and the League of Nations Union, the American League to Enforce Peace, French juridical internationalists who envisaged a more robust, and exclusive, *société des nations*, yet also German liberal and social democratic moderates who eventually became more assertive in their struggle for "peace of understanding" and a universal "organisation of international law". But the war also spurred less radical yet in many ways more consequential reorientations, which manifested themselves in more evolutionary and more unequivocally hierarchical conceptions for a League of Nations. Most significant here were the schemes developed by Cecil and other British postwar planners, which came to focus on the aim of establishing a League as framework for a reconfigured – and essentially transatlantic – concert of the great powers.

All of these conceptions and aspirations came to compete with – and were *in part* formulated against – other, more radical ideas for a recast European and world order that were reinforced during the war – namely those of the more radical socialists who sought to reconstitute the International and hammered out a first common programmatic platform at the Zimmerwald conference in September 1915 – and then, above all, those of Lenin, Trotsky and the vanguard of the Bolshevik revolutionaries of 1917. What eventually exerted the most powerful influence – though it never became as decisive for shaping the postwar order as has often been suggested – was the ideological counter-vision Lenin propagated in line with his earlier maxims. Like Trotsky, he saw the "imperialistic war" as a world-historical opportunity to incite a revolutionary class war, or "civil war", in which instead of fighting against each other, workers and peasants were to unite against their real enemies, the leading "capitalist" classes, overthrow the entire liberal-bourgeois-capitalist order and build a novel Soviet world system. Crucially, Lenin claimed that only in such a "new order" would it be possible to realise genuine "self-determination".[22]

Thus, one crucial consequence of the war's political-ideological struggle was that conceptions both of self-government and of national self-determination, which had already been developed before 1914, gained a newly powerful *and global* significance as a key precept of a "modern" international order. What by the end of 1918 had gained decisive ground was the general – though contested – notion that all "nations" or national groups that could present a credible claim should have the "right" to determine their own affairs and, essentially, establish an independent state. Soon Wilson's championing of republican self-*government* would have a crucial impact here. Yet Lenin's earlier and far more unequivocal call for "self-determination" had already reverberated in and beyond Europe long before the American president's rhetoric.[23] And leading social democrats and socialists had in fact long advocated a negotiated peace that guaranteed "National Self-determination" or where this applied the "Autonomy of Nationalities".[24]

By the end of the war, a vast array of governmental leaders, strategists and publicists on both sides of the European trenches and, in particular, leading figures of the Polish and other east European national movements had taken up the demand for self-determination and used the concept to advance their respective political interests.[25] And the vanguards of nationalist, anti-imperialist independence movements in the extra-European world had begun to do the same. This held true for those who challenged British imperial rule like the Indian nationalist leader Bal Gangadhar Tilak and the leader of the nationalist Wafd Party in Egypt, Sa'd Zaghlul; yet it also held true for Sun Yat-Sen and those who struggled to establish a sovereign democracy in China and Korean nationalists who desired to end Japan's colonial regime.[26] For the most part, all of these actors had developed their own "self-determination" agendas, drawing on pre-war ideas. They did not need Wilson's, or Lenin's, inspiration. But all would seek to enlist the American president as a powerful supporter of their cause.

Nonetheless, in a more general perspective the First World War thus indeed also gave rise to a clash between a Wilsonian and a Leninist conception of future order. But it marked not the beginning of but rather a prequel to the sustained Soviet-American competition that would gain decisive momentum

---

[22] Zimmerwald Resolution, September 1915, International Socialist Commission at Berne, *Bulletin* No. 1 (21 September 1915); Lenin (1914), pp. 208, 210.

[23] See the Bolshevik six-point peace programme, December 1917, Degras (1951–53), I, pp. 1–3.

[24] Stockholm memorandum, 12 June 1917, Scheidemann (1929), II, pp. 342–50.

[25] See Leonhard (2014), pp. 525 ff.

[26] For the global context, see Manela (2007); Gerwarth and Manela (2015).

after 1945 and then dominate world politics.[27] What mattered more in the actual historical context of the Great War was that the aspirations of Wilson and other "progressives" came to clash with other, more "traditional" power-political and imperial conceptions of order, which had also become more comprehensive, expansive or even radicalised during the war.

In other words, it is indeed essential to understand that the crisis of the war also spurred different kinds of reorientation processes. In short, it not only reinforced but also radicalised pre-war ideas of power politics, especially in Germany and France; and it gave rise to conceptions of a postwar international system that were either governed by core precepts of balance-of-power thinking or by radicalised ideas of imperial or neo-imperial hegemony. Leading "*realpolitical*" and imperialist strategists also alluded to a League or "self-determination" for tactical and propaganda purposes. But the conceptions they concocted were essentially based on the premise that, ultimately, not novel international institutions or norms but only power-political means and preponderance could guarantee peace, security and independence within a recast but fundamentally unaltered system of power states that, in their eyes, would continue to dominate the world after the war.

On the side of the *Entente*, particularly key French policymakers – including the resolute wartime premier Clemenceau, his key adviser André Tardieu and the influential commerce minister Clémentel – clearly did not abandon the conviction that it would be crucial to rely on power-political maxims to establish a postwar system that protected vital French security interests vis-à-vis Germany more effectively than before. Yet they realised that in view of the newly critical American influence – and British priorities – it would be necessary to find new ways to safeguard France in the longer run. They would essentially view support for a League of Nations as a means to construct a robust Atlantic alliance system of security and containment. And they would invoke not only considerations of security but also "self-determination" to push ahead with – neo-imperialist – schemes to alter the strategic balance vis-à-vis Germany, not least through the creation of "buffer states".[28] By contrast, while power-political concerns remained integral to how key policymakers in London defined Britain's essential war aims, only a minority – and notably the seasoned strategist Eyre Crowe – argued expressly that future peace and stability would chiefly depend not only on containing German power but also on establishing a viable balance of power in Europe – and in the world.[29]

Strikingly more far-reaching and more unambiguously imperialistic or neo-imperialistic were the postwar visions advanced by the advocates of a more or

[27] Cf. the influential interpretation advanced by Mayer (1964) and (1964), and its most recent restatement in Westad (2018), pp. 1 ff., 43 ff.

[28] See Stevenson (1982), pp. 36–56; Tardieu note, 20 January 1917, Tardieu Papers, vol. 417.

[29] See Crowe memorandum, 7 December 1918, FO 371/3451.

less radical *Siegfrieden* or "victorious peace" in wartime Germany. In essence, such visions were remarkably backward-looking and Eurocentric. Yet, influenced by the war's escalatory dynamics, they also became far more radical than the pre-war conceptions on which they obviously drew. By and large, they all were premised on the assumption that the German Empire had to fight on until it had achieved a decisive victory that would allow it to ensure its future security and development as Europe's geopolitically central power, not by seeking an accommodation with the western powers within a League of Nations but rather by attaining a position of imperial-hegemonic predominance on the European continent. In more "moderate" conceptions, notably those devised by Friedrich Naumann and Walther Rathenau, this was to be achieved by creating a German-led central European economic and customs union. Proponents of a more uncompromising power-political agenda pushed for a more far-reaching agenda, calling for the annexation of substantial strategically important territories in the west and the creation of a far-flung "eastern empire" of vassal states under the banner of "self-determination". Eventually, these neo-imperialist visions would become even more radicalised in reaction to the novel challenge that the military and political-ideological intervention of the United States presented.[30]

A core premise that all of these schemes had in common was that international relations after the war would continue to be dominated by the inexorable competition between imperial power states. This was conceived as a struggle in which notably the British Empire and the United States would be Germany's pivotal competitors – and that compelled Germany to impose on Europe a more or less expansive system of imperial domination to ensure its future as a world power. Such German imperialist visions of international "order" clearly had pre-war antecedents. Yet the more radical schemes that now emerged also anticipated core elements of more far-reaching or even totalitarian "visions" of empire and imperial order that would be hatched in the 1920s and 1930s. And they would only be superseded by the qualitatively different ideas of the German "Peace Resolution" parties once Ludendorff and Hindenburg reckoned that they could no longer win the war.

In their own ways French policymakers also came to develop neo-imperialist schemes to gain control over the Rhineland. In general, however, neither French nor British conceptions for postwar Europe were based on imperialist premises. The designs of imperial "consolidation" and expansion the *Entente* Powers *did* develop during the war focused on the extra-European sphere and above all the Middle Eastern provinces of the embattled Ottoman

---

[30] See Naumann (1915), pp. 40–2; Rathenau to Bethmann Hollweg, 7 September 1914, Rathenau (1929), p. 12; Hildebrand (1998).

Empire. Both powers originally made a traditional power-political deal to divide the expected spoils and extend their spheres of control and influence through the Sykes-Picot agreement of May 1916. Subsequently, however, strategists working for Britain's Imperial War Cabinet, notably the South African general and eventual prime minister Jan Christiaan Smuts, would try to pursue the same objective in a new way. Not least in response to Wilson's growing influence, they came to devise strategies that sought to secure and legitimise extra-European "liberal empires" in the postwar world as "tutelage powers" that "aided" populations that were not (yet) deemed capable of governing themselves to prepare for eventual self-rule. It was with these objectives in mind that Smuts would eventually propose the creation of a neo-imperial mandate system under the auspices of the League of Nations whose core purpose was to extend the control of "civilised" imperial states, particularly in the Middle East, under a new guise.[31]

III. The Great War as a Germination Period – Antecedents, Continuities and Transformative Developments

As should have become clear by now, overall, the escalating Great War and what became the transatlantic political struggle at its core were *not* a transformative period in which *novel* conceptions of a different, more peaceable, durable and legitimate international order emerged, in which novel, original norms, rules and principles of international politics were conceived, or in which blueprints for a League of Nations or, more broadly, for international institutions or organisations appeared for the first time. Nor, as will be seen, did the peacemaking processes of 1919 spawn genuinely novel conceptions. Rather, the war years can be seen as a germination period in which ideas and conceptions that had already been developed *before* the war and sometimes had a very long pre-history – reaching all the way back to ancient Greece – were seized upon, revived, in some cases rediscovered, and then elaborated further and welded into more comprehensive blueprints and more expansive visions. At the same time, and crucially, it was a period of catalytic crisis in which such concepts and ideas could acquire unprecedented significance and power – that seemed to create conditions under which it appeared possible to build, for the first time, a "modern" international system whose structure and underpinnings were informed by broadly speaking "progressive" norms and principles. These ideas and visions were advanced and debated in what had become a far more genuinely global context; crucially, however, they were advanced, at the core, in the newly central transatlantic force-field of power and political and ideological struggle.

---

[31] Smuts, "The League of Nations", 16 December 1918, CAB 29/2.

The Great War thus indeed became a decisive germination period for "liberal" and progressive visions that directly or indirectly also had a massive impact on all future attempts to create a modern global order in the twentieth century. Yet much the same can and has to be said about other, alternative conceptions that the war generated, both the imperialist varieties and, indeed, socialist and Bolshevik schemes. They too drew heavily on ideas that had been developed before the war. Yet it was the war that seemed to create unprecedented possibilities, first for hyper-imperialist schemes, then, with more long-term repercussions, for Bolshevik aspirations. As noted, the underlying assumption that, irrespective of the precise outcome of the war, the future "global order" would continue to be dominated by imperial "world powers" and that it was thus imperative to expand one's imperial sphere of influence by conquest or by economic forms of domination in order to survive in a never-ending inter-imperial struggle of the future – in which the United States would play a key role – of course derived directly from the pre-war era of global imperialist competition.[32] And so did ideas focusing on how to modernise imperial states and how to make them more effective to compete in the postwar world.

But more "progressive" conceptions of international order and politics that became prominent during the war and critical in 1919 – from different notions of "self-determination" and "self-government" to ideas to promote peace through international arbitration and notably a League of Nations" – also had a rich and variegated pre-history. As we have seen, more explicit demands for *national* self-determination, "the emancipation of all nations" – of Europe – had been made during the revolutions of 1848.[33] And subsequently, around 1900, leading socialist thinkers, and above all Lenin, had played a crucial role in turning the "right of self-determination" of *all* peoples into a powerful *global* principle and catchphrase.[34] The notion that the extension of democracy and democratic "self-government" would have a pacifying effect on international relations had already been advanced by Mazzini and then become particularly prominent on both sides of the Atlantic since the 1890s, particularly in progressive and social democratic circles.[35]

Yet such ideas of course had important antecedents especially in the era of Enlightenment when eminent European thinkers like Rousseau and Kant and leading minds of the American revolution like John Adams and Thomas Jefferson – who all built on classic Greek conceptions of political order –

---

[32] See Darwin (2008), pp. 365 ff.

[33] See Proclamation of the French Provisional Government, February 1848; Lamartine (1848).

[34] See Chapter 4; Lenin (1960); Lenin (1914), pp. 208, 210; Meissner (1970), pp. 245–61; Fisch (2010), pp. 133–9.

[35] Scheidemann *Reichstag* speech, 30 March 1911, in Scheidemann (1929), I, pp. 154–5.

had posited that "perpetual peace" was inconceivable without the establishment of *republican* – rather than democratic – forms of constitutional government.[36] The idea that more authoritative international law and effective rules of arbitration held the key to preventing war had become newly influential in the pre-war period of the Hague Conventions; but, as noted, it too had a very long pre-history, reaching back to the maxims of Grotius and, beyond that, to the Greek *polis* world of Thucydides' *Peloponnesian War*.[37]

Finally, Wilson and all the British, American, French and German minds who conceived plans for a League of Nations during the Great War clearly drew on ideas that had gained contours in the years before its outbreak, notably those informing Bourgeois' scheme for a *société des nations*.[38] But they also wittingly or unwittingly built on conceptual foundations that had been laid much earlier, by Penn's 1693 proposal to guarantee the "Future Peace of Europe" through the "Establishment of an European Dyet, Parliament, or Estates", Abbé de Saint-Pierre's *Projet pour rendre la Paix perpétuelle en Europe* of 1712 and above all Rousseau's and Kant's seminal treatises on "perpetual peace".[39]

In his powerful "Philosophical Sketch" of 1795 Kant reasoned that "peace can neither be inaugurated nor secured without a general agreement between nations" that resulted in binding articles of a "Law of Nations". In his assessment, a lasting peace required the creation of "a particular kind of league" – not a monolithic "international state" but rather a "Federation of Free States" that espoused republican – rather than democratic – government (i.e. a federal union that introduced the rule of law and a separation of powers rather than a potentially tyrannous "rule of the majority"). Significantly, Kant also argued that an association of states conceived on this basis could form the "focal point" of a universal peace order. It could lead other peoples to determine that they also desired to espouse republican government and join the federation, thereby "extending it gradually to encompass all states and . . . leading to a perpetual peace".[40] Though conceived in a republican tradition rather than for a "democratic age", Kant's treatise thus nonetheless prefigured core premises of the League conceptions that Wilson and other liberal and progressive proponents of a new international organisation would champion after 1914.[41] But the crucial difference was of course that now, finally, the

---

[36] Rousseau (1761); Kant (1795); Adams (2003); Jefferson (1999).

[37] Thucydides (2009); Grotius (2005), pp. 277–8; Penn (1726) II, 838–48; Fraser (1926), pp. 182–3.

[38] Bourgeois (1910), pp. 265 ff., 276–85.

[39] Rousseau (1756); Kant (1795), pp. 93–115.

[40] *Ibid.*, pp. 102–3, 104–5.

[41] To be mentioned too here are, of course, the aforementioned schemes for an internationalist league that social democrats developed before 1914 – and Lenin's more radical conception of a transnational union of Soviet republics. See Chapter 4.

transformative historical constellation seemed to have been created to turn such visions into reality.

IV.   Key Actors and Emerging Visions in the War's Transatlantic Struggle

Above all, then, the Great War had a decisive *political* impact. For while it did not quite destroy the pre-war international "order", it came to shake it up violently. And it came to shake up the power-political and imperialist rules, norms and practices that had been prevalent up until 1914 so violently that it created openings for systemic change – and also some room for changes in individual and collective mentalities. Put differently, the war's very escalation discredited or at least cast sufficient doubt on what had been practised and thought by the dominant "players" of international politics before. And it created a degree of crisis and urgency that made qualitative changes in the reigning paradigms of international politics conceivable and the emergence of new ground-rules and mechanisms of order possible. Yet the strength of the counterforces that sought to block such changes or canalise them to preserve older hierarchies and modes of "order" had not been decisively weakened yet either. Indeed, more traditional power-political ideas and approaches had by no means disappeared or been entirely devalued – and in some quarters, particularly in Germany, they even became more radical during the war.

But not only an ever greater number of non-governmental actors but also some key political decision-makers came to believe that the catastrophe of the war made it imperative to reorder Europe, and the world, more fundamentally and to create a different, "modernised" international order. Wilson would become the most influential champion of such aspirations. Eventually, Lenin would emerge as an important "counter visionary". Yet, as noted, what long dominated, especially from 1916, was the transatlantic competition between Wilson's evolving peace programme and the war-aim agendas of the principal European belligerents. It was in the context of this competition that the first contours of the most influential conceptions took shape, the distinctive American, British and French conceptions that would eventually leave their imprint on the Paris Peace Conference. Essentially, they all can be seen as different attempts to answer the question of how a new *Atlantic* system of peace and order could be established – for Europe and as *the* key element of a new world order.

More fundamentally, what its official and unofficial protagonists engaged in was not only a struggle over what would be the rules and norms of this reconfigured postwar order – of security as well as of finance, economics and social order. It also, and crucially, was a competition over who would have the authority to set these rules and norms and to shape the process through which they would be set. Would it be the leaders of whatever coalition emerged victorious from the war? Would it be European statesmen or an aspirational American president? Or would an unprecedented transnational configuration of governmental and non-governmental actors determine the making and character of a novel kind of peace?

At the core, it was thus a struggle over the premises, rules and parameters of postwar international *politics* – as it were, the *political* in international politics – which to an unprecedented degree was bound up with the constraints of domestic politics in all the belligerent states and, as noted, with the new dynamics generated by the transnational ideological competition – the "war for the world's mind" or more precisely the struggle to influence a "world opinion" that fell apart into a multiplicity of "public opinions", especially but not only in the different societies that actually fought in the war. The core concepts and aspirations of the most influential political leaders and governmental strategists, yet also of the most important non-governmental actors who had a part in this conflict, deserve a more thorough re-appraisal, because their influence would reach far beyond 1919.

V.   Wilson's Americanist Aspirations for a New *Atlantic* Order

Unquestionably, the aspirational peace programme that the American president Woodrow Wilson developed and eventually presented to the world had a crucial impact on the unprecedented transatlantic process that gained momentum during the Great War. Yet both his programme and the influence it exerted were also distinctly ambivalent. Wilson's was an evolutionary rather than revolutionary vision for a "peace to end all wars". Originally, he sought to realise this ambitious aim by creating, under American leadership, a novel, progressive *and integrative* peace order that was based on an essentially political form of "collective security", the expansion of self-*government* and, crucially, a new institution that was to become its "superstructure", which he too eventually came to call a "League of Nations".

Arguably, what Wilson advanced – first under the heading of a "peace without victory", then, on different premises, as leader of the power that decided the war – became the most influential scheme for a "new world order" that emerged during the Great War. The governments and opinion-makers of all European belligerents thus faced the novel challenge of having to grapple with the power of the United States *and* the impact of what its president proclaimed. And they indeed came to adapt their ideas and strategies to these new forces – some more reluctantly, some more proactively, and some only in the shadow of defeat. Rhetorically, Wilson indeed offered maxims for a universal and egalitarian "new order" for the world. Essentially, however, what he developed was the conception of a new *Atlantic* order – and distinctly hierarchical.

It was in his landmark speech to Congress of 22 January 1917 that the American president most forcefully presented his original programme, which hinged on the premise that to be durable *and legitimate* the peace ending the Great War must be "a peace without victory". He argued – presciently – that the victory of one side "would mean peace forced upon the loser, a victor's terms imposed upon the vanquished", only "accepted in humiliation, under duress, at an intolerable sacrifice, and would leave a sting, a resentment, a bitter memory upon which terms of peace would rest, not permanently but only as upon quicksand". Instead, Wilson made the case for an integrative peace whose foundations and rules were to be negotiated on terms of equality. He claimed that "(o)nly a peace between equals can last – a peace the very principle of which is equality and a common participation in a common benefit".[42] It is hard to overstate how essential the maxim of a negotiated "peace *without* victory", rather than a peace imposed by whoever would "win" the war, was for Wilson's entire conception of how to progress towards what he in 1915 had called a "modern" peace – and a "modern" international order, anchored in a "universal" yet hierarchical League of Nations.[43] And it has rightly been stressed that this conception in part sprang from the lessons that he as a southerner had drawn from the humiliating terms that in his view the victorious Unionists had forced on the Confederates at the end of the American civil war.[44]

Crucially, Wilson had by this time also formulated his own idealising conception of the new role he envisioned the United States to play in the world – namely the role of a novel hegemon of peace and "neutral arbiter" that would mediate a peaceful end to the "colossal struggle" and thus pave the way for a new, progressive equilibrium in the world. Already in April 1915 the president had declared that the American republic was destined to become "the mediating nation of the world" that, acting on behalf of all mankind, would initiate "processes of peace" in and beyond the war-ridden Old World. In Wilson's stylised vision, America was not only becoming the world's new "mediating nation" with a view to "its finance" but also in "a broader sense". Though far from having departed from the racist and segregationist worldview that he had formed in the South, he conjured up the image of a nation "compounded of the nations of the world", mediating "their blood", "their traditions", "their sentiments" and therefore "able to understand all nations".[45]

---

[42] Wilson Senate address, 22 January 1917, *PWW*, XL., pp. 533–9.

[43] Wilson to Bryan, 27 April 1915, *PWW*, XXXIII, pp. 81–2.

[44] Wilson Prolegomenon, ca. 25 November 1916, *PWW*, XL, pp. 67–70, 67, 68, 69. On Wilson's Southern background and racist leanings, see Cooper (2009), pp. 23–5, 79–88; Yellin (2013); O'Toole (2018).

[45] Wilson remarks, New York, 20 April 1915, *PWW*, XXXIII, pp. 38–9; Wilson address, 4 November 1915, *PWW*, XXXV, p. 168.

The progressive "new order" the American president began to lay out and champion publicly as self-styled new arbiter of world politics was to be premised on two principles. The first was indeed "the equality of nations", which he defined as an "equality of rights", stressing that while inequalities in power could not be eradicated the new peace "must neither recognize nor imply a difference between big nations and small, between those that are powerful and those that are weak". The second, even "deeper" than first, was "the principle that governments derive all their just powers from the consent of the governed". In other words, Wilson argued that there could be no durable peace unless the principle of self-government was made a universal precept.[46] These were to be the underpinnings of a new, more sustainable "equilibrium" in the world and, above all, between the United States and Europe.[47]

Unquestionably integral to what Wilson envisioned was the creation of what he in 1917 termed a "League for Peace". It is thus all the more remarkable how general and unelaborated his League plans remained until the very end of the war. In many ways, the same can be said of the entire peace programme of a president who until the outbreak of the war had clearly concentrated on domestic priorities, his New Freedom Agenda. Having only begun to sketch some basic ideas by the late 1914, Wilson in February 1915 for the first time privately sketched a four-point peace agenda that comprised the call for "an association of nations, all bound together for the protection of the integrity of each" and providing for automatic "punishment" of "any one nation breaking from this bond".[48] By the time of the presidential election campaign of 1916, which he would narrowly win against his Republican opponent Charles Hughes, Wilson had made a forceful public commitment to the establishment of the new institution, proclaiming that it was the United States' "duty to lend the full force of this nation – moral and physical – to a league of nations".[49]

When he presented his far-reaching aspirations to the American Congress and world opinion in January 1917, Wilson explained that the League he desired was to institutionalise an "international concert" and thereby establish a permanent "community of power" that would hence guarantee a "stable equilibrium" and an "organized, common peace". In his view, it thus was to play a critical role in superseding the European-dominated "old order". Significantly, he stressed that it had been the European "balance of power" system of "entangling alliances" that had drawn nations "into competitions of

---

[46] Wilson address, 22 January 1917, *PWW*, XL, pp. 536–9.
[47] Wilson to McCormick, 5 January 1917, Wilson Papers, Series 3, vol. 37.
[48] Wilson remarks, autumn of 1914, in Bacon and Scott (1924), p. 244; Baker memorandum of conversations with Stockton Axson, 8, 10, 11 February 1925, Baker Papers; Baker (1927–39), V, pp. 73–5. See Knock (1992), pp. 35–8.
[49] Wilson speech, 5 October 1916, *PWW*, XXXVIII, pp. 346–8.

power" and thereby caused the outbreak of the war.[50] Though he did not use this term, Wilson argued that a core purpose of the new organisation thus had to be to replace European-style "selfish" rivalries with an unprecedented system of "collective security". As he put it, the League had to act as "the organized major force of mankind" and as such guarantee not only "the permanency of the [peace] settlement" but also the security and integrity of all of its member states. And he proclaimed emphatically that it would command a power and legitimacy "so much greater than the force of any nation now engaged, or any alliance hitherto formed or projected, that no nation, no probable combination of nations, could face or withstand it".[51] But for a long time the American president developed only very general ideas about how the League would actually deal with aggressors; and he would insist that peace and international security would be safeguarded most effectively by moral and political rather than by military sanctions.

At bottom, Wilson's quest for a "peace to end all wars" was informed by the essentially political – and ideological – aspiration to transform not only the norms, principles and ground-rules but also the framework or "super-structure" of international relations, and international order. At the same time he aspired to foster – by promoting self-government – a pacifying reform and in his view an "Americanisation" of political order within states. And in all of these respects Wilson clearly was, and remained, focused on reforming the European states-system, and states. And he remained focused on recasting relations between the United States and Europe with the aim of founding a new Atlantic order at the centre of a new global order. Wilson's was the most aspirational yet also the historically and strategically most uninformed attempt to draw consequences from the unprecedented catas-trophe of the Great War and the pathologies of pre-war imperialist power politics. And it was at the same time not only far too ambitious, raising expectations that he could not fulfil, but also distinctly *unilateral* and high-handed vis-à-vis the representatives of *all* other powers and peoples.

It should also be stressed, however, that Wilson was not mistaken in diagnosing the core challenge of the post–First World War era – namely that of creating a fundamentally reformed international order that transcended the *indeed* war-prone balance-of-power system of the pre-war years. And the eventual failure of his aspirations should not obscure the fact that he began to embark on a remarkable yet also strikingly limited and unfinished learning process, which ultimately remained constrained by his ideological view of the world and of international politics. For better or worse, this process would culminate at the Paris Peace Conference.

---

[50] Wilson address, 22 January 1917, *PWW*, XL, pp. 536–9.
[51] *Ibid.*, pp. 536–9.

Generations of "realist" critics have portrayed Wilson as the misguided prophet of a "new order" premised on illusory foundations who dangerously disregarded the realities of power. But he has also been presented as a key figure of progressive internationalism whose overall laudable aspirations were frustrated by his domestic opponents and, especially, the ploys of European *realpoliticians*.[52] Yet both interpretations are misleading. For all his internationalist and egalitarian rhetoric, Wilson's approach to peacemaking, his vision of the future international order and his underlying worldview were fundamentally Americanist, distinctly top-down and informed by a very expansive conception of American power – not just financial, economic and military but also political and civilisational. In turn, these ideological proclivities informed his conception of a new, progressive global *and Atlantic* hierarchy. Wilson was convinced that the time had come for the United States to turn from an exceptional to an "exemplary" power – the world's new leading, "mediating" and "tutelage" power.[53] In his eyes, the American federal republic had acquired not only unprecedented strength but also a vanguard position as the world's most progressive democratic state. Hence he derived the claim to play a hegemonic role in transforming international *and* inner-state order after the Great War along American lines, first in Europe, then, in hierarchical gradations, in those parts of the world that were less advanced or still under imperial rule or domination.

In short, the American president thus essentially set out to pursue internationalist *ends*, above all the creation of the League, by Americanist and essentially unilateral *means*. Put differently, he insisted on recasting the international system on – his – American terms. Essentially, this was to be achieved by promoting the internationalisation of what he regarded as exemplary rules and practices of the American republic – or rather of what he presented as the progressive "ideal type" of this republic. They were to become the new standards of the international system, superseding old-style international politics. More specifically, Wilson sought to build a lasting peace and bolster a transnational reform process by internationalising core elements of the domestic reform agenda he had pursued under the banner of "New Freedom".[54]

Under the impact of the Great War, Wilson tried to distance himself from some of his earlier progressive imperialist leanings, and he changed the tone of

---

[52] Cf. Ambrosius (1987) and Knock (1992); Cooper (2009); Ikenberry (2020), pp. 100–40.

[53] Wilson remarks, New York, 20 April 1915, *PWW*, XXXIII, pp. 38–9; Wilson address, 4 November 1915, *PWW*, XXXV, p. 168. On Wilson's Southern background see Cooper (2009), pp. 13–55.

[54] See Wilson Senate address, 22 January 1917, *PWW*, XL, pp. 536–7, 533–9; Wilson address, 4 November 1915, *PWW*, XXXV, p. 168.

his rhetoric. But he never fully transcended his earlier assumptions. He did not undergo an "intellectual metamorphosis" towards progressive international-ism.[55] Rather, he essentially adhered to a hierarchical understanding both of civilisational advance and America's new international responsibilities. As he would assert after the armistice, the new American mission he envisaged was to "organize the moral force of the world" to "preserve" peace, to "steady the forces of mankind, and to make the right and the justice" to which "great nations" like his own devoted themselves "the predominant and controlling force of the world".[56]

It was on these premises that Wilson in January 1917 proposed a trans-formation at two levels – the international and the domestic – which he clearly regarded as interdependent. In the sphere of international relations, the new institution of the League was to inaugurate not only new principles, but also new processes of rational cooperation and conflict resolution. It was to establish not just a newly comprehensive covenant of international law but also, even more importantly, new *political* rules that not only safeguarded the "equality of rights" between "powerful" and "weak" member states but also protected their "political independence" and development prospects in a more effective way. Essentially, this was to be achieved by committing all members, yet especially the most powerful states, to explicit "mutual guar-antees" to this end but also to the organisation's new system of "collective security" through which its members would join forces against an aggressor. Yet the American president did not yet state how precisely the members of the League would intervene to deter or counter aggressors. At a deeper level, he placed his faith in political and moral sanctions rather than military deterrence. And what mattered at least as much in his view was that the League's novel "international concert" would become the key mechanism for the peaceful resolution of international disputes – under the pacifying scrutiny of what he later called "the moral force of the public opinion of the world".[57]

Crucially, despite his allusions to a future when the "rights of humanity" might take precedence over the "rights of sovereignty", Wilson never intended the League to become a new kind of "super state" or global federation that would curtail essential elements of state sovereignty – including the United States' self-accorded "rights" under the Monroe Doctrine.[58] Rather, he envis-aged it as an association of essentially sovereign nation-states that committed themselves to a covenant of common rules and principles but retained the

---

[55] Cf. the different interpretation in Knock (1992), p. 105.
[56] Wilson remarks at Buckingham Palace, 27 December 1918, *PWW*, LIII, p. 523.
[57] Wilson address, 28 December 1918, *PWW*, LIII, p. 532. For Wilson's evolving ideas see his speech to the League to Enforce Peace, 27 May 1916, *PWW*, XXXVII, pp. 113 ff.
[58] Wilson address, 19 October 1916, *PWW*, XXXVIII, p. 488.

authority to make sovereign decisions, notably about the use of force.[59] It is crucial to highlight, however, that Wilson originally conceived the League as a universal and essentially *integrative* mechanism of order. He argued that it could only be really effective if it included *all* relevant states and, in particular, all the belligerents, the *Entente* as well as the Central Powers. And this meant, in the final consequence, that at this point he contemplated incorporating them in the new institution *regardless* of their form of government.

But Wilson also proclaimed that, and in the longer run, a lasting and legitimate peace was inconceivable without substantive changes in the sphere of domestic politics. It required the spread of democratic, American-style self-government. What thus emerged, at least in his rhetoric, was the guiding maxim of a new order of self-governing states that would form, and be protected by, the League. Here too, however, the American president mainly thought of Europe. He had earlier stated that the eventual postwar settlement should be made "for the European nations regarded as Peoples" rather than "for any nation imposing its governmental will upon alien peoples", and he had opined that, in particular, Austria-Hungary "ought to go to pieces for the welfare of Europe". But not only did Wilson still fail to specify what constituted a "nation" or "people" with rightful claims. He also had barely begun to consider the complex implications of any attempt to reorganise central and eastern Europe along "national" lines.[60]

Yet despite his universalist rhetoric, Wilson's underlying ideas about self-government and "national development" were still informed not only by racist notions but also by philosophical precepts he had internalised during his intellectual-political formation in the first decades of the long twentieth century. Like other American progressives, he by and large clung to the premise that peoples with a less fortunate history than the United States could only gradually progress towards American-style democracy. They had to undergo "long processes of historical development" and required "a period of political tutelage" to enable them to assume "entire control of their affairs".[61] And he continued to believe that a further "all-important" condition for the success of democratic institutions was "homogeneity of race and community of thought and purpose among the people".[62]

Though with some modifications, such ideas would still guide Wilson's thinking after the war. They would still shape his outlook on European and global progress, the extension of self-government and, crucially, the question

[59] See Wilson speech, 27 May 1916, *PWW*, XXXVII, pp. 113 ff.; Wilson address, 22 January 1917, *PWW*, XL, pp. 536–7.

[60] Brougham memorandum of interview with Wilson, 14 December 1914, *PWW*, XXXI, pp. 458–9.

[61] *Ibid.*, pp. 71–5.

[62] Wilson, "The Modern Democratic State" (1885), *PWW*, V, p. 74.

of who had a claim to participate in the making of the new Atlantic and global order. Significantly, it was only at a very late stage, in February 1918 – and mainly in response to Lenin's championing of the concept – that the American president came to espouse the principle of national "self-determination" as an "imperative principle of action" in the eventual peace settlement. Yet he immediately cautioned that only "well defined national aspirations" should be satisfied – without creating new or perpetuating old sources of discord that would over time "break the peace of Europe and consequently of the world". And he still interpreted "self-determination" essentially in terms of self-*government*, stressing that henceforth peoples should be "governed only by their own consent".[63]

What Wilson proclaimed would have an unprecedented transnational impact on a global scale; and it would particularly affect governmental strategies and non-governmental aspirations on both sides of the European trenches. Both propelling and impeding qualitative advances in the sphere of international politics, it would provide essential reference-points and impulses for the daunting reordering processes that would unfold in 1919. But neither Wilson's League ideas nor his more general maxims could offer, in themselves, realistic answers to the complex question of how Europe and the world were to be stabilised and pacified after the Great War. And it still was highly uncertain how far the American president would actually learn to do what he had not even begun to do since 1914, namely to devise realistic *political strategies* not to impose vision but rather to *negotiate* the rules and shape of a more durable and legitimate peace system with the representatives of other states, particularly the weakened but still powerful European states that were still determined to fight on until one side won the war. At the same time, Wilson's tendency to act like a high-handed "prophet of peace" who sought to mobilise popular support rather than build a broad coalition where it mattered most, in the US Congress, cast doubt on his ability to gain crucial domestic-political backing for his far-reaching world-political aspirations.

It is worth reiterating that Wilson's "peace without victory" programme encapsulated the essentials of his vision of a new international order and the exemplary "neutral" guardian role the United States should play within it. Yet the president would alter – and have to alter – his approach significantly after the United States intervened in the war on the side of the *Entente* in the spring of 1917 – which he had long sought to avoid. He came to elaborate *and* reorientate his conception in a series of programmatic speeches that culminated in his Fourteen Points address of 8 January 1918 and the Four Principles speech of 11 February 1918.[64] And the impact of these pronouncements was

---

[63] Wilson, "Four Principles" speech, 11 February 1918, *PWW*, XLVI, pp. 321–3.
[64] Wilson, "Fourteen Points" address, 8 January 1918, *PWW*, XLV, pp. 534–9; Wilson, "Four Principles" speech, 11 February 1918, *PWW*, XLVI, pp. 320–3.

now heightened by the work of a newly established agency, the American Committee on Public Information, headed by George Creel, which effectively functioned as the official American propaganda machinery and disseminated Wilson's maxims widely across the United States, Europe and the wider world.

The new guiding maxim of what became Wilson's crusade as president of an exceptional belligerent – which only "associated" with the *Entente* – was to "make the world safe for democracy".[65] What he thus came to unfold was an ambitious ideological-cum-political agenda for a democratic peace that, rhetorically, went beyond the trenches of the war and its European epicentre. When seeking a declaration of war from Congress, the president had proclaimed on 2 April 1917 that the United States would fight "for democracy" and the "liberation" of the world's peoples, "the German peoples included". And the vision he subsequently propagated was that of an inclusive Atlantic order – and League – of democratic states. It was predicated on the notion that a "steadfast concert for peace" could "never be maintained except by a partnership of democratic nations".[66]

Most famously, and with most resonance, Wilson would present his recalibrated "program of the world's peace" in his Fourteen Points address of 8 January 1918, which would indeed become one of the central reference points for the eventual peace negotiations in 1919. In his speech, which he characteristically presented without any prior consultation with the *Entente* Powers, Wilson for the first time made more concrete proposals for the political and territorial reorganisation of Europe after the war. In particular, he called for the establishment of an "independent Polish state", including "the territories inhabited by indisputably Polish populations" and assured of "a free and secure access to the sea". And, using very ambivalent and deliberately imprecise language, he called for an – utterly unrealistic – "free, open-minded, and absolutely impartial adjustment of all colonial claims, based upon a strict observance of the principle that in determining all such questions of sovereignty the interests of the populations concerned must have equal weight with the equitable claims of the government whose title is to be determined".[67]

But in terms of his ideas for the postwar order the Fourteen Points broke hardly any fresh ground. Wilson reiterated the American maxim that the "freedom of the seas" had to be guaranteed. And he reasserted core maxims of the long-standing US "Open Door" policy, demanding the "removal, so far as possible, of all economic barriers and the establishment of an equality of trade conditions among all the nations consenting to the peace". Further, he

---

[65] See e.g. Wilson address to Congress, 2 April 1917, *PWW*, XLI, p. 525; Wilson's annual message to Congress, 4 December 1917, *PWW*, XLV, pp. 196–8.

[66] Wilson address to Congress, 2 April 1917, *PWW*, XLI, p. 525–7; Wilson, "Fourteen Points" address, 8 January 1918, *PWW*, XLV, pp. 538–9.

[67] Wilson "Fourteen Points" address, *PWW*, XLV, pp. 536–8.

asserted that there were to be no "punitive damages" in any eventual peace settlement. Behind this demand lay a hardly elaborate but clearly powerful economic agenda for the postwar period that the Wilson administration had adopted by this time. It centred on the aim to prevent "closed" economic blocs or "selfish and exclusive economic leagues" of any kind, which was directed not only against the various German plans for a central European customs union that had been put forward since 1915 but also against schemes for an Anglo-French economic bloc that had emerged from the *Entente*'s economic conference in Paris in 1916.[68]

Wilson now indeed pushed for a globalisation of the "Open Door" precepts that, as we have seen, successive American governments had already championed before the war, particularly in China. The newly predominant economic power thus sought to use its influence to ensure unrestricted access to all of Europe's and the world's markets – while the majority in the American Congress still adamantly insisted on protectionist tariff policies. But it should be emphasised that Wilson himself – though by no means unaware of America's leverage as new principal creditor and dominant economic power – never paid close attention to the financial and economic underpinnings of the postwar order; and economic or financial factors were never central to his progressive peace design.

Yet the American president in fact said remarkably little in his Fourteen Points about the *political* architecture of the peace he sought. He merely declared once again, in very general terms, that "a general association of nations" had to be formed "for the purpose of affording mutual guarantees of political independence and territorial integrity to great and small states alike".[69] Wilson's seminal address is thus more significant as a manifest of ideological warfare and as a statement about the parameters of peacemaking – about how and by whom the eventual peace actually was to be made. The American president underscored that "processes of peace, when they are begun" had to be "absolutely open" and "involve and permit henceforth no secret understandings of any kind". And, seeking to dissuade Lenin from making a separate peace dictated by Germany, he also opened up the tactical perspective of an accommodation with the Bolshevik regime while obliquely expressing support for the Russian people's right to self-determination. Wilson thus pledged his support for "obtaining" for Russia "an unhampered and unembarrassed opportunity for the independent determination of her own political development and national policy" and assured it "of a sincere welcome into the society of free nations under institutions of her own choosing". Far more consequential, however, was what the president stated about how he intended to approach peacemaking with the key enemy state, the German Empire.

---

[68] See House, *Intimate Papers*, III, pp. 32 ff., 167 ff.
[69] Wilson, "Fourteen Points" address, 8 January 1918, *PWW*, XLV, p. 538.

Essentially, Wilson proposed a peace that would give Germany "a place of equality among the peoples of the world" – on the condition that it was prepared to "associate" itself with the United States and "the other peace-loving nations of the world in covenants of justice and law and fair dealing".[70] Behind closed doors, he had by this time adopted the rationale that a progressive peace could only be made once the German Empire's "military party" and autocratic leaders, whom he now blamed for the war's outbreak, had either been toppled by reformist forces within Germany or, if necessary, decisively defeated. Wilson thus offered Germany a stake and a place in the new order he envisaged; but he tied this "offer" to what was *de facto* an exhortation of regime change. In January 1918, the president avowed not to "presume to suggest to [Germany] any alteration or modification of her institutions". But he insisted that serious peace negotiations could only proceed if there was clarity about "whom her spokesmen speak for when they speak to us, whether for the Reichstag majority or for the military party" and those who sought "imperial domination". And he clearly conveyed that a peace "of justice and law and fair dealing" could only be envisaged if Germany was represented by the leaders of a parliamentary government.[71]

Clearly, Wilson's crusade on behalf of democracy was thus also a form of ideological warfare, intended to weaken the war efforts of the Central Powers by driving a wedge between their "autocratic" political and military leaders and proponents of democratic reforms – as well as the wider populations. And this raised particular challenges for those who actually fought for a democratisation and "parliamentarisation" of the German Empire against a semi-dictatorial High Command – the Social Democratic, Centre and liberal parties in the *Reichstag* that in July 1917 had passed the "Peace Resolution" and those who rallied behind their call for a "peace of understanding".[72] One leading figure, the later Social Democratic chancellor Philipp Scheidemann, observed that the world was sympathetic to the Allied side because they had a "form of democracy, more or less developed" and that it was thus all the more imperative for German reformers to break the stranglehold of the old anti-democratic elements of "Prussia".[73] In the eyes of the resolution's main instigator, the leading Centre politician Matthias Erzberger, the adoption of parliamentary democracy would lend real credibility to a German call for a peace of understanding. And for him and those who thought like him, Wilson's aspirations were indeed highly significant – yet also a double-edged sword.

---

[70] *Ibid.*, p. 538.

[71] *Ibid.*, pp. 538–9.

[72] Peace Resolution, 19 July 1917, Matthias and Morsey (1959), I, pp. 6–10, 93; Scheidemann (1921) pp. 80 ff.; Jarausch (1973), pp. 260–2; Miller (1974), pp. 304–9.

[73] Scheidemann (1929), I, pp. 308–9.

Seeking to assert their own democratic credentials, and to avoid the opprobrium of being branded traitorous collaborators of Germany's enemies – the
leaders of "Peace Resolution" parties took pains to distance themselves from
the American president's rhetoric. They insisted that no outside pressure or
influence was required to "force Germany to [establish] free state institutions"
and that it was "was the task of the German people alone to develop its
institutions in accordance with its convictions".[74] At the same time, not only
official German propaganda but also proponents of liberal political reforms
like the historian Friedrich Meinecke castigated Wilson's pursuits as a dangerous strategy to make the war ever more "unlimited".[75]

Yet the American president not only intended to set the terms of peacemaking vis-à-vis Germany. He also essentially sought to seize on what he
perceived as the United States' new power and prestige to persuade *and if
necessary to compel* the *Entente* leaders to accept his peace design. What came
to the fore here – as in his domestic-political conduct – was a highly problematic Wilsonian unilateralism. In short, the American president not only
refrained from any serious efforts to coordinate his peace plans with Lloyd
George and Clemenceau. He also clung to the view that eventually he would be
in a position to make a peace on his terms – as it were, over the heads of the
governments of the other belligerents – by rallying "the peoples" and particularly the more progressive forces in and beyond Europe behind his cause. Like
Lenin, Wilson thus entertained the – illusory – expectation that by mobilising
a transnational coalition of "right-minded" forces, he would be able to shape a
new kind of peacemaking and reordering process. In 1919 he would have to
learn the hard way that it was impossible to found a legitimate modern order
by such means – and that the cardinal challenge was to negotiate complex
comprises with those who represented the other key powers.

VI.   Towards a New Atlanticism? Lloyd George and the Evolution
of British Conceptions of Peace and Postwar Order

Of less immediate ideological impact but ultimately no less significant for
post–First World War peace negotiations and reordering processes were the
conceptions of postwar order that decision-makers and strategists of the
British wartime governments developed. Most important here were the essentially hierarchical-liberal peace plans that key actors within Lloyd George's

---

[74] Resolution of the SPD Extended Party Committee, 19 April 1917, in Dowe (1980), I,
pp. 504–5; Scheidemann speech, Reichstag, 15 May 1917, Scheidemann (1917), pp. 3–4.
See Niedhart and Dülffer (2011), pp. 67–8.

[75] See Niedhart and Dülffer (2011), p. 68; Meinecke notes, 7 and 13 October 1918, Meinecke
(1969), pp. 307 ff.

coalition government and notably in the Foreign Office and the newly established Imperial War Cabinet, had begun to work on since the spring of 1917. Especially since the American intervention in the war – and partly in response to Wilson's programmatic offensive – these plans had acquired a dominant Atlantic orientation. And contrary to what has long been asserted about essential continuities in British approaches to international order, they actually signalled a significant reorientation. More precisely, they marked a departure from the "balance-of-power" strategies that had dominated British conduct up until 1914 and a shift towards the pursuit of a new international equilibrium and, crucially, a commitment to the guiding idea of creating a modern institutionalised international concert.[76]

Eventually, a majority of the most influential policy- and decision-makers, including Lloyd George himself, adopted the underlying rationale that substantive reforms of the international system were imperative to ensure peace and safeguard the security of Britain's – yet again expanding – imperial world system after the immensely costly cataclysm. This led them to support the creation of a League of Nations, and it led some, notably the aforementioned Cecil and Smuts, to develop the most comprehensive blueprints for a new international organisation that emerged during the war. Crucially, more explicitly than Wilson, British strategists came to envisage the League essentially as an institutional framework for a reconfigured, at the core Atlantic, concert system. Yet like the American president they envisaged an *integrative* system that was to include not only the Allied and Associated Powers but also the Central Powers – above all, eventually, a defeated and reformed Germany. At the same time, they came to view the organisation as framework for an informal partnership, and burden-sharing, with the United States in overseeing a new Atlantic – and global – order after the war. They thus revived and developed further ideas that stood in a longer British tradition reaching back to the Vienna system. But the novel conception that emerged was that of a shared Anglo-American hegemony, a compact in which Britain was to assume the role of a decisive steering and "tutelage power".

Throughout the war, British peace concepts were based on one central premise that clashed markedly with Wilson's original design – namely that an essential prerequisite for a stable peace was an unequivocal victory over the Central Powers and above all German "Prussianism". Ever since 1916, Lloyd George had turned the slogan that the "fight must be to a finish – to a knockout" into his rallying cry as charismatic wartime leader.[77] And British

---

[76] For more traditional appraisals of British policy see Steiner and Neilson (2003); Lowe and Dockrill (1972); Charmley (2009).

[77] Lloyd George interview with Howard, 26 September 1916, *The Times*, 28 September 1916; Lloyd George (1933–36), II, pp. 852–9.

propaganda, eventually orchestrated by Beaverbrook's Ministry of Information, had propagated this maxim widely.

By 1917, the protagonists of Lloyd George's government and the Imperial War Cabinet came to envisage a settlement that, after the defeat of "Prusso-German" ambitions to dominate Europe, created conditions for a postwar accommodation with a German state that was to be chastised and "reduced" to the status of a European power. Crucially, however, it was to be incorporated in a reconfigured Atlantic concert of powers. British planners thus only sought to impose minor territorial losses on the enemy – the "restitution" of Alsace-Lorraine to France and, eventually, the cessation of some predominantly Polish provinces to a newly established Polish state. All the more sizeable, by contrast, would be demands for reparations, which came to be based on the claim that Germany had to pay for the "offence" of causing the war. Yet the key British interest lay in eliminating Germany as a world power that could again threaten the Empire – by depriving it both of its overseas colonies and its navy.[78] This priority was only one part of a more expansive extra-European war-aims agenda that imperialists like Lord Curzon advanced and sought to shield from unwanted American interference. Curzon, who became a driving force behind the War Cabinet's postwar planning efforts, proposed in 1917 that Britain should seize both Mesopotamia and Palestine from the Ottoman Empire in order to safeguard the vital Middle Eastern nexus of the British imperial world system. As noted, Smuts would eventually transform this agenda into a neo-imperial programme of expanding Britain's sphere of influence in this strategically vital region under the cloak of a League-administered mandate system.[79]

Preceding the Fourteen Points, Lloyd George himself put forward his own vision of a liberal-progressive peace in in a speech to the Trade Union League at Caxton Hall on 5 January 1918, which was doubtless intended to ensure Labour support for his "knock-out blow" policy – and to respond to the newly critical Bolshevik threat – but can also be seen as his response to the challenge that Wilson's peace programme presented. What Lloyd George outlined with the distinctive hyperbole and vagueness of wartime rhetoric was the conception of an essentially inclusive postwar order and a "broad democratic peace" – in Europe and the Atlantic sphere. He argued that a more permanent peace had to be premised on a re-established "sanctity of treaties", a more legitimate "territorial settlement" based on "the right of self-determination or the consent of the governed" and, finally, the creation of an "international

---

[78] Minutes of the Imperial War Cabinet, 15 August 1918, CAB 23/7; Lloyd George (1933–36), II, 833–41, pp. 877 ff.

[79] See Darwin (2009), pp. 305–57.

organization" that would "limit the burden of armaments and diminish the probability of war".[80]

On the one hand, the British premier thus made a more explicit commitment to "self-determination" than Wilson had been prepared to make up to that point. But he also introduced important qualifications, favouring outright "self-determination" where it suited British interests and favouring an emphasis on "consent of the governed" and democratisation when this appeared preferable because it was deemed compatible with the consolidation of – liberal – empire. Accordingly, he pledged Britain's support for "an independent Poland" that comprised all "genuinely Polish elements". Yet, still entertaining hopes of detaching a liberalised Austria-Hungary from Germany, he supported the preservation of an internally reformed Austro-Hungarian Empire. Lloyd George thus called for "genuine self-government" on "true democratic principles" for all "Austro-Hungarian "nationalities who have long desired it".[81] And he indeed highlighted the fundamental challenge that an "extreme" interpretation of the self-determination principle posed, not only with a view to creating a stable "new order" in eastern Europe but also for the future cohesion of the British Empire. Here, he eventually resorted to the defensive formula that the Empire already constituted an exemplary "league of nations" in its own right.[82]

But in his Caxton House address Lloyd George not only sought to put forward Britain's main war and peace aims. He also for the first time outlined publicly how he envisaged making a "democratic peace" and dealing with the Central Powers, especially Germany. Anticipating Wilson's rationales at this critical juncture of the war, the British premier underscored that Britain did not intend to "destroy Austria-Hungary" or to "question or destroy" Germany's "position" in Europe or to seek "the break-up of the German peoples or the disintegration of their state or country". Rather, its underlying aim was to thwart German "hopes and schemes of military domination". Ostensibly, Lloyd George also mapped out the perspective of negotiating a "democratic" peace settlement with Germany. While denouncing the German Empire's military autocracy as a "dangerous anachronism in the Twentieth Century", he insisted that Britain had not entered the war "to alter or destroy [its] imperial constitution" and that the matter of internal reforms was "a question for the German people to decide". But he also clearly stated that the "adoption of a really democratic constitution by Germany would be the most convincing evidence that in her the old spirit of military domination had indeed died" – and would thus "make it much easier" for the western powers to conclude a "democratic peace" with it.[83] Behind closed doors, however, the British premier would remain committed to two

[80] Lloyd George (1918), p. 1–2, 3; Lloyd George (1938), II, pp. 495–6.
[81] Lloyd George (1918), p. 3.
[82] Lloyd George speech, 12 September 1918, in *The Times*, 13 September 1918.
[83] Lloyd George (1918), p. 3. See Newton (1997), pp. 113–21.

distinctly different maxims: first, that a stable peace could only be made after an unequivocal military victory over the Central Powers that dealt a decisive blow to the legitimacy of Prussianism; and, second, that the victorious western powers would then fundamentally impose the terms of peace on the vanquished without any real negotiations.

In January 1918, Lloyd George also anticipated Wilson in outlining how the reconfigured international order he envisaged actually was to be supervised – and how peace actually was to be preserved. But he said very little of substance. He merely re-affirmed his government's support for the establishment of an "international organization".[84] But by this time influential policymakers in the Foreign Office and the Imperial War Cabinet had in fact already begun to develop more substantive schemes for an essentially Atlantic League. The British premier had first committed himself to the creation of some kind of postwar League in the spring of 1917, and he had subsequently obtained the War Cabinet's backing for this goal.[85] Lloyd George not only responded to growing political pressure – not least that exerted by pro-League pressure-groups, from the left-liberal Union of Democratic Control to the so-called Brice Group and the League of Nations Society – and public support for a "peace league". He also, and crucially, responded to Wilson's aspirations; and he came to envision the new institution mainly as an instrument to ensure Anglo-American cooperation and burden-sharing in the management of a reconfigured peace order.

But actual official plans for a new international organisation were made by others. British preparations would be masterminded by Smuts and Cecil, who came to head Foreign Office planning for the League. Both began to develop what would evolve into the League blueprints that had the greatest impact in 1919 – at the core, schemes for an unmistakeably hierarchical and in key respects conservative rather than progressive international organisation that was intended to integrate all relevant major powers and – crucially – built on the pivot of the new Anglo-American hegemonic partnership. What they conceived, with different emphases, was neither a "super state" with extensive supranational or "supra-imperial" powers nor a novel egalitarian institution, but fundamentally a more permanent framework for a new concert of the great powers. The League they outlined was to be formed by sovereign states on a footing of equality under international law; yet all key decisions would be made by representatives of the "civilised" great powers, which were to be granted special authority as permanent members of a League Council. Both in Cecil's and in Smuts' conception, finalised in 1918, this council was thus envisaged as the new key mechanism of a new global system, a mechanism

---

[84] Lloyd George (1918), p. 3.
[85] Imperial War Cabinet, 20 March 1917, CAB 23/43.

dominated by the United States and the key European powers that was to provide "collective security" and the wherewithal to settle international conflicts and preserve "world peace".[86]

Cecil then also instigated the creation of a British expert committee, set up in January 1918 and chaired by Sir Walter Phillimore, that would play an important role in concretising official British League plans. The Phillimore Committee's influential report of 20 March 1918 followed Cecil's conceptual lead and put forward a very narrow scheme, essentially proposing a League that was not much more than an institutionalised alliance modelled on the wartime compact of the western powers. It was to safeguard peace by committing all alliance members to a peaceful settlement of all disputes between them. In addition, all were to pledge not to go to war without previously submitting disputes or grievances "to arbitration or to a Conference of the Allied States". Should a state violate these commitments, the others would take "jointly and severally" all such measures against it "military, naval, financial, and economic – as will best avail for restraining the breach of the covenant". Further, the report envisaged basic "collective security" provisions, stipulating that if a member state was attacked by another state then "any of the Allied States may come to its assistance". But what the Phillimore Committee outlined was essentially an exclusive league formed by the wartime allies and incorporating neutral states but making no provisions for the eventual admission of "enemy powers".[87] Yet Cecil himself – like Smuts – came to advocate a different, essentially *inclusive* League conception. He consciously drew on the example of the nineteenth century's European concert, proposing to refashion it to cope with the challenges of the twentieth century – and arguing that in order to be effective, the new League-based concert also had to comprise Germany.[88]

Significantly, Cecil was the first influential policymaker who recommended British support for a League as the best way to foster a conceptual reorientation that he deemed imperative, namely to draw the newly powerful United States into a strategic partnership based on what he saw as both parallel interests and shared "political ideals". In his conception, the Anglo-American powers were not only to be pre-eminent in the League, but also the pivotal actors in creating and overseeing a more durable and essentially liberal international order after the war. And like other British policymakers, he considered it crucial to make an effort to "tutor" Wilson, whom he saw as a "Gladstone liberal", and the wider elites of a state that for the first time took

---

[86] "Cecil Plan", 14 December 1918, in Miller (1928), II, pp. 61–4; Smuts, "The League of Nations: A Programme for the Peace Conference", 16 December 1918, CAB 29/2.

[87] Phillimore report, 20 March 1918, FO 371/3483.

[88] Cecil memorandum, circulated to War Cabinet on 18 September 1917, CAB 24/26/2074; Smuts memorandum, 16 December 1918, CAB 29/2.

"a part in international European affairs". The aim was to teach them to use their new power "rightly" – in accordance with British "ideas of right and justice". For Cecil, then, the new organisation was to be the key instrument through which a more western-orientated international system was to be created and European peace was to be kept once the war had been won.[89]

Lloyd George long remained more equivocal towards the League project and distinctly more sceptical towards the notion of reaching a substantial understanding with Wilson. While deeming the American president's more far-reaching aspirations unrealistic, he was also more acutely aware of the challenges Wilson would face in legitimising his league designs at home and overcoming entrenched American objections to "being drawn into the complex of European politics". But by the autumn of 1917 the British premier had come to espouse the maxim that it was nonetheless in Britain's strategic interest to explore on what premises it might be possible to build a more long-term partnership with the United States. And he basically came to support Cecil's core idea of a league inspired by "the character of the Concert of Europe formed after 1815" that would now include the American power.[90]

Parallel, the Great War caused an – albeit episodic – reorientation of British ideas about the future economic order. For a time, notions of establishing a more protectionist and, broadly speaking, regulated economic order came to prevail. This marked a significant departure from the "free trade" conceptions that had long dominated British pre-war policies and even from earlier schemes to establish an "imperial preference" system. In June 1916, at an economic conference of the *Entente* held in Paris, the Conservative Party leader and Colonial Secretary Andrew Bonar Law played a leading role in drawing up an Anglo-French agenda for a "veritable reconstruction of the world economy" after the war. Its main aim was the establishment of a trade regime, and economic system, that would be regulated and controlled by the *Entente* Powers to a significant degree – "to the detriment of Germany". This agenda was intended to counter the perceived threat of different German *Mitteleuropa* schemes, i.e. plans for a German-dominated European economic and customs union. British support for it was also motivated by the concern that after the war Germany would resume what was seen as its aggressive pre-war "campaign of universal [commercial] penetration" and its alleged under-handed "dumping" methods.[91]

---

[89] Cecil memorandum, 18 September 1917, CAB 24/26/2074.
[90] Lloyd George was here also influenced by his adviser Maurice Hankey. See Hankey statement, War Cabinet 67/9, Appendix I, 17 February 1917, CAB 23/1.
[91] *Conférence économique des gouvernements alliés tenue à Paris les 14. 15. 16 et 17 juin 1916* (Paris, 1916). See Soutou (1989), pp. 261–7.

Seeking to protect British industry and trade from such threats, Bonar Law backed a programme that essentially foresaw the establishment of a comparatively loose Anglo-French economic bloc which was to introduce not only a – vaguely defined – set of common protectionist and punitive policies but also "permanent measures of mutual aid and collaboration". One of its main purposes was to control the access to and distribution of essential raw materials – and to restrict Germany's access to these commodities. Yet British attitudes towards the more far-reaching French project of creating not just a fully-fledged Anglo-French economic union but also a firmly regulated economic and trading system after the war – with built-in discriminations against Germany – remained lukewarm.

By the spring of 1917 the Imperial War Cabinet deemed the Paris resolutions no longer applicable, and by the autumn of 1918 the Lloyd George government had clearly disassociated itself from the ambitious agenda of 1916. And this was not least due to entrenched American opposition to this agenda. By and large, it again adopted a more liberal approach, which gravitated back to British "free trade" maxims of the pre-war era and was broadly compatible with American "Open Door" preferences. Emphasising the "most-favoured-nation principle" British plans now foresaw that "normal", unhampered trade was to resume after a short transition period in which restrictions were to be imposed on Germany to give the *Entente* Powers a "head start" in postwar reconstruction and positioning themselves for the global economic competition of the future.[92]

VII. Campaigns for a New International Order. Formative Ideas and Impulses of Non-Governmental Actors during the War

Yet of course not only the leaders of governments and strategists and planners within the different governmental bureaucracies were engaged in efforts to conceive and propose more comprehensive peace plans. One of the salient developments that took place on the war's changing playing-field of international and transnational politics – not only but particularly in Europe and the United States – was the exponential increase in the number of non-governmental actors – individual activists and well-established or newly formed pressure-groups – that sought to influence the political and ideological "war within the war" over the shape of the postwar order. In doing so, these actors came to generate and propagate an unprecedented multiplicity of diverse ideas of how to build peace on new and better foundations and how to create a more "just" and secure international order. Though to different

---

[92] This reflected preferences that the decisive British Board of Trade had asserted all along. See Board of Trade memorandum, November 1918, CAB 29/1/P-33; Board of Trade report, 27 October 1916, CAB 29/1/P-12; Glaser (1998), pp. 375–6.

degrees, non-governmental actors and associations played their part in changing the political force-fields of all the principal belligerents.

But what proved most consequential for the eventual peacemaking process was that both in Britain and in the United States liberal-progressive and to a lesser extent reformist-socialist parties and activists came to have a newly prominent influence on public and inner-governmental debates. And they came to play a newly prominent part in both propagating and disseminating ideas for a new kind of international politics – a "new diplomacy". These included not only various league schemes but also proposals for a more effective international arbitration regime and the expansion of both democratic government and self-determination. Unsurprisingly, though, what these individuals and groups lobbied for tended to be more radical and far-reaching than what the heads and planners of the various governments contemplated. The most significant conceptual and political impulses for the creation of a "peace league" came from a phalanx of pressure-groups in Britain and the United States – the only countries where also a substantial "pro-League" movement emerged during the war. The most important of these groups – notably the Union of Democratic Control, the Brice Group and the League to Enforce Peace – not only formed different transatlantic networks but also advanced the most widely noted unofficial blueprints for a new international organisation, and a novel international order.

Essentially, the non-governmental protagonists of this crisis period did not develop any new ideas or original conceptions. Rather, just like Wilson, Cecil and other decision-makers, they built on concepts that had been developed before 1914, in the context of the Hague processes, in the debates of the Second Socialist International and elsewhere – or much earlier. Their main significance lies in the fact that they sought to expand these concepts to meet the novel challenges the war had created – and that they made more concerted efforts to seize on the opportunity the fundamental crisis of the "old order" presented to *see their ideas actually implemented*. Activists on both sides of the war's trenches indeed struggled to find more effective ways of influencing national policies and international politics. And some of what they proposed had a noticeable, though ultimately never a decisive, hearing on the policies and eventual peace agendas of the belligerent governments. Arguably, however, their main impact has to be sought elsewhere. Essentially, they shaped the wider national and transnational debates that ensued between 1914 and 1918 about the meaning of the war and about what would constitute a better, more peaceable order in its aftermath. The decision-makers who eventually faced the task of making peace would have to take this into account.

It must also be noted, however, that the war of course also became a political battlefield for many propagandists and pressure-groups that agitated for entirely different, namely nationalist, imperialist and expansionist war aims and visions of postwar order. And their influence in different national force-fields was often even greater than that of liberal or socialist internationalists – particularly in continental Europe, and above all in France and the German Empire. Influential groups of this kind included, on one side of the trenches, the French *comité de la rive gauche du Rhin* and the French steel industry's *comité des forges* and, on the other, the Pan-German League and, from 1917, the "Fatherland Party" and expansionist *Siegfrieden* movement.

Overall, the Great War thus also became a formative phase for the rise of non-governmental activists and associations in twentieth-century international politics. But it was a period not only of high aspirations but also of profound frustration. What appears particularly remarkable in retrospect is the degree to which many of the most committed liberal, progressive and socialist peace activists actually came to believe that the war had actually created an opening for realising their elaborate designs – that it would actually be possible to make international relations more rational, pacific, and governed by universally accepted covenants of international law. And the fact that one of the most powerful actors, the American president, seemed to take up their cause reinforced such expectations. They would thus be all the more brutally disappointed by the outcomes of the "real" peacemaking processes of 1919. A systemic analysis can show, and it is indeed essential to highlight, that only very few non-governmental actors, and ideas, really came to have a notable impact on how the different governments prepared for peace, and then on the actual peace negotiations – while thousands of other appeals and manifestos, which not seldom were more substantial, had no or at best a very marginal influence.

VIII. The Critical Impetus of British Liberal and Labour Internationalists

In Britain, Ramsay MacDonald and other protagonists of the left-liberal Union of Democratic Control, formed in August 1914, argued that the carnage of the war should be stopped as soon as possible through a negotiated peace. And, supported by leading figures of the Bloomsbury group, among them John Maynard Keynes, Virginia Woolf and E.M. Forster, they called for far-reaching domestic and international reforms, which they deemed indispensable if a recurrence of the catastrophe was to be prevented. Early on, they thus became the most vocal and influential promoters of a "democratic control of foreign policy" and a new form of international politics that eschewed "alliances" for the purpose of maintaining the "Balance of Power". What they championed instead were efforts directed towards "concerted action between the Powers determined by public deliberations in an International Court" and the peaceful settlement of international disputes through mandatory arbitration and conciliation.[93]

Embodying these demands, the UDC manifesto for a negotiated peace, published in November 1914, was the first statement on behalf of what became known as "New Diplomacy". Of particular import too, not least because it became an early inspiration for Wilson, would be the manifesto "The War and the Way Out" that the UDC member and Cambridge classicist Goldsworthy Lowes Dickinson drafted soon after the war's outbreak and that was then widely publicised on both sides of the Atlantic. Dickinson proposed the establishment of a "permanent League of Nations" in and beyond Europe, becoming the first to use the term in the English-speaking world. Crucially, taking up ideas of the Hague movement, he envisaged a league that was to inaugurate a general system of compulsory arbitration, overseen by a central council in which all recognised states could participate. This council also was to exert control over the armed forces of all member states. And, reflecting a core precept of the UDC's "New Diplomacy" platform that Wilson would make famous, Dickinson stipulated that all League members also had to commit themselves to practising "open diplomacy", thus accepting the ultimate control of the people.[94]

On behalf of the Independent Labour Party, MacDonald sought to revive the pre-war solidarity of the Second International and renew cooperation with other European socialists on both sides of the trenches, notably with German social democrats. He desired to "keep the foundations of the International intact so that at the earliest possible moment they may begin to rebuild upon these foundations what the war has destroyed".[95] While aspiring to a socialist-internationalist rather than Wilsonian postwar order, MacDonald, who in 1914 had favoured neutrality, thus remained one of the chief advocates of a negotiated "peace without victory" in Britain. In early 1918, he tried to persuade Lloyd George, in vain, to permit him and other Labour representatives to meet with German and Austrian social democrats, arguing that because the present was not "an old-fashioned war" its "settlement" could not be "old fashioned" either; it had to be approached with the support of progressive forces from all sides.[96]

By contrast, Arthur Henderson, the chairman of the Labour party who had entered the British War Cabinet as minister without portfolio, initially

---

[93] See Records of the UDC, Box 2; Swartz, (1971), pp. 28–45.

[94] Dickinson "The War and the Way Out", *Atlantic Monthly*, 14 (December 1914), pp. 820–37; Dickinson (1915). Wilson was alerted to it by his friend Newton Baker. See Baker to Wilson, 6 January 1915, *PWW*, XXXI, p. 24.

[95] MacDonald (draft letter) to Lloyd George, 1 January 1918, MacDonald Papers, 30/69/1162; "Labour and War Aims", *The Times*, 29 December 1917; Marquand (1977), 164–85; Imlay (2017), 20-1.

[96] MacDonald (draft letter) to Lloyd George, 1 January 1918, MacDonald Papers, 30/69/1162.

championed a more robust approach. In early 1917, when Wilson called for "peace without victory" he still insisted – like Lloyd George – on a peace premised on defeating German "tyranny" and aspirations for "world domination". Soon thereafter, however, Henderson came to pursue a different course. He urged the Labour Party to accept the Petrograd Soviet's invitation to an international socialist congress, which was supposed to be convened in Stockholm, as long as Labour would not be bound by its decisions.[97] This was to initiate a process through which, with the help of combined socialist pressure, a breakthrough to peace negotiations was to be achieved. Yet Henderson's scheme would be frustrated at an early stage because both Lloyd George and the Ribot government in Paris prevented socialist representatives from going to Stockholm.

But Labour did not relent its efforts to push for negotiated peace. By December 1917, the Labour Party had joined the UDC in calling for the creation of a "Super-National Authority, or League of Nations" – with more substantial authority, powers and inclusiveness than anything Wilson or Cecil would ever envision. The league Labour proposed was to comprise an international high court, an international parliament with proportional representatives from all European states and the United States, which "every other independent sovereign State in the world should be pressed to join". Labour's manifesto also emphasised that the League's members were to commit themselves to settling all international disputes by arbitration – and use "any and every means at their disposal to enforce adherence".[98] By late February 1918, an inter-allied socialist conference in Paris passed a resolution that echoed Labour's earlier call for "united action of the working classes" to bring the "monstrous conflict to a summary conclusion conformably to the principles of the International". While renewing the demand for an internationalist league, the resolution also called for a peace settlement based on the principle of self-determination for the peoples of Europe (not extending it to the colonies).[99]

At an earlier conference of the inter-allied socialists in London, MacDonald had again gone further than Henderson in arguing that a peace based on "justice and liberty" could not be made through a "simple military victory" or the "secret diplomacy" of governments. He thus proposed that socialists from all sides – who could not simply rely on Wilson – ought to organise an inclusive international conference that brought together the feuding majority and minority factions to deliberate "the peace conditions that will bring a final

---

[97] *Report of the Seventeenth Annual Conference of the Labour Party*, 23 January 1917; Henderson (1917), pp. 49, 87–8; "British Labour Conference", *The Times*, 11 August 1917, 4; Imlay (2017), pp. 31–4.

[98] Labour Party and Trades Union Congress, *Memorandum on War Aims* (London, 28 December 1917).

[99] "Labour War Aims", *The Times*, 25 February 1918; Imlay (2017), pp. 34–42.

end to militarism". Anticipating one of the most consequential questions that would arise after the armistice, MacDonald especially called for cooperation with the German social democrats to this end, stressing that it would be much better not to keep them isolated but to "bring them back" to "grace" and confront them with the "truth of democracy".[100]

Liberal internationalists in Britain were less concerned with how a peace would be negotiated – and most of them broadly supported the core maxim of governmental policy and propaganda that a defeat of Prusso-German militarism represented the fundamental precondition of a stable peace. They focused more on the question of how the west European powers and the United States could cooperate in reforming the postwar order and, above all, on the demand for a League of Nations. Already in March 1915 the so-called Bryce Group, made up of liberal and socialist critics of pre-war international politics and headed by the historian and erstwhile ambassador to the United States, Lord Bryce, had published what became one of the most influential schemes for a "peace league" in British and American government circles. The Group's *Proposals for the Avoidance of War* presented a detailed plan for an essentially transatlantic league that initially was to be formed by the six European great powers, the United States and Japan – as well as all other European states that were willing to join it. Its central purpose would be to foster the peaceful settlement of international disputes. These were divided into "justiciable" disputes, to be settled by the Permanent Court of Arbitration at The Hague, and non-justiciable disputes, to be settled by a permanent council of conciliation. Though setting out to effect a "real and radical change" in the way international relations were organized, the programme advanced by the Bryce Group, which built on the Hague Conventions, was in fact relatively conservative. Not least, it was intended to be more palatable for the political leaders of the different belligerents and the still neutral American power – and thus did not envisage an authoritative international organisation that curtailed the sovereignty of states in any meaningful way. In pursuit of its mission, the Group successfully established numerous links with like-minded individuals and associations in the United States, particularly the League to Enforce Peace, to advocate "the idea of a peace league" more effectively.[101]

Another elite association, the League of Nations Society (LNS), formed in the spring of 1915, not only sought to put pressure on the British government and educate the public about the need to create a new international organisation. It also took a further qualitative step and presented a basic conception of general "collective security", stipulating that all of the organisation's members had to "make provision for Mutual Defence, diplomatic, economic, or

---

[100] "Labour War Aims", *The Times*, 25 February 1918.
[101] Viscount Bryce, "Proposals for the Avoidance of War", 24 February 1915), Bryce Papers. See Kaiga (2018).

military" in the event that any of them was attacked by a state that was "not a member of the League" and refused to respect the rulings of "an appropriate Tribunal or Council".[102] The League of Free Nations Association (LFNA), whose founders broke away from the LNS in the summer of 1918, came to emphasise different political priorities, some of which anticipated those of key decision-makers at Versailles, including Wilson. It demanded that the Allied and Associated Powers should go ahead and form as soon as possible a union or league of "free", "democratic" nations. And it demanded that this union should dispose of an "international force to guarantee order in the world". Significantly, in contrast to the UDC and more left-leaning league proponents, the League of Free Nations Association insisted that the Central Powers were to be *excluded* from the new organisation until – following their defeat – they were prepared to undergo substantial democratisation processes.[103]

This agenda would subsequently be taken up by the League of Nations Union into which the LNS and the LFNA fused in October 1918. What became the most influential British pro-League organisation thus explicitly advocated the creation of an *initially exclusive* "world organization" with considerable authority and immense responsibilities. The league it envisioned was to oblige all of its members to use "methods of peaceful settlement" to resolve international disputes, institute a "permanent Council" as well as a "Supreme Court", "guarantee the freedom of nations", act as "guardian of uncivilized races", "maintain international order" and "thus finally liberate mankind from the curse of war".[104] Both Wilson and Lloyd George would acknowledge the rising public and elite pressure for a new international organisation that was reflected in the growing support for the LNU and other British and American pressure-groups; but both leaders would only be marginally influenced by the conceptions these associations put forward when it came to developing their own League agendas.

IX.   Progressive American Impulses – and the Political Battles over the United States' Role in War and Peace

In the United States, the soon highly controversial debate about the project of a League of Nations and, more broadly, the American role in efforts to make peace and forge a more pacific international order became inseparable from the "war for the American mind" that had ensued ever since 1914. This "war" revolved around the question of what attitude the American government and

---

[102] League of Nations Society (1916), p. 4; LEP "League Bulletin", No. 31, 20 April 1917, Bryce Papers, 243. See Egerton (1978), pp. 11–13.
[103] See minutes of provisional LFNA executive committee, 24 July 1918, Murray Papers, 178.
[104] LNU programme, November 1918, in Winkler (1952), p. 77.

people should adopt vis-à-vis the war in Europe – whether they should stay neutral, as Wilson demanded, or intervene on the side of Britain and France in a "war for civilisation". The competing agendas of senators and members of Congress in Washington of course played their part in this intense political and ideological fight, in which all sides endowed their positions with a higher patriotic purpose; and the president himself obviously came to play a pivotal role. But it also involved activists who lobbied for their own, often conflicting agendas.[105]

A very vocal minority of more radical internationalist progressives and socialists had urged Wilson ever since the war's outbreak to stay out of the conflict and use America's authority as a neutral vanguard power of peace both to mediate an end to the mass slaughter at the earliest opportunity and to advance radical international and domestic reforms. Building on their programmes of the pre-war years, leading progressives now intensified their campaigns on behalf of a more "rational" and cooperative peace order. Among those who spearheaded such campaigns were the charismatic leader of the American Socialist Party, Eugene Debs; the protagonists of the American Union Against Militarism, notably the editor of *The Nation*, Oswald Garrison Villard; and the lawyer Hollingsworth Wood. They too advocated the creation of an authoritative international association that hence was to settle all inter-state conflicts and foster general disarmament. Yet in their eyes such an association could only usher in a more permanent peace if it could be made into an instrument of both political and economic internationalism. As such, they argued, its mission had to be the promotion of broader political, economic and social reforms that tackled not only German authoritarianism but also the iniquities of western societies and, at bottom, the capitalist system. It was thus only logical that progressive pacifists like Jane Addams stepped up parallel campaigns for domestic reforms, democracy promotion and, notably universal suffrage and women's rights. To make their work more effective, Addams and the suffragist Carrie Chapman Catt in April 1915 founded the Woman's Peace Party.[106]

But progressive opinion in the United States would become deeply divided during the war. By early 1917 a new vanguard of standard-bearers of a more assertive – and interventionist – Americanist progressivism had emerged. It was headed by Croly and intellectuals like the young publicist Walter Lippmann who founded the *New Republic* in November 1914. Both Croly and Lippmann had also initially prodded Wilson to promote an "American

---

[105] See Kennedy (2004), pp. 45–92.

[106] Addams to Wilson, 29 January 1915, *PWW*, XXXII, p. 162; Addams (1922), p. 7. Peace and mediation initiatives were also launched by transnational church organisations like the Church Peace Union and the "World Alliance for International Friendship through the Churches". See Marchand (1972), pp. 362–3.

Peace Idea", the design for a "just settlement" proposed by a neutral "Third Party" – "not from the point of view of victory but from the point of view of Right". And they too had argued that as a powerful neutral power the United States had to "lead the effort" to create a "League to Enforce Peace".[107] Yet they would change their attitudes and eventually were among the most influential opinion-makers who criticised the president's policy of "neutrality" and pushed for an American intervention in the war.

It was with the aim of endowing this intervention with a higher moral purpose that Croly and especially Lippmann would strive to define an ideological agenda that both anticipated and marginally influenced Wilson's eventual crusader's rhetoric. And, significantly, they would for the first time introduce conceptions of a – transatlantic – "western world" and an "Atlantic order" into the wider American debate. They posited that the American republic not only had a duty to defeat the autocrats and militarists who had led the German Empire into an "offensive war" against the "western world" but also to defend liberal western "civilisation", which in their eyes required the expansion of American-style democracy. Essentially, they thus sought to translate the progressive programme they had developed before the war to fulfil the "promise" of the "Land of Democracy" into a far more ambitious Americanist war *and* peace agenda.[108] Above all, both Croly and Lippmann now argued that the United States had to enter the Great War and decide it in favour of the "western" powers, so that it could then set the terms of a "just" peace and decisively influence the construction of a progressive – Atlantic – "world order" that ended the reign of European power politics. And Lippmann now declared that an American intervention was also essential for realising Wilson's revolutionary plan to create a novel "international organization", which offered the best hope of "substituting security for insecurity as the basis of international relationships".[109]

At the very moment when controversies over a possible American entry into the war came to a head, Lippmann became the first influential intellectual who explicitly advanced the conception of an "Atlantic community". In February 1917 he defined this community not only in geopolitical terms but also in terms of a common political "civilization" whose hallmark was a predominant "liberalism". Lippmann noted that the American people and the peoples of Europe should realise that by the early twentieth century

---

[107] Croly, "An American Peace Idea", *New Republic*, 8/103 (21 October 1916), pp. 289–90; Lippmann to Wilson, 31 January 1917; Wilson to Lippmann, 3 February, *PWW*, XLI, pp. 83 (and ft. 1), 113.

[108] Lippmann, "The Defense of the Atlantic World", *New Republic* (17 February 1917), pp. 59–60; Croly (1909), pp. 2–3.

[109] Lippmann, "America's Part in the War", *New Republic* (10 February 1917), pp. 33–4; Lippmann to Wilson, 11 March 1917, *PWW*, XLI, pp. 388–9; Croly, "An American Peace Idea", *New Republic* (21 October 1916), pp. 289–90.

the United States had become a "member" and integral "part" of one "great community of nations" linked by the Atlantic Ocean. In his interpretation, what had "grown up" on the ocean's "two shores" was a "profound web of interests" and a shared liberal "civilization" of what he called "the West". It joined together, on the one hand, Britain, France, Italy, "even" Spain, Belgium, Holland and the Scandinavian nations and, on the other, "Pan-America", led by the United States, making all of these nations members of "one community in their deepest needs and purposes". Lippmann demanded that because they were "to-day more inextricably bound together than most even as yet realize", they all had to develop a transatlantic consciousness and recognise that they belonged to one "western world", which they had to defend and develop further. And, crucially, he posited one further specific premise that would become integral to all subsequent attempts to construct an Atlantic community in the long twentieth century. He argued that it also had to be understood as a *security* community, in which an attack on one member was tantamount to an attack on all. Consequently, he asserted that by invading France, violating Belgian neutrality, "striking against" Britain and attempting to cut the "vital waterways" of the "Atlantic world" through its unrestricted submarine warfare, the German Empire had not only severed its links with this community but also threatened its future existence – and thus ultimately America's national security and the future of western "civilisation" itself.[110]

To prevent such a scenario, Lippmann thus called on Wilson to lead his country into the war on the side of the *Entente*. Yet he also outlined more far-reaching aspirations, underscoring that America's "entrance" in the war would make the organisation of a "league for peace" an "immediately practical object of statesmanship". Significantly, he recommended that this "league" should become not only the superstructure of the "Atlantic community" but also the "cornerstone" of a wider international "federation". And he insisted that Germany – which "(b)y rights" ought to be a "powerful and loyal member" of the western-orientated "Atlantic world" – should not be excluded from the new international institution. But, he maintained, it was only to be admitted once it no longer committed its "destiny" to those who waged an "offensive war" against the "western world". Accordingly, America's higher war aim should be "not to conquer Germany as Rome conquered Carthage", but to "win Germany as Lincoln strove to win the South" – by discrediting "those classes who alone are our enemies", its current rulers and military masters, and taking steps to "force and lure her back to the civilization in which she belongs".[111]

By contrast, Lippmann regarded both Russia and Japan as powers that did not belong to the "western" community he delineated. Lippmann would strive

---

[110] Lippmann, "The Defense of the Atlantic World", *New Republic* (17 February 1917), pp. 59–60.
[111] *Ibid.*, p. 60.

hard to persuade Wilson to adopt his ideas, both as a publicist and later as member of the president's Inquiry group of informal advisers.[112] Wilson would never speak of an "Atlantic community"; but in substance the peace agenda he came to pursue as wartime president indeed reflected Lippmann's rationales. Much to the latter's chagrin, however, the president would depart from them in 1919.

The philosopher John Dewey also played an important role in preparing the ground for the shift towards interventionism in one segment of the American progressive spectrum. Dewey came to see the war as a historical watershed that had the potential to instigate collective learning processes – to make the world more susceptible to the guidance of reason and a more rational organisation of both national communities and the international order. He held that Wilson's aspirations reflected an underlying American "desire for stable peace and an established amity of peoples through a comity of democratic nations", which could open up the "prospect of a world organization and the beginnings of a public control which crosses nationalistic boundaries and interests". Yet he also argued that what pacifists like Trueblood desired – "a "vitally energetic [American] role" in the reorganization of the world" – first of all made it imperative to play a leading part in defeating the German Empire and the autocratic backwardness it represented.[113] Already in 1915 the sociologist Thorstein Veblen had provided highly effective ammunition for American and British propagandists by putting forward a notion that would then reverberate through the long twentieth century, which centred on the thesis that Imperial Germany had veered onto a "special path" during the industrial revolution, a path of backwardness dictated by Prussian authoritarianism and militarism that deviated from those of the advanced western states, which he glorified as bastions of freedom-loving civilisation and progress.[114]

Lippmann, Dewey and other progressive interventionists would be severely criticised by anti-war progressives for betraying the cause of American internationalism and undermining the United States' moral stature as possible mediator of a progressive peace. Randolph Bourne, a young disciple of Dewey, castigated the latter for advocating a misdirected war mission based on the erroneous conviction that America was "ordained" to "lead all erring brothers towards the light of liberty and democracy". Bourne doubted that it would be possible to "mould" the war "in the interests of democracy" and

---

[112] Lippmann to Wilson, 11 March 1917, *PWW*, XLI, pp. 388–9; Lippmann et al. memorandum to Wilson, December 1917, *PWW*, XLV, pp. 458–73. See Gelfand (1963).

[113] John Dewey, "The Future of Pacifism", *New Republic*, 11/143 (28 July 1917), p. 358; J. Dewey, "What America Will Fight For" (1917) in Dewey (1980), vol. 10, p. 275; Kennedy (2004), p. 50.

[114] Veblen (1915). See also Veblen (1917).

"civilization". And he argued that the "League of Peace" that Wilson and other progressives propagated was "neither realizable nor desirable" and in fact "reactionary". In his assessment, it would create "a world-order founded on mutual fear" and contained "no provision for dynamic national growth or for international economic justice", which the world needed far more than "political internationalism".[115] But this remained a marginal view at this juncture – as well as in 1919.

A diametrically opposite position was advocated most forcefully by Theodore Roosevelt. Consistent with the maxims he had championed as president, Roosevelt became one of the fiercest critics of Wilson's neutrality policy and "peace without victory" philosophy. And he emerged as one of the most influential advocates not only of war-preparedness and intervention against the Central Powers but also of a martial vision of a "righteous peace".[116] In his widely read book *America and the World War*, published in 1915, Roosevelt denounced the "kind of "neutrality" which seeks to preserve "'peace' by timidly refusing to live up to our plighted word" and "take action against such wrong as that committed [by Germany] in the case of Belgium". In contrast to this, he reiterated his pre-war creed that the only peace "of permanent value" was "the peace of righteousness", a peace in which "highly-civilized small nations" like Belgium had to be protected "from oppression and subjugation". And he reasserted that this could only be done by the civilised great powers and ultimately through the righteous use of military force. Roosevelt now thundered that "the actions of the ultrapacifists of the generation past, all their peace congresses and peace conventions" had "amounted to precisely and exactly nothing in advancing the cause of peace". He exhorted America's political leaders to draw consequences from this blatant failure. In his eyes their duty was twofold: they had to prepare for defending "the vital honor and the vital interest of the American people"; and they had to devise a League "scheme" that went beyond Wilson's pacifist proclamations – a scheme by which the "civilized military powers" would commit themselves to "securing the peace of righteousness throughout the world" by agreeing "*to back righteousness by force*".[117] Roosevelt's demands resonated in interventionist circles but were essentially ignored by Wilson.

Of greater influence, especially with a view to American thinking about the League, were the conceptual blueprints and organisational activities of the

---

[115] Bourne (1917), "The War and the Intellectuals" (June 1917), in Capper and Hollinger (1989), II, pp. 167 ff.

[116] Roosevelt (1915), pp. 42–3.

[117] *Ibid.*, pp. xi–xii, 3–4, 42–3. In the autumn of 1914 Roosevelt also proposed that neutral powers should enter into an agreement that committed them to join forces in a *Posse Comitatus* with the other great powers against an aggressor state. See Roosevelt to Grey, 3 October 1914; Grey to Roosevelt, 18 December 1914, in Grey (1925), II, pp. 139–43.

League to Enforce Peace (LEP) that Taft and more conservative "international-ists", for the most part Republicans, had founded in June 1915. Clearly building on the efforts that Taft, Root and others had earlier made on behalf of international arbitration, the League to Enforce Peace sought to promote a more ambitious agenda. It championed a conception that was more elaborate and distinctly more juridical than Wilson's; and in contrast to the president, it demanded from early on that the new League should be formed by the United States and the "civilised" nations of the *Entente*. The League to Enforce Peace came to be backed by a wide array of relatively more conservative political, financial, business and educational leaders, including the former Secretary Of State Root, the influential banker Thomas Lamont of J.P. Morgan and Co. and the President of Harvard, Lawrence Lowell. Comprising 4,000 chapters in nearly all US states by 1918, it became the most powerful American pro-League pressure-group; and it also established close links with like-minded British associations, notably the Bryce Group and eventually the League of Nations Union.[118]

In its founding declaration the LEP demanded that the United States should "join a league of nations" that bound its signatories to four principles. One core principle was that all "justiciable questions" that could not be settled by negoti-ation were to be submitted to a new international "judicial tribunal", while all other questions should be decided by a new "council of conciliation"; another core principle was that all signatories should "jointly use forthwith both their economic and military forces against any one of their number who goes to war". Further, the LEP proposed that regular conferences of the member states ought to be held "to formulate and codify rules of international law".[119]

Taft emphasised that the League he sought was "only applying to the international community the same principle that has been applied to the domestic community, that of using the force of all to suppress the lawless force of the few for the common good".[120] But the LEP's programme was actually based on explicitly hierarchical notions of how the international community was to be organised, which reflected longer-standing assumptions about civilisation and "righteous power". Its leading figures were convinced that the United States, Britain and other "civilised" great powers had to lead the new organisation and contribute their share to "an international police force to suppress the disturbers of peace". And while Taft had initially insisted that the League had to comprise "all the great nations of the world", and

---

[118] See *New Republic*, 9/117 (27 January 1917), p. 340.
[119] See LEP Proposals, 17 June 1915, Gerrity (2003), VII, pp. 3–4; Goldsmith (1917), pp. xx–xxi; *Proceedings of the First Annual Assemblage of the LEP, Washington, 26–27 May 1916* (New York, 1916); Bartlett (1944).
[120] Taft speech, 20 January 1917, Gerrity (2003), VII, p. 76; Goldsmith (1917), pp. x–xi; LEP pamphlets, Records of the League to Enforce Peace, 1915–21.

"minor stable nations", the LEP soon changed its emphasis.[121] Having pushed for a US intervention in the spring of 1917, it subsequently adopted the position that an effective League to Enforce Peace could only be founded after the "military autocracies" of the Central Powers had been defeated. As Taft put it, the "Allies" had to take the lead in founding the new organisation; and they could "not make the military autocracies of the world into nations fit for a World League, unless they convince them by a lesson of defeat".[122] The League to Enforce Peace came to exert a considerable influence on US public opinion and moderate Republicans in Congress. But Wilson not only pointedly disregarded the recommendations of the predominantly Republican association when he began to develop his own League plans. He also came to reject what he saw as misguided LEP ideas to create a "militarised" League with a "hard and fast constitution" that placed undue emphasis on the use of force.[123]

What has to be stressed, however, is that in the wider spectrum of American politics – and public opinion – engagement on behalf of some kind of League, and of new American leadership in international politics and peace-building, remained essentially the cause of a small elite, or rather of competing elite actors and groups. And one constant never changed: Wilson and other League proponents indeed faced a political up-hill battle, especially in the critical force-field of Congressional politics. For their aspirations also galvanised the opposition of those, particularly in the US Senate, who either for partisan-political reasons or on ideological grounds came to reject the entire thrust of what Wilson, progressive League supporters and the leading voices of the LEP advocated. And these actors sought to counter and contain this thrust by re-asserting what they presented as time-honoured American practices and traditions of non-entanglement and "insulation" from – European-style – alliance and power politics. This became particularly obvious when Wilson embarked on his – futile – "peace without victory" initiative in the autumn of 1916.

Henry Cabot Lodge, who at this time began to emerge as a key opponent of Wilson in the Senate, would play a critical role in what hence escalated into a profoundly divisive political battle that would reach its climax in the "treaty fight" of 1919/1920. Chiefly because of partisan political considerations – and with the underlying aim to weaken Wilson and the Democratic Party, Lodge fiercely criticised what he called the president's dangerous "experiment" to broker a "peace without victory". In January 1917, he publicly stressed that the United States still had "nothing to do" with the war in Europe "legally and nationally". And, still considering Britain America's natural ally, he warned that Wilson's initiative would actually be "friendly" towards Germany and

---

[121] Taft speech, 20 January 1917, Gerrity (2003), VII, pp. 73–7.
[122] Taft address, 26 September 1917, Gerrity (2003), VII, pp. 87–8.
[123] Bullitt diary, 9 [10] December 1918, *PWW*, LIII, pp. 350–2.

position the United States against the *Entente* Powers, which were waging the "battle of freedom and democracy as against military autocracy". But Lodge also seized the opportunity to underscore his opposition to Wilson's entire peace programme. Earlier, he had briefly supported the idea of a League. Now he accused Wilson of leading the American people down a path of "peril" and abandoning "long and well-established policies" of "separation" and non-entanglement. He declared that "future cooperation in a league for the preservation of the world's peace" was unlikely to succeed. And he argued that such a multilateral undertaking would force the United States to commit to "the doctrine of general cooperation with the powers of Europe" – not only in European but also in American affairs – which would bring with it both dangerous infringements of American sovereignty and unwarranted international commitments. Lodge's categorical rejection of such a "very momentous step" foreshadowed his future determination not just to re-affirm Senate prerogatives and US independence but ultimately to thwart the realisation of Wilson's League aspirations by all means.[124]

Even more fundamental opposition to the concept of a League and Wilson's call for a new American engagement in the world came from leading Progressive senators in the ranks of the Republican party who later came to be known as his "irreconcilable" opponents. The most prominent among them, and one of only five senators who had voted against the war resolution in 1917, was Robert La Follette from Wisconsin. He accused Wilson of fighting a war "for the benefit of the dominant economic classes" and to the detriment of the vast majority of the American people. La Follette had earlier endorsed Wilson's aim to act as a neutral mediator between the European belligerents. But he strictly opposed American involvement in a peace league that in his view would compel the United States to enforce a regime of economic, political and military sanctions. He maintained that such commitments would invariably lead the American republic into perilous international entanglements and, particularly, the machinations of European power politics. And, reviving traditional tenets of exeptionalist isolationism, he warned that such entanglements would compromise America's "precious heritage" of sovereign self-government, threatening instead to turn the American republic into a European-style military state.[125]

Another progressive opponent of the war resolution, Senator George Norris of Nebraska, advanced very similar arguments when calling on the Senate to

---

[124] Lodge Senate statements, 3 and 4 January 1917, Congressional Record, 64th Congress, 2nd session, pp. 793–7, 830–3; Lodge address, February 1917, in Lodge (1917), pp. 278–80.

[125] La Follette speech, Senate, 4 April 1917, Congressional Record, 65th Congress, 1st session, 4 April 1917, 224–225.
    La Follette speech, Senate, 19-20 July 1916, in Holmes (1920), pp. 192–3.

heed Washington's "advice" and "keep out of entangling alliances".[126] And while he originally voted in favour of intervention, the future leader of the "irreconcilables", Senator William Borah of Idaho, likewise remained staunchly opposed to both Wilson's and the LEP's League plans. He too vindicated his opposition by stressing that an American involvement in the envisaged international organisation would require abandoning salutary long-standing maxims of US foreign policy, notably that of avoiding "entangling alliances". In response to Wilson's "peace without victory" address Borah had thus in January 1917 introduced a Senate resolution intended to affirm that Washington's Farewell Address and the Monroe Doctrine still guided US international conduct.[127] While a majority of more moderate Republican senators did not share such views and were more sympathetic to the general idea of a peace league, the positions of progressive "insulationists" like La Follette, Norris and notably Borah represented sentiments that were not only quite widespread in the American public, particularly in the western and mid-western states, but would also carry considerable weight when the controversies over the League and America's place in the postwar order reached a climax in 1919 and 1920.

X.   Power-Political Conceptions of Order, the Radicalisation of Neo-Imperialist Visions and the Search for Alternatives. Evolving Ideas of Peace and Postwar Order in France and Germany

Yet, as noted, what had also become more pronounced, far-reaching or even radical the longer the war lasted, and the more the political competition within the war escalated, were different power-political – and more or less overtly imperialist – war-aims agendas and "visions" of postwar order. Most relevant in the context of the ideological struggle during the war and consequential for the eventual peacemaking process were the fundamentally antagonistic concepts and "visions" that came to the fore, and became prevalent, in France and in Germany. Those who developed them were not unaffected by the changes in the ideological and political environment that the war generated and in various ways sought to legitimise their aspirations by invoking principles of international law, "self-determination" and, in the French case, democratic values. Essentially, however, they tended to seize on such ideas and principles in a more obviously instrumental fashion – in pursuit of what they regarded as overriding strategic interests.

What these war-aim imperialists envisaged and pursued thus collided more or less fundamentally with Wilson's aspirations and evolving British ideas for

---

[126] Norris speech, Senate, 4 April 1917, Congressional Record, 65th Congress, 1st session, 4 April 1917, 224, 228.
[127] Borah to Roosevelt, 29 December 1916, Borah Papers; Nichols (2011), pp. 240–1.

a postwar Atlantic concert; and it clashed even more violently with the ideas of committed internationalist activists and advocates of a League of Nations.

This held true for the *essentially defensive* strategies and conceptions for a robust postwar Atlantic security system that were formulated by leading French policymakers, particularly after the energetic Georges Clemenceau had become premier in November 1917. And it applied even more starkly to the more overtly imperialist-hegemonic "designs" that the official and unofficial protagonists of the German war-aims movement put forward – and that would be taken to new extremes by those who, not least in response to Wilson's challenge, propagated ever more expansive visions of a German "victorious peace". But both in France and Germany there were also notable counterforces – liberal internationalists, social democrats and more radical socialists who championed alternative ideas for a "peace of understanding", a strengthened regime of international law, a League of Nations, democratisation and "self-determination". While these forces were politically marginalised or on the defensive during most stages of the war they would play an important role in its aftermath, especially in the fledgling Weimar Republic.

XI. First French Visions of an Exclusive Atlantic Alliance and Union of Democracies – and Changing Attitudes towards the League

The core aim of all relevant conceptions of peace and of postwar order that emerged within the different French wartime governments was to find more effective ways to ensure the long-term security of the ever more exhausted French state, and empire. Almost without exception, French strategists sought to secure a "peace to end all threats", not by aspiring to a League of Nations and counting on a transformation of international politics but rather by working towards a more resilient international security system. What they envisaged was a system based on long-term alliances, a forcible "restructuring" of Europe's "balance of power" and, at a different level, on power-political containment and deterrence. The cardinal purpose of French plans, which intended to create an *exclusive* rather than integrative western "security community", was not only to contain but also maximally diminish the threat posed by an inherently more powerful German state, which they viewed as inherently antagonistic in any postwar scenario that was contemplated. And one of the most influential French policymakers, André Tardieu, concluded that, to this end, it was in France's vital interest to seek to forge a *transatlantic* community of democratic states – and to draw the United States into it as a key guarantor of French postwar security vis-à-vis Germany.

It was thus chiefly due to overriding security concerns, and a profound distrust of German intentions, that French wartime governments never departed from the rationale that France would only make peace once the

Entente Powers had "broken Prussian militarism".[128] This would also be the key maxim of the remobilisation agenda Clemenceau came to pursue in the autumn of 1917. By this time a French war-aims movement had formed that brought together nationalist parties, business associations, intellectuals and newly formed pressure-groups like the *comité de la rive gauche du Rhin* and the *comité des forges*, which represented the interests of the French steel industry. The various groups within this movement agitated not only for a return of Alsace-Lorraine and the imposition of major indemnity on the German aggressor but also for a *de facto* annexation of the Rhine's left bank and the industrial region of the Saar. And they justified these demands by stressing France's existential need for a safety zone on its eastern border and an expansion of its industrial power at Germany's expense.[129]

The new and soon authoritative wartime leader Clemenceau had not sub-scribed to narrow conceptions of *Realpolitik* or maxims of balance-of-power diplomacy before 1914, even during his first premiership in the wake of the first Moroccan crisis. But in the course of the war he had made his name as a fierce critic of socialist pacifism and champion of a policy that rejected all notions of a negotiated "peace without victory" and emphasised instead the need to mobilise all moral and physical resources to achieve a complete victory over the Central Powers in the greatest "moral war" of all times.[130] This was essentially the mission on which he embarked as prime minister. At the same time, however, Clemenceau was even more reluctant than his predecessors to present far-reaching war aims and peace programmes to the French public and the wider world, seeking instead to concentrate public attention on the claim for Alsace-Lorraine.

But behind closed doors the French premier and those who came to shape France's peace strategies, notably Tardieu and the commerce minister Étienne Clémentel, had begun to develop a very ambitious postwar agenda whose underlying purpose was to guarantee France's longer-term security, national development and survival as an empire through a combination of more traditional and novel methods. This came to extend to a willingness to endorse, mainly for tactical reasons, Wilson's aspiration to create a League of Nations. But that should not distract from the fact that the underlying French concern was, and remained, to effect and gain Anglo-American sup-port for a substantial restructuring of the postwar balance of power in France's favour, all to constrain German power. With this aim in mind, the French General Staff had in 1916 gone so far as to propose that the German Empire

[128] Poincaré message and Viviani speech, 4 August 1914; Viviani speech, 22 December 1914, *Journal Officiel (Chambre)*, 1914, 3110–13, 3124–5; Poincaré (1926–33), V, p. 522; VI, pp. 67–71.

[129] See Jackson (2013), pp. 112–14.

[130] Clemenceau speech, 1917, cited after Winock (2007), p. 431.

should be broken up into nine independent states. But this was never a realistic option. From early 1917, two leading Foreign Ministry officials, the brothers Jules and Paul Cambon, had begun to prepare more targeted schemes whose objective was to establish a strategic frontier on the Rhine – either by outright annexation or by ending German sovereignty over the Rhineland in other ways. Championing the idea of an "international frontier of liberty" on the Rhine, Tardieu strongly supported this overall aim and devised a plan to create a Rhenish "buffer-state" to gain control over the strategically vital territory.[131]

Even more significant, however, was that Tardieu came to develop – as a complement – the wider and far more ambitious conception of an unprecedented Atlantic alliance and the ideological vision of a postwar community of shared values that was to unite the "civilised democracies of the west" – France, Britain and the United States – against the long-term danger posed by the German Empire.[132] Crucially, Clemenceau endorsed Tardieu's plans and developed concomitant ideas of his own. And it was in order to advance this scheme for an exclusive transatlantic alliance and security community that both Clemenceau and Tardieu would eventually adopt a more constructive attitude towards American and British League proposals. But this only really occurred *after* the end of the war. And both essentially came to view the *société des nations* in an instrumental fashion: as a means to draw Wilson and Lloyd George as far as possible into a more substantial postwar alliance. At the same time, once they had lost the crucial Russian ally in the wake of the October revolution French policymakers came to prioritise the creation of a "barrier" of new states to contain German ambitions in eastern Europe. They would seek to outbid the Central Powers in their support for east European national movements and their calls for "self-determination". But their chief concern throughout was power-political. Above all, they thus strongly backed from early on the establishment of an "independent Poland", pledging to guarantee its "free political, economic and military development".[133]

In pursuit of a parallel strategy, Commerce Minister Clémentel sought to expand the Anglo-French agenda of the Paris Conference of 1916 and elaborated plans for an exclusive "economic union" among the "allied democracies", which he had hatched with the assistance of his adviser Henri Hauser and the young lawyer Jean Monnet. Clémentel's union was to comprise "joint programmes for the importation of raw-materials" and, notably, a "redistribution" of the "means of credit", all ostensibly to foster Europe's revitalisation after the war but in fact mainly intended to redress the postwar economic balance of forces. Accordingly, the union was conceived as an exclusive

---

[131] Jules to Paul Cambon, 12 January 1917; Tardieu note, 20 January 1917, Tardieu Papers, vol. 417.

[132] Tardieu note, 20 January 1917, Tardieu Papers, vol. 417. Stevenson (1982), pp. 36–56.

[133] See Stevenson (1982), pp. 190–1.

combination of the victors – and selected "free peoples" – and designed to place tangible restrictions on Germany to prevent it from "pursuing anew its dream of economic domination" by way of various *Mitteleuropa* schemes.[134]

It is indeed worth emphasising that the ideas and conceptions that leading French policymakers developed and debated in the course of the war were in many ways no less aspirational than Wilson's League designs or emerging British plans for a reconfigured Atlantic concert system. But despite efforts to accommodate British and American priorities, they were ultimately based on very different premises. Crucially, they were all geared to the overriding objective of forging an exclusive rather than integrative postwar order. Exclusivity and containment were supposed to protect France. Any thought of eventually seeking some kind of accommodation with Germany, from a position of strength, was subordinated to this priority. While adapting to changing transatlantic realities, French conceptions were thus still fundamentally shaped by balance-of-power thinking.[135] They thus were in many ways incompatible both with Wilson's and prevalent British approaches; and it remained to be seen whether the far-reaching security commitments that French decision-makers desired from their counterparts in London and Washington were realistic, not least in view of the domestic constraints the latter faced. But an even more important question was how far – understandable – French security concerns and the ways in which French leaders sought to assuage them could eventually be reconciled with the requirements of a realistic peacemaking process and, in a wider perspective, the creation of a sustainable international system after the war.

XII.   Changing Attitudes towards the Idea of a League and Alternative Peace Conceptions in France

In contrast to British and American political leaders, France's wartime governments were markedly suspicious of initiatives to promote a League of Nations, regarding them as dangerously pacifist and detrimental to fighting *morale* and national unity, the often evoked *union sacrée*. They thus took measures to prohibit them and to censure pro-League propaganda – just as they sought to suppress all discussion about peace or possible peace terms. Similar official attitudes prevailed in the German Empire. And partly on account of such restrictions, yet also because the political cultures and prevalent traditions were not conducive to it, neither in France nor in Germany a more substantial pro-League movement emerged during the war. As noted, what dominated the tone of public and more private debates as well as

---

[134] Clémentel letter to Clemenceau, 19 September 1918, in Clémentel (1931), pp. 343, 346–7.

[135] For a different interpretation see Jackson (2013).

propaganda were, rather, the demands of the respective war-aims movements, which also of course propagated their often utopian and excessive "visions" of the grand aspirations that were to be realised through a victory of their side. A much smaller number of activists, associations and liberal yet chiefly social democratic and socialist politicians eventually began to make more concerted efforts to advance their own proposals for a League. But they did so only at a late stage – essentially from the spring of 1917. And more substantial governmental and non-governmental efforts to develop a League platform began even later, in France only in the summer of 1918 and in Germany only in the autumn of the same year.

The overwhelming majority of official French policymakers, including Clemenceau, and the most influential opinion-makers indeed maintained a dismissive or even hostile attitude towards the project of a "peace league" throughout the war. But a small and distinctive group of "juridical internationalists", led by Bourgeois and the president of the French Human Rights League, Ferdinand Buisson, took up the cause – and thus in fact revived their pre-war efforts to push for a stronger regime of international law and compulsory arbitration. In 1915, the venerable *association de la paix par le droit* (APD), which by then represented only a small minority of mostly pacifist internationalists, was the first to demand publicly the "constitution of a free League of pacific Nations". In a declaration chiefly authored by its president, the pacifist Théodore Ruyssen, the *association* postulated that all members of this League would have to "submit their differences without exception to arbitration and to place their allied forces at the service of general peace". But it was the *ligue des droits de l'homme* (LDH), in which Ruyssen also played a leading part, that became the most important non-governmental organisation that sought to promote an alternative, liberal-pacifist conception of peace in wartime France. The *ligue* not only organised the first public debates about the "conditions of a durable peace" but also circulated more elaborate schemes for a new association of nations. In November 1916, it issued a declaration demanding that what had to arise from the war, "through the victory of the Allies", was "a new international order founded on justice" and "a durable peace through the creation of a 'Société des Nations'". Significantly, all of the *ligue*'s blueprints foresaw an organisation whose initial core was to be formed by the states of the *Entente* and, following its intervention, the United States.[136]

The core ideas French internationalists developed about the remit and powers of a peace league were distinctly more ambitious than those of

---

[136] APD pamphlet "Peace through Justice" (January 1918), in Ingram (1991), pp. 30–1; "Congrès de la Ligue (1916) – Résolutions adoptées – Les conditions d'une paix durable", *Bulletin officiel de la ligue des droits de l'homme*, janvier 1917, p. 5. See Guieu (2006), pp. 90–6.

like-minded British and American activists. They included the demand to introduce compulsory arbitration for *all* forms of international disputes as well as the demand to provide the League with an international force strong enough to deter or counter all forms of aggression. While some *ligue* protagonists, including Ruyssen, favoured a more "realistic" concept that limited infringements of the member states' sovereignty, others joined Jean Hennessy in advocating an outright "federation of states" – initially formed by the "civilised" states of the *Entente* – that was to have an international parliament, a supreme court and an executive council "powerful enough to ensure the swift execution of its decrees". Hennessy even argued that the war manifested the urgent need for a "supra-nation" (*"surnation"*) or for a "global constitutional assembly" that had to frame a "global constitution".[137] From 1917, such "global" conceptions would also be promoted by new associations that were specifically formed to advocate a League, such as the *Ligue pour une Société des Nations basée sur une constitution mondiale.* Finally, it should be underscored that in contrast to the vast majority of their British or American counterparts, virtually all French pro-League activists subscribed to the maxim that new covenants of international law could not be effective without means to enforce them. And, being no less concerned about the German threat than leading government officials, they also emphasised that an international organisation could only safeguard peace and security if it was empowered to adopt "coercive measures", including "economic boycott" and "concerted action of international army and naval forces", to prevent or "repress" any attempt of aggression.[138]

It was only after the United States had entered the war that, compelled to react to Wilson's priorities, official French policy assumed a more favourable posture vis-à-vis the League. Premier Alexandre Ribot made the establishment of a *"Société des Nations"* an official French war aim and prevailed on the French parliament in June 1917 to adopt a declaration on behalf of the "organization ... of a League of Nations" that was to provide "durable guarantees for the peace and independence of great and small [states]".[139] Subsequently, the Ribot government established an inter-ministerial study commission for a *société des nations*, which came to be chaired by Bourgeois and charged with the task to prepare French plans for possible future negotiations with Britain and the United States. The League blueprint the study commission presented in June 1918 was clearly influenced by Bourgeois' prewar conceptions – and essentially outlined an organisation that was far more

---

[137] Ruyssen speech, 2 November 1917, *Bulletin officiel de la ligue des droits de l'homme*, 1er-15 avril 1918, p. 239; Hennessy (1917), p. 40; Guieu (2006), p. 95.

[138] *Bulletin officiel de la ligue des droits de l'homme*, 1er-15 août 1918, p. 456; Guieu (2006), pp. 95-6.

[139] Declaration of the French Parliament, 4 June 1917, cited after Blair (1993), p. 278.

authoritative, far more of a League *to enforce peace* than the organisation Wilson or British policymakers had in mind. And contrary to prevalent British and American conceptions it was also unequivocally designed as an instrument to guarantee a long-term containment of Germany, which was to remain outside the organisation for the foreseeable future. The organisation the Bourgeois commission proposed was to be established around an "International Council", made up of the leaders of governments of "free nations". It also was to feature an international judicial tribunal, which was to set international law and adjudicate it, and a secretariat. But the most distinctive feature of the commission's blueprint was an elaborate system of compulsory arbitration and sanctions that ultimately was to be controlled *and enforced* by the League's council and obliged member states to use force against aggressors and "violators" of international law. To ensure this, the commission proposed another radical departure: the creation of an international army to be employed under the executive council's authority.[140]

A French pressure-group that sought to gain support for the League idea in the French public and the halls of government would only be founded on 10 November 1918. The *Association française de la Société des Nations* (AFSDN) brought together a wide array of political and public figures, trade union leaders and prominent members of the *ligue des droits de l'homme*, among them Buisson. Yet it was Bourgeois who, as its president, dominated its programmatic vision. Following his lead, the *Association* came to lobby for far-reaching League schemes that essentially mirrored the internal proposals of the Bourgeois commission. It mapped out a *société des nations* conceived as an essentially "western" league of democratic states that would institute a forceful regime of obligatory arbitration and sanctions. And it championed the demand for an international force under the auspices of the League, whose key purpose would be to protect France against future German aggression.[141] But the mission Bourgeois and his collaborators pursued would turn into a prolonged political struggle. For a long time, Clemenceau and Tardieu only offered lukewarm support for his aspirational plans, which they considered unrealistic and hardly likely to meet France's existential security needs. Eventually, however, they would seize on Bourgeois' proposals to realise their cardinal aim of forging a fully-fledged postwar alliance with Britain and the United States.

Yet in France, like Britain, socialists and trade unionists actually led the way in mobilising wider support for the League, though it remained comparatively small and only gained momentum in 1917. At the same time, only a minority

---

[140] Commission report, 8 June 1918, AN, F12 8106; Miller (1928), II, pp. 238–46; minutes of the Bourgeois commission, 8 October 1917, Bourgeois Papers, PA-AP 29 (17).

[141] AFSDN programme, submitted to the French government, 18 December 1918, MAE, SDN, vol. 7; Buisson, Thomas and Prudhommeaux (1918).

among French socialists sought to re-forge internationalist bonds with German and Austrian social democrats, which the majority of the French socialist party and the trade union organisation CGT rejected. Albert Bourderon and Alphonse Merrheim, trade union leaders who backed this minority position, even attended the Zimmerwald Conference in September 1915 and participated in efforts to hammer out a common platform for a negotiated peace. But the majority among French socialists and trade unionists endorsed the argument that a defeat of German militarism had to precede any attempts to forge a socialist postwar order.

In February 1915, representatives of the French Section of the Workers' International and the CGT, notably Jean Longuet and Marcel Sembat, had participated in the first conference of *Entente* socialists in London. But they were not yet prepared had reach out across the war's trenches, vetoing Labour initiatives to invite German and Austrian representatives. Instead, the French delegates ensured that the assembled *Entente* socialists stipulated as their first task to show solidarity in the effort to defeat "German imperialism" and "Prussianist militarism". Only then could a "pacific federation of the United States of Europe and the world" be created that would guarantee "the liberty of peoples" and "the unity, independence and autonomy of nations".[142] Subsequently, the majority of the French socialist party committed itself to an agenda of "robust internationalism" that placed a far greater emphasis on security and enforcement than Wilson or the British Labour Party. It not only included the call for disarmament and extended democratic control of foreign affairs, but a system of compulsory international arbitration enforced through a "an arbitration court of the nations" and both military and economic sanctions.[143] Despite much debate and some initial moves towards a more cooperative approach, Pierre Renaudel and the majority among French socialists clung to these positions till the end of the war.

Nonetheless, the Socialists were the only party in France that came to advocate a more conciliatory approach to peacemaking and the German problem – *after* the defeat of the German Empire. This in part explains their eventual support for Wilson's peace programme and their hopes that the American president would manage to prevail over what they regarded as Clemenceau's backward-looking approach to peace. Eventually the majority also gravitated towards the position that French socialists should join their British counterparts and seek to build new bridges with the German Social Democratic Party. Yet they formulated stringent conditions that German social democrats had to meet to be considered partners in a negotiated peace, demanding that the latter had to repudiate their *de facto* support for German

---

[142] London conference resolution, February 1915, *Le Parti socialiste* (1918), pp. 7–8. Resolution, Congrès National, 29 December 1915, *ibid.*, pp. 129–33.

[143] "Manifeste du Congrès national", 29 December 1915, *Le Parti socialiste* (1918), pp. 129–33.

imperialism and acknowledge Germany's sole responsibility for the escalation of the war.[144] By the end of the war, only Longuet and a few other determined internationalists tried to push the party in the direction that MacDonald championed in Britain and that Wilson had by then abandoned, namely away from a "peace through victory" platform and towards a conciliatory peace agenda that built on "solidarity" with those German socialists who struggled against "absolutism" and "pangermanism".[145] Yet while gaining ground within the French socialist party, such aspirations remained extremely marginal in the wider spectrum of French wartime politics.

XIII. Radical and Less Radical Aspirations for a "Greater German" Imperial Hegemony over Europe

The war-aims programmes that came to prevail in the German Empire during the war, and the ideas of postwar order that informed them, were strikingly more expansionist and more overtly imperialistic. While differing in some fundamental ways, they shared a set of underlying characteristics. They stood in an underlying continuity with pre-war notions of German *Weltpolitik* insofar as they were clearly based on power-political assumptions according to which the war represented a new stage and intensification of the inherent struggle between the great powers that lay at the heart of international politics; yet they were also marked by a qualitative shift: the espousal of the core premise that in order to assert itself, and maintain its "independence" as a great power in the future, Germany had to attain a hegemonic position in continental Europe by imperialist means.

In more "moderate" conceptions, which were espoused by Chancellor Bethmann Hollweg and by and large dominated in the Foreign Office, this was to be achieved by creating a German-dominated economic and political "association" in and beyond central Europe. In the more radical visions that were first propagated by the more extreme protagonists of the burgeoning "war aims movement" and later even came to be expanded in the circles around the increasingly predominant Supreme Army Command, Germany was to create, by conquest and force, not only an "eastern empire" at the expense of Russia but a wider imperial system in which it would dominate its western and eastern neighbours and reduce them to mere "vassal states". And it should be emphasised that all of these visions of a German-dominated postwar Europe became even more radical, if not utopian, once its leaders had manoeuvred the German Empire into the unprecedented struggle against the United States.

---

[144] *Report of the Sixteenth Annual Conference of the Labour Party*, 26 January 1916.

[145] "Manifeste du Congrès national", 29 December 1915, *Le Parti socialiste* (1918), pp. 129–33; Imlay (2017), pp. 23–6.

Guiding ideas that came to inform official German war-aims programmes and general postwar conceptions had first been laid out in Chancellor Bethmann Hollweg's secret – and decidedly Eurocentric – "September Programme" of 1914, essential parts of which had been drafted by his assistant Kurt Riezler. The main objective of Bethmann's programme was to secure Germany's future as an independent great power by establishing not only "its economic predominance over *Mitteleuropa*" but an overall preponderance on the European continent. What Bethmann envisaged would have altered the status quo of July 1914 decisively. He sought to annex the northern parts of Lorraine, transform Belgium into a "vassal state" and incorporate not only Luxembourg but also a strategic zone of French coastal territories, including Dunkirk, Calais and Boulogne, into the German Empire. In the east, Russia was to be pushed away from German borders and its rule over all non-Russian "vassal peoples" to be ended. Beyond this, the German chancellor mapped out the contours of a German imperial-hegemonic order in Europe: not only Austria-Hungary, and eventually Poland, but also France, Belgium, the Netherlands and Denmark were to be compelled to join a "central European economic association", nominally on a footing of "equal rights" but "in fact under German leadership".[146]

What Bethmann Hollweg proposed had been markedly influenced by the *Mitteleuropa* conception of Rathenau, who now directed the Raw Material Department of the German War Ministry. Building on the ideas he had publicised in 1913, Rathenau argued that the higher purpose of the German war effort should be to bring about a fundamental reorganisation of Europe by creating a customs union and, more generally, an economic community that was to comprise Germany, Austria-Hungary, and the current enemy-states France and Belgium. The "final objective" of this economic imperialist design was to establish a "Mitteleuropa unified under German leadership, politically and economically consolidated against England and America, [and] on the other side against Russia".[147] Yet it was the *Mitteleuropa* conception of the national-liberal publicist and parliamentarian Friedrich Naumann that would have a greater impact on the postwar conceptions espoused by more "moderate" liberal imperialists in Germany. In 1915, Naumann called for the creation of a "world power *Mitteleuropa*", which was to constitute itself around an extended union of the German Empire and Austria-Hungary and thus revive the liberal notion of a "greater Germany" of 1848. In Naumann's conception,

---

[146] Bethmann Hollweg programme, 9 September 1914, Reichskanzlei Nr. 2467 Bl. 54 ff.; Bethmann Hollweg to Delbrück, 16 September 1914, in Fischer (1961), p. 100. See *ibid.*, pp. 98–101. See Winkler (I/2000), pp. 340–1; Jarausch (1973). Bethmann's private secretary Kurt Riezler contributed central ideas.

[147] Rathenau to Bethmann Hollweg, 7 September 1914, Rathenau (1929), p. 12; Rathenau diary (1967), 25 July 1912, p. 169. See Gall (2009), pp. 176–7, 185–6.

German pre-eminence in the new European order was to be *primarily* based on economic dominance. But it was essentially, like Rathenau's, an imperialist project in which Germany would use its economic-cum-political power to coerce the "consent" of other, in fact subordinate states and peoples. And like all other imperialist visions hatched in wartime Germany, it was predicated on a decisive German victory.[148]

Yet what actually set the dominant tone in inner-German debates were the nationalist and right-wing "war-aims parties" in the *Reichstag* and the leading voices of what had grown into an expansive war-aims movement in which the Pan-German League became most influential pressure-group. These parties and groups propagated distinctly more far-reaching imperialist and annexationist visions of a new "German order" in Europe. By the autumn of 1917 the Pan-Germans, the newly founded "Fatherland" Party and the industrial and agricultural associations behind it, and other agitators for a "Greater Germany" had rallied behind the agenda of a "Greater Germany" and a "*Siegfriede*", a German "victorious peace" – or "Hindenburg Peace" – that was to be imposed after Germany had decisively defeated its enemies, which by then included the United States. And, crucially, what they demanded reflected the outlook of the heads of the Supreme Army Command, Hindenburg and the politically decisive figure Ludendorff, who had come to assume all but dictatorial roles after Bethmann's forced resignation in July 1917. Broadly speaking, the proponents of a *Siegfriede* agenda asserted that only a peace of conquest and imperialist domination could justify the sacrifices of the war and, crucially, secure Germany's future as a world power. The underlying aim was to make the German Empire the undisputedly predominant power in Europe, particularly by annexing key strategic territories not only in the west – in Belgium and France – but also in the east. Here Russia was to be pushed back "to Asia" and the German Empire was not only to dominate but also to "Germanify" Russian Poland, the Baltic provinces and northwestern Russia. Further, the British Empire, regarded as Germany's most dangerous enemy, was to be constrained by the imposition of a sizeable indemnity.[149]

One leading proponent of an annexationist peace programme and a "Greater Germany of the future" was the National Liberal politician Gustav Stresemann. He was also one of the most notable German actors who began to develop a deeper understanding of the critical relevance of American power – on decidedly antagonistic premises. Stresemann argued that the wider objective of the German war effort had to be nothing less than the establishment of an "economically and militarily unassailable" German predominance over Europe. He thus called for an annexation of the coastal provinces of

---

[148] Naumann (1915), pp. 31, 40–2, 101; Winkler (I/2000), pp. 343–4.
[149] See "Gründungsaufruf der Deutschen Vaterlandspartei", 2 September 1917, in Mommsen (1960), pp. 420–1; Winkler (I/2000), pp. 352–3.

northern France as far as Calais, a westward "correction" of the entire French–German frontier, the reduction of Belgium into a colonial vassal state and the consolidation of a German-dominated central European economic "union". And he justified this expansionist programme by underscoring time and again that its realisation was critical for Germany's future as a great power in what he imagined as the all-defining postwar competition both on the world market and in the international system: the stand-off between a "Greater Germany", the British Empire and, above all, a newly preponderant United States whose economic power had been decisively "strengthened" as a result of the war.[150] In the 1920s, Stresemann would develop a more cooperative and realistic conception of a new Atlantic order – and concert.[151] During the war, however, his outlook epitomised the prevalent German penchant for neo-imperial designs that clashed with the most basic requirements of a stable and legitimate postwar order.

Indeed, what prevailed among those who tried to develop ideas of postwar order were either more traditional or radicalised *realpolitical* or more precisely *power-political* assumptions about the future international relations. What they envisaged was a future "order" in which the military, political and economic struggle between the great powers would continue, and the race for imperial domination would merely enter a new phase. The emphasis thus lay on fortifying Germany's position in this struggle by asserting its continental preponderance – and this could only be achieved through an unequivocal "victory" in the war.[152] And what proved crucial was that virtually all of the actors who actually influenced the often byzantine decision-making processes in wartime Germany both misjudged and underestimated the influence of the United States and its messianic president. Consequently, they never developed outlooks, let alone conceptions, that would have allowed them to come to terms with the new realities of what had essentially become a Euro-Atlantic theatre of war – and international system.

Neither Bethmann nor the wartime protagonists of the German Foreign Office – the secretaries of state for foreign affairs Jagow and Zimmermann – ever developed approaches that pointed beyond a radicalised Wilhelminian *Weltpolitik*. Only at a very late stage would Zimmermann's successor Richard von Kühlmann tentatively pursue a different conception – namely during the German–Bolshevik peace "negotiations" in the wake of the October revolution. Kühlmann's aspiration was to return to Bismarckian balance-of-power

---

[150] See memorandum, 7 November 1914, Stresemann Papers, vol. 139; Stresemann speeches, 26 May 1916 and June 1917, in Berg (1990), p. 44; Wright (2002), pp. 73–6; Edwards (1963), pp. 34 ff.

[151] See Cohrs (2006), pp. 121–5.

[152] See e.g. Bethmann statement to Cambon, Cambon report, 28 July 1914, in Herwig in Hamilton and Herwig (2003), p. 164. See *ibid.*, pp. 163–4.

strategies and conclude a comparatively moderate peace with the Bolshevik regime. Essentially, he thus tried to prepare the ground for eventual negotiations with the western powers and, ultimately, a restoration of the core of Europe's pre-war great power system. Collaborating with the Austro-Hungarian foreign minister, Count Ottokar Czernin, Kühlmann sought to bypass the hardliners of the German Supreme Command and forge a "modern" peace settlement that appeared to conform to western and notably Wilsonian principles. His core rationale was to invoke respect for the "right of free self-determination" of the populations of Poland, Courland, Lithuania and others that had lived under Russian rule and to encourage them to declare their independence while accepting the "protection" of the Central Powers. Thus, not only a *cordon sanitaire* vis-à-vis Russia but also a German order for eastern Europe was to be founded in which the new states were formally independent but in fact ultimately vassals of Germany.

The wider aim of Kühlmann"s backward- rather than forward-looking *and strikingly Eurocentric* scheme was to pave the way for an "honourable peace" with the western powers and thus to create conditions for rebuilding a functioning European order after the war. Kühlmann held that even though they had become antagonists it was "still a common interest of all great states" to ensure that the European states-system would "not perish".[153] But by the end of 1917 this was wishful thinking. Neither French nor British leaders were prepared to countenance an "honourable peace" on these premises. And for all his references to self-determination Kühlmann had only a limited grasp of the new transatlantic and global realities the war had created – and no concept at all of how to fit American power and Wilson's aspirations into his restorative scheme. More fundamentally, it was no longer possible to seek a peace based on the premises of the "old European order" and somehow return to the *status quo ante* of 1914.

In any case, Kühlmann's hopes were crushed when Ludendorff prevailed and, following the offensive of mid-February and occupation of large parts of Ukraine and Belarus, imposed core elements of his far more draconian "peace" agenda in March 1918. The resulting treaty of Brest-Litovsk, signed on 3 March, was a hybrid that also contained "modern" elements but was dominated by Ludendorff's militarist expansionism. Through this treaty he and those who agitated for a "Hindenburg Peace" appeared to have taken decisive steps towards realising the vision of a "Greater German" imperial hegemony over Europe that was to allow the key Central Power to shift its forces to the west, win the war against the western Allies through a decisive offensive, and thus

---

[153] See Kühlmann statements, 20 December 1917 and 1 January 1918, Matthiass and Morsey, *Der Interfraktionelle Ausschuß*, II, pp. 4, 640; Kühlmann note, autumn 1917, in Hildebrand (1998), p. 113; Kühlmann (1948), pp. 523–4; Hertling speech, 29 November 1917, Fischer (1961), pp. 414–20; Czernin (1919), pp. 217–18.

position itself for the inexorable future struggle against the British and American world powers.

The "peace" of Brest-Litovsk indeed seemed to fulfil the hopes of those who had aspired to build a German "eastern empire". The Bolshevik regime, on whose behalf Trotsky had acted as chief negotiator, in the end ceded what had been "Russian Poland", Courland, Lithuania and, crucially, Ukraine where a Ukrainian People's Republic had already declared its independence from Russia in January 1918. While Kühlmann and others still insisted that one had thus aided the "self-determination" of the peoples between Germany and Russia, what had really shaped the "peace" were Ludendorff's militarist-strategic rationales. And the outcome was a soon untenable German imperial system of formally independent but *de facto* subordinate satellite states.[154]

In some ways, the aims Ludendorff and his acolytes pursued at Brest-Litovsk indeed prefigured the more totalitarian projects of hyper-imperial domination that would lie at the heart of National Socialist notions of expanding a Greater German Empire in the east. For they not only desired to conquer "living space" for the Germanic people but also to "Germanify" it. In contrast to National Socialist plans, however, what shaped the rather inchoate German ideas of 1918 were not visions of ethnic cleansing but rather more "traditional" notions of expanding a German imperial sphere of influence.[155] For Lenin, who soon told his inner circle that he would only honour the terms of Brest-Litovsk as long as it served his strategic aims, the treaty marked an essential success insofar as it gave the Bolshevik regime a critical "breathing space" for consolidating its power, which he then would accomplish through tactics of "equivocating, waiting and receding". With the benefit of hindsight, Lenin would argue that the agreement was "significant" because it showed that the Bolsheviks had for the first time found a way "under extremely difficult circumstances" to "use the contradictions" between the imperialist powers, or more precisely between "German" and "American imperialism", in such a way as to "ensure the ultimate victory of socialism". By making concession to one "imperialist group" they had managed to "protect" themselves against the "persecutions" of the other, western "imperialist groups".[156]

The frustration of Germany's great western spring offensive of 1918 and the subsequent defeat of the Central Powers shattered not only

---

[154] See German High Command proposals, 3 December 1917, Der Friede von Brest-Litovsk (1971), pp. 19 ff. The German Empire indeed imposed Carthaginian terms on the Bolshevik regime. Russia lost roughly a third of its territory, half of its coal production and was left with only a narrow access to the Baltic Sea. Through supplemental treaties, finalised in August 1918, it was then settled with an indemnity of six billion Goldmarks.

[155] See Münkler (2013), pp. 661–74; Liulevicius (2005).

[156] Lenin speech, 27 November 1919, Degras (1951–53), I, pp. 221–2.

all aspirations to consolidate a German "eastern empire" but also, for the foreseeable future, all prospects of establishing a German imperial hegemony in and beyond *Mitteleuropa*. Yet the "peace" of Brest-Litovsk still had important implications for the way in which peace negotiations would eventually be approached after the Great War. Of particular import here was the fact that the treaty had been endorsed by a majority in the *Reichstag* on 22 March, although it blatantly violated the principles set forth in the "Peace Resolution". Only the Independent Social Democrats had voted against it, while the Majority Social Democrats eventually abstained. Unsurprisingly, this would tarnish the credibility of later appeals by German liberals and leading centrist social democrats for a moderate negotiated peace – not only in the eyes of the *Entente* leaders but also in Wilson's perception. And it would thus further constrain the German room to manoeuvre to open up a path towards "equitable" peace negotiations and a place in a new Atlantic order after the war.

XIV.   Between Opportunism and the Search for Alternative Conceptions of Postwar Order. German Reorientations towards the League – and the United States

In view of the power-political priorities and assumptions that continued to govern the mind-sets and actions of even the more moderate German policymakers – and of course those of the more radical expansionists – it is hardly surprising that in these quarters no postwar conceptions emerged that were *not* premised on some form of German domination. Nor did any forward-looking ideas gain contours here for addressing the problem of Germany's "central position" and the structural challenges of creating a less conflict-prone international system. No plans for anything resembling a peace league were hatched. Only Kühlmann and a few other Foreign Ministry officials mused about the desirability of somehow reconstituting a pre-war European states system whose bases had been largely eroded by the war; and even they had nothing or very little to say about how to deal with the new power and influence of the United States.

In fact, both German wartime decision-makers and the propagandists who clamoured for far-reaching war aims rejected the idea of a League of Nations and denounced British and American League proposals as tactical ruses intended to conceal Anglo-Saxon aspirations for global predominance. At the same time, German authorities reacted with marked suspicion and repressive measures when some German liberals and particularly social democrats began to call for a League. It was only to prepare the ground for his initiative to secure a negotiated peace when conditions appeared favourable for the Central Powers that Bethmann Hollweg publicly signalled, in November 1916, that

Germany was ready to *"enter a League of Nations at any time"* and even to *"lead an organization which curbs those disturbing peace"*.[157]

But this overture was not backed up by concrete German proposals; nor did it lead to any serious efforts to define what authority the League was to have and how a German membership could be reconciled with the Central Powers' stated war aims. Fundamentally, Bethmann – who in principle supported the idea of an international "order based on law" – never actually believed that a peace league could guarantee Germany's future security and development as a great power. More importantly, that the German Empire would join an international organisation never entered the strategic calculations of those who really were in charge at this stage, Ludendorff and Hindenburg. They were hardly prepared to sacrifice their vision of a German-dominated European "order" for the sake of entering into what they regarded partly as an Anglo-American ploy and in general terms as an illusory project.[158]

Yet there were also other political actors within Germany who could not gain decisive influence during the war but nonetheless constituted an increasingly coherent and important counterforce – namely the reformist forces of the Liberal, Centre and Social Democratic majority parties in the *Reichstag*. Their protagonists were, among others, the Centre politician Matthias Erzberger and the aforementioned centrist social democrat Philipp Scheidemann, who from 1915 had become the key proponent of a negotiated "peace of understanding" – or "Scheidemann peace" – in Germany.[159] Behind them a multifaceted and initially loose coalition of interests had emerged that included more forward-looking representatives of German industry and high finance, yet also trade union leaders. Particularly influential within this coalition was a Hamburg-based Hanseatic faction led by the bankers Max Warburg and Carl Melchior and the shipping magnate Albert Ballin, who were profoundly concerned about ensuring that after the war Germany would be able to operate in an "open" world economy unimpeded by political barriers and at the same time still believed in the power of intertwined economic and financial interests between the most advanced states. They thus underscored early on that the German government was well-advised to turn towards the United States and build on what they regarded as the common German-American interest in rebuilding a "liberal" world-economic system after the war.[160]

Since the spring of 1917 the *Reichstag* majority parties and those who supported them in wartime Germany's divided political force-field, had rallied around two sets of demands that were intimately connected. On the one hand,

---

[157] Bethmann Reichstag speech, 9 November 1916, Thimme (1919), pp.163–4; Jarausch (1973), pp. 250–3.

[158] See Pyta (2007), pp. 227 ff., 244 ff.; Nebelin (2010), pp. 401 ff. 461 ff.

[159] Scheidemann speech, Reichstag, December 1915, Scheidemann (1929), I, pp. 296–7; Scheidemann speech, Reichstag, 15 May 1917, Scheidemann (1917), pp. 3 ff.

[160] See Warburg (1952); Philipson (1984).

they demanded substantial internal reforms, essentially a democratisation of the German political system and above all steps to strengthen the authority of the parliament. On the other, they advocated, also in reaction to Wilson's proclamations, a conciliatory compromise peace – a demand that was most resonantly expressed in the "Peace Resolution" of 1917. What informed this resolution, which had been instigated by Erzberger, was the idea that a reformed Germany had to contribute to the forging of a new international order by seeking to reconcile and cooperate with those states that were now its enemies. Significantly, taking up Wilson's demands, the "Peace Resolution" parties had made the commitment to the establishment of a League an integral part of their reform programme. The authors of the resolution emphasised the need for a *universal* international "organisation of law" that set binding rules for arbitration and the peaceful settlement of disputes. And in a way that echoed the American president's earlier "peace without victory" rationales they had also called for a negotiated peace of "understanding and lasting reconciliation among peoples" that ruled out "enforced territorial expansion and political, economic or financial violations".[161]

It has to be stressed that as long as Ludendorff and Hindenburg held the reins of power and there was still a dominant expectation that a victorious Germany would be able impose a "peace of victory" the parties of the *Reichstag* majority could not speak for a majority of the German public or gain any real influence on German decision-making processes. But their leaders became the actors who would seek to chart a more cooperative and western-orientated course against the backdrop of a looming German defeat, most notably Erzberger. And they were indeed the crucial forces that then stood behind the attempt to pursue a new, republican German foreign policy and to lead the new German republic into a reformed international order after the war.

From August 1918, when the spectre of a possible defeat became more concrete, Kühlmann's successor Admiral Paul von Hintze and those in the Foreign Office who saw the need for a more than tactical reorientation of German international policies also began to seek common ground with the *Reichstag* majority. Based on a distinctly sober assessment of German interests and possibilities, Hintze argued that the German government should propose a peace agreement on the basis of the American president's Fourteen Points programme. And with the support of both Erzberger and Scheidemann, who backed the new "American orientation", Hintze then prevailed on the weak chancellor Georg Hertling to commit to this strategy.[162] Unquestionably, such eleventh-hour efforts to align with Wilson's agenda were thus intricately

---

[161] See Peace Resolution, 19 July 1917, Matthias and Morsey (1959), I, pp. 6–10, 93; Scheidemann (1921), pp. 80 ff.; Winkler (I/2000), pp. 348–50; Jarausch (1973), pp. 260–2; Miller (1974), pp. 304–9.
[162] See Krüger (1985), pp. 34–6.

bound up with the hope of opening the door to a moderate peace; but particularly the aspirations of the reform proponents in the *Reichstag* went beyond such tactical considerations.

The same can be said of the numerous German plans for a League of Nations that were drafted in this changing political context. In the summer and autumn of 1918, reformist politicians and opinion-makers who sought to prepare a German response to Wilson came forward with ambitious League designs. Hintze reasoned that more substantial support for a League could strengthen Germany's appeal to Wilson – and his successor Wilhelm Solf even invoked Kant's *Perpetual Peace* to convey to the American president that the new German League enthusiasm built on a long tradition. Only in September the Foreign Office and a cross-party committee of the *Reichstag* then began more serious discussions about what kind of German conceptions for an international organisation should be put forward. Shortly thereafter, Foreign Office planners formulated elaborate legalistic blueprints. But the main impulses for Germany's evolving League policies came from Erzberger, who had become an increasingly pivotal actor since the "Peace Resolution", and later from Walther Schücking, a committed internationalist and authoritative international-law expert who had been marginal in the Foreign Office during the war but now seized his opportunity and would eventually put his stamp on the League conceptions the German delegation presented in 1919.[163]

In late September 1918, Erzberger seized the initiative and advanced an elaborate scheme for a universal League of Nations. Seeking to build bridges to Wilson and underscore the internationalist commitments of those in Germany who desired a negotiated peace, he also invoked the authority of Kant and outlined an organisation that included all "states", was founded on the premise of an "equality of rights of all peoples" and established "international guarantees of justice" by means of a "comprehensive" regime of international law" and collective security. Erzberger's guiding aim was to place "the relations between states on the basis of lawfulness" in the same way that a "*Rechtsstaat*" – a "state based on the rule of law" – guaranteed lawfulness for "individual persons". And, reflecting the concerns of Warburg and economic internationalists in and beyond Hamburg, he also demanded that the League had to guarantee "free economic development" and equal commercial "rights" for all states. To underscore what he saw as common German-American interests he explicitly called for a universal application of the "Open Door" and unrestricted global trade and traffic.[164] As will be shown, after the war Schücking would develop even more aspirational League conceptions.

[163] See Schücking (1915); Hoeres (2004), pp. 483–5.
[164] See Erzberger programme, 30 September 1918, in Erzberger (1920), pp. 309–10. Erzberger (1918), esp. pp. 3–4; 90–144, 161–71, 184 ff.; Erzberger (1919).

The far-reaching designs of Erzberger and Schücking reflected the difficult but remarkable attempts of the *Reichstag* majority forces to modernise German international policies – not just to improve the prospects for a lenient "Wilsonian peace" but with the intention of overcoming core deficiencies of Wilhelminian *Weltpolitik* and addressing the structural problems that had led to the war *and* stifled Germany's inner liberalisation. But this was a process that could only really gain momentum in the aftermath of the war. And, revealingly, it was only then that, through an initiative launched by Erzberger and the liberal Ernst Jäckh, steps would be taken to found a specific pressure-group to promote the idea of a League in Germany. This mirrored developments in France. The "German League for the League of Nations" would be established in December 1918 – with the backing of the German Foreign Ministry and clearly in an effort to highlight the new German government's internationalist credentials vis-à-vis Wilson. But the "League" did not merely serve tactical purposes. Erzberger intended it to become a rallying point for influential German League supporters that allowed them to refine their ideas not just for a new international organisation but also for an international "order of law".[165]

Of even greater political significance was the fact that particularly from the summer of 1917 the general aim to found a League had been strongly supported both by leading majority social democrats Ebert and Scheidemann and by Hugo Haase, the leader of those who had voted against further war credits in early 1917 and formed the Independent Social Democratic Party (USPD). All German social democrats could invoke their long-standing commitment to the idea of an international organisation, which after all had already been an important feature of their pre-war agenda. Especially Scheidemann now renewed the call for a social democratic "League of Nations".[166] He and other leading social democrats stressed the need for a universal and inclusive organisation that replaced power politics with arbitration and thus safeguarded the security and independence of its members. But the ideas they formulated remained comparatively undeveloped, hardly going beyond the level of general policy manifestoes.[167]

What Haase and the USPD focused on was a campaign both for a renewal of internationalist cooperation and solidarity among socialist parties from all the belligerents, and for a peace without annexations. Though far more restrained because of the fear of being labelled unpatriotic, the Majority

---

[165] Jäckh (1928), p. 22; See Wintzer (2006), pp. 47–50.

[166] Scheidemann speech, Reichstag, December 1915, Scheidemann (1929), I, pp. 296–7; Scheidemann speech, Reichstag, 15 May 1917, Scheidemann (1917), pp. 3 ff.; Scheidemann (1929), II, pp. 342–50.

[167] Scheidemann RT speech, 9 December 1910, in Scheidemann (1929), I, p. 151. See Gellinek (1994), pp. 24–36.

Social Democrats had presented, in the Stockholm memorandum of June 1917, their own proposal for a negotiated peace without annexations or indemnities. They called for a re-establishment of the status quo of July 1914 yet also a fundamentally reformed international order in which, under the auspices of a League, self-determination became a guiding principle and both arbitration and disarmament were to be made mandatory.[168] In the autumn of 1918, Scheidemann and Ebert would re-accentuate the Social Democrats' demand for an authoritative League of Nations.[169]

Yet it was only at this very late stage of the war – when armistice negotiations were already underway – that the leaders of the Majority SPD deemed it politically possible to state expressly that Wilson's Fourteen Points should form the "basis for a democratic peace". They now proposed the convocation of an International Socialist Congress to unify socialist forces against those who opposed peace negotiations "on this basis". On 2 November, Scheidemann declared that the "fate of the world" depended on the reunification of all socialist and progressive forces on behalf of a conciliatory peace.[170] His appeal would fall on fertile ground among leading Labour politicians, particularly MacDonald and Henderson, and even met with a positive echo among some French socialists. But Scheidemann's underlying hope of gaining Wilson's support for charting path towards a social democratic "peace of understanding" would soon be frustrated.

XV. Radical Socialist Counter-Visions and the Rise of the Bolshevik Challenge

What deserves to be highlighted, then, is that the most important social democratic majority parties in Europe – Labour and the SFIO on the side of the *Entente* and the MSPD in Germany – came to develop peace agendas during the war that, although they long remained markedly Eurocentric, were fundamentally compatible with Wilson's aspirations. Potentially, this could make these parties and the forces they represented important allies in the making of a "progressive peace". But because the majority factions long refused to renew transnational cooperation across the war's dividing-lines, the most significant steps to establish a new International and a common peace platform *across* the war's trenches were taken by the more radical socialists. They represented minority positions. But what they advocated came to constitute the most important ideological counter-vision, and challenge, to Wilsonian as well as more evolutionary social democratic aspirations to

---

[168] Stockholm Memorandum, 12 June 1917, *Protokoll* (1973), pp. 39–44; Imlay (2017), pp. 45–7.
[169] Scheidemann, "Der Frieden und die Internationale", *Vorwärts*, 2 November 1918, p. 1.
[170] *Ibid.*

reorder Europe and the wider world. The vanguard of what now became a more potent communist movement included the exiled leaders of the Russian Social Democratic Labour Party's Bolshevik faction, Lenin and Trotsky, and the future heads of the German Spartacist movement, Karl Liebknecht and Rosa Luxemburg, who sought to form a revolutionary International "on the ruins of the old" and accused the "false" pro-war socialists of allying with the capitalist ruling classes.[171]

First steps to this end were taken at the First International Socialist Conference at Zimmerwald in September 1915. At one level, the Zimmerwald socialists united behind Trotsky's demand for a "peace without indemnities or annexations". Yet the underlying aim that he and Lenin pursued, in line with their earlier thinking, was to seize on the crisis of the war to incite a trans-European revolutionary process – as the first stage of a global revolution. The so-called Zimmerwald resolution, which underscored these aspirations, was chiefly drafted by Trotsky. It stipulated that "the war which has produced this chaos" was "the outcome of imperialism", of the attempt of "the capitalist classes of each nation" to "foster their greed for profit by the exploitation of human labor and of the natural treasures of the entire globe". And it proclaimed that by transforming this "imperialist war", which pitted workers, and peasants, against one another, into a "civil war" between the working classes and the "capitalist classes", it would not only be possible to end the war but also to overthrow the entire liberal-bourgeois capitalist system. The Zimmerwald socialists thus appealed to the workers on all sides to take up the struggle for a "peace among the peoples". And they renewed the demand that the "right of nations to self-determination" must hence be "the unshakable foundation" of international relations. But they also emphasised that a "real" peace could only be created if, led by the radical-socialist vanguard, workers and peasants erected a new order based on "international proletarian solidarity". And like their German comrades, Lenin and Trotsky considered violence a necessary and legitimate means to instigate the world revolution history commanded.[172]

Following their successful coup d'état in Petrograd and the historical *caesura* of the October revolution, the Bolsheviks would unquestionably place themselves at the head of a burgeoning communist movement and socialist aspirations for a "new world order". And while it was still very uncertain whether they would actually prevail against the forces of the old order, the fact that they managed to topple Kerensky's provisional government and seize power in Russia in November 1917 lent new weight to their cause and indeed

---

[171] Liebknecht letter, September 1915, Lademacher (1967), pp. 55–6.

[172] Zimmerwald Resolution, September 1915, International Socialist Commission at Berne, *Bulletin* No. 1 (21 September 1915); Lenin, Works, XVIII, pp. 207, 235. See Priestland (2009), pp. 85–8; Koenen (2017), pp. 656–743.

added a new dimension both to the war and to the ideological war within it. For they not only took Russia out of the war but were now also in a far stronger position to pursue their wider world revolutionary agenda, which relied on the power of ideology and propaganda more than on the force of arms. By the time Wilson presented his Fourteen Points Lenin had thus indeed become an important counter-figure in the wider struggle over the shape of the postwar order. Yet it is worth stressing again that it would be erroneous to say that from the watershed year of 1917 this struggle mainly turned into a competition between liberal-progressive "Wilsonian" and Leninist-Bolshevik visions.[173] What proved far more decisive both for the reordering of Europe and on a global scale was the competition between Wilson's aspirations and the priorities of the eventual European victors of the war, Britain and France.

Like Lloyd George and Clemenceau, the American president eventually supported a limited intervention against the Bolsheviks in the escalating Russian civil war. And he also came to see and present his peace programme as a means to counter the appeal of Bolshevik ideology. But Wilson never came to view Lenin as his crucial political adversary. He mainly aspired to prevail over the forces of the "old order" on both sides of the European trenches. And in the war's aftermath he would mainly invoke the "Bolshevik threat" to underscore the urgency of making a progressive peace.[174] By contrast, Lenin indeed came to perceive Wilson as a key antagonist. For a long time, he had one dominant concern that other radical socialists, notably Rosa Luxemburg, also voiced. He feared that the wider appeal of revolutionary socialism could be stifled because the leaders of the warring powers would make all kinds of rhetorical concessions, promise "democracy", "self-deter-mination", "peace" and "reforms of every kind" to induce the workers to continue fighting the war. And in this context Lenin came to regard the American president as a particularly dangerous enemy of the revolution who, with his "hypocritical phrases" about "democracy" and a "union of nations", merely provided an insidious cover for the interests of American and European capitalist oligarchies.[175]

To counteract such unwelcome influence and gain the propagandistic upper hand the Bolshevik leadership on 8 November 1917 – one day after starting the uprising in Petrograd – issued its famous peace decree. It called for the "immediate opening of general negotiations for a just and democratic peace". And while Lenin had earlier only heaped scorn on Wilson's "peace without victory" formula and centrist socialists like Morel and Kautsky who had

---

[173] See Mayer (1964).

[174] Wilson "Fourteen Points" address, 8 January 1918, *PWW*, XLV, pp. 538–9. See Chapter 10.

[175] Lenin (1960–70), XVIII, pp. 207, 235; Lenin, "Letter to the Workers of Europe and America", 21 January 1919, Lenin (1970), pp. 375–8.

embraced it, he and Trotsky for tactical reasons now proposed something akin to a "peace without *military* victory". Yet in their calculation this, of course, was to pave the way for something fundamentally different from what Wilson desired, namely a transnational triumph of socialism. In competition with the American president, the Bolsheviks also appealed directly to the "belligerent peoples", notably to those of "the most advanced nations" – England, France and Germany. They called for the abolishment of "secret diplomacy", publishing all secret treaties the Tsarist regime had made with the *Entente* governments. And they not only renewed the call for a peace of "self-determination" but also stressed that this principle had to extend not only to Europe but also to all "distant, overseas countries", so that the peace terms would be "equally just for all nationalities, without exception".[176] The Bolsheviks' subsequent six-point programme of December 1917, mainly authored by Lenin, basically reiterated these maxims and demands while also containing more elaborate, yet still sweeping, proposals for a fundamental reorganisation of Europe – and the world – on the basis of "self determination". It stipulated that wherever a people had been under imperial rule or otherwise oppressed, it should be allowed to decide its future through a free referendum.[177] This transformative agenda indeed posed a radical threat to which Wilson, Lloyd George and all other wartime leaders had to respond.

The proclamations of Lenin and Trotsky would not set the stage for general peace negotiations – nor as yet for a dynamic world-revolutionary process. Rather, as we have seen, they initiated the remarkable process of Brest-Litovsk. Yet Lenin had of course not lost sight of his core revolutionary agenda. For him, the new "peace of Tilsit" was indeed only a preliminary peace, a tactical necessity imperative to ensure, first of all, the survival of the Bolshevik regime and *then* to instigate an *all-European* revolution. Whether the revolutionary spark could be carried into the United States was a lesser concern at this stage.[178]

But the Bolsheviks' propagandistic barrage against Wilson would not abate. In October 1918, Georgi Chicherin, who came to act as Commissary for Foreign Affairs, submitted a "peace proposal" to the American president that in fact contained a blistering Bolshevik critique of his peace programme. Chicherin contrasted the high-minded rhetoric of the Fourteen Points – notably the pledge to respect Russia's "independent determination of her political development" – with the reality of the actions Wilson had taken, above all his authorisation of America's participation in the western intervention in the Russian civil war.

---

[176] Bolshevik peace decree, 8 November 1917, Tucker (1975), p. 545. See Mayer (1967), pp. 262–5.

[177] See Degras (1951–3), I, pp. 1–3.

[178] Appeal for the Formation of the Communist International, 24 January 1919, Degras (1951–3), I, p. 136–7; Lenin, Letter to the Workers of Europe and America, 21 January 1919, Lenin (1970), pp. 375–8.

Further, Chicherin castigated the double standards of Wilson's League proposals, asking why the American president, who purported to seek a "free league
of nations", demanded freedom only for Poland, Serbia and Belgium yet not for
"Ireland, Egypt or India". On behalf of the Bolsheviks, Chicherin asserted that if
it was to serve the higher purpose to make future wars "impossible", the league
had to be established, not on Wilson's terms but as a Soviet "league of mutual
aid of the working masses" that brought the "expropriation of the capitalists of
all countries" and universal disarmament.[179]

However tenuous their grip remained at first, the Bolsheviks' seizure of
power, the revolutionary maxims that Lenin and Trotsky advanced and the
strategies they pursued to realise them, which eventually extended to the
formation of a Third International in January 1919 – all of this created novel
challenges not only for Wilson but also for the governments of all the other
belligerents. And it would have a multifaceted long-term impact on twentieth-
century international history. More immediately, it would have a distinctly
ambivalent but clearly significant influence on the Paris Peace Conference. For
hence a more than theoretical alternative, indeed revolutionary vision of how
Europe – and the wider world – might be reordered after the catastrophe had
arisen. And, as will be shown, at least for a time most western leaders and
opinion-makers came to see the spread of the Bolshevik revolution as a
distinct possibility – particularly once Germany and central Europe were cast
into a state of turmoil. More diffuse yet potentially also more powerful still was
the transnational influence and gravitational pull of Bolshevik ideology.

But the "Bolshevik threat" could and would also be exaggerated and instrumentalised in various ways – by Wilson and others who sought to push for more
far-reaching progressive reforms and, eventually, by the representatives of the
vanquished who sought to attain a more "lenient" peace. In the end, Lenin,
Trotsky and other leading communists would fail to spur a trans-European and
ultimately a global revolution. And what really becomes clear in retrospect is
that the actual impact of the Bolshevik factor on the reordering processes after
the Great War was never as critical as has later often been claimed.[180] The
Bolshevik challenge remained real and politically virulent in the aftermath of the
war. Initially, however, it seemed as if – after Greater German ambitions had
been defeated, not just on the battlefield – the western powers and especially the
United States had not only won the military conflict but were also poised to win
the political-ideological war that had raged since 1914.

---

[179] Chicherin note to Wilson, 24 October 1918, Degras (1951–3), I, pp. 112–17.
[180] Cf. Mayer (1967); Westad (2018), pp. 43 ff.

8

No "Peace without Victory"
And the Making of the Frail Atlantic Armistice of 1918

Ultimately, it proved impossible to end the First World War through a negotiated peace – either at an early stage or, later, through some kind of "peace without victory". In many ways, the more the war escalated beyond all previous wars, and the higher the stakes and the heavier the sacrifices became for all sides the harder it became politically to bring it to an end through some form of compromise settlement based on a common realisation of the futility and unbearable price of its further escalation. Rather, when the cataclysm finally came to an end – in the west – it did so because of the sheer exhaustion of one side, or more precisely after Ludendorff and Hindenburg concluded that the Central Powers no longer had any hope of winning against the superior manpower and resources of the Allied and Associated Powers. And, as should be stressed, this occurred at a point – in mid-September 1918 – when above all the by then ever more palpable American contribution made the war seem unwinnable in their eyes.

Both in the most significant attempt to attain a negotiated "peace without victory" – around the turn of 1916–17 – and in the process that then actually led to the armistice of November 1918, Wilson and the new power of the United States came to have a pivotal part. In a wider sense, as will be shown, re-appraising why and how the *Great* War was brought to an end can serve to highlight yet again the degree to which not only militarily but also politically and ideologically it had become an essentially transatlantic conflict. Understanding its specific transatlantic dynamics and interdependencies is particularly important if one wants to fathom why the war ultimately did not end with a more unequivocal defeat of the Central Powers, especially Germany. Yet it is even more vital for illuminating the more salient question of why the armistice agreement that would be concluded at Compiègne on 11 November 1918 could only furnish such a tenuous and in many ways problematic basis for eventual peace negotiations and, ultimately, for establishing basic underpinnings of an Atlantic peace order that had prospects of enduring.

I. The Elusive Quest for a "Peace without Victory"

Wilson became the most powerful but by no means the only actor who sought to impress on the belligerents, most urgently in the autumn of 1916 and early

1917, that precisely because the conflict had turned into an unprecedentedly costly and blood-letting "systematised" mass slaughter – and into a conflict that no side could win without paying a price that no victory could justify – it was imperative to end it as soon as possible through a negotiated peace.[1] Similar arguments were made before and after him, particularly by liberal and socialist internationalists and pacifist associations on both sides of the trenches and in Europe as well as in the United States. They came forward with numerous appeals to end the war through some kind of negotiated peace, which they also saw as a first step towards a new international order.

As we have seen, appeals of this kind were notably made by the liberal and labour protagonists of the Union for Democratic Control, the leading activists of the Woman's Peace Party and other American Progressives, the German social democrats who supported Scheidemann's call for a negotiated "peace of understanding" and later the Stockholm memorandum of 1917, and the reformist parties behind the Reichstag's "Peace Resolution" of July 1917.[2] More strident demands for a "peace without annexations and contributions" had been made by the more radical socialists who backed the Zimmerwald resolution of 1915 and eventually – as a tactical measure – by Lenin and the inner circle of the St Petersburg Soviet who in November 1917 issued the Bolshevik peace decree.[3] But all of these initiatives remained essentially fruit-less. They had little to no effect on the strategies and war-aims policies of the governments of the various belligerents, and their resolve to carry on the war until their side had prevailed. On 1 August 1917 Pope Benedict XV had added his voice, issuing a peace note and a seven-point peace plan to each of the belligerent powers. Yet his exhortations likewise fell on deaf ears – except in Austria-Hungary.

Earlier, there had also been a few largely tactically motivated peace initia-tives by the governments of the Central Powers, yet revealingly none by the *Entente* Powers. The most important German initiative had been the peace note Bethmann Hollweg submitted on behalf of the Central Powers on 12 December 1916. Drawing on proposals by the Austrian Foreign Minister Stephan Freiherr von Burián and the Progressive parliamentarian Conrad Haussmann, Bethmann proposed immediate negotiations to find "a suitable basis for the establishment of a permanent peace" and appealed to Wilson to back his initiative. Bethmann claimed that his overture was driven by the will

---

[1] Wilson Prolegomenon, ca. 25 November 1916, PWW, XL, pp. 67–70, 67, 68, 69; Wilson note, 18 December 1918, PWW, XL, pp. 273–5.

[2] Scheidemann speech, Reichstag, December 1915, Scheidemann (1929), I, pp. 296–7; Stockholm Memorandum, 12 June 1917, Protokoll (1973), 39–44.

[3] Zimmerwald Resolution, September 1915, International Socialist Commission at Berne, Bulletin No. 1 (21 September 1915); Bolshevik peace decree, 8 November 1917, Tucker (1975), p. 545.

to prevent a further escalation of a "catastrophe" that threatened to ruin Europe's "moral and material advance". It was also motivated by the desire to unite "all the discordant voices of Wilhelmine Germany". But what dominated were tactical concerns. Essentially, his was a rather transparent attempt to make peace from a position of strength and assert German preponderance in Europe at a time when the Central Powers had just seized Bukarest – and the United States still remained neutral.[4] Predictably, however, Bethmann's proposals came to nothing; they irritated the American president and were categorically rejected by the *Entente* governments.

Shortly thereafter, Wilson himself embarked on a more genuine quest to end the war through a negotiated peace. And the bid for a "peace without victory" that he launched in the wake of his re-election in November 1916 indeed became the most significant initiative to this end between 1914 and 1918. By this time, three fundamentals of Wilson's peace policy had been reinforced which would all soon prove untenable. He was still determined to keep a "neutral" United States out of the war. He was still convinced that only by acting as a "neutral arbiter" he would be able to pave the way for a durable peace. And he still reckoned that he actually had the authority and political and financial leverage to succeed. It was on these premises, yet without having developed any effective mediation *strategies*, that Wilson on 18 December 1916, sent a peace note to the governments of the *Entente* as well as to the Central Powers.[5]

While asking both sides to clarify their war and peace aims, Wilson's note sought to impress on all European belligerents that the time had come to enter into discussions about a negotiated peace so that "millions upon millions lives will not continue to be sacrificed" and an irreparable "injury" to "civilization itself" would be avoided. Further, Wilson called on the European governments "to settle the issues of the present war upon terms" that would "certainly safeguard the independence, the territorial integrity, and the political and commercial freedom of the nations involved". But the overriding task he defined pointed to the heart of his progressive peace agenda. He argued that it was in the "higher" common interest of all states to transcend the "uncertain balance of power amidst multiplying suspicions" and to "consider the formation of a league of nations to ensure peace and justice around the world".[6]

[4] German note, 12 December 1916, in Lansing to Wilson, 14 December 1916, *PWW*, XL, pp. 231–2. See Zelikow (2021), pp. 81–106.
[5] Beforehand, Wilson had sent his informal emissary Colonel House on numerous but inconclusive "sounding missions" to the different European capitals. See Zelikow (2021), pp. 17–47.
[6] Wilson, "Appeal for a Statement of War Aims", 18 December 1918, *PWW*, XL, pp. 273–5. See also Wilson's draft note, 25 November 1916, *ibid.*, pp. 70–4.

In a confidential Prolegomenon or introductory essay to the peace note the American president had put down his thoughts about the preconditions for "a lasting peace" after a conflict that had escalated into a "vast, gruesome contest of systematized destruction". He argued that if the German Empire achieved a decisive victory and came to dominate Eurasia, this would only set the stage for future conflict – as even Germany's "unmatched genius for military organization" could not "keep the whole of Europe in military subjection". Yet a defeat of Germany would only create on a greater scale the kind of scenario France had experienced after 1870: it would inevitably lead to "the annexation of her colonies", "an indemnity for the rehabilitation of Belgium" and "the reimbursement in part of the military expenses of the Entente". And "such an outrage to her pride" would not be forgotten, it would "rankle in her breast as did the rape of Alsace-Lorraine to the French". Wilson thus concluded that a victor's peace for either side would not make for an "enduring peace".[7] And he noted that even after two years of escalation, the Great War still presented the "statesmen of the world" with an "unparalleled opportunity" to avoid such a scenario. For never "in the world''s history" had two warring sides been so "equally matched", and "the slaughter been so great with as little gain in military advantage" so that both sides should realise that victory could only be brought about "by the attrition of human suffering" for which the eventual victor would pay as high a price as the vanquished. The American president reasoned that under such conditions – when there was no longer any "glory" to be gained "commensurate with the sacrifice of the millions of men required in modern warfare to carry and defend Verdun" – only a negotiated peace without victory would furnish the "psychological basis" for a durable "peace structure". His – elusive – hope was that it would thus even be possible to eliminate war "as a means of attaining national ambition".[8]

Had it succeeded, Wilson's initiative would not only have kept the United States out of the Great War but also produced a completely different outcome than that of 1918. Yet it is highly doubtful that it could indeed have become, as Wilson desired, the starting-point for a fundamental recasting of the international system. At one level, it might have led to something resembling a *status quo ante* settlement in which many of the main features and players of the pre-war system, including the eastern empires, would have been preserved. On another, it might have set processes in motion that would have led to the creation of a different kind of transatlantic postwar order in which not only the United States and the *Entente* Powers but also the German, Austro-Hungarian and Russian Empires would have joined a very different kind of League of Nations – while independent east European states may not have

[7] Wilson Prolegomenon, ca. 25 November 1916, *PWW*, XL, pp. 67–70, 67, 68, 69.
[8] *Ibid.*, XL, pp. 69–70.

come into existence (yet). But all of this pertains to the realm of counter-factual history because Wilson's quest would remain futile – as futile as all other attempts to end the war through negotiations. In fact, it was to be the last substantive bid of this kind before the autumn of 1918. Ironically, it was at a time when it had already become abundantly clear that his initiative would fail that the American president made his most powerful appeal for a "peace without victory" to the world in his address before Congress on 22 January 1917. In fact, his globally transmitted speech was essentially a last-ditch attempt to put public pressure on all of the European belligerents to accept his proposal – and thus to keep the American republic out of the war.[9]

For by then both the British and the French governments had rejected the American initiative more or less categorically. Together with their Italian and Romanian allies the *Entente* Powers on 10 January 1917 responded to Wilson's appeal by presenting a carefully sanitised statement of their common war aims, which included "the reorganization of Europe" founded on "respect of nationalities and full security and liberty [of] economic development" for all nations, "great or small"; the "liberation" from "foreign domination" of Italians Poles, Czechoslovaks, Southern Slavs, Romanians and "populations subject to the tyranny of the Turks"; the evacuation of all "invaded territories"; the restoration of Belgium, Serbia and Montenegro; and "equitable compensations and indemnities for damages suffered" through the war.[10] But neither Lloyd George nor the French premier Aristide Briand were actually prepared to negotiate about a cessation of hostilities. Fundamentally, both leaders and a clear majority within their cabinets remained committed to the rationale of fighting on until Prusso-German imperialism had been decisively defeated – and they would then be in a position to impose peace terms that guaranteed what they considered to be fundamental political, economic and security interests. Thus, both governments were mainly concerned about ensuring the continued mobilisation of their populations. And, crucially, both held out for an American intervention, expecting that eventually Wilson would no longer be able to maintain his policy of "neutrality" and the American power and its immense resources would tip the war's scales decisively in their favour.

As noted, the British Empire had reached its worst financial impasse in the autumn of 1916 and its ability to prosecute the war was hence critically dependent on further American loans. In May 1916, the bleak financial outlook had already led Chancellor of the Exchequer Reginald McKenna to urge Asquith to accept American mediation to explore a peace of accommodation on the basis of what Colonel House and Foreign Secretary Grey had outlined in a

---

[9] Wilson Senate address, 22 January 1917, *PWW*, XL, pp. 533–9.
[10] Allied response to Wilson's note, 10 January 1917, *PWW*, XL, pp. 439–41.

common peace memorandum.[11] Keynes, who favoured the idea of a negotiated peace, hoped that the spectre of a looming bankruptcy would compel the British government to end the war – and sweep away the old caste of British leaders, including the increasingly dominant "crook" Lloyd George.[12]

By mid-November 1916, wider financial and political considerations had prompted the former Conservative Foreign Secretary Lord Lansdowne to propose immediate peace talks. Lansdowne, who emerged as the most prominent "appeaser" in Asquith's faltering government, argued that in view of the strains the war put on British resources and the immense casualties it had caused – by then more than one million – the prospect of a decisive victory seemed "remote". Yet, echoing the concerns of Cecil and other leading Liberals and Tories, Lansdowne also argued that a further escalation of the war would inflict far greater damage – it would unravel "the fabric of our civilization" and what remained of the European state-system, fomenting instead chaos and anarchy.[13] But Lloyd George, then heading the Ministry of Munitions, adamantly opposed Lansdowne's initiative; and once he had succeeded Asquith as head of a new coalition government in December 1916, he blocked any further move towards "appeasement" and a negotiated peace. Ever since September, the rallying cry with which Lloyd George had established himself as a charismatic wartime leader had been that the "fight must be to a finish – to a knockout". And what he hence concentrated on – with remarkable success – was to ensure the British Empire's continued mobilisation and remobilisation.[14]

Consequently, the new British premier had no interest in a success of Wilson's "peace without victory" initiative and effectively repudiated it in a first programmatic speech in the House of Commons on 19 December.[15] In retrospect, he would stress that he feared that the "resolutely pacifist" American president could have "contented himself" with attempting to "balance" what he regarded as utterly irreconcilable: the likely terms German leaders would have proposed and the "proposals of the Allies". In his eyes, what Wilson proposed thus threatened to lead to "an inacceptable and inconclusive peace".[16] And while the Independent Labour Party welcomed that "the head of the greatest neutral Power in the world" had "come to the support of the same ideas" they had "long advocated" and Henderson favoured a more conciliatory course, a majority in the Cabinet sided with the prime

[11] Hankey diary, 24 May 1916, in Roskill (1970), p. 274.
[12] Skidelsky (1994), pp. 335–6, 346–8.
[13] Lansdowne memorandum, 13 November 1916, CAB 29/1.
[14] Lloyd George interview with Howard, 26 September 1916, *The Times*, 28 September 1916; Lloyd George (1933–36), II, pp. 852–9.
[15] Lloyd George speech, House of Commons, 19 December 1916, Hansard, Commons, 5th series, vol. 88, cols. 1334-5.
[16] Lloyd George, (1933–36), IV, p. 1779.

minister.[17] Following the eventual American entry into the conflict, Lloyd George would adhere all the more uncompromisingly to his "knock-out blow" maxims and reassert that no peace could be made until "Prussian military despotism" had been overcome and the Allied Powers "could dictate terms". The British premier insisted that this constituted the only "effective starting-point" for a lasting peace settlement.[18]

The leaders of France's wartime governments had been at least as determined as their British counterparts to rebuff all American initiatives for a negotiated peace.[19] Soon after the outbreak of the war, the assertive foreign minister Delcassé had set the tone in summarily rejecting any notion of peace that was not based on a decisive victory over the German Empire. These were fundamentals from which the Briand government would not depart in December 1916. In fact, from the vantage-point of French decision-makers, Wilson's demands and House's earlier peace feelers had posed a threefold challenge. Domestically, they threatened efforts to preserve national – and imperial – unity during the bloody struggle. This had remained the overriding domestic priority ever since President Poincaré, in August 1914, proclaimed his *union sacrée*, which was to bring and keep together all the major forces in French politics until victory had been achieved.

As it turned out, France's "sacred union" proved more durable than its German equivalent, the *"Burgfrieden"*, only beginning to fray during the "terrible year" 1917. And in 1916 the prevalent consensus to maintain it effectively marginalised the relatively few proponents of a negotiated peace that could be found among French socialists and radicals.[20] Further, in the eyes of French leaders Wilson's peace initiative also constituted an acute threat to inter-allied unity, which they resolutely sought to preserve. What mattered more, however, was that it clashed with the overriding priority that not only a majority of France's political elites but also the most relevant pressure-groups – and the wider French public – shared: the concern to ban what was perceived as the existential threat posed by the aggressive German Empire. The core maxim of French wartime ideology and propaganda remained that, as Briand had reiterated in the spring of 1916, the only peace the French republic could accept was one based on "the conclusive defeat of Germany's ... ambition to dominate" Europe.[21]

Because of these core domestic, strategic and ideological concerns the Briand government would essentially close ranks with its British *Entente*

---

[17] *Report of the Sixteenth Annual Conference of the Labour* Party, pp. 134–5; Mayer (1964), p. 161; Egerton (1978), pp. 54–5.

[18] Imperial War Cabinet Meeting 32, 15 August 1918, CAB 23/7.

[19] See e.g. House diary about talks with Delcassé, 13 March 1915; Hodgson (2006), pp. 104–9.

[20] See Becker and Krumeich (2008), pp. 77–81.

[21] Briand to Jusserand, 28 May 1916, Jusserand Papers MSS (31).

partner to obstruct the American president's peace initiative in January 1917. Then, once the United States had entered the war, Briand's eventual successor Clemenceau would insist as adamantly as Lloyd George that the war had to be carried on until German designs to subjugate Europe had been unequivocally squashed.[22]

In Germany, Wilson's appeal had been welcomed by Scheidemann and all those who had clamoured for a negotiated peace since 1914. But the official German response was lukewarm and ambivalent. While for tactical reasons signalling his readiness to consider Wilson's overture even the relatively conciliatory chancellor Bethmann Hollweg, whose own peace initiative had just been rebuffed, was ultimately not prepared to consider serious negotiations – and to agree to a process in which the American president would play a mediating role. Yet even if he had assumed a different attitude, his authority would have been far too weak to ensure the requisite domestic support for entering a negotiation process, let alone for some kind of moderate peace settlement. Fundamentally, Bethmann and the protagonists of the German Foreign Office – Secretary of State Jagow and the ascendant Zimmermann – came to agree that Germany had no interest at that point in American mediation and the prospect of "general peace conference" in which the United States participated. For they reckoned that it would hardly be possible in such a setting to safeguard what they saw as vital German interests. By and large, they remained committed to the aims Bethmann had set out in his September programme of 1914, and which remained irreconcilable both with Wilson's and the *Entente* Powers' essentials. Most fundamentally this applied to the assertion of Germany's political, strategic and economic preponderance in Europe, which still included strategic control over Belgium.[23]

What ultimately proved even more consequential, however, was that those who really came to hold the reins of power in the byzantine German leadership structure around the turn of 1916–17 and would become even more dominant after Bethmann had been ousted in July 1917 – Ludendorff and Hindenburg – rejected any notion of a negotiated peace even more categorically than Lloyd George or, eventually, Clemenceau. For they continued to assume that a decisive military victory both in the east and on the western front lay yet within their grasp – and that this would ultimately put them in a position to impose a *Siegfrieden* and realise their far-reaching ambitions to establish a German "super-empire" in and beyond Eastern Europe.[24] In the end, the Supreme Command's profoundly misguided decision to resume

[22] Lloyd George statement, Imperial War Cabinet Meeting 32, 15 August 1918, CAB 23/7; Clemenceau speech, 11 November 1918, *Journal Officiel* (Chambre), 1918.
[23] Bethmann Hollweg to Bernstorff, 18 August 1916, Bernstorff (1920), pp. 279–80.
[24] Ludendorff (1919), part X; Nebelin (2010), pp. 343–400.

unrestricted submarine warfare in the Atlantic on 1 February 1917 brought Wilson's campaign for a "peace without victory" most obviously to a halt – and undermined it for good. Yet it of course also marked the beginning of the end of Ludendorff's and Hindenburg's imperialist ambitions.

At one level, that no way of pre-empting a further escalation of the war could be found through Wilson's or any other endeavours for a negotiated peace was thus indeed due to the tactical considerations and strategic priorities of the principal European decision-makers. Both the leaders of the *Entente* and those of the Central Powers clung to the underlying rationale that only winning the war would put them in a position to achieve a peace that satisfied what they defined as existential aims and interests – by ultimately imposing their terms from a position of strength. And, crucially, the key actors on both sides of the trenches *actually still expected* that they could achieve a decisive victory – and thus neither had the political will nor felt decisive pressure to envisage substantial negotiations.

Yet there were also deeper reasons that went beyond the aims, calculations and expectations of individual leaders or governments. What had a decisive influence was precisely that, as noted, the longer the war lasted, and the costlier it became for all sides, the more all the different governments became chiefly preoccupied with the need to ensure the continued mobilisation of their soldiers and wider populations and a basic domestic-political unity and cohesion. And this led political leaders and propagandists to enunciate war aims, and raise expectations, that only a decisive victory, not some kind of compromise peace could possibly fulfil. Ultimately, they all came to be shackled by the consequences of their wartime ideologies whose common core message had become that only a decisive defeat of the enemy could justify the war's ever increasing exertions, and bring the kind of peace and compensations that, not only in material terms, vindicated the sacrifices that had been made. As has rightly been stressed, in this crucial respect too decision-makers on all sides thus found themselves caught in a trap of rising and eventually uncontrollable *and conflicting* expectations that, if at all, they could only hope to meet after their troops had prevailed on the battlefield.[25] And once the United States had entered the war, Wilson too would have to confront the core mobilisation challenges facing a wartime leader. In responding to these challenges he would depart from core premises of his "peace without victory" agenda and emphasise ideological war and peace aims that in fact militated against it. Above all, this applied to his new core rationale that it would only be possible to make a progressive peace once Germany's "military party" and the political and military "masters" of the Wilhelmine empire's old regime had been ousted – or defeated.[26]

---

[25] See Leonhard (2014), pp. 809–10.
[26] Wilson address to Congress, 2 April 1917, *PWW*, XLI, pp. 525–7.

In view of all this, it was no coincidence that the processes which actually led to the end of the Great War were set in motion when the key decision-makers of one side, indeed the military "masters" Hindenburg and Ludendorff, reckoned that they no longer had any realistic prospects of winning it. In the wake of the "peace" of Brest-Litovsk, Ludendorff had committed himself to a *vabanque* game. Pursuing an all-or-nothing strategy, he placed all his bets on breaking the Allied front in the west through a great summer offensive; and he surmised that if this offensive were to be repulsed, the German Empire would be bound to lose the war. By mid-September the failure of Ludendorff's all-or-nothing approach became evident, and by the end of that month he informed the Kaiser that only a rapid call for armistice negotiations could prevent a massive breakthrough of the enemy. By this time both he and Hindenburg were convinced that the Central Powers were so exhausted that they would soon be defeated by an enemy coalition that was reinforced by a rapidly growing military presence and of course the seemingly inexhaustible resources of the United States. In fact, they anticipated that their collapse was only a matter of time. While recommending that Wilson should be approached as a mediator, Ludendorff now also demanded that domestic reforms, steps towards a parliamentary monarchy, should be initiated. While he argued that this would make German overtures to the American president more credible, his plan was mainly intended to shift responsibility for the fiasco of his own "strategy", and what *de facto* would be a German defeat, onto the "defeatist" reformist forces that had long called for a negotiated peace and that, as he and Hindenburg would soon claim, had stabbed Germany's valiant soldiers in the back.[27]

Ludendorff's move created the decisive pressure for the formation of the reformist government under Max von Baden in early October, which was backed by the *Reichstag* majority parties. They had been rallied by Erzberger to step in and seize responsibility both to foster Germany's democratisation and to end the war on acceptable terms. The new protagonists immediately confronted daunting tasks on the home as well as on the international front. Both von Baden and Erzberger were aware that in order to put the new government into a not entirely hopeless negotiating position it would have been necessary to begin by consolidating it, announcing a new programmatic course centring on constitutional reforms and the goal of a negotiated peace on the premises of Wilson's programme – and only *then* propose an armistice. Yet because of the pressures the Supreme Command exerted, they felt compelled to take rapid action and did exactly the opposite. In a note sent to Wilson on 3 October, von Baden launched a precipitate appeal for an

---

[27] See Nebelin (2010), pp. 461–508.

armistice and thus indeed presented the American president with an opening to shape the way in which the Great War ended – on the western front.[28]

II. No Wilsonian Victory. The Paths to the Armistice of November 1918

The tumultuous and ever accelerating process that led to the armistice signed at Compiègne on 11 November 1918 unquestionably set crucial parameters for the peace negotiations of 1919 and the remaking of international order in the aftermath of the Great War. But the outcome and significance of this process – which carried on for five weeks, first revolved around the dramatic exchange of notes between Wilson and the von Baden government and only at the eleventh hour extended to minimal consultations between a self-styled American arbiter and the leaders of the *Entente* – have been interpreted in very different ways. Affirmative interpreters of Wilson's "internationalist" design have portrayed the armistice agreement as a programmatic foundation-stone of a "Wilsonian" peace that ensured the creation of the League of Nations and established standards for a "new order" which were then corroded by the *realpolitical* strategies of the *Entente* governments. And they have portrayed the making of the agreement overall as a victory of the diplomacy the American president and his key collaborator Colonel House pursued.[29] By contrast, "realist" critics have claimed that Wilson's misguided pursuits led to a premature ceasefire and end to the war and thus ultimately thwarted the chance of forging a more durable peace, one based on a complete victory of the Allied and Associated Powers over Germany that then would have put them in a position to force a decisively constraining peace on the defeated power.[30]

It is worth emphasising at the start that both the timing and the nature of the armistice that brought an end to the *Great* War only highlighted the extent to which it had essentially turned into a Euro-Atlantic war in which American power and the political-cum-ideological influence Wilson had acquired now played a determining role in this respect too. But the armistice process also revealed that the American president, who came to pursue a strikingly unilateral and high-handed approach, was in fact *not* in a position to impose his terms and visions on the *Entente* Powers – or could do so only in a very shallow manner. More importantly, though, the main deficiency of the by no means "Wilsonian" armistice of November 1918 was *not* that it prevented a more "total" defeat of Germany and thus undermined the prospects of a stable peace. For while it would have changed the power-political preconditions of peacemaking – and "brought home" to the German elites and wider public the

---

[28] See Krüger (1985), pp. 36–7.
[29] Keynes (1919), p. 60; Knock (1992), pp. 169–84; Walworth (1977).
[30] See Tooze (2014), pp. 222–3, 231.

reality of defeat – even a more unequivocal victory of the western powers would not have "eliminated" Germany as the state with the greatest demographic and power potential on the European continent. Even then, it would have remained a key element in a highly interdependent Euro-Atlantic state-system, and world economy. And because none of the western leaders – including Clemenceau – ever seriously contemplated breaking up the Bismarck state, one of the key questions of the eventual peacemaking process would also have remained fundamentally the same, namely: how to come to terms with the defeated but still powerful German state – by power-political coercion and containment or, once initial guarantees had been assured, through more realistic policies of negotiation, accommodation and integration.

What really was most problematic about the armistice and the way in which it was concluded was something else. In short, both the agreement and the process that led to it provided only a very fragile basis for the eventual peace settlement and, at a deeper level, for advances towards a sustainable Atlantic order. For they manifested that there was actually only a very superficial consensus between Wilson and the *Entente* leaders about approaching peace negotiations on the basis of the president's Fourteen Points agenda – and that, more profoundly, they were still far from any real agreement about how peace was to be made and a durable new order would be created. At the same time, the outcome of 11 November indeed encouraged exaggerated hopes for a moderate "Wilsonian peace of justice" among those who struggled to negotiate on behalf of the new German government. And it encouraged tendencies to rely too much on Wilson's power and insist too narrowly on what they came to interpret as quasi-legal claims for such a peace. All of this created very inauspicious preconditions for a *more deeply realistic* modern peacemaking process: one in which the victors first reached a firm consensus about the parameters of the peace settlement and then the ground was prepared for substantial negotiations between them and the vanquished and thus, ultimately, for a more legitimate outcome.

The German note of 3 October reflected the hope of a majority of German reformist politicians and diplomats that Wilson could still be approached as a quasi-impartial umpire or mediator between the Central Powers and the *Entente* governments – and, strikingly, it addressed the American president as though he was actually in a position to play such a role. It should be noted, however, that von Baden himself originally had not favoured a one-sided appeal for an armistice on advantageous "Wilsonian terms". He not only distrusted Wilson's underlying motivations but also argued that the new government should prove its commitment to a credible peace policy by offering negotiations to all the Allied and Associated powers – rather than pursue a course that could be interpreted as an attempt to drive a wedge between the United States and the *Entente* states.

But the new chancellor ultimately went along with the "strategy" favoured by the leading figures of the *Reichstag* majority parties, and above all by

Erzberger, who by this time had espoused a decidedly American or Atlanticist orientation. They too had their suspicions vis-à-vis what they regarded as Wilson's double-edged pursuit of progressive peace designs and propaganda warfare. Yet, fearing a draconian "Clemenceau peace" and harsh British demands, they had come to view the peace programme he had outlined in January 1918 and elaborated thereafter as the best possible basis for an eventual peace settlement that kept the *Entente*'s vindictiveness in check and safeguarded essential German interests. But it is important to stress that they also regarded it as the most auspicious platform on which a reformed Germany could find a new place in a recast postwar order – and, crucially, in a League of Nations – the making of which, they assumed, would be decisively influenced by Wilson's vision. It was at this point that Erzberger presented his own "German plan" for a "league of peoples" and argued most cogently that in order to build bridges to Wilson and enhance its credibility the new German government should highlight its commitment both to a domestic agenda of democratisation and a strong, universal League of Nations.[31] The new "American orientation" of German policy was also steadfastly backed by the new secretary of state for foreign affairs in von Baden's government, Wilhelm Solf.[32]

Von Baden's note appealed not only for an immediate armistice but also for actual peace negotiations that then were to lead to a formal peace treaty. Paving the way for such negotiations – with Wilson's support – would remain the key priority of German policymakers in the coming weeks and months. What the protagonists of the new government hoped for at this stage was essentially a status quo peace, premised on the restoration of Belgium and, in the east, full autonomy for all the territories that had been "liberated" from the Russian yoke. Further, they hoped to make sure that Germany would be among the founding members of a universal League. Following the recommendations of Erzberger and Solf, the note explicitly recognised Wilson's Fourteen Points of January 1918 and the peace programme he had advanced in subsequent speeches as the cardinal reference points for the armistice as well as the eventual peace, alluding particularly to what the American president had specified in his widely noted "Liberty Loan" address on 27 September. Should its armistice offer be rejected, the von Baden government envisaged calling for a "people's war" to carry on the fight until a military decision had been reached.[33]

In the address he delivered in New York to launch the Fourth Liberty Loan, Wilson had made a point of reasserting and even elaborating his progressive conception for "a *secure* and *lasting* peace" – and, remarkably, he had

---

[31] Erzberger statement, 12 September 1918, IFA, II, p. 530.
[32] Erzberger, League design (1918). See Krüger (1985), pp. 34–6.
[33] German note to Wilson, 3 October 1918, Ludendorff (1920), p. 535.

re-accentuated fundamentals of his "peace without victory" vision. The president had stressed once again that a "permanent" peace had to be premised on a fundamental equality of rights of all nations, irrespective of their power, and on the freedom of all peoples to have a government of their own choosing. And, significantly, he had renewed his commitment to the creation of a universal League of Nations that notably had to comprise all belligerents. Calling such a League the "indispensable instrumentality" of a durable peace, he had emphasised that it could not be "formed now" while the war was still raging. For then it would be "merely a new alliance confined to the nations associated against a common enemy". Rather, in order to "guarantee the peace" in a new, more effective way it had to be founded as a "general alliance" that would then foster "common understandings and the maintenance of common rights". Wilson thus declared that the League should be established at a general peace conference convened after the war – and become "the most essential part of the peace settlement". Finally, the American president had again committed himself to one cardinal demand that had been central to his earlier "peace without victory" programme and was to acquire critical political significance in the coming months. It was the demand for a peace that brought the "ultimate triumph of justice" because it was based, not on terms that one side imposed on the other but on "fair negotiations" and a common effort to exercise "impartial justice in every item of the settlement, no matter whose interest is crossed" and thereby ensure "*the satisfaction of the several peoples whose fortunes are dealt with*".[34]

Wilson had thus re-accentuated his claim to act as arbiter of a novel kind of "just peace" that was to be negotiated between representatives of all the states and peoples whose "fortunes" were affected by the war, including those of the Central Powers. Yet he had also stated more unequivocally than before that he would not negotiate with those who in his view represented the old militaristic and autocratic Germany. He had proclaimed that the "German people must by this time be fully aware" that he could not "accept the word" of those who "forced this war upon us" – and who by forcing a "peace of conquest and force" on the Bolsheviks at Brest-Litovsk had shown that they did "not intend justice . . . observe no covenants, accept no principle but force and their own interest".[35] But there was an even more fundamental tension or contradiction in Wilson's approach, which now became palpable. It was the tension between, on the one hand, ideas of a "peace of justice" *through negotiations* and, on the other, notions of acting as a pre-eminent, essentially unilateral "*arbiter* of justice". This fundamental inconsistency had in fact characterised the American president's pursuits ever since 1916; yet it now acquired critical

---

[34] Wilson address, 27 September 1918, *PWW*, LI, pp. 127 ff., 132–3.
[35] Wilson address, 27 September 1918, *PWW*, LI, p. 129.

political significance in his conduct towards both the *Entente* and the Central Powers. This first became apparent in mid-September 1918, in Wilson's reaction to an initiative of the Austrian government to hold, under his supervision, peace talks on neutral ground. While stressing the need for a newly "fair" and inclusive negotiating process, he also conveyed rather uncompromisingly that he had already worked out the terms and conditions of a "just" peace – terms and conditions that were essentially non-negotiable. Yet however stubbornly he resisted it, the American president would eventually have to recognise that he was simply not in a position to "decree a just peace".[36]

Essentially, then, Wilson saw von Baden's note of 3 October as an opportunity to assume the role to which he had aspired ever since 1916. He now endeavoured to act as the progressive arbiter of global politics who ultimately compelled *all* the European belligerents, including the *Entente* Powers, to accept his peace design – not by force of arms but by political and ideological means. More precisely, he sought to bring to bear the United States' new political and financial might and, above all, the power of his own programmatic vision. Against the background of a military situation on the western front that in his assessment was changing decisively in favour of the western powers, the American president soon adopted an increasingly harder line and an ever more imperious tone vis-à-vis Berlin. Without consulting Lloyd George and Clemenceau, he reacted to the German appeal with an exploratory yet also agenda-setting note that his Secretary of State Robert Lansing transmitted on 8 October. Its core purpose was not only to ascertain whether the German government accepted the Fourteen Points and Wilson's subsequent proclamations as a basis for negotiations but actually to push for an unequivocal German commitment to the president's peace agenda. Further, it set important preconditions, demanding that as proof of good faith German authorities should withdraw all forces from the French and Belgian territories they still occupied. Yet, asking "the Imperial Chancellor" to clarify for whom he spoke, and whether he still spoke for the old authorities that had "so far conducted the war", the note also reflected Wilson's underlying distrust of the newly formed government in Berlin. And, crucially, it signalled that he refused to accept it as a negotiating partner.[37]

In its response, drafted by Solf, the von Baden government not only confirmed its unconditional acceptance of Wilson's programme as "foundations for a lasting peace of justice". It also declared that Germany was prepared to withdraw from all occupied territory, proposing that this process should be supervised by a "mixed commission". And it took pains to distance itself from

---

[36] See Leonhard (2018), p. 229.
[37] Lansing to Oederlin, 8 October 1918, *PWW*, LI, pp. 268–9; Schwabe (1985), pp. 44–7.

the "old order" of the Wilhelmine Empire by stressing that it had been formed with the "consent of the vast majority of the *Reichstag*" and that von Baden thus legitimately represented the will and could speak on behalf of "the German people".[38] Yet such assurances were far from satisfactory for the American president at a juncture when he felt he had to act decisively not only to overcome domestic opposition against anything but a policy of "unconditional surrender" but also to prevail on the *Entente* leaders to accept his terms. While professing that he wanted to avoid an "undue humiliation" of Germany, Wilson now actually sought to raise the stakes and put forward more stringent demands.

A second American note, sent to Berlin on 14 October, laid down significantly more uncompromising conditions. To respond to core objections of America's European "allies", whose political and military leaders had reacted with profound irritation to Wilson's unilateral pursuits, it demanded that instead of a "mixed commission" solely Allied military experts would be in charge of overseeing the evacuation of German troops from Allied territories and determining the military conditions of the armistice. This was to make it impossible for Germany to renew hostilities. More importantly, Wilson now insisted on a precondition that simply could not be fulfilled in the short term: he required *guarantees* that Germany was really taking decisive steps on the road to a democratic government.[39] The president's unilateral escalation tactic culminated in the subsequent note of 23 October. It stated in categorical terms that if the American government had to continue exchanges with the military leaders of Germany, "it must demand, not peace negotiations, but surrender". To conclude an armistice and enter into negotiations about a peace on the basis of the Fourteen Points it had to be assured that it would deal with "the veritable representatives of the German people" – "assured of genuine constitutional standing". Most immediately, this implied that nothing less than the abdication of the Kaiser would suffice.[40]

It is important to understand that Wilson did not place such an emphasis on decisive constitutional reforms because he actually believed that there could be substantive changes towards a "genuine democracy" within Germany in the near future. He had actually developed sceptical and decidedly hierarchical and simplistic views about the prospects of a German democratisation process. This view reflected his underlying Americanist outlook and would also have a marked effect on how he would approach the eventual peace negotiations and deal with those who came to represent the fledgling Weimar Republic. In short, Wilson held that in view of Germany's long-standing proclivities for

---

[38] German note, 8 October 1918, Schwabe (1997), pp. 55–6.
[39] Lansing note, 14 October 1918, Schwabe (1997), p. 56; draft of US note, *PWW*, LI, pp. 333–4; House diary, *ibid.*, pp. 340–2.
[40] Wilson to Lansing, 23 October 1918, *PWW*, LI, pp. 416–19.

authoritarianism and militarism, significant changes would require a long time and men like Erzberger and Scheidemann could at best take some first minor steps. Unquestionably, the American president's distrust of the key actors who now sought to gain trust as the "spokesmen" of a democratising Germany had been deepened when, in his eyes, they had acquiesced in the "peace of conquest" of Brest-Litovsk. But what had an even more decisive influence were his deep-seated hierarchical assumptions. And these assumptions had one crucial consequence: they led him to refuse to accept those who would soon strive to consolidate a German republic as equal, legitimate negotiating partners in the process of making peace and establishing a progressive postwar order.

At the same time, the tactic Wilson pursued during the armistice exchanges had a highly problematic impact on the inner-German power struggles that were now taking place. That he had explicitly made democratisation and "regime change" a condition of armistice *and* peace negotiations came to poison the very attempts of the *Reichstag* majority forces to foster substantive democratic reforms, because their opponents could now portray them as mere puppets of the enemy. In fact, this was an underlying problem that notably Scheidemann and other Social Democrats had recognised ever since the American entry into the war. As it was intended to do, Wilson's approach effectively pushed the frail new German government into a corner, ever more constraining its ability to resist his armistice agenda. Indeed, though he had decided that he needed a less than completely defeated Germany as a political counterweight to compel the *Entente* Powers to commit to his peace design, Wilson also sought to render those who sought to negotiate on Germany's behalf so powerless that they would have to accept whatever terms he set.

In Berlin, the third American note caused shock and dismay and decisively sharpened the conflict between von Baden's government and the *Reichstag* majority parties on the one hand and the Supreme Command, the Kaiser and the forces of the "old order" on the other. Both Hindenburg and Ludendorff insisted on a rejection of Wilson's demands, claiming they amounted to an "unconditional surrender", and Ludendorff travelled to Berlin to rally support for a "fight to the bitter end". But von Baden and his government remained committed to the pursuit of negotiations with Wilson – and prevailed. On 26 October, William II dismissed Ludendorff at von Baden's behest; on 29 October, the emperor himself left Berlin for the military headquarters at Spa, after having signed the laws changing the German constitution to that of a parliamentary monarchy.[41]

What united von Baden, Erzberger, Solf and leading Social Democrats in the midst of growing unrest, first revolutionary uprisings and a rapidly escalating state crisis in Berlin was the conviction that ultimately an armistice

---

[41] See Winkler (I/2000), p. 366; Schwabe (1972), pp. 95 ff.

concluded on the premises of Wilson's peace programme would offer the only real chance to come to an eventual peace settlement that, crucially, preserved the basic integrity of the German state. While some stressed that a literal application of the Fourteen Points threatened to deprive Germany not only of Alsace-Lorraine but also of essential territories in the east – Upper Silesia, the area around Posnan and Western Prussia – most assumed that it would not be impossible to negotiate an eventual agreement that applied Wilson's terms, and the principle of self-determination, in Germany's favour.[42]

The von Baden government thus did everything it could to address Wilson's demands and prevent a failure of the armistice process. In the note of 27 October, Solf emphasised that "fundamental changes" in Germany's "constitutional life" had already taken place and argued that it had already been assured that those would enter peace negotiations on the German side were the representatives of a "people's government" who now held the decisive constitutional powers in their hands and also controlled Germany's military power.[43] Von Baden himself – who actually sought to salvage a parliamentary monarchy as an "anchor of stability" – had resolved to hold out for what still had to be clarified, the actual armistice terms of the Allied and Associated Powers, and to keep the option of instigating a *levée en masse* if they seemed unacceptable.

Most striking about Wilson's conduct during these critical weeks was the extent to which, although he was the leader of a power that fought *in a coalition*, he stubbornly clung to his role-conception as superior progressive arbiter. His guiding rationale was that only by playing this role and by essentially compelling "allies" as well as "enemies" to go along with his programmatic vision he would be able to prepare the ground for a "just" progressive peace. And only thus, he maintained, would it be possible to come to an agreement that prevented "a renewal of hostilities by Germany" but at the same time was "as moderate and reasonable as possible". This reasoning also lay behind his equally adamant rejection of the idea of prosecuting the war until the Central Powers had been forced into an unconditional surrender – a position that, as will be seen, he then defended against strong domestic opposition, particularly among his Republican opponents in the Senate.

Fundamentally, Wilson adopted his own kind of balance-of-power maxim, telling his key diplomatic envoy Colonel House that "too much success or security on the part of the Allies" would make "make a genuine peace settlement exceedingly difficult if not impossible" because it would put the *Entente* Powers in an excessively powerful position, enabling them to insist on imposing harsh terms and curtailing his own influence.[44] As the president

---

[42] Krüger (1985), p. 41.
[43] German note, 27 October 1918, Schwabe (1997), pp. 61-2.
[44] Wilson to House, 28 October 1918, *PWW*, LI, p. 473.

impressed on the Democratic senator Henry Ashurst, one of his party's most outspoken proponents of "unconditional surrender", by pursuing an armistice that kept British and French power in check he was "thinking now only of putting the United States into a position of strength and justice" – and "playing for 100 years hence".[45]

Remarkably, Wilson thus largely spurned warnings by House and members of his own Cabinet that it would be futile to try to force the *Entente* governments to accept armistice terms they did not desire. Instead, he insisted that if necessary, they ultimately had to be "coerced". While never developing a clear strategy to this end, the American president acted on the assumption that Lloyd George, Clemenceau and the Italian premier Sonnino could not afford an open breach with him because they depended on the United States: Britain could not "dispense with [American] friendship in the future" – and "the other Allies" needed American support to "get their rights as against England".[46] There was unquestionably an idiosyncratic, personal dimension to Wilson's high-handed unilateralism, which harmomised ill with his insistence that the world required above all a new "international concert" in the form of League of Nations.[47] But in a wider context it merely epitomised wider proclivities of the policy- and decision-making elite of an aloof exceptionalist-exemplarist power that in its entire history had never cooperated or entered into commitments with other states and peoples on a footing of equality.

Essentially, however, the tumultuous developments of October showed that Wilson's power and leeway to pursue a unilateral course at this decisive point was actually markedly limited. He soon came up against weighty constraints on his own home front, which foreshadowed future domestic-political challenges he would face in the quest to make America into the world's principal progressive power. And, more importantly, his pursuits aroused not just major irritations but also tangible objections on the part of the *Entente* Powers, whose leaders first and foremost insisted on *consultation* and originally threatened to reject the president's entire agenda – and to continue the war. One necessary though by no means sufficient precondition for a success of Wilson's aspirations was to build a strong platform of domestic support. Yet here he had to struggle to maintain at least some room to manoeuvre. In the middle of a heated campaign for the Congressional elections that were to take place in early November, only progressives supported more or less wholeheartedly what they saw as Wilson's endeavour to chart a path towards a forward-looking peace settlement and warned against the militarist alternative of waging war until not only "the decisive defeat but the destruction of Germany" had been assured. The leading progressive commentators of the

---

[45] Ashurst diary, 14 October 1918, *PWW*, LI, pp. 338–40.
[46] Wilson to House, 29 October 1918, *PWW*, LI, pp. 504–5.
[47] Wilson address, 22 January 1917, *PWW*, XL, pp. 536–9.

New Republic demanded that America's aim had to be "to remake, not to rehash Europe" and to build a new order in which there should also be "a place for the German people evolved by the horrors of war beyond their slavery and barbarism". And in their view this could only be accomplished on the basis of Wilson's peace programme, and through the implementation of his plan for a League of Nations.[48]

Politically more important, however, were the strong counter-currents Wilson faced in the American Congress – and in the wider spectrum of public opinion.[49] Colonel House warned the president that most American voters were essentially "against anything but unconditional surrender". And, crucially, Wilson and the Democratic chairman of the Senate's Committee on Foreign Relations, Gilbert Hitchcock, had to reckon with the fact that a majority of Senators on both sides of the aisle distinctly opposed a cessation of hostilities before the Allied victory was unequivocal and German troops had been pushed back to German soil – or even all the way to Berlin. Particularly disconcerting for Wilson was that some Democratic senators emerged as vocal advocates of "unconditional surrender", with Henry Ashurst, the aforementioned senator from Arizona, even going so far as to demand that the Allied Powers should drive "a wide pathway of fire and blood from the Rhine to Berlin".[50] More consequential, however, was that Wilson's Republican antagonists championed the call for a complete victory and sought to instrumentalise it to defeat the Democrats and thus constrain the president.

It was at this juncture that Henry Cabot Lodge emerged as Wilson's key domestic opponent. As Lodge noted on 2 October, he felt "sure that the American people want a complete victory and an unconditional surrender ... to win this fight on German soil".[51] And subsequently he stepped up his efforts to avert what he saw as "the constant danger of a negotiated peace" with Germany. Laying out Republican war aims during a Senate debate on the Man-Power Bill in mid-October, Lodge explicitly demanded a harsh "dictated peace", asserting that "(n)o peace that satisfies Germany in any degree" could satisfy the Republican Party.[52] Following his lead, other prominent Republican senators, like Miles Poindexter of Washington, also denounced any notion of a "compromise peace" and asserted that negotiating peace terms with Germany was out of the question.[53]

---

[48] "The Republicans and Germany", *New Republic* (19 October 1918), pp. 327–9; "A Victory of Justice Vs. A Victory of Power", *New Republic* (5 October 1918), pp. 271–3.

[49] *Literary Digest/Current Opinion*, LXV, no. 4 (October 1918), p. 208.

[50] See Congressional Record, 65th Congress, 2nd session, 11,155–167. See Knock (1992), pp. 170–6.

[51] Lodge to Roosevelt, 2 October 1918, in Redmond (1925), II, p. 540.

[52] Lodge to Roosevelt, 19 October 1918, in Roosevelt and Lodge (1925), II, p. 542; *Literary Digest/Current Opinion*, LXV, no. 4 (October 1918), p. 208.

[53] See *Literary Digest*, LIX (19 October 1918), pp. 8–10; Knock (1992), pp. 171–2.

And Lodge and Poindexter went one step further. They now also attacked Wilson's peace agenda as such more vigorously than before, going so far as to claim that a peace settlement premised on the Fourteen Points would amount to an Allied defeat in the war.[54]

The Republican critics of Wilson essentially continued the assault and adopted arguments of the man who had become his sternest public critic during the war, Theodore Roosevelt. Roosevelt protested vehemently against Wilson's exchange of notes with the German government. He argued that America should not act as "an umpire between our allies and our enemies" but rather agree on common terms with the former. And he too demanded that the war should be continued until a complete victory had been achieved and the Allied powers could impose their terms. Crucially, however, Roosevelt renewed his effort to delegitimise Wilson's peace programme, lamenting that some of the so-called fourteen points were "couched in such vague language" as to "have merely rhetorical value" while others were "absolutely mischievous". What he championed instead, adapting his ideas of the pre-war era, was a militarily robust League that was to be formed, firstly and principally, by the United States and its "present allies" – yet which in his eyes could only complement, not replace the security guaranteed by American military "preparedness".[55]

The inner-American disputes over the armistice indeed prefigured those that would rage during and after the Paris Peace Conference. Adamantly defending his progressive essentials, Wilson sought to persuade Ashhurst and other critics that only his approach would assure that American power and justice would prevail and shape the world in the aftermath of the war.[56] Dismayed by what he saw as the effect of Republican agitation for a harsh peace, Wilson privately expressed his concern that most Americans were "on the verge of yielding to the sort of hate which we are fighting in the Germans" and noted he was "beginning to be fearful lest we go too far to be in a mood to make an absolutely and rigorously impartial peace".[57] But the president not only failed to sway his Republican opponents but also a majority of American voters – and the Democrats would lose the November elections. That the Republicans now controlled both the Senate and the House of Representatives would alter the American political playing-field; and it would turn Wilson's attempt to gain essential domestic backing for his vision of a "new world order" into an uphill struggle.[58]

---

[54] See Congressional Record, 65th Congress, 2nd session, 10 October 1918, 111171–72; "A Review of the World", Literary Digest, LXV (November 1918); Literary Digest, LIX (October 1918), pp. 7–8.

[55] See Congressional Record, 65th Congress, 2nd session, 10 October 1918, 1171–72.

[56] Ashurst diary, 14 October 1918, PWW, LI, pp. 338–40.

[57] Wilson letter, 26 October 1918, Wilson Papers, Series 3, Vol. 54.

[58] See Chapter 10.

III.   Frail Foundations for a Progressive Peace. Wilson, the *Entente* Powers and the Finalisation of the Armistice Agreement

But Wilson did not just confront tangible domestic obstacles. He also, and crucially, had to find ways to address the concerns of those on whose attitudes the success of his design depended to a critical extent – and more than he was willing to acknowledge: the political leaders of the European *Entente* Powers. The American president continued to treat them, not as the elected leaders of the United States' *de facto* allies who had at least as strong a democratic mandate has he did, but rather as antagonistic actors who had to be compelled to abandon their old-style imperialistic war aims and power-political agendas.[59] On these questionable premises, he remained determined to push ahead and, if necessary, to use coercive methods to commit them to the premises and principles of his "higher" Fourteen Points agenda. But the limits of his approach soon became clear. In fact, he would be compelled to seek a basic consensus with Lloyd George and Clemenceau. And it soon became obvious how hard and complicated this would be.

For their part, Lloyd George and Clemenceau, who represented powers that had been in the war much longer than the United States and still bore the brunt of the fighting in 1918, confronted not only a very unexpected situation but also the danger of a *fait accompli* – of being implicated in an armistice *and* peace agenda that ended the war without ever having a real say in shaping it. Initially, following a meeting in Paris in early October, the *Entente* leaders and Sonnino thus tried to impede further exchanges between the German and American governments and, predictably, insisted that Wilson had to confer with them before any further steps were taken. They signalled that they were not prepared simply to fall in line behind the Fourteen Points programme, even threatening to present a catalogue of their main objections – and thereby to make an armistice in the near future illusory. Essentially, though, the German–American exchange of notes created a dynamic that compelled the *Entente*'s key political and military decision-makers to consider within a very short time and under immense pressure not only *whether* they should accept actual armistice negotiations but also on what conditions they ought to insist if such negotiations were to be pursued. For, as they realised, all of this would have major implications for the character and terms of the eventual peace settlement.

The German appeal and Wilson's initial unilateral reaction raised profound concerns and suspicions, not only among leading policymakers. In the light of their estimate of Germany's capacity to fight on, which they still regarded as very considerable, British and especially French military leaders doubted the sincerity of the German offer. They therefore demanded from early on that at

---

[59]   Wilson to House, 29 October 1918, *PWW*, LI, pp. 504–5.

the very least it would be essential to formulate military conditions for the armistice that would make it impossible for German forces to resume the war.

What mattered more, however, was that Wilson's approach ran counter to what were the then still prevalent *Entente* conceptions of how to end the war – namely only after a decisive defeat of the Central Powers. In France, particularly the assertive president Poincaré argued – on grounds that reflected those of Lodge and Roosevelt – that it was strategically imperative to carry on the war and block an armistice that prevented what he deemed critical for a lasting peace and future French security: not only an undisputable defeat of Germany but also the occupation of strategically vital German territory.[60] Time and again Lloyd George had asserted his commitment to fighting the war until a decisive victory guaranteed the end of all German "schemes of military domination" over Europe.[61] In September, seeking to placate Liberal and Labour opinion in Britain and to incite inner-German opposition against the German Supreme Command's "military masters", he had publicly proclaimed that with a Germany "freed from military domination" a moderate peace could be made – a peace that would "lend itself to the common sense and conscience of the [British] nation as a whole", was "not dictated by extreme men on either side" and would not "arm Germany with a real wrong".[62]

But the position Lloyd George originally adopted after von Baden's appeal for an armistice was shaped by other, sterner priorities. He not only questioned whether the new German government really had the power to end the dominance of Ludendorff and Hindenburg. He also expressed long-term considerations that were diametrically opposed to Wilson's. On 13 October, the British premier wondered whether an early armistice might encourage German elites and the German public to conclude that they had not really been defeated, and thus provoke another war in the future. And he mused whether the analogy of the final Roman victory over Carthage in the Punic Wars could actually provide a valuable lesson: namely that the Romans had insisted on carrying the war to and achieving an unequivocal victory on the enemy's soil.[63] Remarkably soon, however, not only Lloyd George shifted his emphasis. Both *Entente* governments effectively came to agree that an armistice should be pursued – and would hence focus on ensuring that it met certain military *and* political conditions they deemed essential.

Clemenceau stressed that because of France's overall exhaustion the war should not be continued one day longer than absolutely necessary and, seizing on the authority he had accumulated as wartime leader, he prevailed over

[60] Cabanes and Duménil (2014), p. 1294.
[61] Lloyd George (1918), p. 3.
[62] Lloyd George speech, 12 September 1918, in *The Times*, 13 September 1918. See Grigg (2002), pp. 590–2.
[63] Lloyd George comments, meeting at Danny, 13 October 1918, CAB 24/66.

Poincaré and other critics. Concerns of imminent exhaustion were less acute on the British side yet also influenced the Cabinet decisions in London. Both governments also dreaded the risks of an actual conquest and occupation of Germany, fearing that it would be very difficult to keep troops mobilised not only to prevail militarily but also to act as occupying forces. And the leading generals – Foch and Pétain on the French side and Henry Wilson on the British side – voiced similar concerns rather than insisting on a prolongation of the war.[64] Further, not only British but also French leaders reckoned that after years of extreme and ever more straining mobilisation public opinion in their countries would actually *not* be in favour of fighting on to "unconditional surrender" but rather desire to end the war sooner rather than later – if there was a prospect for a peace that met prevalent expectations.

Undoubtedly, the calculations of Lloyd George and Clemenceau were also influenced by the expectation that the longer the war went on, the more the weight of the economic, financial and military contribution of the United States would grow – and thus progressively strengthen Wilson's position in an eventual peacemaking process and his capacity to impose his kind of "American peace". Yet it is crucial also to recognise the significance of more fundamental political rationales of a different order that now came into play. In short, in their different ways Lloyd George, Clemenceau and the policy-makers and advisers who now shaped British and French peace strategies sought to accommodate Wilson and his peace and League agenda – *within certain limits* – because however dismayed they were by his conduct, they were also acutely aware that they ultimately would have to work out a peace settlement with him; and that they would require his and wider American goodwill to meet cardinal postwar challenges. Fundamentally, both sides had indeed begun to reorientate their outlooks and strategies in an Atlantic direction.[65]

What the *Entente* leaders thus concentrated on was to induce Wilson to enter into consultations with them and, first of all, to accept that Allied military experts would have the final authority in setting the military terms of the armistice.[66] At the same time they began deliberating the salient political question of how far they could actually countenance the Fourteen Points as the basis of a future peace. In France, all the main actors agreed that the armistice had to guarantee the return of Alsace-Lorraine. But what dominated the debate were precisely those security concerns that would also loom largest in 1919. Marshal Foch, commander-in-chief of the Allied armies since the spring of 1918, urged Clemenceau to ensure that the armistice terms would include

---

[64] Stevenson (2012), p. 477.
[65] Cecil memorandum, circulated to War Cabinet on 18 September 1917, CAB 24/26/2074; Tardieu note, 20 January 1917, Tardieu Papers, vol. 417
[66] See Lloyd George to Geddes, 12 October 1918, *PWW*, LI, p. 313.

provisions for Allied control of key strategic bridgeheads on the Rhine, a military occupation of the Rhenish territories on its left bank and the establishment of a roughly 30 kilometre-wide demilitarised zone on its eastern bank. Yet Foch also put forward more far-reaching political-cum-strategic aims when underscoring that in his assessment a permanent control of the hitherto German provinces on the Rhine's left bank was critical for France's longer-term security.[67] Though angered by the marshal's attempt to influence French policymaking so directly, Clemenceau agreed with the basic terms Foch proposed – and thus to conditions that were in fact essentially strategic and political, intended to enable France, as far as possible, to contain Wilson's agenda and redress the balance of power vis-à-vis Germany.[68]

From the perspectives of Clemenceau and leading officials in the French Foreign Ministry the underlying challenge was to respond to Wilson's wider peace agenda, which they overall viewed with deep scepticism, in such a way as to maximise their ability to safeguard what they deemed cardinal French security interests. Echoing the views of other senior officials at the Quai d'Orsay, notably the influential strategist Philippe Berthelot, the French Foreign Minister Stephen Pichon deemed Wilson's programme not only ill-defined but actually dangerous. He warned that making them the basis of peace negotiations carried one major risk, namely that the French government would not be in a position to impose the restrictive military, territorial, political and financial terms on Germany that he deemed vital to protect France against renewed German "aggression" in the future.[69] Clemenceau himself was no less concerned. He resented what he saw as Wilson's attempt to impose his peace agenda and had by no means abandoned the warily sceptical attitude vis-à-vis the American president's League plans and lofty moralistic proclamations that had hardened since 1916. It was only after tense exchanges with House and Lloyd George in Paris on 29–30 October that the French premier would eventually signal that he was prepared to accept the Fourteen Points as *general* parameters for the armistice and subsequent peace negotiations – and to confirm his government's earlier public commitment to the creation of a League of Nations. Yet he would insist that, in return, Wilson – and Lloyd George – had to accept vital amendments: Foch's military terms.

It is critical to note, though, that neither Clemenceau nor any other French policymaker ever contemplated adopting Wilson's premise that the armistice would set the terms on which the actual peace agreement would be negotiated with German representatives. Placed in a wider context, the inner-French deliberations of October 1918 thus can be seen as an early stage within a more complicated and drawn-out reorientation process. At this point, as has

[67] Foch note, 8 October 1918, in Jackson (2013), p. 192.
[68] See Stevenson (1982), pp. 125–32.
[69] See Jackson (2013), pp. 193–5.

rightly been stressed, more traditional power-political ideas and conceptions of security still clearly prevailed – above all vis-à-vis Germany – and thus markedly clashed with Wilson's call for transformative changes in international politics. Yet there was also a nascent awareness that French policy-makers would have to develop new approaches to come to terms with a power, and president, on whose support they ultimately depended.

On the British side, Lloyd George, his foreign secretary Arthur Balfour and a majority of his ministers had by 26 October adopted the view that it was in Britain's interest to conclude an armistice and to make "a good peace if that is now attainable". Here too, if less unequivocally than in Paris, the underlying assumption was still that the peace would ultimately not be negotiated with but imposed on the enemy. And while British ideas of what would constitute the essentials of a "good peace" still had to be clarified, the prime minister obtained the Cabinet's support for his new course vis-à-vis Wilson. Lloyd George had proposed to accept the Fourteen Points as the political framework of the armistice agreement and, in very general terms, of a future peace settlement if they could be modified in two important respects. He categorically rejected Wilson's demand for a complete "freedom of the seas", arguing that his government could not compromise its "right" to impose blockades, as this was an essential strategy for safeguarding the security of Britain and its empire. And, crucially, in order to establish a British claim for reparations, he insisted that the armistice terms had to ensure that Germany would be obliged to make "compensation" for "all damages done to the civilian population of the Allies" by its "aggression ... by land, by sea and from the air".[70]

Yet both in the Cabinet and in the Foreign Office cautious attitudes prevailed. As noted, the Lloyd George government had made the creation of a League of Nations an official war aim, and Cecil and the protagonists of the Phillimore Committee had devised plans designed to transform Wilson's aspirations into a more "workable" scheme which would allow Britain and its empire to protect core political and security interests in new ways.[71] But they by no means assumed that it would be easy to forge a mutually acceptable framework for the envisaged international institution with the American president. Reflecting prevalent concerns in his Cabinet, Lloyd George's outlook at this juncture was decidedly more sceptical yet. While he by now backed an official British commitment to the League, he still considered the ideas Wilson had thus far advanced on the subject disconcertingly aspirational. He still judged the general visionary peace agenda the president had mapped out in much the same way, deeming it anything but a realistic blueprint for building a stable postwar order. At the same time, Wilson's imperious

[70] See British memorandum, in House to Wilson, 30 October 1918, *PWW*, LI, p. 515.
[71] Cecil memorandum, circulated to War Cabinet on 18 September 1917, CAB 24/26/2074.

conduct following the German armistice appeal had reinforced his sense that negotiating some form of cooperative Anglo-American partnership in the making and maintaining of peace after the war would be a very challenging task.[72] But the underlying rationale of his conduct would now be reinforced too – and this rationale was that it was in Britain's strategic interest not just to accommodate and rein in Wilson's aspirations for tactical purposes but actually to hammer out a more substantial Anglo-American accord, and strategic bargain.

For his part, the American president entertained no notions of this kind (yet). It was only after nearly three weeks of bilateral exchanges of notes with the von Baden government that he took a first meaningful step to respond to the irritations and demands of the *Entente* leaders. He agreed to send Colonel House, who had already acted as his main envoy to Europe during earlier stages of the war, on another mission – this time to Paris. On the surface, House was to pursue consultations with the heads of the British, French and Italian governments. But his real mission, as Wilson saw it, was to ensure – if necessary by coercion – that they "consented" to the political essentials of his armistice agenda and thus, more fundamentally, to his peace programme.

Seeking to control this process from afar as much as possible, Wilson instructed House carefully, impressing on him his essential aims and concerns. Still vehemently opposed to a policy of "unconditional surrender", he emphasised that the United States must throw its "whole weight" behind an essentially "moderate" armistice that did not humiliate the enemy power. He noted that he strictly opposed deliberating the actual peace terms with the *Entente* Powers prior to an eventual peace conference, because this would convey the impression that they were intent on "dividing the spoils" among themselves. And, significantly, Wilson emphasised not only that at the general conference he envisaged German representatives had to be given the opportunity to "state their case". He also underscored that the Germans "ought to be present" when the League of Nations was constituted. He thus still maintained the maxim that the League had to be founded as an inclusive organisation.[73] Finally, warning that "too much *severity* on the part of the Allies" would "make a genuine peace settlement exceedingly difficult", the president demanded that the military terms Foch had proposed – and similar recommendations that the commander-in-chief of the American expeditionary forces, General John Pershing, had made – should be significantly scaled down. Notably, he opposed plans for an occupation of strategic bridgeheads and the eastern bank of the Rhine, calling them "practically an invasion of German soil under [the] armistice".[74]

[72] Lloyd George to Sir Eric Geddes, 12 October 1918, *PWW*, LI, p. 313.
[73] Wilson to House, 28 October 1918, *PWW*, LI, p. 473.
[74] Baker (1927–39), VIII, p. 521.

But during the decisive deliberations in Paris, House would actually pursue a more accommodating approach vis-à-vis those whom he, in contrast to Wilson, referred to as America's "allies". Misinterpreting the president's instructions or deliberately disregarding them, he came to pursue a bargaining strategy of his own. Ultimately, he would make concessions to Clemenceau and Lloyd George on specific points – crucially, the French military terms – in order to achieve what he considered to be the overriding aim, namely to commit them to the general programme of "American war aims", that of the Fourteen Points.[75] Already in mid-September House had noted that while he had endeavoured to foster "political unity" among the "Allies", Wilson seemed determined to show to the world that the United States was "acting independently". In his eyes, this would have been a reasonable course if the "purpose" was to "stand aloof from world politics". But it was "wholly wrong" if the president desired to establish a League whose "essence" was to foster "close political and economic unity throughout the world".[76] He thus had urged Wilson to pursue a more cooperative strategy to "commit the Allies" to the essentials for which "we are fighting".[77] Now he made this his own mission.[78]

How difficult and complex it would actually be to forge a basic agreement between the Allied and Associated Powers was revealed when House met with Lloyd George, Clemenceau and Sonnino on 30 October to agree on the content of what would be the decisive American armistice note to Germany.[79] The British premier submitted a draft proposal which explicitly stated that the Allied Powers would be prepared to accept the peace conditions that Wilson had outlined in his Fourteen Points and the "principles" he had proclaimed in his subsequent speeches as the basis of the armistice and the subsequent peace negotiations. But he demanded that the American president had to accept in return the two reservations he had formulated with the backing of his Cabinet: objections to the "freedom of the seas" clause – i.e. the demand for exemptions for the British naval-blockade doctrine – and, to assert British indemnity claims, the demand for German compensation for "all damages" that had been inflicted on the civilian populations of the Allied Powers.[80]

On the first issue, no compromise could be reached. While voicing some understanding for British strategic concerns, Wilson insisted that he could not

---

[75] House to McAdoo, 18 October 1918, House Papers. See Schwabe (1985), p. 91.
[76] House diary, 16 September 1918, *PWW*, LI, p. 23.
[77] House, *Intimate Papers*, IV, pp. 65–6.
[78] House's mission also threw into relief the improvisational character of Wilsonian diplomacy at this time. Once in Paris, House enlisted the services of Walter Lippmann to provide "a precise definition" of each of the Fourteen Points, which he then – with Wilson's authorisation – used during his talks with the *Entente* leaders. See Walter Lippmann, oral history, Lippmann Papers.
[79] House to Wilson, 30 October 1918, *PWW*, LI, p. 511.
[80] See British memorandum, in House to Wilson, 30 October 1918, *PWW*, LI, p. 515.

conclude a peace that did not include "freedom of the seas", and House duly transmitted the president's position.[81] Yet the British premier refused to withdraw his demand, eventually conceding merely that the issue should be discussed again at the eventual peace conference. By contrast, neither House nor later Wilson raised objections to Lloyd George's indemnity clause, and thus the armistice came to include a provision that both *Entente* governments would seize on to assert expanded reparations claims vis-à-vis Germany at the eventual peace conference.

Yet, as his envoy reported to Wilson, Clemenceau and Sonnino still threatened "not to accept [the American president's terms but to formulate their own" – and thus to not only to prevent an armistice in the near future but to derail Wilson's entire peacemaking agenda. In the face of these threats, House at first resorted to an assertive version of "open diplomacy". He posed a quasi-ultimatum, warning that if no agreement could be reached, Wilson would make *Entente* demands public by presenting them to the American Congress, underscoring that neither members of Congress nor the American public would then be prepared to carry on a war in pursuit of what in the light of the Fourteen Points they would regard as "selfish", imperialistic objectives. House here merely followed Wilson's lead. The latter had earlier impressed on him that if "the Allied statesmen" intended to "nullify" his influence he would be prepared "to repudiate any selfish programme openly".[82]

Clemenceau relented. He signalled that he was willing to back the British compromise proposals. But he insisted on something in return that would be of great import for the eventual peace negotiations. The French premier underlined his most fundamental concern: the need for firm guarantees against renewed German aggression. And he fought hard to ensure that the armistice agreement comprised in an essentially unaltered form the military conditions Foch had stipulated, including the establishment of strategic bridgeheads and a "neutral zone" on the Rhine's eastern bank. He warned – not for the last time – that he would be forced to resign unless these essential French conditions were accepted.[83] Raising core British concerns that would re-appear in 1919, Lloyd George argued that what the French premier demanded would be regarded as too severe in Germany and complicate not only the armistice but also the eventual peace settlement. House pointed to the danger of a "red revolution" in Germany that could then spread westward. But none of these concerns impressed the French premier. And it was at this point

[81] Wilson to House, 30 October 1918, *PWW*, LI, p. 513.
[82] House to Wilson, 30 October 1918, *PWW*, LI, pp. 511–17; Wilson to House, 29 October 1918, *PWW*, LI, pp. 504–5.
[83] House to Wilson, 30 October 1918, *PWW*, LI, p. 511; Foch memorandum, 26 October 1918, House, *Intimate Papers*, IV, pp. 143–5; House to Wilson, 27 October 1918, *PWW*, LI, p. 463.

of crisis that House switched to the more accommodating approach he had favoured all along and played an instrumental part in crafting – largely on his own authority – a diplomatic bargain. At the core, he came to acquiesce to the military provisions for which Clemenceau had fought so vigorously in order to pave a way for an overall *Entente* acceptance of Wilson's peace agenda.

In the end, House advised Wilson to agree to an armistice on the basis of Lloyd George's proposal and the French military terms in order to secure what he saw as the decisive breakthrough: the Allied endorsement of the *political* essentials of the Fourteen Points.[84] Wilson was aware of the problem arising from occupying positions on the eastern bank of the Rhine, and he rejected the idea of a longer-term occupation of German territory.[85] But his priority was indeed to ensure the *Entente* Powers' consent to his overall peace programme. And he acted on the assumption that the armistice's military provisions were of a temporary nature and that once a progressive peace had been concluded and the League had been set up, they would swiftly be superseded. He thus raised no objections to incorporating Foch's terms. In Paris, Lloyd George had ultimately acquiesced as well. In return, Clemenceau solemnly promised that France would withdraw from the Rhenish territories – once the French government had concluded that its demands had been met. In the end, then, an armistice document had been agreed upon which essentially constituted a hybrid, uneasily combining a – superficial – commitment of all Allied and Associated Powers to Wilson's progressive political "superstructure", Lloyd George's "exceptions" and a set of military conditions that were dictated by French security concerns and traditional power-political considerations.

The results of the arduous negotiations in Paris were transmitted to the German government in the "Lansing note" of 5 November. In Berlin, particularly the far-reaching "French provisions" caused some consternation. Yet the main reaction the "Lansing note" produced when it arrived on 6 November was a sense of relief. For by this time not only von Baden's government but the entire German state was about to disintegrate. By 9 November, the mutinies and unrest that had expanded since mid-October escalated into what became the – unfinished – German November revolution of 1918. Shortly after Erzberger had travelled to Compiègne as head of a small German delegation, seeking to pursue final negotiations over what could no longer be negotiated, the Kaiser finally stepped down, both the moderate Scheidemann and the radical Liebknecht proclaimed a new German republic – on 9 November – and a Council of People's Deputies, led by Ebert, formed by the Majority and Independent Social Democrats but only provisionally legitimised by workers' and soldiers' councils, took over. And it was this Council that on 11 November

---

[84] House to Wilson, 30 October 1918, *PWW*, LI, pp. 515–17.
[85] Baker (1927–39), VIII, p. 521.

urged Erzberger not to wait for further concessions but to sign the armistice agreement, which he did, under duress, at 5 a.m. on the same day. This is how the Great War came to an end in the west.

What House had reported to Wilson on 5 November as "a great diplomatic victory" for him and the president was in fact at best a superficial victory. It by no means assured that peace negotiations would actually proceed on the premises of Wilson's peace programme.[86] For the *Entente* leaders had indeed only committed themselves superficially to his political terms, insisting on important reservations and still harbouring more profound misgivings in private; and the president's unilateral conduct had weakened rather than strengthened his position. In fact, the final agreement Lloyd George and Clemenceau had negotiated with House could only conceal momentarily that they and Wilson were still far apart when it came to the most salient questions of peacemaking. These differences did not just relate to the nature and signifi-cance of the envisaged League of Nations, reparations and the key question of future international security. They also pertained to something more fundamen-tal: the core ideas each of these actors had begun to form about what kind of postwar order he envisaged and about the way in which it was to be established – ideas that were still evolving at this critical stage. Crucially, they had not even tried yet to reach a preliminary consensus about how to deal with Germany. They still had to decide whether they should seek to forge a "peace order of the victors" that they would then impose on the vanquished, which notably Clemenceau favoured – and Lloyd George seemed to favour too – or whether they should aim to work out preliminary terms and then also allow German representatives to "state their case", as Wilson had insisted.

If one takes into account the extremely adverse conditions under which they had to operate, the agreement of Compiègne can in retrospect indeed be seen as a relative success for Erzberger, von Baden and those who had struggled to negotiate on Germany's behalf. Yet it also stimulated what soon hardened into a prevailing expectation that was not only destined to prove illusory but would also impede subsequent efforts to develop a more realistic German approach to the actual peacemaking process. Essentially, the armistice came to be interpreted as a *pactum de contrahendo* under international law, a treaty that "legally" obliged all the signatories to conclude a future peace agreement on its terms. And behind this lay even more far-reaching, and even more illusory political hopes, which so far even Wilson's high-handed conduct had not dispelled, namely that the armistice could serve as the foundation-stone for a "Wilson peace", a "peace of justice" that would allow them not only to protect what they saw as existential German interests but also lead a

---

[86] House to Wilson, 5 November 1918, *PWW*, LI, p. 594; House diary, 4 November 1918, House, *Intimate Papers*, IV, p. 188.

"democratised" German state into the League as a power with "equal rights". Yet, like a good part of the German public, they clearly overestimated American president's leverage; and more importantly they were still far from developing a more realistic conception of the likely dynamics and complexities of the future peace negotiations.[87]

Overall, then, the hybrid armistice could only lay brittle foundations for peacemaking after the First World War. Most of the key parameters for how the negotiations of 1919 would actually proceed were only set in its aftermath; and the key compromises that would eventually underlie and shape the peace "settlement" of Paris still had to be negotiated.

[87] See Krüger (1985), pp. 41; Payk (2018), pp. 151–64.

9

No Prospects for a Lasting Peace?

The Urgent and the Systemic Challenges of Peacemaking and the Need for a New Atlantic Order

The armistice brought the Great War to an unexpectedly sudden end – or more precisely the war ended in the west while violence and conflict continued across Central and Eastern Europe, in what turned into a zone of revolutionary and nationalist unrest, instability and often chaotic conditions following the collapse of the continental European empires. What the war left in its wake in Europe – and on different premises in the United States and the world outside Europe – was a prevalent sense that there could be no return to the past, to some kind of *status quo ante* of 1914; that the world prior to the July crisis could – and in the eyes of many should – not be recreated; and that the political conditions, cultural norms and mentalities that had dominated in the pre-war era had been had been battered so violently by the storm of the war that something different had to take their place. This went hand in hand with a heightened a sense of profound insecurity, disorientation and a further intensification of the search for new orientations that had already been going on during the war – the search for different political structures, modes of order and norms that could not only fill the void of what had been destroyed or discredited but actually pave the way for a less violent future and indeed a "peace to end all wars".

Fears and profound scepticism abounded. Yet what also intensified, particularly among those who championed a progressive renewal in the United States and on both sides of the European trenches, was a sense of historical opportunity. For here the notion came to prevail that (only) a catastrophe on the scale of the Great War could open up real prospects for transformative reforms both within and between different states and societies – for the creation of a peace league that would really banish war, for new modes of more democratic, participatory politics, for far-reaching social reforms. Others saw the opportunity to fulfil their aspirations for statehood and "self-determination". And the leading Bolsheviks and radical socialists of course saw an historical opportunity of a different kind, namely that of a revolutionary overthrow of the entire system of belligerent imperialist capitalism.[1]

---

[1] See Mayer (1967), pp. 90 ff.; Leonhard (2018), pp. 372–5.

It was in this context that one particular question arose and would now be intensely debated on both sides of the Atlantic – though on the whole by intellectuals more than by policymakers. It was the question of whether the war had not only ushered in the overall decline of Europe and a new world-historical era in which the future of Europe and the wider world would be decided by a newly predominant American power and its political and economic civilisation. Friedrich Meinecke was not the only European observer who wondered whether as a consequence of the war, "the era of the [European] great powers" had irrevocably reached its end and Germany and Europe would hence come under a new kind of "world domination, under a pax americana". Like others clearly shaken by the scale of the European catastrophe, Meinecke mused whether what he described as a hitherto essentially anarchical great-power system, in which in the last instance conflicts had been "settled" through war, would and could hence be superseded by a liberal world order in which, he implied, the United States would clearly be the pre-eminent power on account of its superior financial and economic potential, yet also its political-ideological strength as the pre-eminent power of liberal democracy.[2]

Similarly, Max Weber noted in late November 1918 that while the days of a "*world*-political role of Germany" were over, "America's domination of the world was [now] as unavoidable as in classic times that of Rome after the Punic War".[3] Yet had Europe, the United States and the world indeed reached such an epochal juncture? Had the time come for a Wilsonian *Pax Americana* – and was the scene set for a confrontation between Wilson's and Lenin's visions, inaugurating the US–Soviet competition that eventually, after 1945, would play such a clearly dominant part in the remaking of world order? In retrospect, the contemporary assessments of Meinecke and Weber appear as strikingly exaggerated as later interpretations of this kind, mainly advanced during the era of the Cold War, appear misleading.

It is important to understand why that is so. Yet it is even more important to widen the focus and gain a deeper understanding of something more fundamental, or rather a whole range of interlocked fundamental questions: How far was it at all politically possible under the circumstances to chart a path from the Great War and the turmoil and disintegration it had produced to a durable peace and a new, more legitimate order – both between and within states? How far could a modern peace order be created that fostered national *and* international stabilisation while also buttressing economic reconstruction? How far could political reforms be initiated, and sustained, that actually met the core demands of the different populations after the immense hardships of the war? And how far could the newly critical aspirations for

---

[2] Meinecke (1969), pp. 307 ff. See Niedhart (2011), p. 68.
[3] Weber letter, late November 1918, in Weber (1926), p. 648.

national self-determination in different parts of Europe and the "colonial world" not only be satisfied but also addressed in ways that at least minimised the potential for new international conflicts? Arguably, however, the crucial problem lay deeper still. In the end, everything hinged on whether the key actors would manage to negotiate norms, rules and mechanisms of international order that could actually prove more effective than those that had existed before 1914 *and thus forestalled another, potentially even Greater War.* Could anything even approaching such a new international architecture be founded after 1918 – a modern order for the long twentieth century?

Essentially, contrary to what many had hoped, though it had undoubtedly been a profound and in some respects transformative crisis the Great War left behind a constellation in which it was *neither* possible to return to the past – to the power politics and hierarchical imperialism of the pre-war era – *nor* to forge a radically different international system through and around the League of Nations. Put differently, it was as impossible to restore the "old world order" as to build a transformative "new world order" that would really merit that characterisation. But what could be achieved, what could be built instead? In order to answer this question, explain why there could be no "Wilsonian peace" and, crucially, elucidate why there was an overriding need for a new Atlantic order – a *Pax Atlantica* – on different premises, it is essential to re-appraise not only the most obvious problems but also the underlying and systemic challenges that confronted those who sought to make peace after the Great War. And it is no less essential to gain a clearer understanding of the altered and extremely challenging conditions under which they had to operate – on a political playing-field that the war had transformed – and essentially *widened.*

I. The Key Actors, the Key Questions They Faced and the Key Requirements of Peacemaking

It is no exaggeration to say that in the tumultuous aftermath of the Great War, the year between the armistice and the immediate aftermath of the Paris Peace Conference constituted the most complex and in many ways the most overburdened *and fraught* period in the history of modern international politics. It was in many ways far more complex and daunting than the years after the revolutionary and Napoleonic wars or the Second World War. This was due both to the scale and to the *simultaneity* of the pressing issues and more profound systemic challenges that the leading actors had to confront – and the fact that they not only had to deal with the multifaceted and often overwhelming consequences of the war itself but also, in many ways, with the onerous long-termer legacy of the war's pre-history, the developments in the first third of the twentieth century that had led to its outbreak in the first place and had then been further intensified and radicalised since 1914.

What the war left in its wake was a disheartening array of challenges, not only in terms of their multitude but also in terms of their novelty and indeed their intractability. These ranged from concrete and urgent problems such as that of countering the ongoing violence in the post-imperial spaces east of the Rhine and providing food supplies to ailing populations to the most profound, and immensely challenging, systemic problems – all the way to the arduous tasks of constructing nothing less than a new system of states in and beyond Europe, finding underpinnings for a new world economic and financial order and, crucially, laying the groundwork for a new system of international politics, and security, for Europe and the wider world.

Contrary to what has long been the prevalent view, the main problem after the Great War was *not* that it proved so difficult and ultimately impossible to create a robust postwar system of the victors that provided the wherewithal for an effective containment of the vanquished, notably Germany – which ultimately relied on force. For such a system was essentially unsustainable under the conditions the war had created. Rather, the only realistic path towards a durable new order could be charted through a more balanced and ultimately inclusive negotiating process that essentially yielded a compromise peace – a settlement that far as possible balanced the interests, concerns, needs and expectations of all key actors, notably not only those of the victors but also those of the vanquished. How to pave the way for such a process, and such settlement, was the cardinal challenge after the armistice. But at the same time the character of the war – and of the transatlantic ideological war within it – had made advances towards such a peace harder than ever before in the history of modern international politics. This was the fundamental dilemma.

Crucially, both the scale of the catastrophe and the escalating ideological struggles within it had not only unsettled but indeed begun to transform the playing-field of international, domestic and transnational politics and generated unprecedentedly deep political and ideological antagonisms between the opposing sides. They had also given rise to an unprecedented range of not only heightened – often even millennial – but also often *conflicting* expectations of what kind of peace was to be founded and what it was supposed to bring. Notably, collective transnational expectations for a universal League and a progressive, democratic "peace to end all wars" collided with more traditional security expectations; expectations of material and immaterial compensations for the war's hardships among the populations of the victorious states collided with expectations of a lenient "Wilsonian peace" on the part of the vanquished; expectations of different national movements in eastern Europe that their aspirations for statehood and self-determination would be fulfilled not only often clashed with one another but also with core German and Austrian expectations that their claims to self-determination would be recognised; and the expectations of those of anti-imperial nationalists in the "colonial-imperial world" outside Europe of course collided with the expectations of the remaining imperial powers, above all Britain and France, that they would be able to reassert their imperial prerogatives.

Further, it is essential to understand that some of the most critical, under-lying postwar challenges did not just stem from the destructive and radicalis-ing impact of the Great War itself but had roots that reached deep into the nineteenth century and the formative decades of the long twentieth century. In particular, they were bound up with the wider legacy of the pre-war era of high imperialism and the dynamics, mentalities and assumptions that it had created. Essentially, the Great War had not only led to the collapse of the eastern empires; it had – in a world-historical perspective – destroyed not all but most of the "old order" of the pre-1914 era – the "order" of European imperial power-states and the world system that they had still dominated despite the ascent of the United States and Japan. The fact that the British and French empires had emerged victorious from the war – only with essential American help – did not really change this basic outcome. In short, by the end of 1918 there was a both urgent and fundamental need to establish, finally, the groundwork for what had been lacking ever since the demise of the Vienna system and the escalation of globalising economic and power-political compe-tition, namely a functioning *international* system that provided effective restraints, ground-rules and guarantees of general peace and security.

But taking any substantial steps towards building such a system was a daunting task amidst the disorder and disarray of late 1918. And this task became even more complicated because it had to be approached for the first time through a process that could no longer be inner-European, could not – yet – be global in a meaningful way but had to be essentially *transatlantic* – the first attempt to build a modern *Atlantic* order at the core of a reconfigured global order. As will be seen, this required immense learning processes from the key actors – and major reorien-tations from elites and wider publics – on both sides of the Atlantic. In many ways, the struggles not only over the future of Europe but also over the future of the international order that had escalated during the war now reached their climax. An unprecedented multiplicity of actors now strove to have voice in the peace and reordering processes, to influence the ways in which peace would be made and the world reordered – which in itself constituted one of the novel challenges of 1918–19.

The political leaders and experts who prepared for the peace negotiations on behalf of the western powers would not only have to deal with those who sought to represent the vanquished powers as well as with the leaders of smaller European states – belligerents and neutrals – and with the representatives of the newly proclaimed east European states, notably Poland and Czechoslovakia. They would also have to wrestle with the Ukrainian, Ruthenian and other east European nationalists who still sought to gain recognition for their claims to self-determination and statehood – and of course with the leaders of anti-colonial nationalist movements outside Europe who now also put forward their claims and strove to have a voice in the reordering process.

Further, those who occupied leading positions in governments and state hierarchies now had to contend with the vast array of non-governmental actors who had campaigned for their causes, lobbied for their various, more or less internationalist peace-building and reform plans, and advanced their schemes for a League of Nations during the war. These activists and pressure-groups now stepped up their efforts, seeking to influence both governments and "world opinion". Yet so did of course all those who pursued more particular national interests, nationalist aims, and national or nationalist causes. And, significantly, whoever sought to set the terms of peace and postwar order now had to grapple with the unprecedented challenge posed by Lenin and those who sought to spread Bolshevik ideology and to foment revolutionary changes, particularly across the unsettled political landscapes of Eastern and Central Europe – to Germany and even further to the west. At a critical juncture when most of these old and new actors sought to exert influence not only on national publics but also and crucially across national and continental boundaries, the complex international politics of peacemaking thus also had acquired a newly critical *transnational* dimension.

Essentially, however, while many hitherto more powerless or peripheral actors tried to reshape post–First World War international politics, the key decisions about how peace negotiations would actually be approached and the first key parameters of the new order would be set – and about which expectations would be fulfilled or disappointed – would be made, to a striking extent, by those who acted on behalf of the most powerful states: the political leaders of the war's principal victors and those who advised them. Indeed, the months following the armistice and then, even more so, the peacemaking processes of 1919 would clearly manifest that they were the players who, though facing complex constraints, had most systemic leverage. And they would also play the most critical role in recasting and reshaping the playing-field of modern international politics under most conflict-prone circumstances.

At the same time, this intense period would not only throw into relief how relatively constrained the agency and influence of those who represented the vanquished and other, smaller states was; they would also highlight how limited the influence of most of the non-governmental actors was and how relatively ineffectual their newly or re-formed transnational networks proved when it came to the most vital decisions of peacemaking. This proved especially sobering for the leading policymakers of the defeated powers, above all the fledgling Weimar Republic; yet it also particularly frustrated the most "progressive" and radical activists in Britain and the United States who had counted on Wilson's support for their aspirations to initiate a newly transparent and inclusive peace process and thus to build a genuinely *new* world order. Finally, the aftermath of the war would ultimately also reveal the limits rather than the pervasive power of the Bolshevik regime and its revolutionary clout – though "the Bolshevik menace" would affect the eventual peace process in various ways.

But post–First World War peacemaking was also, and significantly, complicated by the fact that in striking contrast to their predecessors of 1814–15 by the time the armistice was concluded the pivotal actors, those who shaped the policies of the victors, had not even begun to reach a consensus on the most important issues they now faced – and, more fundamentally, on the architecture and the rules and norms of the refashioned international order that hence was to guarantee a stable peace. None of the protagonists had made more than basic, preliminary preparations for peace negotiations. And they had not reached any agreement yet on how to treat the beaten enemy, on what terms and to what extent it would have to pay reparations and, above all, how Germany and the successor states of the Austro-Hungarian Empire were to fit into the postwar order. Nor did they yet see eye to eye about how to guarantee future international security, what part the envisaged League of Nations was to have in this context – and how it was to be constituted. They had no common approach when it came to the question of how to constitute and secure the new nation-states in central and eastern Europe to which they had committed themselves in various ways. They did not agree on what was the best strategy to respond to the Bolshevik regime and its aspirations to fan the flames of communist revolution across and beyond Central Europe. And they differed on numerous other lesser but no less intractable matters.

What is more, the victors had not even begun to reach agreement on the crucial question of *how* they would seek to make peace – and notably whether the eventual peacemaking process would ultimately comprise negotiations with the vanquished powers, above all Germany, or remain essentially a process that was exclusively determined or at least essentially dominated by the western powers. All three western governments thus still had to develop more fleshed-out agendas and conceptions for the envisaged general peace conference – and it was still an open question to what extent they could actually coordinate these agendas. The lack of consensus among the victors was in part due to Wilson's insistence on pursuing a unilateral mission on behalf of his version of an "American peace". But it also reflected the basic fact that the three principal victors pursued peace aspirations, interests and agendas that conflicted in crucial respects – and that would have been very difficult to reconcile before the end of the war. This is why the two months between the armistice and the opening of the Paris Peace Conference were such a critical phase – and why peacemaking in 1919 became such a complex and in many aspects overburdened process.

II.   The Most Pressing Challenges – the Cardinal German Question, the Reorganisation of Central and Eastern Europe, and the Novel "Bolshevik Threat"

First, however, it is imperative to have closer look at the challenges themselves – and indeed to reassess what were most acute and the most salient challenges of peacemaking in the wake of the First World War. At the outset, it is important to underscore the relative "openness" of the historical constellation after the Great War as it presented itself to the actors at the time. And it is no less critical to retain in retrospect, from a distance of 100 years, a perspective of relative openness as well, i.e. not to presuppose – with the benefit of hindsight and the knowledge of how the first would relatively soon be followed by a second world war – that it was impossible to forge a more lasting peace settlement after the catastrophe of the Great War. Put differently, it is crucial to resist the temptation to "over-determine" the failure of peacemaking in 1919 – to amass, in retrospect, an overwhelming number of not only contingent factors but also profound structural and systemic reasons for why the efforts to create a new international order at this juncture could only produce ephemeral results. Indeed, just as the outbreak of the Great War was *not* inevitable, as we have seen, the reordering processes after 1918 were *not* bound to fail or yield only an inherently unstable and contested "scaffold of peace".

Yet in order to grasp what *could* be achieved at this juncture it is even more essential to gain a clearer understanding of the tremendous challenges that those who sought to make peace had to grapple with – not only both the acute and the massive *structural* problems the war itself had created but also the longer-term systemic dynamics and problems that had produced the cataclysm. For these challenges, and particularly the *underlying* structural or systemic challenges, were actually quite different from what has long been asserted, both in 1919 and thereafter, particularly by "realist" observers. And only if they are properly understood it is possible to gauge what prospects and room to manoeuvre the peacemakers of Versailles really had, or thought they had, to forge a "peace to end all wars". And only then it is possible to gauge, ultimately, why it proved so extremely difficult for all sides, yet especially the leaders of the victorious powers, to lay foundations for a "rational", balanced peace settlement that could be considered as basically legitimate by *all* relevant parties, including the vanquished – and for a functioning postwar order.

Further, comprehending these underlying systemic challenges can help to illuminate why it proved so challenging even to begin to repair the torn fabric of a deeply fractured international society in and beyond Europe – and to found, as liberal and socialist internationalists had hoped, a universal League of Nations and a new kind of international community that transcended the divisions of the war. Ultimately, it can thus serve to elucidate why, under the circumstances, making any progress towards a more sustainable international system, at the core a Euro-Atlantic order for the long twentieth century, would require considerably more time, changing conditions and, crucially, more substantive reorientations on all sides.

It is worth highlighting again that never in the modern – or ancient – history of conflict had any war *caused* or *catalysed* a more intractable and inauspicious array of problems and challenges. The very *simultaneity* of so many immediate and structural, short-term and long-term problems made the task to "make peace" unprecedentedly demanding. Nonetheless, it seems helpful to distinguish between two kinds of challenges that the Great War had left in its wake: on the one hand, the most salient and pressing *immediate* problems that now appeared on the peacemaking agenda; and, on the other hand, the *underlying structural* and *systemic* challenges with which the different actors now had to contend. What also and crucially features under these latter challenges are the profoundly altered domestic, international *and* transnational conditions under which the peacemakers operated and, in particular, the conflicting *demands* and *expectations* they confronted. Especially these wider challenges become more easily discernible with the benefit of hindsight; but they have not been properly illuminated yet.

1) The Crucial German Question – and Its Transatlantic Dimensions

Unquestionably, the most pressing and obviously critical problem the victors had to tackle was how to deal with the principal defeated power. And it was, in a broader sense, *the German question* in its manifold dimensions. This was the question around which French peace planning revolved; it would also come to be at the centre of British peace policy; and – eventually – Wilson would also be compelled to face it squarely. On very different premises, it was of course also a problem that the originally isolated and powerless policymakers who acted on behalf of a fledgling German republic had to address in new ways. Subsequently it would lie at the heart of the tumultuous peace negotiations of Versailles. Yet what exactly was the German question after the Great War? Was it essentially the problem of how to contain German power and keep Germany in check most effectively – as generations of "realists" have argued, based on the assumption that this was vital to forestall an otherwise "inevitable" *revanchist* assault of the defeated power on the postwar order?[4]

Arguably, on a more fundamental level the critical question was a different and broader one. It was the problem of how to find a proper place for a vanquished but still inherently very powerful German nation-state *within* a recast international order. More precisely, the real challenge after the war, especially but not only because it had ended with a less than total defeat, was to find ways to construct a peace system that, as far as possible, made the continued existence of a German state reconcilable with the security and development interests of its old and new neighbours – and, in a broader context, with European, transatlantic and global peace and stability. And this essentially required a system that fostered, not a precarious new "balance of power" but rather advances towards a new equilibrium of security, rights, satisfactions, possibilities *and restraints*, above all between the principal victors

---

[4] See MacMillan (2002); Keylor (2011), pp. 73–9; Marks (2013); Tooze (2014), pp. 271–7; and the more even-handed interpretations of Steiner (2005), pp. 67–70; and Sharp (I/2008), pp. 199–207.

and the principal vanquished power of the war. Understood in these terms, the German problem was thus also one of the most critical *systemic* questions that arose after the war – in the sense that the manner in which it was addressed was bound to have a decisive bearing on the stability and viability of the entire postwar international system. It was thus intimately bound up with the question of whether a sustainable Atlantic order could be established in 1919.

In a wider sense, this German question had existed in different guises and had remained unsettled since the foundational stages of the European state-system and the Peace of Westphalia of 1648.[5] As noted, the protagonists of the Congress of Vienna had found relatively successful *temporary* solution: a German Federation guaranteed by the European great powers and interlocked with European international law. But this construction could eventually no longer accommodate the strength and formative power of German nationalism. Bismarck's "blood and iron" revolution from above and the founding of the German imperial state in 1871 had created Europe's and eventually the world's "modern" German problem, which had never been "resolved" thereafter.

Between 1914 and 1918 it had taken the combined power of the western powers and Russia and ultimately the decisive American intervention to defeat the German Empire – and its Austro-Hungarian ally – and to prevent a suffocating German predominance over the European continent. Yet what now had crucial implications both for the peace process and the longer-term stabilisation prospects of Europe was the decidedly challenging combination of factors that has already been discussed, namely that the war had not ended with an unequivocal western victory; that it had left the German state largely unscathed and the German power potential largely intact; and that at the same time it had precipitated the collapse of the Wilhelmine regime, revolutionary turmoil and a political transformation process – towards a German republic or possibly a German soviet republic – whose outcome was highly uncertain.

In the aftermath of the armistice, the German question thus re-appeared both with new urgency and in a new form. At one level, the victors not only had to decide what terms they would put forward for the "settlement" with the defeated power. In particular, they had to agree on what kind of compensations – mainly in the form of reparations for war damages – and what kind of penalty – in terms of economic yet also military, territorial *and political* restrictions – were to be sought from Germany after a war for which, as all victors now claimed, the regime of the German Empire – or even the German people – bore the sole responsibility. Behind this lurked what was essentially a deeper, not only political but also moral question: who would be held accountable for the all but incomprehensible catastrophe of the war, and who would have to "pay" for it, not only in financial but also in moral terms.

[5] See Krüger (1985), pp. 2–6; Schroeder (1994); Doering-Manteuffel (2010); Simms (2014).

At another level, the victors had to agree on how they would seek not only to contain the threat of Germany's still massive war-machine but also come to terms with the underlying problem of its abiding military and economic potential. The German question thus clearly lay at the centre of the postwar security problem, which will be examined in greater depth below. Essentially, they had to find effective ways to prevent the defeated power from seeking to reverse the outcome of the war and challenging the new international order they sought to establish. And, closely connected with this, they confronted two no less fundamental questions: not only what shape, and borders, Germany was to have but also, and crucially, what status the vanquished power was to be accorded in the reconfigured international system.

Did the only realistic "solution" to the German problem lie in seizing on the victory of November 1918 to impose a peace of containment, diminution and control on the defeated power – as Clemenceau and key French strategists contemplated? Did it lie in constraining and controlling German power by force, and thus altering the fundamental structural imbalance between Germany and France, by enforcing not only far-reaching military restrictions and rigorous disarmament controls but also curtailing German territory and sovereignty and imposing both tangible economic limitations and heavy reparations on the postwar German state? And was the only "realistic" longer-term strategy to ban the German threat not only through a perpetuated alliance of the victors but also by isolating the defeated power for the foreseeable future? Or were there – in spite of the highly adverse conditions the war had created – prospects for a different, more "modern" and potentially more sustainable approach to the vexing German problem?

Was there any possibility of actually advancing towards what Wilson had still favoured during the armistice process and what many more committed internationalists had long clamoured for: a negotiated peace or, more precisely, negotiations with those who now sought to assume political responsibility amidst the revolutionary turmoil in Germany? Could a peace settlement that sought to accommodate not only the interests and concerns of the victors but also those of the defeated power create better prospects for a sustainable order? Might more deeply realistic paths to peace be opened up by trying to integrate Germany not only in the League but also in a novel, more integrative "Atlantic order"? And could it be more advantageous to try to bind not only the victors but also the vanquished to new common ground-rules and principles of international politics that could then serve to manage the inevitable postwar disputes? In November 1918, all of these were still open questions. But in view of the French government's fundamental resistance to envisaging any kind of negotiated peace with Germany, any progress in this direction would critically depend on the attitudes and approaches of the key British and American actors – and above all on how far Lloyd George and Wilson were willing, and able, to assume pivotal hegemonic responsibilities and provide effective strategic and political *reassurance* to France.

Ultimately, then, one, if not *the* key challenge after the Great War was to forge a settlement that fostered Germany's integration into the postwar order on terms that ensured the security of France and the stability of western Europe – and that at the same furthered rather than jeopardised the consolidation of the most unsettled region, Central and Eastern Europe, and the security and development prospects of the new states that were emerging there. Yet any attempt to address this challenge and the critical German problem in a balanced manner encountered immense obstacles that the increasingly "total" character of the war had created. And among the greatest obstacles were the unprecedentedly deep divisions, the chasms of distrust and political-psychological enmity that the virulence of wartime nationalisms and ideological warfare had opened up, especially between the western powers and Germany – and above all between Germany and France. Yet what also mattered here, what could either complicate this process further or enable a new kind of "solution", was the fact that for the first time dealing with the German problem was no longer merely a European affair; it had to be approached in a new transatlantic force-field in which the policies of the United States and notably the priorities of its president were crucial in every way.

These wider international dimensions of the German problem were in fact closely bound up with a crucial domestic question that would have to be decided within Germany, but that would also be significantly influenced by the policies and behaviour of the victors. It was the question of what kind of constitutional-political order could be created and stabilised in the postwar German state. This was of immense importance for the future of European and global stability. Essentially, it had to be decided who would have control and legitimate authority over the German state and its levers of power. Would those who had earlier backed the *Reichstag*'s Peace Resolution now be able at least to lay the groundwork for a stable parliamentary democracy, a German republic, under the shadow of an unacknowledged defeat? And would they be able and in a position to develop a new, coherent republican approach to German foreign policy – and realistic strategies for what they expected and prepared for: eventual peace negotiations with the western powers? Or would they be frustrated? And would this open up new political possibilities for those who had earlier clamoured for a "victorious peace", were now on the defensive but already began to contemplate how to turn the "shameful collapse" of November 1918 into an ultimate German victory? Or would it create opportunities for new, even more radical authoritarian *revanchists*?

What is more, an even "greater" German question resurfaced in the aftermath of the Great War – for the first time since 1848. It was brought to the fore by the mainly socialist and liberal forces who after the dissolution of the Habsburg Empire campaigned for a union of Germany and German Austria – or the *Anschluß* of the newly proclaimed Austrian republic to Germany – in the name of "self-determination". It remained to be seen how the victors would react to these aspirations, which raised the spectre of creating a potentially even greater concentration of German power at the centre of Europe. Yet the *Anschluß* question nonetheless also raised the wider normative question of how far the postwar order would and could indeed be consistently based on the principle of "self-determination" or whether overriding considerations of power and international stability would take precedence.

2) The Imperative Reorganisation of Central and Eastern Europe and the Critical Polish-German Question

Yet the German question was also in many ways bound up with a far vaster and even more intricate complex of problems that now had to be urgently addressed: the reorganisation of Central and Eastern Europe in the wake of the collapse of the three empires – the Wilhelminian, the Romanov and the Habsburg Empires – that had long dominated and structured this part of the European continent. Essentially, what now arose was the question of how far it would be possible at all to create not only viable states but also a geopolitical environment – and an international "superstructure" – that would allow them to consolidate.

What made this question particularly virulent, intractable and potentially unsettling for Europe as a whole was not only the fact that the war had created a power vacuum and left this region in a state of acute turmoil – with violent conflict in Central and Eastern Europe not only continuing but even escalating after the armistice. The more profound challenge was indeed to deal with the Pandora's Box of newly vehement Polish, Czech, Slovak and numerous other national and nationalist claims for statehood and "self-determination" that had arisen during the war. These had been further encouraged not only by Wilson's – and Lenin's – rhetoric but also by the promises that both the *Entente* and the Central Powers had made to different national movements for largely tactical purposes. For more often than not, the unsurprisingly often maximalist and strikingly ethnocentric agendas and claims of these movements extended to the same territory and thus conflicted in a region whose historical evolution had produced an often intricate intermingling of different populations and ethnic groups. And, crucial for the wider stabilisation prospects of postwar Europe, this not only fuelled conflicts between the claims of the different east European nationalist causes, e.g. the Polish and the Czech, but was also bound to generate clashes between their aspirations and German "self-determination" claims.

Thus, Wilson and the other principal peacemakers would not only have to grapple with the question of how far it would be at all possible even to approach an "equitable" application of the "self-determination" principle in a highly unstable constellation marked by radicalised nationalisms, inter-ethnic enmity and profound mistrust. They also confronted the wider challenge of somehow reconciling as far as possible the politically critical satisfaction of hardly reconcilable national expectations and the requirements of not just eastern European but more general Euro-Atlantic peace and stability. This was a gargantuan task. And it became even more challenging because the victors would have to deal with leaders of provisional governments of "states in process of formation" as well as heads of national movements who were trying their utmost to create "facts on the ground" prior to any formal peace conference.

By the time of the armistice, the most important of these – Marshal Józef Piłsudski on behalf of Poland and Tomáš Masaryk on behalf of the provisional Czechoslovak government – had indeed already proclaimed the birth of new independent nation-states. And that the former southern Slav minorities of the Austro-Hungarian Empire – Croatians and Slovenes – would in some way join with Serbia in a new Yugoslavian state, a Kingdom of the Serbs, Croats and Slovenes – was also already clear before the peace conference even began, though this state had not yet been recognised. Yet it was far from clear how far the different and often conflicting claims for territory could be settled or at least de-escalated. Those who formed the vanguards of the east European national causes would now confront the enormous longer-term task of building states, of consolidating what were as yet necessarily fragile "states-in-formation" that were situated in a most problematic geopolitical environment, namely between two temporarily weakened but inherently more powerful post-imperial states, Germany and Russia. Western "peacemakers", however, would now face the challenge of not only trying to redraw Eentral and Eastern Europe's geopolitical map – as far as it was in their power – but also coming to grips with the numerous short- and longer-term conflicts that were bound to ensue in this region and, crucially, to establish something akin to a security and stabilisation framework for Central and Eastern Europe. Here, too, the question arose how far the League of Nations could serve this purpose.

Arguably, the most critical and explosive question in the context of eastern Europe's unavoidable reorganisation was the Polish question, which in central aspects can more accurately be characterised as a Polish-German question. Like the Franco-German problem in the west, it had a crucial systemic significance for the post–First World War era. The manner in which it was addressed would have a decisive bearing on the stability of the postwar system and the pacification of Europe as a whole – and indeed global implications – in the shorter as well as the longer term. Crucial decisions about the shape and borders of the new Polish state still had to be made. While Piłsudski and the more moderate elements of the Polish national movement were relatively restrained in their aims, the more expansionist Polish National Committee, led by Roman Dmowski, advanced rather far-reaching claims about the territory a "viable" Polish state should have. And particularly these claims extended to provinces that had been part of the German Empire and comprised sizeable German populations. They thus collided head-on with the claims and interests of a defeated but still powerful German postwar state – and would be fervently refuted by German politicians, publicised opinion and propaganda. On a smaller scale, the same problem arose in conjunction with Czech claims to the Sudeten area, which had been a predominantly German-speaking province of the Habsburg Empire. And similar problems were caused by Slovak, "Yugoslav" and Romanian claims to territories that had been part of the Kingdom of Hungary, including large areas in which ethnic Hungarians constituted the majority. Further, they arose in the still very volatile border regions of the former Russian Empire, where notably a burgeoning Ukrainian national movement now advanced claims for a Ukrainian nation-state.

But the Polish-German problem was of far greater import for the peace-making processes of 1919 – and the future prospects of a new Euro-Atlantic order. Essentially, the leaders and policymakers of the western powers faced immensely complex political questions: How far could the creation of a "viable" Polish nation-state with access to the Baltic Sea, to which Wilson and the *Entente* governments had generally committed themselves, be effected while *limiting* what could not be avoided in the historical constellation of 1918: the creation of seedbeds of future Polish–German conflicts over boundaries and minorities? And how far could they establish any mechanism and rules to address these conflicts in the longer run to prevent them from destabilising the entire postwar order? It was no coincidence that the disputes over the future borders and relations between Poland and Germany also raised with particular acuteness fundamental normative questions that would have to be addressed at the peace conference and were to have crucial implications for future international politics: How far would it be possible to apply with any measure of consistency the principle of national self-determination that both sides invoked? Was there any realistic prospect of working out something resembling a mutually acceptable settlement? Or should the settlement be based on other, overriding political and strategic considerations?

In the constellation the war had left behind, the real challenge lay in finding ways both to minimise and to manage these problems as far as possible by negotiating complex compromises and applying basic principles in the most equitable manner conceivable. And the real question was how far the different visions, aims and interests of the victors would allow this. Beyond this, new ways had to be found – not only but especially in this case – to deal with one issue that now became particularly virulent: the issue of ethnic minorities in the newly established nation-states. The challenge was to establish effective protections for the political and cultural rights of minority groups – such as the Jewish and German minority populations that the recreated Polish state would comprise to a greater or lesser extent. And, crucially, it had to be decided through what kind of processes these explosive problems would be addressed. Could they be adequately "settled" by the western victors? Or was there any prospect of a negotiating process that also involved not only Polish but also German representatives? A lot was at stake here. The larger challenge was to prevent the emergence of a precarious structural antagonism between a new Polish state intent on asserting itself while seeking security and a defeated, volatile but inherently still far more powerful German neighbour that would hence harbour irredentist grievances vis-à-vis Poland and contest essential aspects of its sovereignty and integrity.

Yet the unavoidably conflict-prone delineation of a new border between Poland and Germany was in many ways merely the most troublesome aspect of a far wider systemic question – the question of how far – and how – such a profound recasting of the political and territorial map of what had long been a region dominated by multinational empires could be pursued without creating a vast area of structural conflict and instability for a long time to come. In many ways, this depended not only on the processes through which the new states were established and the precise boundaries they would have. It also, and crucially, depended on the extent to which it was approached with close attention to what had an even greater bearing on the prospects of longer-term European peace and stability: the requirements of a sustainable settlement of the German problem. It still remained to be seen to what extent the victorious powers could actually exert a tangible influence on the ways in which the political map of Central and Eastern Europe was reorganised. But of even more import was their capacity to lay the groundwork of an international system that provided a critical security framework for this structurally unstable region – and that in particular provided both reassurance to the fledgling eastern states – above all against possible German revisionism or Bolshevik–Russian challenges – and effective mechanisms to address what were certain to be long-term *and structural* inter- and inner-state conflicts. Here, too, it remained to be seen what role the League could play. And, as will be shown, these immensely demanding challenges now had to be addressed, and could only be addressed, through a transatlantic process in which Wilson and other American policymakers would play a critical part.

3)   The Novel Challenge of the "Bolshevik Threat" – and Its Limits

What further complicated the situation in Central and Eastern Europe – and was to affect the eventual reordering processes of 1919 in numerous ways – was that further east another novel, unpredictable and potentially enormous challenge had arisen – that posed, on the one hand, by the Bolshevik regime and the spectre of a Bolshevik-dominated Russia and, on the other, by what the western governments saw as the threat of a dynamic westward spread of Bolshevik revolutionary ideology and unrest across a war-torn continent. While the future of the Bolshevik regime was still far from certain in the winter of 1918–19, the victorious powers, which thus far had intervened indecisively in the ongoing Russian civil war with troops and military aid for the "White forces", now had to deliberate whether they should, and could, expand their intervention and actually try to defeat the Bolsheviks by military means – or whether they should seek to negotiate and work out some kind of "truce" or even a basic *modus vivendi* with the Bolshevik leaders.

At the same time, they had to respond to the much wider transnational impact of a Bolshevik threat whose extent and repercussions for future domestic and international politics they had only begun to comprehend. It soon became clear that on a continent that was so profoundly unsettled and devastated by the Great War, the ideology and propaganda of the Bolsheviks indeed constituted a novel, qualitatively distinct challenge. What Lenin, Trotsky and others proclaimed had by this time hardened into a potent alternative vision that challenged older as well as more progressive "western" concepts of both international and domestic order. And, in particular, it challenged Wilson's essentially liberal vision of a League of Nations and the hierarchical spread of American-style democracy. This added a new, if still somewhat diffuse, dimension both to the preparations for the peace conference and then to the peacemaking process itself.

III.   The Underlying Challenges – Limited Prospects for Global Transformations and the Need for a New Atlantic Order

In many ways even more daunting and critical – yet also less easily discernible both for the protagonists of Paris and later analysts – were the deeper systemic challenges of making peace and building or rebuilding order after the Great War: the profound challenges of insecurity and instability that arose from the fact that war had brought about a systemic collapse and reconfiguration of world-historical proportions. In short, it had shattered not only the eastern continental European empires but also undermined the entire pre-war system of high-stakes competitive power politics and essentially unbounded globalising competition and *Weltpolitik* in which, despite the United States' dynamic ascent, the modes and rivalries of the European imperial powers had still essentially shaped international politics. And it had at the same time largely undermined the political, financial, economic, cultural *and mental* preconditions for a restoration or recreation of the "old order".

At a deeper level, then, peacemaking in 1919 would be unprecedentedly difficult because, as we have seen, the Great War had brought about more momentous changes in the overall configuration and power structure of the international system than any previous modern war – changes that indeed generated new global dynamics but especially affected the relations between the European states that fought or were drawn into the war and, crucially, the relations between the United States and Europe. And it is important to note that the leading political actors of 1918 and 1919 only began to comprehend the scale and repercussions of these transformative changes. In retrospect, the novel challenges that arose from them indeed warrant a systematic re-appraisal because they would not only have a profound effect on the peace negotiations but also a formative long-term influence on the second half of the long twentieth century.

1)   The Collapse of the Old European "Order" of Empires

The war both deepened and radicalised the polarising processes that, as we have seen, had already shaped the relations between the two different camps of European power states before 1914; and the political and ideological war within the war between the western powers and the Central Powers created far deeper divisions than previous wars. Of even more fundamental import, however, was that by the time it ended it had also in essential respects shattered the old European international system of the era of high imperial-ism, a system that had been shaped and dominated by the political interests and rivalries between the five preponderant empires.

While the *Entente* Powers Britain and France emerged from the war deeply exhausted and weakened, but also as yet resilient, great powers – whose victory had come at a high price and had ultimately only been possible because of American support – it proved highly consequential that neither the Russian nor the Austro-Hungarian empires survived the war – and that the Ottoman Empire would collapse soon thereafter. Even more consequential, however, was the fact that although the German state survived the defeat the German Empire collapsed in the wake of the war. As a consequence, all imperialist-hegemonic aspirations of those who since 1914 had clamoured for a *Siegfrieden* had been stymied for the foreseeable future.

2)   Towards a New System of Self-Governing States?

The war thus brought about a wider shift that not only had major conse-quences for the future of Europe but also was to have far-reaching global repercussions. It created a constellation in which the core question became how far it would be possible to replace the competitive system of the pre-war era, which essentially had been a system dominated by more or less multi-national empires, and to create a durable modern international system of *states* – i.e. a system in which more or less unified and more or less sovereign nation-states, not multinational empires, were to be the crucial units and actors. And by the end of 1918 this question had unquestionably been made more acute and politically charged by a transatlantic political-ideological struggle that turned the notion of "self-governing" or "self-determined" state-hood, which had existed before 1914, into a *prevalent* concept on the changing playing-field of international politics. Indeed, what now became a key rationale that the – often competing – nationalists and national movements in and beyond Europe adopted was that the only way to ensure independence, security and *recognition* in the international sphere was to acquire a (nation-) state. Yet it remained to be seen how far such a reconfigured system of states could be created in an equitable manner – and in such a way as to further rather than hinder Europe's postwar pacification. And it remained to be seen how far, as its proponents envisaged, the League of Nations would furnish more effective safeguards for the sovereignty and integrity of states than had existed in the past – which meant, above all, guarantees for smaller states against threats or infringements by more powerful states whose leaders invoked strategic necessities or civilisational prerogatives.

In this context, one further critical political question arose – and posed itself in ways that were qualitatively different from previous instances when order had been recast after major wars. It was the question of what kind of criteria – apart from being nation-states and recognised as such – states had to fulfil to become part of the new order – and who would set these criteria. Crucially, it had to be decided how far "membership" in this order, and in the League, would hence no longer merely depend on the willingness of a state's representatives to commit to international treaty obligations, but essentially on the state's form of government – and more specifically its *democratic* form of government. Put differently, what became acute was the question of whether "equal" rights and representation in the postwar order would only be extended to states that met the essentially "western" criterion of being democratic or self-governing. And this had a direct bearing on one of the most critical problems, namely that of how far the principal vanquished power – the fledgling German republic – should be included in a reconfigured Atlantic order.

3) Persistent Power Hierarchies and Limited Prospects for Advances towards a New Global Order

In a broader perspective, the war and its outcome unquestionably created major *global* challenges and reordering needs. Yet while in a *longue durée* perspective it marked the beginning of the end of the European-dominated imperialist "world (dis)order" that had taken shape in the first third of the long twentieth century, it by no means as yet led to a dissolution of this system. Put differently, it brought down some empires – those that ended up on the losing side – but not the system as such.

From a distance of 100 years, one can discern more clearly that the Great War had indeed not only generated demands but also created a fundamental systemic need for substantial changes – steps towards a refashioned global order or, more realistically, steps to at least initiate – as non-violently as possible – what some, though comparatively few actors at the time regarded as paramount: the necessarily more long-term transition from the pre-war "order" of empires towards an essentially post-imperial system of more or less sovereign and self-determined states *on a global scale*.

As we have seen, the developments of the war, the political-ideological struggle it fomented and not only Lenin's proclamations but also, and crucially, Wilson's rhetoric had raised hopes that a more universal transformation process would be within reach in its aftermath. Following the armistice, the leading figures of nationalist anti-imperialist independence movements in the colonised or "imperialised" world – those who sought to end colonial rule or imperialist domination by the European powers, the United States and Japan – also intensified their efforts to gain a political platform for their demands for "self-determination" and independent statehood. And all of these actors expanded their attempts both to seize on Wilson's pronouncements and to enlist the American president as a powerful ally for their cause. On behalf of the growing Indian nationalist movement Bal Gangadhar Tilak asked the American president to espouse his call for *Self-Determination for India*. His Egyptian counterpart, Sa'd Zaghlul, sought to do the same in order to put pressure on the Lloyd George government to grant independence to Egypt. In East Asia, Korean nationalists intensified their efforts to push their self-determination agenda. And the leading Chinese reformer Sun Yat Sen appealed to Wilson in November 1918 "to save democracy in China" as he had "done in Europe", calling on the American president to support inner-Chinese efforts to bolster the republic that had been established in 1912 and at the same time to restore a sovereign China.[6] And these were only some of the most audible voices who essentially demanded an end to colonial rule and imperial domination.

But the pivotal question was how far the war had not only begun to transform the political playing-field and the hierarchy of prevalent norms – particularly strengthening the political power of "self-determination" – but also shaken up or even altered the actual power structures and power hierarchies beyond Europe to such an extent that the conditions for a substantial reordering process existed. A retrospective analysis can underscore that in the constellation the war left behind, the prospects for such a process and significant advances towards a genuinely recast or modernised *global* order after the Great War – an order in which basic ground-rules, norms and principles of order, e.g. the principle of self-determination, were respected not just in the transatlantic sphere (as well as, within certain limits, in Latin America) but universally, without marked hierarchical gradations, were in fact distinctly limited. And so were, consequently, the prospects of founding anything approaching a truly universal, global League of Nations.

---

[6] Sun Yat Sen missive, enclosed in Lansing to Wilson, 20 November 1918, *PWW*, LIII, p. 140.

Potentially, that a powerful figure like the American president had rhetorically espoused the cause of self-determination – and that the power balance
between the old and the new world had shifted – seemed to create new
opportunities for far-reaching changes in the global sphere. But the
American president had thus far neither developed any policies to this end;
nor had he departed from his underlying liberal-hierarchical assumptions that
he had developed before the war – which centred on the notion that some
more civilised peoples were more capable of governing themselves than "less
advanced" peoples, and that the former had a claim to tutor the latter. And,
revealingly, in the fifth of his Fourteen Points, Wilson had used far more
restrained, cautious and ultimately highly ambivalent quasi-legal language
when calling for a "free, open-minded, and absolutely impartial adjustment
of all colonial claims, based upon a strict observance of the principle that in
determining all such questions of sovereignty the interests of the populations
concerned must have equal weight with the equitable claims of the government whose title is to be determined".[7]

In fact, however, the disparities in power and influence between the "title
holders" of the colonial claims and those who contested them were simply too
enormous to permit anything even approaching an absolutely "impartial"
adjustment – whatever this meant in a concrete context. And both in terms
of his power and in terms of his own liberal-hierarchical mindset and proclivities – the American president simply was not in a position to act as a decisive
impartial arbiter here. In short, what was confirmed in 1918–19 was that the
Great War had shaken and affected but by no means undermined the pre-war
system of imperial rule and domination. It had created a constellation that was
marked by one essential tension: the heightened hopes of those who clamoured for substantial political change and self-determination outside Europe
came up against a power structure that in essential respects had *not* been
transformed – and in which those who sought to maintain and even expand
the remaining imperial systems, above all the British, the French and the
Japanese, still had decisively greater leverage than those who were determined
to cast off the yoke of empire and determine their own affairs.

This made it all but unavoidable that the expectations of the different anti-
colonial vanguards would be disappointed. While Germany had been eliminated as a global imperial power for the foreseeable future, the two key imperial
powers that had come out on the winning side, France and Britain, had been
weakened but by no means lost their power and capacities to defend their
imperial interests through incentives – including promises of reform – yet if
necessary also through coercion and the suppression of dissent and unrest.[8]

---

[7] Wilson, "Fourteen Points" address, 8 January 1918, *PWW*, XLV, pp. 538–9.
[8] See Darwin (2009), pp. 358 ff.

And while particularly British imperial rule was challenged by the self-determination agendas of nationalists in India and Egypt, leading British imperial strategists also proved especially adept at adapting old and developing new strategies to renew the legitimacy of what they confidently saw as an exemplary empire that, as Lloyd George proclaimed in 1918, already constituted a "league of nations" in its own right and could indeed serve as a model for the new international organisation Wilson and others envisaged.[9]

In view of this alignment of the "realities of power" there was actually very little room on the post–First World War playing-field for *general* shifts towards a global post-imperial order. What thus came to lie at the centre of the global reordering problems the principal victors *had* to address was a comparatively much narrower question, namely what would be done with the territories and peoples that had formerly been part of or controlled by the empires that had lost the war – the hitherto German colonies and territories that, like the Chinese province of Shandong, had been in the German sphere of influence, and what had been the Arab provinces of the Ottoman Empire. By the end of 1918, all of these provinces and all former German colonies were occupied by Allied forces. At the same time, Japan controlled not only the formerly German-held islands in the north Pacific but also Shandong, which its forces had seized as early as November 1914 and which Tokyo had forced the weak Chinese government to cede formally in 1915. The deeper question that arose was, in a nutshell, whether the future of these peoples and territories would still essentially be decided on old premises – by the "right of victory" and according to "spoils-to-the-victors" maxims – or how far – especially because of Wilson's influence – considerations of "self-determination" and the interests of local populations would come into play in ways they had not prior to 1914. Further, here too it would have to be decided what role, if any, the League could play in this process.

Since 1916, the prevalent sentiment in leading circles in Britain and the Dominions had been that the British Empire should simply retain and if necessary annex the German colonies that British and Dominion forces had captured. And through the secret agreement negotiated between the French colonial diplomat François Georges-Picot and the British expert of Middle Eastern affairs Mark Sykes, which was finalised in November 1916 – and would provoke immense criticism after the Bolsheviks published it in 1917 – the *Entente* Powers had originally distributed the Ottoman Empire's Arab provinces among themselves. They had thus extended their respective imperial spheres of influence through a classic power-political bargain that divided the spoils of conquest. According to the agreement, France was to acquire control of Lebanon and the coastal regions of Syria while Britain was to control

---

[9] Lloyd George speech, 12 September 1918, in *The Times*, 13 September 1918.

southern Mesopotamia and most of Palestine was to be placed under inter-national control; further, an Arab state or a confederation of Arab states was to be established – yet that too would be divided into a British and a French sphere of exclusive rights.[10] Following the armistice, key French policymakers still insisted at the end of the war that both powers should find ways to implement the Sykes-Picot agreement. Yet what proved decisive now was that in response to Wilson, and liberal and Labour pressures at home, the British government had concluded that it would be impossible or at any rate impolitic to proceed on this basis. And, drawing on more long-standing liberal imperi-alist traditions and ideas of imperial tutelage and trusteeship, it had from 1917 reorientated its policy. It now began to adopt a different, imperial-internationalist approach that sought to accommodate the American president by proactively espousing the promotion of "self-determination". The under-lying ultimate aim, however, was to expand Britain's sphere of imperial influ-ence by new, internationalist means.

By June 1917, Lloyd George himself had proclaimed that the "desires" and "interests" of the peoples of the former German colonies had to be the "dominant factor" in determining their "future government"; and in his Caxton House address, he had underlined in January 1918 that the peoples of the Middle East had a claim to have their "separate national conditions" recognised.[11] As has rightly been stressed, however, the core assumption that the British premier shared with all other key imperial policymakers was that such pronouncements were indeed entirely compatible with an extension of British imperial rule or oversight because local populations would actually desire to become part of Britain's imperial system. In their view, the promo-tion of self-determination outside Europe was thus entirely congruent with a further expansion of this system.[12]

Arch-imperialists like Curzon argued in categories of strategic expedience that the Imperial War Cabinet should use "self-determination for all it is worth" to secure imperial gains. But other, eventually more influential officials advocated a different approach, which took up ideas of liberal intellectuals and progressive Labour figures like MacDonald – namely to build bridges to Wilson yet ultimately take the lead as a champion of self-determination. By the autumn of 1918, this was to congeal into to a new prevalent strategy, most elaborately advocated by the aforementioned South African politician Jan Christiaan Smuts. It sought to make the envisaged League of Nations – modelled on an idealised, hierarchically progressive vision of the British Empire – into the framework for a new kind of neo-imperialist mandate

---

[10] See Pedersen (2015), pp. 21–3.
[11] Lloyd George speech, *Manchester Guardian*, 30 June 1917; Lloyd George, Caxton House speech, in *The Observer*, 6 January 1918.
[12] See Pedersen (2015), pp. 24–5.

system through which the "civilised" powers could exercise trusteeship sanctioned by international law, above all in the Middle East.[13] The realisation of this conception critically depended on Wilson's consent and, in a wider context, it hinged on a kind of broader Anglo-American accord in the management of the postwar global order. What thus remained to be seen was how far such a bargain could indeed be struck, how far the assumed underlying congruence between British and Wilson's liberal hierarchical thinking would reach – and how far an essentially hierarchical Anglo-American "internationalism" would indeed dominate at the Paris Peace Conference.

In East Asia the western powers faced one critical question that raised particularly uncomfortable complications for Wilson – namely how to deal not only with Japanese demands to retain control over the Chinese province of Shandong but also with the more fundamental question of Chinese future status in the postwar order. For although Chinese authorities had been compelled to confirm the 1915 cessation arrangement by a secret treaty in September 1918, Japan's imperial demands thus obviously clashed with the Chinese republic's aspiration to restore "national sovereignty". And after the armistice the Chinese government would feel both compelled and emboldened to seek not just the return of Shandong but a more general resettlement of relations with the western powers and Japan, which was intended as a decisive step towards a restoration of Chinese sovereignty and notably included the abolition of the entire pre-war imperialist system of extraterritorial privileges and an extension of China's control over its tariffs and railroads.[14] While British and French leaders had committed themselves to supporting Japans's claims, Wilson thus faced the question of how he would deal with these colliding sets of demands, which clearly raised fundamental issues of self-determination yet also of course affected vested US interests in China.

4)   The Need for a New Transatlantic Order

Thus, the only region or geopolitical arena in which the war had created the necessary preconditions for more fundamental changes was Europe – and the newly critical transatlantic sphere. And it was in Europe, where the war had originated and produced the most destructive consequences, that the urgency of creating a new order was greatest. What mattered decisively from a systemic point of view was that the war had also in essential respects destroyed the pre-war system of European international politics – or, more precisely, the system of competitive balance-of-power politics into which it had degenerated in the first decades of the long twentieth century. It cannot be stressed enough that

---

[13] Smuts, "The League of Nations: A Programme for the Peace Conference", 16 December 1918, CAB 29/2.

[14] See MacMillan (2002), pp. 330–6.

the outcome of 1918 made any attempt to restore or recreate this system essentially inconceivable – not only because the geopolitical constellation had been so fundamentally altered, i.e. three of the system's five key players had collapsed or been incapacitated, but also because the underlying understandings and rules of the system had been challenged and devalued by the catastrophe of the war.

\First attempts to draw consequences from the pre-history of the war and its unexpected scale and destructiveness had in fact begun to propel formative reorientations. In short, the premises and practices of pre-war *Realpolitik* had indeed come to be discredited to a significant degree, not only by Wilson, Lenin and the critiques of liberal and socialist internationalists but also by the impact of the war itself. As we have seen, they had by no means been abandoned by all actors who mattered – notably, despite first reorientations, in France. Crucially, however, the main American and British actors had drawn different consequences. The maxim that European-style power politics had to be transcended remained integral to the American president's vision, and key British policy- and decision-makers now also deemed decisive *evolutionary* steps in this direction imperative.[15] And because Wilson now played such a crucial role, and British attitudes would be critical too, there was no realistic scope for making a peace and remaking international order on the basis of balance-of-power maxims. Not only different principles and modes of peacemaking but also different foundations for a postwar systemic architecture would have to be negotiated. This posed particularly profound challenges for French policymakers.

Indeed, it was now, in the weeks following the armistice, that both sides – the different European governments and non-governmental actors and the key players on the American side – had to grapple in earnest with the full implications of the United States' emergence as a pivotal power. Was it even, as it appeared to observers like Meinecke and Weber at the time, on the cusp of being the power that would hence *dominate* Europe and the world?[16] That the United States had become the key creditor power, above all because of its decisive loans to Britain and France, and that it was poised to become the ever more clearly predominant power in the global economy, was bound to have a critical bearing not only on the peace negotiations but also, in the longer run, on Europe's stabilisation after the war. Even more significant was the new *world political* role and influence the war had conferred on the American republic and its president in the midst of an unprecedentedly unsettled international situation. And through his crusade on behalf of a "new world order" during the latter stages of the war, Wilson had gained an

---

[15] Wilson address, 22 January 1917, *PWW*, XL, pp. 536–7; Wilson, Free Trade Hall address, 30 December 1918, *PWW*, LIII, pp. 550–1

[16] Meinecke notes, 7 and 13 October 1918, Meinecke (1969), pp. 307 ff.; Weber letter, late November 1918, in Weber (2012), p. 648.

unprecedented, though highly ambivalent political and ideological influence. He had pushed himself – and had been pushed by the expectations and calculations of many others – into the position of a pre-eminent, if not "messianic" protagonist in the search for a new international order. But, as should be underscored once again, the American republic and its president were far from having attained a new and undisputed pre-eminence in the world – notably vis-à-vis Britain and France. And for all of the United States' novel political-cum-financial power and the remarkable appeal of Wilson's general "vision", it was far from a foregone conclusion that the peace and postwar order would be founded on his terms.

In fact, while Wilson clung to his role-definition of an elevated progressive arbiter his power and authority were actually markedly *limited*. At one level, the novel patterns of transatlantic interdependences and the requirements of modern peacemaking were far too complex to permit a clear American preponderance – or, simply put, a quasi-automatic translation of American financial power and ideological capital into a Wilsonian *Pax Americana*; on another, Wilson and those who sought to aid him at this juncture were ill-equipped to exercise effective leadership – nor was the president at all assured of a strong domestic mandate for the transformative changes he sought.[17] The struggles over the armistice had already thrown this into relief. The post-armistice period thus became all the more critical.

For it was now that the American president and those who advised and eventually accompanied him to Europe had to confront one unprecedented challenge head-on, namely that of having to learn how to act, not as a *primus inter pares* but rather as *one* among *several* leading powers in immensely complex reordering processes.[18] For although they had been far more severely affected by the war, Britain and France still had the capacity to exert a powerful influence too. First and foremost, he would thus have to find ways to negotiate mutually acceptable terms with their political leaders. Not least, it was on their cooperation that the realisation of his "grand design" and particularly of his plans for a League of Nations depended. In a wider context, it is thus essential to note once again that the aftermath of the Great War did

---

[17] For a different interpretation see Tooze (2014). For the wider context see the aforementioned Kennedy (1988).

[18] Not only policymakers, officials, and experts but also intellectuals and activists on both sides of the Atlantic began to perceive and draw consequences from this transformative development. For notable examples see Wilson address, 5 March 1917, *PWW*, XLI, p. 334; Lippmann editorial "Peace without Victory", *New Republic*, 9/112 (23 December 1916), pp. 201–2; Keynes memoranda, 10 and 24 October 1916, in Keynes (1978), XVI, pp. 197–201; Cecil memorandum, 18 September 1917, CAB 24/26/2074; Clémentel letter, 19 September 1918; Hauser memorandum, summer 1918, AN, F12/8106; Tardieu recommendations, 26 November 1918, Fonds Clemenceau, 6N 137-3, SHD-DAT. For German perspectives see Krüger (1985), pp. 31–7.

not (yet) mark the turning-point when political hegemony and the decisive influence over who would set the terms of peace and international order actually passed from the European powers to the United States and the stage for a qualitatively different *Pax Americana* was set.

From a European perspective, it has been argued that Wilson's powerful influence and universal designs for a League of Nations and a "new world order" in fact overpowered and stifled European attempts to find more appropriate ways and mechanisms to stabilise Europe after the Great War – and that what would really have been necessary were efforts to revitalise the European states-system and to create a kind of resuscitated European concert.[19] But in the radically altered transatlantic configuration of power, influence and interdependence that the war had created it was extremely difficult and in critical respects simply no longer possible for European decision-makers to make peace and establish a new international order for Europe on their own – and "in a European way". It was no longer possible to stabilise Europe and to address the crucial systemic problems – those of security and German power, financial and economic reconstruction and, more broadly, the consolidation of a modern and legitimate system of states *without the United States*. This marked the crucial *caesura*, and European policymakers, particularly those who represented the main victors – and the vanquished – would have to learn how to come to terms with the new transatlantic realities.

Essentially, what the catastrophe of the Great War thus made imperative was something else, something unprecedented that only very few had imagined before 1914: not merely a readjustment of relations between Europe and the United States, but the first serious bid to lay the groundwork for a functioning *Atlantic* international order. More precisely, the key American and European actors had to find ways to agree on the mainstays of a transatlantic system of international politics and security – and, inseparable from this, the transatlantic nucleus of a new world financial and economic order. For at the end of the war, not even rudiments of such a system existed. There were as yet neither mechanisms nor common ground-rules that allowed actors on both sides of the Atlantic to come to terms with the new forms of Euro-American interconnectedness and interdependence that had emerged.

More fundamentally, advances towards a transatlantic system were critical, indeed indispensable not only for addressing the most pressing postwar challenges – the German question, the Franco-German antagonism, the reordering and stabilisation of Central and Eastern Europe, and the Bolshevik challenge. They were also vital for coming to grips with the crucial problems of *systemic insecurity and instability* that now afflicted Europe. And in a wider context they were equally critical for coming to grips with the

---

[19] See Krüger (1985) and (2006), pp. 123–7.

longer-term structural developments that had led to the conflagration of 1914 – the legacy of decades of ever more narrowly defined European and escalating global imperialist competition.

5)   The Crucial Security Problem and the Need for an Effective Transatlantic Security System

Indeed, transatlantic approaches were particularly needed to come to terms with what was arguably the most critical systemic problem after the Great War: the immensely complex and multidimensional security problem. Especially in this vital sphere it was simply no longer possible to establish a functioning *European* security system – because of the war's destructive consequences, the role the United States had played in ensuring the Allied victory, and the pivotal influence Wilson now exerted.

Both the breakdown of the pre-war European "order" and of course the war itself – the unprecedented escalation of violence on an industrial scale – created enormous and profound *insecurity* on many levels. Unquestionably, the multifaceted security questions and forms of insecurity that decision-makers confronted in its aftermath had global dimensions. Violent conflicts would continue not only in eastern Europe but also in the Middle East as the disintegration of the Ottoman Empire reached its final stages. The potential for further conflicts and violence in East Asia was considerable, as Japan's imperial ambitions and the demands of Chinese – and Korean – nationalists who struggled for "self-determination" continued to clash. On a wider scale there was a major potential for a violent collision between the interests of the remaining imperial powers, above all Britain and France, and the aspirations of those who aspired to achieve independence. Arguably, however, security problems were most profound and urgent on the continent, where the catastrophe of 1914 had originated and produced its most destructive consequences. Here, the war created not only newly complex but also indeed novel challenges – at bottom a core problem of *endemic* insecurity and a prevalent *sense* of insecurity. And more than ever the security question now transcended the boundaries between international and domestic politics. Insecurity not only affected the sphere of inter-state relations but also social relations within states.

Not only in the perception of the leading actors of 1919, the crucial security problem was and remained that of international or inter-state security; but this was now influenced to an unprecedented degree not just by inter-state rivalry and threat perceptions but also by domestic-political factors and developments – as well as transnational developments – that had existed before the war but would now influence international relations to an unprecedented degree. While the situation within the "victorious states" was relatively stable, violent revolutionary unrest and conflicts that often crossed the threshold to civil war swept through Europe east of the Rhine. Structural insecurity was particularly pronounced in the unsettled post-imperial landscape of eastern Central Europe, where, after the collapse of the eastern empires, competing nationalist agendas clashed and violence even intensified after the armistice. Most precarious was the collision of Polish national claims and German claims for "self-determination". But even more menacing in the longer run was the wider threat posed by violent *revanchism* on the part of the vanquished. Of a different nature, but no less unsettling, was the novel spectre of a violent Bolshevik-inspired revolution; and in Russia the full-blown civil war between the Bolsheviks and their White opponents still raged on.

Systemically, however, one question clearly towered above all others: the question of how to prevent the escalation of another general industrial war. And unavoidably connected with it was – especially from the perspectives of the victors, above all France – the question of how to come to terms with the German threat or more precisely the threat that the defeated but still powerful central state of Europe would seek to revise the outcome of 1918 by force. It is therefore not surprising that these questions would be right at the forefront of the eventual peace negotiations. As the armistice negotiations had shown, the political leaders of the victorious powers basically agreed that a far-reaching disarmament of Germany was one necessary precondition for safeguarding European security and preventing another major war. Yet one of the most critical questions of peacemaking was whether they would be able to find common ground in establishing, beyond this, an effective security architecture that allowed them to come to terms with the German problem. For their approaches were still far apart.

Leading French policymakers defined security primarily in terms of *national* security needs and, at the core, as protection against renewed German "aggression". And from their vantage-points achieving this overridingly important security aim – ultimately by military and power-political means – clearly took precedence over efforts to seek a peaceful accommodation with the defeated neighbour, which in their eyes indeed risked *compromising* French security. From the perspectives of British and American policymakers the German aspects of the security problem were central too. Yet so far they had only addressed them in the context of the more general proposals for a League and some kind of postwar system of collective security. Now, they thus faced the critical challenge of developing more substantive approaches to Euro-Atlantic security – approaches that dealt with the issue of Germany's overbearing power on terms that reassured its neighbours, and above all France. And it of course also remained to be seen how far those German policymakers who sought to chart a new course after the catastrophe would find ways to address not only the problem of German power but also the wider problem of postwar insecurity in Europe. Yet the vexing German problem also highlighted a much broader change, namely that the unprecedented escalation of violence, destruction and loss that the Great War had brought with it had given rise to expanded security *needs* and security *expectations* among elites but also wider populations of the states that had been involved in the war.

These political-psychological needs and expectations – whose main common denominator was the longing for guarantees against a recurrence of the carnage and losses the war had inflicted – were particularly profound in societies that had been most directly and most strongly affected by the war, societies such as the French; yet they were palpable on all sides – and became a critically important factor. They were also strikingly different in terms of their intensity – and in terms of the political significance they had. Much depended, not least, on perceptions of future threats and dangers to national security – or more precisely on how far – in the perception of decision-makers, opinion-makers and wider publics – the future security of different states was endangered by the situation the war had created. The crucial question of what threat Germany still posed was viewed very differently in France, Britain and the United States, and this in turn was also connected with the geopolitical positions of these states. In short, the German threat seemed distinctly more ominous from the French perspective than from the vantage-points of the relatively distant British power and an American power that could retreat to a seemingly unassailable "hemispheric fortress" – particularly once Germany was no longer a global naval power. Of critical import, however, was how leading political actors *perceived* and *interpreted* not only the core security needs and interests of their respective states but also the concerns and expectations of the societies they represented. Ultimately, then, no pacification of Europe after the Great War was possible without finding new – and essentially transatlantic – ways of addressing the profound and complex security problems the war had left behind.

Yet the war and the political struggles it sparked had also begun to alter something more fundamental: underlying ideas about the relationship between security and peace. Prior to 1914, despite the efforts to secure peace through regimes of international law like the Hague Conventions, states had ultimately been seen as the crucial guarantors of security – externally against threats by foreign enemies, internally through their enforcement of a monopoly on the legitimate use of violence. And political leaders had assumed that as *ultima ratio* they had a "right" to resort to war to protect national or imperial security. Particularly after the disintegration of the Vienna system, the safeguarding of security, and vital interests, had thus ultimately been considered as more important than the preservation of peace *per se*. After the catastrophe of the Great War, what had gained ground, though by no means prevalence (as yet), was the notion that in view of the disastrous consequences they had produced older conceptions of national security – and notably balance-of-power thinking – had to be abandoned. Hand in hand with this another salient development had gained momentum: the ascendance of the idea that from now on the preservation of overall peace, or "world peace", had to take precedence, and that this would require new mechanisms of *collective* security and a new willingness to subordinate sovereignty and other nation-state concerns to the overriding priority of preventing *all wars*.[20]

What thus arose was the question of how far it would now be possible and lie in the interest of the most powerful players to establish a different, more effective international security system on these premises. And what was needed above all in view of the situation the war had created was a system that met two purposes: it had to satisfy the understandable security concerns of France and Germany's other neighbours by guarding against the threat posed by its largely undiminished power and possible revanchist tendencies; yet it also, and crucially, had to provide a framework for a stabilising *integration* of the defeated power into the recast international order.

But the debates about how such a system was to be created, how far it should really curtail state sovereignty when it came to vital security questions, and whether it should rely on collective force or rather on the collective power of "world opinion" and *political* conflict-resolution were far from over. They indeed reached a new intensity following the armistice. And, as noted, the war had also spurred momentous changes in ideas and perceptions of what "security" actually comprised. These not only pertained to the prevention of war between states through arbitration, new rules for the peaceful settlement of disputes and, more fundamentally, the aspiration to "civilise" international politics by means of authoritative international law. They also extended to reforms of inner-state and social order – notably the pacification of domestic politics through democratic reforms. As we have seen, both social democratic and liberal reformers thus sought to enhance overall security by pushing for advances towards an international society of democratic states committed to far-reaching covenants which set new, pacifying standards of international law and politics. But more traditional *realpolitical* ideas and assumptions had by no means disappeared, notably in France and Germany. These still centred on the notion that the only effective way of ensuring national security was to maintain deterrent military power, effective alliances, and astute balance-of-power politics. And those who clung to such notions insisted that the war had by no means devalued them – and that the real task now was to forge stronger alliances and a more efficacious balance of power.

The key question that thus arose after the armistice – and that chiefly the political leaders and strategists of the victorious powers had to answer – was not only *whether* any real advances towards a new transatlantic security system could be made but also, and crucially, what *kind* of system it was to

---

[20] See Conze (II/2018), pp. 238 ff.; Conze (I/2018).

be and on what foundations it would be built. This question would indeed dominate the peace conference.

The main problem that now crystallised was *not*, as has often been argued, that the victors failed to reach a consensus that would have permitted the establishment of a forceful and exclusive balance-of-power system that preserved peace by ensuring a long-term containment of Germany. For attempting to create and enforce such a system was not only elusive; very likely it would also have produced precisely what it should have prevented: insecurity, a further deepening of antagonistic divisions and eventually the escalation of another major war.[21] Yet was there a realistic prospect after the Great War to safeguard European peace and security by pursuing a radical reform of the international order, as Wilson's rhetoric suggested and progressive internationalists demanded? Would it be possible to create "deeper" peace and security by constructing a Euro-Atlantic system of self-governing states anchored in a new League of Nations? and establishing a tight system of collective security? Could the profound, structural problem of insecurity be tackled by relying on a new international covenant with strong provisions of collective security and rules and norms that in crucial respects limited what had been at the core of the pre-war system, namely state sovereignty and particularly the sovereignty of great powers? And crucially, would all of this indeed provide guarantees that were really more effective and satisfied core security needs and expectations, especially in Europe?

After the armistice, it was essentially clear that in one form or another a League of Nations would be established. Apart from the support this idea had gained not just among pro-League activists and associations but also among and political parties and wider societies – notably in Britain and the United States – the fact that the American president had made it his priority and that the British government backed it created the essential conditions for this departure. But it was not clear yet at all what kind of League would be established – how authoritative, how hierarchical, how universal, how integrative it would be. To the chagrin of all the pro-League activists who had called for more fundamental changes, it soon became apparent that the most powerful political actors – the leaders of the victors, including Wilson – were *not* prepared and did *not* see a need to cede core attributes of national or state sovereignty to the envisaged organisation.

The prospects for taking transformative steps and establishing the League as an essentially supranational mechanism of security and order were thus distinctly limited from the start. The real question became how far an effective league *of* or rather *between* states could be founded. And here another critical problem arose. Whatever form and authority it would eventually acquire, the new institution would still have to be consolidated and gain credibility, which

---

[21] See notably Clemenceau speech, 29 December 1918, *Journal Officiel* (Chambre), 1918, 3732–3; Tardieu memorandum, 20 January 1919, Tardieu MSS 49, MAE; Tardieu (1921), pp. 202–32.

even in a best-case scenario would require time. By itself, a general and theoretically global institution could thus not (yet) provide the wherewithal to pacify Europe, *especially in the critical shorter term, the immediate aftermath of the war.* In particular, it could not furnish guarantees that Clemenceau and a majority of French policymakers deemed sufficient to protect cardinal security interests vis-à-vis Germany.

Therefore, what was required to come to terms with both the pressing and the structural challenges the Great War had left behind was something qualitatively different: steps to create, for the first time, a more *specific* transcontinental system that provided a new and more effective architecture of inter-state security and a robust mechanism to manage and *regulate* relations between the rising American power and the old and new European states. In short, it was imperative to found what can best be characterised as a modern transatlantic concert for the long twentieth century. The wider challenge was to create a system in which smaller states were accorded equality under international law and more tangible guarantees for their integrity, but in which the more powerful states still could meet pivotal responsibilities in maintaining peace and international order – while accepting restraints through a recognised covenant of rules. Yet the crucial challenge was to establish a system that was essentially integrative, i.e. designed to include not only the victors – and hitherto neutral states – but also the vanquished. For what Europe's longer-term pacification required most urgently were concepts and efforts to overcome the war's divisions and to prevent the hardening of a structural antagonism between the western powers and Germany. More generally, it was imperative to forestall conditions and dynamics that, sooner or later, would give rise to a new and even more destructive stage in the competition between power states that had led to the war in the first place. Arguably, only a robust Atlantic concert could meet these challenges. And, in a wider context, only advances towards such a concert could establish a possible core for a more sustainable *global* order.

Unquestionably, to found – through the League – a fully-fledged concert system that comprised the victors and the vanquished on more or less equal terms was hardly realistic in the immediate aftermath of the Great War – precisely because it had created such deep political and ideological divisions. But the willingness and capacity of the principal victors to *lay the groundwork* for such a system was critical not only for Europe's stabilisation but also for the consolidation of a legitimate postwar order. More precisely, what mattered most was the extent to which they were willing and able to establish, not an exclusive regime of the western victors but rather the *nucleus* of a hence more western-orientated Atlantic system of international politics that permitted the swift inclusion of the defeated powers, above all the fledgling German republic; that allowed – *over time* – a settlement or at least management of the daunting array of problems the war had created; and that overall furthered a peaceful accommodation between the victors and the vanquished.

In the final analysis, only through a modern concert of this kind a way could be found to foster what was most essential for a legitimate peace at this juncture, a historical watershed when all the key players were democratic or democratising states: the negotiation of complex *political* compromise agreements – and indeed strategic bargains – that as far as possible accommodated and balanced the interests and concerns of *all* the different governments and societies and that, crucially, the different decision-makers could hope to legitimise in their respective domestic force-fields.

Advances towards an integrative Atlantic concert system could thus potentially open up more realistic prospects for a durable post–First World War order than any regime of enforced containment. The key lay in giving the principal defeated power incentives to accept and participate in maintaining the postwar order; and it lay in binding it to *mutually accepted* security obligations and ground-rules of peaceful conflict resolution. It is worth stressing that the envisaged League of Nations could actually provide an essential institutional frame for a renovated concert. Conversely, only a functioning transatlantic concert could enable the League to fulfil the core purpose its main proponents desired it to meet, namely to safeguard European and world peace. Yet there was another important requirement for the longer-term stabilisation of Europe – and the world – that should not be forgotten: the western powers had to find a place for Russia in a novel Atlantic system and to decide how they would deal with the Bolshevik regime – if Lenin and Trotsky were to prevail. But, as will be seen, in the face of the ongoing Russian civil war it proved impossible for them to agree on a common approach, let alone to take decisive steps to come to terms with either the Russian or the Bolshevik question. Systemically, however, forging a postwar system that could incorporate Germany was clearly more vital for Europe's pacification.

In the constellation the war had created, the policies and approaches of the political leaders of Britain and the United States would be crucial for any meaningful advances towards an effective Atlantic concert. For only they had the means to provide what constituted the essential prerequisite: the guarantees and strategic re-assurance that were required to satisfy the pre-eminent security concerns of France and Germany's other western and eastern neighbours. That is why so much depended on the extent to which they were prepared and domestically in a position to make tangible security commitments. Beyond this, a lot depended on whether British policy-makers could develop effective strategies to promote their evolving ideas of a reconfigured concert of powers.[22] Even more depended on whether Wilson would be willing and able to translate his vision of a universal

---

[22] Cecil had a decisive influence on British conceptual planning here. See the "Cecil Plan", 14 December 1918, in Miller (1928), II, pp. 61–4.

"international concert" into a more workable conception, and strategy, for a new transatlantic order.[23]

Ultimately, however, real progress towards a more integrative Atlantic concert also required the fundamental consent of those who determined French postwar policies. Here, the main question was how far French decision-makers were at all prepared and had the domestic leeway to countenance such steps – and how far they might come to see it in France's longer-term interest to envisage a process of accommodation with Germany that enmeshed the troublesome neighbour in a system of *mutual* obligations. By contrast, those who had to reorientate German international policies after the war faced the underlying, essential challenge of overcoming postwar isolation and developing realistic policies to prepare the ground for Germany's eventual inclusion in a recast international order – as a reformed power with "equal" rights *and* duties.

6) The Need for a New Atlantic Financial and Economic Order

Ever since Keynes published his famous *Economic Consequences of the Peace* in December 1919, what has exerted an enormous influence on assessments of post–First World War peacemaking is the thesis that even more decisive for European and global stabilisation after the Great War than traditional security issues or national and nationalist concerns was the need to deal with the financial and economic repercussions of the conflict.[24] While this thesis is exaggerated and ultimately misleading – for political questions far beyond the realm of the economic, notably those pertaining to security, status and indeed self-determination, mattered even more – it can certainly be confirmed that the war had created an overriding need for agreeing on new basic underpinnings, and ground-rules, for an economic *and* financial peace. This was indeed a critical task after a war that, as we have seen, had been marked by escalating economic and financial warfare and had profoundly damaged the deeply entangled and interdependent economic structures that had existed in pre-war Europe.

More precisely, what really had become imperative was to lay nothing less than the groundwork for a reconfigured financial and economic system for Europe, and the world, that allowed the different states to come to terms with the massive economic and financial fall-out of the war. And because economic and financial factors had by this time gained a more vital significance in the realm of international politics – and for the postwar stabilisation of domestic order – than ever before, the way in which this was approached would indeed have decisive consequences for Europe's *political* pacification. At the same time, financial and economic issues had become unprecedentedly *politicised* –

---

[23] Wilson address, 22 January 1917, *PWW*, XL, pp. 536–7. See also Wilson's statements, 8 December 1918, Grayson diary, 8 December 1918, *PWW*, LIII, p. 339.

[24] Keynes (1919), pp. 9–10, 35 ff.

they were influenced by conflicting political concerns and rationales of the different states and the different elites within these states.

Essentially, as Keynes had been one of the first to recognise, in view of the revolution of economic and especially financial relations between the old and the new world – above all, the new financial-cum-economic interconnections between the *Entente* Powers and their American lender and supplier – this required something unprecedented as well, namely a transatlantic architecture – agreements, and a system, that were supported and ultimately underwritten by the world's newly pre-eminent financial and economic power – and creditor – the United States, which was in many ways indispensable but also ill-prepared for the new role it was supposed to play. And what now had to be seen was how far Wilson and the other American political actors and financial experts who came to Europe would be in a position to use US power to push, essentially, for a globalisation of the United States' hitherto less than reciprocal "Open Door" policy – and notably its extension to Europe.

More broadly, it had to be decided whether an "open", liberal, largely unregulated and unfettered world economic system could be reconstituted, which in essential respects reflected American and now re-accentuated British preferences for a relatively speedy return to unhampered trade within a "most-favoured-nation" system – or whether some form of more "organised", regulated regime of economic and trade relations would emerge. As outlined, notably French planners and some of their British counterparts had advocated such a more "organised" system ever since 1916. Yet the schemes they proposed had in crucial aspects been designed to contain German financial and economic power and place tangible restrictions on future German access to resources and the world's markets.[25]

Indeed, one of the most critical questions thus became how far and on what terms Germany – which had been one of the most important and dynamic economies in the pre-war world of imperialist globalisation, integral to a deeply intertwined European economy, and a key trading "partner" of the United States – would be permitted to re-join a reconfigured postwar economic order. These essentially political questions were inseparable from that of how far any advances could be made towards a new, at the core transatlantic system of international finance and agreements to come to terms with the newly critical problem of inter-allied debts after a war that had cast the United States into the position of an in many ways ill-prepared financial hegemon and pivotal creditor power.

Undoubtedly, in the aftermath of the Great War financial and economic questions were thus more central to the peacemaking and reordering processes

---

[25] Wilson, "Fourteen Points", *PWW*, XLV, pp. 536–8; British Board of Trade memorandum, November 1918, revised in December 1918, CAB 29/1/P-33; Clémentel letter to Clemenceau, 19 September 1918, in Clémentel (1931), pp. 343, 346–7; See Soutou (1989); Boyce (2010), pp. 3–4; Boyce (2009).

than ever before in the history of major modern postwar settlements, and notably more critical than one hundred years earlier, at the Congress of Vienna. They were distinctly more complex. And they would have a significant, though not decisive bearing on the making and longevity of any post–First World War "order".

At one level, even more than before 1914 financial and economic factors were more intricately bound up with core questions of international politics and security – with decisions over the future distribution of power, leverage and possibilities in the international system. This had global implications, but it particularly affected Europe and the now so densely interconnected transatlantic sphere, above all the relations between the newly dominant United States, the principal European victors and Germany, which, though defeated, still had the potential to re-emerge as Europe's economic powerhouse. And this in turn affected two other major questions: How was Europe's economic and financial reconstruction to be organised – or more precisely: How would those areas of Europe that had been devastated by the war be rebuilt, how would the economies of the different European states, which had all been turned into war economies, be revitalised as peacetime economies, and how would one deal with the wider financial and economic fall-out of the war? One fundamental problem that now had to be addressed, was bound to cause profound controversies and essentially required a political rather than a "rational" financial and economic answer was: who in the end would have to pay for the catastrophe, and on what grounds?

At a different level, financial and economic concerns were thus indissolubly bound up with crucial pressures and dynamics of domestic politics within all of the different states that had fought in the war. On the side of the victors, not only but particularly the political leaders of Britain and France faced strong pressures and demands for compensation on their home fronts – compensations for the sacrifices and hardships of the war, improved living conditions and social and economic reforms; such demands had a distinct political and psychological connotations – and went hand in hand with the call for a financial and economic punishment of a defeated enemy that, as wartime propaganda had insisted for four years, had forced the war on the rest of Europe and the world. Yet those who sought to negotiate on behalf of the vanquished of course also faced demands for compensation and a return to better economic and living conditions after years of warfare, which here became politically more explosive because of the shock of defeat.

This wider context has to be illuminated in order to understand why it proved so difficult to come to terms with one the most intricate and ultimately frustrating problems on the peacemaking agenda of 1919 – the reparations problem. At its core lay the dispute not only over the extent and modalities but also over the political and moral *justification* of the indemnity payments that the victorious European powers would demand from Germany for the human and material costs of what they interpreted and presented as a war caused by

German aggression. The core question was whether it was at all conceivable to thrash out a reparations agreement that not only satisfied the politically highly sensitive demands and expectations of the European victors but would also be acceptable to the vanquished – and could actually be fulfilled. Because the reparations problem was *de facto* so closely connected with the aforementioned and indeed unprecedented indebtedness of Britain and France to the United States, the position and policies of the American creditor power was indeed highly significant in this context.

A lot hinged on the question of how far the Wilson government, which came to propose a "scientific settlement" of indemnities, was not only willing to countenance but also in a position to gain domestic – and especially Congressional – support for a more comprehensive settlement of the debts and reparations, which also raised the domestically sensitive issue of debt relief. In a wider context, the reparations question complicated, but could not be separated from, the much bigger question of how far any substantial advances towards a new *transatlantic* framework for postwar European reconstruction, fundamentals of economic and financial peace, and indeed a new superstructure for a global financial and economic order could be made. If there was no or little progress in this direction, the longer-term consequences for Europe were bound to be severe. But the main challenge was to find ways to replace the war-prone and now defunct European balance-of-power system of the pre-war era with a more sustainable transatlantic system of order that provided a new, more effective "superstructure" for the long-term stabilisation of Europe and, potentially, a new international equilibrium. And the manner in which this challenge was approached, would not only have decisive implications for the future of Europe but also significant repercussions for the extra-European world.

7)   The Crucial Problem of Transatlantic Asymmetry

At the same time, however, the Great War had also created conditions that structurally impeded more substantial advances towards a new Atlantic order. For it gave rise to a pattern of interdependence between Europe and the United States that was distinctly *asymmetrical*. On the one hand, European states – and national movements – desired or needed US commitments, concessions, continued engagement and support, or at least cooperative behaviour. The *Entente* Powers – and especially France – were interested in the firmest possible security commitments, the reduction or even cancellation of debt obligations, and fresh American capital; those who strove for "self-determination" and statehood clamoured for US support and Wilson's patronage; those who represented the vanquished powers sought to hold Wilson to what they interpreted as his promise of a lenient and integrative "American peace".

On the other hand, Wilson indeed required European support, especially that of the main European victors, if he wanted to realise his aspirations for a

League-based "new order". And there was now a newly pronounced interest, not only on Wilson's part and among the newly prominent American League and peace activists but also among important segments of US political and financial elites, in creating conditions for a leading American role in Europe's long-term pacification and stabilisation, and in helping to create conditions which ensured that the New World would not have to intervene in another world war precipitated in the Old World. By and large, they shared an interest in stabilising and revitalising Europe as a sphere of financial investment and economic expansion – while safeguarding US debt claims. And they reckoned that the world's newly dominant economy would benefit substantially from the "openness" of European markets and favourable political conditions for such an expansion.

In the prevalent American perception, however, the future security, prosperity and development of the United States appeared to be *comparatively* far less dependent on future developments in Europe – especially after the threat posed by German naval power, and imperial aspirations, seemed to have been eliminated for the foreseeable future.[26] And, as will be seen, those who argued that in view of this the American republic not only *could* but also *should* return to more traditional or "normal" policies of aloofness still found considerable resonance in the American political spectrum. All sides – Wilson as well as Lloyd George and Clemenceau, those representing the victors as well as those representing the vanquished – would have to find ways to deal with this challenging asymmetry.

IV. Scant Prospects for a Legitimate Peacemaking Process? The Altered Conditions and Playing-Field of Peacemaking and the Core Problem of Exaggerated Expectations

The actors who sought to make peace after the Great War thus faced immense urgent and longer-term challenges. And their success in meeting them, and in founding a durable postwar order, would critically depend on *how* or more precisely *through what kind of processes* a peace settlement would be approached. Indeed, this was one of the most fundamental political questions that had to be answered in the aftermath of the armistice – because, more than has hitherto been recognised, it was essentially still an open question.

It was by no means clear yet how the peacemaking process was to be organised, how hierarchical, how inclusive, how "modern", how transparent

---

[26] For influential contemporary assessments of such transatlantic interconnections and their significance for the United States and Europe, see Hoover to Wilson, 20 December 1918, O'Brien (1978), pp. 22–3. Davis/Lamont proposals, May 1919, in Baker (1923), III, pp. 352–56; memorandum of Wilson's conference with US experts, 19 May 1919, Lamont Papers, 163–13; Keynes memorandum, 22 October 1918, Keynes Papers PT/2/3.

or confidential it would or could be. And, crucially, the victors still had to decide whether it would involve negotiations with those who represented the vanquished powers, above all Germany, or essentially remain a process exclusively determined by them.

1)   The Requirements of a Modern Peacemaking Process and the Changing Parameters of International Politics

In this critical context it is vital to highlight one fundamental point that generations of "realist" historians have either disputed or simply disregarded.[27] In view of how the Great War had ended – in the west – namely *not* through an unequivocal victory of one side over the other (that all sides perceived as such), in view of how complex the requirements of peacemaking were and in view of the far-reaching *expectations* the transatlantic ideological war and notably Wilson's rhetoric had nourished it would be extremely difficult, if not impossible, to impose a victors' peace on the vanquished that was actually sustainable.

More precisely, it would be extremely difficult, if not impossible, to sustain a peace based either on more traditional "right of victory" conceptions or on progressive claims of higher authority. It would be as inconceivable to build a durable postwar order this way because, ultimately, it would not meet basic "modern" requirements of legitimacy. And, in particular, it would be impossible to pacify Europe this way. For under the conditions the Great War had created, the only way to uphold a victors' peace was through a coercive regime and ultimately by force; and against the background of the peace visions Wilson and Lloyd George had laid out during the war it was highly unlikely that the powers they represented would support such an approach. More fundamentally, post–First World War Europe could not be stabilised, and no stable international system could be created, without or even against the power that remained the most powerful and populous state at the centre of the continent, Germany.

This is why systemically so much hinged on the question of whether it would be possible to initiate a peacemaking and reordering process that could be considered more or less legitimate or at least acceptable by all the main actors, including those who acted on behalf of the vanquished. And here, nothing mattered more than to come to actual *negotiations* in which all sides could represent and fend for what they considered essential. For only such a negotiation process could potentially lead to what was actually the only kind of peace through which a more sustainable order could emerge – essentially,

---

[27]   Notable examples of this are MacMillan (2002); Marks (2002); Keylor (2011); and even Steiner (2005).

a compromise peace, a settlement that was based on some form of accommodation not only between the interests of the victors *and* the vanquished but
also between their underlying concerns, perceptions and expectations.

More precisely, what was required was the initiation of a process that, as far
as possible, *began* to settle the most pressing issues yet also, and crucially,
established a framework and mutually accepted ground-rules to negotiate
difficult compromise agreements that could only be worked out *over time*
and that were so crucial after 1918 – agreements that policymakers on all sides
could then hope to legitimise in the different national force-fields. And only
the leaders of the victors could potentially initiate such a process – if they
found ways to overcome their own differences and came to have the common
will to do so. While from a systemic point of view the concerns of the victors
and the most powerful vanquished were crucial, the same need to balance
interests and expectations of course applied in many other cases, notably when
it came to the clashing national claims and nationalist aspirations in central
and eastern Europe.

On a wider, global scale such processes were fundamentally no less important. But, as we have seen, it was highly doubtful at this juncture that the
remaining imperial powers would allow them and make meaningful concessions where their interests and prerogatives came into conflict with the claims
of anti-imperialist nationalists. Yet it was particularly critical to seek wider
compromises in Europe because – in spite of the war – its different peoples
and societies, old and new states, were and remained politically, economically,
socially, and culturally interconnected and interdependent in so manifold
ways and to such a remarkable extent. In fact, Europe remained a more highly
complex and dense system of interconnections and interdependencies than
any other part of the world; and Germany remained at its centre. Essentially,
however, because the war had created such a newly dense web of connections
between Europe and a newly powerful United States, more inclusive, integrative ways of peace-building could only be opened up with American support.[28]

In short, then, what the creation and stabilisation of a "modern" international order after the Great War required more than anything were integrative processes and the search for a peace of mutually acceptable compromises.
Yet the altered conditions of international politics that the Great War had
created, the complexity of the problems it left behind and the depth of the
ideological divisions it caused made precisely such a process and such a
settlement immensely difficult. This difficulty was compounded by the original
lack of consensus between the victors.

Indeed, it soon became clear that those who confronted the task of peacemaking had to act on a playing-field that had been fundamentally recast

[28] See Krüger (1986); Nolan (2012); Cohrs (2018).

through the war – in Europe, on a global scale, yet particularly between Europe and the United States. This playing-field, which was characterised by an *intricate intertwining and interdependence* of international, domestic and transnational politics, had not only *expanded* in various ways but also become much harder to navigate. On it, as we have seen, the political leaders and experts who prepared for the peace negotiations on behalf of the western powers would have to deal with a newly vast and diverse range of both governmental and non-governmental actors and groups that sought to advance their different interests and agendas. Indeed, the struggle over the shape of this playing-field, over who had a claim to be a player on it and, crucially, over who had the authority to set the "rules of the game" that was being played on it now entered a decisive phase. This was the underlying struggle which in many ways shaped the preliminary manoeuvrings and then the actual peacemaking processes of 1919. And it was to have more important national-domestic dimensions and more distinctive transnational dimensions than any previous reordering process after a major war.

To begin with, the boundaries between international and domestic politics had become distinctly more permeable than before 1914. At a juncture when all of the key decision-makers operated in a new configuration of profoundly unsettled, evolving or fledgling mass democracies, international politics and the eventual peace negotiations were bound to be influenced to an unprecedented degree by domestic-political considerations, the demands and expectations of elites and wider publics, of parties, pressure-groups and other political forces, heightened by the struggles of the war and amplified by organs of publicised opinion that had hitherto engaged in the war's boundless propaganda battles. The need to ensure domestic legitimacy and support thus became both extremely challenging and paramount. Conversely, the way in which international politics was actually conducted and, above all, the peace negotiations would unfold was to have massive repercussions for postwar domestic politics, the stability of governments and entire systems of political order. This affected all states and societies, but some far more than others – especially those where, as in the case of Germany, the domestic-political situation was highly volatile.

But the dynamics and parameters of international politics had changed on an even larger scale. Essentially, the aftermath of the Great War thus became a period in which, building on the famous metaphor Max Weber coined in 1919, one could say that actors had to learn how to drill through not only very thick and hard but also extremely complex, unwieldy – or sometimes precariously brittle – boards. Some of these boards had hardened and become increasingly unwieldy over decades or centuries, others were novel and it was not clear yet at all how one could ever drill through them.[29] On the one hand, those who

---

[29] See Weber (1919) in Weber (1994), p. 369.

had to perform the act of drilling and were called upon to hone their judgement confronted problems that were immensely intricate in themselves – such as agreeing on basic parameters for the League of Nations, establishing underpinnings of postwar security or negotiating complex border settlements where different self-determination claims collided. On the other hand, their drilling efforts themselves had changed in character. In many ways, they had turned into something that many actors no longer pursued with a sense of realism and rational judgement but rather on the basis of ideological postulates, utopianisms and overreaching simplifications. They envisioned or at any rate promised grand results and thus raised expectations that far exceeded the realm of the possible.

What is more, the drilling efforts that lay at the heart of the long twentieth century's international politics had to be conducted in a changed environment in which ideologically charged controversies about any given issue spilled across national boundaries. In this new environment, relatively few actors actually sought transnational common ground. What mainly occurred was something else, not just a clash between "Wilsonianism" and "Leninism" but in fact a much broader transnational process of escalation. In the newly widened, ever more global public sphere, different ideas, demands, expectations and propagandistic ploys clashed and indeed radicalised each other.

It is essential to understand, though, that in spite of all these important structural changes the protagonists of the Paris Peace Conference were still mainly accountable to their national electorates. But it is no less important to understand that, ultimately, drilling processes in the sphere of modern international politics could only be considered successful if they led to outcomes that not only "settled" the core problems through some kind of agreement that the drillers themselves, and their electorates, found acceptable. What mattered more than ever was that these processes and outcomes could also find acceptance on the part of the other states and actors that had something at stake – including the vanquished powers – and that they could eventually gain legitimacy in an array of different, often highly polarised domestic forcefields. This was an extremely tall order.

Those who would be the main peacemakers in 1919, the key decision-makers of the victorious powers, thus faced unprecedentedly complex tasks under unprecedentedly complex conditions. They had to deal with novel transnational challenges and dynamics. Because they were the elected leaders of more or less democratic powers, *domestic-political* constraints and the pressures exerted by different political parties, interest groups and newly relevant mass media mattered even more. And crucially, they had to ensure that their policies and decisions would be backed by majorities in their respective parliaments – or, in Wilson's case, a majority in the American Congress, especially the Senate. Ultimately, however, they confronted an even more daunting and complex task – indeed a core challenge of modern international politics in the twentieth century that became especially acute after the Great War. In short, they had to develop policies and practices that allowed them to forge international agreements and basic underpinnings of a new international order that not only balanced, as far as possible, their different aims and agendas but for which *all* the relevant actors could then gain support on their respective home fronts. And in 1918 and 1919 this too included not only the victors but also the vanquished. As will be seen, each of these actors had to meet very distinctive domestic legitimation requirements, needs and expectations.

Even beginning to meet these challenges was unquestionably made harder by the aggressive varieties of radicalised nationalism that had come to dominate on all sides during the war. These now threatened to turn into vindictive nationalisms on the part of the victors, overly assertive nationalisms on the part of those who sought to assert or reassert their nation-state claims in Central and Eastern Europe and, on different premises, nationalisms of humiliation and revenge on the part of the defeated. These radicalised nationalisms fundamentally complicated any efforts to make headway towards some kind of balanced peace. And they of course collided head-on with the progressive agendas of American and European internationalists. They indeed placed massive obstacles in the way of any effort to initiate necessarily longer-term pacification processes – efforts to prevent future wars and build a "deeper" peace through international reconciliation and advances towards a new internationalist consciousness and sense of transnational solidarity.

Further, postwar politics was – unsurprisingly – characterised by a profound lack of *trust* not only between those who had been engaged in the war on opposite sides, but also among those who had been allies. And there was hardly any room for confidence-building measures. Even more problematic was that, as we have seen, the war's political and ideological struggles had created unprecedentedly profound ideological divisions between the opposing camps, particularly between the western powers and Germany. It is no exaggeration to say that they had inflicted harsh blows on the complex fabric of the European and the fledgling Euro-Atlantic international society that had existed before 1914. And these struggles had one further significant consequence for peacemaking in 1919. They had furthered not only to a newly impactful *ideologisation* but also to a newly prevalent *moralisation* of international politics, of conceiving of politics in moral categories of "good versus evil", of "good democracy and civilisation" versus "evil militarism and authoritarianism" – to which Bolshevik ideology added yet another dimension.

While countless politicians and propagandists on both sides of the Atlantic had also played their parts here, these trends had notably been furthered by Wilson's rhetoric. Hence arose the notion of a morally higher authority that could be used to vindicate, in the final consequence, the imposition of a qualitatively new and "superior" peace settlement. At the same time, however, the Wilsonian notion that the victory of democratic civilisation over the forces of the old order would pave the way for a novel *common* and *progressive* "peace to end all wars" had raised immense and profoundly unrealistic hopes in the opposite direction, particularly on the part of the vanquished, yet also among liberal and socialist internationalists in both Europe and the United States. All of this made it very hard to look ahead and take the necessary steps towards a peace based on political compromises and a rational, dispassionate accommodation of state and national interests, especially between the western powers and Germany.

2) The Key Problem of Expanding, Excessive and Conflicting Expectations

Yet there was one particular problem that not just the hardships and sacrifices of the war but also the unprecedented mobilisation of the different populations and, particularly, the escalation of the transatlantic competition between increasingly expansive war and peace agendas, and promises, had pushed to the forefront of international politics. It was to have far-reaching repercussions for the peacemaking process and its aftermath. And it can best be character-ised as the fundamental problem of immense, heightened, often exaggerated *expectations*.[30] Here the wartime rhetoric, propaganda and postwar visions of political leaders were particularly significant because they had been instru-mental in partly creating, partly expanding the scope of at times millennial expectations of what a victory in and the end of the Great War would usher in. Towering above all others were different expectations of a "peace to end all wars". Yet these expanded expectations tended to clash; or they simply exceeded the realm of the possible and were thus bound to produce dangerous disappointments.

At one level, as we have seen, the war had given rise to unprecedented expectations of what states – and imperial systems – were supposed to provide in its aftermath: essentially, different forms of compensation for the exertions and sacrifices populations made as long as the conflict lasted. The longer the war had lasted, the higher these expectations had become. And they took different forms. Compensation could be expected in the form of economic and social reforms and improvements and, in particular, the expansion of state-organised welfare – including new measures to meet the needs of war veterans. All of this involved immense financial costs for the exhausted and indebted European belligerents. As noted, on the side of the European "exhausted victors", particularly in Britain and France, yet also in Belgium, such expectations came to spur demands for far-reaching indemnities from Germany – demands "to make Germany pay" that were connected with

---

[30] On this see Leonhard (2018), part II.

political-psychological expectations to be compensated for the material and immaterial sacrifices they had endured during the war.

But compensatory expectations could also turn into something else, namely calls for more far-ranging political reforms that met demands for wider political participation – in the form of democratisation or "republicanisation" – or more radical, namely Bolshevik or radical socialist alternatives. In the case of different "national" groups and minorities within the collapsed multi-national empires – and the remaining empires – they found expression in demands for "self-determination" and statehood. This posed complex challenges for political leaders and governments on all sides. To some extent, the demands and expectations of the different populations had remained relatively restrained while the war was still being fought; but they were building up and, in different ways, came to the fore all the more forcefully in the aftermath of the struggle – among the victors, yet also on the part of the vanquished and on the part of those who now strove to build new states of their own. With renewed urgency, this raised the question of which states, and which kinds of political order, would be most capable of meeting these often contradictory expectations – whether liberal-democratic states could do so, and set an example, or whether a situation might arise in which either communist or more authoritarian regimes could appear as serious, attractive alternatives.

In a broader perspective, the transatlantic ideological struggle had indeed also spawned more far-reaching and indeed dangerously inflated expectations of a new kind of peace and a new kind of international order that would vindicate the sacrifices of the war and hence safeguard Europe and the world against the horrors of industrial mass warfare. These also escalated, as it were, all the way to quasi-millennial expectations that somehow it would indeed be possible draw more fundamental consequences from the unprecedented calamity of the Great War and make a peace that would "end all wars". Undoubtedly, such hopes and expectations had especially been raised by, and projected onto, the American president, and they were indeed spurred by his wartime rhetoric. Yet, as noted, different internationalist activists and pressure-groups had gone even further in developing and spreading such expectations.

Among the most committed internationalists there were many who now in fact expected that the time had come not only to embark on a novel peace-making process informed by "open" or "new diplomacy" – but also to found a genuinely progressive "new order" that established an authoritative and universal international institution, a peace league, that inaugurated new and binding norms and rules of international relations, particularly arbitration and "collective" security, ensured the equality of bigger and smaller states under a strengthened, codified regime of international law, enshrined the principle of national "self-determination" and brought about general disarmament. This went hand in hand with the prevalent expectation that a novel peace system of this kind would both promote, and be reinforced by, domestic reform and democratisation processes either along liberal or social democratic lines.

But what also reached a preliminary peak at this juncture were quite different, more radical expectations, namely those Lenin and the vanguard figures of the Bolshevik regime had raised – that now, because the war had undermined the "old" capitalist order, a world-historical opportunity had arisen to accelerate revolutionary changes and to Bolshevise Europe – and the world. But all of these hopes and expectations all had one thing in common, namely that they were impossible to fulfil after the Great War – especially in its immediate aftermath – which in turn generated profound disappointments and disenchantments that, as will be shown, were to have manifold political consequences, contributing significantly to postwar instability in and beyond Europe. Yet there were not only different "millennial" notions and expectations of a "peace to end all wars" and a "new world order". Crucially, progressive aspirations also came into conflict with more traditional or particular expectations that important actors or particular national publics had, for example with the prevalent French security expectations and concerns vis-à-vis Germany.

What mattered, of course, was how far those who had formulated and raised expectations were able to translate them into concrete political demands or, better still, effective political agendas that could be implemented and influence the complex peacemaking process. And what mattered, too, was whether they had the power, influence or political acumen to assert them. Yet, as will be shown, the extent to which also more general or vague expectations – *that were perceived as relevant by political decision-makers who were accountable to electorates and public opinion* – influenced the peace negotiations should not be underestimated either. Broadly speaking, one can indeed say that in the altered constellation of power and influence the war had created some expectations clearly had greater *political* weight than others. Indeed, what emerged after the Great War can be called a new *hierarchy of expectations*. First of all, what should not be neglected are the expectations that the key political actors themselves had as they approached the peacemaking process, particularly the political leaders of the victors; and it is vital, too, to assess which more general expectations – of their national publics or other actors – they themselves *perceived* as most essential, and how they interpreted them.

All of this would have critical implications for the peace negotiations. Yet in many ways no less essential was what the leaders of the vanquished expected, and thought their publics expected. Likewise, the expectations of pressure-groups and "public opinion" of the principal victors had a greater bearing than those of others, including the defeated powers. But in the longer run, what key parties, interest groups and wider publics on the part of the latter expected was also relevant. Further, the claims and expectations of "self-determination" of stronger or more effectively organised national movements – like the Polish and that of Czechs and Slovaks – which had already created "facts on the ground" and whose aspirations corresponded with the aims and interests of the victors had more "purchase" than those of weaker or as yet less powerful national movements – such as those that challenged British and other imperial interests in the extra-European sphere.

Of overriding significance for the eventual peace negotiations were doubtless those expectations that had become dominant in the domestic force-fields of the victors – and which collided in crucial respects. But in many ways, no less important were the hopes and expectations that came to dominate the public debates on the side of the defeated, and that in crucial respects stood in diametrical opposition to those dominating in the west. As noted, in France, Clemenceau would have to deal with far-reaching expectations related to financial yet also political "reparations" for the blood-toll and the devastations the war had caused.[31] Yet there was also, far more pronounced than in the British and American contexts, the widespread expectation that the peace settlement had to bring the firmest possible guarantees against renewed German aggression.

In Britain, the Lloyd George government had to deal with equally prevalent expectations of the public to gain compensation and reparation for the unprecedented casualties and sacrifices of the war. Influenced by wartime propaganda, these expectations were also linked – not just among right-wing parties and segments of the British press – to the demand for a chastising peace that punished German transgressions and banned the threat of Prusso-German militarism. Lloyd George himself would raise such expectations considerably further through the promises he made after the armistice. But what had also gained ground in wartime Britain was a different set of expectations – above all the expectation, not just in liberal and Labour circles, that with essential American support a more far-reaching reform of the international order could be initiated and a League would be created that also welcomed a reformed Germany. And there was also the wider expectation that a peace would be made that ensured above all that Britain, the Dominions and the other subjects of Britain's imperial system would never again have to intervene in Europe at such great cost.[32]

For his part, Wilson had not only raised vast expectations across Europe – and the world. He also had to deal with a range of different, often incompatible expectations in his own country. There were those – the vocal but nonetheless politically marginal minority of Americanist internationalists of different stripes – who expected him to lead the world towards a progressive American peace – without punitive indemnities or annexations – and to play

[31] See Chapter 12.
[32] See Chapter 11.

a crucial role in founding a universal League of Nations that would also include the democratic forces in Germany. There were more moderate Republican internationalists who also demanded that a League should be founded but combined this with the expectation that it should be at the core a league of the victors and part of a stern peace that punished the now defeated power for its transgressions. Yet Wilson would also have to reckon with an influential set of expectations that would eventually be seized upon by the "irreconcilable" opponents of his progressive aspirations. These would congeal into the demand that after an unwarranted and dangerous intervention in the "European" war, the American government should refrain from making any "un-American" commitments to a new international institution and instead return to what they regarded as salient American traditions of hemispheric isolation and pronounced "freedom of action" in international affairs.[33]

This daunting array of prevalent and partly colliding expectations on the side of the victors met with the – profoundly unrealistic – expectations that came to inform the public – and confidential – debates on the side of the vanquished powers, particularly in Germany, after the hitherto dominant expectations of the "victorious peace" movement had brutally collapsed. These were expectations that Wilson's wartime pronouncements had furthered – and that those who sought to pursue a new, republican foreign policy in Berlin would accentuate rather than moderate. At their core lay the hope that, on the basis of the armistice and in return for the German commitment to establish a republic, it would be possible to negotiate a lenient Wilsonian "peace of justice" on the premises of the Fourteen Points that would allow Germany to escape the consequences of its defeat and re-emerge as a great power with "equal rights" in the reformed postwar order and, notably, in the League of Nations.[34] Similar expectations were raised in Vienna and Budapest.

Essentially, what had thus emerged was a politically highly precarious constellation. It was indeed inconceivable not to end up in some way with a peace settlement, and reordering process, that disappointed all sides to a greater or lesser degree. It was thus all the more vital not just for the victors but also for the representatives of the defeated powers to avoid as far as possible what Wilson began to dread after the armistice, namely to spin a "net" of unrealistic expectations from which it would be impossible to "escape".[35] One crucial political challenge they thus faced after the armistice was one intrinsic to modern international politics but amplified through the war. It was the challenge to "manage" and as far as possible to moderate expectations, particularly the various expectations they faced in their own national force-fields yet also those that had acquired transnational significance.

[33] See Chapter 10.
[34] See Chapter 13.
[35] Creel (1947), p. 206.

This required learning processes and determined leadership. For precisely because the stakes of peacemaking were so high after the catastrophic war, the obstacles to moderation and restraint were also immense – and the political costs of pursuing moderate aims could be immensely high. And to some extent shaping or limiting expectations was indeed beyond the control of political leaders at this juncture. To some degree they were simply overwhelmed by expectations. Further, the temptation to cater to exaggerated expectations or to instrumentalise them for political purposes could be greater than the readiness to invest political capital in restraint. And, of course, a crucial prerequisite for furthering more realistic outlooks all around was that the political leaders themselves developed more realistic conceptions of what could and what could not be expected from the peacemaking process.

Finally, though, it also has to be pointed out that the "management" of expectations was not a "one-way-street"; it did not only concern the chief "producers" or amplifiers of expectations. What also mattered was the extent to which different elites and wider publics allowed themselves to be influenced or manipulated by what the different leaders promised – and the extent to which they too were willing and able to scale back excessive expectations they had formed during the war.

Yet it is important to recognise that there were certain key actors in 1918 who not only had to deal most directly with the problem of boundless expectations but also wrestle most head-on with the daunting multitude of short- and long-term challenges that the war had left behind. They were also the only actors who, if any, were in a position to come to terms with these expectations and challenges. And these actors were, ultimately, the leading decision- and policymakers of the main victors of the Great War. And whether it would be possible to lay foundations for a new Atlantic world order would depend above all on how they approached these challenges, how far their underlying assumptions and outlooks were at all compatible and how far they could find common ground. It is thus still imperative to assess more precisely how – and how far – they perceived these challenges and to what extent they actually could develop policies and strategies to meet them – and to cooperate. No less important, however, is an assessment of how those who now repre- sented the vanquished saw these challenges, how they tried to address them under conditions of relative powerlessness and isolation – and how far they could build bridges to the victors.

PART III

Reorientations and Incipient Learning Processes

The Dominant – Atlantic – Approaches to Peace and Order after the Great War

Despite the unprecedented range of official and unofficial actors who strove to influence it, what actually proved decisive for the way in which peacemaking after the Great War would be approached and for how the momentous reordering process of 1919 then unfolded were, indisputably, the prevalent aims, visions and *evolving* conceptions of the principal political leaders of the three principal victors – Britain, France and, notably, the United States. Yet the crucial question was how far these actors could now – in the aftermath of the armistice – concretise and if necessary *reorientate* the ideas and approaches that had gained contours during the war. Put differently, what mattered most was how far Wilson, Clemenceau, Lloyd George and their key advisers could now actually develop more substantial conceptions and effective strategies that lent themselves to constructing a durable peace and postwar order.

Even more decisive, however, was something else. In essence, the quality of the peace settlement hinged on the protagonists' capacity to accomplish now, in the midst of a very turbulent post-armistice period, what they had not even attempted during the war, especially because of the American president's insistence on a unilateral crusade: namely to find a modicum of common ground between their different interests, agendas and ideological priorities. Indeed, Wilson and the *Entente* leaders even still had to reach a basic understanding about how the peacemaking process itself was to proceed. And they had to accomplish all of this while also finding ways to manoeuvre on a both unsettled and rapidly changing transatlantic playing-field of international, transnational and domestic politics.

It is thus crucial to recognise that particularly the most powerful decision-makers now had to embark on complex and challenging learning processes under very adverse circumstances. They not only had to flesh out and adapt their concepts in the light of the evolving postwar realities they perceived; they also had to learn to pursue effective transatlantic approaches. More fundamentally, what now had to be seen was what deeper lessons they had drawn from the catastrophe of the war, how they sought to build on these *different*

349

lessons, and how far this enabled them to approach the massive reordering tasks that lay ahead of them in a realistic and constructive manner. All of this would have a decisive bearing on the nature of the eventual peace negotiations, and it would especially influence the victors' attitudes to the vital question of whether the fundamentals of the peace and the postwar order would be negotiated with, or without, the vanquished.

But immense learning and readjustment processes were also required from those who now sought to take responsibility on behalf of the defeated power, although or rather *because* they were originally cast in the role of an isolated "object" of international politics. This was a challenge that particularly the Weimar Republic's first foreign minister Ulrich von Brockdorff-Rantzau and the Social Democratic leaders of the Ebert-Scheidemann government would face when they began to chart a new, essentially Atlantic course. Whether they would be able to draw more profound consequences from a defeat that most Germans failed to acknowledge and, crucially, to develop realistic peace strategies – this remained an open question. But it would have crucial implications for the prospects of European and global peace, not just in 1919 but also in the longer term.

All in all, the two months between the armistice of November 1918 and the opening of the peace conference in mid-January 1919 thus were indeed a decisive phase of *learning* both for the victors and for the vanquished. And it was a phase in which the key actors not only elaborated but also in critical respects *came to reorientate* their approaches to peacemaking and the making of a new international order. In the following, all of this will be examined in greater depth. And it will be re-appraised from four dominant perspectives – the American, the British, the French, and the German – which are most essential to gain a clearer understanding of what could and what could not be achieved during what promised to become the most challenging reordering process in modern history.

10

Towards a Progressive Atlantic Peace of the Victors
The Reorientation of American Approaches to Peace and International Order

In his annual message to Congress on 2 December 1918, Wilson announced that he would embark on a mission no American president had ever undertaken before. He would travel to Paris and join the representatives of the powers the United States had associated with during the war to discuss "the main features of the treaty of peace". Significantly, Wilson claimed that both the *Entente* and the Central Powers had "accepted the bases of peace" he had proposed in his Fourteen Points address and subsequently re-affirmed and elaborated. And he stressed that it was thus incumbent upon him to be personally present at the envisaged peace conference to translate these "bases" into "peace settlements" that were "of transcendent importance both to us and to the rest of the world".

By conveying that the substance of his peace design had already been endorsed by the other victors Wilson raised high expectations. He emphasised that he would strive to "give order and organization" to a peace based on "new foundations of justice and fair dealing". To achieve this, he noted, he first of all had to ensure that "no false or mistaken interpretation" was placed on his proposals. Then, his critical task would be to "assist in arriving" at "common settlements" with the heads of the associated governments, notably Lloyd George and Clemenceau. The American president did not clarify at this point how this was to be achieved; nor did he have a clear idea of what he would face on the other side of the Atlantic, above all in Paris and London.[1] But fundamentally he was still resolved to act as arbiter who ushered in a modern "American peace".

Crucially, Wilson did not specify whether the "common settlements" to which he aspired would also be negotiated between the victors and the vanquished. He did not rule such negotiations out, but left this critical question open. Nor did he indicate how he planned to confront the Bolshevik challenge. And just as unclear remained how far, and in what form, the peace process he envisaged would include the participation of smaller powers and, notably, of those who were clamouring not only for

---

[1] Wilson, Annual Message to Congress, 2 December 1918, *PWW*, LIII, pp. 276–9, 284–6.

self-government but also for self-determination and statehood in and beyond eastern Europe. Instead, the president expressed his general hope "to translate into action the great ideals for which America has striven".[2] What he thus essentially announced – mainly addressed to Congress and his domestic audience, yet eagerly followed in Europe and the wider world – was *not* the beginning of an arduous struggle to negotiate principles of peace and terms of order with the representatives of other powers and causes; it was, rather, a mission to ensure that American principles and rules would be converted into a novel settlement on *his* American terms.

Yet how did Wilson – and the experts and policymakers who sought to assist him – actually come to define the American peace agenda at this juncture? How far did they actually come to develop more coherent and concrete designs not just for a League but for the entire novel order the president had proclaimed – as they grappled with the multifaceted challenges that arose after the armistice? Initially, Wilson himself adhered to the general maxims of a peace premised on "international justice" and of an inclusive peace process that had been integral to his Fourteen Points and the Four Principles, and which he had reasserted during the armistice negotiations. While clearly turning his attention to Europe and the Euro-Atlantic sphere, he still emphasised publicly that the time had come to lead humanity towards a new *global* system of order based on universal principles. And in the aftermath of the armistice he insisted all the more fervently that the "superstructure" of this order had to be the novel League of Nations.

Though still offering no specific plans for the new organisation, Wilson underscored again how critical it was to supersede the pathologies of balance-of-power politics by inaugurating, through the League, a novel system of "collective security". With remarkable optimism, he maintained that the organisation he envisioned would be strong enough to guarantee the sovereignty and integrity of its members and acquire sufficient authority to set binding rules not only for the pacific settlement of international disputes but also, and crucially, for *peaceful change* in what he saw as an evolving postwar system rather than one "set in stone".[3] The American president also argued with renewed vigour that the League would be instrumental for establishing what he continued to regard as the key foundational principle of a new *progressive* international order: the principle of self-determination or, in his underlying conception, self-government. In his speeches and statements, he still declared that the spread of self-government had to be a universal aspiration. But here too the focus of his unchangingly hierarchical outlook was ever more clearly on Europe.

[2] *Ibid.,* pp. 284–6.
[3] *Ibid.,* pp. 276–9.

Significantly, although he now spoke as the leader of one of the victorious powers Wilson still essentially upheld the claim that the United States was the only power that could act as a disinterested umpire of peacemaking. And he was more convinced than ever that he had the authority, prestige and political, financial and moral leverage to pave the way for the transformative peace he had mapped out. He asserted that he was called upon to initiate and oversee a new kind of peace process. It was to be a process in which he and the other plenipotentiaries would, as representatives of their peoples, make a "peace of the peoples" that then would enjoy an unprecedented popular legitimacy on all sides. Further, he proclaimed that it was to be a process of "open diplomacy" whose yardstick had to be "the very simple and unsophisticated standards of right and wrong" of the common people.[4] It should be noted, however, that Wilson's definition of "open diplomacy" was far from implying total transparency in international politics. As he had explained in his Fourteen Points address and thereafter, he did not rule out "confidential diplomatic negotiations involving delicate matters". But he also stressed that the results of such negotiations could not be "binding" unless they were made "public to the world" and could thus be scrutinised by "world opinion".[5]

Demonstratively casting himself in the role of an arbiter, the American president initially signalled that he was determined to mediate between the principal European victors and a by now essentially powerless Germany. He thus rejected confidential negotiations with the *Entente* governments and the idea of settling peace terms with them ahead of the actual peace conference. His underlying concern at this point was still that this would not only create the impression of "dividing the spoils" in advance but also ultimately lead to an imposed peace, which he clearly regarded as irreconcilable with his progressive agenda. Wilson thus stated explicitly that representatives of the defeated power should eventually be invited to the peace conference to "state their case". And he also maintained that Germany "ought to be present" when the League of Nations – which had to be "at the very centre of the Peace agreement" – was founded, thereby placing renewed emphasis on the maxim that the League should not be constituted as an exclusive institution of the victors.[6]

In retrospect, what seems most noteworthy is how confident Wilson was that he would actually be able to steer the peacemaking process and realise his pre-eminent aims: to found the League as an authoritative and *inclusive* "superstructure" of a renovated international system and to arbitrate a "just"

---

[4] Wilson, Annual Message to Congress, 4 December 1917, *PWW*, XLV, p. 198.
[5] Wilson, "Fourteen Points", *PWW*, XLV, pp. 536–9; Lippmann-Cobb memorandum, 26 October 1918, *PWW*, LIII, p. 495.
[6] Wiseman memorandum of conversation with Wilson, 16 October 1918, *PWW*, LI, pp. 347–52. Wilson remarks, 10 December 1918, Swem memorandum, Wilson Papers.

settlement on the basis of the Fourteen Points. As the president had earlier told House, he notably sought a peace agreement with the defeated power that prevented a renewal of German "hostilities" but was, essentially, "as moderate and reasonable as possible".[7] This is how he still presented *and defined* his mission when he embarked for Europe in early December.

Ahead of his first encounters with the *Entente* leaders Wilson told newspaper correspondents on 8 December that his earlier statement "that this should be a 'peace without victory' [held] more strongly today than ever". And he declared that "the peace that we make must be one in which justice alone is the determining factor".[8] On the passage to Europe he would impress on the members of the Inquiry that if peace was not made "on the highest principles of justice" it would be "swept away by the peoples of the world in less than a generation". He warned that both the peace settlement and the governments that made it would rapidly lose legitimacy, and this in turn was bound to heighten the "susceptibility" of the "people of Europe" to Bolshevism's poisonous appeal.[9] Wilson never explained precisely what he meant by a "just peace". Yet he conveyed that what he meant was essentially a settlement consonant with the "progressive" principles and rules that he had put forward, i.e. one that met basic standards of "fairness" and "equitability". Crucially, however, he reserved for himself the authority to decide which process and which outcome could be called "just".

But what remained integral to Wilson's conception was the explicit commitment not to invoke the "right" of the victor and use the winning side's superior power to force terms on the vanquished. Rather, he suggested that peace had to be made through negotiations that fundamentally observed American principles of "due process" and specific principles such as that of "self-determination". And he pointedly distinguished what he presented as the American conception of a "just peace" from notions of a peace of bargaining and compromise that he identified with outmoded traditions of European *Realpolitik*. He noted that the *Entente* governments would discover at the peace conference the American delegation would "stand for no bargaining" and a "peace of loot and spoliation" but rather "hold firmly by the principles" he had set forth.[10] Earlier he had observed that the disposition to make an "absolutely and rigorously impartial peace" was "growing less and less on the other side of the water", particularly in Britain and France.[11]

---

[7] Wilson to House, 28 October 1918, *PWW*, LI, p. 473.

[8] Grayson diary, 8 December 1918, *PWW*, LIII, pp. 336–7.

[9] Bullitt diary, 9 [10] December 1918, *PWW*, LIII, p. 352.

[10] Grayson diary, 8 December 1918, *PWW*, LIII, pp. 336–7; Swem memorandum of Wilson remarks, 10 December 1918, Wilson Papers.

[11] Wilson letter, 26 October 1918, Wilson Papers, series 3, vol. 54.

Yet he had underscored all the more how determined he was to insist that the settlement following the Great War "must be a peace of justice to the defeated nations" or it would be "fatal to all the nations in the end".[12]

Crucially, Wilson continued to believe that a peace dictated by the victors without any negotiations would lack legitimacy in essential respects. When first meeting Lloyd George in London on 27 December 1918, the American president still emphasised that a settlement predetermined by the victors and then "simply presented" to Germany would be a "sham". And he had not abandoned this fundamental premise when the Paris Peace Conference commenced.[13] At the same time, though, the "just" process Wilson envisaged actually restricted the scope of meaningful negotiations between the victors and the vanquished. For his conception was and remained essentially unilateral: he never departed from the conviction that ultimately he had the authority to judge, as arbiter of the peace, what was truly "just". He thus never set out to foster deliberations in which different conceptions of what was just and appropriate could be balanced as far as possible. Rather, he now even accentuated his resistance to peace negotiations whose primary aim was a "pragmatic" accommodation of interests and concerns, also with the defeated power. Moreover, he made clear that he strictly opposed the search for bargain agreements that linked political and financial-cum-economic aspects, notably when it came to cardinal questions of security, reconstruction and reparations.

At Versailles, the American president would thus have to learn the hard way that he had little choice but to set aside these maxims and engage in hammering out what were indeed very complex *quid pro quo* bargains, above all with the leaders of Britain and France. Yet he would not seek to pave the way for more far-reaching compromises between the victors and the vanquished. Essentially, then, Wilson only began to realise at a very late stage, at the peace conference itself, that he would have to depart from his original ambition to make a scientific and impartial peace. In fact, he would be forced to acknowledge that he had neither the political and financial means nor the authority to prevail on the representatives of the other powers, notably Britain and France, to accept the parameters of his peace programme. At the same time, it became obvious that it would not be possible for him to fulfil his aspirations by making himself the leader of a novel kind of transnational coalition of liberal and progressive forces.

[12] *Ibid.*

[13] Minutes of Imperial War Cabinet meeting, 30 December 1918, memorandum no. 47, CAB 23/42; Hunter/Miller "skeleton" US draft of peace treaty, 30 December 1918, *FRUS-PPC*, I, pp. 308–9.

I. Significant Reorientations. Towards an Atlantic Nucleus of the "New World Order" – and a Peace of the Victors

Yet Wilson had actually begun to reorientate his approach to peacemaking long before the opening of the Paris proceedings. And this reorientation, which occurred in the gestation period after the armistice, was very significant. Though he still held up the maxims of his earlier designs in his rhetoric, it was now that he retreated from his long avowed priority of making an integrative peace between the victors and the vanquished. And it was now that he gravitated towards an approach that eventually led him to acquiesce – however reluctantly – in a peace process dominated by complicated arrangements between the principal victors of the war and, in the end, a victors' peace. Unsurprisingly, he would later defend the outcome of this process as both "just" and appropriately severe.

Though this was not the only reason, Wilson initially altered his course to ensure that he would reach his primary goal: to establish a League of Nations, on his terms, as the core of a "new world order". Yet here too he changed his approach. In short, he still insisted that the "general programme" of the League had to be an integral part of the peace settlement. But he now stressed that the "nucleus of the league" could and should be established by the United States, Britain and France as well as Italy and Japan.[14] Thus, to lay the groundwork for a new universal system – to which he still aspired *in the longer run* – Wilson came to prioritise the creation of a *transatlantic nucleus* of order (despite the strategic need to include Japan as the only East Asian, and non-western, world power at the time). More precisely, he proposed a nucleus formed by the principal victors and excluding the vanquished. In effect, he hereby came to adopt a course his key adviser House had long advocated.[15]

At one level, Wilson's reorientation can be seen as a reaction to external pressures, chiefly the need to gain support for his League plans from his most powerful European counterparts, and domestic constraints, especially the need to avoid alienating the oppositional Republicans in the Senate who insisted on a draconian peace. But it was also the outgrowth of a more fundamental change in his peace *conception*, which brought to the fore his underlying hierarchical outlook on international politics. To justify what in fact was a departure from core premises of the Fourteen Points and his earlier "peace without victory" agenda, the American president advanced a fundamental rationale that he would also propound at Versailles. He now stressed that he envisaged not an immediate but only an *eventual* integration

---

[14] Grayson diary, 8 December 1918, *PWW*, LIII, p. 339.
[15] House to Wilson, 5 and 16 November 1918, *FRUS-PPC*, I, pp. 129 ff.

of Germany into the reformed postwar order. And he argued that it was appropriate to impose a period of probation and rehabilitation on a country that had only just shed its old regime, did not yet have a new democratic constitution and was engulfed by revolutionary turmoil. As Wilson told American correspondents in early December, "Germany's present chaotic state would make it necessary to put her on probation, as it were, until she showed herself fit for reception into the League", essentially by undertaking credible democratic reforms.[16]

Wilson adopted the same rationale to justify a second significant reorientation, and departure from fundamentals of the Fourteen Points, which began in November 1918 yet would ultimately only be confirmed at Versailles. It concerned the core parameters of the peace process itself. Essentially, he now claimed that it was not – yet – possible to negotiate the terms of peace and order with German plenipotentiaries as long as there were, in his interpretation, no representatives of a legitimate German government with whom he and the other victors could "make peace".[17] Initially, the president had been in favour of delaying the opening of the actual peace conference until a new government had been established in Berlin – precisely to create conditions for a negotiated peace. But after he had decided to travel to Europe, he came to espouse the formula that "official dealings" and substantive negotiations could only be envisaged once a "constituent assembly" had been convened and "a definite form of government" had been "agreed upon and set up" in Berlin. Wilson thus did not consider the provisional government headed by Ebert, the Council of People's Commissars, a legitimate, i.e. *democratically legitimised* government and negotiating partner.[18] This argument he could and would subsequently also invoke to exclude the vanquished power from the initial peace negotiations.

In the most critical phase, once a constituent assembly had gathered in Weimar in January 1919 to work out a republican constitution and elect the first democratic government, Wilson was no longer willing or in a position to lead efforts on behalf of a negotiated peace. His altered approach still left open the possibility of *eventual* talks with German representatives. But his real priority by then was to ensure the foundation of the League and to forge the requisite agreements with the *Entente* Powers. The American president thus retreated to his "probation" rationale.[19] Wilson's new course contributed decisively to setting the stage for the hierarchical peace process of the victors that then ensued at Versailles – and for its far-reaching consequences.

---

[16] *Ibid.*, p. 338.
[17] Wilson statements, 28 December 1918, *PWW*, LIII, p. 576.
[18] Wilson to Lansing, 25 November 1918, *PWW*, LIII, p. 194.
[19] Wilson adopted the same approach towards German Austria and Hungary.

II.   The American Actors. Wilson, His Peacemakers
and Their Peace Programme

A more substantial American peace programme was only elaborated at a very late stage – before, during and after Wilson's historic voyage to Europe. In crucial respects, it retained an improvised character. It remained the programme of a power that did not have government structures prepared to take on complex international negotiations and peacemaking efforts and, for better or worse, saturated with a long history of experience in such affairs like the British or French governments. On central points, notably the constitution of the League, the American essentials were only worked out on the eve of the peace conference in early January. Overall, Wilson was and remained the principal architect of the US agenda. While Lansing remained on the periphery, the American president still mainly drew on Colonel House's advice. The professional diplomat Henry White, who had attended the Algeciras Conference of 1906 as Theodore Roosevelt's observer, became the only Republican in the US peace delegation – and would offer prudent, if often unheard counsel. General Tasker Bliss, who had been the official American military representative on the Supreme War Council, was appointed as the fifth peace commissioner and came to advocate a lenient peace as well as actual negotiations with Germany.

The experts of the reconfigured Inquiry, headed by Sidney Mezes and including authorities like the geographer Isaiah Bowman, drew up an impressive collection of more "conservative" recommendations on both general and specific issues. It contributed detailed blueprints for a league covenant – the domain of the legal adviser David Hunter Miller – but above all self-assured expertise on questions relating to the political and territorial reorganisation of eastern Europe. In mid-January 1919, this would be gathered in a "Black Book" for the American Peace Delegation. Yet Wilson would never pay consistent attention to what his experts recommended. On financial and economic issues – as well as, eventually, on reparations – Treasury representatives like Norman Davis, yet also semi-official experts like the influential financier and chairman of the War Industries Board Bernard Baruch and the Morgan partner Thomas Lamont, supplied advice. And Herbert Hoover, who during the war had chaired the Commission for Relief in Belgium and would soon spearhead the efforts of the American Relief Administration, came to advance his own vision of how the United States could not only provide postwar relief but also a distinctly American concept for Europe's longer-term reconstruction in the wake of its self-inflicted catastrophe.[20]

---

[20] See Walworth (1986), pp. 7–105.

III. The Centrality of the League of Nations. Evolving Conceptions of the "Superstructure" of the New Order

Before embarking for Europe, Wilson made unequivocally clear that the overriding aim he would pursue during the peace negotiations was the creation of a League of Nations on his terms. He had once again called it the "indispensable instrumentality" that would "guarantee the peace" and stressed that it had to become "the most essential part of the peace settlement itself".[21] He was adamant that the "general programme of the league of nations" had to "constitute part and parcel of the peace treaty" and could not "be left to any later consideration".[22] The American president thus sent a clear signal against what he perceived as *Entente* pressures to postpone discussions over the League. And he also rejected the warnings of Lodge and other Republican critics who insisted that the founding of the new institution should be kept separate from the real priority: the peace treaty to be imposed on Germany. British and French peace planners were clearly ware of Wilson's priority and made it part of their evolving bargaining strategies. Wiseman conveyed the prevailing perception when emphasising that Wilson had come to Europe with one central goal, "the formation of a League" or at the very least "a definite agreement as to its form among the great Powers" because he believed that the thorniest postwar questions could "only be satisfactorily settled on the basis of a LEAGUE OF NATIONS".[23]

By the time he travelled to Paris, Wilson could indeed count on what looked like an impressively broad, if uneven, transnational coalition of governments yet also of individuals, parties, and pressure-groups on both sides of the Atlantic – and around the world – that backed the establishment of a League in one form or another. While the *New Republic* demanded that the new organisation had to be established as a "supernational agency of international fair play", these forces in fact all had different ideas about what kind of League could and should be constituted.[24] Yet all of them looked to Wilson as the pivotal figure in the founding process. Crucially, however, if he wanted to implement his as yet vague designs, the American president needed to gain the consent of the other principal peacemakers – and chiefly that of Lloyd George and Clemenceau. The degree to which this gave the British and French delegations – as well as the Japanese – critical bargaining power vis-à-vis the United States throughout the peace negotiations should not be underestimated. At the same time, Wilson of course still faced the no less daunting challenge of gaining the support of a majority in the Republican-dominated

---

[21] Wilson address, 27 September 1918, *PWW*, LI, pp. 127–33.

[22] Grayson diary, 8 December 1918, *PWW*, LIII, p. 339.

[23] Wiseman to the British Foreign Office, Paris, 15 December 1918, *PWW*, LIII, pp. 394–5.

[24] *New Republic*, 5 October 1918, p. 272.

Senate to ensure that the United States would break with its most hallowed foreign-policy traditions and actually join the new organisation.

Although the League was still at the very centre of Wilson's aspiration to create a novel international order, he remained distinctly guarded about his plans. In private he had already departed from his earlier preference for an "organic growth" of the envisaged institution and drawn up his own covenant blueprint in August 1918. Yet even in the months preceding the opening of the peace conference, when he would have had an opportunity to seize on his prestige and present a more concrete design, the American president, wary of exposing himself to criticism and debate, made a point of confining himself to reiterating the general maxims he had already proclaimed during the war. And he remained similarly non-committal in his preliminary discussions with House and Inquiry experts on board the *George Washington*. Thus, American ideas for the actual architecture of the new "association" were only fleshed out once Wilson had reached Europe and indeed further revised immediately before and at the peace conference.

On the critical question of *how* the League would be established Wilson, as noted, altered his approach significantly after the armistice. Beginning to face up to the *realpolitical* necessities of reaching an understanding with Britain and France, and under the impression of the turmoil in Germany, he abandoned his original premise that the League should not be founded as an exclusive institution of the victors.[25] By early December, the new maxim of Wilson's policy was that the victorious powers ought to go ahead and form the "nucleus" of the new organisation. Other states would then "of necessity come in to preserve their own interests".[26]

On 20 November 1918, Wilson had outlined his adjusted plans to the influential Swiss professor and diplomat William Rappard, who would eventually be instrumental in persuading the American president to establish the League in Geneva. Wilson had stressed that "the foundation of the Society of Nations" was "to be constituted at the peace conference by the belligerent allies alone" and provide them with "mutual assurance against war" and "the benefits, not of free trade, but of freer and equal economic intercourse". And he had argued that once established, the League was to "remain open to such neutrals as may seek and be granted admittance". Significantly, however, he had also indicated that only a "*reformed* Germany *may later on be admitted also*".[27] This hardened into the president's hierarchical "probation" maxim. As he told members of the Inquiry on 9 December, he had come to conclude that it was "necessary for Germany to pass through a probationary period" before

[25] Wiseman memorandum of conversation with Wilson, 16 October 1918, *PWW* LI, pp. 347–52.
[26] Dr Grayson diary, 8 December 1918, *PWW*, LIII, p. 339.
[27] Wilson's ideas cited in Rappard to Wilson, 26 November 1918, *PWW*, LIII, pp. 209–10.

being admitted to the League "because it must still be proved that the German people have a responsible, decent government".[28]

At the same time, a shift had occurred within the American Peace Delegation as well. In the circles around Wilson there were no longer any prominent voices who questioned the wisdom of his reorientated approach. House had clearly favoured a "victors' strategy" all along and in fact sought to persuade the president to pursue it, not only to commit the *Entente* Powers to the American League programme but also to reach a preliminary understanding with them on the fundamentals of the peace settlement itself.[29] And among the experts, those who advocated a similar course, notably David Miller and James Scott, came to prevail, while those who still argued that the League should be founded as a universal organisation in accordance with earlier American proclamations either now played a more peripheral role, like Bullitt, or, in the case of Lippmann, had left the president's circle of advisers.[30]

Thus, with the backing of his most influential experts Wilson now insisted that the path to the League had to lead via an agreement with the other principal victors. Yet he was still confident that he could compel the latter to accept essentially American terms of reference. Nonetheless, he now made some tactical concessions to France – and Britain; and he indeed managed to ensure that the elaboration of the League Covenant would be the first item on the agenda of the peace conference. Following the armistice, particularly the Clemenceau government had put pressure on the American president to abandon the aim of including Germany in a *société des nations*. Ambassador Jusserand conveyed Clemenceau's verdict that the new German leaders could not be trusted: Germany could not "change its heart" as quickly as it had "changed its constitution".[31] Wilson also responded to changes in the constellation of US domestic politics after the Republican Party's victory in the Congressional elections in November. He now required the backing of at least part of the Republican majority, which remained at least reserved or even profoundly hostile towards his League aspirations. Yet he was also aware that key senators like Lodge were, if at all, in favour of a League conceived as an exclusive organisation of the victors that grew out of their wartime alignments.[32]

But Wilson's shift was not merely a tactical concession or response to changing international and domestic constellations. In fact, he sought to

[28] Bullitt diary, 9 [10] December 1918, *PWW*, LIII, p. 352.

[29] House to Wilson, 5 and 16 November 1918, *FRUS-PPC*, I, pp. 129 ff.

[30] Miller memorandum, 22 November 1918, *FRUS-PPC*, I, pp. 355–63; House to Wilson, 5, and 16 November 1918, *FRUS-PPC*, I, pp. 129 ff.; Bullitt memorandum, 8 November 1918, *PWW*, LIII, pp. 6–9; *New Republic*, 21 December 1918, pp. 212–14.

[31] Jusserand to Pichon, November 1918, MAE, A Paix 292, A 1163.2.

[32] See Lodge memorandum, 2 December 1918, Lodge Papers.

pursue a new path to come to grips with the daunting task of committing the other crucial powers to his League scheme and, more broadly, the underpinnings of his "new world order". He essentially reckoned that this task would have be rendered distinctly more difficult, if not impossible, if German representatives were "present at the creation". For then conflicts between the European victors and the defeated power would have threatened to block the necessary initial agreements. In effect, Wilson thus made a strategic choice. Ever since 1916 he had suggested that an integrative "peace without victory" and the creation of a League of Nations were *both* essential to a "new world order" – and could be achieved at the same time. Now, he came to pursue his overriding objective – the constitution of "his" League – at the expense of his integrative agenda.

En route to Europe and then even more emphatically once he spoke to the peoples of the "old world", Wilson re-affirmed his progressive ambition to replace what he saw as the dysfunctional European "balance-of-power" system of the pre-war era with a new order of fundamentally equal self-governing states. And he underscored once again how indispensable the novel institution was to this end. In his evolving conception, he still saw as the League's main purpose that it would guarantee the "sovereignty" and "territorial integrity" of its "component states". But, beginning to grasp the gigantic challenges that especially the political reorganisation of Eastern Europe raised, he also stressed more than before that it would be critical to establish binding League rules and procedures for the peaceful settlement of international disputes and crucially, if necessary, for the *peaceful change* of a given political or territorial status quo. As he outlined, the new association had to be empowered "to readjust frontiers" if the people of a certain "territory" appealed for such changes – or if they were deemed imperative in the interest of peace.[33]

The American president thus sought to establish the League not only as the main guarantee mechanism of the new order that provided unprecedented protections for its members, including the new east European nation-states. He also intended it to become the key mechanism that fostered the *evolutionary* consolidation of a recast European and global system of states in the longer run. According to Bowman, Wilson stressed that the League "implied political independence and territorial integrity plus alteration of terms and alteration of boundaries if it could be shown that injustice had been done or that conditions had changed". In the president's judgement, such consolidating adjustments and "alterations" would be easier to make at a later stage, when the passions of war had subsided and matters could be viewed "in the light of justice rather

---

[33] Bullitt diary, 9 [10] December 1918, *PWW*, LIII, pp. 350–2. See also Bowman memorandum of Wilson remarks to Inquiry on 10 December 1918, *ibid.*, p. 354.

than in the light of a peace conference at the close of a protracted war".[34] Yet what Wilson envisaged were in fact extremely far-reaching responsibilities for an organisation that still had to gain authority, legitimacy and the consistent support of its member states, particular the principal victors of the war.

It was only after he had made the critical decision to construct the League around an essentially transatlantic "nucleus of the victors" that Wilson finally elaborated, and revised, his own blueprint for the novel organisation at the beginning of 1919. He did so in a characteristically self-reliant manner, paying scant attention to the more sophisticated blueprints developed by David Hunter Miller. Yet the president did draw on two proposals that had been submitted to him during his stay in London in December 1918, the plan prepared by Cecil and notably Smuts' *Practical Suggestion* for a hierarchical League.[35] The revised Covenant Wilson would present at Versailles would indeed reflect Smuts' and Cecil's recommendations, but at the core it represented a crystallisation of the conceptions the president himself had formulated during the war.[36] Wilson now also proposed a bicameral League system, including a stronger permanent council that was to take on the settlement of international disputes. While still envisaging a general assembly as the main forum of international discussion and deliberation, he thus sought to make sure that the great powers, which in his view bore the main responsibility for maintaining the League and enforcing its "collective security" regime, would be granted a permanent and higher authority.[37]

In his rhetoric, Wilson still emphasised the need to break with the past and create a truly egalitarian institution that established new equilibrium between "strong" and "weak" states. But his thinking about how to make the League an effective organisation and how to reconcile basic international equality and particular "responsibilities" of the "advanced" great powers had undergone a marked change. Ever since 1916, he had declared that the League's foundational principle had to be "an equality of rights" that "must neither recognize nor imply a difference between big nations and small, between those that are powerful and those that are weak".[38] Now, to justify the elevated role and new prerogatives of the United States – and other civilised great powers – Wilson came to adopt a more hierarchical conception, based on the rationale that only the "power of the strong" could protect the rights and security of the weak in

---

[34] Bowman memorandum of Wilson remarks to the Inquiry on 10 December 1918, *PWW*, LIII, p. 354.

[35] See Cecil memorandum, 17 December 1918, *PWW*, LIII, pp. 415–17; memorandum for Wilson, 26 December 1918, including passages from Smuts' *The League of Nations*, *PWW*, LIII, pp. 515–18; Miller (1928), I, chapter 7.

[36] Protocol of Plenary Session of the Inter-Allied Conference for the Preliminaries of Peace, 25 January 1919, *PWW*, LIV, p. 266.

[37] Wilson, Draft of a Covenant, ca. 8 January 1919, *PWW*, LIII, pp. 678–86.

[38] Wilson Senate address, 22 January 1917, *PWW*, XL, pp. 536–7, 533–9

the new world order he envisaged.[39] This rationale underlay his call for an authoritative League Council, which indeed prefigured that of the UN Security Council. The permanent members of the council thus were to form the core of what he had earlier described as a new kind of international "concert". They were to have the ultimate authority to decide what constituted "aggression" and violations of the Covenant, how international disputes were to be settled and what sanctions were appropriate. And they would also decide when and on what terms changes of the political and territorial status quo were advisable to further overall peace and stability. The American president thus effectively proposed making the "advanced" great powers the de facto hegemons of the new international system – yet hegemons bound by the rules and restraints of the League Covenant. But he clearly regarded the United States as the most advanced and indeed pivotal power within this new, essentially transatlantic concert system. What he still had to confront, however, was the challenge of legitimising this new vision of order, and of America's exemplary role, not only internationally but also on the home front.

One of the most critical questions that Wilson's aspirations raised was whether, in exercising their particular "responsibilities", those who represented the great powers, including the United States, would indeed commit themselves to the new rules he proposed – and whether they would thus accept both more far-reaching international obligations and essential limits on hitherto prevalent conceptions of great-power sovereignty. Indispensable, therefore, was the willingness of not only the principal western victors and Japan but also – eventually – the vanquished and the future Russian state to abide by *self-imposed* responsibilities and obligations, and to legitimise them domestically. How far not only Wilson but also his principal counterparts at Versailles would actually be prepared to do so would be a crucial political question in 1919. Put differently, it was a litmus test indicating how far the post–First World War constellation opened up real prospects for a novel League-based international system and for superseding the "old order" and the privileges and prerogatives that the exclusive club of imperialist powers had asserted before 1914.

In the eyes of Wilson and other American and European proponents of the League, both the – pacifying – impact of "world opinion" in a new era of "open diplomacy" and the internal liberalisation and democratisation of states were to furnish essential assurances and restraints. In fact, though, the far-reaching transformation process they sought to foster required nothing less than fundamental learning processes and qualitative changes in individual and collective mentalities not only in Europe but also in the United States – as well as outside the transatlantic sphere. For Wilson represented a new American world power that still insisted on "special rights" in Latin America, the western hemisphere and East Asia, under the Monroe and "Open Door" doctrines. A cardinal problem that arose, not only for Wilson, was to make the exercise of a new kind of shared hegemony compatible with, and indeed conducive to, the League's consolidation into an *effective* and *more broadly legitimate* organisation – an institution that actually addressed the structural problems that had to be confronted after the Great War and decades of high imperialism. Not least, Wilson, Lloyd George and Clemenceau would have to reach an agreement about which states would qualify as members of the League and on what criteria they would be admitted. Here, no decision would be more significant and explosive than the timing and conditions of Germany's admission. A further question Wilson and the other victors faced, and for which the president's blueprint offered no solution yet, was that of how far the League should and could accommodate Bolshevik Russia.

Yet the even more fundamental question Wilson now had to tackle head-on was one that not only the unprecedented catastrophe of the war itself but also the manifold crises of the pre-war era had bequeathed to him and the other peacemakers. It was the question of how peace and international security could be guaranteed in Europe, and the world, in new and more salutary ways after all previous diplomatic practices and "remedies" had so disastrously failed. On his journey to Europe, the American president essentially reaffirmed his "vision" of what had to be achieved. He again rejected all notions of special alliances and combinations – particularly the notion of creating, in one form or another, a new "Holy Alliance" among the victors to contain the vanquished. What he underlined instead was that under the conditions humanity now faced, a "peace to end all wars" could only be secured through a novel regime of League-anchored "collective security" – though he used neither the terms "security" nor "collective". Like his key advisers, Wilson still counted on the pacifying influence of "world opinion"; and he still pursued the vision of buttressing peace and security in the longer term by promoting political reforms and democratisation in and beyond Europe. At the core, however, he outlined the contours of a system whose guiding "idea" was, as he told his experts, that "we should make sure that the world will combine against an outlaw in the future just as it has combined in the present war against Germany".[40]

Essentially, the American president thus saw no need to envisage any kind of alternative, more regionally specific security arrangements for Europe that could complement an as yet untested international organisation. Nor did he contemplate more specific American commitments, e.g. to an alliance of the victors to guard against renewed German threats. He even stressed that he

---

[40] Bullitt diary, 9 [10] December 1918, *PWW*, LIII, pp. 350–2. See also Bowman memorandum of Wilson remarks to Inquiry on 10 December 1918, *ibid.*, p. 354.

ruled out such commitments, because in his eyes they would harm efforts to establish an effective League regime. And while his key adviser House was more sympathetic to French security concerns vis-à-vis Germany, neither he nor any other of the other American experts and delegates offered any alternative suggestions.[41] They by and large agreed with the president and with the priority of avoiding "old-style" entangling commitments in Europe and the risk of being drawn into outmoded European alliance and security politics.[42] As a result, there was no further debate, and no American plans for a more specific regional security "architecture" for Europe and the transatlantic sphere emerged at this stage. Particularly the notion of entering into a postwar alliance of the victors remained anathema to Wilsonian thinking. And it was rejected by the experts who advised him as a break with long-standing US traditions that could not be justified vis-à-vis Congress and the American people, particularly because there seemed to be no serious future threats to US security.

Though he came to consider them excessive, Wilson was not oblivious to French fears of renewed German aggression. But he remained very suspicious of what he perceived as French attempts to turn the League into a militarised quasi-alliance of the victors and an instrument designed to enforce the postwar status quo against the vanquished power. De facto, however, the American president espoused the premise that initially the United States and the principal European victors would play a dominant part in making the organisation's new system of "collective security" work – a system in which the vanquished power would not (yet) be included. In his assessment, this would provide more powerful and reliable re-assurance and deterrence than old-fashioned "shifting alliances" and thus also guard against new German challenges to European peace more effectively.

Wilson indeed signalled in his own way that he desired a robust League of Nations. In Article X of his revised League draft of January 1919, he accentuated that in order to serve its purpose the League's security regime had to have "teeth", i.e. clear and strict enforcement provisions that placed far-reaching obligations on the organisation's members, above all the great powers. Significantly, he adhered to the maxim that in case of actual hostilities, or if any power outside the League took "hostile action" against a member state, all the Contracting Powers would be obliged to impose commercial sanctions on the aggressor, close its frontiers and, crucially, use "jointly any force that may be necessary" to accomplish their objective. Ultimately, they would have to "unite in coming to the assistance" of the attacked member of the League,

---

[41] House diary, 7 January 1919, *PWW*, LIII, pp. 652–3.
[42] See e.g. Lansing to Wilson, 23 December 1918, Wilson Papers.

"combining their armed forces on its behalf".[43] Wilson argued that certain constraints on the sovereignty of each power were necessary for the greater common good. Yet he would insist, then and thereafter, that there would be *no automatism*. In his interpretation, the proposed key Article X of the Covenant stipulated a "moral", not a "legal obligation". Ultimately, decisions over sanctions and the use of force as part of collective action would be subject to the political approval of each government – and, in the United States, the Senate.[44] In fact, the American president had only begun to grapple with the problem of how an effective system of "collective security" could be set up and then operate effectively.

In late December, Lansing voiced fundamental concerns, urging Wilson to abandon any notion of substantial "positive" international guarantees and sanctions, which he deemed irreconcilable with the American constitution. As an alternative he proposed that each sovereign state should give the "negative" guarantee to exercise self-restraint, under which he subsumed the pledge not to violate another state's territory, integrity or independence. Lansing also argued that the American delegation could best serve the cause of peace by making the promotion of self-government and democracy its priority. Lansing observed that whereas a League Council in which each member could veto decisions would be highly ineffective one that operated on the principle of majority decisions would raise the danger of obliging the United States to participate in economic and military sanctions against its will – and of breaching the US constitution, and US sovereignty, if actions were taken without the approval of Congress. The secretary of state thus pointed to important constitutional issues that had to be addressed if the United States was to play a leading role in the new international organisation.[45]

But Wilson discarded Lansing's caveats and would largely ignore his further interventions at Versailles. Because in his conception protecting the sovereignty and integrity of its members and especially of "weaker" states against overt and less overt forms of aggression was to be a such a central function of the League, he maintained that political conflict management and deterrence had to be complemented by economic sanctions and, as a last resort, collective military measures *authorised by the individual governments*. Yet the president and his advisers confronted still further and even more complex problems. How far could and should the League protect the rights and security of minorities in its "component states", particularly the new or "reborn" *multi-ethnic* states that were being formed in eastern Europe? And how were the

---

[43] Wilson, Draft of a Covenant, ca. 8 January 1919, *PWW*, LIII, p. 684; Lansing memorandum, 11 January 1919, *PWW*, LIV, pp. 3–4.
[44] Wilson statement, 19 August 1919, *PWW*, LXII, pp. 339–411.
[45] Lansing to Wilson, 23 December 1918, Wilson Papers.

interests and "rights" of peoples to be safeguarded that could not (yet) gain recognition for their claims to "self-determination" and statehood – particularly in the colonised world beyond Europe? As will be shown, the president himself had only begun to face up to these problems; and he had yet to provide conclusive answers – for Europe, yet even more so in a global perspective.

IV.   Universal Rhetoric and Transatlantic Priorities. The Limits of Wilson's Global Vision and the Maxim of a New Atlantic "Partnership of Right"

Particularly since 1916, Wilson had proclaimed maxims and principles for a new *world* order. And he had come to argue that a new European system of self-governing states had to be embedded in such an order. But neither before nor after the armistice had he developed an actual, coherent *global* conception of how this order was to be created. What he began to elaborate prior to the peace conference was rather, essentially, a more limited and hierarchical approach that centred on the United States' relations with Europe and the reorganisation of Europe itself. What he thus brought to Versailles was far from a substantial programme for a renovated global system that not only delegitimised but actually fostered decisive steps towards overcoming imperialist practices and colonial rule in the extra-European world. And because he realised more acutely than before how essentially he depended on British, French – and Japanese – support for his League designs, he largely refrained from seriously challenging the claims and interests of the most powerful remaining empires.

Thus, there would be no constructive response to the efforts of Sa'd Zaghlul to engage the American president as a patron of the Egyptian national cause. Nor would Wilson endorse or actually seek to further the self-determination agenda advanced by Bal Gangadhar and the Indian National Congress. Similarly. He remained very circumspect in response to Sun Yat Sen and never intervened decisively to "save democracy in China".[46] Instead of mapping out a global agenda of self-determination in accordance with his wartime rhetoric, which would have been bound to fail at this juncture, Wilson came to focus on something else. Clearly influenced by the proposals Smuts had advanced in his *Practical Suggestion*, he began to devise his own version of a distinctly hierarchical system of trusteeship, to be instituted under the auspices of the League, for those extra-European territories and peoples that had formerly been ruled by the Eastern empires, including the Ottoman Empire. In his conception, this system was to be administered by League agencies,

---

[46] Sun Yat Sen missive, received on 19 November 1918, enclosed in Wilson to Lansing, 20 November 1918, *PWW*, LIII, p. 140. See Manela (2007).

which in turn could delegate mandates to appropriate "advanced" powers. The president explained that the German colonies in Africa "should become the common property of the League", to be administered by a smaller member state "primarily in the interest of the natives". Unsurprisingly, however, he never made a serious effort to consult with representatives of the peoples whose destinies were to be determined.[47]

An important mediator between British and American ideas for a new kind of Anglo-American collaboration after the war, particularly in establishing a mandate system, was the Inquiry member George Louis Beer, an expert on the history of British colonial rule. Following the American entry in the war, Beer had published a book on the "English-speaking Peoples", their "future relations" and "joint international obligations". He did not envisage a "political reunion" of the "two great branches of the English-speaking people" but rather proposed that they should jointly foster "new forms of political organization" that could "permanently unite" different nations in "a common co-operative purpose" predicated on "law and justice", which would also extend to acting as trustees of former German colonies. Beer saw the "necessity of a co-operative democratic alliance" and "Community of Policy" between the United States and Britain that could over time be developed into a "new type of permanent political association" between the most civilised and "culturally kindred peoples" in what he called a "markedly interdependent world". In his view, this would be vital for the "re-establishment of peace" after the defeat of the German Empire. Wilson did not espouse Beer's vision of an Anglo-American special relationship. But he drew on his advice when the League's trusteeship system was finalised at Versailles.[48]

Essentially, however, the American president built on his own hierarchical assumptions and notions he had developed before the war, especially with a view to the Philippines. As noted, he had consistently stressed the tutelage duties of the more "advanced" powers, and particularly the United States, to aid less "civilised" peoples in developing the prerequisites for *eventually* determining their own affairs. Building on such ideas Wilson, in his covenant draft of 8 January 1919, proposed making the League the "residuary trustee with sovereign right of ultimate disposal or of continued administration" of territories outside Europe that formerly had been under the "dominion" of the German and Ottoman empires. He stressed that these were *not* to be annexed by any state "either within the League or outside of it". And, opting for a characteristically flexible formulation, he suggested that, with a view to the "future government" of the different peoples in question, "the rule of self-

---

[47] Bullitt diary, 9 [10] December 1918, PWW, LIII, p. 351; Bowman memorandum of Wilson remarks to Inquiry on 10 December 1918, ibid., p. 355; Hankey notes of meeting of the Council of Ten, 28 January 1919, PWW, LIV, p. 326.

[48] See Beer (1917), viii, ix, x, pp. 169 ff., pp. 201 ff., 250–71; Beer (1923).

determination, or the consent of the governed" should be "fairly and reasonably applied".[49]

Fundamentally, adopting a formula that Smuts had offered to please him, Wilson underscored that the League was to be the "successor to the Empires" and as such "empowered" to "watch over the relations *inter se* of all new independent States arising or created out of Empires" and to settle differences among them to provide for the "maintenance of settled order and the general peace".[50] The American president thus clearly signalled that the United States would share in these new League responsibilities. But during the first meetings with Lloyd George and Balfour in London in late December he then resisted British attempts to induce him to take on carefully selected *specific* obligations of guardianship. Wilson would never espouse the notion of a kind of neo-imperial Anglo-Saxon civilising mission that would centre on the successor states of the Ottoman Empire. He underscored that he was very much "opposed to any intervention in these territorial questions". And he notably distanced himself from the idea that the United States would take over mandatory responsibilities in Armenia or, as Balfour indirectly proposed, as a "mandatory at Constantinople". While sympathetic to the Armenian plight, Wilson emphasised his doubt that either the US Senate or the American public would accept a mandate far beyond the western hemisphere.[51]

In the final analysis, the focus of Wilson's evolving peace policies was and remained on Europe; and his ideas of a new international system *de facto* came to revolve around the transatlantic nucleus of a "new world order". What had not changed, however, were the president's fundamental approach to international politics and his assumptions about the distinction between progressive US conceptions and outmoded European practices and rules. He never tried to understand or draw lessons from the longer history of European international politics and the search for a stable equilibrium and standards of a *ius Europaeum*, particularly in the era of the Vienna system. Rather, he would on numerous occasions publicly denounce the "covenants of selfishness and compromise" that had been entered into at the Congress of Vienna and stress that they offered no guidance for peacemaking in the twentieth century.[52]

Speaking at London's Free Trade Hall on 30 December 1918, Wilson clearly signalled that the United States had "no interest" in becoming a "European power" and part of a European postwar system that returned to the pathologies of pre-war balance-of-power politics. What he proposed instead was

---

[49] Wilson, Draft of a Covenant, ca. 8 January 1919, *PWW*, LIII, pp. 678 ff.

[50] *Ibid.*; Lansing memorandum, 11 January 1919, *PWW* LIV, pp. 3–4.

[51] Minutes of the Imperial War Cabinet, 30 December 1918, CAB 23/42. For the wider context see Laderman (2019), esp. pp. 111 ff.

[52] Wilson, Annual Message to Congress, 4 December 1917, *PWW*, XLV, p. 198; Hankey's Notes of Two Meetings of the Council of Ten, 28 January 1919, *PWW*, LIV, p. 314.

a new "partnership of right between America and Europe". And he emphatically affirmed his universal mission, stating that the United States was "not
interested merely in the peace of Europe, but in the peace of the world". As he
emphasised, creating and preserving a lasting global peace made it imperative
to accomplish what had never been attempted before, the formation of a
"genuine concert of mind and purpose" led by the victors. Ultimately, it was
to become a universal "combination" of "all" nations in the framework of the
League. Yet the novel transatlantic "partnership of right" had to come first and
lie at the centre of this "combination" and a fundamentally reformed international system.

Though he never explicitly adopted a specific regional conception, what
Wilson thus implicitly advanced under an umbrella of universalist rhetoric,
and with global implications, was essentially his vision of a new Atlantic order,
and concert, *on progressive American terms*.[53] The president's "Americanist"
assumptions were shared by all other key members of the American delegation
and the Inquiry. While House persisted with his efforts to broker preliminary
understandings with the *Entente* governments he essentially subscribed to
them as well – and would hence seek to act as a mediator on behalf of
Wilson's design.[54]

V. How to Found a New Atlantic Order? American Approaches to Peacemaking and the Complexities of Creating a New International System

Yet how did Wilson and those who would become the other American "peacemakers" of 1919 actually envisage translating the president's "principles" into an
actual peace settlement? And how did they actually seek to lay the groundwork
for a new "Atlantic world order"? How far did they develop actual strategies to
this end, and what kind of peacemaking process did they expect? How did they
assess America's new position in the world, its unprecedented political leverage
and financial power in this context? And how far did they recognise essential
limits of US power? To what extent did they understand the complexity of the
tasks they faced? And how acutely were they aware of the dangerously
heightened expectations Wilson's rhetoric had raised?

When the president had outlined to Congress in December 1917 the basic
aims and principles for which the United States fought in the war, he used
harsh words to distinguish them from what he presented as the outdated ideas
and maxims of 1815. He stressed that the war had to lead to a new order based
on "a partnership of peoples, not a mere partnership of governments". And he

---

[53] Wilson address, Free Trade Hall, 30 December 1918, *PWW*, LIII, pp. 550–1.
[54] House diary, 16 December 1918, *PWW*, LIII, p. 402; Wiseman to Foreign Office, 15 December 1918, *ibid.*, p. 395.

asserted that "(s)tatesmen must by this time have learned that the opinion of the world is everywhere wide awake and fully comprehends the issues involved"; no "representative of any self-governed nation" would "dare disregard it". In his view, a peace forged through a series of "selfish" compromises between the great powers was thus no longer admissible, and bound to crumble.[55] Before his first actual encounters with Lloyd George and Clemenceau in December 1918, Wilson reaccentuated this theme, declaring that he had not come to Europe to "bargain" with the leaders of the Allied Powers. He thus signalled unequivocally that he was not prepared to accept *quid pro quo* agreements that revived what in his eyes were discredited traditions of European diplomacy and accommodated their narrow national and imperial interests at the expense of the vanquished power – and world peace.[56] Intent on leading the world in a different direction, and to put pressure on his interlocutors, he renewed the call for a peace process that met novel standards of "impartiality", "justice" and "open diplomacy".[57]

Essentially, the American president thus showed his resolve to approach the reordering process after the Great War in a distinctly unilateral, indeed high-handed manner. Following two years of wartime speeches in which he had argued that the world required American "principles" and American "policies" and claimed that they represented what all "forward-looking men and women" of "every modern nation, of every enlightened community" desired, he was now determined to fulfil the mission of a progressive arbiter of peace at the forthcoming conference. Although he began to realise that their support would be vital, he refrained from seeking any substantial consultations with the *Entente* governments.[58] He continued to regard both Lloyd George and Clemenceau, with whom he only had brief and inconsequential encounters during his tour of the European capitals, as representatives of the "old order" and old-style power politics that he sought to overcome.

As self-styled prophet of a new order Wilson was resolved to pursue neither a victors' peace nor the role of a mediator between the victors of the vanquished; rather, he would aspire to bring his elevated authority to bear, and essentially set the terms in line with his interpretation of what was "just". At the same time, this was his way of trying to cope with what lay ahead and represented entirely uncharted terrain for him and the nation he represented: the challenges of highly complicated international negotiations with powerful interlocutors. Crucially, however, as it had done ever since 1917, Wilson's approach again blocked any attempts to coordinate the peace agendas of the

---

[55] Wilson, Annual Message to Congress, 4 December 1917, *PWW*, XLV, p. 198.
[56] Swem memorandum, Wilson Papers; Grayson diary, 8 December 1918, *PWW*, LIII, pp. 336–7.
[57] Wilson, "Fourteen Points", *PWW*, XLV, pp. 536–9.
[58] Wilson Senate address, 22 January 1917, *PWW*, XL, pp. 536–9.

principal victors and to reach prior understandings on fundamental issues. All of this would have to be thrashed out at the peace conference itself, which added significantly to its problems and complexities.

In his own judgement, which had been reinforced by this time, Wilson was in a strong position, if not predestined, to put his stamp on the peacemaking process. As he saw it, he was cast in a commanding role by virtue of the political, financial and strategic leverage he had as leader of the power that had decided the war, as leader of the new "world creditor", and as the peacemaker who had put forward the most compelling blueprint for a "new world order".[59] Wilson had no qualms about stressing that he would be prepared to push for the largest naval construction programme in history if no agreement on the "freedom of the seas" could be reached and Britain insisted on its right to naval blockades and preponderance. On 8 December, he observed that the Lloyd George government found itself "in the peculiar position of submitting to the principle of disarmament" by agreeing to the Fourteen Points while at the same time announcing that it "meant to retain naval supremacy". The president stated that if necessary the United States "could and would build the greatest navy in the world" to make British elites more cooperative. Yet he also intended to use this "naval threat" in a wider context: as a lever to compel British – and French – leaders to accept the American peace agenda.[60]

In general terms, Wilson also intended to seize on the United States' leverage as the world's newly pre-eminent financial power and war-debt creditor to bolster his position as arbiter of the peace conference, particularly vis-à-vis Britain and France. He still acted on the assumption that the *Entente* Powers were "financially in [American] hands" and reckoned that he would be able to capitalise on this, particularly to compel them to accept his League design. He also contemplated putting financial pressure on his British and French counterparts to induce them to accept a "scientific" and moderate settlement of their indemnity claims vis-à-vis Germany. With these overriding aims in mind, and while calculating that their financial shortfalls and dependence on America would *de facto* place severe limits on their ability to make sovereign decisions, Wilson was all the more intent on maintaining American independence when it came to financial and economic decision-making.[61] But neither he nor key financial advisers like Davis, Baruch or Lamont developed

---

[59] Bowman memorandum, 10 December 1918, *PWW*, LIII, pp. 353 ff. See Walworth (1986), pp. 25 ff.

[60] Grayson diary, 8 December 1918, *PWW*, LIII, p. 337; Murray to Wiseman and Reading, 5 December 1918, Wiseman Papers; Geddes memorandum, 7 November 1918, *PWW*, LI, pp. 633–4.

[61] See State Department instructions to US representatives in Paris and London, 19 November 1918, Department of State, RG 59, 600.001.591/606a; Hoover to Wilson, 11 November 1918, O'Brien (1978), pp. 4–5.

effective strategies to bring the potential leverage of the aspiring financial hegemon to bear on the peace process. Wilson himself did not see the need to pursue strategies that parlayed American power into targeted political influence. And he would steadfastly oppose more ambitious political-cum-financial bargains that could have altered the outcomes of 1919.

As will be shown, the rigid axioms of American policy on inter-allied debts, which precluded incentives in the form of debt relief or cancellation, and even more importantly the constraints that Congressional opposition to any such schemes created, placed strict limits on American leverage from the start. And these constraints would not change in the course of the peace conference. At the same time, Wilson had to acknowledge that in many ways he was at least as dependent on the political support of the Allied leaders as they were on his goodwill, particularly if he wanted to realise his League aspirations. At a deeper level, however, Wilson simply was not willing to depart from his basic approach. He had not come to Europe to make peace through a series of complex *do ut des* bargains that linked American incentives, or concessions, in the financial and economic spheres to conciliatory *Entente* behaviour in the political sphere. He still rejected such an approach as a matter of principle. And his advisers followed suit.

VI. A Novel Method? Wilson and the Notion of a Transnational Coalition of Progressive Forces

Yet there was another – novel – dimension to the American approach to peace under Wilson. In the immediate aftermath of the armistice, the president and some of his closest advisers still had high hopes that they would be able to seize on the unprecedented transnational appeal of the president's wartime pro-nouncements, American propaganda and the Fourteen Points agenda itself to form a new kind of transnational coalition – a phalanx of liberal and progressive forces *from both sides of the trenches* – that was to pave the way for a new kind of integrative "progressive peace". Soon, however, Wilson came to limit his ambitions. His new focus would be on rallying liberal and progressive opinion in Europe in order to compel Lloyd George and Clemenceau to endorse not only his League plans but also the other essentials of his peace programme.

In the second half of November, in the face of revolutionary developments in Central Europe and the rising Bolshevik challenge in the east, Wilson at first sought to persevere with the approach he had pursued as self-appointed "leader of the liberal idea" during the war and that Lippmann had emphatic-ally recommended ever since 1917.[62] Raising the banner of the Fourteen

---

[62] Baker (1927–39), VIII, p. 562; Lippmann memoranda, ca. 15 and 22 December 1917, *FRUS-PPC*, I, pp. 27–8, 43–8.

Points, he aspired to create momentum for a peace settlement in their spirit, and to strengthen his position as arbiter, by galvanising a broad and essentially inclusive, yet also markedly heterogeneous, coalition of "forward-looking" liberal and left-progressive forces. It was supposed to exert influence not only on the side of the victorious powers, smaller states and neutral countries but also on Germany and the other defeated powers.[63] At this point Wilson thus still entertained the notion that such a novel transnational coalition could also encompass liberal and both moderate and more left-leaning social democratic forces in Germany. And he still hoped that it would allow him to bring off a progressive settlement that would contain the appeal of more radical – Bolshevik – alternatives.

Among those who sought to aid Wilson, House was the only one who assumed a distinctly sceptical attitude. By contrast, Ray Stannard Baker and William Bullitt, sent to Europe to intensify contacts with liberal and labour leaders, nourished even greater hopes than the president that the days of European diplomatic machinations and Europe's *"ancien régime"* of aristocratic privileges and reactionary politics had come to an end, not just on the part of the defeated Central Powers. And they anticipated that the Wilsonian mission could give decisive impulses, not just to a novel "internationalist" peace but also to far-reaching political and social reforms across Europe – reforms that would also stem the Bolshevik tide if they were pursued in accordance with the progressive American example. Hoover, who also travelled to Europe in November to oversee major postwar relief efforts, sympathised with this new American mission as well.

In a memorandum on "The Bolshevist Movement in Western Europe", which reached Wilson on 9 November, Bullitt – drawing on reports from Germany but also France, Italy, and Scandinavia – came to the "inescapable conclusion" that "social democracy throughout the continent of Europe is inevitable". In his assessment, the question "still before the world" was only "whether the evolution to social democracy shall be orderly and peaceful under the leadership of the moderate leaders" or "disorderly and bloody under the dominance of the Bolsheviki". In view of these developments, Bullitt recommended that Hoover should immediately be dispatched to Switzerland to organise food relief in Central Europe. And he proposed that House should lean on Lloyd George and Clemenceau to "call into consultation the labor leaders and moderate socialists of their countries" to establish "a basis of cooperation against Bolshevism". He warned that if the governments of the victors formed "a holy alliance against social democracy in Europe" this would drive moderate socialist leaders – which in his view included figures like Albert

---

[63] See Wilson message to Congress, 2 December 1918, *PWW*, LIII, pp. 284–6; Wilson to Tarbell, 29 November 1918, Wilson Papers.

376 REORIENTATIONS AND INCIPIENT LEARNING PROCESSES

Thomas, Renaudel, Henderson and Webb, yet also Scheidemann, Haase and Victor Adler – into the arms of "Bolshevist forces". This would lead to "definite class war" and bring about "the ultimate bloody triumph of Bolshevism".[64] Bullitt thus called on Wilson to take the lead in forming a broad "alliance" with the leaders of moderate socialism that transcended the dividing-lines of the war. While his warning proved overstated with a view to western Europe, where bourgeois order would be recast rather than cast aside, the president's emissary captured a critical challenge that American policy now faced, particularly vis-à-vis Germany.

That Wilson should adhere to the Fourteen Points, lead a progressive coalition and push for a transformative peace settlement and a "new era" of progressive reform on both sides of the war's dividing-lines was certainly what Lippmann and other liberal commentators demanded, particularly in the United States and Britain. On the eve of the peace conference, the leading voices of the *New Republic* called for a new kind of solidarity between progressive forces among the victors. They warned that "the act of imposing a peace" on Germany should not sow dissent "among friends" and make them lose sight of the real priorities: to overcome reactionary and imperialist forces in their own countries, as whose representatives they identified Lodge, Milner and Clemenceau; and to sustain progressive reforms that also bolstered democratic "self-government" in Germany and brought a reformed enemy power into the new order.[65]

By the time he embarked for Europe Wilson still believed that it would be vital *and possible* to rally a potent liberal-progressive coalition behind his mission to forge a novel order. He underscored that the peace terms "must have the support of the progressive elements in the world", including those within Germany, or they would not "last for a generation".[66] And, remarkably, he still clung to the conviction that he would be in a position to implement his design "over the heads" of the *Entente* leaders and those who would represent other important powers at the peace conference.[67] Significantly, however, by the time he arrived in the "old world" Wilson had begun to distance himself from the more aspirational elements of his progressive peace agenda. Rather than renew the

---

[64] Bullitt memorandum, 8 November 1918, enclosed in Lansing to Wilson, 9 November 1918, *PWW*, LIII, pp. 8–9.

[65] See notably the editorials the "Dissensions among the Allies" and "Pivotal Germany", *New Republic*, 21 December 1918, pp. 211–12, 212–14. See also *The Nation*, 14 December 1918, p. 718.

[66] Fosdick diary, 11 December 1918, *PWW*, LIII, p. 366.

[67] One member of the Inquiry, Frank Cobb, had even made the utterly unrealistic proposal that in order to retain his status as unchallenged arbiter of peace Wilson ought to stay in the United States and from there direct the peace process "over the heads" of the assembled plenipotentiaries. Cobb memorandum, 4 November 1918, *PWW*, LI, pp. 590–1.

call for a settlement involving the most forward-looking forces from all sides, including the vanquished, he now concentrated on using the transnational support he commanded as a *background force* to compel the political leaders of Britain and France to fall in line with his peace essentials. Following his first meetings with Clemenceau and Foch in Paris, the American president found his negative perceptions confirmed. He deplored "the general lack of understanding of the world situation" among the Allied governments and emphasised all the more how necessary for the future "well-being and orderly conduct of all governments" the realisation of an American-style "liberal program" was.[68]

Wilson began to fathom that he would have to come to some kind of understanding with Lloyd George and Clemenceau if he wanted to implement the core elements of his programme. But he stubbornly refused to abandon the idea that he was called upon to lead Europe and the world towards a "peace to end all wars" that, in his eyes, the peoples of Europe and the world genuinely desired. And he still believed that he could act as the "spokesman of humanity" who, for the first time in history, would represent *and* direct the pressure of the people – and "world opinion" – to persuade or if necessary force all other governments to follow his lead. As the president told his advisers on 10 December, the up-coming peace congress would be "the first conference in which decisions depended upon the opinion of mankind, not upon previous determinations and diplomatic schemes of the assembled representatives". If the latter failed to head "the opinions of mankind and to express the will of the people" they would "soon be involved in another breakup of the world" which "would not be a war but a cataclysm".[69] And it would be his mission to prevent this apocalyptic scenario.

Undoubtedly, the unprecedented manifestations of mass public support that Wilson encountered after his arrival reinforced his belief that he had the mandate of "the people" across Europe. This seemed to be borne out by the rapturous reception he received on the streets of Paris, which in Poincaré's words "stood alone among the welcome given any previous visitor", as well as in London, Manchester and later in Rome.[70] Particularly the overwhelmingly positive reactions his visit to Britain provoked, from crowds in the streets yet above all from labour leaders and liberals like the editor of the *Manchester Guardian*, C.P. Scott, confirmed Wilson's belief that he would be able to play a decisive role as patron of a progressive postwar order.[71] This belief was

---

[68] House diary, 16 December 1918, *PWW*, LIII, p. 402.
[69] Bowman memorandum, 10 December 1918, *PWW*, LIII, pp. 353–6, Bowman Papers.
[70] Grayson diary, 14 December, *PWW*, LIII, pp. 382–3; Wilson remarks to a delegation of French socialists, *PWW*, LIII, pp. 387 ff.
[71] Wilson conversation with C.P. Scott, 29 December 1918, Walworth (1977), p. 152. See *ibid.*, pp. 150 ff.; editorial, *Manchester Guardian*, 31 December 1918.

bolstered further by the reports he received from Germany and eastern Europe. As will be seen, the surge of both genuine and opportunistic sympathy for Wilson's peace agenda was especially strong in a German political spectrum in the grips of revolutionary disarray. It was most sincere among those who led the new provisional government, i.e. independent socialists, majority social democrats and progressive liberals and Centre politicians like Erzberger. In a wider context, what manifested itself across Europe was the – short-lived – culmination of a development that had gained momentum since 1916: the rise of dangerously inflated, yet also often tactically exaggerated, expectations that were projected onto the American president and that he himself had done much to encourage – expectations that were bound to be disappointed. In some quarters, Wilson was by now indeed regarded as a quasi-messianic figure, a "saviour" or "prophet" who would usher in an era of progressive renewal.

But it would simply prove impossible for Wilson to implement his peace design by relying on the ultimately diffuse power of "world opinion", transnational networks and his own charismatic prestige, which in any case would wane quite rapidly in 1919. All of this could provide some leverage, but its effect was distinctly limited. At the core, the American president would have no choice but to find ways to come to terms, and make compromises, with the elected leaders of the other key powers, notably Lloyd George and Clemenceau. He could not make a modern peace "over their heads". The more Wilson *began* to face up to this, the more his aspiration to pursue a transformative approach to peacemaking receded into the background. House had assumed a different, more realistic attitude all along. He shared Wilson's liberal convictions to some extent, and also thought it politic to keep up the pressure on Lloyd George and Clemenceau. Chiefly, however, he now intensified his efforts to meditate between the president and the *Entente* governments. And his main aim remained to work out basic preliminary agreements so as to prepare the ground for a peace settlement that was workable *and* incorporated Wilson's essentials. House notably tried to build bridges to the British government and to re-assure Lloyd George that Wilson had no intention "of laying down the law" and imposing "his own solutions" at the peace conference. For tactical purposes he emphasised that in his assessment American and British views on the peace and the shape of the postwar order were essentially in harmony. But in view of Wilson's persistent penchant for unilateralism and unchanging opposition to preliminary "inter-allied" accords, the success of House's endeavours was extremely limited.[72]

In retrospect, it has to be stressed that Wilson's notion of paving the way for a novel "American peace" and international order as the leader of an

---

[72] See Wiseman to Foreign Office, 15 December 1918, *PWW*, LIII, p. 395.

unprecedented transnational phalanx of liberal forces and popular support proved not only elusive but essentially counterproductive. Most counterproductive was the notion that he would thus have the power to impose his aspirations and terms on the (more or less) legitimate representatives of other states or peoples. The array of liberal and socialist forces that supported Wilson's general programme across the Great War's divides could never be transformed into a coherent coalition with a definite impact on the way peace would be made. In fact, beyond rhetorical appeals, Wilson never pursued any concrete initiatives to this end.

Nor had the American president's appeals decisively altered the internal balance of political forces in those countries whose leaders would have a decisive influence at this juncture. Leading Labour and liberal voices in Britain remained forceful proponents of Wilsonian positions; but, as will be seen, Lloyd George would win a strong new electoral mandate in December 1918, which brought a shift to the right and by and large led him to pursue a more assertive British peace agenda. In France, the liberal internationalists who called for a *Société des Nations* and Wilson's only other steadfast supporters, the Socialist Party, were still a distinct minority, while Clemenceau enjoyed strong prestige and had a clear mandate to pursue an even more hard-fisted course as "father of the victory". Unsurprisingly, the influence of forces who adopted Wilsonian premises – or had a tactical interest in doing so – was most pronounced on the part of a defeated power seeking the most lenient peace that could be obtained under the circumstances. Yet it was highly uncertain whether these forces would actually have any voice in the peace negotiations – not least because Wilson himself had decided to exclude them from the negotiating process, at least initially.

VII. The Challenges of a Complex Peace Process – and Dangerous Expectations

The longer he was on European soil, the more unequivocally Wilson thus had to confront the "reality" that in spite of America's new prestige and clout he was *not* in a position to decree the terms of peace or the architecture of the postwar order. Crucially, he did not have the power to force his terms on Britain and France. As he and House had to realise, those who represented the interests of Europe's remaining world and imperial powers retained serious reservations about the American peace programme; and they were by no means so dependent on US political and financial support or under such pressure from their populations that they simply had to accept the Wilsonian agenda. Moreover, Wilson had to acknowledge that he would not be able to act as an "impartial" arbiter that stood above the other victors, adjudicated a "just peace" and saw to the fulfilment of the "rightful" claims of the vanquished. And he had to recognise that he was not in a position to fulfil the conflicting expectations of those who represented the different east

European national causes – or the high hopes he had raised among those who clamoured for self-determination outside Europe.

While only beginning to own up to all of this the American president would in fact have to learn to play a different role: the role of not *the* but of *a* leading actor who had to find ways to forge and legitimise precisely the kind of difficult compromises and strategic bargains that he had rhetorically shunned – above all with Lloyd George and Clemenceau. This was a task for which neither his own formation nor any traditions of US international conduct had prepared him. Wilson would only *begin* to grapple with it during the actual peace negotiations of 1919; yet he would never quite comprehend, let alone master it. In contrast to House, the president had hardly developed a deeper understanding of the vital aims, interests, and domestic constraints of his key negotiating partners by the time he first met Clemenceau and Lloyd George in December. In particular, he still failed to grasp the extent and political implications of underlying French security concerns. Wilson still interpreted the policies and agendas of the *Entente* governments through the lens of his own ideological preferences, believing that he knew better what lay in the real interest of the different European peoples than their elected leaders. This assumption also informed his attitudes towards the representatives of all other states and causes in 1919.

In the final analysis, however important it was for Europe's reconstruction it was not financial or economic strength (alone) that accounted for the novel systemic power Wilson and US peacemakers could potentially exercise after the Great War. What mattered most was, rather, the degree to which they could fulfil, not only in the financial but also and crucially in the political and strategic sphere, the far-reaching leadership responsibilities that its new stature conferred on the United States – as a pivotal hegemon and guarantor of a reconfigured international system. The new American world power could indeed play a decisive part in fostering Europe's reconstruction, consolidating a new security system and making the League into an effective agency for conflict-resolution and the promotion of peaceful change. But all of this hinged on the American president's capacity not only to *make* but also to *legitimise at home* consistent long-term commitments to this end, which then of course also would have to be honoured by those who followed him at the reins of US foreign policy.

To a significant extent, then, what influence Wilson could exert on the peacemaking process derived not so much from the inherent quality of his peace designs, or America's financial and economic clout, but rather depended on his ability to master these unprecedented challenges. At the same time, it derived from the shared interest of British and French decision-makers to commit the American president to a longer-term strategic burden-sharing in postwar Europe – and their desire to gain US concessions on war debts and other vital financial and economic issues. And the American president could of course also count on the fact that, for different reasons, those who sought to

negotiate on behalf of the fledgling German republic and those who represented the older and newer national causes in eastern Europe also desired his
support and longer-term US engagement.

Wilson was not unaware of the exceedingly high and politically explosive
expectations that his aspirational rhetoric had raised and Creel's "publicity"
campaigns had amplified around the world – expectations that no American
president nor even the most the most transformative peace process imaginable
could have fulfilled in the aftermath of the Great War. During his voyage he
had wondered whether he had not "unconsciously spun a net" of exaggerated
expectations "from which there is no escape". And he reflected on the millennial hopes he had stirred, musing that the "whole world" was now turning to
America "not only with its wrongs, but with its hopes and grievances". He had
recognised that the "expectations" directed at him had "the quality of terrible
urgency", noting that people would "endure their tyrants for years, but they
tear their deliverers to pieces if a millennium is not created immediately". Yet
he had also rightly emphasised that "these ancient wrongs, these present
unhappinesses" could not "be remedied in a day". Nor, however, could they
be remedied by a presidential prophet who laid down a visionary American
peace design. But this was the expectation that Wilson had created.

In many ways, the American president had thus decisively contributed to
setting the stage for precisely the "tragedy of disappointment" he dreaded.[73]
Indeed, once he arrived in Europe he did nothing to pre-empt such a "tragedy", however difficult this would have been at such a late stage. On the
contrary, by emphatically reasserting his world-historical mission wherever
he went, and by seeking to mobilise "world opinion" in support of his design,
he further heightened expectations rather than scale them back to more
realistic proportions. At the same time, he did not even begin to prepare the
American public or the wider world for what would be a far more likely
peacemaking scenario, namely an unprecedentedly complex negotiating process that would make the realisation of an "American peace" an elusive
prospect.

VIII. Wilson and the Newly Decisive Nexus of International and Domestic Legitimacy

The period following the armistice thus threw into relief what would become a
vital and indeed unprecedented challenge for Wilson and his peacemakers –
the challenge of having to engage, for the first time in US history, in multifaceted and essentially inter-governmental negotiations with other powerful
actors. At the same time, this was only one dimension of the wider legitimacy

---

[73] Creel (1947), p. 206.

problem the American president had confronted ever since he had first championed a "peace without victory" and that now presented itself with new urgency. In short, he now had to tackle concretely the twofold problem of gaining *international* backing for his aspirations and of preparing the ground for eventually ensuring vital *domestic* support, above all in the Senate. On the home front, Wilson not only had to redouble his efforts to persuade the American public and its representatives in Congress that the time had come to assume a radically different role in the world and far-reaching responsibilities in the new international organisation he intended to establish. He also had to prepare his domestic audience for a scenario that he himself only began to fathom, namely an extremely difficult peacemaking process that would require numerous compromises and make it impossible to forge a League or an overall settlement on *his* American premises. And, no less crucially, he had to build a broad and as far as possible bipartisan base of domestic-political support. But the president neglected these tasks, insisting instead that he could not compromise his peace mission and pursuing it, also vis-à-vis the US Senate, in a very high-handed fashion.

But it was precisely at this time, just before his departure for Europe, that the domestic constellation changed in ways that made Wilson's task of legitimising his vision distinctly harder. He could no longer count on a significant segment of his base of progressive supporters, notably the leading figures of the Woman's Peace Party, the Union Against Militarism and the Socialist Party, who had turned away from him since he had led the United States into the war and opted for what they castigated as repressive wartime policies. Yet they had represented a minority all along. More important was that not only Wilson's domestic position but also his international authority had been weakened by the Democratic defeat in the Congressional elections of 5 November 1918 – though it did not inevitably foreshadow the president's eventual defeat in his fight with the Senate. Launching an appeal to the American voters, Wilson had made the election a referendum on his peace policy. He had asked the American people to support the Democratic Party so that the United States' "inward unity of purpose may be evident to all the world" and he could continue to be the American people's "unembarrassed spokesman in affairs at home and abroad". And he had stated very frankly that a Republican victory would be interpreted in Europe as nothing less than a "repudiation" of his efforts on behalf of a new international order.[74]

Yet the outcome of the elections "disturbed" Wilson and led him to rely all to the more on his "implicit faith in Divine Providence". The fact that the Democratic Party lost control of both the Senate and the House of

---

[74] Wilson, "Appeal for a Democratic Congress", 25 October 1918, *PWW*, LI, pp. 381–2. See also *New Republic*, 26 October 1918, pp. 360–1.

Representatives could be seen, and was indeed interpreted, as a "repudiation" of his global leadership aspirations and peace policies. And, as the president noted, it would "create obstacles" to the settlement of the key questions, notably the creation of the League and the treatment of Germany.[75] The election setback did not make the domestic legitimisation of Wilson's aims impossible; but it weakened his authority at home and abroad and considerably constrained his domestic and international room to manoeuvre. In the domestic context, it obviously made some kind of bipartisan approach all the more imperative.

Essentially, this raised the question of how far Wilson – who had hitherto taken no substantive steps in this direction – would be willing to negotiate some kind of compromise arrangement with the Republican leadership in the Senate. Yet it also raised the question of whether the key Republican senators and especially the president's main political adversary, Lodge, would at all be interested in seeking common ground. Unsurprisingly, however, Wilson persisted with his imperious approach. He did not make any meaningful effort to develop a bipartisan peace agenda. And after he had decided that he would actually attend the peace conference, he pointedly refrained from including prominent Republicans in the American delegation. Earlier, Wilson had considered taking along two seasoned Republican "internationalists", Root and Taft.[76] But then he had only appointed the respected diplomat but political outsider Henry White. Lodge did not regard White's appointment as more than a symbolical gesture. It was not a step towards bridging the political divides in Washington, which were deep and would in fact become even deeper in the months ahead.

Wilson's domestic difficulties had serious international implications. European governments, particularly those in London and Paris, began to question not only whether the American president still had sufficient backing for his peace programme in Washington but also how far he would be in a position to make binding commitments, notably in the critical sphere of security and with a view to the League. There was a growing concern that whatever Wilson underwrote would later be contested, or even repudiated, by the oppositional majority in the Senate.[77] Following the Republican victory, Lodge became the chairman of the Senate's Committee on Foreign Relations and thus acquired a new power base. As had been become clear during the election campaign, he not only opposed Wilson because of domestic-political calculations. He had also developed a markedly different conception of the United States' role in the postwar world and what would constitute a desirable

---

[75] Wilson to Logan, 8 November 1918, Wilson Papers.

[76] House diary, 27 January 1918, *PWW*, XLVI, pp. 115–16.

[77] See e.g. Crowe memorandum, 7 December 1918, FO 371/3451, and Wiseman's reports on the American political situation in November and December 1918, Wiseman Papers.

peace and a "good" League. Lodge adamantly opposed any notion of a "negotiated peace" with the vanquished. With Theodore Roosevelt's approval he demanded in the Senate that the armistice had to be followed by a "dictated peace", declaring once again that no settlement that "satisfies Germany in any degree" could satisfy the Republican Party, because it would only lead to renewed German threats to world peace. And he clearly spoke for a majority among Republican senators who had likewise criticised Wilson's willingness to make a "compromise peace" with the enemy and who subsequently claimed that the Republican election victory manifested strong popular support for their uncompromising stance.[78]

What Lodge – and Roosevelt – thus focused on was keeping up the political pressure to force the president to make a peace that was both appropriately harsh and duly imposed on the vanquished foe. Lodge's outlook was dominated by geopolitical and power-political considerations. The main requirement of peace, and overriding American interest, the senator from Massachusetts identified was to put "Germany in a position where she cannot break out upon the world again".[79] He desired to ensure that Europe's geopolitical map and balance of power would be decisively recast in order to contain future German ambitions. The terms he wanted to see imposed on the Central Powers were, apart from the restoration of Belgian sovereignty and the return of Alsace-Lorraine to France, the creation of an "independent Poland" and the establishment of "independent States" for the "Jugo-Slavs" and the Czecho-Slovaks" that ended the domination of Austrians and Germans "whom they loathe".[80] The *New Republic* had earlier criticised Lodge for desiring a "victory of power" rather than a "victory of justice" and proposing a peace of "discrimination against Germany" that would sow the seeds of another war. It warned that the Republican senator spoke for those who sought to move towards "a new world of territorial arrangements and *Realpolitik*, where new states are legislated into existence for the convenience of great powers, and where a dangerous state is merely crushed to her knees". It insisted that America's aim had to be "to remake, not to rehash Europe" and in this new Europe there should be "a place for the German people evolved by the horrors of war beyond their slavery and barbarism". Wilson was urged to be steadfast in pursuing this mission against Republican opposition.[81]

Lodge's general views did not change after the armistice. He continued to advocate a peace settlement that ensured that Germany was not only disarmed

[78] Lodge speeches, Senate, October 1918, *Literary Digest/Current Opinion*, LXV, no. 4 (October 1918), p. 208; Congressional Record, 65th Congress, 2nd session, 11, 155–67.

[79] Lodge to Roosevelt, 19 October and 26 November 1918, in Roosevelt/Lodge (1925), II, pp. 542, 547. See also Lodge to Trevelyan, 20 January 1919, Lodge Papers.

[80] Lodge speech, Senate, October 1918, *Literary Digest/Current Opinion*, LXV, no. 4 (October 1918), p. 208.

[81] See *New Republic*, 19 October 1918, pp. 327–9; *New Republic*, 5 October 1918, pp. 271–3.

and subjected to draconian peace terms but also kept in check thereafter. To ensure this, he actually favoured a continued American engagement in Europe rather than a withdrawal into hemispheric isolation. But it was not to be an engagement on Wilson's terms. In private and in public, Lodge made clear that he considered the "League for Peace" that Wilson and his supporters proposed a "very dangerous thing". Essentially, he opposed an authoritative international organisation that would curtail US sovereignty and threaten to override fundamental Congressional powers. In his judgement, the United States should not consent "to join any international body which would arrange our immigration laws or our tariff laws, or control the Monroe Doctrine or our actions in our own hemisphere, or have power to order our army or navy". Because of these reservations, Lodge also emphasised that the League "ought not to be attached to the treaty of peace". He argued that the real priority should be to "get a decent treaty" which contained the German threat for good.[82]

Behind closed doors, Lodge actually favoured not only a peace of the victors but also a quasi-alliance that preserved the unity between America, Britain and France. He envisaged "a good league", by which he meant an extension of the wartime "league" of "the Allies and the United States" that already existed, fortified to maintain a "world order" that served cardinal US interests. While publicly speaking out against the unlimited universal obligations that, in his interpretation, Wilson's ill-defined vision of the League would entail, Lodge in private asserted that the United States should agree to specific guarantees in postwar Europe – guarantees that protected France and the new East European states against renewed German aggression.[83]

Closing ranks with Lodge, Theodore Roosevelt remained – until his death on 6 January 1919 – one of the most relentless critics of what he denounced as Wilson's impractical schemes for a democratic League and illusory ideals of an equitable peace with the vanquished. After the armistice he elaborated counter-proposals that built on the ideas he developed as president and then elaborated during the war. Roosevelt argued with renewed vigour that American peace policy should focus on creating a different kind of League, an institution of the western great powers that was to enforce a peace of the victors and police the postwar order while safeguarding their "vital interests". And he demanded that in order to fulfil its obligations as a policing power the United States should maintain a posture of military preparedness and expand its naval strength further.[84] Shortly before his death he impressed on Lloyd

---

[82] Lodge to Roosevelt, 26 November 1918, in Redmond (1925), II, p. 547.

[83] Lodge to Bryce, 14 October 1918, Lord Bryce Papers; Lodge to Roosevelt, 26 November 1918, in Redmond (1925), II, p. 547.

[84] Roosevelt to Beveridge, 15 October 1918; Roosevelt to Wood, 2 November 1918, Theodore Roosevelt Papers; Roosevelt editorials, 17 November and 2 December 1918, in Roosevelt (1921), pp. 263, 279.

George that he categorically rejected Wilson's approach to peacemaking and felt that the United States should act, not as an umpire "between our allies and our enemies" but as power whose "prime duty" was to stand by Britain and France, agree with them on the peace terms and then force these terms on Germany.[85]

On the conservative side of the American political spectrum, Taft and the "conservative internationalists" of the League to Enforce Peace remained the most audible and unequivocal proponents of a new and authoritative international organisation. Drawing on the schemes they had prepared since 1915, they also advanced the most elaborate proposals for a League that, as they saw it, would actually have the power to enforce what peace was made after the Great War. With this cardinal aim they stepped up their efforts to influence the American and international debate – and to push Wilson to adopt essentials of their agenda. In important respects these still differed markedly from what Wilson envisaged. But the LEP's "internationalists" had long emphasised one crucial premise that, as noted, the president now also came to adopt, namely that the League was to be founded as an institution of the victors. In its "Victory Program" of November 1918, the LEP's executive committee consequently called for a peace agreement made by the victors whose key purpose had to be the establishment of a "League of Free Nations with judicial, administrative, and executive powers and functions", including – above all – clearly defined, and extensive, enforcement and sanction powers. And it recommended that its "initiating nucleus" was to be formed exclusively by "the nations associated as belligerents in winning the war". Reasserting its hierarchical conception, the LEP also demanded that the League should be given "an administrative organization" to manage "affairs of common interest" and ensure "the protection and care of backward regions and internationalized places". But its centrepiece was to be a robust "collective security" regime. The "resort to force by any nation" was to be "prevented by a solemn agreement that any aggression will be met immediately by such an overwhelming economic and military force that it will not be attempted".[86]

Taft remained the most authoritative champion of the programme proposed by the League to Enforce Peace. He had consistently maintained that only a clear defeat of the "German military caste" would really discredit the old autocratic order and lead the German people to question "the false philosophy of the state and German destiny, with which they have been indoctrinated" and to change their government. In his view, the "allied" victory of November

---

[85] Roosevelt to Lloyd George, 10 December 1918, Lloyd George Papers, F/24/3/81.
[86] LEP "Victory Program", 23 November 1918, Gerrity (2003), pp. 5–6; New York Times, 25 November 1918; Taft speech, 6 December 1918, Gerrity (2003), pp. 143–6.

1918 was thus an essential prerequisite for eventual democratic reforms that would deprive "the Prussian military caste" of the "power to control the military and foreign policy of Germany" and lead it into a "union of the democratic states of the world". But Taft argued that this could not be relied upon – initially, and for the foreseeable future, a League of the victors had to ensure "permanent" peace and also guard against renewed German aggression.[87] Yet Wilson, more determined than ever to implement his own League conception, would keep a conspicuous distance from Taft and the LEP. He refrained from endorsing or even acknowledging their recommendations. In early December, he impressed on his advisers that a "hard and fast constitution of the 'League to Enforce Peace' variety" neither could nor should be established at this point. In the president's judgement, proposals to "militarise" the new organisation by granting it far-reaching enforcement and sanction powers would not prevent future wars but rather provoke new conflicts by emphasising the use of force; moreover, they would impose undesirable military obligations on the American government.[88]

Particularly the governments of the *Entente* Powers, yet also German diplomats and other European observers, were well aware of these inner-American controversies. As will be seen, the alternative conceptions Lodge and Roosevelt advocated corresponded quite closely with French postwar priorities. Yet like Lloyd George, Clemenceau recognised that, for better or worse, he would have to negotiate with Wilson and take his programme as the main frame of reference. The fact that the American president came to Europe against the backdrop of strong domestic opposition to his peace agenda unquestionably weakened his negotiating position at the peace conference. Yet it would be misleading to conclude that this had a critical impact on what he could or could not achieve at Versailles. What mattered more were the dynamics and constraints of the ensuing *international* negotiating process. But the difficulties Wilson faced on the home front, and particularly the Republican campaign for an imposed and demonstratively harsh settlement, which reflected prevalent public sentiments, had one important effect before this process had even begun. It put additional pressure on Wilson to turn away from any serious attempt to pursue a negotiated peace with Germany and draw the vanquished into the new "comity of nations" he envisaged. For this threatened to expose him to Republican criticism that he was unduly lenient with the defeated power and thus jeopardised his main objective: to found "his" League.

---

[87] See Taft address, 26 September 1917; Taft remarks, 9 November 1918, Gerrity (2003), VII, pp. 80, 85–7, 128–9.

[88] Bullitt diary, 9 [10] December 1918, *PWW*, LIII, pp. 350–2. See also Bowman memorandum, 10 December 1918, *ibid.*, p. 354.

IX.   What New Order for Europe? Towards a Europe of Self-Governing Nation-States

In Wilson's conception, the League of Nations was to play a pivotal role not only in guaranteeing international security but also in pacifying Europe after the Great War. Yet how did he and his advisers actually envisage founding a new order for Europe and coming to grips with the acute and the structural problems that had arisen through the war, particularly the overriding necessity to reorder Central and Eastern Europe after the demise of the eastern empires? Essentially, Wilson and his "peacemakers" would propose general principles for such an order – notably "self-government" and "self-determination" – and the League as the "super-mechanism" to maintain it. But they did not elaborate any more specific conceptions for it in the wider context of Wilson's universal aspirations – conceptions that addressed Europe's most salient postwar challenges. And they were even further from developing specific strategies for Europe's stabilisation in the longer term. Crucially, they only began to realise at the peace conference itself that a more comprehensive approach was required to address the pivotal systemic *and* geopolitical problem: the German question. And by the time they came to Paris they were still grappling with the question of how to cope with the Bolshevik regime and the transnational appeal of Bolshevism.

At the end of 1918, the American president reasserted that he categorically rejected the notion of making a peace settlement, and envisaging a reorganisation of Europe, in which balance-of-power considerations overruled self-determination concerns.[89] He underscored his determination to resist a settlement that, on such premises, centred on the curtailment of Germany's territory and power and the creation of "buffer states" on its western and eastern borders. But neither Wilson nor his key advisers had worked out a convincing alternative strategy. The American "peacemakers" came to Versailles without a clear idea of how to deal with the problem of German power and, more importantly, of how to find a place for the defeated power in the new order on terms that could be reconciled with the security of its old and new neighbours – and that would be conducive to a new international equilibrium in Europe and the transatlantic sphere.

Wilson clung to the maxim that in order to be durable and peace-enforcing the postwar order had to become a system of self-governing states. In his view, this was to have a determining influence on the future configuration of Europe. He continued to demand that the League had to be formed by states whose governments were legitimised by the consent of the governed. And he continued to emphasise that one of the organisation's cardinal purposes would be to promote the spread of democracy – across the world but above all in

---

[89] Wilson address, Free Trade Hall, 30 December 1918, *PWW*, LIII, p. 550.

Europe.[90] But when he was more immediately exposed to the tumultuous developments in Germany and eastern Europe around the turn of 1918–19, the American president in fact developed a distinctly more sceptical outlook on the prospects of democratisation and its pacifying effect, notably in Germany, the new Polish state and eastern Europe more generally. Most consequentially, this shaped his increasingly wary attitude towards the German revolution and his decision to put postwar Germany on "probation".

What came to the fore here were Wilson's long-standing assumptions about which peoples were capable of "responsible" self-government and worthy of being "equal" partners in his "new world order". Fundamentally, however, and particularly in his rhetoric, he did not depart from his championing of democracy – nor from presenting the United States as the vanguard power of a new democratic internationalism.[91] The president's progressive supporters on both sides of the Atlantic urged him to maintain precisely this kind of internationalist approach, particularly vis-à-vis Germany, and not to compromise it.[92] And for different reasons, chiefly to avoid far-reaching commitments in the League, even a hitherto pessimistic Lansing now adopted the view that the promotion of democracy in Europe should be the core American priority at the peace conference. The secretary of state impressed on the president that successful democratisation processes – also in Germany – would establish better safeguards against future aggression than the most elaborate regime of international sanctions.[93]

But, as noted, since February 1918 Wilson had also publicly committed himself – most clearly in his "Four Principles" address – to another "imperative principle" of postwar order, the principle of "self-determination".[94] After the end of the war, the American president reaffirmed that all questions pertaining to Europe's future territorial order and political organisation had to be decided, not by the dictate of power-political interests but in accordance with the "principle of self-determination". Yet although he underscored that statesmen would "henceforth" ignore it "at their peril", he had never clearly defined since then what he precisely meant by "self-determination" and how exactly it was connected with his crusade on behalf of "self-government".[95] Indeed, it would be misleading to conclude that Wilson came to Europe determined to recast the territorial and political order of Europe – and the

[90] Grayson diary, 8 December 1918, *PWW*, LIII, pp. 338–9; Wilson speech, 28 December, *ibid.*, pp. 535–6.

[91] Wilson message to Congress, 2 December 1918, *PWW*, LIII, pp. 284–6; Wilson speech, 28 December, *ibid.*, p. 535.

[92] See e.g. *New Republic*, 21 December 1918, pp. 211–14.

[93] Lansing to Wilson, 23 December 1918, Wilson Papers.

[94] See Wilson address, 11 February 1918, *PWW*, XLVI, pp. 320–3.

[95] Grayson diary, 8 December 1918, *PWW*, LIII, pp. 338–9.

wider world – by implementing a *strict* interpretation of self-determination. He did not stipulate that every people that could be recognised as such should in future have the right to determine its own affairs by fulfilling the desire to acquire a state of its own. Fundamentally, though he did not spell this out, Wilson's approach to self-determination was still informed by his conception of self-*government*. And central to this conception was and remained the maxim that every "people" should have the right to choose, and consent to, its own government *but not necessarily the right to choose its own nation-state.* The real emphasis of his aspirations thus continued to lie on paving the way for an expansion of democratic self-government across Europe – in existing states as well as in those that were to be formed after the war. Eventually, a democratic "new order" was to be consolidated.[96] But Wilson maintained a very hierarchical outlook on how this process was to unfold, based on the notion that not just in Asia or the Middle East but also in Europe some peoples, and "civilisations", were more capable of advancing towards genuine self-government than others. Thus, what he envisaged for the foreseeable future would be a distinctly stratified international system.

Due to these underlying preferences, the American president remained noticeably circumspect in his public advocacy of "self-determination" after the armistice. He still underestimated the complexity of the situation in eastern Europe and the degree to which different national movements, or elites, seized on his pronouncements to further their usually conflicting aims. But he was by no means oblivious to the massive and clashing expectations he had raised and to the problems that any attempt to satisfy what he had called "well defined national aspirations" would entail. As he had emphasised in February 1918, the – daunting – challenge was to satisfy different legitimate claims without "introducing new or perpetuating old elements of discord and antagonism" that would over time "break the peace of Europe and consequently of the world".[97] This was particularly difficult, of course, when there were different "national" claims for the same territory, as would often be the case.

Nonetheless, Wilson was far from sharing the sense of foreboding that his secretary of state expressed in the run-up to the peace conference. On 30 December 1918, Lansing warned that invoking the "right of "self-determin-ation" and "putting such ideas into the minds of certain races" was bound to lead to "impossible demands on the Peace Congress, and create trouble in many lands". Noting that the "phrase" was simply "loaded with dynamite", he argued, presciently, that it would "raise hopes which can never be realized" and was, in the end, "bound to be discredited, to be called the dream of an idealist who failed to realize the danger until too late to check those who

---

[96] See Wilson address, 22 January 1917, *PWW*, XL, pp. 536–7; Wilson address, 11 February 1918, *PWW*, XLVI, pp. 320–3.
[97] Creel (1947), p. 206; Wilson address, 11 February 1918, *PWW*, XLVI, p. 323.

attempt to put the principle into force".[98] But neither Wilson nor any other leading statesman still had the power at this stage to put the genie back in the bottle or to close this particular compartment of the Pandora's Box the Great War had opened. Essentially, not least because of the American president's proclamations it would henceforth be inconceivable to create a stable international order in and beyond Europe without finding convincing ways to deal with "self-determination" claims.

Wilson thus now had to prepare for a role and responsibilities he had long desired to avoid. He would not only have to "interfere in European affairs" but also be called upon to act as an "arbiter in European territorial disputes" – as well as in disputes between antagonistic nationalist agendas (while also having to find common ground with the British and French protagonists on these issues).[99] He would have to deal with the leaders of a plethora of national movements in Central and Eastern Europe, yet also of course in the extra-European world, who clamoured for their "right" to self-determination and looked to him as a key supporter of their claims for *states*. Both Wilson and his advisers realised ever more acutely that satisfying all of these aspirations, and doing so in an equitable manner, would be impossible in the tumultuous aftermath of a war whose violent aftershocks continued to ripple through eastern Europe. Yet they had barely begun to think about how to set priorities and balance concerns of self-determination with overriding considerations of geopolitical stabilisation.

At the same time, the American president and the experts who sought to create a more sustainable ethnic-territorial order in Europe now had to grapple with even more vexatious problems "on the ground" that often defied a straightforward application of the principles they proposed. The members of the Inquiry who came to focus on these challenges – men like the historian Archibald Coolidge, who came to head the Inquiry's East European Division – were actually quite cognisant of the fundamental challenges; and even Wilson himself began to fathom them, though he maintained a penchant for abstract general "solutions". To a greater extent than many later critics have acknowledged, they realised that one core problem was that against the background of its complicated history Eastern Europe's ethnic-political map was immensely complex and marked by an intricate intermixture of ethnicities and "nationalities". And they realised that, more often than not, the different nation-state claims collided because they concerned the same territory, and that it would be extremely difficult to draw mutually acceptable borders – and impossible to establish states that did not contain one or several ethnic minorities. In turn, this led them to address more rigorously than before the newly critical

[98] Lansing memorandum, 30 December 1918, in Lansing (1921), pp. 97–8. On the wider problem see Fisch (2010), pp. 153–4 and ff.
[99] Wilson address, 11 February 1918, *PWW*, XLVI, pp. 320–3.

question of how the security and rights of such minorities could henceforth be protected more effectively than they had been – according to their assessment – in the defunct empires. In Coolidge's judgement, Europe's future peace and security could only be ensured if the principle of self-determination was applied as rigidly as possible. It could also be relied upon to "create" the smallest possible number of new national minorities.[100] Nonetheless this critical problem would have to be tackled on an unprecedented scale.

But the American "peacemakers" had to confront yet another complication. They had to acknowledge that the newly prominent principle of "self-determination" could be invoked not only by the leaders of the most influential nationalist movements in Central and Eastern Europe, the Polish and the Czecho-Slovak movements, but also by the vanquished powers, notably Germany, to stake or defend claims to particular territories. What they only began to realise, however, was that one of the most critical problems they faced – and which would then have long-term repercussions for Europe's postwar stabilisation – would arise where the aspirations of Polish, Czech and Slovak nationalists on the one hand and German claims and interests on the other came into conflict. They would propose different answers but never elaborated a balanced strategy to address this problem. Particularly the American president tended to point to the League as the mechanism through which conflicts that he deemed unavoidable in this context could be resolved over time. What he contemplated threatened to burden the fledgling international organisation with immense responsibilities.[101]

X. The Creation of a New Polish State and the Future of Eastern Europe

In approaching the reorganisation of Eastern Europe both Wilson and leading American experts devoted most attention to one particular issue which the latter had long regarded as the "most complex" of all the postwar challenges in Europe: the future shape and ethnic composition of Poland – and, particularly, the settlement of its borders with Germany.[102] Following the armistice, Wilson remained fundamentally committed to the premises of his Fourteen Points. Official US policy called for the creation of a *new* independent Polish state. It thus still opposed historic claims for the resurrection of a Poland in or beyond the pre-partition borders of 1772 that were advanced by Dmowski, the head of the Polish National Committee, who had made considerable lobbying efforts on behalf of his programme for a "Greater Poland" in the United States in the summer of 1918. In mid-November, Wilson impressed on

---

[100] Miller (1924–26), I, p. 267; VII, pp. 366–8. See Fink (1998), p. 262.
[101] Bowman memorandum, 10 December 1918, *PWW*, LIII, p. 354.
[102] Inquiry memorandum, 4 January 1918, *PWW*, XLV, pp. 470–1.

Dmowski that he would not change his position.[103] He in fact considered the Polish National Committee's aims excessive and continued to oppose some of its core demands, notably that for the strategically vital port city of Danzig. In general terms, the American president still desired to create a new Poland whose borders were decided according to ethnic criteria and that was to be "inhabited by indisputably Polish populations". But by the autumn of 1918, his awareness of the virulence of the problems posed by the unavoidability of sizeable German, Jewish and other minorities in any conceivable Polish state had grown.

Earlier Polish lobbying activities in the United States – which soon concentrated on the aim of an independent state – had intensified since the well-known artist Ignacy Paderewski had come across the Atlantic as honorary chairman of the Polish National Department. In late 1916, Paderewski had presented House with a memorandum addressed to Wilson which called for the re-establishment of a Polish state defined in political and historical, not ethnic terms – in the form of a multi-national federation that was to comprise the previous kingdoms of Poland, Lithuania, Polesia and Galicia, which roughly corresponded to the borders of pre-partition Poland. The new state would pledge to guarantee complete equality for all nationalities, and Jews, who were to be classified as "Poles". Paderewski came to espouse a conception of a future Poland that the socialist leader and future leader of postwar Poland, Józef Piłsudski, championed. Dmowski had come to the United States in the summer of 1918 to advance a different concept and a distinctly more expansive territorial programme. He particularly sought to gain Wilson's support for Polish claims to territories that had been part of the German Empire. His proposals included the demand to make East Prussia part of a federation under Polish control, which was to eliminate the problem of a Polish "corridor". Dmowski argued that many Poles in the United States came from these areas and would be disappointed if they were not given to Poland.

Wilson never supported Dmowski's vision. As noted, he and Lansing had been reluctant to follow France in recognising the Polish National Committee as the sole representation of the Polish people, doubting its legitimacy to speak on behalf of a majority of Poles. They had more sympathies for Paderewski and Piłsudski, who in their view represented more liberal forces and a more liberal conception of a future Poland. Wilson had met both Dmowski and Paderewski in mid-September 1918. And he had impressed on the former that the new Polish state should only include territories inhabited by Polish populations.[104]

Yet by the time he was on his way to Europe, Wilson still had not committed himself to any clear blueprint for Poland's borders and above all

---

[103] See Dmowski to Zamoyski, 15 November 1918, *Sprawy Polskie*, I, p. 266; Wandycz (1980), pp. 112–13.

[104] See Wandycz (1998), p. 314; Wandycz (1980), pp. 122–5.

to a definition of what would constitute a free and secure Polish access to the Baltic sea. He still favoured a Polish state that as far as possible conformed to the "self-determination" principle and that postwar Germany could learn to accept. Wilson argued that while the province of Poznan should go to Poland – because it was predominantly Polish – "east Prussia should not be detached from the rest of Germany" because this would cause undesirable political instability. At the same time, the American president still contemplated an arrangement that would ensure Polish access to the sea, not through a territorial "corridor" but by making Danzig a "free port" and providing international guarantees for Poland's use of the railroads and waterways – chiefly the Vistula – that led to the Baltic.[105]

All of these issues also remained the subject of controversial debate among the American experts whose recommendations would have some impact at Versailles – although here, too, Wilson would ultimately pursue his own course. Significantly, the expert who would be most influential, the Harvard professor Robert Lord who headed the Inquiry's Polish section, had come to an assessment that differed from that of the president. And he proposed a different approach, which also came to be supported by the authoritative geographer Isaiah Bowman. Essentially, their emphasis clearly lay on ensuring the creation of a viable Polish state that could maintain its independence between Germany and Bolshevik Russia. They argued that in order to achieve this, strategic and economic considerations had to take precedence over ethnic considerations and the application of the self-determination principle. And they advanced the rationale that the "vital interests" of the new Polish state they envisaged, which by and large corresponded with Dmowski's "Greater Poland", had to outweigh those of roughly two million Germans who would form a minority within it – and who were to be accorded some form of minority protection. What the two experts did not address in any substantive way, however, were the consequences this would have for Poland's future relations with its western neighbour and how to cope with the unsettling force of German irredentism.

As noted, the Inquiry had begun to grapple with the Polish question at the end of 1917. The Cobb-Lippmann memorandum on the Fourteen Points of October 1918, which House recommended to Wilson as a set of guidelines for American peacemaking, had underscored that the "chief problem" was whether the Polish state was to "obtain territory west of the Vistula" as that would "cut off the Germans of East Prussia from the Empire" – or whether Danzig could be "made a free port and the Vistula internationalized"; in the east, it argued, Poland should not receive any territory in which Lithuanians or

---

[105] Bullitt diary, 9 [10] December 1918, PWW, LIII, p. 351. See Schwabe (1985), p. 172.

Ukrainians dominated.[106] Within the Inquiry, the views on how to settle this problem changed. What came to prevail on the eve of the peace conference were Lord's views and underlying assumptions. They would eventually be reflected in the Inquiry's "Black Book" of recommendations for the American Peace Delegation that was put together in mid-January 1919. Lord was the main author of a special report that proposed an expanded Polish state. It was to comprise not only parts of East Prussia and the strategically important industrial region of Upper Silesia but also Poznania and Pomerania, thus incorporating areas that would include significant German minorities. Most importantly, Lord also drew up a scheme under which both Danzig and major parts of West Prussia would be given to Poland. He thus in fact proposed the creation of what came to be known as the Polish "corridor" separating East Prussia from the rest of postwar Germany. He and other Inquiry experts argued that while this constituted a serious problem, and both Polish and German concerns had to be taken into account, on balance it was more important, and just, to give priority to the interests of 20 million Poles in having a secure access to the sea than to satisfy German interests in this matter, which they deemed "aside from Prussian sentiment" as "quite second-ary".[107] Lord and Bowman anticipated that the League would have to deal with future Polish–German conflicts. But they clearly underestimated how unsettling the consequences of the "corridor" arrangement could be.

A related question that received far less attention from Wilson, and in the fledgling American peace programme, was that of what shape the other major east European "state in formation", the new Czechoslovakia, was to have. This was closely bound up with a wider problem that American peace planning never addressed in its entirety, namely that of not only reconfiguring but also stabilising Central Europe after the demise of the Austro-Hungarian Empire. In his Fourteen Points address, Wilson had still spoken of granting the different national minorities of Austria-Hungary, whose "place among the nations" he had wished to see "assured", the "freest opportunity to autonomous development". Thereafter, he had contemplated the advantages of preserving a reformed Habsburg Empire in some form. But in the autumn of 1918 he had abandoned this option. On 3 September, the American government had officially recognised the claim for a new Czecho-Slovak state that the torchbearers of the Czech and Slovak national aspirations, the future foreign minister Edvard Beneš and the "founding father" and future first president Thomas Masaryk, had asserted. Beneš had been instrumental in instigating the revolution that ended Habsburg rule. Wilson conveyed to Masaryk on

---

[106] Cobb-Lippmann memorandum, 29 October 1918, *PWW*, LI, pp. 503–4.

[107] See Berle to Lord, 26 December 1918, Records of American Commission to Negotiate Peace, NA185.1127/18; Lord memorandum "The Polish-German Frontier", undated, *ibid.*, 185.1127/11; Lord and Bowman in House and Seymour (1921), pp. 71 ff.

10 January 1919 that he was gratified "that the Czecho-Slovak people" recognised him as "their friend and the champion of their rights".[108]

Yet by this time Wilson had not given much thought to the problems that the creation of a Czecho-Slovak state raised – as in the Polish case, problems connected with an equitable application of the "self-determination" principle, minority issues and the spectre of future German irredentism.[109] Notably, he only had a vague notion of the fact that in the form that Beneš and Masaryk desired – and that the Clemenceau government supported – the new state would include a German-speaking minority of roughly three million, in what had been the Austrian province of Bohemia, above all the Sudeten German minority in northern Bohemia. The Inquiry had considered these challenges in greater depth. Its expert on the "states in formation", Charles Seymour, had recommended that the American peace delegation should propose a different boundary arrangement, under which the historical German–Bohemian border would be altered and at least a part of the Sudeten Germans end up living under German rule. Archibald Coolidge also warned of the danger of sowing seeds of future German irredentism.[110] But Wilson did not heed the recommendations and warnings of his experts; and prior to the peace negotiations there was no consensus in the American delegation about how to address the most problematic aspects of the Czecho-Slovak question.

More generally, it should be emphasised that what Wilson and the key US experts proposed in order to reform Central and Eastern Europe was *not* based on efforts to develop a specific peace conception for the region. Rather, it derived to a large extent from attempts to apply the "remedies" of the general Wilsonian concepts for a progressive peace. For all their laudable efforts to comprehend and address the complexities of the east European situation, what is truly remarkable in retrospect is the extent to which not only the president but also most of his experts believed that it would be possible to work out a "scientific" peace settlement that recast significant parts of Europe, essentially on the basis of the "self-determination" principle. Equally remarkable is their assumption that it would be possible to craft on this basis "just" settlements that took into account not only the claims of east European national movements but also the concerns of Germany – without envisaging substantial negotiations with German representatives. Ultimately, they were confident that they would have a decisive say in redrawing the map of Europe – and that if this was done the American way it would be possible to keep irredentist pressures, future minority problems and future conflicts over territory to a minimum.

---

[108] Wilson to Masaryk, 10 January 1919, *PWW*, LIII, p. 711.
[109] See Bullitt diary, 9 [10] December 1918, *PWW*, LIII, pp. 350–2.
[110] Seymour (1951), pp. 9 ff. For the background see Perman (1962).

Where such conflicts were unavoidable the League of Nations was to play a crucial role. All of the American protagonists agreed that it was to become the core instrument for the protection and re-assurance for the Central and East European "states in formation", safeguarding Poland and Czechoslovakia against potential German revisionism. Yet it also was intended as the mechanism through which, in the longer term, conflicts over territorial claims and minority rights were to be adjudicated and, wherever and whenever this proved necessary, a process of "orderly" peaceful change could be instigated, including the "readjustment" of frontiers.[111] These were immense, indeed daunting responsibilities. It was not clear whether any international organisation would be able to meet them. Whether the League could do so would depend on the extent to which it would be possible to make it into an effective and legitimate institution. In turn, this depended on the commitments the principal victors – including the United States – would actually make.

A further critical question, also in this context, was when and on what terms Germany would actually be brought into the League system. In effect, neither Wilson nor the other protagonists of the US peace delegation had a precise idea at this point of what role the United States would actually play in all of these developments, and in the longer-term processes of peace-building *and peaceful change* the president foresaw in postwar Europe. It was still very unclear how far, apart from assuming general obligations under the new League Covenant, the American power would actually engage as a guarantor and mediating power in such processes *after* the initial peace conference.

The League also played a central role in American attempts to address one particular problem that was not new but had never before been so pressing and potentially explosive, precisely because of the new emphasis on national "self-determination" and "nation-states" – the aforementioned problem of protecting the security and rights of minorities in the newly-formed multinational states. Not only the experts of the Inquiry but also Wilson himself realised the gravity of this task and saw the need to find new ways of approaching it. Nowhere did they deem this more crucial than in the case of Poland. The Cobb-Lippmann memorandum had urged that if territories like Poznan and Silesia were to be ceded to Poland, it would be imperative to provide "rigid protection" for the German and Jewish minorities who would live in these provinces.[112] But by the time the peace conference opened the president and his advisers had only begun to outline how this was to be achieved. Wilson's original "solution" centred on the League of Nations and the general idea of instituting a *universal* system for the protection of minority rights. In his revised covenant draft of mid-January 1919 he added a

---

[111] Bowman memorandum of Wilson remarks to Inquiry on 10 December 1918, *PWW*, LIII, p. 354.

[112] Cobb-Lippmann memorandum, 29 October 1918, *PWW*, LI, pp. 503–4.

significant new provision that obliged new states – and here he especially had those of Eastern Europe in mind – to grant equal treatment to all ethnic and religious minorities.[113] The president had embarked on this path under considerable pressure from Jewish interest groups, notably the American Jewish Committee and the American Jewish Congress, whose main concern naturally was to establish new safeguards and a "Bill of Rights" for Jewish minorities.[114]

On behalf of the Inquiry, Coolidge recommended that minorities that would come to live under the rule of a different ethnic majority should be ensured of what he termed their "human rights" of "life, liberty, and the pursuit of happiness" by requiring the states in question to make binding declarations to this effect, which would then be underwritten by the principal powers. Like Wilson, he proposed that this form of minority protection was to be instituted under the authority of the League.[115] Yet it was in fact highly doubtful whether such universal schemes, which again conferred enormous duties on a yet-to-be-established institution, were at all realistic under the prevailing conditions – and, more importantly, whether they would offer effective remedies to the post–First World War minority problems of eastern Europe, particularly those that threatened to poison Polish–German relations.

Looking at the larger picture, however, there is no way around the conclusion that by the time they came to Paris, neither Wilson nor the protagonists of the Inquiry had taken the full measure of the wider challenges posed by the aspiration, and necessity, of creating a new order in Central and Eastern Europe, which was bound to affect the entire Euro-Atlantic system. Crucially, they had only begun to address the international ramifications of the Polish–German problem. On a larger scale, the same applied to the wider reorganisation of Eastern Europe and the relations between the newly created states, Germany and Russia.

No integrative concepts had been developed to address two problems that were in fact intimately connected: the consolidation of eastern Europe and the treatment of the vanquished power. No strategies had been developed to cope with the fact that Germany was likely to retain a superior power potential and share contested borders with unconsolidated neighbour states that would comprise, to a greater or lesser extent, German-speaking minorities. At the same time, no decisive steps had yet been taken to deal with what remained a cardinal factor of uncertainty, the Bolshevik regime. Yet Wilson was more convinced than ever that only an ambitious progressive "cure" – a peace and fundamental reforms on American premises – would not just contain but eventually

---

[113] Wilson covenant draft, ca. 18 January 1919, *PWW*, LIV, pp. 138–48.
[114] See Marshall to Wilson, 7 November 1918, *PWW*, LI, pp. 226–7; Fink (1998), pp. 254–74; Fink (2004), pp. 153–4.
[115] See Miller (1924–26), I, p. 267; VII, pp. 366–8.

eliminate what he came to describe as the "greatest danger" in postwar Europe: the spread of Bolshevism's transnational influence to the west.[116]

XI. Wilson and the Revolutionary Challenge of Bolshevism

Against the backdrop of a continuing civil war in Russia, whose outcome was unfathomable, Wilson continued to grapple with the problem of formulating a coherent policy both to deal with the Bolshevik regime and to counter what he saw as an ever more acute challenge, the proliferation of its ideology and concrete Bolshevik aspirations to incite further revolutionary upheavals across profoundly unsettled Central and Eastern Europe. On 20 November, the president had asked Lansing whether it would be "feasible, in view of the present at least temporary disintegration of Russia into at least five parts, Finland, the Baltic Provinces, European Russia, Siberia, and the Ukraine, to have Russia represented at the peace table". Subsequently, he would decide against admitting the "white" Omsk government to the peace negotiations as representative of a "part" of Russia.[117]

At the same time, Wilson persistently opposed an expansion of the western powers' intervention in the Russian civil war on the side of the "white" forces, reckoning that such a move would carry incalculable risks, lack domestic support and be very unlikely to have a decisive effect.[118] Countering French interventionism he thus retreated to the position that the Russian people themselves would ultimately have to decide the outcome of the war, and their political future. At the outset of the peace conference, Wilson would impress on the other plenipotentiaries that the western powers would be "fighting against the current of the times" if they "tried to prevent Russia from finding her own path in freedom". And he would support a British suggestion to "allow as many groups as desired" to "send representatives to Paris", including the Bolsheviks, on the condition that the latter "refrained from invading" Lithuania, Poland, and Finland. Eventually, however, he distanced himself from any further attempts to come to terms with the Bolshevik regime, falling back on the assertion that its leaders could not be recognised as legitimate representatives of the Russian people, whose democratic aspirations still awaited the establishment of "orderly free government".[119]

On the wider, transnational battleground Wilson was determined to combat Bolshevism, which he saw as symptom of more fundamental deficiencies of

---

[116] Wilson remarks, Supreme War Council meeting, 24 January 1919, *PWW*, LIV, p. 245.

[117] Wilson to Lansing, 20 November 1918, *PWW*, LIII, pp. 136–7.

[118] Minutes of Imperial War Cabinet meeting, 30 December, memorandum no. 47, CAB 23/42.

[119] Hankey notes of meetings of the Council of Ten, 16 and 22 January 1919, *PWW*, LIV, pp. 102–3, 205–6.

Europe"s "old order", by means of successful progressive peacemaking and the initiation of American-style reforms in Europe. To the members of the Inquiry he stressed that he could only attribute "the susceptibility of the people of Europe to the poison of bolshevism" to the fact that their governments had "been run for wrong purposes". And he warned that "if this peace is not made on the highest principles of justice it will be swept away by the peoples of the world in less than a generation".[120] In his assessment, Bolshevism had become attractive because it was "a protest against the way in which the world has worked". The task of the American delegation was thus "to fight for a new order 'agreeably if we can, disagreeably if necessary'".[121]

While condemning the brutality of Lenin's regime, Wilson thus interpreted Bolshevism as an undesirable but inevitable consequence of misguided European imperialism, autocracy and outmoded forms of economic and social organisation that no longer corresponded with the legitimate interests of the people. Consequently, he argued that the real remedy lay in a political, economic and social renewal of Europe along American lines of progressive democracy and liberal capitalism. And he emphasised that the more far-reaching such advances were, the more decisively they would not only push back but also erode the Bolshevik threat in and beyond Europe. By 1919, this confident notion, informed by a belief in the superiority of the American model of the New Freedom era, had indeed become a core feature of Wilson's conception of an "American peace". Adapted to the challenges of their times, it would also be espoused and proclaimed by all of his successors in the long twentieth century, notably Franklin Roosevelt.

XII. The Pivotal German Question – and the Place of the Fledgling German Republic in Wilson's "New Atlantic Order"

But Wilson and American peace planners were ever more acutely aware that the pivotal problem they confronted was the treatment of Germany. In many ways, it had been the central concern of Wilson's peace designs during the war, notably the agenda of the Fourteen Points. On the basis of the armistice, which he had decisively influenced, the president was called upon to provide an American answer to a twofold question: the question of what were to be the terms and underlying premises of the settlement with Germany – and, crucially, the question through what kind of process this settlement should be made. In a wider context, it was in this critical phase that Wilson had to decide how far he would, and could, act on the premise he re-accentuated in early December, namely that he still sought a "just" settlement on the premises of a "peace without

---

[120] Bullitt diary, 9 [10] December 1918, *PWW*, LIII, p. 352.
[121] Bowman memorandum, 10 December 1918, *PWW*, LIII, p. 355.

victory". And it was now that he also had to decide how far he would still make it a priority to pursue a core maxim of his Fourteen Points agenda, namely to assure Germany "a place of equality among the peoples of the world" if it was prepared to accept "covenants of justice and law and fair dealing".[122]

After the victory over the Central Empires, the underlying problem the American president faced, and saw, was not only to prevent future German challenges to what was to be a "peace to end all wars". It was, indeed, to work out what place the vanquished power, the fledgling and crisis-ridden German republic, was to have in the new, essentially transatlantic system he sought to found. Essentially, Wilson adhered to the medium- and long-term outlook of his progressive peace conception – to the underlying aim of not only preserving Germany's basic integrity and fostering its democratisation, but also integrating the defeated power in his "new order" and, notably, the League. But, as noted, by the time he embarked for Europe in early December he had significantly altered his approach to this end and changed not only the short-term priorities but also core rationales of his peace agenda. He distanced himself from the prospect of immediately admitting Germany to the League and began to emphasise that its new leaders, and people, would first have to prove their willingness and capacity to pursue substantial democratic reforms *and* abide by the new international rules he championed; only then would they be allowed to join the comity of democratic nations.[123] This lay at the core of the "probation policy" he would henceforth pursue vis-à-vis the provisional government in Berlin and, crucially, also vis-à-vis the first elected government of the Weimar Republic in 1919. On the same grounds, Wilson also began to distance himself from what had been central to his progressive conception of peacemaking during the war and initially re-affirmed after the armistice: the rationale that actual negotiations with German representatives had to be an essential part of the "negotiated peace" through which the new international order was to be constituted.[124]

More fundamentally, Wilson remained conviced that by acting as an "impartial" arbiter at the peace conference he would be in a position to ensure a fundamentally "just" peace that would also satisfy legitimate German concerns and interests – or what he regarded as such. It was on this overriding aim that he now came to focus his attention. He thus also maintained his opposition to a peace settlement in which the treatment of Germany was dominated by power-political considerations – or demands for discriminatory economic restrictions and punitive indemnities.[125] While the president was committed

---

[122] Grayson diary, 8 December 1918, *PWW*, LIII, pp. 336–7; Wilson, "Fourteen Points", 8 January 1918, *PWW*, XLV, p. 538.

[123] Grayson diary, 8 December 1918, *PWW*, LIII, p. 338.

[124] Wilson statements, 28 December 1918, *PWW*, LIII, p. 576.

[125] Wilson note, 5 November 1918, *PWW*; LIII, pp. 25–6, 456–7; *FRUS 1919*, I, pp. 340–2; War Cabinet minutes, 31 December 1918, CAB 23/42.

to enforcing the far-reaching disarmament clauses of the armistice and imposing significant military restrictions on the defeated power he still intended to
make this the starting-point for universal disarmament within the new League
system (focusing on land rather than naval forces). More profoundly, Wilson
still held that the German problem could not be "solved" by enforcing a long-
term containment and ostracisation of the vanquished power and diminishing
its power by forcing it to cede strategically vital territory on its western and
eastern borders. He never contemplated a dissolution of the German nation-
state or entertained the idea of compelling it to return to a looser pre-
Bismarckian federation – because all of this was incompatible with his conception of self-government. Significantly, Wilson thus intended to preserve, in
essence, the integrity of the German state of 1871 and he came to invoke, also
in this case, the primacy of the principle of self-determination.

While by and large accepting that the "matter" of Alsace-Lorraine should be
"righted" in favour of France – and ultimately without a plebiscite – Wilson
continued to oppose an Allied occupation of the Rhineland and rejected
French demands for further revisions of Germany's western border for strategic reasons. This notably applied to the cessation of the Saar basin and the
proposal to transform the provinces west of the Rhine into an autonomous
"buffer-" state, which he opposed on grounds of self-determination. With a
view to the east, as we have seen, he acted on the basic – if hardly realistic –
assumption that German nationality claims had to be respected and that it
would be possible to settle the new Polish–German border without major
violations of the self-determination principle.[126] But the American president
opted for a different approach when in late November he was apprised of
aspirations for a republican union between Germany and German Austria.
Departing from his general maxims, he came to see these aspirations chiefly in
terms of their impact on how power in postwar Europe would be distributed
and a future equilibrium within the envisaged League system could be created.

In early December, the president told his advisers about an "interesting
problem" that had "arisen under this same principle of self-determination"
because of "the purported decision" of German Austrians to affiliate themselves with "the original German Empire". As he saw it, this "would mean that
the new Germany would be one of the most powerful countries in Europe"
and "a great Roman Catholic power". In his judgement, this problem was a
"hard knot to unravel" if the victors "were to apply the principle of self-
determination literally". Significantly, however, he did not rule out a

---

[126] See Lloyd George (1938), I, p. 193; Wilson remarks, 10 December 1918, Swem memorandum, undated [December 1918], Wilson Papers; Bullitt diary, 9 [10] December 1918,
PWW, LIII, pp. 352–3. Intent on nipping German imperialist aspirations in the bud,
Wilson also rejected a return of the former German colonies. As noted, he originally
proposed that they should become League-supervised mandates.

German–Austrian union at a later stage – once both states had successfully gone through a period of probation. He observed that it "might be handled by the associated powers demanding that Austria and Germany act separately until they proved their sincerity and worth".[127] Yet he would not return to this proposal, because the *Entente* Powers, and above all France, vehemently opposed any scheme of this kind.

It would thus be erroneous to conclude that Wilson simply disregarded or underestimated the problem of German power – the problem posed by preserving a German nation-state as potentially the most powerful actor in Europe. More generally, he indeed became more conscious of the need to take the future distribution of power in the Euro-Atlantic sphere into consideration. But he never developed a more substantial concept and even less a targeted strategy to address it – at least not on premises that would have been acceptable to French decision-makers and to more conservative policymakers and observers in Britain and the United States. Essentially, the American president saw no need for such a concept or strategy. For he clung to the maxim that it could and should be addressed by transcending the dangerous logic of balance-of-power politics. In his view, the real, progressive solution lay in making a peace that was so "just" that it would also be acceptable to the vanquished power; and it lay in creating a League and a new system of collective security that would permit a "safe" international integration of Germany and, more broadly, the stabilisation of a new, progressive equilibrium within a reformed Atlantic world. In turn, he reckoned, all of this could serve to buttress a pacifying inner democratisation of the defeated power that was to re-assure its neighbours and provide a further, and important, underpinning of peace.[128]

The core task Wilson thus came to define for himself was to lead efforts to forge a "scientific" and equitable peace settlement that would also gain legitimacy in a consolidated German republic. He saw this as the most effective way to counter two dangerous tendencies: that Germany would either succumb to Bolshevism, which would entail a breakdown of "order" in Central Europe – or that, fed by resentment against an unjust "victor"s peace", there would be a resurgence of anti-western nationalism, militarism, and authoritarianism, which would give rise to *revanchist* challenges to the international order he sought to build. In Wilson's evolving conception, the same purpose would be served by *eventually* including a reformed Germany in this new order and the League. At the same time, and particularly in the initial postwar period, the League also was to provide an answer to the twin problem of German power and potential revanchism. As the American president saw it,

---

[127] Grayson diary, 8 December 1918, *PWW*, LIII, pp. 338–9; Swem memorandum [December 1918], Wilson Papers.
[128] Grayson diary, 8 December 1918, *PWW*, LIII, pp. 336–7.

the system of "mutual assurance against war" he envisaged would be far more effective than old-style alliances in deterring future German aggression and protecting the security of the defeated power's western and eastern neighbours.[129] Wilson anticipated that the League would furnish an even better framework of security and stability for Europe once a "rehabilitated" Germany had been allowed to enter it and accepted its rules and obligations.

These underlying rationales and assumptions remained central to Wilson's approach to the German question and would inform his actions at the peace conference. By and large, they were supported by a majority in the American peace delegation. But they were not fully espoused by all peace commissioners, nor by the more conservative experts of the Inquiry. Yet no other American peacemaker really dared to challenge Wilson at this stage by strongly advocating a different approach. Though never departing from his commitment to the president's peace programme, House was the only influential figure at this juncture who had begun to develop a more geopolitically informed outlook on the challenges that Germany and German power posed for Europe's stabilisation. Notably, he had become more cognisant of the need to address France's "unhappy" geopolitical situation and French concerns vis-à-vis Germany. At Versailles, House would thus try to promote compromise solutions that allowed Wilson to preserve his essentials while providing greater re-assurance to Clemenceau that his security demands would be met.[130] Ultimately, however, House would not propose any alternative policies. He rejected the option of a fully-fledged alliance of the victors against Germany as politically unfeasible and also opposed the creation of "buffer states" and the strategic curtailment or long-term occupation of German territory. And he would adapt his recommendations and actions to what he believed to be the president's preferences.

Lansing, whose influence on American policy remained very limited, also on this issue, had earlier proposed a distinctly more draconian and traditional power-political strategy to come to grips with Germany. In the autumn of 1917, he had noted that any "stable peace" was unthinkable without "rendering the German power impotent for the future". He had stressed that that he was losing "faith" in achieving this by "discrediting Prussianism with the German people" because they would "never change their code of morals or be worthy of trust and confidence". He had thus concluded that "a peace founded on their promises would be worthless" and that the "democratic nations" would have to "maintain for their own safety a superior physical force to compel compliance". And he had recommended that the "surer" way to draw the "teeth" of the "Beast" would be to use any means necessary to

---

[129] Wilson's ideas, cited in Rappard to Wilson, 26 November 1918, *PWW*, LIII, pp. 209–10.
[130] See House diary, 16 September 1918, *PWW*, LI, p. 23; House diary, 9 February 1919, House Papers.

"render powerless the physical might of the nation" that was "responsible for this awful crime against humanity". To this end, Lansing had drawn up an agenda of territorial curtailments that were to provide natural checks on German power and to foster a new balance of power in Europe. In particular he had proposed a strategic adjustment of frontiers in the west – including the restitution of Alsace-Lorraine to France – and the creation of sizeable buffer states in Eastern and South-Eastern Europe.[131] By the end of 1918, the secretary of state had not changed his outlook. But he pointedly refrained from advancing any schemes of this kind. Rather, as noted, he now recommended to Wilson precisely what he had earlier questioned, namely the promotion of democracy as the most effective safeguard against future aggression and war – also with a view to Germany. Clearly, Lansing's chief concern by this time had become to prevent incalculable American commitments in postwar Europe. He thus urged Wilson to avoid any obligations to enforce either a "power-political" peace or far-reaching sanctions against Germany through the League.[132]

In the aftermath of the war, one of the most prominent conservative members of the Inquiry, the medieval historian Charles Haskins, thus emerged as the only American peace planner who actually recommended an explicitly geopolitical approach to the settlement with Germany. Haskins, who headed the Inquiry's West European section, essentially side-lined considerations of "self-determination" and basically proposed to assess the question of Germany's future western – and eastern – borders in strategic and economic terms. His underlying concern was the future balance of power and economic resources not only between Germany and France but in Europe as a whole. And he shared the basic assumption that Lansing had expressed earlier, namely that even if it formally became a democracy, Germany could not be expected to pursue a more pacific foreign policy than the previous Empire.

Haskins thus argued that the future security of Europe – and the United States, depended on the creation of a new, more viable balance of power and resources. And in his assessment this could only be achieved by giving France not only Alsace-Lorraine (without plebiscite) but also the resources of the Saar basin. But Haskins' ideas went further. Before the end of the war he had suggested that the Rhineland should be separated from the German Empire and converted into an autonomous buffer state, either as a direct protectorate of France or linked to it through a customs union. After the armistice he no longer envisaged a "compulsory" French control of the strategically vital region; but he still proposed making the Rhineland a demilitarised zone and encouraging the "(a)utonomous political organization of the Left Bank" of the

---

[131] Lansing memorandum, "Certain Essentials of a Stable Peace", 24 October 1917, Robert Lansing Papers.
[132] Lansing to Wilson, 23 December 1918, Wilson Papers.

Rhine and a Franco-Rhenish customs union. Haskins invoked similar strategic and economic necessities to call for a substantial revision of Germany's eastern borders. Here, he notably argued that the new Polish state should be granted not only the province of Posen but also the important industrial region of Upper Silesia.[133] What Haskins proposed dovetailed with the more far-reaching schemes of French postwar planners. And it echoed the demands of Lodge and other leading Republicans in Washington. But, more importantly, the geostrategic maxims Haskins articulated never gained a noticeable influence on Wilson's actual pursuits in 1919. They remained peripheral at this formative stage of American reorientation vis-à-vis Europe and the rest of the world.

XIII.   A Significant Reorientation. Wilson, the German Revolution and the Challenges of Making Peace with Germany

In his Fourteen Points, which he continued to present as the essential basis for the peacemaking process, Wilson had effectively tied his offer of a "place of equality" for Germany in the postwar order to the "suggestion" that meaningful negotiations could only be envisaged if, in the final consequence, the path for regime change and towards the foundation of a democratic German polity was cleared.[134] Even after his profound disappointment about the draconian settlement of Brest-Litovsk the American president had renewed his call for "a *secure* and *lasting* peace" on these premises, notably in his landmark address of 27 September 1918. And during the exchanges over the terms of the armistice, he had reasserted his determination to act as an umpire between the *Entente* Powers and Germany as well as his refusal to settle peace terms with Britain and France in advance, insisting on an integrative peace process in which German representatives would also be invited to "state their case".[135] What now mattered decisively, however, was not only how far Wilson remained committed to pursuing a negotiated peace between the victors and the vanquished, but also how far he actually made it a priority to prepare the political ground for such a peace process – and to commit Lloyd George and Clemenceau to it.

Between the armistice and the opening of the Paris proceedings the American president did not radically recast his approach. But he felt compelled to develop a new strategy, and he began to alter some of his underlying

---

[133] Haskins report, 14 November 1918; Haskins memorandum [December 1918], Inquiry nos. 210, 208; Inquiry Report, "Possible Territorial Changes in the German Empire" [December 1918], Wilson Papers; Gelfand (1963), pp. 190–7.

[134] Wilson, "Fourteen Points" address, 8 January 1918, *PWW*, XLV, pp. 538–9.

[135] Wilson address, 27 September 1918, *PWW*, LI, pp. 127–33; Wiseman memorandum, 16 October 1918, *ibid.*, pp. 347–52.

assumptions about how to make peace with Germany and incorporate it in the new Atlantic order. He essentially came to espouse the idea of a peacemaking process in two stages: a *preliminary* process of consultations among the principal victors, followed by a *formal* peace conference at which the victors' preliminary terms were to be presented to the enemy powers.[136] More fundamentally, however, Wilson now came to accentuate the notion of a hierarchical process of peacemaking in which those who represented the nascent and crisis-ridden German republic were initially treated as probationers. At the core, he thus sought to legitimise a process in which the victors – and ultimately he – made the essential decisions about the peace settlement and the fundamentals of the new international system – and in which they also retained the power to decide two crucial questions: whether the plenipotentiaries of the Weimar Republic would *eventually* be admitted to the peace negotiations; and when and on what conditions a "rehabilitated" Germany would qualify for "admission" to the League and the reconstituted postwar order.

This marked and consequential reorientation resulted not only from Wilson's attempt to adapt to important international and domestic constraints he now faced, notably the preferences of the *Entente* governments and the Republicans' staunch opposition to a negotiated "progressive peace". It was also motivated by his appraisal of the German November revolution, which he came to see as less of a *caesura* than its protagonists, and by his changing outlook on the capacity of the German people to construct a lasting democratic order.[137] In his armistice address to Congress, Wilson had observed that "with the fall of ancient governments" had "come political change not merely, but revolution". And he had wondered "(w)ith what governments" the victors were "about to deal in the making of the covenants of peace", with "what authority" they would meet the victors and "with what assurance that their authority will abide and sustain securely the international arrangements" that had to be made. He had thus proclaimed that the western powers should "hold the light steady" until the peoples that "have but just come out from under the yoke of arbitrary government" had found their path and "themselves". The main responsibility of the victors was to "establish a peace that will justly define their place among the nations, remove all fear of their neighbours and of their former masters, and enable them to live in security and contentment when they have set their own affairs in order". At this point, Wilson still saw "some happy signs that they know and will choose the way of self-control and peaceful accommodation".[138]

---

[136] Wilson to Lansing, 22 November 1918, Wilson Papers.

[137] For different interpretations see Schwabe (1985), esp. pp. 161–81, and Sedlmaier (2003).

[138] Wilson address to Congress, 11 November 1918, *PWW*, LIII, pp. 35–43, 42–3.

The new German government that was formed in the wake of the revolution indeed lost no time to appeal to Wilson to act as patron of a "peace of right" on the premises of the Fourteen Points. Shortly after he had assumed responsibility as head of the Council of People's Commissars, Ebert declared that the new leaders were fully committed to establishing a republican form of government and assembling "all Germans for constructive work of peace" in conformity with the ideals and principles the American president had enunciated.[139] This would set the tone for all subsequent German efforts to win the backing of the new American hegemon in their increasingly desperate search for a Wilsonian peace. Bullitt, who had been charged by Lansing to assess the Bolshevik danger in Central Europe, had concluded on the eve of the armistice that "social democracy throughout the continent of Europe is inevitable". Yet he had also underscored that the "question still before the world" was whether the "evolution to social democracy" would be "orderly and peaceful" under the leadership of moderate leaders or "disorderly and bloody under the dominance of the Bolsheviki". Bullitt thus had no doubt about what Wilson's mission ought to be. Observing that Hoover's food relief measures were vital but not sufficient to stem the Bolshevik tide, he recommended that the American president should prevail on Lloyd George and Clemenceau to consult with the moderate socialists and labour leaders in their own countries but also in Germany and Central Europe. Above all, however, he urged him to prevent the victorious powers from forming a new "holy alliance against social democracy" that would deliver Central Europe to "class war and the ultimate bloody triumph of Bolshevism". In his view, Wilson thus essentially had to step up as a patron of social democratic reform who supported moderate leaders like Ebert and Scheidemann against "the Liebknecht-Bolshevist menace" by cooperating with them in his efforts to build a new order.[140]

Progressive opinion-makers in the United States, notably Lippmann, made a similar case. They sought to push Wilson to stay true to his ideals of a liberal and essentially integrative peace that promoted "order and a steady progression towards political and social democracy" as well as Germany's "rehabilitation". And they urged him to support the "conservative Socialist" forces in Germany who dominated the provisional government and backed such an orientation – as well as "unity, cohesion and orderly commerce with foreign lands" – against the minority socialists who desired a "proletarian dictatorship" and "world revolution".[141] Based on his more economically orientated

[139] Ebert statement, transmitted by Bliss to Lansing, 11 November 1918, *FRUS 1918*, I/1, p. 493.

[140] See Bullitt memorandum, 8 November 1918, *PWW*, LIII, pp. 6–9. Bullitt to Lansing, 2 November 1918, NA 862.0017.

[141] *New Republic*, 21 December 1918, pp. 212–14. See also *ibid.*, pp. 211–12; *The Nation*, 14 December 1918, p. 718.

analysis of the situation, the future czar of American food relief, Herbert Hoover, felt the need to issue stern warnings of his own. He impressed on Wilson that the most urgent and "fundamental necessity" in Germany and Central Europe was to "prevent anarchy" and thus to contain the spread of Bolshevism, which pried on instability and chaos. And he considered it a key American interest to prevent the disintegration of Germany and thus to bolster the provisional government in Berlin against separatist movements. For Hoover, the essential instrument to counter such tendencies was an orderly provision of food and vital supplies to the defeated power. He thus strongly recommended including it in food relief programmes; and he under-scored that to be effective such programmes had to be organised under American auspices and effectively under his control.[142] Wilson agreed. At the outset of the peace conference, he would insist that the provision of food relief to Germany was essential. And, against French opposition, he would authorise Hoover to initiate major relief measures, arguing that "any delay in this matter" could be "fatal" and bring "the dissolution of order and govern-ment" through the forces of Bolshevism.[143]

In the early phase of the revolutionary developments Wilson had privately expressed considerable hope that the German people "had shaken off the imperialistic rule and the military autocracy", noting that as they were "an industrious people, and naturally orderly" they might "if properly treated, ultimately be a bulwark for peace in Europe". And he had underlined that fostering "order" in Germany – a stable republican order, led by social democrats and liberals – was a key prerequisite for a lasting peace.[144] By mid-November, however, the president already shared Bullitt's concerns about what both saw as a dangerous deterioration of the political situation in Germany and the threat posed by Bolshevik influence. Yet he remained reluctant to endorse an active policy of building bridges to Ebert and Scheidemann. And, more importantly, he still refused to recognise the Council of People's Commissars as a legitimate government and potential negotiating partner – or even to issue a statement of solidarity on its behalf. Wilson thus essentially declined to act as a patron of moderate social democratic forces.

The utmost Wilson was prepared to do was to propose a joint *démarche* of the victors, notifying the "German authorities" that there could be "no official dealings with them" regarding "the final settlements of the peace" until "a constituent assembly has been brought together and a definite form of government agreed upon and set up". In his calculation, this mainly was to

---

[142] Hoover to Wilson, 20 December 1918, *PWW*, LIII, pp. 453–4.
[143] Hankey notes of meeting of the Supreme War Council, 13 January 1919, *PWW*, LIV, p. 40.
[144] Cummings memorandum, 8 November 1918, *PWW*, LI, p. 647.

"bring the uncertainties in Germany to a head and clear the way" for a stable republican government.[145] Due to French opposition, however, such a *démarche* would never be issued. More importantly, Wilson had hereby established essential preconditions that Germany's new political leaders had to fulfil before any kind of negotiations could be envisaged: not merely the formation of a new and "definite" government but nothing less than the elaboration of a new constitutional order. These were far-reaching and indeed unprecedented preconditions in the history of major peace settlements. Conversely, the criteria the American president advanced could also be used to exclude Germany at least from the initial negotiating-process for as long as they had not been met. And this is essentially the position Wilson had come to adopt by the time the peace conference opened – after he had predictably encountered staunch French resistance to any negotiations with the van-quished and ambivalent but ultimately negative British attitudes towards this vital issue.[146]

In late December, mistakenly believing that the Council of People's Commissars had been ousted, Wilson complained that he found it "difficult to see with whom we shall make peace".[147] But it is noteworthy that he nonetheless still kept the option of *eventually* having actual negotiations with German representatives open.[148] When discussing essential terms of reference during his first meeting with Lloyd George and Balfour on 27 December, he had agreed that the principal victors should hold *informal* talks to agree on a *preliminary* framework. Yet he had also impressed on his British interlocutors that "the general Peace Conference would be a sham if definite conclusions were simply arrived at beforehand and then presented to Germany".[149] Effectively, however, by accepting the core procedural terms on which Lloyd George and Clemenceau had settled by this time, Wilson had consented to parameters that, while not predetermining the nature and outcome of the peace process of 1919, made it very likely that there would be no meaningful negotiations between the victors and the vanquished of the Great War. In retrospect, it should also be emphasised, however, that even if Wilson had decided to persevere with the pursuit of an integrative peace on the premises

---

[145] Wilson to Lansing, 25 November 1918, *PWW*, LIII, p. 194. Similar arguments were advanced to refuse peace negotiations with Austrian representatives.

[146] Jusserand note for Wilson, 29 November 1918, *PWW*, LIII, pp. 292–8; Jusserand to Lansing, 1 December 1918, *FRUS-PPC*, II, pp. 106–7; minutes of Imperial War Cabinet meeting, 30 December 1918, CAB 23/42.

[147] Wilson statements [to Edward Bell], 28 December 1918, *PWW*, LIII, p. 576.

[148] The Inquiry's Scott-Miller peace treaty draft of 30 December 1918 still stated that Wilson's "Program" seemed to involve the participation of Germany in a general peace conference. See *FRUS-PPC*, I, pp. 308–9.

[149] Minutes of Imperial War Cabinet meeting, 30 December 1918, memorandum no. 47, CAB 23/42.

of the Fourteen Points, he would not have had the power to prevail over British and especially French opposition.

In part, Wilson's new course can be indeed attributed to his realisation that it would be impossible to overcome French – and British – opposition to an alternative approach. As we have seen, he was also aware of profound Republican and wider domestic opposition to negotiating a "Wilsonian peace" with Germany. Tactically, he had made a concession to achieve his overriding aim. In return for agreeing to the *Entente* Powers' procedural terms, he had ensured that the elaboration of the League Covenant would be the first item on the agenda of the peace conference. Yet Wilson's essential reluctance to pursue a negotiated peace with the vanquished power also owed to underlying changes in his outlook on Germany's political future. By the end of 1918, he had become increasingly sceptical about the prospects of a swift and substantial German democratisation process; and by the spring of 1919 he would even begin to question whether a democratic form of government was indeed appropriate for Germany. His perception of the – inevitably – arduous efforts to establish a republican order on the ruins of a semi-authoritarian Empire combined with his distrust of Ebert and the forces he represented, and brought to the fore growing doubts about German aptitudes for democratic government. And what also came to the fore was Wilson's version of the notion of a "special path" in modern German history. In his interpretation, it was the notion that since the mid-nineteenth century German advances in the development of political order and institutions had not kept pace but rather been overshadowed by rapid economic development and the formation of an essentially authoritarian "power state". The American president surmised that even in the most auspicious scenario, coming to terms with this burdensome legacy would require a long time.[150]

It was against this background that one new axiom of Wilson's policy became ever more significant, namely the axiom that Germany would have to pass through a "probationary period" – of unspecified length – to prove its capacity to form a "responsible, decent government" and, more broadly, its commitment to democracy before it could enter the League.[151] During the armistice exchanges he had still insisted that Germany had to be among the organisation's founding members.[152] But by early December he had committed himself to the different and decidedly high-handed "probation" rationale, which hence indeed came to shape his rigidly hierarchical approach to the core challenge of how, and when, Germany was to be integrated in the transatlantic

---

[150] For Wilson"s assessment and "image" of Germany see Sedlmaier (2003), pp. 34–41, 74–5, 118–21.

[151] Bullitt diary, 9 [10] December 1918, *PWW*, LIII, p. 352.

[152] Wiseman memorandum, 16 October 1918, *PWW*, LI, pp. 347–52.

comity of democratic nations he envisaged.[153] In hindsight, it has to be stressed that – in contrast to some of his advisers – the American president failed to recognise the importance of what were in fact remarkably swift and decisive steps towards the establishment of a new republican order in Germany, which reached a first peak with the drafting of the Weimar Republic's constitution and the election of the first "Weimar coalition" government under Scheidemann in January 1919.

XIV.   Towards an Economic Peace on American Terms? Essential Limits and Constraints of American Aspirations

Before his resignation in November 1918, Wilson's Treasury Secretary McAdoo had underscored that a "permanent and satisfactory peace" could hardly be realised unless "financial conditions" were created that permitted "the various nationalities to prosper materially and reap the rewards of industry and frugality". As McAdoo outlined, settling reparations would be one of the critical problems affecting these conditions that had to be addressed at the peace conference; the other main challenge would be the organisation of postwar "reconstruction", which would raise the question how far the United States should participate through the supply of relief provisions, material aid and financial resources.[154]

As noted, while Britain remained an important power in this respect the United States had by the end of 1918 unequivocally become the dominant and indispensable creditor power in the transatlantic sphere – and the world. Following JP Morgan's initial private credits, the American government had by this time extended massive war loans amounting to $8 billion (and allocated $2 billion for loans that had not yet been used) that had mainly gone to Britain, which, now owed the United States nearly $4 billion, and France, which had incurred obligations of ca. $2 billion.[155] At the same time, the war had also accelerated America's ascent to the position of the world's newly preeminent economic power. And the policymakers and financiers who acted on its behalf were intent on setting the postwar rules of the world economy, notably by globalising the paradigm of the "Open Door". Wilson thus represented a power with significant financial and economic clout, although the United States was still far from reaching the level of predominance it would command after the Second World War.

But the critical question that arose after the armistice in view of these seismic changes was essentially political. It was the question of how far

[153] See Chapter 12.
[154] McAdoo to Wilson, 27 October 1918, *PWW*, LI, pp. 468–70.
[155] See Moulton and Pasvolsky (1932), p. 426.

Wilson and other leading US decision-makers would be willing, and in a position, to commit the United States – as the only power that had the requisite financial resources – to play a hegemonic role in laying the financial and economic groundwork for a "permanent and satisfactory peace". As will be shown, to a significant extent this hinged on their political will, and ability, to promote more comprehensive schemes of financial revitalisation and economic reconstruction that would alter the playing-field not just for a "solution" to the reparations issue but also for decisive advances towards a financial and economic *pax Americana*. In turn, this raised further salient questions: Would American decision-makers be willing, and have the leeway, to put effective pressure on their war debtors, yet also to offer incentives – notably in the form of debt reduction or even cancellation – to lead the way towards a workable reparations settlement? Would they be willing and able to lead efforts to build a functioning new economic system that fostered effective postwar reconstruction? And how far would Wilson, McAdoo and his successor Glass – if they *were* to pursue such priorities – be in a position to gain the indispensable Congressional and wider public support for financial incentives, concessions and more far-reaching commitments to further Europe's rehabilitation?

Essentially, what Wilson, those who directed US financial policies in the Treasury and key financial experts actually deemed appropriate and consonant with American interests at this stage, and what they thought they could legitimise domestically, left little or no room for more ambitious political-cum-financial schemes to foster Europe's financial and economic revitalisation. In particular, it left no room for schemes that either would depend on American concessions, above all debt reductions, or require the American government to assume, and justify, far-reaching *official* guarantees and liabilities. Those who determined US financial and economic policies in this phase reckoned – rightly – that the Republican-dominated Congress would not be prepared to countenance such guarantees and liabilities. And they acted on the assumption that it would not be possible to gain the support of the American taxpayers, and voters, for measures of this kind.

At the same time, however, and at a deeper level, the president who had driven forward the progressive "New Freedom" agenda and his key financial experts also shared a core ideological predilection that placed strict limits on the *international* responsibilities of the American government. Essentially, they favoured private rather than intergovernmental and government-driven approaches to Europe's financial revitalisation and its short-term and long-term reconstruction. And they all espoused the basic assumption that relying on private actors – bankers, experts and the "regular channels of commerce" – and limiting governmental oversight and coordination not only minimised political risks and liabilities but was also, and essentially, more effective. This was notably what US experts like Hoover, Norman Davis, Thomas Lamont and Bernard Baruch propounded – though with different emphases – as the "American way" to stabilise and reform Europe.[156]

Thus, rather than take a lead in developing ambitious multilateral designs for postwar Europe, the clear priority of the Treasury, which Wilson shared, was and remained to protect what were regarded as vital national interests of the United States: the financial interests of the newly preponderant creditor power, which had never been in this position and only recently modernised its own banking system; and the core interest of the most dynamic economic power to expand the "Open Door" regime. This went hand in hand with a determination to block or discourage any British, French – or German – proposals that were regarded as detrimental to these fundamental interests. Unquestionably, therefore, one underlying interest that not only Wilson but also his main advisers pursued was to make the world safe for the expansion of US liberal capitalism, transnationally operating US high finance and capital export. But it would be misleading to suggest that the policies Wilson pursued in 1919 were mainly determined by such common elite interests and the premises of the "Open Door".[157] As we have seen, what chiefly informed Wilson's peace agenda were political aspirations and ideological assumptions, which crystallised in his blueprint for a League of Nations.

In retrospect, it is worth emphasising that, though constrained, the American government would have had more means and leverage than any other "player" to advance and lead international efforts to implement more forward-looking designs for a financial and economic peace after the First World War. But Wilson and those who oversaw US financial and economic policies did not see any need to develop such designs, or to prepare the ground for them, domestically or internationally. Three years after the peace conference the leading financial expert Norman Davis would acknowledge that the American planners "did not offer any detailed plans for the economic revival of Europe". Rather, he stressed, they "stood for sound economic principles", notably those of the "Open Door" and a liberal trade regime, and "fought for the adoption of political and economic settlements" – notably regarding Germany – without which "no plan would work".[158]

The domestic constraints to which Wilson and his financial peacemakers responded – distinct forms of economic nationalism yet also an emphasis on the protection of more narrowly defined financial interests – indeed placed tangible restrictions on their potential to provide significant "systemic" leadership in the financial and economic sphere. Yet their capacity to play such a role was also

---

[156] See memorandum of conference Wilson – US experts, 19 May 1919; Lamont, Davis to Sec. State for Leffingwell, 27 May 1919; Lamont to Brand, 10 June 1919, Thomas W. Lamont Papers, 163–13, 165–10.

[157] Cf. the different interpretations in Williams (2009); Bender and Geyer (2008), pp. 32–3.

[158] Davis to Baker, 26 July 1922, Davis Papers, Box 3. See Van Meter (1974), p. 162.

limited by the assumptions and ideological preferences that informed their outlook. They thus were neither prepared nor in a position to bolster what would have been critical for a sustainable peace: indispensable efforts to hammer out in negotiations with the other relevant governments some kind of financial *and political* programme for Europe's longer-term stabilisation – a programme that even went qualitatively beyond what some French strategists envisaged at this juncture, anticipating the thrust of the Marshall Plan.

The combination of self-imposed limitations, ideological convictions and towering domestic constraints would also distinctly limit Wilson's ability to seize on America"s new financial and economic power to advance his *political* design for a "new Atlantic order" at the peace conference. Above all, it limited his capacity to induce or compel the *Entente* Powers to accept it. Yet it had one even more important consequence. It severely curtailed the ability of Wilson and his financial advisers, notably the financiers Baruch and Lamont, to act as "disinterested arbiters" and promote a moderate – and "scientific" – settlement of the explosive reparations question, which in the American perception had unduly dominated deliberations over peace terms, and domestic politics, in Britain and France – but in fact could not be divorced from the towering transatlantic problem of inter-allied war debts.

XV. The Essentials and Essential Constraints of American Reparations Policy

In Wilson's assessment, what was required, *and could be achieved*, was an indemnity settlement that restrained *Entente* demands and did not compromise the implementation of his broader progressive peace agenda. In February 1918 the American had reaccentuated what would essentially still be his fundamental position after the war, namely that he sought a peace with "no contributions, no punitive damages".[159] Following the armistice agreement, and influenced by the need to find common ground with the European victors, Wilson had tried to clarify the American position on the reparations issue. And, with the unstated aim of ensuring that Britain and France would be in a position to repay their wartime obligations to the United States, the American president came to draw a clear line. He now asserted the maxim that Germany had to pay indemnities "for all damage done to the civilian population of the Allies and their property by [its] aggression."[160]

Wilson showed some understanding for the domestic pressures that British and French leaders confronted. He understood "the strong demand in Allied countries that Germany be made to pay for the cost of the war", though he was

---

[159] Wilson speech, 11 February 1918, *PWW*; LIII, pp. 25–26.
[160] Wilson note, 5 November 1918, *PWW*, LIII, pp. 456–7; *FRUS 1919*, I, pp. 340–2; War Cabinet minutes, 30 December 1918, *PWW*, LIII, p. 563; 31 December 1918, CAB 23/42.

not too "disturbed by the Election speeches" of Lloyd George and other leaders.[161] But he made clear that he would "oppose any indemnity except for the damage actually done by Germany". Originally, he thus rejected any British claims that went beyond this category, i.e. claims to be indemnified for war *costs*. Wilson vowed to block excessive British demands, having read that Lloyd George would ask for £8 billion. In early December, he again signalled this unequivocally and at the same time, echoing prevalent attitudes in the American delegation and among US experts, expressed his conviction that the exact amount Germany owed should and *could* be "determined scientifically".[162]

In accordance with Wilson's general guidelines, the American financial experts who were mainly charged with this task, Davis and Baruch, developed what in their view amounted to "definite program" to settle the reparations problem. The "principles" they proposed were based on the terms of the armistice agreement. In their interpretation this meant that Germany had to compensate the allied powers for the damage that had resulted from actions that were "clearly in violation of international law". As such, they particularly highlighted the German violation of Belgium's neutrality. More generally, they concluded that Germany was liable to pay *reparations* for "all damage to the civilian population and their property" that had been caused by German forces on the Belgian and French territories they had occupied. Baruch proposed that the extent of the *direct* damage the German "aggression" had caused should be assessed through "field examinations" in the devastated areas. These could then provide a "definite" and objectively accurate scheme – and a definite total sum of reparations.[163] By contrast, the programme of the American experts excluded more extensive *indemnities* for other categories of damages the war had caused and, crucially, for general war costs – which from the start pitted their recommendations particularly against prevalent British "conceptions", yet also against French demands for a more extensive *"réparation intégrale"*. Wilson endorsed the recommendations of Davis and Baruch, and in the initial stages of the peace conference he would insist that the victors were "honor bound" to negotiate a settlement that conformed with the limits his experts had set.[164]

The main interests and underlying rationales that informed the American stance on reparations are not difficult to discern. But it is important to note that they transcended more narrowly-defined financial and economic interests – and were indeed connected to overall political concerns and

[161] Wiseman to the British Foreign Office, Paris, 15 December 1918, *PWW*, LIII, p. 395.
[162] E. Benham diary, 8 December 1918; Bullitt memorandum, 9[10] December, *PWW*, LIII, pp. 341, 351.
[163] See Baruch (1920), pp. 18–20; minutes of meeting of American economic advisers, 11 February 1919, cited after Walworth (1986), p. 172.
[164] Wilson to Lansing, 23 February 1919, *PWW*, LV, p. 231.

considerations pertaining to the future stabilisation of the League-based new political order in Europe. A core rationale was that while Germany would have to be punished by paying for actual war damages what had to be avoided was to saddle it with politically inflated indemnity obligations of such magnitude that they would cripple it financially, and economically. As the Treasury expert Paul Cravath observed, the United States had become the nation that exported more to Germany than all others and had no interest in wrecking indefinitely the purchasing power of its best customer, which potentially could become again its key trading partner in Europe.[165] Yet there was also a more general political rationale that became increasingly prominent in Wilson's thinking and which also informed the approaches of US experts and important figures like Hoover. It concerned not just the reparations problem but also the broader question of Germany's recuperation *and political stabilisation* – which in their view was intricately bound up the stabilisation of Europe as a whole.

At one level, American policymakers acted on the premise that immediate postwar relief had to be extended not just to the Allied Powers and the fledgling east European states but also to Germany and German Austria. They thus demanded that the Allied blockade of Germany had to be lifted as soon as possible. Yet Wilson, Hoover and others also believed that in the medium and long term a sustainable financial and economic recuperation of Europe was simply inconceivable if Germany was burdened by excessive reparation demands – and forced to accept a discriminatory financial and trade regime. Further, they shared a growing concern that unless the more far-reaching British and French schemes were contained, financial and economic conditions would be created that undermined political order in Germany and opened the door to Bolshevik influence. And they feared that this would have far-reaching repercussions not just for the peacemaking process but for also the longer-term prospects of creating a stable postwar order on American terms.

In this sense, the evolving American reparations policy was inseparable from what remained a core premise of the Wilsonian peace design: the premise that Europe's longer-term consolidation required the stabilisation of a republican system of government *and* a liberal-capitalist political economy in Germany. Eventually, a reformed German state was not just to be integrated in the new political order Wilson sought but also in an American-led world economic order on liberal-capitalist terms. Hoover would express these underlying aims more unequivocally and forcefully than the American president himself during the volatile post-armistice period. But Wilson fundamentally shared them.[166]

As noted, Wilson had some understanding for the desire of the *Entente* governments – and peoples – to make Germany pay for the war; and he was

[165] See Walworth (1977), p. 105.
[166] See Hoover to Wilson, 20 December 1918, O'Brien (1978), pp. 22–3.

not oblivious to the immense fiscal and reconstruction challenges which French policymakers confronted – and that fused with the desire to "make le Boche pay".[167] US experts like Baruch were even more keenly aware that in view of the sacrifices and losses the war had brought for the *Entente* Powers the reparations question was not only closely bound up with pressing financial and economic problems that beset Britain and a French state that hovered on the verge of "bankruptcy". They recognised that it also had to be understood as a *political* question – a question whose "settlement" was not merely or mainly a matter of financial and "legal" calculations but would be profoundly affected by the nationalist fervour and political-psychological expectations the war had engendered, and which official post-armistice rhetoric in Britain, France and elsewhere had further heightened.

Like US Treasury officials and financial experts, Wilson regarded the promises of Lloyd George and Clemenceau as politically highly irresponsible, because in his view they raised the expectation that financial problems would be addressed by imposing vast indemnities on the enemy rather than through efforts to balance budgets and turn war economies to more efficient peace economies.[168] Yet nor were the president or his advisers oblivious to the actual constraints and far-reaching domestic demands the *Entente* leaders confronted. Nonetheless, Wilson and the US experts who would sit on the Reparation Commission in Paris would enter the peace negotiations with the expectation that it would be not only be proper but also possible – with the help of American expertise – to effect a moderate and "scientific" reparations settlement. And they expected as well that such a settlement could actually be made acceptable to the *Entente* Powers. This became part of the Wilsonian aspiration to oversee a "scientific peace". But it would soon become clear that such expectations were highly unrealistic. The United States' new status as key creditor power gave Wilson a pivotal role, but it did not translate into decisive influence in the reparations dispute. And this was not least due to the rigidity and narrow limits of the Wilson administration's approaches to two other essential issues on the postwar agenda: inter-allied debts and the financial-cum-economic reconstruction of Europe.

XVI.   No "Grander Schemes". US Approaches to Debts, European Reconstruction and the Postwar World Economic Order

Both before and after the armistice, US diplomats in Europe and policymakers in Washington were bombarded with British "inquiries" and French schemes that in different ways sought to link the reparations question, the issue of war

---

[167] Wiseman to the British Foreign Office, 15 December 1918, *PWW*, LIII, p. 395.
[168] *Ibid.*

debts, and European reconstruction. British "inquiries" had focused on the "cancellation" or reduction of US loans and an "equalization of loans" between the different belligerents and the idea of a coordinated approach to American debt relief vis-à-vis Britain in return for British debt relief vis-à-vis France and other continental European countries. And, notably, they had raised the irksome issue of "linking" American loans and the question of Allied reparation demands vis-à-vis Germany.[169]

While also keen to reduce or eliminate his country's war-debt obligations, Clemenceau's commerce minister Étienne Clémentel approached Wilson with more aspirational schemes, which revolved around the idea of extending the remit of the League by also creating a kind of financial – and economic – *société des nations*. Within it, the victors and selected neutral powers would cooperate, in the "financing" of the necessary reconstruction of devastated areas in France – and Belgium – yet also, in a wider perspective, to deal with the financial fall out of the war and the challenges of European reconstruction.[170] All of these French plans excluded Germany and were geared to France's wider objective of recasting the structural balance vis-à-vis its eastern neighbour. What proved crucial from the American standpoint, however, was that they threatened to entangle the American creditor power in far-reaching political commitments – ultimately, the commitment to assume a large share of the war's financial costs and to become the main underwriter of Europe's recuperation.

In response to a first wave of *Entente* inquiries and proposals, McAdoo proposed very restrictive guidelines for American policy; and Wilson would essentially confirm these guidelines.[171] Essential for the opposition of Wilson, the Treasury and American experts to any *direct* and *official* involvement in "grander schemes" for Europe's postwar rehabilitation – let alone a financial League of Nations – were two cardinal axioms that had crystallised by the end of 1918. The first axiom had already been laid down by William McAdoo before the armistice. He had impressed on Wilson that for the sake of America's "financial safety" it was imperative to "deprecate the suggestion" that the United States should "cancel the indebtedness of the Allied governments" that it held – or even consider reducing war debts.[172] On 11 December, McAdoo underscored that the Treasury would not "consider or discuss suggestions to cancel our foreign loans" as it had "no power to make such cancellations". The final decisions here rested with the American Congress. To block any further negotiations, the Treasury would not even be officially

---

[169] See McAdoo to House, 11 December 1918, *FRUS-PPC*, II, p. 538.
[170] See Clémentel letter to Clemenceau and Wilson, 19 September 1918, AN, F12 8104.
[171] McAdoo to House, 11 December 1918, *FRUS-PPC*, II, pp. 538–40.
[172] McAdoo to Wilson, 27 October 1918, *PWW*, LI, pp. 468–9.

represented at the peace conference; Davis was to act as a more or less unofficial representative of Treasury interests.

The overriding concern for the newly pre-eminent "lending nation" was to ensure that Britain and France honoured their obligations. McAdoo and his successor Carter Glass had assured Congressional representatives that US loans would be collected in due course; and they thought that this was clearly the main interest in Congress. McAdoo warned that even "suggestions of cancellation of our loans" had raised "concern as well as opposition in some quarters of Congress", notably the Republican opposition, with a view to granting any further loans to European countries. More generally, he was convinced that cancellation, which would have to be balanced by tax increases, would be a highly unpopular proposition for the American electorate. The utmost the Treasury was prepared to discuss – yet in Washington, not in Paris – was a "conversion" of its "demand obligations" into "long time obligations". Significantly, McAdoo thus recommended that *all* discussion regarding existing and possible future US loans "for war and reconstruction purposes" should be "kept out of" the peace conference as far as possible – which he found "desirable from the standpoints of international and internal policy alike".[173]

The president fully agreed with McAdoo's assessment both of the international and the domestic constellation. And both he and Glass would later confirm this basic premise of US policy, stating unequivocally that the American government would make no concessions on war debts but insist on their repayment, contemplating at most a moratorium on interest payments.[174] Wilson would assure Glass that he saw no "proper basis" for negotiations over either American debt claims or fresh US loans to Britain and France. The same essentially applied to wider reconstruction schemes that raised the issues of debt relief or new long-term financial engagements.[175] All of this would have a tangible and distinctly constraining impact on the peace negotiations.

Pursuing narrower priorities, the new Treasury Secretary finalised a *bilateral* arrangement to extend further short-term loans to France. With the approval of Congress, and drawing on funds allocated under the original Liberty Loan Act, the American government would lend an additional $800

---

[173] McAdoo to House, 11 December 1918, *FRUS-PPC*, II, pp. 538–40; Glass to Wilson, 19 December 1918, *ibid.*, p. 544; McAdoo to Wilson, 27 October 1918: *PWW*, LI, pp. 468–70.

[174] Wilson speech, 11 February 1918, *PWW*, LIII, pp. 25–26; Wilson note, 5 November 1918, *ibid.*, pp. 456–7; *FRUS 1919*, I, pp. 340–2; War Cabinet minutes, 30 December 1918, *ibid.*, p. 563; War Cabinet minutes, 31 December 1918, CAB 23/42.

[175] Glass to Wilson, 19 December 1918, *FRUS-PPC*, II, pp. 544–6; Wilson to Davis, 6 January 1919, forwarded to Glass, 9 January 1919, *FRUS-PPC*, II, p. 556; Wilson to Davis, 5 February 1919, Wilson Papers; Davis to Wilson, 12 February 1919, *ibid.* See Walworth (1977), pp. 244–7.

million to the French government in February 1919. Yet it stipulated that these funds were only to be used to purchase relief supplies, not for the reconstruction of devastated areas.[176] US policy vis-à-vis Britain, which in American eyes did not face pressing financial problems on the scale of France, followed a different course. House informed the new British Chancellor of the Exchequer, Austen Chamberlain, on the eve of the peace conference, that the American government would terminate its official loans.[177]

The second and essential axiom of US financial policy was that the issues of inter-allied war debts and reparations were to be treated in a strictly separate manner. In December, McAdoo underscored that the Treasury "opposed in principle" the "use of our foreign loans" at the peace conference to "conciliate rival claims for indemnities and other advantages". More broadly, the Wilson administration rejected all British and French suggestions of "linking" their obligations with "questions such as reparation by Germany". Essentially, one was not prepared to "finance" a more moderate reparations settlement – i.e. allow Britain and France to scale down their demands – by making concessions on American debt claims.[178] In early January 1919, Norman Davis, now Assistant Secretary of the Treasury, would reiterate to Keynes the fundamental American opposition to any form of "linkage".[179] This position would be adamantly maintained throughout the negotiations in Paris – and significantly narrow the *Entente* Powers' room to manoeuvre in the reparations debate.

For his part, Wilson was intent on maintaining the United States' economic room to manoeuvre in order to further his political agenda at the peace conference.[180] Yet he also endorsed this maxim because he and other American policymakers held that US economic interests and the ideas they had formed about the postwar world economic order mandated this course. The American president thus pursued a course that Herbert Hoover had advocated most forcefully at this juncture: to steer clear of any commitments that would involve the United States in any – French – schemes to convert inter-allied wartime organisations into mainstays of the postwar economic order.[181] After his administration had rejected the discriminatory economic war-aims agenda the *Entente* governments had finalised at the Paris Economic Conference of 1916, one important plank in the platform of Wilson's peace programme had indeed been the universal extension of American rules and principles that were to underpin a liberal, essentially non-discriminatory

---

[176] See Soutou (1989), p. 838.
[177] See Skidelsky (1983), p. 360.
[178] McAdoo to House, 11 December 1918, *FRUS-PPC*, II, pp. 538–9.
[179] Davis to Keynes, 7 January 1919, Keynes Papers, RT/1/24.
[180] Instructions to US representatives in Paris and London, 19 November 1918, NA, State Department. 600.001.591/606a.
[181] Hoover to Wilson, 11 November 1918, O'Brien (1978), pp. 4–5.

world economic order, and trade regime: the rules of the "Open Door" and the "most-favoured nation" principle. Crucially, in the prevalent American conception these rules and principles essentially were to apply universally, not just to the victors and neutral powers but also to the enemy powers.

Following consultations with the leading economic expert of the US Tariff Commission, Frank Taussig, Wilson and House had also confirmed in the autumn of 1917 that the administration would maintain a distance from attempts to perpetuate a discriminatory regime and to develop schemes for an inter-allied economic *entente* and customs union, all geared towards an economic exclusion and "containment" of the Central Powers, and above all Germany, that had been endorsed at the Anglo-French Economic Conference of 1916, and that Clémentel had vigorously pursued ever since then. After the armistice, Wilson and the leading American economic experts would re-affirm what the president had stipulated, in general terms, in the Fourteen Points, namely the core aim to push for the "removal, so far as possible, of all economic barriers and the establishment of an equality of trade conditions among all the nations consenting to the peace and associating themselves for its maintenance".[182]

The cornerstones of US foreign economic policy after the war and the American economic peace agenda, would indeed be the "Open Door" precepts and the ambition to promote unfettered trade conditions. There were no American plans to empower the League to set and oversee new rules for global commerce as a kind of new world trade organisation, or by ambitious inter-governmental plans for a transatlantic economic union, as French planners envisaged. Rather, the main aim was to prevail on Britain and France to accept a postwar trade regime on American terms, under which the most-favoured-nation status would be expanded rather than restricted to the victors and neutral states. More precisely, the underlying US interest was to ensure an acceptance of the premise that states would not erect discriminatory trade barriers against particular other countries – including the former Central Powers – but rather pledge that if they granted specific trade conditions or concessions to one trading partner they would also extend these conditions to all other countries that were part of the "most-favoured-nation" regime. This remained a central feature of American ideas about the postwar economic system: and it was one of the cardinal rules for global trade after the war that the US experts would seek to impress on their British and French counterparts at the outset of the peace conference.[183]

But Wilson could not present the United States as a credible champion of "free trade" and advances towards an "equality of trade conditions". In pursuit of his "New Freedom" agenda, he had effected the first reduction of US tariffs

---

[182] Wilson, "Fourteen Points", *PWW*, XLV, pp. 536–8.
[183] See Soutou (1989), pp. 539 ff.; Glaser (1998), p. 376.

since the Civil War through the Underwood-Simmons Tariff Act of 1913, altering a "tariff" which, in his words, had cut the United States off from its "proper part in the commerce of the world".[184] But he now had to wrestle with a Republican Congressional majority – and Democratic interests – that opposed further reductions, let alone a fundamental revision of the US tariff regime.

Integral to American approaches to economic peacemaking, and order, was and remained the assertion of economic and commercial independence. This was one of the main motivations behind the resistance to any ambitious schemes for the establishment of an inter-allied system of governmental controls and economic redistribution after the war – and, more generally, the recasting of the economic playing-field, and balance of forces, by creating a victors' regime and imposing longer-term commercial discrimination on Germany. Wilson thus pointedly refrained from offering any constructive response to the far-reaching and in some respects revolutionary and forward-looking plans for an "economic union" among the "allied democracies" that Clémentel had presented to him in September 1918.[185]

On the eve of the Paris Peace Conference, some American protagonists – notably Baruch – saw the need to establish some form of *temporary* control over the access to and pricing of raw-materials. Prior to the armistice, when he was still the chairman of the US War Industries Board, Baruch had proposed granting the League the authority to enforce equal economic opportunities. He stressed that the war had taken a heavier toll on the economic life of the *Entente* Powers. And he voiced understanding for French concerns vis-à-vis a German neighbour whose "machinery and factories" had remained intact during the war and that was "ready immediately" to resume "competition for the world's market". In October 1918, Baruch had thus suggested that the United States should require Germany to supply not only France but also Belgium and Poland with industrial products and essential raw materials at reduced prices – and to agree with the *Entente* governments on instrumentalities to ensure German compliance.[186]

Yet Wilson did not follow Baruch's advice. More generally, the US delegation would not seek any preliminary agreements with Britain and France on postwar economic order. And neither the American president nor his key advisers, including Baruch, would subscribe to the wider aims of what Clémentel recommended as a concept germane to an "organised peace", an "economic union" of the victors. US decision-makers and experts would not just pour cold water on French designs but effectively block them.[187] Crucially,

[184] Wilson, Inaugural Address, 1913, PWW, XVII, p. 150.
[185] Clémentel letter, 19 September 1918, AN, F12/8104.
[186] Baruch to Wilson, 23 October 1918, PWW, LIII, pp. 419–20; See Baruch (1920), p. 79.
[187] Clémentel (1931), pp. 337–48; Glaser (1998), pp. 374–6.

the thrust of US economic policies and interests could thus provide a powerful *integrative* impetus of a different kind, with potentially far-reaching economic and political implications. It opened up the perspective of including – *in the longer run* – not only the *Entente* Powers, the other West European states and the new states of Eastern Europe but also a liberal-capitalist German republic in a postwar economic system in which the United States would be the most powerful actor.

11

The Search for a New Equilibrium – and an Atlantic Concert
The Reorientation of British Approaches to Peace and International Order

In contrast to the American constellation, there was not only a wide public debate in Britain after the armistice about the essentials of the peace and postwar order – which intensified during the immediately ensuing election campaigns. There was also a far-ranging strategic debate *within* the governing circles, both in the Imperial War Cabinet and between its protagonists, the Foreign Office and the Treasury. Nonetheless, to a remarkable extent it was ultimately Lloyd George himself, influenced by a small circle of advisers, chiefly his closest confidants Philip Kerr and Maurice Hankey, who would shape what gradually crystallised into a distinctly British peace policy. At its core lay the pursuit of a new Atlantic order, and equilibrium, that also was to make the world "safe for liberal empire" or, more precisely, safe for the consolidation *and expansion* of Britain's imperial system. Once re-elected, the prime minister felt exceedingly confident that he would be able to broker a "British peace" of this kind at the peace conference, and he would clearly become the dominant British decision-maker in 1919.

Undoubtedly, Lloyd George's aspiration to act as the statesman and consummate democratic politician who mediated a just and durable peace after the Great War was often overshadowed by his proclivity for tactical manoeuvres and opportunistic vacillations. These indeed were salient characteristics of his "pragmatic" approach to domestic and international politics.[1] But this should not obscure the fact that, in the aftermath of the war, Lloyd George and those who aided him actually developed an increasingly coherent – and essentially transatlantic – peace conception, which incorporated essentials of British peace planning during the war. Indeed, they also began to craft more comprehensive strategies to implement their designs.

Yet nor should one overlook the problematic and at times contradictory assumptions on which this conception and these strategies were based, above all the assumption that through a process of negotiations, and bargaining, with Wilson and Clemenceau it would be possible to make, and *impose*, a victor"s

---

[1] For influential critiques of Lloyd George's pursuits, see Keynes (1978), X, pp. 23–4; Nicolson (1931), p. 209. For a recent more favourable portrayal see Fry (2011), pp. 3–192.

peace that was so "equitable" and "just" that it would also be accepted by the vanquished.[2]

In many ways, Lloyd George's peace policy only gained decisive contours in the course of the Versailles negotiations. It was articulated most clearly in the Fontainebleau memorandum that he and his closest advisers drafted in March 1919, which represented the closest approximation of a British "grand design" for a firm yet "moderate" peace that not only the victors but also Germany could deem legitimate.[3] But the core elements of this design had already emerged by the end of 1918. And so had the guiding rationale of fostering a new Anglo-American partnership to promote a substantial reform of the international order and a new hegemonic burden-sharing *on British terms*. After the armistice, the hierarchical internationalists Smuts and Cecil were the most emphatic and influential advocates of this newly dominant Atlantic orientation. Crucially, elaborating their wartime schemes they now stepped up their efforts to commit Lloyd George to a strategy of close cooperation with Wilson – with the key objective of creating an effective League of Nations. In their conception, the League was to serve above all as framework for a new compact with the United States – and a new transatlantic concert.

I.   Beyond the Balance of Power, towards a New International Concert – and a Legitimate Equilibrium?

Unquestionably, a core premise on which Lloyd George and those who masterminded Britain's peace preparations acted was that fundamental British interests had already been satisfied by the armistice agreement. Crucial had been the provisions that de facto would banish the threat Germany posed to the British Empire as an imperialist rival and global naval power. One of the Lloyd George government's main aims thus simply became to ensure that the eventual peace settlement would confirm these essentials. But its evolving agenda for the peace conference went considerably further. It has often been asserted that British policy after the Great War reverted to the traditional strategy of promoting a largely self-regulating "balance of power" in Europe and a peace of limited liabilities to concentrate on imperial consoli- dation and the reinvigoration of Britain's financial and economic power.[4] Yet this is misleading. What came to characterise British pursuits under Lloyd George was not the revival of balance-of-power precepts but rather a

---

[2] See Lloyd George speech, 12 September 1918, *The Times*, 13 September 1918; Lloyd George address, 29 July 1917, *New York Times*, 30 June 1917.

[3] Lloyd George, Fontainebleau Memorandum, 22 March 1919, in Lloyd George (1938), I, pp. 403–16.

[4] See Stevenson (1988), pp. 247–8; Keylor (2011), pp. 83–4; MacMillan (2002), pp. 42–4. For the imperial dimension, see the nuanced analysis in Darwin (2009), pp. 358–64.

significant reorientation. It centred on the attempt to draw lessons from the catastrophe of the war and create a different, essentially transatlantic yet still markedly hierarchical international system, which over time was to foster a new, more legitimate international equilibrium. And, in crucial aspects, it was driven by conscious efforts to build on the precedent of British policy at the Congress of Vienna and to renovate it to the meet requirements of the long twentieth century.

One of the most salient consequences Lloyd George had drawn from the war was that it had become imperative to find new ways to build a system that pre-empted another catastrophe of its kind – and thus to avoid another immensely costly intervention like that of 1914. Not only seasoned policy-makers in the Foreign Office like Eyre Crowe but also the prime minister and protagonists like Cecil recognised the necessity to pay attention to balance-of-power concerns. And they concluded that it would be in Britain's interest to try to recalibrate the distribution of power and influence in and beyond Europe after a war that had so radically recast the geopolitical map. In particular, they deemed it essential to reduce Germany's military power to a minimum and to constrain it in the longer term. Yet they also sought to prevent what they regarded as an unsustainable and potentially destabilising French predominance in continental Europe.[5]

More significant, however, was that neither Lloyd George nor his key advisers intended to pursue these aims by resorting to old-style balance-of-power *policies*. Rather, the policies they had begun to develop were based on the premise that neither Britain nor the world could afford to go back to the conflict-prone politics that had dominated before the war. Yet nor did they assume that a revolutionary transformation along Wilsonian lines was either possible or desirable. Like a majority in the War Cabinet, Lloyd George had by no means simply accepted that Wilson's peace programme would set the parameters for the peace negotiations. He continued to view the American president's aspirations as both too vague and too radical – or even as danger-ous. This notably applied to the latter's universal rhetoric of self-determination and, fundamentally, to the idea of a negotiated peace with Germany. Nor did the British premier ever believe that a League of Nations represented the decisive answer to the massive challenges the war had left behind. He would never espouse the conception of a powerful "internationalist" League that he associated with Wilson's plans and the demands of more radical pro-League associations in Britain – rejecting any steps towards organisation that would require him to accept significant infringements of national and imperial sovereignty *and* prerogatives.[6]

---

[5] See Crowe memorandum, 7 December 1918, FO 371/3451.
[6] Lloyd George statements, Imperial War Cabinet, 24 and 30 December 1918, CAB 23/42.

Rather, Lloyd George sought to play a, if not *the* leading role in negotiating peace terms and laying the groundwork for a postwar order that fostered a different kind of equilibrium in the Euro-Atlantic sphere, and the world – an equilibrium of security, status, rights and the satisfaction of "legitimate" claims and interests, chiefly but not only between the principal powers. And he came to act on the premise that this – rather than aloofness or the pursuit of an elusive "balance of power" – would be the best way to safeguard Britain's security and its vital interests as a global imperial power.[7]

In the peace order Lloyd George came to envisage, the integrity and security of France – as well as of Belgium and the Netherlands – would have to be assured; yet what had to be moderated were those French territorial and security aims that he deemed excessive and counterproductive because they would unnecessarily humiliate the beaten enemy, provoke German *revanchism* and thus threaten to create seedbeds of future conflict. At the same time, he insisted that Germany ought to retain its integrity as a *European* power. And he argued that it lay in Britain's interests to promote, in the longer run, its stabilisation not only as an indispensable trading partner but also as a functioning republic – and thus to forestall a victory of Bolshevism or a resurgence of militarist-authoritarian "Prussianism". Yet a core premise of Lloyd George's policy was that the vanquished power first had to be chastised and deterred from ever challenging the international order again. Fundamentally, he reckoned that German postwar elites, and the German people, had to recognise that as a consequence of their defeat their country had lost the claim to be a world power with colonial and naval aspirations.

On these premises the British premier sought to pave the way for Germany's *eventual* rehabilitation and integration into the postwar order. Crucially, however, his core axiom remained that a "just" *and* chastening peace had to be imposed on the key enemy power of the Great War.[8] Backed by a majority in the Imperial War Cabinet, Lloyd George thus envisioned a peacemaking process in which the terms and rules would be set through negotiations and strategic bargains between the principal victors. They were not to be negotiated with German plenipotentiaries – and whether they represented a legitimate republican government was ultimately of little consequence.[9] In his view, the new German leaders and the wider German public had to prove not only their commitment to democratic reforms; they also, and more importantly, had to prove that they would accept the terms of the victors and ultimately, as the price of defeat, the abandonment of previous world-power aspirations. In this sense, Lloyd George and his closest advisers

---

[7] For a different interpretation see Fry (2011), pp. 68–74.

[8] Lloyd George speech, 12 September 1918, *The Times*, 13 September 1918.

[9] For Lloyd George's underlying assumptions, see his statements in the Imperial War Cabinet Meeting 32, 14 August 1918, CAB 23/7, and the meeting at Danny, 13 October 1918, CAB 24/66.

advanced their own, sterner rationales for putting postwar Germany on probation.[10] More generally, their search for a new equilibrium was by no means irreconcilable with the hard-fisted pursuit of what they regarded as essential British interests. In particular, they were determined to make a defeated power whose old elites in their judgement had caused the catastrophe of 1914 pay for the cost of the war.

By contrast, the British premier was in favour of inviting Russian representatives to the peace conference and giving them a voice in the proceedings. He argued that the victors could not ignore the concerns and interests of a "great people". Crucially, he also favoured including representatives of the Bolshevik regime, and thus recognising what he called Russia's "*de facto* Government", though it did not represent the Russian people.[11] While future relations with the Bolsheviks remained uncertain, concerns over the future international equilibrium also came to have a dominant impact on British approaches to the reorganisation of Central and Eastern Europe. What gained prominence here, notably among the relevant experts in the Foreign Office, was the idea that peacemaking efforts should focus on an "equitable" application of the principle of self-determination in balancing the claims of those who now aspired to nation-states with the concerns of the vanquished powers. Ultimately, however, different political rationales came to prevail. Lloyd George's principal concern became to avoid outcomes that placed sizeable German minorities under foreign – especially Polish – rule, provoked future German irredentism and thus, in his eyes, would make it extremely challenging to stabilise the postwar order.[12]

One core assumption of Lloyd George's essentially evolutionary approach to postwar order should be highlighted in particular. It was the assumption that while it would be essential to lay the groundwork and set the basic rules for a new order at the peace conference, it could only be consolidated through *a longer-term* process. This made the pursuit of what emerged as one of most significant objectives of British peace policy all the more crucial, namely to create a renovated international concert, which included the United States, as the key mechanism of a reformed Euro-Atlantic system – and global politics. Building on ideas that he had begun to develop during the war, and drawing on the recommendations of his key confidants Hankey and Kerr, Lloyd George came to envision this concert, not as a system of strict supranational regulations and legalistic procedures, but essentially as a more flexible mechanism of international politics that, essentially, was to permit the political leaders of the

---

[10] See Lloyd George speech, 12 September 1918, *The Times*, 13 September 1918.

[11] See Cabinet deliberations, Imperial War Cabinet 48, 31 December 1918, CAB 23/42; Lloyd George statement, Council of Ten, 12 January 1919, *FRUS-PPC*, III, p. 491; MacMillan (2002), pp. 68–9.

[12] See Headlam-Morley memorandum, 15 November 1918, FO 371/4353/f23/PC55; Lloyd George statement, 27 March 1919, *FRUS-PPC*, IV, pp. 415–17.

great powers to consult and cooperate to prevent the escalation of crises, settle international conflicts and oversee the longer-term evolution and peaceful adjustment of international order.[13] The emphasis thus lay on British political and diplomatic engagement within the envisaged concert system. This also was to allow the British government to avoid other, more traditional commitments in continental Europe, notably the conversion of the wartime *Entente* into a long-term postwar alliance with France to keep Germany in check. After the end of the war, only a small number of strategists in the Foreign Office, and notably Eyre Crowe, recommended making a clear commitment of this kind to the Clemenceau government, not least to restrain French policy.[14]

At a deeper level, what thus came to inform British aspirations was the notion of drawing on the precedent of the Vienna settlement of 1815 and the nineteenth century's Concert of Europe to foster an expanded concert system for the tewntieth century. By the end of 1918, the British premier had adopted Cecil's rationale that the League could serve as a useful institutional platform for a new concert – if it could be set up on the basis of British plans.[15] It is important to note that while both Cecil and Smuts proposed more ambitious and *essentially integrative* designs, Lloyd George's policy came to centre on the idea of first establishing the *transatlantic nucleus* of such a "concert within the League" – a nucleus formed by Britain, France and the United States.[16] But the underlying rationale was to integrate Germany in the foreseeable future – though only after it had accepted the victors' terms and begun to "rehabilitate" itself. Cecil even recommended that in order to make the new system effective, the vanquished power should be included from the outset.[17]

Crucially, the pursuit of a new international concert was thus closely connected with the culmination of another significant reorientation of British policy that had begun in 1914 and gained momentum since 1917. In short, Lloyd George and a majority in the Imperial War Cabinet came to favour the *qualified* pursuit of a strategic partnership with the United States. Thus, they also came to espouse a basically cooperative strategy vis-à-vis Wilson – though, as the prime minister had put it earlier, "with every caveat in place" – that at the same time sought to redirect the American president's aspirations in accordance with what

---

[13] See Lloyd George speech, 12 September 1918, *The Times*, 13 September 1918; Hankey memorandum, 16 January 1918, CAB 24/39; Kendle (1975), pp. 250–3.

[14] Crowe memorandum, 7 December 1918, FO 371/3451; Crowe minute, 30 December 1918, FO 371/4353/f29/PC152.

[15] Lloyd George statement, 16 November 1918, Lloyd George Papers, F 237; Imperial War Cabinet minutes, 24 and 30 December 1918, CAB 23/42; Hankey memorandum, 16 January 1918, CAB 24/39

[16] See "Cecil Plan", 14 December 1918, in Miller (1928), II, pp. 61–4; Smuts (1918), pp. 5–9, 26–40, 41–63; Smuts, "The League of Nations: A Programme for the Peace Conference", 16 December 1918, CAB 29/2; Hankey memorandum, 16 January 1918, CAB 24/39.

[17] Cecil memorandum, 17 December 1918, CAB 23/42; Cecil (1941), pp. 60–2.

they defined as core British interests. Not least in order to reinforce this partnership, and the British Empire's bargaining position vis-à-vis Wilson, they reaccentuated official support for a League of Nations.[18]

This less than radical but nonetheless profound change was based on the premise that despite ideological differences and unresolved bilateral problems – notably British war debts and the future of Anglo-American naval relations – Britain and its Empire had a fundamental interest in sharing hegemonic responsibilities and burdens with the United States, above all in Europe yet also beyond the European continent. What thus also gained ground was the aspiration, most forcefully advanced by Smuts, to promote hegemonic cooperation between the "two great democratic Commonwealths" – and contain the challenge of Wilson's self-determination rhetoric – by engaging the American president in an ambitious civilising mission. On a global scale, this mission was to be pursued through the League of Nations; in particular, it was to bring new order to the strategically vital regions in the Middle East that had formerly been under Ottoman rule.[19]

Unquestionably, the reconfigured international order that Lloyd George, his advisers and the key members in the Imperial War Cabinet envisaged in broad outlines was still conceived as a distinctly hierarchical system of states – rather than a radically new, egalitarian world order. Within it, the integrity and political independence of smaller states were to be safeguarded more effectively through the League and a new intergovernmental concert, yet not though ironclad guarantees and compulsory sanctions. But Britain and a few other "advanced" great powers clearly were to retain pre-eminent roles and prerogatives. Beyond Europe, the new order was conceived as an even more hierarchical system that, crucially, was to buttress the consolidation – and even expansion – of the most advanced empires, above all the British Empire, which – as noted – Lloyd George praised as "league of nations" in its own right.[20]

II. A Moderate Peace or a Punitive Peace of the Victors? Essential Domestic and Political Parameters of the British Approach to Peacemaking

Important parameters for British peace policy were set by the way in which the wartime leader Lloyd George would seek – and gain – a new and broader

[18] Imperial War Cabinet deliberations, 30 and 31 December 1918, CAB 23/42; Lloyd George statement, Imperial War Cabinet, 11 October 1918, CAB 23/8; Imperial War Cabinet, 5 November 1918, CAB 23/8.
[19] Smuts memorandum, 3 December 1918, Cabinet Paper P. 39, CAB 29/2; Smuts, "The League of Nations: A Programme for the Peace Conference", 16 December 1918, CAB 29/2; Smuts (1918).
[20] Lloyd George speech, 12 September 1918, in The Times, 13 September 1918.

domestic mandate as "peace leader" during the campaign for what became known as the "Khaki Elections" of December 1918. Essentially, the British premier would shift from championing a moderate peace settlement to calling for a "sternly just" peace of deterrence, which clearly clashed with core premises of Wilson's programme. Though he insisted that he would not seek a settlement of revenge and retribution, the prime minister came to commit himself to peace terms that left little scope for constructive negotiations with Germany, especially, but not only, because he vowed to make the defeated enemy pay for the "entire cost" of the war. Overall, Lloyd George's rhetoric did little to manage public expectations. Rather, his quest to fortify his basis of domestic legitimacy for the forthcoming peace conference contributed decisively to heightening further what were already dangerously high expectations in many quarters. He thus made the challenge of delivering a peace that would bring due punishment *and* compensation for the sacrifices of the war even more daunting.

When the armistice was concluded Lloyd George had declared that its terms rightly amounted to a "stern reckoning" for a German nation that had caused the war. But he had also stressed that it was now incumbent on the victors to exhibit leniency and fairness in settling the terms of the eventual peace and to refrain from provoking a German thirst for revenge.[21] In the early stages of the election campaign, the prime minister then indeed presented himself as a neo-Gladstonian champion of a moderate and "just" peace and – particularly to appeal to Liberal and Labour audiences – he emphasised another guiding theme: his support for a "real" League of Nations. To Labour delegates he proclaimed that he favoured a peace settlement in the spirit of the Fourteen Points – except for the "freedom of the seas" – and that he had sympathies for Labour's demand to found a "League of Free Peoples". To Liberal audiences he insisted that the time had come to draw lessons from the pre-history of the war. He promised that he would not repeat the mistakes that Bismarckian Germany had made in forcing the "settlement of 1870" on France, which had been an "outrage upon the principles of liberty and fair play". This time, he underscored, the victors had to treat the defeated power with moderation and abstain from inflicting a peace marked by a spirit of revenge and greed.[22]

At this point, Lloyd George clearly committed himself to the creation of "real League of Nations", though he revealingly defined it as "a real concert of Europe instead of a sham one". He argued that the main purpose of such a League, which would be assisted by a comparatively disinterested United

---

[21] Imperial War Cabinet minutes, 10 and 11 November 1918, CAB 23/8 and 14.
[22] Lloyd George statements, Labour delegation meeting, 6 November 1918, Lloyd George Papers, F217/6; Lloyd George comments, meeting with Liberals, 12 November 1918, Lord Lothian Papers.

States, was to safeguard European stability and the integrity and security of the successor states of the Russian and Austro-Hungarian empires. But he also highlighted that it would be crucial to protect Europe and the world from renewed crises such as those that had escalated in the Balkans and produced such disastrous consequences in 1914. While never abandoning his more conservative conception, the prime minister would present himself as a staunch advocate of the League throughout the campaign, vowing to go to Paris to make it "a reality" and calling it "more necessary than ever" in the face of Europe's postwar turbulences.[23] The election manifesto of pro-coalition Liberals and Conservatives contained the pledge to "promote the formation of a League of Nations" to "avert a repetition of the horrors of war" and "ensure society against the calamitous results of militarism". And, though with caveats, even Bonar Law and prominent Unionists thus publicly endorsed the cause of the League. In the War Cabinet, the prime minister underscored that any government that did not take up this cause in earnest would "be sternly dealt with by the people", implying that he had to reckon with Wilson's popular appeal in Britain, which extended beyond Liberal and Labour circles.[24]

Lloyd George thus responded to a significantly altered domestic climate. What by this time had become a veritable British pro-League movement was now spearheaded by the League of Nations Union. The LNU mounted a wide-ranging campaign, appealing to all parties to adopt its programme for a League of free – democratic – peoples and to join forces with Wilson. It renewed the call for a powerful "world organization" that obliged its members to use "methods of peaceful settlement" to resolve international disputes, instituted a "permanent Council" as well as a "Supreme Court" to "maintain international order", "guarantee the freedom of nations", act as "guardian of uncivilized races" and "thus finally liberate mankind from the curse of war". And it demanded that the new organisation should admit "all peoples able and willing to give effective guarantees of their loyal intention to observe its covenants".[25]

In the changing spectrum of British party politics the most fervent calls for an authoritative League unsurprisingly came from Asquith's Liberal Party and from Labour. In presenting the election manifesto of anti-coalition Liberals, Asquith proclaimed that a cardinal purpose of the peace, for which the "Allies" had fought the war, was "bringing into being of a League of nations" that was to "secure the peace of the world and the reign of international justice and humanity".[26] George Barnes and the leadership of the Labour Party still

[23] Lloyd George comments, meeting with Liberals, 12 November 1918, Lord Lothian Papers.
[24] Coalition Election Manifesto, November 1918, in Dale (1999), p. 20; War Cabinet, 26 November 1918, CAB 23/42.
[25] LNU programme, November 1918, in Winkler (1952), p. 77.
[26] Asquith address, November 1918, in Dale (2000), p. 34.

championed their own version of a "League of Free Peoples" that comprised not just the western democracies but also Germany and thus fostered a "peace of reconciliation" between the enemies of the Great War.[27]

Prior to the end of the war, when he had still been a member of the War Cabinet, Barnes had urged the prime minister to take a clear stand on the League. And he had publicly championed a transformative "League to Abolish War" that would guarantee the independence and integrity of its members, dispose of effective military sanction powers and require also the great powers to relinquish core attributes of sovereignty, not least by contributing to an international army that was to execute its sanctions. While also demanding that the new organisation should implement far-reaching disarmament schemes, Barnes highlighted one aspect that had only received marginal attention in other British League plans: the need to make provisions for an admission of the enemy powers. More generally, the Labour party remained committed to the concept of a universal and essentially inclusive League and the idea of a conciliatory peace that strengthened social democratic forces in Germany.[28] Yet such conceptions would only gain decisive influence in the aftermath of the Paris Peace Conference. In the winter of 1918–19, leading Labour politicians maintained the hope that Wilson could play a key role in realising their aspirations. Shortly after the American president's visit to Britain in December, Labour and the Trade Union Council would sponsor demonstrations on behalf of his League programme and a resolution calling for a "Wilson peace".[29]

Lloyd George continued to pay heed to the currents of Liberal and Labour internationalism. Yet as the campaign reached its final stages, different themes came to dominate his agenda. Responding to what he perceived as prevailing tides of opinion, he not only fanned the flames of an already widespread anti-German sentiment. He also advanced arguments on behalf of a different kind of peace – and made commitments he would then find very hard to fulfil at the peace conference. Speaking in Newcastle on 29 November, the prime minister pledged that he would pursue a "sternly just" and "relentlessly just" peace settlement, declaring that its higher purpose had to be to deter German leaders, and the German people, from ever repeating the "crime" of 1914. Crucially, however, he infamously pledged – in Bristol on 11 December – that he would compel the vanquished to pay to

---

[27] Labour election manifesto, 1918, Labour Party, *Report of the Nineteenth Annual Conference* (Southport, 1919), p. 185.

[28] Barnes lecture, 5 August 1918, Cabinet Paper G.T. 5364, CAB 24/60; Barnes, War Cabinet 481, 2 October 1918, CAB 23/8.

[29] Brand (1964), pp. 244–5; Walworth (1977), p. 153.

the utmost of its capacity – to the "last penny" – to indemnify Britain and the Empire for "the whole cost of the war".[30]

As in France, the inner-British and inner-imperial debates over "reparations", which came to dominate the wider discussion about the peace settlement, not only had financial and economic but also essential political and psychological dimensions. Lloyd George responded, and had to be responsive to, widespread demands for material – and immaterial – compensations for the sacrifices that had been made during a war that British propaganda had presented as a defensive struggle against the onslaught of Teutonic militarism. Indeed, the Great War had proved unexpectedly and unprecedentedly costly, not only in financial terms but also and above all in terms of its human toll, resulting in the death of roughly 900,000 soldiers and more than 3 million casualties within the Empire.[31] Lloyd George, who had gained authority as the Empire's charismatic wartime leader, was keenly aware of the magnitude of such compensation demands and the political pressures they created. Yet he did not consider it politic at this stage to channel or moderate them.

Rather, the prime minister stressed that Britain and its Dominions had "an absolute right" to demand full reparations for the toll the war had taken. At the same time, he suggested that this could be arranged without damaging Britain's trade interests and prospects of economic recovery: the economy of what could again become Britain's most important trading partner would not be ruined; yet nor would Germany be allowed to pay its obligations by furthering its exports through "dumping methods". The core argument he now advanced was that he had to consider the interests of the people "upon whom Germany has made war", not those of the German people "who have been guilty of this crime against humanity". Lloyd George thus presented a clear *moral* claim, not only against the old elites of "Prussian" militarists but against the entire German population who, as the guilty party, had to be held accountable for the war's consequences. Parallel, he renewed his – highly popular – demand that the Kaiser should be put on trial for high treason against humanity. The Conservative leader Bonar Law used the same arguments to justify the call for punitive indemnities and a punitive peace – and, politically, he would reap even more benefits from this rhetoric.[32]

The Khaki Elections of 14 December 1918 brought a landslide victory for Lloyd George and his coalition, which was confirmed two weeks later.

---

[30] Lloyd George speech, Newcastle, 29 November 1918; Lloyd George speech, Bristol, 11 December 1918, Lloyd George Papers, F246, F326.

[31] For new and comparative perspectives, see the contributions to Winter (2014), vols. II and III.

[32] Lloyd George speech, 29 November 1918; Lloyd George speech, 11 December 1918, Lloyd George Papers, F246, F326. Bonar Law speech, 12 December 1918. See Fry (2011), pp. 179–85; Newton (1997), pp. 291–5.

They indeed provided him with a far stronger domestic mandate at the peace conference than Wilson had, which further accentuated the prime minister's confidence that he, not the American president, would be poised to act as the decisive arbiter of peace at Versailles. In fact, however, the elections – which decimated the Asquith Liberals and made Labour the main opposition party – were mainly a triumph of the largest coalition partner, the conservative Unionists. During the peace negotiations Lloyd George would have to deal with conservative backbenchers who vowed that they would hold him to his election promises, particularly regarding indemnities. He would still have considerable room to manoeuvre; and he would invoke his domestic concerns at decisive stages of the negotiations to minimise concessions to Wilson and Clemenceau. But the new domestic-political constellation in Britain, and the scale of the expectations Lloyd George had raised, would significantly complicate the pursuit of an actual policy of "moderation" in Paris – not only with respect to the touchstone issue of reparations. And, significantly, the outcome of the election reinforced Lloyd George's rationale that the peace had to be forced on Germany, for it signalled that such a course was supported by a majority of political parties and British voters.

III.   Contradictory Objectives and Unprecedented Limitations British Reparations Policy, Debts and the Search for an Economic Peace "Fit for Heroes"

The inner-governmental deliberations over British reparations policy that took place in the shadow of the election campaign revealed a clash between markedly different approaches and resulted in a distinctly ambivalent strategy. The Treasury concentrated on crafting an indemnity policy within the parameters of Wilson's Fourteen Points and the essentials of the pre-armistice agreements. Keynes, who became the main architect of Treasury policies, had recommended a moderate sum of "reparation" for direct damages to civilian life and property, proposing a preliminary claim of £4,000 million. The young expert expected Germany to be able to pay a total of ca. £3,000 million. Yet he stipulated that a payment of £2,000 million, to be made in annuities over a number of years, would constitute "a very satisfactory achievement" under the circumstances – and the "limit" of what Britain could "safely exact, having regard to our own selfish interests only".

Keynes emphasised that Allied claims had to consider Germany's capacity to pay. He warned against imposing excessive liabilities that would either crush the defeated power's productive capacity or force it to strive for an export surplus that would harm British commerce and constitute a "drastic disturbance" of world trade. What Keynes desired to promote was the stabilisation of a German republic that would remain crucial power in the postwar economic order. He argued that a policy that furthered "starvation" and "general anarchy" in Germany would only result in crippling its ability to pay reparations, noting that, "an indemnity so large as to leave the German population without hope" was "liable to defeat itself". The underlying rationale Keynes thus proposed was that if Germany was "to be 'milked', she must not first of all be ruined".[33]

Lloyd George shared the Treasury's concerns to some extent, and he was notably concerned about Germany's actual capacity to pay. But under his leadership the War Cabinet came to pursue a different course. It set up a committee on indemnity, chaired by the Australian premier Billy Hughes, one of the most vociferous advocates of a harsh peace, and the equally unrelenting Lord Cunliffe. The committee's final report on 2 December recommended that the government should demand a far more enormous sum from Germany – a total of £24,000 million or 220 billion Goldmarks (which roughly amounted to five times the pre-war German annual national income). The Cabinet rejected this recommendation as a "wild and fantastic chimera". But the prime minister drew precisely on this report to make his far-reaching election pledges. His government would eventually endorse the formula that Britain should "endeavour to secure from Germany the greatest possible indemnity she can pay consistently with the economic well-being of the British Empire and the peace of the world, and without involving an army of occupation in Germany for its collection".[34]

Although he deemed their proposals excessive, Lloyd George actually chose to make Hughes and Cunliffe the main British representatives on the Reparations Commission that would be created at Versailles. He thus essentially barred Treasury experts from the formal reparations negotiations and put his political weight behind a punitive rather than a more moderate approach. This would set essential parameters for British pursuits in 1919 and clash with the prime minister's loftier *political* rationales for a "just" peace. And, crucially, it contributed decisively not only to making a "rational" reparations settlement exceedingly difficult but also to preventing advances towards a negotiated peace of accommodation with Germany.

Yet it should be clear by now that the problematic reparations policy of Lloyd George and his government was also significantly influenced by another factor: Britain's unprecedented indebtedness to the United States. Following his first discussions with Wilson in late December, Lloyd George stressed that

[33] Treasury memorandum, 26 November 1918, Keynes (1978), XVI, pp. 344–82. See also Keynes memorandum, *ibid.*, p. 341; Keynes memorandum, November 1918, Keynes Papers, PT/7/2. British war costs were calculated to total £8,000 million (while the Treasury estimated £6,660 million). See Skidelsky (2005), pp. 217–19.
[34] Cabinet Committee on Indemnity report, 2 December 1918, paper P. 38, CAB 29/2; Minutes of the Imperial War Cabinet, 24 December 1918, CAB23/42; Bunselmeyer (1968), p. 103; Skidelsky (1983), p. 356.

it was particularly on the "question of indemnity" that Britain could expect "really hard resistance" from the American president.[35] Not only the prime minister but also the leading Treasury experts were acutely aware of how substantially Britain's position as a financial power had changed since 1916. Of critical significance was that while it remained a key creditor to its European wartime allies, above all France and Russia, it had become, for the first time in its history, a major debtor by the end of the war. In Keynes' calculation it owed far more to the United States than it could claim from its own debtors, roughly £4,000 million.

In November, Keynes had proposed a radical "solution", a scheme that not only tackled the war-debt problem but also was to permit a moderate reparations settlement and, crucially, bold advances towards meeting what he saw as the pre-eminent challenges: Europe's "reconstruction" and the resumption and revital-isation of trade. Yet Keynes' comprehensive plan hinged on the cooperation – and financial concessions – of the newly predominant American creditor power. In short, he recommended that the British government should suggest at the opening of the peace conference that "all debts incurred between the Governments of the Associated Powers" prior to 1 January 1919 "should be cancelled". This was to rid the world of "a net-work of heavy tribute" that was "a menace to financial stability everywhere". Under his scheme Britain would "forgo the whole of her share", yet the American government would be asked "to make a somewhat larger nominal sacrifice". Reasoning in financial and moral terms, Keynes argued that unless such a general debt-cancellation agreement could be made the "new world" would hence not only "own the principal undeveloped resources of the world" but also "draw tribute from the greater part of Europe". And he stressed that Germany would be the only power "free" from the American "financial grip". In his judgement, the United States' "financial contribution to the war" had not been sufficient to "justify such a state of affairs", and profound American interference with the Allied Powers' financial-cum-political sovereignty, which he deemed "injurious to the future of Europe".[36]

In the War Cabinet, Winston Churchill, now secretary of state for war, proposed a rougher bargaining approach. According to him, the only "point of substance" Britain ought to pursue vis-à-vis the American government during the peace negotiations was to induce it "to let us off the debt we had contracted ... on the understanding that we should do the same to the Allies", above all France. Churchill proposed if this could be ensured the British government should in return support Wilson's position on "the matter of indemnity".[37] The British delegation would indeed pursue initiatives along the lines Keynes and Churchill suggested. Yet all efforts in this direction would

---

[35] Imperial War Cabinet minutes, 31 December 1918, CAB23/42.
[36] Keynes memorandum, November 1918, Keynes Papers, PT/7/2.
[37] Imperial War Cabinet minutes, 30 December, CAB 23/42.

meet with the uncompromising opposition of Wilson and the US Treasury and ultimately remain futile.

The issues of reparations and British debts to the United States also had a critical bearing on the overriding aims of Lloyd George's domestic postwar agenda: to ensure Britain's financial and economic revitalisation and to pursue far-reaching reforms. Essentially, he needed resources to fulfil his election promise to make Britain a "fit country for heroes to live in".[38] Having created a Ministry for Reconstruction under the Liberal Christopher Addison in August 1917, the prime minister was resolved to use state power to pursue an unprecedented programme of reconstruction, housing and social reform as well as, notably, measures to aid the re-integration of demobilised soldiers. And he pledged to achieve this without raising taxes. Yet he had to cope with the onerous financial consequences of the war. The British government not only faced rapidly growing budget deficits but also had to service a national debt that exceeded £7.4 billion. At the same time, the coalition government had pledged to convert the wartime economy into a newly competitive peacetime economy to reassert Britain's leading position in a recast global economy in which the United States had surpassed the former financial centre and "workshop of the world". And Lloyd George realised that Britain's revitalisation was critically dependent on the recovery of Europe, and that this recovery would be jeopardised by imposing peace terms that severely disrupted the German economy.[39]

Prior to the armistice, Keynes had pointed to the "imperious claims" that postwar "reconstruction" and "the establishment of a secure and stable international order" imposed. In his analysis, Europe's reconstruction and the creation of such an order were inconceivable without integrating Germany and making sure that its economic power remained intact. Keynes recommended that British policy should be "directed to facilitate as early a return as possible to normal trade conditions" after the war. He also emphasised, however, that following a "definitive peace" it was imperative to create a "nucleus of international organisation" in the financial and economic sphere, which could then be extended to include the enemy powers, potentially under the auspices of the League. Keynes in fact envisaged an "international machinery" that anticipated the ideas that would later underpin the Bretton Woods system, notably that of a "world bank" whose main purpose was to be to grant credits to countries in need. And he proposed that for a transition period a "closer international control" of the distribution of "certain essential commodities" should be established, including wheat, meat and oil-seeds.

Keynes insisted that in all of these respects – and in order to create a new "international order" that would actually foster the "reconstruction" of

---

[38] Lloyd George speech, Wolverhampton, 23 November 1918, *The Times*, 25 November 1918.

[39] Imperial War Cabinet minutes, 24 December 1918, CAB 23/42.

Europe – finding ways of engaging the American government was the crucial challenge for British policy. He noted that in view of the prevailing American tendency to "refuse to enter into arrangements of a formal character" the "difficult diplomatic task" was to "secure that close co-operation between the British Empire and the United States which must form the effective power in reconstruction policies". To this end, he suggested a policy of small, pragmatic steps first focused on providing immediate postwar relief in Europe rather than the pursuit of a theoretical grand design.[40]

Following the armistice, the British government did not espouse ambitious plans for the establishment of international "machineries" to organise lending, reconstruction and the controlled distribution of vital commodities. And British policymakers found it very difficult to implement a "diplomatic" strategy of pragmatic cooperation with the United States in these areas. But those who formulated the essentials of Britain's economic peace policy, above all on the Board of Trade, took important steps in this direction by proposing a significant departure from its previous agenda of economic war aims. Following their recommendations, the Lloyd George government distanced itself from the more far-reaching – and essentially discriminatory – Anglo-French programme that had been agreed at the Paris Conference of 1916. It refused to commit Britain to Clémentel's plans for an inter-allied economic union after the war and their wider aim of establishing a "regulated" economic regime geared towards constraining German economic power. Not least, it was acutely aware of the pronounced American hostility to such plans.

At the same time, the Lloyd George government confirmed that it would maintain some preferential tariffs within the Empire that the War Cabinet had approved in the summer of 1918 – though official support for a protectionist "imperial preference" system would wane rapidly thereafter.[41] What proved more significant, however, was that it reaccentuated more long-standing traditions of British trade policy – and gravitated towards American preferences. It signalled that it would favour the creation of a postwar economic order premised on the most-favoured-nation principle and the resumption of "normal", unhampered trade at a relatively early stage. All of this corresponded with the Board of Trade's directives. The Board's experts merely envisaged *temporary* restrictions, proposing that the Allied Powers should be given a "head start" during an initial phase of reconstruction by withholding

---

[40] Keynes memorandum, 22 October 1918, Keynes Papers PT/2/3. See also Keynes memorandum, November 1918, *ibid.*, PT/7/2.

[41] See Drummond (1972), pp. 17 ff., 143 ff.; Boyce (2009), pp. 3–4.

most-favoured-nation status from Germany for five years or until the defeated power was admitted to the League.[42]

This would become the underlying rationale of British policy at Versailles. Essentially, the British delegation thus came to pursue maxims that the Board of Trade had already formulated as early as 1916. Then, it had concluded that to "impose terms of peace" on the defeated enemy that would lead to a "permanent crushing of the commercial and industrial power of Germany" would not only harm Britain's economic interests but also "outrage the moral sense of the civilised world".[43] Overall, in contrast to the alignment of interests in the explosive reparations dispute, the evolving – and readjusted – British approaches to "economic peacemaking" after the Great War were far more compatible with American than with French essentials when it came to the basic rules of the future economic order, the reconstruction of Europe and, notably, Germany's eventual re-integration into the world economy.

Financial, economic and wider domestic concerns thus had a marked impact on the reorientation of British peace policies in the aftermath of the armistice. But how precisely did Lloyd George and other protagonists intend to establish a new, more sustainable order? What core lessons had they drawn from the Great War and its origins? How far had underlying assumptions really begun to change as a consequence of the cataclysm? And on what premises did British policymakers eventually decide to pursue an essentially Atlantic orientation and a strategic partnership with Wilson and the United States?

IV. Towards a *Pax Anglo-Americana* on British Terms? A Formative Strategic Debate – and the Reorientation of British Peace Policies

The essentials of Britain's peace policy and strategy vis-à-vis the United States were only worked out after a far-ranging strategic debate, which had begun during the election campaign but reached its decisive stage in its aftermath. The inner-governmental and inner-imperial policy- and decision-making processes differed significantly from those of Britain's allies. Lloyd George and his closest advisers had to weigh an array of different recommendations, which came not only from the – still rather marginal – Foreign Office but also from an array of special committees. But the basic guidelines for the peace conference would ultimately be hammered out – under the prime minister's lead – in the Imperial War Cabinet in late December 1918. In contrast to Wilson, the key members of this Cabinet could draw on extensive preparatory planning that had been carried on during the war. Yet their deliberations

---

[42] Board of Trade memorandum, November 1918, revised in December 1918, CAB 29/1/P-33. See Glaser (1998), pp. 375–6.

[43] Board of Trade report, 27 October 1916, CAB 29/1/P-12; Percy note, December 1918(?), FO 371/4353. See Goldstein (1991), pp. 19306.

represented the culmination of what had gained momentum after the armistice: the most formative discussions yet about the fundamental aims and strategies Britain and the Dominions should pursue not just at the peace conference but, more broadly, in the new world the Great War had left in its wake. They yielded three alternative and indeed distinctive approaches, which were also informed by distinctive assumptions, lessons and outlooks on the challenges and possibilities it had created.

The proponents of a newly prominent and eventually dominant Atlantic orientation – notably Cecil, Smuts and Foreign Secretary Arthur Balfour – argued that it was in Britain's, and the Empire's, interest to opt for an unprecedented strategy: to give priority to collaboration with the Wilson administration and to envisage creating a new order, and pacifying Europe, on the basis of a kind of *Pax Anglo-Americana*. To this end, particularly Cecil and Smuts urged Lloyd George to make a clearer commitment to the creation of a League of Nations. But they also recommended using Britain's influence to amend Wilson's general designs and to pave the way for a more workable international organisation, essentially one that served to institutionalise a new concert of great powers.[44]

Those who advocated a different, more unequivocally neo-imperial orientation – notably Milner, who in December became Colonial Secretary, and the protagonists of the *Round Table* group, including Lloyd George's closest adviser Kerr – also sought to involve the United States – in a "global civilising mission". Yet they were profoundly suspicious towards the League project, or even regarded it as harmful to what they regarded as Britain's overriding imperial interests. While their clear emphasis lay on the consolidation, defence *and expansion* of the Empire, they proposed the alternative idea of a considerably looser and distinctly more hierarchical concert system. Within it, led by the British Empire and the United States, the great powers were to resolve conflicts and maintain the peace within a neo-imperial world order. In their view, involving the American government in such a system would also blunt the challenge posed by Wilson's espousal of "self-determination". At the same time, they not only favoured relying on naval superiority for purposes of national and imperial defence but also insisted on maximal aloofness from postwar Europe. They thus rejected any binding commitments and advocated instead the creation of a viable "balance of power", which in their eyes meant the preservation of a relatively strong Germany as a counter-balancing

---

[44] See Balfour to Lloyd George, 29 November 1918, Lloyd George Papers, F/2/4-7; "Cecil Plan", 14 December 1918, in Miller (1928), II, pp. 61–4; Smuts, "The League of Nations", 16 December 1918, CAB 29/2.

European power vis-à-vis France – while they stressed that further German global aspirations had to be permanently denied.[45]

Seeking to expand the Empire's sphere of influence, notably in the Middle East, Conservative imperialists like Curzon and Leopold Amery laid even greater stress on the need for imperial aloofness. Yet they also recommended keeping a distance from Wilson's aspirations. For they ultimately considered a postwar policy that relied on co-operation with the United States and made too many concessions to Wilson's League plans both precarious and potentially dangerous. Amery anticipated a future "world order" in which ever larger Empires and imperial states would prevail and "balance" each other. He thus opposed League schemes that would enshrine the premise of equal rights for smaller states and lambasted Wilson's "facile slogan of self-determination".[46]

Yet there were also still proponents of a third, in different ways more conservative strategy – essentially, a minority of policymakers in the Foreign Office whose most authoritative representative was the relative outsider Eyre Crowe. They concentrated on European rather than imperial concerns and advocated a European rather than transatlantic orientation. Disagreeing with the Atlanticist foreign secretary Balfour, Crowe sought to highlight not only what he saw as the uncertainties and risks inherent in the quest for an Anglo-American partnership, and far-reaching League designs. Yet he also stressed the dangers of imperial detachment from Europe. What he recommended instead, was a renewed emphasis on what he considered essential long-standing traditions: a prudent policy that aimed to negotiate a firm postwar *entente* with France, which he regarded as Britain's de facto most important strategic partner after the war, and to create and control a viable "balance-of-power" system that contained and constrained German power on a European continent whose geopolitical map had radically changed.[47]

It is noteworthy that Crowe's strategic recommendations would hardly have any bearing on British policies at the peace conference. Yet neo-imperial approaches would not dominate either – even though all members of the Imperial War Cabinet of course shared the pre-eminent aim of making a peace that furthered the – expanded – Empire's consolidation and security. Rather, Lloyd George and a majority in the Imperial War Cabinet would ultimately decide to pursue what could be called a circumspect transatlantic approach – and an equally circumspect pro-League policy. The British peacemakers would thus give priority to a strategy whose underlying objective was to moderate

---

[45] Milner committee report, 1917, Lloyd George (1933–36), IV, pp. 1799–1800; Kendle (1975), pp. 250–1.

[46] Curzon statements, Imperial War Cabinet, 24 and 30 December 1918, CAB 23/42; Amery (1953), II, pp. 162–3; Rothwell (1972), pp. 68–75.

[47] Crowe memorandum, 7 December 1918, FO 371/3451; Crowe minute, 30 December 1918, FO 371/4353/f29/PC152. See also Headlam-Morley memorandum, 15 November 1918, FO 371/4353/f23/PC55.

Wilson's progressive agenda and to commit him, and the United States, as far as possible to a postwar order and an Anglo-American "burden-sharing" on British premises.

After the armistice, Cecil had reasserted himself as the most forceful proponent of what in his view was a crucial prerequisite for any advances towards a stable postwar order: the pursuit of the closest possible cooperation with the American president and, ultimately, a *Pax Anglo-Americana* system in which Britain played a commanding role. At the same time, he remained the crucial advocate of a *relatively* strong League of Nations in the government. Cecil still essentially envisaged an inter-governmental institution, at the core a platform for a new concert of the European great powers and the United States – plus Japan – that was modelled on the nineteenth century's Concert of Europe yet would have a sturdier institutional structure and more far-reaching collective responsibilities for peacekeeping and postwar security. In his eyes, a key purpose of the League was to commit the United States to sharing the responsibilities of managing the international system and, above all, consolidating the peace in Europe. At the same time, he argued that British policy-makers could use their influence to refine American League conceptions.

Cecil built on rationales for collaborating with Wilson, whom he essentially considered a "Gladstone liberal", and a new kind of joint hegemony that he had outlined to the War Cabinet in September 1917. His premise was that while the American people were "very largely foreign, both in origin and in mode of thought" their "rulers" were "almost exclusively Anglo-Saxon and share our political ideals". In his judgement, the pre-eminent British task was to play the part of a steering and tutelage power in a partnership with American counterparts who were "entering upon an entirely fresh chapter of their history", for the first time "taking a part in international European affairs" and bound to realise soon "what vast power they have". Essentially, however, more experienced British elites had to ensure that Americans "make use of it rightly" – "in accordance with [British] ideas of right and justice" and vital British interests.[48]

In late November 1918, Cecil assumed the lead in Foreign Office planning for the League, and he would be appointed, with Smuts, as the British representative for League affairs at the peace conference. By mid-December, he submitted the so-called Cecil Plan, which built on the recommendations of the Phillimore report and incorporated conceptual ideas developed in the Foreign Office's Political Intelligence Department, notably by the classical scholar and historian Alfred Zimmern. The League the "Cecil Plan" proposed – in the spirit of a distinctly hierarchical and to some extent paternalistic "internationalism" – was to be established around the "pivot" of a refashioned

[48] Cecil memorandum, 18 September 1917, CAB 24/26/2074.

and regularised concert of the great powers in which representatives of the British Empire and the United States were to play key roles, initially sharing responsibilities with their counterparts from France, Italy and Japan. In private, Cecil maintained a more aspirational impetus. But what he and leading Foreign Office planners proposed was markedly more conservative than what Wilson envisaged, and far from any aspiration to create a "supra-national" organisation that would have placed significant restrictions on great-power sovereignty. Essentially, it was a conscious attempt not only to revive and expand on the rules and practices of the Vienna system but also to draw consequences from its eventual disintegration – and from the fact that by 1914 there had no longer been any effective mechanism to settle disputes between the principal powers and prevent the escalation of regional conflicts into a general war.

The organisation Cecil and his collaborators mapped out was to provide an institutional framework for a more regularised concert system that operated through regular conferences between the contracting powers and in which, crucially, the United States was to be integrated for the first time. It was a system overseen and largely controlled by those who led the great powers. Aided by a permanent secretariat, the heads of state and leading decision-makers, who remained accountable to their national parliaments and publics rather than any higher authority, were to steer the diplomatic processes required to settle disputes, maintain peace and deter aggressors. They would make the key decisions, and their decisions had to be unanimous; smaller states would not exercise "any considerable influence". In the event of a crisis or the threat of war a great power, or any other member of the League, would have the right to demand the convocation of a special conference.[49]

In Cecil's conception, an important purpose of the new organisation would be to protect smaller states like Belgium and the newly created east European states against aggression and to safeguard their rights under international law. But his plan was designed to distance Britain from a League Covenant that would contain explicit guarantees for the territorial integrity and political independence of all member states, which Wilson and many American and British League proponents deemed imperative. Further, in line with prevalent Foreign Office thinking, the "Cecil Plan" did not propose an elaborate system of compulsory arbitration. It rejected clearly defined "*automatic*" sanctions against aggressors. But Cecil himself insisted that the League could only be an effective mechanism of peace and security if all of its member states – yet above all the great powers – committed themselves to taking collective action not merely against any member state but also against states outside the

---

[49] "Cecil Plan", 14 December 1918, in Miller (1928), II, pp. 61–4; Cecil memorandum, 17 December 1918, CAB 23/42; Zimmern, "The League of Nations", Cabinet Paper P. 68, 20 December 1918, CAB 29/2. See Egerton (1978), pp. 95–100.

organisation that threatened peace and did not accept its procedures for peaceful conflict-resolution.[50] And, significantly, Cecil was more unequivocal than any other British policymaker – and Wilson – in demanding that the League had to be established not as a victors' organisation but essentially as an integrative institution. He recommended that the defeated powers, notably Germany and Austria, should be included from the outset. Fundamentally, he sought to integrate a reformed Germany in the recast concert of great powers, and he maintained that the new League system could only operate successfully if this could be achieved.[51]

The other pivotal strategist in the Imperial War Cabinet, Jan Christiaan Smuts, came to advance an even more ambitious design not just for a "Practical" League of Nations but also for an Anglo-American peace. Smuts' core premise was that as the war had ended with the demise of not just the Romanov and Habsburg Empires but also of the German Empire, only three first-rate powers were left that would have a decisive say over the postwar order: the British Empire, France, and the United States. In his assessment, the Imperial War Cabinet thus faced a strategic choice with far-reaching implications. Smuts argued that it would be ill-advised to return to traditional balance-of-power policies and focus on a perpetuation of the *Entente* with France. For in his appraisal, French decision-makers aspired to a position of continental dominance and would tie Britain to a postwar system in which the vanquished foe was kept in "a state of humiliating subjection". To avoid such a scenario, which clashed with the requirements of the "future peace and international cooperation", Smuts emphatically recommended a strategy of cooperation with the United States and support for Wilson's peace programme in all matters of "large policy", including the League – as far as this was "consistent" with the British Empire's "own interests". The underlying assumption of Smuts' conception was that the interests and civilisational "ideals" of the "Anglo-Saxon" powers were essentially congruent – and that the same applied to "all fundamental considerations of policy". This made a new partnership of what he emphatically called the "two great democratic Commonwealths" in the "new world order" he envisaged both possible and eminently desirable.[52]

Like Cecil, Smuts recommended that because the League was the pivot of Wilson's entire peace programme, Britain should unequivocally endorse the new organisation at the outset of the peace conference. At the same time, British policymakers had to act as instructors of the American president and his advisers in order to "give substance to his rather nebulous ideas".[53] After

---

[50] "Cecil Plan", 14 December 1918, in Miller (1928), II, pp. 61–4.
[51] See Cecil (1941), pp. 60–2.
[52] Smuts memorandum, 3 December 1918, Cabinet Paper P. 39, CAB 29/2.
[53] *Ibid.* See Egerton (1978), pp. 83–8.

the armistice, Smuts had declared that the Great War was "the greatest of all revolutions" mankind had experienced and caused a world-historical *caesura*. In his eyes, the "old Europe, the old world" was "dead" and a "whole world order" was "visibly passing away before our eyes". Yet he had also stressed that the "greatest" and "most fruitful" result of the "great world crisis" was "the coming together of Europe and America". And he had asserted that in the "building up" of "the future peaceful order", which he pictured as a new world order emerging around a transatlantic hub, the cooperation of the United States was "essential" – it now had to bear its "fair share in the great burden of world politics". On these premises, Smuts made an ideological case for a new Anglo-American mission, arguing that if America and the British Empire, which were bound together by the same "principles of political freedom" and the same "regard for the rights of the human personality", joined forces this would "form the best guarantee for the future peaceful development of civilization".[54] As Smuts saw it, their pre-eminent task now was to collaborate, and include the former enemy, in fostering advances in the "political organiza-tion of the world" and making the world "safe for democracy in a great organization", the League of Nations. He thus argued for wider *systemic* changes in the international order. For in his diagnosis the Great War had been "as much the result of outworn international law and organization as of German imperial ambitions".[55]

In mid-December 1918 Smuts presented the War Cabinet and then the world with one of the most comprehensive and impactful blueprints for a League of Nations that came out of the Great War. What Smuts put forward internally and in his widely noted treatise *The League of Nations: A Practical Suggestion* was conceived in a spirit of hierarchical internationalism and with an eye to "world opinion". But it was mainly, and successfully, designed to influence British policymaking and, notably, the American president.[56] Adopting Wilson's priorities, Smuts proposed that the League should be the "starting point" of all "peace arrangements" and become nothing less than "the foundation of the new international system" that had to be erected "on the ruins of this war" – and the "ever visible, living working organ of the polity of civilization".

The organisation Smuts outlined was not designed to become a new "super-state" nor a "federation" or even a "confederation". For his premise was that no new "super-sovereign" was either desired or desirable. Rather, the new "system of world-government" was to be a system of *states*, which would be "controlled not by compulsion from above but by consent from below". And for all his concessions to Wilsonian rhetoric Smuts clearly did not envisage an

---

[54] Smuts speech, 14 November 1918, *Smuts Papers*, IV, pp. 8–11.
[55] *Ibid.*, p. 15.
[56] Smuts (1918); Smuts, "The League of Nations", 16 December 1918, CAB 29/2.

448 REORIENTATIONS AND INCIPIENT LEARNING PROCESSES

egalitarian organisation. He foresaw a "Parliament" of representatives from all member states that would mould "international public opinion". But he argued that the only way to make the League an effective instrument of "world government" was to create as its central "organ" a council with real executive authority. This council, modelled on the "Versailles Council of Prime Ministers", was to do the "real work", perform the responsibilities of keeping world peace, organise collective responses to security threats and promote far-reaching general disarmament. Similar to Cecil, Smuts proposed an "organ" in which the great powers, represented by their premiers and foreign ministers, were to have a strategic majority.[57] And, significantly, he argued that not only the British Empire, the United States, France, Italy and Japan should become "permanent members" – Germany too should be included "as soon as she has a stable democratic Government".[58]

In Smuts' assessment, the crux of the League system of peace-keeping and security lay in developing an effective regime of sanctions both to deter and act against those who threatened regional or global peace. Yet while he considered this the "most important question of all" he actually proposed limiting the actual obligations of member states and notably the great powers. The Covenant he envisioned was not to comprise guarantees for the protection of political independence and territorial integrity of all members. Reflecting prevalent assumptions in the Imperial War Cabinet, Smuts emphasised that the League chiefly had to provide a framework for what in his thinking remained indispensable to cope with "the most dangerous and intractable causes of war": political processes and diplomatic practices of meditation and conflict-resolution. He emphasised that "large questions of policy, of so-called vital interests, and of national honour" around which national and international "passions" gathered like "storm-clouds" were simply not amenable to rigid judicial procedures and arbitration. In his judgement, addressing such questions required expert advice but above all "tactful diplomatic negotiation and conciliation between the disputants" which "great statesmen [knew] best how to bring to bear". Essentially, the League was to allow them to act in concert in order to settle disputes by peaceful means – and to "guide" world public opinion "correctly" and thus to "mobilize its forces on the side of peace".[59]

Smuts proposed one central mission for the new organisation. It was to become the "successor" of the "defunct" Eastern Empires. More precisely, it

---

[57] Smuts (1918), pp. 5–9, 26–40, 41–63; Smuts, "The League of Nations", 16 December 1918, CAB 29/2.

[58] Smuts (1918), p. 32. Earlier, Smuts had argued that after Prussian militarism had been defeated the western powers should turn to "the great creative tasks ahead" and draw the former enemy into a "better order". Smuts speech, 14 November 1918, Smuts Papers, IV, pp. 10–12.

[59] Smuts (1918), pp. 41–63. See also Smuts, memorandum, 16 December 1918, CAB 29/2.

was to be given the "colossal task" of not only maintaining peace and order in what he regarded as a geopolitically crucial region but also overseeing a fundamental recasting of its political map, fostering – hierarchically structured – advances towards "self-government" and, ultimately, the formation of independent states. According to Smuts, the victors here had to give priority to the principle of self-determination even in cases of conflicting strategic considerations. He reckoned that in cases like Poland, Czechoslovakia and "Yugoslavia", formerly oppressed nationalities would probably be "sufficiently capable of statehood to be recognized as independent states" from the beginning. And he warned that a peace settlement that did not meet their expectations would only add to the appeal of Bolshevism and, more generally, "open the fountains" of profound popular discontent that would "overwhelm victor and vanquished alike in the coming flood".[60]

By contrast, Smuts judged that outside Europe – in the former "Transcaucasian" and "Transcaspian" provinces of the Russian Empire and in the "ex-Turkish territories", notably Syria, Lebanon, and Mesopotamia, local populations were "as yet deficient in the qualities of statehood"; they were at best – and in varying degrees – capable of "internal autonomy". Here, then, a different solution had to be found. And, drawing on what he saw as exemplary practices of the British Empire, the South African strategist proposed that the League was to provide "external authority" – and effectively oversee "state-building" processes – by establishing a system of mandates. Within it, the organisation was to delegate oversight and tutelage responsibilities to "advanced" states. This mandate system was also to be extended to Germany's former colonies in Africa and the Pacific, which in his view were "inhabited by barbarians" who could not "possibly govern themselves" and where it would thus be "impracticable to apply any idea of political self-determination in the European sense".

Smuts suggested that not only Britain and the Dominions but also the United States were to act as principal mandatory powers. In his eyes, close cooperation with Wilson in the spirit of a new Anglo-Saxon "internationalism" was thus by no means incompatible with the expansion of the British Empire's influence and global role.[61] In effect, he aspired to engage the United States in a global civilising mission under the League's auspices. More important, however, was his rationale to induce the rising American power to share hegemonic responsibilities in creating a new Euro-Atlantic order. Despite their ambitious scope, Smuts' suggestions fell on fertile ground in the Imperial War Cabinet. What he mapped out corresponded with many of Cecil's aims, was fundamentally backed by Balfour and clearly had an effect on Lloyd George's evolving peace strategy.

---

[60] Smuts (1918), pp. 6–25.
[61] *Ibid.* For a critical appraisal see Mazower (2009), pp. 28 ff.

But what also still carried weight by the end of the war was a different imperialist "vision" of how peace and stability could be secured and how a new compact with the United States was to be approached. It had emerged since 1917 and first been advanced by Lord Milner, who had headed the War Cabinet's committee on war aims. Subsequently his political ally Philip Kerr and the members of the aforementioned *Round Table* group developed it further. In the conception of Milner and Kerr, which also drew on nineteenth-century traditions, a consolidated British Empire that was advancing towards a Commonwealth was to serve as a model for renewed concert of the great powers. They envisaged a concert based on a loose constitution yet above all common ideals, which would operate through regular conferences allowing statesmen to discuss and resolve the most contentious international and inter-imperial disputes. Milner's committee had already recommended in 1917 to discuss a "scheme" along these lines especially with the United States "before the conclusion of the war". And it had explicitly proposed it as an alternative "any too comprehensive or ambitious project to ensure world peace" – such as the peace league Wilson contemplated – which "might prove not only impracticable, but harmful".

The exclusive concert Kerr had in mind would neither require an ambitious institutional architecture nor oblige its members to follow a certain course of action or impose sanctions. Rather peace and stability were to be secured more organically, by fostering voluntary cooperation, consultation, and common understandings among the representatives of the great powers.[62] Yet Kerr emphasised, in contrast to Milner, that a key purpose of the new concert system would be the containment of German power. Already before 1914 he had warned that the aggressive German Empire and "Germanism, in its want of liberalism, its pride, its aggressive nationalism" posed the most dangerous threat to Britain's continued benign "supremacy".[63] And now, in late 1918, Lloyd George's adviser reckoned that despite the revolutionary developments in Berlin, underlying German proclivities and mentalities would at best change slowly.

What Milner and Kerr advocated beyond this was also emphasised by conservative imperialists like Curzon and Amery, namely to concentrate on Britain's traditional naval strategy. Following the armistice, they thus insisted that everything had to be done to protect the Empire and its strategic lines of communication by maintaining British naval pre-eminence, also vis-à-vis the United States. And they categorically rejected Wilson's call for "freedom of the seas", defending the prerogative to impose blockades as essential for imperial security. Naturally, they also insisted on eliminating the German naval threat.

---

[62] Committee report, 1917, Lloyd George (1933–36), IV, pp. 1799–1800. See Kendle (1975), pp. 250–1.

[63] Kerr (anonymous), "Foreign affairs: Anglo-German rivalry", *The Round Table*, I (1910), pp. 7, 26–7.

At the same time, their common priority was not merely the consolidation but actually the expansion of the British Empire, or at least of the sphere of imperial influence and control. The emphasis lay on safeguarding imperial security, above all the security of the Suez Canal and, more generally, the vital lines of communications between India and the Mediterranean. Crucially, because of their focus on global imperial concerns, both "Milnerites" and more conservative imperialists sought to extricate Britain as far as possible from further commitments in continental Europe. In their view, British policy merely had to ensure that, somehow, a more or less "self-regulating" balance of power was established on the continent. And except for Kerr they shared a penchant for leaving Germany in a comparatively strong position in Europe but making sure that it would not regain its colonies, which as far as possible were to be administered by the Dominions. Yet particularly Curzon also preferred imperial aloofness in a different sense. He did not consider Wilson – or the United States – a possible or desirable strategic partner and was wary of his far-reaching League schemes.[64]

In the eyes of critics within the cabinet, notably Balfour and Cecil, an "Empire first" strategy appeared not only unrealistic. They argued that instead of improving imperial security it was prone to create new hazards and liabilities, particularly because it suggested that Britain could afford to avoid meaningful international commitments – and because it extended the Empire's vulnerabilities in an unprecedentedly connected and complex world.[65] They thus continued to advocate a transatlantic approach. But even the most fervent Atlanticists in the Imperial War Cabinet were aware that forging a strategic partnership with the United States presented a considerable challenge. They had to operate with uncertainties that had not changed since America's entry into the war and become even more acute in the wake of the Democratic defeat in the November elections.

These uncertainties stemmed not only from Wilson's as yet general pronouncements about his peace programme but also from the open question of whether he would actually be able to rally the requisite domestic support for his League plans and the unprecedented international commitments he advocated. British diplomats had closely followed domestic developments in the United States. And leading policymakers were well aware of Lodge's serious reservations. This further complicated what had been a fundamental question from the British standpoint ever since 1916: how far the American government could become a reliable partner in the postwar international order – a

---

[64] Rothwell (1972), pp. 68–75; minutes of the Imperial War Cabinet, 24 December 1918, CAB 23/42.
[65] Ibid.

partner that actually accepted wider responsibilities and made, and kept, longer-term commitments.[66]

Concerns of this kind were far more pronounced on the part of those who still had serious misgivings in the first place about basing British postwar policy, and imperial defence, on a compact with Wilson and the "great experiment" of the League. They had drawn different lessons from the war and based their recommendations on more traditional assumptions about the requirements of international order and the best way to protect Britain's interests as a European *and* imperial power. Eyre Crowe, the half-German veteran who now headed the Foreign Office's Western European Section and oversaw its peace planning, emerged as the most forceful advocate of a recalibrated but fundamentally unchanged *and Eurocentric* balance-of-power strategy. He recommended that Britain's overriding aim should be a tried and tested one: to re-create and maintain a workable "equilibrium" of power in Europe – even under significantly changed conditions. Crowe warned that the fulfilment of Wilson's promises was subject to the vagaries of US domestic politics and that the United States was in any case far removed from Europe's troubles. More fundamentally, however, he was convinced that what Wilson and British League proponents demanded would undermine any prospect of establishing an effective system of postwar security and stability. Crowe conceded that the terms of the armistice would dramatically reduce Germany's military power and thus provide assurances in the immediate future. But he maintained that in the longer term British and imperial security still depended critically on the creation of a sustainable European balance of power.

The main danger Crowe saw was that the British government, lured by the prospect of an Anglo-American partnership, would prioritise unrealistic League designs of "collective security" and disarmament. In his view, it would thereby neglect what was essential: the forging of strategic alliances to contain Germany's power, also in the longer run. As Russia was no longer available as a potential balancing-power, and as long as the United States remained a very uncertain candidate, there was only one strategic partner Britain could rely upon – France.[67] Crowe thus recommended converting the Anglo-French wartime alliance into an effective peacetime *entente*, observing that "our friend America lives a long way off; France sits at our door". One of his rationales was that by providing reassurance, Britain would be able to restrain French postwar policies vis-à-vis Germany. Fundamentally, however, he was concerned with keeping the vanquished in check.

---

[66] Wiseman memorandum, 16 October 1918, *PWW*, LI, pp. 347–52; Lodge to Balfour, 25 September 1918, Lodge Papers; Roosevelt to Lloyd George, 10 December 1918, Lloyd George Papers, F/24/3/81; Minutes of Imperial War Cabinet meeting, 30 December, memorandum no. 47, CAB 23/42

[67] Crowe memorandum, 7 December 1918, FO 371/3451; Crowe note, 30 December 1918, FO 371/4353.

In Crowe's assessment, the revolutionary turmoil in Germany posed incalculable problems – and it was far from certain whether radical left-wing forces, moderates or a reactionary old guard would ultimately gain the upper hand. He thus saw a critical common Anglo-French interest in guarding against possible revisionist ambitions of a German power whose potential was likely to remain superior to that of France and all of its other neighbours. Essentially, then, the main consequence Crowe had drawn from the Great War was diametrically opposed to what Wilson and internationalists of different stripes asserted. He deemed it crucial to salvage, rather than jettison, maxims of a circumspect balance-of-power politics. As he had emphasised earlier in criticising Cecil's plan for a "peace league", the "balance of power" re-appeared as the "fundamental problem"; nothing but "adequate force" could prevent a state or a group of states from pursuing "through war and bloodshed, a policy of aggression and domination". In Crowe's judgement, "a solemn league and covenant" could only make a difference in the longer term, "with the development of modern political thought".[68]

The historian James Headlam-Morley, who as assistant director of the Foreign Office's newly created Political Intelligence Department played an important role in developing postwar plans for Germany and Eastern Europe, came to similar conclusions. In his view, it was in Britain's interest to work with Wilson as far as possible and to take his peace programme seriously, but he warned that it would be dangerous to make British postwar security dependent on the success of such a strategy. Headlam-Morley argued that even if the League was actually created the balance of power would remain "a fundamental point" in international affairs. And this would apply even more unequivocally if Wilson's grand design were to fail. Fundamentally, he too thought that British interests still commanded to forestall the dominance of one single power on the European continent – and, in particular, to prevent either Germany or France extending their control to the strategically vital coastline along the Channel. Yet he agreed with Crowe that pre-empting a renewal of German aspirations to gain pre-eminence in and beyond Europe had to be the primary concern.[69]

But what Crowe, Headlam-Morley and other Foreign Office strategists recommended failed to exert a significant influence on British policies at Versailles – or even on the foreign secretary himself. In fact, Balfour strongly opposed a strategy that hinged on perpetuating the Anglo-French *Entente* and tied Britain too closely to what he regarded as counter-productive French peace plans. Instead, he too advocated the pursuit of an Anglo-American concord both during the peace negotiations and overseeing an overhaul of

[68] Crowe note, 12 October 1916, Cabinet Paper G.T.404a, CAB 24/10.
[69] Headlam-Morley memorandum, "The Settlement: Europe", 15 November 1918, FO 371/4353/f23/PC55; Cabinet Paper P. 53, December 1918, CAB 29/2.

the international order. On 29 November, Balfour told Lloyd George that he had been alarmed by the Clemenceau government's insistence on pre-emptively settling between Britain and France all essential "questions in which they were in any way interested" before Wilson had even arrived in Europe. He also informed the prime minister about the "apocalyptic" postwar scenario Ambassador Paul Cambon had elaborated – of a "future great war in which England and France would find themselves fighting side by side in a death struggle with a German and an American Republic". Balfour deemed such a scenario "little short of insanity" and considered the French government's economic and territorial aims vis-à-vis Germany "so greedy" as to be unacceptable.

At the same time, the foreign secretary observed that France's "deliberate effort to exclude the Americans from any effective share in the world settlement" was "neither in our interest nor in that of the French themselves". He insisted that it was essential to coordinate British peace efforts with the American government and above all with House, who was "undoubtedly anxious" to work with the British government "as closely as he can". Balfour warned that it would be "fatal" to give Wilson the impression that Britain and France "were settling, or had the least desire to settle, great questions behind his back".[70] He saw even more reason to assert his Atlanticist position during the inter-allied conference that took place in London in early December. Accepting his basic rationale, Lloyd George distanced himself from the more far-reaching schemes Clemenceau and Marshal Foch presented on this occasion. And he cold-shouldered Clemenceau's proposal of a prior Franco-British understanding about the modalities of the peace conference that could then be presented to Wilson as a *fait accompli* and thus contain the American peace agenda.[71]

V.   Setting a New Course. The Imperial War Cabinet and the Decision to Pursue an "Atlanticist" Strategy – and a League on British Premises

Nonetheless, when the Imperial War Cabinet held its final deliberations before the peace conference – and under the impression of Wilson's "triumphal" reception in Britain – it became clear that no strategic consensus had been reached yet. The Australian premier William Hughes spoke for quite a few members of the cabinet when he warned that those who would negotiate on behalf of the Empire should beware of finding themselves "dragged behind the wheels of President Wilson's chariot". Hughes argued that while the American "part" in the war had been considerable "it was not such as to entitle [Wilson] to be the god in the machine at the Peace Settlement, and to lay down the

---

[70] Balfour to Lloyd George, 29 November 1918, Lloyd George Papers, F/2/4–7.
[71] See minutes of Anglo-French and Allied meetings, 1 and 2 December 1918, CAB 28/5.

terms on which the world would have to live in future"; and he suggested that while humouring him Lloyd George and Clemenceau could, and should, "settle the peace of the world as they liked". Curzon likewise stressed that Wilson should not be regarded as "the sole arbiter" of peace and that Lloyd George would go to Paris "with an authority fully equal, and indeed superior" to that of his American counterpart.[72]

At the same time, what clearly still prevailed in the War Cabinet – as in the Foreign Office – was a sceptical outlook on the League. Especially leading Conservatives – among them Curzon, Chamberlain, and Bonar Law – voiced profound misgivings. They were not prepared to rely on a novel, untested system of "collective security" to meet the essential security interests of the British Empire. Nor were they prepared to accept far-reaching curtailments of national and imperial sovereignty that, in their interpretation, Wilson's ideas and even the proposals of Cecil and Smuts would entail. And they also doubted that, as Austen Chamberlain observed, any American government would be willing to place US armed forces under the higher authority of an "International Council". Churchill and Hughes shared these doubts. Churchill argued in favour of a reduced League of the victors premised on a "complete and intimate understanding" between Britain, France and the United States. But he mainly warned that in whatever form it took a League could be "no substitute for national defences".[73]

But a majority in the Cabinet – led by Balfour, Cecil and the Canadian premier Sir Robert Borden, eventually including Lloyd George himself – in the end opted for a transatlantic peace strategy and a clear commitment to the League. Seeking to ensure a clear Cabinet endorsement of his plans Cecil reiterated that the "greatest guarantee" for "a settled peace" lay in "a good understanding with the United States", which could only be secured if Britain clearly backed "the idea of the League of Nations".[74] The prime minister basically supported these rationales, even though he was far less emphatic in his commitment. But he ultimately decided that it was in Britain's fundamental interests to avoid antagonising Wilson and that cooperation with the United States would be vital at the forthcoming peace conference.[75]

Thus, Lloyd George would become the first British prime minister who after a major war pursued an Atlantic approach to come to grips with the challenges of peacemaking and reordering Europe and the world. And he gradually came to develop his own distinctive conception of a new Atlantic order in which Britain was to regain a pivotal hegemonic role. Yet he never championed an

---

[72] Minutes of Imperial War Cabinet meeting, 30 December 1918, CAB 23/42.
[73] Minutes of Imperial War Cabinet meeting, 24 December 1918, CAB 23/42.
[74] Minutes of Imperial War Cabinet meeting, 30 December, memorandum no. 47, CAB 23/42.
[75] Ibid.

Anglo-American "special relationship" and in fact retained considerable doubts about the prospects of negotiating mutually satisfactory outcomes with an American president whom he had criticised for his unilateral pursuits ever since 1916 and whose ideological rhetoric he had long viewed with disdain. His first actual encounter with Wilson on 27 December led him to develop a more positive outlook. But he was still determined to proceed with "with every caveat in place" to safeguard cardinal national and imperial interests.[76] Essentially, Lloyd George came to pursue a strategic *and* tactical policy that combined elements of qualified co-operation, bargaining, tutelage and "containment" vis-à-vis the American president and his aspirations. And he clearly agreed with Curzon that Wilson "was not to be regarded as a sole arbiter" in setting the terms and rules of the postwar order.

On these premises the prime minister also defined the role he intended to play at the peace conference: that of the essential peacemaker who would confidently employ his negotiating skills and powers of persuasion to broker a "British peace". As such, he would chiefly seek to forge strategic bargains with Wilson, but he was resolved to retain the option of siding with Clemenceau if that promised to serve what he regarded as underlying British interests. Based on their first "general measuring-up of aims and hopes" with Wilson, both he and Balfour concluded that it would be possible to reach a basic understanding with the American president on essential points, including the League. And they deemed it expedient to support Wilson's wish to discuss the foundation of the League first at the forthcoming conference, calculating that this would make it easier to come to a subsequent understanding with him on matters of vital concern to Britain and the Empire.[77] In the prime minister's view, which others shared, the only salient issues on which there were major disagreements between Britain and the United States after the armistice – apart from general concerns over Wilson's rhetoric of "self-determination" – were reparations and the "freedom of the seas".[78] In particular, he was aware that the essentials of Britain's ambitious reparations agenda collided with the American resolve to reject punitive indemnities and to craft a "scientific" reparations settlement. As Lloyd George pointed out, the main threat stemmed from Wilson's insistence on "pure reparation", which would "practically" rule out indemnities for the British Empire's war costs while France and Belgium would "get every thing". And he clearly intended to avoid such American strictures.[79]

---

[76] Lloyd George statements, Imperial War Cabinet, 30 and 31 December 1918, CAB 23/42. For his underlying assumptions, see Imperial War Cabinet, 11 October 1918, CAB 23/8.

[77] See Lloyd George and Balfour statements, Imperial War Cabinet, 30 and 31 December 1918, CAB 23/42; Grayson diary, 27 December 1918, *PWW*, LIII, pp. 519–22.

[78] Minutes of the Imperial War Cabinet, 5 November 1918, CAB 23/8.

[79] Minutes of Imperial War Cabinet meeting, 30 December, memorandum no. 47, CAB 23/42.

The other divisive issue had a direct bearing on Britain's core strategic interests and was not confined to different attitudes towards the "freedom of the seas". More profoundly, what created tensions between British and American policymakers was the question of who would set the rules of the future global naval regime and thus determine the future strategic equilibrium of an interdependent world – at a juncture when the German naval threat seemed to have been neutralised for the foreseeable future. And what had arisen was the core challenge to recalibrate relations – and the balance of forces – between the world's long-predominant naval power and a dynamically rising challenger with an increasingly superior financial potential. With a view to the "freedom of the seas" it seemed possible to agree on an Anglo-American *modus vivendi*. When meeting with Wilson in late December, Lloyd George underscored the British resolve to retain the prerogative to impose blockades as a key instrument of imperial defence; and the American president indicated that he would not insist on his Fourteen Points agenda in this respect, consenting to further discussions once the League had been established.[80]

But more fundamental problems persisted. Both the Imperial War Cabinet and the British Admiralty had paid close attention to Wilson's threat to use an envisaged naval construction programme as a strategic lever to push through his peace agenda, and they noted what they saw as American aspirations to outspend and surpass Britain in this vital sphere with growing concern. The First Lord of the Admiralty, Sir Eric Geddes, had warned in early November that Wilson was actually "pursuing the 'Balance of Power' theory" yet was applying it to "world politics" only in the sphere of "sea power". In Geddes' assessment, Wilson's aim was to build up American naval power until it exceeded "the sea power of the British Empire" – and then to establish a League that would allow America to "control recalcitrant members" by "the exercise of sea-power".[81]

Essentially, those who oversaw the Empire's naval policies were determined to resist the American challenge and preserve its status as the world's pre-eminent naval power. At a time of relatively scarce resources, however, they sought to achieve this by prevailing on the American government to scale down its naval construction plans. In the longer run, this aim would inform a more general British interest in establishing a global regime of naval arms control after the Great War.[82] During the decisive discussions in the Imperial War Cabinet, Lloyd George stressed that he was "not pessimistic about inducing President Wilson to agree ultimately, though possibly under protest" to

---

[80] *Ibid.*

[81] Geddes memorandum, 7 November 1918, *PWW*, LI, pp. 633–4.

[82] War Cabinet minutes, 26 October 1918 and 10 November 1918, CAB 23/14; House diary, 4 November and 19 December 1918, House, *Intimate Papers*, IV, pp. 180–1; *PWW*, LIII, p. 448.

accept British essentials not just regarding the "disposal of the German colonies" and economic issues but also on indemnities and the "freedom of the seas" – if British policy helped Wilson to "secure his League of Nations", which "politically, was a matter of life and death to him". Yet he also underscored that should the American president prove "obstinate", he would not hesitate to close ranks with Clemenceau, observing that the "sacrifices of France and Great Britain were such that they were entitled to have a final say".[83] In fact, the British premier would find it harder than expected to forge strategic agreements with Wilson at Versailles. What escalated into a "naval battle" and growing tensions over reparations would severely strain Anglo-American relations and impede co-operation between the two powers on both on core aspects of the German settlement and the finalisation of the League Covenant.

But what kind of League did Lloyd George actually envisage? Following his discussion with Wilson the prime minister concluded that in substantive terms it would not be difficult to accommodate the president's League plans as his thoughts appeared to point in the same direction as the proposals Smuts and Cecil had advanced.[84] But in spite of his public commitment to *a* League during the election campaign, the British premier actually remained reserved towards Cecil's and Smuts' more ambitious proposals. He was far from espousing Wilson's aspirational ideas. And – like the overwhelming majority in the War Cabinet – he was even more opposed to an international organisation with far-reaching supranational authority. Lloyd George had by this time developed a distinctly conservative idea of what he desired the League to become. Essentially, he favoured the creation of an intergovernmental mechanism that would not require the British government to relinquish core prerogatives of national and imperial sovereignty.

At the core, influenced by Cecil's and Smuts' ideas yet mainly by what his confidants Kerr and Hankey had suggested, Lloyd George envisaged the League to take shape as framework for a renovated international concert of the great powers that, crucially, would hence lock the American government into assuming shared responsibilities, above all in postwar Europe. The prime minister also espoused the idea of beginning with a nucleus formed by the principal victors which could later be extended to include the vanquished power, yet only once its leaders, and people, had accepted a "just and chastising peace" – and consolidated a democratic system of government (though the latter was not an essential precondition in his view).

In a broader perspective, the key purpose of the League Lloyd George desired was to regularise cooperation and negotiations between the political

---

[83] Minutes of the Imperial War Cabinet, 30 and 31 December 1918, CAB 23/42.

[84] Minutes of Imperial War Cabinet meeting, 30 December, memorandum no. 47, CAB 23/42.

leaders of the great powers, allowing them to consult and act in concert to manage the international order, resolve crises and remove the seedbeds of future conflicts. This way, it was also to offer better protections for the integrity and security of smaller powers, including the successor states of the Eastern Empires. But its pre-eminent purpose was to become the main safeguard of overall European and global stability which, not least, prevented regional crises from again escalating into a general war. To this end, the British premier also desired the League's concert to provide the wherewithal to foster peaceful change and negotiate readjustments that might prove necessary over time. Further, he hoped it could create conditions for decisive steps towards a general disarmament – of land forces. Lloyd George's general conception thus remained distinctly more limited than the vision Wilson had begun to flesh out on the eve of the peace conference.[85]

During the formative Cabinet discussions in late December, the prime minister unequivocally opposed taking the decisive qualitative step of making the League a "body with executive power" and endowing it with a sanction regime and mandatory obligations of "collective security" that would take final decisions about war and peace out of the hands of the British government. Rather, he underscored that he desired to build on the "admirable precedents" of the Imperial War Cabinet and the Supreme War Council to establish the nucleus of a new international concert. He declared that if a mechanism of this kind had existed in 1914 it could have prevented the outbreak of the Great War. And Lloyd George had actually come away from his encounter with Wilson with the re-assuring impression that the American president did not actually intend to challenge the fundamentals of state sovereignty either. In his assessment, Wilson did not contemplate "giving executive powers to the League of Nations".[86]

In a wider context, however, what was most significant and had the most formative effect on British policy at Versailles was that Lloyd George had indeed embarked on a reorientation process and, with the Cabinet's approval, committed himself to an approach to peacemaking whose main aim was to lay the groundwork for a new transatlantic order and to engage Wilson in this process. The pre-eminent British decision-maker had decided to pursue a new course predicated on the rationale that it was in Britain's – and the Empire's – interest to prioritise a guarded cooperation with Wilson and thus to try to establish basic parameters, not for a radically different world order but for a profoundly reformed international system. What he aspired to create was a system no longer dominated by balance-of-power politics but constructed – by

---

[85] See Hankey memorandum, 16 January 1918, CAB 24/39; Fry (2011), pp. 85 ff.; Billington (2006).

[86] Imperial War Cabinet, 24 and 30 December 1918, CAB 23/42.

way of the League – around a reconfigured Atlantic concert that functioned as a new international directorate and clearing-house. Significantly, not only the prime minister but a clear majority of British decision-makers had thus opted against the continental strategy that Crowe and other Foreign Office strategists had recommended. They did not contemplate specific security commitments on the European continent, especially to France; and they clearly did not envisage transforming the wartime *Entente* into a muscular postwar alliance to deter Germany. Clearly, a pre-eminent concern they shared was that Britain might be dragged into another European conflict by tying itself too closely to France and potentially conflict-prone French policies. Fundamentally, how-ever, they did not think that a reversion to more traditional, essentially power-political strategies would be conducive to the stabilisation of Europe.

Thus, for Lloyd George and other important British policymakers first attempts to draw lessons from the Great War and its origins had not led to a fundamental change of paradigm. But they had spurred a significant degree of qualitative reorientation. Like others, the prime minister had persuaded himself that British leaders had genuinely struggled in 1914 and the preceding years to prevent the outbreak of a general war. But they also began to acknowledge that preventing the recurrence of another catastrophe like the Great War, or even greater calamities, required advances towards a different *system* of international politics – one that departed from the logic of competi-tive alliances, balance-of-power diplomacy and chronic insecurity and fur-thered instead concerted conflict resolution and collective efforts to secure a more durable peace.

VI.   Imperial Preoccupations and the Wilsonian Challenge. Adjusted Strategies of Imperial Consolidation, Legitimation – and Expansion

Yet Lloyd George and a majority in the Imperial War Cabinet also were and remained preoccupied with wider imperial concerns at this stage. These concerns pertained not only to the consolidation and reform of the British Empire after the "war for empire" had been won but also to the question of how, and on what terms, Britain's imperial influence could best be expanded in the Middle East, to strategically important territories that had been under Ottoman rule. What British policymakers came to pursue was an approach that was less aspirational than what Smuts had proposed but followed some of his core rationales. On the one hand, it came to centre on what could be called the strategies of "imperial defence, adaptation and legitimation" that were designed to ensure that British and Dominion leaders would be in a position to preserve and reform the Empire without undue external or internal inter-ference – and thus also to counter the challenge posed by Wilson's quest for a "new world order" and its world-wide influence. On the other hand, it came to focus on a *targeted* pursuit of Smuts' strategy of involving the American president in a "civilising mission" that actually furthered the expansion of British imperial influence.

During their first encounter with him, Lloyd George and Balfour suggested to Wilson that the United States should assume specific – and carefully selected – obligations of guardianship, namely as a mandatory power outside Europe. Balfour raised the vague idea that the United States could act as a "mandatory at Constantinople".[87] Lloyd George had desired early on that the newly important American power should share mandatory responsibilities. But he did not intend to allow "an absolutely new and crude Power" to interfere with the British Empire's "complicated interests in Egypt, Arabia and Mesopotamia". He therefore proposed to Wilson that the United States should assume a mandate in Armenia – a suggestion to which, in spite of the American president's reservations, he would return at Versailles.[88] But other influential Cabinet members had developed more ambitious designs.

By December 1918, Balfour and Cecil had concluded that one of the main dangers the British Empire faced was that of imperial overstretch. They thus warned against extending the Empire's commitments and liabilities even further.[89] But the War Cabinet's most assertive imperialists, led by Curzon and Amery, now came forward with a grand vision of neo-imperial expansion that centred on the Middle East. Their guiding idea was to abandon the Sykes-Picot agreement with France and to invoke, in the spirit of Smuts' proposals, the principles of self-government and self-determination that both Lloyd George and Wilson had proclaimed. On this basis, they intended to grant superficially a large degree of self-government to different Arab and Levantine provinces that had been part of the Ottoman Empire – with the exception of Palestine – and to transform them into "mandates". What they actually sought to establish this way, with Wilson's acquiescence, was a system of de facto protectorates in which Britain's influence would dominate. This system notably was to include the oil-rich territories around Mosul (which eventually would become part of the British mandate Iraq).[90] During the peace conference, such schemes would encounter fierce French opposition – and American reservations. It was only under pressure that Britain's plenipotentiaries would eventually scale down their expansionist programme when the League's mandate system was hammered out.

---

[87] Minutes of the Imperial War Cabinet, 30 December 1918, CAB 23/42.

[88] Barnes and Nicholson (1980), I. p. 239; Imperial War Cabinet minutes, 30 December 1918, CAB 23/42.

[89] See Imperial War Cabinet minutes, 24 December 1918, CAB 23/42.

[90] Curzon even proposed to extend this system to Persia, the Caucasus and Central Asia, but a majority in the Cabinet drew a line here, fearing an "over-stretch". See Darwin (2009), pp. 317–18.

Initially, the War Cabinet had also pledged its support for the Dominions' demand to control former German colonies in their vicinity. But as a concession to Wilson, Lloyd George would later back a League-administered system. This provided an opening for a scheme Smuts and Cecil had prepared to establish a more "forward-looking" mandate system. They proposed a hierarchy of mandates, ranging from "A" mandates, which were "almost" prepared to determine their own affairs – e.g. Middle Eastern "nations" – via "B" mandates, less advanced and in need of a mandatory supervision – e.g. territories in sub-Saharan Africa – to "C" mandates, which were situated close to potential mandatory powers and could thus best be administered by them. Conveniently, this rationale could be applied to bolster South Africa's claim to administer the former German colony of Southwest Africa.[91]

In principle, if less radically than Lenin's call for a new order of Soviet republics, Wilson's rhetorical espousal of the "self-determination" principle as a universal precept of a new international order of course shook the fundamental premises of every form of traditional empire, including those of the British Empire. And one underlying aim of the strategies of "imperial defence, adaptation and legitimation" that Lloyd George and both liberal and conservative British imperialists had developed during the war was to meet precisely this challenge.[92] On the eve of the peace conference, all leading British and Dominion politicians remained wary of the repercussions of the American president's speeches, not only in Egypt and Ireland but also, and particularly, in India. But by this time they had basically concluded, erroneously, that it would be relatively eassy to contain the threat posed by Wilson and, above all, the rise of nationalist movements within the (non-white) Empire that demanded unequivocal and swift advances towards self-determination.

Already in the spring of 1917 Lloyd George and the Imperial War Cabinet had endorsed Milner's doctrine that "matters affecting the vital interests of the British Empire" were not to be subjected to an international mechanism like a peace league.[93] After the war, they confirmed the claim to an exclusive imperial sphere of prerogatives – effectively, though not explicitly, asserting a Monroe Doctrine for the British Empire. In late December 1918, Balfour spoke for a majority in the Cabinet, including Lloyd George, when he insisted that "in the case of the British Empire" – where Egypt and Ireland "would certainly claim at the Peace Conference to be granted their independence" – it was "obvious" that one "could not permit outside interference with our own domestic affairs" either by the American president or, eventually, the League.[94]

---

[91] See Imperial War Cabinet minutes, 30 December 1918, CAB 23/42; Council of Ten, 24 January 1919, *PWW*, LIV, pp. 249–51.

[92] Darwin (2009), pp. 305 and ff. For the wider background see Manela (2007), pp. 55–98.

[93] Imperial War Cabinet, 26 April 1917, CAB 23/40.

[94] Minutes of the Imperial War Cabinet, 24 December 1918, CAB 23/42.

At the same time, Lloyd George and both liberal and conservative imperialists in the War Cabinet searched for new ways to fortify and legitimise the Empire. They envisaged a global postwar order in which a reformed British imperial system would actually remain a central building bloc – and again serve as a civilisational model. It was to set an example of how to make evolutionary progress on the paths of enlightened political and economic reform – and the promotion of self-determination. As noted, by early 1918, in response to the cumulating challenges of Lenin's radical proclamations, Wilson's rhetoric and unrest in India, Egypt and other parts of the Empire, Lloyd George had emphatically proclaimed that he intended to make the British Empire the vanguard power of "self-determination", "self-government" and "democratisation".[95] But his government in fact came to pursue a neo-imperial and distinctly "stratified" approach to this end.

In 1917, the Lloyd George government had responded to the influence of Milner and his followers and to the pressures of Dominion leaders to be compensated for the Dominions' ever more vital support for the war effort. It had agreed that Britain's relations with the governments of the white Dominions would be placed on a new basis after the end of the war. It had pledged to grant them in the foreseeable future "full recognition" as "autonomous nations" in an "Imperial Commonwealth" and "an adequate voice in foreign policy" and "foreign relations". And it had promised "continuous consultation", also – eventually – about the terms of the peace, which was then instituted through the Imperial War Cabinet. But in the crisis-ridden aftermath of the Great War, Lloyd George, who had always been opposed to Milner's more ambitious ideas and clearly rejected even more radical visions of an "imperial federation", was reluctant to implement the promises of 1917; and major reforms towards an "Imperial Commonwealth" would be put on hold. At the same time, while formally engaging in consultations with the Dominion governments, the British premier actually kept a tight rein on the Empire's peace policies.[96]

The language of promises in the direction of non-white dependencies – above all India – that the imperial centre would support advances towards self-government – remained markedly more ambiguous. In the summer of 1917, the new Viceroy, Edwin Montagu, had persuaded the War Cabinet to accept a

---

[95] Lloyd George speech, 5 January 1918, Lloyd George (1918).

[96] Resolution IX of the Imperial War Conference, April 1917, in Madden and Fieldhouse (1985–2000), VI, p. 42. In a parallel move, Milner and his followers promoted the idea of a modernised, more self-sufficient imperial system that emphasised "closer unity" with the white Dominions and allowed the British Empire to survive in the continuing struggle with other imperial "world states" – including the United States – they anticipated after the war. But the influence of such ideas had waned by the end of 1918, and Lloyd George was not prepared to back them. See Darwin (2009), pp. 328–30, 334–61.

reform scheme for the British Raj that promised "the gradual development of self-governing institutions". It was designed to preserve India as "an integral part of the British Empire" and to counter demands of Tilak's Indian Home Rule League and Mohammed Ali Jinnah's Muslim League for more far-reaching constitutional reforms and, essentially, self-government on par with the white Dominions. But these and subsequent British reform schemes envisaged only very slow progress towards self-rule and no significant Indian participation in governing the Raj. And they were rejected by the Indian National Congress and by Muslim nationalists. In the spring of 1919 a new phase in the history of Indian nationalism would begin – and culminate, for the time being, in Gandhi's Non-Cooperation movement in 1920, which inaugurated "the last phase of British rule" in India.[97] Thus, Lloyd George actually defended a distinctly hierarchical conception of "liberal Empire" – and glossed over massive inner-imperial tensions and challenges – when in September 1918 he proclaimed that the British Empire already constituted "a League of Nations" that could inspire the rest of the world.[98]

The Imperial War Cabinet's preoccupation with imperial concerns and aggrandisement had another critical consequence: it meant that less attention was paid to cardinal questions of the European settlement, above all the settlement with Germany. Nonetheless, despite these preoccupations, the central aim Lloyd George and other key policymakers pursued was to create a viable postwar order for Europe – with the help of the United States. Yet what kind of order did they actually seek to establish? And what kind of peace settlement did they precisely envisage?

VII.   How to Found – and Consolidate – a Stable Order. Lloyd George and the Pursuit of a New International Equilibrium for Europe

Though Lloyd George and his advisers would only formulate it more coherently during the peace conference – mainly during their retreat to Fontainebleau in late March 1919 – what emerged between the armistice and the end of 1918 can indeed be seen as core elements of a British peace conception for Europe. Its guiding rationale was to foster – through a peace-making process dominated by the victors – a new international equilibrium in Europe and the transatlantic sphere. Crucially, this conception was *not* based on the premise that a stable postwar order required the creation of a new and self-regulating "balance of power" – that it required a political, economic and territorial settlement that curtailed German power and resources as far as possible and would then have to be effectively enforced by the victors. Rather,

---

[97] See Madden and Fieldhouse (1985–2000), VI, pp. 678–9; Darwin (2009), pp. 353, 346–53.
[98] Lloyd George speech, 12 September 1918, in *The Times*, 13 September 1918.

it was premised on the assumption that it would be difficult but possible to craft a settlement that created conditions for what would then have to be consolidated over time: a new, overall legitimate equilibrium, a balance of security, status, rights, and the satisfaction of different sets of core national interests – including those of the vanquished powers, once certain essential conditions had been met.

While notably Foreign Office experts still used "balance-of-power" terminology, it was the pursuit of a such a more comprehensively conceived equilibrium that came to shape British approaches – and particularly Lloyd George's approach – to all the questions that were deemed vital and that were clearly regarded as intricately connected: the question of how the security of France and the smaller states of western Europe was to be assured; the question of how the unavoidable reordering of Central and Eastern Europe was to be effected, which also raised the problem of how the Bolshevik challenge should be treated; and, above all, the question of what status and shape Germany was to have in the postwar system. Undoubtedly, evolving British plans were influenced by the aim to minimise the potential for future conflict – and the need for renewed military intervention on the European continent. But they reached beyond this aim. Fundamentally, Lloyd George agreed with Foreign Office strategists that it was in Britain's interest to prevent the re-emergence of a marked imbalance of power in Europe. Above all, this meant that Germany had to be denied the possibility to regain its inherent military superiority and embark on another quest for "world power". But nor was the French government to be allowed to seize on the outcome of the war to establish a continental preponderance – which in British eyes was impossible to sustain and bound to have destabilising effects.

Yet the prime minister's general assumptions about peacemaking and the future Atlantic and global order clearly transcended such concerns. One of the main lessons he had drawn from the war and the fact that Britain had finally been compelled to intervene on the side of France and Russia was that a reliance on narrowly defined alliances and power-political remedies had been counter-productive. In his assessment, this had in fact exacerbated the structural problems of the pre-war international system. What thus became one of Lloyd George's core maxims was that different ways had to be charted so that Britain would never have to intervene in Europe again to redress the "balance of power" – that basic parameters and rules for a new kind of peace system, and equilibrium, had to be established. To this end, he deemed it crucial to reassure the elites and wider populations of France and the smaller West European states.

The prime minister unquestionably recognised the cardinal importance of French security concerns for the entire peacemaking process; and he intended to preserve a fundamental alignment and understanding with Britain's wartime ally in the longer term. But, as noted, he – like Balfour – was not prepared to predicate British security policy on an actual alliance with France, which would necessarily be directed against Germany. Rather, he would seek to address the question of French and wider European security and re-assurance by forming a new concert – in which the United States was to play a vital role – and by imposing far-reaching military restrictions on the vanquished power.

This way, Lloyd George and Balfour also aimed to counter or at least moderate what they came to view as self-defeating French aspirations to reverse the balance of forces on the European continent, particularly by gaining control over the Rhineland yet also by draconically reducing Germany's economic potential or even undermining its political and territorial integrity. For in their judgement such aspirations threatened to create a precarious status quo and dangerous sources of instability and future conflict – by provoking precisely the kind of German resentment and revisionist ambitions the victors ought to nip in the bud. Lloyd George thus categorically rejected the far-reaching schemes that Clemenceau and Foch presented during the inter-allied consultations in London in early December. He notably distanced his government from Foch's proposal to establish a new strategic frontier on the Rhine by supporting the creation of an independent Rhenish state that was to be guaranteed by Britain and France. His concern, which Balfour shared, was that such a strategy would ultimately produce exactly what it purported to prevent: renewed German aggression. Nor was the British premier willing to take up Clemenceau's suggestion to strike a grand bargain that would have linked an accommodation of British and French imperial claims in the Middle East – in Britain's favour – with British support for a prolonged occupation of the Rhineland.[99]

More fundamentally, Lloyd George had by this time developed the conception of a stern and punitive yet at the same time just and redemptive peace that, as he saw it, was required to pave the way for a stable and ultimately *integrative* postwar order.[100] Reflecting the prevalent outlook in the War Cabinet, the prime minister was clearly convinced that the victors had a moral claim to impose chastising peace terms on Germany – after a cataclysmic war that, in his view, Wilhelminian militarism had caused and in which German leaders had violated "the law of nations". Ultimately, these terms had to be tantamount to a redemptive reckoning for the German people, which he regarded as a necessary precondition for discrediting the "old order" and accommodating a chastened Germany in the postwar order. Essentially, Lloyd George adhered to the rationale that if it "repudiate(d) and condemn (ed)" the "perfidy of her rulers" a Germany "freed from military domination"

[99] Minutes of the Imperial War Cabinet, 30 December 1918, CAB 23/42. Balfour memorandum, 18 March 1919; Balfour notes, 5 March 1919, Lloyd George Papers, F/3/4/19 and 15.

[100] Lloyd George speech, 12 September 1918, *The Times*, 13 September 1918.

and with a reliable democratic government would *eventually* be "welcome into the great League of Nations".[101] What he thus came to pursue after the armistice – influenced by Kerr – can be characterised as a "policy of redemption". It was essentially a harsher version of Wilson's probation policy and, like it, designed to vindicate a victor's peace. Its core rationale was that the political leaders of postwar Germany, and the German people, had to demonstrate not only that they had repudiated Wilhelmine militarism and embraced democratic renewal but also, and crucially, that they would abide by the peace terms the western powers would decree. These were the cardinal prerequisites for Germany's eventual integration in a new international concert – and the comity of nations.[102]

These rationales and considerations would inform Lloyd George's peace-making efforts in 1919. But what became increasingly dominant, and integral to his pursuit of a new equilibrium, was the ambitious idea to use whatever leverage Britain had to make what he defined as a *balanced* peace: a peace on terms that – while satisfying core British interests – were so "just" and consonant with "the principles of liberty and fair play" that they could also be accepted by the vanquished power. As he impressed on the Imperial War Cabinet, it was imperative to seek a settlement that would not arouse a "spirit of revenge" in Germany or arm it with "a real wrong".[103]

As noted, what the British premier regarded as essential, and essentially justified, was the fulfilment of substantial British reparation demands – while he subjectively opposed excessive indemnity claims that could undermine the German economy and also rejected long-term measures to restrict German trade or curtail its economic power. A further priority he considered entirely justified after his crusade against militarist "Prussianism" was a substantial disarmament of Germany and its elimination as a major military and especially naval power for the foreseeable future. He thus insisted on a strict application of the military terms of the armistice, and he attached particular importance to the prohibition of a German conscript army.

Essentially, however, the British premier – like Wilson – sought to preserve Germany's territorial and political integrity as a European power. He in fact deemed this a fundamental precondition not just for pre-empting German irredentist and revisionist pressures but also for the longer-term stabilisation of Europe – and the consolidation of a new equilibrium. And, though with

---

[101] *Ibid.* See also Lloyd George statements, Imperial War Cabinet, 14 August 1918, CAB 23/7.

[102] Lloyd George speech, 12 September 1918, *The Times*, 13 September 1918; Kerr to Lloyd George, ca. 19 February 1919, Kerr Papers, GD 40/17/1223.

[103] See Lloyd George comments, 12 November 1918, Kerr Papers; Lloyd George statement, 16 November 1918, Lloyd George Papers, F 237; Imperial War Cabinet deliberations, 10 and 11 November 1918, CAB 23/8 and 14.

different accentuations, this premise was shared by the protagonists of the Imperial War Cabinet and relevant experts in the Foreign Office. While accepting the restitution of Alsace-Lorraine to France the British premier and other influential policymakers thus opposed what they regarded as both unwarranted and counterproductive French aspirations to alter the status quo on Germany's western border, which obviously clashed with German self-determination claims.

Appreciation for the new power of the self-determination paradigm and ultimately decisive concerns for the future Euro-Atlantic equilibrium also informed British attitudes towards the *Anschluß* question that arose after the dissolution of the Austro-Hungarian Empire. Significantly, the Foreign Office's permanent under-secretary, Charles Hardinge, actually recommended that Britain should support the union of German Austria and Germany, which in his assessment was impossible to prevent in the longer run anyway. While acknowledging the concerns the emergence of a more powerful German state raised, he and the Foreign Office expert Lewis Namier dismissed them "both on the grounds of principle and expediency". They pointed to the political difficulty of opposing Austro-German invocations of self-determination; and they argued that an accession of the predominantly Catholic Austria would actually dilute the still dangerous influence of protestant Prussianism.[104] In retrospect, Lloyd George would voice sympathies for such arguments. But after the armistice his emphasis lay on preventing an *immediate Anschluß* because in his judgement the creation of a greater German-speaking power would unsettle Europe's postwar balance of forces and complicate advances towards a stable equilibrium. At the same time, the British premier was well aware of Clemenceau's vehement opposition to an Austro-German union. Eventually, he would agree with Wilson on the formula that such a union would not be "permanent(ly)" prohibited but made dependent on the "good conduct" of both Germany and Austria. The final decision was to be made by the League of Nations.[105]

As noted, till the autumn of 1918 Lloyd George had upheld his pledge not to seek the "break-up" of the Austro-Hungarian Empire. Similar to Wilson, he had thus also merely called for greater autonomy – and "genuine self-govern-ment" – for "those Austro-Hungarian nationalities who have long desired it".[106] Once the demise of the Habsburg Empire had become irreversible, however, the Foreign Office had come out in favour of an independent Czechoslovakia and recommended that Britain should at last back the cause

---

[104] Hardinge note, undated, FO 371/4354/ f65/PC65; Namier memorandum "German Austria", December 1918, FO 371/4355/f90/PC90.

[105] Lloyd George (1938), II, p. 23; Mantoux (1992), I, pp. 459–60. See Low (1974), pp. 40–1, 324–5.

[106] Lloyd George speech, 5 January 1918, Lloyd George (1918).

of Beneš and Masaryk unequivocally.[107] Though far less emphatically, Lloyd George had also come to support the creation of a Czechoslovakian state. During the armistice negotiations he had stressed that the question of which nations were to be founded on the territory of the former empire had to be "very judiciously arranged with a view to the sentiments of the different populations". But he subsequently took no particular interest in this problem. And he would ultimately be forced to deal with the *faits accomplis* that Beneš and Masaryk created with decisive French support ever since their provisional government had issued a "Declaration of Independence of the Czechoslovak Nation" on 28 October 1918. Lloyd George remained critical of what he considered to be the new Czechoslovak government's excessive territorial claims. And in principle one of the concerns animating his revised peace strategy at Versailles – namely to minimise the size of *German* minorities in the new states of Central and Eastern Europe – also applied to the roughly 3 million Sudeten Germans that Beneš's demand for Bohemia's "historic frontier" would place under Czechoslovak rule.[108] Yet, preoccupied with other priorities, notably the Polish–German settlement, he would not take any steps to meet the "self-determination" claims of the Sudeten Germans.

VIII.   A "New Europe" in the East? Self-Determination, Overriding Strategic Concerns and the Equilibrium Paradigm

More generally, not only leading experts in the Foreign Office but also Lloyd George and his Cabinet were clearly aware by the end of the war that "settling" the German question in the east and creating a stable status quo on Germany's eastern borders would be among the most daunting challenges of the entire peacemaking process. And they recognised too that the way in which this challenge was met would have major implications for the consolidation of some kind of postwar equilibrium. At the same time, they realised that it was indissolubly bound up with a wider and no less fundamental question that they now had to tackle, namely how to establish a new kind of order in the geopolitically critical region of Eastern Europe that had been dominated by the three Eastern Empires. And they were also cognisant of the fluidity of the constellation they confronted – a constellation in which armed conflicts persisted after the armistice and different nationalist movements, particularly those striving for new Polish and Czechoslovak states, had already begun to create "facts on the ground".

---

[107] Seton-Watson memorandum, November 1918, FO 371/4354/f52/PC52.

[108] Notes of Lloyd George–House conversation, 2 November 1918, House Papers; Lloyd George memorandum, 25 March 1919, *PWW*, LVI, p. 260. See Perman (1962), pp. 63–96.

While seeking to come to grips with this complex situation, British policy-makers had barely begun to develop strategies to deal with the uncertainties of the Russian civil war, in which Lloyd George – in contrast to Churchill and others – did not want to become further embroiled, and to address the even more critical question of what place Russia – and potentially a Bolshevik Russia – was to have in the new order. The premise of Lloyd George's evolving approach was that the western powers had to consider the legitimate interests of the "great people" of Russia in all decisions that affected the territory of the former Russian Empire. And while he saw the need to involve the representatives of Lenin's "White" opponents in an eventual peace process he also was actually in favour of negotiating with the Bolshevik regime, which in his eyes represented Russia's "*de facto* Government" at this stage.[109] The British prime minister was convinced that in the longer run the western powers could find ways to contain the Bolshevik threat by political means – not least by implementing forward-looking political, economic and social reform measures.[110] But his more immediate concern was to counter the spread of Bolshevik influence in Germany and Eastern Europe and the looming threat of a future Bolshevik–German alliance. Yet on the eve of the peace conference it still remained highly unclear how and to what end negotiations with Bolshevik representatives could be conducted – and whether some kind of *modus vivendi* with Lenin's regime was conceivable. And it was even harder to foresee for British policymakers how far any agreement with the Bolsheviks could be concluded that actually furthered Lloyd George's underlying aim of fostering overall European stability.

In the meantime, those who shaped Britain's "eastern policies" came to focus on the complex problems that arose in connection with the inevitable restructuring of Eastern Europe. The protagonists of Foreign Office planning efforts for the region, who brought to bear considerable historical expertise, developed an ambitious strategy to transform this part of a shattered old world into a "New Europe". The most important impulses here came from the members of the Foreign Office's Political Intelligence Department, which had been set up in March 1918 to provide recommendations to the government in anticipation of an eventual peace conference. Building on schemes he had drawn up during the war, Headlam-Morley, who had become its assistant director, argued that peace and stability would best be assured by reconfiguring Eastern Europe as far as possible on the basis of the principles of self-determination and nationality. In his assessment, the aim to "establish nation States" in accordance with these principles "entirely coincide(d)" with what he

---

[109] See Cabinet deliberations, Imperial War Cabinet 48, 31 December 1918, CAB 23/42; Lloyd George statement, Council of Ten, 12 January 1919, *FRUS-PPC*, III, p. 491.

[110] Lloyd George (1938), I, pp. 330–1.

saw as Britain's strategic interest in fostering a more viable balance of power in Europe; for this balance now hinged on the creation of East European "nation States" – like a viable Poland – that would hence prevent the predominance of any one power on the continent. Headlam-Morley noted presciently that "the method" by which the East European "territorial problem" was settled would affect "the future peace of the world". And he proposed a "method" that would be exceedingly difficult, if not impossible to implement at the peace conference, namely an *equitable* application of the self-determination principle. He emphasised that it had to be applied to Germans and "Magyars" just as much as to Poles, Czechs, Slovaks and Romanians. Headlam-Morley thus recommended that the British government should in "cordial co-operation" with the United States take the lead in restructuring Eastern Europe on premises that Wilson championed. At the same time, this was to bring a "legitimate extension of British influence" in the region.[111]

Lloyd George indeed intended to act as an "honest broker" in the process of remaking Eastern Europe. But he only made very selective use of Foreign Office expertise and recommendations in approaching this task. Like his foreign secretary, the prime minister acknowledged the need to pay unprecedented attention to the self-determination principle. But he regarded a rigid application of this principle as highly problematic – not only when this affected the future of the British Empire but also with a view to the complex situation in Eastern Europe. He thus agreed with Balfour's verdict that it was unwise to "carry" the "principle of self-determination" to "its extreme point".[112]

Overall, Lloyd George tried to find a compromise between ethnic, historical and economic considerations; but he ultimately gave priority to overriding strategic imperatives and, above all, to what he regarded as the requirements of a new international equilibrium. On these premises, the prime minister's basic rationale was to promote the creation of viable and, as far as possible, democratic states that actually had the potential to consolidate – and could thus also contribute to the consolidation of a regional order whose preservation would not require constant interventions in the future. Above all, his approach would be guided by the maxim that while Polish and Czechoslovak aspirations to found nation-states had to be satisfied, the main emphasis

---

[111] Headlam-Morley memorandum, 15 November 1918, FO 371/4353/f23/PC55. See Goldstein (1991), pp. 124–5. Developing an ambitious programme, Foreign Office experts recommended a reorganisation of South-Eastern Europe along similar lines to prevent it from becoming again the powder keg setting off a major war. British policy was to foster the establishment of multi-ethnic states – Romania, Bulgaria, Albania, and the new state of Yugoslavia. They proposed "international guarantees" for their "independence and territorial integrity". See Leeper and Nicolson memorandum, 13 December 1918, FO 371/4355/f68/PC68.

[112] Minutes of the Imperial War Cabinet, 24 December 1918, CAB 23/42.

should lie on accommodating German interests and self-determination claims in order to pre-empt future German irredentism. In his judgement, this priority had to be pursued not only for the sake of Europe's future equilibrium but also to safeguard the future security and development prospects of Germany's less powerful eastern neighbours.

Like their American counterparts, Foreign Office experts clearly regarded the establishment of a viable Polish state as both the most critical and the most complex question awaiting the peacemakers in Eastern Europe. They had long favoured an approach that on the one hand underscored ethnic criteria in determining Polish boundaries and, on the other, was informed by overriding geopolitical and strategic concerns. Yet they did not reach a consensus on essential points, notably the new state's precise boundaries, its access to the Baltic Sea and the future status of Danzig. Esme Howard, who would provide significant advice at Versailles, regarded the "creation of a strong compact Poland" with appropriate access to the sea as the "first necessity" in the reordering of Eastern Europe. He argued that the decisive criterion in determining Poland's boundaries had to be respect for Polish self-determination claims – even if that meant severing East Prussia from the rest of Germany. He recommended, however, that Danzig should remain a German city; and he would subsequently propose that, along with Hamburg and Stettin, the predominantly German city should be made into an international "free port" under the authority of the League.[113]

Another expert scholar, Charles Oman, Professor of Modern History at Oxford, argued more unequivocally that not the interests of postwar Germany but those of the new Polish state should take precedence. Echoing the demands of the London-based Polish Association – which eventually also the most renowned Polish immigrant, the novelist Joseph Conrad, made his own – Oman held that a strong Polish state needed uncontested access to the Baltic Sea and that this warranted support for a "Polish corridor", including Danzig. But Lewis Namier – who was of Jewish origin and had grown up in Galicia – urged the Foreign Office to veto what he regarded as the Polish National Committee's excessive – and chauvinistic – ambitions. And he was deeply sceptical about granting the new Polish state access to the sea via a corridor, observing that for "the sake of Poland's own future" Britain had to "oppose exaggerated Polish claims" that would place sizeable German minorities under Polish rule and thus only fuel German irredentism. Weighing in on the internal debate, Cecil also insisted that the scheme of a Polish corridor ought to be rejected for reasons of overall European stability, because it would "only create a sore place which will never heal". He thus favoured providing Poland with special transit rights to the sea – through what was to remain

---

[113] Howard memorandum, "Poland", November 1918, FO 371/4354/f46/PC70.

German territory – and suggested that the League should review the new *status quo* in ten years' time.[114]

Paying some attention to Foreign Office recommendations, Lloyd George came to pursue priorities that echoed Cecil's and were in fact relatively compatible with Wilson's. Following the armistice, he confirmed his support for an "independent Poland", which de facto had come into existence in mid-November 1918. At the same time, he adhered to the premise that the new Polish state had to be formed in accordance with the "general principle of national self-determination" and, crucially, limited to territory inhabited by "genuinely Polish" populations.[115] Both the prime minister and his foreign secretary retained a distinctly paternalistic outlook on the Polish national movement. And they came to adopt a very critical attitude towards the nationalist agenda pursued by Dmowski and the Polish National Committee, and what they saw as their outrageous aspirations to expand Polish claims to territories with mixed populations or even a majority of non-Polish ethnicities. When the armistice was finalised, Balfour had underscored that the British government would not support a reconstitution of Poland in its historic borders of 1772. And he urged Dmowski and his followers not only to form a coalition government with Paderewski's more moderate faction but also to prove their "fitness for independence" by showing "self control and orderliness".[116]

While actually harbouring liberal sympathies for the cause of an independent Polish state, Lloyd George came to view the complex Polish question chiefly under the aspect of its wider geopolitical ramifications and, above all, its implications for Europe's general pacification after the Great War. And the more he had to countenance Dmowski's growing influence, and French pressure on his behalf, the more his predominant concern became to prevent, with American support, a constellation that in his view threatened to cause endemic instability and even contained the "seed of future war": the creation of a new Poland that would be "alienated" from its powerful western neighbour from the start because it comprised sizeable German minorities and formerly German territory. On similar grounds, he would oppose schemes for a "Greater Poland" that clashed with Russian interests and threatened to produce similarly unsettling effects on the new state's eastern border.[117]

---

[114] Oman memorandum, 14 November 1918; Namier memorandum, "Poland", 6 December 1918; Cecil minute (undated), FO 371/4354/f46/PC46, 73; Joseph Conrad, "A Note on the Polish Problem", in Conrad (1921), pp. 175–84.

[115] For Lloyd George's essentials see his Caxton Hall speech, 5 January 1918, Lloyd George (1918).

[116] Balfour to Cambon, 30 November 1918, FO 371/3277; Balfour to Wade, 5 January 1919, FO 608/68.

[117] Council of Four, 27 March 1919, Mantoux (1992), I, pp. 36–8; FRUS-PPC, IV, pp. 415–17.

While seeking to minimise them, Lloyd George thus clearly appreciated the unprecedented relevance of minority problems for future peace and stability in Europe. The relevant experts in the Foreign Office also clearly expected that it would be impossible to avoid such problems in the "New Europe" of nation-states – even if new states could be established with the most scrupulous attention to "lines of allegiance and nationality". They also concluded that minority conflicts could become particularly virulent in the new Polish state; but they reckoned that such conflicts were bound to arise across all of Eastern and south-eastern Europe. They thus emphasised that finding effective ways to protect the rights of ethnic and religious minorities in the region would be critical.[118] Like the Wilson administration, the British government had long been pressured to address this issue by Jewish advocacy and interest groups that sought to highlight the plight of Eastern Europe's Jewish minorities and the urgency of establishing a new regime of protections for them after the war. Most influential here was the Joint Foreign Committee, which had been founded at the end of 1917 and was headed by the journalist Lucien Wolf. Joining forces with the American Jewish Congress, Wolf lobbied energetically on behalf of minority rights and autonomy provisions for Jewish populations in Eastern Europe, above all in a future Polish state.[119]

Though their main concern clearly pertained to the future of the German-speaking minorities, Lloyd George and Balfour did not ignore the concerns of Jewish organisations. Essentially, however, they were as wary as the relevant Foreign Office experts of any ambitious new schemes to protect minority rights. They notably opposed the idea of establishing a universal regime of minority protection under the auspices of the League that would have entailed far-reaching commitments and challenged the premises of state sovereignty they sought to uphold. Instead, they proposed to fall back on a more trad-itional approach that had been codified at the Congress of Berlin: the "new and independent States" were to be compelled to agree to specific "territorial treaties", formally guaranteed by the principal victors, that would require them to safeguard the political, cultural and religious rights of minorities who lived within their borders. Further, the British experts recommended the establishment of independent regional commissions that were to provide oversight and enforcement. Thus, neither the League nor the great powers would be obliged to intervene to protect minorities or to enforce minority rights.[120] Overall, however, minority problems only received scant attention while the British government prepared for the peace conference.

---

[118] Leeper and Nicolson memorandum, 13 December 1918, FO 371/4355/f68/PC68.
[119] See Fink (2004), pp. 98–9.
[120] Headlam-Morley minute, 20 November 1918, FO 371/4353; Zimmern memorandum, undated, FO 371/4353; Percy note, January 1919, Miller (1928), II, p. 130. See Fink (2004), p. 154.

IX. Fundamental Premises. "Imposing a Just and Desirable Peace" – and the Eventual Integration of Germany into a Renovated International Order

A fundamental premise of Lloyd George's peace strategy was that forging an "equitable" settlement at the peace conference was only a first, though decisive, step on the longer path towards a new European and transatlantic equilibrium. And at the core of the *medium- and longer-term* strategy he pursued lay the rationale to foster stability by accommodating and *eventually* integrating an appropriately reduced and chastised Germany in the postwar order. This went hand in hand with the medium-term aim to buttress the consolidation of a stable republican order in Germany – and thus to contain both Bolshevik and reactionary forces. Fundamentally, the British premier still insisted that the price the new German decision-makers, and the German people, had to accept was to abandon the *Reich*'s ambitions to be a world power. But he also reasoned – within the limits of his "redemptive peace" definition – that the more acceptable the initial peace terms could be made for Germany the easier it would be to draw it, at a later stage, into a renovated international concert – and the comity of nations. All of this was relatively compatible with the outlook and priorities Wilson had come to adopt by the end of 1918; but it collided with the core rationales behind Clemenceau's pursuit of a peace that ensured France's longer-term security vis-à-vis Germany.

But Lloyd George's peacemaking conception was based on one crucial – and problematic – axiom that he not only upheld but actually reinforced after the armistice. It was the axiom that, following a war on the scale of the Great War, it was not only imperative but also possible to "impose a just and desirable peace" on the defeated power. Again echoing Wilson, the British premier indeed acted on the assumption that, with him in the role of an "honest broker", the victors would be able to lay foundations for a legitimate peace settlement – and a legitimate international order – by first dictating terms and rules to the defeated power, regardless of who represented it.[121] Confidentially, Balfour had earlier formulated the underlying premise of this approach when noting that once its authorities had accepted the provisions of the armistice, notably its military clauses, Germany would no longer have any real bargaining power and "practically ... have to accept any terms that we chose to dictate to her".[122]

It was on these premises, espoused not only by Lloyd George but also by an overwhelming majority in the War Cabinet, that the British government rejected the prospect of any substantial negotiations with the representatives

---

[121] See Lloyd George speech, Manchester, 12 September 1918, *The Times*, 13 September 1918; Minutes of Anglo-French and Allied meetings, 1 and 2 December 1918, CAB 28/5.

[122] Derby diary, 31 October 1918, Derby Papers, 28/1/1.

of the new provisional government in Berlin. And it was on the same premises that, at the Inter-Allied Conference of 2 December, Lloyd George essentially accepted the Clemenceau government's procedural "terms of reference" for the forthcoming peace conference. He thus basically agreed that the Allied Powers should deliberate the "Preliminaries of Peace" amongst themselves and then present them to German plenipotentiaries, but only in order to compel them to accept what the victors had already decided.[123] The British premier closed ranks with Clemenceau to contain what he still regarded as a potential threat at this stage, namely that Wilson would insist on a negotiated peace with Germany. On 31 December, the Imperial War Cabinet confirmed its endorsement of his decision.[124]

On the eve of the peace conference, Lloyd George signalled to Wilson that he did not rule out some kind of discussion with Germany at a later stage of the proceedings. But he was not prepared to negotiate with the German government in the decisive first stages of the peace conference when the essential conditions were to be determined, including those of the indemnity settlement. And, revealingly, the War Cabinet dismissed the American president's argument that a peace whose terms were merely presented to the defeated power would be a "sham".[125] In short, though British positions were less unequivocal than those of the French government, what Lloyd George envisaged essentially precluded a substantial negotiating process between the victors and the vanquished.

These priorities and underlying assumptions of Lloyd George's pursuit of a "just" peace also account for what at first glance appears to be a fundamental ambivalence at the heart of British policy towards Germany – and of British reactions to the tumultuous inner-German developments during and after the November revolution. On the one hand, concerns over Bolshevism's destabilising effect on Germany and Central Europe were growing. And there was an underlying interest in fostering the emergence of a moderate social-democratic or centrist government and a stable republican order, not only to ward off Bolshevik incursions but also to prevent a resurgence of "chauvinist" and reactionary forces that would seek to reverse the outcome of the war. On the other hand, the Lloyd George government uncompromisingly adhered to a policy of "shunning" the embattled Council of People's Deputies under Ebert and Haase. It took no steps that could have aided or stabilised the new government in the domestic-political struggle it faced. It did not send any signals that would have implied its recognition as a legitimate authority with which negotiations could be

---

[123] French "Proposals for the Preliminaries of Peace with Germany", 26 November 1918; French note, 3 December, CAB 1/27/24 and 26.
[124] Imperial War Cabinet, 31 December 1918, CAB 23/42.
[125] Minutes of the Imperial War Cabinet, 30 December 1918, memorandum no. 47, CAB 23/42.

pursued in the future – and even refrained from spelling out what criteria a legitimate German government would have to fulfil to this end.

Not least, this policy was pursued to pre-empt pressures – from Wilson, from Liberals and Labour at home, and from Berlin – to act in accordance with Lloyd George's wartime rhetoric, his Caxton Hall platform of early 1918, and "reward" German advances towards democracy by way of a lenient peace settlement. For this would have required above all to moderate the official British reparations agenda, which was ruled out. In league with Clemenceau, Lloyd George thus rebuffed all attempts by Ebert to invoke the new government's social democratic credentials to appeal for a moderate peace on Wilsonian terms. And he took all necessary measures to ensure that the Ebert–Haase government would be excluded from the peacemaking process.[126]

In Britain, the government's course was sharply criticised by prominent Labour figures like Henderson and MacDonald, who sought to push the government to promote democratisation in Germany, aid the new government in Berlin and bring a democratic Germany into a "League of Free Peoples". And it was equally criticised by Liberals and Radicals who had long argued that Britain should build bridges to the proponents of democracy and concili-ation in Germany by offering a moderate peace and who now advocated a similar policy to bolster liberal and social democratic forces in Germany – and the prospects of a new democratic order in Europe.[127] But Lloyd George and the Conservative protagonists of what had been the "knock-out blow" coali-tion dismissed criticism of this kind; and they never considered offering such incentives or pursuing such a peace. The pledges they had made during the Khaki Election campaign and the harsher peace programme to which the prime minister had committed himself at the end only hardened their resolve further. Formally, the Lloyd George government came to back the French proposal that the Allied Powers could only have official dealings with Germany once a "constituent Assembly" and then a new government had been elected "freely by universal, secret and direct suffrage". But the main rationale behind its assent to this formula was to justify a postponement of any such official dealing while the victors hammered out the terms of the peace settlement.[128]

Essentially, Lloyd George and his closest advisers Kerr and Hankey remained profoundly sceptical about the prospects of swift and decisive

---

[126] Thus the apt characterisation in Newton (1997), pp. 309–15.

[127] See Labour Party (1919), p. 185; MacDonald editorial, *Labour Leader*, 27 February 1919; Marquand (1977), pp. 248–9; Murray to Balfour, 29 March 1918, Murray Papers, 36; Newton (1997), pp. 130 ff.

[128] French Proposals for the Preliminaries of Peace with Germany", 26 November 1918, CAB 1/27/24; Headlam-Morley note, December 1918(?), Headlam-Morley Papers, Acc. 727, Box 11.

progress towards a stable democratic government in Germany. And they equally retained doubts about the prospects of a wider democratisation process, particularly in the short term. They were not prepared to count on transformative advances in the immediate aftermath of the war, arguing that even in the best-case scenario more substantive steps towards a viable German democratic order would take time in view of the country's authoritarian past. Crucially, however, they were not prepared to further the fortunes of a fledgling German republic at the price of renouncing core British peace aims.

In the final analysis, what mattered most was Lloyd George's determination to "impose a just peace" irrespective of which government ruled in Berlin – and regardless of how he assessed the trustworthiness and democratic credentials of leading actors like Ebert. Even after the constitutional assembly in Weimar had passed a new constitution and elected the first democratically legitimised government under Scheidemann, Kerr continued to counsel the prime minister that in his judgement Germany was still "fundamentally unrepentant" and required "very firm and uncompromising handling".[129] And Lloyd George essentially concurred with this assessment. At this critical stage, his main concern was, ultimately, not to buttress a moderate democratic government but to ensure that whatever government emerged in Germany was sufficiently stable to sign the peace the victors would decree, and to ensure its ratification.

---

[129] Kerr to Lloyd George, ca. 19 February 1919, Kerr Papers, GD 40/17/1223. See Newton (1997), pp. 367–8.

12

The Search for Security and an Atlantic Alliance of the Victors

The Reorientation of French Approaches to Peace and International Order

Undoubtedly, the dominant theme of the Clemenceau government's approach to peacemaking in the aftermath of the Great War was the search for security – and as far as possible "complete security" – from renewed German threats. And the fact that this objective overrode and shaped all other considerations set the French approach apart from those pursued by the British and American protagonists. In the perception of the leading French policymakers, theirs was a quest to guarantee for France and the entire world that Germany would "not repeat her offenses" of 1914 – and 1870.[1] And the underlying rationale espoused by those who came to devise and indeed reorientate French policies after the armistice was no less unequivocal: to ensure their nation's long-term *sécurité* and development prospects by charting old *and* new paths to redress the structural disequilibrium between a war-battered France and a German power that had emerged from the war hardly unscathed but with a still far superior economic, demographic and strategic potential.

A fundamental premise of French pursuits was that it would *not* be possible to turn back the clock of history, break up the German nation-state and return to a status quo akin to that which had existed under the nineteenth century's Vienna system. In effect, Clemenceau and the strategists who advised him recognised this and never actually pursued such radical objectives, not least because they were aware that this would provoke forceful Anglo-American opposition and thus undermine what they sought to preserve above all after the hard-won victory: "Allied unity". In a wider context, for all their resolve to protect the French Empire and expand France's imperial influence by implementing the Sykes-Picot agreement, the focus of the key decision-makers in Paris was thus far more unambiguously on Europe, and Germany, than that of Wilson and British policymakers.

It has to be emphasised that Clemenceau and those who developed the French agenda for the peace conference operated in the shadow of a war that had affected France more profoundly than Britain or, naturally, the United

---

[1] Thus Tardieu (II/1921), p. 78. See Clemenceau speech, 29 December 1918, *Journal Officiel (Chambre)*, 1918, 3732–3; Tardieu memorandum, 20 January 1919, Tardieu Papers, vol. 4; Stevenson (1982); Soutou (1998), pp. 168–9; Jackson (2013), pp. 235 ff.

States. It had not only devastated France's eastern provinces and the eastern heartlands of French industry but also turned the country into the most heavily indebted victor – indeed a power on the verge of bankruptcy, with massive obligations both to Britain and the United States totalling 35 billion gold francs and an overall public debt that had risen to more than 200 billion gold francs by the end of 1918. Above all, however, the war had taken a colossal human, mental and psychological toll. Official estimates would tabulate a French death toll of roughly 1.4 million; and they would confirm that more than a quarter of all French soldiers had died and almost half of them had been more or less seriously wounded. More than 2 million war victims, including incapacitated veterans, widows and affected families had to be accommodated. All in all, it was estimated that the French population had shrunk by roughly 3 million people, to less than 40 million.

Shaping the French postwar outlook, these developments further exacerbated the imbalance vis-à-vis Germany that so preoccupied Clemenceau and his main advisers, who at the same time underestimated the war's consequences for the defeated power *outre-Rhin*. Not only the strategic but also the political and psychological implications of France's very costly victory were thus immense. And consequently its political leaders – like their British counterparts – faced unprecedented public demands for a financial and political "peace dividend": demands not only for material – and immaterial – compensations but also for re-assurances against a further calamity on the scale of *la grande guerre* that were exceedingly difficult to moderate, let alone to satisfy.[2]

I.   Essential Assumptions and Aims: The Priority of a New Atlantic Alliance, "Structural Re-Balancing" and the Pursuit of a Community of Western Democracies

Against this background, the main architects of what evolved into France's ambitious peace and security programme for Versailles – Clemenceau, his key strategic adviser André Tardieu and, in the financial and economic spheres, Commerce Minister Étienne Clémentel – essentially pursued aims and acted on assumptions that had informed French policies since 1917. In critical respects, however, they revised and adapted their peacemaking strategies after the armistice – particularly once it was confirmed that Wilson would actually attend the peace conference, and that he and the power he represented would thus play a decisive part in negotiating the parameters of the postwar order. Essentially, they came to develop their own conception of a new Atlantic order. What they envisaged was a hierarchical system of order chiefly designed

---

[2] See Becker and Krumeich (2008), pp. 294–5; Becker (1986). For new comparative perspectives see the relevant contributions in Winter (2014), vols. II and III.

to contain Germany and dominated by what Clemenceau described as France's "political, economic and military union" with Britain and the United States and what Tardieu conceived as an exclusive community of "Western democracies".[3]

On these premises, and under the *leitmotif* of an "organised peace", the French protagonists indeed came to pursue a transatlantic strategy to realise their wider and intimately connected objectives: not only to establish a robust security system that checked and constrained German power, but also to found an "economic union" of the western democracies that remedied France's structural problems.[4] What thus became a key aim of Clemenceau's policy was to preserve the wartime alliance with Britain and the "associated" American power and to transform it into something unprecedented – a peacetime alliance of the principal victors that would commit not just Britain but also and notably the United States to guaranteeing French security and safeguarding a restructured European order against "inevitable" German challenges in the longer term.[5]

In the interest of maintaining "unity" and solidarity among the victors and to pave the way for a successful process of strategic bargaining, Clemenceau had even eventually taken up Tardieu's recommendation and altered his official position on the League of Nations. While not hiding his underlying scepticism, he committed France more unequivocally to the goal of creating a new international organisation. More importantly, however, he came to espouse the maxim that the League was to be established, not as a "Wilsonian" institution or platform of a new international concert but, essentially, as a framework for the firmest possible postwar alliance of the victors.

Unquestionably, in the conception that Clemenceau and Tardieu developed, the organisation's chief purpose was to draw the United States and Britain into such an alliance. They thus envisaged the League as a means to an end: an instrument to forge an exclusive rather than integrative postwar system that was controlled by the victorious western democracies, included other "free nations" but isolated Germany for the foreseeable future – and that at the same time allowed the victors to contain the vanquished power. In the longer term, they calculated, this could create essential conditions for *eventually* pursuing efforts to "find an accommodation" with Germany from a position of strength and, crucially, within a system that provided essential safeguards for French security.[6]

---

[3] Clemenceau statement to the Foreign Affairs Commission of the *Assemblée Nationale*, 29 July 1919, CAE, *Assemblée Nationale*, CTP, C/7773; Tardieu memorandum, 25 February 1919, Tardieu, (II/1921), pp. 156–61.

[4] Clémentel letter to Clemenceau, 19 September 1918, in Clémentel (1931), pp. 343–7.

[5] Tardieu to Clemenceau, 26 November 1918, Fonds Clemenceau, 6N 137–3, SHD-DAT; Clemenceau speech, 29 December 1918, *Journal Officiel (Chambre)*, 1918, 3732–3.

[6] Clemenceau speech, 25 September 1919, *Journal Officiel (Chambre)*, 1919.

Clemenceau's and Tardieu's new transatlantic priorities thus created a – limited – opening for the ideas of Bourgeois and the members of the Bourgeois Commission, who had played such a marginal role during the war yet now saw a chance to gain support for their idea to found a League on French terms. More generally, they seemed to give a boost to the aspirations of the French liberal "internationalists" who had lobbied for this cause through the *Association française de la Société des Nations*. Following the armistice the French pro-League activists expanded their lobbying efforts. But the League blueprints they promoted were still hardly reconcilable with Wilson's evolving conceptions and prevalent British schemes. For they insisted on a robust *société des nations* that would institute a forceful regime of international law and, crucially, a system of compulsory arbitration and sanctions backed up by force, even calling again for an international force under League auspices.[7] Yet neither Tardieu nor Clemenceau would ever subscribe to this ambitious agenda. They would continue to see the League essentially as a mechanism to realise their alliance plans.

Nonetheless, it became evident by the end of 1918 that the French premier and his key collaborators had to react and to a certain extent accommodate the progressive norms and "internationalist" ideas that had gained new prominence during the war and found their most powerful champion in the American president – including those underpinning the call for a League, norms of international law and arbitration, and of course ideas of "self-determination" and democratisation. The French protagonists had indeed concluded that it was necessary to pay heed to these normative precepts in the altered international environment the Great War had left in its wake. Essentially, though, they would seek to seize on them, and redefine them, to further what they regarded as overriding French security interests vis-à-vis Germany and, closely connected with them, imperative prerequisites of France's economic revitalisation.

At a deeper level, those who devised France's postwar policies had drawn lessons from the existential catastrophe of the war that differed from those informing Wilson's pursuit of a "peace to end all war" or British conceptions of a new international equilibrium. While they were searching for new methods and instrumentalities, the war had not altered but rather reinforced their basic assumptions about the nature of international politics and the requirements of security and stability in its aftermath. They were still not prepared to rely on what they saw as illusory but potentially hazardous Wilsonian notions of "new diplomacy" and universal "collective security". Nor were they prepared to entrust French security even to the most robust *société des nations* – or a novel Atlantic concert. Rather, they held that a

---

[7] Bourgeois Commission report, 8 June 1918, AN, F12 8106; AFSDN programme, 18 December 1918, MAE, SDN, vol. 7.

prudent application – and adaptation – of well-understood maxims of balance-of-power politics and *Realpolitik* were essential to secure France's long-
term future – above all, but not only, vis-à-vis the "structural" German enemy.
It was on the basis of these assumptions that they sought to lay secure
foundations for what could *over time* become a stable "edifice" of international
order in which it would then be possible to transcend "selfish" power politics –
and to accommodate the troublesome *voisin outre-Rhin.*[8]

Fundamental balance-of-power rationales not only informed Clemenceau's
priority of pursuing a postwar "union" with Britain and the United States.
They also lay behind another ambitious programme that, on his instruction,
Tardieu elaborated in December 1918 and early 1919. The core objective of
this far-reaching programme, which built on earlier French schemes, was
nothing less than to change the structural balance of forces and to level the
systemic playing-field in postwar Europe. It was to reinforce the declining
power of France, which in his and Clemenceau's perception had been severely
affected by the war, while at the same time decisively weakening the power and
possibilities of its inherently superior eastern neighbour. Tardieu's comprehensive "re-balancing" agenda, which was complemented by plans developed
in the Commerce Ministry, came to comprise an impressive array of military,
territorial, political, and economic measures.

In line with the French Foreign Ministry, Clemenceau's adviser stressed the
necessity of enforcing an almost complete disarmament of Germany, to be
achieved through an uncompromising execution of the armistice terms and by
establishing a strict regime of military control. Beyond this, he proposed to
sever the strategic coal-and-steel regions of the Saar and Upper Silesia from
postwar Germany. He also adopted the idea, advanced by Foreign Minister
Pichon and the experts of the Quai d'Orsay, to forge a *cordon sanitaire*
between Germany and Bolshevik Russia, demanding the creation of a system
of buffer-states in Eastern Europe, which could become France's allies and
compensate for the lost Russian "counterweight" until the Bolshevik regime
was defeated. Here, the principle of self-determination was only to be invoked
where it furthered these overriding strategic imperatives, i.e. against Germany.
Tardieu's key priority, however, was to create an autonomous Rhenish buffer-
state and thus establish a strategic frontier on the Rhine. An integral part of his
strategy, which Clemenceau backed, was to suggest that France's strategic aims
could be achieved in accordance with Wilsonian precepts, i.e. without violating the self-determination claims of the Rhenish population. More generally,

---

[8] Clemenceau speech, 29 December 1918, *Journal Officiel (Chambre)*, 1918, 3732–3;
Clemenceau speech, 25 September 1919, *Journal Officiel (Chambre)*, 1919. For Tardieu's
underlying assumption see Tardieu memorandum, 20 January 1919, Tardieu Papers, PA-
AP 166 (49).

he presented the Rhine as the new frontier of the civilisational community of "Western democracies".[9]

Tardieu's "structural" agenda rested on three core assumptions: that it would not be possible to dissolve the "Bismarckian" state; that it would be necessary to complement whatever guarantees France could obtain from the Anglo-American powers; and that it might prove necessary to ensure French security by alternative means if such guarantees were ultimately unobtainable or remained limited. Tardieu's blend of power-political imperatives and an ideological emphasis on common western values derived quite seamlessly from ideas he had formulated during the war to aid France's ideological struggle against the German Empire. At the very time when Wilson had launched his appeal for a "peace without victory" between all belligerents, Tardieu had begun to elevate the Rhine into the "international frontier of liberty" that divided the "civilised democracies of the west" from the autocratic and militaristic German *Reich*.[10] Following the armistice, he seized on these ideas to elaborate his conception of a western alliance system. Because he was aware of how different British and American security conceptions and threat perceptions were, he strove to develop an ideological superstructure for the transatlantic security community he deemed vital for France's future. Tardieu thus sought to emphasise not only common security interests – essentially the common threat posed by Germany – but also common values and civilisational standards, notably those connected to traditions of republican or democratic government. These were to provide the "glue" for a longer-term unity of the "Allied Powers". Tardieu insisted that what he defined as the "common security" of the "western democracies", including the United States, required above all to keep postwar Germany in check and to deprive it of the "means" to mount another aggressive attack on what he defined as "the west".[11]

The core interest that Clemenceau and Tardieu thus came to pursue in 1919 was to gain Anglo-American support for their ambitious agenda. Both realised that it would be difficult to reconcile their Rhenish aspirations with the priority of creating a new Atlantic alliance. And they calculated that making some compromises with Wilson and Lloyd George would be unavoidable. Remarkably, however, they thought that it would actually be possible to forge essential strategic bargains despite the profound differences that, as they acknowledged, existed between what they sought and what the latter, and notably the American president, envisaged. What they thus prepared for was a complex bargaining process among the principal victors. And, as has to be

---

[9] *Ibid.*; Tardieu notes, 20 January 1919, Tardieu Papers, PA-AP 166 (417); Tardieu memorandum, 25 February 1919, in Tardieu (II/1921), pp. 163–70. See McDougall (1978), pp. 120 ff.; Pichon to Beneš, 29 June 1918, Beneš (1928–29), II, pp. 231–2.

[10] Tardieu note, 20 January 1917, Tardieu Papers, vol. 417.

[11] Tardieu memorandum, 25 February 1919, in Tardieu (II/1921), pp. 154–5.

noted in retrospect, they were excessively confident that they would manage to find a critical modicum of common ground with their principal "allies".

The same impetus – the idea both to "restructure" the balance of power vis-à-vis Germany *and* to establish mainstays of a new Atlantic order *à la française* – also informed the ambitious economic and financial peace programme that, with the backing of Clemenceau, Clémentel developed with with the assistance of his adviser Henri Hauser and the young Jean Monnet. This pogramme became an important component of the wider French agenda for the peace conference. Most significant was the plan for an "economic union" among the "allied democracies" that was to become an integral part of an "organised peace" and, eventually the nucleus of a new "economic organisation of the world". This union was to comprise "joint programmes for the importation of raw-materials" and, notably, a "redistribution" of the "means of credit" to foster Europe's revitalisation and, above all, to meet France's structural needs. To this end, and to redress the economic balance after the war, it was conceived as an exclusive combination of the victors and selected "free peoples"; and it was designed to constrain Germany. An essential purpose of French schemes was thus to restrict German access to and possibilities within the postwar financial and economic order – if possible in the longer term, but at least for a transition period of French reconstruction – so as to "prevent Germany from pursuing anew its dream of economic domination".[12]

More aspirational still was Clémentel's plan to extend the remit of the League of Nations by establishing an – equally exclusive – financial and economic section of the organisation. Under its umbrella the victors, and selected neutral powers, were to cooperate not only in financing the rehabilitation of devastated areas in France – and Belgium – but also in coping with the wider financial consequences of the war. French planners, who strove to present their schemes as a logical extension of Wilson's aspirations, were keenly aware that their success depended on the willingness of the American government to underwrite them as the main financier and allocate requisite funds that no other power could provide. Yet they misjudged not only the domestic-political constraints but also the priorities of Wilson and the US Treasury. The frustration of Clémentel's ambitions would have major repercussions for France's evolving reparations policy and the way in which leading actors – Clemenceau and eventually the assertive Finance Minister Louis-Lucien Klotz – came to put forward far-reaching demands for a "*réparation intégrale*" for the damages and losses France had suffered.[13]

The core premise of the Clemenceau government's peacemaking strategy, which followed quite naturally from the imperatives of its ambitious

[12] Clémentel letter to Clemenceau, 19 September 1918, in Clémentel (1931), pp. 343, 346–7.
[13] This is convincingly shown in Trachtenberg (1980).

programme, was that the terms of the settlement and the ground-rules of the postwar order had to be dictated by the victors and forced on the vanquished without any negotiation. The uncompromising pursuit of this axiom led French policymakers to view Wilson's persistence on a "peace without victory" and an eventual negotiated peace as a strategic threat; and it led them to make vigorous efforts to close ranks with the British government and prevent such a scenario by setting the procedural parameters of the peace conference. Essentially, in Clemenceau's and Tardieu's eyes it was neither possible nor prudent but actually dangerous to try to make a peace that could also find acceptance in Germany – regardless of whether a republican government could be consolidated in Berlin.[14] They adamantly maintained that the ideas of the victors and German conceptions of what constituted a "just" peace settlement were inherently irreconcilable and any attempt to seek a compromise between them at the peace conference would be detrimental to French security and European stability.[15]

It should be noted that, like their British and American counterparts, the main French decision-makers envisaged the initial negotiations among the victors about the parameters of the settlement only as the beginning of a longer process through which a stable postwar order was to be established. But, in contrast to Wilson and Lloyd George, they primarily looked ahead to a process that centred on the enforcement of the terms and rules the western powers would set and the fortification of a transatlantic balance-of-power system that contained Germany. This was to be the dominant concern in the short and medium term, and it was the endeavour to which they primarily sought to commit the Anglo-American powers. In their conception, only a successful process of this kind would permit what they deemed crucial *in the longer term*: to entangle Germany within a system of checks and obligations whose main purpose was to ensure that the problematic *voisin outre-Rhin* remained effectively constrained. It was in this sense that Clemenceau would call the peace process of 1919 only "the beginning of a beginning".[16]

The French peace programme that thus took shape after the armistice represented in many ways the most clearly defined agenda of any of the principal victors, particularly when it came to the future "order" of Europe and the underpinnings of postwar security. It was a maximalist agenda designed to obtain, in the best-case scenario, complementary and mutually reinforcing guarantees – a firm alliance with the United States and Britain

---

[14] Clemenceau to Allied governments, 11 November 1918, MAE, Paix 47. Clemenceau statement, Council of Ten, 12 February 1919, *FRUS-PPC*, III, p. 975; Tardieu memorandum, 25 February 1919, Tardieu, (II/1921), pp. 156, 161–2. Cf. Jackson (2013), esp. pp. 5–8.

[15] Clemenceau statement, Council of Four, 28 March 1919, Mantoux (1992), I, pp. 62–5.

[16] Clemenceau speech, 25 September 1919, *Journal Officiel (Chambre)*, 1919.

as well as maximal advances towards the construction of a new balance of power in continental Europe. But at the same time, and despite their efforts to take them into account, what the key French actors envisaged constituted the most powerful *counter-design* to Wilson's aspirations and British peace ideas. More importantly, it represented not the only but the most important impediment to anything approaching a balanced or "moderate" peace settlement with Germany.

Yet it is worth accentuating once again that both Clemenceau and Tardieu regarded a peacetime alliance with the United States and Britain France's overriding strategic interest after the war. It was an interest that took precedence over all other concerns. But it did not fundamentally alter the "structural agenda" they had developed. In early February 1919, the French premier underscored the central predicament he saw when observing that the defeated power would be in a position to regain not only its economic and financial superiority but also its strategic preponderance in Europe within a short time unless the victors took measures to prevent this.[17]

Indeed, it can be said that the strategies Clemenceau and his principal collaborators came to pursue were based on some cardinal "systemic" assumptions, above all the assumption that in an "open", integrated postwar system the Franco-German imbalance would reappear, and evolve even more to the advantage of the stronger power. What French policymakers thus had to assert were regulations and restrictions that recast the rules and parameters of the system in ways that benefited the weaker power. This also meant, as Clémentel stressed, that they had to try to regulate the "free interplay of economic forces" and offer alternatives to the "Open Door" rules that those who represented the newly dominant American power sought to globalise.

All leading French actors recognised that it would be impossible to effect such systemic changes without Anglo-American support. More generally, they were aware of France's diminished weight not only vis-à-vis Germany but also vis-à-vis the United States. And they were remarkably conscious of a formative change that created particularly daunting challenges for them. In short, they foresaw how exceedingly difficult, if not impossible, it would be to address the German problem and other key issues *within a European framework*, i.e. without a constructive American engagement not only in the financial and economic but also in the political and strategic spheres. Crucially, they thus realised that France depended far more than the United States or even the potentially vulnerable British Empire on the cooperation of others, particularly the postwar world's potential hegemons, to create an international system through which it could satisfy its strategic needs. In this respect, France's position can indeed be compared to that of Austria at the time of the Vienna Congress.

---

[17] Clemenceau interview, *Action française*, 10 February 1919.

In the judgement of Clemenceau, Tardieu and Clémentel the main consequence of this dependence was that they had to prevail on American and
British decision-makers to back their ambitious containment and enforcement
schemes. But a more comprehensive systemic analysis can underscore that
France's future security and prosperity in fact hinged on something else: the
construction of a functioning and more broadly legitimate international order
in which not only the problems the Great War had caused but also the
structural challenges of an era of complex international and transcontinental
interdependence could be tackled. Above all, it had to be a system of order that
indeed opened up secure avenues for a peaceful accommodation with
Germany and that allowed for a constraining yet also stabilising integration
of the defeated power. In turn, this required strategies to come to an understanding with moderate republican forces in Germany that were willing to
chart such a path. All of this can be seen more clearly in retrospect; but it could
be grasped and was grasped by some actors at the time. Yet what Clemenceau
and the other French peacemakers actually sought to pursue threatened to
impede or even block such extremely difficult but necessary processes and,
ultimately, advances towards a more sustainable order.

The preoccupation of key French policymakers with national security was
understandable under the circumstances; and their distrust of Wilsonianism
and the intentions and reliability of German decision-makers was hardly
surprising. But their strategies could produce unintended consequences and
fundamental dangers. Even if they succeeded in the short term in asserting
French essentials through tough negotiations with American and British
representatives, this could turn into a Pyrrhic victory if relations with the
Anglo-American powers were overly strained. The gravest risk was that an
overburdened French power would eventually be left without key allies *and*
with the impossible task of enforcing an unenforceable settlement – indeed a
settlement that could only last as long as it was backed by superior power. At
the same time, French policies threatened to provoke precisely what they were
intended to counter: aggressive German revisionism and irredentism.

Undoubtedly, the path towards some kind of accommodation with
Germany was extremely hard to navigate because of the horrors and ideological battles of the war and the conflict-ridden Franco-German relations
before 1914. But making progress here was, as Clemenceau would later
acknowledge, the "central challenge".[18] Yet although the French premier
sought to prepare the ground for such progress *in the longer run*, the main
danger was that what he and Tardieu prioritised in 1919 would create new,
and immense, obstacles. Finally, though, it should also be highlighted that the

---

[18] Clemenceau statement to the Foreign Affairs Commission of the *Sénat*, 29 July 1919,
CAE, *Sénat*, vol. 1893. See also Clemenceau speech, 25 September 1919, *Journal Officiel
(Chambre)*, 1919. See Jackson (2013), pp. 310–12.

extent to which French policymakers *could* pursue different, more integrative approaches was significantly influenced by two essential factors: the degree to which American and British decision-makers found ways to make, and legitimise, effective commitments that fostered French security and Europe's stabilisation; and the domestic room to manoeuvre they had to gain support for more cooperative or even reconciliatory policies.

II.   A Forceful Mandate – and a Wide Spectrum of Expectations. Clemenceau and the Domestic Parameters of French Peace Policies

Owing to his role in securing the ultimate victory over the German Empire Clemenceau had gained immense prestige and indeed a dominant position in his government, both chambers of parliament and the broader French political spectrum. Widely acclaimed as *père la Victoire* he had emerged as a charismatic wartime leader on a par with Lloyd George. The French premier's renown was only rivalled – temporarily – by that of the "father" of the military victory, Marshal Foch. More generally, he had as clear a democratic mandate was conceivable in the Third Republic to pursue an assertive course at the peace negotiations. This was confirmed when in late December he obtained overwhelming support for the general maxims of his peace and security policy in the French parliament – with a clear majority of 398 to 93 votes.[19]

Thus, like Lloyd George – and in contrast to Wilson – Clemenceau would come to the peace conference with a resilient base of parliamentary and public support, not for specific peace aims – which he still had not revealed by the end of 1918 – but for the guiding rationales of his agenda. Consequently, he in fact had considerable room to manoeuvre, if not a free hand, to pursue hard-fisted negotiations for tangible security guarantees and other key French objectives, notably regarding the Rhineland and, eventually, "integral reparations". Crucially, for all the weight of public expectations that he had to bear his strong domestic standing also made Clemenceau and his government relatively impervious to external pressures. This meant that despite the outpouring of public support for Wilson during his visit, the influence of the American president on the French political process and his ability to push Clemenceau by appealing to French public opinion were actually extremely limited.[20]

After the armistice, only the socialists and the trade union CGT, flanked by a small number of left-wing intellectuals and pacifists, challenged Clemenceau and prevailing ideas with some force. They campaigned for an alternative peace programme along the lines of Wilson's Fourteen Points. And following

[19] See Mordacq (1930), III, pp. 191; House diary, 19 December 1918, *PWW*, LIII, p. 448. Minutes of the parliamentary debate, 29 December 1918, *Journal Officiel (Chambre)*, 1918; Duroselle (1988), pp. 721–8.

[20] See Stevenson (1998), pp. 93–5; Miquel (1972).

the armistice, they initially placed high hopes in the American president. A welcoming committee headed by Albert Thomas, Pierre Renaudel and Marcel Cachin presented him with an address of support and solidarity on his arrival in France and the Socialist Party and CGT only called off a planned mass rally in Wilson's honour on 14 December when he told them that he did not want to be identified too closely with "any single element" in French politics. Yet by the spring of 1919, when the American president was perceived as a weak negotiator who abandoned genuine internationalist positions and made flawed compromises at Versailles, widespread disillusionment with Wilsonianism set in on the French left.[21]

For their part, French socialists adhered to the programmes they had developed during the war and renewed their call for a new international order based on the principle of self-determination and a powerful League that was to introduce strict security guarantees and a novel regime of international arbitration. Crucially, theirs were the only voices in the French debate that insisted that a genuine peace league had to incorporate Germany from the start. And only they argued that it was in France's interest to aid the German social democrats in their efforts to create a republic. In January 1919, the Socialist Party even advocated that the peace should be based on actual negotiations with the newly formed Scheidemann government. Its leaders espoused a vision that would later be pursued by the socialist premier Édouard Herriot but remained marginal at this stage, namely that it was possible to work not only towards a *modus vivendi* but actually towards a new pattern of postwar relations with a reformed Germany. They saw this as a critical step towards realising their wider aim: to promote a genuine reconstruction of Europe on socialist-internationalist premises. Although they regarded demands for reparations as justified and reconcilable with such lofty ambitions, they held that they should be strictly limited to compensations for actual war damages.[22] But while leaving a mark on the public debate socialist influence on actual French peace policies remained very limited, because Clemenceau essentially did not require the Socialist Party's backing. Overall, the socialists clearly represented only the positions of a vocal minority, both in parliament – where the Radicals and the other *union sacrée* parties rallied behind Clemenceau's general course – and in France's wider political force-field.

Closer to the centre of this force field, Bourgeois, Buisson and other French "liberal internationalists" now intensified their efforts to mobilise public and particularly party-political support for their agenda. They favoured imposing a relatively harsh peace settlement on Germany and placing strict reins on its

---

[21] See Mayer (1967), pp. 176–7.

[22] See minutes of the parliamentary debate, 29 December 1918, *Journal Officiel (Chambre)*, 1918; Miquel (1972), pp. 419–32; Ducoulombier (2010), pp. 205–17; Soutou (1998), pp. 185–6.

power. But their chief concern remained to lobby for an authoritative League of Nations. As noted, in contrast to Britain and the United States the war had not given rise to a powerful pro-League movement in France. But after the armistice the vanguard of the newly formed *Association française pour la Société des nations*, a core group comprising Buisson, Bourgeois, Jules Prudhommeaux and other prominent members of the *ligue des droits de l'homme* embarked on a campaign for a League of Democratic States that was to protect "human rights" yet chiefly establish and enforce a rigorous regime of international law.[23] Whereas French internationalists had not established any strong links with like-minded British and American activists during the war, the protagonists of the *Association française* now took the lead in organising an "inter-allied" conference of pro-League pressure-groups, which then took place in Paris in late January 1919. They thus sought to widen public support for their cause in and beyond France. But their first priority was to commit the Radical Party and, ultimately, Clemenceau to a more than symbolical support for their idea of a *société des nations* and their aspirational aim to ensure a "durable peace" by replacing "the existing rule of force with a regime of organised law".[24]

But Bourgeois, Buisson and those who backed their cause still represented a small avantgarde and lacked the political power to sway a majority in the Radical Party. Notably the influential chairman of the *Chambre*'s Foreign Affairs Committee, Henry Franklin-Bouillon, supported a distinctly more old-fashioned policy that sought to guarantee France's future security not by means of elaborate League schemes but rather by diminishing the German through substantial territorial and economic guarantees. In particular, Franklin-Bouillon demanded that the "Rhenish people" should be granted far-reaching autonomy so that the Rhine could become the "barrier of the occident" protecting the "common fatherland of Democrats and Democracies" against the "Prussians".[25] Crucially, however, the protagonists of the *Association française* could never prevail on Clemenceau to place the creation of a forceful *société des nations* at the centre of his peace agenda.[26] French "juridical internationalists" thus fought an uphill battle in their own country.

---

[23] AFSDN programme, 18 December 1918, MAE, SDN, vol. 7. Buisson, Thomas and Prudhommeaux (1918); Guieu (2008), pp. 46–51.

[24] Bulletin de la AFSDN, 2 January 1919; AFSDN programme, 18 December 1918, MAE, SDN, vol. 7.

[25] Franklin-Bouillon speech, 24 November 1918, *Bulletin du Parti radical et radical-socialiste*, 14 December 1918; minutes of the parliamentary debate, 29 December 1918, *Journal Officiel (Chambre)*, 1918; Guieu (2008), pp. 39–49; Candar (2010), pp. 205–17; Soutou (1998), pp. 185–6.

[26] House diary, 19 December 1918, *PWW*, LIII, p. 448; Clemenceau speech, 29 December 1918, *Journal Officiel (Chambre)*, 1918, pp. 3732–3; Tardieu to Clemenceau, 26 November 1918, Fonds Clemenceau, 6N 137-3, SHD-DAT.

And in view of their emphasis on enforcement and sanctions, they would also be sorely disappointed when it became clear at the outset of the peace conference that Wilson clung to a very different vision of the League and was not prepared to make substantial concessions to theirs.

In wider context, the foundation of a League of Nations remained a comparatively marginal issue in France. What dominated both the public and the parliamentary debates after the armistice were demands and general expectations that can be subsumed under two themes: how a peace could be made that brought tangible reassurance against renewed German "aggression"; and, as in Britain, how to ensure that the settlement would yield adequate reparations for the human and material losses France had sustained during the war.[27] Unsurprisingly, the most assertive calls for a draconian peace came from pressure-groups and parliamentary representatives of the nationalist right. The *comité de la rive gauche du Rhin* stepped up its agitation for punitive indemnities and, above all, the restoration of France's frontier of 1814, an Allied protectorate on the Rhine's left bank and the annexation of the Rhineland. Further, foreshadowing French designs of the 1920s, it demanded that the strategically vital Ruhr area should be occupied to enforce French reparations demands.[28] In the French parliament, nationalist *députés* like Jules Delahaye also demanded an outright annexation of the Rhineland. The *Ligue française* and its influential leader Maurice Barrès proposed a somewhat subtler approach. Barrès called for an autonomous, demilitarised Rhineland, suggesting that it could initially become a buffer-state but later serve as a political and cultural bridge between France and Germany. Another influential propagandist, the nationalist-monarchist historian Jacques Bainville, presented an even more ambitious programme. He proposed a settlement that would eliminate the German threat by creating a Rhenish state linked to France and, in Eastern Europe, a system of new client states to compensate for the lost Russian alliance partner.[29]

The positions of the nationalist right tended to be extreme and never had a dominant impact on the French government's decision-making processes of the. But they reflected more widespread anxieties and expectations. What mattered most, however, was that the main currents of French public, publicised and parliamentary opinion favoured not only an imposed peace that ensured sizeable reparations. They also, broadly speaking, favoured a traditional approach to postwar security. In particular, a clear majority saw the need for firm guarantees and demanded the creation of some kind of safety zone between France and *l'ennemi outre-Rhin*. The French Chamber and Senate and remained divided on the Rhineland question. But Franklin-Bouillon's priorities

[27] See Stevenson (1998), pp. 93–5; Miquel (1972), pp. 37 ff., 419–32.
[28] Babelon (1917).
[29] See Barrès (1922); Bainville (1920), pp. 24, 10–61; Miquel (1972), pp. 306–14.

probably reflected those of most who rallied behind Clemenceau and his government. He opposed nationalist demands for an outright annexation. Yet true to the Radical Party's platform he favoured some form of neutral-isation, championing a scheme to expel "Prussian" influence and then incorporate an autonomous Rhineland into a community of western democ-racies. Only the Socialist party rejected such demands. On its behalf, Cachin declared that any attempt to limit German sovereignty on the left bank of the Rhine, let alone to annex German territory, was irreconcilable with what should be France's real priority: to encourage the formation of a strong German republic.[30]

Clemenceau had to pay some attention to the ongoing parliamentary and public discussions – and, temporarily, to the "Wilson factor". But overall the French premier could operate far more aloof from domestic politics and public opinion than either Wilson and or Lloyd George. And he could be quite confident that the policies and aims he would pursue were consonant with what most French voters, parties and opinion-makers expected.[31] By contrast, Wilson's popularity in France proved short-lived, turning into disenchant-ment and alienation when it became obvious that the kind of peace he sought would not tally with prevalent French demands for "restitutions, reparations, guarantees, sanctions".[32]

III. Towards a New Atlantic Order – and League – on French Terms?

Clemenceau was thus in a remarkably strong and unchallenged position when it came to determining his country's core aims and strategies for the peace conference. In this process, he came to rely on the advice of key confidants – above all on Tardieu and, eventually, Louis Loucheur, the newly appointed Minister of Industrial Reconstruction – rather than on Pichon and the experts of the Quai d'Orsay, who were largely bypassed after the armistice. Outside his government, the French premier made a point of *not* consulting in any substantial manner with President Poincaré or Marshal Foch, who both favoured a more draconian approach. Yet they would initially support the premier's programme when its contours became apparent during the early stages of the Versailles negotiations.

Building on the conceptual groundwork that Tardieu had laid and Clémentel's plans supplemented in the economic and financial spheres, the Clemenceau government came to pursue two core and essentially defensive agendas. As noted, the main objective of the first was to forge the most solid

---

[30] Franklin-Bouillon speech, 24 November 1918, *Bulletin du Parti radical et radical-socia-liste*, 14 December 1918; Duroselle (1988), pp. 755–6.

[31] See Stevenson (1998), pp. 93–5; Miquel (1972).

[32] See *Bulletin du Parti radical et radical-socialiste*, 14 December 1918.

peacetime alliance with Britain and the United States that could be obtained – as the key instrument to control the postwar order, safeguard French security and contain Germany. The second was to achieve something even more difficult: to craft a settlement that would recast the balance of power and possibilities in Europe in France's favour.

Fundamentally, both agendas were based on power-political rationales; yet they also incorporated elements of a distinctive French "internationalism". The leading French policymakers assumed that they could be pursued in parallel and were even complementary. In fact, however, it would prove very hard to reconcile them. Clemenceau and Tardieu of course recognised as clearly as Clémentel that Anglo-American backing or at least acquiescence was critical for a success of France's far-reaching "re-balancing" programme. And they calculated that they would have to countenance certain compromises for the sake of inter-allied unity. Precisely because of this they developed a maximalist strategy, devised to safeguard cardinal French interests in the tough bargaining process with British and American leaders they expected. In fact, the pursuit of this strategy would have a profoundly unsettling effect on the peace negotiations – and postwar international politics.

It has long been asserted that Clemenceau clung to an "old-style" security policy after the war.[33] But the French premier not only recalibrated his approach and underlying conceptions after the war; he actually developed them further. In this process he even came to adopt a more constructive attitude towards the League project – although he remained profoundly unconvinced by Wilson's ideological precepts and the recommendations of Bourgeois and French "internationalists". Nonetheless, what lay at the core of Clemenceau's reorientation was a changing outlook on transatlantic relations and the vital future role of the United States for which Tardieu provided important impulses. While the French premier would still aim for tangible territorial and economic guarantees as well, his "directing thought" for the peace negotiations became to convert the wartime coalition that had ensured the victory over Germany into a long-term postwar alliance in which the United States was to be a pivotal partner.[34] On this basis, Clemenceau would seek to construct a new transatlantic order – and security community – of democratic states united by the common aim to contain the German threat. And, however reluctantly, he would adopt Tardieu's rationale to seize upon Wilson's League aspirations to advance this design.

As noted, Clemenceau had become deeply irritated by what he saw as Wilson's high-handed pursuit of his Fourteen Points agenda during the latter stages of the war and the armistice negotiations. And his irritation grew

---

[33] For still influential older interpretations see Duroselle (1988); Soutou (1998); Stevenson (1982). For a different, more nuanced analysis see Jackson (2013), pp. 203–34

[34] Clemenceau speech, 29 December 1918, *Journal Officiel (Chambre)*, 1918, 3732–3.

further when the American president signalled thereafter that he would persist with his unilateral approach and quest for a progressive peace. The French premier initially regarded this as so threatening that he sought to neutralise Wilson's influence and explored options to organise the peace conference without him. Even after Wilson's decision to travel to Europe, Clemenceau still pushed for a prior understanding with Lloyd George during the Anglo-French summit meetings in early December. And he tried – in vain – to commit the British government to essentials of France's evolving security strategy, notably a long-term occupation of the Rhine's left bank – before the American president could interfere.[35]

Earlier, the French Foreign Ministry had prepared a procedural plan for the peace negotiations whose hierarchy of priorities clashed with Wilson's, because it proposed to begin with the settlement of the conditions to be imposed on Germany and only then to deliberate the Covenant of the League. And it had drawn up a programme, chiefly developed by Philippe Berthelot, that was designed to base the peace settlement on a prior understanding with the British government – and to contain the undesirable aspects of Wilson's Fourteen Points agenda. The Quai d'Orsay leading strategist indeed sought to make sure that key French interests were not compromised by incalculable Wilsonian "internationalism" and what he saw as the American president's dangerous penchant for vague formulae of "new diplomacy" and, crucially, a negotiated peace with Germany. Foreign Minister Pichon essentially agreed with Berthelot and, building on his recommendations, he too insisted that the concrete terms of the peace could not be premised on Wilson's principles.[36]

On 29 November, the long-serving French Ambassador Jusserand used more diplomatic language to convey the Quai d'Orsay's essential concerns to the American president. He underscored that the French Foreign Ministry had based its determinations not on abstract principles but an "examination of the precedents of the Congresses of Vienna 1814–1815, Paris 1856, and Berlin 1878". And he stressed above all that in the French interpretation, Wilson's voyage to Europe would "enable" the principal victors "to agree among themselves upon the conditions of the peace preliminaries to be imposed severally on the enemy without any discussion with him". Jusserand noted that these preliminaries would "shape the way for the settlement of the main territorial restorations: Alsace Lorraine, Poland, the Slav countries, Belgium, Luxemburg, the cession of the German colonies, the full recognition of the protectorates of France over Morocco and of England over Egypt".

---

[35] French "Proposals for the Preliminaries of Peace with Germany", 26 November 1918; French note, 3 December, CAB 1/27/24 and 26.

[36] French "Proposals for the Preliminaries of Peace with Germany", 26 November 1918, CAB 1/27/24; French Foreign Ministry commentaries, in House to Lansing, 15 November 1918, *PWW*, LIII, pp. 86–91.

Yet the French proposals also stated unequivocally that the peace conference was to be divided into "two main series: the settlement of the war properly so-called" and only then "the organization of the Society of Nations". They stipulated that this distinction was not least "made necessary" by the fact that "the enemy has no right to discuss the terms that will be imposed on him by the victors". Using a language that utterly failed to convince the American president, the Quai d'Orsay's peace planners argued that even though the Allied Powers had *generally* accepted them under the armistice agreement, those of "Wilson's principles" that were "not sufficiently defined" to be "taken as a basis for a concrete settlement of the war" could only be applied "in the matter of the future settlement of [international] law" – namely in elaborating the League's Covenant. They were not to be applied when deciding the salient questions of peace in and beyond Europe, above all the treatment of Germany.[37]

In effect, Clemenceau and Tardieu would not espouse the Quai d'Orsay's defensive approach and instead seek to hammer out a strategic compact with the American president – on their terms. But they too were cognisant of the vast gulf that separated Wilson's aspirations from their essentially still "*realpolitical*" outlook on the nature of international politics and requirements of peacemaking. Notably the French premier still regarded essential elements of Wilson's programme and the ideological premises of his "new diplomacy" as highly problematic. This especially held true for his League schemes, which in Clemenceau's judgement rested on dangerously optimistic assumptions about human nature, the prospects of "collective security" and the pacifying effect of democratic reform – especially but not only with a view to Germany. He simply considered what Wilson proposed too vague and "toothless" to satisfy specific French and European security needs. Further, like Pichon and Berthelot, the French premier still feared that Wilson would persist with his campaign for a "moderate" peace under the banner of the Fourteen Points and insist on actual negotiations with German representatives. More fundamentally, Clemenceau now faced the challenge of finding new ways to respond to Wilson's vision and to defend what he still considered vital: the pursuit of a prudent, modernised balance-of-power approach to postwar security and international order.

Clemenceau's approach remained circumspect. But, partly due to Tardieu's advice, he would alter not only his policy vis-à-vis the American president, and the United States, but also his peacemaking strategy on the eve of the peace conference. Not just for tactical reasons he came to pursue a policy of constructive engagement vis-à-vis Wilson; and he came to emphasise – internally, yet also to the French public – the overriding importance of maintaining a

---

[37] Jusserand note for Wilson, 29 November 1918, and enclosed French memorandum, *PWW*, LIII, pp. 292–8, 293; 295. See also French Foreign Ministry commentaries, in House to Lansing, 15 November 1918, *ibid.*, pp. 86, 90, 91.

close concord and forging a durable *entente* not only with Britain but also and especially with the United States. In private, Clemenceau impressed on his closest advisers that the French people must not forget that "without America and England, France would perhaps no longer actually exist". And publicly he now underscored – in the Chamber of Deputies – that his guiding aim at the forthcoming peace conference would be to maintain unity among the victors. At the same time, he signalled that to ensure this the French government, and the French people, would have to be prepared to make concessions. Though he did not specify what this meant, he clearly implied that his government could not afford to make demands that would undermine vital "allied solidarity".[38]

At one level, the French premier's more affirmative attitude towards Wilson was clearly motivated by the desire to improve his position in the bargaining process he expected once he had confronted the American president with the essentials of France's territorial and economic peace programme, above all the Rhineland agenda (which they took care not to disclose to him before the negotiations at Versailles). And he of course also calculated that Wilson would depend on French goodwill if he wanted to realise his League aspirations. But the strategy Clemenceau now came to pursue, and that Tardieu would elaborate further, reached beyond such concerns. Its core rationale was to engage with the Wilsonian League agenda in order to refashion it – and ultimately to remould the League itself – to draw the United States into the firmest possible alliance of the victors.[39]

The French premier's new course was reinforced by what he regarded as an unexpectedly amicable and pragmatic first meeting with Wilson in Paris on 15 December. He came away from it with the impression that despite his different ideological proclivities and limited grasp of the complexities of the European situation, Wilson was a leader with whom he could come to terms – and who could be prodded in a direction that served French interests.[40] At a deeper level, Clemenceau's reorientation was not only influenced by his long-standing interest in the dynamic development of the American republic and first-hand experience of working and travelling in the United States. It was also informed by the essentially "Atlanticist" outlook on the future of world politics he had developed. In short, like Tardieu, he had acquired a keen understanding of how decisively America's newly dominant strategic, political and financial power could shape the postwar order – and a keen sense of how vital it would be for France to commit the American government to more permanent responsibilities and guarantees in Europe – on French premises.

[38] Clemenceau speech, 29 December 1918, *Journal Officiel (Chambre)*, 1918, 3732–3.
[39] See Tardieu memorandum, 20 January 1919, Tardieu Papers, PA-AP 166 (49).
[40] Derby to House, 16 December, House Papers; House diary, 19 December 1918, *PWW*, LIII, p. 448; House diary, 21 December 1918, House Papers.

On these grounds, the French premier also adjusted his position and outlook on the League. He still doubted that an organisation of the kind the American president envisaged could ever gain the authority and provide effective mechanisms to secure the peace. But he realised that the League might be the only available "vehicle" for obtaining the Anglo-American commitments he deemed critical for France's long-term security. When Clemenceau met Wilson again on 19 December, he used cautious and concili-atory language. He voiced his underlying concerns, underscoring that he was not "confident of success" when it came to "forming" the new organisation or "its being workable after it was formed". But he conceded that the establish-ment of a League of Nations should nonetheless be attempted.[41] To House, the French premier admitted that he regarded this as the best way to obtain what might otherwise remain elusive: an American promise to aid France against an attack by an "outlaw nation". And it should not be overlooked that in his thinking, and that of Tardieu, securing such a promise was directly linked with a further cardinal strategic aim: to ensure that an as yet equivocal government in London would also commit itself to guaranteeing France's security. With these imperatives in mind, Clemenceau underscored his willingness to work with the American peace delegation to create, as far as possible, a viable international institution, and he even distanced himself, for the moment, from Bourgeois' demands for a more robust League that had armed forces and its own general staff.[42]

The main strategic challenge Clemenceau now faced had two dimensions. On the one hand, he had to pave the way for a concord with the Anglo-American powers and to persuade the French public, and notably critics in parliament, that this would require concessions. On the other hand, he had to be all the more assertive in justifying – for domestic reasons, yet also in the court of "world opinion" – why he still adhered to fundamental principles of balance-of-power politics. It was indeed essential for his entire peace policy to insist that these principles had not lost their validity and could not simply be discarded. But it should also be noted that Clemenceau sought to build on them to achieve something he considered not only unavoidable but necessary against the background of a transformed global constellation: namely to construct a *new*, essentially Atlantic "edifice" of order after the Great War. He did *not* advocate a return to the precepts and practices of the pre-war international system, in which French decision-makers had ultimately not been able to "solve" their country's strategic dilemmas.

To clarify his stance was the challenge Clemenceau sought to meet on the only occasion after the armistice when he actually made a public statement

---

[41] House diary, 19 December 1918, *PWW*, LIII, p. 448.
[42] House diary, 7 January 1919, *PWW*, LIII, pp. 652–3; Poincaré (1926–33), XI, pp. 283, 390–6; Duroselle (1988), p. 728.

about his approach to peace, in a speech to the French parliament on 29 December. This speech was partly intended to reinforce his claim as the French "father of peacemaking" and to widen his room to manoeuvre vis-à-vis proponents of a more hard-line approach, particularly Franklin-Bouillon, who had renewed his demand for "material guarantees". Yet what Clemenceau outlined was also intended to counter the aspirational message of Wilson's earlier Guildhall address. He emphasised that at the peace conference he would remain "in part faithful" to an "old system which appears to be discredited today" – a "system of alliances" in which states were ultimately "responsible for their own defence and strove for 'solid and well defended frontiers, armaments and something called a balance of powers'". And he presented this system as the outgrowth of long common history and experience of peoples in Europe who "since time immemorial" had "engaged in constant struggles for the satisfaction of their appetites and their selfish interests".

Clemenceau conveyed that it would be extremely difficult to rise above such traditions, conceptions of state interests and basic human drives – even or especially after a catastrophe like the Great War – and to build peace on radically different premises, such as those that Wilson advocated. Notably, the French premier stressed his profound doubts about "international guarantees" that were yet to "be defined" and that would be harder "to establish in reality than in speeches and writings" – and his unspoken assumption was of course that such guarantees would not suffice to cope with the cardinal German threat. He thus "praised" Wilson's – naïve – "candour" but also underscored that his lofty aspirations were influenced by the reality that the United States was "a long way away from Germany".[43]

In one respect, Clemenceau thus sought to vindicate an approach to peace and postwar security that was informed, not by faith in a new integrative "internationalism" but by what he presented as time-honoured fundamentals of *Realpolitik*. Significantly, however, he also impressed on his audience that it would not only be unwise but actually impossible to realise cardinal French peace aims by pursuing an aggressive unilateral approach. He declared that "nothing must happen" at the peace conference that "might separate after the war the four Powers that were united during it" (thus also including Italy among the victorious great powers). And he emphatically stressed that the key lay in preserving a united front and longer-term "unity" with Britain and the United States – and that this unity had to take precedence over the realisation of concrete French peace aims if both came into conflict.

In a wider perspective, Clemenceau signalled – in a gesture to Wilson – that French security and a stable postwar order demanded a departure from the "sentiments" that had prevailed in pre-war international politics. He observed

---

[43] Clemenceau speech, 29 December 1918, *Journal Officiel (Chambre)*, 1918, 3732–3.

that the victors could not *only* rely on the "traditional procedures of the old architecture" but were *also* called upon to pave the way for a "new spirit in international relations" and build a new "edifice" of order that comprised a "superior authority" to regulate conflicts and transcended the power-political manoeuvres of states and pursuit of "selfish interests". Yet the French premier refrained from committing himself to a more "concrete vision" of how this was to be accomplished, and how this "edifice" could be constructed. Ultimately, his overriding interest was and remained to lay foundations for a new transatlantic "edifice" built around an alliance of the victors.[44] Clemenceau was criticised, not only by French socialists, for failing to present a more comprehensive and forward-looking peace agenda. And he was also accused of heaping scorn on the "noble candour" of Wilson's novel approach in liberal-progressive circles in the United States and Britain, where his statement was interpreted as a profession of faith in the wisdom of old-style power politics. But more consequential was that, as already noted, he obtained the backing of a clear majority in parliament – and indeed a strong public mandate – for the general course he had outlined.[45]

Undoubtedly, Tardieu spurred the reorientation of Clemenceau's approach to peace. He shared the prime minister's underlying assumptions, and fundamentally the war had not altered his long-standing conviction that it was crucial for France's future development and security not to discard fundamentals of balance-of-power politics. As he saw it, French peace policies had to be based on a sober analysis and appreciation of the altered power-political challenges and necessities the war had left in its wake. But he had also become increasingly convinced that French diplomacy had to pursue new strategies to create an unprecedented *Atlantic* security "architecture" that not only preserved a favourable balance of forces but also introduced more reliable guarantees than the pre-war system had ultimately provided – guarantees that, in short, would make a recurrence of the scenario of 1914 unthinkable.

Tardieu's main premise was that a durable peace would require above all a "lasting union of the forces which had won the war". The "unity of the Allies" not only had to be maintained; it had to be "made closer". For they had to be prepared for "common action" in what he regarded as a long-term endeavour, the "execution" and enforcement of the – severe – peace terms that had to be forced on the vanquished power – including stringent disarmament obligations – to ensure that Germany would "not repeat her offenses".[46] In his view, this made a consolidation of the *Entente* with Britain indispensable. But it chiefly called for a new strategy towards the Wilson administration. Tardieu

[44] *Ibid.*
[45] See minutes of the debate on 29 December 1918, *Journal Officiel (Chambre)*, 1918, 3732–3; Mordacq (1930), III, pp. 191, 206; Duroselle (1988), pp. 721–8.
[46] Tardieu, (II/1921), p. 78.

argued that it was imperative to respond constructively to Wilson's aspirations, notably his championing of the League, in order to persuade the American president to accept on behalf of his nation not only a de facto alliance with France but also *longue durée* responsibilities in Europe.[47] Essentially, he thus sought to foster, not a "new world order" but a viable transatlantic balance-of-power system designed to contain Germany. In his conception, consolidating a system of this kind could also – over time – create "safe" conditions for what he deemed inevitable yet sought to delay as far as possible: Germany's eventual admission to the *société des nations* and the negotiation of a more cooperative *modus vivendi* with France's problematic neighbour.[48]

To legitimise his aspirations, and to endow them with a higher purpose, Tardieu introduced the ideological concept, or construction, of a "community" of "Western democracies", at whose core stood France, Britain and the United States. He presented it as an exclusive "community" of advanced western states whose civilisational frontier had to be defended on the Rhine. The defeated power was to remain outside this community for "an indefinite length of time". It would only be allowed to accede to it once it had accepted and fulfilled the victors' peace conditions and proved its attachment to the rules of "civilised" international conduct and democratic order. In Tardieu's judgement, this was bound to take a "long time".[49]

During the war, Tardieu had closely observed the evolution of Wilson's peace policies as French commissioner in the United States. And he had already studied the traditional principles, practices and constraints of US foreign policy before 1914. He realised that Theodore Roosevelt and some leading Republicans, notably Lodge, actually favoured something approaching an alliance with France. But he was also conscious of the abiding relevance of the long-standing tradition of non-entanglement in European affairs that he identified with the Monroe Doctrine.[50] Nor did he underestimate Wilson's commitment *not* to break with this tradition but rather to transcend old-style alliance politics. But although he saw all of these problems, and although he retained profound doubts about Wilson's earlier conceptions of the League, "open diplomacy" and "collective security", he nonetheless urged Clemenceau to avoid everything that could alienate the American president and his advisers – and to pursue a constructive course.

Essentially, Tardieu's experience as commissioner in Washington had reinforced his conviction that, if duly guided, Wilson and those who determined US policies could play not only a dominant but also a salutary role in

---

[47] See Tardieu to Clemenceau, 26 November 1918, Fonds Clemenceau, 6N 137-3, SHD-DAT.
[48] See Tardieu to Wilson, 10 June 1919, in Tardieu (I/1921), p. 135.
[49] Tardieu memorandum, 25 February 1919, in Tardieu (II/1921), pp. 156, 161–2.
[50] See Tardieu (1908), pp. 266 ff.

setting the rules of the postwar order – in a manner that was conducive to French interests. After his return to Paris, Tardieu thus took pains to impress on Clemenceau the historic importance of America's "entry into world affairs". He argued that because of the war this "entry" had occurred "two generations earlier" than it would have done in the absence of the Great War. And he insisted that consequently the French government now simply had to come to terms with the leader of the newly pre-eminent power. Tardieu warned that it would be disastrous for France and its future position in Europe if the American president and the American public were to conclude after the peacemaking process that "Washington and Monroe were right after all" and the United States was "better off" returning to its pre-war traditions and "leaving Europe to its own affairs".[51]

On these premises, Tardieu proposed his strategy for forging a long-term Atlantic alliance of democracies under the guise of the League of Nations. And he also proposed a reorientation of French policy towards the League itself. He recommended that French influence should be brought to bear on the preparatory process in which the parameters of the new organisation were hammered out: French experts finally had to participate in preparatory negotiations with their American and British counterparts, and their task should be to *improve* earlier American and British designs. All of this was to further the aim of establishing a more forceful *société des nations* that could at least *contribute* to meeting French security needs vis-à-vis Germany. Concretely, Tardieu would draw on the work of the Bourgeois Commission to advance schemes for a powerful League. And, in an attempt to accommodate Wilson's preferences, he urged Clemenceau to endorse the president's position that the main task of the peace conference was to found "a new organisation of international relations".[52] Yet Tardieu never altered his view that even if all of the French recommendations were adopted by its allies, the resultant international organisation would still need time to consolidate and gain the necessary authority. And he never changed his verdict that by itself a League would not be able to provide sufficient guarantees, especially for the immediate postwar period – while the need to control and contain Germany was urgent.[53]

Earlier, Tardieu had sought to coordinate peace preparations with the members of the Inquiry and in October had dispatched Professor de Martonne, the general secretary of the *Comité d'études*, to Washington to further this process. But he had to countenance that Wilson did not desire to enter into a process of "inter-allied" coordination, particularly with French representatives, that threatened to compromise his still unrefined League plans

[51] Tardieu to Clemenceau, 26 November 1918, Fonds Clemenceau, 6N 137-3, SHD-DAT.
[52] Tardieu memorandum, 5 January 1919, Tardieu Papers, PA-AP 166 (412), MAE.
[53] See Tardieu memorandum, 20 January 1919, Tardieu Papers, PA-AP 166 (49); Tardieu memorandum, 25 February 1919, in Tardieu (II/1921), pp. 147–67.

before the peace conference had even begun. French policymakers, and notably the experts of the Bourgeois Commission, remained excluded from what then evolved into an essentially Anglo-American process of hammering out a preliminary platform, and covenant, for the new international organisation.

In retrospect, it is difficult to see how the profound differences between as yet vaguely defined American, the comparatively elaborate British and the qualitatively distinct French schemes could have been reconciled prior to Versailles. The fundamentally divergent conceptions underlying them would then clash at the peace conference itself. In Tardieu's retrospective assessment, what lay behind these tensions were approaches to international politics and mentalities that were separated by "centuries of history".[54] With the benefit of hindsight, it is thus all the more remarkable that both he and Clemenceau, despite their relative familiarity with US domestic politics and the constraints that any American president faced in this respect, still deemed it a viable option to bargain for far-reaching American security commitments in Europe. And it seems no less remarkable that they underestimated just how committed Wilson would remain to *his* conception of the League, which was and remained fundamentally at odds with their pursuit of a de facto alliance.

Nonetheless, it is indeed worth emphasising that the new strategic priorities of Clemenceau and Tardieu's formative impulses bestowed a new, if largely instrumental significance on the hitherto peripheral French League conceptions that Bourgeois and the members of the *Commission interministérielle d'études pour la Société des Nations* had developed since September 1917.[55] Until the end of the war, both Clemenceau and Pichon had adopted a reserved and dismissive attitude towards the work of the Bourgeois Commission. In contrast to official – and unofficial – British efforts to promote the Phillimore report, the Clemenceau government simply transmitted the Bourgeois Commission's no less comprehensive report to Washington in the summer of 1918 without endorsing it. By the end of 1918, Clemenceau, Tardieu and senior officials at the Quai d'Orsay had not fundamentally changed their outlook. They still doubted that it could become the main mechanism guaranteeing peace and international order, notably in Europe. But they had concluded that by supporting the project of a *société des nations* they would not only be able to influence its character but also, and crucially, further the underlying aims of their alliance strategy and their search for more tangible "material guarantees", particularly on the Rhine.[56]

---

[54] See Tardieu (II/1921), pp. 85–6, 95–6.
[55] See Bourgeois Commission, minutes of 1st meeting, 28 September 1917; minutes of 4th meeting, 19 December 1917, MAE, SDN, vol. 1; Bourgeois Commission report, 8 June 1918, AN, F12 8106.
[56] See House diary, 19 December 1918 and 7 January 1919, *PWW*, LIII, pp. 448, 652–3; Tardieu comments on Foch note, January 1919, Tardieu Papers, vol. 422; Tardieu

Bourgeois and those who collaborated with him essentially adhered to the ambitious League ideas that his commission had presented in its authoritative report of 8 June 1918. What they advocated, and what Bourgeois himself would forcefully champion at the peace conference, thus was and remained qualitatively distinct from, and indeed conflicted with, the schemes that Wilson and American experts elaborated – and it equally clashed with the evolving British plans authored by Cecil and Smuts. It was an elaborate blueprint for a *société des nations* that was not conceived as a supranational organisation but rather as a union of the principal victors and associated "free nations" whose core institutional features would be an "International Council", aided by a secretariat, and a judicial tribunal. Bourgeois himself insisted that the League's real cornerstone had to be a firm regime of compulsory arbitration that, in contrast to the evolving American and British schemes, placed the emphasis not only on strictly defined sanctions but also on military enforcement. He thus proposed endowing the council with far-reaching authority and instrumentalities to enforce the rulings of the judicial tribunal against those who violated the "law of nations". The Bourgeois Commission's scheme not only obliged each member to use "its economic, naval, and military power" to this end but also, as noted, foresaw the formation of a supranational army, overseen by a permanent general staff. Thus, its principal aim was to empower the League both to provide effective protections but also to deter potential aggressors, particularly by enabling the organisation to act swiftly in imposing sanctions or intervening militarily against states that acted against its rules, failed to abide by the tribunal's decisions or posed a threat to one of its members.[57]

Unquestionably, Bourgeois and his collaborators had drafted their recommendation with one underlying purpose in mind, namely that the League would have to be equipped to address fundamental French security concerns and secure the postwar *status quo* in Europe. Above all, they thus saw the need to create an international mechanism that provided solid guarantees, safeguards and sanctions to prevent renewed German aggression. And, in particular, they desired to establish a mechanism that would ensure that Britain and the United States would aid France – by committing themselves to arbitration *and* the participation in military sanctions, or even by pledging to contribute to an international military force whose core mission would be to protect and police Europe's postwar order.

Nonetheless, it would be misleading to conclude that those who drafted French League plans merely intended to extend France's wartime alliance "in the guise of

---

memorandum, 20 January 1919, Tardieu Papers, vol. 49; Berthelot memorandum, 18 December 1918, Fonds Clemenceau, 6 N 72, SHD-DAT.

[57] Commission report, 8 June 1918, AN, F12 8106; Miller (1928), II, pp. 238–46; minutes of the Bourgeois commission, 8 October 1917, Bourgeois Papers, PA-AP 29 (17). See Jackson (2013), pp. 262–4.

a league of nations".[58] What they proposed went qualitatively beyond this. They had developed concepts for a powerful international organisation that was to establish a far-reaching system of international commitments, sanctions and "collective security". Like other French internationalists, Bourgeois paid reverence to traditional French conceptions of state sovereignty and was careful to stress that he did not call for the establishment of a "supranational" organisation that would override the sovereign rights of its member states. In his conception, their commitment to respect and enforce international law was to be voluntary, and subject to the political approval of state governments. In principle, however, his plans for a *société des nations* on French terms went much further than Wilson's ideas or prevalent British schemes in actually challenging core attributes of state sovereignty, particularly when it came to decisions about sanctions and the ultimate control over armed forces.

The entire thrust of what the Bourgeois commission recommended conflicted with Wilson's vision of what the League was to become, notably his rejection of "hard and fast sanctions" and emphasis on the *political* settlement of international disputes. At Versailles, both he and Cecil would harshly criticise what they regarded as French ambitions to "militarise" the League. In a wider context, however, the French proposals made important conceptual contributions. And they pointed to fundamental challenges that had to be addressed in the search for effective international organisations and an effective system of "collective security" – problems that would resurface in the 1920s and then again during the formative discussions that led to the creation of the United Nations in the 1940s.

At the same time, though, French conceptions were not only particularly hierarchical but also invoked universal principles to legitimise, essentially, a League of the victors rather than a universal and integrative organisation – at least in its foundational phase. The Bourgeois Commission's emphasis on a League of "free nations" was also intended to link the French republic to Wilson's crusade "to make the world safe for democracy". But it was primarily motivated by the interest to justify that the organisation would essentially be established and controlled by the democratic western powers – and initially exclude Germany. And yet Bourgeois remained the only senior French policymaker in this critical phase who not only regarded a future German membership in the new organisation as inevitable but actually argued that it could have a positive, peace-enforcing impact. As he saw it, the League could further a process of habituating German elites, and the German population, to the primacy of international law and to respect for the rules and obligations of a civilised *société des nations*.[59]

---

[58] See Egerton (1978), p. 74.
[59] Bourgeois speech to AFSDN Constitutive Assembly, 10 November 1918, MAE, SDN, vol. 7.

For all their willingness to cooperate with Wilson and to pledge their support for a League of Nations, neither Clemenceau nor Tardieu were prepared to entrust the guarantee of French security to a new international organisation – even if it could be endowed with the strictest enforcement provisions. As an institution, the League remained peripheral in the wider context of Clemenceau's peace and security policy. He never espoused Bourgeois' idea that peace and stability could be guaranteed through an elaborate regime of international law. And he was certainly not prepared to relinquish essential elements of French sovereignty and great-power preroga-tives. In a speech to the French parliament just before the opening of the peace conference, the French premier emphasised that in his judgement only funda-mental changes in mentalities and "spiritual dispositions" in "every state" would "permit" a *société des nations* to "live and function".[60]

But the implication of what Clemenceau said was clearly that even under the most favourable circumstances such changes would require a long time; they could not be relied upon in the foreseeable future. In his thinking, more traditional underpinnings of security and international stability thus remained imperative. Tardieu fundamentally agreed with this outlook. Accordingly, the approach that he recommended and Clemenceau came to pursue was and remained dominated by overriding strategic considerations. They intended to cooperate in setting up the League not only to realise their transatlantic alliance plans but also to obtain Anglo-American support for what was still an integral element of their security policy: the quest to obtain "material" guarantees against renewed German aggression.[61]

IV.   A Strategic and Civilisational Frontier on the Rhine? The Quest for "Material Guarantees" and a New Balance of Power and Security

Essentially, all senior French policymakers acted on the premise that even if they succeeded in forging a de facto peacetime alliance with Britain and the United States this would still not suffice to "solve" the French security dilemma. What thus continued was the search for structural guarantees against the German threat. This search entered a new and decisive phase at the end of 1918, after Clemenceau had authorised Tardieu to elaborate a

---

[60] Clemenceau speech, *Chambre*, 16 January 1919, SDN (16), MAE; Tardieu memorandum, 20 January 1919, Tardieu Papers, PA-AP 166 (49).

[61] See Tardieu comments on Foch note, submitted to the Allied governments on 10 January 1919; Tardieu memorandum, 20 January 1919, Tardieu Papers, PA-AP 166 (422, 49); House diary, 7 January 1919, *PWW*, LIII, pp. 652–3; Berthelot argued on similar grounds that France should back the League to perpetuate the wartime alliance and make the victors the "gendarmes of Europe" under its "authority". Berthelot memorandum, 18 December 1918, Fonds Clemenceau, 6 N 72, SHD-DAT. See Jackson (2013), pp. 266–8.

complementary and indeed rather radical security programme as a basis for negotiations with the other principal victors. Tardieu would present what essentially amounted to a comprehensive scheme to improve France's defensive posture and recast the strategic balance between France and Germany. At its core lay his older aspiration to create a "frontier of liberty" on the Rhine. But he now proposed a new strategy to end German sovereignty over the Rhine's left bank and establish an autonomous Rhenish buffer-state on terms that, in his view, were consonant with the self-determination principle and acceptable to the Anglo-American powers.

After the armistice, Clemenceau had originally contemplated less ambitious designs. While insisting on the return of Alsace-Lorraine – without plebiscite – he had long favoured a return to the frontier of 1814 and thus French claims to significant parts of the Saar and its resources. Beyond this, he had broached in his conversations with Lloyd George in early December a *do ut des* arrangement under which, in return for French concessions in the Middle East under an amended Sykes-Picot agreement, the British government was to back an extended Allied occupation of the Rhineland.[62] But this came to nought, and by mid-December the French premier conveyed to his British counterpart that he had significantly expanded his ambitions. He now not merely sought to secure a long-term occupation of the Rhine's left bank and the establishment of strategic bridgeheads across the river, but actually a change of the pre-war status quo. He proposed the creation of an "independent [Rhenish] State" whose "neutrality" was to "be guaranteed by the Great Powers".[63] Further, Clemenceau now backed French attempts to loosen the Rhenish population's bonds with the German state by providing economic inducements. He thus gravitated towards an agenda for which Marshal Foch had begun to campaign.

In the aftermath of the war, Foch, who was now in charge of enforcing Germany's disarmament, emerged as a forceful proponent of a re-balancing strategy that hinged on an assertive French Rhineland policy. Casting his prestige as military *père la Victoire* into the balance, and arguing on military grounds, Foch also desired to demarcate a new strategic frontier on the Rhine. He called it a "common barrier of security essential to the society of democratic nations". Foch urged Clemenceau to go beyond the boundaries of 1814 and incorporate the entire Saar basin – and thus more than one million German citizens – into the French state. And, crucially, he underscored that it was in France's overriding strategic interest to create permanent buffer-states on the left bank, which were to be brought into a "customs union" with France and other west European states. Further, he demanded the occupation of a "neutral zone on the right bank". A critical element of Foch's plans was the

---

[62] Clemenceau thought that he had gained Lloyd George's consent to his scheme, but the latter subsequently denied this. See Lloyd George (1938), I, pp. 132–6.

[63] See Derby to Balfour, 14 December 1918, Lloyd George Papers, F/52/2/52.

provision to guarantee the new status quo – not just for a transition period – by "Allied forces". The marshal insisted that French and European security required depriving Germany of "all territorial sovereignty on the left bank of the Rhine" – both on account of its "material and moral situation" and its continuing "numerical superiority" over "the democratic countries of Western Europe".[64]

Though he deemed it too radical, Clemenceau took heed of Foch's proposals. But he charged Tardieu with preparing a more elaborate Rhenish programme and reinforcing it with a compelling strategic, political, economic and historical justifications. This would shape what became the French government's highly divisive Rhineland policy at Versailles. Tardieu would only finalise his strategy once the peace proceedings had already begun. He deemed it crucial to underscore that French policy did not seek an outright annexation of the Rhineland, which he called irreconcilable with French political "ideals" – and which was bound to alienate France's allies. What he proposed instead, in line with Clemenceau's thinking, was the creation of nominally neutral "free Rhine state" on the left bank. It was to have an independent "political system" and would come "under the protection of the League of Nations". Yet it also was to be linked to France by means of a "Western European Customs Union" – which also would include Belgium – and thus *de facto* come under French economic and political domination. Tardieu's key arguments on behalf of this arrangement echoed those of Foch and were essentially geopolitical. He stressed that only an "independent" Rhine state could act as an effective "buffer" between Germany and the democratic western powers, furnishing guarantees that neither German disarmament nor the League could provide. Fundamentally, Tardieu argued that France required an essential "safety-zone" on land, to counter the potential threat of "millions of Germans trained to war", just as the Anglo-American naval powers, already protected by the sea, claimed naval safety zones and insisted on eliminating the German naval threat. In his interpretation, the French government thus had a strong claim to prevent the Rhineland from "again becoming a base for German aggression". To the same end, he demanded not merely a temporary but an indefinite inter-allied occupation of strategic bridgeheads across the Rhine.[65]

Tardieu's core strategic premise was that France urgently required a natural strategic frontier on the Rhine because even a Germany reduced in territory and deprived of some of its economic potential was still inherently more powerful and demographically far superior. He stressed that the "limitation" of Germany's

[64] Foch note, 21 November 1918, Tardieu Papers, vol. 43, MAE; Foch note, 10 January 1919 in Tardieu (II/1921), pp. 145–7; Foch (II/1931), p. 490.

[65] Tardieu memorandum, 20 January 1919; Tardieu notes, 20 January 1919, Tardieu Papers, PA-AP 166 (49, 417); Tardieu memorandum, 25 February 1919, in Tardieu (II/1921), pp. 163–70. See McDougall (1978), pp. 120 ff.

military power did not provide sufficient guarantees, as German elites would try to re-convert their country's economic strength into renewed military might. At the same time, he reiterated that the League, particularly in its inception phase, would not provide sufficient guarantees or the means for a rapid reaction to German aggression; and he calculated that while Russia no longer provided a power-political "counter-weight" in the east "the States recently created" in Eastern Europe, notably Poland and Czechoslovakia, did "not yet count". In his conception, a "physical guarantee" in the west thus constituted not only an essential complement but indeed a vital French interest.[66]

Yet Clemenceau's chief strategist also felt the need to present France's Rhineland policy as an approach that was essentially compatible with Wilson's Fourteen Points agenda. To deflect British and above all American objections, he even argued that it would actually foster the spread of newly relevant norms of international politics and democratic order. Tardieu argued that promoting Rhenish independence would not disregard the local population's claims to self-determination but actually reflect and further them. In his assessment, the Rhineland's more than 5 million inhabitants had a long history of independence in modern times, notably from Prussia; and, based on reports the French occupation forces had submitted about prevalent attitudes he felt confident that German nationalism could be mitigated and that the Rhenish people could be induced to embrace autonomy and even switch national allegiance. Tardieu calculated that much could be achieved by offering economic incentives. He therefore proposed granting the Rhineland more favourable economic peace terms than the rest of Germany and "advantages" under the proposed customs union.[67]

What Tardieu elaborated was a set of rationales – and overall outlook – that Clemenceau came to espouse, and it would inform the forceful "Rhineland campaign" both would pursue in the spring of 1919. The French premier even entertained the more far-reaching hope that following an initial occupation period the Rhineland would be "willing to unite itself with France".[68] Undoubtedly, Tardieu's Rhineland agenda must be understood as a maximalist programme, drawn up for expected bargaining with the United States and Britain at the actual peace conference. At the same time, it was an agenda that French policymakers could fall back on should it prove difficult or impossible to forge a firm postwar alliance of the victors. On the eve of the peace conference, both Clemenceau and Tardieu still hoped that they would be able

[66] Tardieu memorandum, 25 February 1919, in Tardieu (II/1921), pp. 156, 161–2.

[67] Tardieu notes, 20 January 1919, Tardieu Papers, vol. 417.

[68] Ribot, *Journal*, 16 February 1919, p. 259. The French government sought to complement the envisaged western security system by fostering both military cooperation and economic integration with Belgium. Further, it unequivocally supported Belgian claims for the hitherto German provinces Eupen and Malmédy.

to gain British and American support for the project of a Rhenish buffer-state. In late December, they presented their basic ideas to House in the hope of engaging him as an intermediary who would impress their concerns on Wilson. But this did not bear fruit.[69] Internally, they had also begun to think about ways of committing the Anglo-American powers to an alternative scenario that the French premier had already contemplated in early December: a prolonged occupation and enforced demilitarisation of the strategically vital region. Notably, Clemenceau was prepared to envisage compromises to salvage "unity" and the prospect of a firm alliance between the victors. Yet precisely because it could prove difficult to gain Anglo-American consent to such an alliance, the more far-reaching aims he and Tardieu pursued in the Rhineland could also be *accentuated* to obtain concessions from Wilson and Lloyd George. In fact, such tactical imperatives would indeed shape French actions at Versailles.

Neither Clemenceau nor Tardieu dwelled on the potential political risks and destabilising repercussions of their Rhineland schemes. To some extent they accepted these risks. But in retrospect it has to be stressed that they underestimated the power of German nationalism, the strength of the ties and allegiances that had been forged since 1870, particularly through nationalist education, and the effect of the common experience of fighting in the trenches of the Great War. More importantly, French policies carried the risk of provoking nationalist resentment and irredentism in the rest of Germany. Thus, they not only threatened to sow seeds of structural instability in the heart of postwar Europe. They also threatened to create distinctly unfavourable conditions for any advances towards a longer-term accommodation with Germany. And despite Tardieu's legitimation efforts, they threatened to place immense strains on inter-allied solidarity and relations with British and American leaders who had a different outlook on the future of the Rhineland – and future relations with Germany.

V.   "Self-Determination" and the Prevalence of Power-Political Imperatives. The Pursuit of a *Cordon Sanitaire* in Central and Eastern Europe

While focusing on Western Europe, the French government also approached the reordering of Central and Eastern Europe with one overriding objective: to weaken Germany's potential and to construct on the ruins of the eastern empires an essentially complementary *cordon sanitaire* between a reduced German and an incalculable Russian power – even though Clemenceau

---

[69] See House diary, 19 and 21 December 1918 and ff., House Papers.

remained determined to topple Bolshevik regime. The Quai d'Orsay, which had dominated conceptual planning in this area during the war, pursued this ambition in a distinctly unilateral manner, with little consideration for British and American preferences. And so did Clemenceau and Tardieu in the aftermath of the armistice. Both with a view to the crucial Polish question and the general restructuring of Eastern Europe's post-imperial space, French policymakers did not hesitate to invoke the principle of national self-determination, not only but also to placate Wilson and to legitimise their pursuits in the court of "world opinion". Yet they clearly did so in an even more instrumental fashion than their British counterparts, using normative conceptions – in conjunction with historical, economic and strategic arguments – to advance overriding power-political and security interests. And they also defined the interests of the new East European states – France's future allies – along these lines.

At a deeper level, geopolitical prerogatives thus clearly dominated in French official planning, and thinking, when it came to the creation of a "new order" in Central and Eastern Europe. And this gave rise to an unmistakeable double-standard. In short, French experts and decision-makers accentuated the "self-determination" principle in support of the claims of the leaders of Polish, Czecho-slovak and other national movements, particularly when they conflicted with German counter-claims. At the same time, they denied or downplayed its relevance when it concerned the interests of German populations in contested areas – or aspirations that threatened French security interests, notably those for an Austro-German union.

The creation of a strong Polish state was and remained the cornerstone of what Foreign Minister Pichon had in June 1918 characterised as France's strategy to build an "insurmountable barrier to German aggression" in Eastern Europe that compensated for the defunct alliance with Russia. This "barrier" was to take the form of a "close union" that also comprised a Czechoslovakian state and a "Yugoslav State".[70] After the "peace" of Brest-Litovsk, Pichon had sought to obtain from London and Washington an unequivocal public commitment to the resurrection of a "free, self-governing, and independent Poland" that had to be capable of ensuring "its own economic, political and military development". In June 1918, the French government had finally persuaded its European allies Britain and Italy to join in a common declaration stipulating that "the creation of a united and independent Polish State, with free access to the sea" constituted "one condition of a just and solid peace". This went a long way towards meeting the expectations of Dmowski's Polish National Committee and those who supported its cause in

[70] Pichon to Beneš, 29 June 1918, Beneš (1828–29), pp. 231–2. See Stevenson (1982), pp. 106–8.

the French Foreign Ministry.[71] In September 1918, Clemenceau had publicly renewed this promise.

On these premises, Tardieu and the experts he convened from the Quai d'Orsay, the *Comité d'études* and Foch's staff to hone France's eastern policy in early 1919 recommended that the French government should back the establishment of a Polish state that could act both as a "buttress against German expansion" and a "screen between Russia and Germany". What the French delegation then advocated at Versailles was largely congruent with the demands of the Polish National Committee. Essentially, Poland was to be "reborn" in the frontiers of 1772 and thus comprise sizeable territory along the Baltic coast, including Danzig. The creation of a "Polish corridor" and the "internationalisation" of Danzig were contemplated as fall-back options should it prove necessary to make concessions to Britain and the United States. But this was never regarded as the preferred "solution". Significantly, French policymakers also supported Polish demands for the strategically important coal-and-steel region of Upper Silesia, though they were aware that it contained a complex and unevenly distributed mixture of German and Polish populations. Here, as in general French concepts for the future Polish state, prevalent strategic concerns and balance-of-power calculations took precedence over the interests of the affected German populations. The danger of creating virulent minority problems and sources of future German irredentism was downplayed. The underlying assumption was that Germany would have to be contained by force in any case – and that the best way to further Polish and French interests was to create the strongest possible Polish state in terms of territorial reach and economic resources.[72] Obviously, this stood in marked opposition to American and, notably, British rationales.

On similar grounds, French policy- and decision-makers firmly backed the demands that Beneš and Masaryk made on behalf of a consolidated Czechoslovakian state that both for economic and strategic reasons was to include the predominantly ethnically German province of the Sudetenland.[73] Essentially, this merely confirmed the adjustments Clemenceau and Pichon had already made in the summer of 1918. Earlier, they had still contemplated detaching the Austro-Hungarian Empire from Germany and

---

[71] Pichon to Cambon, Jusserand and Barrère, 7 March 1918 MAE (Guerre) 732; Allied Declaration, Versailles, 3 June 1918, in Stevenson, p. 107. See Stevenson (1982), pp. 106–7.

[72] See French Foreign Ministry memorandum, 26 November 1918, transmitted to Balfour, FO/371/3446; "Pologne" committee minutes, 29 January 1919, Europe 1918–29, Pologne (68).

[73] See committee minutes on the frontiers of Czechoslovakia, undated, Tardieu Papers, PA-AP 166 (77).

preserving it as a possible counterweight to German influence in postwar Europe. But by June, Pichon had been authorised to endorse the agenda of the Czech National Council. As he assured Beneš, France would hence officially support claims for an independent Czechoslovakia "within the historic limits" of its provinces – and thus, in the Czech interpretation, also the Sudetenland region. Pichon had taken this step to encourage not only the Czech war effort but also the new state's adherence to the French "barrier" system in Central Europe.[74]

It should be emphasised, however, that while Pichon was attached to his eastern policy the concept of an eastern *cordon sanitaire* only played a secondary, complementary role in the new security system that Clemenceau and Tardieu envisaged. In their assessment, the eastern "barrier" could never compensate for the essential security guarantees that Britain and the United States were supposed to provide – or for the "physical guarantees" of the Rhineland regime they desired. But the French balance-of-power approach in the east could have onerous consequences, which would be particularly severe if the Anglo-American powers refused to make tangible commitments. It could create a highly unsettling scenario in which the French government – and the new states in this region – would have to bear a heavy strategic burden in safeguarding the new status quo against irredentist pressures, not only but chiefly from Germany. During the peace conference, the interest in forestalling such a scenario would give rise to British and American efforts to find different, more sustainable ways of restructuring national and international order in Eastern Europe. But it would prove immensely arduous to come to terms with this challenge.

Unsurprisingly, fundamental concerns over the postwar balance of power also motivated Clemenceau and Pichon to underscore early on their uncompromising opposition to the proposed *Anschluß*. The French premier simply refuted the desire expressed by representatives of the newly founded Austrian Republic to be united with Germany as "absolutely inadmissible". And he and his foreign minister essentially contested the legitimacy of this desire, seeking to brush off Austrian and German invocations of "self-determination". The official French position was that the Austrian parliament's vote for a union with Germany of 12 November 1918 was not representative. In the perception of all key French decision-makers, an Austro-German union that threatened to create a German-speaking power block in the heart of Europe contradicted the entire thrust of the French re-balancing strategy. Only the Socialist Party opposed the government's policy, pleading for an acceptance of *Anschluß* on the basis of Wilsonian principles – at a time when the American president

---

[74] Pichon to Beneš, 29 June 1918, Beneš (1928–29), II, pp. 231–2.

himself, as noted, had already decided that power-political considerations would take precedence in this case.[75]

In a wider context, not just France's policy towards Eastern Europe was determined by the search for a postwar system that offset the loss of the critical ally Tsarist Russia – even if the pre-war Franco-Russian alliance had neither prevented the German offensive of 1914 nor had the desired impact during the war. In the constellation of late 1918, and in the face of the ongoing Russian civil war, French decision-makers had to confront with renewed urgency the question of how to deal with the Bolshevik regime. Clemenceau still harboured a profound ideological antipathy towards Bolshevism. And in contrast to their British and American counterparts, not only the French premier but also the strategists at the Quai d'Orsay and in the French military command maintained the hope that there was still time, and opportunity, to intervene decisively in the Russian civil war and defeat Lenin's forces. In Clemenceau's eyes, Lenin and Trotsky had abetted German imperialist designs by signing the Brest-Litovsk treaty; and he feared that their regime would in the future become a de facto ally of German aspirations to reverse the outcome of the war and regain a predominant position in Europe. Both Clemenceau and Foch thus remained fervent advocates of an interventionist policy. But they would not be able to overcome the resistance of their reluctant British and American "allies".[76]

The degree to which leading French decision-makers remained wedded to the essential premises of French pre-war diplomacy seems remarkable. And their expectation that Russia would shake off the Bolshevik scourge and could once again be engaged to counterbalance and constrain Germany seems, in retrospect, far-fetched. Berthelot explicitly recommended that French postwar policy should be based on this assumption that Russia would re-emerge as a "conventional" European great power. Clemenceau fundamentally agreed, noting at one point that the re-emergence of a cooperative Russia would be critical for French efforts to "re-establish the European balance of power" and secure the peace – as important as the desired alliance with the Anglo-American powers.[77] Yet such attitudes not only reveal the vicissitudes of wishful thinking; they also point to fundamental problems. For the prospect of decisively expanding the western powers' intervention and bringing about a

[75] Clemenceau to Lloyd George, 10 November 1918, Lloyd George Papers, F/50/3/47; Pichon statement, 29 December 1918, *Journal Officiel (Chambre)*, 1918, 3334; Poincaré (1926–74), X, p. 258. See Low (1974), pp. 262–71.

[76] See Pichon to Clemenceau, 1 October 1918; Clemenceau to Pichon, 11 October 1918, MAE, Série Z, URSS, vols. 208, 210; memorandum on "Germano-Russian co-operation", 8 December 1918, Fonds Clemenceau, 6N 73, SHD-DAT.

[77] Clemenceau to Pichon, 23 October 1918, MAE, Série Z, URSS, vol. 208; Quai d'Orsay memorandum, 4 December 1918, *ibid.*, vol. 210. See Stevenson (1982), pp. 163–4; Jacobson (2013), pp. 235–7.

"white" victory in the Russian civil war, which was slim to begin with, all but disappeared at the outset of the peace conference – when both Wilson and Lloyd George rejected moves in this direction. Clemenceau and Pichon thus had to concentrate on far less ambitious priorities: to prevent German–Bolshevik collaboration and to stem the westward spread of Bolshevism, particularly by intensifying their efforts to create an East European *cordon sanitaire*.

VI.   No French Blueprints for a New World Order. The Continuities of French Imperial Policy and the Centrality of Euro-Atlantic Concerns

While French conceptions for a new Euro-Atlantic order were gaining contours and pointed beyond traditional understandings of power politics, the ways in which leading policymakers approached extra-European questions and, broadly speaking, "global" aspects of peacemaking were informed by power-political priorities. And they were informed by a decidedly unreconstructed outlook on imperialism and the interests of the French Empire, which particularly applied to the reordering of the Middle East. There were not even any significant tendencies to move towards the kind of neo-imperial "internationalism" that the British Empire's leading minds espoused at this juncture. At the same time, although Clemenceau and other protagonists were keen to expand France's sphere of imperial influence, extra-European issues and global concerns were at no point vital or even particularly relevant to French peace strategies. In contrast to what influenced British priorities, the centre of gravity of French preparations and preoccupations clearly lay in Europe and in the transatlantic sphere.

Nonetheless, Clemenceau, who had been a critic of France's imperial expansion before the war, now played his part in what turned into a neo-imperialist "dividing of spoils" in the Levant and the Middle East that unmistakeably harked back to pre-war practices. Fundamentally, he did not question the continued existence of the French Empire, or its justification. And he acknowledged that *France d'outre-mer* had significantly contributed to the French war effort. In fact, more than half a million soldiers from the French colonies had been mobilised during the war, and more than 200,000 colonial workers had served in war industries in metropolitan France. The French government was not prepared to relinquish these sources of strategic support in the future. For his part, Pichon had been an enthusiastic imperialist all along and now emerged as an emphatic proponent of an assertive imperial and colonial policy after the war. But his influence remained limited.[78]

---

[78] See Thomas (2005), pp. 17–18.

With Clemenceau's backing, but often left to their own devices, those who essentially devised France's imperialist policies for the postwar era were Gaston Doumergue and Berthelot, who led an inter-ministerial committee that had been set up to this end. They were far from doubting either the legitimacy or the wisdom of French-style colonial rule. Their common aim was to assert French interests by not only consolidating but also expanding the sphere of French imperial control. Yet they did not develop any "grand vision". To all appearances, they were less aware than their British counterparts of the potentially far-reaching repercussions that the Great War, Wilsonian rhetoric and Lenin-inspired calls for universal "self-determination" could have for the future of imperial rule and, in particular, for the French Empire. And failing to grasp these challenges, they did not see the need to develop more sophisticated or comprehensive strategies to fortify and legitimise imperial domination in new ways. By and large, they focused on re-asserting pre-war justifications of France's *mission civilisatrice*, defining it still essentially as a paternalistic mission of political and cultural tutelage and progress.

Clemenceau and those who oversaw French imperial policies shared the British interest in "re-assigning" the former German colonies. And, more fundamentally, they also desired to end German colonial rule and further imperialist aspirations after a war in which, in their view, they had repulsed the German Empire's bid to dominate Eurasia. The French Colonial Minister, Henry Simon, advocated a consolidation and unification of France's African Empire, which in his view required extending French rule over what had been German West Africa. Thus recurring to arguments and language of the era of the Fashoda crisis Simon insisted that imperial consolidation measures of this kind were essential to guarantee France's survival as a political and economic great power in the postwar world.[79] But the real focus of the French government lay on asserting French claims on the Middle Eastern territories that had been "liberated" from Ottoman rule. As before and during the war, the aims and ideological underpinnings of its imperial and colonial policies were partly influenced by pressure-groups – notably the *Congrès français de la Syrie*, the *Comité de l'Afrique française* and the venerable *Société de géographie* – that aimed to promote the imperial cause in France, disseminated propaganda and now urged Clemenceau to implement a far-ranging programme of imperial expansion. In the French parliament, these groups were supported by the Colonial Alliance Party. But they never had a significant impact on the official policymaking process or the government's wider extra-European priorities.[80]

---

[79] See Andrew and Kanya-Forstner (1981), p. 168.
[80] *Ibid.*, pp. 164–72; Thomas (2005), pp. 17 ff., 38–9.

What French policymakers basically envisaged was a process of redistributing peoples and territories between the two principal imperial powers that been victorious in the war, Britain and France – or, in short, they envisaged a division of the spoils of victory. They did not desire the League to play a role in this process and developed no concepts for making it an agency of neo-imperial oversight and "tutelage". Nor did they see any sense in involving the United States in a wider neo-imperial mission in the Levant and the Middle East. Rather, they now sought to implement the confidential accords with Britain – the Sykes-Picot agreement of 1916 – and incorporate formerly Ottoman-held Syria and Lebanon into France's imperial system. Consequently, they tried to shield these accords from any American interference and to pre-empt future interference through the League. They thus approached the "settlement" of a new, post-Ottoman status quo in the Middle East more or less in the manner their predecessors had proceeded at the height of the global imperialist competition in the earlier decades of the long twentieth century. And, significantly, they acted on the – by and large unquestioned – assumption that, as an exhausted great power, France had to pursue an all the more hard-fisted policy of imperial consolidation and expansion not only to keep up with Britain but more generally to bolster its position as a world power.

The main concern was to use the victory to put the French Empire in the best possible position to succeed in what was expected to be a new phase in the worldwide imperialist competition in which, after Germany's defeat, it now seemed set to play a dominant role alongside Britain. The French protagonists began to fathom but did not really comprehend that globally too the dynamics of international politics would change significantly in the aftermath of the Great War – and that the war had particularly altered the nature and challenges of both formal and informal imperialism. More than their British counterparts, they underestimated the political costs of maintaining or even expanding empire after a conflict that had propelled anti-colonial and anti-imperialist nationalism, also in the French imperial system.

Those officials who took an active interest in extra-European and colonial affairs thus adhered, to a remarkable extent, to mind-sets and worldviews that had been shaped by decades of imperialist competition. Leading strategists like Berthelot and Doumergue sought to justify their expansionist aims by reverting to arguments that had long been used to vindicate France's "civilising mission". They showed scant regard for the desires or "self-determination" of extra-European populations and, more fundamentally, made clear hierarchical distinctions between European and non-European levels of "civilisation". They considered, and presented, those who had lived under Ottoman rule and even more so those who had lived under German rule in Africa as not sufficiently "civilised" and advanced to be capable of determining their own affairs. Therefore, they ruled out applying or even referring to the self-determination principle. In their eyes, the peoples in question would require

French guidance, instruction and oversight for a long time to come. While extending its influence, the French republic would oversee and train local elites and raise the level of development in the territories that it would administer.[81]

Based on such assumptions, Berthelot, in mid-December 1918, came to propose a more ambitious scheme to dismantle the Ottoman Empire and repartition the Levant and the Middle East. In his judgement, its history of misrule, exploitation and the "period massacre of its people" had shown that the Ottoman Empire was "the most diametrically opposed of all the belligerents to the principles for which the Allies have fought". It thus had to be broken up and replaced by new political entities and a revised regional regime. Yet this could not be achieved by applying the "same method" that was to be adopted in Europe, i.e. by forming new independent states. Because the local populations had no experience of self-rule, having been subject to imperial rule since Persian times, it would be unavoidable to envisage a long-term regime of "European tutelage and control". Turkey itself was to be turned into a kind of international protectorate, controlled by an "international gendarmerie" and placed under European "surveillance". At the same time, the Straits were to be internationalised, under Anglo-French control, while Constantinople and the territories around it were to become a neutral zone of its own, protected by the European great powers until, at some point, the League might administer it.

In contrast to Smuts, Berthelot did not foresee either an American contribution to this regime nor a central role for the League, particularly in the shorter term. Significantly, neither he nor any other French policymaker ever envisaged anything like a League-administered mandate system. Rather, their core rationale remained that Britain and France were to divide direct or indirect control over Arab and Levantine territories in accordance with the Sykes-Picot accords. Echoing Jules Ferry, Berthelot argued that this way France's "material interests" in consolidating its influence in a region that was an "important part" of its "hereditary patrimony" would go hand in hand with the "moral" interest of extending the "benefits of civilisation".[82]

But Clemenceau essentially discarded Berthelot's far-reaching plans. His focus was and remained on Europe. And he was prepared to make concessions to Britain in the Middle East to gain Lloyd George's support for what was far more important: France's Rhineland agenda. Without consulting the Quai d'Orsay, the French premier seized on the basic understandings of the Sykes-Picot agreement to pursue strategic bargaining at the highest level.

---

[81] See Berthelot memorandum, 12 December 1918, Fonds Clemenceau, 6 N 72, SHD-DAT. For French policies of imperial consolidation and expansion after 1918, see Andrew and Kanya-Forstner (1981), pp. 28–63, 146–79; Thomas (2005), pp. 38–41; Fieldhouse (2006), pp. 36 ff., 245 ff.

[82] Berthelot memorandum, 12 December 1918, Fonds Clemenceau, 6 N 72, SHD-DAT.

When meeting Lloyd George in early December he proposed a bartering arrangement under which France would relinquish claims to Palestine and to Mosul (though still sharing access to oil and expected oil revenues) in return for Britain's recognition of French "rights" in Syria and Lebanon – and, crucially, British support for his evolving plans to neutralise the Rhineland. As Clemenceau saw it, Lloyd George had actually agreed to an arrangement of this kind but subsequently reneged on the promises he had made.[83]

At Versailles, France's plenipotentiaries would confront not only British attempts to supersede the Sykes-Picot agreements but also combined British and American pressures on behalf of a League-administered mandate system. They would oppose Anglo-American mandate ideas, clinging instead to the older notion of creating outright protectorates. But they would eventually have to concede that they could not prevail with their conception – and that they would have to pursue their imperialist interests, like Britain, under the guise of the League's mandate regime. Anglo French imperialist skirmishes over the post-Ottoman "settlement" for the Middle East would indeed cast a long shadow over the peace conference and make attempts to find common ground on vital European issues even more difficult. And Berthelot's plans to establish a European control regime over Turkey in Asia Minor would eventually be superseded – like all British schemes, vaguer American notions and, ultimately, the terms of the Treaty of Sèvres – by Atatürk's nationalist revolution and the creation of a "modern" Turkish state.[84]

VII. Towards a New Economic and Financial Order on French Premises? French Schemes for an Exclusive "Atlantic Union" and a "Financial League of Nations"

From the outset, the Clemenceau government's overall approach to the peace negotiations and postwar security was significantly influenced by profound economic and financial concerns, both domestic and international, which were intricately intertwined. Such concerns also lay behind the ambitious strategies that were chiefly developed by Commerce Minister Clémentel and his key collaborator Henri Hauser and elaborated between June and December 1918. Their underlying aim was ambitious indeed: to lay the groundwork for a new – and essentially transatlantic – economic and financial order on French premises. The aspirational conceptions they advanced built on the French agenda for the Paris Economic Conference of 1916 and were crystallised in the Clémentel plan. It proposed the creation of an "Atlantic union", a new kind of economic union that was to be controlled by the victors, accessible for

---

[83] See minutes of Anglo-French and Allied meetings, 1 and 2 December 1918, CAB 28/5.
[84] See MacMillan (2002), pp. 381–409.

smaller and neutral states – as well as the new states of Eastern Europe – but excluding Germany. It thus was designed to place severe limits on German access to this core sphere of the world market after the war. Ideally, this new systemic status quo was to be maintained not just for a short transition period after the war.

What Clémentel and his influential adviser envisaged was in fact an unprecedented system of "economic organisation" that was to ensure France's economic security and solvency by establishing new rules to regulate postwar competition and "re-balance" the distribution of economic power, resources and access to the world economy. Undoubtedly, this system was chiefly intended to prevent renewed German aspirations to achieve "economic domination" in Europe. But it was also designed to tie and rein in the newly predominant American power. Clémentel's scheme foresaw that *eventually* a constrained Germany could be integrated in the economic order he hoped to establish – if it proved that it was willing to abide by the French rules. Yet he and other French policymakers had even more far-reaching aspirations. They hoped to address the challenges of postwar reconstruction and France's daunting financial problems by not merely relying on German reparations but also creating an essentially transatlantic economic regime in which financial resources were to be "pooled" and redistributed, and which also was to facilitate debt relief – all under the auspices of the League of Nations.

The concerns and ideas of those who shaped French policies thus went far beyond the rallying cry *"l'Allemagne paiera"* and the priority to reconstruct the provinces devastated by the war, which had been the eastern heartlands of French industry. They sought to address fundamental and deeply disconcerting structural challenges that the Great War had left in its wake. At one level, they confronted an unprecedented fiscal malaise. As noted, France's public debt had risen sixfold since 1913, to more than 200 billion gold francs, while debts to Britain and the United States amounted to 35 billion gold francs. At the same time, the Clemenceau government faced a spiralling budget deficit and was in fact critically dependent on further American short-term loans to escape the risk of bankruptcy.[85]

In a wider context, Clémentel and Hauser sought to prevent what they regarded as a potentially very threatening international scenario, namely that the dynamic pre-war process of globalising economic competition between the advanced powers would resume and even accelerate under America's newly decisive influence. In their assessment, such a development was bound to favour the intrinsically strongest powers, including Germany. It thus had to be channelled and, as far as possible, regulated to the advantage of a

---

[85] Only about half of French liabilities were long-term debts, the rest was "floating debt" that could require short-term repayment. See Jackson (2013), pp. 218–20.

French power that, because of its inferior economic potential, was otherwise bound to fall behind.

The underlying fear, which Jean Monnet, then a junior official in the Commerce Ministry, diagnosed astutely, was that a swift return to essentially unfettered competition under the liberal "Open Door" maxims that Wilson championed would have very dangerous consequences for France. It would threaten its postwar recovery and allow Germany to regain predominance in Europe, with unsettling political and strategic consequences. Clémentel shared these concerns and recommended that Clemenceau should impress on Wilson that such a scenario would inevitably lead to a new phase of economic warfare in postwar Europe – with "customs barriers" and "economic coalitions" – that would again endanger the "peace of the world".[86] French policymakers realised that British but above all American support for their designs was indispensable – that they were even more dependent on it than in the sphere of postwar security. But they did not sufficiently grasp how profoundly their *dirigiste* proposals not only clashed with US "Open Door" conceptions but also challenged prevalent American approaches to all critical issues: war debts, reparations, and postwar reconstruction. What is more, French ideas were deeply at odds with fundamental American preferences for a an organisation of the economic and financial peace that minimised state controls – and the new financial hegemon's official responsibilities and liabilities.

In the summer of 1918, the French commerce minister had revised the design for a future inter-allied economic league that he had originally presented at the Paris Economic Conference. But his conceptual approach, and the assumptions that informed it, were fundamentally unaltered. In mid-September, Clémentel had then sent a letter to Clemenceau and Wilson in which he presented a revised programme for a postwar economic order on French terms. It was still conceived as a scheme to counter the dangerous spectre of a German-dominated economic bloc in *Mitteleuropa* in the aftermath of Brest-Litovsk. Clémentel renewed his call for an "Atlantic union" between the "allied democracies". He stressed that it was to form the "nucleus" of an "economic union of the free peoples". At the core, however, it was meant to provide the most "durable cement" for the desired peacetime alliance between western powers. The underlying purpose of Clémentel's schemes was twofold. At one level, there was the aspirational intention to create a novel international and in some respects supranational economic regime. The new "union" would not only rest on mutual agreements to lower tariffs. A special emphasis was placed on maintaining the inter-allied commissions, controls and mechanisms that had been established during the war to regulate

[86] Monnet to Clémentel, 2 November 1918, in Roussel (1996), pp. 73–5; Clémentel to Clemenceau, 31 December 1918, AN F12 / 8104.

shipping and the distribution of food and essential primary resources. In fact, these were to be converted, and extended, into something unprecedented: far-reaching "joint programmes" not only for "the importation of raw-materials" but also, and crucially, the "redistribution" of the "means of credit" for Europe"s revitalisation – which would meet cardinal French needs. This was to be an integral part of what Clémentel, in an appeal to Wilson's "principles", would call an "organised peace".[87]

Crucially, however, what the commerce minister proposed also was to serve another cardinal aim, which gained new prominence after the armistice. In short, he sought to commit Britain yet above all the United States to a system that protected France against the threat posed by a German power "pursuing anew its dream of economic domination" – and using once again "economic power" and illicit practices of "dumping" and "camouflage" to attain its "imperialist goals" in and beyond Europe. Clémentel thus not only insisted on excluding Germany from the "Atlantic union" but also proposed depriving it of the most-favoured-nation status that had ensured its commercial prepon-derance before 1914. Originally, he and Hauser therefore desired to establish the new "economic union" as a discriminatory regime. And they did not only envisage temporary changes but sought to instigate longer-term structural changes in world economic system.[88]

Clémentel had been aware all along that realising his plans required British backing but that the most daunting challenge he faced was to commit the United States as the by now "greatest economic power of the world". And he was not oblivious to the fact that fundamentals of US foreign economic policy – which clashed with his designs – had not changed since the Paris Economic Conference. As he had informed Clemenceau in September 1918, both Wilson and American experts not only continued to oppose "all meas-ures of economic coercion" directed against Germany but were also hostile to the entire idea of a postwar economic order regulated by inter-governmental agreements and founded as a "closed" system.[89] Nonetheless, he at first remained confident that the French government would be able to build bridges to the Wilson administration, and in fact find ways to co-opt American power, by pursuing a new strategy. Essentially, he followed Tardieu's suggestion to advance France's design "under the aegis of Wilson's principles" and to

[87] Clémentel letter, 19 September 1918, AN, F12 8104; Hauser memorandum, summer 1918, AN F12/8106; Monnet (1976), pp. 106–7. For different interpretations see Soutou (1989), pp. 766–9; Trachtenberg (1980), pp. 15–22; Glaser (1998), pp. 374–5; Jackson (2013), pp. 249–55.

[88] Clémentel letter, 19 September 1918, in Clémentel (1931), pp. 343, 346–7. In this respect, it seems not too far-fetched to characterise Clémentel's scheme as a "long-term concept for an economic war after the war". See Glaser (1998), p. 375.

[89] Clémentel letter, 19 September 1918, AN, F12/8106.

suggest that it was not only reconcilable with the president's peace aspirations but actually extended their scope. At this stage, Clemenceau and Tardieu had whole-heartedly endorsed Clémentel's strategy.[90] But it would not bear any fruit. As we have seen, French designs met not only with British reservations. They also encountered fundamental American resistance, spearheaded by Hoover, which was barely disguised by a non-committal official attitude. This resistance did not just concern the plan for a transatlantic raw materials consortium but indeed the overall thrust of Clémentel's ambitions.

Forced to adapt, Clémentel proposed a revised approach, which he presented to Clemenceau shortly after Wilson's visit to Paris in December 1918. While still advocating an "economic league", he now sought to gain American support for inter-allied economic agreements and discriminatory provisions at least for a *transition period* – arguing that this was essential for France's reconstruction after the war. And he now devised a scheme of temporary economic controls and "probation" that, as he saw it, could protect cardinal French interests while addressing American concerns. He impressed on Clemenceau that it should not be France's official aim to crush Germany economically – once a "just peace" had been imposed it would be incompatible with the ideals of the victors to "deprive" the beaten foe of "the means to live and get back to work". But he deemed it imperative to ensure – through the League – a *controlled* "socialisation" of postwar Germany. An effective League-administered regime of economic sanctions was to compel it to honour its "obligations as a civilised power". In Clémentel's conception, this discriminatory regime would only be altered once Germany had proved that it had embraced the standards of the "community of free nations". Until then, the victors would have the prerogative to form "favourable commercial combinations" such as a "customs union" – while the defeated power would be forced to grant "most-favoured-nation" status to them.[91]

Yet it would soon become clear in the early stages of the peace conference that also Clémentel's revised plans would founder on the rock of entrenched American opposition. Essentially, while they in some ways offered a forward-looking vision of how to come to grips with the challenges of reconstruction *and* interdependence after the Great War what Clémentel and his assistants elaborated in 1918 remained a distinctly hierarchical – and exclusive – conception of how the economic order was to be reorganised in the postwar world. It accorded the victors decisive control and discriminatory powers. And it was designed to give a profoundly exhausted French power a decisive say, and veto, in determining who was allowed to participate in this new order. In essential respects, it would thus be misleading to conclude that Clémentel's

---

[90] *Ibid.*; notes of meeting, 28 September 1918, AN, F12/8104; Trachtenberg (1980), pp. 14–18.
[91] Clémentel to Clemenceau, 31 December 1918, AN, F12/8104.

proposals prefigured the schemes of supranational economic – and political – organisation and integration that Monnet would advance in the 1940s. Undoubtedly, though, one of the most critical problems in the first half of the long twentieth century was and remained – apart from the behaviour of the newly dominant American power – the vexing question on what terms Germany could be constructively integrated into the European, transatlantic and world economy.

VIII.   The Rationales and Transatlantic Dimensions of French Approaches to the Reparations Question

The Wilson administration's attitudes towards the postwar economic and financial order also had a crucial bearing on the *changing* rationales of the French government's approach to reparations. Yet its evolving policy was of course also influenced by the far-ranging and politically delicate public expect-ations in France about the price Germany would have to pay for a war that in the opinion of an overwhelming majority it had forced on France. Similar to Britain, these expectations made the reparations question not merely a finan-cial but also and essentially a political and psychological issue. And yet it was inseparable from France's unprecedented fiscal problems and indebtedness. These concerns were forcefully articulated by Finance Minister Klotz, who became one of the most outspoken proponents of immense indemnity demands and subsequently one of the French protagonists in the "reparations battle" at Versailles. Ultimately, however, French reparation policies were also decisively shaped by underlying power-political "re-balancing" and control considerations vis-à-vis Germany.

When he sought to formulate a coherent French reparations programme in early January, Tardieu had to deal with two conflicting sets of recommenda-tions: one developed by Clémentel and the chief planners of the Commerce Ministry, the other presented by Klotz on behalf of the Finance Ministry. The commerce minister recommended that, provided it could obtain Anglo-American backing for his scheme to found an "economic union", the French government should seek a comparatively moderate settlement that only assured "integral reparation" for the actual damages sustained in the occupied and devastated areas.[92] Using formulations that echoed those of Keynes Clémentel argued that it was not in France's interests to "ruin" Germany, observing that forcing it to pay for the entire cost of the war would "destroy the defeated party" and reduce it "to a state of economic servitude that would deprive humanity of all hope for a durable peace".[93] Like Hauser, he also

---

[92] *Ibid.*
[93] Clémentel letter, 19 September 1918, AN, F12/8104.

opposed major cash transfers from Germany, stressing that they could spark inflation and thus harm the French economy. What Clémentel proposed instead was a two-phase policy. First, Germany had to be forced to pay appropriate indemnities; later an international "pool", a *"caisse mondiale"*, was to be established under the auspices of the League whose funds would be used to finance reconstruction measures. The commerce minister of course realised that most of the funds for this "pool" would have to come from the United States. Like his other schemes it hinged on Wilson's political will to assume and legitimise potentially far-reaching financial responsibilities that would effectively make the American government the principal sponsor of European reconstruction. But of course this too collided with the premises and self-imposed limits of the Wilson administration's approaches to postwar reconstruction, not to mention the limits set by the US Congress.

Equally predestined to come into conflict with American essentials were French plans to establish a linkage between reparations and war debts and to justify the cancellation or reduction of French obligations to both Britain and the United States. In a futile attempt to persuade American decision-makers, Clémentel argued that the promotion of France's restoration and Europe's recovery required a significant alleviation of the enormous debt burdens. At the same time, he asserted that France could only afford to limit its reparation demands vis-à-vis Germany if its chief creditors agreed to a "revision and reduction" of their demands. This proposal became part and parcel of a broader debt-cancellation scheme under which Britain and the United States were to write off their wartime loans to France – and Italy. To gain Lloyd George's backing, the French government would offer to support an annulment of most of Britain's obligations to the principal American creditor power. All was presented as serving the "common" interest of all the victors to boost Europe's revitalisation.[94] Yet French schemes of this kind, which like parallel British designs ultimately put the "onus" of debt relief on the American government, stood no chance of overcoming unwavering US opposition.[95]

When it became clear that the American veto to his plans would not be rescinded, Clémentel's influence on France's reparations policy waned rapidly. It would subsequently be determined, not by Tardieu but rather by Klotz and, notably, the newly appointed Minister of Industrial Reconstruction, Louis Loucheur. And they, in short, would advocate a different approach and seek to attain core aims of the French "re-balancing" strategy by pursuing a *harsher* reparations agenda. Whether or not he actually coined the slogan

---

[94] Clémentel to Clemenceau, 31 December 1918, AN, F12/8104.
[95] Clémentel note to Clemenceau and "Avant-projet", [late] December 1918; Commerce Ministry memorandum, 31 December 1918, AN, F12/8104.

"Germany will pay" after the war, Klotz had indeed espoused an uncompromisingly maximalist interpretation of what constituted rightful French demands, with scant regard for Germany's capacity to pay. He asserted that the defeated power had to be forced to compensate France not only for the damages in the territories it had occupied but also for its complete war expenses, including veterans' and widows' pensions. And he also demanded a restitution of the entire indemnity that the Bismarck Empire had imposed on France in 1871.[96]

Behind the finance minister's harsh posture lay not only the pressing fiscal constraints but also towering domestic-political pressures. His foremost concern was to reduce the massive French budget deficit and to address the daunting debt problem as swiftly as possible. And though he had done nothing to moderate public hopes through his own rhetoric he – like Clemenceau – was indeed tangibly constrained by what was already the dominant expectation in the French public, and press, namely that Germany would pay massive reparations. Influenced by wartime propaganda and official justifications of the war effort, the sweeping demands that followed from this expectation had acquired a distinctly moral and symbolical connotation, which President Poincaré emphatically reasserted after the armistice and again at the outset of the peace conference. In short, the reigning notion was that the French nation was entitled to demand from the power that was responsible for the catastrophe of the war "full reparation" for the sacrifices it had made in defending the cause of western civilisation and democracy.[97]

Expectations and constraints of this kind would have a significant impact on French strategies at Versailles. Loucheur himself would favour fixing a moderate total sum; and he would seek to work out a compromise with American experts. But the fact that exaggerated public notions of what qualified as "réparation intégrale" were impossible to satisfy made it exceedingly difficult for Clemenceau or his main negotiators to commit France to a definite or restrained reparations settlement – particularly as long as they could not obtain any American concessions. Yet he and Tardieu would also seize on the obvious domestic difficulties they faced, and insist on far-reaching reparations demands, in order to drive a hard bargain at the peace conference – and to realise their overriding objective of recasting the strategic balance vis-à-vis Germany and to impose maximal constraints on the vanquished power. Here, as will be shown, reparations could be used as a lever, especially to justify towards France's difficult Anglo-American allies (at the very least) a long-term occupation of the Rhineland.

---

[96] See Finance Ministry memorandum, 18 November 1918, Tardieu Papers, PA-AP 166 (3).
[97] See Poincaré speech, 18 January 1919, in Horne and Austin (1923), VII, pp. 37–43; Miquel (1977), pp. 424 ff.

IX. No Negotiations with the "So-Called German Democracy" The Imperative of a Dictated Peace – and a Future Accommodation with Germany?

In view of the far-reaching strategic, economic and financial aims of the evolving French peace programme, and the assumptions on which it rested, it was only logical that not only Clemenceau but virtually all relevant French policymakers insisted more unequivocally than even their British counterparts on one key premise as they approached the actual *process* of peacemaking. They were adamant that the only way to ensure a satisfactory peace was to force it on Germany. And they were equally adamant that the victors had to decree the ground-rules and set the basic parameters of the postwar order without German interference. They never envisaged even partial or even symbolical negotiations with the *ennemi outre-Rhin* that could have challenged the "unity" of the victors or compromised the French government's essential interests. More fundamentally, Clemenceau and those who shaped French policies shared the conviction that the very idea of even *seeking* a settlement that would be acceptable not only to the victors but also to the vanquished was not only flawed but indeed dangerous. As they saw it, such an approach was not only bound to fail; it would also prevent the western powers from forging a peace, and establishing a postwar system, that really contained and constrained the defeated power.

At Versailles, Clemenceau would assert that even if the victorious powers tried to make a "just" settlement the Germans would never "forgive" them and "only seek the opportunity for revenge", as nothing would "extinguish the rage of those who wanted to establish their domination over the world and who believed themselves so close to succeeding".[98] Ultimately, he maintained, the vanquished would have to resign themselves to "a peace imposed by the stronger who has justice on his side on the weaker who has been the aggressor".[99]

This outlook led French policymakers to pursue, ever since the conclusion of the armistice, a vigorous policy of containment vis-à-vis what they regarded as Wilson's unchanging ambition to push for a negotiated peace settlement with Germany on progressive premises. In sharp contrast to the American president's interpretation, Clemenceau and Tardieu contended that the terms of the armistice amounted to an "unconditional surrender" of Germany that would "permit the Allies to impose their terms of peace".[100] Not only Foch but also Pichon and Berthelot shared this assessment. Consequently, aided by the Quai d'Orsay, Clemenceau subsequently made it his priority first to close ranks with Lloyd George but ultimately to commit both him and Wilson to

---

[98] Clemenceau statement, Council of Four, 28 March 1919, Mantoux (1992), I, pp. 62–5.
[99] Tardieu (I/1921), p. 134.
[100] See Tardieu (II/1921), pp. 43, 60, 76.

the French terms of reference for what essentially was to be a peacemaking process of the victors. And because the overriding priorities of all the principal victors were de facto compatible regarding this crucial procedural issue, the French government would succeed not only in forestalling any moves towards initial negotiations with the provisional government in Berlin but also, eventually, in preventing a substantive negotiating process with German plenipotentiaries at the actual peace conference.

Prior to the inter-allied consultations in London in early December, the Clemenceau government had formally proposed that the Allied Powers should deliberate peace terms amongst themselves and then present them to German representatives, but only to "compel them to accept without any discussion" the "conditions already arrived at" between the victorious powers.[101] French decision-makers thus unequivocally rejected any preliminary discussions with Ebert and the Council of Peoples' Commissars. On 11 November, when the revolutionary turmoil had just begun in Germany, Clemenceau had proposed that the "Allied Governments" should come together "as soon as possible" to settle the "preliminaries of peace" without "any consultation" with the defeated power.[102] Later, once Wilson's participation in the peace conference had been confirmed, the French premier switched to a different tactic and sought to delay peace negotiations, not in order to create conditions for eventual discussions with the leaders of the fledgling German republic but to ensure that a new government would be formed in Berlin that would be stable enough to "accept" and execute the peace terms decreed by the victors. The core aim was and remained to keep the new German authorities isolated from the peacemaking process and to ward off challenges that could arise from German appeals to Wilson and Wilsonian terms of reference.

The French government now declared that the Allied Powers could only deal with "a constituent Assembly elected freely by universal, secret and direct suffrage". But it basically did so in order to delay any dealings with German representatives until after the German elections, which then would be held in January 1919. Clemenceau told House that it would be "absurd" to make "hard and fast arrangements with governments as shaky as those of Lenin and Ebert". Earlier, he had impressed on Lloyd George that it was advisable to "let the German Revolution settle itself a little" so that the *Entente* leaders would know whom they would have to "confront".[103] Yet Clemenceau never

---

[101] French "Proposals for the Preliminaries of Peace with Germany", 26 November 1918, CAB 1/27/24.

[102] Clemenceau to Allied governments, 11 November 1918, MAE, Paix 47.

[103] "French Proposals for the Preliminaries of Peace with Germany", 26 November 1918; French "Note Verbale", 3 December, CAB 1/27/24 and 26; House to Wilson, Paris, 15 November 1918, *PWW*, LIII, pp. 84–5; House diary, 5 December 1918, House Papers; Clemenceau to Lloyd George, undated, in Lloyd George (1938), I, p. 88.

abandoned his rationales for a dictated peace. Essentially, he was even more determined than the British prime minister to impose peace terms on Germany regardless of who represented it or how legitimate its representatives would be.

The French premier took the revolutionary upheavals in Germany seriously and at one point observed that they could have far-reaching consequences, exposing the victors to "the unknown". Essentially, however, he evaluated the German situation, the future of Franco-German relations and, crucially, the requirements of peace on the basis of deeper, long-held assumptions about German mentality and "the German character". In turn, these assumptions were shaped by decades of critical engagement with *le voisin étrange outre-Rhin*. In short, they reinforced Clemenceau's conviction that the revolution did not represent a fundamental break with the Empire but only a superficial and indeed deceptive development. Reflecting the views of Tardieu – and a clear majority among French elites – he swiftly concluded that there were fundamental and disconcerting continuities between the Wilhelmine Empire and the nascent Republic of Weimar. In his eyes, Ebert and the leaders of the Council of People's Commissars did not pursue a qualitatively new approach to foreign policy and peace but rather the same fundamental – and profoundly threatening – objectives as the old Wilhelmine elites; and the same would later hold true for the Scheidemann government and the new foreign minister Brockdorff-Rantzau. As Clemenceau saw it, they all shared the underlying aim of not only preventing a harsh peace but also preserving the bases of German power so as to regain, over time, the means to establish a German hegemony over Europe and thus pose a renewed threat to France.[104]

Like his key advisers, the French premier in part emphasised such continuities and deliberately denigrated the advances of German liberals and social democrats for tactical reasons, namely to discredit the new German government and to counter any German or Anglo-American arguments on behalf of negotiations or a lenient peace that aided the fledgling German democracy. But his underlying concerns and suspicions were genuine and ultimately decisive. In Clemenceau's assessment, which revealed an even more hierarchical outlook on what distinguished the western democracies from the German power state than those of Wilson and Lloyd George, it was illusory to expect swift and decisive changes in prevalent German thinking and international behaviour – even if the defeated power adopted a republican constitution. And it was thus not only imprudent but outright hazardous to pursue a policy that aimed at accommodating a German republic and sought to strengthen moderate republican forces on the other side of the Rhine. Even in the medium

---

[104] Clemenceau notes to Lloyd George and the Italian and Belgian prime ministers, 9 and 10 November 1918, MAE, Paix, 47.

term, Clemenceau considered such an approach misguided. Behind this lurked a fear that most French policymakers shared: the fear that forces of the "old order" would find ways to seize the reins of power once again – and could then capitalise on any concessions the victors had made to those who claimed to represent a "new Germany".[105]

Consistent with this outlook Clemenceau early on accused the new authorities in Berlin of exaggerating the danger that Germany would succumb to Bolshevism and France would also be "infected by the same scourge", either of which he deemed unlikely. He thus regarded German pleas as a ploy to wring concessions from the Allied Powers. For his part, Pichon suspected that the German Social Democrats chiefly intended to "obtain more moderate peace conditions" from Wilson by suggesting that Germany's fate lay in his hands. Both Clemenceau and his foreign minister thus warned that the western powers must not be manipulated by German efforts to conjure up the spectre of Bolshevism. For them, the potential menace of a revitalised German power bent on revenge clearly outweighed that of a "Bolshevisation" of Germany.[106] On these grounds they also opposed US proposals for targeted interventions to stabilise the German situation – either through diplomatic support for the provisional government or expedited food relief, which Hoover recommended as the most effective means to combat Bolshevism. Pichon argued that any support for the Council of People's Commissars would only strengthen the "centralising tendency" of Prussia against the "autonomous and federal tendency of other States, notably Bavaria". The French government indeed sought to encourage "federal" and separatist tendencies – especially but not only in the Rhineland. While French policymakers realised that a dissolution of the Bismarck *Reich* was beyond their grasp, the underlying aim was clearly to the weaken the German state as far as possible.[107]

Tardieu shared Clemenceau's fundamental assumptions and outlook on the German problem. His entire security strategy and conception of a community of western democracies was based on the premise that it would be both futile and risky to negotiate with the leaders of what he termed the so-called German democracy and to count on significant qualitative changes in Germany, either towards a stable republican order or towards a more cooperative foreign policy. Tardieu tried hard to impress his pessimistic outlook on the Wilson administration and those American and British "liberals" who in his eyes

---

[105] *Ibid.*; Clemenceau to Allied governments, 11 November 1918, MAE, Paix, 47. For his underlying assumptions see Clemenceau (1916).

[106] Clemenceau to Allied governments, 11 November 1918, MAE, Paix, 47; Clemenceau statement, Council of Ten, 12 February 1919, *FRUS-PPC*, III, p. 975; Pichon to Paul Cambon, 7 December 1918, in Stevenson (1982), p. 142. See Köhler (1980), pp. 324–7.

[107] Pichon to Jusserand, 1 December 1918, Jusserand Papers, MSS (42); Clemenceau to Foch, 11 January 1919, in Bariéty (1977), pp. 51–3; Stevenson (1982), pp. 141–3.

advocated a dangerously conciliatory approach. Like Clemenceau, he insisted that those who had become leading figures in the wake of the revolution – men like Ebert, Erzberger and Brockdorff-Rantzau – represented a deceptive democratic renewal and had by no means abandoned the aggressive and duplicitous behaviour that the old elites of the Wilhelmine Empire had displayed before them. He pointedly accused them of having been "the most active agents of militarism and imperialism". And he categorised them as essentially untrustworthy. Underscoring that they all had up until recently supported the "old order", he claimed that they too represented a Germany "whose word cannot be trusted for a long time to come".[108]

The implication of Tardieu's assessment was unequivocal: the victors would have to keep a check on Germany for the foreseeable future while its new leaders – as well as the German people – would have to demonstrate over time that they were committed not only to reforming their system of government but also to amending Germany's international conduct. He remained profoundly sceptical. What came to the fore here, as in the case of Clemenceau, were entrenched notions of civilisational hierarchy and gradations of civilisational progress. Such notions also informed Tardieu's essentially defensive conception of an exclusive community of "Western democracies" to which Germany did not (yet) belong and whose frontier indeed had to be defended on the Rhine.[109]

How then did Clemenceau, Tardieu and other leading French policymakers envisage the future of Franco-German relations and the longer-term stabilisation of the victor's peace they sought to impose? The French outlook differed rather drastically from those of Wilson and the protagonists of British peace policies. What Clemenceau and Tardieu envisioned was partly an uncompromising "probation policy" vis-à-vis Germany. But at the core it was a longer-term struggle whose main emphasis lay on enforcing stringent peace terms and an effective control and containment of the defeated power. Yet it should also be noted that the underlying rationale was to create secure conditions for an *eventual* accommodation and ultimately perhaps even a mutually beneficial cooperative relationship with Germany. As Clemenceau would emphasise *after* the Paris Peace Conference, France was bound to confront this task one day. But in his view this could only be done once the victors' fundamental conditions had been fulfilled and, crucially, a strong and functioning alliance with Britain and the United States had been forged and provided essential re-assurance.[110] Both he and Tardieu recognised that in

---

[108] Tardieu memorandum, 25 February 1919, Tardieu (II/1921), pp. 156, 161–2.
[109] *Ibid.*
[110] See Clemenceau statement to the Foreign Affairs Commission of the *Assemblée Nationale*, 29 July 1919, CAE, *Assemblée Nationale*, CTP, C/7773; Clemenceau speech, 25 September 1919, *Journal Officiel (Chambre)*, 1919.

the longer run it would be impossible to exclude Germany either from the League or from the recast international order.[111] And they reckoned that at some point a new understanding and *modus vivendi* with France's long-time "structural enemy" would have to be worked out. But the question of what form such a process could take was not on their agenda as they prepared for the peace conference.

One maxim the main French actors agreed on was that any kind of accommodation process had to be postponed as far as possible and, crucially, that it could only take place once the victorious great powers had created, and Germany had agreed to meet, essential preconditions. The Clemenceau government eventually acquiesced in the formula that the new German leaders and the German people had to prove their commitment to democracy and a republican system of government to become eligible for admission to the *société de nations*. But neither Clemenceau nor Tardieu or the Foreign Ministry's senior strategists set great store by this. And they mainly used categories like "democratic standards" to justify why – for the foreseeable future – Germany had to be ostracised from the "comity of nations".[112] The real criterion they emphasised was a different one: German willingness to comply with the terms and to fulfil the conditions of the peace that the victors would decree.

According to the French design, those who represented Germany thus had to accept not only substantial power-political and territorial curtailments, economic restrictions and indemnity obligations but also, essentially, an unequal status in the postwar system. What mattered even more, however, was that British and American leaders agreed not only to support the French peace programme but also to engage in its enforcement. In the eyes of Clemenceau and Tardieu, only a strict enforcement of the victors' terms and, crucially, the formation of an effective "union" of the victors could create an environment in which it would be "safe" for France to pursue *eventually* a more cooperative course towards Germany.[113] Significantly, it was only after the Versailles negotiations that the French premier would explicitly stress the necessity of preparing for such a significant reorientation. In August 1919 he would impress on French senators that the "central challenge" the French nation faced in the medium term was not only to ensure Germany's demilitarisation but, more fundamentally, to negotiate "an accommodation" with its

[111] *Ibid.*; Tardieu to Wilson, 10 June 1919, in Tardieu (I/1921), p. 135.
[112] See Tardieu memorandum, 25 February 1919, Tardieu (II/1921), p. 156; Berthelot memorandum, 18 December 1918, Fonds Clemenceau, 6 N 72, SHD-DAT.
[113] See Clemenceau statement to the Foreign Affairs Commission of the *Assemblée Nationale*, 29 July 1919, CAE, *Assemblée Nationale*, CTP, C/7773.

more populous eastern neighbour.[114] Yet before or during the peace conference he would pointedly refrain from making such arguments, in private or
in public.

In the aftermath of the armistice Bourgeois thus emerged as the only
notable policymaker who actually proposed rationales for a more cooperative
and integrative long-term strategy towards Germany. What he developed, and
publicly outlined in mid-November 1918, can be characterised as a distinctive
internationalist – and decidedly paternalistic – variant of a French "probation
policy". In many ways, Bourgeois shared the prevalent pessimistic outlook on
the prospects of establishing a viable democracy on the ruins of the
Wilhelmine Empire and advancing towards a peaceful coexistence with
Germany. In his view, the German Empire had been a state in which the
"tragic doctrine of force" had acquired the significance of a "sacred precept of
state policy", and he expected that those who sought to establish a German
republic would find it a daunting challenge to depart from such traditions.
Nonetheless, Bourgeois anticipated that in the longer run integrating Germany
in the *société des nations* could indeed have a pacifying and "civilising" effect
by giving future German decision-makers, and the wider German population,
a stake in a system of mutual rights *and* obligations under a strong covenant of
international law. He reckoned that they could thus, over time, become
accustomed to respecting the pre-eminence of law and lawful procedures in
international relations.[115]

But France's most influential League proponent insisted no less adamantly
than Clemenceau that the new German government first had to meet essential
preconditions. Above all, it had to accept the victors' peace "settlement"
without any substantial negotiations and execute it faithfully. Further, the
German people and their new leaders had to prove that they were "fit" for
membership in the new postwar "community" of civilised states he envisaged.
As Bourgeois reasoned, in a language that echoed Wilson's, the Germans not
only had to establish a stable republican order but actually undergo a "moral
revolution" in their values and civilisational standards that went far beyond
superficial reforms of the "political system".[116]

---

[114] Clemenceau statement to the Foreign Affairs Commission of the *Sénat*, 29 July 1919,
CAE, *Sénat*, vol. 1893. See also Clemenceau speech, 25 September 1919, *Journal Officiel
(Chambre)*, 1919. See Jackson (2013), pp. 310–12.

[115] Bourgeois speech to AFSDN Constitutive Assembly, 10 November 1918, MAE, SDN,
vol. 7.

[116] *Ibid.* See also Bourgeois commission report, 8 June 1918, AN, F12 8106.

13

A New Beginning?

German Pursuits of a Wilsonian "Peace of Justice" and First Steps towards an Atlanticist Foreign Policy

Those who had been thrust into the position of having to develop peace strategies on behalf of the vanquished power and, eventually, a fledgling German republic faced challenges and constraints that were both more pressing and more existential than those the protagonists of the victorious western powers confronted. In the international sphere, they had to act under conditions of powerlessness and drastic isolation in the wake of the rapid German collapse and the far-reaching armistice agreement. Domestically, they confronted acute revolutionary turmoil and, in a wider context, a transformational process at whose outset it was far from clear whether the November revolution would escalate into an uncontrollable civil war between those who aspired to a Bolshevisation of Germany and the forces of the "old order" – or whether a path towards the foundation of a parliamentary democracy could be charted.

It was under these adverse conditions, and the multiple constraints they imposed, that the new German protagonists – first, the Social Democratic leaders of the new provisional government, later the new Foreign Minister Ulrich von Brockdorff-Rantzau – had little choice but to embark on immense learning and reorientation processes. They not only had to work out a realistic approach to peacemaking from a position of immense weakness. They also had to find ways to initiate a fundamental reorientation of German foreign policy – in the shadow of an insufficiently acknowledged defeat and onerous traditions of Wilhelmine power politics that, as noted, had become radicalised during the war, especially under Ludendorff and Hindenburg. What the new protagonists conceived never quite evolved into a coherent German strategy for the envisaged peace negotiations. Nonetheless, it came to be marked by two core characteristics: a distinctly one-sided turn towards Wilson, his peace programme and, in a wider sense, the United States; and a rigid focus on the priority of preventing a debilitating *Entente* "peace of force" by insisting on a Wilsonian "peace of justice". In the German interpretation, such a peace not only was to guarantee the fundamental integrity of the German state but also to ensure the nascent German republic's inclusion in a new League-based world order and an "open" world-economic order that both were expected to be dominated by the United States.

Unquestionably, this fledgling peace strategy was in part informed by opportunistic considerations and short-term tactical imperatives under conditions of powerlessness. It lacked a convincing conception for the stabilisation of Europe. It provided no cogent answers to the core question of how Germany was to make peace with the *Entente* Powers and more broadly its western and eastern neighbours – and at least *initiate* a process of postwar accommodation and reconciliation.[1] And it was profoundly unrealistic, raising expectations of peace that no German government could hope to fulfil in the post–First World War constellation.[2]

And yet what deserves to be highlighted is something else, namely that now – under extremely adverse conditions – first, limited and yet remarkable attempts were made to place German international policies on new foundations, to reorientate not only their aims but also their methods and indeed to develop a distinctive republican foreign policy that clearly departed from the power-political maxims of the Wilhelmine era.[3] Crucially, German pursuits acquired a distinctive Atlanticist orientation. They can be interpreted as the first serious attempt to create conditions for the eventual integration of a republican Germany in a reconfigured Atlantic order in which, in the perception of the new German key actors, the United States would hence play a preponderant role. And they indeed provided starting points for such an integration process, which held the key to a durable peace after the Great War. Under the circumstances, it could only unfold as an extremely challenging *longer-term* process. But it could not be initiated by the defeated power; it had to be instigated by the western victors of the war.

This new German approach and the conceptions that informed it only gained clearer contours after the war. But both had emerged before the German collapse. First significant steps had been taken by the heterogeneous coalition of actors and forces that had advanced the *Reichstag*'s Peace Resolution and called for a negotiated "peace of understanding" in the summer of 1917. Following the armistice, this coalition could be maintained in a radically changed environment. Its key elements thus were still the *Reichstag* majority parties, which would eventually form the first Weimar coalition government: as the most significant force the Majority Social Democrats under Ebert (which for a time cooperated with Haase's more left-leaning Independent Socialists), Erzberger's Centre party, and the liberal-progressive German Democratic Party (DDP). This coalition rallied behind it an even more heterogeneous array of forces from left-wing liberals to social democrats and the major trade unions. Further, it included the representatives of German business circles and high finance – notably the banker Max Warburg and a liberal Hanseatic faction. In the German Foreign Office,

---

[1] See Krüger (1985), pp. 17–71; Niedhart (2012), pp. 46 ff.

[2] See Leonhard (2018), pp. 458–9.

[3] The ground-breaking work here is Krüger (1985), esp. pp. 17–37, 45–72. See also Niedhart (2012), pp. 46 ff.; Winkler (2018), pp. 87–8.

those who like Hintze saw the need for a renewal of German foreign policy had early on cooperated with the "Peace Resolution parties". And eventually the actor who would be charged with formulating an actual agenda for the peace negotiations, Brockdorff-Rantzau, built on their programmatic premises.

Those who led this new coalition not only shared a determination to lead postwar Germany onto an "orderly" path of inner reform and democratisation, which soon concretised in intense efforts to create the constitutional framework for a German republic. They were also united in the view that a reformed and essentially disarmed German power should commit itself to two overriding priorities. Most importantly, it had to underscore its commitment to the establishment of an authoritative and all-embracing international "organisation of law" and, connected with this, a regime of arbitration and binding rules for the peaceful settlement of international disputes. This commitment to a universal League clearly went beyond opportunistic calculations; it can be seen as the outgrowth of more serious efforts to draw lessons from the fiasco of the war and to break with hitherto predominant imperatives of Wilhelminian *Machtpolitik*, not least those of keeping a "free hand" and eschewing wider international obligations.

The second hallmark of the new German approach was the championing of an unrestricted world economic system that guaranteed freedom of commercial exchange and fostered the intertwining of world-economic interests. This marked a clear departure from earlier *Mitteleuropa* conceptions and more far-reaching agendas of German economic imperialism that had aimed to establish a "closed" German-dominated system in Europe. The new underlying assumption was that an "open" global economy would be of existential importance for the future development of the German state. It thus was deemed critical to counter French yet also British attempts to place far-reaching economic restrictions on postwar Germany.[4] What is worth emphasising, then, is that in both the new world-political and world-economic priorities they set, German policymakers were influenced by their interpretation of Wilson's progressive peace agenda and what they saw as an essential compatibility between their aims and underlying American interests. And while they too used universalist terms, they in fact put forward their own, limited version of an Atlantic rather than European or genuinely global conception of postwar order.

But a fundamental problem was and remained that these efforts to reform German international policies, which overall pointed in a forward-looking direction, were unavoidably affected and often indeed impeded by the pressing need to prepare for the expected peace negotiations – and to contain what all protagonists saw as the cardinal threat of a "crippling" settlement imposed by

---

[4] See Krüger (1985), pp. 20–23; Krüger (1973); Niedhart (2012) pp. 63 ff.

the *Entente* and, above all, French leaders. Especially once Brockdorff-Rantzau had taken charge, this gave rise to one particularly problematic tendency – the tendency to invoke the new commitment to the League and to progressive ideas of international order and world-economic interdependence all too often in a functionalist manner – namely to further the German demand for a "peace of justice" on the premises of the Fourteen Points. The new German government's unswerving insistence on such a peace effectively bound it to extremely far-reaching – and unrealistic – criteria for what kind of peace settlement it could accept. This not only prevented any meaningful attempt to moderate what became immensely high public expectations, which centred on the ever more illusory hope for a "Wilson peace" that would somehow allow Germany to escape from the consequences of its de facto decisive defeat. It also limited even further the already severely constrained room for manoeuvre that German decision-makers had to try to negotiate some kind of more sustainable compromise peace.

I. Canalising the German Revolution – and the Attempt to Create Conditions for a "Wilson Peace". The Majority Social Democrats and the German Transformation Process of 1918–19

The first efforts of the new provisional government in Berlin to prepare for peace negotiations, which it desired to begin as soon as possible, were overshadowed by a domestic-political transformation process that had begun with the outbreak of the revolution and reached a decisive point just after the opening of peace conference in mid-January 1919. It was a process whose outcome seemed open in its early stages – it indeed not only raised the spectre of a triumph of Bolshevism but also threatened to escalate into an uncontrollable clash between the forces of the radical left and the forces of the nationalist right. Yet it would ultimately bring about an essentially evolutionary rather than revolutionary change of the German political system and constitutional order, which culminated in the founding of the Republic of Weimar, whose constitution would finally come into force in August 1919.

A watershed was reached when in mid-December 1918 the path to elections for a "Constituent National Assembly" was cleared, which then were held on 19 January 1919. While they have often been criticised for their compromises with the old elites and inability to a effect a more unequivocal "new beginning" Ebert, Scheidemann and the Majority Social Democrats actually came to play a pivotal role in this process. By canalising the revolution of 1918 they not only prepared the ground for the first German parliamentary democracy. They also opened up *the possibility* of a negotiated peace between the western powers and a democratically legitimised German government.[5]

---

[5] See Miller (1978), pp. 107 ff. For a critical appraisal see Winkler (I/2000), pp. 382–94.

538 REORIENTATIONS AND INCIPIENT LEARNING PROCESSES

More fundamentally, what ensued and was decided in this critical phase was an uneven power struggle between three very different political groupings that had emerged since 1917: the "Peace Resolution" parties that now essentially sought to chart an "orderly" path towards a parliamentary democracy; the social protest and peace movement that had grown since the January strikes of 1918, organised itself in workers' and soldiers' councils and raised general demands for a socially more just postwar order; and the vanguard of a more radical socialist left that under the lead of Karl Liebknecht and Rosa Luxemburg agitated for a "free socialist republic of Germany" and aimed to join forces with the Bolsheviks in Russia to kindle a wider trans-European and indeed global revolution.[6] The overriding concern of Ebert and the Majority Social Democrats in this struggle was to prevent a further escalation of revolutionary developments. For they feared that such an escalation would not only lead to a complete collapse of the German state but indeed foment a civil war – by provoking violent resistance from the right which then would also be directed against those who struggled to establish a republic. What thus had to be forestalled, in their eyes, was ultimately the danger of a postwar dictatorship in Germany.

Particularly Ebert was motivated by such fundamental concerns, and he thus invoked the example of Russia's descent into chaos after the Bolshevik revolution and warned that the chaos that threatened after a take-over of the *Spartakists* would give the Allied Powers a pretext to intervene and occupy Germany.[7] What appeared on the horizon in November and December 1918 was indeed an ominous scenario, namely that Germany could become the epicentre of protracted political instability and violence in Europe. And while the forces of the nationalist right – broadly speaking, those that had formed the core of the *Siegfrieden* and Fatherland parties till the end of the war – were disorganised and politically paralysed at this stage it was indeed from this direction that in the longer run a more serious challenge to the consolidation of a German republic – and an Atlantic peace order – could arise than from the left.[8]

In order to contain the revolutionary dynamics and the wider dangers of a civil war, Ebert and those who supported him, notably Scheidemann, came to pursue four strategic priorities. They included Haase and the more left-leaning Independent Socialists (the USPD) in the Council of People's Commissars so as to gain the acceptance of the workers' and soldiers' councils for the provisional government. They pursued an accommodating course vis-à-vis the German military leadership to ensure the loyalty of the *Reichswehr* as a

---

[6] See Liebknecht declaration, 9 November 1918, *Vossische Zeitung*, 10 November 1918; Liebknecht statement, 9 November 1918, Liebknecht (1982), p. 389; Communist Party of Germany Programme, ca. 1 January 1919, Weber (1963), p. 38.

[7] See Herbert (2017), p. 178; Büttner (2008), pp. 43–53.

[8] See Troeltsch (1924), pp. 117–18; Krüger (1986), pp. 70–81.

"force of order", which manifested itself in Ebert's pact with Ludendorff's successor Groener on 10 November. They also pursued a compromise regarding Germany's economic reorganisation, supporting the agreement between German industrialists and trade unions that was finalised by Hugo Stinnes and Carl Legien on 15 November. They thus backed an arrangement that, on the one hand, established a "corporative" socio-economic structure in which the participation of trade unions was institutionalised and working conditions and wages were regulated through mutual agreements – yet that, on the other hand, confirmed that there would be no "socialisation" of major German industries and the basic capitalist principle of private ownership would be preserved. Finally, and crucially, the leading figures of the MSPD sought to ensure that the process of drafting a new republican constitution through an elected constituent assembly would begin as soon as possible. Both Ebert and Scheidemann regarded swift advances in this direction as critical for initiating peace negotiations with the western powers, on which they still counted, and imperative for bolstering their claims for a "peace of justice" on the premises of Wilson's programme.[9]

On 19 December, a clear majority of delegates at the decisive General Congress of Workers' and Soldiers' Councils supported their agenda.[10] And it finally became clear that Ebert's course had prevailed when elections for the national assembly were held one month later. Just one week before these elections, the MSPD leaders had confronted the hitherto gravest domestic crisis when Liebknecht and Luxemburg, who accused them of having betrayed the revolution as "henchmen of the bourgeoisie", followed the Bolshevik example and instigated a violent uprising. By then leading the newly founded Communist Party, the *Spartakusbund*, they saw themselves as vanguard forces in "the most enormous civil war in world history". Yet in fact they only represented a very small minority even on the left. That the *Spartakus* uprising would be suppressed by force – and that Liebknecht and Luxemburg would be assassinated by *Freikorps* soldiers shortly thereafter – marked a more than symbolical *caesura*, but it did not pre-empt processes that otherwise would have led to a Bolshevik "councils' republic" in Germany.[11]

In the elections of 19 January 1919, the MSPD confirmed its position as the strongest party, receiving almost 38 per cent of the votes (while the USPD only received roughly 8 per cent) – and the "Peace Resolution" parties gained a combined three-quarter majority and thus a very strong mandate for their constitutional-parliamentary programme. Speaking at the opening of the

[9] See Miller (1978), pp. 188–203; Herbert (2017), pp. 177–8; Ebert statement, transmitted by Bliss to Lansing, 11 November 1918, *FRUS* 1918, I/1, p. 493.
[10] Resolution of the Congress of Councils, 19 December 1918, Allgemeiner Kongreß (Berlin, 1918), Sp. 283. See Miller (1978), pp. 188–203.
[11] Communist Party of Germany Programme, ca. 1 January 1919, Weber (1963), p. 38.

Constituent National Assembly in Weimar on 6 February, Ebert stressed that the Majority Social Democrats had taken on the unenviable task of acting as "liquidators of the old regime". Indeed, they in many ways acted less as confident founders of a new German democracy and rather as stewards of an "orderly", non-violent transition from the old regime to a new constitutional order. With a view to the wider reordering processes of 1919, however, what mattered more is that they had set the course for the formation of the first democratically elected German government, which Scheidemann then came to lead from early February, and for the subsequent, immensely arduous struggle to consolidate a German republic. Potentially, they had thereby also created basic conditions for an eventual negotiating process with the western powers. But according to Ebert, who was elected as the first president of the new republic, Germany's new political leaders had done much more: they had effectively reinforced their claim for a Wilsonian "peace of justice".[12]

II. Social Democratic Claims for a Wilsonian "Peace of Justice" – and First Attempts to Devise an Atlantic Approach to Peace

Indeed, ever since they had committed to this aim during the German–American exchange of notes in October 1918, Ebert, Scheidemann and their political allies had set their sights on attaining a "Wilson peace". In their interpretation, such a peace was to create a novel international order framed by a League of Nations and based on new standards of self-determination and peaceful conflict-resolution – an order corresponding with their own programmatic platform that *from the outset* would include a reformed Germany. They held that Wilson's Fourteen Points agenda provided not only the best possible assurance for preserving Germany's territorial integrity but also the essential basis on which it could become a respected member of a recast comity of nations. And initially they were convinced that by having taken decisive steps towards the establishment of a democratic republic, the new government in Berlin had fulfilled cardinal preconditions to deserve both a peace consonant with Wilson's programmatic essentials and a place of equality in the postwar order.

Rather than try to develop an actual peace *policy*, the leading Majority Social Democrats thus soon came to concentrate almost exclusively on asserting these ambitious claims. And they sought to foster a new sense of national unity by rallying the German public behind them. After decades of having been castigated by their political opponents as "enemies of the *Reich*" because of their internationalist maxims, the Social Democratic protagonists indeed

---

[12] Ebert speech, 6 February 1919, *SB Nationalversammlung*, vol. 326, pp. 2–3. Winkler (I/2000), pp. 384–5.

felt a particular need to underscore in this way their national-patriotic allegiances in a time of acute national crisis and division.[13]

No one pursued this course more stubbornly than Ebert. Immediately after
the signing of the armistice, he set the tone that would dominate all subsequent MSPD proclamations and soon also publicised opinion in Germany. On
11 November, he had declared that the days of "monarchy" and "imperialism"
in Germany had come to an end and "the republic" would be "the future form
of government". And he had proclaimed that this republic was entitled to
insist on a peace on Wilson's terms and to "become an equal member of the
league of nations of all free countries". Ebert had voiced his determination to
unite all Germans behind such a settlement. At the same time, he had invoked
a strong bond of common interests and ideals that, as he saw it, now united the
American republic and Germany, which he called the world's second "largest
republic".[14] Fundamentally, Ebert maintained as fervently as Scheidemann,
Erzberger and leading liberals that the new German republic had a "right" to
belong to the core of the new League system of "free peoples". They refused to
accept, or even to imagine, that Germany could be relegated to a pariah status
outside this system.

But by the time the Constituent National Assembly opened in Weimar in
early February there had been no indications that Wilson regarded the moderate social democrats and their allies as essential partners in the making of his
"new world order" – or that their efforts would be "rewarded" by a "peace of
justice" as they defined it. In fact, Ebert and Scheidemann had become
markedly sceptical about Wilson's willingness to push for such a peace after
he had proved, in their perception, disappointingly unresponsive to their
earlier appeals. And while they never developed a more precise understanding
of the American president's evolving priorities – and constraints – they
assumed that he would find it very hard to prevail against the "plans of
revenge and violation" of the *Entente* Powers against which they publicly
protested. But Ebert insisted all the more adamantly on what he regarded as
legitimate German demands. On 6 February, he declared before the Weimar
assembly that after Germany had "laid down its arms" trusting in "the
principles of President Wilson" now the time had come to be granted "the
Wilson-peace to which we have a claim"; and he thereby gave expression to
prevalent attitudes not only within Scheidemann's new coalition government
but also in the German public.[15]

---

[13] See Miller (1978), pp. 274–87; Leonhard (2018), pp. 438–43.

[14] Ebert statement, transmitted by Bliss to Lansing, 11 November 1918, *FRUS* 1918, I/1,
p. 493.

[15] Ebert speech, 6 February 1919, *SB Nationalversammlung*, vol. 326, pp. 2–3. For a critical
assessment of hopes for a "Wilson peace" and Germany's isolation see the editorial in the
Social Democrats' influential newspaper *Vorwärts*, no. 8, 5 January 1919.

That the social democratic guardians of Germany's democratic new begin-ning focused so uncompromisingly on these demands had very problematic consequences. Essentially, it not only raised but also tied the new government to expectations of a moderate "peace of justice" that were illusory. Official proclamations even refrained from acknowledging that a settlement based on the Fourteen Points would have entailed considerable sacrifices and, notably, the cessation of territory to the new Polish state. And in a wider context the leading Social Democrats failed to prepare the ground for a more realistic inner-German debate about what kind of peace was possible and what kind of place Germany could expect to have in the postwar order. This contributed significantly to setting the stage for subsequent disappointments, resentment and eventual efforts to deflect responsibility by accusing Wilson of having "betrayed" Germany by reneging on the promises he had allegedly made.[16] Against the background of the nationalist-ideological fervour the war had fomented in Germany and the shock the collapse had caused, it would undoubtedly have been extremely difficult to dampen expectations and initiate a more sober public discussion. But this was not even attempted.

Indeed, the preoccupation with clamouring for a "peace of justice" and shoring up what remained a very superficial national unity in many ways took the place of serious efforts to confront the harder questions the war had raised – to take a harder look at the responsibility of those who had led the German Empire not only for the outbreak of the war but also for its escalation and the eventual disaster it had produced; and to debate what political conse-quences were to be drawn from this disaster – not only by those who now sought to build a republic but also by the majority of the German people who had backed the *Siegfriede* agenda until the final stages of the conflict. Such a process of reckoning and genuine discussion would have been essential for creating a broader basis for a new German "policy of understanding and reconciliation" with the states and peoples that had been enemies during the war. But no process of this kind could be initiated in this critical phase.

What further limited a German new beginning was the fact that while the leaders of the new government were making first efforts to deal with the fall-out from Germany's de facto defeat they long deemed it politically impossible to acknowledge it openly – and thereby to counter what, influenced by Ludendorff's and Hindenburg's propagandistic efforts, came to prevail in German published and public opinion: the more or less pronounced refusal to face up to the fact that Germany actually was a vanquished power. When welcoming returning German troops in Berlin on 10 December 1918, Ebert famously proclaimed that "(n)o enemy has defeated you" and thereby aggra-vated the more general problem – even though he then added a more nuanced

---

[16] See Krüger (1985), pp. 47–9; Schwabe (1985), pp. 4, 124–6.

assessment, which indirectly alluded to the impact of America's intervention, stating that one only had "given up the fight" when "the superiority of the opponents in terms of men and materiel" had become "ever more onerous".[17] By early February, when the Constituent National Assembly had begun its deliberations, Ebert had decided that the time had come to declare unequivocally that Germany had "lost the war" – and to stress that this "fact" was not "a consequence of the revolution". But subsequent efforts to come to terms with the defeat remained half-hearted. And ultimately this would only benefit the forces who sought to weaken and delegitimise those who struggled on behalf of a German republic and a policy of reconciliation – by allowing the myth to fester that the latter had "stabbed" Germany's valiant soldiers "in the back".[18]

In retrospect, it is important to underscore just how preoccupied the leaders of the Majority Social Democrats were with towering domestic-political challenges. Having hitherto spent their political lives in opposition, they now had to learn, under highly unfavourable circumstances, how to exercise practical governmental responsibility and shoulder the burdens of power *and* powerlessness. It is thus hardly surprising that their efforts to provide unifying leadership exhibited limitations and no clear and more realistically defined social democratic peace policy emerged that went beyond the appeals for a "Wilson peace". Politicians like Rudolf Breitscheid and the later chancellor Hermann Müller, who sought to give impulses in this direction and, in particular, to formulate a social democratic blueprint for a League of Nations, were the exception and relatively far from the party's leadership. For their part, Ebert and Scheidemann essentially left more specific matters of foreign policy and, crucially, the elaboration of a programme for the expected peace negotiations to the professional diplomats of the German Foreign Office.

So it was here, in the Foreign Office, that after the armistice more concrete preparations for the envisaged peace negotiations began. Under Solf, who continued as secretary of state for foreign affairs, a special unit, entitled "*Paxkonferenz*", was created to this end, headed by the former German ambassador in Washington, Johann Heinrich Count Bernstorff. It became an important discussion forum for experts, notably international lawyers and economists, who were supposed to act as advisers to the German delegation for the peace conference that was now assembled. In a note to Lansing on

---

[17] Ebert remarks, 10 December 1918, Ritter and Miller (1983), p. 139.

[18] Ebert speech, 6 February 1919, *SB Nationalversammlung*, vol. 326, p. 2. The limited acknowledgement of the defeat can be linked to a wider problem that was particularly acute in Germany: the immense difficulty of coming to terms with the massive consequences of a two-front war that caused the highest casualty toll of all the belligerents. As noted, it reached roughly 2.4 million dead and 3 million wounded by the end of 1918, plus an estimated 700,000 civilians who died due to food shortages and diseases resulting from the British blockade. See Hagen (2012), p. 231; Heinemann (1983).

11 November, Solf had early on confirmed the underlying American orientation of Germany's fledgling peace policy. His appeal already featured key elements of the Scheidemann government's subsequent strategy: the commitment to Wilson's peace programme and the attempt to commit the American president to his own "principles"; the invocation of the "commonality of democratic goals and ideals"; and, above all, the attempt to gain Wilson's support as a patron who was supposed to play an instrumental role, first in mitigating the "disastrous" armistice conditions, then in preventing a draconian peace settlement on the terms of the *Entente* and forging instead a "lasting" – and lenient – "peace of justice".[19] Solf also explicitly asked the American president to pave the way for a swift initiation of peace negotiations and proposed the conclusion of a "classic preliminary peace". He thus sought to commit Wilson to the more traditional European diplomatic instrument of a preliminary agreement in which the more general parameters of peace were to be set, and which would then provide the framework for the actual peace conference at which the western powers and Germany would negotiate the specific terms of the settlement.[20]

Yet it was Bernstorff who emerged as the most forceful advocate of a pronounced German orientation towards Wilson and the United States. Having gained first-hand insights into US politics during his time as ambassador in Washington, where he had worked since 1908, Bernstorff had sought to promote Wilson's notion of a peace without victory in 1916 – and engaged in a futile attempt to prevent America's entry into the war. Following his return to Berlin in 1917, he had become a proponent of a peace of understanding as confidant of Max von Baden. From late November 1918, Bernstorff sought to place German preparations on a less ideological footing, proposing a genuine departure based on a sober assessment of German and American interests and the transformative changes the war had brought about. He stressed that the "position" of the unexhausted American power, which had determined the war's outcome, was certain to be "decisive" for the future of Germany and Europe. He was convinced that it would emerge as the hegemon of the postwar world, not least because the "whole world" – yet especially the indebted European victors and Germany – would become financially and economically "dependent" on it.

Bernstorff thus highlighted the vital connections between financial and political power and the unprecedented degree of European dependence on America that, as he saw it, would shape peacemaking and international politics after the war. The consequence he drew from this was that Germany had to try to align with the United States in the envisaged negotiations and to engage

---

[19] Solf to Lansing, 11 November 1918, *ADAP*, A/I, p. 5.
[20] *Ibid.*; Solf note to Lansing, 11 November 1918, Schwabe (1997), pp. 68–9.

Wilson – in his view the only statesman who had advanced a "genuine pacifist programme" – as a guardian of essential German interests against the "open or died-in-the-wool imperialists" who led the *Entente* Powers.[21]

Bernstorff thus recommended that the new German government had to pursue an "indeed pacifist policy" for the foreseeable future and that German representatives should support Wilson on all core issues that were close to his heart, from the League to disarmament – and even "outdo" him – because that was the only way to "compensate the current weakness of Germany" and to "contain the imperialism of [its] other opponents".[22] The "means-to-an-end" approach he proposed – a "pacifist" orientation and unconditional support for Wilson's programme as the means to secure an acceptable peace and further Germany's "reconstruction" and re-ascension as a great power – anticipated important aspects of Brockdorff-Rantzau's pursuits in 1919. As formative was Bernstorff's tendency to assign to Wilson the reduced functionalist role of a pacifist progressive who could be relied upon to act in the German interest. This tendency would make it harder to develop more nuanced German policies that grasped Wilson's *changing* priorities after the armistice and recognised that a progressive German-American alignment at the peace conference was highly unlikely.

Bernstorff's recommendations found a strong supporter in Max Warburg, the Hamburg-based banker and brother of Paul Warburg. He would become the most influential proponent of a more "pragmatic" German approach to peace-making that sought to open up avenues of "intimate collaboration" with the United States on the basis of a sober assessment of underlying economic-cum-political interests.[23] But Warburg also spoke for a newly influential group of more outward-looking bankers, traders and industrialists who represented a Hanseatic or "Hamburgian" Germany – and who advocated both a more economic orientation of German foreign policy and a turn towards Wilson's America. They had cooperated and competed notably with their British and American counterparts in the globalising world of the pre-war era; and they had been part of extensive networks of internationally orientated financiers, businessmen and politicians that had expanded especially across the Atlantic. Having supported the *Reichstag*'s "Peace Resolution" of 1917, they had long favoured a negotiated peace. After the armistice their main fear was that the *Entente* governments would insist on a settlement that cut Germany off from the world economy, or at the very least imposed substantial economic and financial constraints.

The core interest of this group was to ensure that the new German republic would be included in a refashioned, essentially liberal economic system in

---

[21] Bernstorff note, 24 November 1918, *ADAP*, 1918–1919, p. 55.

[22] *Ibid.*

[23] Warburg to Bernstorff, 30 December 1918, *ADAP*, 1918–1919, p. 155. Warburg (1952), pp. 53–60.

which they could trade and operate without restrictions. They reckoned that within a system of this kind the "intertwining" of economic interests that had already redounded to Germany's advantage during the "globalisation" of the pre-war era could be revived and even expanded – particularly in the relations with America and Britain yet also, in the longer run, with France and Germany's other neighbours. And the cooperative policies they proposed hinged on the assumption that the newly pre-eminent American power had an overriding interest in creating precisely such a system, an expanded "Open Door" system for the postwar era.[24]

In the autumn of 1918, Warburg had advocated these views and interests most energetically, and from mid-November he played a central role in German preparations for the financial and economic-cum-political aspects of the peace negotiations. He assembled a circle of financial experts whose task would be to aid the German peace delegation. Yet he would mainly collaborate with Carl Melchior, a "German Wilsonian" and long-time associate in the Warburg banking house who would be instrumental in formulating a more realistic, if ultimately futile, German reparations policy in 1919.[25] Warburg's main concern was to make sure that Germany would "rise again" – as an economic great power with a republican constitution – in what he expected to be a fundamentally recast postwar order. And he had understood earlier than most others that while the war had left all the European belligerents profoundly exhausted, it had turned the United States into the strongest power not only politically but also in economic and financial terms. After the armistice Warburg agreed that it was vital to insist on a peace "on the basis of the 14 Points and the later speeches of Wilson" and to impress on the American president that he now had to act in the spirit of his proclamations if he did not want to lose "his credit before Germany and the world". But what he really emphasised was that the new government in Berlin should concentrate on developing a less ideological approach and chiefly seek to foster "for purely pragmatic reasons" a close cooperation with the United States.[26]

Essentially, Warburg, Melchior and other proponents of a more pragmatic reorientation towards the United States and a new economic orientation of Germany's postwar policies held that one could, and should, bank on fundamental compatibilities between cardinal American and German interests that, in their view, could be leveraged to attain an acceptable peace settlement. They were convinced that Wilson would ultimately be driven by the concern to prevent peace terms that would cause a longer-term enfeeblement or even collapse of a country that had been the most important European trading partner and export market for the United States before the war. And in their

[24] See Krüger (1985), pp, 23–32.
[25] See Haupts (1976), pp. 55 ff.; Schwabe (1985), p. 147.
[26] Warburg to Bernstorff, 30 December 1918, *ADAP*, 1918–1919, p. 155.

assessment the American desire to ensure a swift revitalisation of Germany would be all the more pronounced because American policymakers, including the president, would realise how vital this revitalisation was for furthering a wider US interest, a rapid economic and political stabilisation of postwar Europe, which would allow the new economic hegemon to resume and expand its export of capital and goods. Finally, as noted, they assumed that German and American interests were also congruent when it came to the even more fundamental question on what premises the postwar economic order was to be based. They therefore urged the new German government to back unconditionally Wilson's call for a removal of all "economic barriers" and the creation of a non-discriminatory system of world trade.[27]

It was with these broader concerns in mind that Warburg, on 30 December 1918, recommended fostering cooperative relations with the United States as the "natural" course German policymakers ought to pursue. Yet he also stressed his hope that the new German constitution would be "very similar to the American", because this would provide a basis for "greater mutual understanding".[28] In retrospect, it seems worth emphasising that Warburg and those who thought like him had quite accurately discerned some of the main *longer-term* financial and economic interests that would eventually inform American policies vis-à-vis Europe after the Great War. But what seems more remarkable is the extent to which they – wrongly – assumed that such interests would actually influence Wilson's pursuits at the peace conference – and shape the peace settlement itself. In fact, all German attempts to attain a "moderate peace" on economic grounds would be frustrated in 1919.

III.   Brockdorff-Rantzau's Progressive Atlanticist Peace Strategy – and Its Limits

What Bernstorff outlined and what Warburg proposed can be regarded as first and in many ways limited attempts to define a German approach to peacemaking that took into account both Germany's drastically altered position and the newly crucial power of the United States. Essentially, however, nothing even approaching a more coherent and comprehensive peace strategy had emerged by the end of 1918. The new key actor who faced the core challenge of developing such a strategy was a relative outsider, the career diplomat Ulrich von Brockdorff-Rantzau. After his appointment in late December, the new foreign minister, who would later become the first Weimar government's chief plenipotentiary in Paris, not only asserted himself as an ardent proponent of a new, "progressive" German foreign policy. He also emerged as the

---

[27] See Krüger (1985), pp. 31–2.

[28] Warburg to Bernstorff, 30 December 1918, *ADAP*, 1918–1919, p. 155.

main "architect" of the policy the Scheidemann government would actually pursue to attain a "peace of justice" in the spring of 1919.[29]

Essentially, Brockdorff-Rantzau came to develop a more exclusive, rigid and assertive "Atlanticist strategy" than any of his immediate predecessors had envisaged. Its core rationale was to align the fledgling German republic as closely as possible with what he took to be Wilson's core progressive aspirations – and to bank not only on common economic interests but also on a core of compatible political and ideological concerns. Brockdorff-Rantzau asserted the German claim for a "peace of justice" more stridently and methodically. But the underlying aim of his pursuits was to gain the American president's support for a *negotiated* peace that would allow Germany to re-emerge as a democratic great power within a reconfigured Atlantic order – a great power that was on a par with the leading western world powers.

Brockdorff-Rantzau had acquired a certain, though not very profound understanding of the power-political and ideological shifts the war had caused. And he had some but by no means strong credentials to become the architect of a new "republican" foreign policy. During the war, he had been the German minister in Copenhagen and essentially ensured Danish neutrality. Espousing liberal-democratic principles partly out of conviction, partly because he deemed this imperative to salvage Germany's great-power status, he had from 1917 supported liberal reforms, especially changes to Prussia's election laws, that were to ensure "a greater participation of the people in determining its future". He had also emerged as advocate of a negotiated peace in tune with the aspirations of the "Peace Resolution parties".[30] And it was on these grounds that he had gained the confidence of leading social democrats, particularly Ebert and Scheidemann.

When he was appointed as the new foreign minister on 24 December 1918, Brockdorff-Rantzau immediately declared that his foremost task would be to bring about a "peace of justice"; and he underscored that, in his interpretation, the foundations for such a peace had already been laid through the Fourteen Points and subsequent speeches of the American president, which Foreign Office experts internally referred to as his "Twenty-Seven Points".[31] He shared the conviction that the "limits" this programme set would provide an essential framework for protecting the most existential interests of the new German republic – above all its integrity as a state and "economic body" – against the

---

[29] For different previous interpretations see Wengst (1973); Krüger (1985), pp. 69–75; Schwabe (1998), pp. 42–52.

[30] Brockdorff-Rantzau memorandum, 1 April 1917; Brockdorff-Rantzau memorandum, 18 July 1917, Brockdorff-Rantzau Papers, 6/1; Wengst (1973), pp. 10–13.

[31] Brockdorff-Rantzau declaration, 24 December 1918, Brockdorff-Rantzau (1925), p. 36; Foreign Office memorandum, December 1918, Versailles II, 9105 H/H235565, Brockdorff-Rantzau Papers.

Entente Powers' far-reaching designs for a "peace of force". The official guidelines for Germany's peace delegation of 17 January 1919 clearly confirmed this priority.[32]

Mainly but not only to underscore his support for Wilson's programme, Brockdorff-Rantzau soon presented himself as a fervent advocate of a universal League and the wider aspiration to establish, through such an oganisation, a progressive international order. He emphasised that this order had to be premised on newly prevalent principles of arbitration, the peaceful settlement of inter-state disputes, self-determination, general disarmament and the fundamental rejection of balance-of-power politics – as well as the freedom of economic exchange.[33] To some extent, the new foreign minister indeed sought to reorientate German policy in a "modern", Wilsonian direction. Ultimately, however, his championing of progressive principles was mainly intended to serve the ambitious – and profoundly unrealistic – objective towards which his entire peace strategy came to be geared – namely to prepare the ground for a settlement that permitted Germany's re-emergence as a reformed world power with essentially "equal" rights. Like Bernstorff and Warburg, Brockdorff-Rantzau expected the postwar order to evolve into an essentially Atlantic system that would be supervised by the League and in which the United States would be preponderant. And in his conception Germany was to play a constructive part in this new order – as a progressive republican power that committed itself to the rules and norms of the League, pursued essentially pacific policies vis-à-vis its neighbours and firmly renounced any "war-like" militarist pursuits while limiting its armed forces to the minimum required to maintain domestic order and protect its external borders.[34] Yet the precondition for all of this was, as he saw it, a "peace of justice" that guaranteed Germany's renewed great-power status.

Tactically, Brockdorff-Rantzau's core rationale remained that only the alignment with Wilson and his programmatic essentials could thwart British and above all French plans to impose a "peace of force". His interpretation of the agendas and aims of the *Entente* Powers was distinctly influenced by the political and ideological battles of the war and based on relatively little tangible intelligence about what their leaders and strategists actually envisaged. In his calculation, both the French and the British governments would seek to

[32] Rantzau declaration, 2 January 1919, Brockdorff-Rantzau (1925), p. 37; official German guidelines, published on 17 January 1919, Vorbereitung der Friedensverhandlungen, 9105 H/H234836–38, Brockdorff-Rantzau Papers.
[33] Brockdorff-Rantzau speech, 15 January 1919; Brockdorff-Rantzau speech, 14 February 1919, Brockdorff-Rantzau (1925), pp. 38–9, 57–9.
[34] See Brockdorff-Rantzau note, 14 January 1919; *ADAP*, 1918–1919, pp. 184–6; Brockdorff-Rantzau speech, 14 February 1919, Brockdorff-Rantzau (1925), pp. 57–9. See Schwabe (1998), p. 44.

weaken Germany economically or even to render it "economically powerless" by implementing the programme of the London economic conference of 1916 and forcing "paralysing" or even "annihilating" restrictions on the German competitor. An even graver threat was posed by what he took to be French designs, if not to break up the entire German state then at least to sever from it the most "essential and vital" regions. His main fear was that the Clemenceau government, animated by the underlying aim to weaken Germany, would persevere with the encouragement of "centrifugal forces" and push for an "autonomous Rhenish republic" that would then fall under French domination.[35]

By contrast, the foreign minister assumed that not only compatible definitions of vital interests but also ideological affinities could further a strategic partnership between Wilson and the new German government. He too was convinced that Wilson and his main advisers would not wish to see Germany rendered "politically and economically powerless in perpetuity". And he expected that the American president would be guided by the interest to implement his progressive peace design and to forge a settlement that ensured the inclusion of a newly democratic Germany not only in the League but also in a postwar economic order on "Open Door" premises.[36]

On the one hand, Brockdorff-Rantzau's pursuits were thus marked by a fundamental distrust of the aims and agendas of both *Entente* governments. He made no serious effort to understand the postwar challenges from their perspectives – and especially to comprehend the depth of French security concerns, the wider interests of the Lloyd George government and the profound exhaustion of both powers. On the other, rather than seeking to understand Wilson's *changing* priorities after the armistice, which were in fact ever less compatible with German ideas of a negotiated "peace of justice", the new foreign minister largely acted on general and for the most part erroneous assumptions about the American president's key aspirations, which were distinctly influenced by wishful thinking.[37] At the same time, although he concluded that Wilson's power vis-à-vis Britain and France was weaker than during the war, because they no longer needed US support to the same extent either "militarily or "financially", he still overestimated the influence the

[35] German guidelines, 17 January 1919, Foreign Office memorandum, ca. 23 January 1919, Vorbereitung der Friedensverhandlungen, 9105 H/H234792, Brockdorff-Rantzau Papers; Brockdorff-Rantzau speech, 14 February 1919, Brockdorff-Rantzau (1925), p. 47.
[36] Brockdorff-Rantzau draft, 21 January 1919, Brockdorff-Rantzau memorandum, 21 January 1919, *ADAP*, 1918–1919, pp. 204–7.
[37] *Ibid.* Like other German policymakers, Brockdorff-Rantzau partly based his assessment of Wilson's policies on the Cobb-Lippmann memorandum on the Fourteen Points of 29 October 1918, which German diplomats had obtained and interpreted not only as favourable to German interests but also, wrongly, as actually reflecting the American president's priorities.

American president could actually have on the peacemaking process. And although he was aware that Wilson's position had been weakened by the outcome of the Congressional elections in November, he still underestimated the cardinal domestic constraints the American president would face, which limited the prospects for a German version of a "Wilsonian peace" still further.[38]

But what actually was Brockdorff-Rantzau's conception of a "peace of justice"? He came to define a *distinctly ambitious* set of essentials. Unquestionably the pre-eminent concern of the confidential peace agenda he formulated was the preservation of the German state's territorial integrity – on the basis of an "equitable" application of the principle of self-determination.[39] This principle notably was to be invoked to ward off all French attempts to gain control over the Rhineland or the Saar basin – while a plebiscite was to decide the future status of Alsace-Lorraine. In the east, Germany would only be prepared to cede those provinces of the former German Empire to the new Polish state that could be classified as "indubitably Polish" – which also was to be determined through plebiscites; and Polish access to the Baltic Sea, in accordance with the thirteenth of the Fourteen Points, was to be assured, not by the cessation of territory – West Prussia and the city of Danzig – but rather through international conventions overseen by the League.[40]

Publicly, Brockdorff-Rantzau also argued that on grounds of self-determination the desire of the German-speaking Austrians to form a union with Germany should be respected. But he actually was wary that French decision-makers would invoke the threat posed by these "Greater German" aspirations to push further with their plans to create a Rhenish buffer-state.[41] Finally, he demanded the return of Germany's colonies – while proposing that they would hence be administered under the supervision of the League. Yet the foreign minister also stipulated economic criteria for a "just peace" – namely that Germany's economic freedom and unrestricted participation in the world economy on the basis of the "most- favoured-nation" principle had to be assured. No less important, however, was something else – namely a peace settlement that guaranteed the German republic's immediate entry into the League, not just as a founding member but indeed as a power on the new organisation's executive council – and that thus recognised it as one of the leading powers.[42]

---

[38] Brockdorff-Rantzau memorandum, 21 January 1919, *ADAP*, 1918–1919, pp. 204-7.
[39] Rantzau declaration, 2 January 1919, Brockdorff-Rantzau (1925), p. 37.
[40] See German "Richtlinien", 27 January 1919, Miller, Matthias and Potthoff (1969), II, pp. 319–20.
[41] See Schwabe (1985), p. 187.
[42] Brockdorff-Rantzau speech, 14 February 1919, Brockdorff-Rantzau (1925), pp. 47, 58–9.

A further essential of Brockdorff-Rantzau's "just peace" conception was that the *Entente* Powers' reparations claims vis-à-vis Germany had to be strictly limited to the compensation for "war damages" in the "occupied territories" of Belgium and northern France, which the German government had recognised under the armistice agreement.[43] Indeed, also with a view to reparations the Lansing note, and in a wider sense the Fourteen Points, still remained – in the assessment of Brockdorff-Rantzau and other key policymakers – the essential protection against expanded French and British reparation demands. And this was also the main reason why under Solf's direction the Foreign Office had already in late November decided to make an official declaration on the politically immensely charged war-guilt issue in which it strongly rejected the *Entente* claim of Germany's sole responsibility for the outbreak of the war.

The reasoning behind this declaration was that if it did not formally challenge this claim, the new German government could be deprived of the Lansing note's protective limits – and the *Entente* leaders could then significantly extend the scope of their demands on the basis of Germany's alleged exclusive war guilt. Further, the Foreign Office had proposed that a neutral commission of experts should be created to assess the wider question of how the war had escalated and what kind of responsibility could be assigned.[44] Chiefly for such legalistic reasons, yet also out of the wider concern to defend Germany's reputation as a civilised power, it had thus proactively placed the war-guilt question on the peacemaking agenda. Subsequently, the leading social democrats Ebert and Scheidemann would also pointedly defend Germany against war-guilt allegations. And from January 1919, Brockdorff-Rantzau would make the public contestation of Germany's responsibility for the war a central part of his campaign for a "peace of justice". On 24 January, resorting to arguments that Wilson and other progressives had used earlier, he asserted that the "old system" of alliances of "that questionable European balance [of power]" was more to blame for the escalation of the war than "any single person" or nation.[45]

Yet the German "war guilt offensive" was bound to be counterproductive at this critical juncture. Early on, the western victors simply declared that a war-guilt commission of the kind the German government demanded was not necessary "as the responsibility of Germany for the war has been long ago incontestably proved", and they had refused any further discussion. In the eyes of Clemenceau, Lloyd George *and* Wilson, the new government's refusal to acknowledge this responsibility was proof that it had not distanced itself from the old regime – which by implication it exonerated through its protestations. This indeed weakened its claim for a "peace of justice" insofar as that claim

---

[43] Brockdorff-Rantzau memorandum, 21 January 1919, *ADAP*, 1918–1919, pp. 204–5.
[44] *Quellen*, I, vol. 2, pp. 207–8, 273; Schwabe (1998), pp. 47–9.
[45] Brockdorff-Rantzu speech, 24 January 1919, Brockdorff-Rantzau (1925), p. 41.

was based on the argument that it represented the forces of a democratic new beginning. More importantly, however, it set the stage for a political-cum-ideological battle during the peacemaking process that, if Brockdorff-Rantzau and the other German protagonists persisted with their approach, could only escalate further and in which there was very little to gain and much to lose from their perspective.

These, then, were the essential elements and the most problematic facets of what Brockdorff-Rantzau defined as a "peace of justice", which in fact would largely be supported not only by the leading peace planners in the Foreign Office but also by the Scheidemann government. But he still had to answer one cardinal question – the strategic question of *how* the new German government could seek to attain such a peace. The "new" methods Brockdorff-Rantzau proposed were intended to initiate a marked change in the ways and means of German foreign policy. His conceptions built on the precedent of the armistice "negotiations" and were influenced by Wilson's "new diplomacy" yet also by the example of the Bolsheviks. He came to advocate, first, the pursuit of an assertive campaign to influence "world opinion" and especially public opinion in the "enemy countries" with the aim of mobilising it in support of German claims for a *Rechtsfrieden*. And, second, he sought to present the German republic – to the world, yet above all to the American president – both as a committed supporter of "Wilsonian" conceptions and as a potential key ally in the establishment of a progressive "new world order".

From early January 1919, Brockdorff-Rantzau would pursue this "strategy" chiefly through a long series of public speeches, while experts in the Foreign Office began to prepare an ever more elaborate campaign in line with his instructions. One core rationale that informed these efforts was that by turning Germany's current weakness into a virtue and appealing to the "conscience of the peoples", one could use the newly crucial leverage of public opinion to put pressure on the political leaders of the democratic western powers. Particular hopes were pinned on the mobilisation of liberal and left opinion in Britain and the United States. The other core rationale was to highlight in every possible way how committed Germany's new democratic government was to the "spirit of the Wilsonian points" – and that it was led by "genuine idealism" and the will to "co-operate in the establishment of a moral order among the peoples".[46] The foreign minister would affirm this time and again.[47]

Brockdorff-Rantzau's version of a "Wilsonian" approach was problematic not only because he came to pursue it in a more aggressive manner than his predecessors but also because it was based on profoundly unrealistic

[46] See Foreign Office memorandum, undated [mid-January 1919], *ADAP*, 1918–1919, p. 185.
[47] Brockdorff-Rantzau statement, 15 January, Brockdorff-Rantzau (1925), p. 38; Brockdorff-Rantzau note, undated [late January 1919], Brockdorff-Rantzau Papers, 7/7.

expectations – both about the extent to which Wilson and the *Entente* leaders could be influenced by public opinion in ways he desired and about the extent to which German efforts could actually win over western public opinion in the first place (not least in view of the impact anti-German propaganda had had during the war). Further, as noted, the foreign minister's efforts were based on a misinterpretation of Wilson's attitude towards the new German government at a time when the latter had already signalled that he by no means regarded it as a "progressive partner" and publicly proclaimed his new rationale of putting Germany "on probation". And they were marred by a marked overestimation of the influence that public campaigns of this kind could have on a peacemaking process that, as Brockdorff-Rantzau recognised, would most likely be dominated by complicated negotiations between Wilson and the leaders of Britain and France.

At the same time, Brockdorff-Rantzau's exaggerated emphasis on the new German government's legitimate claim to a Wilsonian "peace of justice" – and his insistence that, in fact, it could only accept such a peace – exacerbated another, even more fundamental problem. It bound him and eventually Scheidemann's government to a highly ambitious *and elusive* set of demands – and it further reinforced expectations in Germany that would be impossible to meet. This decisively constrained the political scope he had to negotiate possible compromise agreements with the victorious powers. Because they saw this danger, some German protagonists, notably Erzberger, would internally criticise Brockdorff-Rantzau's approach as too rigid and recommend that the inner-governmental deliberations should focus more on identifying areas and seeking ways in which practical compromises could be forged.[48] But Ebert and Scheidemann – and then a clear majority within the first Weimar coalition – backed the foreign minister's "strategy" at this point. As noted, they did so also for cardinal domestic-political reasons, namely to rally a majority of the German public behind a common set of demands and thus to strengthen the domestic standing of the new republican government.[49] Yet they thereby also tied the government's future legitimacy to the fulfilment of a fundamentally unrealistic "vision" of peace – and this was to have very onerous long-term consequences for the stabilisation of the Weimar Republic.

The conditions for developing a more realistic peace strategy became even less auspicious, and the German government's room for manoeuvre even more limited, when in mid-January 1919 the peace conference was opened without any German delegates and it dawned on Brockdorff-Rantzau and his advisers that, in the end, Germany could actually face a "dictated peace". To find a way to ensure that there would be actual *oral* negotiations between the victors and

---

[48] Erzberger to Brockdorff-Rantzau, 1 April 1919, Versailles I, 9105 H/ H234779, Brockdorff-Rantzau Papers. See Dürr (2021).
[49] See Leonhard (2018), p. 459.

German plenipotentiaries in the decisive stages of the peacemaking process would remain one of Brockdorff-Rantzau's key aims. But on 14 January, he warned the Council of People's Commissars that they had to be prepared for a very different scenario, namely that "there won"t be any negotiations in the proper sense of the word at all" and that Germany's "opponents" would instead present Berlin with their "project" and then simply demand its acceptance. At this point, Brockdorff-Rantzau could offer little to pre-empt this danger, except for the recommendation to persist with his "Wilsonian" strategy and seek to persuade Germany's "opponents" of the "justice" of its claims and the need for a negotiated "peace of justice". He noted that any attempts to "play" the western powers "off against each other" should only be considered once this strategy had clearly failed. And he underscored his general resolve not to fall back on "the means of previous diplomacy" and seek to sow "discord among the allies" as the "bond" that tied them together was too strong and it was crucial for the new German government to gain trust and credibility as advocate of a new kind of international politics.[50]

Very soon, however, the German foreign minister would actually conclude that German appeals for a "peace of justice" would not suffice to open the door to an actual negotiating process and to prevent, in the final consequence, a crippling peace settlement. He would thus attempt to devise a more comprehensive, if ultimately inchoate strategy whose core aim was to persuade Wilson – and the *Entente* governments – that a negotiated peace that met "rightful" German demands was also in fact in their own well-understood interest. Put differently, he sought to fuse rationales for a "peace of justice" with those for a peace based on overriding common interests that, in his assessment, all sides shared – or should share – and that transcended the antagonisms of the war.[51]

Most persistently Brockdorff-Rantzau would emphasise the common concern to "keep Bolshevism away from western Europe". Time and again, he would declare that the western powers should realise that their real interest lay in stabilising Germany, and a viable German republic, as a bulwark against the spread of the Bolshevik revolution. The Foreign Office even recommended that the German government should seek to gain an understanding with the victors not only about the outlines of a "proper and just peace" that guaranteed Germany's survival but also about an agenda focused on the "(c)ommon fight against Bolshevism".[52] As we have seen, the foreign

---

[50] Brockdorff-Rantzau notes, 14 January 1919; Brockdorff-Rantzau notes, undated, *ADAP*, 1918–1919, pp. 184–6.

[51] Memorandum, 21 January 1919, Vorbereitung der Friedensverhandlungen, 9105 H/ H234798–802, Brockdorff-Rantzau Papers.

[52] Brockdorff-Rantzau memorandum, 21 January 1919, Vorbereitung der Friedensverhandlungen, 9105 H/H234798–802, Brockdorff-Rantzau Papers. The third priority was to effect a "common economic reconstruction of Russia".

minister and his advisers were not mistaken in concluding that the Bolshevik problem became a vital concern for the western powers. But they vastly overestimated the leverage he could gain from this. And Brockdorff-Rantzau's excessive use of the "Bolshevik card" was too obviously informed by tactical considerations and in fact proved strategically counter-productive. Crucially, it also weakened an evolving, more forward-looking "common interest" agenda he developed.

This agenda was influenced by Bernstorff and earlier recommendations by Warburg and other economic experts who aided the peace preparations, but Brockdorff-Rantzau came to place his own political and ideological stamp on it, seeking to invoke the essential interdependence of world-economic *and* world-political interests after the war in pursuit of his core aims. The foreign minister and his collaborators made some attempts to identify common concerns that also could form the basis for an understanding with the governments of Britain and France. But these attempts did not go very far. Essentially, they revolved around two ideas. The first was to persuade the *Entente* leaders that the preservation of Germany as a viable economic power would be crucial for what had to be in their interest as well: the reconstruction of Europe and the revitalisation of international trade. The second was to convince them that they too should be interested in making a settlement that fostered the consolidation of a German republic as a core element of political stability at the centre of Europe and a state that accepted not only far-reaching military restrictions but also the obligations of the League. But these ideas remained undeveloped.

Brockdorff-Rantzau's reorientated strategy thus remained fixated on Wilson. He now sought to appeal more overtly to the "special interest" the American government ought to have in protecting Germany's integrity and thereby preserving "an extremely receptive terrain for the exercise of its financial and industrial power" which had "enormously expanded through the world war".[53] Like Warburg, the foreign minister overestimated the relevance of such financial and economic considerations for Wilson's peace-making agenda. Above all, however, he counted on what he saw as the profound congruence of political interests between the American president and the new republican government in Berlin. He clung to the view that these converged in the overriding interest in forging a progressive peace on the foundations laid by the Fourteen Points – as he interpreted them. This remained the pivot of his expanded strategy on the eve of the peace conference. And this is why he persisted so stubbornly with his efforts to persuade

[53] *Ibid.*; Brockdorff-Rantzau speech, 14 February 1919, Brockdorff-Rantzau (1925), pp. 58–9.

Wilson – and "world opinion" – that the new German republic ardently supported the American president's vision of peace and postwar order.[54]

While in some ways pointing in a forward-looking direction, Brockdorff-Rantzau's wider "common-interest" strategy still had important limitations and was all but bound to fail in the constellation of 1919. One core problem was that he still insisted that a "common-interest" peace had to fulfil his rigid criteria for a "peace of justice". Another was that he held on to the misperception, and misconception, that Wilson's interest in implementing his peace programme would ultimately redound to Germany's advantage. What is more, he persevered with his approach although he began to realise that Wilson's actual leverage vis-à-vis the *Entente* Powers would be constrained in many ways and he would have to depart from the parameters of the Fourteen Points.[55]

But a more important shortcoming was that the foreign minister gave no serious thought to more concrete policies that could potentially create common ground not only with the United States but also with Britain and France. While declaring that he intended to pursue a "policy of reconciliation" with the enemies of the war, he did not try to gain a clearer understanding of British, and especially French, core concerns and to respond to them.[56] This clearly applied to his defensively legalistic approach towards the reparations question. Even more detrimental, however, was that Brockdorff-Rantzau and the leading policymakers at the Foreign Office made only very limited advances towards addressing the crucial postwar problem of security and above all prevalent French fears of a renewed German "assault". The foreign minister was not oblivious to the concerns that dominated Clemenceau's peace agenda. And he developed some understanding of how critical a "solution" to the Franco-German security question was for Europe's pacification. In his programmatic speech of 14 February, he emphasised that as long as Germany and France continued to treat each other as "hereditary enemies" their mutual antagonism would remain a source of inherent instability and insecurity and could not be tolerated by "the world" in the longer run. He thus declared that one of the principal tasks of the peace conference was to "create guarantees" that would remedy this "state of affairs" – while stressing that such guarantees could not be gained by tearing vital regions like the Rhineland away from Germany.[57]

Yet what could constitute different and more effective guarantees? And what contribution could Germany make? Here, the foreign minister and

[54] See Brockdorff-Rantzau statement, 15 January, Brockdorff-Rantzau (1925), p. 38; Brockdorff-Rantzau notes, undated, *ADAP*, 1918–1919, pp. 184–6.
[55] Brockdorff-Rantzau memorandum of discussion with Groener, 4 April 1919, Versailles, IV, 9105 H/H234106, Brockdorff-Rantzau Papers.
[56] Brockdorff-Rantzau statement, 15 January 1919, Brockdorff-Rantzau (1925), pp. 38–9.
[57] Brockdorff-Rantzau speech, 14 February 1919, Brockdorff-Rantzau (1925), p. 51.

German peace planners only advanced very general ideas rather than conceptions that could offer convincing assurances to France and really addressed the underlying problem of Germany's power and threat *potential*. At one level, Brockdorff-Rantzau emphasised that the new German government was not only committed to carrying out its disarmament obligations but also prepared to renounce any aggressive military and armament policies in the future.[58] The assumption that informed his outlook and also prevailed in the Foreign Office was that under the terms of the armistice, and the eventual peace, Germany would for the foreseeable future be so severely constrained as a military power that it would constitute no tangible threat to France or its other neighbours.[59]

At another level, Brockdorff-Rantzau argued that the new German republic would make a *proactive* contribution to peace and security by underwriting the League's new system of *general* guarantees – and by pledging to settle all international disputes by peaceful means and, chiefly, through arbitration.[60] He thus instructed Foreign Office experts to draw up elaborate plans for a League-based universal arbitration regime. Yet general German commitments of this kind were hardly likely to satisfy French decision-makers. Only some policymakers – notably Erzberger – began to face up to the political reality that in one form or another the general resource and demographic potential of the German state – which they sought to preserve – would continue to be regarded as a significant menace, especially in France, and that it was thus imperative to provide more tangible guarantees and re-assurance. Eventually, in May 1919, Erzberger would propose that the German government should guarantee to keep a 50-kilometre-wide "safety corridor" on the eastern bank of the Rhine demilitarised.[61] But this was only an isolated step that had no political impact at the time. In the end, neither Erzberger nor Brockdorff-Rantzau – or any other German protagonist – could as yet formulate a more coherent security policy for the post–First World War era under the pressures of 1919.

More fundamentally, Brockdorff-Rantzau's policies were limited by the fact that he never managed to develop a more clearly defined and comprehensive conception of a new *Euro*-Atlantic order in which a newly republican Germany could find a place. In particular, he never developed substantive ideas about how to open up avenues of accommodation and initiate a pacification process in the *European* substratum of such an order, particularly in the relations with Britain and France. Not unlike Wilson, he remained too focused on abstract "universal" concepts that could not convincingly address the cardinal question of how Germany's re-emergence as a "modern" republican

[58] See Brockdorff-Rantzau note, 14 January 1919; *ADAP*, 1918–1919, pp. 184-6.
[59] Brockdorff-Rantzau memorandum, 21 January 1919, Vorbereitung der Friedensverhandlungen, 9105 H/H234798–802, Brockdorff-Rantzau Papers.
[60] Brockdorff-Rantzau speech, 14 February 1919, Brockdorff-Rantzau (1925), p. 38.
[61] Erzberger proposals, Conger report, 19 May 1919, in Epstein (1955), pp. 430-1.

and non-military great power within a recast Atlantic system, which he desired to promote, could be made reconcilable with the security needs and essential interests of its neighbours – in the west as well as in the east.

IV. Beyond *Realpolitical* Opportunism. German Turns towards the League and the Aspiration to Integrate a Republican Germany into a New Comity of Civilised Nations

In Brockdorff-Rantzau's general conception, the League of Nations came to play a pivotal and by no means only an instrumental role. From the outset, the foreign minister re-affirmed and even accentuated the new German government's fervent support for an authoritative and universal League in the spirit of Wilson's proposals. He declared the German nation stood behind the idea of a "league of nations" and the American president's maxim that it had to be "the foundation of the reshaping of the world" with all the idealism that sprang from "the awakening of the German people to a new form of state". And, employing Wilsonian language, he emphasised that those who had assumed responsibility in Germany were determined to distance themselves from old-style secret diplomacy and play a constructive part in the formation of the new organisation. As he put it, they realised that this could not be done, and "the ultimate victory of democracy in the world" could not be secured, "by way of intrigues and antechamber secrets".[62] That such a demonstrative turn towards the League only occurred against the background of the German collapse predictably led to allegations of tactical opportunism, particularly from French and British policymakers. Distrust also characterised the attitude of Wilson and his main advisers, who for the most part did not take German pro-League proclamations seriously or found them presumptuous. In retrospect, such suspicions seem understandable, but they are in important respects distortive.

Among those who now demonstratively clamoured for a *Völkerbund* in Germany, there were unquestionably numerous opportunists, in the Foreign Office and elsewhere, who simply regarded support for the League as expedient at a time of German powerlessness, whose real interest was to improve Germany's negotiating position and who had by no means abandoned maxims of sovereign great-power politics. There were many who did not believe in "League internationalism"; and there were those who envisaged either instrumentalising or simply side-lining the League and the new "rules" of world politics that Wilson and others championed once Germany had regained a position of power. But all of these were rather marginal actors at this critical stage.

---

[62] Brockdorff-Rantzau declaration, 15 January 1919; Brockdorff-Rantzau remarks to foreign correspondents, 24 January 1919, Brockdorff-Rantzau (1925), pp. 38–9, 40–2.

By contrast, the emphatic commitment of the most influential German decision-makers to a "Wilsonian" League was *also* unquestionably due to tactical and strategic considerations – it was and remained an integral part of their attempt to gain Wilson's support for a "peace of justice". But it would be misleading to conclude that the distinctive pro-League orientation that Brockdorff-Rantzau, Erzberger, the leading social democrats and key experts in the Foreign Office adopted was only or even mainly shaped by motivations of this kind. Rather, the pivotal German actors came to regard the envisaged organisation as an essential framework for a new kind of rule-bound international politics that, in their eyes, could not only serve to safeguard vital German interests but also foster a more durable peace. And, crucially, they came to view it as the key mechanism through which the newly republican Germany could escape isolation and ostracisation after a profoundly divisive war and become part of a reconfigured "comity of nations". That was why the emphasis on being *included in* and *taking part in* the process of creating the League acquired a more than merely tactical or symbolical significance in the Foreign Office, then for the first Weimar government and eventually also in the wider German public debate.[63]

Brockdorff-Rantzau thus captured wider prevalent attitudes when he emphatically declared, on 14 February, that "a people like the German people", which had just established a democratic order, must not be treated as a "second-class people" by the western powers and obliged to undergo a "period of quarantine" before it was admitted to the new organisation. Yet the foreign minister went one step further. He demanded that the new German republic not only had to be admitted forthwith to the League but also be given a place on its executive council. He vindicated this claim by arguing that "a free people" could be asked to "cede a large portion of its sovereignty only if it participates in [the League's] executive and thus provides means for the enforcement [of peace]"; it could not join the new organisation if it remained a mere "object of the executive".[64] More fundamentally, Brockdorff-Rantzau considered a permanent place on the League's Council as integral to the realisation of his underlying aim to regain for Germany a place of equality among the leading world powers. And in a wider context it is indeed difficult to overstate the extent to which he and other German protagonists were guided by the maxim that the new German republic had to be recognised as a *respected* great power with equal rights – and not be treated as a pariah that had not only lost the war but also the claim to be ranked among the first-tier "civilised nations".

---

[63] Brockdorff-Rantzau statement, 15 January 1919, Brockdorff-Rantzau (1925), pp. 38–9; Ebert declaration, transmitted by Bliss to Lansing, 11 November 1918, *FRUS* 1918, I/1, p. 493.

[64] Brockdorff-Rantzau speech, 14 February 1919, Brockdorff-Rantzau (1925), pp. 47, 58–9.

The post-armistice period also saw a – belated – surge of not only governmental but also non-governmental efforts to promote the League idea in Germany and to underscore, vis-à-vis the western powers in general and Wilson in particular, that there was a broader and growing base of support for the envisaged organisation. Above all, as noted, this found expression in the creation of the "German League for the League of Nations" in December 1918. Though sponsored by the German Foreign Office, where notably Simons and Schücking supported its activities, and also created to serve its political aims, it should not merely be seen as a "Trojan horse" of German foreign policy during the peace conference. In line with the mission that its chief instigators Erzberger and Jäckh had defined, the new association would indeed become a central forum for those who sought to develop ideas and even an "ideology" for a "genuine League of Nations" that was "universal and democratic" and, more broadly, for a new international "order of law". And it would be instrumental for disseminating such ideas in and beyond Germany.[65] At the same time, it thus played an important role in initiating what was difficult to achieve under conditions of defeat but long overdue: a more substantial inner-German debate not only about the purposes of a League but also about the core question of what role Germany should play in the postwar international order.

The German League brought together an immense variety of policymakers, experts and scholars. Prominent among them were, apart from Erzberger, both majority and minority social democrats – among them Ebert, Scheidemann as well as Haase. Its supporters also included the financial expert Hjalmar Schacht and the industrialists Robert Bosch and Wilhelm Cuno, who saw a new international organisation as a means to re-integrate Germany into the postwar economic and political order. But the most active members would be liberals who supported the orientation of Schücking and pacifists like Ludwig Quidde and Helene Stöcker. All of them regarded efforts to champion a League as a natural outgrowth of their long-standing struggle to liberalise and pacify German approaches to international affairs.[66]

From early February 1919, a more clearly non-governmental association – the "Heidelberg Association for a Policy of Law" which assembled leading liberal-bourgeois scholars and intellectuals, would also seek to champion the central notion of a "peace of right" – a "Rechtsfrieden" – and the constitution of a League as an authoritative organisation of international law and cornerstone of a new world order. Here too the expectation prevailed that Wilson would be the key figure who realised such aspirations against the opposition of the Entente Powers.[67] Another independent blueprint for a League of Nations

[65] Jäckh, "Die Gründung" (1928), p. 22.
[66] See Wintzer (2006), pp. 47–50.
[67] See draft memorandum of objectives the "Arbeitsgemeinschaft für Politik des Rechts", undated, Haußmann Papers, 12; Leonhard (2018), p. 453.

had been prepared by the German Society for International Law. It also called for a league that guaranteed the "equitability" of the rights and duties of *all* states. The scheme it proposed was actually transmitted to Wilson in February via the German League of Nations Society, but there is no indication that he took any notice of it.[68] That most of the now rapidly growing number of unofficial German League plans made Wilson's declarations their central reference-point was as unsurprising as that those who developed them on behalf of a defeated and isolated state stressed the need for a *universal* and *inclusive* world organisation. But many of the experts and private scholars who now turned their attention to the League were also driven by the resolve to draw wider lessons from the carnage of the war, strengthen precepts and instruments of international law and promote international understanding and reconciliation in its aftermath.

But those who championed the League and a German commitment to a new "international order of law" would not only have to confront the suspicions of the western powers. They also had to gain support and legitimacy for their course within the volatile and polarised domestic environment of post-armistice Germany. And here they faced an array of outspoken nationalists and right-wing extremists who vilified the League as a power-political ploy of the Anglo-American imperialists – or simply ridiculed its premises. These forces were keen to exploit any setback in Germany's League aspirations to discredit the entire conception of a peace of accommodation with the western powers. This inner-German struggle over the League would continue in the decade after 1919. What proved politically decisive in the short term, however, was that all the key figures of the Council of People's Commissars – and then of the first Weimar coalition – were united in their staunch support for a "proactive" League policy and able to unite the parties and forces they represented behind them. And what mattered particularly here was that Ebert, Scheidemann and the Majority Social Democrats, who stressed their long-standing allegiance to the idea of a strong "league of peoples", backed these priorities unequivocally.[69]

From January 1919, endeavours to develop a more coherent official League policy would gain momentum. And these endeavours were marked by a basic parallelism of functional shorter-term aims and more substantial longer-term imperatives of a new German foreign policy. This parallelism had already characterised the approach that proved formative for all subsequent efforts – namely that which Erzberger had pursued ever since October 1918. Following

---

[68] Jäckh (1928), p. 19.
[69] See declaration of the German government, 17 January 1919, Vorbereitung der Friedensverhandlungen, 9105H/H234836, Brockdorff-Rantzau Papers; Ebert statement, transmitted by Bliss to Lansing, 11 November 1918, *FRUS* 1918, I/1, p. 493; Scheidemann (1929), II, pp. 342–50.

his recommendations, two essential elements came to mark evolving German League strategies: on the one hand the demonstrative resolve to back the establishment of a Wilsonian "league of peoples"; on the other, the emphasis on elaborating more refined German blueprints for such a League, which were intended to underscore both the sincerity of the German commitment and the need for an integrative, non-discriminating organisation. As noted, Erzberger had early on presented an ambitious plan for a universal international association that was to foster "world peace" not only through a regime of obligatory arbitration and disarmament but also through covenant that guaranteed economic "equal rights" and a universal application of the "Open Door".[70] And he would step up his efforts on behalf of such a League after the armistice. But the task to prepare an official German League blueprint would eventually be delegated to the Foreign Office.

Under Brockdorff-Rantzau, the German Foreign Office finally established a commission whose specific mission was to formulate League proposals for the expected peace negotiations. This commission also came to include economic experts but would be dominated by rather progressive lawyers and international-law experts. As head of this commission, the foreign minister appointed Walter Simons, a liberal "internationalist" imperialist who would become commissioner general of the German Peace Delegation and one of Brockdorff-Rantzau's key advisers. Simons would play a significant role in shaping the Foreign Office's League plans. In the wake of the armistice he had positioned himself as proponent of a "Wilsonian peace" and adopted the position that a League founded on Wilsonian principles – of which he expected the German republic to be a founding member – could become the essential instrument to further co-operation and reconciliation between the antagonists of the war. Under Simons' direction, the Foreign Office's expert commission had begun preliminary deliberations and may have prepared a preliminary draft by the end of January.

But more substantial work on an official League blueprint would only begin in reaction to the Draft Covenant that Wilson presented on behalf of the victorious powers on 14 February. It would eventually result in an elaborate scheme that the Scheidemann government decided to publish on 24 April. Yet the essential elements on which the Foreign Office's plans focused were clearly discernible from the start: the emphasis on the need for an all-inclusive organisation that guaranteed the equality of all its members under an elaborate covenant of international law; and the emphasis on a far-reaching arbitration regime and, more generally, a new regime of rules to ensure the peaceful settlement of all international disputes, including those involving "political interests" and "questions of honour". Later, German planners would add a third emphasis: the idea to turn the League also into a key institution in the

---

[70] Erzberger (1918), esp. pp. 3–4; 90–171, 184 ff.; Erzberger (1919).

postwar economic order, which was to foster commercial cooperation and ensure above all the "freedom" of international trade on "most-favoured-nation" premises.[71]

The fact that Brockdorff-Rantzau stressed the need for more substantial German League designs created unexpected opportunities for a distinct minority of committed internationalists in the Foreign Office. Most notable among them was the aformentioned juridical internationlist Walther Schücking, who would eventually be charged with preparing the German counter-proposals to the victors' provisional League Covenant. He put forward a distinctly progressive, and legalistic, conception. Schücking had been a fervent advocate of the Hague conventions and drew on ideas that had long been prominent in liberal German legal thinking. In 1915, he had argued that the central task of the future would be to build "an international order of law" that set an end to the influence of "old generals" on the future of Europe. Going far beyond Wilson's aspirations, he desired to establish nothing less than the primacy of law in international relations, including great-power relations. As he saw it, newly binding guarantees, rules and procedures of conflict resolution under an authoritative international covenant held the key to peace.[72]

In the aftermath of the war, Schücking thus emphasised that both the new international organisation and the international "order based on law" it was to create had to be constituted as a "closed system" that provided a "universal guarantee of peace". And he was even more uncompromising than Bourgeois in demanding that arbitration had to become the new standard procedure of international relations and be made compulsory for all forms of international conflict, including those involving core national interests and questions of security. Schücking's ideas would be reflected in the blueprint that was presented to the victors and the wider world on 24 April.[73] But by then they would essentially serve propagandistic purposes – namely to manifest that German League conceptions were more progressive than those of the victors. In substantive terms, they were decidedly more progressive and ambitious than what Brockdorff-Rantzau or Erzberger envisaged, notably when it came to arbitration.

Brockdorff-Rantzau publicly championed "the idea of arbitration" of international conflicts that could not be settled by diplomatic means; but he did not advocate a far-reaching regime of mandatory arbitration. Rather, he argued that for "questions of interests" that were not amenable to legal remedies,

---

[71] See Niemeyer (1919); Wintzer (2006), pp. 143–8; Krüger (1985), p. 71; Krüger (1973).

[72] During the war Schücking had sought to build "spiritual bridges" across the trenches as an activist in the transnational "Central Organisation for a Lasting Peace". See Schücking (1915), p. 5; Hoeres (2004), pp. 483–5.

[73] See Schücking (1915), p. 5; Hoeres (2004), pp. 483–5; Cabinet protocols, 22 and 23 April 1919, AR Scheidemann, nos. 50 and 51; Pariser Völkerbundsakte (1919).

international mechanisms of "mediation and settlement" had to be expanded – following the example of the Bryan treaties – that would allow the political settlement of disputes between the League's member states before they escalated. At the same time, the foreign minister advanced an ambitious vision of his own, arguing that it would be imperative to establish the League as a "firm" international institution not only with a robust administrative structure but also with a "permanent federal parliament".[74] But the real priority he pursued through such proposals was and remained to make sure that when the League was founded, the new German republic would immediately join it and play a leading role within it.

Interestingly, and very likely because this appeared inconceivable in the immediate aftermath of a war that seemed to have destroyed all notions of a common European system, no influential German policymaker used the term "concert" or invoked the precedent of nineteenth-century "Concert of Europe" conceptions in the way British strategists did. But what gained first contours was the idea that the League could become the instrument for creating, over time, a new concert of states that would involve the United States, the *Entente* Powers and Germany, and allow the former enemies to deal with the most critical postwar problems. But the German protagonists of 1919 were still in the early stages of a very difficult readjustment process; they resorted to general "Wilsonian" maxims and had not yet formed more coherent ideas about what the creation and operation of a functioning postwar concert would require, especially from Germany, in terms of reassurance, reliable international conduct and willingness to compromise. They were still far from developing more substantial conceptions to this end – such as those that Stresemann and his key adviser Carl von Schubert would eventually advance, in response to an escalating postwar crisis, in the mid-1920s.[75]

V.   The Priority of Safeguarding the Integrity of the German State
German Approaches to Self-Determination, the Critical Polish Question and Aspirations for an Austro-German Union

When on 2 January 1919 Brockdorff-Rantzau made a declaration about the general principles to which the new German government had committed itself under the armistice agreement, he stressed that it had recognised "the right of self-determination" as a "basic right of peoples". He would renew this general commitment on numerous occasions. His first priority, however, was to appeal to this "right" on Germany's behalf. And it was with this concern in mind that he proclaimed that the new constitutive principle of the postwar order had to be applied to all peoples "in equal measure" and sought to hold the American

---

[74] Brockdorff-Rantzau speech, 14 February 1919, Brockdorff-Rantzau (1925), p. 38.
[75] See Cohrs (2006), pp. 227–31, 347–53.

president, whom he addressed as the most powerful champion of "self-determination", accountable for ensuring "equitability".[76]

By the time a first version of the official guidelines for the German peace negotiators had been drafted, in mid-January 1919, this emphasis had been confirmed. These guidelines stressed that in approaching the reorganisation of Europe and "Nearer Asia", German plenipotentiaries would recognise "the great principle of the right to self-determination" in favour of others who had a legitimate claim as much as they had to insist on it "in favour of the German people".[77] German policymakers thus made an equitable, non-discriminating application of self-determination norms into a litmus test for the new mode of peacemaking Wilson had proclaimed.

Predictably, then Brockdorff-Rantzau and other leading decision-makers, including Erzberger, focused on marshalling the self-determination principle essentially to prevent the loss of territories that had belonged to the German Empire. As they now found themselves in a position of weakness, they no longer invoked this principle, like the architects of Brest-Litovsk, to cloak imperial ambitions in Eastern Europe, but rather defensively. And they did so particularly to counter what they regarded as the main threat: French designs to impose major territorial curtailments on the vanquished power, both along the Rhine and in the east, in order to weaken Germany in the longer run and, as it were, structurally. In the west, they sought to repulse French aspirations to gain control over the Rhineland by arguing that the will of the local population to remain within the German state had to be respected. In the case of Alsace-Lorraine, they demanded a plebiscite on "Wilsonian terms". But they eventually had to acknowledge that this was an elusive aspiration.[78]

In the east, Brockdorff-Rantzau and the leading Social Democrats were keenly aware that the settlement of the future border between Germany and the new Polish state would not only be one of the most critical questions of the entire peacemaking process but also one of the most explosive problems they faced on the domestic front. In fact, the weak German government hardly had any means to defuse the tensions and violent conflicts with the fledgling Polish state that had rapidly escalated since the armistice. On one side, it confronted Polish attempts to assert control over disputed areas amidst nationalist agitation for a "Greater Poland" and notably, since December, an uprising of the Polish population in the Posen province as well as intensifying disputes between Poles and Germans about the future of Upper Silesia. On the other side, it had to deal with the fact that local German resistance against Polish incursions,

[76] Brockdorff-Rantzau declaration, 2 January 1919; Brockdorff-Rantzau speech, 15 January 1919, Brockdorff-Rantzau (1925), pp. 37, 39.

[77] Official German guidelines, published 17 January 1919, Vorbereitung der Friedensverhandlungen, 9105 H/H234836–38, Brockdorff-Rantzau Papers.

[78] Ibid.

in which both workers' and soldiers' councils and, from January 1919, *Freikorps* forces participated, had turned the "defence of Germany"s integrity in the east" into a vital domestic-political issue. And at the same time it had to deal with national-patriotic representatives of the eastern provinces who now demanded that no "German territory" must be ceded and found widespread support for these demands in German public and publicised opinion. What had problematic effects here were, at a deeper level, the longer-term consequences of ethnocentric conceptions of nationalism that had become prevalent in the German Empire and fed a deeply ingrained sense of superiority vis-à-vis "Prussian Polish" populations and the wider Polish national movement.[79]

In view of such immense pressures and constraints it was exceedingly difficult for Brockdorff-Rantzau to develop a realistic, let alone a constructive policy and even to begin to come to terms with "the Polish question" while restraining national demands and expectations.[80] The primary – and unenviable – task he faced was to develop guidelines for how German representatives would address the complex question of the Polish–German border at the peace conference. Unsurprisingly, though he spoke of the need to work out a "*modus vivendi*" with what he described as Germany's "inconvenient" new neighbour in the east, his chief concern was to minimise territorial losses and to ensure, by all available means, that Germany's national claims would be recognised by the western powers. And while invoking the principle of self-determination, the official German guidelines came to be marked by a decidedly one-sided and restrictive use of this principle vis-à-vis Poland – or even, where it suited German interests, its de facto rejection.

Publicly, Brockdorff-Rantzau took pains to underscore his determination to defend Germany's "right of nationality" in the east. He argued that the German government was also prepared to recognise this "right" when it was detrimental to Germany's "current position of power". But he actually set clear limits vis-à-vis Polish claims, stipulating that consonant with Wilson's Fourteen Points only "indubitably Polish territories" were to become part of the new Polish state.[81] Internally, the foreign minister initially proposed that in areas with mixed populations plebiscites overseen by a "non-partisan" body should decide *after the conclusion of the peace treaty* what their future status would be. And he originally envisaged using this procedure in all areas under dispute, including West Prussia, where he anticipated an outcome favourable to Germany.[82] Further, as noted, he suggested that the Polish state's access to

---

[79] See Niedhart (2012), p. 3; Schattkowsky (1994), pp. 21 ff.

[80] Official German guidelines, published on 17 January 1919, Vorbereitung der Friedensverhandlungen, 9105 H/H234836–38, Brockdorff-Rantzau Papers.

[81] Brockdorff-Rantzau speech, 14 February 1919, Brockdorff-Rantzau (1925), pp. 54, 53.

[82] German "Guidelines", 27 January 1919, Miller and Matthias and Potthoff (1969), II, pp. 319–20.

the Baltic Sea should be guaranteed without the creation of a "Polish corridor" that severed East Prussia from the German state – through international access agreements under the supervision of the League of Nations.[83]

But the German experts who were charged with preparing more detailed recommendations for the eastern territorial questions insisted successfully that the official German position should be decidedly more restrictive, demanding that plebiscites should only be held in the eastern parts of the province of Posen but *rejected* in all other areas that were deemed vital, notably West Prussia and the important industrial area of Upper Silesia. Highlighting that "fair" referendums would be impossible in a situation marked by violent conflict and ongoing "attacks" of "proletarian" Poles in Upper Silesia, experts like Friedrich Wilhelm von Schwerin and the scholar Otto Hoetzsch argued that rather than an abstract right to plebiscites other, essentially economic, historical and political criteria should be decisive. While Schwerin proposed that the future economic welfare of the population in a given area should be a key criterion, Hoetzsch proposed focusing on the historical claims of particular groups and their contributions to a particular province's development. Unsurprisingly, in their interpretation all of these criteria commanded that there would be no "Polish corridor" and Upper Silesia would remain part of the German state.[84]

Overall, the foreign minister and his experts thus remained almost exclusively focused on the priority of preventing as far as possible any territorial "concessions" to the new Poland. And because of this priority, it was only at a late stage – from March 1919 – that policymakers in Berlin really turned their attention to another vital issue, the protection of the political rights and "cultural autonomy" of German-speaking minorities in the Polish state, and demanded Polish "assurances" to this end.[85] In retrospect, it becomes even more obvious that, as both British and American experts warned after the armistice, the Polish–German border conflict raised one problem that could have particularly destabilising consequences for the entire postwar order – and that was the problem of German irredentism. Essentially, this problem could not be avoided but only be contained in the aftermath of the Great War. More precisely, what arose was the danger that if sizeable German minorities hence had to live under Polish rule, this could give rise to powerful political pressures. What loomed on the horizon was a scenario in which not only the new minorities but also potent forces within the reduced German state, and by no means only nationalist forces, would demand in the name of "self-determination" that the "lost provinces and countrymen" had to be reunited with the rest of the "fatherland". As a consequence, the unconsolidated Polish state would thus be confronted with strong revisionist tendencies of a still far more powerful German neighbour.

[83] *Ibid.*
[84] See Schwabe (1985), pp. 303–4; Haupts (1976), pp. 200–1.
[85] See Brockdorff-Rantzau memorandum, 21 March 1919, *ADAP*, 1918–1919, pp. 324–6.

In fact, Max Weber had conjured up an even starker doomsday scenario in mid-December 1918 when he warned that if the victors took major territories from Germany, particularly in the east, then after "a period of a mere pacifism of fatigue" even "the last worker" would turn into a "chauvinist", "(h)atred between peoples" would become a permanent feature of the postwar world, the flames of "the German irredenta" would be fanned "with all the usual revolutionary means of self-determination", the League of Nations would be "dead on the inside" and "no 'guarantees' would be able to alter" these destructive developments. Ultimately, Weber prophesied, the entire peace that still was to be concluded would be in grave jeopardy.[86] In a more restrained manner, Brockdorff-Rantzau would likewise point to the "dangers" to which the "creation" of "irredenta" would unavoidably give rise. Yet like other German policymakers in the spring and summer of 1919, he would mainly do so in order to persuade western powers that it was in their interest too to avoid such "dangers" in the first place – by not severing any significant territories and German-speaking populations from the German state.[87] Beyond this, the foreign minister and the relevant experts in the Foreign Office had little or nothing to offer to tackle an incendiary problem that in one form or another was *inescapable* in the constellation the Great War had created.

Challenges of a different nature, and order, had to be confronted by Brockdorff-Rantzau in the context of another central European problem that had become acute after the war: the future of the German-Austrian "rump state" that had been left behind after the dissolution of the Habsburg Empire. From his vantage-point what became the "*Anschluß* question" had both a distinct domestic and a broader international dimension. After the idea of a Danubian Federation had been discarded, the Social Democratic-dominated government of Karl Renner and Otto Bauer in Vienna essentially doubted that an independent Austrian republic would be viable, particularly economically. And on their initiative the Austrian National Assembly had on 12 November 1918 passed a resolution in favour of a union with Germany. Having recourse to the principle of self-determination, and invoking the progressive "Greater German" legacy of 1848, Brockdorff-Rantzau repeatedly declared in 1919 that the wish of the German Austrians to unify with Germany should be granted.[88] In fact, however, he and other policymakers at the Foreign Office came to handle this issue with marked caution. They were wary of pushing for an *Anschluß* of German Austria

---

[86] Weber, 'Deutschlands künftige Staatsform' (15 December 1918), in Weber (1958), p. 444. For Weber's thoughts and positions during war and its aftermath see Ghosh (2016), pp. 205–17.

[87] Brockdorff-Rantzau, 14 February 1919, Brockdorff-Rantzau (1925), p. 55; German memorandum, 30 March 1919, Wkg. 30 geh./I, D 931 100, PA.

[88] Brockdorff-Rantzau, 14 February 1919, Brockdorff-Rantzau (1925), p. 52; *ibid.*, pp. 145–8.

because they expected that the French government would strongly oppose such a scenario. They were not sufficiently aware of the geopolitical threat that in French eyes the creation of a greater German power at the heart of Europe posed. Their main fear was rather that the French government would use assertive German demands for an Austro-German union as a pretext to convince Wilson and Lloyd George to create a buffer-state on the Rhine. Essentially, they thus sought to push back *Anschluß* demands in order to protect the integrity of the "Smaller German" Bismarck state.[89]

But the foreign minister and his advisers had to reckon with the fact that not only in Austria but also in Germany a majority actually desired a union. And of greatest political import was that the Liberals and notably the Social Democrats now saw an opportunity to invoke the "right" of national self-determination to realise the *emancipatory* "Greater German" vision that had been defeated in 1849, namely to found a republican and less Prussocentric German state that could become a bastion of liberal and social democratic order. In their eyes, an Austro-German union on these premises could also provide the new republican system they sought to establish with more domestic legitimacy, taking the wind out of the sails of reactionary and nationalist forces on the right by fulfilling an old national aspiration.

Yet the social democratic proponents of *Anschluß* faced an even more complicated and adverse international constellation than their forebears had encountered in the mid-nineteenth century. They had to find ways to make the aim of building a democratic Greater Germany reconcilable with the wider requirements of Euro-Atlantic stability in a postwar situation marked by tremendous unsettledness and disorder. And, crucially, they had to overcome the suspicions of those who had fought against the Central Powers. Underestimating the geopolitical implications of an Austro-German union, they essentially sought to achieve this by pointing to their democratic credentials and emphasising that their aspirations were compatible with the emphasis on "self-determination" that, in their perception, Wilson and progressive forces in the United States and Britain also espoused. But this obviously did not suffice in the fraught constellation of 1919. The unequivocal French veto, which Lloyd George and Wilson came to back, would frustrate all further social democratic hopes and like-minded liberal aspirations in Austria and Germany before the peace conference had even got underway.[90]

---

[89] It should be noted here that the fate of the about 3.5 million Sudeten Germans who would become a minority in the new Czechoslovak state was no major concern for German peace planners. While the irredentist potential of this issue was recognised, the primary interest of Germany's "new diplomacy" actually lay in developing constructive relations with Czechoslovakia.

[90] See Krüger (1985), pp. 54–8; Miller (1978), pp. 192–3; Judson (2016), pp. 436 ff.

PART IV

No *Pax Atlantica*

The First Attempt to Found a Modern Atlantic Order – and Its Frustration

Ten days after the opening of the Paris Peace Conference, on 28 January 1919, Wilson impressed on his fellow peacemakers that there was not "any historical precedent for the work now in hand; least of all should the Congress of Vienna be cited as such".[1] In fact, the peace negotiations of Versailles not only turned into something unprecedented. They can indeed be interpreted as the most complex and overburdened peacemaking and reordering process in modern history. Notably, they were more complicated and raised more intractable international, transnational and domestic-political challenges than either the proceedings of the Vienna Congress roughly one hundred years earlier or the in many ways more successful subsequent efforts to create a new Atlantic and global order – roughly twenty-five years later – after the Second World War.

Why this was so, why the first, essentially transatlantic attempt to create a modern international order for the long twentieth century turned into such an arduous struggle, and why it was ultimately frustrated in crucial respects – all of this will now be re-examined not only with an eye to the broader systemic dimensions of the processes of 1919 but also with due regard for the immense dynamism and drama of modern peacemaking.

---

[1] Hankey's Notes of Two Meetings of the Council of Ten, 28 January 1919, *PWW*, LIV, p. 314.

14

An Impossible Peace?
The Incomplete Transatlantic and Global Peacemaking Process of 1919

The peacemaking process that commenced in January 1919 had unprecedented global dimensions not only in terms of the actors who came to Paris seeking to have a say in it, the issues that would be fought over and the expectations it raised – and largely disappointed. It also provided a focal point for an evolving global public sphere and, as it were, a multifaceted and profoundly controversial global debate about the future world order. That so much attention focused on the founding of a League of Nations – and that Wilson, its most powerful proponent, had championed it in universal terms – added a further global element. But what evolved in 1919 never actually became, in a stricter sense, a truly global reordering process. In fact, it revealed that there was actually only a very limited scope for significant, let alone transformative changes in the direction of a "new *world* order" in which fundamental norms and rules were applied, if not on a basis of "equality" then at least without significant hierarchical distinctions. Rather, the negotiations manifested and confirmed that the Great War had given rise to a new hierarchy in the world at whose apex stood the United States, the remaining imperial world powers Britain and France – and, in East Asia, the regional imperial power Japan. And they confirmed that, while the most powerful actors pledged to uphold and act as trustees of newly prevalent universal norms such as "self-determination", outside Europe and the transatlantic sphere – and to some extent Latin America – hierarchical and neo-imperialist modes of international politics persisted.

Similarly, it was conceivable that the newly established League of Nations would eventually provide a framework for advances towards a global system of states that were equal under international law. But the way in which the League was actually founded established it as a distinctly hierarchical, exclusive and at the core Euro-American institution, which in many ways was designed to institutionalise the dominance of the war's principal victors.[1] Further, it was clear from the outset that, not least because he required the backing of Lloyd George and Clemenceau to implement his League aspirations, Wilson would cling to the rationale of not openly contesting British and French imperial rule.

---

[1] See Chapter 15.

And subsequent developments would show that both Britain and France still had the means to reassert their prerogatives, consolidate their imperial systems for the foreseeable future and, if necessary, assert control through coercive measures. This meant that the more far-reaching ambitions of the nationalists within these empires who like Tilak and Zaghlul clamoured for actual "self-determination" were bound to be frustrated.[2]

Yet both in what they furthered and what they impeded the processes of 1919 of course had massive globally relevant consequences – not just because they sparked a world-wide debate about "self-determination" that would reverberate through the long twentieth century. And they also had important effects on regional configurations of order beyond Europe and north America. One "innovation" that had a wider significance was the League-supervised mandate system for the former German colonies and Near and Middle Eastern provinces of the Ottoman Empire, which was created on British premises of "trusteeship" that Wilson essentially adopted. This indeed marked a departure from more traditional forms of pre-war colonialism. But it nonetheless established what de facto was a neo-imperialist "internationalised" regime that would allow particularly Britain and France to extend their respective spheres of imperial influence in new ways.[3]

The Paris Peace Conference thus also had significant implications for the reorganisation of the Near and Middle East at a time when the Ottoman Empire was rapidly disintegrating. But this would turn into a far longer and violent process at whose decisive stages the United States would no longer be involved as an "ordering power". By June 1919 only the most basic outlines of a possible Middle Eastern "settlement" had emerged – a "settlement" that hinged on the illusory idea of the American republic acting as a mandatory power for Constantinople, the Straits and Armenia. But this chimera would soon be superseded by events. Indeed, it would prove as ephemeral as the Treaty of Sèvres which, intended to assert British, French and notably Greek interests in Asia Minor, would be imposed on the Ottoman Sultan in August 1920. Following the successful resistance and nationalist revolution led by General Mustafa Kemal Atatürk, and his victory over Allied and Greek forces, only the Lausanne agreements of 1923 would eventually establish a somewhat more durable status quo in the Near and Middle East, where soon thereafter Atatürk's secular Turkish Republic would emerge as a key power.[4]

Last but not least, the Versailles process also had important short- and longer-term repercussions in East Asia. Crucially, what came to a head in Paris

---

[2] See Darwin (2009), pp. 359–417; Andrew and Kanya Forstner (1981), pp. 164 ff.; Thomas (2006), pp. 93 ff.

[3] See Pedersen (2015), pp. 23–35.

[4] See Sharp (I/2008), pp. 176–86; Provence (2017), esp. pp. 68–83, 101 ff.; Laderman (2019), pp. 140 ff.

was the conflict between the treaty-steeled claims of the imperial power Japan for the formerly German-controlled Shandong province and the demand of those who represented the embattled Chinese republic that not only its rightful claims to Shandong but indeed its sovereignty and right to self-determination had to be recognised. Ultimately, Wilson would feel compelled to strike a strategic bargain with the most powerful actor in the region, Japan, which was manifestly at odds with his championing of self-determination. The American president hoped that by ensuring Japanese membership in the League it would be possible, in the longer run, to gain "justice" for China and to pave the way for a truly sovereign Chinese republic.[5] But the outcome of the Versailles negotiations not only bitterly disappointed China's representatives. It also made a fulfilment of his wider hopes seem highly uncertain; and it created a structurally unstable status quo in East Asia.[6]

In a wider historical context, it thus has to be emphasised that in their combined effect British "imperialist-internationalist" conceptions and modern strategies of imperial defence, tacit Anglo-American understandings and the competitive division of the spoils between the British and French imperial powers played a decisive part in constraining or even blocking advances towards a more egalitarian global order. And this created both long-term and increasingly acute problems of legitimacy. In the medium term, it would lead those who continued to live under imperial rule or imperialist domination to seek other, both peaceful and violent paths towards self-determination and independent statehood – while the British and to a far lesser extent the French and other imperial systems underwent successive reforms to accommodate and contain nationalist forces. And it would give rise to a world-historical constellation in which (not only) the expansion of the British and French spheres of imperial influence could provoke other powers to try to expand their own imperial remit – like Japan – or, in the case of Germany, to strive to become an imperial world power once again.

How the newly dominant American power would act – how far it would continue to champion self-government and universal norms but in fact persist with its distinctive combination of hegemony and informal empire – was bound to have a major impact on this conflict- and potentially war-prone dynamism. In retrospect, it was not inevitable but in fact distinctly likely that, unless they were amended in the aftermath of the peace conference, the decisions the western imperial powers and the United States made in Paris would sooner or later lead to a further stage of competition between "liberal" and newly extreme forms of empire such as that which then escalated in the 1930s and 1940s. In a yet wider historical context, the developments and

---

[5] Baker (1923), II, p. 266.
[6] See Manela (2007), pp. 178–82, 192–3; Cohen (2000), pp. 316–18.

outcomes of 1919 marked a critical stage in an even longer dialectical process in which imperial modes of rule and domination that had been profoundly challenged during the Great War were temporarily re-affirmed yet also the counterforces and counter-ideologies emerged that would eventually undermine them. But this process would only reach its decisive stage in the period of decolonisation that followed the Second World War – when, under conditions of a globalising Cold War, the end of traditional empires was sealed, a plethora of postcolonial states was founded and the new, though distinctive American and Soviet "super-empires" came to be dominant.[7]

But for all the global ramifications it had, the peacemaking process of 1919 actually revolved around something else. It revolved around the challenge not merely to reorder Europe, and to come to terms with the overwhelming array of pressing and structural problems that this raised, but to lay a basic groundwork for a novel Atlantic peace order – after the Eurocentric "order" of the pre-war era had irretrievably collapsed. It is worth stressing again that it was inconceivable to "settle" or create a stable peace in the immediate aftermath of a cataclysm such as the Great War had become. Imperative were, instead, efforts try to reach basic agreements on the most critical issues – above all the German problem – and, at a deeper level, to establish first bases of a reformed system of security and international politics and a constituent framework of norms and rules that, essentially, permitted the pursuit of longer-term negotiation and settlement processes and thus, the *eventual* consolidation of a functioning and legitimate postwar order. But only very insufficient foundations for such a system and for such longer-term processes could be laid in 1919.

To understand why this was so, one has to re-appraise the essential nature, dynamics and constraints of the multi-layered processes that began in mid-January and came to a preliminary end in mid-June 1919. What took place during these six months was not a transformative act of peace-building of the kind Wilson had originally envisioned and for which progressives like Lippmann still clamoured – one in which the American president acted as leader of a transnational coalition of liberal and progressive forces that was to compel his counterparts at the peace conference, and particularly Lloyd George and Clemenceau, to accept his design for a progressive League of Nations and "new world order". Yet nor did 1919 witness a return to older forms of power politics and negotiations shaped by British and French attempts to outmanoeuvre Wilson and assert their different national interests and imperial priorities. Rather, the negotiations in Paris became a peacemaking process of a new kind. They evolved into an unprecedentedly world-

---

[7] For different interpretations, see Darwin (2008), pp. 365 ff., 425 ff.; Burbank and Cooper (2010), pp. 369 ff., 413 ff.; Getachew (2019), pp. 37–70, 71–106; Westad (2007), pp. 1–157, Westad (2018).

encompassing and convoluted yet also distinctly hierarchical process that ultimately was dominated by the principal victors. And, through them, this process was quintessentially shaped by a new mode of international politics: a hierarchical mode of democratic peacemaking.

Vital decisions would be made and key parameters would be set through often informal negotiations between the political leaders of the most powerful and more or less democratic victorious powers. And the quality of outcomes of Versailles would essentially be determined by the extent to which they could develop – with the help of advisers and, selectively, experts – modes and ways to hammer out complex balanced agreements. The larger and immensely challenging task in 1919 was to forge broader balanced compromise agreements – not only among the victors but also between them and the vanquished and, in a wider perspective, between the aims, interests and expectations of *all* the states, national movements and causes that were in some way represented – or struggled to be represented – in Paris. But what actually came to determine the reordering process and the eventual peace settlement was, in the end, the tough battle *between* the victors – between Wilson, Lloyd George and Clemenceau – to forge something much narrower but nonetheless extremely difficult: more than ephemeral *inter-victor* compromises that not only reconciled, as far as possible, their often so strikingly diverging aims and interests but also allowed each of them to meet essential legitimacy requirements and expectations in the democratic force-fields that constituted their home fronts. For ultimately they were most accountable not to the wider world or to the vanquished but to their own parliaments and electorates. And first and foremost they thus had to ensure that they would gain sufficient domestic support for whatever decisions and commitments they made at the peace conference.

More fundamentally, it should be emphasised once again that particularly the principal peacemakers of Versailles faced immense challenges of learning under distinctly adverse conditions for more substantive learning – in the face of a vast sea of pressing and weighty challenges, under the pressures of a conference assembling multitudes of actors and unfolding, often in a chaotic fashion, under the glare of excited public interest across the globe. As we have seen, each protagonist had drawn his own consequences from the cataclysm and developed distinct conceptions of how to make peace and establish a more stable and peace-enforcing postwar system. In short, they thus had to learn to find ways to reconcile these conceptions, and the wider aims and interests for which they fought, during the actual peace conference – when they finally had to confront head-on the actual complexities of peacemaking and establishing a new order, which in 1919 involved a daunting array of interrelated and political intricate issues. Above all, they had to learn to find ways to make *complex compromises*. In the end, however, the advances they could make in this direction remained distinctly limited.

In fact, the western leaders only managed to work out very *tenuous* compromise agreements on the essential issues – security, the reparations problem, Europe's financial and economic reconstruction, the reorganisation of Eastern Europe, the "settlement" of the new Polish–German border and, crucially, the wider German question. More fundamentally, they could never reach a workable consensus on what the main underpinnings of the new Atlantic order were to be – and how this order was to be stabilised in the longer run. To a significant extent this was due to the fact that they ultimately could not really reconcile their disparate aims and approaches; yet it was also a consequence of another irreducible constraint: the fact that the specific domestic-political needs they had to satisfy were and remained so hard to balance. In turn, all of this had one particularly problematic consequence. It came to reinforce the resolve of all three principal victors to rule out what would have been crucial in order to make the Versailles process more legitimate, even if it would have been extremely difficult at this juncture: *eventual* substantive negotiations with representatives of the defeated power, and a more broadly conceived compromise peace that opened up prospects for a stabilising integration of the fledgling Weimar Republic into the postwar order.

I.   The New Hierarchy of Actors, the Unprecedented Conditions of Peacemaking, and the Wider Struggle of 1919

But the peacemakers of 1919 had to come to terms with even broader challenges. They not only faced a profoundly unsettled situation, particularly in central and eastern Europe, but also had to operate on a playing-field of international politics that had been significantly altered and essentially *expanded* under the impact of the Great War. The proceedings of Versailles became the first reordering process after a major war that took place under "modern" conditions. What this meant was that peacemaking became significantly more complicated because it had to be pursued in a setting, and in an environment, that had not only become more pronouncedly global but was also marked by a not entirely new but unprecedentedly complex interplay, and interdependence, of international, transnational and domestic politics. And the dynamics, pressures and constraints this interplay created made it even more difficult to "settle" the cardinal issues that had arisen and more challenging still to address the underlying systemic problems the war had created.

Crucially, never before in the history of international politics had there been so many different actors who, on many different levels, sought to influence the making of a peace settlement. And never before had the conceptions, aims, interests, demands and wider expectations of these various actors been so diverse yet also in so many ways incompatible or even violently conflicting. In contrast to the last major general peace congress, the Congress of Vienna, these actors were not just representatives of the European great powers.

Now, not only an American president was to play a pivotal role. In a wider perspective, a global array of actors tried to exert influence – on the ground in Paris or from afar. It included not only government leaders but also the leading figures of different national movements and various non-governmental groups and activists. What thus ensued from mid-January 1919 was an unprecedented competition not just over what kind of peace and order should be established, and how it was to be established, but also over who was to be included, and indeed have a voice, in the process.

Yet what also emerged was a new *hierarchy* of actors, which in turn had a crucial impact on the nature and dynamics of the actual, at the core intergovernmental peace negotiations. Essentially, despite or rather because of the multiplicity of players and agendas, the most powerful among them – the leaders of the victorious great powers – sought all the more to control the overall process and turned it, ultimately, into a strikingly hierarchical and in essential respects exclusive *transatlantic* peacemaking process. As noted, though they had been shaken up, hierarchical distinctions were and remained most pronounced outside the "Euro-Atlantic world". But Versailles also manifested the extent to which the war had altered the distribution of power and influence in the transatlantic sphere.

The preponderant actors in the recast hierarchy were unquestionably the political leaders of the principal victors, the United States, Britain and France. Their pre-eminence was also reflected in the size of the peace delegations that Wilson, Lloyd George and Clemenceau brought with them to Paris. Wilson was accompanied not only by four other plenipotentiaries, including House, but also by a delegation that included dozens of advisers, military officials and experts on various political, territorial and financial issues. Yet the representation of a power whose government and elites had no previous experience in complex international negotiations of this kind seemed small and improvised when compared with the more effectively organised delegations that Lloyd George and Clemenceau brought with them – the British comprising almost 400 members, the French reaching similar proportions. Italy was also granted an elevated status as an Allied great power and eventually included in the pivotal Council of Four. But the Italian delegation, led by Prime Minister Vittorio Orlando and Foreign Minister Sidney Sonnino, pursued narrower aims and agendas, mainly seeking to vindicate the Italian war effort by asserting claims to the southern provinces of the Tyrol and the Adriatic port city of Fiume.

What bestowed a global significance on the peacemaking process of 1919 without making it genuinely global was not least the number and range of extra-European and "non-western" representatives who came to Paris to fight for their various interests, causes and claims. Those who represented the most powerful player here unquestionably came from Japan, which indeed became the first "non-western" power that was recognised as a great power of the first order at a major peace congress. The Japanese government sent seasoned diplomats, the former foreign minister Baron Nobuaki Makino and the ambassador to Britain, Viscount Chinda Sutemi, while Japan's chief delegate, Prince Saionji Kimmochi, only arrived in March. Essentially, however, the Japanese plenipotentiaries would not concern themselves with the general tasks of peacemaking but concentrate on the assertion of more immediate interests and concerns. Apart from the priority of underscoring Japan's claims to the Shandong province, their primary aim in Paris was to gain recognition for their aspirations to take charge of the islands in the northern Pacific hitherto controlled by the German Empire.[8]

The government of the Chinese republic was represented by a delegation led by the foreign minister Lu Zhengxiang and notably including the erstwhile Chinese minister to Washington, Wellington Koo. The ambitious goal of the Chinese delegation was nothing less than to gain a place of equality for China in the envisaged new world order and to gain recognition for their claim that "self-determination" should be extended to the Chinese republic, which hence was to be treated as a fully sovereign state that also was economically independent. China's representatives thus demanded the abrogation of all unequal treaties that foreign great powers had imposed on China; and they in particular sought to gain Wilson's backing for restoring Chinese sovereignty over Kiaochow and the Shandong peninsula. Yet they had to negotiate on behalf of a weak and deeply divided government that struggled to assert even nominal authority in an even more profoundly divided country.[9]

Further, Brazil and other Latin American countries that had been in a state of war or had merely broken off diplomatic relations with the Central Powers would also be represented at the peace conference. Their delegates would particularly seek to ensure that the envisaged League of Nations would incorporate Latin American countries on a footing of equality and thus help to supersede the iniquities in their relations with the predominant US power, which persisted after the failure of Wilson's Pan-American Pact initiative.

The leading figures of anti-imperialist and anti-colonial nationalist movements in India, Egypt, Korea, Vietnam and other parts of the colonised world also travelled to Paris, eager to seize on the world-historical opportunity the peace conference seemed to present and still counting on the American president as a powerful ally in their quest for "self-determination". Those who came to the French capital with their claims, petitions and high

---

[8] Japan also became the most powerful champion of the principle of "racial equality". It demanded that the League Covenant should explicitly recognise the equality of all races. The Hara government was under domestic pressure to lead efforts to combat racial discrimination and concomitant US immigration restrictions. But the Japanese delegation also instrumentalised "racial equality" to strengthen its bargaining position vis-à-vis Wilson. See Shimazu (1998).

[9] See Manela (2007), pp. 112–17.

expectations included the leader of the Indian National Congress, Tilak, who – accompanied by the young Gandhi – sought to underscore demands for Indian self-determination, and Zaghlul, who asserted Egypt's "right to independence" as the head of a delegation of the nationalist Wafd Party.[10] In the words of Colonel House, Paris became during the winter and spring of 1919 "the Mecca for the oppressed not alone of Europe but of the earth", it turned into "the great modern Babylon".[11] But the hopes of "the oppressed" would essentially be thwarted. While some managed to get "perfunctory hearings", their claims would essentially be either ignored or outright rejected by the principal peacemakers; and they would remain marginalised actors outside the perimeters of the actual peace conference.[12]

Smaller European states that had fought against the Central Powers would also seek to represent their claims and concerns, and to play a more "equal" role both in the negotiations and the new international order than they had in the pre-war era. But in practice they would largely be confined to a secondary and relatively peripheral status during the proceedings – and only be consulted by the principal powers in a limited manner, on issues that directly affected them. Two notable examples may suffice here. The main goal of the Belgian delegation, led by Foreign Minister Paul Hymans, was to ensure an adequate share of reparations from Germany for the losses and devastation its forces had inflicted on their country, which had suffered most damage on the western front after France. While Hymans advanced claims to the small German-held territory between the towns of Eupen and Malmédy, the underlying Belgian concern was the creation of an effective postwar security system that provided guarantees against renewed violations of Belgian neutrality. Yet Hymans also sought to press for equality of representation on behalf of the smaller powers, criticising – in vain – what he called the emergence of a new "Holy Alliance" of the great powers at Versailles.[13]

On behalf of the Greek delegation, the grandiloquent prime minister Eleutherios Venizelos meanwhile pursued the grand ambition of gaining the western powers' backing for a significant expansion of the Greek state. Venizelos sought to extend Greek claims not only to the southern part of Albania but also a sizeable portion of western Asia Minor. In 1919, he would

---

[10] *Ibid.*, pp. 93–7, 149–50.

[11] House, "The Versailles Peace in Retrospect", in House and Seymour (1921), p. 431.

[12] Parallel to the peace conference, the formidable Afro-American leader W.E.B. Du Bois and the French-Senegalese deputy Blaise Diagne launched an initiative to boost self-determination across Africa and organised the first "Pan-African Congress" in Paris in February 1919. But their demands were ignored by the principal peacemakers. See Lewis (2000).

[13] See Marks (1981).

thus lobby for an expansionist agenda that clashed violently with Turkish nationalism and ultimately spelled disastrous consequences for Greece.[14]

Arguably more vital for Europe's overall pacification was the manner in which the leading representatives of the east European "states-in-formation" acted and pursued their claims in Paris. This especially held true for the pursuits of those who came to head the Polish delegation, the leader of the Polish National Committee, Roman Dmowski, and the new premier Ignace Paderewski, who in turn had to seek agreement with the key figure in Warsaw, the provisional "Chief of State" Piłsudski. Having ensured the victors' recognition of the revived Polish nation-state, they now also successfully insisted that it was treated as a recognised state at the peace conference. And while the Polish government continued its policy of trying to extend de facto Polish control over disputed provinces on the ground, Dmowski would focus his energies in Paris on lobbying for his expansive conception of a "Greater Poland".[15] More measured aims and expectations were advanced by the main representatives of the recently proclaimed and recognised Czechoslovak nation-state, Tómas Masaryk und Edvard Beneš, who would take part in the peace proceedings on the same footing as their Polish counterparts. Beneš put forward claims to the predominantly German-speaking Sudetenland and defended Czechoslovak "rights" to the Teschen province vis-à-vis Poland; yet he also emerged as an avid supporter of a strong League.[16]

Having assured their seat at the peacemaking table, Serbian envoys would seek to impress on the western powers their expansive conceptions of Yugoslavia, the new state of the Southern Slavs that would join Serbia with the former Southern-Slav minorities of the Austro-Hungarian Empire, Croatians and Slovenes. Those representing the Baltic nations came to Paris mainly to confirm what had already been largely assured: that they would be recognised as independent states. By contrast, the leader of another significant national movement in Eastern Europe – Symon Petliura, who called for "free Ukraine" – sought in vain to win the backing of the principal victors for his cause. In the west, the Irish republican independence movement sent envoys to Paris, seeking to attain recognition – and particularly Wilson's support – for

---

[14] See MacMillan (2002), pp. 350–2. European countries that had remained neutral during the war like Switzerland, the Netherlands or Sweden did not participate in the peace conference. But from these countries came some of the most committed internationalists, figures like the aforementioned Swiss diplomat William Rappard, who now campaigned for a strong League, also as a key instrument for the future protection of neutrals' rights. See Rappard to Wilson, 26 November 1918, PWW, LIII, pp. 210–11; Hertog and Kruizinga (2011), pp. 1–14; Jonas (2019); Ørvik (1971).

[15] Dmowski statements, Council of Ten, 29 January 1919, FRUS-PPC 1919, III, pp. 772–9; Paderewski to Lansing, 28 January 1918, PWW, XLVI, pp. 120–1.

[16] See Sharp (I/2008), pp. 158–60.

the independent Irish Republic that had been proclaimed during the Easter Rising of 1916; but theirs, too, would be a futile quest.

Crucially, however, the protagonists of the German government and those who sought to represent Austria, Hungary and the other vanquished powers were excluded from the opening stages of the conference. Officially, the victors had justified this exclusion by asserting that these powers either had no democratically elected governments or were in such a state of domestic turmoil that they could not send legitimate plenipotentiaries. Remarkably, though, it was at first very unclear whether, following an initial "inter-allied" conference, they would eventually be invited to actual negotiations at a final, more general peace congress – or whether their only option would remain to try to influence the course and outcome of the negotiations from the outside, as pariah powers.[17]

The other key power that was not invited to Paris was Bolshevik Russia; and against the backdrop of the ongoing civil war this had likewise been vindicated by the argument that the domestic situation in Russia was so unsettled that there were no representatives that could legitimately speak on behalf of the Russian people. As noted, by the time the peace conference opened the western leaders still had reached no consensus on how to deal with the Bolshevik regime – whether to countenance negotiations about a *modus vivendi*, as Lloyd George contemplated, or to follow Clemenceau's suggestion and expand the intervention in the civil war in aid of the counter-revolutionary forces under Denikin and Kolchak, which both Wilson and the British premier rejected.[18] Nor did they see eye to eye on how to address the wider Bolshevik challenge to the peacemaking efforts on which they were about to embark – that posed by the transnational influence of Bolshevik doctrines and attempts to fan the flames of revolution in and beyond central Europe.

But on the broadening playing-field of international politics those who represented more or less powerful governments and states at Versailles also had to reckon with the new force of non-governmental actors. They had to contend with the individual activists and associations that now sought to put pressure on the leaders of the principal victors, yet also to influence public opinion in different countries, and indeed "world opinion", on behalf of the different causes for which they fought. Particularly liberal and left-liberal activists and pressure-groups on both sides of the Atlantic that championed a strong League of Nations and, more broadly, a progressive peace settlement persevered with their lobbying efforts during the peace conference. Many of these actors travelled to Paris, others concentrated on raising their voices in

---

[17] See e.g. Brockdorff-Rantzau notes, 14 January 1919, *ADAP*, 1918–1919, pp. 184–6.

[18] Lloyd George statement, Council of Ten, 12 January 1919, *FRUS-PPC*, III, p. 491; Wilson statement, Council of Ten, 16 January 1919, *PWW*, LIV, p. 102. Clemenceau to Pichon, 11 October 1918, MAE, Série Z, URSS, vol. 210.

the wide-ranging debates that now raged within and between different national force-fields.

The British League of Nations Union became a driving force behind efforts to forge a transnational coalition that campaigned to make the foundation of a new international peace organisation – led by the Allied Powers – a priority at the conference. It now joined forces with the *Association française pour la Société des nations* and other likeminded associations to form the Allied Societies for a League of Nations, which would intensify their common lobbying efforts and hold a first major conference in London in March 1919.[19] By contrast, MacDonald and other leading figures of the Union of Democratic Control campaigned for a more marked departure: a peace process in the spirit of "open diplomacy" that was to bring about far-reaching disarmament, strengthen democratic government and social reform on both sides of the war's trenches and, crucially, establish a "democratic" League that represented the peoples rather than governments and became an engine of postwar reconciliation. In their view, efforts to make peace and to found the League thus also had to involve negotiations with representatives of the German and Austrian republics.[20]

In the United States, Taft and the League to Enforce Peace stepped up their lobbying efforts, mainly seeking to prevail on Wilson to incorporate essentials of their League platform in the Draft Covenant that was being negotiated in Paris. Though they were disaffected by this time and hardly hoped any longer that Wilson would champion the cause of radical internationalist reforms at the peace conference, more left-leaning progressive associations like the Woman's Peace Party and the American Union against Militarism did not relent in their efforts to clamour for a "truly progressive democratic peace".[21] The Progressive opinion-makers of the *New Republic*, whom Lippmann had joined once again, mainly sought to keep up the pressure on Wilson, calling on him to forge and lead a transnational coalition of progressive forces with which he could then shape a forward-looking peace settlement. They tried to impress on the American president and "world opinion" that the real conflict that now had to be fought out was no longer one between competing nation-states or between the victors and the vanquished of the war but rather that between the forces of progressive internationalism – or, as they called it, the "American view" – and the forces of reaction and the "old order".

In late December 1918 the *New Republic* proclaimed that "the stage so recently cleared of war" had now "become occupied by a political struggle, the most momentous in history" – a struggle "not between nations but between parties whose constituency transcends all national bounds". In this interpretation, the

---

[19] League of Nations Union (1919).
[20] Robbins (1976), p. 188; Egerton (1978), p. 142; Mayer (1967), pp. 393 ff.
[21] Knock (1992), p. 228; Addams (1922), pp. 65–72.

"progressive wings of the American parties, British labor and liberals, French and Italian and Belgian liberals and socialists" were "for the purposes of the peace conference one party" – and offered a path to a new order that would transcend the old and at the same time push back Bolshevik alternatives. This progressive phalanx would have to face down the "opposing party" whose protagonists were no longer Wilhelminian military dictators but the "Lodges and Milners and Carsons and Clemenceaus and their following of imperialists and militarists and protectionists".[22]

But the actual struggles of peacemaking would not escalate according to this transnational matrix. They would follow a very different script; and a very different peace would eventually be made. More generally speaking, while they continued to influence the wider debates of 1919 in various ways the efforts of opinion-makers and both nationally and transnationally operating activists and pressure-groups would only have a marginal impact on the course of the peace negotiations and its outcomes. And particularly more left-leaning liberal, socialist and progressive activists and publicists would be immensely disappointed by what they castigated as the "Punic peace" of Versailles.[23]

Partly more successful were activists who came to Paris to lobby on behalf of more specific causes. Most relevant here were those who sought to promote the causes of organised labour, Jewish minority rights, and the suffragette movement. The leaders of organised labour in Europe, the United States and the wider world (yet no labour representatives from the defeated powers) came to Paris to put the improvement of labour relations and working conditions on the peace agenda. Samuel Gompers led a delegation of the American Federation of Labour and would be joined by the leaders of the British Trades Union Congress, the French *Conféderation Générale du Travail* and other trade unions from allied and neutral countries. As chair of the peace conference's Labour commission, he then played a leading role in drafting the constitution of the International Labour Organisation, then established as an agency of the League, whose main purpose was to be to promote improved common labour standards by bringing together the representatives of governments, employers and workers.[24]

Among those whose specific lobbying efforts would have a more general impact on the negotiations were Jewish organisations that campaigned for the

---

[22] *New Republic*, 21 December 1918, pp. 211–12.

[23] See e.g. John Hobson, "A New Holy Alliance", *Nation*, 19 April 1919, pp. 626–7; the editorial "Peace at Any Price" and Lippmann, "Mr. Wilson and His Promises", both in the *New Republic*, 24 May 1919, pp. 100–2, 104–5; "A Punic Peace", *New Republic*, 17 May 1919, pp. 71–3; Addams (1922), pp. 66–8.

[24] Pursuing their own peace agenda, socialists from both sides of the war's trenches took first steps to reconstitute the Second International. This was at the top of the agenda of a conference they held in Bern in February 1919. See Mayer (1967), pp. 375 ff.; Imlay (2018), pp. 57–62.

protection of the religious, cultural and civil minority rights – through the League or by other means – of the Jewish populations that would now become minorities in the different new East European states, particularly in Poland. Most important here were the activities and proposals of the American Jewish Congress and particularly the Joint Foreign Committee, which had been founded in late 1917 and was headed by the journalist Lucien Wolf. They would significantly influence the minority treaties that were eventually drawn up in 1919.[25]

By contrast, the strenuous efforts of the leading representatives of the international women's suffrage movement to place the cause of women's political, citizenship and labour rights on the official agenda of the peace conference would be frustrated. The leader of the French suffrage movement and vice-president of the International Woman Suffrage Alliance, Marguerite de Witt-Schlumberger, her British counterpart Millicent Fawcett and others notably appealed to Wilson to this end, stressed that their cause was vital for the creation of a truly democratic League of Nations and urged him to permit the representatives of women's associations to participate in the deliberations of the conference. But their appeals would be denied. De Witt-Schlumberger reacted by organising a parallel conference in Paris, the Inter-allied Women's Conference, which opened in mid-February 1919. Its delegates would persist with their attempts to put pressure on the assembled male plenipotentiaries. But they would essentially remain futile because the latter deemed their demands far too radical. Nevertheless, Paris thus became an important rallying-point for a rapidly expanding transnational women's movement and network of associations that struggled for their rights.[26]

It should not be forgotten, however, that there were at least as many activists and interest groups – as well as, notably, political parties – that did not campaign for the League or various broadly-speaking "progressive" causes but rather sought to exert pressure on behalf of particular *national* agendas and what they defined as vital national interests. Particularly relevant in the decisive months of 1919 were, for example, the British Unionist Party and its demands for maximal reparations and groups like the *Ligue française* and the *Comité de la rive gauche du Rhin*, which continued their campaigns for a draconian peace that brought tangible territorial security guarantees and compensations from Germany for the human and material losses France had sustained during the war.[27]

In a broader perspective, then, it is critical to understand that the political leaders of the victors, the other plenipotentiaries assembled in Paris and those who sought to represent the vanquished powers were only the most conspicuous protagonists in what was indeed a much wider and more encompassing political struggle about the shape of the peace and the essentials of the postwar

[25] See Fink (2004), pp. 98–9.
[26] See Siegel (2019); Rupp (1997).
[27] Stevenson (1982), pp. 150–1.

order that unfolded in 1919. It was a struggle whose epicentre would be in Paris but that also escalated on a much wider scale. In a profoundly changed transnational setting – in what could be called an expanding and indeed ever more *global* public sphere – the peace negotiations became part and parcel of, and inseparable from, a wider battle not only for different "national minds" but also over who would win over "world opinion".[28]

Essentially, this was a continuation of the ideological and propaganda battles that had escalated during and after the war itself. It now reached a new climax, raging across national, regional and continental boundaries. It was an immensely divisive struggle. In it, not only political leaders and governments but also pressure-groups, parties and of course journalists, publicists and opinion-makers from many different national backgrounds and with many different political-ideological agendas – nationalist and internationalist, imperialist and anti-imperialist, revolutionary and reactionary – put forward their conflicting ideas and schemes, advanced specific demands or raised wider expectations about what kind of peace was to be made and what kind of order had to be established. Ultimately, they all can be seen as contenders in a high-stakes competition over who would determine what constituted a "just peace" and a "just world order" after the Great War. In this constellation, it was all but impossible for the principal peacemakers – and notably for Wilson – to avoid the "tragedy of disappointment" that he had already anticipated on his passage to Europe, or more precisely to avoid disappointing most of the exaggerated expectations that he had raised in the first place and that had then been directed towards him.[29]

One feature of this wider battle, and the "modern" conditions of peacemaking, was the new relevance not only of public opinion but also of journalists and "public opinion-makers". This manifested itself most obviously in the fact that 500 reporters, among them roughly 100 American correspondents, came to Paris. They were eager to gain insights into the ongoing negotiations – and tried their utmost to hold Wilson to his promise of "open diplomacy". Yet they not only sought to inform but also to shape different national publics and "world opinion" in accordance with their own worldviews and interests. As noted, before travelling to Europe Wilson had asserted that "(s)tatesmen must by this time have learned that the opinion of the world is everywhere wide awake and fully comprehends the issues involved".[30] And the liberal editor of the *Manchester Guardian*, C.P. Scott, in February 1919 even went so far as to claim that "the organised opinion of the world" had now become

---

[28] See Daniel (2018), pp. 81 ff.; Leonhard (2018), pp. 681–4.
[29] Creel (1947), p. 206.
[30] Wilson, Annual Message to Congress, 4 December 1917, *PWW*, XLV, p. 198.

"a tremendous weapon" and might well "prove also to be a growing one" – because no power would "dare in the long run expose itself to universal obloquy".[31]

But of course there was not *one* "world opinion". Rather, there was an immense array of different "public opinions" that often were still distinctly national or nationalist. And yet opinions were formed, and debates and controversies raged, not only within national contexts but also across national boundaries and influenced one another in many different ways. While this now occurred across the globe, it became particularly intense in what could be called the transatlantic public sphere. And here Wilson was not the only but the most powerful figure who sought to invoke the new power of "world opinion", who claimed to know how to interpret what it demanded, who sought to educate it, but who also used and instrumentalised the term to advance his own agenda.

II.   Towards a Peace of the Victors. The Hierarchical and Exclusive *Modus Procedendi* of the Peace Negotiations – and Their Overall Trajectory

Yet although or probably rather because they took place in such a challenging transnational environment, and under such challenging modern conditions, the actual, substantive peace negotiations became a remarkably hierarchical and exclusive endeavour. When the peace conference opened on 18 January 1919, representatives of a total of twenty-seven states which had been in a state of war with the Central Powers had gathered at Versailles. They included those representing the new East European states-in-formation, like Poland, which were thus de facto recognised; and they also included delegates from the Dominions, as well as British India. But as neither Germany nor the other defeated powers – or Russia – were represented, the delegates who assembled in the Hall of Mirrors were far from representing a universal "league of the world's people". More importantly, the Paris peace conference remained too exclusive and ultimately lacked the authority to act as a "virtual world government".[32]

In fact, it became clear early on that the peacemaking agenda would be set by those who led the victorious powers. Crucial parameters for the subsequent *modus procedendi* had been set six days before the conference's opening ceremony, on 12 January, when the highest representatives of these powers met and decided to form what became known as the Council of Ten, which until late March would function as the main decision-making body of the Paris proceedings. Throwing into relief its inter-allied character, the Council of

---

[31] C.P. Scott, *Manchester Guardian*, 15 February 1919.
[32] For a different interpretation, see MacMillan (2002), p. 57.

Ten emerged from the Supreme War Council of the Allied Powers and the American Associate Power that had been established during the final stages of the conflict to coordinate the common war effort. It now came to comprise the heads of government and foreign ministers of the main victors – Wilson and Lansing for the United States, Lloyd George and Balfour for Britain, Clemenceau and Pichon for France as well as Vittorio Orlando and Sidney Sonnino for Italy and Prince Saionji and one further Japanese representative. And another critical decision had been made on 12 January, namely that the key negotiations over the terms and conditions of a "preliminary peace" would be pursued – in an informal and confidential manner – within this council.

Wilson, who had earlier actually sought to limit the number of states represented at the conference, had emphasised that the "question of represen-tation" of the smaller powers was "largely one of sentiment and psychology". Yet he had also observed that this mattered in a new way. If they wanted to make a legitimate peace, he impressed on Lloyd George, "the Great Powers" must not "appear to be running the Peace Conference" or give "even the appearance of only consulting Nations when the Great Powers considered they were concerned".[33] In practice, however, this is precisely what happened. Those representing smaller states and "states in process of formation" would only be allowed to present their concerns on issues of immediate concern to them. And the wider "solution" that was found to address the participatory claims of smaller powers – the establishment of a Plenary Conference that comprised delegates from all represented states and gave the proceedings the semblance of a wider peace congress – was indeed no less limited. Discussions between great- and small-power representatives remained brief and compara-tively superficial; and the Plenary Conference was only convened eight times, thus hardly coming close to an ad hoc world parliament.

Essentially, then, a clear hierarchy had been created between the members of the Council of Ten and all other participating states, which in many ways reflected the power realities in the aftermath of the Great War. And Clemenceau certainly reflected Lloyd George's position when he insisted that, fundamentally, the powers that by the end of the war had mobilised 12 million men and had borne the brunt of the sacrifice necessary to win it now also had a right to determine the essentials of the peace settlement.[34]

Eventually, however, having failed to reach decisions on any major question after two months of negotiations, the Council of Ten came to be considered as too big and unwieldy. Chiefly because of the far-ranging problems that the German settlement raised, Wilson thus proposed what from late March – after his return from a month of absence, during which he had sought to shore up

[33] Hankey notes of meeting of the Council of Ten, 12 January 1919, *PWW*, LIV, p. 14, pp. 23–4.
[34] Tardieu (I/1921), p. 110.

support for the League Covenant in the United States – would become the crucial informal decision-making body of the peace conference: the Council of Four. It was here that, aided by their advisers, those who came to be known as the "Big Three" – the American president, Lloyd George and Clemenceau – would ultimately make all critical decisions not only about the German treaty but also about the shape of the postwar Atlantic order. The Italian prime minister Orlando was largely relegated to a more peripheral role except when the negotiations turned to cardinal Italian interests in the South Tyrol and regarding Fiume.[35] The directorate of the "Council of Three" epitomised the hierarchism that became such a salient characteristic of the Paris Peace Conference. Reflecting the post–First World War distribution of power and influence, this development was in some ways a logical response to the growing need to reach mutually tenable agreements on complicated issues that involved cardinal interests of the victorious powers. But it only accentuated the marked tension, if not contradiction, at the heart of peacemaking process – that between the novel egalitarian, inclusive and transparent international politics that particularly Wilson had called for and the ever more high-handed and arcane approach that the most powerful "peacemakers" actually came to pursue.

In the face of extraordinary public interest, and precisely because they confronted such unprecedented demands for "open diplomacy", all of the protagonists, including Wilson, came to place a premium on secrecy – or, more precisely, on confidentiality. This indeed became a hallmark of the negotiations between the Big Three. *En route* to Europe, Wilson and the members of the Inquiry had still agreed that they "must tell the United States the truth about diplomacy, the peace conference, the world" and guarantee "the free flow of news" to the United States in the face of European opposition and censorship.[36] And at the outset of the conference, the American president had underscored towards his European counterparts that he doubted "whether anything less than complete publicity" about the conference proceedings "would satisfy the American public" and stressed that all of them were "responsible to public opinion in their own countries, and the public had a right to know what they had said". But, meeting resistance from Lloyd George and Clemenceau, who explicitly defended French censorship, Wilson admitted that "privacy" might be necessary on certain "occasions".[37] And he came to put his stamp on a common declaration of the Allied and Associated Powers on "publicity", which emphasised that they did "not

---

[35] Council of Four, 24 April–6 May, 29–30 May 1919, Mantoux (1992) I, pp. 290 ff., II, pp. 251 ff.; Nicolson (1931), pp. 336 ff.

[36] Bowman memorandum of Wilson remarks to Inquiry on 10 December 1918, *PWW*, LIII, p. 355.

[37] Hankey notes of meetings of the Council of Ten, 16 and 17 January 1919, *PWW*, LIV, pp. 97–8, 120.

underrate the importance of carrying public opinion with them in the vast task
by which they are confronted" but asserted that certain "limitations" would be
necessary, especially to avoid "premature publicity" that could distort public
impressions of the negotiations and cause unnecessary "misapprehensions"
and "*anxiety*". The American president reasoned that such misapprehensions
could only be dispelled once the results of the peace conference could be
"*viewed* as a whole".[38]

In fact, Wilson thus sought to act according to a more restrictive interpretation
of what he meant by "open diplomacy" that he had advanced in the summer of
1918. Then he had emphasised that "delicate matters" could be discussed confidentially yet maintained that a critical requirement of modern peacemaking was
that "no secret agreements should be entered into" and that "all international
relations, when fixed, should be open, above board, and explicit".[39] In 1919, it
soon became clear that just like the British and French leaders the American
president considered essential confidentiality a crucial prerequisite for successful
negotiations. He even became more resolute than them in placing tight restrictions on information about the deliberations of the Council of Ten and later the
tense negotiations among the Big Three. Trying in vain to counter the impression
that he had abandoned his earlier maxims, he thus came to disappoint all those
who clamoured for unqualified "open diplomacy" and "open covenants openly
arrived at" in and beyond the United States.[40]

That decision-making came to lie to such an extent in the hands of the leaders
of the western democracies had one further notable consequence. In contrast to
pre-war international relations, foreign ministers and professional diplomats
who sought to bring their experience and expertise to bear on the proceedings
were comparatively marginalised at Versailles. This particularly manifested
itself in the fact that Balfour and Pichon had as limited an influence as
Lansing. Those who would play far more important roles were the informal
advisers of the pivotal actors: Tardieu, Kerr and Colonel House (though the
latter's influence waned after he lost Wilson's trust following his unauthorised
attempt to reach a compromise on the Rhineland question). As has rightly been
stressed, Versailles thus inaugurated an underlying trend in the politics of
twentieth-century peacemaking after major wars, including the Cold War,
namely that "very few" political leaders made the most critical decisions.[41]

By contrast, a further significant group at the proceedings – experts
on territorial, legal, financial, economic, historical and other relevant questions – arguably came to play a more prominent part than at previous peace

---

[38] Statement on publicity, to be issued to the Press, amended by Wilson, 17 January 1919,
PWW, LIV, p. 122, and *FRUS PPC-1919*, III, p. 622.
[39] Wilson to Lansing, 12 June 1918, Baker (1923), I, p. 46.
[40] See Keylor (1998), pp. 473–5.
[41] See Steiner (2005), p. 17.

conferences, which in part was certainly attributable to the breadth and complexity of the problems that had to be confronted, from reparations to the territorial questions in Central and Eastern Europe. And yet the work of these experts would ultimately often be subservient to political interests or their role would be that of warning voices that were not heard – as in the case of John Maynard Keynes. Many among the legions of international lawyers, historians, geographers and financial and economic experts who came to Paris would stress how essential "objective", scientifically grounded "expertise" was for modern, "rational" peacemaking. Unsurprisingly, however, though some of them took care to proceed with scientific detachment, most of these experts were actually by no means "objective"; they too were influenced by underlying political considerations and various conceptions of national interest. And at the same time the political instrumentalisation of expertise acquired a new dimension *on all sides*, particularly when it came to the controversial reparations problem and, more generally, the different territorial settlements in Central and Eastern Europe, above all that of the Polish–German border.

The comparatively most influential experts could be found in the ranks of the American, British and French delegations and often came from the Inquiry, the British Foreign Office's Political Intelligence Department and the French *Comité d'Études*. At the outset, it had been decided to create five main commissions whose task would be to deliberate and prepare recommendations on core issues on the conference agenda. The two most important of these commissions would be the ones focusing on the establishment of the League of Nations and on reparations. Eventually, more than fifty expert commissions would be established in 1919; yet only very few of their recommendations would actually have a significant impact on the final decisions. As will be seen, Wilson, Lloyd George and Clemenceau would use expert proposals very selectively, modify them or even disregard them completely – depending on their overriding political and strategic considerations regarding the issues at hand.[42]

Yet the protagonists still had to settle a far more fundamental question, on which they had reached no agreement at the outset and which would long remain unresolved. In short, they still had to decide what status and purpose the peace conference was to have. Here, disparate conceptions came to the fore, but while some were more draconian than others they all distinctly limited the room for eventual substantive discussions with representatives of the vanquished. Early on, Clemenceau had indicated that he contemplated "two Conferences, a preliminary Conference of the Allied Powers, followed by the regular Peace Congress". But the underlying French rationale, which he would resolutely uphold, remained that the victors would agree on the terms

---

[42] See Leonhard (2018), pp. 674–81.

of a "preliminary" peace that would then be imposed on Germany, thus making it de facto a definite peace. Only more general aspects of the postwar settlement, such as the League of Nations, were to be deliberated at a general "Peace Congress".[43] Lloyd George had also proposed a "preliminary conference" of the victorious powers and then "more formal Conferences on peace" in which all belligerents, including the defeated powers, would participate. But, as the young diplomat Harold Nicolson noted, the underlying British premise was likewise that the victors would set the terms of the "preliminary peace" and then essentially compel Germany to accept them. The British protagonists thus also ruled out any negotiations on core issues such as territorial questions and German disarmament and only envisaging discussions of minor details and certain financial and economic terms, though not the critical question of reparations.[44] For his part, Wilson had agreed that there should be a preliminary conference of the Allied and associated powers. But he had originally maintained that once the victors had worked out basic agreements it would be essential to proceed to a general peace congress at which German representatives could also "state their case".[45] Crucially, however, he had not specified whether he envisaged actual negotiations with the vanquished power.

But there would never be a general Peace Congress; and the notion of some kind of "preliminary" settlement came to be superseded by the conception, and reality, of an all but *definitive* peace treaty whose terms and conditions the victors had determined in advance and that would ultimately be handed to the German delegation, on 7 May, on the understanding that there would be no oral negotiations of any kind. Essentially, then, while it would have been extremely difficult, if not impossible, to negotiate anything approaching a mutually tenable compromise peace between the victors and the vanquished under the conditions of 1919, this was never even attempted.

The reason for this was not primarily that the victors had never quite managed to clarify in the early stages of the proceedings whether they were preparing a final treaty or only a basis for subsequent negotiations with Germany at a decisive Peace Congress.[46] Nor was it just a consequence of the immense, in their subjective perception even more acute time pressures under which the peacemakers had to operate after Wilson's return from the United States in mid-March. Rather, what played a decisive role was – at one level – precisely that even when they resorted to the hierarchical-confidential mode of the Council of Four Wilson, Lloyd George and Clemenceau found it so exceedingly hard to find even a modicum of common ground.

---

[43] Clemenceau statement, Supreme War Council, 12 January 1919, *PWW*, LIV, p. 25.

[44] Nicolson (1931), pp. 97–8.

[45] Wilson here adhered to earlier positions. See Wiseman, 16 October 1918, *PWW*, LI, pp. 347–52; Wilson remarks, 10 December 1918, Swem memorandum, Wilson Papers.

[46] Nicolson (1931), pp. 100–1.

Consequently, the compromises they managed to forge were so strained that they could all too easily unravel under the pressures of wider negotiations with the German delegation.

Yet what also came into play here, and should not be disregarded, were indeed concomitant underlying assumptions and outlooks that, with some modifications, all the western protagonists shared. Crucial was the assumption that as the highest representatives of powers that had not only been victorious but also represented more advanced – democratic – systems of political and civilisational order, they had a claim and indeed a prerogative to set the essential terms of the peace and the new international order. On the same grounds, they accorded themselves the authority to impose these terms on those who, however fervently they claimed to represent a new, democratic Germany, in their eyes had to be held accountable for the actions of a power that had not only been defeated but also transgressed standards of "civilised conduct" during the war and only effected a "regime change" when defeat seemed imminent. All the victors held that the vanquished now had to accept their rules – and, essentially, a more or less extensive period of "probation". Only their medium- and longer-term outlooks continued to diverge. While Wilson and Lloyd George still envisaged a relatively swift integration of a compliant German republic into the postwar order, Clemenceau's priority was to constrain and isolate France's menacing neighbour as far and as long as possible, irrespective of whatever advances it made towards consolidating a democratic system of government.

What thus ensued in 1919 was and remained a peacemaking process directed by the victors that comprised four distinct stages: (1) a first general inter-allied phase lasting from mid-January until mid-February that centred on negotiations over the Draft Covenant of the League as well as deliberations about the future of the former German colonies and the envisaged mandate system, but remained inconclusive with a view to all other core questions of European, transatlantic and global reordering; (2) an interim phase between mid-February and mid-March during which Wilson campaigned for the Draft Covenant in the United States, and Lloyd George and especially Clemenceau sought to re-set the agenda in accordance with their priorities; (3) the in many ways most decisive phase between 24 March and mid-April when the crucial struggles within the Council of Four took place. This brought the gravest crisis of the entire process – when for a time, in early April, a failure of the entire peace conference seemed possible. But it was also the phase when, after Wilson's endeavours to regain the initiative and Lloyd George's efforts to adopt a somewhat more balanced approach vis-à-vis Germany had met with Clemenceau's determined resistance, the Big Three ultimately managed to forge the conglomeration of compromises that came to lie at the core of the "draft" peace treaty, which would then be presented to the German plenipotentiaries on 7 May. This, then, was also the time when the critical decisions about the original parameters of the postwar Atlantic order were made; (4) and finally a phase of "non-negotiations" between the victors and vanquished that lasted from early May until mid-June. After the victors had insisted that German representatives would only be allowed to submit written reactions and counter-proposals to their draft treaty, these "non-negotiations" took the form of an exchange or rather a "war of notes" that quickly escalated into a mutually alienating stand-off between overall intransigence on the part of the western leaders (challenged but not altered by Lloyd George's eleventh-hour attempts to push for some conciliatory modifications) and Brockdorff-Rantzau's counter-productive attempts to put pressure on the victors through a campaign of "progressive" counter-proposals that were intended to under-score how far their terms departed from those of a "peace of justice" and to rally "world opinion" behind the German cause.

This final phase would confirm that the peace settlement after the Great War would ultimately be forced on the vanquished and thus be marred by indisputably fundamental legitimacy deficits. It would confirm that the original Atlantic international system that emerged after the cataclysm would essentially be a truncated system, marked by inner strains and contradictions. And it would confirm that what was negotiated in 1919 could only mark a *first step* in the search for a more sustainable and more legitimate transatlantic peace order for the long twentieth century – which in many ways made this search even more onerous than it would have been anyway after this century's formative catastrophe. In the following, it will be examined in greater depth why and how this came to be the essential outcome of the Versailles process.

15

Novel Superstructure of a New Atlantic Order?

The Struggle to Found the League of Nations
and the Limitations of the Covenant of 1919

On 22 January, the plenipotentiaries assembled in the Council of Ten resolved that the establishment of the league was "essential to the maintenance of the world settlement" and that it "should be created as *an integral* part of the *general treaty of peace*".[1] In accordance with Wilson's cardinal goal, this would eventually be achieved. And with Lloyd George's support, the American president successfully insisted, against French objections, that deliberations over a covenant for the new international organisation would be given priority at the outset of the conference.[2] In a wider context, it had to be decided how far the League could actually become a universal international organisation – how far it could provide a framework of principles, rules and procedures on a *global* scale – for a "new *world* order" – and how far, and on what terms, it would really be open to all states or "nations" that desired to join it.

But the controversies that hence ensued among the victors – in and outside of the League Commission – mainly revolved around the question of how the League could be established as the "superstructure" of a new transatlantic system of "collective security" and concerted conflict resolution. And they revolved around the wider question of whether a novel organisation of this kind could really become not only an authoritative but also an *effective* mechanism through which Europe's cardinal postwar problems – above all the German problem – could be addressed and European security could be fostered. In turn, this was intimately connected with a further fundamental question. It was the question of whether the League would be founded essentially as an exclusive "victors' institution" or whether it could be set up as a more inclusive institution that either admitted the vanquished powers from the outset or at least offered a clear perspective of integrating and thus committing them to its rules and obligations in the foreseeable future.

I. The Protagonists and Their Converging and Diverging Approaches

The drawn-out negotiations within the League Commission and the controversies surrounding them revealed very soon that the visions and conceptions

---

[1] Hankey notes of meeting of the Council of Ten, 22 January 1919, *PWW*, LIV, p. 206.
[2] Tardieu (II/1921), pp. 88–91; *FRUS 1919*, III, 535–7.

596

of the principal American and British champions of the new organisation who now took the lead, Wilson and Cecil, were substantially at odds both with the more far-reaching legalist ideas of the key French negotiator Léon Bourgeois and, more importantly, with the more traditionalist, fundamentally *realpolitical* outlook and conceptions that Clemenceau and Tardieu asserted on France's behalf.

Relying on British cooperation, Wilson sought to forge a Covenant that embodied his progressive, *evolutionary* and at the core political rather than legalistic conception, whose underlying aim remained to establish the League as a "superstructure" that would not only safeguard peace but also effect a qualitative transformation of international politics. The American president reiterated that the "collective security" system he envisaged also had to include provisions for the use of force as a measure of last resort. But he mainly reasserted that he desired the League to become the institutional framework for a new kind of international concert that was to allow the representatives of states – and, in an elevated capacity, the political leaders of the great powers – to settle disputes and respond to "the collective aspirations of humanity". He thus essentially negotiated on behalf of a vision that made the new institution "a permanent clearinghouse" at the heart of the new international order "where every nation can come, the small as well as the great". It was to "arbitrate and correct mistakes" that were "inevitable" in the settlement the victorious powers were "trying to make" and which could then be remedied "one by one" over time. At the same time, he re-accentuated his vision of the League as a central forum for an emerging international society where the new force of international "public opinion" could exert both a deterring and a pacifying influence.[3]

Yet Wilson was by now also clearly committed to establishing the League initially as an organisation shaped and dominated by the – democratic – victors, an organisation to which the defeated powers, and notably Germany, would only be admitted after they had successfully completed a period of probation. It was with these priorities in mind that he sought to impress on the other representatives that the foundation of the League of Nations was the most critical part of the entire peace settlement and that the new institution would be the "structural iron" of the peace, especially in Europe. Without it, he warned, whatever peace was made would merely be a "house of cards".[4]

Cecil, who would become the other main architect of the League at Versailles, was determined to fend for a similarly political yet more distinctly hierarchical conception. He sought to persuade Wilson, the other negotiators – and not least his own prime minister – that it was imperative to establish a

---

[3] Wilson address, 25 January 1919, *PWW*, LIV, pp. 266–7; Wilson remarks, 14 February 1919, Wilson (1939), p. 239.

[4] Wilson statement to Democratic Committee, 28 February 1919, *PWW*, LV, pp. 317–18.

"solid organisation" which, at the core, institutionalised a new kind of international, essentially transatlantic concert of great powers. He particularly
stressed the need for a strong Executive Council in which Britain and the
United States co-operated, as essential hegemonic powers, with other pre-
eminent powers to safeguard international security and settle international
disputes. Like Wilson, Cecil thus emphasised that the League chiefly had to
establish clearly defined political rules and procedures for the concerted
management and peaceful settlement of international conflicts. But he
remained strictly opposed to the idea of compulsory arbitration and mandatory sanctions, still envisioning the organisation as an inter- rather than
supranational organisation that did not override essential attributes of state
sovereignty. In his view, this was essential not only to ensure that more
powerful states actually committed themselves to the novel institution but
also to turn it into an effective mechanism for the management and supervision of international order. In contrast to Wilson, Cecil also insisted during
the negotiations that the new international concert system he aimed to set up
through the League could only really function if Germany was included from
the outset.[5]

   But the prevalent American and British visions of the new organisation
would soon be challenged at Versailles. And arguably the most substantial
challenge came from Léon Bourgeois in his role as the principal French
representative on the League Commission. At one level, Bourgeois fought for
the far-reaching legalist-internationalist conception of a *société des nations*
that he and his collaborators in the *Association française* had developed; at
another level, he was one actor in the wider French effort to bargain for firmer
Anglo-American security guarantees vis-à-vis Germany. He strove to persuade
his British and American counterparts that the League's cornerstone had to be
a "binding regime of international law" that made the arbitration of international disputes compulsory. And he campaigned for a robust security
regime that included mandatory sanctions against aggressors, renewing his
demand for an "international force" under the authority of the League. In
many ways, Bourgeois' chief concern remained to found an international
organisation that could effectively protect French security and pre-empt
renewed German aggression. Though conceiving it as a "universal" institution
in the longer run, he thus also insisted that Germany should only be allowed to
enter the *société des nations* once its elites, and people, had demonstrated their
adherence to democratic principles and "the rule of law".[6]

   Yet the Versailles negotiations revealed very clearly that in contrast to
Wilson, Cecil and other champions of the League, the political leaders of

---

[5] Cecil Diary, 5 February 1919, Cecil Papers. See Johnson (2013), p. 104.

[6] Bourgeois statements, Minutes of League Commission meeting, 11 February 1919, *PWW*
LV, pp. 74–7; Bourgeois (1919), pp. 50–2; Jackson (2013), pp. 262–4.

Britain and France had formed distinctly different ideas about the merit and purpose of the new organisation and, in different ways, maintained more sceptical and "realistic" outlooks on its potential to guarantee peace after the Great War. And, crucially, they represented widespread attitudes in their governments and among the political elites in their respective countries.

Each in his own way, Lloyd George and Clemenceau would pursue their own League agendas at Versailles and bring their own, more functionalist ideas of the organisation's role and purpose in the postwar order to bear on the negotiations. The British premier basically maintained that the League should be set up as a platform for a new great-power concert that was modelled on the Supreme War Council and serve the core purpose of facilitating the consultation between political leaders in dealing with "international quarrels" and managing the problems and conflicts the war had left behind. At the core, he still envisaged it as an instrument of select cooperation and strategic burden-sharing, above all between the Anglo-American powers through which, ultimately, Britain would be able to play a hegemonic role in the postwar world without making hard and fast general, potentially unlimited commitments or conceding any significant limitations of its national and imperial sovereignty.

Lloyd George's opposition to a more ambitious institutional architecture and any provisions that threatened to curtail the British government's ultimate decision-making power in matters of war and peace became even more pronounced at Versailles. And it was shared by a majority of the members of the Imperial War Cabinet, as well as key advisers like Hankey and Kerr. When he finally focused his attention on the League in late January, the British premier went so far as to suggest that in-depth negotiation over its formation should be postponed until after the end of the peace conference. And he underscored his opposition to any attempt to establish through the covenant a far-reaching system of "collective security" that specified "certain stated conditions" under which its member states were obliged to go to war. Lloyd George argued that no nation would "commit itself" in such a "vital matter" except by the "free decision of its own Government". He warned that disregarding such vital concerns of political sovereignty would not only deter the principal powers – including Britain and the United States – from joining the new organisation but also lead to "the destruction of the League itself". He thus recommended that the Covenant's "paper obligations" should be kept to an "absolute minimum". And he re-accentuated his axiom that the new institution should mainly serve as a framework for "continuous consultation" among the great powers "under a system" that enabled them "to come to prompt and great decisions on world problems" as they arose.[7]

---

[7] Lloyd George statements, 31 January 1919, Cecil Diary, 31 January 1919, Cecil Papers. He drew on Kerr's memorandum on "The League of Nations", 30 January 1919, Lothian Papers, G.D. 40/17/54.

Clemenceau and Tardieu maintained even stronger reservations both vis-à-vis Wilson's conception of the League and Bourgeois' juridical internationalism. They never came to believe that even a robust *société des nations* could become the centrepiece of a new international security system that would stabilise European peace and above all furnish effective guarantees against renewed German "aggression". On the eve of the peace conference, Clemenceau had argued in the French Parliament that a truly vibrant and functioning *Société des Nations* required, not a covenant of legalistic provisions and guarantees but nothing less than a moral transformation; a fundamental change of "spiritual dispositions" in "every state" – including Germany – was needed, which even under favourable conditions would take a long time. He thus insisted all the more that for the foreseeable future French and European security had to rest on different, more tangible foundations.[8] And in his view, which had not changed, these could only be provided by a determined containment of Germany and, crucially, by a firm postwar alliance of the victors. It was in this sense that he insisted that the League "was to be" first and foremost "a League of Defence".[9] Tardieu shared both the premier's outlook and his priorities. Fundamentally, he too was convinced that only "in the indeterminate future" one would be able to count on "the sufficient development of civilisation and on the moral sense of people" to "look to a powerfully organised Society or League of Nations as an obstacle to wars of conquest"; until such a League acquired "the necessary authority" one had to rely on more tried and tested alliance policies – and "the material guarantees of peace" that their victory had placed in the hands of "the Allies".[10]

Essentially, the French premier and his key adviser were determined to use the deliberations over the League to bargain with Wilson and Lloyd George for firmer and more specific security guarantees and to draw the Anglo-American powers as far as possible into a transatlantic alliance – or security community – of the victors. As noted, in early January Clemenceau had assured House of his support for the new organisation for precisely this reason. At the same time, following Tardieu's recommendations, they seized on the League negotiations to bargain for British and American concessions on issues they considered more critical, especially the "material" guarantees they sought through the creation of a *de facto* Rhenish buffer-state.[11]

---

[8] Clemenceau speech, *Chambre*, 16 January 1919, MAE, SDN, vol. 6.

[9] Hankey notes of meeting of the Council of Ten, 28 January 1919, *PWW*, LIV, p. 328.

[10] See Tardieu's revised draft of a note by Foch, 10 January 1919, Tardieu Papers, vol. 422.

[11] House diary, 7 January 1919, *PWW*, LIII, pp. 652–3; Clemenceau comments, 27 March 1919, Poincaré (1926–33), XI, pp. 283–4; Tardieu memorandum, 2 February 1919, Tardieu Papers, vol. 417; Tardieu comments, 25 February 1919, Fonds Clemenceau, 6N 73-2, SHD-DAT.

Wilson would ultimately fulfil his aspiration to lay the groundwork for a League of Nations at the peace conference. At the core, this outcome was unquestionably the result of Anglo-American cooperation and, more precisely, the collaboration between and relatively congruent conceptions of Wilson and Cecil, assisted by the most influential British and American legal experts on the League Commission, Hurst and Miller. This collaboration did not evolve without marked conflicts. Important conceptual differences regarding core provisions of the structure of the organisation, "collective security", the peaceful settlement of disputes and, notably, peaceful change had to be reconciled. But their joined efforts paved the way for the eventual agreements forged in the League Commission. These efforts had begun with private deliberations in January 1919 that gave rise to the Hurst–Miller draft, which in turn represented a compromise between earlier American and British League plans. What essentially evolved as a two-stage process gave rise to the first draft of the Covenant, which Wilson presented on 14 February, and the revised but not substantially altered version that was approved by the Plenary Conference on 29 April 1919, and which indeed became a centrepiece of the peace treaty of Versailles.[12]

The League of Nations would not have been founded in the way it was, and it would not have become an integral element of the postwar system, if Wilson had not made this the absolute priority of his peace agenda – and if he had not put his entire political weight and prestige behind it. But the League's final Covenant and the key provisions and organisational structure it contained were heavily influenced by the British plans that had been drawn up since 1917, particularly those developed by Cecil and Smuts. The American president adopted and adapted essential elements of these designs. Yet he also insisted on what he saw as the key to the League's "collective security" system, a *political* rather than legal commitment of the signatories, then enshrined in the Covenant's crucial Article X, to "preserve" the territorial integrity and political independence of all member states of the new organisation against external aggression.[13]

Essentially, what became the "constitution" of a strikingly hierarchical organisation in which the victorious great powers played key roles and accorded themselves essential prerogatives as permanent members of the organisation's crucial Executive Council – derived from a compromise between Wilson's and prevalent British conceptions. It was thus clearly based on Anglo-American premises rather than qualitatively different and indeed more ambitious "legalist" conceptions of how the League was to enforce "collective security" and the rule of international law that Léon Bourgeois sought to assert in the interest of

[12] Miller (1921), pp. 400–1; Wilson statement, 14 February 1919, *PWW*, LV, p. 160; *FRUS 1919*, III, pp. 210–15.
[13] Wilson statements, session 6 February 1919, Miller (1928), I, pp. 168–70.

France. In all cardinal respects Bourgeois struggled in vain to amend what remained a quintessentially Anglo-American blueprint.

More generally, what soon became clear in the spring of 1919 was that in the post–First World War constellation there was no prospect of founding a League of Nations with significant attributes of supranational authority, a robust regime of compulsive arbitration and far-reaching sanctions against aggressors, and an international force to enforce its decisions. Even less was there a prospect of creating an organisation on radical internationalist premises – something akin to a federation of nations with a higher level of supranational authority and integration, and with powerful novel institutions like an international parliament. For those who had decisive influence on the shaping of the Covenant, the Anglo-American protagonists of the League Commission, did not envision an organisation that imposed any significant infringements on the sovereignty of its member states – particularly the great powers that were designated to play leading roles within the new organisation. Essentially, they considered such infringements neither desirable nor politically feasible. And they maintained that the League could only gain the essential support of its member states *and* would be more effective in guarding peace if it established a different, essentially political system of "collective security". Above all, however, they emphasised that it had to become a permanent framework for the political management and settlement of international disputes that left the final decisions about what course of action would be pursued at the discretion of the political leaders of states, particularly the leaders of the great powers that had won the war.

Yet what mattered more for the future stabilisation of Europe and the possibilities of forging an effective Atlantic peace system after the Great War was something else – namely that because of the complex compromises the victors had to make, and above all because of Wilson's hardening attitude towards the German government and overriding French imperatives, the League of Nations would be established as an *institution of the victors* that excluded the vanquished powers, particularly the fledgling German republic. Indeed, at the end of the peace negotiations there was no certainty, and no consensus among the victors, as to when and precisely on what conditions Germany might eventually be admitted to the new organisation – and, in a wider sense, integrated into the postwar comity of nations. This salient outcome of the Versailles negotiations essentially limited the League's capacity to become the key mechanism of security, stabilisation and conflict resolution within a new Atlantic order. It did not make it impossible to turn the League into what Wilson and British protagonists still desired it to become: the framing structure for a new, essentially integrative transatlantic concert of states that committed both the victors and the vanquished to new principles and ground-rules and through which they could manage and as far as possible settle conflicts over time. But it created significant obstacles for such an evolution of the new institution.

II. Crucial Disagreements: "Collective Security", Arbitration and the Authority of the League

The Hurst–Miller draft and the conceptions it embodied became the basis both of the League Commission's deliberations and the wider debates about the League in the spring of 1919. Faced with an Anglo-American design that in critical respects clearly fell short of what they deemed essential, the French representatives on the commission, Bourgeois and Larnaude, tried their utmost to secure substantial changes. Yet what they advocated actually went beyond mere amendments; it was the call for a fundamentally different, far more ambitious juridical-internationalist League. Bourgeois took the lead and made the case for an organisation with far-reaching authority and capacities. He reiterated that it would only be able to safeguard peace and security if it instituted a tight regime of mandatory arbitration and its members were "legally required to enforce its decisions".[14]

In a narrower sense, the amendments Bourgeois proposed were designed not only to create a "strong" League but also to make it an institution that was dominated by the victors and whose cardinal purpose would be to establish and uphold the firmest possible guarantees against future German threats. Most controversial was his proposal to create a permanent "international force" that was to be "so superior" that "no nation or combination of nations can challenge or resist it". Bourgeois sought to persuade Wilson that a "military organization" that brought together "national contingents" under the authority of a permanent general staff was imperative because it would allow them to be "rapidly co-ordinated against an aggressive State". He warned that without such provisions, the League would become "nothing but a dangerous façade". At bottom, Bourgeois held that an international force was essential because it offered the only effective means either to deter or to ensure a rapid response to another German attack. Like Clemenceau and Tardieu, he emphasised that France guarded the "frontier of liberty" on the Rhine and could not be "tranquil" unless it could "count on the effective help of the other members of the League", above all the United States and Britain. Further, he proposed a League-based "system of international surveillance and verification for both troops and armaments" to control Germany's fulfilment of its disarmament obligations.[15]

Finally, Bourgeois called for provisions in the Covenant that made arbitration mandatory for the settlement of international disputes and established the principle of automatic sanctions against aggressors. This went hand in hand with the attempt to strengthen the authority of both the League Council and

[14] Bourgeois note, submitted on 11 February 1919, Bourgeois Papers, vol. 18.
[15] Bourgeois statements, Minutes of League Commission meeting, 11 February 1919, *PWW* LV, pp. 74–7; Bourgeois to Clemenceau, 7 February 1919, Bourgeois Papers, vol. 18; Jackson (2013), pp. 268–73; Miller (1928), I, pp. 192–5.

the so far only vaguely envisaged International Court of Justice, which in his conception had to be given more far-reaching jurisdiction than the pre-war era's Hague court. His proposals here effectively revived earlier attempts by the Belgian foreign minister Paul Hymans to gain Anglo-American support for a system of compulsory arbitration at the heart of the new organisation's security regime. Hymans had suggested making it obligatory for League members to comply with the decisions the Council had reached, if they had been unanimous, and thus ultimately to enforce any sanctions the Council imposed.

What Bourgeois fought for was a *société des nations* that not only estab-lished a far-reaching system of arbitration and sanctions but also had the military means to enforce its decisions. He impressed on his Anglo-American interlocutors that without such a system and such capacities, the new organ-isation would only be "effective in appearance" but "in reality a trap of nations of good faith".[16] The former French premier thus became the most powerful spokesman of a robust juridical internationalism at Versailles; but he also advocated an agenda that was essentially shaped by essential French interests.

More fundamentally, Bourgeois argued that the preservation of peace after the catastrophe of the Great War would require states to accept that, to a certain extent, their sovereignty would hence be limited. It was the "role" of the League "to specify these limits", to "fix them equitably on the basis of mutuality and reciprocity". His was thus an inherently universal conception. But because he insisted that the League had to be founded *by* the victors and as an organisation *of* the victors, it simply could not (yet) establish the same guarantees and sanctions for all. Bourgeois only envisaged the inclusion of Germany and the other defeated powers at a later stage, once the League had been consolidated and the latter could be integrated under safe conditions.[17] It is important to note that neither Clemenceau nor other senior French policy-makers backed Bourgeois' far-reaching vision during the peace negotiations. Yet the French premier did not rein in his efforts because he considered them useful in two respects: to underscore French security concerns and, eventually, to bargain for "supplementary guarantees".[18]

Yet Bourgeois' struggle would essentially be futile. His proposals called for structural changes and infringements of national sovereignty that none of the governments of the principal victors, including the French, were prepared to accept. At the same time, they challenged the very premises of Wilson's League conception as well as the plans that Cecil strove to implement on Britain's behalf. Both rejected Bourgeois' demands more or less categorically. Yet in

---

[16] Minutes of League Commission meeting, 11 February 1919, *PWW*, LV, pp. 74–7.
[17] Bourgeois address, Fifth Plenary Session of the Peace Conference, 28 April 1919, MAE, PV-SDN.
[18] Clemenceau statement, 27 March 1919, Poincaré (1926–33), XI, pp. 283–4.

response to his challenge they also reasserted their less rigidly binding, less far-reaching and ultimately political rather than legalistic ideas of how the League was to provide "collective security" and safeguard peace. Wilson acknowledged that the French government desired to "obtain the best guarantees possible" before entering the new organisation and acknowledged that a German "menace" could resurface if "the militarist madness has not been destroyed" there. But he did not see the danger of a sudden German aggression and argued that initially the security of France and of Europe would be assured by the "complete disarmament" of the defeated power, which would create a "period of safety". With a view to the League, the American president insisted that it was essential to distinguish between what was and what was not politically "possible" – and he stressed that bringing American forces under international control would be "in direct contradiction" to the US Constitution and American "public opinion".[19]

But Wilson's disagreement with Bourgeois was of a more fundamental nature. He strictly opposed the idea of an organisation that by establishing an "international army" would essentially substitute "international militarism for national militarism".[20] Rather, as he declared again on 14 February, the League he sought would depend "primarily and chiefly upon one great force", the "moral force of the public opinion of the world – the cleansing and clarifying and compelling influences of publicity". Wilson clung to the view that this "force" would play a crucial role in transcending a system of world politics dominated by "intrigues" and sinister "designs". But it would be misleading to conclude that his entire conception rested on this premise. In fact, he now stated explicitly that the League's security system would also rely on "(a)rmed force", asserting that "if the moral force of the world will not suffice, the physical force of the world shall". But he still maintained that "physical force" was only to be used as "the last resort" – that the Covenant was to create a new "constitution of peace", not "a league of war".[21]

At the same time, Wilson insisted on a political conception of "collective security" that essentially did not limit national sovereignty. As he put it, to Bourgeois' dismay, the League had to furnish "definite guarantees of peace" against aggressors, but its provisions had to be "flexible" and "general" when it came to the means that the member states would adopt to honour these guarantees. It was to be a "vehicle" of new international power structure in which power "may be varied at the discretion of those who exercise it" – the governments of the member states – in accordance with the "changing circumstances of the time" and what was politically possible at the national level.[22] Yet Wilson was indeed aware that to be effective the League's

[19] Minutes of League Commission meeting, 11 February 1919, *PWW*, LV, pp. 75–80.
[20] *Ibid.*
[21] Wilson statement, 14 February 1919, *PWW*, LV, p. 175.
[22] *Ibid.*

"concert" would require some relinquishment of sovereignty. And he would make some efforts to gain domestic-political support for what would indeed have constituted a significant departure in the history of US foreign policy.

Meeting members of the Senate's Foreign Relations Committee and the House Foreign Affairs Committee on 26 February 1919, Wilson would argue that as a member of the League the United States should be prepared – like other nations – to "relinquish some of its sovereignty" for "the good of the world". At the core, this was "warranted" because "any concert of action of the nations to eliminate war from the world" could not work without it. But the American president was careful to emphasise that the new Covenant did not imply a "surrender of sovereignty" when it came to the final *political* decisions of how governments would respond to aggression – and notably did not limit the Senate's authority to decide whether the United States would use force and, ultimately, go to war.[23] On similar grounds, Wilson maintained his opposition to compulsory arbitration. He argued that arbitration had to be regarded as only one of several possible modes to settle international disputes. In the "vision" he continued to champion at the peace conference, the League of Nations was to be founded as a mechanism that offered a range of more broadly conceived political processes of concerted conflict resolution in which the members of the Executive Council were to play pivotal roles yet also retain essential political discretion.[24]

Sharing Wilson's outlook on core questions of sovereignty and "collective security", Cecil opposed Bourgeois' proposals even more vigorously, and he herein reflected Lloyd George's positions and the prevalent views in the British government. He admonished that no country, and certainly no great power, would "accept an international general staff that would have the right to interfere in its own naval and military plans". More broadly, Cecil still rejected any significant limitations of state and especially great-power sovereignty on cardinal questions of international security. In his judgement, what lay behind Bourgeois' demands was another, more specific agenda. He held that they were designed to ensure through a novel supranational regime the military superiority of France vis-à-vis an essentially disarmed Germany – and to create an organisation that could primarily be used to contain the defeated power and enforce its compliance with the victors' peace terms.

On the military front, Cecil proposed an alternative that basically reflected British and American preferences yet could hardly be deemed satisfactory from a French perspective, suggesting that a permanent commission should be established to "advise" the League Council on "naval and military questions".[25]

[23] Wilson speech, 26 February 1919, News Report, 26 February 1919, *PWW*, LV, pp. 268, 273.
[24] Wilson statement, 14 February 1919, *PWW*, LV, p. 175.
[25] Cecil statements, League Commission, 11 and 13 February 1919, Miller (1928), II, pp. 296, 290–3; I, pp. 247–8.

In the main, however, he used harsh language to "persuade" Bourgeois and Larnaude to accept the essentials of the Anglo-American Draft Covenant. He impressed on the French delegates that the League was "their only means of getting the assistance of America and England". If they persisted with their obstructionist course France would be "left without an ally in the world". Cecil observed that due to their geopolitical positions the United States and Britain could afford to maintain a distance from continental European affairs after the war; what they offered through the covenant should thus be regarded as a strategic "present" to France. Should the French delegation refuse to accept the essentials of the Hurst–Miller draft and the Anglo-American offer it contained, thus his stern warning, the French government would have no alternative options to obtain firmer guarantees – and have to countenance instead the formation of "an alliance between Britain and the United States".[26]

In what he described as one of their confidential "heart to heart talks" House had earlier sought to impress on Clemenceau in very similar terms why the League provided the best possible solution to French security problems after, in his assessment, Europe's old balance-of-power system had irretrievably collapsed. He argued that there was no longer a "balance of power as far as the Continent was concerned because Russia had disappeared and both Germany and Austria had gone under", so that France was now the only "great military power" left on the European continent. And he noted that this new constellation was also "apparent" to British policymakers, who did not like it because, in his view, they still had a fundamental interest in re-establishing an "equilibrium" in Europe. Crucially, he sought to present the League as the only mechanism that would furnish tangible British – and American – guarantees for France, observing that the alternative of a formal alliance between the victors was undesirable and politically out of the question from Wilson's point of view. House thus urged Clemenceau not to squander the "chance which the United States offered through the League of Nations" as "it would never come again because there would never be another opportunity"; and he sought to re-assure him that the American president was certain to "force [the League Covenant] through" the American Senate.[27]

When speaking in front of the Plenary Conference on 25 January, Wilson had in his own way sought to highlight that the League had to be regarded as the only "superstructure" which could make certain that the United States would commit itself to acting as a guarantor of European peace after the Great War. And he had also pointed to one core challenge that those who sought to establish a League-based system of "collective security" had to address: the asymmetrical security constellation between the United States and Europe or,

---

[26] Cecil Diary, 11 February 1919, Cecil Papers; Miller (1928), I, pp. 216–20; Johnson (2013), pp. 104–7.

[27] House diary, 7 January 1919, *PWW*, LIII, pp. 652–3.

put differently, the marked disparities between American and European – and particularly French – perceptions of future security threats and needs. Wilson noted that the United States had a less acute interest in the League than its European associates because no cardinal American security interests seemed to be at stake any longer; it had now become far "less likely" that America with its "great territories" and "extensive sea borders" should "suffer from the attack of enemies". He therefore impressed on the assembled delegates that the American "ardour" for the League did not spring from "fear" but from the new "ideals which have come to consciousness in the war". And he insisted that the United States "would feel that she could not take part in guaranteeing [the] European settlements" that would be made at the peace conference "unless that guarantee involved the continuous superintendence of the peace of the world by the associated nations of the world". In short, Wilson thus underscored that the American republic would only engage in safeguarding and stabilising Europe's postwar order if a League of Nations was established – on his premises.[28]

III. Institutionalising a Novel International Concert? The Key Provisions of the Covenant and the Envisaged Architecture of the League of Nations

The initial draft of the Covenant of the League of Nations that the American president presented after a very short period of intense and often acrimonious negotiations on 14 February did not entirely correspond with his core aspirations; but it was indeed a constitutional blueprint that would by and large establish the new international organisation on Anglo-American terms, or more precisely on the terms of a compromise between Wilson's and British essentials that the Hurst–Miller draft had prefigured. And these would essentially remain unaltered in the final League Covenant that then became an integral part of the Versailles treaty and system. Only a few minor concessions to Bourgeois' and Hymans' aims and agendas had been made. Yet the draft did not include any provisions for sanctions, a far-reaching arms-control regime, compulsory arbitration or an international army and general staff.

The centrepiece of what was to be the organisation"s novel system of "collective security" was Article X of the Covenant, which can also be seen as Wilson's crucial contribution. As we have seen, ever since he had advanced his first general ideas for a peace league Wilson had insisted that one of the central purposes of such a league had to be to protect the integrity and independence of its members, particularly of smaller states. And during the League Commission's decisive discussions in early February, he indeed

[28] Protocol of Plenary Session, 25 January 1919, *PWW*, LIV, pp. 266–7.

emerged as the most powerful advocate of what the Hurst–Miller draft had proposed as the Covenant's most far-reaching provision: the obligation at the core of Article X that the High Contracting Powers not only had to "respect" but also, and crucially, to "preserve as against external aggression the territorial integrity and existing political independence" of all member states.[29]

Wilson now stressed more unequivocally than before that in his judgement this general guarantee was vital because it manifested that the new organisation meant "business and not only discussion". He even called Article X "the key to the whole Covenant". But the American president also proposed an amendment stipulating that in the event of an aggression the Executive Council would be called upon to "advise the plan and the means by which this obligation shall be fulfilled". He argued that this amendment was necessary to clarify how the guarantee would be implemented. But its effect was to blunt the power of Article X, for the execution of any guarantee obligations was now made dependent on a *unanimous* decision in the executive council, and even then it was merely authorised to *advise* appropriate measures. This gave the members of the Council, i.e. above all the great powers, essential political leeway in deciding how – or whether – they would act. Wilson deemed this qualification essential not only because it accorded with his overall political conception of the how the League was to operate but also because he saw it as a critical precondition for gaining the support of the US Senate for the Covenant. For he was well aware that this support depended on making clear that the Senate's ultimate political authority when it came to authorising, ultimately, armed intervention in response to aggression would not be curtailed, let alone overruled. Wilson's amendment was incorporated in the Covenant after Cecil had backed it on behalf of the British government and Bourgeois had been compelled to follow suit. But in the eyes of the latter and other French protagonists this decisively weakened the League's "collective security" regime.[30]

Aware of the profound reservations within the Imperial War Cabinet, particularly the aversion to rigid and potentially both universal and unlimited obligations, Cecil had sought to "soften" the unqualified guarantee of Article X. He proposed to limit it to the more passive commitment to "respect" the independence and integrity of all members of the organisation. And he warned that if Article X's provisions were not amended, the League Covenant would stipulate an obligation – in the final instance a compulsory requirement for member states to go to war – that was so far-reaching that it could not be "carried out literally and in all respects". In his view, this would effectively weaken or even undermine the organisation's security regime. Further, and

---

[29] Article X, Draft Covenant, 14 February 1919, *PWW*, LV, p. 167.

[30] Wilson statement, session 6 February 1919, Miller (1928), I, pp. 168–70; Draft Covenant, 14 February 1919, *PWW*, LV, p. 167.

again reflecting general British preferences, Cecil sought to ensure that the League would be an institution that, while protecting the integrity of its members, also established procedures for a peaceful change of the territorial or political status quo in cases where this was deemed necessary in the interest of overall pacification.[31] For his part, Wilson had also emphasised that the League's constitution had to permit a peaceful change of the status quo if this was deemed necessary in the interest of the "peace of the world". In his second "Paris draft" of 18 January 1919 he had stipulated – in Article III – that it was "understood" between the Contracting Powers that "such territorial readjustments, if any, as may in the future become necessary" either on grounds of "self-determination" or if a three-quarter majority of the delegates judged that they were "demanded by the welfare and manifest interest of the people concerned". And he had explicitly demanded that all member states had to accept the "principle" that the "peace of the world" was "superior in importance to every question of political jurisdiction and boundary".[32]

Wilson did not entirely abandon his overall conception of making the League an instrument for peaceful adjustments of the postwar order in the longer run. But during the negotiations in early February he changed his priorities. He now adamantly opposed the proposed British amendments, arguing that they would hollow out Article X and compromise the League's ability to secure peace. Unsurprisingly, the American president's veto was seconded by Bourgeois and Larnaude, who sought still sought to turn the new organisation into a mechanism that reinforced the status quo the victors would decree. Consequently, their interest lay in blocking any provisions that in their view could eventually be instrumentalised by Germany and other states that desired to revise the postwar settlement. The only concession Cecil managed to negotiate was a very general and overall insubstantial clause, incorporated in what finally became a separate Article XIX, which Wilson eventually endorsed. It stated that the League Assembly could "from time to time advise the reconsideration . . . of treaties which have become inapplicable and the consideration of international conditions whose continuance might endanger the peace of the world".[33]

The Covenant's provisions specifying what actions or measures member states actually were to take to respond to aggression, or if war threatened, were in fact remarkably general and left the representatives of the different states considerable political leeway. Following Cecil's and Wilson's preferences, Article XI stipulated that any "war or threat of war", whether or not it immediately affected individual members, was declared "a matter of concern

---

[31] Cecil statements, 6 and 11 February 1919, Miller (1928), I, pp. 168–70, 201–11.

[32] Wilson, Second "Paris Draft", 18 January 1919, *PWW*, LIII, p. 140.

[33] Cecil statements, 6 and 11 February 1919, Miller (1928), I, pp. 168–70, 201–11; Article XIX, Final Covenant, p. 4.

to the League" – and to be deliberated in the League Council. Yet it merely stated that its members could then "take any action that may be deemed wise and effectual to safeguard the peace of nations". Hardly meeting French demands to set clear criteria for sanctions and, if necessary, military action against aggressors, this indeed opened up a wide spectrum of possible responses; and it ultimately meant that cardinal decisions about how to react to threats were left at the discretion of the most powerful member states – and depended on their ability to reach an agreement in the Council.[34]

Overall, however, the draft Covenant clearly manifested the Anglo-American emphasis on creating a League that would become the world's new central institution for the pacific settlement of international disputes. But, here also reflecting the maxims of Wilson and the priorities of the British government, it only introduced provisions for *non*-compulsory arbitration, leaving out all mandatory stipulations that Bourgeois and Hymans had sought to include, and in fact largely drawing on the rules and procedures the British Phillimore Committee had originally proposed.[35] Article XII obliged members of the League in the event of "any dispute likely to lead to a rupture" to "submit the matter either to arbitration or judicial settlement or to enquiry by the Council"; and it obliged them not to resort to war "until three months after the award by the arbitrators or the judicial decision, or the report by the Council".[36] But Article XIII stated that the member states of the League agreed to submit to "arbitration" or "judicial settlement" only disputes "which they recognise to be suitable for submission to arbitration or judicial settlement and which cannot be satisfactorily settled by diplomacy".[37]

Fundamentally, this reaffirmed the pre-war premise that in disputes that involved "vital" national interests and political concerns the organisation's member states were at liberty to pursue other – political or diplomatic – processes to settle conflicts by peaceful means. The Draft Covenant did establish a basic sanction regime. But this regime was comparatively loose and, significantly, it was not connected to the far-reaching guarantees of Article X but rather to the enforcement of the provisions for international conflict-resolution in the "covenants under Articles XII, XIII and XV". Article XVI stated that if any League member went to war in defiance of these covenants it would be "deemed to have committed an act of war against all other members of the League". The Council could then impose financial, economic and diplomatic sanctions in the form of an immediate and far-reaching boycott or blockade. Should these sanctions prove ineffective, the Council was empowered to give *recommendations* to individual member states

---

[34] Article XI, Draft Covenant, 14 February 1919, *PWW*, LV, p. 167; Final Covenant, p. 3.
[35] League Commission session, 7 February 19, Miller (1928), I, pp. 192–5.
[36] Article XII, Draft Covenant, 14 February 1919, *PWW*, LV, p. 167; Final Covenant, p. 3.
[37] Article XIII, Draft Covenant, 14 February 1919, *PWW*, LV, p. 167; Final Covenant, p. 3.

as to what military forces they could provide to "protect" the League's covenants; but it had no authority to compel them to supply such forces; it could
only request them. Crucially, the same procedures were to apply if a state that
was not a member of the organisation was involved in a dispute with a
member state and "resort(ed) to war" against it.[38]

All of this fell far short of French demands for a forceful sanction regime
backed and enforced by international armed forces at the disposal of the
League – and for a robust "collective security" regime that permitted swift
and decisive military responses to aggression or threats of aggression – from
Germany. In accordance with American and British conceptions, and interests, the League that would be founded on the basis of the Draft Covenant
would ultimately be dependent on the political support of its member states,
above all the great powers. It would have no substantial authority or instruments of enforcement of its own. Those who represented the most powerful
states had made general commitments that clearly went beyond those of the
pre-war era. But cardinal decisions about how to respond to aggression and
how to secure "the peace of the world", and notably the peace of Europe,
would still lie in their hands. And, as the sovereignty of the greater and smaller
states had not been significantly limited, they still would have considerable
freedom of action in deciding how, and how far, to act in the manner of a new,
institutionalised "international concert".

That the new organisation would have an essentially hierarchical rather
than egalitarian character was clearly reflected in the institutional architecture
of the League that was negotiated in the spring of 1919. This architecture was
essentially based on the conceptions of Smuts and Cecil, which Wilson had
largely endorsed by early January 1919 and the Hurst–Miller draft had elaborated further. In a wider context, it concretised the new international hierarchy that had emerged under the impact of the Great War. The draft
constitution of 14 February confirmed that the new organisation was to be
structured around one core authority, an Executive Council dominated by the
five victorious great powers – France, Britain, the United States, Italy and
Japan – while also comprising representatives of four other members selected
by the League Assembly.[39] It was to be aided by a permanent Secretariat.

On account of its make-up, the Council could thus potentially become the
executive organ of a new transatlantic system. By contrast, the role conceived
for the League Assembly, where all member states would be represented, was
more than merely symbolical but essentially limited. The main drafters of the
Covenant essentially envisaged it as a forum in which urgent or structural
international problems could be debated – and that could bring "conditions"

---

[38] Articles XII–XVI, Draft Covenant, 14 February 1919, *PWW*, LV, pp. 169–70; Final
Covenant, p. 4.
[39] Article III, Draft Covenant, 14 February 1919, *PWW*, LV, p. 165.

that threatened "the peace of the world" to the attention of the Executive Council – and "world opinion".[40] In very general, feeble terms, the Covenant also called for the creation of a Permanent Court of International Justice. It was "to hear and determine any dispute of an international character which the parties thereto submit to it" and to "give an advisory opinion upon any dispute or question referred to it by the Council or by the Assembly".[41]

It is indeed noteworthy that not only Cecil but also Wilson had long insisted on setting up the Executive Council, which both regarded as the decisive body of the new organisation, as an exclusive instrument of the great powers.[42] Having placed such an emphasis on the need for a new "equality of rights" between great powers and smaller states in his wartime speeches, Wilson had at first proposed that the executive council should also include representatives of the latter. But Cecil had insisted – out of conviction yet also because he had to heed Lloyd George's views – that the organisation's structure had to reflect that "the Great Powers must run the League". And the American president had soon essentially accepted this maxim and come to support Cecil's conception of a council exclusively comprised of great powers, which reflected Smuts' design. Consequently, this had become a core provision of the Hurst–Miller draft.[43]

It was only due to the vehement protests of the representatives of smaller states on the League Commission, particularly Hymans, that the Anglo-American protagonists eventually agreed to an extension of the Executive Council. Backed by Bourgeois, Hymans argued that a League whose main council was the exclusive remit of the great powers would fail to gain the support of the other states and lose legitimacy in the eyes of the world. The members of the League Commission worked out a compromise which included concessions to Hymans but essentially ensured that the great powers would retain the crucial decision-making and veto power in the League's highest body. The Council would be composed of the five great powers, as permanent members, and four smaller powers as non-permanent members. The first to be designated as such were Belgium, Spain, Greece and Brazil. Wilson would subsequently seek to justify the establishment of a de facto executive directorate at the top of the League by arguing that the special

---

[40] Article II, Draft Covenant, 14 February 1919, *PWW*, LV, p. 164; eventually the League Assembly's functions were specified in Article III of the Final Covenant, p. 1.

[41] Article XIV, Final Covenant, p. 3.

[42] Minutes of the League Commission, 4 February 1919, Miller (1928), I, pp. 141–8, 158–67. Cecil diary, 4 February 19, Cecil Papers. Cf. Wilson's Senate address, 22 January 1917, *PWW*, XL, p. 536.

[43] Wilson draft, 20 January 1919; Miller memorandum of changes to this draft; Cecil to Miller, 29 January 1919, Miller (1928), I, pp. 57–61.

political and strategic responsibilities the great powers had to assume entitled them to an elevated status within the new organisation.[44]

By contrast, Lloyd George continued to criticise a council design that contradicted his preference for establishing the League more unequivocally as a kind of permanent concert of the great powers.[45] Even after the Draft Covenant had been finalised, he would still impress on the British Empire Delegation that it was "unthinkable" that a system "could last" in which great powers that represented about seven hundred million people had to share executive authority with smaller powers that represented at most fifty million people.[46] Like Clemenceau, Lloyd George thus maintained a distinctly more hierarchical outlook on the future of international politics, particularly with a view to the League. Yet neither the British nor the French premier would insist on a more exclusive League Council in the end.

IV.   A New Regime and Persistent Civilisational Hierarchies
The Creation of the League's Mandate System

The disputes about the League Covenant also became directly linked to the question of how the victors would deal with the former German colonies and "possessions" in Africa, East Asia and the Pacific, because it now had to be decided how far, and in what way, the League would play a novel role in how their future would be administered. In turn, this question would lead to particularly acrimonious debates because the way in which it would be addressed not only had implications for the future of the former Middle Eastern provinces of the Ottoman Empire but also for the future of colonial rule as such.

At a deeper level, these debates and the eventual compromises that created the "internationalising" but clearly neo-colonial mandate system under the auspices of the League showed above all the *limited* extent to which the newly proclaimed principles and rules of international politics, the respect for "self-determination" and ideas of "equitable sovereignty" were applied beyond Europe and the transatlantic sphere. Put differently, they manifested the degree to which core ideas about civilisational hierarchies and "tutelage" persisted, particularly when it came to the "imperial-colonial" world that had been "created" in the first decades of the long twentieth century. In 1919, such ideas were for the most part merely adapted to create

---

[44]   Minutes of the League Commission, 4 February 1919, Miller (1928), I, pp. 141–8, 158–67. Cecil diary, 4 February 19, Cecil Papers. Cf. Wilson's Senate address, 22 January 1917, *PWW*, XL, p. 536; Wilson speech, 19 September 1919, Shaw (1924), II, p. 1017.

[45]   Record of meeting of Lloyd George with Kerr, Cecil and Smuts, 31 January 1919, Cecil diary, Lothian Papers.

[46]   Minutes of British Empire Delegation, 5 May 1919, CAB 29/28.

"internationalised" modes of oversight that allowed the "more advanced" powers to extend their spheres of influence while avoiding the charge of outright "annexationism".[47]

In his Fourteen Points address Wilson had called for a "free, open-minded, and absolutely impartial adjustment of *all* colonial claims" and demanded that in this process "the interests of the populations concerned must have equal weight with the equitable claims of the government whose title is to be determined".[48] Yet the American president's tacit agreement to refrain from directly challenging British and French colonial rule – and the determination of those who represented the remaining global imperial and regional colonial powers to preserve, or even extend, their imperial suzerainty – set very clear limits to anything even approaching a general, global "adjustment process" of this kind in the colonial sphere from the outset. All attention thus focused on the fate of what had been the German Empire's overseas colonies. On 24 January, the members of the Supreme Council quickly reached a consensus on one point: that these colonies would not be given back to Germany. But the discussions about what was to be done with them soon sparked major controversies that brought to the fore not only competing claims but also competing ideas about the future of colonialism – and the authority of the League. On 28 January 1919, Wilson called on the other powers to accept what he described as a "genuine idea of trusteeship" under the supervision of the League. He proposed to turn the former colonies into mandates that were either supervised directly by the new organisation or by mandatory states it designated. And he outlined that the League also was to evaluate the advances these territories made in terms of government, political and economic development and, based on its findings, decide when they would be "ready" for actual self-government. As he had stressed earlier, the "basis" of this proposal was "the feeling which had sprung up all over the world against further annexation".[49]

Yet Wilson's proposals met with considerable resistance. Only Lloyd George supported them, but he too demanded exemptions for the former colonies in southern Africa and the Pacific, with which the representatives of the Dominions, and Japan, fervently agreed. The British War Cabinet had originally backed the Dominions' demand to control former German colonies in their vicinity. And the Dominions now put considerable pressure on the British premier and reasserted their de facto annexationist claims, Smuts and Botha for Southwest Africa, the premier of New Zealand, Robert

---

[47] For different perspectives see Pedersen (2015), pp. 27–35, and Leonhard (2018), pp. 708–18.

[48] Wilson "Fourteen Points" address, 8 January 1918, *PWW*, XLV, p. 536.

[49] Hankey notes of meeting of the Council of Ten, 28 January 1919, *PWW*, LIV, p. 326; Supreme Council Meeting, 27 January 1919, *ibid.*, p. 293.

Massey, for Samoa and, particularly vociferously, the Australian premier
Hughes for New Guinea and smaller adjacent Pacific islands. A fervent critic
of the League idea, Hughes warned Wilson that he should not assume that the
United States' contribution to winning the war put him in a position to dictate
the terms of the peace. Clemenceau left no doubt either about his deep
scepticism towards the League as supervising agency of a mandate and
trusteeship system.[50] The French premier asked his colonial minister Henri
Simon to make a case for French control of Togoland and the Cameroons.
This Simon did while also insisting that France had a sovereign "right" to carry
out its *mission civilisatrice* in Africa, which he contrasted with German
colonial misrule, without League interference.[51] Confronted with this resistance and surge of claims, Wilson warned that if his interlocutors insisted on
their demands "(t)he world would say that the Great Powers first portioned
out the helpless part of the earth, and then formed a League of Nations", which
would discredit the new institution from the start.[52] And to contain the other
powers' annexationist ambitions he now threatened to make their imperialist
claims public. But this had little effect.

Intent on coming to an agreement with Wilson, Lloyd George took the lead
in the search for a compromise that salvaged the basic idea of a League-
administered mandate system, for he had concluded that such a system, if
properly modified, would both serve the interests of the "most advanced
imperial power" and protect the victors against the charge of simply annexing
"spoils of war". The compromise proposal he developed with the help of Cecil
and Smuts centred on the conception of a differentiated system of mandates.
And while Smuts had proposed in his *Practical Suggestion* that a mandate
regime should be limited to the former Middle Eastern provinces of the
Ottoman Empire – whose inhabitants he deemed capable of advancing
towards self-rule – the British premier now proposed that a differentiated,
multi-level system could also be extended to the former German colonies. This
compromise proposal would be accepted remarkably swiftly.

On 30 January, Wilson and the other plenipotentiaries on the Supreme
Council agreed to the fundamentals of a hierarchical – and indeed neo-
colonial – mandate system that would subsequently be incorporated in the
League Covenant under Article XX.[53] Following the earlier suggestions of
Smuts and Cecil three categories of mandates were specified: "A" mandates –
the former Ottoman provinces – that had "reached a stage of development
where their existence as independent nations can be provisionally recognized"

---

[50] Lloyd George (1938), I, p. 294.
[51] Hankey notes of meeting of the Council of Ten, 28 January 1919, *PWW*, LIV,
pp. 318–20, 328.
[52] Supreme Council Minutes, 28 January 1919, *BDFA*, Part II, series I, vol. II, p. 38.
[53] Supreme Council Minutes, 30 January 1919, *BDFA*, II/I, vol. II, pp. 61, 51–68.

and that thus only required "administrative advice and assistance by a Mandatory until such time as they are able to stand alone"; "B" mandates, which were less advanced and in need of various regimes of mandatory supervision that also secured "equal opportunities for the trade and commerce of other Members of the League", which was to apply to Germany's former colonies in West and Central Africa; and finally "C" mandates – territories that due to "the sparseness of their population, or their small size, or their remoteness from the centres of civilisation, or their geographical contiguity to the territory of the Mandatory" could "be best administered under the laws" of the mandatory state "as integral portions of its territory", which conveniently applied to Southwest Africa and the formerly German-controlled Pacific territories.[54]

Following Smuts' suggestion, all mandatory states would be required to submit annual reports to the League Council about their "charges", which indeed introduced a certain element of "internationalisation" as their activities were hence to be measured – in the "court of world opinion" – by the standards the League Covenant set – though it remained very uncertain how far the new institution would be capable of really holding mandatory states accountable. But the language used to define and justify the purpose of the mandate system in the Covenant revealed to what remarkable extent it was still informed by imperialist thinking of the pre-war era and the basic notion of a descending hierarchy of civilisations – which was now, as it were, to be "internationalised" as well. Article XXII stated that as the former colonies and imperial provinces were "inhabited by peoples not yet able to stand by themselves under the strenuous conditions of the modern world", their "tutelage" should "be entrusted to advanced nations who by reason of their resources, their experience or their geographical position can best undertake this responsibility". They were to act on "the principle that the well-being and development of such peoples form a sacred trust of civilisation".[55]

Because Wilson insisted that the mandates should only be distributed once the League Covenant had been formally adopted, protracted negotiations ensued. The Supreme Council finally allocated Germany's former colonies on 7 May. Following informal agreements the British Colonial Secretary Lord Milner made with his French counterpart Simon, Britain would be confirmed as mandatory for most of what had been German East Africa and a stretch of Cameroon adjacent to its colony Nigeria, France for the remainder of Cameroon and Togoland, while Belgium was in the end allowed to retain Rwanda and Burundi. As Smuts had envisaged, South Africa would administer

---

[54] See Supreme Council Minutes, 30 January 1919, *BDFA*, II/I, vol. II, pp. 56 ff.; Article XIX, Draft Covenant, 14 February, *PWW*, LV, pp. 135–6. This subsequently became Article XXII of the Final Covenant.

[55] Article XXII, Final Covenant, p. 4.

what had been German Southwest Africa as a "C" mandate. In the Pacific, Australia would receive New Guinea, New Zealand would get Samoa and Japan would take charge of all formerly German-held islands north of the equator – while, as will be seen, the controversial Shandong question would only be "settled" after the peace conference's most significant crisis with extra-European roots had reached a climax in late April.

By contrast, against the background of ongoing military conflict in the Middle East no decisions about the "A" mandates, the former Ottoman territories, would be made in the spring and summer of 1919. Here, the parameters would only be set at the San Remo conference in April 1920s – after the original Anglo-American project to extend a mandate system in this region had been undermined by the American Senate's rejection of the Versailles treaty, and earlier, particularly British notions that the United States should take over "light" mandatory responsibilities – in Armenia and possibly regarding Constantinople and the Straits – had been swept aside. The San Remo accords would confirm that British and French leaders had reverted to the framework of the Sykes-Picot agreement of 1916. Under the neo-colonial arrangement they made, Mesopotamia and Palestine became British mandates while Syria and Lebanon would be allocated to France.[56]

V.   Towards a League of the Victors. The Crucial Question of Germany's Admission to the "Comity of Nations"

In the European context, the protagonists of the League Commission had to tackle one further, indeed essential question whose significance has often been underrated, namely when and on what conditions Germany and the other defeated powers were to be admitted to the new international organisation. This was far more than simply a symbolical question, because the way in which the victors dealt with it would have vital implications not only for the future structure and relevance of the League but also for Europe's future stabilisation. At a deeper level, it pointed straight to the crucial problem of when and how – if at all – the vanquished and above all Germany were to be integrated in the postwar international order the victorious powers were struggling to establish.

By the time Wilson presented the Draft Covenant, key parameters had been set and prevalent interests and underlying rationales had aligned in such a way that it was highly likely – though not inevitable – that the League would essentially be set up as an institution founded and steered by the principal victors and that Germany would not be included from the outset. What had a decisive bearing here was that Wilson's "probation policy" and his preference

---

[56] See Pedersen (2015), pp. 30–42.

for establishing the League initially as an institution of the – democratic – victors had been reinforced in the spring of 1919 – and that in crucial respects his priorities came to align with cardinal French aims that were advanced, albeit on different premises, by Clemenceau and Bourgeois. This significant congruence of interests and political as well as ideological imperatives would ultimately prevail over the markedly different approach that Cecil proposed – and that Lloyd George by and large endorsed: an approach that was based on the premise that it was critical for the consolidation of a viable postwar order to bring Germany into the League as soon as possible.

During the early stages of the League Commission's deliberations Bourgeois and Larnaude had presented an amendment to the Anglo-American Draft Covenant that reflected Clemenceau's priorities. It was designed to ensure that Germany would remain outside the League for the foreseeable future and only admitted once it had fulfilled far-reaching criteria of internal reform, proved "uprightness" in international affairs and complied with the victors' disarmament demands. The amendment stipulated that no nation was to be admitted to the League unless it had "representative institutions" which made it "responsible for the acts of its own Government", unless it "was in a position to give effective guarantees of its sincere intention to abide by its agreement" and unless it conformed to the League's principles "regarding naval and military forces and armaments".[57] Though he too saw German society as deeply pervaded with militarism and aggressive nationalism, Bourgeois himself still favoured a policy that *eventually* sought to draw a republican Germany into the Society of Nations. He continued to argue that tying the defeated power into a system of mutual obligations would also oblige German decision-makers to respect and uphold a robust regime of international law based on principles of "mutuality" and "reciprocity".

Bourgeois indeed deemed it possible that, over time, a republican Germany could become a responsible member of a *société des nations*, which in his view could open up a more promising path of safeguarding European peace and security than reliance on power-political containment. Yet France's leading League advocate insisted that German elites first had to prove that they were not only committed to developing a democratic political culture but also willing to comply with the core tenets of the League Covenant that the victorious powers were formulating.[58] What Bourgeois envisaged prefigured Briand's more integrative strategies vis-à-vis Germany in the mid-1920s. In 1919, however, his recommendations had no tangible influence on those who determined French policies.

---

[57] Minutes of League Commission meeting, 11 February 1919, *PWW*, LV, pp. 74–7.
[58] See summary of a conversation between Bourgeois and Clemenceau, undated, Bourgeois Papers, vol. 18; Bourgeois speech, 5th Plenary Session of the Peace Conference, 28 April 1919, MAE, PV-SDN, 396; Jackson (2013), pp. 273–4.

Clemenceau and Tardieu maintained an outlook both on the significance of the League and the question of Germany's admission that not only differed from Bourgeois' views but also, and more importantly, remained substantially at odds with the approaches Wilson and notably Cecil and Lloyd George pursued. They reckoned that not least in view of the longer-term aims and interests of the Anglo-American powers a German membership in the League would be impossible to prevent in the longer run. But they deemed it essential to delay it as far as possible, and to constitute the League clearly as an "exclusive" victors' institution. For in their eyes the primary function of the new institution, whose intrinsic value they continued to view with profound scepticism, was and remained to draw the United States and Britain into a transatlantic alliance and security system; and it was to serve as an instrument that aided France in containing the vanquished power.

It followed quite logically from these overriding objectives that Clemenceau and his main adviser were intent on making Germany's *longer-term* compliance with the obligations they intended to impose on it, including those concerning reparations, a cardinal precondition for its *eventual* admission to the League. Fundamentally, the French premier still acted on the assumption that it was not only unrealistic but indeed dangerous to count on more than superficial German advances towards democracy in the shorter term and even more hazardous to expect that such advances would soon alter German international behaviour. It was therefore for strategic reasons – namely to justify Germany's prolonged exclusion – that he consented to making the establishment of democratic institutions a further condition for the defeated power's admission to the *société des nations*. Nor did Clemenceau – or Tardieu – expect at this point that integrating Germany into the League and committing it to mutual rules and obligations could actually serve to pacify German conduct. All of these considerations led the key French decision-makers to insist not only on initially excluding Germany from the League but also on retaining an essential veto regarding its possible future admission.[59]

Not Wilson, but two British protagonists – Cecil and Lloyd George – emerged as the strongest advocates of a very different, more integrative approach at Versailles. In the League Commission, Cecil argued against French attempts to set demanding and in his view excessive and ideologically charged preconditions for German League membership – notably the requirement of proven adherence to democratic government – because he feared that they would be used as a pretext to block or delay the defeated power's admission.[60] Cecil remained one of the most committed proponents of a

---

[59] Tardieu (I/1921), p. 135; Tardieu note on French proposal of 14 March, Tardieu Papers, vol. 418; Poincaré note, 18 January 1919, Poincaré (1919), II, p. 143; Berthelot memorandum, 22 December 1918, MAE, SDN, vol. 6.

[60] See Cecil (1941), pp. 60–2.

League that comprised not only the victors but also the vanquished. He thus stepped up his efforts on behalf of an *early* inclusion of Germany not only in the League but also its Executive Council. And he particularly sought to gain Wilson's support for these priorities. In his assessment, only by integrating Germany early on would the League be able to fulfil what he saw as one of its cardinal purposes, namely to facilitate the peaceful settlement of disputes between *all* relevant powers. Further, Cecil believed that it would be prudent to bind German postwar governments to the rules and procedures of the envisaged League Covenant, providing incentives by offering them the opportunity to re-join the "comity of nations" yet also placing restraints on their policies. And he also reckoned that drawing Germany into the League could contribute to stabilising its new and still frail democratic order.[61]

Lloyd George shared Cecil's underlying rationales in important though not all respects. He also thought that a relatively swift inclusion of Germany into the League was both necessary and advantageous. His underlying aim, however, was to involve the defeated power in the new, more flexible concert of great powers he envisaged. In the controversial Fontainebleau memorandum of 25 March 1919, Lloyd George argued that the new government in Berlin had to fulfil one essential precondition for making Germany eligible for membership in the League: it had to accept the peace terms that the victors considered "just" and "fair" and prove its willingness to abide by them. And he recommended that, once this had been assured, Germany should be "admitted" to the League as soon as it had "established a stable and democratic Government".[62] But like Cecil the British premier actually considered it counter-productive to make Germany's "proven democratisation" an essential criterion that could then be invoked to put off its entry into the League. More fundamentally, he too was convinced that the consolidation of a republican form of government in Germany would be a lengthy and uncertain process. While he was not prepared to provide particular incentives to foster this process, he held that it was critical for Europe's longer-term stability to buttress a moderate government in Berlin that withstood the Bolshevik challenge, accepted the victors' rules and refrained from challenging the postwar equilibrium by force. And to this end, he reasoned, it was "safer" to accommodate Germany in the League at an early stage – whereas a lengthy period of exclusion or isolation threatened to drive the vanquished power into the arms of Bolshevik Russia. On these premises, Lloyd George eventually came to propose that the victors should give assurances that Germany would be allowed to join the League within a year.[63]

---

[61] Cecil memorandum, 17 December 1918, CAB 23/42.

[62] Lloyd George, Fontainebleau memorandum, 25 March 1919, *PWW*, LVI, pp. 264, 261–4.

[63] *Ibid.*, pp. 261 ff.; Lloyd George remarks, British Empire Delegation, 33 and 34, 1 June 1919, CAB 29/38/1.

In view of the conflicting British and French approaches and rationales that came to the fore at Versailles, Wilson's attitude towards the critical question of Germany's admission to the League – and the wider question of its integration into the refashioned postwar system – acquired a pivotal significance. The American president had not altered his longer-term conception. He still considered it imperative that *eventually* Germany and the other vanquished powers of the war had to become members of the League. And his underlying assumption remained that this would have a peace-enforcing effect on two levels: it would commit and habituate German representatives to the rules of the novel "international concert" he sought to establish; and it would further Germany's inner reform and democratisation processes. But by the time the first key decisions about the Covenant were made in mid-February 1919, Wilson emphasised his determination to insist on the "probation" rationales he had come to espouse after the armistice. He argued that Germany's new leaders, and the German people, had to prove not only their commitment to democracy but also their commitment to peaceful and "civilised" international conduct before they would be permitted to enter the new international organisation. More fundamentally, it now became apparent that Wilson's hierarchical approach had hardened, not just rhetorically. He now declared that the world had not only "had a moral right to disarm Germany" but also a right "to subject her to a generation of thoughtfulness".[64]

Yet the American president's tougher stance was also influenced by other important considerations, both international and domestic. He had already signalled in mid-December 1918 that in order to attain "a definite agreement" on the formation of the League with the *Entente* Powers, he was "even willing to agree to the French proposal that the Germans should be excluded from the League for a time".[65] And he had no intention of further inciting Senate opposition to the League by demanding a clear perspective for Germany's admission. To Republican senators he would underscore in late February that he was not in favour of "recognizing that Germany had any immediate right to a place in the League".[66] In the debates of the League Commission, Wilson thus agreed to incorporate Bourgeois' amendment in the final draft, and Cecil would find himself overruled.[67]

Consequently, the Draft Covenant not only confirmed that Germany was not to be among the "original signatories" but also stated that admission to the League would be "limited to fully self-governing countries" and require "the assent of no less than two-thirds" of the member states. And it specified that

---

[64] Hankey notes Council of Ten and Supreme War Council, 12 February 19, *PWW*, LV, pp. 104–5; Miller (1928), I, pp. 279–80.

[65] Wiseman to the British Foreign Office, Paris, 15 December 1918, *PWW*, LIII, pp. 394–5.

[66] *New York Times* news report, 27 February 1919, *PWW*, LV, p. 276.

[67] Wilson statement, 5 February 1919, Miller (1928), I, p. 164. Schwabe, pp. 248–50.

no state was to be admitted unless it was "able to give effective guarantees of its sincere intention to observe its international obligations" and "conform to such principles as may be prescribed by the League in regard to its naval and military forces and armaments".[68] In practice, these far-ranging criteria would place considerable obstacles in the way of Germany's eventual entry – and give the French government ample leverage to resist or delay it. In many ways the victors' preliminary yet formative deliberations in the League Commission and the compromises that underpinned the Draft Covenant of 14 February indeed prefigured how the final League Covenant would be framed and the League eventually be established.

For Brockdorff-Rantzau, Erzberger and the Social Democratic protagonists of the newly formed Scheidemann government, the publication of the Draft Covenant marked the clearest setback yet for their aspirations to ensure Germany's prompt admission to the League as a great power "with equal rights". In the programmatic speech he gave before the Constituent National Assembly on 14 February, Brockdorff-Rantzau thus stressed all the more emphatically that the democratically elected German government had a claim to enter the new organisation, not as a "pariah" after a "period of quarantine" but rather as a founding member, and member of its Executive Council. And he underscored its resolve to "co-operate in building and developing [the] League without reservations".[69]

In Germany, both the debate about and the new enthusiasm for the League, which had gained momentum after the armistice, had reached a peak at this point. But not only the public debate but also German attitudes were characterised by exaggerated expectations. Therefore, the disappointment with the victors' blueprint was all the more pronounced. And what dominated German reactions was by and large a predictable response: one contested or outright rejected essentials of what the main newspaper and organ of the Social Democrats, *Vorwärts*, condemned as a "League of Nations of the Victors"; and one called instead for a "genuine" League of Nations that was to be universal, genuinely "progressive" and, of course, include Germany from the outset.[70] At a rally in support of a "Real League of Nations" that took place in Berlin in mid-March, Erzberger proclaimed that Wilson still had a duty to implement his peace programme and lead efforts to create a truly universal League as anchor of a "peace of justice". And he too underscored that the new

---

[68] Article VII, Draft Covenant, 14 February 1919, *PWW*, LV, p. 166. Wilson had at first insisted making *democratic* self-government the core membership criterion. But he then agreed to omit a direct reference to "democracy" because of British concerns that this would have prevented the admission of the Dominions, which could not be categorised as "democratic" states. See Wilson statement, 5 February 1919, Miller (1928), I, p. 164.

[69] Brockdorff-Rantzau speech, 14 February 1919, Brockdorff-Rantzau (1925), pp. 47, 58–9.

[70] "Völkerbund der Sieger", *Vorwärts*, 17 February 1919.

German republic was entitled to join the new organisation immediately, and as a state with equal rights.[71]

Not only Erzberger's *Zentrum* but all the parties that stood behind the first Weimar coalition government strongly supported these demands. Ebert and Scheidemann declared that they could not support League that had the character of a financial "trust" in which the victors had reserved the Executive Council for themselves and prevented the new organisation from becoming a universal instrument of peace. The influential trade union leader Carl Legien advanced a similar critique, observing that the plans the victorious powers had presented would not create a peace league but rather a "joint stock company of the victors" that was designed to assert their capitalist interests.[72] For communist opinion-makers, the Draft Covenant merely proved that the imperialist victors would seek to impose their will on the imperialist powers that had been defeated. In their view, it was thus all the more imperative to persevere with the struggle for a more radical transformation of the international order along Bolshevik lines.[73] But it was the reaction on the right wing of the German political spectrum – from the forces that the newly founded German National People's Party (DNVP) represented in the new parliament – that foreshadowed a far more serious challenge to the development prospects of the League and the international system it was to create. Leading DNVP politicians like Karl Helfferich and Siegfried von Kardorff categorically rejected the victors' Covenant plans, calling the League itself not merely a "farce" but also a ploy of the enemies to subjugate the German nation. And nationalist commentators agitated against German League membership, arguing that the German government would "shamelessly" betray the *Reich*'s "last vestige of national dignity" if it submitted to the terms of the western powers.[74]

It was against the background of such increasingly agitated public debate that Brockdorff-Rantzau persevered with his "Wilsonian" strategy to ensure what, in contrast to German nationalists, he deemed imperative for Germany's future as a great power in the postwar system, namely a German membership in the League on terms of equality with the world's principal powers. And it was in response to the victors' Paris draft, which they perceived as a crushing blow, that, in collaboration with the legal expert Johannes Kriege and Harry Count Kessler, Schücking drafted a "more progressive" German League

---

[71] Erzberger speech, *Deutsche Allgemeine Zeitung*, 17 March 1919.

[72] "Völkerbund der Sieger", *Vorwärts*, 17 February 1919; Hochschild (1982), pp. 24–7; Legien speech, Berlin, *Deutsche Allgemeine Zeitung*, 17 March 1919. See Wintzer (2006), pp. 143–8.

[73] "Der Völkerbund", *Rote Fahne*, 20 February 1919.

[74] See *Hamburger Nachrichten*, 17 February 1919. For the background see Hertzmann (1963); Jackisch (2012).

blueprint that he would later characterise as a "pronunciamento for liberty, equality, and fraternity among nations". Including forward-looking features like an international parliament, this blueprint – made public on 24 April – was intended to underscore the new German government's progressive commitments and to put additional pressure on the victors to accept Germany as founding member of a "revised" League.[75] But, as will be shown, these efforts would prove as futile and counter-productive as Brockdorff-Rantzau's entire peace strategy.

VI. The Wider Controversies over the League Covenant – and Wilson's Mounting Domestic Challenges

The publication of the Paris Draft Covenant in mid-February 1919 sparked far-ranging debates not just in Germany. It indeed gave rise to intensifying national and transnational controversies around the world – about the draft itself, yet also about the question of what kind of League was really required to secure world peace after the cataclysm of the Great War. In Britain, the Liberal Party and particularly the League of Nations Union (LNU) basically welcomed the result of the Paris negotiations. The LNU leadership called the proposed draft covenant "the longest possible step" that could have been taken under the circumstances, though it stressed that it favoured a more prominent role for the general assembly as well as provisions for an absolute ban on war that left no loopholes for the resort to force. A similarly positive reaction came from the Allied Societies for a League of Nations, which also endorsed the Paris blueprint, proposing only minor amendments. Significantly, its member organisations, including the LNU, also backed the premise that League should be founded as an organisation of the Allied Powers – and of neutral powers that wished to join it – yet exclude the enemy powers of the war for the foreseeable future.[76]

By contrast, more left-leaning liberal and Labour internationalists, both from the ranks of the Labour Party and the Union for Democratic Control, criticised the proposed League Covenant draft sharply and in ways that mirrored German objections. They castigated it as a design to forge a new "Holy Alliance" that enshrined the dominance of the victorious great powers; they considered it to be short-sighted because of its exclusion of the enemy powers and deficient because it failed to include significant provisions for universal disarmament and, above all, a democratic assembly that represented

[75] Cabinet meeting, 22 April 1919, *AR* Scheidemann, p. 205; *Pariser Völkerbundsakte* (1919).
[76] LNU Research Committee, "Observations on the Draft Covenant", ca. 20 February 1919, Murray Papers, LNU Folder; League of Nations Union (1919).

peoples rather than governments.[77] Notably, the leading Labour figures MacDonald and Henderson voiced such criticisms. As delegates at the Conference of the Second International that brought together Labour and socialist representatives from both sides of the war's trenches in Berne in early February they had been instrumental in drafting the so-called Berne resolution. Adopted on 6 February, this resolution stated that a genuine League of Nations could only be built on the basis of a "real peace of justice", that its central organ was to be composed not of delegates of national governments but representatives from national parliaments, "thus ensuring not an alliance of cabinets or governments, but a union of peoples" and that, crucially, the organisation had to be open to all nations, including the enemy states, from the outset.[78] In April, the Labour leader William Adamson renewed Labour's critique in the House of Commons. He demanded that instead of a "League of Allied Nations" there should be a "real League of Nations that will embrace all the countries of the world", declaring that it "would be a grievous mistake if the enemy countries were to be kept outside" the new organisation.[79]

On behalf of the UDC, John Hobson would subsequently publish a very influential critique of the League the victors proposed, which denounced it as a "New Holy Alliance" and argued that it remained a "sham" as long as there were no clear provisions for the admission of Germany and Bolshevik Russia.[80] As Hobson saw it, what the victors had negotiated was no longer the "chief instrument" of a "new world-order" and for the "realization of the great principles of nationality and self-determination, open diplomacy, and equality of economic opportunity" that Wilson had originally promised.[81] The "statesmen of the old order" had distorted the League "into a Holy Alliance of the Entente Powers", "removed every shred of popular or Parliamentary control" and "destroyed effective internationalism by giving every state the separate power to paralyze the action of the League by means of a veto". Hobson concluded the "net result" was "not a league of peoples devoted to peace and fruitful international coöperation, but a conspiracy of autocrats designed to hold down their enemies by superior economic and military-naval force, and to exercise a domination over the whole world". And he emphasised that the essential condition "to convert this sham League into a really international League" was "the admission of the enemy Powers".[82]

---

[77] See Mayer (1967), pp. 389–95, 407–8.
[78] Berne resolution, *Official Bulletin of the International Labour and Socialist Conference* (Berne, 1919).
[79] Hansard, Commons, 5th series, 114, 16 April 1919, cols. 2957–8.
[80] John A. Hobson, "A New Holy Alliance", *Nation*, CVIII (19 April 1919), pp. 626–8.
[81] *Ibid.*, p. 626.
[82] *Ibid.*, pp. 626–7.

Similarly forceful critiques were advanced by prominent observers from neutral countries, where the discussion about the covenant was particularly intense because the League was set to end classically defined neutrality for all states that joined it. Reflecting the views of others, the Swiss diplomat Rappard observed that the so-called *Société des Nations* the victors presented to the world was "only the cristallisation of [their] current alliance" and that its "limited remit, rudimentary organisation" and "badly defined" and "restrained" competences would make it an "organisation that hardly deserves the name League of Nations".[83]

Of greater political consequence, however, was that a marked scepticism towards the proposed Covenant and the League project as such still prevailed among key figures of the Lloyd George government and the political parties and forces it represented. Reservations vis-à-vis a League with far-reaching competences remained particularly pronounced in the leadership and ranks of the largest faction in the government, and parliament, that of the conservative Unionists. While underscoring his general support for a League in the House of Commons on 12 February 1919, Lloyd George himself stressed that no consensus had yet been reached in Paris about the organisation's "functions" and "the extent to which it ought to have the power of committing the great nations to war". And he signalled that in his view the – victorious – great powers had to retain the ultimate sovereign authority to decide such a commitment.[84] Churchill warned that British strategic planning could not be scaled back just because a League was being created. In his view, the new organisation would be "on trial" and have to prove that it could deal with "terrible facts" before it could be confidently regarded as an effective security mechanism.[85] On behalf of the Dominions, the Canadian prime minister Borden, who generally welcomed the creation of the League, registered his fundamental opposition to Article X and what he saw as a security system that would be impractical and create far-reaching obligations. His Australian counterpart Hughes criticised the draft as "halting between two inconsistent principles of international cooperation and supra-national government" – and unequivocally rejected the latter tendency.[86] Yet despite this array of criticisms Lloyd George could be reasonably assured of gaining the backing of a majority in parliament and of the Dominions for the envisaged League Covenant.

In the French debates about the peace settlement the League continued to be a less prominent concern; and by the time the Draft Covenant was published,

---

[83] Rappard to Sulzer, 13 February 1919, *DDS*, 7-I, doc.181. See Wintzer (2006), pp. 147–8.
[84] Hansard, Commons, 5th series, 90, 1919, cols. 192–3.
[85] Churchill speech, House of Commons, 3 March 1919, Hansard, Commons, 5th series, 113, 1919, cols. 69–90.
[86] Borden memorandum, 13 March 1919, CAB 29/97; Hughes, "Notes on the Draft Covenant", 21 March 1919, CAB 29/9.

wary and critical attitudes had come to prevail. No leading politician in Clemenceau's government thought, or sought to persuade the French public, that a new organisation of this kind could really be relied upon to safeguard French postwar security. And there were hardly any opinion-makers with significant influence on the French public, let alone the governmental policy-making process, who were prepared to champion the cause of the League. The *Association française de la Société des Nations* remained the only significant pressure-group that consistently campaigned for the new institution. And its leading members backed the emerging Covenant, even though they shared Bourgeois' misgivings about its Anglo-American limitations. They thus endorsed the affirmative resolution of the Allied Societies for a League of Nations that was agreed upon in London in mid-March 1919. Yet prominent "juridical internationalists" like Buisson and Prudhommeaux still continued with their lobbying efforts for a League that created a more forceful "regime of organised law".[87] By contrast, leading French socialists had by this time begun to become critical of what they saw as Wilson's abandonment of a more radically internationalist League programme at the peace conference. As leading French delegates at the conference of the Second International in Berne, Thomas and Renaudel thus backed the resolution that demanded significant changes to the Paris Draft Covenant and presented as a "Socialist ideal" the alternative of a "genuine" internationalist League of the Peoples that was built around an authoritative international parliament, enforced general disarmament and included the enemies of the war. Yet they also demanded more far-reaching provisions of "collective security" and a more elaborate regime of international arbitration than their British and German counterparts.[88]

Unsurprisingly, the parties and pressure-groups of the nationalist right objected to the Draft Covenant as well, though for very different reasons. Essentially, they maintained their fundamental scepticism, irrespective of the precise form the League would take. Delahay and other prominent nationalist representatives in the *Assemblée Nationale* declared that a reliance on Wilsonian notions of "collective security" and reconciliation would compromise France's future security. And they renewed their calls for far-reaching "material guarantees", particularly in the Rhineland. The leading activists of the *Comité de la rive gauche du Rhin* and the *Ligue française* shared this negative outlook. The League had no place in the agendas they pursued.[89] But neither the nationalist right nor the socialist left could exert any significant influence on either the wider public debate in France or the prevalent attitudes of the Clemenceau government towards the *société des nations*. While hardly

---

[87] League of Nations Union (1919); Bulletin de la AFSDN, 2 January 1919; AFSDN programme, 18 December 1918, MAE, SDN, vol. 7.

[88] Renaudel (1919); Mayer (1967), pp. 393–5; Ducoulombier (2010), pp. 205–17.

[89] See Miquel (1977), pp. 306–14; Barrès (1922).

making any public statements about the League, Clemenceau left no doubt about his abiding scepticism. To him the specific provisions of the Covenant were never essential; what unchangeably dominated was his interest in forging a transatlantic security community of the victors.[90] In the French Parliament, Clemenceau could expect that the Radical Party and the majority that had endorsed his overall course would also back his strategic rationales for supporting the League. But most of the representatives in the *Chambre* and the *Sénat* were not prepared to entrust France's security to a novel international organisation. What dominated were, rather, demands for more concrete British and American guarantees and "material" guarantees against a renewed German attack.

Far more ominous for the League's development prospects, however, were the controversies that Wilson had to face in the United States. Not unaware of the challenges he confronted, the American president had returned to Washington to shore up domestic political support for the Draft Covenant immediately after he had presented it in Paris. The Draft Covenant was overall favourably received by leading conservative and progressive internationalists. On behalf of the League to Enforce Peace, Taft called the Covenant an acceptable basis for a peace-enforcing league, even though he would have preferred a tighter regime of international law and sanctions. Taft particularly emphasised his support for Article X, which he saw as "the heart of League" and the "foundation" on which the League's other "provisions to secure peace" rested. In his interpretation it contained "the primal essence of the League", which was "the union of force in the world to suppress lawless force".[91] He thus came to campaign on behalf of the League Covenant. And he and the chairman of the LEP's executive committee, Lowell, proposed amendments to ensure a modicum of moderate Republican support in the US Senate. Taft impressed on Wilson that it would be crucial to negotiate "specific reservation for the Monroe Doctrine" in the Covenant if he wanted to "carry the treaty" in the Senate.[92]

The leading Progressive opinion-makers of the *New Republic* held that, as it stood, the "constitution of the League" appeared "adequate to the maintenance of the peace" while it in effect perpetuated "the existing alliance among Germany's conquerors" and rightly excluded the defeated powers at the outset, ensuring that that the League would "not be embarrassed from the start by hopelessly discordant elements". They warned that "(i)f the League is really to be beaten, it will not be in the name of a more effective internationalism, but in the name of American nationalism, alleged to be impaired by its provisions",

---

[90] See Clemenceau speech, *Chambre*, 16 January 1919, MAE, SDN, vol. 6.

[91] Taft to Yost, 22 May 1919, Taft Papers.

[92] See Wilson to Taft, 26 February 1919, *PWW*, LV, pp. 201–2; Taft to Wilson, 18 March 1919, *PWW*, LVI, p. 83; Lowell-Lodge debate about the League, Boston, 19 March 1919, *New York Times*, 20 March 1919; Bartlett (1944), pp. 118–21.

pointing to likely nationalist objections against "participation in military and naval measures". To ensure that the League would find the necessary public and Congressional support in the United States they thus called for specific amendments.[93] It was indeed ironic that the criticism of Lippmann and *New Republic* Progressives came to focus on Article X and what they interpreted as the victors' intention to turn it into a bulwark against peaceful change. They argued that in its present form the Covenant's key article was an instrument for cementing a status quo that corresponded with the interests of the principal victors and would make it impossible to correct later on "mistakes" and "injustices" that were bound to be committed in the "hasty settlement" forged in Paris. They thus urged that Article X should be replaced by stronger provisions for arbitration and conflict resolution that guaranteed concerted interventions against an aggressor yet made the League, at the core, an institution that guaranteed "the peaceful settlement of disputes" and, if necessary, peaceful change.[94]

More fundamental objections to the Covenant Wilson had negotiated were raised by the progressive internationalists who had earlier supported Wilson's "Peace without Victory" agenda but by this time found themselves rather isolated in the American political spectrum. Leading figures of the American Union against Militarism, the Woman's Peace Party and the American Socialist Party who had become disenchanted with Wilson's war and League policies now attacked the Draft Covenant on similar grounds as the UDC, arguing that it did not go far enough in the direction of establishing a truly universal League of the Peoples that overcame the politics and hierarchies of imperialism and also integrated the defeated powers in the framework of a negotiated peace. Reflecting the views of other radical progressives, Jane Addams criticised that the League Covenant would permit war and recourse to force "in too many instances", because "its very structure and functioning" was "pervaded by the war spirit, the victorious disciplining the defeated". In her eyes, the League conceived in Paris thus could not become the instrument of a new international order and a "peace between equals".[95] Supported by the Woman's Peace Party, the International Congress of Women that took place in Zurich in mid-May 1919 would pass a resolution which stated that if the League was "to be a real instrument of peace, capable of development rather than one which sets up conditions tending to produce war" the Covenant would have to be significantly amended. In particular, the resolution demanded that membership had to be "freely open, from the time of the establishment" also to the vanquished if they were "willing to perform the duties of membership".[96]

[93] *New Republic*, 22 February 1919, pp. 100–3.
[94] Editorial "Defeat Article X", *New Republic*, 29 March 1919, pp. 263–5.
[95] Addams (1922), pp. 66–8.
[96] Resolution of the International Congress of Women, 17 May 1919, Addams Papers.

Yet such progressive concerns and critiques remained comparatively marginal. In the wider inner-American debate that now regained momentum, the *New York Times* predicted, prematurely, that Wilson's political opponents in the American Congress would "contend in vain" against "an overwhelming public opinion" in favour of the president's cause, and the League Covenant. An opinion poll published in the *Literary Digest* recorded that two-thirds of the American population were in favour of the League. Yet what would really matter politically was the alignment of opinion in the Senate.[97] And here, a full-blown controversy now escalated that would have a major impact on the future of the League and indeed foreshadowed the core challenges Wilson would later face in the "fight" over the League and the Treaty of Versailles in the aftermath of the peace conference. Most senators who belonged to the Democratic minority, and particularly their leader Gilbert Hitchcock, remained behind Wilson's League aspirations and now came out in support of the Draft Covenant.[98]

But when the president returned to Washington in late February, it soon became clear that he would have to wrestle with a still variegated but by then formidable phalanx of opponents in the ranks of the Republican Senate majority. William Borah, Hiram Johnson and others, who would soon become known as "irreconcilable" critics of the League, remained staunchly opposed to any commitments that led the United States further away from pre-war isolationism and salutary non-entanglement. And they now vehemently attacked the Draft Covenant. Borah argued that the unlimited commitment stipulated by Article X would force the United States to become involved in every future conflict in Europe and the wider world – and to preserve "the territorial possessions" of other powers, and notably Britain, "the world over".[99] Then there was a still sizeable group of more moderate Republican senators who had only mild reservations, generally favouring a League but seeking to ensure that certain long-standing traditions and maxims of US foreign policy, notably those of the Monroe Doctrine, would not be compromised. Politically decisive, however, were those who now began to voice more fundamental reservations. Claiming to represent true "Americanism", they desired to protect above all US freedom of action and the traditional prerogatives under the Monroe Doctrine, as they interpreted them. And they were also determined to defend the Senate's final authority in cardinal decisions about war and peace that affected the United States. Lodge now seized the opportunity to rally Republican opposition not just to the Draft Covenant but to Wilson's entire League policy.

[97] *New York Times*, 18 March 1919; Czernin (1968), p. 105; Knock (1992), pp. 228–9.
[98] See Hitchcock to Wilson, 4 March 1919, Miller (1928), I, pp. 276–7.
[99] Borah to Gwinn, 27 February 1919, Borah to Kluck, 28 February 1919, Borah Papers, Box 550. See Ambrosius (1987), pp. 89–90.

Privately, Lodge noted early on that the proposed Covenant was "in the highest degree dangerous".[100] And his critique came to focus squarely on Article X. On 28 February, Lodge proclaimed in the Senate that as it stood the hastily concocted constitution of the League would force the United States to abandon the most salutary traditions of its foreign policy, particularly the Monroe Doctrine. And he began his forceful campaign against Article X, warning that its pledge to guarantee the territorial integrity and political independence of every nation in the world threatened to involve the United States in unlimited obligations.[101] Having concluded that Wilson was unwilling to address his concerns, Lodge decided to send a powerful signal to the president, the American public and the other "peacemakers" in Paris. He joined the like-minded Republican senators Brandegee, Knox and Cummins in drafting a resolution that flatly rejected the proposed Draft Covenant, which he then introduced in the Senate on 3 March. This so-called Round Robin resolution, which also demanded that final deliberations about the League should be postponed until after the settlement with Germany had been made, would be endorsed by more than a third of all senators. It thus indeed signalled to the world how challenging it would be for Wilson to gain the two-thirds majority that would be required to ratify the League Covenant – and the entire peace treaty – in the American Senate.[102] Subsequently, Lodge expanded his efforts to lambast "Wilson's Covenant". In a widely noted debate with the president of Harvard and prominent LEP supporter Lawrence Lowell, which took place in Boston on 19 March, he concentrated again on the sweeping provisions of Article X. He warned his audience in and beyond Boston that "the most important article in the whole treaty" contained a dangerously far-reaching "promise" that ultimately could entangle the United States in multiple conflicts in different parts of the world. And he declared that he did not believe the American people would be prepared to send "the hope of the nation, the best of our youth, forth into the world on that errand".[103]

Lodge indeed positioned himself not only as the most powerful American critic of the Draft Covenant but also as the main proponent of a Republican conception that was intended to rival Wilson's "universal" vision of a progressive new world order. He still did not advocate a retreat to isolationism. But he also rejected Wilson's globalist aspirations, which in his view would require the United States to enter into "a general, indefinite, unlimited scheme of

---

[100] Lowell-Lodge debate, Boston, 19 March 1919, *New York Times*, 20 March 1919; Lodge to Beveridge, 18 and 27 February 1919, Lodge Papers.

[101] Lodge speech, 28 February 1919, Congressional Record, 65th Congress, 3rd session, 4520–4528.

[102] Senate debate, 3 March 1919, *Congressional Record*, 66th Congress, 1st session, 4974.

[103] Lowell-Lodge debate, Boston, 19 March 1919, *New York Times*, 20 March 1919.

always being called upon to meddle in European, Asian and African questions". Instead, Lodge favoured a more regionally focused approach that essentially preserved America's sovereign freedom of action in international affairs. He was intent on protecting the prerogatives of the Monroe Doctrine in the western hemisphere. Yet he also held that the United States could and should pursue what lay in its strategic interest: a *temporary* involvement in establishing order in postwar Europe. More precisely, he advocated a targeted cooperation with the *Entente* Powers in establishing what he deemed vital after a draconian peace had been forced on the vanquished: a system of power-political containment and "barrier states" designed to "fetter Germany" for the foreseeable future.[104]

In the struggle with Wilson, Lodge's priority became to unite Republican opposition to the president's League agenda. And, aided by Knox and the chairman of the Republican National Committee, Will Hays, he developed a strategy to this end that centred on advancing proposals for amendments that ostensibly were intended to make the League's "constitution" more acceptable to the Republican majority. Publicly, Lodge thus claimed that he did not oppose the creation of a League as such, but rather desired to ensure that in its final form the Covenant of the new organisation would be compatible with the American constitution.[105] In the efforts to formulate such amendments, the Republican elder statesman Elihu Root came to play an important role. Root generally favoured the idea of creating a League, but he had also criticised the Draft Covenant sharply. At Hays' request, he would eventually propose significant changes to a League design in which he saw "great value" in some respects but also "serious flaws".[106]

Building on his pre-war championing of arbitration, Root demanded stronger provisions for compulsory arbitration of justiciable questions in the Covenant. He recommended that the Monroe Doctrine – as well as domestic matters such as immigration – should be exempted from the jurisdiction of the League. And, crucially, he proposed that Article X should no longer be a permanent clause but amended "to hold for a limited time" of five years – after which any League member would be free to withdraw from it. Root reasoned that it would be wrong to "preserve for all time unchanged the distribution of power and territory" in the world in accordance with the "views and exigencies of the Allies in this present juncture". Yet he stressed that the United States had a "duty" in the war's immediate aftermath and in view of

---

[104] Lodge to Beveridge, 7, 18 and 27 February 1919, Lodge Papers; Lodge speech, 28 February 1919, Congressional Record, 65th Congress, 3rd session, 4520–4528. See Ambrosius (1987), p. 94; Cooper (2010), pp. 65–6.

[105] Lowell-Lodge debate, Boston, 19 March 1919, *New York Times*, 20 March 1919.

[106] Henry L. Stimson Diary, 15 February 1919, Stimson Papers; Root to Hays, 29 March 1919, Root Papers, Box 137.

"the present chaotic condition of Europe" to contribute to reordering and pacifying the Old World. He also emphasised, however, that the League should be transformed as soon as possible from "an alliance of one half of the active world against or for control of the other half" into a more comprehensive "league of peace" – which could only occur "in a calmer atmosphere".[107] Root's underlying aim was to sketch the basis for a possible compromise between Wilson's positions and those of his Republican critics in order to pave the way for an American membership in a League built on an "improved" Covenant. But while welcoming Root's proposals Lodge pointedly refused to commit himself to endorsing the Covenant, and the League, if Wilson accepted the changes the Republicans' *éminence grise* suggested and ways could be found to implement them. And Knox and other prominent Republican senators did not make any such commitments either.

Wilson responded to the ever more palpable Republican challenge with a characteristic mixture of superficial conciliatoriness and fundamentally uncompromising high-handedness in pursuit of his League agenda. Immediately after his arrival in Washington he had made a gesture towards his Republican critics and on 26 February met with Lodge and thirty-three other members of the Senate's Foreign Relations Committee and the House Foreign Affairs Committee at the White House. Offering to discuss with them the core articles of the proposed "constitution", he made some efforts to show a conciliatory attitude, stressing that he would welcome proposals for amendments. Essentially, however, he defended the Covenant's essential provisions. In response to numerous Republican objections he notably underscored that, in his interpretation, Article X would by no means force the American government to intervene militarily in every conflict – that such action was and remained ultimately "a matter for the United States to the decide" and that the Senate's ultimate authority in questions of war and peace would not be affected.[108]

Unsurprisingly, however, the meeting at the White House remained inconclusive and did nothing to narrow the gap between the president and his Republican opponents. Rather, the frontlines soon hardened. Wilson insisted that the Draft Covenant came "as near to being a guarantee of peace" as one could attain after the catastrophic war and that it was what "the world insists on".[109] And instead of signalling a willingness to compromise, he reacted defiantly to the Republican resolution of 3 March and once gain sought to use the presidential pulpit to put pressure on his critics. In a speech at the Metropolitan Opera House, where he made a joint appearance with Taft shortly before his return to Paris, he castigated them for their "comprehensive ignorance of the state the world". And, more importantly, he insisted that the

[107] *Ibid.*
[108] Wilson remarks, 26 February 1919, News Report, 26 February 1919, *PWW*, LV, p. 274.
[109] Wilson speech, 28 February 1919, *PWW*, LV, pp. 309–24.

Covenant had to remain an integral part of the peace settlement and was connected with it in so many ways that one "could not dissect" it from the eventual peace treaty "without destroying the whole vital structure".[110] Crucially, Wilson here revealed a tendency that would become even more pronounced in the later "treaty fight" with the Republican-dominated Senate: his determination to rely, ultimately, on the support of what he declared to be "an overwhelming majority of the American people" that favoured the League and to mobilise this majority to compel the Senate to approve the Covenant.[111]

Yet despite his defiant rhetoric the American president actually began quite soon to contemplate ways to amend the Covenant to accommodate his critics without, in his eyes, altering its essential character. Hitchcock, who remained his key ally in the Senate, had urged Wilson to prepare the ground for some kind of compromise. He had proposed a number of amendments that, in his judgement, would allow the president to persuade a sufficient number of Republican senators who had supported the Round Robin to endorse the League after all. What the leader of the Democratic minority considered especially critical was an explicit provision recognising the validity of the Monroe Doctrine. Yet he also proposed an amendment that clearly exempted national affairs from the purview of the League.[112] The president considered Hitchcock's recommendations, and he would also consider suggestions for amendments made by Root and Taft, who likewise deemed "a specific reservation of the Monroe Doctrine" critical.[113] Soon after his return to Paris he confidentially met with House, Cecil and his legal adviser David Hunter Miller to deliberate possible changes. Yet in the end Wilson insisted that Article X could not be weakened as this would decisively compromise the League's ability to secure peace – and it was the one article "on which the French relied". But he agreed to exclude domestic questions from the League's jurisdiction. Most of all, however, he indeed came to focus his attention on what predictably proved a highly controversial issue in Paris, namely to seek exemptions for the Monroe Doctrine.[114]

VII.   Amending the Covenant. The Struggles and Essential Bargains between the Principal Victors

By the time Wilson was back in Paris it had thus become even more obvious that he would have to overcome formidable opposition in the American Senate

---

[110] Wilson address, 4 March 1919, *PWW*, LV, p. 418.
[111] *Ibid.*
[112] Hitchcock to Wilson, 4 March 1919, Miller (1928), I, pp. 276–7.
[113] See Lamont to Wilson, 19 March 1919, *PWW*, LV, pp. 99–100; Taft to Wilson, 18 March 1919, *ibid.*, p. 83.
[114] See Miller Diary, 18 March 1919, *PWW*, LV, 78–80; House Diary, 18 March 1919; Cecil Diary, 18 March 1919, *ibid.*, pp. 81–3.

if he wanted to ensure a leading American role in the League and prevent damages to what he saw as the "vital structure" of the postwar order. And in the light of the escalating controversies in Washington the perception gained ground in the British and French delegations – and beyond – that the American president might not be able to overcome the resistance of the Senate majority. This cast doubt not only on the prospects of the League but also on the American ratification of the eventual peace treaties. Albeit with marked reluctance Wilson eventually decided to go ahead and claim reservations for the Monroe Doctrine. And this set in motion a drawn-out and complex bargaining process that involved not only but chiefly the principal victors. This process intensified in the last week of March and would drag on until 10 April.

Wilson was not oblivious to the concerns that other members of the American delegation had immediately raised. Particularly House had warned that if the president insisted on "a special reservation of the Monroe Doctrine" the Japanese delegates could be emboldened to demand a "reservation regarding a sphere of influence in Asia" and other powers would likely press for similar exemptions or other concessions. He feared that this could trigger an endless process that would greatly weaken the League Covenant.[115] Wilson's adviser captured a core problem of the entire peacemaking process that became particularly palpable here. The more the representatives of one state, and notably of a principal power, demanded exemptions and "special rules" for strategic or domestic-political reasons, the more their counterparts would follow suit – and ultimately this could only corrode the credibility of principles and rules that, as in the Covenant, had been formulated in universal terms and were supposed to apply universally. And as the most eminent spokesman of a "universal" League, Wilson of course set a particularly problematic precedent. Another no less fundamental danger that arose here was that rather than a general, universal regime of "collective security" and standards of conflict-resolution the League would merely establish an international system in which, citing the example of the United States, all the most powerful states could still claim their own "Monroe Doctrines" and maintain, or expand, formal or informal spheres of influence that lay beyond the League's purview.

During the controversial discussions that ensued in and beyond the League Commission, Wilson not only sought to persuade the other representatives that what *he* defined as the core maxims of the Monroe Doctrine were entirely compatible with the provisions of the Covenant. He even argued that the Covenant itself could be interpreted as a compact that essentially *universalised* the long-standing American doctrine. For, he claimed, its provisions represented an "international extension" of the principles advanced by the United

---

[115] House diary, 18 March 1919, *PWW*, LV, p. 82.

States when it had pledged, in Monroe's declaration, to protect the "political independence" and "territorial integrity" of other American states.[116] Wilson thus in effect sought to revive a "vision" he had already advanced during the war. In the wake of the – failed – initiative for a Pan-American Pact he had proposed, in his "Peace without Victory" speech of 22 January 1917, that all nations should adopt the Monroe Doctrine as "the doctrine of the world" and thereby subscribe to the principles "that no nation should seek to extend its polity over any other nation or people" and "that all nations henceforth should avoid entangling alliances which would draw them into competitions of power".[117]

Yet the subsequent debates at Versailles soon revealed that, for different reasons, the other plenipotentiaries strongly objected both to exemptions for the Monroe Doctrine *and* its universalisation. On behalf of the Chinese delegation, Wellington Koo voiced the concern that Japan would seize on the American precedent to claim its own "reservations" so as to extend its sphere of power and influence at China's expense.[118] But the most serious and fundamental objections were raised by France's chief delegate. Bourgeois pointed out if one accepted Wilson's claim that the Monroe Doctrine was consistent with the League Covenant there would be no need for any special "reservation" – and stressed that such a "reservation" would thus in fact be "dangerous". His underlying concern was that it would further weaken the collective security provisions of Article X and cast doubt on the American commitment to fulfil its League obligations in postwar Europe.[119]

Crucially, however, the fact that the American president felt compelled to seek an amendment to accommodate the Monroe Doctrine led the most powerful actors with whom he had to negotiate to press for concessions on issues that they deemed vital. In different ways, Lloyd George and Clemenceau made their consent to Wilson's amendment – and to some extent to the League as such – dependent on his willingness to make broader *quid pro quo* agreements. Essentially, both the British and the French premier now seized on the fact that Wilson had made the creation of the League his absolute priority *and* that he faced such powerful challenges on the home front in order to strike harder bargains with him. The struggles over the League Covenant thus came to have important ramifications for the way in which the

---

[116] Minutes of the League Commission, 22, 24, 26 March and 10 April 1919, Miller (1928), I, pp. 327–31, 439–52; II, pp. 360–95.

[117] Wilson Senate address, 22 January 1917, *PWW*, XL, p. 539; See also Wilson speech to League to Enforce Peace, 27 May 1916, *PWW*, XXXVII, pp. 113 ff. See also Wilson remarks, 26 February 1919, News Report, 26 February 1919, *PWW*, LV, pp. 268, 271.

[118] See Clements (2008), pp. 67 ff.

[119] Bourgeois and Larnaude statements in the League Commission, 22, 24, 26 March and 10 and 11 April 1919, Miller (1928), I, pp. 310–53, 439–52; II, pp. 360–95.

negotiations between the Big Three would evolve in the most critical "inter-allied" phase of the peacemaking process, between mid-March and the end of April. They therefore became part and parcel of the wider search for complex compromises between the principal victors that became one of the most salient characteristics of the Paris Peace Conference. Lloyd George saw an opportunity to safeguard a key element of Britain's global strategy of imperial defence, namely its naval preponderance. The French premier now stepped up his efforts to commit the American president to the transatlantic security system that he and Tardieu intended to build; more precisely, he now sought to bargain for Wilson's consent to "material guarantees", chiefly in the Rhineland, and to something that came as close as possible to a de facto alliance of the victors.

Lloyd George's concerns focused on a looming new naval bill in the American Congress that aimed to extend the massive naval expansion programme that the Wilson administration had pursued since the passing of the 1916 Naval Act. He had earlier impressed on the American president that Britain would "spend her last guinea to keep a navy superior to that of the United States." But in view of serious fiscal challenges and retrenchment requirements the real British interest was to pre-empt what could escalate into a postwar naval arms race with a competitor that by then had greater financial resources at its disposal.[120] For his part Wilson was still determined to use the threat to "build the greatest navy in the world" as a lever to compel the *Entente* Powers, and particularly the British government, to accept the essentials of his peace agenda; and the naval bill was intended to serve precisely this purpose.[121] The American president thus initially insisted that steps to limit US naval construction could only be considered once the British government had signed a peace that included the Covenant and guaranteed that the League would actually be established.

But Lloyd George was no less determined to insist on a strategic bargain on his terms. He made the conclusion of a naval agreement that entailed a significant modification or preferably an abandonment of the new American naval programme the essential precondition for Britain's cooperation in finalising the League Covenant. This became a key element of the revised peace strategy that Lloyd George and his advisers Hankey and Kerr developed at Fontainebleau in mid-March. In the decisive memorandum the prime minister stated that the League would be "a sham and a mockery" unless a "firm understanding" could be reached between the British Empire and the United States, as well as France and Italy, that there would be "no competitive building up of fleets and armies between them". Lloyd George not only

---

[120] House diary, 19 December 1918, *PWW*, LIII, p. 448; See also War Cabinet minutes, 10 November 1918, CAB 23/14.

[121] Dr Grayson diary, 8 December 1918, *PWW*, LIII, p. 337.

signalled that if Wilson did not agree to such an "understanding" he would block the amendment to Article X of the Covenant that exempted the Monroe Doctrine and America's self-accorded prerogatives in the western hemisphere; he even threatened that he would prevent the Covenant from becoming part of the peace settlement.[122] To Cecil, he confessed that the "real reason" for pursuing such a hard-fisted approach was that "he wanted to have something to bargain with" in order to compel "the Americans to give up their plan of building ships as against the British".[123]

What thus escalated has aptly been called the Anglo-American "naval battle" of Paris. And this battle was ended peacefully through a bargaining process in which two key intermediaries – Cecil and House – played pivotal roles. They managed to negotiate a compromise after two tumultuous weeks of deadlock and deepening friction between Wilson and Lloyd George. Cecil tried to persuade the British prime minister, from whom he felt increasingly alienated, to refrain from instrumentalising the League to push through core interests of the British Empire, which in his eyes was profoundly "hazardous" to the "cause of the League".[124] But as this fell on deaf ears he sought to encourage Wilson to resort to tough bargaining tactics as well. He suggested that the president ought to put forward a draft peace treaty in the Council of Four that reasserted the parameters of the Fourteen Points, including the centrality of the League, and then compel his European counterparts to sign up to an "American peace" by making assertive use of America's leverage vis-à-vis its debtors – and even using the threat of leaving the peace conference unless they fell in line.[125] Wilson would not go quite that far; he would not revert to his – unrealistic – original aspiration to impose an "American peace". But, frustrated with Lloyd George's obstructionist behaviour – and Clemenceau's parallel recalcitrance on the thorny issues of French security, the Rhineland, and the Saar – he in fact threatened to depart for the United States. Ultimately, Lloyd George was not prepared to risk a complete rupture with Wilson and abandon completely his strategy of seeking to stabilise the postwar order through cooperation and burden-sharing with the United States. And Wilson agreed to seek a compromise rather than risk losing the cooperation of a power that thus far had de facto been his key strategic partner in establishing the League.

The Anglo-American naval conflict could not be resolved in 1919, but it was at least possible to forge a *preliminary* agreement that effectively brought the League process back on track. This outcome would have been inconceivable if Wilson and Lloyd George had not been willing to seek common ground at the

---

[122] Lloyd George, Fontainebleau memorandum, 25 March 1919, PWW, LVI, 259–70.
[123] Cecil diary, 26 March 1919, Cecil Papers; House diary, 27 March 1919, House Papers.
[124] Cecil to Balfour, 5 April 1919, Balfour Papers, Add. Mss. 51099.
[125] Cecil to House, 5 April 1919, House Papers.

eleventh hour. But it was the result of the mediating efforts of two intermediaries who pursued one common priority: to preserve a modicum of Anglo-
American unity and cooperation without which, as they saw it, the entire
League project was doomed to fail. Having obtained Lloyd George's author-
isation, Cecil entered into confidential negotiations with House. And with
Wilson's backing, the latter proposed that if the British government consented
to having the League covenant included in the peace treaty the Wilson
administration would be prepared not only to "abandon or modify" the new
American naval programme but also to enter into annual consultations with
Britain on limits for future naval construction.[126]

On these premises, a bilateral agreement between Britain and the United
States was concluded on 10 April 1919. Wilson now emphasised that he had
an overriding interest in preventing the escalation of competition between the
world's two largest naval powers and that, to set an example, he would support
bilateral arms-control negotiations between them after the peace treaty had
been signed.[127] Lloyd George accepted this compromise formula. And he now
also consented to the amendment to the Covenant that the American delegation proposed on the same day and that would then be enshrined in a new
Article XXI rather than in Article X. It stipulated that "(n)othing in this
Covenant shall be deemed to affect the validity of international engagements,
such as treaties of arbitration or regional understandings like the Monroe
Doctrine, for securing the maintenance of peace".[128] In the end, the Anglo-
American compromise "solution" merely postponed more serious attempts to
address the salient issue of naval arms control. But it was nonetheless significant in that it prepared the ground for a momentous process that would
unfold after the peace conference, and outside the League, and through which
eventually the most significant naval arms-control regime of the postwar era
would be forged – at the Washington Conference of 1921–22.[129]

Of even more import for the dynamics and outcomes of the peacemaking
process was the equally hard-fisted bargaining strategy Clemenceau came to
pursue after Wilson's return to Paris in mid-March. It was a strategy that
Tardieu had significantly influenced and that was shaped by the French
security imperatives vis-à-vis Germany. In short, in return for supporting
the League Covenant and the Monroe Doctrine amendment Clemenceau

---

[126] House to Cecil, 8 April 1919, House Papers. See Egerton (1978), pp. 161–3; Tillmann
(1961), pp. 286–94.
[127] See Anglo-American "Memorandum", 10 April 1919, House Papers.
[128] See Miller (1928), I, pp. 442–61; Article XXI, *PWW*, LVIII, p. 195; Knock (1992), p. 248.
[129] Asserting their hegemonic interests, the British and American protagonists made sure
that naval questions would not be broached during the general disarmament and
security discussions at Versailles. See Council of Four Deliberations, 26 March 1919,
Mantoux (1992), I, pp. 20 ff.

and his principal adviser sought to gain Wilson's backing on two crucial issues: "tangible guarantees" in the Rhineland and, even more importantly, firmer assurances that the Anglo-American powers would to come to France's aid in the event of future German aggression.[130] Because of his unchanged priority of ultimately securing "unity among the victors", Clemenceau never went so far as to threaten to block the entire League project. But he encouraged Bourgeois to obstruct Wilson's efforts to secure a "reservation" for the Monroe Doctrine and to push again for a more robust organisation. And Bourgeois would indeed not only persist with his criticism of the American president's proposals but also renew his call for a "League army" and a stricter sanction regime.[131] In House's assessment, what he demanded again raised the danger that the League would be turned into an "instrument of war" that was directed against Germany instead of becoming an "instrument of peace" and conflict resolution between the victors and the vanquished.[132]

In the end, Bourgeois would be instructed to relent. Clemenceau would be prepared to support an essentially Anglo-American League Covenant and an exemption for the Monroe Doctrine. But the negotiations over the Covenant had only reinforced the profound apprehensions with which he and Tardieu looked upon the League and their view that, in whatever form it was established, the new organisation would not provide "adequate" security guarantees.[133] Thus, the underlying aim they pursued was clearly to obtain the support of Wilson and Lloyd George for the French Rhineland agenda and more *specific* Anglo-American security guarantees. And they only became more conciliatory on the League once they concluded that they had obtained essential concessions and assurances from their British and American interlocutors.[134]

In the final stages of the controversies over the League Covenant Wilson also finally had to confront head on one of the most critical extra-European questions of the peace conference. Japan's representatives chose this moment to reassert their claims to the Shandong province and on 24 April stepped up the pressure by threatening to leave the peace conference and, by implication,

[130] Clemenceau comments, 27 March 1919, Poincaré (1926–33), XI, pp. 283–4; Tardieu memorandum, 2 February 1919, Tardieu Papers, vol. 417; Tardieu memorandum, 25 February 1919, Fonds Clemenceau, 6N 73-2, SHD-DAT.

[131] See Cecil diary, 28 February 1919; Cecil Papers; Cecil to House, 8 March 1919, House Papers; Bourgeois and Larnaude statements in the League Commission, 22, 24, 26 March and 10 and 11 April 1919, Miller (1928), I, pp. 310–53, 439–52; II, pp. 360–95.

[132] House diary, 16 March 1919, House Papers.

[133] Tardieu memorandum, 26 February 1919, endorsed by Clemenceau, in Tardieu (II/1921), p. 158; Clemenceau (1930), p. 179.

[134] Clemenceau comments, 27 March 1919, Poincaré (1926–33), XI, pp. 283–4; Tardieu note to House, 22 March 1919, Tardieu (II/1921), pp. 135–8; Tardieu note, 2 April 1919, ibid., p. 138; Tardieu note on French proposal of 14 March, Tardieu Papers, vol. 418.

to withdraw Japan's support for the League. The Shandong question, which had been left unresolved since it was first debated in late January, not only had important regional repercussions – for the future relations between Japan and China and the future underpinnings of "order" in East Asia. It also became a critical test for the credibility of the self-determination and equality agenda Wilson had championed – and the manner in which it was "settled" would show just how difficult it was for Wilson to avoid major, in fact discrediting concessions if he wanted to found the League as a globally relevant organisation and ensure that it included the strongest non-western power, Japan.

The clash and the essentially unbridgeable gap between Japanese and Chinese claims, which were based on starkly conflicting premises, had already become obvious when the Shandong issue had first been broached in late January. On behalf of the Chinese delegation, Wellington Koo had demanded the return of Kiaochow and the Shandong province to China. Stressing that he acted as "spokesman of a quarter of humanity" Koo had invoked not only self-determination and international law but also historical arguments, maintaining that China had never surrendered its sovereign rights to a province that, as the home of Confucius, was a heartland of Chinese civilisation – and whose original "lease" to Germany had been effected through force.[135] In April, Koo once again strove hard to refute Japan's demands. He reiterated his arguments and now emphasised in particular that the treaties Japan had compelled Chinese authorities to sign since 1915 in pursuit of their Twenty-One Demands were invalid because they essentially had been imposed by force. And he appealed to the values Wilson, Lloyd George and Clemenceau claimed to represent. He argued that China's delegates had come to Paris to attain "justice" and believed in "the justice of the west"; and he warned that if this was refused, the Chinese people would blame "the attitude of the west" and those might gain the upper hand who sought to turn away from the United States and Europe and align with Japan to build a new Pan-Asian order "for the Asians".[136]

But these warnings would have little effect. The Japanese plenipotentiaries refused to yield any ground. The most powerful negotiator, Count Makino, had early on asserted what he saw as Japan's legitimate claims to the disputed province, pointing not only to the treaties Tokyo had concluded with the Chinese government but also to the secret agreement of 1917 in which Britain and France had recognised Japan's suzerainty over Shandong. In effect, Makino thus invoked the sanctity of treaties based on pre-war rationales of imperialist power politics. Pursuing a more "modern" approach, he in late April would also try to seize on the earlier Japanese demand to include a

---

[135] Baker (1927–39), II, pp. 229–31, 241 ff.
[136] *Ibid.*, pp. 256–7; Clements (2008), pp. 81 ff.; King (1959), p. 20.

"racial equality" clause in the League Covenant – which Wilson and British representatives had rejected – in order to heighten the pressure on the American president in the Shandong question.[137] And for overriding geostrategic reasons, Lloyd George had supported and would continue to support the claims of Britain's Japanese ally. He had justified this by underscoring that the sanctity of treaties had to be upheld as a basic principle of international order after the Great War, thus pointedly refuting Wilson's demand to sweep away all secret treaties and power-political agreements.[138]

The American president thus faced a fundamental dilemma. On the one hand, his overall credibility and the United States' future relations with China were at stake. On the other, what loomed was the dangerous scenario of Japan turning away from the League and pursuing an assertive imperialist policy in China or even aligning with another power that would likely remain outside the League system – Germany. In the end, Wilson saw no other option but to give in to Japan's demands and accept, here too, a de facto bargain that combined elements of old and new international politics. Japan's control over Shandong was recognised, and the only gesture the Japanese government had to make was a non-binding declaration in which it promised to restore Chinese sovereignty over the province in the future if China proved its willingness to cooperate with Japan. In return, Japan accepted the Covenant – without an explicit or less explicit "racial equality" clause – and agreed to join the new world organisation. Noticeably embittered, Wilson tried to defend an arrangement that he himself deemed essential not "fair" by stressing that it represented the best possible solution that could be found in view of the "dirty past" of competing imperialisms in China. Characteristically, he thus focused his hopes all the more fervently on the League itself and the capacity it would have, in his view, to bring different states together and foster new standards of international conduct. He argued that once Japan had joined the the League, the United States could take the lead in trying not only to secure "justice" for China vis-à-vis Japan but to restore overall Chinese sovereignty by also ending the privileges the victorious European powers still asserted. Yet the negotiations of 1919 provided few assurances that such processes could indeed be initiated; and Wilson had not addressed America's informal but no less intrusive "Open Door" policy vis-à-vis China.[139]

The bargain over Shandong manifested again just how many difficult compromises Wilson had to make with the other principal powers represented at Versailles if he wanted to salvage the League – on terms he could hope to legitimise at home – and to make sure that it received their fundamental backing. This aim, and the concern to prevent a new phase of power-political

[137] Shimazu (1998), pp. 13 ff., 137 ff.; Burkman (2008), pp. 80–6, 90–4.
[138] Baker (1927–39), II, pp. 241–7.
[139] Elleman (2002), pp. 111 ff.

rivalries and balance-of-power machinations in and beyond East Asia ultimately outweighed his determination to insist on the principles he had proclaimed and concerns over the consequences the acute disappointment of
Chinese expectations might have. Yet the Shandong "deal" would indeed
contribute markedly to weakening the American president's credibility, not
only in China; and it would arouse especially fierce criticism in the United
States, providing his opponents with further ammunition against him.

Finally, the intense debates over revisions of the Covenant also led the
victorious powers to grapple once more with the cardinal question of when
and on what conditions Germany was to be admitted to the League. While
Clemenceau and Bourgeois insisted on criteria designed to create high barriers, Wilson now came to modify his earlier position and sought to make to
Germany's *eventual* entry easier. His priority was and remained to make the
League an integral part of the peace treaty itself. A consequence of this was
that, unless revisions were made, Germany would be required to accept the
peace treaty and the Covenant while at the same time remaining outside the
new international organisation and not even having a clear prospect of
membership. On 22 March, the American president had thus suggested that
rather than a two-thirds majority a simple majority in the League Assembly
should be sufficient to admit new members. And it was only now that he
stressed that such a measure was necessary to avoid turning the League into an
exclusive institution of the victors and neutral powers. Earlier, the American
representatives on the League Commission had collaborated with Cecil to
make provisions for a future expansion of the Executive Council so that when
it joined Germany would be accorded a permanent seat.[140]

But it was only in the final stages of the peace conference, when the victors
had to respond to the German delegation's counter-proposals, that Wilson
really changed his emphasis; yet he would do so largely because of tactical
concerns, above all to ensure that the Scheidemann government signed the
peace treaty. In the final deliberations with Clemenceau and Lloyd George, he
came to argue that if the German government proved its willingness to abide
by the terms of the peace treaty Germany should be admitted to the League
very soon. And he now espoused the British view that it was preferable to
"have the Germans in the League", where they could be restrained, rather than
to "treat them as pariahs" and thereby push them to join forces with other
pariah powers like Bolshevik Russia and Hungary.[141] Cecil now urged the
assembled negotiators to give the Scheidemann government a clear signal that
if it gave satisfactory proof of its "pacific tendency", Germany would be
included in the League within a few months. For his part, Lloyd George

---

[140] Miller (1921), pp. 399, 404.
[141] Wilson, Council of Four, 3 and 7 June 1919, Mantoux (1992), II, pp. 288–9, 347–9;
FRUS-PPC, VI, pp. 251–2.

underscored that the victors should make clear that Germany's entry could be effected in the near future, after roughly one year, provided that the German government had by then shown "good faith" in fulfilling the terms of the peace treaty.[142]

But Clemenceau would oppose even these limited concessions. And neither the British premier nor the American president would be prepared to strain the fraying unity among the victors any further over this issue.[143] In the end, they would accept an agreement that, in accordance with French preferences, not only ruled out an "early admission" but gave no clear assurances at all of a German entry to the League in the foreseeable future. Instead, it stipulated that the vanquished power would have to pass through a probation period during which it provided "clear proofs" not only of the "stability" of its democratic government but also of its willingness to comply with the terms of the peace treaty.[144] These conditions would also have to be met by the other defeated powers that for the time being remained outside the League.

VIII.   A Truncated Concert of Nations to Eliminate War from the World. The Potential and Limits of the League Covenant

The product of multiple compromises – among the victors – the, slightly revised League Covenant that was approved by the Plenary Conference of Versailles on 29 April combined in a strained and at times contradictory manner more traditional ideas of international order, notably adapted nineteenth-century conceptions of a great-power concert, and liberal-progressive principles of international organisation, international law and transnational cooperation that, while having much older roots, had been significantly advanced in the decades before 1914. Wilson praised the Covenant as the fulfilment of his aspirations and, seeking to emphasise its progressive character, argued that it had created a "living thing", an evolving structure that could serve essentially as a "permanent clearinghouse" for international conflicts and problems. Later he would call it a "concert of action of the nations to eliminate war from the world" that through its very existence and operation could transform the character of international politics. He thus indeed still thought that the League would hold the key to transcending the

---

[142] Cecil memorandum, 3 June 1919, Cabinet Paper W.C.P. 916, CAB 29/16; draft reply, 7 June 1919, *FRUS-PPC*, VI, pp. 251–2; Lloyd George remarks, British Empire Delegation, 33 and 34, 1 June 1919, CAB 29/38/1; Council of Four, 2 June 1919, Mantoux (1992), II, pp. 269–71.

[143] Council of Four, 3 and 7 June 1919, Mantoux (1992), II, pp. 289, 347–9.

[144] Council of Four, 12 June 1919, Mantoux (1992), II, p. 403; "Reply of the Allied and Associated Powers", 16 June 1919, *FRUS-PPC*, VI, pp. 926 ff., 934, 940.

onerous legacy of European and global balance-of-power politics of the pre-war era and coping with the consequences of the Great War itself.[145]

In fact, the Covenant founded an organisation of essentially sovereign states, and particularly sovereign principal powers, thus affirming that the latter were and remained the key international actors. At the same time, however, it established more explicitly than ever before the basic premise that all – member – states, regardless of their size and power, would be fundamentally "equal" and have the same "rights" under international law; and it offered not only more participatory possibilities to smaller states but also a more explicit provisions to protect their security and integrity. But, as we have seen, the Covenant also institutionalised hierarchical distinctions between the – victorious – great powers on the Executive Council and the other member states. It created an organisation that in principle was open to all sovereign states but originally not only excluded the vanquished powers of the war but also set criteria that made their eventual accession uncertain. And it inaugurated even starker differences between its sovereign members and the new mandate states under the League's at the core neo-colonial regime.

The Paris Covenant fell distinctly short of the expectations of more radical internationalists, socialists and left-wing progressives on both sides of the Atlantic. What it contained did not live up to their stirring vision of a radically new and authoritative, indeed essentially supranational organisation. Nor was it a blueprint for a "League of the Peoples" that ended the era of great power politics and prerogatives, embodied and created a forum for "new diplomacy", and promoted far-reaching universal disarmament. Yet the Covenant's core provisions also had to disappoint French juridical internationalists like Bourgeois and others who had advocated a more authoritative League "with teeth". Shaped by Wilson's and prevalent British maxims, the League's constitution envisaged an inter-state rather than a supranational institution, establishing neither an ambitious system of compulsory arbitration nor an iron-clad security regime with far-reaching sanction powers that was backed up by an international force. It thus clearly did not have the makings of a new insitutionalised "world government", let alone those of a "superstate". Rather, the organisation that was to be set up in Geneva was essentially conceived as the institutionalised framework of a new *concert of states*, and at the core a concert of the – victorious – great powers, that was to permit them to pursue, manage and oversee the postwar international order, prevent and defuse conflicts, and respond to threats to regional and "world peace". Crucially, all committed themselves to new rules and procedures for the peaceful settlement of international conflicts.

---

[145] Wilson statement, 14 February 1919, *PWW*, LV, pp. 175–6. Wilson remarks, 14 February 1919, Wilson (1939), p. 239; Wilson speech, 26 February 1919, News Report, 26 February 1919, *PWW*, LV, p. 273.

At the same time, the League would create what can best be described as a political rather than juridical system of "collective security". International security was to be safeguarded, and aggressors were to be deterred, not merely by the pacifying power of "world opinion" but by the solemn commitment of all signatories, but above all the great powers, to take appropriate action and, in the last resort, to use force to protect the integrity of the League's member states and to come to their aid in the event of an aggression. Through Articles X and XI, the Covenant for the first time enshrined the principle that a threat to peace and security anywhere in the world was a concern for all members of the League, and particularly for the members of the Executive Council. But, as both the American president and all leading British decision-makers had insisted, the final decisions about what course of action to take in order to safeguard peace had to be made by state governments and national parliaments.

In the most critical areas the Covenant of 1919 thus did not entail any significant infringements of national and particularly great-power sovereignty or hard-and-fast guarantees. And the negotiations of Versailles clearly manifested that none of the governments of the principal powers, including the French, were prepared to countenance such limitations. The effectiveness of the League as an instrument of "collective security" – in Europe and beyond – would therefore depend above all on the willingness of these governments to honour their – limited – commitments under the Covenant to assume responsibilities in settling conflicts in accordance with the principles it prescribed. This fell distinctly short of what the champions of a more robust "collective security" regime had advocated. And it notably fell short of the "tangible guarantees" that Clemenceau and other French policymakers sought. What proved crucial was that the political leaders of Britain and the United States essentially rejected more far-reaching commitments; and when both Wilson and Lloyd George stressed that it would be impossible to gain domestic support for such commitments their *caveats* actually reflected the realities in the countries they represented.

In spite of its inner tensions and contradictions the League Covenant of 29 April 1919 can nonetheless be seen as the closest approximation of a constitutive framework for a new global order after the Great War. Despite all the compromises, problems and frustrated expectations that had accompanied its inception, the League could still become a forum and crystallisation point for postwar internationalism, give important impulses to the development of rules and norms of an emerging international society, and heighten the awareness of common challenges and problems – in the political, economic, social spheres – that required inter- and transnational answers. And once it had been set up and consolidated, the institution itself could essentially become a laboratory for new forms of international cooperation and further the evolution of internationalist outlooks among those policy-makers, administrators and experts who would work for or on behalf of the new organisation.[146]

But in the way it came into being the League could *not* yet serve as the essential framework for peace and security in post–First World War Europe – or the wider world – or as the much needed "superstructure" of a new Atlantic order. First of all, there was still a need to address the fundamental security concerns of France – and of other states with particularly strong security needs – through more forceful guarantees. And in the constellation of 1919 only the Anglo-American powers could provide such guarantees. Even more important, however, was that the League itself still had to be turned into what its original champions had desired all along: an essentially universal and *integrative* rather than *exclusive* institution.

For one of its principal shortcomings, which has not been sufficiently appreciated, was that the Paris Covenant established the League as a *truncated* organisation that excluded, for an indefinite period, the defeated powers, above all Germany. If steps could be taken *after* Versailles to make the League more inclusive then it and particularly its Executive Council still had the potential to become, in accordance with American and British preferences, the platform of a new, institutionalised transatlantic concert of democratic powers, which also drew in the nascent German republic. And it could then also indeed function as what Wilson had all along desired it to become: a "clearinghouse" of international politics in which the most salient problems and systemic conflicts the Great War had left behind could be addressed in a concerted manner.

But the decisions and compromises the victors had made at Versailles actually impeded advances towards a more integrative, universal league – or at least they made them significantly harder. A crucial precondition for any such advances was, of course, that Wilson first of all gained the requisite support for the new organisation in the American Senate, which was by no means assured in view of the Republicans' more or less pronounced reserva-tions against the entire League project. Yet the American president and British proponents of an essentially integrationist orientation also still faced another fundamental problem. In short, the prevalent French conceptions of what the League was to become – namely both the framework for a *de facto* postwar alliance of the victors and an instrument for the control and containment of Germany – still pointed in a completely different direction.

While the French protagonists realised that they would not be able to prevent the defeated power's eventual admission to the League, their principal concern was to ensure that the new organisation remained, as long as possible,

---

[146] See Pedersen (2007), pp. 1091 ff.; Clavin (2013), pp. 1 ff.; Webster (2016).

a victors' institution. At the same time, Clemenceau and Tardieu impressed on Wilson and Lloyd George time and again that they regarded the "guarantees" the new organisation provided as utterly insufficient. Indeed, in their eyes France's core security needs vis-à-vis Germany could not be met through the League, or through the League alone. All of this meant that not only the development prospects of the League as a core mechanism of a modernised world order but also, more specifically, the prospects of creating an effective Atlantic peace system depended decisively on the willingness, and capacity, of the American and British peacemakers to offer more *tangible* and *specific* guarantees to France *beyond the League*. They needed to provide assurances that could eventually induce French policymakers to accept Germany's integration into the League of Nations – and into a reconfigured Atlantic order.

16

No Just Peace without Security

The Pivotal German Settlement and the Struggle
to Found a New Atlantic Security System

At the time Wilson prepared to return to the United States, after nearly a month of deliberations that had mainly centred on the League of Nations, the negotiations about the core problems of the peace process – namely the terms of the envisaged peace settlement with Germany – had not even begun. As not only House emphasised, there was an overriding need to draw up a "program" for the general settlement that was to be presented to German representatives.[1] What the political leaders, strategists and experts of the victorious powers now had to confront, at a deeper level, were the two crucial systemic problems of 1919 – problems that were intricately interconnected, even interdependent: the German question and the question of how far it would be possible to establish, for the first time, an effective transatlantic security system.

Arguably, the quality and durability of the entire peace settlement depended on how far the protagonists found ways to come to terms with these problems. With a view to Germany, they still had to agree on the terms and modalities of the reparations settlement as well as the precise economic terms and military restrictions they would seek. They still had to reach a consensus on what borders the postwar German state was to have in the east. And in view of the far-reaching French schemes for the Rhineland, they had to grapple with the question of how far German sovereignty was to be curtailed in the west.

More fundamentally, the victors now had to decide how they would deal with the problem of German power and the underlying question of what place, and role, the vanquished power was to have in the renovated international order not only in the short but also in the longer term. And further salient questions finally had to be answered: How far would the political leaders of the western powers seek to negotiate a settlement that took into account not only German self-determination claims but also the interests and needs of those who represented the fledgling Weimar Republic? Would they be able to reach solid *preliminary* understandings that could permit actual negotiations with the Scheidemann government after all? Would they be willing to countenance such a process, even in a limited form? Or would it now become clear that the

---

[1] House diary, 14 February 1919, *PWW*, LV, p. 193.

only realistic outcome in 1919 was a victors' peace – with all the consequences this was bound to have?

As the initial negotiations among the Big Three revealed very clearly, there was no prospect of "solving" the German problem and forging a sustainable settlement without first laying the groundwork for a new system of security that above all provided effective assurances to France – and Belgium – yet also to the new East European states against what they perceived as the critical threat: *revanchist* attacks of the power that had been defeated at such immense cost. Because the Clemenceau government did not regard a League on Anglo-American premises as an effective instrument to guarantee France's future security the altercations between the victors that now ensued in many ways concentrated on the dispute over how French concerns vis-à-vis Germany could be addressed more effectively. Yet the really critical question that arose was indeed a systemic one. It was the question of how far the western powers could agree on the basic underpinnings of a more specific transatlantic security architecture – an architecture of agreements, guarantees and rules that not only provided reassurance against the "German threat" but indeed addressed the broader and multi-dimensional security problems that beset western, Central and Eastern Europe in the aftermath of the war.

And it now became even more obvious than before that at this critical juncture Britain and the United States were the only powers that had the means to provide the necessary assurances on which the creation of such a security architecture depended. What thus had a crucial bearing on the further evolution of the peacemaking process and the future development of the international order was the extent to which key British and American decision-makers not only saw the need but also found new ways to make firmer and more specific commitments to European postwar security – commitments that above all calmed understandably profound French anxieties. No less important, however, was the question of how far they could gain the indispensable domestic-political support for such commitments in their own countries.

From a systemic vantage-point it is worth stressing again that the negotiations between the victors were decisively affected by the distinctly asymmetrical security constellation the Great War had created. The fact that France's security needs differed so markedly from those of Britain and the United States had a palpable effect. Both among British and American policymakers the prevalent perception was clearly that once Germany had been deprived of its naval power, it posed no longer even a medium-term threat to the states and societies they represented – because of their geopolitical detachment from continental Europe and their superior naval forces. Their security concerns were thus more general and less existential than those of their French counterparts who perceived the threat posed by a structurally superior German power that was their immediate neighbour as highly disconcerting. The approaches each side pursued indeed reflected this imbalance.

Yet it also has to be emphasised how difficult the conditions and how immense the time constraints were under which the principal peacemakers had to operate when they finally sought to tackle what Wilson rightly termed the "most difficult and urgent questions". As the American president warned after his return to Versailles in mid-March, the western leaders were facing a "real race between peace and anarchy", notably in Central and Eastern Europe.[2] In many ways they thus felt compelled to hammer out agreements as quickly as possible, which did not encourage a search for balanced solutions and contributed to the often make-shift character of the decisions they made in the span of five weeks of heated altercations. It was against this background that Wilson recommended the establishment of the Council of Four. Henceforth, the crucial negotiations would indeed take place in and around this council and at the highest level – essentially between the Big Three. What unfolded can be described as a multi-layered and in many respects strikingly "modern" political negotiating and bargaining process – in which the political leaders and their informal advisers rather than professional diplomats or experts played the critical roles and sought to balance international and domestic concerns. This process would ultimately give shape to the crucial political compromises that were finalised in late April and eventually lay at the heart of the Versailles settlement.

While they struggled, the victors actually managed to forge agreements on innumerable particular aspects and specific territorial, political and financial questions – on the Rhineland, the Saar, the future German–Polish border and, most precariously, reparations. But they never managed to address the German question *as a whole* or the wider European security question in a comprehensive manner. Nor could they reach agreement on how they would deal with the new German republic in the future – on whether to concentrate on containment and exclusion, as the French protagonists demanded, or on making a settlement that would permit its relatively swift accommodation in the postwar order.

At a deeper level, not only the approaches and interests but also the underlying assumptions and outlooks of the principal victors remained incompatible or extremely difficult to reconcile. Put differently, they did not converge or only converged superficially. This the negotiations clearly mani-fested, and this is what has to be illuminated in order to grasp essential limitations of the peacemaking process of 1919. Most profound was and remained, undoubtedly, the conflict between French approaches and outlooks on the one hand and those of the British and American leaders on the other. Consequently, rather than establish the firm nucleus of a new Atlantic security

---

[2] Wilson, Council of Four, 24 March 1919, Mantoux (1992), I, p. 3.

order, the victors could only agree on basic, and disparate, elements of what essentially became a *hybrid* system. It was a system that uneasily combined "material guarantees" through a long-term occupation of the Rhineland and "political guarantees" enshrined in a treaty that was supposed to complement the League and stipulated carefully limited Anglo-American commitments to come to France's aid in case of unprovoked German aggression.

In one important respect, however, the strategies and outlooks of the pivotal peacemakers did converge in the spring of 1919. Though on different grounds, they came to agree on the fundamental premise that there would be no substantive negotiations with German representatives and that the peace terms they negotiated would not be preliminary but essentially final terms. The fact that it proved so exceedingly difficult even to reach a modicum of agreement between their conflicting interests and priorities undoubtedly reinforced this premise. But it is important to understand that it was also based on remarkably similar and distinctly hierarchical assumptions that shaped the actions of the victors. At the core, these were assumptions about civilisational hierarchies, the standards they represented and their legitimate claim, as the political leaders of the victorious *and* most advanced powers, to set the rules of the peace and to *impose* them on the defeated power – even if both Wilson and Lloyd George advanced the – unrealistic – maxim that the peace settlement should be so "just" that the new German government could accept it *without* negotiations.

I.   Securing Peace Through Disarmament – and Military Control?

In the early stages of the peace conference the victors' approaches to postwar security and the treatment of Germany seemed to align in one important area, at least superficially. There was a basic consensus that, based on the terms of the armistice, the eventual peace settlement would have to impose far-reaching limits on Germany's future military capabilities, essentially setting out to disarm what had been Europe's most potent military power and leaving it only with minimal forces. What still had to be settled was the precise extent of the restrictions and the question of what kind of armed forces the defeated power would be allowed to retain. But the main controversy was sparked by another question, which yet again exposed underlying differences between French and Anglo-American outlooks. And that was question of how, and how far, Germany's compliance with the victors' envisaged restrictions would be monitored and controlled.

In mid-February, the Supreme Council had made a first important decision. Extending the armistice for an indefinite period, it established a commission headed by Marshal Foch whose task was to prepare detailed proposals for the peace treaty's military terms. On 3 March, this commission recommended – in line with Foch's preferences – that the defeated power was to be permitted to maintain a small army of 140,000 men, made up of conscripts whose service was to be limited to one year, yet without a general staff or any modern weaponry. The aim of Foch's plan, which lay at the heart of the commission's proposals, was to turn Germany into a power that would no longer be capable of waging or even preparing to wage a modern war.[3]

After he had made the defeat of Prusso-German militarism one of Britain's key war aims, Lloyd George supported strict disarmament provisions. He now demanded that the "military machine" the German Empire had "misused" in 1870 and 1914 had to be effectively eliminated.[4] Yet he argued that the best way to achieve this was to go one step further and prohibit conscription altogether, proposing instead that Germany was to have a small professional army that would just be strong enough to protect its borders, maintain domestic order and fend off Bolshevik forces. Subsequently, his military adviser Henry Wilson proposed a volunteer army of 200,000 men. The British premier praised this as an effective remedy because it would prevent Germany from training over time a large reservoir of conscripts that could later be mobilised to form the nucleus of a mass army. He was evidently less worried that a professional army might become a "state within the state" or a rallying point for those who aspired to reconstitute Germany's military power and challenge the postwar order. And for once, Lloyd George managed to persuade Clemenceau to follow his lead. The French premier abandoned Foch's scheme for a conscript army. By early March, an Anglo-French compromise had thus been reached that would set the terms ultimately enshrined in the Treaty of Versailles. It foresaw a volunteer army whose size had been further reduced, namely to 100,000 men.[5] Wilson, who had earlier stressed that the victors had a moral right to disarm Germany, agreed to this proposal; and he came to espouse Lloyd George's reasoning, concluding that a 100,000-man army was large enough to protect Germany's eastern borders but so small that it would no longer pose a threat to its neighbours.[6]

Both Wilson and Lloyd George thus emphasised that they had a common interest with Clemenceau in ensuring that the German state would never again have the means to dominate Europe militarily and thereby also politically. But both they and their advisers differed from their French counterparts on the vital issue of *how* this was to be achieved in the longer run. Expecting that German authorities would try to circumvent military restrictions by all available means, Foch and Clemenceau pushed for the strictest possible regime of

---

[3] See Stevenson (2006), pp. 195–224; Jackson (2013), p. 282.

[4] Lloyd George, Council of Ten, 10 March 1919, *FRUS-PPC*, IV, pp. 297–8; Sharp (II/2008), pp. 91–2.

[5] Notes of a conversation between Lloyd George, Clemenceau and House, 7 March 1919, Lloyd George Papers F/147/1.

[6] See Wilson statement, Supreme Council, 17 March 1919, *PWW*, LVI, pp. 3 and ff.; Bliss memorandum, 17 March 1919; Walworth (1986), pp. 209–10.

military and disarmament control. According to French plans, this regime was to be supervised by an inter-allied control commission with far-reaching inspection powers, which would be authorised to operate as long as necessary. In a wider context, French decision-makers regarded this commission as one of the main instruments to control the peace of containment for which they fought.

Yet both the British and the American military experts at Versailles voiced serious reservations against a long-term regime of military control. American reservations were particularly pronounced. General Bliss had warned Wilson that the military terms proposed by Foch would "create" rather than "prevent war". He argued that the "harassing control" the French marshal recommended would only provoke continual friction, proposing instead a strict three-month limit for control and inspections measures. And he counselled that relying on the League and a "growing democratic feeling" in Germany would offer "better protection for France". The military adviser Admiral Benson made a similar case. He was determined to prevent a scenario in which the United States not only joined in control measures that would produce "a perpetual series of incidents" but in fact became part of a perpetual treaty-enforcing alliance against Germany, which he deemed entirely undesirable. More importantly, Bliss and Benson pointed to a fundamental strategic predicament that, in their analysis, arose from French aspirations to establish, through the commission, a postwar regime ultimately based on military force. As they saw it, if French leaders, representing a nation of 40 million people, insisted on a long-term military containment of a neighbour with a population of roughly 70 million, it would soon become clear that their country was too weak to maintain this course on its own. France would thus become dependent on American support and consequently seek to involve the American government in upholding a conflict-prone status quo. They thus advised the American president to steer clear of any entangling control commitments.[7]

Wilson emphatically agreed with his advisers on these fundamentals. On 17 March, he declared in the Supreme War Council that he would not assent to terms that would subject Germany to permanent control, using harsh language to warn that this would bring "not peace, but Allied armed domination". Ultimately, the American president was adamant that his government would not participate in any measures that would de facto compel the United States to participate in the military enforcement of a precarious "balance of power" in Europe.[8] Lloyd George and his military advisers had similar reservations, suspecting that what lay behind the French proposals were designs not only to create a mechanism for the long-term control of Germany, but also to

[7] Bliss to Wilson, 14 March 1919, Wilson Papers; Benson to Wilson, 14 March 1919, Baker Papers. See Schwabe (1985), pp. 226–7.

[8] Wilson, Supreme War Council, 17 March 1919, *FRUS-PPC*, IV, pp. 358, 358–63.

establish a power-political preponderance on the European continent, which they regarded as both undesirable and untenable.[9]

Yet Wilson came to overrule his advisers in one important respect. Responding to French pressure, he eventually accepted that German disarmament would be overseen by an inter-allied control commission not just for an initial period of three months but until Germany had fulfilled its obligations. Subsequently, he wavered and backed a provision that would have authorised the League to take over the control of Germany's disarmament. But the French negotiators, who did not want to entrust such critical responsibilities to the new organisation, insisted successfully that an Inter-Allied Military Commission of Control (IMCC) would be in charge. And while a deadline for Germany's compliance with the victors' disarmament terms would be set – namely 31 March 1920 – no end date for the mandate of this commission would be specified.[10] Nonetheless, the negotiations threw into relief marked tension between French and Anglo-American priorities, between the French imperative to enforce a strict disarmament regime and an Anglo-American preference for concluding the control and verification process as soon as possible and avoiding longer-term measures that not only entailed far-reaching responsibilities but also clashed with their political interest in pacifying relations with Germany. This tension would persist in the 1920s.[11]

As noted, both Wilson and Lloyd had actually come to Paris with more far-reaching aspirations in the sphere of disarmament. In short, both envisaged making German disarmament the starting-point for a more general agreement on the limitation of armaments. In keeping with his liberal-radical philosophy, the British premier was broadly committed to this aim, arguing that Europe's peace and reconstruction could be furthered by taking steps towards general disarmament that would also reduce the burden of "wasteful" military spending. It was with this goal in mind that Lloyd George impressed on Kerr that the victors "must disarm Germany" because it would be "good for her as well as for us". Yet he made sure to focus on the reduction of land forces, guarding the right to make sovereign decisions about questions of British naval power and imperial defence and – as we have seen – approaching naval arms limitation as an issue to be addressed through bilateral negotiations with the United States.[12]

---

[9] See Sharp (I/2008), pp. 91–2.

[10] At the same time, British and American naval advisers crafted a preliminary agreement under which Germany was only to be allowed to retain a minimal navy comprising essentially six pre-dreadnought battleships, six light cruisers, and twelve destroyers yet no submarines or naval aircraft. But it proved difficult to reach a final agreement, and on 21 June, all previous arrangements were rendered obsolete when German crews scuttled the bulk of the imperial fleet at Scapa Flow. See Walworth (1986), pp. 209–10.

[11] See Salewski (1966).

[12] Lloyd George to Kerr, 10 February 1919 Lloyd George Papers, F/89/2/8.

For his part, the American president clung to the maxim he had proclaimed in the Fourteen Points, namely that after the war all states were to reduce their armed forces "to the lowest point consistent with domestic safety". Yet he too had his sights mainly set on disarmament "on land" and remained committed to what was at the time the most ambitious naval construction programme in the world.[13] By contrast, Clemenceau and Tardieu were as determined as Foch to resist British and American pressure to limit the size of France's future army. All were resolved to ensure that France would maintain armed forces that could effectively guard against the German threat and serve as a key instrument for controlling and containing France's troublesome neighbour. In turn, this reinforced the prevalent Anglo-American perception that French policy was dominated by a "militaristic" mind-set.[14] At the same time, it is important to understand that from the French perspective, even the strictest regime for the control of German disarmament could not provide sufficient guarantees. For all leading French policymakers agreed that Germany would remain dangerous as long as it retained the war-making potential of what was still Europe's largest and most advanced industrial economy.

But it was not primarily due to such obvious differences and inconsistencies that no meaningful advances towards general disarmament would be made in 1919 – nor due to the fact that neither the British nor the American delegations ever developed concrete programmes to this end. The real problem lay deeper – and was hardly mysterious. Essentially, in the aftermath of a conflict that had been as costly and destructive as the Great War it was impossible to reach a consensus on significant arms-limitation agreements of a general kind without first making tangible progress towards more effective mechanisms and guarantees of international security – mechanisms and guarantees that satisfied the prevalent security concerns of *all* relevant states. Yet no concerns were more relevant at this juncture than those of the French government and, more broadly, French society.

II. Different Paths to a Secure Peace. French Rhineland and Alliance Aspirations and the Reorientation of British and American Approaches to the Cardinal European Security Question

It was no coincidence that Clemenceau and Tardieu began their efforts to reset the agenda of the peace conference and to pursue their assertive bargaining strategy after Wilson's departure from Paris in mid-February. For they indeed sought to establish, as far as that was possible, essential yardsticks for the settlement they desired to impose on Germany, particularly in informal

---

[13] Wilson, "Fourteen Points" address, 8 January 1918, *PWW*, XLV, pp. 538–9.
[14] See e.g. Grayson diary, 21 January 1918, *PWW*, LIV, p. 178.

discussions with House. Originally, their strategy was clearly dominated by the aim to create a Rhenish buffer-state and thereby to block the "historic invasion route" German forces had used in 1870 and 1914. Tardieu stressed that this was the "essential problem" that French policymakers had to tackle at the peace conference.[15] But, as noted, this was only one, if central component of a more ambitious and multi-dimensional policy they now tried to implement – a policy whose aim was to safeguard France's longer-term security by *both* detaching the Rhineland and the industrial region of the Saar from Germany *and* forging an unprecedented transatlantic security community centred on a long-term alliance of the victors. Yet they also sought to create a fall-back option: to gain territorial guarantees in case it proved impossible to obtain satisfactory Anglo-American assurances.

What Clemenceau and Tardieu came to pursue with considerable vigour, even brinkmanship, was an evolving strategy that remained rooted in balance-of-power thinking. But they recognised that especially in order to forge unprecedented peacetime alignments with the United States, the French government had to commit itself to new ideological underpinnings and place a new emphasis on democratic standards and the principle of self-determination.[16] Ultimately, though, the negotiations would clearly show that power-political and security imperatives were paramount, and that principles and ideological concepts were used to serve these overriding imperatives.

It was in the pursuit of such imperatives, and to vindicate them in a new way – particularly vis-à-vis Wilson – that Clemenceau now gave Tardieu free rein to present his conception of a north Atlantic union of the victors. And Tardieu strove hard to persuade his British and American counterparts of the need and mutual benefits of such a union, impressing on them that it was to be based not just on common security interests but also on shared values and civilisational standards, particularly the espousal of democracy and "self-determination", which set the victorious powers apart from Germany. As Tardieu stressed, unsurprisingly, the main purpose of this community was to protect not just France but western civilisation against the defeated power, which he presented as the most serious long-term threat to its future.[17] The exclusive western union for which he and Clemenceau sought to gain Anglo-American support thus only *partly* anticipated the North Atlantic Alliance of

---

[15] Tardieu memorandum, 25 February 1919, in Tardieu (II/1921), pp. 147–67.

[16] Jackson (2013), pp. 276–7.

[17] Tardieu revisions on final draft of Foch note of 10 January 1919, Tardieu Papers, vol. 422. Tardieu drew on the conceptual planning of his assistant Aubert, who had earlier highlighted the fundamental distinction between "the democracies of the North-Atlantic" and Germany. Aubert note, 2 January 1919, Tardieu Papers, vol. 417. See Jackson (2013), pp. 285–6.

the post–World War II era because, unlike the latter, it was *not* conceived as an inherently *integrative* mechanism of collective security that could eventually be extended to include Germany.

Both the French premier and his main adviser realised that it would be difficult to reconcile their Rhineland agenda with the priority of forging a new kind of security community with the Anglo-American powers. And for all the brinkmanship they displayed their overriding aim remained to draw Britain and the United States into a such a community. When it became clear that it would be impossible to overcome British and American opposition to French buffer-state schemes, Clemenceau would be prepared to seek a compromise that centred on a long-term occupation of the Rhineland. In a wider context, he subordinated French Rhineland plans to what remained his overriding priority: to cement longer-term solidarity among the victors. And Tardieu fundamentally shared these priorities. That the French premier initially pursued a tougher course, which dangerously strained the very allied unity he sought to preserve, was in part doubtless due to domestic pressures. During the decisive stages of the peace conference he faced a parliament and public and publicised opinion that, in his perception, were dominated by demands for tangible security guarantees and a buffer zone between France and Germany.[18] A more immediate concern for Clemenceau was the growing criticism that Foch, his political rival Poincaré and other proponents of an – even – more hard-line approach levelled against him as the negotiations entered their decisive phase. And in many ways it was the French premier's pronounced transatlantic orientation – and his eventual willingness to accept a temporary occupation rather than a "permanent" buffer- state – that provoked the most serious challenges from these quarters.

Foch had indeed been instrumental in placing schemes for a Rhenish buffer-state and the creation of a "military frontier" on the Rhine on the French postwar agenda. On the eve of the peace conference, he had presented to the political leaders of the victorious powers his revised scheme to make the Rhine the frontier of a security system in which "the western democracies" would jointly occupy the Left Bank and the Rhenish provinces were to be turned into a neutralised states. Essentially, Foch urged France's wartime allies to understand the disconcerting changes to Europe's balance of power that the war had wrought, despite Germany's defeat, particularly because Russia could no longer serve as a counterweight to German power in the east. He thus reiterated that only a neutralisation of the Rhineland offered a realistic safeguard for French and European security, because it created a security *glacis* against future German invasion

---

[18] See e.g. Franklin-Bouillon speech, 24 November 1918, *Bulletin du Parti radical et radical-socialiste*, 14 December 1918; Duroselle (1988), pp. 755–6.

attempts and offset the abiding superiority of Germany's demographic and power potential.[19]

Increasingly frustrated with what he saw as Clemenceau's failure to maintain a tough stance in the face of Anglo-American opposition, Foch sought to prevail on President Poincaré to put pressure on the French premier. The marginalised president had positioned himself as a severe critic of the Clemenceau's negotiating skills, accusing him of being "incapable" of defending vital French interests. After he had earlier backed a strong League – with an army of its own – as "the only form of alliance that would help France", Poincaré now agreed with Foch that the creation of an autonomous Rhenish buffer-state was crucial to France's postwar security.[20] And he tried to push Clemenceau to pursue a distinctly tougher bargaining strategy and not to compromise on this critical issue.

Clemenceau had to pay some attention to the manoeuvres of Foch and Poincaré. Yet the president never went so far as to challenge him openly and provoke a political crisis in France. Thus, the French premier's position and authority were never seriously threatened, and he could even turn the hardline criticism he faced to his advantage, namely to bolster his bargaining position vis-à-vis Wilson and Lloyd George. In fact, he was in such a strong position that he could largely afford to ignore or deflect Foch's intervention attempts and Poincaré's exhortations. And subsequently he would not find it difficult to gain a clear backing for the Rhineland compromise he made in the French parliament.

Nonetheless, Clemenceau and Tardieu indeed bargained hard. And at the outset of what would be the extended "inter-allied" battle over the Rhineland – and the German settlement – they still insisted on establishing a buffer-state. In preliminary discussions with House, they staked out positions that indeed reflected Foch's demands. On 22 February, the French premier impressed on Wilson's adviser that the only alternative to outright annexation that he was willing to consider was the foundation of a formally autonomous Rhenish republic on the Left Bank. He argued that such a republic could be made so "prosperous" that the local population would not wish to re-join "the German federation". Essentially, however, the premise of his policy was that any consideration for the political wishes of the Rhenish people had to be subordinated to overriding requirements of security.[21] And for the time being,

---

[19] See Foch note, 27 November 1918, *Fonds Clemenceau*, SHD-DAT, 6N 73–2; Foch note, 10 January 1919, prepared with Tardieu's assistance, House Papers. See Jackson (2013), pp. 279–80.

[20] Poincaré, "Notes journalières", 24 and 27 March, BN, NAFR 16033. See Keiger (1997), pp. 256–61.

[21] House diary, 19 and 22 February 1919, House Papers; House to Wilson, 23 Feb 1919, *PWW*, LV, p. 233.

Clemenceau remained uncompromising, signalling to Wilson in early March that the establishment of a buffer-state that "should never be allowed to rejoin Germany" was a *conditio sine qua non* for the French government.[22]

To prepare the ground for an agreement with the Anglo-American powers the French premier had authorised Tardieu to put forward his more elaborate programme and link the demand for a revised status quo on the Rhine with the vision of an unprecedented security community of the "western democracies". By this time, Clemenceau's key strategist had become keenly aware that the French negotiators faced an up-hill struggle in their attempts to overcome the profound British and American reservations about their aims in the Rhineland; and he became concerned that Clemenceau's disregard for the self-determination principle on this vital issue would only increase Anglo-American opposition and ultimately jeopardise the entire French security agenda. He thus proposed a scheme that hinged on the claim that the creation of an autonomous Rhenish republic would actually be compatible with respect for "self-determination" because it respected the political will of the local populations.

The explicit aim of the ambitious programme Tardieu presented in his important memorandum of 25 February 1919 was to transform the Left Bank into an "independent" Rhineland that was to "act as a barrier and buffer between Germany and the Western Democracies". And, significantly, he called for a *permanent* Allied control of the strategic bridgeheads across the Rhine.[23] To leave room for compromise, Tardieu proposed that the precise status of the "independent" Left Bank was still to be determined. But the underlying objective was unmistakably to detach it from Germany. At one level, Tardieu now marshalled the geopolitical arguments he had developed earlier. He observed that while the Anglo-American naval powers could safeguard their security by relying their geopolitical detachment from the European continent and their superior naval forces, France had a vital interest in creating a "zone of security" on the Left Bank. Yet he also sought to present French security interests as congruent with the shared concerns of the "western democracies". His central claim was that the French proposals did not "tend towards the annexation of territories" but rather envisioned a "common protection". In spite of their distinct geopolitical positions, he argued, the victors shared the interest in putting Germany "in a position where she can do no harm by imposing upon her conditions indispensable to the common security of the Western Democracies". And he underscored that this "common security" could not be achieved through the League but only

---

[22] House to Wilson, 7 March 1919, House Papers.
[23] Tardieu memorandum, 25 February 1919, in Tardieu (II/1921), pp. 167, 170.

by recasting the "dangerous imbalance of power" that still existed between France and Germany.[24]

Yet Tardieu and other leading policymakers in the French Foreign Ministry, notably Berthelot, were aware that arguments of this kind would not suffice to overcome Anglo-American objections. And it was for this reason that they now intensified their – futile – efforts to present the scheme of an autonomous Rhineland as a plan that actually was in the best interest of the political aspirations and self-determination claims of the Rhenish population. They reasserted the claim that the bonds of political unity between the Rhineland and "Prussian" Germany were historically weak and could be loosened in ways that took the Rhinelanders' political will and material interests into account. They sought to encourage Rhenish separatism and the formation of an "independent" Rhenish republic by promoting the idea of universal suffrage following the model of the Third Republic. And, like Clemenceau, they reckoned that economic incentives – especially the offer of a "customs union" with France and Belgium – would foster a "different economic orientation" that over time could also create the "conditions for a political reorientation", drawing the envisaged autonomous state into France's orbit.[25]

For tactical reasons, Tardieu signalled to House that the Rhenish republic he proposed would not necessarily be permanently "barred from a union with Germany" and suggested that its inhabitants should be allowed to decide about their political future after a period of five to ten years. But the premise of his proposal was that by then the Rhinelanders would find it more advantageous to remain anchored to France – or the French government would have found other means to keep them detached from Germany.[26] Tardieu thus advanced not only strategic but also normative arguments, but what he asserted was problematic in several respects. In particular, he – and Clemenceau – underestimated the strength of the national-patriotic bonds that bound a majority of the Rhenish population to the German state and which had actually been deepened through the experience and propaganda of the war.

Revealingly, French decision-makers were never prepared to put their arguments to the test and propose that the population of the Left Bank should itself decide its political future. Essentially, they instrumentalised ideas of self-determination for overriding strategic reasons. Yet their schemes carried enormous risks, threatening to create a structural minefield of discord between France and Germany – and it was precisely this threatening scenario that led

---

[24] *Ibid.*, pp. 154–5. See also Tardieu memorandum, 20 January 1919, Tardieu Papers, vol. 49.

[25] Tardieu note, 26 January 1919, Tardieu Papers, vol. 417; Berthelot note, 23 December 1918, Pichon Papers, vol. 6.

[26] House diary, 23 February 1919, House, *Intimate Papers*, IV, pp. 346–7.

the British and American protagonists to oppose the French agenda so vehemently in the spring of 1919.

A further element of the French strategy to re-balance Franco-German power relations was to lay claim to the coal-rich German industrial region of the Saar, which Tardieu did on 8 March. This claim was both presented as an act of historical restitution, namely to re-establish the French frontier of 1814, and as part of France's legitimate demands for "economic reparation" from Germany. Yet what really lay behind it were geopolitical and geo-economic motives: the interest to deprive Germany of industrial resources and to improve France's "military security" by extending the northern border of Alsace-Lorraine and creating a "natural strategic frontier" against German aggression. Conscious that these aspirations, which were to extend French control over roughly one million German citizens, would raise major British and American objections, particularly on grounds of self-determination, Tardieu proposed another ingenious scheme which foresaw that France would gain the entire Saar area and ownership of all mines and related industries but pledge to "respect the rights and interests of the people". They were to be assured that after a period of twenty years they would have the right to decide whether they wanted to become French or German citizens.[27]

It is important to stress, then, that Tardieu's conception of a transatlantic security community was always inseparably connected with – and in fact weakened by – the pursuit of a political-cum-territorial re-balancing agenda. The "western union" scheme for which the French protagonists now sought to win the support of Wilson and Lloyd George was presented not as an *alternative* but as a *complement* to the quest for tangible "territorial guarantees". As Tardieu emphasised to Kerr, the three essential "parts" of the revised French scheme – the "drawing of the German frontier on the Rhine", the "constitution of an independent Rhenish state", and the "Allied command of the [Rhine] bridges" – "stood or fell together". Crucially, they could only be complemented, not replaced, by Anglo-American security guarantees.[28] And territorial guarantees were seen as all the more vital in the worst-case scenario that such guarantees failed to materialise.

These, as it were, were the key initial bargaining position that the French premier came to espouse. Yet neither Tardieu nor Clemenceau could solve the fundamental problem at the heart of their strategy. In short, the pre-eminent aim of forging a strong postwar *entente* with Britain and the United States was in fact seriously *compromised* by their insistence on a Rhenish buffer-state "solution" that, in the eyes of all relevant British and American

---

[27] Tardieu memorandum, 8 March 1919, Tardieu Papers, vol. 415; Tardieu (II/1921), p. 279–89.

[28] See conversations between Tardieu, Kerr and Mezes, 12 March 1919, Cmd. 2169: *Negotiations for an Anglo-French Pact*, p. 64.

decision-makers, not only violated German self-determination claims but was also bound to cause long-term instability. In a wider perspective, French postwar leaders would ultimately have to choose between asserting a balance-of-power approach to security that tended to isolate them and the risky prospect of placing their hopes in Anglo-American assurances and cooperation – and, eventually, the search for a peaceful accommodation with Germany.

The conception Clemenceau and Tardieu now sought to implement was clearly not geared towards creating conditions for a future Franco-German process of accommodation and reconciliation. Rather, it was certain to perpetuate wartime divisions. Yet what they pursued was based on deeply entrenched assumptions about German behaviour that they shared with most other French policy- and decision-makers at this juncture. Both the French premier and his loyal strategist did all they could to impress on their British and American negotiating partners that the key to securing European peace lay not in strengthening moderate Social Democrats and republican forces east of the Rhine, but in reducing German power and depriving the defeated power of the means to challenge the international order the victors sought to build. It thus was not surprising that during the inter-allied altercations of March and April 1919, the main French negotiators resorted to essentialist arguments about civilisational aptitude, the German "national character" and Prusso-German mentality to justify their insistence on a power-political containment and quarantine of the defeated power and to block the path to a different, more accommodating peace settlement.[29]

At the centre of what Clemenceau and Tardieu sought to achieve at Versailles, then, lay the aim of committing Britain and the United States to a peace and a postwar system that not only maximally constrained but also, and crucially, isolated a reduced German state. Both saw the peace negotiations as a first and vital stage at which the basic terms and understandings were forged for what they envisioned as a drawn-out process of containment and "security-building". Because of these priorities, and against the background of the domestic pressures they perceived, neither was prepared even to begin addressing the fundamental question that hung over everything else: namely how the longer-term relations with Germany could be managed. As noted, both Clemenceau and Tardieu deemed an "accommodation" with the *voisin outre-Rhin* eventually unavoidable. But in their eyes the essential prerequisites for such a process were not only a strict German compliance with the victors' terms but also a durable security accord among the western powers.[30]

---

[29] Clemenceau statement, Council of Four, 28 March 1919, Mantoux (1992), I, pp. 62–5; Tardieu memorandum, 25 February 1919, Tardieu, (II/1921), pp. 156, 161–2.
[30] See Tardieu to Wilson, 10 June 1919, in Tardieu (I/1921), p. 135; Clemenceau speech, 25 September 1919, *Journal Officiel (Chambre)*, 1919.

The Rhineland schemes Tardieu presented and the wider French agenda vis-à-vis Germany that now became discernible provoked strong British and American resistance. But they also finally compelled the leading British and American actors to face up to the key challenge of addressing the intricately interconnected problems of French security and the wider German settlement. In many ways it was only now that they began to clarify their approaches to these crucial issues. And notably Lloyd George and Wilson came to *reorientate* their pursuits. In different ways, they came to focus on the priority of securing European peace, and meeting French concerns, not through coercion and an exclusive alliance of the victors but rather through a combination of carefully circumscribed guarantees to France and League-based "collective security". And they came to engage on behalf of a settlement that was so "fair" that it would also be acceptable for the German government; a victors' peace that nonetheless was to permit an accommodation process with Germany in the near future.

Although they regarded French claims as exaggerated, Lloyd George and Kerr acknowledged that Clemenceau had to satisfy particularly urgent and deep security concerns vis-à-vis Germany. Reflecting on France's more precarious geopolitical situation, the British premier stressed that the French government was "entitled to consider [French] fears" because the country it represented was "unprotected by the sea as England and America were".[31] But, expressing prevailing sentiments in the British delegation, he unequivocally opposed all French plans to separate the Rhineland from Germany. In British eyes, Tardieu's schemes were not only highly detrimental to French security but also bound to undermine all prospects of creating a stable postwar order in Europe. As Kerr told Tardieu on 11 March, the British government was thus determined to resist such schemes "to the end". And both he and the prime minster impressed on their French counterparts that British public opinion would simply not accept the deployment of occupation troops to the Rhineland in the longer term, let alone on a permanent basis.[32]

Lloyd George not only interpreted France's Rhineland policy as a misguided attempt to alter the balance of forces and gain a predominant position on the European continent. He also came to regard it as profoundly dangerous. Rejecting Tardieu's arguments, he concluded that the French programme in fact rode rough-shod over German sovereignty and self-determination claims. He feared that it would thus stir up German nationalism and uncontainable domestic pressure to regain the severed territories. In his view, it was thus certain to provoke "endless friction", perpetuating a structural antagonism

---

[31] Lloyd George statement, Council of Ten, 10 March 1919, *FRUS-PPC*, IV, pp. 297–8.
[32] Kerr note of conversation with Tardieu, 11 March 1919, Lothian Papers, 1174; Kerr minute to Lloyd George and Balfour, 13 March 1919, Cmd. 2169, *Negotiations for an Anglo-French Pact*, pp. 68–9.

between France and Germany and thus creating a seedbed of instability in western Europe.[33] For similar reasons, the British premier opposed what he called French plans for an "annexation" of the Saar. He stressed that nothing should be done that repeated the error Germany had committed when it "annexed Alsace-Lorraine". And he insisted that "territorial annexations" constituted a "violation" of the victors' commitments under the armistice, which would give German representatives cause to accuse the western powers of double standards and undermine the legitimacy of the entire peace settlement.[34] But the crucial British concern pertained to the future of the Rhineland.

Here, Lloyd George's views were not only shared by Kerr but also by other senior British actors, notably Balfour.[35] On 18 March, the foreign secretary advanced a fundamental *political* critique of the French agenda that captured essential aspects of the French security dilemma. Balfour concluded that Foch's insistence on creating a buffer-state rested on rigidly backward assumptions, those of "Generals and Statesmen absorbed in the Military memories of 1870 and 1914" – namely that the German populations "will always far outnumber the French"; that Germany would inevitably "organise herself for revenge"; that all attempts to "limit armaments" would be futile; that "the League of Nations will be impotent" and that consequently France had to use all power-political measures available to guard against another German invasion. Balfour argued that these rationales were "one-sided" and would produce the opposite of what they were intended to achieve. He observed that if French assumptions were correct then no "manipulation of the Rhine frontier" could prevent France from becoming "more than a second-rate Power, trembling at the nod of its great neighbours in the East, and depending from day to day on the changes and chances of a shifting diplomacy and uncertain alliances".

Yet the British foreign secretary did not regard this scenario as inevitable – if a more substantive reform of international politics could be pursued. Though he did not entertain high expectations in this direction he argued that the "only radical cure" and the only effective way to prevent a renewed German "policy of world domination" was "a change in the international system of the world" – which French statesmen were "doing nothing to promote". And by this he meant advances towards an order on Anglo-American premises in which, aided by the League, new "methods" of peaceful

---

[33] Lloyd George, Fontainebleau memorandum, 25 March 1919, *PWW*, LVI, pp. 259–61, 267; Lloyd George (1938), I, p. 396. See Fry (2011), pp. 195–223.

[34] Lloyd George statement, Council of Four, 28 March 1919, Mantoux (1992), I, pp. 59–60, 65–6.

[35] Kerr minute to Lloyd George and Balfour, 13 March 1919, Cmd. 2169, *Negotiations for an Anglo-French Pact*, pp. 68–9; Balfour memorandum, 18 March 1919, Lloyd George Papers, F/3/4/19.

conflict management and accommodation came to prevail. Balfour implied that the creation of such a system and a peaceful accommodation with Germany also lay in France's well-understood self-interest. But he did not spell out how this was to be approached, and what contribution British policy could make to this end.[36]

In retrospect, it becomes clear that the priorities of Clemenceau and Tardieu indeed collided fundamentally with what Lloyd George and other British policymakers considered crucial prerequisites for the pacification of Europe. The task the British protagonists thus now had to confront head-on was not just to contain French designs but actually to find an alternative way of assuaging French concerns. What Lloyd George came to advance in mid-March, and what Kerr had a decisive part in conceptualising, never quite amounted to a comprehensive new security strategy. It revealed that the commitments the leading British actors were willing and able to make to European security after the Great War had essential limits. But it nonetheless can be seen as an important departure. The cornerstone of this reorientated strategy was the proposal of a specific Anglo-American security guarantee for France – at the core, the pledge that Britain and the United States would come to the aid of France in the event of an unprovoked German attack. The new British scheme was not only intended to reassure France but also, and crucially, to prepare the ground for a more accommodating German settlement and thus, more generally, for a more sustainable equilibrium on the European continent. And it had a significant impact both on the dynamics of the subsequent negotiations between the victors and on the contours of the – fragile – Euro-Atlantic security "architecture" that emerged at their end – an impact that has not been properly understood.

It is noteworthy – and highly characteristic – that although the Lloyd George government had been aware of different French Rhineland designs at least since December 1918, this proposal was not based on careful planning or the result of a longer policymaking process. Rather, it was devised at the eleventh hour, under the concrete pressure of the peace negotiations. Nor had it been preceded by a process of Anglo-American consultations, even though British policymakers were aware that what they proposed would raise fundamental concerns. For it seemed to require Wilson to depart from the universal "collective security" conception of his League plans – and to conflict with the general American maxim to eschew entangling alliance commitments. The basic idea of a guarantee offer had been developed by Lloyd George and Kerr, who seems to have provided the original impetus. It was then first discussed in the British War Cabinet on 4 March.[37]

[36] Balfour memorandum, 18 March 1919; Balfour notes on French Military Proposals, 5 March 1919, Lloyd George Papers, F/3/4/19 and 15.
[37] War Cabinet minutes, 4 March 1919, CAB 23/15/54.

Undoubtedly, the most immediate British aim was to induce the Clemenceau government to abandon its designs for a Rhenish buffer-state and a strategic frontier on the Rhine. While Balfour, Hankey and other influential policymakers remained wary of making commitments to France, Kerr emerged as the most outspoken proponent of a postwar security compact of the three principal victors. Mindful of Lloyd George's preferences, he advanced a design not for an outright alliance but for a more limited and specific guarantee regime that was to underpin the future "solidarity" between Britain, the United States and France. In his view, its core purpose would be to offer strategic re-assurance to the French government and thus a realistic alternative to its hazardous Rhineland designs. Preparing the ground for Lloyd George's initiative, Kerr impressed on Tardieu that "the real security of France lay in maintaining a complete understanding with Great Britain and America". And he basically presented the British scheme as the centrepiece of a more clearly defined Atlantic system of security and containment. Kerr argued that if the three principal victors "maintained their solidarity with adequate preparations", they would be able to deter any future German attack. He assured Tardieu that the British government would be prepared to commit itself to a policy of vigilance and to "nip" any German attempts to revive militaristic designs "in the bud". Yet he also warned him that the more the Clemenceau government persisted with schemes that undermined inter-allied "solidarity", the more it would harm the very security interests it sought to pursue – because it would diminish the willingness of Britain and the Dominions – and the United States – to come to France's defence in the event of a future German aggression.[38]

Lloyd George adopted Kerr's idea, but he had no intention of committing Britain to anything approaching a rigid transatlantic *entente* designed to deter and contain the defeated power. Rather, he came to view the guarantee offer as an integral part of a more broadly conceived strategy to stabilise Europe, which then took shape in his Fontainebleau agenda. A core rationale behind this agenda would be to re-assure France in order to shift the negotiations between the victors in a different direction and to create, with Wilson's support, conditions not for a peace of containment but for a settlement that permitted a future accommodation of Germany.[39]

It is worth emphasising that the British guarantee proposal was more than a last-resort measure to counter the Rhineland policies of Clemenceau and Tardieu – or Foch's more far-reaching aspirations. The proposal manifested and reflected the prevalent British interest in carefully limiting British security commitments in Europe to where, in their perception, they were strategically

---

[38] Notes of discussion between Kerr, Tardieu and Mezes, 11 March 1919, Cmd. 2169, *Negotiations for an Anglo-French Pact*, pp. 59–62.

[39] Lloyd George, Fontainebleau memorandum, 25 March 1919, *PWW*, LVI, pp. 259–67.

vital – namely to France and western Europe – and even here to insist that Britain would only intervene in the event of an *unprovoked* German aggression. Similar guarantees to the new East European states were never contemplated. At the same time, the guarantee scheme can be seen as one of the clearest manifestations of the new *transatlantic* orientation that had emerged as a dominant feature of British postwar planning at the end of 1918. The core concern was and remained to gain Wilson's consent to a kind of Anglo-American strategic burden-sharing in efforts to secure European peace in the longer run. This burden-sharing was now to focus on targeted political and military commitments to France's security. Significantly, there was no discussion at this critical stage about perpetuating the Anglo-French wartime *alliance* and trying to draw the United States into a combination of this kind. Rather, coupled with a basic endorsement of the League, the perspective of establishing a new – and fundamentally inclusive – international *concert* had clearly come to prevail.

The priorities and *caveats* of Lloyd George's evolving policy also reflected, and were indeed conditioned by, two further prevalent concerns of the British government. Unquestionably important were the domestic constraints that not only the British premier perceived – the British public's aversion to far-reaching new or renewed alliance commitments that could drag Britain and the Empire into another major war (which, in the perception of their leaders, the publics of the Dominions shared); and the need to focus resources on domestic reform and the creation of a "home fit for heroes". No less important, however, were the extra-European *imperial* priorities and constraints that key British actors saw. In short, they all espoused the notion that Britain's now more limited strategic resources had to be concentrated on efforts to ensure the consolidation and defence of its imperial world system.

Nonetheless, within these limits the guarantee proposal represented the most far-reaching British attempt to come to terms with the critical Franco-German security problem that lay at the heart of European insecurity after the Great War. Lloyd George and Kerr first outlined essentials of their plan to Clemenceau and Tardieu while Wilson was still on his way back to Paris. The British premier only informed House on 12 March that he was prepared to "pledge British aid to France in case of unprovoked German aggression".[40] But he then made it a priority of his first meeting with Wilson after the president's return to Paris, two days later, to persuade the American president to agree to a joint Anglo-American guarantee offer. And, remarkably, Wilson gave his consent.[41]

---

[40] House diary, XV, pp. 92–3, House Papers.
[41] House diary, 12 March 1919, House Papers; Grayson diary, 14 March 1919, *PWW*, LV, pp. 497–8.

Contrary to what has often been claimed, the American president was not oblivious to the particular security concerns of the Clemenceau government and the anxieties of the French population that it had to address. In the first press conference he held in Paris, on 14 February, he acknowledged that France had lived "under the dread of Germany" for generations and now the main "fear" was "a recurrence of the horrors from which she had just emerged". In private, however, Wilson considered French fears exaggerated, adopting the view that that the French people "still suffer(ed) from militarism". At the beginning of the peace negotiations he had agreed with the British publicist A.G. Gardiner that "French public opinion had become so hysterical, as a result of the suggestions that an army of 3,000,000 should be kept to protect France against the Germans" that it failed to recognise "the fact that Germany's fangs had been drawn" by the terms of the armistice.[42] Subsequently, he came to regard the ambitious schemes Clemenceau and Tardieu advanced as both excessive and counter-productive. Nonetheless, the American president was willing to go to some lengths to assuage the concerns they presented. And he did so not least to strengthen Clemenceau's position vis-à-vis Foch and other French proponents of (even) more radical measures vis-à-vis Germany.

More generally, Wilson indeed developed a rather nuanced understanding of the more fundamental geopolitical challenges that the victors had to confront in Europe. He also came to analyse the crucial German problem in terms of power, security and geopolitics. In late February, he impressed on the Democratic Committee in Washington that in view of the Austrian desire for a union with Germany, the peacemakers in Paris had to deal with "the prospect of an industrial nation with seventy or eighty millions of people" while they were in the process of establishing "new states" in Eastern Europe – "right in the path of German ambition" – that would remain "weak states" for a long time to come.[43] Yet the president's answer to the security problem the German colossus posed had not changed. He insisted that it could not be mastered by means of territorial curtailments that violated the principle of self-determination, a radical reduction of its power or power-political alliances designed to enforce a rigid regime of containment. And for a long time he maintained that the only way to come to terms with it was to join forces in ensuring Germany's disarmament on the basis of the armistice and, above all, in establishing a functional League of Nations and what he regarded as its ultimately more effective system of universal "collective security". As he tried to impress on the French public, and "world opinion", it was through the League that the "rest of the world" would be able to "reassure France".[44]

---

[42] News report of press conference, 14 February 1919, PWW LV, pp. 162–3; Grayson diary, 21 January 1918, *PWW*, LIV, p. 178.

[43] Wilson address, 28 February 1919, *PWW*, LV, pp. 317–18.

[44] News report of press conference, 14 February 1919, *PWW*, LV, pp. 162–3.

Pursuing these priorities, Wilson remained strictly opposed to all French plans to sever the Rhineland from Germany. He had already warned Clemenceau in the early stages of the conference that if the French negotiators insisted on their more ambitious Rhineland schemes they would sooner or later turn world opinion against France. And he explicitly instructed House to stand "immovably" against what he called France's "programme" for the "western bank of the Rhine" while he was away from Paris. The president stressed that such power-political schemes ran counter to the principles of his peace policy, notably that of self-determination, and threatened to undermine the foundations on which he sought to foster Europe's pacification.[45]

But House decided to disregard Wilson's instructions and pursued a diplomatic initiative of his own on this vital issue. He saw more clearly than the president and other American experts that it would be inconceivable to reach an agreement on a "preliminary peace with Germany" without doing more to satisfy overriding French security demands, noting that "the French [had] but one idea and that is military protection". With the aim of re-assuring the Clemenceau government, furthering French cooperation on the League and paving the way for a moderate German settlement, House thus set out, without consulting the president, to broker a preliminary compromise with Clemenceau and Tardieu on the critical Rhineland issue – a compromise that in his interpretation would not violate Wilson's principles.[46]

Earlier, the president's adviser had sharply criticised French proposals to set up a "Rhenish Republic" as a "buffer-state" between Germany and France, underscoring that doing so "against the will of the [local] people" would run counter to "the principle of self-determination". He feared that it would establish dangerous double standards: the victors "would be treating Germany in one way and the balance of the world in another". And this could have highly detrimental global repercussions, "turning everything from the Rhine to the Pacific, perhaps including Japan, against the Western Powers" and encouraging German propaganda claims that Britain and the United States were aspiring to "form an Anglo-Saxon supremacy of the world", using France merely as a "pawn" to this end.[47]

While House sought to prevent such a scenario, he also emphasised the seriousness of the French security predicament in view of Germany's vastly superior demographic potential. He diligently adhered to Wilson's line that in the longer run, France's "only hope" for the future was the League of Nations. But he came to be swayed by Tardieu's argument that measures had to be taken to afford the French state "a breathing space" and "protection" until it

---

[45] Wilson to House, 20 February, House, *Intimate Papers*, IV, p. 336.

[46] House diary, 14 February 1919, *PWW*, LV, p. 193; House diary, 9 February 1919, House Papers; House to Wilson, 24 February 1919, House, *Intimate Papers*, IV, pp. 345, 346–9.

[47] House diary, 9 February 1919, House, *Intimate Papers*, IV, p. 345.

"recovered from the present war" and the League was "working as a protection
against war". On these grounds, House recommended to Wilson that the
American delegation should back the revised French proposal to establish an
independent "Rhenish Republic" only for "a limited number of years", after
which the local population would "decide for themselves what their future
should be".[48] House's recommendation was supported by the director of the
Inquiry, Sidney Mezes, and the Inquiry's expert on Western Europe, Charles
Haskins. Mezes rejected a permanent separation of the Rhineland from
Germany but saw merit in the scheme to create a Rhenish buffer-state for a
limited duration of maximally ten years. In Haskins' assessment, the buffer-
state scheme corresponded with the explicitly geopolitical approach to the
settlement with Germany that he had recommended all along. He even still
favoured a more long-term strategy that pivoted on the creation of an "(a)
utonomous political organization of the Left Bank" and sought to tie the
Rhineland permanently to France via a customs union, thus structurally
altering the Franco-German balance of power and economic resources.[49]

But Wilson was by no means prepared to support House's initiative. He
would insist on pursuing his own approach to the Rhineland question and the
wider problem of French and European security, having earlier impressed on
House that the American delegates should not be "hurried into a solution"
dominated by the "French official viewpoint".[50] Following his return to Paris,
the American president quickly gained the impression that the preliminary
terms to which House had signalled American assent were essentially incompatible with the premises of the Fourteen Points and his own, still only
generally defined approach to the German settlement. And, overruling his
adviser, he adamantly rejected any compromise on the basis of Tardieu's
Rhineland plans. Wilson argued that any scheme that that drastically curtailed
German sovereignty and separated the Rhineland from Germany against the
desires of the local populations even for a limited time would violate basic
considerations of self-determination. And he warned that this would have
serious repercussions for the legitimacy and sustainability of the entire peace
settlement – for it would expose him and the other peacemakers to the
accusation of deviating from principles they professed to uphold when it
suited their strategic interests.[51]

On the same grounds, Wilson also opposed what he, like Lloyd George,
viewed as French plans for an "annexation" of the Saar region. Here, he

[48] *Ibid.*; House to Wilson, 24 February 1919, House, *Intimate Papers*, IV, pp. 345–9.
[49] For Mezes' view, see McCormick diary, 2 March 1919, McCormick Papers. For Haskins'
recommendations, see memorandum, "The Eastern Frontier of France" [December
1918], Inquiry nos. 210, 208; Inquiry report [December 1918], Wilson Papers.
[50] Wilson to House, 20 February, House, *Intimate Papers*, IV, p. 336.
[51] Wilson statement, Council of Four, 28 March 1919, Mantoux (1992), I, pp. 64–5.

likewise insisted that the western powers had to "hold to the principles" they had "enunciated" and could not interpret them "too generously" to their "own benefit", and "with a lawyer's cunning". Above all, the president stressed, they must not "violate the principle of self-determination". And he warned that if they tried to "establish borders according to historical or strategic" or "economic" considerations there would be "no limit to the claims". He thus considered the treatment of the Saar as an important precedent for the settlements on Germany's eastern border and the question of Danzig's future status.[52] To underline his determination to resist the French designs Wilson also invoked historical precedents. Echoing the British premier, he now emphasised his concern that France's proposals for the Rhineland – and the Saar – would create another Alsace-Lorraine, provoking a national resentment in Germany that would match "the bitterness felt by France against Germany over the lost provinces" after 1871 and thus sow the seeds for another war.[53]

Crucially, however, while the American president was convinced that the Rhineland proposals of Clemenceau and Tardieu would make France and Europe less rather than more secure he still saw no need to develop a more targeted American security policy or to contemplate what he regarded as outmoded European-style security guarantees in order to counter them and to re-assure the French government and public. His vision of an alternative solution remained unequivocally focused on the League of Nations – on turning it into an effective mechanism that could also safeguard French security in a new and better way.[54] Because of this, and because of their basic determination not to entangle the United States in more traditional security politics in Europe, neither the American president nor House – or other relevant US experts – had ever envisaged offering more specific American security commitments to France; and even less had they envisioned anything resembling a "quasi-alliance" of the western powers.

At first glance, it thus seems all the more remarkable that Wilson agreed so swiftly to Lloyd George's proposal of an Anglo-American guarantee agreement with the French government, whose terms House then coordinated with Lloyd George and Balfour. Essentially, however, the American president soon made clear that he regarded this agreement as a supplementary and *temporary* measure rather than a qualitative departure. In his interpretation, it could provide additional re-assurance until the League was ready to function – and at the same time serve to persuade Clemenceau to abandon his Rhineland agenda while strengthening his hand against Foch and other French hardliners. Reflecting British priorities, Wilson thus came to see the Anglo-American guarantee offer as an *auxiliary* means to an end – a means to

[52] *Ibid.*, pp. 60–2, 67.
[53] Grayson diary, 6 April 1919, *PWW*, LVII, pp. 50–1.
[54] See Wilson statement, Council of Four, 27 March 1919, Mantoux (1992), I, p. 41.

re-assure French policymakers and moderate their policies so as to create conditions that would permit the consolidation of a functioning League and, in the longer term, Germany's peaceful accommodation in the postwar order. Significantly, then, the American president had no intention of taking the British proposal as a starting-point for a more fundamental reorientation of his approach to European – and transatlantic – security, let alone for developing a more comprehensive US security strategy for Europe that really addressed the Franco-German power imbalance.

Wilson thus interpreted and justified the proposed guarantee agreement as a temporary *complement* to what he really sought to create, the League's universal system of "collective security". As early as on 18 March, he told Cecil that the agreement he would underwrite "really amounted to very little more than Article 10 of the Covenant".[55] In the Council of Four the American president subsequently underscored that he and his collaborators had "sought to avoid a formula" that "by substituting the action of a group of states on a permanent basis for that of the League" would effectively admit that the new organisation's guarantees would always remain insufficient . And he left no doubt about what was his cardinal aim: not to focus American attention and resources on the specific guarantee for France but to ensure "the effective action of the League of Nations". To this end, Wilson also sought to link the American guarantee pledge explicitly with the League system and proposed that American assistance should be made dependent on an authorisation of its Executive Council – which Clemenceau and Tardieu could hardly take as a re-assuring signal.[56]

House's attitude towards the guarantee agreement was even more ambivalent. Although he had urged to make some concessions to remove one of "chief stumbling-blocks" on the path to a tenable peace agreement – French fears vis-à-vis Germany – he remained distinctly wary of joining Britain in extending a seemingly more traditional security guarantee. In his assessment, it was neither in Wilson's interest nor in America's interest to make such a commitment or to be drawn into an arrangement that could be seen as a de facto alliance with the *Entente* Powers. House warned Wilson that his critics would regard the agreement as "a direct blow to the League of Nations" – for if the western powers deemed it "necessary" to conclude a traditional treaty of this kind would cast doubt on the League's potential to evolve into the new guarantor of international security. House also doubted that the US Senate would actually accept "such a treaty". Ultimately, though, he shared Wilson's interpretation that it "practically" only promised what the United States had already promised under the League Covenant. He thus came to endorse the

[55] Cecil diary, 18 March 1919, *PWW*, LVI, pp. 81–2.
[56] Wilson statement, 27 March 1919, Mantoux (1992), I, p. 41.

guarantee agreement on essentially pragmatic grounds – as a device to come to an understanding with Clemenceau. House noted that as the French premier did not "believe" in the League, it would be "necessary to give him a treaty on the outside".[57]

Of greater consequence, however, was how Wilson himself interpreted the wider meaning of the proposed guarantee treaty. The American president never espoused the ideological concept of an exclusive security union of the victors. Nor did he adopt the language of an exclusive *civilisational* community of the victorious democracies. He thus clearly remained unresponsive to the ideological overtones of Tardieu's proposals. Instead, he regarded the Anglo-American guarantee offer both as an expedient additional re-assurance and, crucially, as a means to draw France into the broader "collective security" system he sought to establish through the League. Though resolved to put Germany initially on probation, Wilson still clung to the idea of a novel, inclusive system that was not directed against any one particular state. What he still counted on was that it would not merely deter aggressors but actually have a transformative impact on international politics. And he had not changed his view that such a transformation, rather than old-style security guarantees or a de facto alliance of the victors, would ultimately furnish the most effective guarantees for French and wider European security after the Great War.

It is important to understand that these priorities were not just the outgrowth of Wilson's progressive ideology. What also lay behind them were, on the one hand, his awareness of still prevalent American reservations against entangling alliance commitments and, on the other, a fundamental concern he shared with other US Progressives. It was the concern that after the American state and society had been mobilised to intervene in the war, the United States would turn into a "military state" that acquired permanent military and strategic capacities to act like a "quasi-European" power. Wilson was determined to ensure that while as a naval power the United States would be second to none and capable of safeguarding its national security and global economic interests, it would not become an "armed hegemon" that mainly relied on military power to maintain peace and order in the world. For he was convinced that this could not only undermine the American republic but also threaten to involve it in precisely the kind of power-political dynamics and dilemmas that in his view had led to the outbreak of the Great War. In many ways, his entire peace and League agenda was intended to prevent a renewed escalation of processes of this kind – and, ultimately, another military intervention of the United States in Europe.[58]

---

[57] House diary, 27 March 1919, House, *Intimate Papers*, IV, p. 395; House diary, 20 March 1919, *ibid.*, p. 394.

[58] See Wilson address, 22 January 1917, *PWW*, XL, pp. 536–7.

In accordance with this logic, Wilson had on 17 March underscored his rejection of measures that, as he saw it, would establish "not peace, but Allied armed domination" in postwar Europe – and refused to back in the Supreme War Council an agreement that would have subjected Germany to a permanent regime of military control. In a wider context, what he and all relevant American actors in Paris agreed on was that the United States would not make any commitments that would involve it in the maintenance and military enforcement of a new Euro-Atlantic "balance of power".[59] Essentially, then, Wilson's "strategy" to deal with the German problem and the geopolitical challenges of postwar Europe had not changed. It continued to centre on the League and the international system that was to be constructed around it. The American president emphasised again that the security of France and the consolidation of the "new states" in Eastern Europe could only be assured if it was supported, through the League, "by the combined power of the world".[60] At the same time, Wilson urged House to impress on Lloyd George and Clemenceau yet again that the League was the only possible mechanism of security in which the United States could participate – that it represented "the only excuse" he could give as American president "for meddling in European or world affairs" at a time when there were no longer any serious threats to US national security.[61] And he insisted that he simply would not be able to gain support in Congress and in the court of American public opinion for something akin to an alliance of the western powers.

In fact, in the US Senate particularly Borah, Johnson and other "irreconcilable" opponents of Wilson would indeed object to the guarantee treaty as strongly as they did to the League and denounce what they regarded as un-American alliance commitments that would inevitably embroil the United States in future European conflicts. But Wilson's main domestic opponent, Henry Cabot Lodge, actually approved of a special treaty to France pledging military aid to ward off German aggression.[62] Kept abreast of the negotiations over the guarantee agreement by White, Lodge impressed on the latter that he essentially desired, rather than a universal League with unlimited global commitments, "a League among those nations with which the United States had been associated in the war" whose main purpose would be to keep Germany in check.[63] This fundamentally conflicted with Wilson's aims.

---

[59] Wilson statement, Supreme War Council, 17 March 1919, FRUS-PPC, IV, pp. 358, 358–63.

[60] Wilson address, 28 February 1919, PWW, LV, pp. 317–18.

[61] Wilson statement, 24 March 1919, House diary, 24 March 1919, House, Intimate Papers, IV, p. 390.

[62] See Borah speech, Senate, 19 November 1919, Borah (1919), pp. 5 ff.; Johnson speech, 2 June 1919, Congressional Record, 66th Congress, 1st session (2 June 1919), 501–9.

[63] Lodge to White, 8 April, White Papers. See Widenor (1980), pp. 318–19, 331–2; Nevins (1930), pp. 438–41.

And because the president never departed from his premise that the guarantee treaty was a complement to the League of Nations, and had to be ratified together with its Covenant and the peace treaty, its political fate became bound up with the wider battle over the Treaty of Versailles and US membership in the League that was to dominate American politics from the summer of 1919.

III. Towards a Severe but Just Settlement? Lloyd George and Wilson in the Face of the German Question

All of the principal peacemakers realised of course that the Rhineland problem was only one, albeit crucial, part of the broader "most difficult and urgent questions" that the settlement with Germany raised, and which they had thus far neglected.[64] And, remarkably, it was only now and in response to the pressure French policymakers exerted that Wilson, Lloyd George and their advisers began to lay out more clearly what kind of settlement they sought. Though on different grounds, they all shared the aim of preventing a peace along the lines Clemenceau and Tardieu advocated, because they clearly reckoned that it would lead to chronic instability and provoke renewed conflict. Instead, they emphasised that in order to create a stable postwar order, it would be vital to agree on terms for a severe but just peace that the government in Berlin could sign and by and large accept – without a negotiating process. Both Lloyd George and Wilson put forward basic parameters and underlying maxims for such a peace. At a deeper level, the decisive negotiating and bargaining process between the victors that now entered its crucial phase can be interpreted as a battle between their conceptions and those for which their French counterparts fought.

The first impulse came from Lloyd George and his closest confidants. Having become increasingly concerned about the full extent and possible implications of the French peace agenda, the British premier and his inner circle, which included Kerr, Hankey, Montagu and the Chief of the General Staff, Sir Henry Wilson, on 22 March retreated to the relative isolation of Fontainebleau. The result of their deliberations was the Fontainebleau memorandum, composed by Kerr, which Lloyd George sent to Wilson and Clemenceau on 25 March. It contained the blueprint for what the British premier presented as a "long-sighted peace". By mid-March, Lloyd George had indeed developed profound misgivings about the direction of the peacemaking process. In short, his impression was that under the impact of French pressure, contours of a German settlement had emerged that appeared fundamentally untenable. The prime minister's unease was reinforced by his principal advisers.

---

[64] Wilson, Council of Four, 24 March 1919, Mantoux (1992), I, p. 3.

Kerr remained the most adamant advocate of a chastising peace. In particular, he insisted on a punitive indemnity that was to serve not only financial but
also political and moral purposes, making the vanquished power pay in more
than just financial terms for a war that, in his assessment, the Wilhelmine
Empire's aggressive policies had caused. Even the German elections in January
had not altered his outlook. He continued to view the intentions and tactics of
Brockdorff-Rantzau and the new German government with deep suspicion.
And he still argued that a "fundamentally unrepentant" German power
deserved "very firm and uncompromising handling".[65] Yet by the middle of
March even Kerr came to conclude that the "accumulation" of the peace terms
that were being discussed would "put Germany in an utterly impossible
position" – even if by itself each "exaction" could be justified.[66]

Hankey had initially shared Kerr's stern outlook. But he altered his view and
came to recommend what could be called a selectively moderate peace. On 19
March, Hankey impressed on the prime minister that the danger he saw was
that Germany would be saddled with "humiliating" peace terms that could
even provoke its "disintegration". He stressed that it was in Britain's interest to
prevent this and to fortify Germany as a "barrier against Bolshevism". In his
judgement, the victors had a right to impose "drastic penalties" on Germany
that brought home to the German people the "enormity" of the "crimes" they
had committed. But he recommended that these penalties should be temporary – that they should be exacted in the form of indemnities rather than the
permanent severing of territory and people from the defeated power. He noted
that this would avoid "the appearance of vindictiveness". Hankey's longer-
term rationale, however, was to buttress the Ebert-Scheidemann government,
aid it in the fight against Bolshevism and expedite Germany's admission to the
League so as to restore German "self-respect". This was to contain the
Bolshevik threat, foster Germany's accommodation in the postwar system
and thereby counteract the destabilisation of Central Europe.[67]

Pursuing his own strategy to redirect the victors' negotiations, Smuts, who
did not participate in the deliberations at Fontainebleau, emphatically
appealed to Lloyd George to steer the victors towards a substantially different
peace settlement – a settlement that sought to make Germany a future partner
and "power of order" within a reformed international order. In Smuts' eyes,
the western powers had not only departed from Wilson's Fourteen Points but
also from Lloyd George's declarations "against the humiliation and dismemberment" of Germany. Using strong language, he warned the prime minster
that the terms they were contemplating would lead to "an impossible peace,

[65] See Kerr to Lloyd George, 19 February 1919 and 13 March 1919, Lord Lothian Papers,
    GD 40/17/1240. See Newton (1997), pp. 367–8.
[66] Hankey to Lloyd George, 19 March 1919, Lloyd George Papers F/24/4/39.
[67] Ibid.

conceived on a wrong basis", which would only provoke "anarchy" in Europe, benefit "the Bolshevists" and "destroy Germany". Smuts especially emphasised that the "territorial arrangements" under discussion – the proposals to assign Danzig and "some millions of Germans" to the new Polish state and the "constitution of a separate state west of the Rhine" – would be "fatal from the point of view of securing present and future peace", for the Germans would never really accept them and thus a "legacy of revenge" would be created that was bound to provoke another war. Instead, he proposed that the peace should be based on the premise that the victors could not "destroy Germany without destroying Europe" and that they could not "save Europe without the co-operation of Germany", which would still be "the dominant factor" on the European continent. Smuts thus implored Lloyd George and the other political leaders to learn from the "wiser" statesmen of the Congress of Vienna who had "looked upon France as necessary to Europe" and then integrated it in the Vienna order. While stressing that Germany would have to "undertake definite liabilities", he went so far as to propose that it should be treated as a "power of order" in a renewed concert of great powers and "be made responsible for part of the burden" of stabilising Europe, which was "clearly too heavy" for the victors to "bear alone".[68]

Lloyd George never went quite as far as Smuts recommended. But the British premier now underscored his determination to prevent "an over-stern peace treaty" that the unstable German government in Berlin would not "dare to sign".[69] And the Fontainebleau deliberations between him and his confidants led to a significant reorientation of the British approach to peacemaking. What they devised was also undoubtedly designed to address multiple tactical concerns – especially the protection of British reparations interests. But it ultimately came closer to a coherent programme for a different, "moderate peace" than anything the American president envisioned at this stage. What Lloyd George soon presented to Wilson and Clemenceau was essentially a British conception for a "long-sighted peace" that was ostensibly based on liberal principles of justice and "fairplay". Its core rationale was that the victors should seek to craft a peace settlement that as far as possible avoided the creation of "causes of exasperation" for the defeated power that would lead future generations to seek "redress" and provoke the outbreak of another war "30 years hence".

Fundamentally, Lloyd George reasserted that the victorious powers were entitled to impose a peace settlement on Germany. And he stressed that its terms could be "severe" or even "ruthless" in the light of "Germany's responsibility for the origin of the war". Yet he also emphasised that they had to be so

---

[68] Smuts to Lloyd George, 26 March 1919, Lloyd George Papers, F/45/9/29.
[69] Lloyd George, "Preface", 23 March 1919, CAB 1/28.

"just" that the German people and their new leaders found them basically acceptable and felt they had "no right to complain". At the core, the British premier thus argued that the victors should "draw up a peace settlement" as if they were "impartial arbiters". And he set them an all but impossible task: to hammer out a settlement that was appropriately "stern" yet not "excessively onerous" and above all so "just" that a "responsible" German government could be expected to "sign [it] in the belief that it can fulfil the obligations it incurs". At the same time, the memorandum advanced an argument obviously intended to challenge the underlying rationales of French policies, namely that it was short-sighted to seek to make Germany so "feeble" that it would never be able to "hit back". It asserted that even if the defeated power's army was reduced "to a mere police force" and its navy to that "of a fifth rate power" it would still find ways of "exacting retribution" – if the prevalent perception in Germany was that it had been "unjustly treated in the peace of 1919".[70]

More specifically, the British premier reiterated that there must be "no attempt to separate the Rhenish Provinces from the rest of Germany". Instead, he now proposed that the Left Bank was to be demilitarised. And he renewed the offer of an Anglo-American security guarantee for France, to be extended "until the League of Nations has proved itself to be an adequate security". At the same time, he stressed that his government would categoric-ally rule out sending a "large army of occupation for an indefinite period" either to force an "unjust" and "excessively onerous" peace on Germany or to enforce it afterwards.[71]

The other pre-eminent concern Lloyd George voiced related to the settle-ment of Germany's eastern borders and the conditions for peace and stability in Eastern Europe. The memorandum underscored that it was crucial to avoid "transferring" German populations from "German rule" to "the rule of some other nation". And it particularly warned against placing more than two million Germans under the rule of a people, the Poles, that had "never proved its capacity for stable self-government". In the British assessment, such a policy would fan the flames of German irredentism and sooner or later spark "a new war". More generally, it would create a highly precarious geopolitical situation – a structural antagonism in which a still "powerful" German nation would be "surrounded by a number of small states" that were as yet weak while at the same time containing large German minorities "clamouring for reunion with their native land".[72] To pre-empt such a scenario Lloyd George proposed as a "guiding principle for the peace" *in Europe* that considerations of national self-determination – or more precisely the maxim that people of a certain

---

[70] Lloyd George, Fontainebleau memorandum, 25 March 1919, *PWW*, LVI, pp. 259–61, 262–3, 267.
[71] *Ibid.*, pp. 266–7, 262–3.
[72] *Ibid.*, pp. 259–67.

nationality should be "allocated to their motherlands" – had to overrule "considerations of strategy or economics or communications".[73]

Unsurprisingly, the Fontainebleau programme was less conciliatory on the thorny subject of reparations. It confirmed that the victors' claims to substantial indemnities were justified. And Lloyd George would invoke the domestic pressures he faced, arguing that he had to deal with a majority in the House of Commons that demanded maximal indemnities and a public that had high, even illusory expectations about what Germany would be made to pay.[74] Following Hankey's recommendations, the Fontainebleau memorandum proposed, ambiguously, that reparations should be so structured and limited in their "duration" that they basically would be borne by the German "generation that made the war", and thus also serve a chastising purpose. Yet it also argued that the victors should ensure that, once the Scheidemann government had accepted their terms, the German people could "get upon their feet again". Clearly confirming the British departure from the harsher Anglo-French economic peace agenda of 1916, the memorandum thus emphasised that Germany was to be included in a liberal world economic system and have "open" access to "the raw materials and markets of the world on equal terms".[75]

Partly out of genuine concern, yet also to put pressure on the French government, Lloyd George and his advisers went to great lengths to invoke the spectre of a Bolshevisation of Germany and Central Europe. Citing the ominous precedent of Béla Kun's proclamation of a Hungarian Soviet republic (on 21 March), Lloyd George warned that "the greatest danger" that an overly draconian peace would produce was that the weak German government would be "swept away", the "spartacists" would seize power in Berlin and then ally with the Bolsheviks. And he conjured up an ominous scenario in which all of Eentral and Eastern Europe was "swept into the orbit of the Bolshevik revolution" and German power and organisational capacity would be put at the disposal of the Bolshevik "fanatics". As he put it, "nearly three hundred million people organised into a vast army under German instructors and German generals" would then be mobilised to launch a renewed "attack on Western Europe".[76] But the relevance of the Bolshevik factor for British policymaking at this critical juncture should not be overstated. What ultimately had a greater bearing was a more fundamental concern – namely that French demands would push the victors towards a settlement that was not only intrinsically unstable but in fact contained "provocations for future wars"

---

[73] *Ibid.*, pp. 259–61, 267; Lloyd George (1938), I, p. 396. See Fry (2011), pp. 195–223.
[74] Lloyd George, Fontainebleau memorandum, 25 March 1919, *PWW*, LVI, pp. 260, 262; Council of Four, 24 March 1919, Mantoux (1992), I, pp. 18–19.
[75] Lloyd George, Fontainebleau memorandum, 25 March 1919, *PWW*, LVI, pp. 260–2.
[76] *Ibid.*, pp. 261, 263

and thus would make it extremely difficult to create, over time, a stable international order in Europe. It was on these premises – and taking his cue from Smuts – that Lloyd George on 27 March pointed to the precedent of the Congress of Vienna. In the Council of Four, he observed that Castlereagh had been guided by the maxim that after the defeat of Napoleon it would have been "a great error to seek to destroy France" because its presence was "necessary for civilization and European stability". He impressed on Wilson and Clemenceau that similar rationales had to guide the victors of 1918 in their conduct towards Germany.[77]

Lloyd George's Fontainebleau aspirations have been criticised for being dominated by tactical considerations and requiring France – and Poland – to make all the crucial concessions while offering no tangible concessions or commitments in return. More importantly, it has been viewed as the first manifestation of a tendency that allegedly came to dominate British policy at Versailles: the shift towards an "appeasement" of Germany at the expense of French and wider European security.[78] But such interpretations are inaccurate. The Fontainebleau programme was undoubtedly shaped and limited by narrower notions of British self-interest, notably on the subject of reparations. Yet it nonetheless provided – at the highest level of the peacemaking process of 1919 – the most coherent vision of a more balanced, in core aspects liberal peace settlement that, however selectively, began to take into account not only the interests and concerns of the victors but also those of the vanquished.

Lloyd George and those who advised him were aware of the crucial systemic problem: the actual imbalance of power and potential that existed between an exhausted France and its structurally superior neighbour. But what they proposed to manage this imbalance, and stabilise Europe, was a policy that, instead of seeking to constrain Germany by force, aimed to foster a new political equilibrium within a reshaped Euro-Atlantic system. This was to ensure, above all, that Britain would never have to fight a major war in Europe again. The underlying rationale that now clearly came to the fore was that longer-term peace and stability could only be achieved if – after the defeated power had accepted an appropriate "chastisement" – the victors set conditions that furthered a relatively rapid accommodation of Germany in the postwar order. The memorandum thus also underlined that once it had agreed to comply with the "just and fair" terms of the victors Germany was to be admitted to the League as soon as possible.[79]

By re-accentuating the Anglo-American guarantee offer to France, the programme Lloyd George presented also demarcated what commitments the British government was prepared make in order to achieve a "lasting peace".

---

[77] Council of Four, 27 March, Mantoux (1992), I, pp. 31–2.
[78] For an illuminating contemporary assessment see Nicolson (1931), p. 109.
[79] Lloyd George, Fontainebleau memorandum, 25 March 1919, PWW, LVI, p. 264.

And not only for this reason it thus also had a pronounced transatlantic dimension. In short, the British premier sought to persuade Wilson to join forces with Britain in laying the groundwork for a peace settlement that, he argued, corresponded with the president's principles; and he sought to commit the United States to the longer-term task of stabilising this new order. Yet Lloyd George's new agenda also had clear inherent limits. Essentially, it was based on two very problematic assumptions. The first was that the proposed Anglo-American security guarantee, his own negotiating skills and Wilson's influence would actually suffice to induce Clemenceau to moderate his more far-reaching aims vis-à-vis Germany – without requiring the Anglo-American powers to make further concessions. The second and even more problematic assumption was that the victors could actually manage to set peace terms that a German government could accept as "just" and "fair" under the conditions of 1919 – *without substantial negotiations*.

There were "more far-sighted moderates" in the British delegation who came to advocate a more decisive shift. They formed a loose circle that comprised Smuts, conservatives like Cecil and Milner, liberals like Churchill, Foreign Office advisers like Headlam-Morley and experts like Keynes. Though on different grounds, they held that it was in the interests of the victors, and future European stability, to bolster the incipient democratisation process in Germany and the standing of what they regarded as a moderate social democratic government in Berlin. And they advocated the conclusion of a peace of accommodation or even of reconciliation with this government that brought Germany into the League of Nations and back into the "comity of nations".[80] Headlam-Morley had already recommended in early January that the western powers should give "active support" to the "moderate socialists" around Ebert and Scheidemann. And in the aftermath of the Weimar Constitutional Assembly, the experts of the Foreign Office's Intelligence Department counselled Lloyd George to adopt a policy that explicitly aimed to strengthen the western orientation of the newly elected Scheidemann government and the reformist forces it represented – by pushing for a settlement that they could accept and thereby pre-empting a nationalist backlash in Germany.[81]

---

[80] See e.g. Cecil to Balfour, 23 February 1919, Cecil Diary, 9 March 1919, Cecil Papers; Churchill speech, 3 March 1919, Hansard, Commons, 5th series, vol. 113, c. 84; Smuts to Lloyd George, 26 March 1919, Lloyd George Papers, F/45/9/29; Keynes to Bradbury and Chamberlain, 4 May 1919, Keynes Papers, XVI, pp. 454–5; Keynes to Mrs Keynes, 14 May 1919, *ibid.*, p. 458.

[81] See Headlam-Morley minute, 3 January 1919, FO 371/3224; Memorandum "The Inner Political Change in Germany", Political Intelligence Department, Foreign Office, ca. 1 February 1919, CAB, A.C.N.P., 484, 862.00/163; Headlam-Morley to Kerr, 5 March 1919, Headlam-Morley Papers, Acc. 688, OS Box 2.

For his part, Milner stressed that following the German elections, which in his view had opened up the most "favourable" prospects for the establishment of a "stable and reasonable government in Germany", the best way to promote stability in Europe was to strengthen the "socialist and democratic parties" that backed Scheidemann's coalition Cabinet. In his assessment, which was clearly coloured by his global-imperialist outlook, it was prudent to support these parties because their approach to foreign policy represented "a sincere repudiation of the aggressive *Weltpolitik* of the old regime". Milner thus urged Lloyd George to make a case for peace terms that were "far more moderate" than those that had hitherto been contemplated.[82] Yet even among the advocates of a peace of accommodation only very few – notably Smuts and Keynes – explicitly argued that in order to conclude a "genuine" settlement it was crucial to pave the way for *actual negotiations* with representatives of the fledgling German republic.[83]

In short, however, the arguments of these "far-sighted moderates" had no measurable influence on the crucial decision-making processes that took place within the British delegation during the crisis month of the Versailles negoti-ations. In the eyes of Lloyd George and his inner circle, bolstering a moderate democratic government in Berlin and a wider inner-German democratisation process was clearly a *secondary concern* at this time. More importantly, they neither now nor later departed from the basic premise of seeking a victor's peace. They never envisaged actually trying to negotiate mutually acceptable peace terms with the "weak" Scheidemann government.

Wilson shared many of the concerns that were expressed in the Fontainebleau memorandum. After his return to Paris the American president quickly concluded that in his absence the deliberations at Versailles had taken a highly disconcerting turn and that this was mainly due to the manoeuvres of Clemenceau and Tardieu. At the same time, he too was affected by reports about Béla Kun's seizure of power as de facto leader of the Soviet Republic of Hungary on 21 March. He and other American delegates became at least as concerned as their British counterparts that this could be the starting-point of a much wider destabilising development: the spread of Bolshevism to Central Europe and, crucially, to Germany.[84] Having thus far focused his attention on the League, the American president now stressed the urgency of addressing

---

[82] See Milner to Earl of Liverpool, 25 January, 22 February and 2 March 1919, cited in Newton (1997), pp. 345–6; Milner to Hamilton-Baynes, 24 March 1919, Milner Papers, 46.

[83] Smuts to Lloyd George, 26 March 1919, Lloyd George Papers, F/45/9/29; Keynes to Bradbury and A. Chamberlain, 4 May 1919, Keynes Papers, XVI, pp. 454–5; Keynes to Mrs Keynes, 14 May 1919, *ibid.*, p. 458; Smuts to Wilson, 30 May 1919; Smuts to Lloyd George, 2 June 1919, *Smuts Papers*, IV, pp. 208–9. 216.

[84] Wilson statement. Council of Four, 26 March 1919, Mantoux (1992), I, p. 20.

"the most difficult and urgent questions" that were not only but mainly connected with the German settlement. And it was at this point that he proclaimed that the victors were facing a "real race between peace and anarchy" amidst growing public dissatisfaction and impatience.[85]

But in contrast to the British premier, the American president never worked out a more coherent approach, let alone a strategy for how to balance an equitable German settlement with the fundamental requirements of European peace and security. Instead, as noted, what Wilson came to advance in response to French designs were merely general maxims for a peace of "stern justice" rather than vengeance that, in his interpretation, conformed with the essentials of the Fourteen Points agenda to which all sides had committed themselves under the armistice. And he initially sought to play the role of an aloof arbiter who adjudicated and made sure that the actual peace terms were indeed consistent with his maxims and what he considered just. Yet the American president would have to learn the hard way – as in the making of the League Covenant – that he had neither sufficient leverage nor prestige to set the terms of a "just peace" in 1919; and that the actual parameters of the German settlement would be set through a multi-layered and often chaotic process of political negotiation and bargaining.

It is worth noting that Wilson hardly consulted with those who were supposed to be his main advisers or with other protagonists of the American delegation. And he often overruled the recommendations of his own experts. For he gained the impression that not only House's manoeuvres regarding the Rhineland question but also the proposals of other American experts on other critical territorial and political issues like the Saar and the German–Polish border stood in conflict with the premises of his own peace agenda. Both the leading US expert on western Europe, Charles Haskins, and the most influential experts on Eastern Europe, Isaiah Bowman and Robert Lord, formulated recommendations that indeed clearly diverged from what Wilson had proclaimed. Essentially, they held that geopolitical and economic considerations had to take precedence over a scrupulous adherence to the progressive principles of Wilson's peace agenda – to which they were clearly less committed than legal experts like Miller. In particular, they argued that such considerations were more important than the concern to do justice to German sovereignty and self-determination claims. And this outlook clearly informed their proposals for different aspects of the German settlement. Essentially, to create a workable balance of power that kept its neighbours secure, they sought to compel the defeated power to cede strategically important territories – even if this meant that sizeable German-speaking populations would hence either live in semi-autonomous buffer-states – in the Rhineland – or directly under

---

[85] Wilson statement, 24 March 1919, Mantoux (1992), I, p. 3.

foreign rule – as in the case of the new Polish and Czechoslovak states they envisioned. In line with his explicitly geopolitical approach, Haskins in effect supported the strategic priorities of Clemenceau and Tardieu. He maintained that the victors should create a postwar order that did not rely on the hope that a democratisation of the defeated power would also pacify its international conduct but rather rested on a recalibrated balance of power and resources between France and Germany. In addition to an autonomous Rhenish state, Haskins thus also recommended that the Saar basin with all of its the coal and steel industries should be given to France.[86]

Bowman and Lord adopted a similar outlook in proposing a substantial revision of the territorial status quo on Germany's eastern borders. Their primary aim was and remained to create a strong Polish state. And in their view it was not only unavoidable but in fact desirable that this state would encompass a significant proportion of formerly German territories and industrial infrastructure – even if this meant placing significant German minorities under Polish rule.[87] By the middle of March, US experts estimated that if the victors insisted on ending German sovereignty over the Rhineland and the projected territorial terms in the east, Germany's population would be reduced by almost one-quarter, and its industrial potential would be markedly reduced. And this was precisely what not only Haskins but also Lord and Bowman recommended in the interest of strengthening Germany's neighbours and creating a more viable European balance of power that would rein in future German ambitions. Fundamentally, the key territorial experts on the American delegation thus all shared more traditional, power-political assumptions about what constituted a desirable solution to the German problem.[88] Interestingly, however, they also agreed with their British counterparts that the "territorial proposals" they had drawn up were intended for a *preliminary inter-"Allied" agreement* and should set "maximum terms" so that "if any negotiation took place with the Germans" – which they still expected – "the result would be to reduce and not to increase the amount to be ceded by Germany".[89]

In contrast to the territorial experts, House had tried to pull together the many different aspects of the German problem the peacemakers had to tackle.

---

[86] See Haskins report, 14 November 1918; Haskins memorandum, "The Eastern Frontier of France" [December 1918], Inquiry nos. 210, 208; Inquiry Report [December 1918], Wilson Papers; Gelfand (1963), pp. 190–7.

[87] See Lord memorandum, "The Polish-German Frontier" (undated), NA PC 185.1127/11; Miller (1924–26), IV, pp. 43–4.

[88] See Inquiry memorandum 609a [March 1919]; Haskins report, 14 November 1918; Haskins memorandum [December 1918]; Inquiry Report [December 1918], Wilson Papers; Haskins statement, 6 March 1919, Miller (1924–26), X, p. 142; Lord memorandum (undated), NA PC 185.1127/11; Schwabe (1985), pp. 251–3.

[89] Minutes of meeting of US and British experts, 21 February 1919, House Papers, 30/165.

He had in fact been the first American actor at Versailles who had seen the need to draw up a comprehensive "program" to prepare a "preliminary peace with Germany". And, crucially, he had proposed something akin to a political strategy to this end. He urged Wilson to reach an understanding with the leaders of Britain and France on the different key issues, by which he meant not only the security problem and the future status of the Rhineland but also reparations and the "delineation" of Germany's western and eastern borders. And he persisted with his efforts to persuade the president that it would be unavoidable to make compromises in order to forge, ultimately, a settlement that was true to American essentials – and guaranteed the establishment of the League.[90] House observed that it would at times be "necessary to compromise in order to get things through". But he was careful to stress that he advocated no "compromise of principle".[91] Yet because of what the president had come to see as a profoundly disloyal act, House's unauthorised Rhineland initiatives, the man who had been his closest adviser would no longer be able to play the role of a crucial broker between Wilson and the *Entente* governments.

Wilson essentially disregarded House's advice and in many ways came to act against the counsel of his territorial experts. In a characteristically aloof and unilateral fashion, he came to pursue his own and markedly different approach – and clearly insisted on pursuing his own conception of peacemaking. As noted, the American president was not at all unaware of the problem that the power potential of a basically preserved German state would pose. But he maintained that the best way of coping with this problem was *not* to follow what he saw as self-defeating balance-of-power maxims – for he too held that the espousal of such maxims with a view to the Rhineland, the Saar and Germany's eastern borders would create an untenable status quo and provoke irredentism and future conflicts that could escalate into a new war.

What Wilson proposed instead were guiding principles and rationales that echoed those Lloyd George had stipulated in the Fontainebleau memorandum, which had actually made an impression on him. Yet the American president placed an even greater emphasis on the necessity to present terms to the German government that fulfilled fundamental requirements of "justice" and "fairness", as he defined them – and that did not compromise principles in the name of overriding national interests or strategic imperatives. Crucially, like the British premier, he assumed that the victors not only should but actually *could* act as if they were "impartial arbiters" – and that it actually would be possible to agree on terms that could be acceptable not only to them but also to the defeated power. But he did still not envisage actual substantive negotiations with those who represented the newly elected government in Berlin.

[90] House diary, 14 February 1919, *PWW*, LV, p. 193.
[91] *Ibid.*

Wilson thus underscored that his main aim was to "prepare a peace founded on justice" – and at the same time a settlement that "Germany can sign". And he argued that if German representatives refused to sign such a "just" peace, then "the entire opinion of the world" would turn against them.[92]

Yet the American president had by this time espoused a distinctly stern conception of justice. Emphasising what had become a firm premise of his peace policy, he noted that he had no objections to a peace that punished Germany severely for the transgressions its imperial masters had committed, and in which the German people had been complicit. He thus distanced himself from the distinction between the German rulers and people that he had made during the war. But similar to Lloyd George Wilson made a distinction between a peace of "stern justice" and a peace of "vengeance" that would sow the seeds of future war. He warned Clemenceau that their main task was to agree on terms that could be considered just rather than vengeful so that the sympathies of the world would not align in Germany's favour in the way they had turned pro-French after the unjustly draconian peace the Bismarck *Reich* had imposed in 1871.[93]

But what were the essential yardsticks for the "just" peace Wilson envisaged? At one level, the American president insisted anew that victors should adhere to the terms of the armistice agreement, those of the Fourteen Points "upon which they had all agreed".[94] And he argued, more generally, that they had to adhere to the principles to which, in his interpretation, they had committed themselves, above all the principle of self-determination. He warned that if they now envisaged terms for the peace with Germany that obviously contradicted their pledges this would undermine the legitimacy of the entire peace settlement, particularly because it would give every discontented power grounds for challenging its validity. Wilson proclaimed that his guiding thought was not to "stray from the path" of what he characterised as a "great world movement towards justice" – as whose leader he evidently saw himself – by agreeing to peace terms that would "allow it to be said" of the victorious powers that they "profess great principles, but they admitted exceptions wherever sentiment or national interest made them wish to deviate from the rule".[95]

It was on these premises that Wilson fundamentally agreed with Lloyd George's professed maxim to exercise "moderation" and display "fairness" vis-à-vis Germany. He underscored that they neither had the power to

---

[92] Grayson diary, 26 March 1919, *PWW*, LVI, p. 284.

[93] House diary, 28 March 1919, House Papers; Wilson statements, 28 March 1919, Grayson diary, Axson memoir, section 49, Wilson Papers; Grayson (1960), pp. 75–6; Walworth (1986), pp. 268–9.

[94] Baker diary, 28 March 1919, *PWW*, LVI, p. 353; Council of Four, 28 March 1919, Mantoux (1992), II, pp. 64–5.

[95] Council of Four, 28 March 1919, Mantoux (1992), I, pp. 64–5.

"destroy" it nor should they attempt to do so. Using terms very similar to those of the Fontainebleau memorandum, the American president underscored on 27 March that the "greatest error" would be to furnish the defeated power with "powerful reasons for seeking revenge at some future time". And, using distinctly moralistic language, he essentially made the case for a "peace of justice" as the best way to avoid this cardinal error. He stressed that it was imperative not to give "even an impression of injustice", be it through "(e)xcessive demands", notably when it came to reparations, or "unfair" settlements of complex territorial questions that involved conflicting claims to self-determination. And he presciently declared that what he feared more than "future wars brought about by the secret plottings of governments" were those conflicts that were "created by popular discontent" – and that would be "inevitable" if the victors were "guilty of injustice".[96]

Following this emphatic plea, Wilson essentially tried to ensure that – in the west – the terms of the peace would leave Germany's political and territorial integrity intact (though he accepted, in line with the Fourteen Points, that Alsace-Lorraine would be returned to France, without a plebiscite). He insisted that separating the Rhineland and the Saar from Germany against the wishes of populations that were "German in character" would violate basic German self-determination claims and provoke the charge that the western powers were pursuing a peace based on double-standards.[97] And he warned that this would stir up nationalism and resentment in Germany, with disastrous consequences for Europe. Clearly irritated by Clemenceau's intransigence during the crisis of early April, the American president exclaimed at one point that if all of France's demands were granted "the world would go to pieces in a very short while". And, as noted, he threatened to leave Paris.[98]

In the east, Wilson's priorities also reflected the concerns Lloyd George had voiced. He evidently found it difficult to depart from the by then unrealistic maxim of establishing, as far as possible, a Polish state that included only "indisputably Polish" populations and to face up to the reality that the new Poland would be a multi-ethic state that encompassed multiple minorities. But the American president did become increasingly concerned that by placing large German minorities under Polish rule, the victors would fan the flames of irredentist nationalism in Germany, which in turn would threaten the security and consolidation prospects of an originally weak Polish state. Though still insisting that it was vital to guarantee Polish access to the Baltic Sea, he now proposed that, consistent with the Fourteen Points, Danzig should be granted the special status of a "free city" under the supervision of the League rather than simply be accorded to Poland. In critical respects, then, Wilson's

[96] Council of Four, 26 and 27 March 1919, Mantoux (1992), I, pp. 20, 31.
[97] Council of Four, 28 March 1919, Mantoux (1992), I, pp. 64–5.
[98] Grayson diary, 6 April 1919, PWW, LVII, pp. 50–1.

priorities aligned with those of the British premier and collided not only with
the French pursuit of a "strong Polish state" – and of course with Dmowski's
agenda – but also with the parameters Lord had earlier proposed in the Polish
Commission.[99]

Finally, like the financial experts on the American peace delegation, notably
Davies and Lamont, Wilson was intent on pushing for a clearly delimited and
"practical" settlement of reparation claims that strictly adhered to the premises
established by the armistice treaty. He essentially sought an agreement that
made Germany pay for the damages its "transgressions" had caused during the
war but would not crush the defeated power and indeed preserve it as an
important American trading partner and key element in the world economy.
The president thus backed a plan proposed by John Foster Dulles and supported by Davies and Lamont which called for the establishment of an expert
commission to assess both war damages and Germany's capacity to pay – and
that pursued the core aim of persuading the *Entente* Powers to settle on a fixed
total sum of indemnities. Yet Wilson also confirmed that he was neither
willing nor in a position to consider any American incentives or concessions,
notably with a view to US war-debt claims, to pave the way for "rational"
reparations settlement of this kind.[100]

When exhorting his European counterparts to intensify their efforts to settle
the most intricate problems of the German settlement, Wilson clearly signalled
his determination to insist on terms that were consistent with his conception
of justice. Yet his pursuits were and remained essentially reactive. He could not
play the role of a decisive arbiter of peace, and he clearly could not shape the
conference agenda. To a significant extent this was due to the fact that,
resisting House's advice, he remained fundamentally averse to what he considered "old-style" European politics of bargaining. He still did not seek a
peace of compromise but a peace of principle. The power of the United States
and the fact that the European victors depended on its support in various ways
undoubtedly were a cardinal factor at Versailles. But the leverage Wilson
actually had to steer the negotiations in accordance with his own conception
of justice – either through incentives or sanctions – was in fact distinctly
limited. And it was reduced further by the fact that, not least for domestic
reasons, he ruled out more robust security guarantees or incentives in the form
of debt relief.

At a deeper level, what Wilson's conduct during the decisive altercations
between the Big Three threw into relief was his distinctly hierarchical – and

---

[99] Council of Four, 27 March and 1 April 1919, Mantoux (1955), I, pp. 41. 198, 201; Miller
(1924–26), I, p. 208.

[100] Meeting of the US economic advisers with peace commissioners, 11 February 1919,
Walworth (1986), p. 172; Lamont (1921), p. 263; Wilson to Lansing, 23 February 1919,
PWW, LV, p. 231.

unilateral – conception of what constituted "justice" and a "just" process in international affairs. Essentially, it was the conception of an elevated arbiter who accorded himself the prerogative to decide what could be deemed just, fair or "justly stern" peace terms. Inevitably, though, he had to recognise in his negotiations with Clemenceau and Lloyd George that each actor of course had his own and distinct conception of what was "just", "fair" or appropriate under the circumstances – and this of course also applied to those who sought to represent the vanquished – as well as to all the other actors who tried to influence the peacemaking process. What he thus was compelled to engage in, and had to learn to engage in, was a strenuous negotiation process in which the representatives of the different key states struggled to find some kind of common ground between their often conflicting notions of what qualified as a "just" settlement – yet also between their different definitions of vital interests and the domestic needs and expectations they had to satisfy.

Under the modern conditions of Versailles, this was the only realistic *modus operandi* for reaching results – as far as this was possible at all – that each side could accept and that, more profoundly, fulfilled basic requirements of "justice" or equitability because they balanced different claims, interests and expectations. In short, only a process of this kind could potentially yield outcomes that could gain more general legitimacy. But what became clear during the most critical phase of the peace conference was that, because of how far apart the main victors were in their conceptions of a "just peace" and definitions of fundamental interests, particularly regarding the German settlement, it was extremely difficult to pursue such a process, and strike such a balance, *even among them*. It was especially difficult because, as we have seen, more or less self-interested British and American notions of a "just peace" collided with a French conception of "victors' justice" that deliberately placed considerations of security and vital strategic interests above considerations of equitability – and justified this in part by asserting that "western" and German ideas of justice simply could not be reconciled.

In view of these profound divisions, it is hardly surprising that the conflict-ridden negotiations of the victors revealed even more starkly how problematic another core premise was that characterised Wilson's approach to peace just as much as that of Lloyd George. And this was the premise that it would be possible for the victors to settle on terms that were so "just" that they would be accepted by the vanquished power as well – without envisaging actual negotiations with German representatives and allowing them to present their claims, interests and concerns. Essentially, then, because Wilson insisted – also publicly – on making "justice" and "fairness" the key criteria by which the quality of the peace settlement was to be measured, he raised expectations that simply could not be met by an imposed peace of the victors. But on this critical issue the American president's attitude had hardened by the time the deliberations in the Council of Four began in earnest in late March. He now basically confirmed the premise on which Clemenceau and Lloyd George had insisted all along, namely that the victors would negotiate not merely a preliminary but for all practical purposes a *definite* peace settlement that the German government would then simply "have to accept".[101]

Unquestionably, the Bolshevik factor also had a bearing on Wilson's outlook; but its significance should not be exaggerated either. Under the impact of the disconcerting developments in Hungary, Wilson's pursuits also became motivated by the concern that a peace whose terms could be regarded as unjust and excessive would raise the spectre of a Bolshevik take-over in Germany. Evidently perceiving the Bolshevisation of Germany as a serious threat at this stage, Wilson emphasised the need for moderation. He noted that the victors confronted a "disorganized and demoralized Germany" and that the new "Weimar government" was unstable and weak – it had "no credit". And he impressed not only on Clemenceau but also on Lloyd George that if the victors' demands were so far-reaching – especially concerning reparations – that they precipitated the collapse of the Scheidemann Cabinet, it would likely be replaced by a government they would not be able to "deal with". Wilson emphatically insisted that the victors could not build a lasting peace by "crushing Germany for thirty-five years" – and that they owed it to "the peace of the world" not to "tempt Germany to plunge into Bolshevism".[102] His fear that the spread of Bolshevism would undermine the prospects of creating stable democratic states in Central Europe was genuine, and it was shared by a majority in the American peace delegation. And while he certainly also invoked the Bolshevik threat to put pressure on his interlocutors, the anti-Bolshevik orientation of Wilson's policy indeed became more pronounced in 1919. Significantly, however, it did *not* lead him to change either his approach to peacemaking or his attitude towards the German government and the challenges it faced in any substantial way.

Making no notable effort to acquire a more in-depth understanding of the domestic-political situation in Germany, the American president maintained a high-handed distance. Even after the Constitutional Assembly had convened in Weimar and a democratically elected government had been formed he still regarded its protagonists as tainted by their links with the old regime rather than as credible representatives of a new republican Germany. More importantly, in approaching the negotiations with Clemenceau and Lloyd George, he never considered the immediate and longer-term needs of the "Weimar government" in a more than superficial manner. Bolstering it never became a primary concern of his, and he now distanced himself even more

---

[101] See Mantoux (1955), I, pp. 14, 79.
[102] Council of Four, 26 March 1919, Mantoux (1992), I, p. 20.

unequivocally from any notion of eventually negotiating with its representatives. Wilson's conduct indeed underscored that he had clearly abandoned his earlier maxim that a durable progressive peace would have to be concluded as a negotiated peace – a peace that, ultimately, had to be negotiated between the victors and the vanquished and also gave the latter a stake in the final settlement and the new order it was supposed to establish. Instead, the American president became preoccupied with a far narrower concern, namely that there would be a government in Berlin that was sufficiently stable to *sign* a peace treaty decreed by the victors.[103]

Facing the concrete task of coming to terms with the other victors, and considerable domestic pressure to impose a severe peace settlement, the American president in fact adopted an increasingly rigorous outlook. Wilson's *longer-term* "vision" of order did not change during the peace negotiations. It still pivoted on the maxim that, by forging a "just" settlement and establishing the League, the victors would create the mainstays of a novel – Atlantic – international order into which they could then draw Germany and the other vanquished powers. In principle, he also clung to the belief that it was in the interest of peace and stability in Europe to foster a process of democratisation in Germany. Yet with a view to the pressing challenges of the immediate future he came to pursue a noticeably tougher approach. He now insisted that before an accommodation or even reconciliation with Germany could be envisaged, those who represented it first had to accept and comply with the terms the victors would decree. And he re-accentuated the key rationale that had already guided his actions after the armistice – the rationale that in view of the "unstable equilibrium" that characterised the situation in Germany, the wisest course of action was to subject the vanquished power to an extended period of probation – and to keep it outside the League – until the western powers could be certain "how the German people were going to behave".[104]

In the spring of 1919, only two important members of the American delegation, Bliss and Hoover, advocated a more affirmative policy towards Germany – a policy that not only took the concerns of its new republican government more seriously but also sought to buttress it and to promote inner-German democratisation more actively. They held that such a policy was in the interest of the victors, not only to contain the spread of Bolshevism. For they had concluded that the pacification of a highly unsettled European continent critically depended upon the consolidation of a stable republican political order – and a liberal-capitalist system – in Germany. And they argued that in order to achieve this it was imperative

---

[103] Wilson, Supreme War Council meeting, 17 March 1919, *FRUS-PPC*, IV, pp. 363, 374–5.
[104] Wilson, Supreme War Council meeting, 17 March 1919, *FRUS-PPC*, IV, pp. 363, 374–5; Council of Ten, 12 February 1919, *PWW*, LV, p. 104–5. See Schwabe (1985), p. 217.

to use US influence to push for a moderate peace of accommodation. General Bliss emerged as a committed proponent of this approach, but he hardly influenced Wilson's thinking.[105]

What carried more weight were Hoover's concerns. He tried to persuade Wilson that it should be a primary aim of American peace policy not only to prevent Germany's disintegration but also to support the newly-formed government in Berlin in its efforts to consolidate a republican – and capitalist – order. In his assessment, this was not only a crucial prerequisite for countering the appeal of Bolshevism but also essential for Europe's economic *and* political stabilisation. And he consistently recommended using the lever of American economic power to this end. At the same time, Hoover continued his efforts to contain Bolshevik and disintegrative tendencies in Germany by ensuring an orderly provision of food and vital supplies.[106] This was the underlying reason for his determination to push for the Brussels agreement, which was then negotiated between delegates of the Associated Powers and German representatives in mid-March 1919. It paved the way for supplying food to all parts of the former enemy power, against German payments in gold marks, through what was essentially an American relief programme organised under Hoover's authority.[107] Hoover thus identified a basis of common interests with the Scheidemann government, and he persistently urged Wilson not only to support it as a de facto ally against Bolshevism but also to push for a peace settlement that would incorporate the German republic in an American-led postwar order on liberal-capitalist terms.[108]

Wilson backed Hoover's Brussels initiative and paid more attention to his recommendations. Ultimately, however, they only had a limited impact on the president's decisions at Versailles. No impact at all had the reports of Ellis Dresel, who had acted as the American government's semi-official observer in Germany since mid-December 1918 and would return to Berlin on a reconnaissance mission in the decisive weeks of April 1919. Becoming increasingly alarmed, Dresel made numerous efforts to convince the American delegation to support the Ebert-Scheidemann coalition, which in his eyes represented the only combination "in sight" that could stabilise a republican order. And through House he eventually called on Wilson to use his influence to induce the *Entente* Powers to pursue actual negotiations with the German government and to make concessions notably on questions that involved German territory and populations on its western and

---

[105] See Bliss diary, 11 February 1919; Bliss to Baker, 14 February 1919, Bliss Papers.
[106] Hoover to Wilson, 20 December 1918, *PWW*, LIII, pp. 453–4.
[107] See Schwabe (1985), pp. 205–10.
[108] See Hoover to Wilson, 20 December 1918, *PWW*, LIII, pp. 453–4; Hoover to Wilson, 11 April 1919, in Bane and Lutz (1942), pp. 400–1.

eastern borders. Yet House declined to back Dresel's appeal; and it never even reached Wilson himself.[109]

IV. The Pivotal Transatlantic Compromises of 1919. The Rhineland and Security Agreements of the Victors – and Their Limits

What began in mid-March and only reached its preliminary conclusion with the presentation of the victors' draft treaty to Germany on 29 April has been called the "French battle" of the Versailles Peace Conference. But it can more appropriately be described as a pivotal stage in the complex transatlantic search for compromises among the victors that had to be pursued under immense international and domestic pressures.

As both Clemenceau and Tardieu had all along pursued the key priority of inducing Wilson and Lloyd George to offer more tangible security guarantees for France, the French premier and his inner circle of advisers welcomed the Anglo-American guarantee proposals. And they indeed regarded them as a crucial step towards the creation of the postwar union of the victors to which they aspired. But it soon became clear that the proposed guarantees would not suffice to satisfy the French government's security concerns. Essentially, Clemenceau and Tardieu were keen to seize on the Anglo-American offer. But they were not prepared to accept the British premise that the "positive" physical guarantees their Rhineland scheme was to provide could be entirely superseded by the *political* guarantees that Lloyd George and Wilson were prepared to give.

It is thus misleading to conclude that, forced to make a choice, the French protagonists decided to pursue an alliance with Britain and the United States instead of seeking to recast the European balance of power.[110] Rather, they now sought to find a new way to obtain such an alliance *and* to create a new, more favourable balance of power in Europe. It was with this aim in mind, and to pave the way for a compromise, that Clemenceau would alter the French bargaining strategy. He would eventually be prepared to abandon the demand for an "autonomous" Rhenish state, seeking instead to gain the support of Wilson and Lloyd George for a prolonged occupation of the Rhineland. Yet he and Tardieu by no means abandoned the core aim of securing a peace settlement that structurally weakened and constrained Germany. This was also the underlying strategic motive behind the insistent French demands for high reparation payments. But Clemenceau supported such demands not only for this reason, nor only because of the domestic-political pressures and expectations he confronted. He also did so for tactical purposes: to bargain for

---

[109] See Dresel-Osborne report, 10 May 1919, *FRUS-PPC*, XII, pp. 111–12, 116–17; Dresel to House, 21 April 1919, House Papers.

[110] See Jackson (2013), p. 294.

Anglo-American concessions in other key areas, particularly with a view to his Rhineland priorities.

All in all, Clemenceau and Tardieu thus had many political and strategic reasons to reject the rationales both of Lloyd George's Fontainebleau memorandum and Wilson's plea for a "stern but just" peace vis-à-vis Germany most categorically. In their perception, what the British premier and the American president proposed challenged the entire French security and "re-balancing" agenda. Clemenceau was aware of how crucial it was for the success of his peace strategy to block and delegitimise any moves towards a "Fontainebleau peace". And he accordingly went to considerable lengths to achieve this, castigating Lloyd George's recommendations as a flawed and dangerous form of "appeasement" that had to be avoided by all means. Clemenceau asserted once again that it was illusory to entertain the very notion that it would be possible to forge peace terms that not only the victors but also the vanquished could deem legitimate. He even argued that it would be dangerous to be unduly influenced by concerns over the possible resentment or nationalist backlash that the victors' decisions could provoke in Germany.

The French premier now stated explicitly that in his judgement it was simply impossible to reconcile the ideas of the western powers and German conceptions of what constituted a "just" peace.[111] And he insisted that it was a "sheer illusion" to believe that the territorial terms of the peace could be adjusted in such a way as to accommodate the defeated power with the new order, calling it a "remedy not equal to the disease". Both he and Tardieu thus warned Lloyd George, Wilson and their advisers that any attempt to forge a peace settlement that could also gain acceptance in Germany was not only misguided but actually incompatible with what they saw as the essential requirements of peace and security in postwar Europe.[112] And they pushed back against Anglo-American policies of "appeasement" that in their assessment compromised cardinal French interests and would also prove futile because, as Clemenceau stressed, it would never be possible to appease German ambitions in Europe once the victors had decided to "cut [it] off from world politics".[113]

It was in this context that Clemenceau now also emphasised underlying French fears that arose from the wider geopolitical shifts the war had brought about – and made a sustainable accord between the principal victors so hard to achieve in 1919. He argued that the cardinal interest of Britain and the United States, namely to eliminate Germany as a "world power" that could threaten their global interests, shifted the burden of countering German

---

[111] Clemenceau statement, Council of Four, 28 March 1919, Mantoux (1992), I, pp. 62–5.
[112] See Clemenceau statement, Council of Ten, 12 February 1919, *FRUS-PPC*, III, p. 975; Clemenceau statement, Council of Four, 28 March 1919, Mantoux (1992), I, pp. 62–5; Tardieu memorandum, 25 February 1919, Tardieu, (II/1921), pp. 156, 161–2.
[113] French note, 28 March 1919, Wilson Papers, VIII-A-29.

power to France – because the defeated power would now concentrate on regaining a predominant position on the European continent. And he dismissed the idea that this could be prevented through moderation and concessions vis-à-vis Berlin.[114] Last but not least, both Clemenceau and Tardieu argued that German attempts to invoke the Bolshevik threat and to suggest that it was in the interest of the western powers to bolster the republican government in Berlin against the novel menace from the east should be viewed with suspicion and must not affect the essentials of the peace.[115] It is worth emphasising again that these views by and large reflected prevalent outlooks and assumptions among French political elites and opinion-makers – outside Socialist circles – about the nature of the German threat, the precarious future of inner-German developments and the need to guard against a resurgence of aggressive German nationalism. These outlooks were marked by an abidingly profound scepticism, which derived not only from the experiences of the war but also by entrenched longer-term perceptions. And, however understandable they were, such outlooks and perceptions made changes in the direction of a less antagonistic postwar approach towards Germany very difficult.[116]

Yet while he adamantly refuted Anglo-American "appeasement" aspirations vis-à-vis Germany, Clemenceau actually used his authority to initiate an important shift of French policy. Discussing the Anglo-American guarantee proposals with Tardieu and Pichon, he declared that the French delegation had to make a vital strategic choice. It could either insist on a Rhenish buffer state, which would "leave France alone on the Left Bank of the Rhine" and risk an irremediable rupture with its crucial allies; or it could seek a compromise – an agreement that, as Tardieu proposed, centred on a long-term occupation of the Rhineland and French control over a significant part of the Saar yet also ensured that the Anglo-American powers would be "allied" to France in the postwar era. Unmistakeably, the French premier favoured the latter option. Presciently, he argued that France would not be able to maintain a permanent Rhenish occupation regime on its own, and he underscored that it could not afford to act unilaterally. More profoundly, then, he and Tardieu realised more acutely than their critics Poincaré, Foch and Joffre that the French state did not have the power to impose a buffer-state "solution" against the opposition of Britain and the United States – and that an overly abrasive bargaining

---

[114] *Ibid.*

[115] See Clemenceau statement, Council of Ten, 12 February 1919, *FRUS-PPC*, III, p. 975; Clemenceau statement, Council of Four, 28 March 1919, Mantoux (1992), I, pp. 62–5; Tardieu memorandum, 25 February 1919, Tardieu, (II/1921), pp. 156, 161–2.

[116] Clemenceau to Allied governments, 11 November 1918, MAE, Paix 47; Clemenceau statement, Council of Ten, 12 February 1919, *FRUS-PPC*, III, p. 975; Tardieu memorandum, 25 February 1919, Tardieu (II/1921), pp. 161–2.

approach indeed carried the risk of corroding the already dangerously strained "solidarity" even further.[117]

That the preservation of an "inter-allied" union mattered most thus became an ever more paramount rationale of the Clemenceau government's pursuits. But the premier and his advisers also agreed that it was imperative to define the desired Anglo-American guarantee obligations more precisely and to make sure that they would come to France's aid not only in the case of an outright German attack but also pre-emptively – if there was *threat* of German aggression. Tardieu emphasised that it was crucial to set out the "*casus foederis*" with "the greatest clarity so that Germany can have no uncertainty as to the precise and immediate consequences of any aggression"; it was to have a "prompt and automatic character". In his assessment, the Anglo-American guarantee agreement thus had to fill exactly the gap, and compensate for the "uncertainty", that the relevant articles of the League Covenant's collective security regime – X and XVI – left.[118] But he and Clemenceau agreed that, regardless of their precise provisions, the agreement's political guarantees would still be insufficient in themselves – and that, consequently, it would be vital to commit the Anglo-American powers to accepting "material" guarantees *in a new guise*.

The French government's response to the Anglo-American proposals, formulated by Tardieu and Pichon, marked the beginning of a new phase of French bargaining efforts. It acknowledged that the envisaged guarantee treaty was of "great value". But it also stressed that France still had "need of a physical guarantee" because in the event of a new German attack, British and American forces could not be mobilised in time to provide effective aid. More interestingly, the note stated that it was not possible for the French government to give up territorial guarantees "for the sake of expectations".[119] What lay behind this formulation were marked doubts about the wisdom of basing France's postwar security mainly on political pledges of the Anglo-American powers. French policymakers had clearly registered the reluctance of British and American leaders to countenance any renewed military involvement in Europe – and the prevalent domestic pressures for demobilisation and against further strategic entanglements that Wilson and Lloyd George confronted. Nor were they oblivious to a problem that could potentially undermine the entire French conception of an Atlantic security community, namely that the ratification of the proposed agreement in the American Senate was far from assured. In fact, the French premier was warned by Lodge – who was

---

[117] See Loucheur diary, 14 and 15 March 1919, Loucheur (1962), pp. 71–2; Jackson (2013), pp. 293–4.

[118] Tardieu memorandum, 29 March 1919, Tardieu Papers, vol. 418.

[119] See Clemenceau to Wilson, with enclosed note, 17 March 1919, *PWW*, LVI, pp. 9–14; French note, 17 March 1919, Tardieu Papers, vol. 418.

actually in favour of the security accord – that the Senate would not support a treaty that conveyed the impression of inaugurating a permanent alliance with France. But Clemenceau evidently placed some trust in Wilson's assurances that the agreement would be ratified along the with peace treaty.

Despite such uncertainties, Clemenceau and Tardieu deemed the guarantee agreement and fundamental concord with Britain and the United States vital for France's future in the post–First World War international system. Yet they were determined to insist, not merely for bargaining purposes, that additional assurances would be indispensable. More precisely, they were determined to ensure that, as a last resort, France would be able to safeguard its security through a long-term control of the Rhineland.[120] Relinquishing their demand for a separate Rhenish state, the French negotiators thus proposed a set of new conditions, which Tardieu had elaborated. They called for an inter-allied "military occupation" of the Rhineland and the establishment of strategic bridgeheads across the Rhine for a period of thirty years; and they demanded that not only the Left Bank but also a fifty-kilometre-wide zone on the Rhine's right bank were to be permanently demilitarised. The decisive French note stipulated that any German breach of these provisions was to be categorised as an act of aggression that would require an Anglo-American intervention – and that France would be authorised to re-occupy the Left Bank and the bridge-heads if the German violation occurred after the initial thirty-year period.

Subsequently, Clemenceau even sought to extend these provisions. He demanded that not only a German breach of the demilitarisation clauses but also of "the military terms of the peace in general" should be regarded as an aggressive act. And, significantly, he and Tardieu would also insist that the occupation was to be maintained not only for security purposes but also to guarantee German compliance with the reparations demands of the *Entente* governments.[121] All of this amounted to a revised French strategy, but its underlying aims remained unaltered. While the pursuit of a "union" with the Anglo-American powers remained paramount, Clemenceau and Tardieu never lost sight of the core objective of making the Rhine the new military and civilisational frontier in Europe and constraining German sovereignty over the Rhineland as far and as long as possible.

While pursuing this hard-fisted yet compromise-orientated approach at the peace conference, the French premier always had to keep a close eye on the

---

[120] See Tardieu statements, 12 March 1919, Cmd. 2169, *Negotiations for an Anglo-French Pact*, p. 64; Cambon (1919), "La paix", *L'écho de Paris*, 29 June 1919; Bonsal (1946), p. 134; Walworth (1986), pp. 326–7.

[121] The French government also renewed its claim to the entire Saar area. See Clemenceau to Wilson, 17 March 1919, *PWW*, LVI, pp. 9–14; French note, 17 March 1919, Tardieu Papers, vol. 418. Tardieu memorandum, 2 April 1919, *PWW*, LVII, pp. 295–6; French note, 2 April 1919, Wilson Papers, VIII-A-29; Tardieu (I/1921), pp. 177–86.

domestic-political front. And it was indeed at this critical point that the most acute pressure arose. It came from Marshal Foch, Poincaré and those forces in the French parliament and political spectrum that rallied behind the demand for more far-reaching territorial guarantees. They now basically accused Clemenceau of being too conciliatory towards the Anglo-American powers. In late March, Foch launched a campaign to force the French premier to end his search for an understanding with Wilson and Lloyd George, who in his view were pursuing a policy to "appease Germany at [France's] expense". Forcing his way into the Council of Four, the marshal claimed once again that French and European security required above all else the establishment of a Rhenish buffer-state and a strategic frontier on the Rhine. Foch viewed the guarantee proposals with profound scepticism, asserting that they would not constitute an effective deterrent and that in case of a German attack, Anglo-American aid would arrive too late. He thus argued that a permanent occupation of the Left Bank and strategic bridgeheads were the only means to avoid an "unreliable peace" and to keep in check a "Germanic mass of around 70 millions".[122] In the public debate, the *Ligue française* and the *Comité de la rive gauche du Rhin* kept agitating for such demands. In mid-April, the Radical senator Paul Doumer and a group of like-minded senators from Clemenceau's own party tabled a resolution calling on the government to make the "military guarantees" Foch had demanded an integral part of the peace treaty.[123] And Foch himself even suggested that an overthrow of the Clemenceau government had to be countenanced to realise his essentials – and urged Poincaré to take charge of the negotiations.

Poincaré too was incensed by what he saw as Clemenceau's willingness to settle for a fifteen-year occupation rather than a potentially permanent buffer-state solution in return for Anglo-American guarantee offers that in his view were far from satisfactory. He demanded that the French government had to "preserve its territorial guarantee" until Germany had executed "all conditions of the peace treaty", envisioning a period of more than thirty years. He urged Clemenceau to procure for France the "right of occupation of the left bank" as a "guarantee" for as long as it still had reparation claims vis-à-vis Germany. And, castigating the proposed Anglo-American pledge as "illusory", he maintained that the only way to ensure that Britain and the United States met their guarantee obligations would be to turn the agreement into a traditional, fully-fledged military alliance reinforced by conventions about "the timetable, the extent and the conditions of the promised military assistance".[124]

---

[122] Foch statement, Council of Four, 31 March 1919, Mantoux (1992), I, pp. 86–9; Poincaré (1926–33), XI, p. 291.

[123] *Journal Officiel (Sénat)*, 1919, 622: 17 April 1919; Miquel (1977), pp. 371–3.

[124] Poincaré draft letter to Pichon, 30 March, in "Notes journalières", BN, NAFR 16033; Poincaré to Clemenceau, 28 April 1919, *Le Temps*, 12 September 1921; Poincaré to

Yet, like Clemenceau and Tardieu, the French president would have to accept that an alliance of this kind was not on the cards in 1919. And he ultimately refused to engage in a "coup" to topple the French premier in the midst of the peace negotiations. In fact, Clemenceau managed to deflect Foch's challenge and contain the looming parliamentary crisis quite rapidly. He issued the threat of calling for a vote of confidence and, as he expected, a majority in both chambers rallied behind him. He thus retained the initiative and indeed expanded his domestic room to manoeuvre. And his domestic troubles even strengthened his position in the negotiations with Wilson and Lloyd George. For he could invoke them to underscore that the new conditions he had put forward in the note of 17 March represented the maximal concessions he could make without provoking a backlash in France.

By early April, the conflict-ridden negotiations over the Rhineland and the wider security question had reached not only a deadlock but indeed "a dangerous pass".[125] For while Clemenceau dug in his heels Lloyd George and Wilson were by no means prepared to accept the new French scheme. The British premier objected most sharply to Clemenceau's demand for a long-term occupation of the Rhineland. He argued that it would not provoke less nationalist resentment in Germany than the earlier buffer-state scheme and become the same "permanent cause of conflict in Europe". And he stressed that no British government would "leave British troops in Germany for fifteen years" – and that it would be impossible to gain public and parliamentary support for an occupation regime that British public opinion would regard as a major obstacle to European peace and stability.[126]

Wilson too grew increasingly irritated by what he regarded as French obstructionism and excessive demands that stood in direct conflict with his peace agenda. He observed that if French negotiators obtained all they claimed France was "entitled" to "the world would go to pieces" and his aspirations for a "just" and "moderate" peace would be undermined. On 6 April, he decided to make a dramatic gesture, telling American peace commissioners that if no tangible progress was made on the decisive issues on the Rhineland and Saar questions he would issue an ultimatum. He would impress on Clemenceau that "unless peace was made according to [the victors'] promises, which were to conform to the principles of the Fourteen Points" he would either threaten to "go home" or "insist upon having the conference in the open". Wilson indeed ordered Admiral Benson to inquire how soon the "George

Pichon, 23 April 1919, Pichon Papers, vol. 7; Keiger (2006), pp. 257–62; Jackson (2013), pp. 298–9.
[125] Bliss to Mrs. Bliss, 3 April 1919, Trask (1966), p. 45.
[126] Lloyd George statements, Council of Four, 22 April, 12 and 13 June 1919, Mantoux (1992), pp. 318–19, 405, 429.

Washington" could be dispatched to Brest.[127] But his ultimatum would not have the desired effect; he would stay in Paris.

The leading voices on security issues in the US delegation, the peace commissioners Bliss and White, were even more apprehensive than the president – and so was Hoover. The objections they raised pointed to some of the most fundamental problems American policymakers had to grapple with in trying to define what kind of world power the United States could become after the Great War. It was the question of what kind of political and security commitments he – or any American president – was in a position to make, especially in view of the fact that the inner-American debates about this vital question had barely begun. Committed to Wilson's League priorities, and still mindful of traditional American antipathies against entangling alliances, the American commissioners remained distinctly wary of extending specific security guarantees to France. In fact, they regarded the French approach to security and postwar order as deeply problematic because in their assessment it threatened to compromise both the League and the prospects of an "American-style" progressive pacification of the Old World.

Bliss and White were not the only members of the American delegation who remained highly critical of the proposed guarantee treaty and shared the view that it would be "most prejudicial to the whole structure of the League of Nations" and its provisions of collective security, which after all intended to replace more traditional security agreements among the great powers. In the eyes of a majority the agreement thus compromised "the ideal" for which the United States had entered the war. The Republican White warned that it would provoke serious domestic opposition, not only from isolationists who were certain to reject what they would see as entangling alliance commitments in Europe, but also from advocates of the League. White advised Wilson at least to disentangle the American from the British guarantee so as to widen the American room to manoeuvre and avoid the impression of a new strategic co-operation with Britain. Bliss confided to his British counterpart Sir Henry Wilson that Wilson had acted irresponsibly in not making clearer to Clemenceau that "neither he nor the Senate nor the people of the U.S.A. would form an Alliance with France".[128]

Bliss also had major doubts about the overall direction of the French government's policies. In his judgement, French leaders had two options: either they could seek to come to an understanding and some kind of accommodation with their arch enemy; or they could pursue a policy of force and deterrence that essentially made France's future security dependent on the willingness of Britain and the United States to come to its aid. Bliss' main fear

[127] Grayson diary, 6 April 1919; House diary, 6 April 1919, PWW, LVII, pp. 50–1, 61–2.
[128] See Minutes of peace commissioners' meetings, 20 and 21 March 1919, FRUS-PPC, XI, pp. 126, 130; H. Wilson diary, 31 March 1919, IWM, cited after Schuker (1998), p. 300.

was that French insistence on keeping Germany contained and isolated for a long time to come would only unsettle Europe further and ultimately increase insecurity, for it was bound to induce German politicians to pursue power-political counter-strategies, form a common front with Russia and challenge the postwar regime that France sought to enforce. He thus recommended that the American government should not make any concessions to Clemenceau's hazardous demands, which in his view threatened to drag the United States into renewed European conflicts.[129]

Yet it was again Hoover who sounded the most emphatic warning. He went to considerable lengths to highlight the detrimental consequences of pursuing a course of compromises that in his view would enable France to co-opt American power in establishing a retrograde and war-prone security regime. As Hoover saw it, Europe could neither be stabilised nor pacified by means of an "armed alliance". He therefore urged the American president to return to his original conception of peace – premised on an effective and inclusive League of Nations – and to distance himself from the schemes of Clemenceau and Tardieu. In Hoover's conception, Wilson thus was to reclaim the role of an independent arbiter who exercised moral leadership in the peacemaking process. This was also the role that Hoover desired the United States to assume in the recast international order. His main concern was that if the United States participated in what was "in effect an armed alliance in Europe" that dominated the former Central Empires, then the League – to which Germany and Russia would not be admitted "for some years" – would essentially become merely a shell for such an alliance, with a few neutral states "gyrating" around it. In turn, this threatened to drive Germany and Russia to form an "independent League", thereby exacerbating the very postwar divisions that American policy should seek to overcome.

Hoover warned that if the president committed the United States to remain in Europe "tied in an alliance", which it had "never undertaken" in the past, and to participate in the "military enforcement" of the peace, it would be forced into "a storm of repression, of revolution" and "dragged into detailed European entanglements" for years to come. And he emphasised that the American people would not be prepared to back such a course. Instead, he urged the president to preserve America's "independence of action" and, above all, its power as "the one great moral reserve in the world today". On these premises, he was to revive his efforts on behalf of an American peace based on the Fourteen Points; and if the *Entente* Powers could not be "brought to adopt" such a peace, the United States should "retire from Europe lock, stock and barrel". Thus Hoover's clarion call in the spring of 1919 in fact

---

[129] See Bliss memorandum, 3 April 1919; Close to Bliss, 31 March 1919, Bliss Papers.

anticipated core maxims, and limitations, of his later pursuit of an "aloof" *Pax Americana* in Europe during the 1920s.[130]

Wilson had sympathies for Hoover's arguments and concerns. But he was determined to hammer out an agreement with Clemenceau – not least because it lay in his interest to come to an understanding about the entire draft treaty as soon as possible, and thus to ensure the founding of the League. Yet the American president now had to recognise that he would not be able to moderate French policies unless he was prepared to make substantial concessions – concessions that in effect would force him to depart from the original parameters of his peace agenda and conflicted both with the fundamentals of his League policy and his earlier approach to the German question. At first Wilson resisted French pressure for a prolonged and potentially indefinite occupation of the Rhineland. He instructed House not to cede any further ground in confidential discussions with Clemenceau and on 12 April conveyed to him and Tardieu "a very solemn warning" that he was not willing to go beyond the commitments he had offered – which, as he reminded them, constituted "an extraordinary step for the United States". At this point, a basic Anglo-American consensus on the most critical issues had emerged. It centred on a re-affirmed pledge to enter into a guarantee treaty and to support a demilitarisation of the Left Bank – where Allied troops would only be allowed to operate under the supervision of the League – as well as the establishment of a fifty-kilometre-deep demilitarised zone on the right bank of the Rhine.

Like Lloyd George, the American president rejected all the amendments Tardieu had proposed. In particular, he objected to provisions that would have required the United States to intervene in case of German violations of the envisaged military and disarmament clauses of the peace treaty. Nor was he prepared to concede to France the right to occupy the Rhine "frontier" and bridgeheads indefinitely if Germany violated the treaty's disarmament or demilitarisation clauses. Wilson made only one significant concession to Clemenceau, which was clearly intended to placate his domestic critics. He agreed that there should no longer be a specific time limit on the security guarantee for France; rather, it was to remain in force until all victors agreed that the League of Nations provided appropriate guarantees. Wilson thus consented to a longer-term yet not necessarily a permanent security arrangement. Fundamentally, he did not depart from the rationale that the guarantee would only be offered until it was rendered unnecessary by what he really sought to foster: a functioning system of collective security anchored in the League.

Significantly, Wilson now accentuated the accord he had reached with Lloyd George on the key issues of the interconnected Rhineland and security negotiations. He underscored that their joint proposals had been made

---

[130] Hoover to Wilson, 11 April 1919, in Bane and Lutz (1942), pp. 400–1.

"after repeated consideration of all other plans suggested" and, crucially, "represented the maximum" of what he deemed "necessary for the safety of France or possible on the part of the United States". And he impressed on Clemenceau that any further amendments would make it impossible for him to obtain support for the proposed treaty in the American Senate.[131]

Wilson's warning had some impact. But the main reason for the eventual final compromise on the Rhineland *and* the security question – which was hammered out between Wilson and Clemenceau on 14 April, while Lloyd George was absent from Versailles – lay elsewhere. Crucial was the French premier's ultimately predominant interest in avoiding a breach and ensuring both that France would obtain what Anglo-American guarantee it could obtain under the circumstances and Anglo-American cooperation in the occupation of the Rhineland. Yet it should be stressed that, ultimately, both Wilson and Lloyd George were prepared to make essential last-minute concessions. And this was chiefly due to their – unwarranted – concern that unless they did so Clemenceau might be replaced by a more hard-line nationalist government, possibly under Poincaré, that would then seek to unravel the agreements they had so painstakingly negotiated and push once again for a Rhenish buffer-state. Thus, some key domestic considerations – regarding the French, not the German situation – had an important impact on one of the most crucial compromises of 1919. And, more generally, it was significantly affected by the perceptions and misperceptions of the political leaders who negotiated it, and the respective challenges they faced on the home front.

In the end, Clemenceau made the decisive move. Relying on House as a mediator, he proposed a strategic *quid pro quo* arrangement. He indicated that he was willing to agree to Wilson's "terms for the protection of France and the west bank of the Rhine". Although they were not "what he wanted", he deemed them "sufficient" in conjunction with the American security "guarantee". Tactically astute, he underscored that he would "fight Foch and his other Marshals". And he asserted that he would also be able to persuade the French parliament to accept the arrangement – on the condition that Wilson accepted a modified occupation regime under which the Rhineland would be divided into three different zones, one to be occupied for five, the second for ten and the third for fifteen years. Significantly, the French premier no longer justified the occupation only as imperative for French security but now linked it explicitly to German compliance with the "indemnity" clauses of the peace treaty, essentially making the withdrawal of French troops dependent on Germany's payment of reparations. Like his

---

[131] Wilson note, 28 March 1919, Wilson Papers, VIII-A-29; House diary, 4 and 12 April 1919, House Papers; Wilson memorandum, 12 April 1919, *PWW*, LVII, pp. 130-1; Wilson to House, 12 April 1919, Wilson-House Correspondence, House Papers.

successors in the early 1920s, he was thus determined to use the Rhineland as a gage to enforce French claims.[132]

Though with obvious misgivings, particularly over the "three five-year periods of occupation", Wilson accepted Clemenceau's proposal while Lloyd George was away to deal with workers' unrest and strikes at home. He thus struck a "deal" that would be at the heart of the Rhineland and security bargain the Big Three finalised on 22 April – and that would be amended in secret deliberations on 30 April. Following his return to Versailles, the British prime minister, who till the end remained vehemently opposed to a prolonged occupation, had first sought to persuade Wilson to reconsider. Once again pointing to domestic constraints, he stressed that as his country was waiting "impatiently" for the "abolition of compulsory military service" no British government would agree to "leave British troops in Germany for fifteen years". But, failing to move Wilson, he ultimately acquiesced in the Franco-American compromise under which, as Clemenceau observed, all France required to manifest allied solidarity was "one battalion and one flag" from each power in the Rhineland.[133]

One controversy that still had to be addressed arose from the French government's demand that the victors should agree on criteria that would justify an extension or renewal of the occupation in the event of German refusal to comply with the peace terms. As all sides realised, for Clemenceau the main purpose of the occupation regime was to furnish a means of last resort to protect French security *and* to enforce the envisaged terms of the peace treaty. He and Tardieu thus struggled to gain a legal basis for prolonging it and, potentially, for retaining the option of establishing a more permanent control over the Left Bank in line with the more ambitious Rhine frontier agenda that they never quite abandoned. When the critical Article 430 of the draft treaty was finalised, Wilson insisted, and Clemenceau conceded, that the occupation could only be prolonged to ensure German reparation payments, not on grounds of security. The formula agreed upon permitted a renewed occupation if the newly established Reparation Commission concluded that Germany "refused to observe the whole or part of her obligations for reparation". Subsequently, Clemenceau told Poincaré that France had gained "the right" to prolong the occupation and control of the Rhineland "if we are not paid". He looked ahead to a scenario that was hardly likely to promote European stability, namely one in which Germany would go "bankrupt" and France would "stay where we are, with the Anglo-American alliance".[134]

---

[132] House diary, 14 April 1919, House Papers.

[133] House diary, 15 April 1919, House Papers; Council of Four, 22 April, Mantoux (1992), I, pp. 318–19.

[134] Notes of Big Three meeting, 9 May 1919, *FRUS-PPC*, V, pp. 519–20. For different perspectives: Bariéty (1977), pp. 62–3; McDougall (1978), p. 59.

But, still under pressure at home, the French premier also persisted with his struggle to create fall-back options for French security policy – and to address one critical concern that he earlier had impressed on Wilson. In short, he strove to put France in a position sanctioned by international law to obtain alternative – physical – security guarantees if because of insurmountable opposition in the American Senate, the envisaged guarantee agreements with Britain and the United States were to fall through. In fact, Clemenceau successfully negotiated an amendment to Article 429 of the draft treaty, which stipulated that the occupation could be extended if after fifteen years "the guarantees against unprovoked aggression" were "not considered sufficient" by the Allied and Associated governments. The French protagonists had thus gained important concessions and extended the options of France's postwar security policy. Crucially, however, under the terms that were agreed on 30 April France was not authorised to act unilaterally. All of the victors would have to agree that a prolonged occupation was necessary to obtain "the required guarantees", which in principle gave the British and American governments the power to veto such a measure.[135] Thus, vital decisions about the future of the Rhineland had been made that would have a long-term impact on the western powers' relations with Germany.

Earlier, the political leaders of the victors had also finally managed to hammer out – with the help of experts – a compromise on the Saar issue, settling a conflict between principles and interests that at one point had almost caused a fundamental rupture between Wilson and Clemenceau. Refuting France's original claims for control of the Saar, Lloyd George had on 28 March proposed a "solution" that British and American experts had worked out. Based on the premise that the only "solid basis" for a "French claim to the Saar basis" was "the principle of compensation", the Saar mines were to become the property of France "by way of reparation" but otherwise the Saar region was to "enjoy complete autonomy", including "its own legislation, its schools, its police".[136] Wilson had essentially agreed with this proposal.[137] Seeking to accommodate these objections, Tardieu had subsequently advanced a revised plan under which France not only was to control the Saar coal mines but also to act as a mandatory power on behalf of the League, while the inhabitants would be allowed to keep their German

---

[135] Tardieu (I/1921), p. 234; Council of Four, 22 April 1919, Mantoux (1992), II, p. 319; Big Three meetings 25 and 30 April 1919, *FRUS-PPC*, V, pp. 244–8, 357; Tardieu (II/1921), pp. 215, 214–17; Schuker (1998), pp. 304–5; Nelson (2019), pp. 243–4, Jackson (2013), pp. 296–7.

[136] Council of Four, 28 March 1919, Mantoux (1992), I, pp. 59–60, 65–6.

[137] *Ibid.*, pp. 64–5.

citizenship – and there would be a vote about the region's future status after a period of fifteen years.[138]

But the American president still opposed what he saw as the scheme for an only formally autonomous buffer-state and resolutely refused to accept an arrangement that established a special political status for the Saar or any form of government to which the inhabitants had not consented; nor was he prepared to grant France permanent control and possession of the mines.[139] Suspecting that the French negotiators merely sought to assert their control under a different guise, Lloyd George now changed his earlier position. He asserted that an arrangement under which France controlled the mines but Germany retained "sovereignty" over the inhabitants of the Saar would "create a perpetual source of friction". Following Headlam-Morley's advice, he insisted that the Saar should instead become an independent region "under the authority of the League of Nations" that would be attached to France through a customs union. And Wilson in the end agreed to work out a compromise on this basis. He proposed the establishment of an administrative commission that would have political authority over the Saar and be accountable to the League. On these premises, he conceded that German sovereignty over the Saar would be suspended. In return, Clemenceau agreed that after fifteen years a plebiscite would be held, under supervision of the League, to decide the future status of the region. And he had to concede that France would not gain permanent possession of the mines; Germany would have the option of buying them back after the end of the initial fifteen-year period.[140]

These were the cornerstones of the Saar compromise that was finalised on 13 April. While both Wilson and Lloyd George had made concessions to the French negotiators they had prevailed in negotiating an internationalised solution that placed the region under the supervision of a nominally independent commission but ultimately ensured that it would come under the responsibility of the League. In Wilson's assessment, French aspirations to create another buffer-state on its border and to exert pressure to draw the Saar into the French orbit had thus been blocked, and conditions had been created that would allow the local population to make, eventually, a by and large independent decision about their political future. On these shaky grounds, he would subsequently defend the Saar settlement as fundamentally "just".[141] Predictably, though, the Scheidemann government did not share this view. Brockdorff-Rantzau would declare that the proposed terms were unacceptable

---

[138] Tardieu proposal, 29 March 1919, Tardieu (I/1921), pp, 266 ff.
[139] Council of Four, 31 March 1919, Mantoux (1955), I, p. 89.
[140] Council of Four, 8 April 1919, Mantoux (1992), I, p. 185; Wilson memorandum, 7 April 1919, Wilson Papers.
[141] Wilson statement, 3 June 1919, FRUS-PPC, II, p. 94. See Schwabe (1985), pp. 273–5, 322–5.

and that an agreement that treated the people of the Saar region like "pawns in a game" was incompatible with the principle of self-determination.[142]

At the same time, and always closely bound up with the altercations over the Rhineland and the Saar, the victors' negotiations over the exact terms of the guarantee agreement reached their decisive stage. Clemenceau and Tardieu had not only persisted with the demand that the Anglo-American guarantees should be made more precise. They also sought to extend the criteria under which Britain and the United States would pledge to come to France's military assistance, aiming to establish a very broad definition of what constituted not only a German *act* of aggression but also a *threat* of aggression that would activate the guarantee. As acts of aggression, Clemenceau's note of 17 March defined not only any German movement or attempted movement into the demilitarised zones on the left and right banks of the Rhine but also German attempts to maintain or restore military fortifications in these areas. Under threats, it categorised any German violations of the demilitarisation and the general disarmament clauses of the envisaged peace treaty.[143]

But both Wilson and Lloyd George resisted. Fearing that these definitions would establish an unduly low threshold for intervention, they insisted that the guarantee commitments they were prepared to make would be limited to one scenario, namely "in cases of plain and unprovoked aggression". And they underscored again that it would ultimately be at the political discretion of the British and American governments to decide what constituted an "unprovoked aggression".[144] Both argued that the main purpose of the guarantee agreement was to deter postwar German leaders from envisaging an attack on France. But the underlying concern they shared was to avoid far-reaching commitments that threatened to draw Britain and the United States into a new conflict on the European continent. They thus impressed on Clemenceau that the states they represented would not come to France's aid if its government pursued provocative or escalatory policies vis-à-vis Germany. Particularly for Lloyd George a key motive for offering a targeted guarantee was not just to re-assure France but also to restrain future French conduct. And the American president essentially adopted the same rationale.

In order to maximise American freedom of action in deciding how and when to honour the proposed guarantee Wilson would insist on a further *caveat*. Claiming that he had never envisaged a joint agreement with Britain, he came to push for a separate guarantee treaty with France, which was then negotiated in confidential talks between him, House and Clemenceau and reflected his search for a compromise formula that did not damage his League agenda. Under the agreement, which was basically worked out on

---

[142] Brockdorff to Clemenceau, 13 May 1919, Luckau (1941), p. 245.
[143] Clemenceau note, 17 March 1919, in Tardieu (I/1921), pp. 197–200.
[144] Wilson statement, Council of Four, 6 May 1919, Mantoux (1992), I, p. 489.

22 April and finalised on 6 May 1919, Wilson pledged that he would seek the approval of the US Senate for an "engagement, subject to the approval of the Council of the League of Nations, to come immediately to the assistance of France in case of unprovoked attack by Germany". And, revealingly, he underscored that the "commitments" must not be given "the appearance of a pact amongst the three powers", as the Senate would "object" to this.[145] The American president thus clearly signalled once again that he would resist any attempt to turn the guarantee offer into anything resembling a more trad- itional military alliance, which he deemed incompatible with the League-based security system he sought to consolidate. This was and remained his overall priority. He never altered his view that the guarantee treaty was a *temporary* measure required to re-assure France and steer Clemenceau away from his original Rhineland plans – and he would always justify it as a *complementary* instrument rather than an *alternative* to the League, whose "effective action" was to secure France, and Europe, in the longer term.[146]

Lloyd George thus had to accept that there would be no joint Anglo- American guarantee. And this only heightened the underlying concern he shared not only with Kerr and Balfour but indeed with a majority in the British Empire Delegation, namely that "the United States might refuse the guarantee". Consequently, the British protagonists deemed it all the more imperative to insure themselves against a scenario in which Britain and the British Empire would have to carry the strategic burden that the agreement conferred all on their own. Following Balfour's recommendation, Lloyd George thus added the important *caveat* that the Anglo-French guarantee treaty would only "come into force" once the Franco-American treaty had been ratified by the American Senate.[147] This meant that the future of one of the most important components of the postwar security architecture that emerged in 1919, if not its centrepiece, would ultimately depend on Wilson's capacity to gain domestic-political support for the eventual peace treaty, and for the League – because the American president insisted that all of these elements of the final settlement had to be ratified jointly.

At the same time, dismissing Poincaré's proposal, the British premier – like Wilson – unequivocally rejected the idea of turning the guarantee agreements into a more fully-fledged military alliance. In keeping with the views prevailing

---

[145] Grayson diary, 14 March 1919, *PWW*, LV, pp. 497–8; House diary, 12 March 1919, House Papers; Council of Four, 27 March and 22 April 1919, Mantoux (1992), I, pp. 41, 319; Wilson to White, 17 April 1919, *PWW*, LVII, p. 430; Wilson statement, Council of Four, 6 May 1919, Mantoux (1992), I, p. 489.

[146] Cecil diary, 18 March 1919, *PWW*, LVI, pp. 81–2; Mantoux (1992), I, p. 41.

[147] See Minutes of the British Empire Delegation, 5 May 1919, Foster Papers; minutes of conversation between Wilson, Clemenceau and Lloyd George, 6 May 1919, *PWW*, LVIII, pp. 480, 489–90; British note, submitted to Clemenceau on 6 May 1919, Cmd. 2169, *Negotiations for an Anglo-French Pact*, p. 104.

in the Imperial War Cabinet, he opposed more far-reaching commitments to France and maintained the official line that the peace could not be secured by a reversion to old-style alliances. Lloyd George therefore emphasised as well that the guarantee treaties had to be "recognized" by the League Council as being "consistent with the Covenant of the League"[148]

When presenting the proposal to the British Empire Delegation in early May, the British premier stressed that it had been essential to "satisfy the French" and permit Clemenceau to assuage the "military party" in in his own country. And like Wilson he reiterated that he regarded the guarantee treaty as a temporary measure intended to meet understandable French security concerns. But the discussions manifested that the British premier had to reckon with a new assertiveness of Dominion leaders who insisted on being consulted on potentially costly decisions of war and peace. And they revealed more specifically that not all Dominion leaders were prepared to accept the guarantee obligations – at least not without making sure that the decision to honour them would ultimately lie in their hands. While the leaders of Australia and New Zealand showed themselves more accommodating, the suspicions of Borden and Botha, who were wary of making commitments to France that carried the risk of involving them in another war in Europe, highlighted deep-seated reservations of the Canadian and South African governments.

To ensure their approval, Lloyd George eventually conceded that the Dominions would each have to ratify the treaty before it could be considered "binding" on them. It was in response to Dominion scepticism that the British premier also made a more substantial case for the special treaty with France, characterising it as an important but carefully limited means to secure the stabilisation of postwar Europe, and "world peace", by manifesting the western powers' resolve to stay together in order to deter renewed German aggression at a time when the European continent was "in disorder" and "broken up into a number of little nations". Yet he was as careful to emphasise the limits of the guarantee offer, underscoring that it would commit Britain and the Dominions to come to France's assistance only in the event of a premeditated and unprovoked aggression on the part of Germany – in a situation "as clear cut as that of 1914". And he asserted too that it was limited to western Europe and thus did not risk dragging Britain into a conflict that resulted from controversies in Eastern Europe – which, as he stressed, were not a primary British concern.[149]

---

[148] Lloyd George to Clemenceau, 6 May 1919, Cmd. 2169, *Negotiations for an Anglo-French Pact*, p. 104.

[149] Minutes of the British Empire Delegation, 5 May 1919, Foster Papers; British note, submitted to Clemenceau on 6 May 1919, *FRUS-PPC*, V, pp. 494–5; Lloyd George to Botha, 26 June 1919, Fry (2011), p. 280.

Distinctly higher on the British agenda were other – extra-European and imperial – preoccupations. In short, as Sir Henry Wilson stressed, the rapidly demobilising British land forces were at this point most urgently needed to maintain "order" at home and safeguard "imperial security" while also combatting unrest in Britain's far-flung and even expanded global imperial system. Against the background of an escalating conflict with the Irish Republican Army and widespread revolutionary tumult in Egypt, Lloyd George's chief military adviser noted in mid-April that his "whole energies" were "bent to getting [British] troops out of Europe and Russia, and concentrating all our strength in our coming storm centres, viz. England, Ireland, Egypt and India". His primary concern had to be to "safeguard our own immediate interests, so that when all the hot air now blowing about Leagues of Nations, Small States, Mandatories, turns to the icy cold wind of hard fact, the British Empire will be well clothed and well defended against all the bangs and curses of the future". Henry Wilson thus unequivocally emphasised the primacy of imperial defence. And Lloyd George could not afford to ignore his warning.[150] At the same time, as noted, he was under pressure to implement his "home fit for heroes" agenda and to proceed with demobilisation, social reform and the reintegration of the demobilised soldiers. Essentially, these constraints, the widespread opposition to maintaining compulsory military service and the predominant aversion to becoming embroiled in another war left him little room to manoeuvre when it came to extending more far-reaching guarantees on the European continent or, for that matter, keeping a sizeable British occupation force in the Rhineland. Apart from tactical considerations, it was the perception of these constraints – both imperial and domestic – that shaped British strategic thinking.

V.   Contours of a New Transatlantic Security System?

The intertwined Rhineland and guarantee agreements that the political leaders of the principal victors had hammered out can be seen as two of the most pivotal compromises of the Versailles negotiations. Yet they can also be regarded as two of the most quintessential outcomes of 1919 – in the sense that in their complexity, their limits and, above all, their inherently strained and inchoate nature, they manifested what was and especially *what was not possible* for the victors to achieve at this juncture. In the final analysis, they barely concealed the conflicting interests, conceptions, assumptions and constraints that continued to divide them or, more precisely, the Clemenceau government and the Anglo-American governments. Moreover, and crucially, they were as yet essentially provisional. In particular it was still far from

---

[150] Henry Wilson to Admiral Cowan, ca. 11 April 1919, Wilson Papers.

assured that the British and American guarantee treaties would actually come into force, as they still had to pass a most critical hurdle in the US Senate.

What thus had emerged were basic – and provisional – contours of an Atlantic security system of the victors whose hallmark would be its hybrid character. For the result of the negotiations was an uneasy combination of circumscribed Anglo-American political guarantees, general collective security – to be provided under the novel regime of the League – and territorial guarantees, furnished through a temporary but longer-term occupation of the Rhineland. The occupation regime did address prevalent French security concerns; but it also was indeed highly likely to become a source of considerable instability and tension. And more importantly it could only be an impediment to any future attempt to foster an accommodation of interests and claims between France and Germany, or even advance towards a Franco-German "reconciliation" or peace process – without which Europe's political stabilisation was inconceivable. More fundamentally, the victors' compromises could only lay a very frail groundwork for a postwar security system because the tense negotiations between them had *not* produced a real consensus about how security in Europe was to be safeguarded and, above all, how the future political and security relations with Germany were to be approached.

Once he had reached the basic understanding with Wilson, Clemenceau had told Poincaré that this was the moment when "peace [was] made".[151] Though they had sought to bargain for more, for him and Tardieu the Rhineland arrangement and notably the guarantee agreement with Britain and the United States represented a highly significant achievement. They saw them as the best possible basis on which French postwar governments could now endeavour to enforce a "peace of containment" and, as far as possible, reinforce a security community of the victors – all to maintain and defend a structurally altered balance of power in continental Europe that offset France's structural weaknesses. They thus essentially regarded the compromises they had negotiated as only the beginning of a longer process of enforcement and reinforcement. At the same time, they were not oblivious to the domestic challenges that notably Wilson would have to confront and indeed aware of the fact that the American – and British – guarantees might not materialise.

In particular, Tardieu warned that in view of the Republican opposition to the president's League aspirations in the US Senate there was a far from negligible "risk of non-ratification". This is why he and the French premier had fought so hard to create "legal" options, under the treaty, to prolong or renew the occupation should this be deemed necessary. And Tardieu did not entirely abandon the hope of promoting an "autonomous" Rhenish state and

---

[151] Poincaré (1926–33), XI, p. 337.

bringing it into France's orbit after all.[152] In any case, the French negotiators realised that even if the guarantee agreements came into force, they and their successors would have to make a constant effort to hold Britain and the United States to the commitments that they had made. Yet they still hoped to build, over time, not just a "union" but an actual alliance of the victors. Significantly, when he later defended his decisions in the French parliament Clemenceau would refer to the guarantee agreements as "alliances".[153] And while he then also argued, for the first time, that France would at some point have to countenance a – controlled – process of accommodation with Germany, he stressed that this could only be envisaged at a later stage – once reliable Anglo-American reassurance and a functioning regime of occupation and control had created safe conditions for such a process.[154]

Wilson, Lloyd George and other important British and American policy-makers maintained distinctly different outlooks. A long-term occupation of the Rhineland clashed with the underlying imperatives of Wilson's peace policy. Like his military and political advisers, he still considered an occupation politically counterproductive, because of the continuous tensions and conflict it would create between France and Germany; and looking ahead, he deemed it equally ineffective in strategic terms because the envisaged occupation regime would be in place while Germany was still weak and was to be ended precisely at the time when Germany was projected to recover from the defeat. He only made concessions out of consideration for Clemenceau's embattled position in his own country, arguing that it was in the American interest to prevent a scenario in which a more assertive right-wing government, supported by Poincaré and the "military party" under Foch, would renege on the hard-won agreements of 1919, revert to the pursuit of the French "buffer-state" agenda and thus threaten to undermine all prospects of a longer-term pacification process in Europe.[155] Yet the American president would still seek last-minute amendments that reflected the profound American misgivings about the occupation. Just before the signing of the Treaty of Versailles, he prevailed on Clemenceau to accept that the occupation could be terminated earlier once Germany had demonstrated its political will to honour its obligations and provided sufficient guarantees to this end.[156]

---

[152] See Tardieu (II/1921), pp. 215, 214–17; Tardieu note, undated [early April 1919], Tardieu Papers, vol. 418.

[153] Clemenceau statement, Council of Four, 13 June 1919, Mantoux (1992), II, pp. 438–40; Clemenceau speech, 25 September 1919, *Journal Officiel (Chambre)*, 1919.

[154] *Ibid.*

[155] Wilson statement, meeting of 3 June, *FRUS-PPC*, XI, pp. 211–12; Wilson to Polk, 15 March 1920, Wilson Papers.

[156] See Council of Four, 12 and 13 June 1919; Mantoux (1992), II, pp. 404–5, 428–31; Convention of the Big Three regarding the Military Occupation, 13 June, *ibid.*, pp. 431–5.

Reflecting the dominant attitudes within the British delegation, Lloyd George continued to see the occupation in an even more negative light. The British premier stressed as well that the only purpose of the occupation agreement was to "protect" the Clemenceau government against its domestic opposition. And he was even more categorical in declaring that strategically the occupation would "serve no use" for it would "only last during the period when Germany is weakest". Even after the compromise had been agreed, he openly denounced it as a "danger for France and for the peace of Europe", impressing on Clemenceau that the very least the victors should do was to make it "as inoffensive as possible".[157] What thus already became obvious in 1919 was that both Wilson and the Lloyd George government had agreed to the occupation as a necessary "lesser evil" in order to prevent the greater evil of a French-dominated Rhenish buffer-state – yet that the core imperatives of British and American policies were all but incompatible with those of the French government. Consequently, American and British reservations at Versailles prefigured salient concerns of British and American stabilisation policies in the 1920s, which would aim to limit both the extent and the duration of the occupation and, essentially, to eliminate it as soon as possible as a source of friction and instability.

At the same time, and crucially, the negotiations had thrown into relief that neither Lloyd George nor Wilson were prepared to make commitments that could lead to a fully-fledged, exclusive alliance with France or, more broadly, to establish a system geared towards a long-term coercive containment of Germany. Rather, though with different emphases, the British as well as the American protagonists of 1919 had made the guarantee offers – and eventually acquiesced in the Rhineland compromise – because they regarded them as means to a different end. They not only sought to assuage French security concerns but also to *moderate* French policies and thus to prepare the ground for a longer-term stabilisation process that was to consolidate a different kind of postwar system: in Lloyd George's "vision", the nucleus of a more loosely configured transatlantic concert system that eventually was to integrate rather than ostracise Germany; in Wilson's "vision", a functioning "international concert" that operated within and through an evolving League of Nations – and would also eventually bind Germany to its common rules and standards.

Arguably, this is where the real potential of the victors' security compromises of 1919 lay. They could provide the starting-point for a wider and more sustainable system that would bring security and re-assurance, not through the occupation of the Rhineland but by a *common* system of binding guarantees, including German guarantees. But any developments in this direction would

---

[157] Lloyd George statement, Council of Four, 12 June 1919, Mantoux (1992), II, p. 405.

not only require further efforts of the victors to work out their abiding differences. They would also require significant reorientations of French security strategies – as well as German postwar policies. Crucially, however, they would require a clear confirmation of the Anglo-American powers' strategic re-assurance for France *and* a forward engagement of both powers in efforts to foster political accommodation and conflict-resolution between France and Germany. A lot thus depended on the extent to which British and American governments were willing, and domestically in a position, to pursue *and sustain* such forward engagement – and to make *and sustain* credible and firm security commitments – or, more precisely, commitments that were perceived by French policymakers and the wider French public as credible. This was indeed a long-term challenge, and how far it could be met would only become clear in the aftermath of the peace conference.

But the controversies in the spring of 1919 had already thrown into relief just how limited the conceptual and political underpinnings of Anglo-American commitments were, and how towering the domestic constraints might prove. Yet before any steps towards the actual consolidation or rather development of what was as yet no more than a frail scaffolding for a post–First World War security architecture could be taken, one critical decision still had to be made first. While Lloyd George could be confident that a majority in the House of Commons would back the Anglo-French guarantee treaty, it was as yet highly uncertain whether Wilson would gain the vital modicum of support for the American guarantee offer, and the League, in the US Senate.

17

The Eastern Frontiers – and Limits – of the New Order

Self-Determination, the Critical Polish-German Question and the Wider Challenges of "Reorganising" Eastern Europe

Not only influential experts like the American historian Robert Lord but also the main political decision-makers of the western powers recognised from the outset that, because of the complex territorial, self-determination and geopolitical issues it raised, the settlement of the border between Germany and the new Polish state would constitute one of the most complicated and consequential problems of the entire peacemaking process. Indeed, the Polish-German settlement had a significance that reached far beyond eastern Europe and its specific geopolitical context. For the manner in which the victors approached it, and the terms they set, would not only have a major impact on the development prospects of the Polish state and its future relations with its more powerful German neighbour; they would also have critical implications for the German acceptance of the peace settlement and, ultimately, the longer-term stabilisation of the postwar order as a whole. This is what set the Polish-German problem apart from all other political and territorial questions that had to be addressed in the east, including the demarcation of the borders of the new Czechoslovak state, where *inter alia* decisions about the future status of the German-speaking population in the *Sudetenland* had to be made.

I. Filling the Post-Imperial Vacuum. The Overwhelming East European Challenges

But the Polish-German question also of course has to be placed in a wider context of a different kind. Coming to terms with it constituted only one, albeit crucial, part of a much more far-ranging challenge that the political leaders, diplomats and experts of the victorious powers now had to grapple with, namely to fill the political and geopolitical vacuum that the disintegration of the multi-ethnic eastern empires had left behind. As we have seen, the Great War had created the need to effect nothing less than a fundamental territorial and political reorganisation of Central and Eastern Europe; but the conditions for establishing a stable regional system of viable nation-states were highly inauspicious.

While not only the civil war in Russia but also multiple armed conflicts across this vast region itself raged on, and they feared the spread of Bolshevik influence from the east, the victors faced an all but overwhelming array of problems. They not only had to deal with what Lord aptly called the very high degree of "intermixture" and "interpenetration" of different ethnicities in this part of the world. They also had to countenance, at the level of politics, the collision of many rivalling nationalist agendas and competing territorial claims advanced by the different older states, the new "states-in-formation" and various national movements that did not yet have a state of their own. And, finally, they had to grapple with the determined efforts of all of these actors to create *faits accomplis*.[1]

Some emblematic examples may suffice to illustrate the larger problem: Both the new Polish and the new Czechoslovak state claimed the coal and industrial region of Teschen, which historically had been part of Bohemia but whose population was mainly ethnically Polish. Further east, Polish claims to Eastern Galicia and Lemberg clashed with the aspirations of those who sought to found a West Ukrainian Republic, the aspirations of those who fought for a Ruthenian state and the interests of White Russian forces. Further north, Poland's claims to the area around Vilnius collided with those of the fledgling Lithuanian state.[2] In South-Eastern Europe, the ambitions of the Romanian premier Ion Brătianu, who had pursued a very successful policy of creating facts on the ground in the final stages of the war, to expand Romania's territory even further at the expense of Hungary and to claim, among others, the entire formerly Hungarian region of Transylvania (including Siebenbürgen), obviously provoked conflicts with the embattled successor state of the Austro-Hungarian Empire. And at the heart of the indeed chronically unstable "powder keg region" of the pre-war period, the Balkans, the claims that former Serbian premier Nikola Pašić made on behalf of the Serbian-dominated – and as yet unrecognised – new Yugoslav state led to disputes with most of its neighbours. Apart from the quarrel with Italy over Fiume, the most explosive conflict constellation resulted from a clash of Yugoslav (or rather Serbian) and Romanian expansionist claims to the multi-ethnic Banat region, which had hitherto been administered by Hungary.[3]

---

[1] Lord (1921), p. 73. For the broader challenges see Prott (2016).

[2] See Wandycz (1998), pp. 328-9; MacMillan (2002), pp. 234-5; Brandes (2001), pp. 174-92.

[3] See Sharp (I/2008), pp. 153-5; Suppan (2019), pp. 66-7; Lederer (1963), pp. 81 ff.; Dahlmann (2001), pp. 193-201.

Although they were indeed – and increasingly – aware of the complexities that the epochal reorganisation of Central and Eastern Europe entailed, particularly American experts and Wilson himself would maintain that the principle of self-determination offered the best possible yardstick for settling conflicting claims and establishing stable borders. And in the course of the peace conference this principle would be invoked to an unprecedented degree – and by all sides: by the western powers in pursuit of their different priorities, by the different east European successor states to justify the particular claims they pursued, and by those who represented the vanquished – Germany, Austria and Hungary – to defend their claims and interests. But the processes of 1919 essentially confirmed what many policymakers and experts had emphasised in advance: namely that it would be impossible to establish a "new order" in Eastern Europe on the basis of a more or less equitable application of a principle whose precise meaning remained highly controversial.

What shaped these processes far more decisively were, ultimately, conflicting strategic imperatives, arguments relating to the future security needs and economic viability of the different states, or more general geopolitical concerns – such as those of French policymakers intent on consolidating an east European *cordon sanitaire*. And what not seldom tipped the balance was simply the power of particular actors to "create facts" and assert control on the ground. Broadly speaking, it thus proved impossible to avoid that most of the new or newly configured East European states of the post–First World War era would from the outset be in conflict with their neighbours on account of contested borders and more or less explosive minority problems. This obviously created very adverse conditions for a longer-term stabilisation of this region. And it was no coincidence that one of the ever more pressing concerns of the western experts who dealt with East European affairs in Paris, and eventually of the political leaders themselves, came to revolve around the question of how the different old and new minorities in Central and Eastern Europe could be effectively protected.

As we have seen, the experts and decision-makers of the victors were not oblivious to the far-reaching problems they confronted in Eastern Europe's post-imperial space. But they had nonetheless underestimated their intricacy. And they had only begun to develop very different concepts and guidelines to deal with them – and came to pursue very different priorities. In short, Wilson and US experts maintained that it would only be possible to forge stable new states if self-determination concerns and the presumed choices of different populations were taken into account as far as possible.[4] While also originally emphasising the need for an equitable application of the self-determination

---

[4] Wilson statement in Supreme Council, 19 March 1919, *FRUS-PPC*, IV, pp. 417–18; Seymour to Coolidge and Davis, 14 February 1919, House Papers; Seymour (1951), pp. 9 ff.; Bowman memorandum, 10 December 1918, *PWW*, LIII, p. 354.

principle, British policymakers and experts like James Headlam-Morley and
Robert Seton-Watson primarily sought to broker border settlements that
established what they regarded as politically and economically viable states
and limited the potential for conflict through future irredentism as far as
possible. The leading British experts had to abandon their earlier plans to
create, as new framework of stability for the region, a Central European
Federation comprising the successor states of the Austro-Hungarian
Empire.[5] By contrast, French decision-makers and experts did persist with
the pursuit of an overarching strategy – namely to create an eastern *cordon
sanitaire* between Germany and Russia – and accordingly gave priority to
strategic and essentially geopolitical considerations. This informed not only
French efforts on behalf of a "strong" Poland and Czechoslovakia but also
French policies vis-à-vis Romania and Yugoslavia.[6]

The differences between the victors' approaches and conceptions were not
irrelevant. But what the Paris Peace Conference showed above all was how
overwhelmed the western "peacemakers" were by the multitude and complexity of the challenges they confronted in Central and Eastern Europe. And,
crucially, it manifested how limited their capacity was to act as "creators" or
"arbiters" of order in this region – especially in parts of it that from their
vantage-points seemed more peripheral. This particularly held true for
Wilson, Lloyd George and the powers they represented. Further, it has to be
noted that only the terms of the new Polish-German border settlement – and
to far a lesser degree those of the new German-Czechoslovak border – were
extensively debated at the highest level, in the Council of Four. Most of the
complex East European problems would be delegated to expert commissions,
and many critical decisions were either made in these commissions or in the
Council of Foreign Ministers. Some of the most controversial issues would
actually be *decided* this way in the spring of 1919. Notably, the Council of
Foreign Ministers eventually resolved to divide the Banat between Romania,
Yugoslavia and Hungary, leaving sizeable Romanian and Slav minorities on
each side of the newly drawn border and proposing to protect them under the
supervision of the League. It was yet another compromise that left all sides
dissatisfied and provoked resentment against League interference and made
future conflicts unavoidable.[7]

---

[5] See Headlam-Morley memorandum, "The Settlement: Europe", 15 November 1918, FO
371/4353/f23/PC55; Headlam-Morley (1972), p. 128; Bátonyi (1999), pp. 13–14.

[6] Tardieu memorandum, 20 January 1919, Tardieu Papers, PA-AP 166 (49), MAE; Pichon
to Beneš, 29 June 1918, Beneš (1928–29), II, pp. 231–2; French Foreign Ministry memorandum on "peace conditions", 26 November 1918, transmitted to Balfour, FO/371/3446;
"Pologne" committee minutes, 29 January 1919, Europe 1918–29, Pologne (68), MAE.

[7] See Sharp (I/2008), pp. 154–5.

Other disputes would essentially be "settled" to the detriment of the van-quished, which had particularly drastic consequences for Hungary. By July 1919, the victors had decided that Hungary, apart from losing most of the Banat, would have to cede Ruthenia to Czechoslovakia and, crucially, Transylvania to Romania. After intermittent negotiations that partly dragged on because of internal turmoil that continued long after the collapse of Béla Kun's Bolshevik regime in August 1919, the victors would eventually compel Hungary to accept terms – in the Treaty of Trianon, signed in June 1920 – that left it reduced to about *one-third* of its pre-war territory and turned roughly *one-third* of its pre-war Magyar population into minorities assigned to its neigh-bours. This would set the stage for Hungarian irredentist revisionism in the inter-war period.[8] But many of the conflicts that had arisen in eastern Europe would not be settled at all, however imperfectly, and were left essentially unresolved in 1919. The Polish–Czechoslovak dispute over Teschen would continue and to further armed conflict. In July 1920 most of the region's coal and industrial areas would be accorded to Czechoslovakia, but relations between the two fledgling states would be poisoned for a long time to come. And under Piłsudski, Poland would be involved in no less than four military conflicts between 1919 and 1921 – not only with Czechoslovakia over Teschen, but also with Lithuania over Vilnius, with West Ukrainian, White and Bolshevik Russian forces in Eastern Galicia and, most consequentially, in the far-ranging Polish–Bolshevik war – before its eastern borders were finally established.[9]

In a wider perspective, what thus became strikingly apparent in the spring and summer of 1919 were, as it were, the eastern limits – or grey areas – of the new Euro-Atlantic order that Wilson and the other principal peacemakers of Paris sought to build in their different ways. And, as will be shown, these limits would become even more obvious further east – in the victors' policies towards the ongoing Russian civil war and the Bolshevik regime.

II. The Complexities and High Stakes of the Polish–German Border Settlement

While their power to shape outcomes in Eastern Europe was thus overall distinctly constrained, there was one issue on which the western leaders could and did indeed exert a significant influence – and that was the cardinal question of the Polish–German border settlement. And it was to this question that not only their leading experts but also the Big Three themselves devoted more sustained attention – and which caused more fundamental controversies between them than any other "eastern question".

---

[8] See MacMillan (2002), pp. 257–70; Suppan (2019), pp. 123–36.
[9] See Porter-Szücs (2014), pp. 79–84; Gerwarth (2016), pp. 192–4; Davies (2003).

Inevitably, the new Polish state would be a multinational state. Whatever its precise make-up and borders would be, it was bound to include to a greater or lesser extent Ukrainian, Lithuanian, Jewish and other minority populations. But the crucial problem they now had to grapple with was not whether but *to what extent* – and according to which criteria – the reconfigured Polish state would encompass territories that had been part of the German Empire and German-speaking minority populations. Because of the complex ethnographic and geopolitical situation the victors confronted it was thus obvious from the start that it would not be possible to reconcile the two – incompatible – aims Wilson had stated in his Fourteen Points address: to establish a Polish state with a "secure and free access" to the Baltic Sea that at the same time only comprised territories inhabited by an "indisputably" Polish population.[10]

More fundamentally, the negotiations indeed threw into relief that it was not only extremely difficult but politically impossible to forge a settlement that even came close to conforming with Wilson's maxim that the victors had to ensure, above all, an equitable application of the principle of self-determination.[11] Yet the really critical systemic task the victors faced was to negotiate an agreement that also met broader political and geopolitical requirements. Essentially, terms and ground-rules had to be worked out that at least *limited* the creation of seedbeds of future conflicts between Poland and an inherently more powerful German neighbour – of conflicts that would unavoidably arise over a contested border and if the Polish state came to comprise a sizeable German minority. Hardly anywhere was it thus more imperative for the victors to try to negotiate, as far as possible, a *balanced* settlement – one that not only considered the self-determination claims and political interests of the new Polish government, and the security and economic needs of the new Polish state, but also the self-determination claims and political concerns of the defeated power and its as yet weak new republican government.

The altercations over the Polish–German border settlement turned into a complex and drawn-out political battle between the principal victors. In its early stages, Polish representatives were given an opportunity to present their interests and claims, which Dmowski used – with French support – to make his case for a "Greater Poland". Subsequently, the experts of the western powers, notably those deliberating in the Polish Commission, again played an important role in setting essential first reference-points. But the negotiations that shaped the outcomes once more took place between the political leaders of the victors – while all that Brockdorff-Rantzau and Erzberger could do was to try to impress on them from afar that the loss of territory and

---

[10] Wilson, "Fourteen Points" address, 8 January 1918, *PWW*, XLV, pp. 538–9.
[11] See Wilson statement in Supreme Council, 19 March 1919, *FRUS-PPC*, IV, pp. 417–18.

populations in the east would be hardest to accept for the German government – and for the German public.

What ensued from mid-March was a multi-layered negotiating-process in which considerations of self-determination had a newly significant influence but that was ultimately dominated by the struggle to find a compromise between the victors' conflicting political imperatives, which pointed far beyond the Polish-German border. Dominant at first were the efforts of Clemenceau and Tardieu to implement their "eastern strategy", a strategy that was unmistakeably informed by classic balance-of-power ideas and strategic priorities that clearly overruled concerns of self-determination and equitability. At its core lay the interest both to deprive Germany of as much territory and industrial as well as demographic assets as possible – and to establish a strong Polish state as a crucial "buffer-state" between Germany and a Russian power that threatened to fall into Bolshevik hands.

Yet these efforts collided with Lloyd George's determination to push for a different settlement – one that was based on the rationale that in order to pre-empt what he saw as the gravest threat to wider European peace and stability, German irredentism vis-à-vis the new Polish state, it was essential to reduce the number of ethnic Germans who would live under Polish rule as far as possible. And what gave the decisive impetus to eventual advances towards a more calibrated compromise was that Wilson would in fact alter his outlook. In short, he too came to adopt the maxim that it was imperative to negotiate a settlement that would "spare Poland the dangers which the existence of a *Germania irredenta* would cause her" and in many ways came to join forces with the British premier.[12]

If one takes into account how complex the ethno- and geopolitical conditions were that they had to deal with, and how conflicting and in many ways irreconcilable the interests and claims were that they had to consider, it should be stressed that the political leaders of the victorious powers, and the key experts who aided them, managed to hammer out terms for a settlement that went remarkably far towards addressing not only Polish but also German concerns – and towards meeting overriding requirements of Europe's postwar stabilisation. Its key components were a reduced "Polish Corridor", plebiscites in some of the most disputed provinces with significant German populations and an "internationalisation" of the port city of Danzig under the auspices of the League.[13] These were the essential terms they would present to the Scheidemann government in early May. By contrast, the pivotal question of what the future status of Upper Silesia was to be had only been superficially

---

[12] Council of Four, 9 April 1919, Mantoux (1992), I, pp. 200, 203.
[13] Council of Four, 18 April 1919, Mantoux (1992), I, p. 271; *FRUS-PPC*, V, pp. 118–22. For different interpretations see Wandycz (1998), pp. 325–7; Tooze (2014), pp. 281–6.

"settled" and would again become the subject of heated controversies in the final stages of the peacemaking process.

But, however noteworthy these efforts were, it was simply not possible under the circumstances to work out a "solution" that not only satisfied Polish aspirations but also gained acceptance in Germany – above all because the victors' compromise terms still required the fledgling German republic to cede considerable territory to its Polish neighbour state and, crucially, they still created a substantial German minority in Poland. And a crucial problem was, of course, that the victors would seek to impose these terms on the defeated power without any substantial negotiations, rather than give the most powerful affected party some kind of voice in the process. Arguably, though, no compromise could be reached in 1919 that was both within the realm of the possible *and* could have been considered acceptable, or even legitimate by German decision-makers and the vast majority of a German public that was encouraged to maintain unrealistic expectations.

Precisely because of this dilemma, however, it was all the more vital for the victors to find ways to cope with a salient longer-term challenge that has not received sufficient attention. In short, they had to develop, and agree upon, policies and mechanisms to manage the structural antagonism that was bound to emerge between Germany and Poland – and to prevent it from escalating and threatening wider European peace and stability. In particular, the western governments were called upon to confront the task that became so critical across eastern Europe: to protect the rights, and security, of minorities. And under Anglo-American influence, they would take some important though less than innovative steps to address this problem, not through a more ambitious League-based regime of minority protection, which could hardly have been effective, but by means of a specific minority treaty that they pressured the Polish government to sign. This treaty would then provide the model for other east European minority treaties; yet it would be resented in Warsaw as a high-handed Anglo-American imposition. But even in the best-case scenario, such a treaty could only offer limited remedies in a period of acutely heightened nationalist tensions; and it could hardly solve the larger problem of – German – irredentism. In this wider context, the key question was whether the victors could at all agree on how they would seek to cope with this problem, protect the security of the as yet very frail Polish state and at least contain the destabilising consequences of the Polish-German conflict. And the underlying question was how far they could create – through or rather beyond the League – a framework of security and order that would allow them and local actors to address these daunting challenges *over time*, and thus to stabilise not only Central and Eastern Europe but the postwar international system as a whole.

Initially, attempts to address the Polish-German question at the peace conference were complicated by the fact that the two main factions that had emerged in the struggle for Polish independence still had very different ideas about the scope of Poland's claims and the strategies to be pursued vis-à-vis the western powers to ensure a recognition of these claims. The more assertively nationalist forces of the Polish National Committee, led by Roman Dmowski, now pushed for their expansive conception of a Greater Poland and chiefly sought to enlist the support of the French government. Piłsudski and the socialist-reformist forces that had become dominant in Warsaw since mid-November, when Polish independence had been declared, adhered to a more restrained "heartland" conception of a strong yet more accommodating Polish state.

Piłsudski, who had held the reins of power as Poland's "liberator" and commander-and-chief – and overseen the reform agenda enacted by the provisional government under Moraczewski – envisaged a multinational federation with Lithuanians and Ukrainians. And he was prepared to leave Polish populations outside Polish borders in order to consolidate the "heartland" and lay the groundwork for constructive relations, especially with Poland's eastern neighbours. Yet he had also dispatched Polish troops into the ethnically mixed province of Poznan to back the uprising of Polish nationalist activists and push out German troops, which had been accomplished by late December 1918. He too thus sought to extend the new state's control and assert its claims vis-à-vis Germany, and he would continue to pursue this *faits accomplis* strategy in the spring of 1919. But Piłsudski was aware that the settlement of Poland's western borders was largely dependent on the western powers' core policies vis-à-vis Germany; and, criticising Dmowski's one-sided orientation towards France, he argued that it was in Poland's interest to intensify cooperation with Britain and the United States and to moderate Polish demands in accordance with their preferences. For he was convinced that Lloyd George and Wilson would have a decisive influence on the decisions affecting Poland's future.[14]

Following the first elections in January 1919, Paderewski, who became both premier and foreign minister, had been instrumental in brokering a political compromise between the opposing camps according to which Piłsudski remained head of state while Dmowski was designated to be Poland's principal representative at Versailles. It was indeed significant that Dmowski became the dominant spokesman for the Polish cause at the peace conference. For he aligned himself with the French government's agenda for a strong Polish buffer-state and, more importantly, came to campaign for his distinctly expansive vision of a "Greater Poland". It was hardly surprising that the leader of an assertive nationalist party would seize the opportunity he was given to pursue maximal aims; but the fact that Dmowski did so in a decidedly unrestrained

[14] See Wandycz (1998), pp. 322, 324–5; Porter-Szücs (2014), pp. 74–9, 85.

manner, and with little or no regard for the implications of his demands for Poland's future relations with Germany, arguably proved counterproductive for the Polish cause. Not least, his conduct increased reservations not only in the British delegation but also on the part of Wilson, who became even more suspicious of what he regarded as Dmowski's excessively nationalistic stance and doubtful commitment to democracy.[15]

It was at Clemenceau's instigation that Dmowski presented his priorities to the Supreme Council on 29 January and subsequently submitted a programmatic memorandum on the "Western Frontiers of the Polish State" to the Commission on Polish Affairs. Essentially, he made the case for a "Greater Poland" not only on historic and ethnic but also, and essentially, on power-political strategic grounds. Dmowski argued that the resurrection of Poland should be regarded as the rectification of an historical injustice, the Polish partitions of the eighteenth century. And he proposed to take the boundaries of the Polish Commonwealth of 1772 as a "point of departure". But, using the language of self-determination, he also urged the victors to pay close attention to the changes in the distribution of different national groups that had occurred since then – which in his interpretation extended Polish claims. Most of all, however, he insisted that the new Polish state had to be strong enough to maintain its independence between Germany and Russia. Dmowski thus underscored Poland's essential need for a secure access to the Baltic Sea – on which Piłsudski and all other Polish protagonists agreed – and its claim to the provinces of Pomerania and Poznan. Yet he also laid claims to two regions that had not been part of the Commonwealth of 1772: the south-eastern districts of East Prussia and, crucially, the industrial region of Upper Silesia, whose population, he claimed, was predominantly Polish following the national revival of the nineteenth century. In sum, the nation-state for which Dmowski campaigned would not just incorporate extended formerly German territories but also large German minorities; and the way in which he sought to ensure Poland's access to the sea was bound to create a "corridor" between East Prussia and the rest of Germany.[16]

Of critical import for the subsequent negotiations in Paris was that the French government in fact encouraged Dmowski's expansive agenda, because his aims were consonant with the overriding strategic interest in constraining Germany that dominated French approaches to the Polish question. And from the vantage-point of Clemenceau, Tardieu and Pichon this interest, and the aim to ensure the formation of a "strong" Polish state, clearly outweighed considerations pertaining to "self-determination" or concerns over creating a future Polish–German antagonism, which they regarded as unavoidable. And

---

[15] See Wandycz (1998), pp. 322; Lundgreen-Nielsen (1979).
[16] Dmowski statements, Council of Ten, 29 January 1919, *FRUS-PPC*, III, pp. 772–9. See Wandycz (1992), pp. 118–20.

their priorities, and underlying balance-of-power axioms, would indeed dominate the early stages of the inter-allied deliberations. Essentially, with Clemenceau's support, Tardieu – who here too gave the decisive impetus – persevered with a strategy whose core objective was to turn the Polish state not only into the key element of an eastern "barrier" between Germany and Bolshevik Russia but also into an important ally in the new system of containment they sought to create on and beyond the European continent. He and Clemenceau resolutely pursued this objective in the spring of 1919. In their eyes, Poland could not replace the Russian Empire but had the potential to become the most important French "second-tier ally" in Eastern Europe.

Drawing on studies prepared by the *Comité d'Études*, the French delegation thus presented its own schemes for a Polish state in the historic frontiers of 1772, even going beyond them where this seemed to serve France's geopolitical interests. As with a view to the Rhineland, Tardieu's pursuits were partly influenced by tactical considerations and the determination to bargain. In private, he reckoned early on that France might eventually have to accept an "internationalisation" of Danzig and even the so-called Polish Corridor for the sake of reaching an agreement with Britain and the United States – and possibly gaining concessions in other, more vital areas. But at the beginning of the bargaining process – and in full agreement with Clemenceau – he thus insisted all the more unequivocally that Poland had to be accorded the broadest possible access to the Baltic Sea and that Polish control over Danzig would be critical for the development of the new state. Likewise, he offered staunch support for Polish claims to Upper Silesia – and here, in contrast to the Rhineland, he left no doubt that the main French concern was to pry away from Germany one of its main industrial regions rather than to champion Polish "self-determination".[17] Essentially, it was this ambitious French agenda that eventually not only raised marked Anglo-American concerns but also led Wilson and Lloyd George to adjust their policies and to push for what they regarded as a more balanced Polish-German settlement – a settlement that minimised foreseeable structural conflicts and pre-empted the danger of future German irredentism.

Those who first tackled the intricacies of the Polish-German border arrangement were the designated experts of the victorious powers who came together in the Commission on Polish Affairs that the Supreme Council had created. Their deliberations revealed that these experts were far from introducing an element of un-biased distance and scientific objectivity into the politically charged peacemaking process. Rather, their recommendations were, consciously or subconsciously, informed by their own political and indeed

---

[17] See Committee meeting, chaired by Tardieu, 29 January 1919, "Pologne", MAE Europe 1918–29, Pologne (68).

civilisational predilections or prejudices – some very personal, others coloured by what they perceived to be core national interests they had to prioritise. Yet the ultimate decisions would yet again be made by the political leaders, who of course added their own biases and preconceptions. Ultimately, they would negotiate a settlement that was chiefly based on – conflicting – political and strategic considerations rather than on a strict observance of the self-determination principle, as Wilson had originally demanded. Nonetheless, the invocation *and* instrumentalisation of this principle would indeed play an unprecedentedly central role in this political process, with each side adapting its use in accordance with its core interests and aims.

The brief of the Commission on Polish Affairs, which came to be chaired by the former French ambassador to Berlin, Jules Cambon, was to elaborate detailed proposals for settling Poland's borders "chiefly upon the ethnographic basis". Yet the leading French, American and British experts agreed that they would also have to give due consideration to strategic factors – notably the control of railways, Poland's access to the Baltic, and the new state's industrial base – as well as broader political considerations. And they indeed found it relatively easy to reach common ground on the essentials of Poland's future borders with Germany and the priority of creating a "strong" Polish state – while either disagreeing about or paying little heed to the implications the settlement they proposed would have for the future of German-Polish relations. Cambon essentially subscribed to the strategic rationales advanced by Tardieu and faithfully represented his programme and what he considered to be overriding French interests in the commission. And the most influential American expert, Robert Lord, essentially supported Cambon's priorities. In line with his earlier schemes for a viable Polish state and the maxim that the "vital interests" of 20 million Poles outweighed German concerns in this matter, Lord recommended Polish control not only over Poznan but also a "corridor" to the Baltic between Pomerania and the Vistula. He emphasised that according to the studies he had made there was also a clear Polish majority in the provinces that would form the "corridor".[18]

But where Polish and German self-determination claims clashed Lord ultimately gave priority to what he saw as the vital political and economic conditions that had to be met in order to establish a "genuinely independent and strong" Polish state; and on these grounds he now clearly favoured the cession to Poland of the predominantly German Hanseatic port city of Danzig – and of the also largely German districts around Marienwerder and Allenstein, both situated east of the Vistula. Reflecting French rationales, Lord impressed on his colleague Isaiah Bowman that they had to insist on "the one right solution": if the new Polish state was to "play the very important role"

---

[18] Lord (Warsaw) to Bowman, 9 March 1919, NA PC 181.2302/70.

that it should play, also in the American interest, of "helping to hold Germany in check and to prevent the Bolshevist or a restored monarchical Russia from joining hand with Germany", then it was indispensable that the new state would have "assured access to the outside world, which nothing but the possession of Danzig" could give it.[19]

Bowman, who was subsequently appointed to serve on a subcommittee charged with making specific recommendations for Poland's future northern and western borders, fully supported Lord's positions, also with a view to the future status of Danzig. Essentially, both American experts first and foremost desired to ensure the creation of a robust Polish state that could preserve and consolidate its independence between Germany and Russia, whatever path the latter power would follow; and they argued that on the most critical issues the strategic and economic needs of Poland had to outweigh ethnic considerations and, in the end, overrule the application of the self-determination principle. It was on the basis of these rationales that they also backed the commission's recommendation that the Polish state should be accorded most of Upper Silesia – without a plebiscite. Neither Lord nor Bowman were oblivious to the problems that an unconsolidated Polish state would face in having to deal with a German minority that in their calculations would encompass roughly two million ethnic Germans. But they essentially argued that these problems could be addressed by providing Germans, like other minority groups in the new Poland, with adequate protections.[20] By contrast, they never seriously considered the crucial issue of future German irredentism and, more generally, the immense political and geopolitical challenges their recommendations would create for Poland in its future relations with Germany. And based on assurances they had received from House they – mistakenly – assumed that Wilson endorsed their recommendations.

Lord had earlier reached an understanding with one of the main British experts on the commission, Esme Howard. What thus had emerged by mid-March was indeed a broad Anglo-American expert consensus along the lines that he and Bowman had proposed. Like his colleague William Tyrrell, Howard had underlying sympathies for the claims of the Polish government. Even though he placed a greater emphasis on the need to respect not only Polish but also German self-determination claims, he still argued that the consolidation of a "strong" and economically viable Polish state ought to be the western governments' primary concern. Having once argued that as a predominantly German city Danzig should remain part of Germany, he now

---

[19] *Ibid.* See Schwabe (1985), pp. 485–6.

[20] See report of meeting of American and British experts and protocol of their recommendations, 21 February 1919, House Papers; Lord memorandum "The Polish–German Frontier", undated, Schwabe (1985), p. 234; Lord (1921), pp. 71 ff.; Nelson (2019), pp. 147–66.

thus backed the commission's verdict that Danzig as well as the Marienwerder region were to be accorded to Poland.[21] The British experts only disagreed on one issue: they successfully insisted that a plebiscite should be held to decide the future status of the Allenstein district. The recommendations of the experts thus went a long way towards meeting Dmowski's demands. This became manifest in the report of the Commission on Polish Affairs that Cambon presented to the Supreme Council on 19 March. On this occasion, he stated explicitly that the commission's proposals were based on the premise that strategic and economic imperatives had to outweigh those of ethnicity and the ideal of self-determination, which could not always be adhered to in practice. He underscored that it was "very difficult" to "make a frontier on purely ethnological lines"; "(e)conomic and strategic requirements" also had to be considered as the new state "should be so delimited as to be capable of life". And he declared that especially the "possession" of Danzig was "a matter of life and death to Poland".[22]

Yet the expert report merely provided the starting-point for the protracted and conflict-ridden negotiations among the Big Three and their main advisers through which not just the main parameters of the Polish-German border settlement but also essential, and overall inauspicious, conditions for Poland's future relations with Weimar Germany would be determined. At first, both Clemenceau and Wilson signalled that they basically endorsed the experts' proposals. Lloyd George, however, set out on what became a sustained campaign to alter a settlement that in his assessment was bound to give rise to an inherently unstable and indeed war-prone constellation, chiefly by provoking inevitable German irredentism, and thus to create massive liabilities not only for the Polish state but also for Eastern Europe and, ultimately, for the western powers themselves. And, significantly, as in the case of the Rhineland, Wilson came to share many of Lloyd George's more fundamental misgivings. Yet in the east it proved even more daunting than in the west to craft a political compromise settlement that reconciled the victors' different interests and priorities. And, more importantly, it proved exceedingly difficult to negotiate terms that at least *limited* the fundamental problems the British premier highlighted and put effective mechanisms in place to deal with them over time.

During the altercations in the Council of Four, Clemenceau vehemently defended the French view that in approaching the Polish settlement the victors simply had to "accept the inevitable difficulties in the principle of self-determination" and in the end give priority to "strategic considerations". And he argued that such considerations notably had to govern their decisions about

---

[21] See report of meeting of American and British experts and protocol of their recommendations, 21 February 1919, House Papers; Howard memorandum, "Poland", November 1918, FO 371/4354/f46/PC70.

[22] *FRUS-PPC*, IV, pp. 413–15.

Poland's access to the sea and the "communications" between Danzig and the "interior" of Poland. Earlier, Tardieu had sought to reinforce the French government's position by emphasising that as the peace conference had set out to "revive ancient States" long subjected to "alien domination", it was inevitable that "the dominating race would be found settled in these areas". In the light of this, he maintained that new frontiers could simply not be settled "on ethnological grounds alone". Instead, the peacemakers should espouse the premise that "(i)f the submerged nations were to be revived a mixed population must be included in them".[23]

Essentially, however, the assertive course of Clemenceau and Tardieu was consistently guided not so much by sympathies for the Polish national cause but by the overriding aims of their strategy to contain and constrain Germany. And in this respect Poland's importance as a "bulwark" state was actually growing in the spring and summer of 1919 as the prospects of a Bolshevik defeat and of regaining Russia as an ally became increasingly elusive. The French protagonists thus sought to support the fledgling Polish state as a new strategic partner. Yet, aware of Anglo-American reservations, they did not yet go so far as to propose either an alliance with or specific guarantees for Poland. By the end of March, French efforts to push for a "strong" Polish state had also become intricately bound up with the aspiration to strike a strategic bargain with Britain and the United States on Anglo-American security guarantees and the occupation of the Rhineland. What particularly Tardieu thus sought to create around Germany had the makings of a system of security and containment whose centre of gravity lay in the west yet that was also supposed to protect the new east European states, which in turn were supposed to play their part as barrier states.[24]

Clemenceau clearly shared these priorities. And this had one important consequence. Essentially, the French strategic imperatives precluded any openness towards a settlement that sought to consider and as far as possible balance Polish and German interests and claims. Rather, Clemenceau reasserted a core maxim of France's containment policy. Just as he had done with a view to the Rhineland, he argued that it was futile to try to stabilise Eastern and Central Europe by seeking to do "justice" to Germany and satisfying the "self-determination" claims of the vanquished, because German conceptions of justice were simply different from those of the western democracies.[25] At bottom, the French premier acted on the assumption that German grievances and irredentist pressure would be unavoidable in the new geopolitical constellation the war had created. And he remained convinced that this was a price worth paying for establishing a Polish state that could

---

[23] Council of Four, 27 March 1919, Mantoux (1992), I, p. 34; FRUS-PPC, IV, pp. 416–17.
[24] Council of Four, 27 March 1919, Mantoux (1992), I, p. 34.
[25] Tardieu (II/1921), pp. 157–67; Wandycz (1998), p. 326.

assist in the containment of Germany. These were the underlying rationales the Clemenceau government pursued at Versailles. They made France into the key patron of the new Polish state; yet they also contributed decisively to pitting the new Poland against the fledgling Weimar Republic.

Lloyd George soon made clear that he objected not only to some of the main recommendations the Commission on Polish Affairs had made but also, more profoundly, to the entire thrust of the French delegation's approach to the Polish–German question. At the same time, he sought to counter and contain Dmowski's demands. Maintaining a decidedly high-handed attitude towards the nationalist aspirations that the latter represented, Lloyd George had concluded – like Balfour – that the main Polish spokesman at Versailles had chosen to pursue a maximalist agenda at France's behest rather than showing his country's "fitness for independence" by exercising "self control". And it soon became clear that not only Balfour but a majority in the British delegation, including Smuts yet also Cecil and Headlam-Morley, shared his concerns.[26]

The British premier came to embark on a veritable campaign to press for a substantially revised German–Polish settlement; and once again it became critical for him to gain Wilson's support. Invoking the maxims of his recently formulated Fontainebleau agenda, he presented his mission as that of a self-styled "honest broker" whose main intention was to negotiate a "fairer" settlement, one that took Polish claims seriously but also accommodated those of a defeated power that had no say in the negotiations yet whose interests had to be considered. But although he emphasised the need for "fairness" towards Germany and respect for self-determination, Lloyd George conveyed rather unequivocally that his most fundamental concerns were of a different magnitude. In short, he persistently warned that the proposed terms would not merely have disastrous consequences for Poland's relations with Germany but indeed undermine all prospects of establishing a "lasting peace in Europe".[27]

When the Big Three began their crucial negotiations in the Council of Four on 27 March Lloyd George argued that the proposed Polish "corridor" to the Baltic not only lacked any real justification – and had to be regarded as a "departure from the principles of the Fourteen Points" – but also constituted an acute danger to European peace. Though he had previously acknowledged that "it was hardly possible to draw a line that would not have Germans on both sides of it", he now emphasised that it was "very dangerous to assign two million Germans to Poland" and thereby to an "allegiance" they were unlikely to accept. Lloyd George particularly opposed transferring the Marienwerder

---

[26] Balfour to Cambon, 30 November 1918, FO 371/3277; Balfour to Wade, 5 January 1919, FO 608/68; Cecil minute (undated), FO 371/4354/f46/PC73; Smuts to Lloyd George, 26 March 1919, *Smuts Papers*, IV, pp. 84–5.

[27] Council of Four, 27 March 1919, Mantoux (1992), I, p. 37.

district with its clear German majority to the Polish state. At this point he also noted that the victors had to acknowledge one particular problem, namely that the German side "had not been heard" in the process; but he never went so far as to call for actually allowing German representatives to make their case before the terms were finalised. What primarily concerned him, however, was neither the fate of German minorities in Poland nor the tactical worry that the German government would not sign a peace on the terms the Polish commission had proposed – or be swept away if it did, opening the door to a Bolshevik take-over. Nor was he preoccupied with the consolidation prospects of the Polish nation-state as such – which he viewed with scepticism. His main preoccupations lay elsewhere; at the core they pertained to the requirements of stabilising a future European equilibrium – and of ensuring that Britain and the Empire would never have to countenance a military intervention on the European continent again.[28]

This is why the British premier insisted so fervently that what was at stake was not only "a question of fairness to Germany" but a problem whose management was critical to the stabilisation of the postwar order as a whole. He argued that if the victors imposed a settlement on the defeated power that deprived it of significant areas that would become "Germania Irredenta", they would effectively sow "the seed of future war". And he raised the provocative yet far from irrelevant question of whether France, Britain and the United States would ultimately be prepared to "go to war to maintain Polish rule" over these areas if disaffected German populations were to "rise against the Poles" and their "fellow-countrymen" came to their assistance. As Lloyd George impressed on Clemenceau, he was certain that "public opinion, both in America and in England, would not support" an intervention "in such circumstances" – an intervention to uphold what he deemed an inherently untenable status quo.[29]

What became palpable at this stage anticipated a more general tendency of British policy in the post–First World War era, which derived from the fear of becoming entangled in far-reaching responsibilities in the volatile region between Germany and Russia that the demise of the eastern empires had left behind. This was closely connected with the prevalent assumption that it would be all but impossible to establish a stable status quo in this region right after the war. It was on account of this fear, and this assumption, that Lloyd George and other British policymakers were extremely reluctant to envisage any qualitatively different, namely *pre-emptive* political or security commitments to the new Polish state – beyond the general commitments under the League Covenant. More generally, no plans were made that would have cast

[28] Council of Four, 27 March 1919, Mantoux (1992), I, p. 37; *FRUS-PPC*, IV, pp. 415–17.
[29] *Ibid.*, pp. 415–16.

Britain in the burdensome role of a guarantor or "power of order" in Central and Eastern Europe.

Instead, the British premier concentrated on using his influence to push for a delineation of the German-Polish border that at least increased the likelihood of making the settlement mutually acceptable in the longer run and that thus lessened the likelihood of another war – or any form of British intervention. And this he sought to achieve by reducing the number of Germans who would live under Polish rule to a minimum and particularly avoiding the transfer of cities and districts where they constituted a clear majority. He warned that the scenario the victors had to avoid by all means was "to create a Poland alienated from the time of its birth by an unforgettable quarrel from its most civilized neighbour". Accordingly, and now drawing on proposals of Headlam-Morley and other worried British experts who urged him to insist on a more equitable application of the self-determination principle, he came to call for a plebiscite in Marienwerder and championed the idea of turning Danzig into a "free port".[30] Later Lloyd George would turn his attention to Upper Silesia, where he also came to call for a plebiscite.

But in the constellation of 1919 not only the essential decisions affecting the future of Franco–German relations and western Europe but also the most controversial aspects of the Polish-German settlement were ultimately a transatlantic affair. And here, too, the attitudes – and reorientations – of the American president himself would have a major influence on the final outcomes. Wilson had earlier left Polish matters largely in the hands of Bowman and Lord and signalled his support for their recommendations. Yet once the critical negotiations began in mid-March he changed his stance and outlook significantly. Unmistakeably he did so in part under the impression of Lloyd George's campaign – and he indeed came to adopt some of the British premier's main arguments.[31]

But the American president actually embarked on a more substantial learning and adjustment process of his own. He now characterised the issue of setting Poland's western frontiers as an essentially "political matter". And he indeed sought to play the role of a mediator – sometimes in cooperation, sometimes in competition with the British premier. His main aim became to strike what he now explicitly described as a compromise or some kind of

---

[30] Council of Four, 27 March 1919, Mantoux (1992), I, pp. 36–8. Davies (1971). Headlam-Morley memorandum, "The Eastern Frontiers of Germany", in Walworth (1986), p. 262; Headlam-Morley, "The Settlement: Europe", 15 November 1918, FO 371/4353/f23/PC55.

[31] Wilson was also evidently impressed by Smuts' arguments on behalf of a settlement that prevented "anarchy" in Central Europe and opened up a path for future "co-operation" with a German power that was set to remain the "*dominant factor*" on the European continent. See Smuts to Lloyd George, 26 March, *Smuts Papers*, IV, pp. 84–5; Council of Four, 27 March 1919, Mantoux (1992), I, p. 36.

"balance between conflicting considerations": the promise of a "free and safe access to the sea for Poland" and the imperative to honour the principle of self-determination. Echoing British concerns, Wilson not only acknowledged that "the inclusion of two million Germans in Poland" was a clear "violation" of that principle but also signalled his determination to seek a settlement that as far as possible limited such a "violation" – and future conflicts between Germany and Poland.[32] Overruling his own experts – and in fact reverting to a "solution" he had already contemplated in December 1918 – he came to back Lloyd George's suggestion to make Danzig a "free city". And in keeping with his overall peace design he proposed that it was to be placed under the supervision of the League. Further, he agreed that the future status of the Marienwerder district ought to be determined by a plebiscite. De facto, he thus sought to curtail not only the size of the envisaged "Polish Corridor", which he still backed in principle, but also the size of the future German minority in Poland.

What lay behind Wilson's reorientation? One of his main concerns was that the victors were "creating" a Polish state that he expected to be "weak" not only "because historically it had failed to govern itself" but also because it was bound to be "divided into factions", both ethnic and religious. Wilson saw eye to eye with Lord and Bowman insofar as he too deemed it imperative to consider not only the economic but also the "strategic needs" of this state, which would have to "cope" with a more powerful German neighbour "on both sides of it". And he also acknowledged that whatever boundaries they drew there was "bound to be a mixture of hostile populations included in either state". Yet he drew different conclusions from those his experts had recommended and in fact pursued his own version of an "equilibrium policy".

At one level, the American president began to pay more attention to the concerns and legitimation requirements of the German government on this vital issue – and the question of what terms would be acceptable for it. At another level, he began to grapple with the cardinal problem of how to negotiate terms that did not create immense liabilities, not just for future relations between Germany and the new Polish state but also for the longer-term pacification of Europe. One of his priorities thus became to reduce the size of the future German minority in Poland and to prevent areas with distinct German majorities from simply being assigned to the Polish state – thereby seeking to curb the problem of future German irredentism under the banner of "self-determination". This created a bond of common interests with

---

[32] Wilson here notably argued that it should not be considered a question in which – French – military considerations vis-à-vis Germany dictated how borders would be determined. See Wilson statement, Supreme Council, 19 March 1919, *FRUS-PPC*, IV, pp. 417–18.

Lloyd George – and Wilson too now stressed his "anxieties" and the cardinal American concern to avoid a scenario in which the desire of Germans "to rescue German populations from Polish rule" would arise – and be "hard to resist".[33]

In the negotiations and political struggle among the Big Three Wilson thus in fact sought to counter what he too had come to see as French designs whose real aim was to weaken Germany and, to this end, extend the domain of the Polish state for power-political reasons, by "giving Poland territory to which she has no right". Here, the American president was also mindful of the wider implications that strategic concessions to Poland would have – if they were made too obviously at the expense of considerations of self-determination and justice. He drew an analogy between the problem of Danzig and the unresolved dispute over Fiume. Asserting that both involved the struggle between national demands and principles that had to be upheld, he stressed that he could not deny Orlando's – in his eyes unfounded – claims to Fiume (which he would then oppose till the end) if he accepted Polish demands regarding Danzig.[34]

Characteristically, Wilson emphasised the fundamental dimension of what was at stake in his view. On 27 March, he impressed on Clemenceau and Lloyd George that what they had to avoid above all was to be "guilty of injustice" and give Germany reasons for "seeking revenge" in the future. And he warned them that unless they adhered to highest standards of scrupulous impartiality in deciding politically contentious questions – standards that *all* sides could subsequently accept – they would effectively "sow the seed of war". The American president reasoned that the victors were "compelled to change boundaries and national sovereignties". He was aware that this was a highly conflict-prone process, noting that the "changes" that had to be made ran "contrary to long-established customs" and would "change the very life of populations". And he clearly had mainly the Polish-German dilemma in mind when voicing his fear that the wars of the future would more likely be caused by "popular discontent" than by future machinations of secret diplomacy.[35] It is worth stressing, then, that the rising tides of acute crisis and foreboding that culminated in late March propelled a more profound, though as yet tentative, reorientation in Wilson's thinking about the *longer-term* and indeed more *fundamental* requirements of peace and stability after the Great War, not just in Central and Eastern Europe.

Undoubtedly, Wilson's stance on the key issues of the German–Polish border settlement was also influenced by the spectre of the communist takeover in Hungary and the growing concern that if the victors insisted on terms

---

[33] Wilson statement, Supreme Council, 19 March 1919, *FRUS-PPC*, IV, pp. 417–18.

[34] See Lundgreen-Nielsen (1982), p. 244; Wandycz (1998), pp. 326–7.

[35] Council of Four, 26 and 27 March 1919, Mantoux (1992), I, pp. 20, 31.

that could be branded as "unjust" or entirely unacceptable in Germany – particularly with a view to the politically sensitive issues involving territory and the future of German populations in the disputed provinces – the Scheidemann government would collapse and be replaced by Bolshevik forces. This concern was heightened by disconcerting reports the American peace delegation received from Berlin. Through the intermediary, Colonel Conger, Wilson had by this time been made aware of a memorandum on "Peace Terms Acceptable to Germany", that Walter Loeb, a confidant and emissary of Erzberger, had prepared. This memorandum was actually based on Erzberger's instructions and also reflected the positions of Foreign Minister Brockdorff-Rantzau and the guidelines for the German peace negotiators of 21 March 1919 that the Scheidemann cabinet had endorsed. It left no doubt about the vital importance the German government attached to avoiding far-reaching losses of territory and population in the east, and it notably contained the demand that plebiscites should be held in all "nationally mixed" territories where German and Polish claims collided (though it here only referred to the Posen province, not to West Prussia).[36]

Brockdorff-Rantzau himself had expressed what was the overwhelming consensus in the cabinet when demanding that Poland's access to the Baltic, conceded by the Fourteen Points, must not be realised through a "Polish corridor to Danzig that would sever East Prussia and parts of West Prussia from the rest of Germany". Desperate to present alternative proposals that could gain British and American support, the Scheidemann government suggested that Poland's access to the sea was to be ensured by creating alternative "free ports" on the Baltic coast – while leaving Danzig in German hands – and by concluding reciprocal agreements on the use of railways and traffic on the Vistula that would guarantee Polish transit rights to the sea.[37] Subsequently, Dresel conveyed to House that all his interlocutors in Berlin stressed that the future status of Danzig was among the issues on which the Scheidemann government would find it hardest to compromise. Based on fragmentary intelligence he had about the proceedings in Paris, Brockdorff-Rantzau had impressed on the American envoy that any German government that accepted the terms the victorious powers were contemplating – including the plan to make Danzig a free port under Polish administration – would be "swept away by public opinion". Erzberger was the only leading German

---

[36] Loeb memorandum, 30 March 1919, Wkg. 30 geh/1, D 931 100, PA; Council of Four, 1 April 1919, Mantoux (1992), I, pp. 100–1; General Nolan memoranda, *PWW*, LVI, pp. 492–4; Brockdorff-Rantzau memorandum on Guidelines for German Peace Negotiators, 21 March 1919, *ADAP*, A/I, pp. 323–4; Erzberger to Brockdorff-Rantzau, Versailles I, 9105 H/H234779, 1 April 1919, Brockdorff-Rantzau Papers.

[37] Brockdorff-Rantzau memorandum, 21 March 1919, *ADAP*, A/I, pp. 323–4.

decision-maker who was willing to accept that Danzig would be given an international status under the guarantee of the League.[38]

Neither the efforts of the German government nor the warnings of intermediaries like Conger or Dresel ever had a decisive bearing on Wilson's position; but they contributed to reinforcing his shift towards a more balanced approach. This also affected the American president's attitude towards the demands of the Polish government – and towards the question of what kind of settlement would be in Poland's longer-term interests. He now sought to convince Clemenceau that their task was to persuade Paderewski and other more moderate Polish leaders that a "fairer" and more mutually acceptable settlement of the issues at hand, which conformed with the parameters of the Fourteen Points, had to be pursued – "without any desire to favour [Poland's] enemies" but rather to "protect [the Poles] from future danger".[39] By early April, Wilson had come to view Dmowski's manoeuvres and demands as decidedly counterproductive. More generally, he came to speak of "our troublesome friends the Poles" and insisted that the western powers should not allow themselves to be "influenced too much by the Polish state of mind", observing that when he had met Dmowski and Paderewski in Washington in 1918 they had presented him with "a map in which they claimed a large part of the earth". And he again underscored his fear that the excessive ambitions of the Polish and other national movements in Eastern Europe could become "an inexhaustible source of disorder and war" unless the victors were "careful" in restraining them.[40] The American president now espoused Lloyd George's maxim that the main danger would emanate from "the existence of a *Germania irredenta*"; and he too now stressed that historical experience had shown that there was "no more serious and lasting cause of international conflict".[41]

III.   The Crucial Compromises of the Victors over Danzig and the "Polish Corridor"

On these premises, Wilson came to play the role of a proactive arbiter who mediated both between Polish and German concerns and between French and British conceptions. And while de facto forming a common front with Lloyd George and relying on British pressure he indeed gave the decisive impetus to forging what in his view became an exemplary and forward-looking

---

[38] Dresel to House, 21 April, House Papers; Brockdorff-Rantzau memorandum of conversation with Dresel, 19 April 1919, *ADAP*, A/I, pp. 423-4; Dresel notes on interview with Erzberger, 26 April 1919, Baker Papers.

[39] Council of Four, 12 April 1919, Mantoux (1992), I, p. 233.

[40] Council of Four, 1 April 1919, Mantoux (1992), I, pp. 108, 110.

[41] Council of Four, 9 April 1919, Mantoux (1992), I, pp. 200, 203.

agreement both on the status of Danzig and a revised "Polish Corridor", which would be finalised in mid-April. Building on an Anglo-American scheme that the head of the Inquiry, Mezes, and Headlam-Morley had worked out the American president proposed that in Danzig and the mainly German territories in its immediate vicinity a "small state" was to be created, which would be autonomous but "economically bound to Poland by a customs union". This state's administration was to be supervised by a high commissioner, appointed by the League, who also was to act as mediator in cases of disputes between Poles and Germans. Wilson noted that he especially favoured a "compromise" of this kind because it would empower the League to "intervene as a guarantor", which in his interpretation meant that the "proposed arrangement" could serve as a model for the future. At the same time, he emphasised again that in Marienwerder "the areas inhabited by Germans would be consulted by plebiscite and could, if they desired it, be united to East Prussia".[42]

Invited to speak in front of the Council of Four on 18 April, the Polish premier Paderewski strongly protested and reasserted his government's view that control over Danzig was "indispensable" for Poland, and indeed an existential necessity for the new state which could not "breathe without its window to the sea". Like all other key actors in 1919, Paderewski also invoked domestic pressures and concerns. Presenting himself as the key moderating force between the Dmowski and Piłsudski factions in Warsaw, he argued that the unstable Polish government, which desired a "complete alliance" with the western powers, would be dangerously destabilised if he failed to get the victors' support on this pivotal issue and returned home without tangible results – and this in turn would threaten the future stability of the Polish state. Clemenceau had once again acted as the main patron of the Polish government and, stressing that the main aim had to be to "reach a solution acceptable to the Poles", resisted any changes to the status of Danzig and the "Corridor". But Lloyd George adamantly opposed any attempts to go back behind the idea of an "independent city of Danzig" that, as he subsequently claimed, he had persuaded Wilson to accept as his own. At the same time, he renewed his call to leave Marienwerder in German hands – before finally settling for Wilson's plebiscite proposal.[43] Facing a realigned Anglo-American common front, Clemenceau eventually relented and reluctantly accepted the revisions Wilson had proposed.[44]

With only slight revisions, the compromise settlement on Danzig and the "Polish Corridor" that the leaders of the victors finalised on 22 April – and

---

[42] Council of Four, 1 and 3 April 1919, Mantoux (1992), I, pp. 106, 124; Mezes memorandum, 1 April 1919, PWW, LVI, p. 505.

[43] Council of Four, 1 April and 12 April, Mantoux (1992), I, pp. 107, 233.

[44] Clemenceau statement, Council of Four, 3 April 1919, Mantoux (1992), I, pp. 123–4.

which would remain essentially unaltered in the final peace treaty – incorporated all the amendments Wilson had suggested.[45] Danzig and the districts surrounding it would thus indeed be placed under a new kind of international regime as a "Free City" under the "guarantee" of the League. The League's main representative would be a high commissioner who was to arbitrate "all differences" arising between Poles and Germans and who would be charged with adjudicating a bilateral agreement on their respective rights and duties that Germany and Poland were to negotiate within one year. The new autonomous city state was to be part of the Polish customs system, and Poland would also be in charge of its "foreign relations" and railways and granted "full and unhampered" use of all waterways and port facilities it required for its trade. While provisions were made to ensure special German rights of communication with East Prussia – through what would be a reduced "corridor" – the Polish government was granted "the control and administration" of the Vistula and all railway and telegraph facilities relevant to its access to the Baltic Sea. Finally, it was confirmed that plebiscites were to take place in Marienwerder and Allenstein, and when they were held in July 1920 an overwhelming majority predictably voted in favour of remaining part of Germany. The final arrangement thus reduced the size of the "Polish Corridor" but did not fundamentally alter it, thus setting terms that overall gave precedence to Poland's vital interest in a secure access to the Baltic Sea – and the outside world – while also going some way towards accommodating German claims and vital interests in particularly disputed areas, including Danzig.

Wilson came to view this agreement as a not only tenable but essentially "just" and in some ways exemplary compromise that struck a balance between conflicting considerations of national interests, complicated geopolitical and ethnographic "realities" and, notably, respect for the underlying principles he sought to uphold. And it is worth underlining again that what the victors hammered out went indeed remarkably far towards constituting the best possible outcome that could be attained under the circumstances. And it may well be true that, as has often been argued, there was no "viable alternative" to this outcome in 1919.[46] Nonetheless, it could not be satisfactory to either of the directly affected parties – and, crucially, it would be outright rejected in Germany. It would have proved extremely difficult – if not impossible – to negotiate and agree on outlines of a mutually acceptable general settlement of border and minority issues with the German government at this stage. But the fact that the victors neither gave nor intended to give German representatives any opportunity to present their positions, and that they would

---

[45] Council of Four, 18 April 1919, Mantoux (1992), I, p. 271; FRUS-PPC, V, pp. 118–22.
[46] See notably Wandycz (1998), p. 334.

refuse any substantial negotiations, made their decisions all the more contest-able from the perspective of the defeated power.

Essentially, then, what the victors had negotiated could only mitigate rather than defuse, let alone resolve, the underlying structural problem that was to become one of the most onerous legacies of the Great War *and* Versailles: the structural conflict between an as yet unconsolidated Polish state with an equally unconsolidated government and approach to foreign relations, which still included (among others) a large German minority, and its inherently most powerful neighbour that was now a no less unconsolidated German republic in which, reflecting the prevalent views of the wider public, an overwhelming majority of decision-makers and elites – from the nationalist right to the republican centre and left – would consider the victors' terms for the new *status quo* on Germany's eastern border unacceptable and indeed illegitimate. How – and how far – the western governments could agree on ways to come to terms with this longer-term, structural Polish–German conflict thus became a pivotal question.

What threatened to add further fuel to this conflict was the struggle over another particularly thorny issue: the future status of Upper Silesia. As noted, from a German vantage-point preventing the loss of Upper Silesia was of special strategic and political importance because after the Ruhr area this region had been the most significant industrial area of Imperial Germany, featuring significant iron and steel mills and accounting for roughly a quarter of the annual German coal, zinc and lead production. For their part, Polish plenipotentiaries continued to base their claims to Upper Silesia on the argument that the province was by then inhabited by a mostly Polish-speaking population and asserted that its resources would be essential for the Polish state's economic development.[47]

The leaders of the victorious powers originally adopted the recommenda-tions of the Commission on Polish Affairs and stipulated in the draft treaty that Upper Silesia was to ceded to Poland without a plebiscite, on the grounds that a clear majority – two-thirds of its population – could be classified as Polish. What had had come to prevail during the commission's deliberations was a fundamental consensus between the French and American key experts, which largely reflected Polish arguments. Lord had agreed with Cambon that Upper Silesia would be of immense economic value for the Polish state – while in French thinking the main consideration clearly was and remained to deprive Germany of a vital industrial and power-political asset. Lord had rejected the ideas of a plebiscite on the grounds that the Polish populations had been dominated by German capitalists and quasi-feudal landowners for

---

[47] Dmowski statements, Council of Ten, 29 January 1919, *FRUS-PPC*, III, pp. 772–9.

such a long time, and were still so economically dependent on them, that it would not be possible to hold a "genuine", unbiased referendum.[48]

Wilson had initially accepted Lord's reasoning and the expert recommendations. And despite growing misgivings, Lloyd George had not contested them at first, concentrating his attention on the "Polish Corridor". But the future of Upper Silesia was as yet far from decided. As will be seen, following vehement German protests the British premier would eventually insist that in the interests of a German signature under the peace treaty and future European stability a different solution had to be found. He would propose yet again to resort to the instrument of holding a plebiscite whose fairness was to be guaranteed by an inter-allied commission, and troops, operating under the supervision of League. In the end, the search for a victors' compromise on Upper Silesia would thus become a crucial part of their eleventh-hour struggles – in early June – over possible changes to the peace terms that made them more acceptable to the defeated power.[49]

IV.   The Czechoslovak Border Settlement, the Future Order of Central Europe and the Vexatious *Anschluß* Question

The need to settle of the borders of the new Czechoslovak state raised many of the same problems that Poland's "rebirth" had caused – albeit on smaller scale and with more limited implications for the stability of the postwar order. Here, too, the western powers essentially faced the challenge of how to balance strategic, economic and political imperatives with considerations of equity, a "fair" application of the self-determination principle and the future treatment of minorities that in one way or another would make up a significant part of the population of the newly-founded Czechoslovak republic.

The new government in Prague not only claimed, in the east, territory inhabited by both Slovak and Hungarian populations, and a southern border that would place around 750,000 Hungarians under Czechoslovak rule. It also advanced claims for the "historic frontier" of Bohemia in the north, even though this meant – as all sides were aware – that Czechoslovakia would have within its borders a large German-speaking minority, the roughly 3 million so-called Sudeten Germans. Having gained western recognition, the protagonists of the Czechoslovak cause at the peace conference – Beneš, now foreign minister, and President Masaryk – were very effective in making the case for a strong Czechoslovak state that was at the same time a western-orientated democracy, a steadfast ally of the victors and bastion of stability in the reconfigured Central Europe, both vis-à-vis Germany and the Bolsheviks.

---

[48] Lord memorandum, 5 June 1919, Wilson Papers; Council of Four, 3 June 1919, Mantoux (1992), II, pp. 279–86. Lord (1921), pp. 71, 73.
[49] Council of Four, 3 June, Mantoux (1992), II, pp. 280–3. See chapter 20.

By the time Beneš presented his government's claims to the Supreme Council on 5 February, the state-in-formation he represented had already asserted authority over most of the territory to which it aspired, comprising the hitherto Austrian provinces of Bohemia, Moravia and Silesia as well as the formerly Hungarian-ruled province of Slovakia. What Beneš now sought above all was the victors' support for the "historic" Bohemian border. He emphasised strategic and economic arguments, underscoring that it would be vital for the future development of the Czechoslovak state to have a defensible boundary vis-à-vis Germany and the economic resources and potential of the borderlands mainly inhabited by Sudeten Germans. As he was assured of French backing, Beneš's strategy was mainly geared towards persuading Wilson and Lloyd George. And he sought to build on the successful lobbying efforts that he and Masaryk had pursued on behalf of the Czechoslovak national cause in 1918, particularly in the United States.

Beneš thus presented Czechoslovakia not just as a state that could play an important role in forming "a barrier between Germany and the East" – where Bolshevism threatened to dominate – but also as a "thoroughly loyal" partner of the western powers in a wider sense, namely as a strong supporter of the League and the new kind of international politics that notably Wilson had championed. He argued that in the light of an historical experience of "300 years of servitude and vicissitudes" that had almost led to its "extermination", those who now represented the Czech and Slovak nation were aware that they had to be "prudent, reasonable and just to its neighbours" and to "avoid provoking jealousy and renewed struggles". More concretely, he pledged that the Czechoslovak government would commit itself to a forward-looking minority policy; it would grant German, Hungarian and other minority populations equal civic rights as citizens of the Czechoslovak republic and ensure that they could have their own political representatives, maintain their own schools and universities, use their own language and enjoy freedom of religion. Not least to pre-empt the western imposition of minority treaties, the first Czechoslovak premier, Karel Kramář, subsequently promised that the new state was "ready to do everything possible for minorities" and to cooperate with the "Great Powers" on this issue in order to have "peace at home".[50]

Czechoslovakia's spokesmen in Paris could count on the firm and consistent support of the Clemenceau government, which had already been their pivotal ally in the final stages of the war. Clemenceau, Pichon and senior figures in the Quai d'Orsay were united in their support for a strong Czechoslovak state,

---

[50] Beneš statement, 5 February 1919, Lloyd George (1938), II, p. 931; Seymour (1951), pp. 155–6; Derby to Balfour, 14 December 1918, Balfour Papers, 184–90; Kramář statement, Plenary Session, 31 May 1919, *FRUS-PPC*, III, p. 402. See Perman (1962), pp. 56–87; MacMillan (2002), pp. 229–35; Bonsal (1946), pp. 46–51.

which they still regarded as a centrepiece of the Central European system of security and containment that they sought to create. In their view, there were sound strategic reasons for according Czechoslovakia a militarily defensible frontier with Germany and, as in the case of Poland, a maximum of economic resources (that thus would not fall under German control). In their wider geopolitical scheme for a new Central Europe, the Czechoslovak state was to be encouraged to link up with Poland, Yugoslavia and Romania and become another key element of the "barrier" system they sought to create between Germany and Russia. Therefore, it was to play a critical role in French designs to fill the power-political vacuum that the dissolution of the Austro-Hungarian Empire had created – and to prevent Germany from ever again pursuing *Mitteleuropa* ambitions and regaining a predominant position on the European continent.[51] It was with these priorities in mind that Cambon impressed on Balfour and Lansing in the Council of Foreign Ministers on 1 April that, as with a view to Poland, the "ethnological principle" could not be the only yardstick in determining the borders of the new states of Central Europe; also in the case of Czechoslovakia economic factors and above all concerns of "national security" had to be duly considered. From a French vantage-point such concerns were indeed, once again, decisive.[52]

Reflecting the earlier positions of the Inquiry, the American experts who chiefly dealt with the Czechoslovak border settlement at Versailles, Seymour and Dulles, were not unimpressed by Beneš's strategic and economic arguments – as well as by the commitments to the protection of minority rights he had made. Nonetheless, when the issue of the "historic" Bohemian frontier was duly debated in the Commission on Czechoslovak Affairs they were the only experts who raised serious concerns. They warned that the "incorporation within Czechoslovakia of so large a number of Germans" – which could turn into a large dissatisfied minority – had the potential not just to impede the consolidation of the Czechoslovak republic but indeed to threaten the very existence of the "new State".[53] In the Council of Foreign Ministers, an isolated Lansing would later raise similar objections, proclaiming that the plan to fix Czechoslovak "frontier lines", determined by military calculations rather than respect for the principle of self-determination, was "directly contrary" to the "whole spirit" that was to animate the League and to the policies of the United States as set forth in Wilson's "declarations".[54] Yet neither Seymour and

---

[51] See French memorandum, "Les Frontières de la Tchécoslovaquie", 22 February 1919, MAE, Série A, Paix, 344 (Tchécoslovaquie); Committee minutes on the frontiers of Czechoslovakia, undated, Tardieu Papers, vol. 77.

[52] Cambon statement, 1 April 1919, *FRUS-PPC*, IV, pp. 544–5.

[53] See Seymour, "Czechoslovak Frontiers", pp. 279–84; Seymour to Coolidge, 14 February 1919, House Papers; Walworth (1986), pp. 263–4; Perman (1962), pp. 146–7.

[54] Lansing statement, 1 April 1919, *FRUS-PPC*, IV, p. 544.

Dulles nor Lansing could offer any convincing alternative solution to the problem they had identified. Minor changes to the envisaged Czech–German border would not alter the basic problem. Because of the geographic separation from Austria, there was no realistic prospect of joining the Sudetenland with the struggling Austrian republic. But particularly in view of the French government's strategic priorities, there was no prospect either of merging it with the fledgling German republic – and the American experts were well aware of the fact that the latter was the successor state of a German Empire to which the Sudeten Germans had never belonged.

In any event, Seymour and Dulles could only register their misgivings. In the commission, they confronted a majority of experts who, following the French lead, passed recommendations that tallied with the demands Beneš had presented, confirming both that the "historic frontier" of Bohemia was to become the northern border of Czechoslovakia and that by and large the Slovak-Hungarian border would also by and large follow the foreign minister's design (only his idea of a southern "corridor" linking Czechoslovakia and Yugoslavia was dismissed). That such a clear majority verdict was reached also owed to the fact that the leading British specialists in this instance came to different conclusions from their American counterparts. Although – as noted – Headlam-Morley had noted early on that it would be vital for the future development of the new Czechoslovak state that "the Germans in Bohemia and the Magyars" had to be "treated on exactly the same principle [of self-determination] as the Czechs", British experts thereafter adopted the view that in order to thrive this state essentially required both the economic resources and the mountain bastion that the *Sudetenland* would furnish. In line with earlier recommendations of the Foreign Office's Political Intelligence Division, they espoused the rationale that a strong Czechoslovak state was likely to prove a great asset. In Seton-Watson's judgement, it could become "the hub of Central non-German Europe" and as such deserved Britain's unequivocal support. Neither he nor Headlam-Morley overlooked the danger of inter-ethnic conflicts in what was set to become a distinctly multi-national state; but they had considerable confidence in the willingness and ability of Beneš and Masaryk to contain this danger, not least by means of the proposed liberal regime of minority rights and protections.[55]

Both Headlam-Morley and Seton-Watson had by this time abandoned the hope of realising their more ambitious schemes for a Central European confederation that was to fill the vacuum the demise of the Austro-Hungarian Empire had left behind – schemes that went far beyond anything their American

---

[55] See Headlam-Morley memorandum, November 1918, FO371/4353; Headlam-Morley (1972), p. 127; Namier memorandum, "The Czechoslovak State", 4 December 1918, FO371/4353; Seton-Watson to Headlam-Morley, 29 May 1919, Seton-Watson Papers, Personal Correspondence, Box 9. See Bátonyi (1999), pp. 162–3.

counterparts ever contemplated. But it is worth noting that in the spring of 1919 they still deemed the creation of some kind of economic union between the new "Danubian" states "desirable". As they envisaged it, such a union would include not only "new" states like Czechoslovakia but also the defeated successor states Austria and Hungary. As they saw it, such a union would not only serve to contain German postwar influence but also and chiefly prevent a fragmentation of Central Europe into weak, separate and antagonistic states, which in turn would spark political and economic chaos and cause starvation on a major scale, thereby preparing the ground for Bolshevism's advance to the heart of Europe.[56] Yet they never developed coherent conceptions for actually creating such a union – and for overcoming the multiple nationalist conflicts and tensions that pitted the older and new states of this region against each other. More importantly, however, preoccupied as they were with other problems, neither Lloyd George nor Balfour ever showed any inclination to pursue more ambitious Danubian schemes of this kind.

When the delineation of the border between Czechoslovakia and Germany was finally deliberated in the Council of Four on 4 April, Lloyd George ultimately acquiesced with Clemenceau's suggestion to follow the majority verdict of the Commission of Czechoslovak Affairs and basically leave the proposed "historical" frontier unaltered.[57] And Wilson would follow suit. The British premier would later claim that he was plagued by major doubts about the wisdom of a settlement that placed such a large German-speaking minority under Czechoslovak rule and could be contested by the Sudeten Germans themselves and more importantly by German governments on grounds of "self-determination". Yet he does not seem to have voiced such concerns at the time; it appears more likely that he did not pay a great deal of attention to the Sudeten question; and he evidently was not prepared to invest political or negotiating capital on what he regarded as a far less explosive issue than the German–Polish problem.[58]

Similarly preoccupied with this and other aspects of the German settlement, the American president never seems to have given much thought either to the intricacies of the Sudeten problem or indeed the future role of Czechoslovakia in a wider Central European context. The American president had some misgivings, which echoed those of Lansing and the American experts. During the negotiations he would complain that Masaryk had left him in the dark about the implications of the Czechoslovak plans for the Sudeten Germans. In fact, however, he had generally been made aware of the aspirations Masaryk and Beneš pursued; and House had earlier signalled to the latter that the US delegation would back his claim for the "historic" Bohemian

---

[56] See Headlam-Morley (1972), p. 128; Bátonyi (1999), pp. 13–14.
[57] Mantoux (1955), I, p. 149.
[58] See Lloyd George (1938), II, pp. 937–41; MacMillan (2002), p. 237.

frontier. Wilson had also received appeals from representatives of the Sudeten Germans and from the newly elected Austrian government in Vienna, both beseeching him to ensure that the former's right to self-determination would be respected and to use his authority to propose a plebiscite. Ultimately, however, the American president basically reverted to a position he had already demarcated in December 1918 when he had observed that while it was preferable in principle to draw a "clear line ... eliminating two million Germans from Czechoslovakia", it would in practice be "too complicated to draw any new boundary in Bohemia". Having subsequently left the matter largely in the hands of the US experts, and of House, he thus went along with what was essentially an Anglo-French settlement that at the same time can be seen as a remarkable success vindicating the western-orientated strategies of Beneš and Masaryk.[59]

It has rightly been stressed that the western powers' handling of the Czechoslovak question in general and the Sudeten issue in particular – while constituting another clear case of imposing double standards regarding "self-determination" that could be contested thereafter – did not necessarily sow the seeds of a major future conflict, let alone a possible new war.[60] While the Austrian government and Sudeten representatives launched futile protests against the victors' decisions, neither the protagonists of the Scheidemann government nor the wider German public – absorbed as they were by other more pressing or fundamental problems – paid any serious attention to the grievances of the Sudeten Germans. Foreign Minister Brockdorff-Rantzau felt obliged to voice his sympathies; but the government's official position was characterised by marked restraint.

Essentially, German policymakers were not prepared to risk further alienating the victorious powers while still holding out hopes for actual negotiations with them; and they concentrated on issues that involved more cardinal national interests, not least the settlement of the border with Poland. Consequently, they did not contest the "historic" Bohemian frontier. And behind the scenes there was even a growing interest to develop good bilateral relations with the new Czechoslovak state and to draw it – like Austria – closer to Germany in an effort not only to improve conditions for the Sudeten German minority but also to prevent the formation of a Danubian confederation, which was seen as harmful to Germany's economic interests.[61] It would indeed take a radically worsened international constellation, a succession of crises akin to those of the 1930s and a pan-German demagogue like Hitler to

---

[59] Wilson statement, 12 December 1918, Bullitt diary, 12 December 1918, Bullitt Papers; House diary, 4 April 1919, House Papers.
[60] MacMillan (2002), pp. 237–8.
[61] See Krüger (1985), pp. 56–7.

turn Sudeten German dissatisfactions into greater German grievances that could be seized upon to destroy the postwar international order.

Following the election of the Austrian national assembly on 16 February 1919, in which the social democrats had won a clear majority, the victors would be compelled to clarify their positions and find a common approach to another controversial and, from their perspectives, vexatious question with potentially far-reaching implications not just for Central Europe – the *Anschluß* question. The Austrian prime minister Karl Renner and particularly his foreign minister Otto Bauer intensified their campaign for a union between the newly established democratic republic of German Austria and Germany, pursued confidential negotiation with the Scheidemann government and renewed their plea for a recognition of this union by the victorious powers in accordance with the principle of self-determination. And while Brockdorff-Rantzau continued to recommend restraint, Scheidemann, invoking the same principle, reasserted the "right" of the new German republic to form a union with Austria.[62] Increasingly concerned that the German and Austrian governments would confront the allied powers with a *fait accompli*, Clemenceau re-affirmed his unequivocal opposition to any form of *Anschluß*, which so evidently collided with French efforts to contain and reduce German power. He impressed on Wilson and Lloyd George that France could not accept aspirations that would add "seven million inhabitants to the population of Germany" and thereby increase the latter's power and recast the continental balance of power "in a manner very threatening to us".[63] And he demanded that the western governments should make their rejection of the Austro-German union explicit and issue a severe warning both to Vienna and Berlin.

Wilson understood that an outright prohibition of an Austro-German union would expose particularly him to charges of acting contrary to the principles he had so insistently proclaimed; and he voiced certain sympathies for the Austrian desire to unite with Germany. Yet he not only recognised that it would be impossible to overcome French objections. He also maintained the view he had formed earlier: that permitting the creation of a large German–Austrian state so soon after the end of the war would pose too much of a challenge for the European postwar equilibrium. Nonetheless, he did not want to preclude the possibility of a future "self-determined" Austrian union with Germany.[64] Harbouring concerns that reflected those of the American president, the British premier also rejected an immediate *Anschluß*, though he too had misgivings about imposing a permanent ban. Under pressure from Clemenceau, Wilson and Lloyd George on 22 April consented to a

---

[62] Walworth (1986), pp. 217–220; Coolidge report from Vienna, 17 March 1919, *FRUS-PPC*, XII, pp. 278–9.

[63] Council of Four, 27 March 1919, Mantoux (1992), I, p. 34.

[64] Grayson diary, 8 December 1918, *PWW*, LIII, pp. 338–9.

resolution which required Germany to acknowledge and "respect strictly the independence of Austria". This would form the basis of Article 80 of the Versailles treaty and also be included in the eventual peace treaty with Austria. Soon thereafter, however, both would raise renewed reservations, and Wilson would ultimately back an amendment proposed by Lloyd George, which then was included in the final peace terms. Essentially, it stipulated that Austria's independence was to be "inalienable, except with the consent of the League of Nations". A future union of Austria and Germany was thus possible in principle, but made dependent on the approval of the League, and this ultimately meant that France would be in a position to veto it in its capacity as permanent member of the League council.[65]

To send a signal of support to the Austrian government, and stave off a "Bolshevisation" of the crisis-ridden rump state, Wilson proposed on 30 April that an Austrian delegation should be invited to Paris to "discuss" the outlines of a peace treaty; and he also argued that the Austrian republic should receive assurances that it would be admitted to the League in the near future.[66] Bauer and the Austrian delegates who travelled to Paris and then had to wait for possible discussions with the victors in the small town of Saint-Germain-en-Laye still hoped that their efforts to establish an Austrian republic would be rewarded by a "Wilsonian peace". In particular, they hoped that their cooperative approach would induce the victors to give serious consideration to their self-determination claims of German-speaking Austrian populations in areas where, as with a view to the South Tyrol, they clashed with the territorial claims of Austria's old and new neighbour states.[67] At the same time, they represented a highly unstable republican government and a fledgling state that, as British and American observers impressed on the peacemakers, was in a state of acute political, social and financial crisis after the collapse and disintegration of the Habsburg Empire.[68] Yet the Austrian delegates would wait in vain for actual negotiations, and their hopes for a lenient peace settlement would be sorely disappointed.

Essentially, rather than setting out to inflict a harsh peace on it the victorious powers largely neglected Austria and never focused on making something akin to an actual Austrian settlement. Rather, particularly the main decisions that would affect Austria's new borders were made by commissions that had been established to prepare other territorial settlements – like those setting Poland's and Czechoslovakia's borders. And they were decisively influenced by

---

[65] Lloyd George (1938), II, p. 23; Mantoux (1992), I, pp. 459–60; Low (1974), pp. 324–5.
[66] Council of Four, 30 April 1919, FRUS-PPC, V, p. 369.
[67] Almond and Lutz (1935), p. 226; Gerwarth (2016), pp. 110–11; Suppan (2019), pp. 90–101.
[68] Report by W.H. Beveridge, 17 January 1919, CAB 24/74/70; Coolidge report from Vienna, 7 April 1919, FRUS-PPC, XII, pp. 287–8.

those who actually had seats at the negotiating table and could stake their claims, as the Czechoslovak representatives did for Bohemia and their Polish counterparts did for Galicia – while Italian leaders of course insisted on their claims to the South Tyrol in the Council of Four.

In the end, on 2 June, Austria's plenipotentiaries would be presented with a largely improvised peace treaty that in core aspects was modelled on the German draft treaty and, in relative terms, distinctly harsher – leaving them shocked and utterly disillusioned. The treaty's terms confirmed not only that Austria would have to cede the South Tyrol to Italy, but that a total of roughly three million German-speaking Austrians would hence become minorities outside the fledgling republic's borders. In a speech he gave after his return to Vienna, Bauer protested that "(n)o less than two-fifths of [Austria's] population are to be subjected to foreign domination, without any plebiscite and against their indisputable will being thus deprived of their right of self-determination".[69]

Eventually, the victors would agree to a plebiscite in one minor case – to decide the future status of the area around Klagenfurt that was under dispute between Austria and Yugoslavia (and when the plebiscite was held in October 1920, a majority would vote in favour of staying with Austria). But overall, what Bauer had decried would come to pass and on 10 September was enshrined in the Treaty of Saint-German, which the Austrian government signed with the greatest reluctance and under duress. In this treaty, the Austrian Republic would be compelled, alongside Hungary, not only to pay back the war debts the Austro-Hungarian Empire had incurred but also to make reparations. In Bauer's verdict, what the victors imposed was bound to lead the "bankruptcy of the [Austrian] state" – and Austria's reparation obligations would in fact be suspended in 1921 on account of its evident inability to meet them.[70]

V.   Limited Advances. The Western Powers, the Minority Problem and the Longer-Term Challenges of the Polish-German Conflict and Eastern Europe's Pacification

The manner in which the political map of eastern Europe was remade in 1919 thus created multiple new conflicts over borders and minorities, and it indeed created deep sources of both local and regional instability. But in the altered geopolitical constellation the Great War had left behind what occurred in the Balkans or other relatively "peripheral" East European regions was arguably less critical for the maintenance of "world peace" than it had been up until 1914. The main danger was no longer that local crises here would

---

[69] Cited after MacMillan (2002), p. 250.
[70] Halstead report, Vienna, 14 June 1919, *FRUS-PPC*, XII, p. 531; Stadler (1966), pp. 136–41; MacMillan (2002), pp. 243–56; Suppan (2019), pp. 102–114.

spark another world war. The new crucial eastern fault line of the postwar Atlantic order would now run through "northern Central Europe". It would be demarcated by the Polish–German border; and the critical structural antagonism that had the potential to cause instability on a much wider scale would be that which divided Weimar Germany and the new Polish state.

In hindsight, it is obviously difficult to avoid assessing the outcomes of 1919 through the lens of the 1930s – in the light of the fact that Hitler would ultimately be able to exploit German grievances vis-à-vis Poland and that it was Nazi Germany's attack on Poland that led into the abyss of the Second World War. In fact, the decisions of 1919 did not inevitably lead to the catastrophe of 1939. But they did create immense *long-term* challenges. It is therefore all the more important to gain a clearer understanding of these challenges. And it is no less important to assess, from the perspective of 1919, not only how the principal peacemakers perceived and interpreted them but also how they actually envisaged coming to terms with them. More broadly, what thus has to be re-appraised is how far those who directed the policies of the western powers could reach a basic consensus on what kind of longer-term engagement the powers they represented should, and could, pursue to stabilise and foster security in one of postwar Europe's most unsettled regions.

It was no coincidence that – as will be shown – Brockdorff-Rantzau and other German protagonists would concentrate their largely futile efforts to negotiate modifications of the victors' peace terms above all on minimising population and territorial "losses" to Poland; and that they would invoke German claims to self-determination most insistently in this case.[71] For they rightly concluded that of all the peace conditions this would be the one the German public would find most difficult to accept. Indeed, though one may argue in retrospect that it was far from draconian and did take German concerns into account, the "settlement" the victors envisaged was bound to provoke irredentist sentiments and concomitant revisionist demands not just in nationalist quarters but across the German political spectrum. These would be intensified by the representatives of those who now protested against becoming minorities under Polish rule and nationalist and other agitators and public opinion-makers who had already raised unrealistic expectations and would now clamour for "righting the wrong" done to Germany. It thus could be expected that, particularly if the victors insisted on imposing them without any substantial negotiations, these "eastern terms" would be at the core of what would make the entire peace settlement illegitimate in the eyes of an overwhelming majority in Germany.[72]

---

[71] Dresel to House, 21 April, House Papers; Brockdorff-Rantzau memorandum of conversation with Dresel, 19 April 1919, *ADAP*, A/I, pp. 423–4.
[72] See Schattkowsky (1999), pp. 524–30.

All of this not only put the new Polish state in a precarious position. It also created immense liabilities for those who sought to stabilise a German republic and to promote its accommodation with the western powers and in a western-dominated postwar international order. It was bound to create immense domestic-political pressure on every German government to contest the new status quo in the east and to commit to a revisionist policy vis-à-vis Poland. On these premises, any advances towards a more constructive German policy, and attitude, towards the reconfigured Polish state – towards a mutual accommodation of interests and concerns rather than simply a "negative" pursuit of revisionist interests – were extremely hard to envisage and to legitimise in Germany. The problem was compounded by underlying nationalist sentiments and a historically shaped, and widespread, German sense of superiority and disdain vis-à-vis "the Poles", which were now suffused with resentments caused by a defeat that many refused to face up to. Undoubtedly, significant political changes, yet also more fundamental changes in mentality, were thus required if any progress towards more constructive relations with Poland was to be made. More ominous still in the longer run was that the new status quo between Germany and Poland was likely to strengthen the appeal of more hard-line German nationalists who could seize on the "plight" of the German minorities to prepare the ground for a more general assault – not only on a "vindictive" and "humiliating" peace settlement but also on the fledgling Republic of Weimar.[73]

While having to struggle to lay the groundwork for a modern Polish state, the new political leaders in Warsaw thus faced the looming threat of a hostile German neighbour, a neighbour that was set to be weakened and constrained for the foreseeable future but nonetheless intrinsically far more powerful. To some extent the future course of Poland's relations with Germany would be affected by Polish conduct vis-à-vis German minorities; and it would also be influenced by the degree to which Polish policymakers either felt compelled to pursue assertive policies that provoked German nationalist reactions – or whether they would find ways to moderate strong the Polish nationalism that had been intensified through the war and to seek, as far as possible, some kind of accommodation of interests with Germany. And it would depend on whether Polish leaders, in their search for security, would be driven to align with France's containment policies, or whether they would feel at all reassured by the kind of guarantees the Anglo-American powers were proposing – essentially through the League. But the means and room to manoeuvre Polish decision-makers had to ensure Poland's future security and integrity were relatively limited.

---

[73] On the general problem see Krüger (1985), p. 58 and ff.; Schattkowsky (1994).

As we have seen, particularly British and American decision-makers saw the danger that minority conflicts and concomitant irredentist and revisionist tendencies would pose, particularly in the case of Germany. At one level, they tried to alleviate the long-term problems the Polish-German settlement created by introducing not radically new but more elaborate and, so they hoped, more effective forms of minority protection. Not least due to the lobbying efforts of Jewish and other pressure-groups, both the political leaders and even more so the leading experts of the Anglo-American powers had come to recognise that it was critical to address the newly virulent issue of how to safeguard the claims and "rights" of the multiple ethnic – and religious – minorities that all newly established east European states would comprise – even if they tried to limit the problem by setting borders with scrupulous attention to "lines of allegiance and nationality".[74]

In retrospect, it has been estimated that the "post-imperial" reorganisation of Central and Eastern Europe that took place in 1918 and 1919 reduced the total number of people considered minorities in this region from roughly sixty million to less than thirty million. But the intensification of conflicts between different national groups and the clash of radicalised notions of ethnic nationalism that the Great War had brought, and that continued after the armistice, created highly inauspicious conditions for future relations between majority and minority populations in de facto multi-ethnic "new" states of Eastern Europe. This made it all the more imperative to create not only a legal but also a political framework to address the claims and secure or protect the "rights" of minorities – but at the same time created conditions in which any such measures would only have a limited effect.

Particularly the leading experts and decision-makers of the Anglo-American powers understood, too, that the way in which they dealt with this issue would have consequences not only for the consolidation of the new states – where inter-ethnic violence flared up time and again in 1919 – but also for the prospects of international peace and stability. It was to be expected that all states that had lost populations to neighbouring states under the new order would seize on the plight and alleged or de facto discrimination of the new minorities to advance their irredentist claims. Yet, as not only Lloyd George and Wilson stressed, nowhere could this problem have more ominous implications for Europe's overall pacification than in the case of Poland and its relations with Germany. While American and British representatives basically agreed on the need for more effective measures to protect minorities, and the French government came to support their efforts, there was no agreement at all about what form such measures were to take – and what role the League was to play in addressing this highly sensitive issue.

---

[74] Leeper and Nicolson memorandum, 13 December 1918, FO 371/4355/f68/PC68.

At the outset of the peace conference – and palpably influenced by the pressure of the American Jewish Committee and the American Jewish Congress to establish a "Bill of Rights" for Jewish minorities – Wilson indeed contemplated a more ambitious approach. He envisioned creating a general regime for the protection of the rights of *all* ethnic and religious minorities, which would be anchored in supervised by the League of Nations. His amended covenant draft of 18 January 1919 had contained specific provisions to this effect – and the real target of these provisions had been the fledgling states of eastern Europe.[75] But the American president would soon distance himself from this far-reaching aim. He began to question how an organisation like the League – and thus ultimately its leading members, including the United States – would be capable of enforcing a universal regime of this kind, which ultimately meant to hold states accountable and to intervene or sanction particular states if the "rights" of minorities were violated. With the benefit of hindsight, it indeed seems highly doubtful that such universal schemes, which again placed enormous responsibilities on the yet-to-be-established institution of the league, were at all realistic under the prevailing conditions – and whether, more importantly, they would offer effective remedies to the post–First World War minority problems of Eastern Europe, particularly those that threatened to poison Polish-German relations. Of more immediate import for Wilson, however, was another concern – namely the fundamental concern to uphold the pre-eminence of state sovereignty also in this vital respect. And this concern led him, as well as American legal experts, to fall back on a different, more conservative "solution". They came to support specific minority treaties that were to be concluded between the principal Allied and Associated Powers and the emerging states of eastern Europe.

Essentially, it became evident during the negotiations that aspirations to advance towards a universal League-based regime for the protection of minorities collided with core attributes of state sovereignty that not only Wilson but also the leaders of the British and French governments sought to preserve. In short, they were not willing to grant the League general authority to act in the manner of a "super state" that protected the rights of minorities and had general authority to interfere in the internal affairs of states. This was another instance in which – as in the case of collective security – 1919 clearly manifested the limits the principal powers set in safeguarding vital aspects of their sovereignty. Instead, the victors came to adopt the more limited and indeed hierarchical approach of working out specific minority-protection treaties that they then compelled certain states to sign. This above all applied to the new Polish state and other fledgling states of Central and Eastern Europe that

---

[75] Wilson covenant draft, ca. 18 January 1919, *PWW*, LIV, pp. 138–48; Marshall to Wilson, 7 November 1918, *PWW*, LI, pp. 226–7; Fink (2004), pp. 117, 153–4

behind closed doors were categorised as "immature" and so untrustworthy in their likely behaviour towards the ethnic and religious minorities within their borders that they required outside interference and an international "code of conduct" underwritten by the "more civilised" principal powers. The provisions of these minority treaties were subsequently worked out in the Committee on New States, where British and American experts took the lead. Decisive for this shift were British pressure and an emerging Anglo-American consensus in which the French delegation eventually acquiesced.

The British government strongly resisted the idea of addressing minority problems through a general League regime. Headlam-Morley insisted that the British delegation could not accept any scheme that empowered the League to interfere in the domestic affairs of every state that had to deal with minority issues, because such a scheme would ultimately annul the sovereignty of states, which still had to be safeguarded as one of the fundamental principles of the postwar international order. Later Headlam-Morley argued that Britain had a legitimate interest in preventing the League from being turned into a "super state" that was authorised to overrule Britain in order to "protect the Chinese in Liverpool" and to deal with the "far more serious problems" that existed in Ireland. Instead, and in accordance with Lloyd George's preferences and the prevalent consensus in the British Foreign Office, British experts recommended building on the precedent of nineteenth-century European great-power practices, particularly those adopted at the Congress of Berlin of 1878. In short, they suggested that the western governments should draft "special" minority treaties that would oblige the "new and immature" states of Eastern Europe, and above all Poland, to guarantee the political, cultural and religious rights of minority populations within their borders.[76]

The US legal adviser Manley Hudson, who also sat on the Committee on New States, fundamentally agreed with Headlam-Morley. Arguing that "as a practical measure", self-determination had "very definite limits". He likewise proposed a less aspirational "solution" and also found it advisable to fall back on pre-war European norms and practices. Hudson argued that specific "minority treaties" were the most effective instruments to "protect the peoples and nationalities concerned" in the wake of the far-reaching "territorial changes" that had to be made in Eastern Europe – and to ensure that the peace did not mean "for numerous discontented groups the exchange of one bad master for another". In his interpretation, such treaties had to include binding provisions for "securing equality in the enjoyment of political, religious, and cultural liberty to all citizens without distinction as to race or language or religion". In Hudson's view, these treaties thus were to prevent

---

[76] Headlam-Morley minute, 20 November 1918, FO 371/4353. See also Percy note, January 1919, Miller (1928), II, p. 130.

the Polish state from embarking on "Polonising" policies in precisely the manner in which Imperial Germany had pursued Germanising policies in Polish-speaking provinces before the war.[77] This was the approach that Wilson would come to back.

The most important result of the emerging Anglo-American agreement was the Polish minority treaty that Lloyd George and Wilson would then – with Clemenceau's grudging consent – impose on the Polish government. Under the terms of this treaty, the Polish state pledged to guarantee "the full and complete protection of life and liberty to all inhabitants . . . without distinction of birth, nationality, language, race, or religion". Minority populations were to be "equal before the law" as Polish citizens and as such "enjoy the same civil and political rights"; they were to be entitled to the "free exercise" of "any creed, religion or belief" not "inconsistent with public order or public morals"; and they were entitled to use their language "in the courts" and to establish and manage schools and "educational establishments" where they also were granted the right to "use their own language" within them. Further, German minorities were entitled to receive financial support from the government in Berlin to preserve their German language and heritage.

Significantly, the treaty conferred responsibility for enforcing its provisions and dealing with "infractions" of its provisions by the Polish state to the League Council, not the League Assembly. At the same time, it stipulated that only a member of the League Council – i.e. one of the great powers or non-permanent members, yet not representatives of the minorities themselves – would have the "right" to bring violations to its attention. If a council member demanded it minority disputes would be treated as international disputes and could "be referred to the Permanent Court of International Justice". Yet decisions about which violations were to be addressed and what measures would be taken to sanction them would thus ultimately lie largely in the hands of the principal victors. All of this was intended to prevent either the minority representatives or, more importantly, powers with irredentist agendas and grievances – like Germany – from using the League as a forum for revisionist "crusades".[78]

The Polish treaty became the prototype for a string of a total of seven further minority treaties that the victors subsequently foisted on the other emerging East European states, including Czechoslovakia. These essentially Anglo-American minority treaties were hailed by some of the proponents of enhanced minority protection as a significant advance, offering in each case a "bill of rights" for minorities. The peacemakers themselves reckoned that the treaties would at least help to foster an accommodation, if not a reconciliation then a bearable and peaceful *modus vivendi* between the different minority

---

[77] Hudson (1921), pp. 203, 216.
[78] Fink (1998), pp. 269–70; Viefhaus (1960), pp. 162 ff.

populations and the states under whose rule they would hence live; and that this in turn – particularly in the German case – would lessen their desires to be reunited with their own kin as well as, crucially, dampen postwar Germany's irredentist ambitions.

In some respects, the minority treaties can indeed be seen as an important and necessary step on the extremely difficult path of coming to terms with the minority problems and the wider problem of inter-ethnic and inter-nationalist antagonisms that the Great War and its aftermath had created or intensified. They could potentially help to lessen the danger of escalating conflicts between majority and minority populations in the East European states – and to make the living conditions relatively more acceptable for specific minorities. But of course they could offer only partial remedies. One important condition for their success was that the governments of the new states basically accepted and had the will to fulfil the treaties' obligations. But they were contested and severely criticised by those who would have to execute and abide by them – above all the representatives of the Polish government, whose positions in turn reflect those of public opinion-makers in and beyond Warsaw.

Dmowski and Paderewski would ultimately sign the Polish Minority Treaty on 28 June, but did so under protest. More importantly, the treaty would be resented in Poland as a dictated "little Versailles", a document that imposed great-power limitations on the new state's sovereignty and was informed by a high-handed western paternalism vis-à-vis the "reborn" Polish nation. Paderewski was not only concerned that it would give German minorities disproportionate influence and strengthen the centrifugal forces that were threatening the cohesion of the Polish state, but also warned that it would create a new "Jewish problem".[79] At the same time, the treaty itself could hardly satisfy those minority populations who were unwilling to accept their new status; nor could they satisfy the Weimar German government or the wider German public and publicised opinion.

In the longer run, even if Polish authorities were willing to fulfil their obligations the minority treaties could only address certain concerns; they could not provide remedies for the more fundamental problem posed by the Polish-German antagonism. Of vital importance was how those who repre-sented the victorious powers envisaged coming to terms with this larger problem in the longer run. For their approaches and decisions would shape not just the geopolitical environment but also the international system, or framework, in which a highly unstable German republic and an as yet frail Polish state would operate. They could significantly widen or lessen the room to manoeuvre that political actors on the German as well as the Polish side had to pursue accommodating rather than antagonistic policies. And they were of

[79] Paderewski to Lloyd George, 15 June 1919, Lloyd George Papers, F57/5/2.

course especially critical for Poland's postwar security. In short, however, the victors could never agree on what policies and what mechanisms would be required to deal with these vital longer-term challenges. At a deeper level, they could never reach a common understanding on how far, and how, they would act as guardians of order and guarantors of international security that oversaw longer-term processes of conflict management – not only between Germany and Poland but also in eastern Europe more generally.

This was not only due to their preoccupation with a daunting array of more pressing issues, not least the delineation of borders. It can also be attributed to the fact that they continued to pursue strikingly divergent longer-term conceptions, conceptions that were influenced by very different sets of interests, political priorities and domestic-political concerns. Here too the divergences were most pronounced between French and, broadly speaking, Anglo-American approaches. And what proved even more critical with a view to Western Europe was the – limited – extent to which the British and American protagonists were prepared to countenance more substantial long-term responsibilities, and the fact that they considered it politically impossible to legitimise wider commitments in the east in their own countries.

The outlook of Clemenceau, Tardieu as well as Pichon and leading strategists at the Quai d'Orsay on France's relations with Poland and the new states of Eastern Europe did not change in the course of the peace conference. In many ways, they pursued the most consistent strategy and indeed a new regional conception of order for Eastern and Central Europe, which was also backed by France's military leaders. At the same time, however, theirs was also the most traditionalist strategy, shaped by classic geopolitical and balance-of-power calculations. In the conceptions of virtually all leading French policymakers, the longer-term role that was ascribed particularly to Poland and Czechoslovakia was that of "barrier states" within the *complementary* East European security system they sought to consolidate around Germany – and in which the League played at best a peripheral role.

Though Tardieu concluded that Poland and Czechoslovakia did "not yet count" as a power-political "counter-weight" that could off-set the "loss" of Russia, French strategists nonetheless planned to fortify them as integral parts of the *cordon sanitaire* they aspired to create between Germany and Russia – for the eventuality that, in the increasingly likely worst-case scenario, the latter would fall to the Bolsheviks. As Clemenceau later put it, the new or revived East European states were thus supposed to provide an "indispensable source of support" against the "eternal pan-German dream of [a German-dominated] *Mitteleuropa*" and renewed "German designs for hegemony in Europe".[80]

---

[80] Tardieu memorandum, 25 February 1919, in Tardieu (II/1921), pp. 156, 161–2; Clemenceau statement, December 1919, cited after Jackson (2013), p. 364. See also Clemenceau statement, Council of Four, 2 June 1919, Mantoux (1992), II, p. 273.

And the new Poland was and remained the most important strategic partner in all French schemes to this end.

The longer-term role Clemenceau and Tardieu envisaged France to play was essentially that of a guarantor and patron power that safeguarded the security and integrity of the Polish state – like that of Czechoslovakia – ultimately by power-political means. In the spring and summer of 1919, their primary interest clearly lay in establishing a longer-term security community with Britain and the United States. And there were not yet any concrete plans to extend more specific guarantees to or conclude actual alliances with Poland – or Czechoslovakia. But this remained the essential fall-back orientation of French policy if the desired Anglo-American guarantees did not materialise. And France would eventually indeed conclude defensive alliances with Poland, in February 1921, and Czechoslovakia, in January 1924.[81]

Crucially, following the logic of balance-of-power politics, the French protagonists deemed it not only futile but actually counterproductive to seek to de-escalate what they saw as an inevitable Polish-German conflicts, let alone to remove obstacles to some form of accommodation between Poland and Germany in the longer run. Rather, they envisaged a sustained cooperation with Poland in efforts to reinforce the status quo the victors had hammered out at the peace conference – where, as they saw it, undue concessions had been made to the defeated power. And they reckoned that the most effective way of improving Poland's – and France's – security and development prospects was to aid the Polish state in consolidating and improving its military capacities, and to encourage it to settle its differences with Czechoslovakia and its other east European neighbours.[82] The main problem the French approach raised was not only that it would burden Poland – like Czechoslovakia, and France itself – with heavy power-political responsibilities but also that it was highly likely to exacerbate the German-Polish conflict scenario.

What the main British and American actors envisaged and sought to achieve was markedly different, and it was essentially incompatible with the Clemenceau government's strategic priorities. The underlying rationale of the longer-term eastern policy Lloyd George and his advisers developed at Versailles, above all with a view to the Polish-German settlement, had been to minimise right from the start the potential for future conflicts that would require future British involvement and possibly another military intervention on the European continent. As the British premier confirmed in late May, the priority he thus pursued was to pre-empt "trouble within the next twenty

---

[81] See Jackson (2013), pp. 364–7, 417–18.

[82] For underlying continuities in French eastern policy see: See French Foreign Ministry memorandum on "peace conditions", 26 November 1918, transmitted to Balfour, FO/ 371/3446; "Pologne" committee minutes, 29 January 1919, Europe 1918–29, Pologne (68), MAE.

years" – and to avoid putting Britain in a position where it would either have to "wage war" to "enforce" the terms of the peace treaty or to accept its "abrogation".[83] But a majority in the British government, and delegation, came to conclude that the preliminary settlement the victors had hammered out would not meet these criteria. In their eyes, it was likely to create a status quo that – despite the modifications Lloyd George had obtained – would prove untenable in the longer run. Particularly the creation of the "Polish Corridor" and the preliminary decision to accord Upper Silesia to Poland caused serious concerns. In contrast to the leading experts Tyrrell and Howard, Lloyd George and other leading politicians viewed the consolidation prospects of the as yet distinctly frail new Polish state with marked scepticism. And they viewed its political leaders with suspicion and some condescension, hardly trusting them to manoeuvre with sufficient restraint vis-à-vis Germany. In turn, this assessment only heightened the fear that the precarious Polish-German constellation would become a seedbed for future conflicts.[84]

First of all, such concerns led influential voices in the British delegation – including Cecil and Smuts, yet also Bonar Law – to urge Lloyd George to seek further revisions to the draft treaty that accommodated German interests and claims. Yet it is important to understand that they also reinforced another underlying tendency, which imposed clear limits on British policies in 1919 and foreshadowed those of future British conduct vis-à-vis central and eastern Europe. Essentially, not only the prime minister himself but a clear majority in the British delegation rejected any wider commitments – *or more direct, tangible guarantees* – that would have obliged Britain to take on the role of a "guardian power" or underwriter of the postwar status quo on the Polish-German border and in the wider East European context. They did so precisely because they viewed it as a region that would remain highly volatile and conflict-prone for the foreseeable future.

In the future scenario the key actors envisioned, Britain might pursue a limited diplomatic engagement as "honest broker" with limited liability. Its decision-makers and diplomats would seek to foster the pacific settlement or at least management of disputes – also in the framework of the League. Yet they would not make commitments beyond those stipulated in the League Covenant. They would not contemplate giving more specific security guarantees to Poland or Czechoslovakia that would have obliged Britain to intervene on their behalf, and in a part of Europe where – and in prevailing perception – no *essential* British economic, political or security interests were at stake. In their assessment, limited British resources had to be concentrated on meeting more vital west European and imperial challenges. And Lloyd George was not the only

---

[83] Lloyd George to Bonar Law, 31 March 1919, Lloyd George Papers, F/30/3/40.
[84] Lloyd George to Bonar Law, 31 March 1919, Lloyd George Papers, F/30/3/40; Cecil to Lloyd George, 27 May 1919, Cecil Papers, Add. 51076.

British politician who argued, and believed, that British "public opinion" would not accept any more far-reaching obligations in Eastern Europe.[85]

Instead of considering more specific regional commitments or guarantees, some British policymakers turned their attention to the League. While Lloyd George maintained a more sceptical attitude particularly Cecil recommended the League as the mechanism that could hence provide framework of order, *general* guarantees to Poland and other east European states and, above all, the wherewithal to settle or at least manage those disputes that had not been resolved or even been aggravated at the peace conference. Cecil held that in order to reduce the danger that German irredentism would provoke another war it was all the more imperative not just to admit Germany to the League in the near future but, more importantly, to accommodate it in a reconfigured concert of the great powers. He argued that this would not only foster the commitment of German political leaders to the ground-rules of pacific settlement but also give them incentives to accept these rules.[86] This was a rationale that Lloyd George espoused as well. More generally, it seems not too far-fetched to conclude that precisely because the key British actors desired to avoid entanglements and obligations in eastern Europe, their emerging "strategy" to come to terms with the longer-term challenges of insecurity in the east focused on Germany. Indeed, the British premier thought that the most realistic way of meeting these challenges was to bring a German state that accepted the victors' terms relatively quickly not just into the League but essentially into a new concert of great powers. The underlying assumption was that promoting such a process could *eventually* create more conducive conditions for de-escalating the Polish–German conflict – and possibly even for peaceful, mutually acceptable modifications of a territorial status quo he continued to regard as precarious.[87]

Cecil, who came to regard the envisaged Polish-German border settlement as incompatible with the requirements of a "solid peace", went one step further. He had earlier sought to make the League into an institution that, while protecting the integrity of its members, actually developed and established procedures and rules for a peaceful change of the territorial or political status quo in cases where this was deemed necessary in the interest of "world peace". And he evidently had the Polish-German problem in mind when he proposed, after the victors' draft treaty had been finalised, that the League

---

[85] Lloyd George, Fontainebleau memorandum, 25 March 1919, *PWW*, LVI, pp. 259–67; Cecil to Lloyd George, 27 May 1919, Cecil Papers, Add. 51076; Smuts letter to Wilson and Lloyd George, 14 May 1919, Lloyd George Papers, F/45/9/34; British Empire Delegation minutes, 33, 1 June 1919, CAB 29/28.

[86] Cecil to Lloyd George, 27 May 1919, Cecil Papers, Add. 51076.

[87] See Lloyd George statements, British Empire Delegation minutes, 33, 1 June 1919, CAB 29/28.

should be given greater authority to act as an agency of peaceful change than had been stipulated in the original Draft Covenant. He argued that it should be empowered, within a postwar adjustment period of maximally five years, to make changes to any terms of the peace treaty that had come to be seen as endangering peace and international stability. Yet such a far-reaching proposal had no prospect of gaining the endorsement of the French government. And, as will be seen, Wilson would also reject it because he concluded that implementing it would actually have more destabilising than stabilising consequences in eastern Europe – and on a global scale.[88]

The American president had indeed become noticeably more cognisant of the wider implications of the Polish-German dilemma – and to a lesser extent he had also become more aware of how massive a challenge the stabilisation and pacification of eastern Europe represented. But, reflecting his overall outlook and the views that prevailed in the US peace delegation, he essentially did *not* change his distinctly general conception of how to come to terms with this dilemma and this wider challenge – which he indeed interpreted as *longer-term* challenge – once the initial peace settlement had been made. Essentially, he adhered to the view that once it was set up the League would play the decisive role. In the future scenario Wilson mapped out, the League would not only guarantee the security and integrity of Poland – and its other new east European member states; it would also become the decisive agency that would enable political decision-makers to pursue step-by-step processes of settling disputes, including those dividing Germany and Poland, and habituate all sides to non-violent ways of managing conflict –within a successively more favourable international environment created by the new organisation's umbrella of "collective security". Wilson clung to the maxim that it would thus be possible, also in eastern Europe, to cope with conflicts that, as he saw it, simply could not yet be settled, or could only be dealt with in a very limited way, in the immediate aftermath of the war.[89] And most US experts, though clearly more conscious of the intricacies of specific border and minority problems, tended to agree with the president.

It is important to understand in this context that Wilson also clung to another core *medium-term* rationale. It concerned Germany's future integration into the progressive order he sought to create – and it was by and large compatible with the aims of Cecil and Lloyd George. While resolved to impose a period of probation on the fledgling German republic he too reckoned that it would be critical for the stabilisation of Central and Eastern Europe, and the security of Poland, to include Germany in the League in the near future and thereby to commit its new political leaders to the organisation's rules and

---

[88] Cecil statements, 6 and 11 February 1919, Miller (1928), I, pp. 168–70, 201–11; Cecil Diary, 20 and 25 May, 1 June 1919, Cecil Papers, 51331.

[89] Wilson statement, 14 February 1919, *PWW*, LV, p. 175.

obligations of peaceful conflict resolution. More fundamentally, for all of his reservations vis-à-vis the Ebert-Scheidemann government the American president still believed that in the longer run this could habituate not only German policymakers but also the wider German public to the "civilised" practices and understandings that were to govern international relations between democratic states. And he assumed that this would also have a moderating impact on German conduct vis-à-vis Poland and its other eastern neighbours.[90]

But in contrast to Cecil, Wilson maintained his distance from earlier conceptions of turning the League into a mechanism of "peaceful change". As noted, in his "Paris Draft" of the Covenant of mid-January 1919 he had still included specific provisions for effecting changes in the international order and, notably, "territorial readjustments", if these seemed warranted on grounds of "self-determination" or if the member states, and *all* of the affected parties, concluded that this was desirable in the interest of "the peace of the world".[91] But by the time the victors argued over the German-Polish border settlement the American president had abandoned this plan and changed his emphasis. He had evidently concluded that in order to foster the stabilisation of the volatile new international order, particularly in Central and Eastern Europe, it was more important to underscore that the League's core purpose was to protect the political independence and territorial integrity of its member states – and especially smaller states. He thus also refuted Cecil's proposal. And he now stressed his fear that if the League was empowered to change territorial or any other provisions of the peace settlement in the interest of global peace, it would be overwhelmed, and postwar stability would be jeopardised, because then all states – or national groups – that had not been satisfied by the settlement would be encouraged to appeal to the League to seek redress for their grievances. This also, and notably, applied to Germany. Wilson thus insisted successfully that there was to be no amendment to the League Covenant that added explicit provisions and procedures for "peaceful change". And he argued that issues like the German–Polish border dispute were to be addressed like all other international disputes, namely through the Covenant's provisions for arbitration and pacific settlement.[92]

Essentially, then, and unsurprisingly, Wilson thus clearly intended to focus future American engagement as guarantor and arbiter of international order in central and eastern Europe on the League. Setting even clearer limits than with a view to France and Western Europe, the American president did *not* intend the United States to assume the role of a "European power" that extended more specific guarantees to Poland or the other new East

---

[90] Council of Four, 1 April 1919, Mantoux (1992), I, p. 106.
[91] Wilson's second "Paris Draft" of the Covenant, 18 January 1918, *PWW*, LIV, pp. 140, 138–48.
[92] Miller (1928), I, pp. 168–70, 201–11.

European states or took on more direct responsibilities as a hegemonic mediator. Still seeking to transform international politics through the League, Wilson did not desire American governments to become more immediately and constantly involved in complex inner-European disputes. Unquestionably, the American president was also influenced by domestic considerations. These were not decisive in this case; but he was clearly aware that it would have been extremely difficult to persuade the US Congress, and the American public, that the United States was called upon to assume more far-reaching commitments in a part of Europe that seemed particularly remote and where no tangible American economic or security interests seemed to be at stake in the foreseeable future.

Finally, it should be emphasised that what the American president envisaged was destined to saddle the novel institution of the League with far-reaching and onerous responsibilities – in Danzig, and on a far grander scale vis-à-vis Poland and eastern Europe. The League would require time, the consistent support of its key members and the inclusion of *all* relevant parties even to have the *potential* to play the role Wilson wanted it to play. And how far the United States would assume a prominent role in any League efforts to pacify Eastern Europe was of course also still dependent on Wilson's ability to gain the requisite domestic support for US membership.

Yet there was an even more fundamental problem. It remained to be seen whether a universal institution like the League could ever become an effective instrument for dealing with complex, multi-layered and high-stakes problems such as the Polish-German question – or whether more specific *regional* mechanisms and approaches would have to be found.

18

A Formative Threat?
The Western Powers and the Bolshevik Challenge

Not only the tasks of reordering Eastern Europe and hammering out the terms of the German settlement but also the broader undertaking of laying foundations for a new Atlantic order were made even more intractable by the unprecedented and incalculable challenges that the existence and aspirations of the Bolshevik regime posed from the perspectives of the western powers. And the peacemakers now also had to grapple with what Wilson called the "curious poison" of Bolshevism's ideological and political challenge not only to Europe's collapsing "old order" but also to his own aspirations to expand a system of democratic *and* liberal-capitalist states in an evolutionary manner.[1] And yet it has to be stressed once again that the significance the "Bolshevik factor" had for the peace negotiations of 1919 – and for the ways in which the basic nature and ground-rules of the newly configured Atlantic order would be determined – should not be overemphasised either. In short, it did affect these processes, but it did not affect them decisively. This was not the "moment" in which the struggle over the shape of the twentieth century's international order essentially turned into one between Wilsonian and Leninist aspirations and, at a different level, into an ever more all-encompassing competition between US modes of liberal and capitalist "order" and Soviet communism.[2]

In concrete terms, the leaders of the western powers first of all had to reach some kind of consensus on a question that had divided them ever since the spring of 1918 – namely what policies they should pursue in the face of the on-going civil war in Russia, a conflict whose outcome was still unforeseeable by the time they first deliberated the issue in the Supreme Council in mid-January 1919. They had to decide whether to expand their military intervention, i.e. commit more troops and step up aid to the – rivalling – counter-revolutionary forces under Denikin and Kolchak. And they ultimately had to assess whether there was any realistic prospect of inflicting a decisive military defeat on the Bolshevik regime. As will be shown, the opposition of Wilson and Lloyd George to an expanded intervention would set decisive limits here. And it

[1] Grayson (1960), p. 85.
[2] For different interpretations, see Engerman (2010), pp. 20 ff.; Westad (2018), pp. 19 ff.; and the classic Mayer (1967), esp. pp. 284 ff.

was only now, when they had to face up to the possibly far-reaching implications of a more interventionist approach – and their own constraints – that the
victors, and notably the British premier, gave more serious consideration to
possible alternatives: initiatives to promote a truce between the different
warring parties in (and beyond) Russia and ultimately even the perspective
of negotiating some kind of *modus vivendi* with the Bolshevik leaders. Lloyd
George went so far as to argue that no durable peace could not be made
without coming to terms with Russia's "*de facto* Government".[3]

But steps to this end remained half-hearted, and futile. That no progress
towards anything approaching a mutually acceptable "agreement" between the
western governments and the Bolsheviks would be made in 1919 was not just
due to the fact that the Big Three could never really agree on a common
approach and on what kind of agreement they should actually seek – not least
because Clemenceau and other French policymakers in fact continued to
oppose negotiations and still preferred a more aggressive approach. More
fundamentally, there was simply no real basis for more than a most ephemeral
truce in the Russian civil war or, in a wider context, for a more than ephemeral
"balance" between the priorities and interests of the western powers and the
tactical imperatives Lenin pursued at this stage to ensure first of all the survival
of the Bolshevik regime and then to instigate a communist "world revolution".

What the developments of 1919 revealed, then, was that the means and
political room for manoeuvre of the western governments either to influence
the outcome of the Russian civil war in accordance with their interests or
somehow to accommodate and contain the Bolshevik regime within a
western-dominated postwar order were distinctly restricted. And from
March onwards the principal "peacemakers" in Paris would essentially refrain
from any further meaningful attempts to interfere in Russia or to negotiate
with the Bolsheviks; instead, they would focus on "insulating" Germany and
Eastern Europe from the "Bolshevik menace". During the decisive phases of
the "inter-allied" negotiations in March and April, the focus of their attention,
and notably of British and American attention, indeed shifted to the transnational and political-cum-ideological dimension of this menace – the threat
of a "Bolshevisation" of Central Europe, which concerned them more than the
impact of Bolshevism in their own countries. And of critical importance here
was the Bolshevik–German nexus.

As noted, in late March – against the background of continued unrest,
armed clashes and general instability aggravated by Béla Kun's take-over in
Hungary – both Wilson and Lloyd George saw for a time a serious danger that
Germany might actually become the first major industrialised power that
succumbed to Bolshevism's appeal – though both leaders also highlighted this

---

[3] Lloyd George statement, Council of Ten, 12 January 1919, *FRUS-PPC*, III, p. 491.

danger to contain French aspirations. In fact, even after the setbacks the German communists had suffered in January not only Lenin but also Spartacists like Max Levien who sought to follow in the footsteps of the assassinated leaders Luxemburg and Liebknecht deemed it crucial to continue the struggle in Germany and thereby to set the stage for a wider communist revolution.[4]

And Bolshevik efforts to internationalise the revolution had in early March gained a new impetus through the formation of the Third – Communist – International. But despite the interlude of the "Bavarian Soviet republic" (in April) the spectre of a Bolshevised Germany soon became less acute – and, crucially, the principal "peacemakers" in Paris soon *perceived* it as less acute. Indeed, what ultimately influenced the course and outcome of the actual peacemaking process most were the different western *perceptions* and *interpretations* of the Bolshevik threat – and the political use different actors, particularly Wilson and Lloyd George, made of this threat to further their own agendas. But most remarkable in retrospect is *how little* any of this really influenced the crucial German settlement of 1919 or any of the other core negotiations among the victors – or, ultimately, the eventual contours of the limited Atlantic order that had emerged by the end of the peace conference. The hope of Brockdorff-Rantzau and other German policymakers that persistent invocations of the Bolshevik danger would boost their campaign for a "Wilson peace" would clearly be disappointed.

I. Conflicting Assumptions and Approaches. The Victorious Powers, Russian Uncertainties and the Bolshevik Question at the Peace Conference

After the armistice had been concluded in the west, Clemenceau and Pichon had sought to persuade their British and American allies to pursue a hard-line policy – namely to step up the military intervention in Russia and aid to the White forces under Denikin and Kolchak with the aim of toppling the Bolshevik regime, which they still regarded as a realistic option at this stage. Both the French premier and his foreign minister remained profoundly concerned about what they saw as the insidious spread of Bolshevik ideas to the west.[5] But the main motive for their interventionism was and remained power-political. In short, while focusing on forging an alliance with the Anglo-American powers they still acted on the assumption that it would be possible

---

[4] Lenin, Letter to the Workers of Europe and America, 21 January 1919, Lenin (1970), pp. 375–8; Lenin Theses, 4 March 1919, Lenin (1970), pp. 382–3; Service (2000), pp. 384–7.

[5] See Pichon to Clemenceau, 1 October 1918; Clemenceau to Pichon, 11 October 1918, MAE, Série Z, URSS, vols. 208, 210.

to regain a Russian power freed from the scourge of Bolshevism as a key ally in the containment of Germany and French efforts to "re-establish the European balance of power".[6]

Foch and the French army's general staff were even more fervent advocates of an ambitious intervention to "destroy Bolshevism" and "restore order and calm in Russia", thus allowing it to become once again "an important factor in the European balance of forces". They would continue to advance various schemes to this end during the peace conference.[7] French troops had been at the head of a small Allied expeditionary force that had set out from Odessa in mid-December 1918. But Clemenceau and Pichon had to recognise that Wilson and Lloyd George, whose consent was obviously critical for a more large-scale and potentially decisive intervention, were not prepared to go along with the risky course they advocated. And by the time the situation in Russia was discussed in Council of Ten in mid-January, the French protagonists had by and large accepted that they would have to pursue far more limited objectives in the short term: to concentrate on forging a *cordon sanitaire* of East European states against the spread of Bolshevik influence and to block what they dreaded most, an "alliance" between the Bolshevik regime and Germany.[8]

Some similarly strident proponents of an expanded allied intervention against the Bolsheviks were also to be found in the British government. Here, Churchill emerged as the leading figure of a small coterie of anti-Bolshevik interventionists, which also included Curzon and Montagu, who were united in the belief that the Bolshevik regime should and could be defeated by military means. Churchill argued that Bolshevism was distinct from other forms of "visionary political thought" in that it could "only be propagated and maintained by violence". And he proclaimed that under the cloak of Marxist-Bolshevik rhetoric, Lenin and Trotsky were building up and ruthlessly using a centralised party and military machinery and pursuing the most destructive and "degrading" kind of "tyranny" mankind had ever seen, bent on destroying whatever stood in their way. Publicly and behind closed doors, Churchill thus campaigned not just for increased military aid to the "White" forces; without giving any convincing reasons he asserted that a targeted expansion of the western powers' intervention would actually turn the tide in the Russian civil war and lead to a decisive defeat of the Bolshevik

---

[6] Clemenceau to Pichon, 23 October 1918, MAE, Série Z, URSS, vol. 208; Quai d'Orsay memorandum, 4 December 1918, *ibid.*, vol. 210.

[7] General staff note, 17 October 1918, MAE, Série Z, URSS, vol. 208.

[8] French Foreign ministry memorandum, 4 December 1918, MAE, Série Z, URSS, vol. 210; memorandum on "Germano-Russian co-operation", 8 December 1918, Fonds Clemenceau, 6N 73, SHD-DAT. See Stevenson (1982), pp. 163–4; Jackson (2013), pp. 235–7.

regime.[9] Crucially, however, both Lloyd George and Wilson became increasingly determined to oppose any schemes of this kind. Like a majority in his Cabinet the British premier considered what Churchill proposed not only too risky and too costly, underscoring that Britain had neither any funds nor any troops to spare for anything approaching a decisive engagement – and that British public opinion would not support it. He also held, fundamentally, that no outside intervention would alter what he saw as the most likely outcome of the Russian civil war, namely a Bolshevik victory.

While opposing the ideological maxims of the Bolshevik regime and condemning its ferocious methods and use of violence the British premier had by this time come to regard Bolshevism as an understandable, albeit extreme and misguided, reaction to the "tyrannical" and "inept" regimes and hierarchies that had dominated continental Europe's "old order" – and to the ways in which the latter had imposed harsh "exactions" on their populations before and especially during the Great War.[10] Yet one of his underlying assumptions was that European states and societies – especially those in the west, and Germany – were comparatively "strong" and resilient and would be able to resist the allure of Bolshevik propaganda. Sooner rather than later, he reckoned, Bolshevism would "die out" – if two conditions could be met. At one, the domestic level, the postwar governments of the different European states had to pursue substantial reforms not only in the political but also in the economic and social spheres – reforms that brought their peoples concrete benefits and removed the causes – the oppressions and inequities – that had heightened the appeal of Bolshevism in the first place.[11]

At another, international level, Lloyd George would invoke the Bolshevik threat to push for a peace settlement that accorded with his ideas of moderation and "fairness", above all with a view to Germany. And, as we have seen, the crucial argument he came to advance here was that a "just peace" along British lines would be vital not only for containing the westward spread of Bolshevism but also for pre-empting what he too presented as the most disconcerting scenario: an anti-western Russo-German combination under Bolshevik auspices.[12] Essentially, then, what the British premier recommended was to contain and isolate the Bolshevik revolutionaries and thus to bring about the regime's eventual demise. Yet Lloyd George also assumed that while a victory of the Bolshevik regime in the Russian civil war was highly probable it would be possible for the western powers to "tame" it in the shorter term if they refrained from antagonising it and reinforcing popular support for it through the pursuit of futile interventionist designs. And he calculated that,

[9] Gilbert (1975), pp. 277–9, 355–6.
[10] PWW, LVI, p. 247.
[11] Lloyd George (1938), I, pp. 330–1.
[12] Lloyd George, Fontainebleau memorandum, 25 March 1919, PWW, LVI, pp. 261–3.

for the foreseeable future, the Bolshevik leaders would be so absorbed by consolidating their hold on power within Russia that they would pose far less of a threat to Britain's imperial interests, notably in Central Asia and the Middle East, than the Russian Empire had posed before the war.[13]

It was on these premises that the British premier seized the initiative at the very outset of the peace conference to call for a significant shift of the western powers' policies: the abandonment of further interventions and the turn towards efforts to begin negotiations with Bolshevik emissaries – as well as with representatives of the "White" forces. In marked contrast to the approach he had adopted towards Germany, Lloyd George now advanced the argument that it would be impossible to create basic conditions for a stable postwar order without coming to some kind of understanding with those who represented the interests of 200 million Russian people at this juncture. Not least to placate Clemenceau, he stressed the need to involve the representatives of the – rivalling – "White Russian" forces under General Denikin in the south and Admiral Kolchak in Siberia in this process. Yet what lay at the heart of the initiative he proposed was the aim of entering into more substantial negotiations and working out, in one way or another, a mutually acceptable *modus vivendi* with the Bolshevik regime, which he now called Russia's "*de facto* Government". The British premier thus signalled that he was prepared to contemplate extending recognition to Lenin's regime. He argued that the victorious powers had to accept Bolshevik plenipotentiaries as representatives of Russia, observing that the idea that they could "pick" who was the "legitimate" representative of a "great people" was "contrary to every principle" for which they had fought the war.[14]

On 16 January, Lloyd George impressed on his counterparts in the Supreme Council that they had three options. They could either expand two policies that they had already tried to pursue – namely to expand their military intervention and the blockade with the aim of overthrowing the Bolsheviks, or to intensify a policy that sought to create a *cordon sanitaire* and insulate the rest of Europe from the Bolshevik-Russian "disease". But in his judgement the former course carried immense and unacceptable risks and had no realistic prospect of success, while the latter would be very hard to maintain, actually strengthen the Bolsheviks' hold over the Russian people andtake a heavy toll on the "ordinary population", leading to death and "starvation" on a massive scale. He thus proposed an alternative two-stage approach. First, all the warring factions in Russia were to be induced to meet and agree on terms for a truce; then, representatives from all sides would be invited to come to Paris for actual peace negotiations. The scope and remit of

---

[13] See Steiner (2005), p. 139.

[14] Lloyd George statement, Council of Ten, 12 January 1919, *FRUS-PPC*, III, p. 491. See also Cabinet deliberations, Imperial War Cabinet 48, 31 December 1918, CAB 23/42.

these negotiations he left open, having evidently formed no clear idea yet of what direction they should take.[15] Lloyd George's proposal would actually be adopted largely because Wilson came to back it, and because he had developed a similar outlook.

The American president continued to grapple with the problem of formulating a coherent policy vis-à-vis Russia, the Bolshevik regime and what he saw as the ever more acute challenge to counter the westward spread of Bolshevism. Wilson agreed with Lloyd George that an expansion of the Allied intervention in Russia was not only futile but actually counterproductive. He too thought that it was highly unlikely to defeat the Bolsheviks – and he too had concluded that it would be politically impossible, and ill-advised, to gain domestic support for such an incalculable and potentially very costly venture. At the same time, he argued that American and British soldiers, as well as the wider publics in both countries, would oppose a "restoration of the old order, which was even more disastrous than the present one". In fact, this assessment reflected his own views of the situation.[16]

Essentially, however, Wilson had come to believe that the outcome of the Russian conflict could neither be determined nor even decisively influenced by outside forces. In many ways, he thus adhered to the maxim that he had formulated in October 1918: that the Russian peoples had to "work out their own salvation" even if this meant that they passed through a prolonged period of civil war and "anarchy". With a view to Russia, Wilson's understanding of "self-determination" thus implied that the parties engaged in the current conflict, including the Bolsheviks, either had to decide on the battlefield or through negotiations how the vast country would be governed in the future; and only once this had happened could others, including the United States, recognise and "do business" with whichever state and government had emerged. In the Council of Ten he thus insisted that the western powers would be "fighting against the current of the times" if they "tried to prevent Russia from finding her own path in freedom". And he re-affirmed what he had stated in his Fourteen Points: that the Russian people had the right to "direct their own affairs" without "dictation" or "direction of any kind from outside" – which of course was far from corresponding with the realities on the ground in view of the persistent presence of western, including American, troops on Russian soil.[17]

---

[15] Lloyd George statements, Council of Ten, 16 January 1919, *FRUS-PPC*, III, pp. 581–3.
[16] Wilson statements, Council of Ten, 16 January 1919, *FRUS-PPC*, III, pp. 591–3.
[17] Wilson drew an analogy between this and his "Mexican policy" – but de facto the United States had in both cases intervened against the forces of revolution. See Wiseman memorandum, 16 October 1918, *PWW*, LX, p. 350; Wilson proposal, 22 January 1919, then incorporated in the "Allied" note of 23 January 1919, *FRUS-PPC*, III, pp. 676–7.

Interestingly, Wilson appears to have assumed that the shape of the future Russian state would essentially be the same as that of the former Russian Empire. He only excepted Polish claims for the predominantly Polish territories that had been under Russian imperial rule. By contrast, he originally resisted a recognition of the independence claims of the Baltic states; and he at no point supported the claims of Ukrainian nationalists for "self-determination" and an independent Ukrainian state. Yet he also maintained a basic policy of non-recognition, based on the premise that the Bolshevik regime could not be recognised as legitimate representatives of the Russian people, whose democratic aspirations still awaited the establishment of an "orderly free government".[18]

Wilson had not changed his underlying assumptions about the challenges the Bolshevik regime and its considerable appeal far beyond Russia posed – and about how they could be met most effectively. In the meeting of the Supreme Council on 24 January he declared once again that Bolshevism presented "the greatest danger" in Germany and Central Europe, though he undoubtedly did so in part to pressure the *Entente* governments to accept his peace programme.[19] The American president condemned the "brutal" practices of Lenin and those who fought with him, their use of violence, "campaign of murder" and "confiscation" and "complete disregard for law".[20] But he still made a distinction between these practices and what he saw as the underlying reasons both for the rise of Bolshevik ideas and their appeal in and beyond Europe. And this distinction also informed his general assumptions about how Bolshevism could not only be contained but overcome as such, which in some aspects anticipated those underlying Franklin Roosevelt's eventual strategy and later American containment policies vis-à-vis the Soviet Union during the Cold War.

Wilson sought to impress on his European counterparts that Bolshevism had developed such a powerful allure because of "genuine grievances" among the peoples of Europe – and the colonised world – vis-à-vis the governments and economic elites of the "old order" that had accumulated before 1914, and that had then been intensified by the war itself. He noted that its "seeds" could not "flourish without a soil ready to receive them". The "cure", he insisted, lay in "constant discussion and a slow process of reform". Alluding to the advances made "in checking the control of capital over the lives of men and over Government" through progressive reforms in the United States, he explained that "some sort of partnership" had to be

---

[18] For the American president's general position, see Wiseman interview with Wilson, 16 October 1918, *PWW*, LX, p. 350; MacMillan (2002), pp. 70–1.

[19] Supreme War Council meeting, 24 January 1919, *PWW*, LIV, p. 245.

[20] See Grayson notes, *PWW*, LVI, p. 247; Wilson statement, Council of Ten, 16 January 1919, *FRUS-PPC*, III, p. 583.

forged between the "privileged minority" who had the capital and "the vast majority who worked and produced" and thought that the minority deprived them of their "rights".[21]

Wilson thus again presented Bolshevism as an undesirable but to some extent inevitable product of the European "old order", misguided imperialist policies, autocratic forms of government and outmoded forms of economic and social organisation that had no longer corresponded with the – legitimate – desires and interests of the people. All of this was to be superseded by advances towards a "new order", on American terms, which would push back the Bolshevik threat. Yet, intent on compelling the British and notably the French government to accept his wider peace agenda, the American president also argued that essential reforms in the international sphere were no less imperative to undermine the influence of the Bolsheviks. And what mattered most here, in his assessment, was not only the formation of an effective League of Nations but also serious efforts to conclude a peace "on the highest principles of justice". Earlier he had warned that if the victorious powers failed to meet this task whatever postwar order they established would be "swept away by the peoples of the world in less than a generation".[22]

What resurfaced here was a constitutive notion of Wilson's vision of a progressive "American peace". It was the – excessively confident – belief that if a rational and "just" peace order on (his) American terms could be founded, and if other states could be induced to emulate the American example and adopt a liberal-democratic political system (which also held the forces of "capital" in check), then the majority of "the people" would come to recognise the superiority of this progressive "order of the future" to Bolshevik alternatives. And in Wilson's view this applied – albeit with marked gradations – not only to the societies of Western and Central Europe but also, *in the longer run*, to the Russian people – and indeed on a global scale.

As we have seen, the vision Wilson had begun to advance during the war built on the premises of his domestic reform agenda, the New Freedom agenda. It revolved around a set of core ideological maxims about the desirability *and possibility* of a progressive transformation of the international system and the internationalisation of progressive American modes of political, social and economic organisation. In competition with exceptionalist and isolationist ideas, these "exemplarist" maxims would hence play an ever more decisive role in the United States' relations with Europe, and the world. In one way or another, many of the most notable policymakers and thinkers who shaped American international policies after Wilson would espouse and develop them further. Among them would be Hoover and Republican "internationalists" in

---

[21] Hankey notes of meeting of the Council of Ten, 16 January 1919, *PWW*, LIV, p. 102.
[22] Bullitt diary, 9 [10] December 1918, *PWW*, LIII, p. 352.

the 1920s, but above all Roosevelt and those who aspired to promote a global "new deal" on the premises of the Atlantic Charter of 1941. And among them would also of course be the protagonists of the Truman administration and all those who sought to advance even more comprehensive – and eventually overreaching – visions of a *Pax Americana* in the systemic competition with the Soviet Union and "world communism" after 1945.

In 1919, Wilson thus clearly concluded that the best way to meet the Bolshevik challenge was not to rely on military means and the pursuit of a confrontational-interventionist approach, but rather to pursue an exemplary peacemaking process and to push for reforms that addressed the root causes of the problem. In the short term, he came to espouse Lloyd George's initiative and the underlying aim of paving the way for some kind of negotiated truce between the different parties of the Russian civil war and of pushing them to "work out their own salvation". And he agreed that both the Bolshevik leaders and their "White" opponents should be invited to "send representatives to Paris" – on the condition that the former "refrained from invading" Lithuania, Poland, and Finland.[23] And what he gravitated towards was a policy that implied both a de facto recognition of the Bolshevik regime as *one* of governments representing the Russian people and opened up the perspective of negotiating, for the time being, a *modus vivendi* with it. Yet he seems to have had no clearer conception than Lloyd George of what such a *modus vivendi* would look like and what it was supposed to achieve, except for the hope that it could mark the beginning of the longer process of "drying out" the sources of Bolshevik influence. With a view to the immediate future, Wilson argued that the Bolsheviks might lose their power to mobilise the masses and even the "support of their own movement" if the western governments gave assurances that there would be no further "foreign aggression" on Russian soil.[24]

Like some of his advisers, the American president had been favourably impressed by the overture that, authorised by Lenin, the Bolshevik government's deputy commissar for foreign affairs, Maksim Litvinov, had made towards him in December 1918. Though never in a position to have a decisive impact on the Bolsheviks' "foreign policy", Litvinov would emerge as the most important advocate of a – temporary – accommodation with the western powers. After the armistice Lenin had dispatched him to Stockholm to explore the possibility of preliminary peace negotiations with the "Allied countries" should their governments "reciprocate" the Soviet desire for "a peaceful settlement of all the outstanding questions". In pursuit of this mission Litvinov, on 24 December, submitted to Wilson what could be interpreted as a first more substantive indication of the Bolsheviks' readiness to enter into

---

[23] Hankey notes of meetings of the Council of Ten, 16 and 22 January 1919, *PWW*, LIV, pp. 102–3, 205–6.

[24] Wilson statement, Council of Ten, 16 January 1919, *FRUS-PPC*, III, pp. 591–3.

negotiations. Litvinov observed that only two courses were open to the "Allied statesmen". One was "continued open or disguised intervention" on the side of the forces of "White Terror" – which would only lead to a "prolongation of war", further "embitterment of the Russian masses" and "interminable revolutions and upheaval"; the other, which he recommended, was to "come to an understanding with the Soviet Government". This had to involve a withdrawal of all foreign troops from Russian territory and a lifting of the economic blockade, yet it could also open up new modes of cooperation in areas of mutual – economic – interest, notably the western powers could "help Russia to regain her own sources of supply" and give "technical advice how to exploit her natural riches in the most effective way". Litvinov's appeal to Wilson included the demand to examine critically the "one-sided accusations" that Russia's former ruling classes and their western allies had made and the "network of lies and calumnies" they had woven round the "activities of the Soviets". What he essentially suggested was that if the American president did so he would realise the essential affinities between his own "peace programme" and the "more extensive aspirations" of the Bolshevik leadership, who after all had been the first who not only "proclaimed" but actually "granted" the "right of self-determination".[25]

Wilson had by no means become less suspicious of the aims and "activities" of Lenin, Trotsky and Chicherin than he had been at the time of the Brest–Litovsk negotiations. Fundamentally, he could never quite decide how far he could rely on any of Lenin's apparent "peace proposals" in view of the latter's parallel and seemingly iron-clad commitment to his revolutionary agenda and what the American president regarded as over-blown Bolshevik propaganda. These suspicions would eventually be confirmed by what he regarded the Bolshevik leader's inherently ambiguous actions and proclamations in the spring and summer of 1919. In late January, however, he and Lloyd George were prepared to respond to the overture Litvinov had made on Lenin's behalf, because it suited their own political agendas. On 21 January, they advanced a joint proposal that followed the British premier's earlier suggestions and, bereft of feasible alternatives, Clemenceau and Sonnino eventually agreed. The western governments thus issued a resolution in which they pledged to "recognise the revolution without reservation" and invited "every organised group" on Russian territory to send representatives to Prinkipo, the Princes' Islands in the Sea of Marmara, where they were to find a way to end the civil war and agree on peace terms that they would then discuss with the western powers in Paris. Thus, "happy co-operative relations" were to be re-established between the Russian people "and the other peoples of the world". Wilson stressed that the

---

[25] Litvinov to Wilson, 24 December 1918, *PWW*, LIII, pp. 493–4; Degras (1951–53), I, pp. 129–32.

peacemakers had to be cognisant of the fact that "Europe and the world cannot be at peace if Russia is not".[26] But while this observation would be borne out in the twentieth century, the prospects for approaching a tenable agreement, let alone for advancing towards a more lasting *modus vivendi* between the western states and the Bolshevik regime, were decidedly slim.

II.   Lenin's Priorities. The Tactical Interest in a Temporary Truce – and the Pursuit of "World Revolution"

At this juncture Lenin actually had a strong *tactical* interest in initiating negotiations and coming to some kind of *temporary* arrangement or *modus vivendi* with the western powers. Unsurprisingly, his cardinal and most immediate interest was to ensure the survival of the "Soviet Government" – and then to assert its hegemony in Russia. By early 1919, the civil war between the Bolsheviks and what Lenin called the reactionary forces of the "White Terror", the former army officers and forces that then operated under the command of Kolchak and Denikin, had reached a climax. After the White forces had come close to defeating them in the summer of 1918, the Bolsheviks had managed to regroup; but half a year later they still only controlled an area not bigger than the medieval Grand Duchy of Muscovy, with Moscow at the centre. Lenin's interest in negotiations was heightened by what he perceived as the very palpable threat to this core of the "Soviet state" – and the future of the Bolshevik movement – that was posed by Kolchak's army, which was expected to launch a major westward offensive in order to seize control of Moscow. Trotsky's efforts to turn the Red Army into a potent mass army had progressed significantly. Nonetheless, the Bolsheviks were under pressure, and he and Lenin had to concentrate all their energies on the struggle to defend the "nucleus" of the Soviet state. Kolchak carried out his offensive, and it was only in May 1919 that the Red Army was finally able to repulse it and to push his army back across the Urals and into Siberia. At the same time, Denikin's forces were still operating successfully in the south, with French support. And in mid-January, the Directorate that steered the affairs of the Ukrainian People's Republic also declared war against the Bolsheviks after Bolshevik forces had invaded Ukrainian territory.[27]

In view of this scenario, Lenin may well have calculated that a temporary truce would be tactically advantageous. But his most immediate goal was to prevent an expansion of the western powers' military involvement in Russia. Further, he of course was interested in a settlement that brought a withdrawal of western – and Japanese – troops from Russia and terminated western aid to

---

[26] Hankey notes of meetings of the Council of Ten, 16 and 22 January 1919, *PWW*, LIV, pp. 102–3, 205–6.
[27] See Service (2009), pp. 237–45; Zhukovsky (1993).

the "White" armies, for he – rightly – reckoned that this would alter the balance of forces decisively in favour of the Bolsheviks. It was in pursuit of these interests and tactical imperatives that Lenin had dispatched Litvinov to Stockholm and authorised him to explore the possibility of peace negotiations with the "Allied countries". And on the basis of the same rationales, he had subsequently authorised Litvinov to approach the American president with the proposal to act as a possible mediator, highlighting not only the Soviet desire for "a peaceful settlement of all the outstanding questions" but also common-alities between more "extensive" Bolshevik aspirations and Wilson's "peace programme".[28]

When the western governments eventually responded with the Prinkipo initiative Lenin essentially reverted to the approach he had pursued to negoti-ate the peace of Brest-Litovsk. In November 1918, Lenin had argued that earlier, when they had been in an extremely weak position, the Bolsheviks had "held out" because in entering into the negotiations that led to the Brest–Litovsk agreement they had "correctly exploited the antagonism between German and American imperialism" by making "enormous concessions" to the German Empire, thus fencing themselves off from "persecution" by all the other "imperialist groups" and opening the door to "Bolshevist disintegration" in Germany. And he had stressed that long as they were weaker than their capitalist opponents, those who now led the wider Bolshevik struggle had to heed the same tactical imperatives.[29]

In the spring of 1919, Lenin would be prepared to offer "weighty", chiefly financial and economic "concessions" to the western victors of the war, whom he characterised as the Bolsheviks' "real adversaries", the capitalist powers, in order to reach an agreement that would once again serve his longer-term agenda; and here the first priority was and remained to end the involvement of western armed forces and military advisers in Russia. In a note Chicherin, the Commissary for Foreign Affairs, transmitted on 4 February 1919, the Soviet government declared that it was prepared to recognise the "financial obliga-tions" that the Czarist Empire had incurred through the loans it had been granted by western creditors. Further, it offered to provide raw materials as guarantee for fresh western credits while also proposing to grant "foreign capital" mining, timber and other concessions to exploit "the natural wealth of Russia"; and it even signalled its readiness to enter into negotiations about "territorial concessions" that could include the "question of the annexation of Russian territories". Crucially, however, Chicherin's note stressed that the "scope" of the concessions the Bolshevik regime was prepared to make

---

[28] Litvinov to Wilson, 24 December 1918, PWW, LIII, p. 493. See Thompson (1966), pp. 82–90.
[29] Lenin speech, 27 November 1919, Degras (1951–53), I, pp. 221–2.

would depend on the "military situation" in Russia – and the western powers' readiness to desist from further interference.[30]

At first glance, the Soviet proposals – and the crude concessions they offered to the "capitalist adversaries" – seemed to manifest a serious interest and willingness to negotiate a "general agreement" and even an arrangement opening up perspectives for a future peaceful coexistence with the western powers. They even included a Bolshevik "undertaking not to interfere in their internal affairs".[31] But Lenin had by no means abandoned his aspirations to instigate a wider "world revolution" – or indeed as yet relegated them to a more distant future. His "peace offers" were clearly dictated by the tactical imperative to conclude a *temporary* ceasefire and seek a *temporary modus vivendi* in order to prepare the ground for a "final victory" not just of the Soviet cause in Russia but of the "socialist revolution" in and beyond Europe. Following the revolutionary upheavals in November, Lenin had indeed come to see Germany as the crucial battleground in the struggle to spread the "world revolution" westwards. Like Rosa Luxemburg, he had originally believed that the German Spartacists and workers' councils would be able to succeed in overthrowing the "old order". From his perspective, it was essential that these forces would prevail over the "social-traitor" parties, the Majority Social Democrats who, led by Scheidemann and Ebert, he regarded as the key opponents in the struggle to advance towards genuine "self-government" and a new order of "proletarian" states. As he saw it, they had not only colluded in the Wilhelmine Empire's war but were now lending their hands to establish a "false bourgeois democracy" and a "parliamentarianism" that ultimately would just be a façade for the "rule of the financial oligarchy".

For a short time, the German developments seemed to confirm the theoretical predictions Lenin had made in his work on *State and Revolution*, which centred on the argument that in the more advanced industrial states it would not be necessary, as in Russia, to rely on a vanguard party and its tight control to instigate revolutions; more mature workers' councils would allow the revolution to "proceed more smoothly". In turn, revolutionary successes in Germany were to spawn concomitant processes in the west as well as in Austria, Hungary and the more unsettled but also less advanced states-in-the-making in Eastern Europe.[32]

---

[30] Chicherin note, 4 February 1919, Degras (1951–53), I, pp. 137–9. Litvinov had earlier presented a similar agenda to the US envoy William Buckler. See *FRUS-PPC*, III, pp. 643–6.

[31] Chicherin note, 4 February 1919, Degras (1951–53), I, pp. 138–9.

[32] Appeal for the Formation of the Communist International, 24 January 1919, Degras (1951–53), I, p. 136–7. See also Lenin, Letter to the Workers of Europe and America, 21 January 1919, Lenin (1970), pp. 375–8; Lenin (1960–70), XXXVI, pp. 189–200; Lenin (1932); "Manifesto of the Communist International", March 1919, in Riddell (1987), pp. 222–32; Priestland (2009), pp. 93–101, 113–19.

But by the turn of 1918–19 Lenin's expectations of a more rapid progress of the revolution, and notably of a Bolshevisation of Germany, had been disappointed and he had come to anticipate a more long-term process. Yet even after the setbacks in Germany, and the murder of Luxemburg and Liebknecht, he was determined to persist with efforts to propel what he regarded as both inevitable and vital, not least to prevent a dangerous international isolation of the Bolshevik forces in Russia: the "internationalization of the entire course of the revolution". This was to be advanced by promoting communist ideology and by taking steps to create an effective transnational network of support, contact and collaboration between Bolshevik parties and "sections" of the "struggling proletariat" in different countries. In the future, a "close alliance" was to be forged between states where the revolution had already triumphed. At the very moment when they sent peace signals to the western governments, Lenin and Trotsky joined others in launching an appeal for the founding of a "new revolutionary International", which then became known and feared in the west as the Third – Communist – International. The appeal stated explicitly that the "basic method" of the revolutionary struggle that the new organisation was meant to further was transnationally coordinated "mass action by the proletariat right up to open armed conflict with the political power of capital". Although Lenin did not envisage the "Comintern" to be led and tightly controlled from Moscow the Bolshevik regime undoubtedly became its key patron.

On the ideological front, Lenin continued to agitate forcefully on behalf of the thesis that the Great War had been an "imperialist, reactionary, predatory war" in which rivalling combinations of "imperialist robbers" – the "German-Austrian" and the "Anglo-American-French" – had engaged in a "furious struggle" that had cost the lives of tens of millions of workers and peasants on all sides. And he continued to assert that the war had both created the conditions for and made it imperative to achieve a proletarian world revolution.[33] At the same time, the Bolshevik leader advanced his own "Leninist" analysis of the power shifts the war had caused and the likely new conflicts it would provoke. He emphasised that the United States had emerged from the conflict as the now pre-eminent liberal-capitalist power, observing that it had made the most "gigantic gains" and that every other state was now "in its debt" and everything "depend[ed] on it". But precisely because of this, he foresaw a growing antagonism "between America and the rest of the capitalist world", and he argued that because "the most profound economic differences" divided them, the United States would not be able to "come to terms" either with Germany or with Britain and France. In short, Lenin predicted the escalation

---

[33] Lenin, Letter to the Workers of Europe and America, 21 January 1919, Lenin (1970), pp. 375–8; Lenin Theses, 4 March 1919, Lenin (1970), pp. 382–3.

of a new transatlantic inter-capitalist antagonism that, in good dialectical fashion, he placed at the centre of a larger context: the "fundamental disagreements in the contemporary capitalist world" that those who struggled to advance the Bolshevik revolution had to exploit.[34]

The ideological and political agenda that Lenin, Trotsky and others developed for the new Communist International in early 1919 thus rested on what they considered a "correct" understanding of overriding historical processes. In the "Appeal for the Formation of the Communist International" they issued on 24 January, they asserted – prematurely, as it turned out – that the "present epoch", the epoch that had culminated in the Great War, was one that would bring "the disintegration and collapse of the entire world capitalist system". And this, they predicted, would lead to the "collapse of European civilization" unless capitalism, with its "insoluble contradictions", was destroyed. To accelerate this process was to be the Communist International's core mission. It was to help and empower the "proletarian masses" to destroy the "State apparatus of the bourgeoisie" and build in its stead a new "apparatus of power" that embodied the "dictatorship of the proletariat" and created the conditions for genuine "proletarian democracy". These "Soviet republics" would then unite to form a revolutionary new order of "proletarian states" that, as Lenin proclaimed, would at last "free mankind from the yoke of capital and the eternal menace of new imperialist wars" that were "inevitable under capitalism". Essentially then, the "Comintern" was conceived as an instrument to expand the "socialist revolution" – and, first of all, to counter the danger that the "alliance of capitalist States" which, led by the United States and Britain, were organising themselves against it "under the hypocritical banner of the "League of Nations" would "strangle" this revolution.[35]

In a "Letter to the Workers of Europe and America" that was made public on 21 January 1919, Lenin actually singled out Wilson as a particularly dangerous adversary; and he condemned him all the more for his "hypocritical phrases" about "democracy" and a "union of nations". According to the Bolshevik leader, these phrases only provided an insidious cover for the interests of American and other western plutocrats – and the victors' schemes for Germany, which centred on a "division of the spoils", were already exposing how hollow they were.[36] Earlier, Chicherin had confronted Wilson with a no less scathing Bolshevik critique of his peace programme.

---

[34] Lenin Theses, 4 March 1919, Lenin (1970), pp. 382–3; Lenin speech, 27 November 1919, Degras (1951–53), I, pp. 221–3.

[35] "Appeal for the Formation of the Communist International", 24 January 1919, Degras (1951–53), I, p. 136–7; Lenin, "Letter to the Workers of Europe and America", 21 January 1919, Lenin (1970), pp. 375–8.

[36] *Ibid.*

Chicherin had contrasted the high-minded rhetoric of the Fourteen Points –
notably the pledge to offer Russia a "cordial welcome into the society of free
nations under a regime of her own choosing" – with the reality of the actions
Wilson had then taken, above all that of authorising America's participation
in the western intervention in the Russian civil war. And he had argued that
Wilson's League schemes were marred by profound inconsistencies and
double-standards, asking why the American president, who purported to
seek a "free league of nations", demanded freedom only for Poland, Serbia
and Belgium yet not for "Ireland, Egypt or India". Reflecting Lenin's positions, Chicherin had then offered an alternative Bolshevik vision. He had
asserted that if it was to serve a higher purpose – not only to "liquidate the
present war" but also to make future wars "impossible" – a genuine league
had to be founded on socialist premises, as a Soviet "league of mutual aid of
the working masses". It was to be based on the "expropriation of the
capitalists of all countries", foster a system of unrestricted trade between
Soviet republics and permit a general reduction of armed forces to "the level
necessary for the maintenance of internal security".[37]

III. The Failure of the Prinkipo Initiative, Futile Attempts to Negotiate with the Bolshevik Regime, and the – Limited – Bolshevik Dimension of the Peacemaking Process

By the time they launched the Prinkipo initiative, Wilson and the other
western leaders thus had ample experience with Bolshevik propaganda,
denunciations of their liberal-capitalist enemies and tactical manoeuvres. Yet
they actually had only scant knowledge on which to base judgements about
Lenin's underlying calculations and wider objectives. Although they hardly
had any reason to trust Lenin and Trotsky as potential negotiating partners the
underlying assumption of the western overture was nonetheless that it was
worth trying to come to some kind of agreement and, as a first step, to
negotiate a truce in the Russian civil war. But the Prinkipo initiative came to
nought. On the one hand, the divisions between the Anglo-American leaders
and the French government persisted, and the victors thus never really
developed a common approach to the Russian situation and future relations
with the Bolshevik regime. On the other, and crucially, there was never a
realistic basis for a truce between the warring factions. Encouraged by the
French government, the leaders of the "White" governments of Siberia,
Archangel, and southern Russia soon rejected the invitation to attend ceasefire
talks; and the French premier then insisted on delaying a response until

---

[37] Chicherin note to Wilson, 24 October 1919, Degras (1951–53), I, pp. 112–17.

Wilson had returned from the United States. By mid-February, any further decision by the victors on Russia had been indefinitely postponed.[38]

In Wilson's absence, House encouraged the plan to send William Bullitt on a secret mission to Moscow to ascertain yet again on what basis the Bolshevik regime would be prepared to enter into peace negotiations with the western governments. With the support of Wilson and Lloyd George, Bullitt would then set out on this mission on 8 March. And, following what he considered constructive talks with Litvinov and Chicherin, the US envoy returned with new peace proposals by Lenin that in core aspects renewed the offers presented in January and now foresaw a two-stage process. Lenin proposed the conclusion of a temporary armistice. This was to pave the way for a "conference" to discuss a "peace" based on the "principles" that all "de facto Governments" on Russian soil were to remain in "full control" of the territories they held at that point and agreed on a demobilisation of their forces. At the same time, the western powers were to pledge to withdraw their troops and cease their military aid to the "White forces".[39] Bullitt regarded Lenin's offer as a promising basis for a peace agreement with the Bolshevik regime. And House subsequently recommended the scheme to Wilson and sought to enlist Lloyd George's influence on its behalf, arguing that a settlement of this kind would allow the victors to approach the key settlement with Germany in a more "positive and satisfactory way".[40]

Yet by then, neither the American president nor the British premier were willing to stake any further political capital on the pursuit of an agreement with Lenin, even though what the latter suggested (formally) corresponded with the premises both had still supported in January. Having had to deal with a mixture of "pragmatic" and what he saw as purely propagandistic proclamations, Wilson had grown distinctly more suspicious of Lenin and Chicherin, seeing them ever less as negotiating partners who would honour any commitments they made. Yet it was for domestic-political reasons that he now distanced himself from the pursuit of any further negotiations. In short, he feared that any further efforts in this direction – and any moves towards a de facto recognition of the Bolshevik regime – would be grist to the mills of the Republican opponents of his peace and League policy.[41] For his part, Lloyd George – who like Wilson was by now fully preoccupied with the German settlement – also calculated that pushing for negotiations with the Bolshevik

---

[38] See Gardner (1984), pp. 233–40.
[39] Lenin "peace proposals", 12 March 1919, Degras (1951–53), I, pp. 147–50. See Mayer (1967), pp. 467–70.
[40] Bullitt to American Peace Mission, 16 March 1919, Wilson Papers; Bullitt memorandum, ca. 14 March 1919, Bullitt Papers, Box 106; House diary, 28 March 1919, House Papers.
[41] See Baker journal, 29 March 1919, Baker Papers; Walworth (1986), pp. 237–8.

government, which would bring the issue of its recognition to the forefront of the debate, was likely to have disproportionally high political costs. One of his main concerns was that it would further increase tensions with Clemenceau and thus further complicate his efforts to negotiate more moderate terms for the treaty with Germany. And while he still had to deal with critics of his earlier approach in his own government, like Churchill and Curzon, he now also had to confront 200 Unionist backbenchers who appealed to him on 10 April to abstain from recognising the Soviet government and making any agreements with it.

Essentially, once the peace conference had entered its crisis period in late March neither Wilson nor Lloyd George made any further efforts to initiate a negotiating process with the Bolshevik regime. And consequently the Allied and Associated powers retreated partly to a "policy of neglect" and partly to different "policies of insulation" whose common denominator was the aim to contain the westward spread of Bolshevism. It has been argued that they thereby missed the most auspicious opportunity after the Great War to establish a mutually "acceptable relationship" with the Bolshevik regime.[42] But it is very difficult to see how it would have been possible to advance towards anything but the most short-lived and artificial agreement – or indeed any agreement at all – between the divided western powers and the Bolshevik regime in the spring of 1919. While there may have been early on a certain modicum of – superficial – common interests between Wilson and Lloyd George on the one hand and Lenin on the other to negotiate a truce and potentially a "general agreement", this was never really supported by Clemenceau. And, more importantly, any such agreement would have been very unlikely to last. For while the British and American leaders sought to create conditions for a political process that intended to undermine the Bolshevik regime in the longer run, Lenin saw any agreement with the western leaders merely as a tactical expedient to the strengthen the position of the Bolshevik government and to align the forces of world revolution for a new stage in the struggle with the capitalist powers that, as he saw it, was bound to follow. It is worth noting here that at this point Lenin had not yet shifted his priorities to the maxim of consolidating Bolshevism (first) in one country, which may have made the perspective of a longer-term *modus vivendi* with the western states more conceivable.[43]

As it was, the western victors of the war ended up with the worst of both worlds: they neither managed to forge an "acceptable relationship" of some kind with the Bolshevik revolutionaries nor ever had the means to defeat them. After having intervened with *small* troop contingents in the summer of 1918,

---

[42] See Kennan (1956), p. 131.
[43] See Mayer (1967), pp. 467 and ff.; Service (2000), pp. 384–405, 421–50.

they did not have the political will or room to manoeuvre to stage a decisive military intervention; nonetheless their pursuits reinforced the perception on the part of Bolshevik leaders that the "capitalist" powers were ultimately determined to extinguish the flames of their revolution – and were portrayed by Bolshevik propaganda in just this light.[44]

In fact, the Big Three did agree in March to withdraw the troops they had sent to fight against the Bolsheviks. This would then be carried out for the most part in the autumn of 1919 – though some US forces remained in Vladivostok till April 1920 and some British forces in Batum till July 1920. A final agreement to end the intervention and to lift the blockade would only be made in January 1921. By this time, the Bolsheviks had prevailed over their enemies. The tide of the Russian civil war had turned markedly in their favour in May 1919 after Trotsky's Red Army had successfully defended Moscow and forced Kolchak's army to retreat to Siberia. The Bolsheviks finally gained the upper hand in the spring of 1920, though the civil war only came to an end in November 1920 with the defeat of the last organised white forces that General Piotr Wrangel had assembled in Crimea. By then, armed conflict, economic chaos and shortages of food, particularly in the cities, had claimed roughly two million lives.[45] In a wider – systemic – context, what indeed seems most striking in retrospect is how *limited* the capacity of the western powers was to influence the outcome of the struggle that took place on the territory of the former Russian Empire – or, for that matter, to exert any significant influence on the processes that would culminate in the founding of the Union of Soviet Socialist Republics, which was confirmed by the First Congress of Soviets on 30 December 1922.

What the western leaders actually came to concentrate on – essentially from March 1919 onwards, i.e. from the time they finally focused on the German settlement – were different attempts to "insulate" the rest of Europe from the "Bolshevik menace". This menace seemed to become even more palpable when, at a constitutive congress that took place in Moscow on 2–6 March, the Third International was founded. This congress was poorly organised and hardly marked the founding act for a powerful organisation; and this fore-shadowed that the Comintern would remain for some time a far from effective instrument for the promotion of the "world revolution". But the delegates of multiple socialist parties and movements who convened in the Kremlin were subjectively indeed convinced that they stood on the threshold of a trans-European and ultimately global revolution that would usher in a Bolshevik new world order. This was also the emphatic message of the programmatic

---

[44] See Steiner (2005), pp. 143–4.
[45] See Neutatz (2013), pp. 152–70; Hildermeier (1998), pp. 105–56.

"Manifesto to the Proletariat of the Entire World" that Lenin, Trotsky and the other protagonists of the First Congress issued.[46]

What mattered politically was that, in and beyond Paris, the creation of the Communist International was *perceived* as a measure that made the "Bolshevik threat" even more acute. As noted, both Wilson and Lloyd George argued that a crucial element of efforts to contain the westward spread of Bolshevism was to forge what they regarded as a "just" and moderate peace settlement that prevented the Bolshevisation of Germany.[47] Yet they also highlighted the threat Bolshevism posed to put pressure on Clemenceau. By contrast, the French premier and his foreign minister Pichon now focused on pursuing their qualitatively different strategy of containment. Their objective was not to counter the expansion of Bolshevism through a more accommodating treatment of Germany, but rather to contain the danger of future German–Bolshevik collusion. This they sought to achieve by, on the one hand, pushing for the imposition of a regime of containment and military control on the defeated power and, on the other, intensifying efforts to create a viable system of East European buffer-states between Germany and a potentially Bolshevik-dominated Russia.[48]

How important, then, was the Bolshevik factor ultimately for the peace-making process and the attempts to create a new Euro-Atlantic order in 1919? And how did it mainly affect them? In the final analysis, it unquestionably had a significant impact but it did not become as decisive for what actually lay at the core of these processes, above all the battles over the German settlement, as has often been claimed.[49] And what affected them most was not so much the *actual* spectre of an imminent Bolshevisation of Central Europe but rather the different western *perceptions of* and

---

[46] "Manifesto of the Communist International", 6 March 1919, in Riddell (1987), pp. 222–32. See also Lenin, "The Third International and Its Place in History", 15 April 1919, Lenin (1960–70), XXIX, pp. 305–313.

[47] Wilson statements. Council of Four, 24 and 26 March 1919, Mantoux (1992), I, pp. 3, 20; Lloyd George, Fontainebleau memorandum, 25 March 1919, *PWW*, LVI, pp. 260, 262; Council of Four, 24 March 1919, Mantoux (1992), I, pp. 18–19. In a parallel initiative, Hoover stepped up efforts to push back Bolshevik influence by organising expanded food aid. He proposed a plan to distribute supplies to the Russian people through an operation headed by the "neutral" Norwegian explorer Fridtjof Nansen. The Council of Four approved Hoover's plan in mid-April. But when the Bolshevik regime rejected any ceasefire until the western powers accepted actual negotiations, the Council refused to pursue the Hoover–Nansen scheme any further. Hoover would launch a more successful famine relief mission in 1921–23. See Hoover memorandum, 28 March 1919, House Papers; Hoover (1961), p. 117; Weissman (1974); Thompson (1966), pp. 263–7; Cabanes (2014), pp. 189–247.

[48] Tardieu memorandum, 20 January 1919, Tardieu Papers, PA-AP 166 (49), MAE.

[49] The most influential work remains Mayer (1967). See also Gardner (1984), esp. pp. 233–56.

assumptions about the significance of the "Bolshevik threat" – and the different ways in which it was politically *instrumentalised*. All of this became apparent when the victors struggled to finalise the essentials of the German draft treaty, and it would be confirmed during the subsequent "war of notes" with the German government.

At one level, particularly American and British policymakers did for a certain time become indeed, and increasingly, concerned about a possible Bolshevik take-over in Germany. These concerns reached a peak in late March after Béla Kun had seized power in Hungary. But the – then short-lived – success of Kun's attempt to establish a Hungarian Soviet Republic only sent *temporary* shockwaves through the venues of the Paris Peace Conference. And the concerns about the situation in Germany waned relatively soon, despite Kurt Eisner's proclamation of a Bavarian Soviet Republic in April (which likewise would only have a very short lifespan).[50] In the political struggles of peacemaking, as we have seen, Wilson and notably Lloyd George – as well as many other prominent British and American actors – often cited and at times dramatised the Bolshevik danger to emphasise the need for a "far-sighted peace" that did not drive Germany into the arms of the Soviet revolutionaries.[51] But this in fact had no tangible impact on Clemenceau and other French negotiators in the complex bargaining processes that took place among the victors. And, as will be shown, that Brockdorff-Rantzau and other German politicians and propagandists continued to invoke the "Bolshevik menace" so persistently in their campaign for a "Wilsonian peace" would ultimately prove counter-productive.[52]

In a longer-term perspective, however, and with a view to the prospects of creating and *consolidating* a viable postwar order, the challenge Lenin's regime and its aspirations to foment a communist world revolution posed was unquestionably relevant. From the vantage-point of Wilson and the other western political leaders, both the existence and the aspirations of the Bolshevik regime constituted a major and abiding factor of uncertainty and still created as yet incalculable risks of future conflict not only in the ideological but also in the geo- and power-political sphere – even if the Bolsheviks were likely to be absorbed for the foreseeable future by consolidating their power in Russia. There was no acute danger that the "horror scenario" Lloyd George presented to his counterparts in late March would

---

[50] See Tökés (1967); Hajdu (1979); Weitz (1997), pp. 179 ff.; Priestland (2009), p. 118.

[51] See Lloyd George, Fontainebleau memorandum, 25 March 1919, *PWW*, LVI, pp. 261, 263; Wilson statement. Council of Four, 26 March 1919, Mantoux (1992), I, p. 20; Smuts to Wilson, 30 May 1919, *Smuts Papers*, IV, pp. 208–9.

[52] Brockdorff-Rantzau memorandum, 21 January 1919, Vorbereitung der Friedensverhandlungen, 9105 H / H234798–802, Brockdorff-Rantzau Papers. See Chapter 20.

actually unfold – the scenario of a disaffected Germany joining forces with a Bolshevik Russia in order to subvert the postwar order.[53]

For all of Brockdorff-Rantzau's speculative musings, the Social Democratic-led German government actually had no intention of pursuing such a course. Particularly the SPD leaders were united in their strong political and ideological aversions to the Bolsheviks and their political allies in Germany; their political efforts were directed at establishing and stabilising an "orderly" republican polity precisely to keep the Bolshevik influence at bay. And neither Brockdorff-Rantzau nor Erzberger or any other policymaker with any influence on the government's foreign policy had developed, or even intended to develop, more or less sophisticated strategies to forge a revolutionary-revisionist alliance with the Bolshevik regime against the western powers.[54] Yet the British premier nonetheless pointed to one of the most dangerous longer-term threats to European stability and a western-dominated Euro-Atlantic order after the Great War. If the victors persisted with an approach to peacemaking that cast not only – a likely Bolshevik-dominated – Russia but also Germany into the role of "pariah powers" – powers that, though for different reasons, essentially remained outside of and even ostracised from the reconfigured international order – this indeed created the *potential* risk that eventually more assertive, un-accommodating German leaders would seek to collude with the Bolsheviks in order to challenge the western victors – or even to reverse the outcome of the war.

In hindsight, it is easier to grasp that in view of this potential risk the "peacemakers" had to heed one crucial strategic requirement. The more obvious it became that it would be impossible for the western powers either to defeat or to find a *modus vivendi* with the Bolshevik regime, the more important it was for them, in strategic terms, to seek ways to negotiate a German settlement that was conducive to stabilising a liberal or rather social-democratic republic in Germany and, above all, to draw this republic into a reconfigured western, Atlantic peace system – and away from ideological or tactical temptations in the east. To some extent, Wilson and Lloyd George had begun to pursue priorities that pointed in this direction. But their pursuits remained limited by all the self-imposed and external constraints that have already been illuminated – and they of course confronted Clemenceau's unwavering determination to bargain for a peace settlement that was based on completely different rationales.

---

[53] Lloyd George, Fontainebleau memorandum, 25 March 1919, *PWW*, LVI, pp. 261, 263.
[54] Brockdorff-Rantzau memorandum on Guidelines for German Peace Negotiators, 21 March 1919, *ADAP*, A/I, pp. 323–4; Erzberger to Brockdorff-Rantzau, 1 April 1919, Versailles I, 9105 H/H234779, Brockdorff-Rantzau Papers.

19

The Political and Moral Stakes of Reparations
And Limited Advances towards a New
Atlantic Economic Order

For all the challenges that the dispute over the Rhineland, the reorganisation of Eastern Europe and the Bolshevik "menace" presented, hardly any other issue the victorious powers had to tackle in Paris caused such protracted controversies among them as the reparations settlement. At its core lay three far from simple questions: *how much* Germany was to pay to satisfy Allied reparation demands; for *what kind* of war damages and *scale* of war costs it was to pay; and *on what grounds* – on what legal, political or moral basis – it would be required make reparations.[1] Unavoidably, the debates about reparations thus also pushed the politically explosive question of how far the defeated power was guilty of having caused the Great War, and therefore responsible for all its consequences, to the forefront of the negotiations among the victors and, eventually, to the forefront of the disputes between them and the German government.

Indeed, apart from the Rhineland issue and the cardinal security question no problem threw into relief so starkly the profound differences between the priorities, approaches and outlooks of the principal victors – differences that above all set the Americans at odds with the British and French protagonists. Ultimately, they would only leave room for a highly complicated and essentially provisional reparations compromise, but no scope for anything approaching a reparations settlement that was also acceptable for the vanquished. Rather, the terms the victorious powers eventually hammered out would contribute decisively to creating what turned into an enormous gap between their imperatives and intentions and German perspectives on what constituted a legitimate peace settlement. And one decisive reason for this was that the political leaders of Britain and France now had to confront head-on the immense, inflated and essentially illusory public expectations that surrounded the politically-charged subject of reparations on their home

---

[1] Hardly any other issue has also caused such heated scholarly controversies ever since Keynes critiqued *The Economic Consequences of the Peace*. See Keynes (1919). Trachtenberg (1980) and Kent (1989) made important contributions to the debate. A concise analysis is provided in Sharp (I/2008), pp. 81–108. For different recent perspectives, see Tooze (2014), pp. 288–304, and Leonhard (2018), pp. 788–812.

fronts – expectations that they, and notably Lloyd George, had decisively encouraged after the armistice. This way, the negotiations over reparations were intricately bound up with the democratic politics of peacemaking that shaped the processes of 1919.

But it is indeed imperative to place the reparations battle of Versailles in its essential transatlantic context. For the acrimonious inter-allied negotiations also threw into relief how inseparable this battle was from the weighty and no less complicated issue of inter-allied debts and, crucially, British and French indebtedness to the United States that de facto tangibly restricted the *Entente* Powers' financial sovereignty. Its outcome would thus also be decisively influenced by the ways in which two other salient questions would be answered in 1919: How far would it be possible at all – despite numerous negative signals from Washington since the armistice – to agree on terms for a postwar debt settlement that, if one followed the arguments of those who represented the financially strapped *Entente* states, brought about a reduction or even cancellation of their obligations to the United States? And was there any scope for even more ambitious British, and French, schemes that in different ways linked debt relief and a moderate reparations settlement, making the latter de facto dependent on concessions from the newly pivotal creditor power? And, finally, what would also palpably affect the reparations battle was the extent to which the principal victors would be able to agree on common parameters for a new, essentially Atlantic postwar economic order. And what would matter decisively here was whether the British, yet above all the American, key actors would at all be inclined to depart from their earlier aversions to French schemes for an "economic union" of the victors at the heart of an "organised" and "internationalised" economic peace settlement that, for the foreseeable future, excluded and constrained Germany.

Both with a view to inter-allied debts and the economic aspects of peacemaking, the developments of 1919 threw into relief just how massively the Great War had recast the power structures in the international financial and economic order – and how dominant *and* pivotal the United States had become. Yet they also manifested the distinct limits that the Wilson administration's debt policy and prevalent American financial and economic maxims set. In short, the axioms from which neither the president nor his advisers would depart ruled out any progress towards a moderate reparations settlement that was achieved by in one way or another making Allied moderation dependent on American debt relief; and they equally ruled out any moves towards intergovernmental agreements that would have laid the groundwork for a novel, more structured economic system for the postwar era. At the same time, however, the negotiations in Paris also revealed more starkly than before the domestic – and essentially democratic – constraints under which the American president and his advisers had to operate, and of which they were only too aware.

Most critical would be the constraints imposed by the evident opposition within the American Congress against granting the European Allied Powers – and indirectly Germany – a kind of "peace dividend" through debt reductions that ultimately would have required tax raises in the United States. In a wider perspective it is worth emphasising that Wilson and the most influential American financial experts never departed from the positions they had already confirmed after the armistice. They never contemplated ambitious American programmes that, as it were, would have prefigured the Marshall Plan – schemes that combined concessions to America's debtors and the provision of fresh US official loans both to aid the *Entente* Powers and to promote overall European reconstruction. Unquestionably, an American engagement of this kind would have recast the entire political playing-field of the reparations dispute. But even if they had seen a need for such initiatives, Wilson and his financial peacemakers would have found it extremely difficult, if not impossible, to gain the indispensable support in Congress – or the wider American public.[2]

I. Financial Reckoning and a Clash of Economic Peace Visions. The Essential Transatlantic Parameters of the Reparations Dispute

As we have seen, in the aftermath of the armistice both the British and the French governments had committed themselves to seeking comprehensive reparations from the defeated power and thus begun to put forward far-reaching claims that went beyond the parameters set by the armistice agreement. Having to respond to growing public demands for reparations that compensated for the losses and sacrifices of the war, Lloyd George now also had to deal with the consequences of the promises he had made during the Khaki Election campaign. The Lloyd George government thus sought "the greatest possible indemnity" and, because Britain and its Dominions had not sustained direct damages to civilian life and property like France and Belgium, the premier himself and the British representatives on the Reparation Commission would essentially insist, in principle, on an *indemnity* that compensated the British Empire for its entire war costs.

Lloyd George based this claim on moral and political rather than legal premises. He would maintain that Germany did not just have to make reparations for particular transgressions of international law like the violation of Belgian neutrality. Rather, thus his core rationale, not only the old Prusso-Wilhelminian elites but the German people as a whole were "guilty" of having plunged the world into the war and thus had to pay for this "crime against humanity" and all the consequences it had produced. In his eyes, this

---

[2] For the wider context, see Silverman (1982), pp. 145–98.

ultimately meant that they were liable to indemnify the Allied powers both for the damages and the costs the Great War had caused.[3] For political reasons, Lloyd George thus asserted a very expansive notion of what could be demanded under the heading of "indemnity". And the British delegation's representatives on the Reparation Commission, notably Cunliffe and Hughes, would justify their demands on the same basis, maintaining the tough lines they had earlier laid down in the British government's indemnity committee.[4]

While Clemenceau had been more careful and refrained from making far-reaching promises, his government too faced immense public pressure to insist on high and indeed also punitive reparations from Germany. And other leading French politicians, notably Finance Minister Louis-Lucien Klotz, who would head the Reparation Commission, encouraged such expectations. Against the backdrop of the French state's catastrophic financial situation, Klotz insisted that Germany had to be compelled to compensate France not only for the damages in the French territories it had to evacuate but also for the "totality" of France's war costs.[5] At the outset of the peace conference, Poincaré had likewise underscored France's claim to "full reparation" or "*réparation intégrale*".[6] And, as in the case of Lloyd George, the core premise on which Poincaré, Clemenceau, Klotz and other French decision-makers based this claim, was – for all their insistence that Germany had to be punished, retroactively, for major transgressions of international law – essentially a moral *and* political one, which was indeed ideologically charged. It was the premise that Germany bore the exclusive responsibility for the outbreak of the war and thus had to pay for all the consequences of an act that they too interpreted as a crime against civilisation.[7]

But, as had become obvious since the armistice, there was another highly significant factor that informed the attitudes of British and French politicians, advisers and experts towards the reparations issue – and accounted for the more far-reaching demands they made – and that factor was the unprecedented indebtedness of the European Allies to the United States. In short, Lloyd George and even more so Clemenceau came to the peace conference as leaders of financially strained and economically deeply exhausted powers. And their

---

[3] Lloyd George speech, Newcastle, 29 November 1918; Lloyd George speech, Bristol, 11 December 1918, Lloyd George Papers, F246, F326. Bonar Law speech, Glasgow, 12 December 1918. See Fry (2011), pp. 179–85; Newton (1997), pp. 291–5.

[4] Cabinet Committee on Indemnity report, 2 December 1918, paper P. 38, CAB 29/2; Minutes of the Imperial War Cabinet, 24 December 1918, CAB23/42; Bunselmeyer (1975), p. 103; Skidelsky (1983), p. 356.

[5] See Finance Ministry memorandum, 18 November 1918, Tardieu Papers, PA-AP 166 (3), MAE.

[6] Poincaré speech, 18 January 1919, in Horne and Austin (1923), VII, pp. 37–43.

[7] See Poincaré speech, 18 January 1919, in Horne and Austin (1923), VII, pp. 37–43; Miquel (1977), pp. 424 ff.

obligations to America not only limited their ability to make sovereign financial decisions. They also of course aggravated the immense problems they faced in view of the fact that, on the one hand, their budgetary room to manoeuvre was severely constrained by spiralling deficits and national debts and, on the other, they had to cover the costs of caring for war veterans and dealing with other consequences of the war, converting wartime to peacetime economies and pursuing overdue domestic reforms.[8] In the face of these challenges, and because of the burdens the war efforts had already placed on the societies they represented, the *Entente* governments deemed it not just undesirable but politically impossible to address their financial woes by raising taxes.

Both the British and the French governments thus persisted with what they had done both before and since the end of the war. They sought ways of inducing the American government to agree to a reduction or preferably an outright cancellation of their debts, and to put forward various, more or less ambitious schemes to this end that established explicit links between debt relief and the issue of reparations. And despite earlier unequivocal signals by US Treasury Secretary McAdoo and other American politicians that even a partial reduction of US claims was out of the question, they persisted with such efforts at the peace conference. British proposals, notably those developed and later refined by Keynes, called for a "cancellation" or diminution of Britain's obligations to the United States as part of a wider inter-allied debt relief scheme that was to permit a moderate reparations settlement – and at the same time promote European postwar reconstruction.[9] On France's behalf, Commerce Minister Clémentel continued his efforts to persuade American decision-makers that it was also in their interest to alleviate or even cancel France's crushing debts. He persisted with the argument that this would be a vital prerequisite for French and wider European recovery after the war. On the eve of the peace conference, the Clemenceau government used similar arguments when it supported an Italian appeal to the Wilson administration to consider a "general reapportionment of the costs of the war". This appeal and Clémentel's earlier proposals followed the same rationale. They sought to impress on the American government that unless it reduced its debt claims it would be financially and politically impossible for France and the other European allies to limit their reparation claims on Germany.[10]

---

[8] Lloyd George speech, Wolverhampton, 23 November 1918, *The Times*, 25 November 1918.

[9] Keynes memorandum, November 1918, Keynes Papers, PT/7/2. See also Wiseman memorandum, 5 April 1919, Wiseman Papers.

[10] Artaud (1978), I, p. 116; Tooze (2014), p. 298; Clémentel to Clemenceau, 31 December 1918, AN, F12/8104.

Undeterred, French policymakers also advanced further proposals that sought to connect debt cancellation, reparations and wider ambitious schemes to involve the United States as principal financier in an internationalised regime to fund not just the reconstruction of devastated areas in France and Belgium but also to aid the Allied Powers to cope with the financial and economic fall-out of the war. In pursuit of such schemes, Klotz would on 27 January renew the call for the creation of a financial section of the League of Nations.[11] And soon thereafter the president of the French Senate, Antonin Dubost, would confront Wilson with even more far-reaching suggestions – though they remained largely symbolical and were not coordinated with the Clemenceau government. Dubost proposed that in the spirit of the American president's call for a new "world harmony", the American government should not only pledge to cover around one-third of the war's overall costs but also join a consortium that would oversee the financial consolidation of Europe and support his – vague – plans to endow the *société des nations* with potentially immense supranational financial authority by creating a kind of international bank that would oversee a global fiscal policy and issue a global currency. But Wilson essentially dismissed Dubost's overture.[12]

Of greater import for the peace negotiations was that, in essence, the British and French governments insisted on explicitly tying the issue of inter-allied debts to the reparation settlement. Their message to Wilson and the American experts in Paris was persistent and clear: if the American creditor power made no concessions they would hold out for high reparations.[13] But the peace negotiations merely confirmed that all hopes of the European Allied powers that either grander schemes or more or less hard-fisted bargaining strategies would change American attitudes were elusive. In accordance with the positions Treasury Secretary McAdoo had asserted and his successor Glass confirmed, Wilson and the leading US financial experts at Versailles unequivocally rejected any form of debt relief. And they of course ruled out a cancellation of British, French – and Italian – obligations. In early March, Glass warned from Washington that any further European appeals for debt relief would be considered as tantamount to a "threat of default" from the part of America's debtors and thus foreclose the possibility of fresh American loans.[14]

---

[11] See Clémentel letter to Clemenceau and Wilson, 19 September 1918, AN F12 8104; Klotz proposal for a financial section for the League, 27 January 1919, Wilson Papers.

[12] Dubost memorandum, 15 November 1918, transmitted to Wilson on 30 January 1919; Wilson to Dubost, 5 February 1919, Wilson Papers; McCormick diary, 21 January 1919, McCormick Papers.

[13] See McAdoo to House, 11 December 1918, FRUS-PPC, II, p. 538; Davis to Keynes, 7 January 1919, Keynes Papers, RT/1/24; Clémentel to Clemenceau, 31 December 1918, AN, F12/8104.

[14] Silverman (1982), p. 32.

At the same time, all American decision-makers maintained their steadfast opposition to any attempts to establish a linkage between "Allied indebtedness" and reparations.[15] As Norman Davis, who came to act as the Treasury's representative in Paris and would become one of Wilson's main financial advisers, had confirmed to Keynes early on, the American government would not accept a "reference to any relation between enemy indemnity obligations and obligations given by the Allied Governments to the United States". And this position would not change during the negotiations of 1919. To ensure that it would be in a position to set the terms, the Wilson administration insisted on dealing with each of America's debtors bilaterally. What also shaped American attitudes was the concern that the United States would in one way or another become a *de facto* creditor of reparations payments that would then be compelled to participate in military or economic sanctions against Germany in case of German non-compliance.[16]

As noted, the political room to manoeuvre Wilson and the American delegation had was actually distinctly limited. They all were aware that a vast majority in the American Congress was and remained opposed to any concessions vis-à-vis America's debtors and strictly rejected any tax raises that would have been necessary to deal with the consequences of debt relief. Yet it has to be stressed again that both Wilson and the key American financial experts themselves rejected the idea that the United States should help the *Entente* governments and potentially pave the way for a more moderate reparations settlement and, more generally, Europe's financial revitalisation by granting debt relief – and thereby, in the end, requiring US taxpayers, and voters, to pay for a significant part of the costs of the Great War.[17]

In a broader context, the peace negotiations thus clearly confirmed that what key American actors actually deemed appropriate, and what they thought they could legitimise domestically, essentially ruled out American support for more ambitious schemes to foster Europe's recovery and financial revitalisation – schemes that would not only have involved debt relief but also required the American government to assume, and justify, far-reaching *official* commitments. On these grounds, the American president and his main advisers rejected Keynes' "scheme ... for the rehabilitation of European credit", that Lloyd George submitted to Wilson in mid-April 1919. The Keynes plan proposed that the German government and its allies would issue reparations bonds worth £1.345 billion and jointly guaranteed by the governments of the victors and the vanquished that were to pay for "all indebtedness

---

[15] McAdoo to Wilson, 27 October 1918, *PWW*, LI, pp. 468–9.

[16] Davis to Keynes, 7 January 1919, Keynes Papers, RT/1/24.

[17] Glass to Wilson, 19 December 1918, *FRUS-PPC*, II, pp. 544–6; Wilson to Davis, 6 January 1919, forwarded to Glass, 9 January 1919, *FRUS-PPC*, II, p. 556; Wilson to Davis, 5 February 1919; Davis to Wilson, 12 February 1919, Wilson Papers.

between any of the allied and associated governments". For ultimately it would have required Washington to act as the official guarantor of last resort and accept a linkage between debts and reparations.[18] Then and at other critical junctures, the leading US experts at Versailles – Davis, Lamont and Hoover – would impress on their European counterparts their preference for private rather than governmental or intergovernmental approaches, recommending to rely on private capital and the "normal" as more effective ways to foster the financial stabilisation, and necessary reforms, in their countries.[19] And Wilson fundamentally shared these views.

Thus, there were no prospects whatsoever in 1919 for the promulgation of anything akin to a "Wilsonian Marshall Plan", a comprehensive programme of debt relief and reconstruction that would have prefigured the European Recovery Program after the Second World War. The unresolved debt problem would continue to burden Britain's and France's relations with the United States – and remain entangled with the unresolved reparations question – after 1919. Agreements that settled but did not reduce, let alone relieve the debts would only be concluded in 1922 (between the United States and Britain) and in 1926 (between the United States and France); the latter, the so-called Mellon-Bérenger agreement, would only be ratified in 1929. The Great Depression would then alter the playing-field of international debt politics radically; both Britain and France would go into default and ultimately only pay back a fraction of their original obligations.[20]

In the spring of 1919, US decision-makers and experts would also effectively block Clémentel's final attempt to bargain on behalf of his agenda for a "organised economic peace" and a postwar economic union of the victors – by also linking this agenda to the reparations settlement.[21] On the eve of the peace conference, Clémentel had realised how averse Wilson and American experts were to his wide-ranging proposals for a "post-war trans-Atlantic raw-material and transport consortium" and a regime of inter-allied commercial agreements with – temporary – discriminatory provisions against Germany.[22] He had thus shifted his course and come to advocate a hard-fisted bargaining strategy to protect France against renewed German economic domination, which Clemenceau endorsed. Outlining French objectives in the Council of

---

[18] Austen Chamberlain to Lloyd George, 17 April 1919, Keynes Papers, RT/16/13-16; Lamont and Davis to Lansing for Rathbone, Leffingwell, Strauss, 1 May 1919, Lamont Papers; Wilson to Lloyd George, 3 May 1919, in Keynes (1978), XVI, p. 441. See Skidelsky (2005), pp. 229–30.

[19] See memorandum of conference Wilson – US experts, 19 May 1919, Lamont Papers, pp. 163–13. Lamont, Davis to Lansing for Leffingwell, 27 May 1919, Lamont Papers; Lamont to Brand, 10 June 1919, Lamont Papers, pp. 165–10.

[20] See Artaud (1978); Silverman (1982), pp. 145 ff.

[21] Clémentel (1931), pp. 337–48; Glaser (1998), pp. 374–6.

[22] See Jackson (2013), p. 255.

Ten on 5 February, Clémentel stressed that the French government would only be able to consent to moderate peace conditions and reparations terms if the other victors agreed to take common "measures" to develop an "economic organization designed to assure the world a secure recovery"; if this could not be achieved, France would have to insist on more substantial security guarantees and a "peace of reprisals and punishments".[23] But Wilson – and Lloyd George – categorically refuted the French commerce minister's bargaining attempt and refused to lend any support to his overall conception.

The American president unequivocally backed the course McAdoo had recommended earlier and Hoover had advocated most forcefully after the armistice: to oppose any plans to create inter-allied postwar institutions that curtailed American control over its own economic decisions and resources – and thus to preserve the United States' essential freedom of action in the economic sphere.[24] Instead, although the economic terms of the peace remained a relatively peripheral concern for him, Wilson maintained his adherence to the "Open Door" paradigm and the maxim to eliminate or reduce, in accordance with the interests of the world's by their pre eminent economic power, eliminate or at least reduce discriminatory trade barriers as soon as possible (while the tariffs the American Congress had legislated would remain in place). In principle, the experts who negotiated on behalf of the US delegation thus pushed for a trade regime on American terms, under which the most-favoured-nation status would not be reserved to the victors and neutral states but also extended to the defeated power on a reciprocal basis. It was only with great reluctance that they eventually conceded that some transitional fetters could be placed on German trade with the victorious powers in the immediate postwar period. And they did so not least in view to Congressional opposition to an immediate extension of "Open Door" terms to Germany.[25]

The underlying rationale of US economic policies was and remained that the elimination of trade barriers would decisively contribute to a general revival of international commerce that in turn would give essential impulses to a restoration of credit and financial solvency in Europe – while of course serving in particular American export interests vis-à-vis countries that had been important US trading partners before the war, which of course notably included Germany. US experts like Hoover and Baruch thus emphasised that,

---

[23] Trachtenberg (1980), p. 34. Clémentel note to Clemenceau and "Avant-projet", [late] December 1918; Commerce Ministry memorandum, 31 December 1918, AN, F12/8104.

[24] See McAdoo to House, 11 December 1918, *FRUS-PPC*, II, pp. 538–40; Hoover to Cotton, 7 November 1918, Pre-Commerce File, Box 3, Hoover Papers; Hoover to Wilson, 11 November 1918; Hoover to Wilson, 20 December 1918, O'Brien (1978), pp. 4–5, pp. 22–3.

[25] See Baruch to Wilson, 29 March 1919, Wilson Papers; Soutou (1989), pp. 539 ff.; Glaser (1998), p. 376; Schwabe (1985), pp. 293–4.

because in their eyes Europe's general economic recovery depended critically on Germany's recovery, it would be imperative not to strangle the defeated power through discriminatory measures. And notably Hoover maintained the view that it was in interest of the United States to promote in the longer term the consolidation of a liberal-capitalist German republic and its inclusion in a postwar economic order on American terms.[26] That these imperatives indeed clashed fundamentally with those Clémentel pursued was obvious, and it also sparked inevitable tensions in the Economic Commission that, under the French commerce minister's chairmanship, had been given the task to prepare the clauses of the "economic peace" and submitted first substantial recommendations on 1 April. In fact, its efforts only received marginal attention from the political leaders in the Council of Four, because they were so preoccupied with other issues that they deemed more critical.

What eventually provided a basis for yet another strained compromise between the disparate positions and rationales of the victors was, this time, a set of proposals that British experts had developed. Turning away from the agenda of the Anglo-French economic conference of 1916, the economic experts who shaped British trade policies after the armistice, notably for the Board of Trade, had generally re-accentuated more traditional British "free trade" maxims that aligned with American preferences, recommending a future regime of international trade without any more permanent restrictions, based on a general application of the most-favoured-nation principle. But they maintained that for economic and political reasons it would be appropriate to accord the Allied Powers a "head start" vis-à-vis Germany. They thus proposed that during an initial phase of postwar recovery the defeated power should not enjoy most-favoured-nation status in its commercial relations with the western powers.[27]

Although they contradicted the maxims he had championed earlier, Wilson would eventually accept economic clauses of the draft peace treaty that reflected these British proposals and that, essentially, aimed at a *temporary* recasting of the economic and commercial power relations in the world. And although they fell decidedly short of fulfilling Clémentel's aspirations, the Clemenceau government would in the end accept them as well. The transitional system of discriminations on which the victors agreed would in fact restrict Germany's commercial room to manoeuvre significantly – though it hardly cut the German republic off from the world economy, as Brockdorff-Rantzau and other protagonists of the Scheidemann government had feared. The victorious powers stipulated that the defeated power was obliged to grant

---

[26] Hoover to Wilson, 20 December 1918, O'Brien (1978), pp. 4–5, pp. 22–3; Baruch to Wilson, 29 March 1919, Wilson Papers.

[27] Board of Trade memorandum, November 1918, revised in December 1918, CAB 29/1/P-33.

the Allied and Associated Powers most-favoured-nation status and forbade it for a period of five years to impose any tariffs on allied trade. By contrast, Germany would indeed be denied the same status, and for the same transition period of five years the victors would have the right to levy tariffs on German exports. Further, it was decreed that the defeated power would lose 90 per cent of its commercial shipping.[28]

II. The Reparations Battle, the Political Question of Germany's Responsibility for the War and the Political Consequences of the Victors' Makeshift Compromises

In fact, the economic terms on which the victors had agreed barely concealed the profound differences between their underlying interests and economic "philosophies" for the postwar era, particularly the differences between those who represented the "Open Door" interests of the ever more predominant American power and those who struggled for more regulated and *dirigiste* approaches on behalf of a profoundly challenged France. Yet what had far more important consequences for the peacemaking process itself were the transatlantic divisions that opened up during the acrimonious negotiations about the reparations settlement. And these divisions became more acute precisely because the American determination to veto any "solutions" that involved debt cancellation or a linkage between inter-allied debts and reparations set such constraining parameters. In the early stages, these negotiations were mainly pursued in the Reparation Commission. But ultimately here too the critical decisions would be made by the political leaders of the western powers – and they would also forge the politically motivated compromises that would ultimately lie at the core of the "makeshift" reparations agreement of 1919.

The deliberations in the Reparation Commission and its three subcommittees, which began in early February, soon revealed how far apart American positions and British and French essentials were when it came to the most fundamental, and controversial, question on what – legal, political or moral – basis the Allied Powers would require Germany to pay reparations, which of course was indissolubly bound up with the question of what amount or rather on what scale it would be required to pay. With Wilson's backing, the American experts Davis and Baruch now proposed the "program" they had worked out to come to terms with the reparations question. They stressed that it would be essential to adhere to the terms of reference that the armistice agreement had set – to which all sides had agreed. And they stipulated that these terms did not permit the inclusion of the *Entente* Powers' war costs in

---

[28] See Glaser (1998), pp. 384, 380–6; Soutou (1989), pp. 840–3.

the demands for reparations. Rather, they insisted, Germany had to "make good the damage resulting clearly in violation of international law" that had been established and valid at the time of the offence, which notably applied to the German violation of Belgian neutrality in 1914, and to provide "compensation" for all the "direct physical damage" to the civilian population and property that had been inflicted on Belgian and French territories. On these grounds, the American experts on the Reparation Commission, notably the under-secretary of the Treasury Norman Davis and the legal expert John Foster Dulles, would maintain their opposition to more expansive *Entente* claims for punitive indemnities or an indemnification of all of their war costs. And they would submit proposals for a "definite" settlement that was to set a carefully calculated fixed sum of reparations for the damages that were covered by what they interpreted as the – narrow – terms of the armistice agreement. In their assessment, the defeated power would have the capacity to pay the total for these damages within a relatively short time.[29]

Thomas Lamont, the J.P. Morgan partner who had come to Paris as financial adviser, argued that a settlement on American terms "would soonest bring about settled financial conditions in Europe" – and thus also contribute decisively to Europe's political stabilisation.[30] While some US experts, particularly Dulles, were chiefly concerned with the legal rather than the financial or political parameters of the reparation settlement, not only his colleague Davis but also Hoover and Wilson himself accentuated wider concerns. These pertained not only to the economic but also the political stabilisation of the fledgling German republic – and, closely bound up with that, the pacification of postwar Europe. Above all, they feared that if the European Allied Powers insisted on burdening Germany with massive indemnity obligations that were inflated for political reasons and far exceeded its capacity to pay, this would not just threaten to drive the defeated power into insolvency – with far-reaching repercussions for Europe; it would also threaten to undermine its weak government and fledgling republican order, ultimately driving Germany into the arms of the Bolsheviks.[31]

But both the British and the French representatives on the Reparation Commission – as well as their Italian counterparts – rejected the American proposals and their underlying rationales more or less categorically. What they emphasised instead had one common denominator, namely that the countries they represented were entitled to claim a *"réparation intégrale"* from the

[29] Minutes of meeting of American economic advisers, 11 February 1919, cited after Walworth (1986), p. 172. See Baruch (1920), pp. 18–20.

[30] Lamont (1921), p. 263.

[31] See Davis to Rathbone, 12 March 1919, NA-PC 102.1/169E, Wilson statements, Council of Four, 25 and 26 March 1919, Mantoux (1992), I, pp. 6, 20, 27–8; Hoover to Wilson, 20 December 1918, O'Brien (1978), pp. 22–3; Walworth (1977), p. 105.

defeated power. With Lloyd George's backing, the Australian prime minister Hughes used harsh language to justify very high reparation demands on behalf of Britain and the Dominions. Significantly, he based these demands on the argument that Germany had committed "criminal" offences against civilisation. At bottom, Hughes and the two British "hard-liners" on the commission, Sumner and Cunliffe, maintained the position that Britain and the other victorious powers had a "just" claim to make the vanquished provide compensations for the entire cost of a war for which it bore the responsibility.[32]

On France's behalf, Finance Minister Klotz, who had been made chairman of the Reparation Commission, stressed that – contrary to the American interpretation – the reservations included in the armistice agreement allowed the victors to demand a "*reparation intégrale*" for their war costs. But the main thrust of his arguments was – like the British – political and on a deeper level moral or rather ideological. He declared that Germany had to be forced to pay for the totality of the costs that it had "caused" by launching a war of aggression – that for this transgression it had to fulfil, as he put it, "the totality of its debt", also to set a warning example for the future.[33] But Wilson at this stage signalled unequivocally that he would not accept a reparations settlement on such premises. When the frustrated American financial experts appealed for his support, the president cabled from the *George Washington* on 23 February that they were "honor bound" to reject the "inclusion of war costs in the reparation demanded." And in terms that encapsulated the principles he struggled to uphold, he impressed on them that they should "dissent and dissent publicly if necessary" not because of the "intrinsic injustice of it" but "on the ground that it is clearly inconsistent with what we deliberately led the enemy to expect and can not now honourably alter simply because we have the power".[34]

Thus, a fundamental gap had opened up, and the result was a protracted stalemate in the Reparation Commission. As is well-known, it was the young American legal counsellor Dulles who, with the help of Davis, would devise a compromise "solution" that eventually formed the basis of the Treaty of Versailles' infamous, and misnamed, "war guilt clause", Article 231. The formula Dulles proposed, and first circulated on 21 February, had two essential components. On the one hand, the victors had to affirm that Germany was *morally* responsible for the war and that they derived from this a *legal* claim to demand, in principle, reparations for "the entire cost of the war". On the other

---

[32] Geyer (2014), p. 795; Sumner to Balfour, 20 February 1919, Balfour Papers, 49479; Kent (1989), pp. 35–8.

[33] Klotz statement, 15 February 1919, House Diary, 16 February 1919, House Papers; Klotz memorandum, 3 February 1919, cited after Schulz (1969), p. 206; Trachtenberg (1980), pp. 32–55.

[34] Wilson to Lansing, 23 February 1919, *PWW*, LV, p. 231.

hand, they would recognise that Germany's capacity was de facto too limited to make indemnities for all of these costs – and thus commit themselves only to insist on reparations for damages that were explicitly defined in the eventual peace treaty. Dulles' compromise formula was intended to allow the European Allied Powers to fulfil – formally – the promises that had been made on the home fronts since the end of the war while at the same time preventing a settlement that would far exceed German capacities. Refraining from using the term "guilt", Dulles actually had no intention of passing moral judgement on Germany's responsibility for the war. Rather, he sought to find a tenable legal basis for the reparations settlement that also met practical political necessities.[35]

But what Dulles suggested would indeed be interpreted very differently in Germany and give rise to a far-reaching controversy that would develop a dynamism of its own – in 1919 and for a long time thereafter. Most immediately, it would be vehemently rejected – by the Scheidemann government and wider German opinion – as an unwarranted moral verdict of the victors. More precisely, it came to be regarded as a stipulation of Germany's exclusive "guilt" for the war – the stipulation that Germany was "guilty" of having embarked on a war of aggression and thus responsible for the Great War and all its consequences. Eventually, particularly those in Germany who came to advocate an outright rejection of the victors' peace terms would seize on the provisions of Article 231 to challenge the political legitimacy of the *entire* peace treaty.[36]

In the more immediate context of the inter-allied negotiations in Paris, Dulles' "solution" would allow the governments of Britain and France to insist on far-reaching reparation claims. Yet there were still cardinal aspects to be settled that bore immense potential for explosive conflict. From early March, controversies came to centre on two issues in particular: What was to be the amount of the actual reparation demands – and should such an amount be fixed? And how would the categories of damages – and costs – actually be defined? What would be included? Behind these latter questions lurked the politically critical problem of how the German payments were to be distributed among the victors. A striking number of vastly divergent figures for what was to be the final reparations bill would be put forward during the negotiations. They were based on remarkably disparate calculations and sets of political aims – and, particularly in the French case, on bargaining considerations that pointed far beyond the remit of reparations.

As noted, the initial figure Cunliffe had proposed was the staggering sum of 220 billion Goldmarks (ca. $52 billion), which represented the equivalent of

---

[35] See Dulles, Preface, in Burnett (1940), pp. XI–XII; Walworth (1986), p. 288.
[36] See Fabian (1925); Dreyer and Lembcke (1993); Leonhard (2018), pp. 800–1; Krüger (1986), pp. 9–15, 70–80.

roughly five times the entire German national income of 1913.[37] While privately contemplating more modest demands, Louis Loucheur, who became Clemenceau's closest economic adviser at the conference and the pivotal French reparations negotiator, even argued that Germany should – and could – pay the gigantic total of $200 billion, over a period of fifty years. By contrast, the highest total sum the American experts estimated was distinctly lower: $30 billion, to be paid over a period of at least thirty years.[38] Because it proved impossible to come to any agreement in the Reparation Commission, Lloyd George, Clemenceau and House on 10 March appointed a special committee and assigned Davis, Loucheur and the more moderate British representative Edwin Montagu the task of working out recommendations that all sides could accept. On 20 March, Davis submitted a memorandum on behalf of the committee that, based on its assessment of Germany's capacity, recommended a maximal figure of $30 billion and a minimal figure of $20 billion that would be paid over a longer-term period of twenty to thrirty years – and an immediate payment of $5 billion.[39]

Lloyd George originally endorsed these recommendations, but he would soon change his course again and distance himself from them. Ultimately, it was – unsurprisingly – yet again an interplay of overriding *political* concerns and considerations – concerns and considerations that shaped Lloyd George's and Clemenceau's priorities in the dispute over reparations – that would render Davis' recommendations futile. More importantly, this interplay would lead to a different, hard-won and essentially provisional compromise that, crucially, avoided any final sum – and that in the end Wilson would accept for political reasons of his own. As French claims to gain reparations for the reconstruction of the areas directly affected by the war were undisputed – and estimated at 64 billion Goldmarks ($15 billion), the priorities of the French government's negotiators were, at one level, to ensure swift first payments to meet urgent reconstruction needs and, overall, the largest share of reparations – at least 55 per cent of the total.[40] Yet, as we have seen, for Clemenceau – as for Tardieu – reparation demands also served wider political and strategic purposes. They were instrumentalised both to further their agenda to recast the longer-term structural balance between France and Germany and to bargain for Anglo-American concessions in other areas, notably with a view to the Rhineland settlement.[41]

At the same time, Clemenceau not only had to deal with France's acute financial crisis and the impasse created by the Wilson administration's

---

[37] See Lentin (II/2001), pp. 23–46.
[38] McCormick diary, 25 and 26 February 1919, Walworth (1986), p. 174.
[39] Davis memorandum, 15 March 1919, in Burnett (1940), I, pp. 688 ff.
[40] Loucheur notes, 14 and 26 March 1919, Loucheur (1962), pp. 69–70, 70–3.
[41] Tardieu memorandum, 5 April 1919, Fonds Clemenceau, 6N 74, SHD-DAT.

uncompromising stance on debts. He also remained under intense pressure in the court of French public opinion, and in parliament, to meet demands and satisfy inflated expectations for a sizeable "*réparation intégrale*" – expectations that were clearly beyond his control. No longer being able to count entirely on the credit he had built up as charismatic wartime leader, Clemenceau was thus inclined to avoid a definite sum that almost inevitably would be perceived as inadequate in the agitated atmosphere of French domestic politics at this juncture.[42]

By contrast, while he sought to "impose a final total that was impressive", the main aim of Lloyd George at this critical stage was to ensure that the *distribution* ratio of reparation payments that was ultimately thrashed out between the victors would satisfy what he and other protagonists defined as essential British, and imperial, interests and needs. In interpretation that prevailed in the British government and among its experts, this meant that Britain would have to receive at least 25 per cent of whatever total Germany would eventually have to pay. Behind these aims lay conflicting calculations. While Britain had not suffered any significant damage on its territory, it not only sustained massive shipping losses but also, as noted, depleted its capital and incurred unprecedented debts to the United States. And it had been confirmed in March, and would again be confirmed in early April, that attempts to negotiate with the Wilson administration about more or less ingenious ways of combining debt relief with a moderate reparations settlement led nowhere.[43] All of this reinforced the underlying interest in imposing indemnities that were high enough to lighten the "burden of the Empire" not only in the shorter but also in the longer term; and it went hand in hand with a concomitant interest to ensure that Germany would not re-emerge after the war as an (even) stronger competitor than it had been before 1914.

These considerations collided with, but ultimately outweighed, the concern not to impose a debt burden on Germany that crushed it and thus jeopardised the revival of a re-balanced European and world economy after the war. And it also conflicted with, and equally outweighed, the underlying political rationales of Lloyd George's Fontainebleau agenda and the maxim that Britain sought a settlement that would essentially be acceptable to the government in Berlin – and that overall fostered the stabilisation of the fledgling German republic. Further, and crucially, the British premier now indeed had to deal with the consequences of the domestic-political expectations that his promises during the Khaki Elections of 1918 had encouraged. In late March, Lloyd George impressed on Wilson that neither he nor Clemenceau would be able "to dispel the illusions which surround the subject of reparation". And he

---

[42] See Jackson (2013), p. 257; Miquel (1977), pp. 424 ff.
[43] See Tooze (2014), pp. 292–3.

stressed that he had to deal with "(f)our hundred members of the British Parliament [who] have sworn to extract from Germany the very last penny to which we are entitled".[44] On 8 April, more than 200 of them, mainly from the Unionist Party, would demand, in an open telegram addressed to the prime minister, that he had to insist on maximal indemnities and a formal declaration that left no doubt about Germany's responsibility for the war.

When the French government resisted British pressure to reduce France's share of the reparation demands, Lloyd George (in)famously changed his tactics and, following a suggestion by Smuts, came to insist that payments for British and Dominion military pensions had to be included in the bill presented to Germany. This was not just criticised by American experts as utterly incompatible with the terms of the armistice. It also inevitably raised the problem that if one indeed considered all pension claims the resulting sum would be enormously expanded, which in turn created a risk of which Lloyd George was indeed aware, namely that the German government would refuse to accept the victors' demands. Eventually Wilson would be urged by his own advisers to act as a referee. By this time, Davis, Lansing and notably the president himself had become profoundly concerned not only about the economic but also about the political consequences that the enormous reparation demands the European Allies contemplated would have in Germany – and for the prospects of Europe's postwar stabilisation. Davis wondered whether the German government might simply refuse to accept a treaty that imposed harsh obligations on the defeated power and would restrict its financial sovereignty for several decades. Lansing expressed the underlying American fear that Germany's new leaders would be provoked to reject the entire peace treaty and join forces with Bolshevik Russia.[45]

Sharing these concerns, Wilson had impressed on Clemenceau and Lloyd George in late March they must "do nothing which would have the consequence of completely destroying Germany". He argued that the allies could not base their calculations on "prewar Germany", whose regime had been "determined to lead the country to economic mastery of the world". By contrast, he observed, the "Weimar government", on which they sought to impose their very high demands, was weak and had "no credit in the world" while Germany itself was "disorganised and demoralised" and its "capacity to pay" much "reduced". Wilson thus warned against "pushing" reparation claims "to a point which would allow no German government to sign the peace" and declared that the victors "owe(d) it to the cause of world peace not to tempt Germany to turn to Bolshevism".[46]

---

[44] Council of Four, 26 March 1919, Mantoux (1992), I, p. 19.
[45] Davis to Rathbone, 12 March 1919, NA-PC 102.1/169E; Lansing memorandum, 20 February 1919, Lansing Papers. See Schwabe (1985), pp. 247–8.
[46] Council of Four, 25 and 26 March 1919, Mantoux (1992), I, pp. 6, 20, 27–8.

But on 1 April the American president departed from these maxims and, though voicing his deep frustration, decided to accept Lloyd George's demand to include military pensions, however brazen and misguided he considered it. He did so at a juncture when, as we have seen, the accumulation of controversies over the Rhineland, Italian claims for Fiume and Japanese demands for Shandong had created a crisis scenario that raised the spectre of a failure of the entire peace conference and thus also of Wilson's League aspirations. He therefore chose to bend the principles on which he had long insisted to overriding political necessities. Now arguing that it would be impossible to settle the vexatious matter at hand "in accordance with strict legal principles", Wilson clearly departed from the premises of the armistice and the positions he had maintained since the outset of the conference – and he would be severely criticised for this, especially by Keynes, who saw it as the moment when the American president revealed his underlying tendency for casuistry and when his "moral position" in the peacemaking process disintegrated.[47] In fact, however, Wilson merely played his part in the process through which the political leaders of the victorious powers would hammer out the reparations "settlement" they presented to German plenipotentiaries in early May.

Once he had gained Wilson's consent, Lloyd George shifted from the stance he had adopted earlier and now stressed that it would be preferable not to stipulate a fixed total sum of reparations – and he thus came to join forces with Clemenceau, who had preferred this option all along. Originally, the dominant concern of both the British and the French premier had been that if they agreed to a concrete figure that in view of exaggerated expectations would be seen as too modest this would enrage public opinion and lead to a backlash on their respective home fronts. Now, Lloyd George's main fear was that a grand total that would be decisively higher through the inclusion of war pensions would provoke a German rejection of the terms – and the eventual peace treaty. The British premier thus supported an Anglo-French compromise "solution" on which both he and Clemenceau would insist – and which Wilson ultimately felt compelled to accept even though it meant that he had to abandon yet another essential of US reparation policy.

It was decided that rather than presenting the Scheidemann government with a concrete figure, an inter-allied reparations commission was to be established that would be charged with determining Germany's total reparation liability by 1 May 1921 and with fixing a schedule of payments – which, when it was eventually worked out, would extend to a thirty-year period, ending in 1951. Further, to satisfy French demands, it was decided that

---

[47] Lamont, "Note of a Conversation with Woodrow Wilson", 3 April 1919, Lamont Papers, pp. 168–4; Burnett (1940), I, pp. 776–7. Keynes (1919), pp. 95–6; Skidelsky (2005), pp. 227–8.

Germany would have to pay 20 billion Goldmarks ($5 billion) in 1919 and 1920 for immediate reconstruction purposes, a substantial part of which would be deliveries in kind.[48]

Keynes, who became the most influential critic of the reparations agreement, which he would castigate as the centrepiece of the "Carthaginian Peace" of 1919, noted as early as 4 May that what the western powers had concocted was merely "a paper settlement which even if it is accepted cannot possibly be expected to last".[49] In fact, a compromise agreement had been forged that postponed some of the thorniest decisions; and apart from the imposition of immediate payments for the initial two-year period, the victors had merely agreed on the premise that they would have to negotiate further and come to an agreement later, once the polarised atmosphere of the immediate postwar period had subsided. After an exceedingly high reparations bill of 269 billion Goldmarks had been set by a conference of the Allied Powers in Paris in January 1921, at a time when the United States was no longer officially involved in the discussions, the then binding total sum that was agreed upon at the subsequent London conference in May 1921 came to 132 billion Goldmarks (ca. $31 billion), which still represented not only a considerable financial and economic burden – more than twice the German national income of 1913 – but also and above all an immense political burden for the unstable German republic.

In retrospect, it is tempting to argue that for all its limitations the inter-allied reparations compromise of 1919 went to the limits of what "momentary settlement" was politically possible for the victorious powers – given how conflicting their aims and needs were, and particularly in view of the financial strictures and political constraints that, each in his own way, the leading political actors faced.[50] But both in the short and in the longer run the terms of the victors' makeshift agreements of 1919 made it all but inevitable that the in core respects unresolved reparations issue – in tandem with the equally unresolved problem of inter-allied debt settlements – would become a crucial problem not just of the postwar financial and economic order but also of postwar international politics and here, above all, the relations between the western powers and Germany. Both would indeed overshadow European politics and transatlantic relations in the 1920s.

In purely financial and economic terms, Germany's capacity to fulfil Allied reparation demands was dependent on a stable currency, a German economic recovery – particularly increased exports that provided a surplus of funds –

---

[48] Lloyd George draft proposal, 29 March 1919, in Burnett (1940), I, pp. 754–5; *ibid.*, pp. 857–8.

[49] Keynes letter, 4 May 1919, Keynes (1978), XVI, pp. 450–6; Keynes (1919), pp. 9–10, 35 ff.

[50] See Keynes (1921), pp. 3–4; Tooze (2014), p. 295. For a different appraisal see Sharp (I/2008), pp. 106–8.

and, in short, a restoration rather than corrosion of the defeated power's financial solvency. In turn, it would soon become apparent in the protracted period of crisis which followed the Great War that Germany's recovery – and capacity to pay – to a critical extent depended on foreign capital or, more precisely, on American loans. Eventually, such loans would be provided, not by the American government but by private American bankers, above all the erstwhile "financier" of the *Entente*'s war effort, J.P. Morgan.[51] Essentially, however, the reparations question was and remained a political problem. And in the political sphere it would only be possible to develop a more workable mode of dealing with this conundrum if the victors found ways to pursue something they did not even contemplate in Paris: to negotiate mutually acceptable, or at least bearable, modalities with representatives of the Weimar government. Decisive steps in this direction would only be taken after the cathartic Ruhr crisis of 1923 and culminate in the London reparations agreement of 1924, which marked a real watershed in transatlantic politics.[52]

In the spring of 1919, the tenuous nature of the victors' agreement, and particularly the political imperatives that had driven Lloyd George and Clemenceau to seek to "placate a public whose expectations had been deliberately overinflated", added a further, capital obstacle to possible negotiations with the Scheidemann government.[53] No attempt would be made at least to *try* to reach a broader compromise that would have given the Allied leaders enough to satisfy public demands at home and German leaders a sum for which they too could hope to gain sufficient domestic support. And particularly the Anglo-French imperatives would also rule out any serious negotiations about a qualitatively different peace settlement – a settlement based on a political-cum-financial "grand bargain" such as that which the German financiers Melchior and Warburg would propose, at the eleventh hour, in May 1919. As will be seen, what they envisaged was a *do ut des* arrangement under which the German government would agree to pay a high "lump sum" of 100 billion Goldmarks in return for concessions from the victors on territorial and political terms of the peace that were deemed essential from the German perspective.[54]

But ultimately the leaders of the victorious powers neither had the political will nor enough political room to manoeuvre to pursue alternative paths that could have led towards a more workable or "pragmatic" reparations and peace agreement. As it was, the terms the victors presented, and above all the stipulations regarding Germany's responsibility for the war, were bound to

---

[51] See J.P. Morgan to Schacht, 12 October 1924, Morgan Papers, Box 195; Kent (1989), pp. 103 ff.
[52] See Chapter 23 and Cohrs (2006), pp. 154–86.
[53] Sharp (I/2008), p. 107.
[54] See Chapter 20.

provoke strong reactions in Berlin. And, more importantly, they were bound to shift the dispute to the level of a moral-ideological contest in which Brockdorff-Rantzau and other German representatives had most to lose but no one could really emerge as an undisputed winner when the fraught peacemaking process of Paris entered its final stage.

20

The Imposed Peace
The Missed Opportunity of a Negotiated Settlement
with Weimar Germany?

In mid-April, the political leaders of the victorious powers decided that the time had come to summon German representatives to Paris in order to present them with the result of their arduous negotiations – the peace terms contained in the draft treaty. By 25 April, it was confirmed that Brockdorff-Rantzau would travel to Paris at the head of a sizeable German delegation. But the Big Three had by this time agreed on a very constraining *modus procedendi* for the subsequent exchanges with those who sought to negotiate on behalf of the vanquished power. It was a *modus procedendi* that would impose essential limits on all that was to follow – and, indeed, on the peace settlement itself. In short, Wilson and Lloyd George endorsed Clemenceau's proposal that there were to be no direct, oral negotiations with the German plenipotentiaries about the victors' peace terms. Rather, there would only be exchanges in written form. The German delegation would only be given a short time to submit in writing their responses to the draft treaty and their own counter-proposals, and the victors would reserve to themselves the prerogative to respond to them in accordance with their own interests and priorities.

This decision, and the fact that the political leaders of the western powers would adhere to it uncompromisingly till the very end, would have a decisive bearing on the final stage of the peacemaking process of 1919. It essentially foreclosed any possibility of initiating now what had become increasingly elusive since the armistice and what would indeed have been extremely challenging at this juncture: actual, substantial *face-to-face* negotiations between the victors and the vanquished. It thus ruled out any advances towards the only kind of process – a then necessarily more extended process of oral negotiations and discussions – through which, *potentially*, the representatives of the different sides could have begun to build up a modicum of trust and to gain a deeper understanding of the aims, interests *and constraints* of those they were facing. And it thereby blocked the only conceivable path, if there was any, to negotiate a more rational and politically balanced peace of accommodation that both sides, not only those who represented the victors but also those who represented the vanquished, could hope to legitimise domestically.

What actually took place between early May and the middle of June – the "war of notes" of 1919 – rapidly escalated into an unsolvable conflict of principle. More precisely, both sides, the victors and the vanquished, turned what fundamentally was a conflict between different conceptions of order, national interests and concerns into a confrontation of different ideological visions of peace and competing moral claims, especially claims about the responsibility of the defeated power for the war. And that was a dispute which simply could not be settled, let alone resolved, under the circumstances – especially not under the extremely tense conditions and time constraints that characterised the endgame of the most complex peace negotiations in modern history.[1]

This escalatory endgame not only reduced to an absolute minimum whatever political room for manoeuvre there still may have been for accommodating competing aims and interests in a more sober, rational fashion. It even widened and deepened the divisions between the different sides further. And it culminated in a final note and ultimatum of the victors, issued on 16 June, that ultimately gave the peace treaty itself and the manner in which it was imposed, and presented to "world opinion", a far more draconian and in core aspects humiliating character than notably Wilson and Lloyd George had earlier envisaged. In the end, both turned the settlement into a punitive victors' peace that was being forced on the vanquished.

That following British and some American pressure the final peace treaty had been modified in minor respects to accommodate German concerns did not really change either the overall nature of the settlement or the way in which it would be perceived on both sides of the Atlantic. This had far-reaching repercussions. It threw into the starkest possible relief that the frail new Atlantic order that took shape in 1919 would be established as an incomplete system, a system of the victors that would not be regarded as legitimate by the vanquished – and also come under severe criticism in Britain and the United States (not only by liberals, socialists and left-leaning progressives). And it would raise a crucial question that those who followed in the footsteps of the peacemakers of Versailles would have to answer: How far would it be possible, not to enforce the victors' system of Versailles but to *transform* it into a more stable and more legitimate peace order – an Atlantic order that also included and accommodated Germany?

It is important to emphasise that, although in hindsight it may seem that way, this outcome was not inevitable. It was not inevitable that the peacemaking and ordering process of Paris remained a victors' process and that it ended with a treaty that was foisted on the vanquished. For all the domestic, internal

---

[1] For different interpretations of the "war of notes", see Schwabe (1985), pp. 299–394; MacMillan (2002), pp. 460–83; and Leonhard (2018), pp. 946–1050.

pressures and constraints they had to deal with – if they had had the political will, the key decision-makers of the victors also could have created the political room to manoeuvre to pursue some form of negotiations with those who represented the defeated power. And it would have been extremely challenging but not *per se* impossible to *try* to negotiate a settlement that came closer to representing compromise peace and that, crucially, committed not only the victors but also the vanquished to common ground-rules of international order in the aftermath of the Great War.

The crucial question that needs to be re-assessed, then, is why the peacemaking process of 1919 ended in the way it did – why it escalated in such an antagonising manner? Undoubtedly, the confrontational strategy the German foreign minister Brockdorff-Rantzau came to pursue – particularly his misguided attempt to put pressure on the victors by underlining the discrepancies between the terms of the draft treaty and the "Wilsonian peace of justice" they had allegedly promised – contributed significantly to the escalation process. Brockdorff-Rantzau's pursuits had some impact, notably on the British and American delegations, and public opinion in Britain and the United States. But in the final analysis they only manifested how extremely narrow the political options of German policymakers were, and it would harden rather than soften the common front of the victors and their resolve *not* to pursue negotiations. It thus also undermined any prospects of success of an eventual German initiative to strike a "grand bargain" involving substantial German reparation payments in return for concessions of the western powers on critical territorial and political issues. At the same time, it reinforced illusory expectations in Germany about what peace was still possible.

But the actors who had, and retained, the decisive power to set the basic parameters, and limits, of the final stage of the peace negotiations were doubtless the political leaders of the victorious powers. And once they had decided not to allow actual negotiations, they had essentially set the stage for the final confrontational "showdown" and battle of principles of 1919. The Big Three would respond to Brockdorff-Rantzau's strategy in kind and ultimately assert in a harsher and more explicitly high-handed manner their *right* to impose a "stern but just peace" on those who represented a power that, as they now declared (even) more categorically than before, bore the sole responsibility for the outbreak and escalation of the Great War.

Arguably, the reasons for their ultimately uncompromising course have not been satisfactorily illuminated. A wider, transatlantic explanation is required. In systemic terms, what had a decisive impact here were the unprecedented dynamics and complexities that had arisen during the first attempt to negotiate an Atlantic peace and, at the same time, the foundations of a new Atlantic international system. More concretely, the political leaders of the victors rejected negotiations with the vanquished precisely because they had found it so extremely difficult to agree on the terms and underpinnings of such a peace *amongst each other*. They did not want to risk that the highly strained

and brittle compromises they had forged – and that barely concealed the
underlying differences – would come undone and that the superficial unity
they maintained with so much effort would be broken up. In this sense, the
nature and difficulties of the newly transatlantic inter-victor process – and the
fact that it had acquired a momentum of its own – indeed left hardly any scope
for a broader negotiation process between the victors and the vanquished.

While Lloyd George would try hardest to push for some modifications of
the peace terms – to be effected *among the victors* – ultimately none of the Big
Three wanted to jeopardise the intricate and tenuous edifice of complex
bargains they had put together, and to upset the balances between their aims,
interests and domestic legitimation requirements they had sought to strike as
political leaders of democratic powers. None of them wanted to risk either a
complete breakdown or a significant prolongation of the peacemaking process
with all the incalculable problems this would raise. Particularly Wilson eventually insisted on a speedy conclusion of the process. And the fact that as
democratic leaders they all had to grapple with particularly strong domestic
pressures and constraints (of their own and of their counterparts) played a
significant role too. It not only curtailed their room to manoeuvre but also
predisposed them to insist all the more categorically on their authority as
victors to set the final terms. This mattered more than the dynamics of the new
transnational playing-field, all attempts to influence public opinion across
national borders and, concretely, the impact of German attempts to put
pressure on the western governments by appealing to "world opinion" and
particularly left-liberal opinion in Britain and the United States.

Yet what also proved crucial now, and should not be neglected, was that
Clemenceau, Wilson and even Lloyd George were fundamentally united in a
different respect: they did not or no longer *have the political will* to countenance actual negotiations with the German government or, more broadly, to
embark on a process of negotiating a qualitatively different *peace of accommodation*. And this is not only attributable to the constraints under which they
operated or to the concern to salvage the tenuous compromises they had
forged among themselves. What played a significant role too were the overall
approaches to peacemaking they came to pursue and certain cardinal assumptions and maxims that informed them, which in fact had been reinforced
during the peace conference. At the core, they all came to espouse the
fundamental position that, as leaders of the principal victors *and* most civilised
states, it was their essential prerogative to impose a "stern but just" victors'
peace on Germany and to establish a postwar order from which the latter
would initially be excluded for a "probationary" period.

The "war of notes" thus brought to the fore – as if under a magnifying-
glass – not only fundamental systemic factors and problems but also underlying assumptions and attitudes that made some kind of accommodation and
a more balanced peace between the western powers and Germany ultimately

impossible in 1919. Yet it should not be overlooked that the altercations between the victors and the vanquished also brought to the fore different tendencies, ideas and outlooks that could not change the course of events at the peace conference but anticipated those that became formative for international politics and subsequent attempts not only to amend but to reform the "Versailles system" and the post–First World War international order in the 1920s. These altercations led influential policymakers and experts, especially in the British and the American delegations, to intensify what they had already begun while the draft treaty had been finalised, namely to take a harder look at its most problematic features and to think harder about what a sustainable peace order and an effective League of Nations would require.

What escalated in Paris sparked not only further massive propaganda battles but also far-ranging public debates about the most contentious issues – both in the different affected states and in the transnational sphere. For obvious reasons, French decision- and opinion-makers clung most resolutely to the imperatives they had espoused since the end of the war and the cardinal aim of imposing a maximally constraining peace on Germany. For similarly obvious reasons, only very few German policymakers began to develop more realistic conceptions and approaches to prepare the ground for an accommodation with the western powers and finding a place for the newly constituted republic in the western-dominated postwar order. Most German decision-makers, and the overwhelming majority of those who set the tone of the wider German debate, still clung to illusory expectations and, when disillusioned by the actual outcomes, reacted with helplessly violent protests against what they viewed as the shattering "peace dictate" of Versailles.

I. Moral Confrontation with the Victors. The Foreseeable Failure of Brockdorff-Rantzau's Wilsonian Strategy to Push for a Negotiated "Peace of Justice"

After a long period of waiting, enforced passivity and futile attempts to influence the deliberations of the victors from the distance of Weimar and Berlin, Brockdorff-Rantzau and a German delegation of all in all 180 members – including the actual plenipotentiaries, diplomats, legal and financial experts – had finally travelled to Paris on 26 and 27 April. Yet what followed was another tense waiting-period in which – emblematic of the realities of power and of exclusion and inclusion in 1919 – the German delegates were more or less confined to the isolated *Hôtel des Réservoirs* in Versailles (officially because the French government could not guarantee their safety) until they were, at last, summoned to Trianon on 7 May to be confronted with the victors' terms.

By the time they finalised their preparations for the peace conference ahead of their journey to Paris, Brockdorff-Rantzau and other key actors in the German delegation actually assumed that the prospects for actual negotiations with the victorious powers were slim. A core premise of the revised "Guidelines" for the German plenipotentiaries of 21 April was that, as had already been predicted in March, the "opponents" would probably present the German side with a "complete draft of a peace treaty" and declare that it could "only be accepted or rejected".[2]

At the same time, neither the German foreign minister nor Erzberger expected any longer that Wilson could be induced to play the part that from their vantage-point he should have played all along, namely that of an arbiter who used his influence to press the *Entente* Powers to accept an "American peace" on the basis of the Fourteen Points – or more precisely a settlement that fulfilled the inflated German expectations of such a peace.[3] A disillusioned Brockdorff-Rantzau had concluded that he would most likely have to face a "phalanx" of victors that included Wilson; and he observed that because the American president could not "realise his Fourteen Points in their ideal form" he would now "try to achieve what is best for America and the Entente".[4] Yet in spite of all this the German foreign minister would not seek to adapt his approach to the realities and dynamics of the victor-centred negotiating process. He was not prepared to adjust, let alone fundamentally reorientate the basic "strategy" he had developed while being forced to wait for the outcome of the victors' deliberations from the distance of Berlin – and for which he still had the backing of the Scheidemann Cabinet.

What Brockdorff-Rantzau came to pursue, in line with the basic rationales he had advanced ever since January, can be characterised as a – profoundly detrimental – Wilsonian-Trotskyite campaign of "open diplomacy". Its aim was to put pressure on the victors to concede actual negotiations after all and to conclude what he interpreted as a "just" peace on Wilsonian terms. To this end he hoped to arouse public opinion, particularly left-liberal opinion in Britain and the United States. His strategy centred on putting forward German counter-proposals to the victors' peace terms, which all relevant German policymakers by this time expected to be harsh, that were elaborated "in the spirit" of Wilson's original peace programme of the Fourteen Points. Above all, these proposals had the aim to demonstrate to the "peacemakers" and to "world opinion" that what the victors envisaged departed from the premises of this programme and thus, in the German interpretation, from the premises of the armistice and the Lansing note – and was consequently unacceptable both

---

[2] German "Guidelines", 21 April 1919, *AR Scheidemann*, p. 193.

[3] Brockdorff-Rantzau found this confirmed through discussions with Colonel Conger on his journey to Paris. Brockdorff-Rantzau memorandum of conversation with Conger, 29 April 1919, Versailles I, 9105 H/H 235232-256, Brockdorff-Rantzau Papers.

[4] Memorandum of discussion between Brockdorff-Rantzau and Groener, 4 April 1919, Versailles I, 9105 H / H234106, Brockdorff-Rantzau Papers. See Schwabe (1985), pp. 301–2.

on moral and legal grounds. At the same time, they were intended to show that the victors' terms were not only impracticable but also bound to produce political consequences that could not be in their well-understood self-interest – namely that they would undermine the stabilisation prospects of the new German republic and provoke either a nationalist backlash or a triumph of Bolshevism.[5]

The German foreign minister set the stage and the tone for his campaign with the defiant remarks he made during the politically, symbolically and psychologically charged ceremony at Trianon Palace at which the victors presented the draft treaty to the German delegation on 7 May. This ceremony was of particular significance because it would remain the only occasion in 1919 when representatives of the victors and the vanquished, the most important belligerents of the Great War, actually encountered each other face-to-face. And it witnessed a collision of French and German interpretations of the war and the nature of the peace to be made in its aftermath that would foreshadow the profundity and scale of the confrontation that lay ahead. As chairman of the assembly at Trianon, Clemenceau made use of his short opening speech to assert the prevalent French view, laying the emphasis squarely on the guilt Germany had incurred by launching an aggressive offensive war, which he called a "crime against humanity". He deliberately placed German actions in a wider historical context, alluding not only to the sacrifices the French nation had made since 1914 but also to humiliation inflicted on France though the founding of the Bismarck Empire at Versailles and the peace the newly formed German Empire had imposed in 1871. The French premier left no doubt that, as he saw it, now the time had come for the civilised powers that had united to defeat the aggressor not to negotiate with it but to pass judgement on it, to "settle our accounts" and to "give" Germany a peace commensurate with the crime it had committed. And he stressed that what he called "this second Treaty of Versailles" had "cost us too much not to take on our side all the necessary precautions and guarantees" to ensure that the new peace of Versailles would be "a lasting one".[6] Remarkably, neither Wilson nor Lloyd George spoke on this occasion.

The statement Brockdorff-Rantzau had prepared thus in part turned into a defensive reply to Clemenceau's accusatory remarks. But it was also addressed to the American and British leaders, to "world opinion" and, not least, to a deeply unsettled domestic-political audience in Germany. The foreign minister acknowledged that Germany bore *part* of the responsibility for the war but strongly refuted the thesis of German "guilt" for the war, arguing that the

---

[5] See Brockdorff-Rantzau memorandum, 21 March 1919, *ADAP*, A/I, pp. 322–4; Minutes of the Cabinet Meeting, 21 March, *AR Scheidemann*, pp. 74–83; Brockdorff-Rantzau to Scheidemann, 22 March 1919, *ADAP*, A/I, pp. 332–3.

[6] See Baker (1923), II, pp. 501–2; Tardieu (1921), pp. 1–14.

German people had believed they had to wage a "defensive war" to protect their nation against the attack of others. He emphasised that the representatives of Germany's new republican government did not deceive themselves about "the scale of our [the German] defeat" or the "degree of our powerlessness", given that the power of German arms had been "broken". And he expressly emphasised that they also were aware of "the intensity of the hatred" that they confronted in Paris – and of the "passionate demand" that the victors should "make the defeated pay and punish [them] as the guilty party". Yet while acknowledging the German violation of international law vis-à-vis Belgium, he emphatically underscored that Germany did not bear exclusive "guilt" for the war.[7]

What Brockdorff-Rantzau really sought to do was to reassert Germany's claim to a "peace of justice". He declared that while Germany no longer had any "allies", the western powers themselves – and notably Wilson – had provided it with an ally of a new kind – the "lawfulness" that had been assured through the armistice agreement and the terms of the Lansing note, which furnished the only legitimate "premises of peace" and marked a departure from a "peace based on might". And he reiterated the German interpretation that "the principles of President Wilson", as encapsulated in the Fourteen Points and subsequent speeches, had become binding for all signatories of the armistice and thus now had to inform the peace settlement.

On this basis, the German foreign minister not only renewed the German commitment to a "free and comprehensive League of Nations" that was to usher in a new social and economic solidarity between democratic states. He also demanded, on Germany's behalf, a peace that was concluded in the spirit of justice and just such solidarity. And he warned that a settlement that "[could] not be defended before the world in the name of justice" would not last because it would "always provoke new resistance against it".[8] Brockdorff-Rantzau's brusque and provocative speech would indeed be interpreted by the victors, and notably by Wilson, as the statement of a German representative who embodied the arrogant habitus and spirit of the old Wilhelminian order. And the confrontational manner in which his "counterproposal strategy" would then be executed proved in many ways self-defeating. Rather than open avenues of communication, further de-escalation and prepare the ground for possible discussions, it was bound to make the victors even less inclined than they were already to countenance any substantial negotiations with German plenipotentiaries or changes of the peace terms that addressed key concerns of the Scheidemann government.

The victors' actual peace terms then exceeded Brockdorff-Rantzau's worst expectations, and his reaction reflected those of all members of the German

[7] Brockdorff-Rantzau speech, 7 May 1919, Brockdorff-Rantzau (1925), pp. 71–3.
[8] Ibid.

delegation and the Scheidemann Cabinet. He immediately concluded, on 7 May, that what the draft treaty represented was a "peace of force" that in all essential aspects deviated from Wilson's "basic premises" and whose acceptance would be tantamount to an "enslavement" of Germany and its "political elimination" as a great power.[9] Like others, the foreign minister focused on the territorial and political terms of the treaty that had vital implications for the integrity, and sovereignty and development prospects of the German state – and that would be particularly difficult to alter in the future.

While the deliberations of the western powers reached their decisive stages, Brockdorff-Rantzau and his advisers had come to view with rising concern what they saw as the French government's attempt to separate the Rhineland from Germany, by direct annexation or support for separatists' ambitions to establish "an independent republic" in the Rhineland that "would soon fall under French leadership". And they had been determined to contest all of these aspirations – and, especially, the foundation of "an international buffer-state" – on the grounds that they directly clashed with the principle of self-determination.[10] When Dresel subsequently informed him that the western powers had settled on a fifteen-year occupation of the Rhineland, the foreign minister condemned this as a "badly disguised annexation". But he decided that it would be futile to try to prevent the occupation. Instead of contesting it as such, his emphasis now lay on ensuring that the political and economic ties between the occupied areas and the rest of Germany would not be severed – and that the occupation regime was not instrumentalised by France to incite separatism and corrode German sovereignty over time.[11]

The foreign minister and those who aided him in formulating the guidelines for the German delegation in the Foreign Office thus concentrated all of their attention on the Saar and on the German–Polish border, where the future of Upper Silesia and Danzig was by now the eminent concern. They stubbornly invoked Wilson's maxims in order to limit the loss of German territory, demanding that the new Polish state should comprise only "indisputably Polish territories" as the American president had enunciated in the Fourteen Points. In provinces with ethnically mixed populations plebiscites were to be held, but this should only apply to the area around Posen; Upper Silesia, the industrial area deemed most "indispensable" to the German economy as it provided 22 per cent of German coal production, was to remain German – without plebiscite – because it had never been "under Polish rule". In the case of Danzig, German policymakers also pointed to the Fourteen Points but

---

[9] Brockdorff-Rantzau to Langwerth, 7 May 1919, *ADAP*, A/II, p. 4.
[10] Brockdorff-Rantzau memorandum, 21 March 1919, *ADAP*, A/I, pp. 322–4; Minutes of the Cabinet Meeting, 21 March, *AR Scheidemann*, pp. 74 ff.; Brockdorff-Rantzau memorandum of discussions with Dresel, 19 April 1919, *ADAP*, A/I, pp. 422–6.
[11] See revised German "Guidelines", 21 April 1919, *AR Scheidemann*, p. 194.

insisted that Poland's access to the Baltic, promised therein, must not be effected through the creation of a politically destabilising "Polish corridor to Danzig" that would separate East Prussia and parts of West Prussia from the rest of Germany; instead, they proposed the creation of "free ports" and guarantees of Polish access by means of reciprocal agreements on transit rights both for railways and shipping on the Vistula. And they demanded that clear "assurances" had to be given by the Polish government that the "cultural autonomy" of those who would now become German minorities would be guaranteed.[12]

While these concerns dominated his agenda, it is worth noting that the core premises, broader aims and more long-term rationales – as well as expectations – of Brockdorff-Rantzau's peace policy had been reinforced rather than altered by the frustrating constellation he confronted in the spring of 1919. He still rejected any notion of reviving Wilhelminian maxims and seeking to regain Germany's power-political clout and alliance options, particularly in the east. And, like a majority in the Scheidemann government, he would have been willing to accept even more far-reaching reductions of German military power than the victors envisaged.[13] But, like all relevant German policymakers at this stage – with the exception of Erzberger – Brockdorff-Rantzau never really grasped the vital security dimension of the peacemaking process. And, in particular, he failed to recognise that it was a core task of postwar German policy to find new ways of addressing predominant French security concerns vis-à-vis its defeated but still potentially more powerful eastern neighbour.

Seeking to capture the underlying Franco-German problem, the foreign minister had earlier underscored that France had a "political interest in every [possible] weakening of Germany" as long as "these two great nations" saw one another as "hereditary enemies and faced one another 'armed to the teeth' – each 'in fear of being attacked by the other'". He had emphasised that "the world" could not permit this unstable and explosive state of affairs to continue in the longer run and thus proposed as one of the central tasks of the peace conference to "establish guarantees" that would make such continued state of fear and armed opposition "seem senseless".[14] But he never developed a coherent conception of how Germany could contribute to meeting this task – and, especially, offer France specific *German* guarantees.

---

[12] Brockdorff-Rantzau memorandum, 21 March 1919, *ADAP*, A/I, pp. 324–6; Brockdorff-Rantzau notes, 27 April 1919, *ADAP*, A/II, p. 4. See also German memorandum, 30 March 1919, Wkg. 30 geh./I, D 931 100, PA; Erzberger to Brockdorff-Rantzau, 1 April 1919, Versailles I, 9105 H/H234779, Brockdorff-Rantzau Papers; Dresel minutes of interview with Erzberger, 26 April 1919, Baker Papers.

[13] See *AR Scheidemann*, pp. 379–81; Krüger (1985), p. 74.

[14] Brockdorff-Rantzau speech, 14 February 1919, in: Brockdorff-Rantzau (1925), p. 51; *AR Scheidemann*, pp. 379–81.

Rather, Brockdorff-Rantzau confined himself to the argument that, apart from its far-reaching disarmament, the guarantees and obligations the German republic would accept once it entered the League would provide the necessary reassurance. In many ways, he thus proposed a Wilsonian remedy to the Franco-German problem, which clearly could not assuage underlying French fears at this juncture. Remarkably, even at this stage Brockdorff-Rantzau still deemed it conceivable to forge a peace of accommodation that would permit him and the government in Berlin to "reunite" the newly republican Germany with the western powers and to integrate it into the League and the new international order as a great power "with equal rights". And he still thought that the appeal to the mutual interest in forming a common front against Bolshevism could prepare the ground for such developments. In an important Cabinet meeting on 24 April, he had gone so far as to argue once again that Germany's "main aim" in approaching "the settlement of peace" had to be "the fight against Bolshevism" and to align with the western powers in this fight.[15]

At the same time, the foreign minister was in fundamental agreement with the key financial experts of the German delegation, Melchior and Warburg, that it was and remained essential to preserve what they saw as Germany's one remaining lever and strength, its economic strength. Like them, he thus deemed it vital to negotiate a settlement that served two cardinal interests. It had to preserve, as far as possible, Germany's "economic integrity" – i.e. allow it above all to keep its most relevant industrial areas, including the Saar and Upper Silesia. And, crucially, it had to ensure that the German access to the *American-dominated* postwar world economic system would not be significantly restricted. This set of core interests lay behind German invocations of the interconnectedness of world economic interests and the argument – now repeated in successive German counter-proposals – that allowing Germany to revitalise and develop its economy *within* an interdependent European and global system was a vital prerequisite for Europe's reconstruction after the war – and a viable reparations settlement.[16]

Even more critical for Brockdorff-Rantzau's pursuits remained the fundamental *political* concern to prevent Germany from becoming a "pariah state" that was placed into "quarantine" for the foreseeable future – a concern that Erzberger and in fact all key members of the German delegation and the Ebert-Scheidemann

---

[15] Cabinet meeting, 24 April 1919, *AR Scheidemann*, p. 221. But Brockdorff-Rantzau also maintained that Germany had to act as a mediator between the western powers and Russia, arguing that it had "the choice to mediate between the west and the east or to furnish the battlefield for their struggle". Brockdorff-Rantzau to Langwerth, 3 May 1919, Versailles I, 9105 H/ H234980–87, Brockdorff-Rantzau Papers.

[16] Brockdorff-Rantzau to German Foreign Office, 19 May 1919, *ADAP*, A/II, pp. 54–6; Warburg to Dernburg, 19 May 1919, *ADAP*, A/II, pp. 56–8.

government shared. The German foreign minister insisted that the fledgling German republic had to be recognised as a great power "with equal rights" in the new international order and renewed the demand for an immediate entry into the League of Nations – and a seat on the League Council.

The key procedural aim of Brockdorff-Rantzau's strategy had not changed. It was and remained to induce or "compel" the western powers to enter into actual – oral – negotiations with Germany. For he still believed that such negotiations represented "the only way" to bring their "diverging standpoints" closer together and, ultimately, to forge a peace settlement that met German demands – and preserved Germany's fundamental political, territorial and economic integrity.[17] Essentially, then, he was determined to push for a wider negotiation process with the victors, and rather than seek minor modifications of the draft treaty he adhered to a maximalist conception of the "just" peace the German government could accept. He impressed on Scheidemann that the Cabinet had to be prepared to reject the victors' peace terms and to refuse to sign any peace treaty that did not meet the far-reaching criteria he had defined – and that the German notes would now present to the world. In his view, only a hard-nosed approach of this kind could give Germany the leverage to achieve what he really desired: a breakthrough to "practical negotiations". But it was an approach that carried enormous risks – and was bound to fail in the constellation of 1919.[18]

What the German delegation embarked on under Brockdorff-Rantzau's lead can best be described as an ill-judged moral-political offensive that confronted Wilson and the other western leaders with "modern" methods that the American president himself – as well as Lenin and Trotsky – had earlier used with such enormous effect. It not only submitted an avalanche of notes to the Allied and Associated Powers that criticised the terms of the draft treaty and offered more "Wilsonian" or "practical" counter-proposals; it also made these notes public. One aim of this tactic was indeed to mobilise left and liberal opinion in the west, especially in Britain and the United States, against an "unjust" treaty that stood in opposition to the principles of a liberal-progressive peace Wilson had enunciated. And for a time Brockdorff-Rantzau and other protagonists clung to the – illusory – expectation that, stirred up by the German campaign, these leftist and liberal forces – and "world opinion" – could put such pressure on the political leaders of the victorious powers – above all Wilson and Lloyd George – that they would eventually feel compelled to engage in a process of negotiations with Germany and agree to a different, "progressive" peace.[19]

---

[17] Brockdorff-Rantzau memorandum of discussions with Dresel, 19 April 1919, *ADAP*, A/I, pp. 422–6.

[18] Brockdorff to Scheidemann, 12 May 1919, *ADAP*, A/II, p. 33.

[19] See Brockdorff-Rantzau's guidelines for "Instructions for the Press", 7 May 1919, *ADAP*, A/II, p. 3; Brockdorff-Rantzau to German Foreign Ministry, 8 May 1919, *ibid.*, pp. 19–20.

It is vital to understand that the approach Brockdorff-Rantzau pursued, and that Scheidemann, Ebert and others complemented in their different ways, also had important domestic mainsprings. In short, all of these actors insisted on a Wilsonian "peace of justice", and thus on a fundamentally unrealistic conception of what would constitute an acceptable peace, not least because they wanted to shore up the domestic legitimacy of what was and remained a very feeble government – and to rally German public opinion behind a common cause. Particularly the foreign minister was convinced that his "open diplomacy" strategy would serve to unify the German public behind the government. And because of this both he and the other protagonists of the Ebert-Scheidemann government essentially persisted with the course they had pursued since the tumultuous turn of 1918–19. They took no steps now to moderate the expectations and demands of a volatile German public. And one of the most problematic consequences of the German notes, and of the strongly worded public declarations that Ebert and Scheidemann made at this stage, was that they confirmed national expectations that had already become not just exaggerated but illusory. Crucially, while tying the government's fate to the fulfilment of such expectations they significantly contributed to creating an overall mood that was bound to make the disappointment with the actual peace terms on which the victors were likely to insist all the greater – and all the more damaging both for the future stability of the Weimar Republic and its future relations with the western powers.

Most of all, the main German decision-makers continued to encourage misleading expectations of what Wilson had pledged and was in a position to "deliver" and, ultimately, the propagandistic simplification of the thesis that the American president had broken his promises to a newly democratic Germany and, as the American observer Dresel put it, "proved himself the greatest hypocrite in all [of] history".[20] This would harden into the notion of Wilson's "great betrayal" of Germany that would be instrumentalised by German nationalists and those who sought to prevent a postwar accommodation of the Weimar Republic with the United States and "the West" in the decade after Versailles. Dresel captured important aspects of the psychological situation and prevalent attitudes in May 1919 when reporting from Berlin about the "crushing effect" the publication of the victors' peace terms had had on the German public. He commented that the German people "did not expect such peace terms" because they had been "consistently encouraged" in the notion that peace would be made "on the basis of President Wilson's Fourteen Points" and that such a peace would "not establish Germany's guilt and the necessity of atonement and reparation". And they had been "led to believe"

---

[20] Dresel to American Peace Commission, 10 May 1919, *FRUS-PPC*, XII, p. 119.

that ultimately Wilson could be "appealed to, and would arrange a comprom-ise peace satisfactory to Germany".[21]

But it should not be forgotten how immense the domestic pressures and constraints were under which Brockdorff-Rantzau, Erzberger and notably the Social Democratic protagonists of the Ebert-Scheidemann government had to operate and justify their actions.[22] And it is as crucial to underscore that these actors *perceived* these constraints and expectations as immense and immensely important. Essentially, they acted on the premise that the government, whose base and hold on power were fragile, would lose its domestic legitimacy and be swept aside by domestic opposition if it agreed to peace terms that, in their judgement a majority of the German public would find unacceptable, above all the loss of territories and German-speaking populations.[23] Brockdorff-Rantzau and others did not merely use such arguments to gain concessions from the western powers. In a wider perspective, they feared that signing a peace treaty on the victors' premises would not only discredit those who sought to establish a republican order in Germany but also jeopardise the development prospects and indeed the survival of the fledgling republic – and strengthen those, particularly nationalist and right-wing forces, that sought to undermine it and had no interest in an accommodation with the western powers. It was against this background that Scheidemann declared on 12 May that he and his government could not accept what he castigated as a peace dictate, emphatically proclaiming: "What hand would not wither that binds itself and us to these fetters?"[24]

It is worth underscoring once again that especially the leading Social Democrats faced daunting domestic challenges that made it very hard for them to contemplate a different approach to peacemaking. They still felt under enormous pressure not only to stabilise the new republican order but also to obtain what they had demanded ever since the armistice: a "Wilson peace". And Scheidemann and Ebert deemed it crucial in both respects to maintain their authority as political leaders who staunchly and patriotically defended what they considered basic interests of the German state and nation. Yet it should also be stressed again that, like Brockdorff-Rantzau, Scheidemann and Ebert fundamentally still believed that in return for their efforts to lead Germany on the path of democracy and for their commitment to the League and the new international rules it was to inaugurate, they were entitled to a

---

[21] *Ibid.*, pp. 118–19.

[22] See Krüger (1993), pp. 323–35.

[23] See Brockdorff-Rantzau remarks to Conger, Conger report to Bliss, 30 April 1919, Wilson Papers; Cabinet discussions, 8 and 9 May 1919, *AR Scheidemann*, 303–5, 308; Scheidemann speech, 12 May 1919, Scheideman (1929), II, pp. 626–8.

[24] Scheidemann speech, 12 May 1919, Scheidemann (1929), II, pp. 627–8.

"peace of justice" as they interpreted it.[25] And this led them to persist all the more categorically with their demands for such a peace – even after the victors' draft treaty had shattered many of the hopes they had earlier entertained.

II.   The Escalation of the "War of Notes" and Belated German Reorientations

The moral-political confrontation of the "war of notes" quickly escalated following the publication of the first German note of 9 May. And, after weeks of antagonising and polarising "exchanges", it reached its climax with the massive compendium of German counter-proposals of 29 May, to which the victors would respond with their newly draconian note and final ultimatum of 16 June. Some of the German notes sought to challenge the moral and legal foundations of the victors' peace terms; other notes targeted the inconsistencies of specific provisions, often precisely those that had been the result of the most hard-won compromises between the Big Three.

The first note of 9 May underscored the central German claim that on "essential points" the "basis of the Peace of Right" on which the belligerents had agreed in the armistice had been "abandoned" in the victors' draft treaty and alleged that it contained provisions that "no nation could endure" and that "could not possibly be carried out".[26] From Berlin, President Ebert sought to do his best to mobilise American public opinion and underscore Germany's moral claim to a Wilsonian peace. Speaking to reporter of the Associated Press, the German president advanced a moral appeal that was intended to press Wilson to fulfil the "sacred promise" he had made in the Fourteen Points but turned into a stinging critique of the American president's conduct at Versailles. Ebert declared that it was the duty of the American people to push their president to effect a revision of the draft treaty's "peace of force" and that the fledgling German republic was "depending on America to hold to its word". He went so far as to argue that if the promise of the Fourteen Points was broken, then the American public would be "approving the fact that their name was misused to deceive a great nation that had fought bravely into laying down its arms".[27]

The first German note on the future of the Saar district asserted that, contrary to their assurances, the underlying aim of the proposed settlement was to sever the Saar basin from Germany. For in the German interpretation it was designed to block a re-acquisition of the Saar mines even if Germany had the means and even if the proposed plebiscite after fifteen years brought a

[25] See Miller (1978), pp. 276–8; Winkler (2001), pp. 212–13; Schwabe (1998), pp. 66–7.
[26] German note, 9 May 1919, *FRUS-PPC*, V, p. 564.
[27] Ebert interview with AP correspondent, 13 May 1919, *Deutsche Allgemeine Zeitung*, 13 May 1919.

pro-German result, because it gave the Reparation Commission the power to block German aspirations by vetoing the release of the gold marks necessary to purchase the mines. More fundamentally, the note criticised in harsh – Wilsonian – language that under the terms of the draft treaty German populations would be "bartered about from sovereignty to sovereignty as if they were mere chattels and pawns in a game" whose purpose was to give "guarantee for financial and economic claims" of Germany's "adversaries" – a game that thus blatantly contradicted the principle of self-determination that Wilson had enunciated. A second note on the Saar issue then presented German proposals that were intended to offer alternative ways of satisfying French economic interests and claims, while avoiding the undesirable political implications of the victors' proposals.[28] Issuing stern warnings of a more general kind, the German notes also sought to highlight the disastrous economic consequences that, in their assessment, the draft treaty's peace terms would have. The German delegation marshalled all available German economic expertise to underscore that the proposed restrictions and severing of vital industrial areas from Germany, notably Upper Silesia, would not only cripple the German economy but also have a highly adverse effect on Europe's postwar recovery and reconstruction.[29]

Earlier, a particularly vehement note had sought to reassert Germany's political and moral claim to a prompt admission to the League of Nations. It highlighted the "discrepancy" that lay in the "fact" that while under the draft treaty Germany was "called upon to sign the statute of the League", it had not been invited to join the new organisation. And it was accompanied by a German programme for a truly "universal" League, mainly authored by Schücking, that was distinctly more radical and progressive than the victors' draft covenant – and intended to underscore the German republic's credentials as a progressive power.[30] Not all German policymakers had deemed it prudent to present an official counter-proposal of this kind. Still seeking to pave the way for an actual negotiating process, the head of the Foreign Office's League Commission, Walter Simons, had advised against this approach. He had stressed that, in view of the Scheidemann government's weak negotiating-position, it would be counter-productive to "present our opponents with an entire system as basis for the discussion" and proposed that Schücking ought to publish his League blueprint in a private capacity.[31] But both Brockdorff-Rantzau and Erzberger favoured a different approach. Particularly Erzberger considered the presentation of an official German "counter-blueprint" not

---

[28] Brockdorff-Rantzau to Clemenceau, 13 May 1919, Luckau (1941), p. 245; Brockdorff-Rantzau to Clemenceau, 16 May 1919, *ibid.*, pp. 248–50.

[29] Brockdorff-Rantzau to Clemenceau, 13 May 1919, Luckau (1941), pp. 242–4.

[30] German note and proposals, 9 May 1919, *FRUS-PPC*, VI, pp. 765–74.

[31] Simons note to Brockdorff-Rantzau, 4 April 1919, Brockdorff-Rantzau Papers, 7/7.

only reasonable but imperative. He reckoned that the new German government could thus underscore its commitment to becoming a responsible member of a universal Society of Nations that was prepared to honour the rules and obligations that it presented. Yet – like the foreign minister – he also argued that a German blueprint that could be presented as more progressive and universal than their original Draft Covenant would serve to put pressure on the governments of the principal victors. It could appeal to "world opinion" and, in particular, help to win the support of socialist and liberal opposition parties in the victorious nations as well as of neutral states. Erzberger's "strategy" would be pursued. In mid-April, the Scheidemann Cabinet decided to authorise Schücking to take the lead in finalising "a German blueprint for a League of Nations".[32]

What Schücking proposed was indeed a far-reaching legalist-internationalist blueprint for a league conceived as an authoritative and universal organisation whose chief purpose was to establish the dominance of international law in relations between states. At the heart of Schücking's proposal lay an elaborate system of arbitration that enumerated detailed procedures for the settlement of different categories of disputes under a newly reinforced regime of international law and sanctions. This clearly reflected his resolve to build on the rules and understandings of the Hague Conventions and, in their emphasis on the primacy of arbitration, his ideas were more compatible with Bourgeois' conceptions than with those of Wilson or Cecil. Yet like the latter, Schücking essentially envisaged the League as a mechanism that was to regulate disputes and also – in the German interest – peaceful change rather than cement a particular status quo. Predictably, his blueprint also made the case for creating a comprehensive League in which Germany was to be included from the outset, on terms of mutuality and equality under international law. To underscore its representative and democratic character, Schücking proposed the establishment of a League "world parliament" whose members were to be appointed by national parliaments rather than governments. Finally, reflecting Warburg's ideas, the German blueprint emphasised that the League had to be empowered to uphold equitable economic relations between states, further economic co-operation between them and aid advances towards a global trade regime that abolished all forms of discrimination. This was supposed to appeal in particular to Wilson and the American delegation.[33]

Though unmistakably revealing the tactical purposes they served, the German notes thus not only threw into relief how preoccupied Brockdorff-Rantzau and a majority of German decision-makers were with preventing both a political and economic exclusion and both a moral and political

---

[32] See Cabinet protocols, 22 and 23 April 1919, *AR Scheidemann*, nos. 50 and 51.
[33] Schücking, League blueprint, 9 May 1919, *Die Pariser Völkerbundsakte* (1919); Wintzer (2006), pp. 152–7.

ostracisation of Germany from the reconfigured postwar order. They also underscored the German foreign minister's preoccupation with the moral and ideological dimensions of the peace settlement and questions of status and "honour". What proved particularly problematic was the way in which the foreign minister focused his attention on a moral-political battle in which he had nothing to gain at this juncture and struggled to refute what he considered the victors' unwarranted assertion of the "exclusive guilt of Germany for the world war" in Article 231 of the draft treaty. Echoing what Brockdorff-Rantzau had argued during the ceremony on 7 May, the German notes of 13 and 24 May not only sought to counter the thesis that the German people could be held responsible for the actions of the leadership of the German Empire. They also rejected the underlying claim that the German Empire's government of 1914 bore sole responsibility for the outbreak of the war.[34]

In Brockdorff-Rantzau's view, it was essential to challenge the "war guilt" clause, which he regarded as the "starting-point" or basic premise of the entire peace settlement the victors had put forward, in order to emphasise that the eventual peace settlement had to be based on different premises, i.e. those of a Wilsonian "peace of justice".[35] But what was intended as a pre-emptive offensive against the "war guilt" premise effectively pushed a politically and morally fraught question to the top of the agenda that could not possibly addressed in a balanced manner under the circumstances. And the effect Brockdorff-Rantzau's offensive was bound to have was to provoke strong reactions from the western powers – which now closed ranks and would insist more unequivocally than before on Germany's exclusive responsibility for the war. Ultimately, all of this would sharpen the public confrontation between the victors and the vanquished.[36]

More fundamentally, it was inherently problematic to turn the exchanges with the victors into an ideological and moral competition. And it was no less problematic to try, as it were, to "beat Wilson at this own game" while accusing him more or less bluntly of having broken his promises, as this was bound to have an antagonising effect on the American president. For he could rightly perceive this as a direct assault on his political and moral integrity. At the same time, Brockdorff-Rantzau's campaign was based on profound mis-calculations regarding the inner dynamics of the victors' negotiation processes and the leverage he or any German actor could have either to induce or "compel" them to agree to substantive negotiations – or to induce Wilson or Lloyd George to intercede on behalf of a German-style "Wilsonian peace". And it clearly vastly overestimated the *immediate* impact that left-liberal

[34] Brockdorff-Rantzau to Clemenceau, 13 and 24 May 1919, Luckau (1941), pp. 240–1, 271.
[35] Brockdorff-Rantzau to Bernstorff, 15 May 1919, *ADAP*, A/II, p. 26.
[36] For a balanced assessment of the "war guilt" problem in 1919, see Krüger (1985), pp. 61–5.

opinion and domestic pressures could have on the American president – yet also on the British premier.

In the end, what the foreign minister pushed forward and what Ebert and others seconded reinforced not only Clemenceau's but also, and especially, Wilson's opposition to any kind of more substantial negotiations with the German delegation; and while the German notes had a particularly strong impact on the British delegation, reinforcing misgivings about the draft treaty that had already existed before, they ultimately did not lead Lloyd George to advocate actual negotiations either – or to push for *fundamental* changes of the peace settlement. Arguably, however, a different, more diplomatic or tactically astute German approach would not have led to a significantly different outcome in 1919 – let alone to a negotiated "Wilsonian peace" that would have met German expectations. For, as we have seen, the victors continued to determine the basic parameters and limits of the peacemaking process; and, as will be shown, their prevalent interests, core constraints and underlying assumptions would leave no room for a qualitative transformation of this process at that stage, or rather: it even *precluded* any transformative changes towards a negotiated "peace of accommodation".

Yet German approaches to peacemaking actually underwent a significant reorientation while the "war of notes" escalated. This reorientation only began to gain momentum at the eleventh hour and – when assessed with the benefit of hindsight – came far too late to make a decisive difference in the constellation of May 1919; but it should nonetheless be highlighted. For it marked the – difficult – early stage in a longer-term reorientation and indeed learning process in which those who sought to develop a "republican" German foreign policy attempted to find more realistic ways of furthering an accommodation and coming to an understanding with the western victors of the war. This recalibrated approach could not bear fruit under the immensely adverse conditions of Versailles, and Brockdorff-Rantzau's confrontational campaign for a "Wilsonian peace" had by this time created the worst possible preconditions for its successful pursuit. But it is indeed noteworthy, because it anticipated *in some respects* the future western-orientated policy of accommodation that would be pursued by the Weimar Republic's pre-eminent foreign minister Gustav Stresemann in the mid-1920s – and eventually foster Weimar Germany's integration into a nascent Euro-Atlantic peace order.

In short, what Brockdorff-Rantzau eventually came to back was an attempt to strike an accommodating "grand bargain" with the victors, which incorporated ideas he and Erzberger had already outlined in April but whose core elements were elaborated by the financial experts Melchior and Warburg. It hinged on the idea of offering substantial financial concessions – in essence, a fixed sum of 100 billion Goldmarks to meet Allied reparation demands – in order to pave the way for a negotiated *quid pro quo* agreement with the victorious powers that preserved Germany's territorial integrity and economic development prospects. The underlying aim was to ensure that the German republic would be accorded a place in, rather than barred from, the new western-dominated political and economic order.

One of the many factors that impeded the formulation of more realistic and level-headed German policies in 1919 was indeed that those who sought to negotiate on Germany's behalf had to act largely in isolation, barred from interaction or direct exchanges with the representatives of the victorious powers. And that they basically had to rely on whatever – very sketchy – information and insights about the deliberations of the victors they could gain through informal channels and intermediaries like Conger and Dresel. The only real exception here were the exchanges that Melchior and Warburg had, particularly with Keynes and other British experts, during preliminary financial negotiations they had pursued at Château Villette in April. It is thus not particularly surprising that they found it difficult to respond and adapt to the political "realities" they confronted and to gain a more accurate understanding both of their own room to manoeuvre and of priorities, interests and constraints of the victors. And it is equally unsurprising that they, and particularly Brockdorff-Rantzau, found it particularly challenging to develop more "realistic" peace strategies – and aims.

Yet by mid-May, little more than a week after the campaign of notes had been launched, not only Erzberger and a majority of the Scheidemann Cabinet in Berlin but also the protagonists of the German delegation in Paris, including the foreign minister himself, had begun to realise that it was very unlikely to have the desired effect. Particularly after the controversies Brockdorff-Rantzau's first "war guilt" note had created, important Cabinet members – foremost among them Erzberger and the Social Democratic minister Eduard David – became acutely concerned about the consequences of the foreign minister's confrontational approach. While David emerged as the most vocal critic in the Cabinet's deliberations Erzberger, who had long objected to the entire thrust of the foreign minister's pursuits, became the real driving force behind the push for a new policy.

On 7 May, Erzberger had still thought that the draft treaty could not represent Wilson's final word and that the American president could yet be persuaded to take the lead in revising the victors' terms.[37] But in his view this was only conceivable if German representatives, instead of antagonising the governments of the victors, pursued a more conciliatory approach and made concrete and constructive proposals that accommodated what he regarded as the victors' key interests. Fundamentally, he pursued the same overriding objective as Brockdorff-Rantzau, namely to negotiate an agreement that prevented territorial losses, long-term economic restrictions and Germany's

---

[37] Erzberger to Bernstorff, 7 May 1919, Pol. 4., 1919, PA.

political isolation. But he advocated a different approach to this end – an approach whose underlying aim was to open up more pragmatic avenues towards a *peace of accommodation*.

On 19 May, Erzberger laid out his plans to Colonel Conger. His thinking centred on proposals to come to a political arrangement of the reparations question and on offering France voluntary German security guarantees, also for its reparation payments. What he proposed were the basic outlines of a *quid pro quo* agreement under which the victors would accept an immediate German entry in the League and pledge that the occupation of the Rhineland would be terminated within six months; in return, Germany would pledge that "no military forces would be maintained within a distance of 50 kilometres of the east bank of the Rhine". This prefigured core elements of Stresemann's security policy of the mid-1920s and the Locarno pact of 1925. Like Melchior and Warburg, Erzberger calculated that in order to make such an agreement possible the German government would have to come up with a substantial reparations offer. Yet he also came back to his idea that Germany should offer support for the reconstruction of devastated areas in France and Belgium. He had earlier submitted detailed proposals for sending 100,000 German workers and, after half a year, 500,000 more workers, estimating that they could complete their task in a "modern and sanitary" fashion.[38] Erzberger's proposals were deemed "very reasonable" by some American peace commissioners. But Wilson never gave them any serious consideration.[39]

By now, however, Brockdorff-Rantzau also conceded that the German note campaign was unlikely to reach its intended objective, noting that despite German efforts the draft treaty had not "met resistance" on the part of the "enemy peoples" that could be expected to have a "tangible impact" on the peace negotiations in the foreseeable future. On behalf of the German delegation he thus sought to gain the Scheidemann Cabinet's approval for a change of strategy. The new approach was based on the assumption that "the enemy governments" could only be "compelled to enter into negotiations over the modification of the draft treaty" if the German government offered "concessions" that were "so clear and substantial" that the political leaders of the victorious powers would not be able to justify to their peoples to "cut negotiations short" and use means of force to impose their terms. The foreign minister urged the Cabinet to adopt the rationale that if Germany desired to "limit concessions in the territorial sphere to a minimum" – and thus to prevent "irretrievable losses" that clearly would be hardest to bear – then "far-reaching sacrifices in the financial and economic sphere" would be

[38] Erzberger proposals to Colonel Conger, Conger report, 19 May 1919, in Epstein (1959), pp. 430–1.
[39] See Schwabe (1985), pp. 350–2.

"necessary".[40] Following heated discussions between the delegation and the Cabinet, and two rounds of consultations between representatives of both sides at Spa on 18 and 23 May, this rationale indeed came to inform what was the most significant German attempt to strike an ambitious strategic bargain and to forge a mutually acceptable negotiated peace in 1919.

This bargain offer became an integral part of, yet would also almost be buried within, the enormous compendium of notes the German delegation submitted to the Allied and Associated Governments on 29 May. While Brockdorff-Rantzau had contemplated an approach of this kind in general terms, Melchior and Warburg had developed a more concrete plan. They proposed that Germany should offer to pay what in their assessment would meet or even exceed the highest reparation demands the *Entente* governments were contemplating: the astronomical total of 100 billion Goldmarks, made as an interest-free payment. A first tranche of 20 billion was to be paid until 1926 and include payments in kind and contributions to reconstruction efforts; this was in fact inconceivable without raising fresh capital, which ultimately meant: American loans. Then annual payments of at least 1 billion were to be pledged, yet they were to be correlated to a certain percentage of the German annual budget, thus taking into account Germany's financial situation and capacity to pay.

As Warburg emphasised, one important premise of the envisaged scheme was that the German government would no longer insist that its liability was limited by the "legal premises" of the Lansing note, but rather make "practical proposals" that the "enemy governments" could accept and justify to "their peoples". Seeking to appeal to British interests, the German experts recommended that Germany should offer to pay not only for direct war damages in Belgium and northern France but also to cover other kinds of damages – such as pension payments.[41] Melchior and Warburg thus essentially advocated a departure from the insistence on a Wilsonian peace or "peace of right". Rather, they sought to address what they identified as core financial and political interests of Britain and France. At the same time, they reckoned that Wilson and other American representatives would have an interest in a "fixed sum" reparations settlement that settled this problem and created favourable conditions for an economic recovery of Europe. They thus pinned their hopes on gaining Wilson's support.

Both Melchior, who was the main architect of the scheme, and Warburg, who had a critical influence on its final elaboration, fundamentally agreed with Brockdorff-Rantzau that it was essential not only to prevent irretrievable

---

[40] Brockdorff-Rantzau to AA, 19 May 1919, *ADAP*, A/II, pp. 54–6. See also Brockdorff to Cabinet, 18 May 1919, *AR Scheidemann*, pp. 338–45.

[41] See Warburg to Dernburg, 19 May 1919, Pol. Ib/1, 1919, PA; Max to Fritz Warburg, 20 May 1919, Max Warburg Papers. See Krüger (1973), pp. 181–91.

territorial losses but also to preserve what they regarded as Germany's one remaining strength after the defeat and a crucial prerequisite for its re-ascension as a republican great power: its economic clout. A further cardinal objective they thus pursued was to induce the victors, through the generous reparation offer, to refrain from imposing longer-term economic discriminations and restrictions on Germany and thus to ensure that postwar Germany would regain unfettered access to the world market and what they envisaged as an American-dominated world economic system after the war. Melchior and Warburg argued that the German government should essentially be prepared to countenance substantial financial liabilities (in the form of long-term reparation payments) in order to pursue these overriding political and economic objectives. In Warburg's view, making a substantial financial offer even represented the only way to prevent a completely unacceptable peace treaty. He at this point warned that an outright German refusal to sign a treaty unless it was substantially revised would have disastrous consequences – it would seal the "*finis Germaniae*".[42] Eventually, however, he would be so incensed by what he saw as the victors' irresponsible intransigence that he came to advocate a rejection of the final treaty terms in June.

In a wider context, what Melchior and Warburg hoped to advance was a distinctly ambitious – indeed transformative – world-economic agenda. At one level, they sought to promote the idea that allowing Germany to recover and trade without restrictions was a key prerequisite for Europe's postwar reconstruction but also for a workable reparations regime that satisfied British, French and Belgian demands, which – they argued – ultimately depended on Germany's ability to achieve on-going export surpluses. This corresponded with the recommendations of Keynes and leading US experts like Davis. But the "visions" of Melchior and Warburg went further. They argued that it was in the common interest of Germany, the *Entente* Powers and the United States to establish new world-economic mechanisms, rules and understandings that were to further a general economic upturn in and beyond Europe. Crucial elements of this framework were to be – apart from the aforementioned liberal regime of world trade – funds to stabilise currencies and mutual credit systems not just for the procurement of goods and raw materials but also to deal with the newly pressing problem of international indebtedness. And, in line with his earlier conceptions, particularly Warburg envisaged giving the League a key function in this respect, namely that of a kind of superstructure for the new postwar economic system and, above all, a "clearing house" for the re-establishment of credit in Europe and on a global scale. These ideas would find their way into the German League proposals of 9 May.[43]

[42] Warburg to Dernburg, 19 May 1919, Max Warburg Papers.
[43] German note and proposals, 9 May 1919, *FRUS-PPC*, VI, pp. 765–74; Mr to Mrs Warburg, 24 April 1919, in Warburg (1952), pp. 76–7.

Yet – like those of Keynes – the more ambitious plans of the German experts essentially misjudged the American government's interest and willingness to support League-based or other "clearing house" schemes that ultimately would have required the American government to make substantial commitments – notably for loans to Germany – or to act as the main underwriter of a new international regime of loans and financial "consolidation".

In a slightly modified form, the Melchior–Warburg proposal became the pivotal part of what turned out to be the final major German counter-proposals to the victors' draft treaty of 29 May 1919. Yet, unavoidably reflecting the different priorities and philosophies of the key actors in the Cabinet and in the delegation that had contributed to it, the 100-page note not only exceeded all reasonable scale, hardly lending itself to focusing the victors' attention on the crucial German proposals and concessions. It also became a hybrid in terms of its underlying rationales and overt emphases, inchoately encompassing both accommodating language and renewed moral-political challenges to the victors. Outlining the far-reaching reparation proposal, the note stressed that, by way of a *quid pro quo*, the German government would demand a substantial modification of the peace terms that essentially preserved Germany's political and territorial integrity in the borders of 1914 and allowed it to regain its "freedom of economic movement at home and abroad". In particular, it restated German claims not only to the Saar district but also to Upper Silesia, which were categorised as "unquestionably German". Following Brockdorff-Rantzau's rather than Erzberger's arguments, the note even rejected plebiscites in these areas. It only called for them in cases where Germany could "consent to the surrender of territory", which applied to Alsace-Lorraine and some districts with mixed populations in Posen.[44]

To reinforce German claims to Upper Silesia, the note not only invoked the principle of self-determination but advanced a combination of historical, economic and geopolitical arguments. It maintained that the region had "belonged to the German state", had been developed by Germans and acquired a "predominantly German character" while having no "political connection" with Poland since 1163. Under the heading "Germany cannot spare Upper Silesia. Poland does not need it", it emphasised that the region's industries were central to Germany's "economic structure" and warned that without it Germany would not be in a position to "fulfil the obligations arising from the war". Interestingly, however, it also advanced a wider political argument, designed to appeal especially to Lloyd George and Wilson. It argued that imposing a decision in favour of Poland would not be in the interests of the local populations or "of the other states of Europe and the World". For it would create "new elements of dispute and enmity" – and, for Germany,

---

[44] German note, 29 May 1919, *FRUS-PPC*, VI, pp. 821–2, 854.

"an ever-open wound". As the "recovery" of Upper Silesia would be the "glowing desire of every German", this would put enormous pressure on any German government and ultimately "endanger seriously the peace of Europe and of the World".[45]

It should not be neglected, however, that the note also re-accentuated what in the German interpretation amounted to a mutually advantageous vision of a political *do ut des* agreement. It argued once again that a German republic that committed itself to a democratic form of government and to disarmament "in advance" of the other powers had to be permitted to enter the League "as a Power with equal rights" immediately on the signature "of the agreed Treaty of Peace". And it argued that on the basis of these commitments, Germany's acceptance of the new organisation's Covenant would not only furnish the "best possible proof" that it was "once and for all renouncing all military and imperialistic tendencies" – and prepared to co-operate in a new international concert – but also provide the most effective guarantee for its willingness to comply with the terms of the peace treaty. This was to render all further political and territorial guarantees – and especially the occupation of the Rhineland – superfluous.[46]

Brockdorff-Rantzau and those who had contributed to drafting the massive German note considered these proposals both compelling and accommodating; and they clung to the hope that they would at last instigate negotiations with the western powers. Yet this overriding aim was hardly furthered by the cover note that introduced the German convolute of offers and demands. Mainly formulated by Schücking, it reiterated Germany's legal and moral claim to a "peace of justice" on Wilsonian terms – and in fact resumed and even amplified the provocative tone that had characterised Brockdorff-Rantzau's earlier strategy. Schücking's cover note once again deplored that the terms the Allied and Associated powers had presented stood "in sharpest contradiction with the agreed basis for a lasting Peace of Right" that the armistice had provided. It once again contrasted these terms with the publicly proclaimed war and peace aims of Wilson and the *Entente* leaders, highlighting in particular the "solemn pledge" the American president had allegedly made that in return for inner reforms and democratisation, Germany would be assured of a "peace of justice" along the lines of the Fourteen Points. And it emphatically demanded that the western powers had to honour the "idea of national self-determination" in their dealings with Germany.

Schücking proclaimed that it was an idea that had guided those who had won American independence and those who "shook off" the fetters of absolutism in western Europe – and that the "heirs of such sacred traditions" could

---

[45] *Ibid.*, pp. 833–5; Lord (1921), p. 80.
[46] German note, 29 May 1919, *FRUS-PPC*, VI, pp. 797–8, 819–21.

not now "refuse this right to the German people, who have only just attained in their internal affairs the capacity to live in accordance with their free will for justice". He thus sought to impress on the victors – and "world opinion" – that a conflict of the destructiveness of the Great War required nothing less than "the establishment of a new order in the world", an order in which "the great idea of democracy" was realised and that was maintained by a "real" and universal league of democratic nations that included Germany. The German cover note reached its remarkable crescendo in a fierce condemnation of the victors' draft treaty, declaring that it utterly failed to meet these requirements and represented instead "the last dreadful triumph" of a "moribund conception of the world, imperialistic and capitalistic in tendency".[47]

Essentially, then, the German protagonists had scrambled to put together what in effect was a contradictory approach, which at the same time sought to provide incentives for immediate – confidential – negotiations with the political leaders of the victorious powers and to put – public – pressure on them. For a majority still believed such pressure could either make the victors more accommodating, or create conditions for a more fundamental revision of the treaty s terms at a later stage. But this "strategy" proved self-defeating. As Simons observed, the main weakness of the German "exposé" was that while it should have conveyed "the overall impression of enormous concessions" of the German government – and listed them in a concise manner – what it actually conveyed was an "impression of accusation and criticism" that overshadowed the decisive offer of a "grand bargain".[48] On 19 May, Brockdorff-Rantzau had voiced his conviction that if the German government could "persevere for two more months" – and if it was possible to keep the German public united behind a policy of perseverance – it would be able to obtain an "acceptable peace".[49] But it was precisely such a prolongation of the peacemaking process, which could expose or widen divisions between them and unravel their hard-won compromises they had forged, that the political leaders of the victors, and particularly Clemenceau and Wilson, were determined to prevent.

III. Reinforcing the Peace of the Victors. French Efforts to Refute and Contain the German Challenge

Predictably, Clemenceau and Tardieu reacted most sternly and uncompromisingly to the flood of German notes and what the latter called Brockdorff-Rantzau's "evil reasoning".[50] And they concentrated all their energies on preventing any kind of general negotiations with the German plenipotentiaries

---

[47] German note, 29 May 1919, *FRUS-PPC*, VI, pp. 817–18.
[48] Simons note, May 1919, in Krüger (1973), p. 193; Luckau (1941), p. 124.
[49] Brockdorff-Rantzau statement, 19 May 1919, in Krüger (1973), p. 192.
[50] Tardieu (I/1921), p. 278.

and any significant changes to the draft treaty. From their vantage-point, which reflected the dominant French attitudes at the time, opening the door to negotiations threatened to undermine the core elements of their hard-won agreements with the Anglo-American powers on the Rhineland, the Saar, Germany's eastern borders and reparations, which they deemed integral to their strategy of securing France by achieving a maximal containment of German power. And making any concessions to the Scheidemann government, particularly on the territorial and political issues that German decision-makers deemed vital, was precisely what they considered utterly irreconcilable with the underlying aims of this strategy. On the same grounds, envisaging some kind of mutually acceptable *quid pro quo*-bargain with Germany appeared even more inconceivable. They thus sought to prevent any such scenario by available means.[51] This was and remained the decisive consideration for Clemenceau and Tardieu, and the main impetus behind their pre-emptive pursuits in May and June 1919.

Essentially, the French premier and his main adviser staunchly adhered to the basic assumptions and maxims that had informed their approach to peacemaking all along. They insisted all the more adamantly that it was not only futile but highly risky to envisage modifications that made the peace more acceptable to the German government and might buttress what they saw as Germany's superficial democratisation process. And they impressed on the Anglo-American counterparts that if necessary the victors had to be prepared to use force to coerce the German government into signing a stern victors' peace.[52] Brockdorff-Rantzau's confrontational strategy reinforced these assumptions. But the French protagonists had already formed their views of and *préjugés* against him and the government he represented long before they encountered the German delegation face-to-face. And politically, the German foreign minister's conduct actually proved useful for them, allowing them to portray the German foreign minister as an embodiment of the old regime and fundamentally unaltered German attitudes that could only be met by a resolute determination of the victors to maintain a common front, refuse any compromise and ultimately impose a justly punitive "second Treaty of Versailles" on the defeated power.[53] The French premier could be assured of a fundamental consensus within the French delegation and government on these essential points, while his main domestic critics, notably Poincaré, of course opposed any negotiations with or concessions to the German government even more stridently.

In the escalating "war of notes" Clemenceau and other key members of the French delegation thus took the lead in ensuring – all in all successfully – that the German notes received strongly worded responses and that the claims and

---

[51] See Clemenceau remarks, Council of Four, 7 June 1919, Mantoux (1955), II, p. 336.
[52] Council of Four, 2 June 1919, Mantoux (1992), II, pp. 272–6. See also Clemenceau remarks, Council of Four, 28 March 1919, *ibid.*, I, pp. 62–5.
[53] Clemenceau remarks, 7 May 1919, Baker (1923), II, pp. 501–2.

demands they advanced were more or less categorically refuted. The victors' reply to Brockdorff-Rantzau's first "war guilt" note, mainly authored by Klotz, emphatically declared that Germany bore exclusive responsibility for the outbreak and escalation of the war – and that not only William II and the imperial government of 1914 but the German people as a whole had to be held responsible and accept the consequences of the German "crime against humanity and civilisation".[54] This indeed highlighted the extent to which the moral-political stand-off between them and the vanquished not only reinforced *but also hardened* the stance all of the victors officially adopted on Germany's culpability for the Great War, which in turn ultimately had to reinforce their insistence on imposing a peace on the defeated power that was justified as a "peace of judgement".

The French protagonists also set the tone for allied responses to more specific German grievances. Tardieu formulated an unyielding note on the Saar question. Going beyond political and economic arguments, he now sought to justify French claims to the Saar by underscoring that a significant proportion of the local population was essentially "as French in their hearts and in their aspirations as the Alsatians and Lorrainers". Seeking to deflect both German and Anglo-American criticism, he insisted that what the French government proposed was by no means an "imperialistic solution" of the Saar problem. And he defended the idea that a plebiscite would be held only after fifteen years by insisting that an immediate plebiscite would be illegitimate and sacrifice "the French of the Saar" because it would have to be held under conditions shaped by "a century of Prussian oppression".[55]

To justify his uncompromising attitude and to counter eventual British calls for significant changes in the draft treaty, Clemenceau once again invoked the pressures of French "public opinion". He told Wilson and Lloyd George that he could make "no concession" on the critical question of the Rhineland occupation or with a view to reparations because he was "attacked on all sides" in the French parliament and in the French public because he *had already made* "excessive concessions". And he warned that his government would risk being toppled if he agreed to any modifications that could be interpreted as a betrayal of cardinal French interests for the sake of "appeasing" Germany.[56] The domestic constellation and pressures the French premier confronted at this stage indeed differed markedly from those his British and American counterparts were facing. Only a distinct minority of Socialist politicians and left-wing opinion-makers argued that the conditions of the draft treaty were too draconian and that a different kind of peace should be made with Germany – a

---

[54] See Tardieu (1921), pp. 14–26.

[55] See Tardieu's draft reply to the German note of 13 May 1919, 15 May 1919, *FRUS-PPC*, V, pp. 823–4; Tardieu (I/1921), p. 278.

[56] Council of Four, 2 June 1919, Mantoux (1992), II, pp. 272–6.

settlement that strengthened German democratisation efforts and prepared the ground for a reconciliation process with France's long-term enemy, also by facilitating Germany's admission to a more genuine League of Nations. Yet the effect of such views and criticisms on the general French debate was minimal, and they had no bearing on Clemenceau's pursuits.

The direct or indirect impact of the German notes was even more limited. Overall, they met with a decidedly hostile reception. The French premier could thus undoubtedly act on the premise that his government's intransigent reaction to the German counterproposals – and particularly to the German note of 29 May, which an influential French opinion-maker castigated as a "monument of impudence" – was widely backed in France. And, crucially, the same applied to his refusal to allow any kind of actual negotiating process with German representatives. What Clemenceau had to take more seriously was pressure from Poincaré, Foch and nationalist critics who accused him of having been too conciliatory to the Anglo-American powers and who asserted that the terms of the draft treaty did not go far enough, essentially falling short of protecting France against the German menace.[57] As noted, in April Clemenceau had faced not only Foch's opposition to the Rhineland compromise but also a parliamentary crisis after numerous Senators and over 300 members of the *Assemblée* had signed a manifesto in which they demanded that Germany had to be obliged not only to pay indemnities for the full cost of the war but also to accept "territorial guarantees".

Yet the French premier had actually reasserted his authority by the time the "war of notes" with the German government escalated. He was thus in a comparatively strong position – and not, as he claimed, in acute danger of being replaced by a more assertively nationalist government that would insist on a more draconian peace.[58] Nonetheless, Clemenceau still had to reckon with considerable public and parliamentary opposition – not only in nationalist quarters – to any modifications of the victors' peace terms that could be seen as "softening" French guarantees and making undue concessions to Germany. Fundamentally, however, it was for overriding strategic reasons and because of his deeply entrenched assumptions about German behaviour that he persisted with his own hard-line approach. He had no intention of using his reinforced authority to make the case for a different, more accommodating settlement with Germany.

IV. Towards a "Stern But Just Peace". Wilson's Hardening Outlook

Arguably, no actor had done more – both during and after the Great War – to push moralistic categories and questions of principles and norms to the

---

[57] See Miquel (1977), pp. 548–55; Duroselle (1988), pp. 758–66; Noble (1935), pp. 353–63.
[58] See Stevenson (1982), pp. 187–8.

forefront of international politics than Wilson. Yet it was hardly surprising that he reacted sternly and defensively to a German "open diplomacy" campaign that so directly contested his authority as a "just" peacemaker and that accused him so undiplomatically of no longer acting in accordance with the principles he had proclaimed. The American president in fact chose to ignore most German notes. But in one of only two direct replies he drafted, he emphatically declared that the Allied and Associated Powers had formulated their peace terms "with constant thought of the principles upon which the Armistice and the negotiations for peace were proposed". At the same time, however, he basically repudiated any further German appeal to the Fourteen Points and asserted that it was the prerogative of the victorious powers to decide what constituted the appropriate legal basis of the peace settlement. Wilson demanded that the German plenipotentiaries should confine themselves to submitting "suggestions of a practical kind".[59]

Overall, Wilson now came to adopt an increasingly tougher and uncompromising approach towards the German government, and this was to have a crucial impact on the dynamics and course of the final stage of the peacemaking process. And this change was indeed reinforced by the strategy of Brockdorff-Rantzau, who in the president's – superficial – judgement represented the attitudes of the old German regime rather than a republican new beginning – and "an extreme opposition to [the western powers'] views".[60] In late April, when waiting for the arrival of the German delegation, Wilson had still impressed on Clemenceau and Lloyd George that Berlin's plenipotentiaries represented "a very unstable government". And he had warned that it would be discredited if they agreed to peace terms that were "absolutely unacceptable to the nation they represent". As he emphasised, the danger that then could arise was that Scheidemann's Cabinet would be replaced by a government that represented "far more dangerous" tendencies, either reactionary or Bolshevik.

Wilson had even argued that the western powers had to pay attention to the requirements of what he characterised as a kind of new international and political "equilibrium" that they had to foster in and beyond postwar Europe.[61] By this the American president did not mean a recast balance of power but a new kind of inter- and transnational equilibrium that had to be maintained by and between democratic states. In his interpretation, the main requirement of peace was that the states and forces that rejected both reactionary *and* Bolshevik alternatives and espoused democratic self-government and the rules of the League had to prevail and maintain this equilibrium. Wilson noted that from "a dynamic point of view", the western powers had to "see what will

---

[59] Note of 10 May 1919, *FRUS-PPC*, V, p. 564.

[60] Wilson remarks, Council of Four, 24 April 1919, Mantoux (1992), I, pp. 354–5.

[61] Wilson remarks, Council of Four, 25 April 1919, Mantoux (1992), I, pp. 372–3.

unleash the least force against the equilibrium" he sought to establish. What he clearly implied was that the settlement had to be made so acceptable to the defeated power that it would reduce oppositional "force" of this kind as far as possible – and that this would constitute an essential prerequisite for creating a stable overall equilibrium in the longer term.[62] And in private he even conceded that the "results" of the draft treaty that would be presented to Germany were "far from ideal" – although he also insisted that he had managed to keep them "tolerably close to the lines" he had laid down in his peace programme.[63]

By mid-May, after the "war of notes" had gained momentum, Wilson had come to espouse a distinctly different premise, which he would basically maintain till the very end of the peacemaking process. Essentially, he adopted the rationale that the establishment of the League, the nucleus of what he still regarded as a "new world order", and the necessity to prevent an unravelling of all the complex compromises he had forged with the British and French leaders on which these advances depended, warranted the *de facto* imposition of a victor's peace.[64] Characteristically, however, while also stressing such tactical and strategic concerns, he mainly vindicated this approach in moral terms and, ultimately, in terms of justice *as he saw them*. He stated that he would eventually consider minor amendments to the draft treaty if it could be "shown" that particular provisions were "unjust". Fundamentally, however, he now declared, and had by all appearances begun to convince himself, that while the victors' peace terms were "undoubtedly very severe indeed", they were also appropriately "harsh" and – crucially – overall met his standards of a "just peace".[65]

It was on these grounds that the American president rejected any notion of more substantive negotiations with the German delegation – and any moves towards a compromise settlement with Germany. He clearly opposed the idea of a peace of accommodation that took into account the victors' interests and needs but also sought to address the most pressing political concerns and legitimation requirements of the unstable Scheidemann government. And he did not want to alter the hard-won terms of the victors merely for the sake making the peace more acceptable for the defeated power or buttressing moderate republican forces in Germany. On 10 May, Wilson emphasised to Clemenceau and Lloyd George not only that he considered the terms they had "prepared" among themselves fundamentally "just" but also that the German perception that he was "ready to favour a compromise" was misleading, and

---

[62] *Ibid.*

[63] Wilson to Herron, 28 April 1919, in Briggs (1932), p. 162.

[64] See Wilson remarks in meeting with US peace commissioners, 3 June 1919, *FRUS-PPC*, XI, pp. 219–20.

[65] Wilson to Smuts, 16 May 1919, Wilson Papers.

that he certainly had "no intention of favouring them".[66] He had thus had clearly abandoned the rationales that had earlier led him to envisage a more integrative "peace without victory" and impress on the British premier that a peace that would simply be decreed by the victors would be a "sham"; and he had departed from earlier maxims of fostering a more durable postwar "equilibrium".[67] His main concern now was far more limited: to ensure that the German government would sign a basically unaltered peace treaty.

Wilson's hardening attitude was also reflected in the more categorical and one-sided stance he adopted – in response to Brockdorff-Rantzau's campaign of notes – on the question of Germany's responsibility for the war. Exasperated by the tone and assertions of the German "war guilt" notes, yet mainly with the aim of reinforcing the legitimacy of the victors' peace terms, he now asserted that they constituted a proper and justified response to "the very great offense to civilisation which the German state committed" and underscored that it was necessary to make "evident once and for all" that such an offence could "lead only to the most severe punishment". Later he would argue in internal debates of the American Peace Delegation that the German people had "earned" severe peace conditions and that it would be "profitable" for them "as a nation" to "learn once and for all what an unjust war means" – and what severe consequences it had. Having to cope with the immense and concrete pressures of the complex negotiating process at Versailles, the American president had thus by now clearly distanced himself from his original emphasis on the decisive role of European balance-of-power politics and the systemic origins of the Great War. And he had abandoned the distinction between the German leaders and the German people that had been central to his Fourteen Points agenda.[68]

On the most fundamental level, Wilson's turn towards a more severe approach was thus informed by hardening assumptions, above all the assumption that the victorious powers had a rightful claim to impose a "stern but just" peace. Yet the extent to which the American president's resistance to negotiations and compromises with the German government was also influenced by weighty political considerations and constraints – both in the international and the domestic spheres – should not be underestimated. In the international sphere – which mattered most – they indeed pointed to the core of the dynamics and inherent momentum and constraints of the complex bargaining process among the victors that had dominated the peace negotiations ever since mid-January. In the domestic sphere, they were bound up with the

[66] Wilson remarks, Council of Four, 10 May 1919, Mantoux (1992), II, p. 19.

[67] Minutes of Imperial War Cabinet meeting, 30 December 1918, PWW, LIII, p. 564.

[68] Wilson to Smuts, 16 May 1919, Wilson Papers; Wilson remarks in meeting with US peace commissioners, 3 June 1919, FRUS-PPC, XI, p. 218. See also Mantoux (1955), II, pp. 121–2.

crucial task of eventually ensuring Congressional and wider public backing for his League and peace priorities.

In response to Hoover and other critical voices in the American peace delegation who held that he had distanced himself too far from his original peace platform and made too many concessions to the *Entente* governments, Wilson emphasised that "the great problem of the moment" was to preserve basic unity and consensus among the three principal victors of the war. He warned that it would be "fatal" for the future development of the postwar order and the realisation of the aspirations to found a functioning League of Nations if this unity was sundered.[69] Like House, he feared that seeking more significant modifications of the treaty (which he deemed unwarranted) and even more so actual negotiations with German representatives would expose the victors precisely to this risk.[70]

By comparison, domestic factors and concerns seem to have had a less tangible influence on the American president's pronounced shift towards a "harder" course vis-à-vis Germany. But based on the information and appraisals they received, he and other members of the American peace delegation were undoubtedly aware that a clear majority of the American public – and publicised opinion – seemed to be broadly in favour of a stern treatment of Germany and the imposition of a punitive peace settlement. What clearly still had a bearing here were the repercussions of both wartime propaganda and what had become a highly polarised postwar debate. Intelligence reports stressed that the American public "approved of the [draft] peace treaty" and that at the same time "the intensity of anti-German feeling" still continued to "grow more feverish". What reinforced such attitudes was that most of the most widely read papers evaluated the draft treaty "only in terms of Germany's punishment" and endorsed it as an appropriate instrument to this end. At the same time, an official survey of the American press underscored that most opinion-makers argued that the victors' terms were in fact very different from those of Wilson's Fourteen Points programme, but it presented this as a strength rather than a weakness of the treaty.[71]

Politically more significant was that Lodge and other leading members of the Republican majority in the Senate now asserted that the conditions of the draft treaty essentially fulfilled the core demand they had made ever since the armistice, namely that a draconian peace settlement was to be forced on Germany that served both as punishment for the offences it had committed and to deter future

---

[69] Wilson remarks in meeting with US peace commissioners, 3 June 1919, *FRUS-PPC*, XI, p. 219.
[70] See Bullitt memorandum of conversation with House, 19 May 1919, Bullitt Papers.
[71] Current Intelligence Division, Weekly Review, 18 May 1919, Bliss Papers. A disillusioned Lippmann impressed on Baker that "over here" there was "a general approval of the treaty as an instrument of punishment". Lippmann to Baker, 15 May 1919, Baker Papers.

German challenges to international order. In Lodge's view, the terms on which
the victorious powers had agreed were as "severe" as they had to be. He was "in
hearty accord" with them and the key purpose they would serve: to ensure that
Germany was "chained up". And he insisted, as he had all along, that they had to
be imposed on the vanquished power without any further negotiations.[72] Wilson
was not oblivious to Lodge's views or the prevailing currents of American public
and publicised opinion. But he did not change his outlook on the peace settlement because he sought to adapt to these views and currents. What ultimately
determined his actions was, rather, his own judgement of what constituted an
appropriately severe but essentially "just" peace.

The American president thus also remained impervious to, and by and
large unaffected by, the fundamental and often scathing critique of the draft
treaty that was advanced by the left-liberal and progressive parties, associations and opinion-makers who had once been the most fervent supporters of
Wilson's original "peace without victory" programme and who now saw their
expectations, which had already been deflated after ever since the armistice,
utterly disappointed by the result of the Big Three s negotiations. Lippmann
and the editors of the New Republic voiced the sentiments of many other
disillusioned progressives when, in a language that encouraged German
hopes, they castigated the draft treaty as a vindictive "treaty of peace" that
had been forged "in the spirit of the traditional diplomacy of Europe" and
rendered peace "impossible". In their appraisal, it was "less in accord with the
Fourteen Points than . . . the peace of Brest-Litovsk" and would "impose on the
German nation the ultimate humiliation of solemnly consenting to its own
abdication as a self-governing and self-respecting community". It thereby
rendered inconceivable what they deemed imperative: a settlement that
strengthened the forces Ebert and Scheidemann represented and buttressed
both Germany's democratisation and its inclusion in an American-led "liberal" postwar order.

Lippmann emphasised that the treaty draft thus was far from embodying
the peace that Wilson had "promised to make", observing that "for reasons of
state" he had agreed to a settlement that violated his promises in cardinal
respects, notably by excluding Germany from the League and sealing the
"surrender" of its "economic independence". He warned that the treaty's
discriminatory clauses and blatant double-standards would undermine all
prospects of forging a stable "liberal" order. Lippmann thus called on liberals
and progressives in and beyond the United States to launch a vigorous
campaign of protest against the victors' peace terms. While he did not expect
that such a campaign would be able to prevent the "ratification" of the "Treaty

---

[72] Lodge to Bryce, 27 and 30 May 1919, Lodge Papers; Lodge to Morse, 2 May 1919; Lodge
to Lord Charnwood, 2 July 1919, Lodge Papers.

of Versailles", he argued that it had to be pursued to preserve "the moral foundation" of western civilisation.[73]

More radical progressives criticised the draft treaty in equally sharp terms and urged the American president yet again to return to the premises and "ethics" of his "peace without victory" agenda. Encapsulating their positions, William MacDonald declared in *The Nation* that the victorious powers had been "morally under obligation" to make a "Wilson peace" that embodied not merely "the substance" but also the "political ethics" of the Fourteen Points. And he asserted, through his own ideological lens, that the American people yet also the people of Britain, France and other nations still "demanded" such a peace. In his judgement, the terms the victors had actually proposed essentially failed to meet the principal "obligation"; they contained "scarcely a trace" of the "ethical principles" Wilson had proclaimed and instead had only one "central purpose" – "the obliteration of Germany". MacDonald concluded that this was not only due to the machinations of Lloyd George and the "reactionary programme" of Clemenceau but also the result of the American president's abandonment of his progressive peace agenda and willingness to enter into negotiations that were marked by "high-handedness, secrecy, and subterfuge". Yet, like other progressive voices, MacDonald had not only grown disillusioned with the American president. He also held that there was no longer any hope that even modifications of the treaty and concessions to Germany, which the "counter-propositions" of Brockdorff-Rantzau suggested, would remedy the settlement's fundamental flaws and "restore the moral principle that the treaty has lacked from the beginning". In desperation, he thus pinned his hopes on a different, transformative peacemaking process that could only begin *after* the flawed victors' peace of Versailles had been imposed on Germany – a process in which, propelled by a "swelling tide of opposition", particularly in Britain and the United States, a genuine progressive "peace of the peoples" would be made.[74]

The arguments of the German counter-proposal campaign thus clearly resonated with those who tried to rally progressive opposition to the draft treaty in the United States. But they and the political and social forces they appealed to were simply not in a position to exert a palpable influence at this stage – either directly on Wilson and the other "peacemakers" at Versailles or, indirectly, by altering the balance of "public opinion" in and beyond the United States. For one basic "reality" had not changed in the course of the

---

[73] See editorial "Peace at Any Price"; Lippmann, "Mr. Wilson and His Promises", *New Republic*, 24 May 1919, pp. 100-2, 104-5; editorial "A Punic Peace", *New Republic*, 17 May 1919, pp. 71-3. See also Lippmann to Baker, 15 May 19919, Baker Papers; Lippmann, "Bolshevism", *New Republic*, 22 March 1919, pp. 12-13.

[74] W. MacDonald, "A Conference Unrepentant", 30 May 1919, *The Nation* (21 June 1919), pp. 978–80.

peace proceedings: they still only represented a distinct minority faction in the American political spectrum. And because of Wilson's decision to distance himself from his "peace without victory" agenda and seek a broader base of domestic-political support, they were becoming less rather than more relevant as a political force during the decisive months of the peacemaking process. The opposition of Labour and liberal opinion in Britain to what came to be seen as a victors' "peace to end all peace" would have a more tangible, though still far from decisive impact – first on Lloyd George's pursuits, then on the final negotiations at Versailles.

V.   British Soul-Searching and Pursuits of an Amended Atlantic Peace

Although some of the British protagonists were appalled by the tone and far-ranging claims of Brockdorff-Rantzau's campaign, the German counter-proposals overall provoked not only a strong but also distinctly more favourable reaction both in the ranks of the British delegation and in the Imperial War Cabinet. For in key respects they touched upon or amplified fundamental concerns and misgivings that a majority of key British actors, including Lloyd George himself, *already* harboured about the terms and character of the draft treaty.

The dispute and the reorientation process that gained momentum in the course of May and reached a climax in early June, when Lloyd George called a series of meetings of the British Empire Delegation and key ministers of his government, has been portrayed as a formative stage in the history of British "appeasement" of Germany in the aftermath of the Great War. And they have thus been placed in the pre-history of the Second World War. According to the prevalent interpretation, they set the stage for subsequent British unease with the Treaty of Versailles, a lack of willingness to enforce its provisions and further endeavours to "appease" Germany in the inter-war period – which then culminated in Neville Chamberlain's misguided attempts to pursue a policy of "appeasement" vis-à-vis Hitler.[75] But it is more appropriate to characterise what ensued among the representatives of the British Empire in the pivotal days of the peace conference as the most substantial debate within any of the delegations, and governments, of the victorious powers of 1919 about the validity – and sustainability – of the peace terms that had thus far been negotiated. More precisely, for all the different tactical and short-term considerations that played a role, it became a formative debate not just about the question of how far the draft treaty had to be modified in order to be more acceptable to the German government but also about a more fundamental question. It was the question of what changes would be required to turn the

---

[75] See Lentin (1984); Lentin (II/2001), pp. 51–2.

envisaged settlement into a more sustainable basis for a stable *and legitimate* international order – into an amended Atlantic peace.

And what this dispute threw into relief was one paramount set of concerns. It revealed that in the eyes of most of those who sought to make peace on behalf of the British Empire the draft treaty had to be substantially modified. Essentially, it had to be reworked into a settlement that, in their judgement, came closer to a "Wilsonian peace" – because they believed that, as it stood, it was bound to create dangerous sources of conflict in postwar Europe. Like most of their colleagues from the Dominions, the British delegates were especially concerned about the occupation regime in the Rhineland, the unlimited reparations terms and the decisions about the Polish-German border. They feared, more broadly, that a peace on the terms of the draft treaty would create legitimate grievances and provoke lasting nationalist resentment in Germany. And they argued that this would not only produce chronic insecurity but also place immense obstacles in the way of what they considered a crucial prerequisite for Europe's pacification, namely an eventual accommodation with the vanquished power and its re-inclusion into the comity of nations.

It was mainly because of this underlying concern that a majority now also came to advocate Germany's early admission to the League of Nations. The most important initial impulses for what by early June had turned into a full-blown and wide-ranging controversy were given by Smuts, Cecil and, indirectly, Keynes. Essentially, they all deemed the draft peace fundamentally flawed and called for far-reaching changes. Notably Smuts and Cecil urged Lloyd George to take the lead in negotiating a qualitatively different peace of accommodation that, in their interpretation, returned to the basis that the victorious powers had vowed to respect: the armistice agreements and, essentially, the Fourteen Points. In the end, however, Lloyd George would manage to gain a mandate for a more limited "revisionist" agenda, which in most respects corresponded with his own tactical and political priorities.

Thus, the upshot of nearly a month of deliberations and soul-searching was a significant yet ultimately limited initiative: the most significant initiative on the part of the victors, not to effect an outright "transformation" of the peace settlement but rather to make substantial changes of specific terms, which were to make the peace more acceptable to the German government. Yet, reflecting the views of a majority, Lloyd George never departed from the axiom that there would be no actual, face-to-face negotiations with German plenipotentiaries. Ultimately, the British premier would seek an amended peace *of the victors*, not a negotiated settlement with the vanquished that would have required more tangible concessions, especially with a view to the crucial reparations issue. He too was conscious of the risk that the entire intricate web of compromises he had forged with the American president and the French premier might come apart if they agreed to direct discussions with the German government. Fundamentally, however, he insisted on the victors' "right" to impose a peace settlement just as uncompromisingly as Wilson and Clemenceau.[76]

Once they had for the first time seen the *entire* draft treaty, most key members of the British Empire delegation quickly came to regard it as a profoundly problematic agglomeration of terms and conditions that, in their cumulative effect, were not merely excessively onerous – or, as some thought, vindictive – but bound to make it impossible to consolidate a stable postwar order. Keynes captured prevalent views when he noted that the proposed "Peace" was "outrageous" and "impossible" and warned that it would have disastrous economic and political consequences because it was both unworkable *and* certain to provoke tremendous, and justified, opposition in Germany.[77] Resigning from the Treasury in protest on 19 May, Keynes criticised that the result of the victors' deliberations contained "much that is unjust and much more that is inexpedient". In particular, he argued that the proposed reparation scheme could not "possibly persist as a solution of the problem", as it showed "a high degree of unwisdom in almost every direction" – not satisfying those who still "had illusions about indemnities" in Britain and France while being entirely unacceptable from the German point of view. Further, he stressed that the terms of the Rhineland occupation lent themselves to "the most terrible abuse" by the French government. Overall, Keynes deemed it inconceivable that the Scheidemann government would "sign the treaty in the form in which it now stands". More importantly, he augured that unless it was significantly modified – in actual discussions with Germany – it would bring "nothing but misfortune", "general order and unrest" to Europe, which would also have a profound impact on Britain and its empire. What came to the fore here were elements of the highly influential critique that Keynes would later on expand in his immensely influential tract on *The Economic Consequences of the Peace*.[78]

But what had a more powerful impact in the immediate context of the peace negotiations was the intervention of Smuts. Building on his earlier arguments, Smuts now advanced a far-reaching appeal. He argued that the peace settlement had to be "recast and transformed" to be "more in accord" with the "solemn undertakings" and "public declarations" the victors had made – and

---

[76] Lloyd George remarks, British Empire Delegation minutes, 33, 1 June 1919, CAB 29/28.

[77] Keynes to Mrs Keynes, 14 May 1919, Keynes Papers, XVI, p. 458. Like many others Headlam-Morley also found the treaty "indefensible", impossible to carry out and in need of a "thorough revision". Headlam-Morley to Smuts, 19 May 1919, *Smuts Papers*, IV, pp. 168–70. For general attitudes in the British delegation see Lentin (1984), pp. 83 ff.

[78] Keynes to Austen Chamberlain, 26 May 1919, Keynes Papers, XVI, p. 459; Keynes to Bradbury and Austen Chamberlain, 4 May 1919, Keynes Papers, XVI, pp. 454–5; Keynes to Mrs Keynes, 14 May 1919, *ibid.*, p. 458; Keynes (1919).

the requirements of a stable peace in Europe. On 14 May, Smuts sought to impress on Lloyd George and Wilson that the "combined effect of the territorial and reparation clauses" would make it "practically impossible for Germany to carry out the provisions of the Treaty". He warned that "occupation clauses" which would "plant the French on the Rhine indefinitely" and the fact that in the west and in the east large "blocks of Germans" were to be "put under their historic enemies" was "full of menace for the future of Europe". And he argued that if the draft treaty was imposed on Germany, Europe and the world would "know no peace".[79]

In Smuts' assessment, it was thus vital for the durability and legitimacy of the peace settlement to return to the political and moral foundations that the American president had proposed and to honour the "solemn obligation" the victors had accepted in November 1918 to "make a Wilson peace" – a peace in keeping with the Fourteen Points. He underscored that this required an alteration of all "one-sided provisions" of the draft treaty that "exclude reciprocity or equality". And this included virtually all the essential compromises the Big Three had forged, notably the Saar agreement, the occupation of the Rhineland, the settlement of the Polish-German border and the reparations clauses. No less critical for Smuts was an immediate inclusion of Germany in the League of Nations. And, significantly, he urged Wilson and Lloyd George not only to use their influence to press for these changes but also to seize on the German counter-proposals to initiate actual negotiations with the Scheidemann government. Convinced that the German proposals would have a major impact on "world opinion", Smuts prophesied that if the victorious powers failed to take these steps and insisted on the terms of the draft treaty they would have to deal with the "terrible disillusion" of the "peoples" whose expectations they had disappointed – in Germany, wider Europe and the United States – and the peace could "become an even greater disaster to the world than the war" had been.[80]

Cecil, who by this time had also become highly critical of Lloyd George's handling of the negotiations, echoed Smuts' core concerns. He too impressed on the British premier that "in its cumulative effect" the draft treaty would prevent "a lasting pacification of Europe" and criticised in particular the envisaged Polish-German border arrangements – notably regarding Upper Silesia – and the Saar compromise as "not really defensible as elements in a solid peace". And he too emphasised that the terms of the draft treaty were more fundamentally "out of harmony with the spirit, if not with the letter" of

---

[79] Smuts to Lloyd George, 2 June 1919, *Smuts Papers*, IV, p. 216; Smuts letter to Wilson and Lloyd George, 14 May 1919, Lloyd George Papers, F/45/9/34. See also Smuts to Lloyd George, 5 and 22 May 1919, *ibid.*, F/45/9/33 and 35.

[80] Smuts to Wilson, 30 May 1919, *Smuts Papers*, IV, pp. 208–9; Smuts to Lloyd George, 2 June 1919, *ibid.*, p. 216.

the Fourteen Points as well as with the war aims Lloyd George had enunciated in his Caxton House speech in January 1918. Cecil's main concern was that the treaty provided a very "unsound basis" for the League. He thus demanded that not only substantial changes to its territorial and reparations clauses should be made but also, and crucially, that Germany should be admitted to the League within "a few months" once the Scheidemann government had given re-assurances of its "pacific tendency".[81] For Cecil, then, a thorough revision of the peace settlement was imperative in order to establish the League as an effective framework for a new, inclusive international concert. He deemed it essential to ensure that the League not only committed the United States to the pacification of postwar Europe but also integrated the vanquished power as soon as possible. He warned that otherwise Germany would be driven to establish some kind of counter-League.[82]

From London, Churchill now also weighed in on behalf of a peace of accommodation with Germany. The secretary of state for war argued that the series of German counter-propositions should be considered "with patience and goodwill" and that the British premier should then seek a revised settlement and "endeavour to split the outstanding differences" between the victors and the vanquished, all in order to "get a genuine German accept-ance".[83] Finally, following the submission of the German note compendium of 29 May, even key Unionist ministers in Lloyd George's Cabinet joined the ranks of those who expressed growing unease and argued that the German counter-proposals had to be taken seriously. Deputy Prime Minister Bonar Law deemed the German note a "very able one" and "in many particulars difficult to answer". In particular, and significantly, the Unionist leader now actually backed the idea of a fixed-sum reparations settlement, proposing a total amount – £5,000 million – that was far lower than the exorbitant figure Hughes and Cunliffe had proposed, and in fact not far from that of the Melchior-Warburg offer. Influenced by Keynes, Austen Chamberlain, the Chancellor of the Exchequer, held that the German government had offered "important concessions" that should be reciprocated; and he too supported a fixed-sum solution to the reparations problem.[84]

Thus, by the end of May a clear majority within the British Cabinet and the delegation, including not only Smuts, Cecil, Churchill and Barnes but also the key Conservative ministers as well as Milner and Montagu were all, as the latter put it, "in agreement" that the German counter-proposals had "made out

---

[81] Cecil to Lloyd George, 27 May 1919, Cecil Papers, Add. 51076.

[82] Cecil Diary, 31 May 1919, Cecil Papers; Cecil memorandum, 3 June 1919, CAB 29/16.

[83] Churchill to Lloyd George, 21 May 1919, Keynes Papers, PT/32.

[84] Bonar Law to Lloyd George, 31 May 1919, Lloyd George Papers, F/30/3, 71; Mantoux (1992), II, p. 270.

a case requiring considerable modification of the Treaty" – even if there was no consensus about the extent of this modification.[85]

Lloyd George was clearly affected by the rising tide of concerns in the ranks of the British Empire Delegation and his government, which of course also represented a thinly veiled criticism of what he had negotiated in the Council of Four. And in a wider context the British premier was not unaffected either by Cecil's warning that "large sections" of the British public were "very uneasy" about the envisaged peace terms and would not back a treaty that was seen as not only too harsh but also essentially unjust and unlikely to lead to a "lasting settlement" of peace in Europe.[86] For Lloyd George shared Cecil's perception that the general "feeling" of public opinion in Britain had begun to change, notably since the publication of the victors' peace terms on 8 May, with Liberal and Labour voices that called for moderation beginning to outweigh those clamouring for a harsh peace. Widely regarded as an early indication of this change had been the decisive victory of the oppositional Liberal candidate Commander Kenworthy over his Conservative opponent in a by-election in mid-April. For Joseph Kenworthy's election platform had centred on the pledge to seek a "non-revengeful peace". Subsequently, he and other Asquith Liberals would openly attack the draft treaty in the House of Commons, declaring it would not bring peace but rather lead to a "just and durable war".[87]

Meanwhile, leading liberal opinion-makers stepped up their efforts to pressure Lloyd George to moderate the terms of the settlement. Reflecting wider liberal misgivings, the editor of the *Manchester Guardian*, C.P. Scott, urged the victorious powers to refrain from imposing a "peace of violence" and called on them to pursue, at last, a "peace of appeasement" vis-à-vis Germany that paved the way for future reconciliation. J.L. Garvin, the editor of *The Observer*, likewise called on the victors to take steps towards a more conciliatory "Real Settlement". Both he and Scott gave voice to the growing liberal demand to "mend" peace terms that contained the seeds of a future European war – and to return to the principles of what was still identified as a "Wilsonian peace".[88]

By contrast, the Labour Party was divided. Under the leadership of an indecisive Will Adamson, the weakened Parliamentary Labour Party maintained a cautious or even affirmative stance. Yet the leaders of the party's National Executive, notably Henderson, deemed the proposed peace deeply

---

[85] Montagu note, 4 June 1919, in Waley (1964), p. 211.

[86] Cecil to Lloyd George, 27 May 1919, Cecil Papers, Add. 51076.

[87] House of Commons debate, 6 June 1919, Hansard, Commons, 5th series, vol. 116, col. 2474.

[88] C.P. Scott editorial, *Manchester Guardian*, 10 May 1919; J.L. Garvin, "First Steps to the Real Settlement" and "How to Mend It", *The Observer*, 18 and 25 May 1919.

flawed and began their own campaign for a peace of conciliation with Germany. And their views came to dominate. This became manifest in an official Labour declaration, published in early June, that criticised the draft treaty as being "based upon the very political principles which were the ultimate cause of the war" – namely those of secret diplomacy and power-political bargains. In particular, the declaration admonished that the "military occupation" of the western bank of the Rhine would have highly detrimental consequences and that the victors had failed to take steps to "secure general disarmament and demilitarization".[89]

One of the key Labour demands was the immediate admission of Germany to the League of Nations. It was most forcefully advanced by Henderson, who argued that this was an essential prerequisite for making the new organisation a genuine instrument of pacification and international reconciliation, an institution that could serve to settle disputes, overcome the divisions of the war and, as far as necessary, revise the most objectionable provisions of the peace settlement.[90] The Labour representative in the British delegation at Versailles, Barnes, whole-heartedly supported Henderson's agenda and pursued his own efforts to persuade Lloyd George of the need for a conciliatory peace that brought Germany into the League of Nations.[91] But all of these efforts and tendencies have to be viewed in a wider context. Even if overall opinion in Britain on the emerging peace settlement may have been in the process of changing, what leading liberal and Labour voices articulated was still far from having a decisive influence where, politically, it mattered most – namely in the House of Commons. And, crucially, it did not alter the prevalent constellation of expectations when it came to the one question that had acquired more significance than any other in the parliamentary and public debates in Britain: the reparations question.

However seriously the British premier took Liberal and Labour critiques, which he did, his primary pre-eminent concern was and remained to satisfy or at least not to disappoint the demands and expectations he himself had contributed to raising further ever since the Khaki Elections. And these expectations of course still collided with the notion of a moderate peace settlement. They had been amplified by the Conservative and particularly the Northcliffe press, whose main organ, the *Daily Mail*, kept up the press baron's campaign to make Germany pay a very high price for its "war of

---

[89] Report of the Nineteenth Annual Conference of the Labour Party, 1919, p. 217.

[90] Henderson to Barnes, 16 May 1919, Lloyd George Papers, F/4/3/16; Henderson (1919). Subsequently, the "revision" of the "harsh provisions" of the Treaty of Versailles and a substantive reform of the postwar order would become core Labour foreign policy aims in the 1920s. See Report of the Nineteenth Annual Conference of the Labour Party, 1919; Callaghan (2007), pp. 61 ff.

[91] Barnes to Lloyd George, 18 May 1919, Lloyd George Papers, F/4/3/16.

aggression". Yet what influenced the prime minister's course most decisively, till the very end of the Versailles negotiations, was his preoccupation with satisfying the far-reaching indemnity demands for which a majority of Unionist backbenchers clamoured.[92] In response to these demands, Lloyd George had in mid-April again publicly committed himself to a peace settlement that, while not being "vindictive", essentially made Germany pay "full" reparations, stressing that it was imperative to prevent a "repetition of the horrors of this War, by making the wrongdoer repair the wrong and the loss which he has inflicted by his wanton aggression". During the subsequent deliberations in Paris, the British premier would not be able to extricate himself from these partly self-imposed constraints. Ultimately, this would lead him to reject once again a "fixed sum" arrangement that could only fall short of meeting the exaggerated expectations that prevailed in Britain.[93]

Nonetheless, once he realised how widespread and profound the misgivings about the peace terms had become within the British Empire delegation, his own Cabinet and important segments of British public opinion, Lloyd George strove to accommodate them. At the same time, however, he would seek to channel and direct these currents towards a less ambitious campaign on behalf of amendments that by and large corresponded with the essentials he had already put down in the Fontainebleau Memorandum. He would come to pursue substantial yet targeted changes of the victors' terms that left the reparations compromise untouched but revised salient political and territorial provisions of the treaty.

To take stock of the prevailing balance of opinions – and to gain a clear mandate for the subsequent negotiations – Lloyd George summoned the most important ministers of his Cabinet to Paris and convened three drawn-out meetings with them and the entire Empire delegation on 31 May and 1 June. In the course of these decisive discussions, only the prime ministers of Australia and New Zealand, Hughes and Massey, argued in favour of not veering from a settlement that "made Germany pay" and insisted on conceding as little as possible, particularly with a view to British reparation demands. For his part, Balfour also cautioned against envisaging major changes. He now accentuated that he doubted Germany had undergone a "conversion" from the state and society that had "caused the war", asking what "faith" one could have in the newly republican Germany's assurances that it would pursue a different course. But it soon transpired that an overwhelming majority of those present was in favour of pushing for significant changes of the peace terms – changes that in one way or another were supposed to make them not only more

---

[92] See Thompson (1999); Lentin (1984), pp. 96–7.

[93] Lloyd George speech, House of Commons, 16 April 1919, Hansard, Commons, 5th series, vol. 114, col. 2950; Lloyd George remarks, Council of Four, 9 June 1919, *FRUS-PPC*, VI, pp. 261–2.

reconcilable with the parameters of the armistice agreement and the Fourteen Points, but also more conducive to the requirements of a stable and legitimate postwar order in Europe.[94]

At the outset of the deliberations Smuts had repeated his comprehensive critique of the draft treaty, reiterating his core argument that whereas the victors had committed themselves to "a Wilson peace", the treaty was full of provisions that were "inconsistent with the Fourteen Points". And he had again demanded in emphatic terms an *overall revision* of what he called an "impossible" peace that was bound to "produce political and economic chaos in Europe" for which "in the long run" the British Empire would have to "pay the penalty". Churchill emphasised that the draft treaty was dangerously dominated by France's "hatred" for Germany and renewed his call for a "split-the-difference peace" that accommodated German concerns and thus ensured that the German government and people "genuine(ly)" accepted the final settlement.[95] Barnes, Chamberlain, Milner, Montagu and others also argued on behalf of significant concessions to the defeated power. Significantly, however, most of those present – including Lloyd George himself – were not prepared to back what lay at the heart of Smuts' emphatic plea, namely the call for a more general re-negotiation of the entire draft treaty. Nor was there support for direct negotiations with German representatives. What came to prevail was, rather, a consensus in favour of an agenda of more targeted, though still substantial, agenda of revisions which the prime minister was mandated to place at the centre of further negotiations with Wilson and Clemenceau.

On 2 June, Lloyd George impressed on them that he had been unanimously authorised to insist on changes in four critical areas. The first concerned the "eastern border" of Germany. Here, he stressed, the "fate" of Upper Silesia could not be determined without a plebiscite – as the region had been part of Poland "for several centuries". The second related to the reparations settlement. Here, the premier noted, the British Empire delegation had been mainly concerned about the "indefinite and unlimited character of the debt" that was to be imposed on Germany and demanded that a definite – and reduced – sum should be agreed upon (which corresponded with American rather than Lloyd George's own preferences). The third demand was that the occupation of the Rhineland was to be shortened and the size of the occupation army was to be reduced so as to minimise its potential to become a destabilising "source of irritation" – and Lloyd George sought to put pressure on Clemenceau by insinuating that Britain's willingness to honour the guarantee treaty would depend on French concessions on the occupation. Finally,

---

[94] British Empire Delegation minutes, 33 and 34, 1 June 1919, CAB 29/28 and 29/38/1.
[95] British Empire Delegation minutes, 33, 1 June 1919, CAB 29/28.

the British premier conveyed his delegation's plea for assurances that
Germany would be admitted to the League of Nations "as soon as possible",
on the condition that the German government showed "good faith" in executing the eventual peace treaty. To underscore the urgency of these British
demands Lloyd George stated that if they were not met, he had been
empowered to withdraw the British Navy from the blockade of Germany
and to refuse British participation in a renewal of hostilities should it become
necessary to force the vanquished power to comply with the terms of the
victors. And he invoked British "public opinion", stressing that the British
people desired "peace" and would not support a government that resumed the
war "without very substantial reasons".[96]

In the end, the British prime minister had thus received a strong mandate
for negotiating significant amendments to the draft treaty rather than its
fundamental overhaul. Lloyd George indeed emphasised that he was not
prepared to go as far as Smuts and others had urged and pursue "such far-
reaching concessions as to amount to a general reconsideration of the whole
Treaty".[97] Rather, his immediate priority was to press for changes that satisfied
key German concerns – as he interpreted them – to such an extent that the
Scheidemann government would not refuse to sign the treaty. The British
premier indeed sought to avoid by all means a situation where it would
become necessary to renew hostilities in order to force the victors' terms on
Germany, because he thought that it was extremely difficult to gain the
backing of the British public for such a course of action. But it would again
be misleading to conclude that Lloyd George's revisionist pursuits were merely
or mainly informed by domestic factors and considerations of short-
term expedience.

Lloyd George's penchant for excessive tactical tergiversations should not
obscure that what really informed his attempt to revise the peace settlement
was essentially the same underlying concern that had already animated the
Fontainebleau approach in March. It was not the fear that the draft treaty's
terms would tilt the postwar balance of power in France's favour and thus go
against time-honoured maxims of British power policies. It was, rather, the
fundamental concern that they would indeed cause long-term instability in
Europe by creating, on Germany's western and eastern borders, conditions
that, as Lloyd George had warned in parliament, would give rise to "a
legitimate sense of wrong" in Germany and would "excite national pride
needlessly to seek opportunities for redress". And in his view, and the prevalent British assessment, this would create massive obstacles for what was most

[96] Lloyd George remarks, Council of Four, 2 June 1919, Mantoux (1992), II,
pp. 269–71, 275.
[97] Lloyd George to Smuts, 3 June, *Smuts Papers*, IV, p. 217.

critical: a longer-term process of postwar accommodation with Germany and the consolidation of a new Euro-Atlantic equilibrium.[98]

Further, while he clearly considered the League less vital than Cecil, Loyd George also backed the call for Germany's early admission to the new organisation, eventually arguing that this should be effected within one year after the signature of the peace treaty. His longer-term aim remained to pre-empt a further deepening of divisions between the victors and the vanquished in the postwar era – and to promote Germany's eventual re-integration into a new concert of powers. Yet in his vision, this could only occur *after* the German government had accepted a – modified – victor's peace and shown its willingness to abide by its obligations.[99]

To vindicate his approach, Lloyd George advanced his own formula for turning the draft treaty into a more workable *and* "just" peace. In the meeting on 1 June, having congratulated the members of the British Empire delegation on a discussion that had taken the form of "an earnest and sometimes passionate plea for justice for the fallen enemy", he emphasised that he would seek to modify those terms of the peace that were deemed wrong or unjust; but he also had to make sure that "the terms imposed . . . were expedient as well as just". In his interpretation this notably called for a modification of the political and territorial terms that he and a majority of the Cabinet and delegation deemed most problematic. Yet it also meant that the power that in his view bore the responsibility for engulfing the world in the immensely costly war had to "pay" for its consequences – rather than "the British taxpayer". Lloyd George thus insisted that the British government should not "water down" what he considered its legitimate – and politically vital – reparations claims. Not least to defend these claims the British premier insisted on underscoring Germany's exclusive "war guilt" and refuted all German attempts to challenge the verdict of the victors.[100]

Crucially, Lloyd George was never willing to explore the option of negotiating a "grand bargain peace" with Germany. He rejected such an approach not only because this would have required a change of British reparation policy that he continued to consider politically undesirable – essentially the acceptance of a "fixed-sum" arrangement that could be seen as dissatisfactory by British voters. He also adhered to the fundamental premise that the victors ultimately had the authority to set and impose the terms of the peace. Yet the British premier also had to pay attention to the complex requirements of inter-allied bargaining. Based on his experience of many weeks of hard negotiations in the Council of Four, he stressed that Clemenceau would practically have to be forced to make

---

[98] Lloyd George speech, House of Commons, 16 April 1919, Hansard, Commons, 5th series, vol. 114, col. 2950.

[99] British Empire Delegation minutes, 33, 1 June 1919, CAB 29/28.

[100] *Ibid.*

any concessions on terms he deemed vital for French security; and he argued that modifications had to be negotiated among the victors, as any attempt to open up a negotiating process with German representatives would only intensify French intransigence and obstructionism. In the final analysis, as noted, Lloyd sought to effect targeted changes, not to undo the entire structure of complex compromises that underlay the draft treaty.

But Clemenceau's intransigence was already on full display after Lloyd George had outlined the British proposals for specific changes. He declared that any move towards concessions would lead the victorious powers down a dangerous slippery slope. And he warned that Brockdorff-Rantzau must not be allowed to draw them into negotiations that might go on for "an incalculable number of months". From his – and Tardieu's – perspective, such negotiations would raise cardinal dangers. In one respect, he argued, with reference to his knowledge of the German mentality, the more the victors conceded "the more [the Germans would] ask". At the core, however, he saw the danger that negotiations with German representatives would open up divisions between him and the political leaders of Britain and the United States – who, as he was well aware, still pursued priorities and conceptions of peace that were fundamentally different from his – and that they would ultimately undermine the critical compromise agreements he had fought so hard to obtain, chiefly the Rhineland compromise yet also the agreements on the Saar and Poland's future border. Moreover, he feared that such wider negotiations could strain or even disrupt the postwar unity between France and the Anglo-American powers on which he and Tardieu had founded their entire conception of French postwar security. Significantly, however, the French premier was not prepared to make – for the sake of inter-allied unity – any real concessions to Lloyd George that addressed the concerns the latter had presented. Rather, Clemenceau urged his counterparts to "rush matters" and force Germany to sign an unaltered peace treaty as soon as possible.[101]

In order to contain Lloyd George's pressure, Clemenceau re-accentuated the argument that in view of the criticism he faced in the French parliament and in French "public opinion" the future of his government would be at stake if he made any further concessions, especially on the crucial issue of the Rhineland occupation, yet also with regard to France's reparation demands. He thus sought to impress on Wilson and Lloyd George that they should close ranks and stand firm vis-à-vis German demands if they wanted to retain him as a relatively accommodating partner in the peacemaking process. Clemenceau argued that he had made "the entente with England and America" the

---

[101] Clemenceau remarks, Council of Four, 2 June 1919, Mantoux (1992), II, pp. 272–6. For the unchanging underlying assumptions, see Clemenceau remarks, Council of Four, 28 March 1919, ibid., I, pp. 62–5; Tardieu memorandum, 25 February 1919, Tardieu (II/1921), pp. 156, 161–2.

"essential foundation" of his policy – but should he be forced to resign they would have to deal with French leaders that would steer a far more uncompromising course.[102] While the British premier was less impressed by these arguments, they would have a palpable effect on the American president.

VI.   American Debates about the Peace – and Incipient Reorientations

Because of the clash between British calls for revisions and French intransigence, Wilson's role once again became pivotal in early June. In fact, the American president was extremely irritated by the British delegation's "unanimous ... funk" and what he saw as Lloyd George's essentially tactical manoeuvres. But in the interest of re-establishing a modicum of unity among the victors he reluctantly agreed to give the British proposals serious consideration. Yet Wilson also reacted this way in part because, in conjunction with the German note of 29 May, the British delegation's proposals brought to the surface criticism of the draft treaty that had accumulated in the American Peace Delegation ever since late April. Discontent reached a highpoint in early June. Leading members of the delegation, notably Bliss and Hoover, now came forward and presented their grave concerns; and, like the financial experts Davis and Lamont, they showed themselves impressed both by the British arguments and by essential parts of the German counter-proposals.

To address these criticisms and misgivings, Wilson eventually agreed to a suggestion Hoover had made and, on 3 June, held the first and only general meeting of all commissioners and experts who had accompanied him to Paris. By this time, Lansing had emerged as the fiercest critic of Wilson's course in the delegation. Embittered by having been relegated to the side-lines of the negotiations, he noted that the president had been driven to abandon the basis of the Fourteen Points, made too many unwarranted concessions to the *Entente* Powers and in the end agreed to peace terms that were not just unduly harsh and humiliating but also in core respects impossible to execute. Earlier, the secretary of state had gone so far as to argue that only a determined German resistance to the draft treaty could take the peacemaking process in a new and more promising direction. He had reasoned that only direct negotiations between the victors and the German government could pave the way for a fundamental revision of the terms he found most objectionable, including the Rhineland regime and the reparations settlement. In early June, Lansing was still in favour of seizing on the new German counter-proposals to this end.[103] But he remained a marginal figure. What carried more weight were the concerns that Bliss and particularly Hoover now voiced openly. Both urged

---

[102] Council of Four, 2 June 1919, Mantoux (1992), II, pp. 272 ff.
[103] See Lansing memorandum, 5 May 1919; Lansing to Polk, 4 June 1919, Lansing Papers.

Wilson to return to the "wisdom" of his original peace programme and push for a substantially modified settlement. And they argued that the objections and demands of the German government had to be addressed not only in the interests of stabilising the fragile German republic but also in the interest of creating a viable postwar order.[104]

Both Hoover and Bliss were influenced by assessments of the Scheidemann government's precarious situation that Dresel had sent from Berlin – yet of which Wilson took no note. On Hoover's instructions and with House's approval, Dresel had been sent on several reconnaissance missions to Berlin between mid-April and early May. He became the US official who gained the most extensive insights into the dynamics of the German domestic-political force-field and the aims and constraints of the embattled government. Following discussions with Brockdorff-Rantzau, Erzberger and other political figures and leading bankers, Dresel had emphasised that the Scheidemann Cabinet would most likely "not accept" the peace terms as they stood and that it would be discredited and lose all public support if it simply bowed to what was widely regarded as dictates of the victors that were "in conflict with President Wilson's principles as interpreted by official Germany". Dresel had recommended that the US delegation should give "such moral encouragement as is possible" to Scheidemann's government, essentially by initiating negoti-ations with the German plenipotentiaries and pushing for changes in the treaty that would make it politically possible for the governing coalition in Berlin to accept it. He had stressed that this coalition represented the "only combination in sight" that was stable enough to guarantee the execution of the peace terms and "representative of the German people". And he had warned that if the western powers persisted with their uncompromising course they would strengthen reactionary and nationalist forces in Germany, observing that a "reactionary uprising" seemed far more likely than "the danger of a new Spartacus revolt". Earlier, Dresel had – somewhat presciently – observed that unless a different peace was made, a new reactionary-nationalist movement could gain momentum and "a leader, as yet undiscovered, would be found to lead a great popular uprising" against the "dictate" of the victors.[105]

Impressed with Dresel's reports, Bliss urged Wilson to take heed of the German counter-proposals, warning that in five years' time "the world will condemn the conference if it does not listen to them". In his view, it was essential to address the concerns of the democratic government in Berlin and

---

[104] Hoover to Wilson, 4 June 1919, O'Brien (1978), pp. 169–70; Bliss to Wilson, 1 June 1919, Baker Papers.

[105] Dresel-Osborne report, 10 May 1919, FRUS-PPC, XII, pp. 112, 116; Dresel to American Peace Mission, 3 May 1919, ibid., pp. 88, 92; Dresel to American Peace Mission, 20 April 1919, Wilson Papers; Dresel to House, 21 April 1919, House Papers. See Schwabe (1985), p. 317.

make changes in the treaty that bolstered its domestic standing as well as the incipient democratisation process in Germany. Bliss noted that there was – around Ebert and the Social Democrats – a "considerable element" in German politics that was "striving for better things" and had to be "strengthened". He too considered actual negotiations with German representatives critical. And he argued that it would be a "good policy" to push for Germany's prompt admission to the League so as to avoid perpetuating its status as a "probable enemy" yet also because it was safer to integrate Germany into the new organisation, while leaving it excluded could have dangerous consequences.[106]

In Hoover's assessment, the draft treaty clashed not only in its core provisions but in its entire character with what he regarded the essentials of a sustainable and forward-looking peace – by which he still meant an essentially "American peace" on Wilsonian terms. He thus appealed to Wilson to seize on the "British change of heart" and take the lead in negotiating – among the victors – "important modifications" that, in his view, were imperative not only to make the peace more acceptable to the German government but also, and essentially, to return to what the president himself had defined as the principles of "far-sighted statesmanship", namely those of his own "original" peace programme.[107]

During the general meeting with Wilson on 3 June, Hoover argued that while "the weighing of justice and injustice" in the context of complex peace negotiations was "difficult", it would be politically wise to alter core provisions that the German government found unacceptable – among them "the Saar basin terms" and those concerning "the Silesian coal mines", the "period of occupation" in the Rhineland, and reparations. Yet he also observed that in his view such alterations would "not contravene the principles of justice". In a letter he sent to the president the following day, Hoover stepped up his campaign for the return to a progressive "American peace" agenda. He declared that after a war in which the United States had fought against "autocracy" and "militarism" a paramount task of American peace policy had to be to foster the "stability" of democratic government across Europe. And he insisted that a success of this policy – and the creation of a stable postwar order – depended above all on decisive steps to "secure the establishment of democracy in Germany". Hoover thus impressed on Wilson that the time had come to return to the "wisdom" of his "original positions" and use his power to effect changes in the peace terms that served this aim.[108]

In April, Hoover had still suggested that Wilson should press for the creation of an "Independent Socialist cabinet", as this would be capable of

[106] Hoover (1961), p. 241; Bliss to Wilson, 1 June 1919, Baker Papers; Bliss memorandum on German proposals, 6 June 1919, in Baker (1923), III, pp. 506, 508.
[107] Hoover to Wilson, 4 June 1919, O'Brien (1978), pp. 169–70.
[108] Hoover remarks, Meeting of Wilson with US Peace Commissioners, 3 June 1919, FRUS-PPC, XI, pp. 217, 220–1; Hoover to Wilson, 4 June 1919, O'Brien (1978), pp. 169–70.

"preserving order" and come "nearer" to "presenting the yearnings of the German people". By early June, however, he had clearly concluded that the Ebert–Scheidemann government represented "the only alternative to either Reactionary or Communistic Government" and played a vital role in fostering a stable democratic system in Germany.[109] Hoover underscored that a prompt admission of Germany to the League would serve the same purpose. And, significantly, he argued that it was a critical prerequisite for creating a genuine, universal League as Wilson had originally envisaged it – an organisation that would be "able to further correct the international wrongs that have accumulated over centuries and deter them in the future".[110]

It is worth noting that House was the only prominent member of the US delegation who defended Wilson's policy of making compromises with the *Entente* leaders and clearly backed the president in the final phase of the conference. Justifying a course that he had in fact recommended from the beginning, and agreements that he had been instrumental in bringing about, Wilson's by now somewhat estranged adviser emphasised the need for a "realistic" outlook and approach. He insisted that in view of the complex challenges the president had confronted in Paris, he had had no choice but to seek compromises and make concessions to Lloyd George and Clemenceau. House also deemed the draft treaty "too severe" and – unlike Wilson – thought it was "far afield" from the Fourteen Points. But the priorities he saw – similarly to the president – were to maintain a modicum of unity with the *Entente* Powers and to ensure that the German government would sign the treaty without any major changes. He underscored that both would be vital for achieving what remained his highest priority: the establishment of the League.

Echoing Wilson, House argued that once it had been set up the new organisation could serve as the key instrument to remedy some of the treaty's main shortcomings and most egregious flaws, particularly regarding the German settlement. He was concerned that any real attempt to meet German demands and negotiate significant amendments would lead to an interminable process of revisions that would not only threaten to unravel the imperfect but essential compromises that the Allied and Associated Powers had painstakingly forged, but conjure up the risk of a failure of the entire peace conference. The only change House advocated was a clear commitment to Germany's swift inclusion in the League. He too reasoned that it would be in the interest of European – and particularly French – security to bind the German government to the rules and obligations of the League Covenant.[111]

---

[109] Hoover to Wilson, 21 April 1919, Bane and Lutz (1942), pp. 384–6; Hoover memorandum, 5 June 1919, O'Brien (1978), pp. 171-3.

[110] Hoover to Wilson, 4 June 1919, O'Brien (1978), pp. 169–70.

[111] Bullitt memorandum of conversation with House, 19 May 1919, Bullitt Papers; House, Confidential Diary, 30 May 1919, House Papers.

Supported by House, Wilson responded to the fundamental concerns Bliss and Hoover had raised, and that a majority in the American delegation shared, in a characteristically high-handed manner. Rather than take them on board or engage in a serious debate, he focused on justifying the sterner, essentially uncompromising approach he had adopted since the beginning of the "war of notes". He clearly signalled his determination to persist with this approach or, put differently, his unwillingness to push for significant changes to the draft treaty. And he continued to reject the entire notion of opening a path towards direct negotiations with the German government which went beyond limited discussions between US financial experts and their German counterparts about a more workable reparations agreement. He never even considered using American influence to work out a more balanced settlement with the vanquished, let alone a "grand bargain" along the lines the German note of 29 May had proposed.

Essentially, Wilson adhered to two important rationales that had informed his pursuits at Versailles all along. He was not prepared to press for concessions "merely" for the sake of buttressing the Ebert Scheidemann government in Berlin and, in a wider context, the stabilisation of a democratic form of government in Germany. In other words, he refused to espouse Hoover's views. More important, however, was something else, namely that he resolutely clung to his unilateral conception of how to make "just peace", which ultimately meant that he deemed it legitimate to impose on Germany a settlement that corresponded with *his* understanding of what was just. This obviously ruled out any engagement on behalf of a – negotiated – compromise peace. On these premises, Wilson's actions came to be guided by two different priorities: on the one hand that of salvaging a basic consensus among the victors and, on the other, that of making sure that the German government would actually sign a peace treaty – and do so as soon as possible. Wilson's essentially unyielding attitude was reinforced by Colonel Conger's – misleading – assessment of the German government's positions. Conger had conveyed to the president that according to his sources in Berlin leading figures including Ebert, Scheidemann, Erzberger and Bernstorff were – in contrast to Brockdorff-Rantzau – ultimately prepared to rescind prior demands and sign a relatively severe peace on the terms the victors had put forward.[112]

On 3 June, Wilson impressed on the American delegation how critical it was for the stabilisation of the postwar order to preserve "agreement" among the United States, Britain and France – and to avoid any further negotiations that could expose "sharp lines of division" among them. He even argued that it was America's task to hold the victorious powers together "if it can be reasonably

---

[112] Conger to Bliss, with enclosed reports, 30 April 1919; Bliss to Wilson, 1 June 1919, Wilson Papers.

done" – at a time when problems like the Rhineland settlement looked "almost insoluble" given that the British delegation was "at one extreme" and the French at the other.[113] Yet the American president also maintained that his negotiating efforts had already "got very serious modifications out of the Allies" and that, fundamentally, he deemed the peace terms of the draft treaty not only appropriately "hard" but also "just". However, partly to placate the critical voices in the American delegation Wilson now formulated a new guiding maxim. He stressed that while he had no intention to "soften the treaty", he had a "sincere desire" to alter those parts of it that were "shown to be unjust" or "contrary to the principles" that he and the other western leaders had "laid down".[114] Crucially, however, the American president insisted that ultimately the political leaders of the victorious powers would decide which modifications would be justified.

Broadly speaking, Wilson had by this time adopted the position that the core political and territorial stipulations of the draft treaty – including the Saar agreement, the essentials of the Polish–German border settlement – all in all met his standards of a "just peace" and were not be altered.[115] In particular, influenced by the assessment of Lord, his leading expert on the issue, Wilson originally opposed the idea of a plebiscite in Upper Silesia because he held that conditions in this region would not permit "a truly free and genuine vote" as the local population had been "so long in a state of vassalage" and was dominated by a small number of "German capitalists" who controlled the coal-mines and the land.[116] At the same time, though he had not changed his underlying view that France's Rhineland policy was misguided, the American president now opposed British demands to shorten the occupation – and he did so mainly because he feared that pressing Clemenceau for any further concessions on this issue would precipitate the collapse of his government.

Moreover, and significantly, the American president initially repudiated the demand of Cecil, Hoover and many others for an early admission of Germany to the League. In the inner-American discussion, he re-accentuated his position that the western powers were justified in keeping the vanquished power outside the new organisation and insisting on a probation period because it was necessary for them to ascertain first whether "the change in government

---

[113] Wilson remarks in meeting with US peace commissioners, 3 June 1919, *FRUS-PPC*, XI, p. 219.

[114] *Ibid.*, p. 218.

[115] Wilson remarks in meeting with US peace commissioners, 3 June 1919, *FRUS-PPC*, XI, p. 221. The leading US expert on the Saar issue, Haskins, had condemned the counter-proposals' "demagogic" pan-German arguments and instrumentalisation of self-determination to nationalist ends. He thus rejected any concessions to the Scheidemann government. Haskins memorandum, 3 June 1919, Wilson Papers.

[116] Council of Four, 3 June 1919, Mantoux (1992), II, pp. 279–86. For Lord's recommendations see Lord memorandum, 5 June 1919, Wilson Papers; Lord (1921), pp. 71, 73.

and the governmental method in Germany" was "genuine and permanent".[117]
It was only with a view to reparations that, in line with overriding US interests
rather than considerations of justice, Wilson responded more favourably to
the German counter-proposals, but here too he set strict limits. Eventually, he
would follow the recommendation of Davis and Lamont and seize on the
Warburg–Melchior scheme to renew the American call for a more practicable
fixed-sum solution to the reparations problem.[118]

VII.   No Transformative Changes. The Final
Negotiations – among the Victors

The final stage of the core peacemaking process of 1919 thus was not, even in a
most rudimentary form, a wider negotiating process between the victors and
the vanquished. Rather, what ensued in the first half of June and then
culminated in the victors' ultimatum to Germany on 16 June became, at the
core, the final phase of the top-level negotiations between the political leaders
of the victorious powers that had dominated the proceedings since the end of
March. And these negotiations by and large centred, not on a fundamental
rewriting of the peace terms but rather on the critical issues that Lloyd George
had raised on behalf of the British Empire delegation: reparations, the occupation of the Rhineland, the Upper Silesia question, and Germany's admission
to the League of Nations. Significantly, these issues were considered separately
rather than as elements of a peace of accommodation. In the end, the final
struggles between the western leaders yielded no substantial changes; rather, it
reinforced the determination of all of the Big Three to compel the German
government to sign an essentially unaltered victors' peace.

The final round of the reparations battle – of 1919 – proved particularly
fruitless. Ultimately, it only confirmed their inability to find common ground.
Concretely, it confirmed that in view of the prevalent interests, strategic and
domestic-political constraints and considerations of Clemenceau and Lloyd
George – and the constraints and self-imposed limits of American loan and
debt policy – it was impossible for them to agree on a "definite" settlement that
might at least have limited the destructive impact of the reparations problem
on postwar international politics. This and the essential common interest of
the victorious powers in *not* negotiating with the German government also
thwarted any remaining German hopes that the offer of 100 billion Goldmarks
could become the starting-point for some kind of "grand bargain". Instead, the
final discussions among the political leaders and experts of the victorious
powers came to focus, once again, on the much more limited question of

---

[117] Wilson remarks in meeting with US peace commissioners, 3 June 1919, FRUS-PPC, XI,
pp. 212, 215.
[118] Council of Four, 3 and 9 June 1919, Mantoux (1992), II, pp. 284–5, 353–6.

whether it would be possible – and politically feasible – to agree on a "fixed sum" of indemnities after all. Once again, the main impetus came from Wilson and the American financial experts.[119]

It was only now, when confronted with what they regarded as the untenable reparations compromise of the draft treaty and a worsening European crisis situation that, with Hoover's support, the American experts Davis and Lamont developed a more comprehensive "American plan" for Europe's financial revitalisation, which they presented to the American president in mid-May. It was designed to prevent the escalation of a full-blown financial crisis and economic depression in postwar Europe – which, they argued, would have serious consequences for US export trade. And it was intended to relieve America's debtors and promote the general economic and political stabilisation of Europe – without abandoning the key premises of US debt and reparations policies. The American experts thus advocated neither debt relief at this stage nor any schemes linking debts and reparations. Yet they of course had not forgotten the crucial connection between the debt and reparations questions, and their proposal was also intended to suggest a way out of the reparation impasse, providing incentives for more moderate Allied reparations demands and an arrangement that did not undermine Europe's postwar reconstruction.

To respond to the imminent crisis they expected, Davis and Lamont suggested that Wilson should seek from Congress further short-term loans for those European countries that required urgent assistance, particularly France, and the authorisation to grant a three-year moratorium on the repayment of interest on their existing obligations to the United States. The longer-term financial stabilisation and revitalisation of Europe, however, was to be promoted "so far as possible" by relying on long-term credits extended by private American banks and underwriters – through "the normal channels of private enterprise". Davis and Lamont argued that every "consideration of humanity, justice and self-interest" commanded that the administration and private financiers worked together to cultivate, "through the establishment of joint interests", a greater readiness in the United States to engage in Europe's reconstruction.[120]

Wilson took note of what his experts recommended and showed himself persuaded that it was in America's interest to take measures to promote Europe's financial and economic revitalisation. But he set clear limits, particularly when it came to measures that could have altered the parameters of the

---

[119] Council of Four, 2 June 1919, Mantoux (1992), II, pp. 269–71.

[120] Baker (1923), III, pp. 352–56; memorandum of conference Wilson – US experts, 19 May 1919, Lamont Papers, 163–13. Lamont proposed the establishment of a non-governmental Finance Corporation in the United States that would lend American capital in cooperation with the British "banking machinery". See Lamont, Davis to Lansing for Leffingwell, 27 May, Lamont Papers; Lamont to Brand, 10 June 1919, Lamont Papers, 165–10: Walworth (1986), pp. 401–2.

reparations dispute. The utmost concession he made was to agree that he would eventually ask Congress to give Britain and France some respite by refunding the interest on their debt payments for the following three years. Essentially, the president thus confirmed that he was neither willing nor in a position at this stage to concern himself with wider, ambitious schemes that addressed fundamental challenges of European recovery and the United States' longer-term role in fostering it.[121]

Wilson was thus all the keener to seize on the German proposals of 29 May. For they seemed to present an opportunity to make a last attempt to gain Anglo-French support for a "fixed-sum solution" to the reparations problem that reined in Allied demands *without* requiring American concessions that he deemed politically impossible.[122] The president here followed the advice of Davis, who had been impressed with the German reparations proposal. In his assessment, it not only offered a chance to avoid "the mistake not to fix in the Peace Treaty a definite amount" that Germany "may reasonably be expected to pay within one generation"; it could also pave the way for a more practical, business-like reparations settlement.[123] This was the specific aim Wilson came to pursue in early June. And to realise it, he came to back the idea of targeted discussions between US, *Entente* and German financial experts about the specifics of a "definite" agreement.

Yet when the American president finally suggested that in the light of the German proposals the governments of Britain and France should settle on a total sum of 100 billion Goldmarks that would be "subject to interest" Lloyd George was quick to distance himself from what the majority in his own delegation, and government, had demanded. And he was as quick to re-affirm his earlier position that, for domestic-political reasons, he could not consent to a fixed-sum agreement. In fact, the British premier ultimately relied on the recommendations of Sumner and Cunliffe, who had been the most uncompromising hard-liners on the indemnity issue in the British delegation all along – and who deemed the German proposals entirely unacceptable.[124] To justify what Wilson saw as yet another *volte-face* of his British counterpart, Lloyd George again pointed to the high expectations he confronted in the British parliament and in the British public, impressing on the American president that any figure that "would not frighten" the Germans would be "below the figure with which he and M. Clemenceau could face their peoples

---

[121] For a critical evaluation of American schemes, and their limits, see Keynes to Bradbury, 22 May 1919, Keynes Papers, RT/1/104.

[122] Council of Four, 3 and 9 June 1919, Mantoux (1992), II, pp. 284–5, 353–6.

[123] Davis memorandum for Wilson, 1 June 1919, Lamont Papers, 169–1; US Project for Reply to German Counter-Proposals, 9 June 1919, *FRUS-PPC*, VI, pp. 267–71.

[124] See Sumner memorandum, 31 May 1919, Lloyd George Papers, F/213/5/36; Cunliffe memorandum, 1 June 1919, Lothian Papers, GD 40/17/62.

in the present state of public opinion". At the same time, he argued that settling a definite sum also carried the risk of re-opening the inter-allied disputes regarding the distribution of indemnity payments that had barely been contained by the draft treaty's compromise formulae. On these grounds, Lloyd George on 10 June rejected Wilson's proposal and vetoed any further deliberations with German financial experts.[125]

Unsurprisingly, Clemenceau concurred. He now went so far as to argue that if the victors followed the American suggestion of a "lump sum" settlement they would do nothing less than "destroy the Treaty", invalidating all the principles and procedures on which they had earlier agreed. The French premier had earlier stressed, once again, that he spoke for the country that had "suffered most from the war" and he too invoked the pressure of public opinion, maintaining that the French public was – mistakenly – under the impression that his government had not "demanded all that we should have from Germany" and that any actual sum fixed at this stage would be deemed too low and cause an outcry in France.[126] Yet Clemenceau and Tardieu also re-asserted their opposition to a fixed-sum "solution" of the reparations question because it of course still stood in conflict with overriding aims of their postwar strategy vis-à-vis Germany.

At one level, as Tardieu observed in retrospect, the French government sought to avoid "an arbitrary sum which might in thirty years raise a Germany free from debt and prosperous at the door of a France deeply involved" in financial problems. More importantly, however, a fixed-sum arrangement would have deprived France of the essential strategic leverage that the control and enforcement instrument of the Reparation Commission was supposed to provide; and it ran counter to the French strategy of using the reparations regime to constrain Germany's economic and financial power potential – and, if necessary, to justify a prolongation of the Rhineland occupation.[127] In the face of the combined and determined opposition of both *Entente* leaders to the American plans Wilson eventually gave up any further attempt to push for an American "solution" to the reparations problem. In the end, he declared with a good measure of resignation that it was simply impossible to reconcile the positions of the American government with those of the British and French governments on an issue that, as he stressed, was of far more immediate importance to them.[128] And this meant that the tenuous reparations compromises of the draft treaty would not be altered.

---

[125] Lloyd George remarks, Council of Four, 9 and 10 June 1919, *FRUS-PPC*, VI, pp. 261–2, Mantoux (1955), II, pp. 351–6.

[126] Clemenceau remarks, Council of Four, 2 and 10 June 1919, Mantoux (1992), II, p. 273, Mantoux (1955), II, pp. 351–6.

[127] Tardieu (I/1921), p. 307.

[128] Mantoux (1955), II, pp. 363, 365.

In the final act of the Rhineland battle of 1919, Lloyd George pursued one last-ditch attempt to persuade Clemenceau to shorten the occupation of the Rhineland and make it less offensive to Germany. He reiterated the underlying British concern that "a prolonged occupation" would constitute "a prolonged peril to the peace of Europe", as it was bound to provoke German resistance and fuel nationalist resentment against the western powers. And he argued that strategically the occupation would "serve no use" in placing an effective check on German power because it would "only last during the period when Germany is weakest".[129] But the British premier's leverage was limited; and he was neither willing nor in a position to offer any further incentives – notably in the form of reinforced security and alliance guarantees – that could have had a decisive impact on Clemenceau.

The French premier successfully fended off the British challenges and vetoed any significant changes. He was simply not prepared to go back behind the compromises he and Tardieu had fought so hard to hammer out on an issue that he deemed so vital for French postwar security. He resolutely opposed shortening the occupation by even one day. To the end, he maintained that it constituted an essential "guarantee for the payment of the indemnity". He also still insisted that it could even be extended if after fifteen years the western powers still deemed "the guarantees against unprovoked aggression" that Germany provided insufficient. And he effectively invoked the domestic constraints he had to grapple with, insisting that in view of the criticisms he faced on the home front he could not make any further concessions.[130]

Clemenceau reiterated that "the union between France, England, and America" was and remained the cornerstone of his security policy and vision of the postwar order. Essentially, however, he – like Tardieu – still saw the occupation and control of the Rhineland not only as a means to ensure German reparations payments but also as a fall-back option to safeguard French security in the event that the Anglo-American guarantees to France would not materialise. And in his interpretation the agreements he had wrested from Wilson and Lloyd George sanctioned the "right" of future French governments to reinforce or even to prolong the occupation if this was considered vital to national security. In confidence, the French premier told Poincaré that France would still be "on the Rhine" in fifteen years and "remain there".[131]

---

[129] Lloyd George remarks, Council of Four, 2 and 12 June 1919, Mantoux (1992), II, pp. 269–71, 405; Council of Four, 12 June 1919, FRUS-PPC, VI, p. 329.

[130] House Diary, 31 May 1919, House Papers; Clemenceau remarks, Council of Four, 2 and 13 June 1919, Mantoux, II, pp. 272–6, 438–40; Council of Four, 12 June 1919, FRUS-PPC, VI, pp. 328–9.

[131] Clemenceau remarks, Council of Four, 13 June 1919, Mantoux, II, pp. 438–40; Mermeix (1922), pp. 229–30.

Once again, Wilson sought to act as a mediator between the conflicting British and French imperatives. But the American president ultimately reinforced Clemenceau's position. A long-term occupation of the Rhineland still clashed with the underlying rationales of Wilson's aspirations to safeguard French and European security through a League-based system of collective security. Like Bliss and Hoover, he still considered the occupation politically counter-productive because he shared the British concern that it was bound to create conditions for interminable tensions and conflict between France and Germany; and he likewise considered it misguided in strategic terms because he too reckoned that the envisaged occupation regime would be in place while Germany was still weak and was to be terminated precisely at the time when the vanquished power was projected to have recovered from its defeat. Yet by this time the American president was no longer prepared to press for a curtailment of the occupation, let alone challenge it in principle. And the main reason for this was, unquestionably, concern about Clemenceau's embat-tled position in France. In short, he deemed it vital to strengthen the latter's hold on power and thus to prevent a scenario in which a more assertive right-wing government, dominated by President Poincaré or the "military party" under Foch, would abandon the hard-won Rhineland agreement and revert to the pursuit of the French "buffer-state" agenda. From Wilson's perspective, such a scenario would have dealt a very serious blow to Europe's stabilisation prospects and, in particular, hopes of eventually initiating a longer-term accommodation between France and Germany.[132]

What Wilson thus focused on instead was to gain Clemenceau's acceptance of minor amendments that were intended to make the occupation less objec-tionable from the German point of view. Following his suggestions, the victors gave assurances that they did not intend to "cut" the Rhineland "off from the rest of Germany", and they pledged that the occupation troops would be confined to their barracks except "in cases of exceptional necessity". Finally, in one last effort to mediate in the persistent Anglo-French confrontation over the length of the occupation, the American president proposed one further amendment that both Lloyd George and Clemenceau came to endorse. It became the basis of a secret and not officially binding "Declaration" that the Big Three signed on 16 June and which stipulated that the Allied and Associated Powers would be "ready" to agree on an "earlier termination" of the occupation if Germany had "given proofs of her goodwill" and "satisfac-tory guarantees to assure the fulfilment of her [reparation] obligations".[133]

---

[132] Wilson remarks in meeting with US peace commissioners, 3 June 1919, *FRUS-PPC*, XI, pp. 211–12; Wilson to Polk, 15 March 1920, Wilson Papers.

[133] Council of Four, 12 and 13 June 1919; Mantoux (1992), II, pp. 404–5, 428–31; Mantoux (1955), II, p. 393; Convention of the Big Three regarding the Military Occupation,

This declaration became the final element of the victors' final compromise on the crucial Rhineland question in 1919. But it was yet another formula compromise that did not qualitatively alter the tenuous agreement they had forged in April. What mattered more in the long run was that the final altercations once again threw into relief the fundamentally conflicting attitudes of the political leaders of three principal victors towards the occupation regime, which made it a distinctly conflict-prone regime from the start. And these attitudes pointed to a far more profound problem that has already been highlighted, namely the persistent divergences in the victors' approaches to the crucial question of how international security was to be guaranteed in the fledgling postwar Atlantic system – by containing or ultimately by integrating Germany.

The victors' final battle over the Polish-German settlement indeed came to centre on the political future of Upper Silesia. Lloyd George now insisted that Upper Silesia's fate had to be decided through a plebiscite. The arguments he advanced in favour of this approach echoed his Fontainebleau rationales. Essentially, stressing that the question of Upper Silesia was "the one that most concerns the Germans", the British premier sought to persuade Wilson and Clemenceau that holding a plebiscite was in the interest of Europe's long-term stabilisation. He argued once again that all sides, including the Polish government, should be interested in pre-empting the danger of future German irredentism. To guarantee "the independence of the vote", Lloyd George proposed that a commission of the League of Nations should supervise the proceedings and a small Allied force should occupy the disputed territories. He dismissed the concern that the outcome of the plebiscite would be unduly influenced by the power of local German magnates and capitalists – while also noting that the German negotiators did not represent "the capitalists" but a government in which "the Socialists are in a majority" Nonetheless, like most British policymakers and experts, he expected that under the proposed conditions a majority would vote in favour of remaining part of Germany.[134]

Predictably, Clemenceau opposed Lloyd George's plan. He maintained that it could not be carried out in a fair manner under a German administration and in view of the prevalent German influence in the region – even if the Polish population was numerically in a majority. Yet in an effort to block the idea of a plebiscite as such he also observed that if the victors followed Lloyd George's proposal and occupied Upper Silesia, the German side would claim that the vote had not been "free" and consider the result illegitimate. What lay behind Clemenceau's resistance, however, were the same geopolitical rationales that had dominated France's "eastern policy" all along – and that

13 June, Mantoux (1992), II, pp. 431–5; "Declaration" signed by Clemenceau, Lloyd George and Wilson, 16 June 1919, FRUS-PPC, VI, p. 522.
[134] Lloyd George remarks, Council of Four, 3 June, Mantoux (1992), II, pp. 280–3.

commanded supporting Polish claims especially where they served the over-riding strategic aim of depriving Germany of critical industrial assets and resources. In the end, the French premier thus once more resorted to the argument that in certain cases the "ethnographic principle" had to "yield to other considerations" and stressed the need to strengthen Poland "as the natural barrier between Germany and Russia".[135] Invited to present the Polish position on 5 June, Paderewski used dramatic language to impress on the leaders of the victorious powers that they had a duty to keep what he called their promise to accord Upper Silesia to Poland without a plebiscite. He warned that if that promise was broken, the Polish state would become "ungovernable" and he would be forced to resign.[136]

At first, Wilson also maintained his opposition to a plebiscite and sided with Clemenceau in emphasising that in view of the region's German-dominated power structures it would be impossible to hold a fair and "free" referendum. In response to Lloyd George's challenge, the American president insisted that he adhered to the "principle of self-determination" but did not want to call on a Polish population to vote under the sway of German "capitalist" power and "under the aegis of German officials". Making a case for what he saw as the historically underprivileged and weaker party in the dispute, Wilson pointed to the negative example of the industrial region of Pittsburgh and politics in Pennsylvania to underscore that, as he saw it, overbearing "capitalist influence" could compromise a voting process. On the other hand, he dismissed the suggestion of an Allied military supervision of a possible plebiscite, arguing – like Clemenceau – that this would only be regarded by the German side as an "arbitrary intervention" of the victors on behalf of Polish interests. Like Lloyd George, Wilson did consider the wider political implications of the Upper Silesian question for the German government's acceptance of the peace treaty, the future of Polish–German relations and Europe's stabilisation in the longer term. But in contrast to the British premier – and Dresel or Hoover – he concluded that, on the basis of what US observers reported, the cession of Upper Silesia was not an issue that provoked "any popular sentiment in Germany". He thus doubted that it was critical for the Scheidemann government's willingness to sign the peace treaty and, in a wider perspective, the legitimacy of the peace in Germany.[137]

But the American president eventually relinquished his resistance and backed a compromise: a plebiscite to be held under such conditions that, in his view, it would remove "any pretext for a German irredentist movement in

[135] Clemenceau remarks, Council of Four, 2 and 3 June 1919, Mantoux (1992), II, pp. 272–3, 283–4; Mantoux (1955), II, pp. 382, 430–3.
[136] Paderewski remarks, Council of Four, 5 June 1919, Mantoux (1992), II, p. 311.
[137] Wilson remarks, Council of Four, 3 June 1919, Mantoux (1992), II, pp. 279–86; ibid., p. xxv; Wilson remarks in meeting with US peace commissioners, 3 June 1919, p. 217; Lord (1921), pp. 71, 73.

the future". Significantly, he did not alter his fundamental assessment; nor did he pay particular attention to the wider regional and geopolitical implications of the Upper Silesian question. Rather, he responded in part to Lloyd George's threat that British troops would not take part in military measures in case of a German refusal to sign the treaty. And he seems to have been influenced by reports that underscored that the local population, and particularly Polish working-class milieus, actually desired a plebiscite and that in the industrial areas a majority would vote in favour of a "union with Poland". Wilson thus agreed to establish an ad-hoc commission that was to propose terms for a plebiscite. Clemenceau now had to follow suit and accepted the plebiscite proposal "so as not to create difficulties" among the victors. On the basis of the commission's recommendations, the Big Three decided that a plebiscite would be held after a cooling-off period of six to eighteen months – under the supervision of an inter-allied commission and policed by Allied troops.[138]

But the way in which the plebiscite would eventually be carried out and decided was neither conducive to containing German irredentist pressure nor germane to the Polish state's security and consolidation prospects. It would aggravate rather than resolve the problem of Upper Silesia and thus, in a wider context, compound the destabilising effect of the decisions of 1919 on eastern Central Europe. The referendum was finally held in March 1921, at a time when the American government had already withdrawn from political respon-sibilities in Europe, ever deeper divisions had emerged between Upper Silesia's different ethnic communities and thousands had died as a result of violent clashes between Polish and German nationalists. Effectively, the plebiscite intensified both this struggle and the violent polarisation it brought. While, overall, 60 per cent voted in favour of Germany and 40 per cent in favour of Poland, votes were split according to regions, with clear majorities for a union with Germany in most of the towns and, in the northern and western districts, clear majorities for union with Poland in the southeast and an "inextricable meld of votes" in the industrial heartland. What followed were further negoti-ations in the inter-allied commission, where British representatives overall supported German claims and French representatives took the Polish side – while the French government supported Polish nationalists who launched what became known as the Third Silesian Uprising.

As there was no prospect for a compromise "solution", the matter was eventually referred to the League Council and, under French pressure, a commission of non-interested powers – composed of Belgian, Spanish, Brazilian and Chinese representatives – decreed a somewhat arbitrary new border, awarding 70 per cent of the territory to Germany but most of the

---

[138] Council of Four, 5, 11 and 14 June 1919, Mantoux (1992), II, pp. 307–12, 385–93, 452–5.

industrial areas and mines to Poland. Significantly, however, in 1922 a basic agreement on how to deal with the Upper Silesia problem would not be reached through the League but through a bilateral Polish–German treaty in which both countries agreed on basic rules for the protection of their respective minorities and pledged to engage in political and economic cooperation.[139] But the Upper Silesian problem remained part and parcel of the wider structural Polish–German conflict-constellation that had been created in 1919. It remained part of the massive liabilities that had been created for the emergence of a secure and liberal Polish nation-state and, no less, for a postwar accommodation between Germany and its newly constituted eastern neighbour – and, in a wider perspective, the integration of the as yet frail Weimar Republic into the new international order.

The German counter-proposals of 29 May had underscored yet again how much importance the protagonists of the Scheidemann government attached to securing the inclusion of a "reformed" Germany in the reformed international system that was being established in 1919. Put differently, what they sought to prevent by all available means was being excluded and *ostracised* from this system. That is why they placed such emphasis on Germany's immediate admission to the League on terms of "equality".[140] This comparatively narrower question indeed became a central issue of the final controversies among the victors. Yet it would be misleading to conclude that the German League strategy had produced the desired effect. Under the circumstances, the political leaders of the western powers regarded Brockdorff-Rantzau's high-minded declarations and Schücking's elaborate blueprint for a "universal" League not as expressions of a sincere desire to play a constructive part in the new international organisation and contribute to its development, which they indeed *also* were, but rather as essentially tactical manoeuvres.

Instead, the decisive impetus came from those in the British delegation who had already argued much earlier, ever since the armistice, that it would be crucial for the pacification of Europe and the formation of a new international concert to bring the vanquished power into the League as soon as possible. The most influential advocate of this policy, Cecil, now proposed a reply to the German proposals which was to assure the Scheidemann government that if it gave satisfactory proof of its "pacific tendency", Germany would be included in the League in the immediate future, i.e. within a few months.[141] But Lloyd George was unwilling to use what bargaining power he had left to back Cecil's

[139] See the balanced analysis in Porter-Szücs (2014), pp. 85–7; Campbell (1970), pp. 361–85; Schattkowsky (1994).
[140] German note, 29 May 1919, *FRUS-PPC*, VI, pp. 797–8, 819–21.
[141] Cecil memorandum, 3 June 1919, Cabinet Paper W.C.P. 916, CAB 29/16; draft reply, 7 June 1919, *FRUS-PPC*, VI, pp. 251–2.

proposal. Fundamentally, the British premier still believed that it was "safer" to accommodate Germany within the League at an early stage; and he still considered the alternative of a longer period of exclusion dangerous because it might drive the vanquished power into the arms of Bolshevik Russia. But he maintained his preference for an intermediate solution, favouring Germany's admission after roughly one year – provided that the German government had by then shown "good faith" in fulfilling the terms of the peace treaty.[142]

Somewhat unexpectedly, it was Wilson who re-emerged – at the eleventh hour – as the most powerful proponent of Germany's swift inclusion in the League. In the final deliberations with Clemenceau and Lloyd George, the American president indicated that he would no longer insist on a longer "probation period". He now demanded that the government in Berlin should receive a clear signal that if it proved its sincerity in fulfilling the obligations of the peace treaty, Germany should be admitted to the League "in a short time". Wilson adopted the argument that it was in the "interest" of the victorious powers to include "the Germans" in the League of Nations rather than leave them "outside", not least because they would thus be in a better position to "restrain" them. And he stressed that it was more advantageous to signal to the German people that the western powers did not intend to "treat them as pariahs" – and thereby push them into undesirable combinations with other powers that would be excluded from the League, namely Bolshevik Russia and Hungary. In fact, however, Wilson had changed his stance not because he had substantially altered his political outlook or out of a profound concern to revive his vision of a "universal League" but rather for tactical reasons – namely to give the Scheidemann government an incentive to sign the peace treaty.[143] It was on these grounds that Wilson came to support the draft reply to the German League proposals that Cecil had formulated with the help of House. It held out the promise that Germany would be admitted as soon as the Allied and Associated Powers were assured that it possessed a "stable" government that had given "clear proofs" of its willingness to meet its international obligations – particularly its disarmament obligations – indicating that this should permit a German entry "within a few months".[144]

Ultimately, though, the American president would not insist on a more clear-cut commitment of this kind. He would fall back on his "probation" rationale, stressing that what he desired was that the League would admit Germany once it had become evident that democratic government there had

---

[142] Lloyd George remarks, British Empire Delegation, 33 and 34, 1 June 1919, CAB 29/38/1; Council of Four, 2 June 1919, Mantoux (1992), II, pp. 269–71.

[143] Wilson remarks, Council of Four, 3 and 7 June 1919, Mantoux (1992), II, pp. 288–9, 347–9.

[144] Council of Four, 7 June 1919, Mantoux (1992), II, pp. 347–9; draft reply, 7 June 1919, FRUS-PPC, VI, pp. 251–2.

been firmly established. He thus re-introduced a criterion that left endless room for different political interpretations. And this allowed Clemenceau to reassert French essentials and fend off anything approaching a binding commitment to the German government.[145]

The French premier conceded that the vanquished power could not be "excluded" in the longer term and had to be admitted "one day". But he warned that it was illusory to assume that Germany's power and international behaviour could be restrained more effectively by drawing it into the League. In fact, an early inclusion of the defeated power of course ran counter to the underlying French aim of turning the League into a platform for the postwar "alliance" of the victorious powers and an auxiliary instrument for the control and containment of Germany. Clemenceau thus re-affirmed his own version of a probation policy, which set very broadly defined conditions for a German entry and, crucially, was intended to give France the power to veto or delay it. He insisted that the victors had to require the German government to give "proof of good faith" that it was complying with the terms of the peace treaty and honouring its obligations before its membership could be considered. And what mattered most was that the French government would ultimately have the power to decide at what time sufficient "proof" had been given. Clemenceau spoke of a probation period of "years". On this basis, he prepared an alternative reply to the German note that did not offer Germany "hope of early admission" and set the basic terms for the victors' official reply of 16 June. As he saw no further prospect of effecting significant changes at this stage, Lloyd George acquiesced in the end.[146]

Consequently, the official reply of the Allied and Associated Powers of 16 June gave no assurance, nor did it provide a clear perspective of a future German entry to the League. Instead, it not only stipulated in a distinctly moralistic language that it was "impossible to expect the free nations of the world to sit down immediately in equal association with those by whom they have been so grievously wronged". It also declared that Germany had to pass through a probation period before it could be considered for admission – a period whose duration was to depend on the future actions of the German government and "the German people". The emphasis had shifted. Now, Germany would have to give "clear proofs" not only of the "stability" of its democratic government but also and crucially of its "intention" to meet the obligations arising from the peace treaty.[147]

---

[145] Wilson remarks, Council of Four, 7 June 1919, Mantoux (1955), II, p. 347.

[146] Clemenceau remarks, Council of Four, 3 and 7 June 1919, Mantoux (1992), II, pp. 289, 348–9; Council of Four, 12 June 1919, *ibid.*, p. 403.

[147] Reply of the Allied and Associated Powers, 16 June 1919, *FRUS-PPC*, VI, pp. 926 ff., 934, 940.

This put the protagonists of the Scheidemann government in the difficult position of being expected to accept and comply with the Covenant and the ground-rules of a new international organisation from which the country they represented remained excluded. What is more, there was no longer even any certain prospect that Germany would be allowed to join what was to be the core organisation of the new international order in the foreseeable future. The sweeping formulations of the Allied note of 16 June gave the victorious great powers substantial political leeway in determining when the fledgling German republic would be eligible for membership in the "Society of Nations" – and they gave each of them ample room to define what constituted German fulfilment of the broadly defined criteria in accordance with its political and strategic imperatives.

Therefore, to a large extent the future of the League and the new order it was to create hinged on the priorities the political leaders of the victors – and the vanquished – would set *after* the peace conference. Potentially, Wilson could still make it a priority to press for Germany's expedited admission in order to realise his longer-term aspiration of a "universal" League. Lloyd George could still push for Germany's entry within one year in order to create the framework for a more viable concert of powers. Yet the final compromise of the victors on the League also gave the French government the power to veto or at least to delay Germany's eventual inclusion in the *Société des Nations*. At the same time, the German republic's weak government now confronted the unenviable prospect of having to pursue and legitimise a policy of "fulfilment" with a view to a peace treaty that its protagonists and a majority of the German public would regard as illegitimate, in order to enter a League of Nations that would be founded as an institution of the victors.

VIII. The Final Ultimatum and the Imposition of the Peace

As is well-known, the victorious powers ultimately proceeded to force the German government to sign the settlement they had forged. On 16 June they issued what Wilson called an "absolute ultimatum", giving the Scheidemann government five days – then one week – to declare that it would accept the victors' terms and making clear that in the event of a German refusal they would take all necessary measures to "enforce their will". Both Wilson and Lloyd George now closed ranks with Clemenceau in backing Foch's contingency plan of leading a combined advance of Allied and Associate troops into Germany – as far as to the Weser river – and to use whatever force necessary to compel the government in Berlin to sign and ratify the peace treaty. They also backed the threat of re-imposing the blockade – that Wilson had earlier striven to lift – if military measures should fail to have the desired effect.[148]

---

[148] Baker journal, 22 June 1919, Baker Papers; Walworth (1986), pp. 427–30.

The heated debates about the response to the ultimatum that now ensued in the delegation and in the Cabinet in Berlin revealed the depth of the predicament in which the Scheidemann government found itself. Even though their expectations had already been greatly reduced by this time, virtually all German protagonists regarded the final note of the victors as both deeply disappointing and offensive. Returning to Berlin on 18 June, Brockdorff-Rantzau urged the Cabinet to reject the peace treaty outright – a demand that was backed by the overwhelming majority of the German peace delegation, including Melchior. And the foreign minister now advocated, as it were, a further escalation of the Wilsonian strategy he had so unsuccessfully pursued since early May. He argued that a republican Germany that refused to sign a draconian peace treaty and was then "oppressed" by the western powers could yet present itself as the true standard-bearer of progressive and "democratic" ideals, and thus rally the masses – particularly in Britain and the United States – against the policies of their own governments. Ultimately, this was supposed to force the western powers to abandon their coercive course. In the illusory scenario the foreign minister outlined to Ebert and the Cabinet, the tenuous coalition of the victors would crumble – within a period of roughly two months – and conditions would be ripe for actual peace negotiations and, in the end, a fundamentally altered "progressive" peace settlement.[149] Simons staunchly supported the foreign minister's course, professing his "invincible belief" that it was now the German government, and no longer Wilson, that was "fighting for the ideas of the future" and that it would win the "conflict of ideas" with the western states.[150]

Most members of the German peace delegation also rallied behind the foreign minister's position. On the one hand, they emphasised the disastrous economic repercussions that the victors' terms would have. As one delegate put it with characteristic hyperbole, one could not sign a treaty that would bring the assured "destruction of the German economy and thus the destruction of the German people".[151] Yet important figures like Warburg also highlighted what they saw as the disastrous political consequences an acceptance of the peace treaty would spell. In fact, they voiced concerns that were also shared by the leading figures of the Social Democrats and the German Democratic Party, notably Friedrich Naumann and Scheidemann himself. Essentially, they all feared that signing the treaty would discredit not only the present government but, in a broader perspective, all those who stood at the forefront of the effort to establish and consolidate a republic in Germany.

[149] Brockdorff-Rantzau to Ebert, 9 June 1919, Pol. 13-4, 1919, PA; Brockdorff-Rantzau remarks to the cabinet, 18 June 1919, AR Scheidemann, pp. 505–7.
[150] Simons to Mrs Simons, 30 May and 14 June 1919, Luckau (1941), pp. 127–8, 131.
[151] Schmitt report, 18 June 1919, Geschäftsstelle für Friedensverhandlungen, Protokolle, vol. 99, PA.

Ultimately, they argued – presciently –, it would thus deal a heavy blow to the development prospects of the newly founded Republic of Weimar itself. For it would allow reactionary and right-wing forces to blame the "Weimar coalition" for failing to stand up for vital German interests and bowing to the pressure of the western powers in signing a treaty that so profoundly disappointed the expectations of a "Wilsonian peace" which the government itself had raised. Warburg warned Ebert that if the Scheidemann government accepted the treaty, "we [would] dig our own grave, demoralize the entire nation, [and] destroy democracy and socialism"; because once its effects – "hunger and misery" – became palpable, "the German people would turn against those who signed the treaty" and there would be "a swing to the right or a revolution from the most radical quarter".[152]

But what gained the upper hand in the Cabinet was a different course, which – supported by David – Erzberger advocated most forcefully. Erzberger warned that following Brockdorff-Rantzau's recommendations would have incalculable and ultimately far more dangerous consequences for Germany. In his assessment, it would not open up a path to negotiations and a more acceptable settlement but lead, on the contrary, to "a still harsher peace" that the Allied and Associated Powers would impose even more harshly after they had invaded and occupied German territory.[153] Through American intermediaries, Erzberger had attempted to negotiate some last-minute concessions, *inter alia* the assurance of an earlier admission of Germany to the League. But when these attempts remained futile he insisted that the Cabinet in Berlin had only one realistic choice, namely to sign the treaty on which the victors insisted.[154] Crucially, though he had still declared publicly on 18 June that Germany would "never sign" what he called "this peace of enslavement", Ebert reconsidered and came to cast his weight on the side of dutiful acceptance. In a statement he made on 24 June, which manifested the profound ambivalence that marked not only his attitude, the German president appealed to all Germans to support the government in fulfilling the conditions of the peace treaty "as far as it is possible to carry it into effect"; yet even then he still argued that this should be done to pave the way for "ameliorations", "revisions" and potentially even a "final removal of the gigantic burden".[155]

By contrast, Scheidemann declared that he could not act in blatant contradiction with the public commitments he had made and become the

---

[152] Warburg to Ebert, 6 June 1919, Pol. 16, 1919, PA.

[153] Dyar memorandum, 11 June 1919, Wilson Papers; *AR Scheidemann*, pp. 417-20; Erzberger (1920), pp. 371-4.

[154] Erzberger remarks, meeting of the peace delegation, 19 May 1919, Pol. 2a, 1919, PA; Conger memorandum, 20 May 1919, *FRUS-PPC*, XII, pp. 127-8.

[155] Ebert speech, 18 June 1919, in Harmer (2008), p. 97; Ebert statement, 24 June 1919, *The Times*, 26 June 1919.

"henchman" of the victorious powers in signing and executing a dishonour-
able peace treaty that "could not be fulfilled" and would bring "the disintegration of Germany".[156] Consequently, he tendered his resignation. Having
failed to persuade a majority in the Cabinet, Brockdorff-Rantzau also resigned.
Thus, the heavy duty of travelling to Paris and putting the German signature
under the Treaty of Versailles in the Hall of Mirrors on 28 June 1919 fell to his
successor, the Social Democrat Hermann Müller, and to the steadfast Centre
Party politician Johannes Bell.

[156] Warburg to Ebert, 6 June 1919, AA, Pol. 16, PA.

21

The Truncated Atlantic Peace Order of 1919
A Re-appraisal

The First World War and the peacemaking process of 1919 recast the global order. And they had both profound and ambivalent effects on regional spheres of order in many parts of the world outside Europe. This notably applied to East Asia – as thrown into relief by the flawed *quid pro quo* settlement of the Shandong question. And, most dramatically, it applied to the Middle East – though here the conflict-ridden reordering processes only came to a preliminary end with the Lausanne agreement of 1923. As has been highlighted, what unfolded at and around the Paris Peace Conference thus had significant global dimensions *and* repercussions. And in the longer run the founding of the League of Nations, whose remit was *supposed* to be universal, could potentially provide a crystallisation-point for more far-reaching or even transformative changes on a global scale. Not least, it could become a crucial institution both for those who had managed to gain and those who still strove to gain recognition for their self-determination demands and aspirations to found independent states.

But, as we have also seen, the aftermath of the Great War did not witness the dawn of a new *world* order. More precisely, no new global order had been created in the sense that, despite the demise of some empires and the general exhaustion of the European powers, the hierarchical imperialist structures of influence and power that had emerged in most of the world outside the Euro-Atlantic sphere in the formative pre-war decades of the long twentieth century were not significantly altered, let alone radically transformed. And, more fundamentally, no such order had been created in the sense that, despite the new precepts enshrined in the League Covenant, the hierarchical processes of Paris had in fact – and unsurprisingly – not (yet) given rise to new constitutive principles and norms that actually had *universal* validity. Essential hierarchical gradations and blatant double-standards persisted, not just with a view to self-determination but also with a view to who had a voice in international politics.

What had emerged can thus best be described as a new global hierarchy, which was also reflected in the ultimately and necessarily hierarchical anatomy of the League. The novel world power, the United States, and the weakened but as yet resilient global imperial powers, Britain and France, were set to play predominant roles for the foreseeable future – and so was, though mainly in

East Asia, Japan. But it still remained to be seen how they would act in these roles and how they would and could actually meet the new and expanded responsibilities they confronted. In some respects, the negotiations in Paris had given clear indications. Acting on the premise and perception that they represented not only the most powerful states but also the most advanced civilisations, the protagonists of the western powers, including Wilson, had in effect found new ways to assert and justify core prerogatives, not only those accruing to them as permanent members of the new League Council but also that of deciding who was entitled to self-determination and who still was to be placed under guardianship and tutelage, or to remain under imperial rule.

It is thus worth re-accentuating that, in a global perspective, 1919 did not mark a real *caesura* in the long twentieth century's *longue durée* processes of decolonisation and advances towards a post-imperial international system. Rather, it marked a point of reassertion and "push-back" on the part of the remaining imperial powers – and a time of reckoning for the vanguards of anti-colonial nationalist movements who, seeing their aspirations rebuffed, would subsequently push their struggles for self-determination in new directions. As noted, with Wilson's acquiescence the British and French decision-makers were overall successful in pursuing adjusted strategies of imperial defence to consolidate and shore up the legitimacy of their imperial systems – holding at bay those who called for self-determination within the British and French empires and in the wider "colonised world". And the mandate system that was established for the former German colonies and provinces of the Ottoman Empire under the aegis of the League (largely following Smuts' blueprint) was geared towards becoming an instrument for the expansion of "internationalised" neo-imperial oversight and, above all, the British and French spheres of influence in the Near and Middle East.

I.   The Problematic "Beginning of a Beginning". The First Attempts to Build a Viable Atlantic Peace Order

Essentially, however, those who became the decisive peacemakers were not, or only fleetingly, focusing their attention on these questions or other global concerns. Rather, they were chiefly occupied with the challenges that had arisen where the war had originated and wrought most havoc, in Europe. Yet they were also grappling with another task that, because it was so unprecedented, represented a particularly immense learning challenge: they had to learn how to come to terms with the massive, indeed transformative changes the war had caused in the relations between Europe and the United States.

As this re-appraisal has sought to show, the complex negotiations, power struggles and political-ideological battles of the Paris Peace Conference in fact pivoted on two questions: whether it would be possible to found, for the first time, a functioning transatlantic international order; and what were to be the shape, foundations and essential ground-rules of this order. But, as it has also sought to underscore, the peacemaking efforts of 1919 could only constitute an in many ways problematic "beginning of a beginning" of attempts to build a viable Atlantic peace order for the long twentieth century.[1]

The settlement that emerged was far removed from the progressive, democratic and inclusive "peace of justice" that Wilson had mapped out in his wartime speeches and still called for after the armistice. It was not, and could not be, a peace that transcended traditional power interests, initiated an accommodation or even reconciliation between the belligerents and established not only an authoritative League but also a new order of international law, arbitration and self-determination. The outcome of the peace conference thus particularly disappointed all those who for a variety of reasons had clamoured for a transformative "Wilsonian peace" and continued to place their hopes in the American president – from progressive internationalists in the United States and Britain, who castigated the Treaty of Versailles as a deeply flawed "peace to end peace", to reformist forces (yet also opportunists) in Germany and other vanquished nations.[2]

Yet such hopes and expectations were profoundly unrealistic from the start. The realities, constraints and prevailing power constellations of peacemaking simply did not allow for transformative breakthroughs in 1919. Wilson himself had to learn how to make compromises. And, as we have seen, when having to face up to the immense pressures and complicated negotiating scenarios of Paris, he came to alter his priorities and approach significantly, eventually becoming one of the main architects of a victors' peace that was distinctly less progressive, more punitive and more one-sidedly dominated by the victors than what he had originally envisioned. Yet nor was it possible to forge the kind of peace for which Clemenceau and Tardieu had struggled, a peace that inaugurated a close military-cum-political alliance among the western victors, placed maximal constraints on the vanquished and curtailed its sovereignty to a significant degree, not least through the creation of a

---

[1] As will be elaborated below, most key actors of Versailles, including Wilson, Lloyd George and Clemenceau, in fact saw the peace settlement as the beginning of a longer-term pacification process; yet they judged this beginning, and the nature of what still had to be done, in very different ways. See Clemenceau speech, 25 September 1919, *Journal Officiel (Chambre)*, 1919; Wilson speech, 19 September 1919, in Shaw (1924), II, p. 1017; Lloyd George speech, Commons, 3 July 1919, Hansard, Commons, 5th series, vol. 117, cols. 1211–32.

[2] MacDonald, "Outlook", Socialist Review (July 1919), captured wider liberal Labour attitudes in Britain. See also Keynes (1919). For influential American progressive verdicts, see the editorials "Peace at Any Price", "For a Fresh Start" and "Mr. Wilson and his Promises", *New Republic*, 24 May 1919, pp. 100–2, 102–3, 104–6, and the declaration of the Women's Peace Association at the "Women's International Conference for Permanent Peace", Zurich, in the *New York Times*, 15 May 1919.

Rhenish "buffer-state". And this owed to essential British and American reservations and the fact that both British and American decision-makers maintained different, overall more liberal approaches to peacemaking.

Instead, what was forged became a victor's peace of a different kind. The settlement and the system it "created", the so-called Versailles system, were more than anything else – and unavoidably – the outgrowth of an accumulation of *complex compromises* – compromises between the conceptions, aims, vital interests and domestic concerns of the principal victors, which in crucial respects remained very difficult or even impossible to reconcile. That in spite of these differences, in spite of the conflicting demands and expectations they had to grapple with, and in spite of the massive array of problems and crises they faced, the victors found ways to avoid a total breakdown of the peace conference and, in the end, to hammer out a settlement – this can can indeed be called a remarkable feat. It is thus tempting to conclude that the peace of Versailles represented the precisely the kind of settlement that could be reached in the challenging constellation of 1919.[3] Yet is it indeed appropriate to go one step further and conclude that the settlement was the *best possible* compromise that was attainable under the circumstances?

The main question that should be asked if one wants to arrive not only at a more nuanced but also at a more accurate appraisal of the peace of Paris is not whether, as Jacques Bainville famously declared in 1919, it was "too gentle for what is in it that is harsh, and too harsh for what is in it that is gentle".[4] Nor should it be evaluated on the basis of narrow and often ahistorically applied "realist" or "neorealist" categories – i.e. it should not be faulted for failing to generate a firmer alliance of the victors and a more efficacious regime of enforcement to keep German power contained and Germany constrained in the longer run. Yet it should not be measured either by the all too aspirational yardsticks that Wilson's rhetoric had introduced, that progressive and liberal critics used at the time, and that their successors have recurred to ever since.

Rather, the peace of 1919 ought to be judged by other, more essential criteria. It has to be judged on how far the peacemakers had pursued, and could pursue, approaches and processes that met fundamental requirements of legitimacy and yielded outcomes that *all* the relevant actors, including the vanquished, could find acceptable in the longer run. It has to be judged on how effectively the peacemakers met, and were in a position to meet, not only the more obviously pivotal problems that had to be addressed after the Great War – such as the remaking of Eastern Europe and, above all, the German question – but also the deeper *structural* problems the war had left behind. And it has to be judged on how well they managed, and could manage, to lay

---

[3] See Leonhard (2018), pp. 1049, 1265; Sharp (2010), pp. 211 ff.
[4] Bainville (1920), p. 24.

the groundwork for a new international system that above all provided effective mechanisms and *modes of international politics* to deal with the challenges that simply could not yet be addressed at the initial peace conference. Finally, it has to be judged on how far they managed to found a system that permitted the pursuit of necessarily more drawn-out stabilisation and accommodation processes that were imperative after 1918, not only but especially between the western powers and Germany. How far did, and how far could, the pursuits of the peacemakers meet these criteria?

To begin with, it is essential to recognise how distinctly limited the power and ordering capacities of the western states were in some critical respects. As has been shown, this became particularly apparent with regard to the massive and multifaceted problems that were raised by the need to reorder Central and Eastern Europe so fundamentally after the collapse of the eastern empires. And it became even more obvious with a view to the situation in Russia, where the prospect of defeating the Bolshevik regime was as elusive as that of negotiating a sustainable *modus vivendi* with it against the backdrop of an ongoing inner-Russian civil war and power struggle. In view of all the complicating factors that had to be dealt with – the complex patterns of ethnic intermixture in this vast region, the clash of conflicting national claims for the same territory, the conflicting strategic and economic rationales of the victors, and the competing agendas of local actors and their often critical bids to create new "realities" on the ground – establishing a *stable* new East European system of states on the basis of a "scientific" recourse to the principle of self-determination was simply out of the question.

In the final analysis, it was essentially beyond the means of the western policy- and decision-makers to set parameters that would have prevented what proved to be one of the most precarious and conflict-prone outcomes of 1919, namely that while some states – like Czechoslovakia – had better consolidation prospects than others, virtually all the new or newly configured states of Eastern Europe that now were supposed to join a League and order of democracies were not only inherently unstable "from within", as decidedly non-homogenous nation-states with strong war-induced nationalist leanings; they were also divided from their neighbours because of numerous disputes over borders and multiple, politically incendiary minority issues.

And where the western peacemakers *could* make a significant difference – with a view to the structurally most unsettling problem of the Polish–German settlement – they still ended up creating a scenario that, in spite of the different American and especially British attempts to work out a less precarious "solution", generated a structural antagonism over borders and minorities between a still powerful German state and a necessarily still very fragile Polish "state-in-the-process-of-formation". Here, the fact that the western powers had compelled the Polish government to accept a minority-protection treaty could at best only provide partial remedies for profoundly intractable problems that had not only ethnic-nationalist but also wider geopolitical dimensions. And the same held true for the impact the other minority treaties of 1919 could have for the pacification of Central and Eastern Europe – however important and even exemplary they were in many ways.

But the most consequential shortcomings of the peace of Versailles lay elsewhere. As this analysis ought to have shown, of crucial import was indeed, at one level, that those who shaped the policies of the victors had not been able to settle the wider German question in a far-sighted manner. More precisely, they had not found ways to deal with the vanquished power on terms, and through processes, that were actually conducive to postwar stability and the consolidation of a new, more durable *and legitimate* equilibrium of rights, security, satisfied interests, responsibilities and obligations. The underlying problem was twofold. It had not been possible to initiate what would have been critical after the Great War: a more comprehensive and more broadly legitimate negotiating process between the victors and the vanquished. And this in turn contributed decisively to the fact that in the end the settlement of 1919 became a precarious and truncated peace of the victors rather than a modern peace of accommodation. It contributed decisively to the fact that the settlement which emerged in Paris essentially sought to balance the interests, claims and domestic requirements of the victors but considered those of the vanquished only in a very limited manner or not at all. Ultimately, it thus proved impossible to forge a peace that not only the western powers but also the fledgling German republic could accept. And what the victors came to impose was a settlement that in fact made it very difficult for the Weimar Republic to accommodate itself with, and be accommodated within, the recast international system in the longer run.

As this Atlantic re-appraisal ought to have made clear, the victorious powers' limited success in forging a sustainable German settlement was pivotally influenced by the fact that they found it so hard to come to terms with the crucial *underlying* systemic challenge of the post–First World War era. In short, they had only managed, and in many ways *could* only manage, to lay very volatile foundations for a new Atlantic order. Only very limited steps had been taken towards an Atlantic economic peace. American British and French representatives could not reach substantive agreements about how come to terms with the massive economic and financial consequences of the war. Advances towards more comprehensive programmes for European post-war reconstruction and the financial revitalisation of the states that had been most affected by the war were inconceivable without the capital and political consent of the new financial-cum-economic hegemon across the Atlantic. Yet such advances had been decisively impeded not only by the domestic and notably Congressional constraints Wilson and the US delegation faced but also by the core maxims they espoused, which committed them to limiting the role and liabilities of the American government in this sphere to a minimum.

The upshot of these constraints and maxims was that the American peace-makers essentially vetoed all schemes that might have entailed the reduction or even cancellation of inter-allied debts or that, more broadly, raised the danger that, in one way or another, the American government – and thus ultimately US taxpayers and voters – would have to pay for the enormous financial fall-out of a war of unprecedented destructiveness that had originated in Europe. Undoubtedly, the absorbing controversies about the modalities and extent of Allied reparation demands vis-à-vis Germany, which were de facto inseparable from these wider concerns, had stifled or even taken the place of more constructive negotiations between American, British and French plenipoten-tiaries about the underpinnings of the postwar financial and economic order – and particularly the settlement of inter-state debts. Yet that there was hardly any room for advances here, and no room for the kind of debt reductions or cancellations that British and French decision-makers sought, in turn made a more conclusive and moderate *political* settlement of the morally and ideo-logically charged yet essentially *political* reparations question even harder than it would have been anyway.

Even more consequential, however, was that it had proved impossible for the victors to create a firmer and more coherent nucleus of a transatlantic system of *security* and *international politics*. It had proved impossible to create the nucleus of a system that could soon be expanded into a new, more viable Atlantic concert of democratic states that provided more effective safeguards of peace by including the fledgling German republic and, crucially, binding it to *mutual* security guarantees and *mutual* commitments to the peaceful settlement of international disputes. Instead, the principal western decision-makers and their main advisers had only been able to establish very tenuous underpinnings of what could be called an as yet very *unfinished* Atlantic security architecture for the postwar era.

What the Big Three had negotiated inchoately combined old-style "material guarantees" provided by the temporary and conflict-prone Rhineland occupa-tion and the far-reaching disarmament provisions for Germany; the general "collective" security guarantees and rules for the peaceful settlement of inter-national conflicts that the League of Nations was supposed to provide; and the – essential – political reassurance that was to be furnished by the British and American guarantee treaties with France. Conceivably, these hard-won agreements could provide a first, if distinctly hybrid, framework of security, which especially addressed fundamental French concerns. Conceivably, they could thus over time create more favourable conditions for what was in fact most critical for the longer-term pacification of Europe: not a hardening Atlantic alliance of the victors but rather the construction of a more integrative transatlantic system of collective security that accommodated, and restrained, Germany. But at the end of the peace conference it was still far from clear whether it would be possible to consolidate what so far was merely the frail nucleus of such a system – and this of course required first of all that Wilson found a way to persuade a majority in the American Senate to back the commitments he had made in Paris.

It is necessary here to emphasise once more that it would be misleading to argue, in retrospect, that a more or less straight line can be drawn from the outcomes of 1919 to the rise of Hitler, the disintegration of international order in the 1930s and ultimately to another world war. The peace of Versailles was not predestined to produce such consequences. Much would depend on how not only the peacemakers but also their successors would act and seek to stabilise the postwar order on the basis of decisions that had been made and the parameters that had been set in Paris; and it would also depend on how those who directed the policies of Germany and other dissatisfied powers would act. But it also seems fair to underscore that the original system of Versailles provided a very problematic basis for building a durable *post–First World War* order and that the protagonists of Paris left behind massive challenges for their successors. Indeed, the principal problem of the system that had taken shape in 1919 was that – just like the original League of Nations – it was not only inherently frail but also essentially an *incomplete* system.

Not just the question of what place – Soviet – Russia was to have in the postwar system remained fundamentally unresolved. Crucially, the unfinished Atlantic order of 1919 not only excluded Germany and cast it in the role of a "pariah power"; it also failed to establish effective instrumentalities and clear common understandings on which the victors could build to foster a stability-enhancing integration of a vanquished power that was reduced but remained essentially unified – and thus also remained the inherently most powerful state on the European continent. Fundamentally, the original "system of Versailles" lacked a spirit of "higher realism". It was not informed by the realisation that in order to secure peace and stability in the longer term it had to be adaptable and amendable – indeed, that it would have to be *developed further*, not only but especially with regard to the relations between the western powers and Germany. This is why the peacemaking process of Paris and the settlement it yielded could only be the "beginning of the beginning" of the search for a more durable transatlantic order. In fact, both the process and the settlement even created new obstacles that made this search even more of an uphill struggle than it was bound to be anyway after the catastrophic Great War.

On a more fundamental level too, the process of 1919 was only a beginning. Though some important advances had been made, particularly since 1916, it could still only be the beginning of more far-reaching individual and collective learning and reorientation processes, on both sides of the Atlantic, that would be necessary to build a more sustainable peace system – a system that could evolve and endure and that could cope not only with the massive consequences of the war but also the wider legacy of the challenges that had arisen since the imperialist dawn of the long twentieth century. In this sense, it can indeed be said – especially with a view to the transatlantic context – that, given

how enormous the changes and challenges were that it brought, the Great War
had been too short – too short to give the actors who confronted and sought to
comprehend these changes and challenges sufficient time not only to draw
lessons but also to accrue learning experiences – to try and fail and try again,
to dismiss unrealistic assumptions and approaches and eventually to progress
towards more tenable solutions.[5] Those who succeeded the peacemakers of
Versailles in the 1920s would be compelled to embark on such processes –
and, as will be shown, they would eventually lay basic foundations for a
qualitatively different, more viable Atlantic peace order.

II.   An Unavoidably Ill-Founded Peace?

The crucial characteristics and limitations of the truncated process, settlement
and order of 1919 warrant a more extensive final appraisal. What the Treaty of
Versailles embodied was not merely a victor's peace but also deliberately
conceived by the political leaders of the western powers as a justly severe
peace – a peace of a punitive character that was intended to sanction the
defeated power for having plunged Europe and the world into the Great War,
for the "war of aggression" it had pursued and for the transgressions it had
committed during the conflict. It was a peace settlement that was supposed to
deter those who led the new German state, and its people, from contemplating
future aggression while at the same time imposing far-reaching constraints on
German power. And it had also become a distinctly hierarchical settlement
insofar as it put the fledgling German republic on probation, left it not only
outside the League but also outside the original postwar order, subjected it to
incisive military and temporary economic restrictions, and made its future
"rehabilitation" and "admission" to this order dependent on potentially far-
reaching criteria: not just the proven compliance with the victors' terms but
also substantive advances towards the consolidation of a democratic system, as
judged by the western powers.

But the settlement of 1919 was by no means a Carthaginian peace. The
terms the victors ultimately decreed not only imposed drastic military restrictions and disarmament obligations but also reduced Germany's population by
more than seven million and its pre-war territory by more than 25,000 square
miles. And most Germans would indeed regard the territorial losses in the east
and especially the fact that sizeable German minorities would hence live under
Polish rule as particularly objectionable. The occupation of the Rhineland
curtailed German political sovereignty and affected a strategically vital region.
Further, the settlement saddled the defeated power not only with economic

---

[5] On learning conditions and requirements in international politics, see the illuminating
   comparative analysis of the peace of Vienna and the postwar settlements of the twentieth
   century in Schroeder (1994), pp. 580–1.

restrictions but also with as yet unspecified but likely very high reparations demands, which not only curtailed Germany's financial sovereignty but could also be used for all kinds of strategic purposes, notably by French policymakers who were keen to extend "material guarantees" to or even beyond the strategic Rhine frontier. Finally, Germany not only lost its colonies but also, in a broader sense, the status of and the means to act as a world power for the foreseeable future.

It is indeed crucial to underscore, however, that the Versailles settlement essentially preserved the unity of the German nation-state and left its basic strategic and economic potential intact. Given that the treaty's economic restrictions were of a temporary nature and set to be rescinded by the mid-1920s, the battered and demoralised German state of 1919 could indeed re-emerge as the predominant economic power in Europe and as a key power in what remained a structurally interconnected European and world economic system. How to come to grips with German power thus would remain one of the most critical challenges in the post–First World War era. A more immediate challenge the victors would face after the conference was that of ensuring that Germany would comply with their terms, particularly when it came to disarmament and reparations. And here the debates at Versailles already foreshadowed future conflicts, between French insistence on forceful enforcement and British and American reluctance to pursue strict or even coercive control and sanction measures.

But the main deficit of the peace of Versailles was not, as has often been argued, that it failed to establish a firmer regime to enforce compliance and keep the vanquished power in check.[6] Nor was the underlying problem that the settlement was too harsh for being so lenient and too lenient for being so harsh. Of decisive importance was something else, namely that what had taken place in Paris fell so decidedly short of a more comprehensive negotiating process in which a serious effort was made to strike a balance between the aims, interests and legitimacy concerns of the victors *and* those of the vanquished – and that, consequently, what it yielded fell so markedly short of a mutually acceptable settlement, and fell far shorter still of a viable peace of accommodation.

Undoubtedly, in the deeply fraught constellation of 1919 it was extremely difficult to take even some first, limited steps towards a peace settlement of this kind – and much harder still to achieve decisive breakthroughs. As should have become clear, this was not only due to the complexity, intractability and multiplicity of the contentious issues that were at stake. It was also due to the fact that on both sides of the trenches the war itself and the transatlantic political-ideological "war within the war", which had come to involve governmental leaders and scores of non-governmental actors, had given rise to such

---

[6] See e.g. Morgenthau (1952), pp. 4–27; Keylor (2011), pp. 73–9; and Marks (2013).

enormous and in critical aspects clashing *expectations* regarding the security, compensations and political changes the peace settlement was supposed to bring. And it owed to the fact that the war and this struggle had at the same time significantly expanded the legitimacy requirements for the eventual peace. More precisely, they had expanded the requirements that the leading politicians of the victorious powers and those who represented the vanquished had to try to meet, or felt they had to meet, on their respective home fronts – and, as we have seen, they too were extremely difficult to reconcile.

The conflict between what was needed to satisfy prevalent French demands for security and British and French demands for compensation on the one hand and what was required to fulfil German hopes for a "peace of right" on the other epitomised this problem. But it is only one important part of a far wider legitimacy problem that beset the peace of Versailles. The impact of Wilson's wartime rhetoric and postwar proclamations unquestionably had a decisive significance in this context. But it too only threw into relief a much broader problem. And it has to be stressed again that the hopes that came to prevail in Germany after the armistice and which Brockdorff-Rantzau and leading Social Democrats actually encouraged – hopes that a Wilsonian settlement was within reach that would spare the new German republic territorial losses and other consequences of a never fully acknowledged defeat – were particularly unrealistic and bound to be disappointed.

The conditions of 1919 were thus profoundly inimical to a negotiated peace of accommodation that could have stood a greater chance of gaining mutual acceptance, and the political room to manoeuvre that would have been needed to forge such a peace was in fact decidedly limited. Yet one of the most salient characteristics *and limitations* of the peacemaking process of Versailles was that those actors who by comparison had most agency and room to manoeuvre, the leaders of the victorious powers, *never even tried* to take any substantive steps in this direction; and that they came to rule out actual negotiations with the representatives of the newly elected government in Berlin. Consequently, they *never even tried* to negotiate something approaching a more broadly conceived compromise settlement *with* the vanquished – agreements over the terms of the peace itself and, no less importantly, over the ground-rules that were to govern the relations between the western powers and Germany in the recast inter-national system. They therefore *never even tried* to forge a settlement that was based on the difficult search for compromises between the different parties' conflicting aims, claims and interests – and on the will to acknowledge that a negotiated peace of this kind represented the most realistic way of approaching, not a reconciliation but as far as possible an accommodation of the inevitably very divergent notions they had of what a "just peace" meant.

It is clearly important to recognise that to a significant extent the limitations of post–First World War peacemaking were a consequence of the dynamics and constraints the victors confronted in the course of the unprecedentedly complex process of 1919 – and notably of the difficulties they encountered when they finally had to try to reconcile their, in crucial aspects, conflicting concepts, priorities and domestic-political needs. What really has to be high-lighted, then, is the degree to which the actual, so profoundly hierarchical politics of "modern" peacemaking in Paris were shaped by the fact that those who played pivotal roles in this process were not only democratically account-able leaders. who each had to deal with very particular pressures and expect-ations in their domestic force-fields, but also the first peacemakers after a major war who had to grapple with the complexities of forging a new transcontinental order and, at the core, a new transatlantic order. As we have seen, this simultaneity posed tremendous challenges for each of the main actors and those who advised them – and it required steep learning curves on all sides. The problem was compounded by the difficulty to find a modicum of common ground between the often highly disparate assumptions and ideological proclivities of Wilson, Lloyd George and Clemenceau.

This combination of factors gave rise to the distinctive mode of democratic peacemaking among the western powers that became the dominant mode in Paris. It lay behind most of the most important compromises and bargains they struck – while also accounting for the tenuous quality of these bargains. And ultimately it had one underlying effect: it reinforced the resolve of all the protagonists to make a victors' peace and then to justify it in a new, modern way as a "peace of higher justice". And, in the final phase, it hardened their determination to insist all the more peremptorily on imposing this peace on Germany. For their part, lacking any real leverage, Brockdorff-Rantzau and the other protagonists of the Scheidemann government insisted for far too long on the illusory maximalist thesis that Germany could only accept a "Wilson peace", and on an equally illusory Wilsonian strategy of "public diplomacy" behind which they also sought to rally the German public.

Undoubtedly, then, what had a decisive influence on the final anatomy of the peace was that eventually the victors – and even Lloyd George – did not want to jeopardise the volatile edifice of compromises they had managed to thrash out amongst themselves. But it should be emphasised again that this is only part of the explanation. What mattered too was that in one crucial respect the western leaders' overall approaches and ideas of what constituted a "just peace" had converged. They ultimately came to agree that their status as highest representatives of the powers that had won the war – and that embodied the most advanced democratic order – conferred on them the "right" to force a "justly severe" peace settlement on the representatives of the nascent Republic of Weimar. Considerations about the repercussions this would have for the future stabilisation of a democratic order in Germany played a distinctly secondary role in the victors' deliberations.

That the peace made in Paris did not even come close to a modern peace of accommodation would have far-reaching consequences, both for postwar international politics and for the consolidation and development prospects of what came to be known as the system of Versailles. In short, it would be marred by significant legitimacy deficits. Most consequential was that the peace was regarded – with exaggerated resentment – as profoundly illegitimate by the defeated power. And the humiliating way in which the Treaty of Versailles had been imposed compounded this problem. The outcomes of 1919 would also be rejected by other elites and wider societies who found themselves on the side of the vanquished, including majorities in Austria and Hungary; but the German reactions would clearly pose the most serious challenges for postwar stability in and beyond Europe. It is also critical to note, however, that while in France many observers, and not just nationalists, criticised it for not going far enough in banning the German threat, the settlement of Versailles would also soon come to be considered by many influential political actors and opinion-makers in Britain and the United States as profoundly unsound – as a settlement that marked only a very problematic beginning of peace-building after the Great War and still had to be amended or even be replaced by a real, more comprehensive and concili-atory peace. And, significantly, this also became a prevalent perception in the sphere of "public opinion" in both countries.

At a deeper level, the way in which the victor-dominated process of 1919 had unfolded gave rise to a problem that also pointed far beyond the treatment of the vanquished but became most palpable and acute with a view to Germany. Essentially, the peace of Versailles was marked by a glaring discrepancy between the claims the leaders of the western powers, and notably Wilson, had put forward about the principles and norms that were to inform the settlement – principles of lawfulness and norms like "self-determination" that were to make this a "peace to end all wars" – and the actual terms of the eventual peace. To some extent, this was unavoidable. But it exacerbated the settlement's fundamental legitimacy problems, most obviously but not only from the perspective of the vanquished and others whose claims had not been satisfied.

Especially through the Covenant of the League, the peace of 1919 for the first time established pillars of what was to be a universal "order of international law". Going beyond the Hague Conventions, it enshrined the constitutive premise that what were to be the key units of the new order – states – would have (more or less) equal rights, and obligations, in this order – regardless of their size and power. In principle, it introduced binding rules of "collective security" and for the peaceful settlement international disputes. And though leaving the empires that had been on the winning side essentially untouched, it enshrined new international standards that from now on could be used to challenge them and particularly their legitimacy. Indeed, it for the first time incorporated in a general postwar settlement principles that had already been championed before 1914 but gained a decisive political significance during the war – and that from now on would become crucial normative reference-points. This especially held true for the powerful but also inherently problematic principle of national self-determination, which had been tied to notions of democratic legitimacy but remained subject to conflicting interpretations.

But one of the cardinal problems was that these principles, standards and norms had been very unevenly or one-sidedly applied at the peace conference and that consequently the outcome was a settlement that was characterised by profound double-standards. For, unsurprisingly, not only the western protagonists' hierarchical conceptions, e.g. about who was entitled to "self-determination", but also their power-political considerations and notions of overriding strategic and economic interests had often exerted a decisive influence on the actual decisions that had been made. Thus, in short, different sets of rules had been applied. In particular, where conflicts had arisen, the self-determination claims of the vanquished (just like, for other reasons, those of anti-colonial nationalists) had been treated as claims of lesser validity or actually been overruled. Arguably most consequential was that the bending of principles had affected the settlement imposed on Germany, and that this could and would be seized upon by those in Germany who rejected the Treaty of Versailles as well as by those who would actively seek to undermine it. But it had also affected something closely bound up with the German settlement, namely the reorganisation of Central and Eastern Europe – even if, as has been shown, in the complex case of demarcating the new Polish–German border key British and American actors had made considerable efforts to find more even-handed solutions.

It would be difficult to overstate how burdensome the consequences were that the "dictate of Versailles" had for the as yet precariously unstable Weimar Republic. And the same can be said for the obstacles it raised to any advances towards more constructive postwar relations between Germany and the western powers. Not only because of its terms – that were *perceived* as both harsh and unjust – but also because of the manner in which it had been forced on the defeated power, the peace settlement was deemed unacceptable not just by nationalists and right-wing opponents of the government but by an overwhelming majority, both in governing and elite circles and in the wider public. And what doubtless made the outcry over the "humiliating terms" of Versailles all the greater was the fact that Brockdorff-Rantzau's strategy, yet also the policies of the Ebert-Scheidemann government, had kept up such profoundly unrealistic expectations until the very final stages of the peace conference. This obviously heightened the disillusionment and tendencies to view the actual terms of the peace as especially Carthaginian and unjust. In an atmosphere of excessive, emotionally charged reactions the allegation that Wilson had "betrayed" the German nation could fall on fertile ground far beyond nationalist circles. And this distortive claim would subsequently be instrumentalised by those who sought to prevent an accommodation of the Weimar Republic with the United States and "the West" in the decade after Versailles.

What was seen as the evident failure of the efforts of the Weimar coalition government to come to an understanding with the western powers signified a major setback for the entire conception of a new republican policy of accommodation with the western powers and for the idea that the new German republic should strive to find its place in an Atlantic, western-orientated order of democracies. The unconcealable futility of the Ebert-Scheidemann government's exertions was grist to the mills of those nationalist and right-wing forces in and beyond the German National People's Party who fundamentally rejected such an approach and began to think about ways to avenge the defeat and cast off the "yoke of Versailles". They would seize upon what they presented as the iniquities of the peace treaty in order to rally support for their anti-western agenda, which was closely aligned with the ambition to restore the German Imperial *Reich* and to make it once again into a dominant world power.[7]

While there was hardly any realism in the agitated inner-German debate about the terms of the peace or any real understanding of how extremely limited Brockdorff-Rantzau's room to manoeuvre had been, the settlement went far towards discrediting him and the protagonists of the Weimar coalition. They were held responsible both for not preventing and then for accepting the "shameful dictate" of the western powers. In a wider perspective, the peace settlement came to cast a shadow over the consolidation prospects of the new republic itself. With the votes of the Weimar coalition parties, the National Assembly ratified the Treaty of Versailles on 9 July 1919. But Ebert lamented that the conditions that had been imposed, "with their economic and political impossibilities", were "the greatest enemy of German democracy and [provided] the strongest impetus for communism and nationalism".[8] What followed was a period of profound domestic-political turmoil. Under immense domestic and external pressure, the beleaguered Weimar coalition government managed to suppress Kapp's attempt to stage a *coup'état* and overthrow the republican order at the head of *Freikorps* forces in March 1920 within a short time. But in the *Reichstag* elections in June 1920 the coalition would lose its majority. And hence there would no longer be a basis for a stable republican government in Weimar Germany. Further uprisings of the left and the extreme right would follow. By 1923, the crisis of the fledgling republic would reach existential dimensions.

Under such adverse conditions, it became very challenging for those who clung to this aim to develop and gain the requisite support for a western-orientated policy of accommodation. And what unavoidably placed marked constraints on their pursuits was that an overwhelming majority in the

---

[7] See Krüger (1986), pp. 70–81.
[8] Cited after Simms (2014), p. 322.

German public and political spectrum came to espouse the view that the "system of Versailles" had to be revised as quickly and as far as possible. In the realigning force-field of political elites and among the less unsettled bureaucratic elites revisionist sentiments came to focus on all provisions and restrictions of the treaty that prevented Germany from re-emerging as a great power with "equal rights" (though here the emphasis mostly lay on equal political and economic rights rather than on the rescinding of military restrictions). Crucially, this underlying demand for revisions, which in the wider public debates tended to take diffuse forms and find expression in vague slogans like "ridding Germany of the yoke of Versailles", became the decisive yardstick by which the foreign policy of German governments would hence be measured; and it in many ways constrained those who sought to pursue forward-looking republican international policies.[9]

Against this background, and informed by a sense of powerlessness, acute dependence on the future policies of the western powers and vulnerability to French coercive pressures, the Bauer government struggled to develop a coherent approach in the aftermath of the peace conference. Essentially, it set out to follow the guidelines that the new foreign minister Müller had put forward in a programmatic speech in the National Assembly on 23 July 1919. Müller had emphasised that Germany still had a vital interest in a League of Nations that accepted Germany as a member "with equal rights" and could thus "become a true instrument of progress" and "point a way out of the difficulties" that the peace treaty had created. He renewed the German government's commitment to a peaceful accommodation of interests with the western powers. And while leaving no doubt that in his view the treaty contained much that was unbearable *and* impossible to fulfil, he underscored that "under the force of the prevailing conditions", Germany had to be committed to "fulfilling the treaty loyally . . . up to the limit of our ability". Yet he also emphasised his determination to "aspire to a revision of this treaty", not by force but "by loyal means" – through diplomatic agreements with Britain, France and the United States, and in accordance with international law.[10]

Later, in October 1919, Müller would establish another maxim that would be become an important constant in the further evolution of Weimar Germany's foreign policy in the post-Versailles era. He argued that despite all subjective disappointment about Wilson's conduct, it would be vital to renew efforts to open up avenues of cooperation with the predominant political-cum-economic power, the United States – and to seek to cultivate perceived parallel interests. In his view, these lay in ensuring a German League membership in the near future and in reducing the peace treaty's trade

[9] See Salewski (1980), pp. 14–25; Niedhart (2012), pp. 11 ff., 70–9.
[10] Müller speech, National Assembly, 23 July 1919, in Heilfron (1920), VII, p. 72.

restrictions and "reopening of the world market for German goods" so as to pave the way for Germany's recovery, also as an essential American market and trading partner. In a medium-term perspective, he observed, it would be essential to ensure as far as possible that the United States as the power with most capital and resources would play an active part in the "economic recuperation of Germany". And this maxim also was to be adopted to pave the way for Germany's political return to the comity of nations.[11] All in all, Müller and like-minded social democrats and liberals thus tried to commit an isolated and struggling German republic to moderate and still decidedly western-orientated policies that sought to effect amendments and revisions of the treaty system by way of a peaceful accommodation with the key treaty powers of 1919.

Yet if one assesses the post-Versailles situation from a bird's-eye perspective, both in political and geopolitical terms, it becomes clear that the process and settlement of 1919 had left behind a structurally unstable and profoundly conflict-prone constellation in Europe. In the west, it gave rise to an inherently antagonistic and confrontational scenario. Here, at the core, two powers that too long had been "arch enemies" were again pitted against each other: on one side, an as yet inherently unstable German republic whose government was to a large extent compelled to pursue revisionist policies – and in which, ominously, a wide array of nationalist, reactionary-monarchist and right-wing extremists propagated a far more assertive or even radical revisionism; on the other side, a French state whose leaders saw it as their primary task to enforce the new status quo the Treaty of Versailles had demarcated – and in which numerous more assertive politicians and opinion-makers even argued that it would be vital for national security to revise this status quo in a different way, by expanding French strategic control, possibly even beyond the Rhineland. At the same time, the Versailles settlement had addressed the underlying problem posed by the structural Franco-German *imbalance* of power only in a very limited and problematic manner. While the terms of the peace markedly weakened and constrained the German state *in the short term*, it was set to retain its inherently superior power potential *in the longer run*.

In the east, the settlement of 1919 had left behind a recast and profoundly unsettled political landscape and created a constellation that was even more precarious. Here, as noted, the key problem was that now a fundamentally revisionist German state in which a clear majority did not accept the newly-drawn borders confronted a still very unconsolidated Polish state – and that despite the imposed minority treaty, the likelihood of conflicts over the future of the German minorities within the new Poland was immense. How far could the instruments and mechanisms of the Versailles system offer the wherewithal to come to terms with these challenges?

---

[11] Müller circular, 18 October 1919, *ADAP*, A, II, pp. 369–70.

III.   No Robust Nucleus. The Frail Underpinnings of the Fledgling Atlantic Order of 1919

Essentially, the principal peacemakers of 1919 had only managed to create a comparatively fragile, in some aspects makeshift and indeed potentially fissiparous nucleus of a new transatlantic international system. It was a system that in many ways was not only in need of consolidation but still had to be developed further, and *extended*, if it was to be effective in coping with these challenges and securing European and Euro-Atlantic peace and stability in the longer term. Above all, the original system of the victors had to be consolidated in such a way that it could be extended to include Germany in the foreseeable future. Within this fledgling and as yet inchoate system there was no principal hegemon. Rather, it hinged on the cooperation of the three principal western democracies. But while no progress towards a more durable postwar order could be made without or against France, the pivotal powers in this system, the only powers that could act as essential providers of security and reassurance, were Britain and the United States.

In their very different ways, those who shaped the peace policies of these powers had all tried to draw lessons from the catastrophe of the Great War and what they interpreted as its main causes. Even though Wilson called for more transformational changes than his British and French counterparts, in their distinctive ways each of the protagonists of 1919 – and their most influential advisers – had concluded that significantly altered approaches and mechanisms were needed to prevent another cataclysm and to build a more durable international order after the massive, transformative changes the war had wrought. And not only the American president but also those who made British and French policies had come to advance distinctive conceptions or even "visions" of order that had one essential common denominator: they were at the core conceptions and visions of a new Atlantic order.

Indeed, what they came to pursue after the war can and should be interpreted as the first attempt at the highest level of political decision-making to provide answers to the underlying challenges that not just the war itself but also the formative decades of the long twentieth century had created. And in particular, it can be interpreted as the first attempt to come to terms with the tectonic changes in transatlantic relations – the unprecedentedly expanded, though still asymmetrical interdependence between Europe and the United States – that the war had brought about. But what proved critical was that while Wilson's vision of a League-based new Atlantic order was relatively compatible with emerging British conceptions of a novel Atlantic concert and a targeted Anglo-American strategic partnership in a postwar system anchored in the League, both were and remained fundamentally at odds with French aspirations to forge a firm alliance and security union with the Anglo-American powers in order to contain and constrain Germany. At the same time, as noted, against the backdrop of conflicting national interests and philosophies in these spheres, American, British and French ideas about the fundamentals of the "financial and economic peace" after the Great War remained substantially apart as well.

During the complex, turbulent and overburdened negotiations in Paris, the main decision-makers of the victorious powers found it impossible to weld their differing ideas and priorities into a coherent and resilient new systemic "superstructure" and, above all, an effective security architecture for Europe and the Euro-Atlantic sphere. The hybridity of the security agreements the victors made – the fact that they in the end could only manage to agree on three very disparate core elements or building blocks of what was to be a new Atlantic security order – not only reflected the abiding tensions between their conceptions and strategies. It also reflected quite accurately how different their security *needs* (and what they perceived as these needs) were after the defeat and projected far-reaching disarmament of Germany. Following the French insistence on more old-style "material guarantees", Wilson and Lloyd George had eventually agreed to a temporary occupation of the Rhineland; but they essentially regarded this measure as counter-productive. While the occupation could provide psychological more than effective strategic reassurance to France, it was by nature a transitional measure. More importantly, the longer it lasted the more it would come into direct conflict with advances towards more constructive relations with Germany, or indeed the initiation of a possible Franco-German reconciliation process.

The guarantees furnished by the Anglo-American guarantee agreements with France were of a different, essentially political nature. These agreements fell short of the kind of fully-fledged military alliance of the victors for which Clemenceau and Tardieu had campaigned. But they – and the crucial pledge that Britain and the United States would intervene on the side of France in the event of an unprovoked German aggression – could provide an essential element of re-assurance in postwar Europe. Last but not least, the Covenant of the League established more general guarantees of "collective security" and provisions for the peaceful settlement of international disputes – all of which were supposed to apply on a global scale but had in many ways been formulated for the core purpose of securing European peace on new premises and ensuring that the United States would play its part in this process.

It has often been argued that the treaty system of 1919 was sufficiently flexible both to keep Europe safe from future German aggression and to accommodate the vanquished power – as long as it was jointly enforced by the victors.[12] But this is misleading. Because of Wilson's and Lloyd George's

---

[12] This argument is advanced in a particularly nuanced manner by Steiner (2005), pp. 69–70. See also Krüger (1985), pp. 84–8.

opposition, and the different conceptions and priorities both leaders pursued, French decision-makers had only succeeded in obtaining distinctly *limited* enforcement provisions. In a wider sense, while the Inter-Allied Military Commission of Control (IMCC) had been established to control German fulfilment of the disarmament obligations, the peace of 1919 had not established an enforceable regime of containment. The negotiations at Versailles had already provided clear indications that the leading politicians of Britain and the United States would not be willing to join their French counterparts in maintaining and enforcing a long-term regime of this kind (not least because they did not expect to gain the requisite domestic support).

Essentially, however, the enforcement of a peace of containment and exclusion would have aggravated rather than alleviated insecurity and instability in Europe. The real problem was that the principal peacemakers of Paris had not yet been able to create a security architecture that provided a robust framework of re-assurance for three salient processes on which Europe's pacification depended above all: a stabilising inclusion of Germany in the postwar order, advances towards an accommodation between the western powers and the fledgling Republic of Weimar and, most importantly, the initiation of an immensely difficult but vital peace process between Germany and France.

Potentially, what the victors had negotiated at Versailles – and especially the Anglo-American guarantee treaties – could nonetheless at least provide a *starting-point* and a *modicum* of security and reassurance, which was indispensable for any steps in this direction. But substantive advances depended not only on the attitudes of French decision-makers, whose first priority remained to make sure that the defeated power would be effectively contained and constrained. They also required that those who directed the policies of Britain and the United States not only fulfilled the guarantees and commitments that had been made at Versailles – and ensured the requisite domestic support for this – but would also actually assume their hegemonic responsibilities, actively engage as promoters of postwar accommodation and, indeed, foster a qualitative evolution of the original "Versailles system".

What role could the League play? As we have seen, the prevalent conceptions and outlooks of the most influential architects of the League – and their resolve to maintain core attributes to state and notably great-power sovereignty – ruled out the creation of an organisation with truly far-reaching, let alone supranational authority as the hub of a new "superstructure" of peace and international security. What is more, chiefly because of Anglo-American reservations the collective security provisions of the Covenant had not been sufficiently fortified – particularly through stronger provisions regarding measures to counter aggressors – to satisfy French security concerns vis-à-vis Germany. And it may well be true that as an institution whose remit was to be global, the League could only be of limited value in coming to terms with the profound conflicts and problems of insecurity that beset Europe after the

Great War. It was not inconceivable either, however, that the new organisation and notably its Executive Council could indeed become, in accordance with American and British preferences, the platform of a new Atlantic concert of democratic powers through which, under the altered international and domestic conditions of the postwar era, leading American and European actors could seek to settle disputes and foster peace and longer-term stability.

But as it had been conceived in 1919, the League could *not yet* function in this way, let alone as the effective "superstructure" of a new transatlantic peace order. Not only time and a consistent commitment of its principal powers – particularly the United States – would be required to prove its effectiveness. One of its most obvious deficiencies was and remained that it too was founded as a truncated institution that was one-sidedly dominated by the victors but excluded, for an indefinite period, not only Russia but also the defeated powers, above all Germany. And although both Wilson and Lloyd George considered Germany's timely admission essential, the Treaty of Versailles provided no clear criteria or assurances to this end. In short, then, if it was to bring effective "collective security" and become the instrument through which the core problems and conflicts of postwar international politics could be tackled, the League not only had to be consolidated; it also had to be transformed from an exclusive into an essentially integrative organisation that bound not only the victors but also the vanquished to the norms, rules and obligations laid down in its Covenant.

In essence, then, what a systemic appraisal of the Versailles settlement reveals is that many of the hardest and most critical tasks that had to be met to stabilise Europe and the world, come to terms with the German problem and build a viable Atlantic order, still had to be addressed *after* the peace conference. And what, finally, has to be emphasised again as well is that the fledgling Euro-Atlantic system and security architecture of 1919 only extended to Eastern Europe in a very superficial way. By becoming members of the League, Poland and the other new and older East European states had committed themselves to the Covenant's rules and obligations; and they were to contribute to and be protected by its general regime of guarantees under Article X. Through the minority treaties, they had been obliged to observe rules and standards of minority protection that had largely been set by American and British decision-makers. But when it came to the question of how they would actually seek to pacify the profoundly unsettled geopolitical landscape of Central and Eastern Europe the leaders of the western powers had not reached any real agreement and continued to pursue very different priorities.

French policymakers already contemplated the conclusion of alliances with Poland and Czechoslovakia in order to engage them as strategic allies and buffer-states in a *cordon sanitaire* of containment between Germany and Bolshevik Russia that was supposed to prevent further "German designs for

hegemony in Europe".[13] By contrast, neither Wilson nor the British government had been prepared to extend further, more specific guarantees or
assurances to Poland and other East European states. British policymakers
did not want to make more tangible guarantee commitments because they
feared that Britain would then have to intervene in foreseeable Polish–German
conflicts over minorities and contested borders – and more broadly because
Eastern Europe was of comparatively peripheral concern in a wider picture
dominated by West European and global-imperial preoccupations. The
American president never considered more specific guarantees because of
his underlying emphasis on the League of Nations and the need to build up
its system of "collective security" and conflict prevention.[14]

But any success in at least containing what could never be entirely eliminated – the danger that minority disputes would escalate into wider German-
Polish conflicts that destabilised the entire postwar order – would not only
require an ongoing Anglo-American engagement. It would also require
advances towards something that the system of Versailles did not yet provide:
common rules for the peaceful settlement of conflicts – and for *peaceful change*
in accordance with international law – that were also negotiated with, and
accepted by, German representatives. Thus, here too, and here especially, the
Atlantic peace order of 1919 remained distinctly unfinished.

---

[13] Clemenceau statement, December 1919, cited after Jackson (2013), p. 364.
[14] Wilson statement, 14 February 1919, *PWW*, LV, p. 175.

EPILOGUE

The Political Consequences of the Peace

*The Aftermath of Versailles and the Making of
the Unfinished Atlantic Peace of the 1920s*

22

Peace Undermined

The Divergent Outlooks of the Victors, the Consequences of Wilson's Defeat and the Escalation of Europe's Postwar Crisis

From the outset, then, the ill-founded and essentially truncated Atlantic order of 1919 was not just in need of consolidation. It not only had to be developed further. In fact, it needed to be substantially *reformed* if it was to foster a lasting peace. Indeed, the longer-term stabilisation and pacification of Europe, the north Atlantic sphere and, ultimately, the global order did not depend on how effectively the original "system of Versailles" could be implemented and enforced. Rather, both ultimately depended on whether the successors of those who had tried to make peace in Paris – the European and American politicians and non-governmental actors who would shape international politics in the decade after the Great War – could find ways to *transform* this system over time into a more inclusive and legitimate international order.

Operating through their own distinctive networks, financiers, peace activists and champions of war renunciation and disarmament made important contributions here. And so did other non-official actors who sought to prevail over those who favoured either "renationalisation" in various guises, radical communist alternatives or, most ominously, a continuation of the war by other means, be it to fortify the unstable status quo of 1919 or to overturn it. But in all of these processes the role of governmental leaders and policy-makers, the actors who still had the greatest influence on the policies and strategies of states, would once again be critical, at least as critical as at Versailles.

In the immediate aftermath of the peace conference the most essential impulses would be given by those who had been the protagonists of the Paris negotiations. And each in his own way Wilson, Lloyd George and Clemenceau would indeed set crucial orientation-marks. More generally, any substantial advances towards a more viable postwar order hinged on the capacity of those who directed British, French and American international policies to achieve now what in crucial respects they had found impossible in Paris, namely to work towards a firmer basis of common understandings about how peace and the fledgling order actually were to be stabilised in the longer run.

It should be stressed again that all the principal peacemakers of 1919 saw the Paris process and the settlement it had yielded only as the the first stage of a much longer reordering and stabilisation process that had to be pursued after the Great War. Yet all the rhetoric they used to affirm their unity and the need to close ranks after the conference could not conceal that their outlooks on this process and on the kind of order it was supposed to sustain were still very much in conflict. And the aftermath of Versailles also soon threw into relief the sharp contrasts between the domestic-political constellations to which the victorious leaders returned, and in which they not only had to account for the decisions they had made but also to organise political majorities for the long-haul peace-building efforts they anticipated in their different ways. All of this meant that the stage was set for further struggles not only between the western powers and Germany but also among the dominant treaty powers of 1919.

I.   The Different Outlooks and Challenges of the Peacemakers after the Paris Peace Conference

During the ratification process in the French parliament Clemenceau and Tardieu defended the peace of Versailles as the maximum that could be achieved under the circumstances: a settlement that would bring France crucial benefits, above all because it recast the balance of power in its favour and placed French security on new, better foundations. Both argued that the treaty furnished the terms and instrumentalities to ban the German threat and, while stressing that the Rhineland compromise went to the limits of what Wilson and Lloyd George had been prepared to accept, both emphasised how vital the Anglo-American guarantees and the maintenance of a close union with Britain and the United States were for France's future.

Tardieu underscored that the terms of the peace treaty not only provided more traditional safeguards against renewed German aggression by strictly limiting German armed power on land and at sea, imposing a demilitarisation of the Rhineland and reducing the German population by almost twelve million. He also impressed on the *Chambre*'s peace treaty commission that the guarantees extended by "the world's greatest financial, industrial and commercial powers" would give France "a decisive advantage in the European balance of power that no physical guarantee can replace". In his interpretation, there was a realistic perspective of maintaining and even deepening, within the new League of Nations, an alliance community with "the two greatest liberal powers", premised on an ideological "unity of views", through which the terms of the peace could be enforced and German power could be contained. And he warned that the alternative to cultivating such a union would be something France could not afford: "political and military isolation".[1]

---

[1] Tardieu statement, Commission du Traité de paix, *Commission des affaires étrangères de l'Assemblée nationale*, séance 29 Julliet 1919, C/7773. See Jackson (2013), pp. 306–7.

Clemenceau likewise insisted that the close cooperation with the Anglo-American powers and the consolidation of what he too still conceived as a *de facto* Atlantic alliance of the victors, the closest possible "political, economic and military union" with Britain and the United States, was what mattered most for France's longer-term security in the postwar world. The French premier underlined that it simply had not been an option to achieve what many centre-right and nationalist members of the *Sénat* and the *Assemblée* longed for: a settlement that banished the German menace by dismembering the Prusso-German state and somehow to return to the status quo ante 1870, which he considered an illusory endeavour. More realistic, he argued, was a policy that accepted the continued existence of a – reduced – German state as a given fact, imposed and enforced a maximally constraining peace and enabled France to deal with its problematic eastern neighbour from a position of strength. And here the "union" with the Anglo-American allies was of cardinal importance.[2]

Significantly, it was only in the aftermath of the Versailles negotiations, and when he sought to defend the compromises he had made, that Clemenceau would explicitly argue that the *longer-term* rationale of French pursuits had to be to create secure conditions for an *eventual* accommodation and ultimately perhaps even a mutually beneficial relationship with Germany. As noted, the French premier realised as much as Tardieu that it would not be possible to keep Germany isolated from the league or the postwar order forever. While not quite foreseeing a "conciliation" with France's "arch enemy", he would declare to French senators in August 1919 that the "central challenge" the French nation faced was not only to ensure Germany's demilitarisation but, more fundamentally, to "find an accommodation with Germany and its 60 million inhabitants while we have only 40 million".[3]

But Clemenceau's basic premise remained that the inevitable accommodation process he foresaw could only take place once France had been assured that it could be pursued in an environment, and on terms, that did not compromise its security. He insisted that the German republic first had to prove its willingness to fulfil the peace conditions of the victors. Yet he also emphasised once again that it was even more essential that the Anglo-American powers would join France in uncompromisingly enforcing the victors' peace terms and, crucially, prove their resolve to maintain a firm postwar alliance with France. Clemenceau thus sought to impress on all factions in the French parliament that "with all its complex clauses" the treaty that had been negotiated at Versailles was in many ways "not even

[2] Clemenceau remarks, Commission du Traité de paix, *Commission des affaires étrangères de l'Assemblée nationale*, séance 29 Julliet 1919, C/7773.
[3] Clemenceau statement, 29 July 1919, *Commission des affaires étrangères du Sénat*, vol. 1893. See also Clemenceau speech, 25 September 1919, *Journal Officiel (Chambre)*, 1919; Tardieu to Wilson, 10 June 1919, in Tardieu (I/1921), p. 135.

a beginning" – it was "the beginning of a beginning" of a long process of securing the peace in a spirit of "vigilance" in which present and future generations would have to engage.[4]

In the end, Clemenceau would not have to overcome major obstacles in securing the ratification of the Treaty of Versailles, which was confirmed by October 1919. But it is worth stressing that among the centre and centre right senators and *députés* on whose approval he depended, there were many who criticised openly that he had not been able to achieve a settlement that satisfied more traditional balance-of-power requirements and guaranteed the future security of France by at least creating a Rhenish buffer-state or even by breaking up the Bismarck state. While Foch denounced the peace treaty as a "capitulation" and even spoke of a shameful "betrayal" of France's vital interests, ferocious criticisms of this kind notably came from Poincaré and those who sought to move the *Bloc National* coalition both towards the right and towards a more assertive foreign policy in the postwar period. Meanwhile, nationalist opinion-makers like Jacques Bainville and Maurice Barrès castigated the premier for having failed to eliminate the German state as a future threat and called for far-reaching revisions of the peace settlement that remedied these mistakes.

More generally, Clemenceau – and his successors – had to direct French postwar policies in a political and public climate in which the idea of any kind of future accommodation with the "arch enemy" *outre-Rhin* remained highly controversial after the experiences of the war – and where the notion of staking the future security of France on the support and political guarantees of the Anglo-American powers elicited many sceptical reactions.[5] Finally, it must be noted that Clemenceau's career as leading French statesman ended very soon after the ratification of the Treaty of Versailles. Following his failed bid for the French presidency (in the wake of the elections of November 1919, which had resulted in a decisive victory of the *Bloc National*), he resigned as premier in January 1920. His successor Alexandre Millerand would reorientate French postwar policy, advocating a stricter and more confrontational policy of treaty enforcement and containment vis-à-vis Germany.[6]

For his part, the British prime minister Lloyd George defended the Treaty of Versailles during the ratification debates in the House of Commons as a rightly severe but just peace, later adding that in his view the peacemakers had "redressed many old wrongs" and that he could not "think of any new ones" they had "created". Intent on vindicating his conduct at the peace conference, and to ensure the support of the more hard-headed Unionists,

---

[4] Clemenceau speech, 25 September 1919, *Journal Officiel (Chambre)*, 1919.
[5] Bainville (1920), pp. 52–3; C. Maurras, "La Politique", *Action française*, 24 September 1919; Miquel (1977), pp. 377–412; Becker and Audoin-Rouzeau (2012), pp. 302–3, 350–1;
[6] See Keiger (1997), p. 267–8; Roussellier (1999), pp. 53 ff.; Jackson (2013), pp. 303–4, 323–7.

he argued that what he praised as the most far-reaching and all-embracing settlement in history by no means constituted a Prussian-style Carthaginian peace that placed a crushing burden on the defeated power and was set to undermine postwar stability. Rather, he asserted, it was a victors' peace that wisely and justly imposed terms that while preserving a unified German state would teach the German people, who had supported a war of aggression, what consequences they would face if they plunged the world into another war. He thus also justified again his insistence on an expansive definition of British reparation claims. More importantly, the British premier emphasised that the peace settlement furnished essential safeguards and means of "discouragement" or deterrence, especially by obliging the Germany to disarm and through the British and American commitments to come to France's aid in the event of "wanton German aggression". He now even declared that the occupation of the Rhineland could act as a useful further deterrent, even if he also stressed that it could be terminated early if Germany met its treaty obligations. Yet he also he made a point of emphasising his support for the League, proclaiming that this "great and hopeful experiment" merited Britain's engagement – and that it would furnish "the greatest guarantee of all".[7]

But for all his politic emphasis on the merits of the treaty system of 1919, Lloyd George too came to act, in his own way, on the assumption that the peace of Versailles was by no means flawless and complete and, crucially, that it marked only the starting-point of a process of stabilisation and pacification that still had to be pursued and would require time. What he came to consider vital was an *evolutionary* consolidation and step-by-step qualitative amendment of the treaty system of 1919. And he reckoned at this stage that the United States would play a critical role in this process as Britain's difficult but essential strategic partner. In the debate in the House of Commons, the British premier had eventually conceded that the settlement comprised unavoidable "crudities, irregularities, and injustices", and he had underscored that one of the essential tasks of the League would be to serve as a mechanism of political consultation and conflict resolution through which these deficiencies could be addressed and as far as possible redressed.[8]

At the core, however, what Lloyd George envisaged once the ratification of the peace treaty was assured was a process in which Britain and the United States would share the burdens of acting as guarantors and hegemonic arbiters of accommodation, the reassurance they provided would moderate French postwar policies, and thus a new "order of equilibrium" could be stabilised. He looked ahead to an order in which France was led away from confrontational, destabilising pursuits of continental hegemony and steered towards an

---

[7] Lloyd George speech, Commons, 3 July 1919, Hansard, Commons, 5th series, vol. 117, cols. 1211–32.
[8] *Ibid.*

accommodating approach vis-à-vis its eastern neighbour. And he envisioned an amended peace system in which a reformed German state that accepted the military limitations set by the treaty, proved its willingness to fulfil its obligations and committed to pacific policies – particularly renouncing forcible revisionism in the east – would be brought into the League and a "genuine comity of nations". The British premier thus came to impress on his French counterparts that the consolidation of a German republic in which liberal and social democratic forces prevailed would be in their interest as much as in the *general* interest of securing peace after the Great War.[9]

What has to be taken into account here is that Lloyd George came to pursue these priorities against the backdrop of marked changes in the prevalent attitudes towards the peace of Paris within the British political spectrum, and public. In late July 1919, it had been no major challenge for the British premier to make sure that the Treaty of Versailles was ratified in the House of Commons where, ultimately, he could count on the decisive majority of his coalition government. Yet quite soon – under the influence of Keynes and other influential opinion-makers – a different outlook on the settlement came to gain decisive ground far beyond liberal and Labour circles. What came to prevail were the profound misgivings that have already been discussed. These crystallised in the view that Smuts had already expressed at the end of the peace conference – that the peace was flawed in essential respects, not only but particularly with respect to the treatment of Germany, and that a genuine "work of peacemaking" and "appeasement" still had to be done, or more precisely that the peace settlement had to be substantially amended.[10]

It is crucial to understand, then, that despite the hard-fisted bargaining at Versailles, notably about the future naval balance of forces in the world, and despite his continued reservations towards Wilson's high-handed progressivism, fostering cooperation and a hegemonic burden-sharing with the United States remained central to Lloyd George's vision of how a new "order of equilibrium" was to emerge and a reconfigured Atlantic concert of great powers was to be formed after the Great War. At the same time, he regarded Anglo-American cooperation – and eventual US concessions on British war debts – as an important prerequisite for a successful pursuit of his domestic reform priority to turn Britain into a country "fit for heroes to live in". Accordingly, the British premier stressed that the League could only be effective in preventing future wars if its members, and especially its principal powers, were actually willing to engage, commit to disarmament and enforce respect for the essentials of the Covenant. He warned that otherwise it would be merely "something that would be blown away by the first gust of war or any

---

[9] See Nicolson (2005), p. 82; Fry (1998), pp. 598-601; Fry (2011), pp. 280 ff.
[10] Smuts statement, 28 June 1919, *Smuts Papers*, IV, p. 256; Keynes (1919).

fierce dispute between the nations". This was a message that was specifically directed at Wilson and even more so at his critics in the American Senate.[11] Not only key advisers like Kerr, who deemed a close Anglo-American partnership within the League vital for a substantive "process of appeasement", shared this outlook. It was also supported by a majority in Lloyd George's government.[12] Cecil, who after his return from Paris resumed lobbying work for the League – supporting wide-ranging campaigns of the League of Nations Union – considered Anglo-American collaboration and US engagement in the League even more indispensable. He feared that without America's participation in the new organisation, it would be impossible to effect the transformation of international politics and departure from old-style balance-of-power traditions that he deemed imperative.[13]

Unsurprisingly, Woodrow Wilson, the actor on whose decisions and political fate still so much depended, came to advance a distinctly Wilsonian interpretation of the peace settlement. He insisted that chiefly by establishing the League of Nations it provided a novel basis for a durable peace order that indeed had the potential to "end all wars". And seeking to shore up the image of an arbiter of peace who had stayed true to the principles he had proclaimed, the American president adamantly clung to presenting the peace treaty – and the League Covenant – not so much as the imperfect results of a necessarily difficult negotiating process with the *Entente* Powers in which he had to make compromises, but rather as achievements that despite some shortcomings were essentially congruent with his Americanist-internationalist vision of peace – and the Fourteen Points. It was on these premises that he would seek to win Congressional support.

Once again, Wilson also focused squarely on the League of Nations when outlining what he envisaged as a longer, essentially evolutionary process of peace-building and the consolidation of a new, progressive international order in which he desired the United States to act, not as a European-style military power but as an exemplary progressive hegemon. He reiterated how crucial the League's new ways of settling conflicts and providing common guarantees for the integrity of all member states would be for securing European and global peace and preventing the resurgence of European-style secret diplomacy and power politics. And he placed renewed emphasis on the centrality of what he saw as the Covenant's pivotal Article X, while still arguing that it bound the

---

[11] Lloyd George speech, House of Commons, 3 July 1919, Hansard, Commons, 5th series, vol. 117, cols. 1211–32.

[12] Kerr to Lloyd George, 12 July 1919, Lloyd George Papers, F/89/3/6.

[13] Cecil speech, Commons, 17 November 1919, Hansard, Commons, 5th series, vol. 121, col. 689. See Egerton (1978), pp. 173–5, 189. The influential league advocate Bryce even warned that without the United States the League would simply "fail". Bryce to Smuts, 2 July 1919, *Smuts Papers*, IV, p. 121.

United States and other members of the organisation morally rather than legally when it came to the ultimate decisions about what action was to be taken against an aggressor. In his view, Article X was and remained an essential cornerstone of the entire League edifice, indispensable for ensuring that the power of the strong (and civilised) states, which now had become the permanent members of the League Council, would finally be used not to trample on but to protect the rights of weaker states.[14]

By contrast, Wilson continued to regard the guarantee accords with France as a not unimportant but decidedly transitional agreement. When he belatedly submitted the guarantee treaty to the Senate in late July 1919, the president underscored once again that in his interpretation it was not only bound up with but also subordinated to the League's "collective" security regime. He declared that the treaty constituted "a temporary supplement" to the peace treaty. Wilson conceded that re-assuring France required an American pledge to provide swift assistance "without waiting for the advice" of the League Council. Yet he also stressed that this "special arrangement" was not "inde-pendent" of the League "but under it" – and that it was not intended to lead to a permanent American special commitment to French and European security. It would only be in force until the League Council "upon the application" of one of its members – likely the United States – had agreed "if necessary, by a majority vote", that the provisions of the League Covenant afforded France "sufficient protection".[15] It was not accidental that Wilson thereafter essen-tially refrained from any major efforts to salvage the guarantee agreement with France during the Senate controversies over the Treaty of Versailles and the League Covenant. He insisted on the primacy of the League.

Crucially, Wilson had maintained the conviction that only the League of Nations could create a "permanent concert" of nations through which con-flicts could either be resolved peacefully or prevented from escalating in the first place. And he now declared more emphatically than before that the League had to become the essential "permanent clearinghouse" of the new order, the forum and mechanism that would permit its members – and especially the principal powers – to "arbitrate" and come to terms with the problems that had not yet been settled at the peace conference and to "correct [the] mistakes" that had been "inevitable" in a peacemaking process that took place so soon after the war. With the help of the League – and under the beneficent influence of "world opinion" – the original order was to be

---

[14] Wilson to Tumulty, 23 June 1919, *PWW*, LXI, p. 115; Wilson remarks to members of the Senate's Foreign Relations Committee, 19 August 1919, *PWW*, LXII, pp. 339 ff.; Wilson speech, 19 September 1919, Shaw (1924), II, p. 1017.
[15] Wilson statement, 29 July 1919, *PWW*, LXII, pp. 27–8.

amended and consolidated step by step, once the passions of war had subsided.[16] In line with *his* evolutionary approach, Wilson thus still envisaged the
League as an evolving organisation, which would grow and expand over time
and in the process stabilise a new order of democratic states that adhered to its
rules and principles. And he indeed clung to the belief that what was really
required was a "gradual deepening" of the commitments of the member states
to "a set of commonly embraced postwar principles" rather than a hard and
fast regime of obligations codified by international law.[17]

In this context, it is worth underscoring how essential it remained in
Wilson's "vision" to turn the League in a *medium-term* perspective into an
institution that also bound the vanquished powers to its principles and
involved them in the evolutionary "clearing" and adjustment processes that
he foresaw. But he obviously considered it politic not to dwell upon this in the
midst of the intensifying inner-American controversies over the ratification of
the peace treaty. More fundamentally, he had by this time committed himself
to a two-stage approach. He held that it was necessary to establish and solidify,
on the basis of the peace treaty, both a functioning nuclear League and an
essentially Atlantic "nucleus of order", which had to be done by way of a
modicum of cooperation with Britain and France; then these nuclear structures were to be extended to integrate the vanquished – yet only once the
fledgling German republic had proven its willingness to comply with the treaty
terms and the German people had shown that they could establish a stable
democratic form of government and were committed to the standards set by
the League Covenant.

But this was not what Wilson stressed to American audiences in the
politically charged atmosphere of the summer of 1919, when it served his
tactical interest to emphasise the severity of the peace. What he proclaimed
instead was that the League would enable the American republic to play the
leading role in international affairs to which it was predestined. In confidence,
he avowed his conviction that the League would give the United States
"leadership of the world".[18] Yet it remained to be seen how far he – and his
successors – would indeed be prepared *and in a position* to exercise such
leadership – and, more importantly, how far they would be prepared *and in a
position* to assume practical responsibilities in dealing with the multiple
conflicts that would arise in Western, Central and Eastern Europe.

Clemenceau's hopes to work towards a novel Atlantic alliance *after* the Paris
Peace Conference thus continued to clash with the thrust of Wilson's

---

[16] Wilson speech in San Diego, 19 September 1919, in Shaw (1924), II, p. 1017. For his
evolving outlook, see Wilson address, 25 January 1919, *PWW*, LIV, pp. 266–7; Wilson
remarks, 14 February 1919, Wilson (1939), p. 239.

[17] Ikenberry (2001), p. 146.

[18] Wilson to Tumulty, 23 June 1919, *PWW*, LXI, p. 115.

aspirations. It was more conceivable that these aspirations could interlock with what Lloyd George and leading British strategists sought to achieve. And, systemically, Anglo-American cooperation and the confirmation of British *and* American commitments were and remained critical not only for establishing an effective League – and, sooner rather than later, an effective concert of powers – but also for assuaging French fears and thus creating essential preconditions for a process of accommodation between the western powers and Weimar Germany. But as all of the key actors realised, any conceivable scenario of how the treaty system 1919 was to be transformed into a more durable peace order was still shrouded in uncertainty. The reassurance of France, the implementation of British postwar plans and of course the realisation of Wilson's ambition to turn the United States into the key power within the "permanent concert" of the League depended on the outcome of what soon escalated into an epic inner-American political battle: the fight over the ratification of the peace treaty – and the League Covenant – in the US Senate that would rage between July 1919 and March 1920.

II.   Wilson's Fiasco in the Treaty Fight and Its Far-Reaching Transatlantic Consequences

What became known as the "treaty fight" centred not only on the Treaty of Versailles but also and chiefly on the question of whether and on what conditions the United States would join the League of Nations. As Wilson insisted to the very end that the peace treaty, the League Covenant and the guarantee agreement with France all had to be ratified together it turned into an all-or-nothing contest in which both domestically and for the wider world the stakes were immensely high. At one level, the "treaty fight" became a political power struggle between the president and his main Republican opponents in the Senate, above all his principal antagonist Henry Cabot Lodge. At a deeper level, it can be seen as another, decisive phase in the struggle that had gained momentum during the war, especially from 1916, the struggle over what was to be the United States' proper role in a dynamically changing world, what kind of international commitments were to be made, and who would ultimately have a decisive say in these matters, the president or those who had a majority in Congress.

The way in which the "treaty fight" played out and ended is of interest here not only because it had major repercussions for the political power-relations within the United States and the inner-American debate about the republic's future international conduct. It also has to be analysed because of the far-reaching international consequences Wilson's eventual defeat would have – and, most of all, because of how this defeat would affect the future of the United States' relations with Europe. In short, it dealt a massive, if not irremediable, blow to the fledgling Atlantic order of 1919. Without the

United States assuming responsibilities as a key hegemonic guarantor, it simply was no longer possible to consolidate an order on the premises set in Paris. In the shorter term, Wilson's fiasco put enormous pressure on the remaining treaty powers Britain and France to shore up what was left of the Versailles system. But what it really heightened, as soon became clear, was the pressure for more fundamental reforms.

The basic battle-lines in the soon highly acrimonious treaty fight – those demarcated by an uncompromising president and his de facto equally compromise-averse opponent Lodge – had already been drawn by the end of July 1919. And these battle lines hardened after a fruitless meeting between Wilson and the members of the Senate's Foreign Relations Committee on 19 August, which merely highlighted how intense the partisan polarisation had become by then – and how limited the willingness to seek common ground was on either side. Indeed, it should be stressed that the eventual fiasco Wilson experienced was mainly due to his own intransigence, and notably his penchant to rely on public pressure rather than explore avenues of bipartisan compromise with more moderate Republicans. But the tactical imperatives of Lodge, who ultimately was mainly interested in inflicting a decisive political defeat on the president, also played a significant and ultimately destructive part.

Determined to confront Wilson head-on, the Republican senator Philander Knox had on 10 June tabled a resolution that proposed to separate the ratification of the Treaty of Versailles from deliberations about the League Covenant, whose key provisions in his view were incompatible with the American constitution. Knox had declared that instead of accepting the unlimited obligations of Article X, it should be the – unilaterally – "declared policy" of the US government that if "any power or combination of powers" (by which he meant Germany and its potential allies) should again threaten the "the freedom and peace of Europe", it would join once again with its "cobelligerents" of the war to remove this "menace" and defend civilisation.[19] But as he considered this resolution too extreme to gain the backing of more moderate Republican senators, Lodge had subsequently sought to unite the Republican opposition behind a different approach – and to confront Wilson in a different way. Essentially, he insisted that the president would have to accept numerous reservations if he wanted to win Republican consent.

Lodge here chiefly drew on recommendations that the Republican elder statesman Elihu Root had made. Re-accentuating positions that he had already outlined in spring, Root counselled that the Republicans should set three preconditions for supporting the League Covenant, which in his interpretation

---

[19] Knox speech, Senate, 10 June 1919, Congressional Record, 66th Congress, 1st session, 10 June 1919, 894.

would preserve the benefits of the new institution while ridding it of undesir-
ably far-reaching and counter-productive provisions. Crucially, he argued that
Article X and the ill-defined and dangerously "vague universal" obligations it
entailed – to intervene in conflicts and to preserve the present status quo on a
global scale – should be expunged from the Covenant. Instead, the Republican
senators should call for a more limited commitment that "every man and
woman in the country will understand" and that actually protected cardinal
US strategic interests.[20]

At the core, Root posited that if it was "necessary for the security of western
Europe", the United States should pledge to "go to the support" of France in
case of an unprovoked German attack. Second, Root proposed that the United
States should be able to withdraw from the League without requiring the
approval of other member states. And third, he insisted that "purely
American questions" – under which he not only categorised matters such as
immigration but also the essentials of the Monroe Doctrine – would be
exempted from the League's "jurisdiction". Seeking to counter the wider concerns Wilson had raised earlier, Root also argued that such reservations would
not require an international re-negotiation of the League Covenant, noting that
other signatory states could simply indicate their consent by not raising official
objections.[21] In fact, however, this only threw into relief the Americanocentrism
of his outlook – and his lack of regard for the danger that, if the United States
claimed not only essential exemptions to protect particular national prerogatives
but also the right simply to discard a pivotal article of the League Covenant,
other states could be emboldened to act similarly. Unquestionably, such developments would emaciate or even undermine the entire "collective security"
system the League was supposed to establish.

Criticising Wilson for his inflexible stance, the second most influential
champion of the League in the American spectrum, William Taft, also came
to advocate milder reservations in order to ensure that the United States would
actually join the new international organisation. He too focused on exemptions for the Monroe Doctrine and, above all, Article X, though he suggested
that it should not be eliminated but merely be amended to leave in no doubt
that the American Congress would ultimately decide what course of action
should be taken.[22] But the LEP's executive committee refused to endorse the
recommendations of its president. The League to Enforce Peace actually came
to lobby for a full, unqualified US membership of the League and a ratification
of the Covenant without amendments or reservations. It even organised a
petition on behalf of what were effectively Wilson's essentials.[23] The American

---

[20] Root to Lodge, 19 June 1919, Lodge Papers.
[21] Ibid.
[22] Taft to Hays, 20 July 1919, Taft Papers, Series 3, Box 452.
[23] LEP Resolution, 31 July 1919, Wilson Papers, Series 4, F 4767.

president welcomed the LEP's support. Yet what had a far more decisive bearing on the political process in Washington was that Lodge managed to rally all Republican senators behind Root's incisive set of reservations. It was a platform that by and large reflected Lodge's own preferences, which he had already outlined in his keynote speech in the Senate on 28 February 1919.[24]

Still accusing Wilson of intending to supplant genuine "Americanism" in international affairs with an un-American "internationalism", the senator from Massachusetts remained most adamantly opposed to Article X and adhered to his view of the dangerous obligations it created. Time and again he underscored his "vital objection" to "any legal or moral obligation upon the United States to enter into war or send its army and navy abroad" – or to impose economic boycotts on other nations – without the "unfettered" consent of the US Congress.[25] What Lodge still really favoured was a more circumscribed commitment to France and a de facto alliance of the victors. In private, he underscored that what he preferred was a "simple proposition", made without reference to the League, that it was the United States' intention "to aid France", which he characterised as America's "barrier and outpost" in Europe, should it be "attacked without provocation by Germany".[26]

By early October Lodge had rallied all Republican senators behind a catalogue of no less than fourteen reservations; yet those that concerned the United States' right of withdrawal, the exemption of domestic affairs and the Monroe Doctrine and, above all, the crucial Article X remained at the heart of Republican objections. Not only more moderate "mild reservationists" who actually were in favour of an amended League – like Wilson's opponent in the elections of 1916, Charles E. Hughes – backed Lodge's agenda.[27] For tactical reasons, namely to defeat the president, also "irreconcilables" like Borah, Brandegee and Johnson came to accept the reservations, even though they remained implacably opposed to "Wilson's Covenant" and rejected any "deal" that, as Johnson put it, would leave the United States "in an alliance or league with European or Asiatic powers".[28]

The way in which Wilson responded was undoubtedly high-handed. The president reasserted that the Treaty of Versailles, the League Covenant and the American guarantee agreement with France would have to be ratified together

---

[24] Lodge, Senate speech, 28 February 1919, Congressional Record, 65th Congress, 3rd session, 4520–30.

[25] Lodge remarks, 10 September 1919, U.S. Senate, *Proceedings of the Committee on Foreign Relations*, 1919, pp. 170–4.

[26] Lodge to White, 23 June 1919, Lodge Papers; Lodge to Beveridge, 11 August 1919, cited after Widenor (1980), p. 332.

[27] Hughes address, 26 March 1919, Hughes Papers, Box 172; Root to Hays, 5 July 1919, Root Papers, Box 137.

[28] Borah to Beveridge, 26 Vol. 58, 3441–2; Borah to Lodge, 24 January 1920, Lodge Papers, file 1920.

and without any substantial amendments. He underlined his "conviction" that if he agreed to the Republican reservations regarding the League, this would "put the United States as clearly out of the concert of nations as a rejection" of the entire peace treaty. And he stressed that a stark choice had to be made: either to "go in" and act as the new hegemon or to "stay out", noting that the latter course would be "fatal to the influence and even to the economic prospects of the United States" whereas the former "would give her the leadership of the world".[29]

With a view to Article X, Wilson basically reiterated – during his only meeting with the Senate's Committee on Foreign Relations on 19 August – what he had already argued when defending the Draft Covenant in spring. He emphasised once again that in assuming a leading role in the League, the United States would make "very grave and solemn" commitments to the preservation of peace but that at the core of Article X lay a "moral, not a legal obligation" – and that nothing restricted the right of Congress to determine which measures the American government would finally take to meet its responsibilities.[30] At the same time, as noted, he stubbornly held on to the view that the American guarantee agreement with France was merely a complementary "special arrangement" that would be ended once the security system of the League provided "sufficient protection".[31]

Wilson still expected at this stage that he would be able to persuade more "independent" Republican senators to side with the Democratic minority. And minority leader Hitchcock, who was still his most important ally in the Senate, unwaveringly backed the president's peremptory "all-or nothing" approach, even though he was more conscious of the need to search for a compromise across the aisles. What proved crucial, however, was that the president assumed that a clear majority of the American voters supported his priorities – and that he thus once again resorted to the "strategy" of acting as a high-handed arbiter and *praeceptor* of the American nation that he had pursued with such ambivalent results in the past. Wilson made no serious effort to engage with the Republican reservations and to try to negotiate some kind of compromise solution. Instead, after the meeting on 19 August had predictably brought no *rapprochement*, he sought to use the bully pulpit that his office afforded to compel the Republican majority, and particularly more moderate Republican senators, to fall in line with his course by essentially mobilising public opinion.

It was with this underlying intention that Wilson in early September embarked on a gruelling and, in this form, unprecedented four-week *tour de force* of public engagements on behalf of his vision of America's future

---

[29] Wilson to Tumulty, 23 June 1919, *PWW*, LXI, p. 115.

[30] Wilson meeting with Foreign Relations Committee, 19 August 1919, *PWW*, LXII, pp. 339–411.

[31] Wilson statement, 29 July 1919, *PWW*, LXII, pp. 27–8.

leadership in the League and in the world. This remarkable tour took him to the mid-western and Pacific states. Predictably, though, his efforts failed to reach their objective. And it was shortly after his return from this exhausting trip that he suffered, on 2 October, the massive stroke from which he would never really recover and that would indeed limit his capacity to act as an effective presidential leader. But, contrary to what has often been claimed, the president's failing health did not play a *decisive* part in his final defeat. For it is very difficult to imagine that he would have been willing, or able, to change his entire approach and make essential concessions he deemed unacceptable in order to address the core Republican reservations, and overcome the deadlock, even if he had been in full possession of his physical and mental capabilities – or indeed that Lodge would have espoused a more constructive approach and allowed meaningful progress in this direction.[32]

The "treaty fight" would be followed by a global audience but nowhere more attentively than in Europe. Much depended on its outcome. Especially the governments in London and Paris were keenly aware of how much was at stake and sought to influence the struggle in accordance with their key strategic interests. In September, authorised by the Lloyd George Cabinet, the former liberal foreign secretary and committed league proponent Grey went on a mission to Washington, intending to use his reputation as an ardent Atlanticist to promote the ratification of the peace treaty. Grey came to stress the need for efforts to accommodate the Republican reservations in order to break the deadlock and forge a compromise that ensured an American participation in the League, which he deemed vital for giving the organisation a "fair start".[33] Yet his mission was ill-fated and would indeed prove futile, not least because he arrived in the American capital just before Wilson's physical collapse. Subsequently, the government in London would send different signals. On 11 November, Balfour voiced grave concerns over the Republican reservations, warning that the League could only function if all of its principal members made the same commitments and carried an equal share of the burden. He argued that if the United States was granted exemptions, other powers would follow suit and the future of the new organisation would be "dark indeed". And he underscored that the Republican protagonists in Washington had to understand that unless they were prepared to "bear an equal share in an equal task" they "would be threatening with ultimate dissolution the whole of the new system" the League was meant to establish. This could hardly impress the fierce Republican critics of the League, but was intended to persuade "mild reservationists".[34]

---

[32] For different interpretations, see Ambrosius (1987) and Cooper (2010).

[33] See Egerton (1978), pp. 182–94.

[34] Balfour speech, League of Nations Union rally, Queen's Hall, 11 November 1919, *The Times*, 12 November 1919, p. 20.

By mid-December 1919, even Lloyd George himself would abandon his reticent attitude and declare that while it remained essential for his government that the United States joined the League, it could not be granted special conditions that exempted it from commitments which bound the other powers. And he too now emphasised that the League had to be constituted as a league of "equal" nations – though what he really still envisaged was an organisation in which the principal powers that led it bore "equal" obligations.[35] Even if the emphasis differed, such pronouncements echoed Wilson's "all in or all out" message; and they were a – vain – attempt to strengthen the American president's position and put pressure on his domestic opponents. By contrast, the Clemenceau government shifted its efforts to influence developments in Washington in a very different direction. Originally, in September, Clemenceau had come out in support of Wilson's agenda and stressed how committed he was to the League. But then, in pursuit of his overriding priority of ensuring American security guarantees for France, he secretly came to side with Lodge. And the chief concern of the premier and French diplomats became to prevail on the pivotal Republican senator to ensure that, with the Treaty of Versailles, the Anglo-American guarantee treaty with France would be ratified.

Essentially, however, the "treaty fight" would be a critical – and not the last – watershed in the long twentieth century that threw into relief how *limited* outside influence was on inner-American processes that would have far-reaching global ramifications. The outcome of this process would be decided in the central force-field of the American republic's political system at a juncture when a power struggle between the president and Congress had become unavoidable. It had become unavoidable, and the stakes were particularly high, precisely because momentous, potentially revolutionary decisions had to be made that could lead to the assumption of unprecedented, potentially very far-reaching international responsibilities. And it became so polarising and ferocious precisely because up to this point the prevailing modes and traditions of US foreign policy, and US political culture, had essentially been geared towards eschewing such responsibilities.

When the first vote in Senate was taken on 19 November 1919, the Treaty of Versailles and the League Covenant clearly failed to gain the required two-thirds majority. The final round of the "treaty fight" then came to an end on 19 March 1920. Following the efforts of more moderate Republican and Democratic senators to prepare the ground for compromise solution, the second vote would be held over a modified proposition, namely the ratification of the Versailles treaty and the League Covenant with a somewhat altered version of the reservations Lodge had proposed. Yet Wilson remained adamant and threatened to use his presidential veto power in order to deter

---

[35] Lloyd speech, House of Commons, 18 December 1919, Hansard, Commons, 5th series, vol. 123, cols. 769–72.

Democratic senators from supporting a ratification on this basis. In the end, the necessary quorum was only missed by seven votes. As has rightly been pointed out, this outcome – and the fact that the United States would neither be part of the Versailles system nor of the League (albeit with the crucial limitations the Lodge reservations would have imposed) – was ultimately a consequence of Wilson's rigid refusal to countenance *any* kind of compromise agreement with the oppositional Senate majority.[36]

In retrospect, it is impossible to avoid the conclusion that by maintaining his intransigent attitude Wilson had played a critical part in massively setting back the prospects of a more constructive engagement of the United States in the post–First World War international system. That from now on there would be no US engagement and leadership in the League when arguably it mattered most, at a time when the new organisation still had to be established and "brought to life", had significant repercussions. It weakened the League and its development prospects, not fatally but decisively. And it made it into a more Eurocentric "global" organisation that initially became dominated by the struggle between French attempts to fortify it as an instrument to protect the status quo of 1919 and British attempts to steer against this and make the League after all into a framework for concerted international politics, conflict resolution and evolutionary peaceful change.

More generally, though, America's withdrawal reduced the relevance of the League, also in the eyes of the French and British governments, when it came to the management of the "big" postwar problems, particularly those connected with Germany. This made it all the more difficult to turn the League into an authoritative instrument of international stabilisation and peace preservation – and, crucially, to turn it from an organisation of the victors into the framework for a more integrative concert of states and system of collective security. At the same time, Wilson's intransigence most definitely eliminated the possibility that the Anglo-American guarantee agreement with France could become, as he and Lloyd George had hoped, an essential means of reassurance that would expedite eventual Franco-German and wider European accommodation processes.[37] Following the Senate's rejection of the peace treaty, the Lloyd George government, clinging to the rationales the British delegation had adopted at Versailles, also distanced itself from its guarantee pledges. It hence had to grapple with the question to what extent it would be prepared to bear the responsibilities of acting as the sole principal guarantor of French security and moderator of French postwar policies.[38]

---

[36] See Cooper (2010), p. 283.

[37] For a different interpretation see Ambrosius (1987), p. 211.

[38] On this, see Lloyd George speech, House of Commons, 18 December 1919, Hansard, Commons, 5th series, vol. 12, cols. 769–72.

Thus, the "Versailles system" had lost what was to have been one of its principal guarantors and "ordering powers"; and as a consequence of this the second principal guarantor power had limited its commitments as well. What was supposed to provide the underpinnings of a new Atlantic security architecture lay in shambles. But Wilson's defeat did not change the underlying fact that the United States remained a power and power factor of the first order. Nor had it changed the fact that the Great War and the peace negotiations of Paris had created newly essential – asymmetrical – interdependencies between the newly dominant, if politically hamstrung, American power and a war-ravaged Europe – and left behind overriding problems that could not be adequately addressed without some kind of American cooperation, or at least acquiescence. This notably still held true for the intertwined problem complexes of reparations, postwar reconstruction and war debts. In a wider sense, however, it also held true for the even weightier systemic questions of how to deal with Germany, how to come to terms with the underlying problem of insecurity and, ultimately, how to build a more viable international order.

Yet what now had become an open question was how far the Republican administration that succeeded Wilson would be willing to become involved in attempts to overcome the profoundly unsettled situation in Europe. It was essentially very unclear what kind of approaches it would pursue, also in collaboration with leading US financiers, after the Republican majority in the Senate had played such a critical part in defeating Wilson's agenda. The fact that the nondescript Republican candidate Warren Harding scored a landslide victory over his Democratic opponent James Cox in the presidential elections of November 1920 can indeed be seen as a referendum over Wilson's aspirational quest to assume progressive global leadership. And at the same time it confirmed a major qualitative shift. For Harding had campaigned under the banner of a "return to normalcy", by which he meant, among other things, the return to the alleged "normalcy" of a US aloofness from more substantive international commitments – and, at the bottom, a revival of pre-war US unilateralism on the premises of the Monroe Doctrine.

It is hard to overstate, therefore, what a crucial *caesura* the "treaty fight" was, even beyond the immediate rejection of "Wilsonianism". And it is tempting to suggest with the benefit of hindsight that it was inevitable that the United States would never become a member of the League. But it is important to recognise that at the time it was by no means deemed certain, let alone inevitable, that America would remain outside the new international organisation for a long time to come. Nor was it a foregone conclusion that US governments would continue to reject other political or security commitments in Europe for the foreseeable future. Pro-League activists and other internationalists both in the United States and in Europe would persevere with their efforts to effect a change in prevalent American attitudes. Yet major leaps were certainly unlikely in the near future.

In fact, it soon became palpable that under Harding, at the dawn of what would be an era of Republican administrations in Washington that lasted until the Great Depression, the official American approach to international questions and foreign affairs would be shaped by markedly different priorities and assumptions. The United States by no means withdrew either to pre-war traditions or an even more pronounced version of unmitigated isolationism – neither in general terms nor, in particular, vis-à-vis East Asia or Europe. But what now crystallised into a fundamental premise of US policies towards the Old World – which came to prevail for a long time, until the transformative debates during the Second World War – was the notion that vital American interests could be most effectively protected, and peace and stability could be promoted most effectively, if the American government kept a safe distance from any formal multilateral commitments and instead pursued essentially *informal* stabilisation strategies.

The Republican administrations of the 1920s thus never retreated to complete isolationism. In fact, after a period of self-absorption and political insulation from the European continent's postwar troubles, the peculiar American world power would play once again a pivotal role in efforts not just to stabilise Europe but also to consolidate a peace-enforcing transatlantic order – yet this time as an *informal hegemon*. Before this occurred, however, post-Versailles Europe descended into a deep and protracted crisis. What eventually reached its peak in the cathartic Ruhr conflict of 1923 was in many ways a continuation of the war by other means – as a fierce and indeed violent political struggle.

III. A Continued State of War. Europe's Descent into Crisis in the early 1920s

While the situation in Eastern Europe remained unstable and conflict-ridden, too, what lay at the epicentre of the crisis that kept Europe in a structural state of war rather than peace after 1919 was unmistakeably the unresolved German problem. And it was the clash between German revisionism and increasingly assertive, and desperate, French attempts to fortify the precarious status quo created at the Paris Peace Conference. Yet what lay behind this clash was the wider structural instability and insecurity that prevailed after Versailles and that had been exacerbated by the fact that neither the United States nor, in consequence of America's withdrawal, Britain, had come to act as hegemonic guarantee powers and providers of security in a profoundly unsettled postwar situation.

Both the ongoing Franco-German antagonism and this wider structural problem also accounted for the virulence of the conflict over reparations that soon re-escalated after Versailles and came to dominate European and transatlantic politics up until 1923, making an already volatile and unusually violent period of international history even more turbulent. In turn, the dispute over reparations pointed far beyond the fraught question of who would ultimately pay for the immeasurable costs of the Great War. It indeed became the battlefield on which the future of the embattled peace order and the future distribution of political, financial and economic power in Europe – and in the by now so intricately interdependent Euro-Atlantic world – were fought out. This struggle and its outcome would have decisive implications not only for the economic but also for the political stabilisation of Europe and the wider world. And it was inseparable from the two other salient questions that still had to be "resolved" after Versailles: the aforementioned and indeed still paramount problem of massive insecurity; and the question of Germany's proper place in the shaky new order. Even in the sharply altered constellation brought about by Wilson's defeat one fundamental had not changed: if they were to be settled at all, all of these questions required some kind of transatlantic solution.

What continued to be a principal impediment to any more comprehensive settlement was that, determined to forestall the formation of a wider European coalition of debtors, the Harding administration reasserted Wilson's axiom that war debts and reparations were to be treated strictly separately. And what continued to put immense pressure on Britain and France was that, as had to be expected, the Republican government also strictly adhered to the position that not even a partial reduction of American war-debt claims could be contemplated – which still reflected majority opinion in Congress – and that no fresh private loans would be authorised until the *Entente* governments agreed to debt settlements on US terms.[39] Leading members of the Republican administration, like Secretary of State Charles E. Hughes, Treasury Secretary Andrew Mellon and Hoover, who had become commerce secretary, agreed with influential Wall Street financiers that what held the key to Europe's stabilisation, and was decidedly in the American interest, was to create conditions for its "successful financial and economic rehabilitation". And in view of the fact that "Allied Europe was financially indebted to the United States" – with the total debt rapidly approaching 13 billion dollars – its economic rehabilitation was not only, as Dulles noted after Versailles, crucial for "her ability to repay what she owes and to from us what we wish to sell". More broadly, American decision-makers believed, economic recuperation and a resumption of largely unfettered trade were also critical for Europe's political stabilisation and the promotion of new interconnected interests between the states that had fought against each other in the Great War.[40]

Yet the Harding administration at the same time strictly adhered to the maxim of rejecting any official involvement in the European reparation dispute. And it re-affirmed Wilson's insistence on a strict separation between reparations and the repayment of allied war debts to the United States. Until

---

[39] See Artaud (1978), pp. 363–73; Silvermann (1982), pp. 186–93.
[40] Dulles memorandum, 8 August 1919, in Pruessen (1982), p. 143.

the Hoover Moratorium of 1931 (and even beyond it), no Republican government in the post–First World War era would depart from the position that
Wilson had reiterated to Lloyd George in November 1920, namely that there
was no room to manoeuvre because neither Congress nor US public opinion
would "ever permit cancellation of any part of the debt" that Britain and
France owed to the United States "as an inducement towards a practical
settlement of the reparation claims".[41]

Essentially, this limited the scope for a "practical settlement" just as decisively
as the non-negotiable positions and constraints of Wilson had done at
Versailles. In the verdict of Keynes, who in 1921 again called for a comprehensive revision of the entire Versailles treaty system, the limitations and erroneous
assumptions of Anglo-French reparation policies *and* US debt policies were
bound to undercut all possibilities of effecting a forward-looking European
reconstruction. And thus they were bound to sow instead the seeds of future
conflict and war. Keynes noted: "Who believes that the Allies will, over a period
of one or two generations, exert adequate force over the German government,
or that the German government can exert adequate authority over its subjects,
to extract continuing fruits on a vast scale from forced labour?" And he left no
doubt that he deemed this not only unrealistic but also a scenario that would
"endanger the peace of Europe". At the same time, he argued that the American
"exaction" of "the debts which the Allied governments owe" was also counter-
productive because it prevented them from purchasing "from America their
usual proportion of her exports". Keynes thus renewed his demand for a
comprehensive transatlantic debt reduction and reconstruction scheme. Yet
while provoking considerable public debate, this demand again fell on deaf ears
in Washington's – and London's – corridors of power.[42]

The decision-makers who sought to steer France through the unsettled postwar period had to confront head-on the constraints that the uncompromising
US debt and loan policies imposed at a time when the French state teetered on
the edge of "bankruptcy" and was in desperate need of capital. And most of them
were even more conscious than Clemenceau had been of the precariousness of
France's overall postwar position – despite the apparent, yet in fact deceptive,
preponderance in Europe that the terms of Versailles had brought. Indeed, their
pursuits were equally shaped by a distinct awareness of how particularly badly
France had suffered during the war, what a high price it had paid for the victory
of 1918 and how hard-won the compromises of the peace conference had been.
In the wake of the American withdrawal from the treaty system not only
Millerand, but then also Briand and Poincaré thus felt, each in his own way,
that they had to struggle all the harder to enforce what remained of the edifice of

[41] Wilson to Lloyd George, 2 November 1920, in Turner (1998), pp. 29–30.
[42] Keynes, *A Revision of the Treaty*, in Keynes (1978), III, pp. 105–14, 115–30.

1919. And all of them were determined to attain, finally, more solid, long-term security guarantees against a German neighbour whose future development was regarded as incalculable but in any case menacing.

This on the one hand led French governments to prioritise the conclusion of a full-blown defensive alliance with Britain to replace the defunct Anglo-American guarantee, which remained a profound frustrating pursuit. In a parallel manoeuvre, France now came to conclude compensatory containment alliances with Poland, Czechoslovakia and other Eastern European states, which built on the groundwork laid in 1919.[43] On the other hand, French decision-makers insisted all the more on forcing Germany to pay substantial reparations. In the grips of a prolonged financial and fiscal crisis, and with no prospect of obtaining fresh US loans, the postwar French state insisted on German payments not only for moral but also for concrete financial reasons. Yet not least because the prospect of a firmer *Entente* with Britain was and remained so uncertain, French reparation policy continued to be dominated by strategic considerations. Essentially, one could threaten to extend the temporary occupation of the Rhineland in order to enforce German compliance; or, more importantly, one could seize on reparation claims as a lever to reinforce France's hold on the Rhineland or even, as some planners envisaged, to extend it to the strategically vital region of the Ruhr.

These and other options would be discussed both in successive French governments and among the higher officials of the Quai d'Orsay. The underlying – offensively defensive – aim remained to find ways to extend France's temporary preponderance in continental Europe into a more lasting hegemony vis-à-vis Germany. And undoubtedly America's disengagement and subsequent British reticence vis-à-vis more far-reaching security commitments played a decisive part in driving French policymakers in this direction. Yet France did not have the means to achieve this. While different multilateral and unilateral options were contemplated, pursuits that went in this general direction threatened to isolate France ever more from the Anglo-American powers, on whose cooperation it still critically depended. And, most of all, they had no prospect of creating a sustainable relationship, or even *modus vivendi*, with Germany or a stable and secure European postwar order. Rather, they provoked conflict and proved profoundly destabilising, effectively undermining rather than fortifying the truncated Versailles system.[44]

While they deemed French fears exaggerated and the French emphasis on coercion deeply detrimental, Lloyd George, his new Foreign Secretary Curzon and leading strategists in the Foreign Office recognised how vital it was after the lapse of the Anglo-American guarantee that, as the remaining key

---

[43] See Wandycz (1961), pp. 29 ff.; Calier and Soutou (2001).

[44] See Trachtenberg (1980), pp. 99–290. For a different, more nuanced analysis, see Jackson (2013), pp. 323–426.

guarantee power, Britain found ways to assuage French security concerns. And in view of the Harding administration's uncompromising aloofness they realised not only that it would be necessary to make alternative, European arrangements but also that these would have to centre, in the first instance, on some kind of renegotiated Anglo-French security compact. Revealingly, however, the overall outlook was essentially optimistic. Confirming the assessment that through the Versailles treaty the German threat had been effectively contained and that no other substantial threats appeared on the horizon, the British War Cabinet decided in July 1919 that Britain's defence policy should hence be based on the assumption that the British Empire would "not be engaged in any great war during the next ten years", thus inaugurating the famous "ten-year rule".[45]

Following America's withdrawal, Lloyd George and especially the arch-imperialist Curzon did not see any reason to alter this posture. Yet they had to think anew about how to meet core security challenges in such a way as to pre-empt the need for any renewed British military intervention. They clearly no longer saw the League as an instrument that could effectively guarantee peace and security in Europe; and they staunchly opposed any notion of extending Britain's collective-security commitments through special amendments to the Covenant. But nor did they regard the idea of a fully-fledged military alliance with France, which French leaders demanded and permanent officials in the Foreign Office favoured, as either desirable or likely to obtain the requisite domestic support. More fundamentally, while the British government sought to execute the treaty stipulations of Versailles with as little coercion as possible, the concern that France's hard-line course vis-à-vis Germany could drag Britain into another continental conflict weighed more heavily than the expectation that an alliance might exert a beneficially reassuring and restraining impact on the difficult *Entente* partner.

Lloyd George was not the only decision-maker who even suspected French leaders seeking to assert a dominance in continental Europe that in his eyes threatened to incite never-ending Franco-German conflict, thus contradicting fundamental British stabilisation interests. Faced with insistent French pleas for an alliance, the British premier would eventually float the idea of a more limited, indeed carefully circumscribed British guarantee, an Anglo-French "defensive pact" that was essentially modelled on the defunct Anglo-American guarantee treaty of 1919 and thus centred on the British pledge of coming to France's aid only in the case of an *unprovoked* German attack.[46] Yet it is important to understand that Lloyd George only saw such a pact as a means to a wider end that he still pursued despite his short-term preoccupations: the

---

[45] War Cabinet minute, W.C. 616a, 15 July 1919, CAB 23/15.
[46] See Steiner (2005), pp. 206–8; Sharp (II/2008), pp. 174–8.

reconstitution of an international concert, now conceived as a European instrument, which drew in Germany and thus became a framework for stabilisation and appeasement in Europe.

But Lloyd George's most pressing concerns lay elsewhere. They pertained to the challenging financial and economic situation that arisen in Britain – and, closely bound up with this, to reparations. Confronting the onset of a sharp recession and rising unemployment – reaching a total of 2 million by the end of 1921 – while it was trying to implement its "home fit for heroes" reform agenda, the Lloyd George government concluded that economic and financial instability lay at the root of the postwar malaise. And it concluded that agreeing at last on a definite settlement of the reparations problem would be essential to restore European and global trade and thus also British prosperity. The first task was to hammer out, finally, a common approach with the French government. Yet British rationales continued to differ sharply from those Millerand pursued and seemed hardly attractive from the French vantage-point. Lloyd George now proposed what he had avoided at Versailles, a fixed sum, and even argued that Germany should set the figure, stressing that all sides should have an interest in a settlement that allowed Germany to recover and that required no or only very limited coercive measures to ensure German compliance.

The British premier and those who oversaw Britain's economic policy were aware of the problem that a revitalised Germany would again become a major competitor on the world market – and would have to increase its exports exponentially to pay reparations. But what counted more at this stage was the realisation that without a German recovery it would be impossible to revive world trade and the interconnected European and world economy, which was certain to harm Britain far more than future German competition. Eventually, the disunited *Entente* Powers accepted, as already noted, the so-called London Schedule of Payments that the Supreme Council had prepared with the help of British and French experts and on 5 May 1921 presented the Fehrenbach government in Berlin with an ultimatum, threatening that if German author-ities refused to accept the Allied claims, now fixed at 132 billion Goldmarks, they would occupy the crucial industrial area of the Ruhr.

Up to this point, German governments had tried to evade substantial reparation payments by stoking inflation and resorting to currency depreca-tion; and they had simply been too weak to pursue any meaningful fiscal and tax reforms to stabilise German finances sufficiently to pay sizeable repar-ations and create conditions for foreign (i.e. chiefly American) loans. The Weimar Republic's fiscal situation continued to be in disarray after the ruinous *vabanque* "strategies" of financing the war through massive borrowing from private sources – and counting on "repayment through victory" – had led to financial disaster at the hour of military defeat. After Versailles, German authorities had tried to blame these difficulties on the horrendous scale of – unwarranted – Allied reparations demands, and in response to the London ultimatum the Fehrenbach Cabinet had promptly resigned. But Wirth, the head of newly formed minority coalition, persuaded a majority of his government to accept the terms of the London Schedule. And he would now pursue a "policy of fulfilment" that in fact was not aimed at making full reparations but rather intended to show that Germany simply did not have the capacity to pay what the *Entente* governments demanded and thereby to prepare the ground for an eventual reduction of their claims.[47] Both Anglo-French hard-headedness and these German tactics essentially sparked what turned into a drawn-out "reparations war" and a protracted financial-cum-political crisis that would reach its climax in the Ruhr conflict of 1923.

As Wirth's minister of reconstruction, Rathenau tried to negotiate a direct Franco-German deal with Loucheur, who by now was minister for the liberated regions, and to revive the older idea of German payments in kind. But when his initiative had failed due to domestic and determined British opposition, Wirth declared that in view of the deepening German financial impasse only a moratorium could "save the situation" and in the autumn of 1921 tried to gain Lloyd George's support for this plan. Yet now the French government vetoed any moves in this direction. Consequently, Wirth informed the Reparation Commission in mid-December that Germany would not be able to pay the instalments that were due in early 1922. This marked the beginning of a worsening pattern of German "non-fulfilment" and ever harsher Anglo-French disagreements about how to react to German default – with Millerand and later Poincaré pushing Lloyd George to agree to coercive measures. As a consequence, hardly any substantial German payments were made to the *Entente* powers. A vicious spiral had begun, which had a highly unsettling effect on postwar Europe as a whole and ultimately only cast a glaring light on what not only Keynes but also American – and of course German – critical observers had long recognised: namely that a fundamentally different approach to the reparations question was urgently needed; and that no practical solution could be envisaged without creating conditions for the flow of – private – American capital to Germany. In the eyes of Hoover, who as secretary of commerce now occupied an increasingly influential position, France's coercive reparations policy rekindled "an atmosphere of war" in Europe both in the political and in the economic sphere.[48]

To overcome the reparation deadlock without having to resort to military enforcement or crippling the German economy, Lloyd George in late 1921 began to develop yet another grand design. This time, it was not a transatlantic but essentially European design to organise a world economic conference with a highly ambitious agenda. One aim of his far-flung and hardly

---

[47] See Krüger (1985), pp. 132–8.
[48] Hoover to Hughes, 24 April 1922, NA RG 59/800.51/316. For British perceptions, see Curzon to British Embassy (Washington), 12 October 1923, *DBFP*, I, XXI, pp. 563 ff.

realistic plans was to create an international consortium for the reconstruction of Bolshevik Russia in which Germany also was to be encouraged to participate. The underlying intention, however, was nothing less than to reintegrate the pariah Germany – and in the longer run Soviet Russia – not only into a reformed European economic system but also into a reconfigured European political order on terms of equality. At the same time, Lloyd George was determined to persuade Poincaré to accept a moratorium on reparations; and he cherished the unrealistic hope of using the conference setting to negotiate a more "workable" reparations agreement. Moreover, and further overburdening the conference agenda, he proposed the conclusion of a general non-aggression pact that was to oblige all signatories, including the German and Soviet governments – to collaborate peacefully in efforts to prevent future wars.[49]

Counting on an American interest to participate in the consortium scheme, the obstinate British premier hoped to prevail on the Harding administration to take part in the envisaged conference. But this was not a realistic expectation as long as there was no convincing British strategy to come up with a reconstruction scheme that the US government could deem acceptable and to assure the difficult but vital American power that involvement in Europe would not expose it to European pressures for debt relief. What Lloyd George had in mind thus remained limited by ineluctably remaining a European design. Yet it was also unrealistically ambitious in itself. It was indeed supposed to bypass and then to reform the Versailles system in ways that his Fontainebleau agenda had foreshadowed – and though he actually sought to maintain the *Entente* it also went against the grain of all that French leaders struggled to do at this stage.

Apart from preparing the ground in relations with Washington, shoring up the partnership with France and working out a *quid pro quo* agreement on how to approach the cardinal issues of reparations and security was a crucial precondition for even a partial success of Lloyd George's plans. This was attempted in protracted and acrimonious negotiations in London, Cannes, Paris and Boulogne in the winter of 1921–22. But the British premier never got anywhere near establishing this indispensable consensus. And for his French counterparts these "consultations" proved even more frustrating. Meeting with him in London in December 1921, Briand sounded out Lloyd George about the possibility of concluding a "broad defensive alliance" in return for French assent to his grand design. But at the subsequent Anglo-French conference at Cannes, the utmost the British premier was prepared to offer was a "ten-year non-reciprocal defensive pact", which again was limited to the scenario of an unprovoked German aggression and only extended to "consultations" if

---

[49] Lloyd George remarks, Genoa, April 1922, *DBFP*, XIX, 340–3. Sharp (II/2008), pp. 191–3; Steiner (2005), pp. 207–12.

Germany violated the demilitarisation clauses regarding the Rhineland. This could hardly satisfy Briand. During an acid encounter with Lloyd George in Paris in mid-January 1922, Poincaré reiterated that his government could only accept a firm Anglo-French security pact that comprised reciprocal guarantees to maintain – in essence – the *status quo* of 1919, the pledge to sanction any German violations in the Rhineland severely and, significantly, a robust military convention. Yet this in turn proved unacceptable to the British Cabinet. Lloyd George made some effort to mediate but Curzon, reflecting the views of a majority, insisted that no British government could sign a pact that would oblige Britain to defend the unsustainable status quo on the Rhine and the equally unstable status quo in Eastern Europe (while thereby de facto propping up an undesirable French hegemony on the European continent).[50]

Following the British government's decision to suspend any further talks about an Anglo-French pact, Poincaré, who harboured a profound scepticism vis-à-vis Lloyd George's entire approach and grand design, underscored that France would only participate in what became the Genoa conference if the entire complex of reparations was kept off the agenda. And he adamantly insisted on this at an even more glacial meeting with the British premier at Boulogne in late February 1922. The British premier nonetheless pushed ahead, and the Genoa conference would take place. But the lack of even a minimal concord with France, compounded by the absence of the United States, meant that his entire scheme, and scheming, was not just premature – it was all but bound to end in failure even if no further complications arose at the conference itself, which of course could not be expected.[51]

The Genoa conference, which Lloyd George praised as "the greatest gathering of European nations which has ever been assembled on this continent", went on from 10 April till mid-May 1922 and was indeed attended by representatives from 34 states, including the new German foreign minister Rathenau and the Soviet High Commissar for Foreign Affairs, Georgy Chicherin.[52] Crucially, however, not a single envoy from the American government travelled to Genoa, and nor did the French premier Poincaré. And Lloyd George's aspiration to negotiate a new relationship between the capitalist powers and Bolshevik Russia remained as stillborn as his plans to boost European reconstruction and reform the Versailles system in one grand move. Essentially, the conference ended in failure, and what followed in the wake of this failure was a further and decisive deterioration of the European post-Versailles crisis.[53]

The ambition of the British prime minister to effect a reparations moratorium and use direct negotiations between the *Entente* Powers and the Wirth

[50] Curzon memorandum, 28 December 1921, *DBFP*, XVI, p. 862.
[51] See Sharp (1984), pp. 22–64; Steiner (2005), pp. 211–12; Jackson (2013), pp. 384–95
[52] Lloyd George remarks, Genoa, April 1922, *DBFP*, XIX, 340 ff.; Steiner (2005), pp. 207–12.
[53] See Fink (1984); Fink, Frohn and Heideking (1991); Steiner (2005), pp. 207–12.

government as a conduit for integrating Germany into a recast postwar order "beyond Versailles" was more or less thwarted from the start by Poincaré's veto against broaching this subject in Genoa. That the latter refused to participate in the negotiations and dispatched instead the deputy premier Louis Barthou, under strict instructions, underscored that Lloyd George's room to manoeuvre to negotiate some kind of compromise was basically close to zero. For its part, the German government had earlier rejected the conditions for a moratorium that the Reparation Commission had proposed. Yet what then essentially undercut all prospects of a turnaround towards more constructive talks at Genoa was that the fundamentals of the then famous and often misinterpreted agreement became known that Rathenau and Chicherin had thrashed out separately, at the nearby sea resort of Rapallo, on 16 April.

Under considerable domestic pressure, the German foreign minister had come to the conference with the general fear that it would prove impossible to negotiate more favourable moratorium terms and the German attempt to re-enter the international arena on equal terms would once again be rebuffed. But his more specific concern was that Britain and France would strike a separate deal with the Bolshevik regime that would bring together Allied reparation and Russian indemnity demands vis-à-vis Germany. To prevent this was the core purpose of the Rapallo treaty in which Germany and the Soviet Union renounced all financial or territorial claims against one another and pledged to assume "normal" relations. Though soon mythicised as such, Rapallo was by no means the starting-point of Soviet–German economic, political and military cooperation that ineluctably led, *inter alia*, to future covert collaboration between the *Reichswehr* and the Red Army. It was by no means a treaty from which a direct line can be drawn to the Hitler–Stalin Pact of 1939. But in western minds it revived the spectre of a German-Bolshevik revisionist alliance that had haunted western statesmen since Versailles. And this proved highly detrimental for the German government and the prospects of a substantive *rapprochement* between the western powers and the Weimar Republic.

In the immediate context of Genoa, Rathenau had to pay a high price for his Rapallo initiative. He not only had to countenance a letter of censure and accept that the German delegates were banned from the resuming negotiations between the *Entente* governments and the Soviet delegation. He also suffered a major setback for his wider agenda, seeing his hope that Germany would re-enter the comity of advanced nations as an equal power dashed.[54] Yet Lloyd George's diplomatic defeat was even more disastrous, and would soon be preceded by his fall from power. While he managed to prevent a complete break-up of the Genoa proceedings, what had been intended as a grand initiative to re-launch Europe on new path to peace and prosperity lay in tatters.

[54] See Krüger (1985), pp. 155 ff., 166–78.

The actors who chiefly influenced the international policies of the Harding administration observed Lloyd George's travails of Genoa from a safe distance. Both Hughes and Hoover thought that the United States had a vested interest in overcoming the old-style power-political considerations that in their view animated France's reparations "war" against Germany.[55] And they held that it was imperative – not least from the standpoint of US creditor and export interests – to chart new paths, first towards an economic revitalisation of Europe, then towards its political pacification. But both were also convinced that it was of cardinal strategic importance to avoid direct political entanglements in Europe's intractable postwar quarrels and maintain a posture of aloofness until they judged the conditions more auspicious, or until the European crisis had reached such a depth that it would be possible to orchestrate a "solution" on American terms as an informal hegemon– without making unwelcome concessions or assuming undesirable political commitments. As noted, their outlook was undoubtedly influenced by their assessment of the narrow leeway Congressional aversions to international entanglements left for US foreign policy in the wake of Wilson's fiasco in the treaty fight. Yet Hughes also sought to make a virtue of necessity. He reckoned that an uncompromising insistence on US debt claims would eventually compel Britain and France to limit their excessive indemnity demands and agree to a workable reparations settlement that would actually allow them to repay their obligations to the United States. At the same time, he reasoned, this would prevent crippling Germany, which remained America's potentially most important trading partner and market for exports and investments on the European continent, and which he also desired to see politically stabilised as a crucial element of a new order of democratic and liberal-capitalist states he envisaged beyond the perimeters of Versailles.[56]

Yet like Hoover – and the influential Treasury Secretary Mellon – Hughes had concluded early on that Lloyd George's far-flung and poorly prepared Genoa scheme offered no realistic way to come to terms with any of Europe's massive postwar problems and in fact bore major risks for the American "world creditor". They thus made sure that the US government would not be co-opted to fund them through debt concessions or fresh capital. And the failure of the Genoa conference only reinforced what had by then become the underlying outlook in Washington: that the European crisis still had to get worse before conditions could get better – and not only the German government but also the leaders and parliaments of the *Entente* Powers would be "ripe" for a remedy on terms determined by the Harding government, terms

---

[55] Hoover to Hughes, 24 April 1922, NA RG 59/800.51/316.
[56] Hughes address, 29 December 1922, in Hughes (1925), pp. 53–7; Schuker (1991), pp. 98 ff.

that would not really cost the administration anything either politically or financially.

Indeed, in the wake of the Genoa debacle the European situation worsened rapidly, and Hughes' calculations would largely been borne out. Driven in part by an accumulation of frustrations with France's British and American wartime allies, Poincaré eventually saw no other alternative but to pursue the French search for reparations and security by unilateral means – and indeed by going beyond of the terms that had been set at Versailles. Seizing on a plan that had been drafted as early as April 1921, he ordered French troops to enter and occupy the German industrial heartland of the Ruhr, which they did, accompanied by Belgian forces, on 11 January 1923. Whether the most assertive French leader of the 1920s merely sought to seize a strategic pawn to compel the German government to resume reparations payments or whether he indeed pursued more far-reaching aspirations of extending French control and influence beyond the Rhine – also through renewed efforts to encourage separatism in the Rhineland – is still the subject of debate. And it is certainly true that he was more "moderate" than other, less influential French actors like the commander of the French army of the Rhine, General Degoutte, who now saw a chance to remedy the shortcomings of Versailles and came forward with even more grandiose schemes to break up Germany's political unity and return to some kind of re-imagined status quo ante 1870.

But regardless of whether the French premier ultimately intended to undermine the German state and establish an "artificial" French hegemony in Europe, what he set in motion would not only provoke a strong German reaction, which culminated in a concerted campaign of "passive resistance" against the French occupation. It would also lead the Weimar Republic towards the brink of political collapse and disintegration while reviving radicalised German nationalism in the defensive struggle against France's excursion. More importantly, however, it provoked unintended consequences in an almost classic fashion. For the French intervention sparked the crucial systemic crisis of the post-Versailles period. It was a disruptive crisis that did not spawn a new era of assertive French predominance but rather a remarkably far-reaching transformation of the postwar international system – the construction of a recast Atlantic order that transcended essential limits of the Paris settlement and was decidedly more conducive to European and global peace than the outcome of 1919.

23

Towards a New Order

Constructive Learning Processes and the Construction
of an Atlantic Peace beyond Versailles

In contrast to the "really-existing" Versailles system, the peace system that now took shape for the first time addressed the underlying systemic established essential underpinnings for what political and economic stabilisation could be achieved in post–First World War Europe. Essential foundations for the new system were created through two salient settlements, the London reparations accords of August 1924 and the Locarno security pact of October 1925. These were the first major agreements that were actually negotiated between the western powers and Germany after the Great War; and they established not only a *modus operandi* to come to terms with the vexing reparations problem but also a fledgling *common* Euro-Atlantic security architecture. At the same time, they laid the groundwork for the stabilisation and international integration of a democratic Germany.

The pathbreaking accords of London and Locarno thus achieved what had proved impossible in 1919: they inaugurated a sea change in the sphere of international politics. The American and European protagonists of the mid-1920s went far towards achieving what their predecessors at Versailles had not accomplished, and in many ways could not yet accomplish immediately after the Great War. They began to work out principles and ground-rules through which the only viable path towards a sustainable and more broadly legitimate order could be opened up – principles and ground-rules that could underpin balanced *and reciprocal* agreements that were forged with, not against, the representatives of the embattled Weimar Republic.[1]

What the agreements of London and Locarno initiated thus really began to supersede the ill-founded Versailles system and to create a new system of international politics. A change of paradigm took place, even if it was more pronounced in Europe than in the United States. What came to be superseded was the earlier postwar politics of French coercion, British "limited liability"-thinking and American aloofness and, on the other side, German resistance, hapless fulfilment and festering revisionism. What came to prevail instead was

---

[1] On the significance of the London and Locarno settlements, see the different interpretations of Steiner (2005), pp. 182–255, 387–410, and Cohrs (2006), pp. 77–270.

a common resolve to take on the hard political task to negotiate mutually acceptable compromises and to develop mutually binding rules and approaches to the big questions the war *and* the peace conference had left behind.

It has to be stressed, of course, that those who shaped American and British policies were and felt comparatively less compelled to recast their pursuits fundamentally; and they had to make fewer concessions – in terms of either strategic commitments or political and financial costs. The most difficult and politically most costly reorientations had to occur, and did occur, in France and Germany. Yet no significant advances would have been possible if those who now became the standard-bearers of peaceful change in London, Washington and New York had not managed to find new and better ways to play the roles that only they could play in the post–First World War international system. More concretely, only they were able to mediate and foster not just a Franco-German peace process but also a wider process of accommodation and conciliation between the western powers and Germany. This they now began to do, and the developments they spurred were more favourable to the creation of a new international equilibrium, and a more mutually acceptable order, than what had been tried in 1919.

I.   A Time to Draw Harder Lessons. The Salient Learning and Reorientation Processes of the mid-1920s

In the final analysis, what made the transformative settlements of the mid-1920s possible and ushered in a new period of relative but remarkable stabilisation and pacification in Europe were more fundamental changes in both individual and collective outlooks on both sides of the Atlantic. Ultimately, what occurred and proved decisive were substantial learning and reorientation processes. In some ways, it was the crucial post-Versailles crisis of 1923 that led the decision-makers and wider elites who now were in charge to reassess and draw harder lessons from the far greater crisis of the Great War, the shortcomings of the Paris settlement and the destructive developments of the early 1920s. And this in turn led them to conclude that the time had come to pursue different strategies and develop new *transatlantic* responses that also set an example for the world.

Of decisive consequence for initiating the transformative processes of the mid-1920s was that, in reaction to the escalating Franco-German conflict over the Ruhr, the American secretary of state Hughes instigated a marked reorientation of US policy vis-à-vis Europe. Earlier, Hughes had adopted the maxim that in order to safeguard core American interests and prepare the ground for an effective intervention in the future, the American government had to maintain an unequivocal posture of aloofness from the European postwar *malaise* – and wait for the European antagonists either to exhaust themselves and reach an untenable deadlock or to create political preconditions and signal that they would accept a "solution" on American terms, as he defined them.

Hughes' priorities were also still conditioned by his keen awareness of the domestic strictures he faced. He had witnessed first-hand the resistance Wilson had encountered during the treaty fight in the Senate, and he continued to act on the premise that his room to manoeuvre to pursue a more proactive stabilisation policy in Europe was markedly constricted.

Reaching beyond earlier, more parochially defined forms of economic diplomacy and "isolation", Hughes advanced a new doctrine of *targeted* US engagement, essentially envisaging the American administration in the role of an informal and "neutral" arbiter that kept a distance from official political commitments. The guiding principles of its pursuits, he declared, should be "Independence" and "Co-operation", by which he meant unofficial cooperation, which notably involved unofficial agents like financiers and financial experts, rather than "alliances and political entanglements". Yet what Hughes actually sought to foster was a more far-ranging evolutionary reform, indeed a transformational process. He aspired to the creation of a new kind of peace system under US auspices that was less ambitiously defined than Wilson's "new order" but in many ways also distinctly Wilsonian. Put differently, he aspired to pursue Wilson's aspirations of creating a new progressive international order based on a superior American model of rationality and modern political and economic standards by other means – where necessary by making some strategic commitments, yet wherever possible without taking on burdensome formal responsibilities.

At one point, Hughes spoke of his aim to foster an essentially transatlantic community of ideals and interests between "liberty-loving and peace preserving democracies" that would comprise not only Britain, France but also, along with other democratic and liberal-capitalist states, Weimar Germany. Within this community, the United States was to act as a new kind of benign informal hegemon. But the rather far-sighted secretary of state also warned that while it was generally assumed that "democracies are disposed to peace" this was yet "to be demonstrated", as the Great War had shown how "deep feeling and a national sense of injury" could also dispose not only autocracies but also democracies to war, particularly when their leaders "inflame(d) popular passion". The task of enlightened statesmanship was thus to strive for reasonable "international agreements" and maintain peace while taking into account "both the advantages and disadvantages of democratization".[2]

While his outlook was global, Hughes did not espouse Wilson's global-universalist language but rather championed a nuanced approach that sought to promote global regimes where this seemed imperative, as in the sphere of naval arms control, but mainly focused on the creation of effective and specific

---

[2] Hughes speech, 12 November 1921, in Hughes (1925), p. 25; Hughes address, 4 September 1923, *ibid.*, pp. 11–12.

regional systems of order, especially the three areas where US interests were most affected: the American hemisphere, where he proposed an "enlightened" Monroe Doctrine; the Far East, where particularly the future status of China had to be renegotiated; and Europe.

In 1921 and 1922 Hughes had played a pivotal role in establishing the Washington system and negotiating with representatives from Britain, France, Japan and Italy the first effective naval arms control and disarmament regime. And he had also led parallel efforts to conclude a nine-power treaty which he hailed as a "Magna Carta" for China that would hence safeguard its sovereignty and set it on a path towards genuine self-determination.[3] In both cases, Hughes was prepared to assume formal commitments on behalf of the United States. In fact, the Washington accords did not mark a real breakthrough to this end, and hardly already established a viable new *status quo* in East Asia at large or in China. Here, the leader of the nationalist Kuomintang forces, Chiang Kai-shek, would soon seek to marginalise a burgeoning communist movement yet in a wider context the stage was set for a long struggle between nationalists and communist forces under Mao. Yet what the protagonists of the Washington Conference thrashed out could potentially become an important stepping-stone for the creation of a less blatantly imperialist "order" in the Far East, not least because the agreements were supported by, and actually strengthened, Japanese leaders like the later foreign minister Shidehara Kijuro and prime minister Hamaguchi Osachi, who advocated a comparatively liberal and cooperative foreign policy – at least in relations with the western powers. And on the margins of the seminal Washington Conference, Hughes and the Lloyd George government joined forces to persuade Japan's representatives to hand back Shandong to the Chinese government, thus reversing one of the most controversial decisions of 1919. All in all, the Washington system thus became one important building-block of the new global order that began to emerge in the 1920s.

Pointing to the rational search for a "just and reasonable basis for accord" that in his view had made these outcomes possible, Hughes subsequently urged the European governments to emulate the model of the Washington Conference to settle the issues that continued to divide them.[4] When he thought the time was ripe for an American solution Hughes then took the decisive step of re-issuing a proposal he had already made on the eve of the Ruhr conflict, in December 1922 – and which in fact revived ideas that Wilson and US experts had sought in vain to implement at Versailles. What became known as the Hughes plan hinged on the premise that the most equitable and efficient way to settle both the reparations dispute and the wider Franco-German

[3] Hughes speech, 12 November 1921, in Hughes (1925), pp. 20–31; Hughes memorandum, 1 July 1924, in Bemis (1928), X, p. 369.
[4] Hughes speech, 29 December 1922, in Hughes (1925), pp. 32–3.

conflict that lurked behind it lay in "depoliticising" both – as it were, to lift the problem out of the sphere of antagonistic politics by authorising an international committee of experts to recommend a workable solution. Hughes insisted that Europe's "rehabilitation" could only be assured if the political integrity of Weimar Germany was preserved and it was allowed to recuperate and to stabilise. And he was aware that his expert proposal was in fact an eminently political act, informed by overriding US interests.

Crucially, the secretary of state now signalled that the American government was prepared, not to play the official "rôle of arbiter" but to cast its political weight behind the expert solution – yet only once all European governments, including the French, had unanimously committed themselves to his terms and created the basic conditions for "effective international co-operation".[5] At the same time, Hughes signalled that he was prepared to use both the carrots and the sticks that the American government had at its disposal. He intimated that the Coolidge administration would be favourably disposed towards facilitating the working of a new reparations settlement through *private* American capital. And he calculated, like Wilson had before him, that by insisting on a repayment of Allied war debts he could de facto compel Britain and France to agree to expert terms that actually worked, permitting Germany to recover and putting them in a position to repay their obligations to the United States.

Hughes' pursuits played a pivotal part in paving the way for deliberations of a US-dominated expert committee that in April 1924 produced the highly consequential Dawes Plan. No less important, however, was that these developments set in motion an even more significant process in the sphere of European international politics – namely, for the first time since 1918, a process of accommodation between the French, British and German governments in which Britain's first Labour premier Ramsay MacDonald came to act as a crucial transatlantic mediator. Aided by a plethora of officials and advisers, MacDonald, the new socialist French premier Édouard Herriot and the new key political actor in Germany, the chancellor and then long-serving foreign minister Gustav Stresemann, succeeded in turning the recommendations of the Dawes Committee into the first politically viable and truly negotiated political compromise settlement after the Great War that all sides could legitimise – the reparations settlement that was then finalised in London in August 1924.

Assuming responsibility at a time when the escalating Ruhr conflict threatened to provoke no less than a disintegration of the Weimar Republic, Stresemann had fervently welcomed Hughes' intervention in the autumn of 1923. He regarded the establishment of an American-backed expert committee as the essential step for

---

[5] *Ibid.*, pp. 55–6; Hughes to Kellogg, 24 June 1924, *FRUS* 1924, II, p 32; Hughes to Howard, 1 May 1924, NA RG 59 462.00 R296/262; Morrow to Hughes, 12 July 1924, Lamont Papers, TWL 176/13; Hughes to Laboulaye, 9 May 1924, Hughes Papers.

a political settlement of the crisis; and he had created essential preconditions for such a settlement by making and implementing the domestically controversial decision to abandon "passive resistance".[6] Subsequently, Stresemann was quick to endorse the recommendations of the Dawes committee For in his view what the experts proposed would not only ensure the preservation of Germany's political and economic unity, and France's withdrawal from the Ruhr – which were his most immediate priorities – but could also serve as a basis for "an economically reasonable solution of the reparations question" that significantly reduced German payments.[7] But an even more important consideration motivating him was essentially political. In short, he reckoned that if a door could be opened to reparations negotiations on American terms, this would allow Germany finally to escape its postwar isolation and enter into a new, mutually advantageous pattern of cooperation and interdependence with the United States – and Britain. Further, and crucially, this was also to create more favourable conditions for what was much harder to achieve, yet imperative in his judgement: an accommodation of interests with France.

Once a strident advocate of far-reaching imperial-annexationist war aims – almost until the final stages of the war – Stresemann had by this time not just gone far towards redefining himself as a "rational republican" and emerging as the Weimar Republic's preeminent statesman. He had also drawn harder lessons from the fiasco of the war, his own wartime illusions and the harsh realities of Europe's profound postwar crisis, which had mercilessly exposed Germany's powerlessness and status as an "object" of international politics. All of this reinforced his conviction that especially those who sought to shape German international policies had the pre-eminent task of finding and pursuing different, more realistic aims and strategies. More systematically and substantially than Brockdorff-Rantzau in 1919 and all his other predecessors of the early 1920s, Stresemann began to conceptualise and pursue a forward-looking western-orientated policy that was informed by core assumptions he had developed about the intricate interdependence of modern international politics, economics and finance. The guiding maxims he formulated were that a pragmatic accommodation and cooperation with the western powers constituted an existential interest of the fledgling German republic, and that in order to make progress in this direction, one had to craft strategies that built on the essential "interconnectedness" of world-economic interests. On these premises, Stresemann sought to pursue a foreign policy that used "the only element which still makes us a great power: our economic power".[8]

[6] See Wright (2002), pp. 203–59.
[7] Stresemann, *Reichstag* speech, 12 August 1923, *SB*, vol. 361, pp. 11839–40.
[8] Stresemann, *Reichstag* speech, 25 November 1922, *SB*, vol. 357, p. 9157. Stresemann speech, *Vossische Zeitung*, 17 December 1920, Stresemann Papers, vol. 216; Stresemann speech, 22 November 1925, in Turner (1967), p. 434.

Like other German liberals before him, Stresemann was convinced that a paramount interest in reviving an "open", interdependent and mutually advantageous system of international trade, capital flows and economic recuperation linked Germany, the United States and Britain – and that this would ultimately foster a common interest in reforming the order of Versailles. Yet he also realised that in view of Germany's structural preponderance finding a way to negotiate changes that were also deemed advantageous in France would be a far harder task. Nonetheless, Stresemann was determined to seize on the powerful nexus of political and economic interests to attain his overriding objective: to integrate a consolidated republican and liberal-capitalist German state into what he conceived of as an essentially Euro-Atlantic postwar order, and to re-establish Germany as a modern great power with equal rights within this system.[9] To this end, preparing the ground for a "return" of the United States to Europe was crucial. Stresemann indeed operated on the premise that "the decisions about Europe's future" lay "essentially in the hands of the United States".[10]

His most important collaborator in the Foreign Office, the later Under-Secretary Carl von Schubert, fundamentally shared these priorities and Stresemann's both European and Atlantic outlook. Schubert had early noted that the aim to return to "the concert of powers as an equal partner" had to be the underlying rationale of a new, republican German foreign policy.[11] All of this echoed what Brockdorff-Rantzau, Erzberger and Scheidemann had begun to formulate in 1919. But it now became part of a much more comprehensive and realistic strategy, which probably could only be developed with at least some distance from the Great War and the German collapse of 1918.

Unquestionably, Stresemann sought to revise the Versailles system. But the core aim of the republican foreign policy that he and Schubert developed was not to put Germany in a position in which it could eventually cast off the yoke of 1919 by aggressive means or even by military force. Rather, they pursued revisionist policy as a policy of peaceful change, international reintegration and the accommodation of interests. And this opened up new avenues for working towards a more durable transatlantic order and anchoring Germany within it. Making his mark as the most significant proponent of such a course in post–First World War Germany, Stresemann would show remarkable resilience in his efforts to pursue and legitimise it in the face of considerable domestic resistance in and beyond the *Reichstag*, and in a very adverse

---

[9] Stresemann, *Reichstag* speech, 28 April 1921, in Stresemann (1926), I, p. 362. Stresemann, *Reichstag* speech, 25 November 1922, *SB*, vol. 357, p. 9157. Stresemann speech, *Vossische Zeitung*, 17 December 1920, Stresemann Papers, vol. 216.

[10] Stresemann to Maltzan, 7 April 1925, Stresemann Papers, H 158699.

[11] Schubert to Haniel, 17 June 1920, Schubert Papers, vol. II.

domestic-political environment characterised by disunity and polarisation rather than a "culture of compromise".[12]

Unsurprisingly, in contrast to Stresemann, Poincaré only accepted the recommendations of the Dawes Committee very reluctantly and under now rapidly increasing Anglo-American pressure. He was simply no longer in a position to hold on to the "productive pledges" France had seized in the Ruhr. And he had no choice in the end but to accept that neither his aim to force Germany to meet its reparation obligations – and Britain to back France's agenda – nor his ill-defined broader agenda to extend French influence and control beyond the limits of 1919 would be realised. Indeed, Poincaré's Ruhr strategy proved disastrous. And reactions in London and Washington threw into relief that, as at the Paris Peace Conference, French attempts to weaken or even dissolve not only the economic unity but also the political integrity of Germany would encounter determined British and American opposition. In fact, he had led France into a situation of dangerous overreach and isolation from those powers on whose cooperation France's future security and development depended. Yet what the French premier pursued was not just incompatible with British and American priorities; more fundamentally, it was indeed irreconcilable with the longer-term requirements of a stable international order in Europe and the Atlantic sphere.[13]

Poincaré's successor, the moderate Radical Socialist Édouard Herriot, whose *Cartel des Gauches* had won a decisive victory in the French elections in May 1924, not least because of widespread public disillusionment with the Ruhr imbroglio, thus confronted a highly precarious situation. And his often hapless pursuits would further weaken the feeble bargaining position he had inherited. Yet Herriot struggled hard to carve out a more constructive policy, early on confirming that his government would accept an "international solution" of the reparations and Ruhr quarrel. By mid-June, he declared that he was determined to depart from his predecessor's "policy of isolation and force", abandon the attempt to seize "territorial pledges" and chart a course that was more accommodating vis-à-vis Germany and, above all, repaired France's strained relations with Britain and the United States.[14] In fact, against the background of France's isolated position and fiscal *malaise* he hardly had a viable alternative; he more or less had to accept the American terms of reference, which the British government had also come to support.

Nonetheless, by trying to contribute to a negotiated "international solution" to overcome the reparations and Ruhr impasse, Herriot actually initiated a necessary process of reorientation, of departing from French postwar strategies

---

[12] See Winkler (2018); Mommsen (1989); Bracher (1978), p. 64.
[13] For different interpretations, see Keiger (1997), pp. 310–11; Jackson (2013), pp. 407–11; Jeannesson (1998), pp. 333 ff.; Fischer (2003), 243–57; McDougall (1978), pp. 360–79.
[14] Herriot speech, *JOC*, Débats, 17 June 1924, pp. 2305 ff.

that had proved to diminish rather than strengthen French security and prosperity. In principle, the new socialist premier favoured a renewed attempt to
solve France's security problem by strengthening the League's arbitration and
sanctions regime. Yet he also desperately sought to obtain – at last – more far-
reaching British security commitments, eventually proposing an extensive
Anglo-French security pact.[15] All of these initiatives would be frustrated.
But – although he was accused by the Poincarist and nationalist opposition of
betraying cardinal strategic interests – it was indeed Herriot who began to
reorientate French policy towards a more cooperative approach, which Briand
would then expand into a more comprehensive new strategy when he returned
to power as foreign minister in April 1925. This shift was aided by leading
officials in the French Foreign Office, notably Charles Seydoux.[16]

Against the background of these incipient changes in Germany and France, it
fell to the new Labour prime minister in Britain, Ramsay MacDonald, to
assume – with Hughes' background support an essential mediating role at
this *caesura* of postwar politics. Because the US secretary of state insisted that
the Coolidge administration would not become officially involved, it was indeed
MacDonald who, with the help of Eyre Crowe and other senior Foreign Office
officials, managed not only to commit the French government to a reparation
settlement on Anglo-American premises but also, and crucially, to pave the way
for the decisive paradigm shift in Euro-Atlantic politics after the First World
War. He instigated a process that led to actual, substantive negotiations between
western and German representatives and, on this basis, the search for a mutually acceptable political agreement. More fundamentally, MacDonald believed
that changes in "psychology" and mentality that he deemed critical for peace
could only be spurred through concrete cooperation between political decision-
makers, not by abstract covenants – and that this could then encourage wider
necessary changes in collective mentalities and attitudes in societies that had so
recently been affected by war mentalities and war-induced nationalism.[17]

As a fervent internationalist, MacDonald had been, as noted, one of the
most strident critics of the peace settlement of 1919, which in his view was
animated by a "logic of war" to which ultimately Wilson had succumbed as
well. He thus had demanded that the unstable "armistice" the peace conference had brought should be superseded as soon as possible by a "real peace",
an internationalist peace negotiated with the newly republican Germany and
transforming the League from an instrument of the victors into the core

---

[15] Herriot statement in the *Chambre*, 19 June 1924, *Journal Officiel (Chambre)*, 1924,
2340–1.
[16] See Jackson (2013), pp. 427–57.
[17] MacDonald minute, 3 July 1924, FO 371/9818; MacDonald statement 15 August 1924,
Proceedings of the London Reparations Conference, II, CAB 29/103–4, pp. 7–8;
MacDonald (I/1923).

institution of international cooperation and conciliation.[18] These were the higher aims he now sought to pursue as prime minister. But his most immediate concern was that of settling a Franco-German crisis that, he feared, could spark another continental conflagration. After the Baldwin government had warned Poincaré in October 1923 that Britain would not tolerate the disintegration of Germany or attempts to sever the Rhineland or other parts from the German state, MacDonald, then a leading figure in the Labour opposition, had been even more emphatic in condemning French actions. He had warned that Germany's political disintegration would have disastrous consequences not only for Britain's prosperity, but also for the peace and stability of Europe.[19]

The most committed Atlanticist among Britain's leading decision-makers in the 1920s, MacDonald was convinced that in order to prevent such a scenario it was imperative to cooperate as far as possible with the American government. And once he had become prime minister he declared early on that an implementation of the American-induced "expert plan" opened up the best prospects for Europe's longer-term pacification.[20] Yet the Labour premier intended to build on the recommendations of the Dawes Committee not to "depoliticise" postwar international relations but rather to foster a newly constructive mode of political conflict resolution, a mode of international politics that transcended the divisions of the war and of the Paris Peace Conference. Above all, this was to bring French decision-makers and the "moral élite" of Weimar Germany's government, whom he considered "sincere spirits who were truly democratic", to the negotiating table on equal terms. And with this aim in mind, the Labour premier was willing to accept in a spirit of pragmatism key terms of reference set by the Republican government in Washington and by representatives of US high finance – even though he continued to criticise American laissez-faire capitalism very harshly.[21]

As a mediator, MacDonald had few concrete incentives to offer when he sought to persuade Herriot to agree to a settlement on the basis of the Dawes report. Committed to his own vision of "general and more universal [League-based] arrangements for ... non-aggression" and conflict resolution, the British premier was not prepared to endorse Herriot's proposal for an old-style bilateral pact. He insisted that he would reject any "sectional alliances" and "give no guarantees of a special kind" to France.[22] Nor were he and his "iron"

---

[18] MacDonald (1919); Miller (1967), p. 86; Labour Party Annual Conference Report 1922, p. 193.
[19] MacDonald to Knox (Berlin), 6 May 1924; MacDonald to Crewe, 26 January 1924, DBFP I, XXVI, nos 462, 344.
[20] MacDonald to D'Abernon, 29 May 1924, MacDonald Papers, MDP 30/69/94.
[21] Ibid.; MacDonald statement, The Free Trader, December 1925, p. 265; MacDonald statements, 8 July 1924, DBFP, I, XXVI, no. 507, pp. 753–6.
[22] MacDonald to Addison, 26 February 1924, FO 371/9801; MacDonald (II/1923), pp. 19–20; MacDonald (1925).

chancellor of the exchequer Philip Snowden willing to countenance scaling down Britain's debt demands vis-à-vis France. Instead, MacDonald exerted considerable pressure and impressed on Herriot in the spring of 1924 that only a workable reparations agreement that was negotiated with Germany would allow France to resort from its present crisis. And he even argued that such a settlement would constitute a decisive step towards placing French security on a sounder footing – by finally laying the basis for a more stable postwar order.[23] More fundamentally, MacDonald aspired to initiate a much more far-reaching reform of the Versailles system, indeed its replacement through a new Atlantic "society" and concert of democratic states, anchored in a reformed League, that not only comprised Weimar Germany but also, in the longer run, a reformed socialist Russia.[24] Yet his most tangible achievement was to prepare the ground for, and convince Herriot to participate in, the seminal London Conference that took place in the summer of 1924.

II.   A Watershed Atlantic Settlement. The Significance of the London Reparation Accords of 1924

The outcome of this conference, the reparations settlement that was signed on 16 August 1924, was a hard-won compromise that can indeed be interpreted as the first genuine peace treaty that was concluded after the Great War. For it was the first agreement that was not more or less unabashedly imposed by the victors on the vanquished but rather the result of real negotiations.[25] And, finalised under Anglo-American auspices, it provided a new groundwork for "the beginning of a real peace" in Europe and, in particular, between France and Germany.[26]

Herriot was later accused of having allowed the Anglo-American powers and Germany to inflict a major defeat on France, undercut the hard-won gains of Versailles and impose a "second Treaty of Frankfurt" as humiliating as the one Bismarck had forced on the Third Republic in 1871. In Germany, those who led left- and right-wing opposition to Stresemann's policies and the "Weimar state" – both the Communist Party's leading ideologue Arthur Rosenberg and the nationalist press magnate and DNVP leader Hugenberg – lambasted the Dawes Plan, with unmistakeable anti-Semitic undertones, as the result of a conspiratorial plot hatched by American

---

[23] MacDonald to Phipps, 24 March 1924, FO 371/9730.

[24] MacDonald statement, *The Times*, 16 February 1924; MacDonald to Grahame, 29 June 1924, *DBFP* I, XXVI, p. 733; MacDonald speech to the League Assembly, 3 September 1924, League of Nations (1924), pp. 41–5; Cmd. 2289: League of Nations (1924), pp. 8–9

[25] See MacDonald statement, 15 August 1924, CAB 29/103-4, Proceedings, II, pp. 7–8.

[26] Herriot statement in the *Chambre* debates, 21 and 23 August 1924 *Journal Officiel (Chambre)*, 1924, 2959, 3076 ff.

Jewish capitalists and their international allies to gain control of the German economy and finance. They thereby introduced themes that Hitler would take up when he raised the National Socialist Party's profile through his vociferous campaign against the later Young Plan at the end of the 1920s.[27]

In fact, however, the watershed accords of London and the Dawes regime had a very different meaning, which those American and European actors who sought to foster a more durable order clearly recognised at the time. They not only ushered in an American "economic peace" but also marked the dawn of a more propitious political stabilisation process in Europe. The London compromise provided no final solution to the reparations dispute that had poisoned postwar politics for such a long time. But it was the first agreement that furnished rules for addressing the issue that had been at the heart of Europe's post-Versailles crisis. The Dawes Plan, whose chief architect was Owen Young, the former chairman of General Electric, furnished a workable preliminary reparations scheme that entailed moderate reductions of German annual payments for a much-needed transition period. And, crucially, it prepared the ground for the decisive initial American 800-million-Goldmarks loan to Germany that was provided through a syndicate led by J.P. Morgan and Co. in October 1924.

What the Dawes regime thus set in motion was a by no means unproblematic unregulated cycle of reparation payments, debt repayment and financial stabilisation through private loans in which US investors came to advance most of what soon became a massive flow of capital to Germany that it then used to meet its obligations to France and Britain, which in turn could be used by them to start repaying the war debts to the United States.[28] That the young US financier Seymour Parker Gilbert became the "king" of the Dawes plan, overseeing its operation as agent general of reparations in Berlin, manifested that the United States now controlled the key mechanism of postwar financial and strategic relations. Clearly, this regime was susceptible to crisis and not the final answer to the post–First World War reparations and debt conundrum. But it provided far better conditions than anything that had been decided in 1919 to make progress in two essential areas: towards setting the Weimar Republic on a path to financial and political stabilisation, and towards setting Europe on a path to consolidation, either of which would have been impossible without a mutually acceptable reparations agreement and American loans.

---

[27] See Rosenberg, *Reichstag* speech, 26 August 1924, *SB*, vol. 381, pp. 944 ff.; Holz (1977), pp. 58–113.

[28] By contrast, the Coolidge administration vetoed further private US loans to France until the French government had followed the British example and both signed and ratified a war-debt settlement on American terms. And, as noted, the Mellon-Bérenger agreement, then concluded in 1926, would only be ratified by the French parliament in 1929. See Artaud (1978).

III. Towards a Euro-Atlantic Security Architecture. The European and Transatlantic Paths that Led to the Locarno Pact of 1925

In a broader perspective, the London settlement and the American economic peace of 1924 had brought about nothing less than a sea change in postwar international politics in Europe and the transatlantic sphere, opening up possibilities for more far-reaching political accommodation and pacification processes. But precisely this sea change also created a new need, and urgency, to accomplish at last what had not been possible in 1919 – namely to come to terms with the unresolved question of security, which had been at the root of European instability ever since the end of the war.

More concretely, what now came to be perceived by leading European policymakers – and, if to lesser extent, their American counterparts – as a both pressing and fundamental necessity was to create, at last, a more effective security system – a system that secured Europe's incipient political-cum-economic stabilisation and that made Germany's incipient revitalisation, and potential re-emergence as a leading power, reconcilable with the security and development needs of France, the states of Eastern Europe and Germany's other neighbours. In a wider perspective, those who now took the lead in instigating a transformational process realised that different paths, ways "beyond Versailles", had to be found. And they recognised that the core task was to create, and secure, a novel, more sustainable *international equilibrium* – by tying Weimar Germany into an architecture of mutual security commitments.

By the autumn of 1925, the basic foundations for such a system had been laid. It would not be predicated on what French leaders had desired since Wilson's defeat, a more robust *entente* or even a fully-fledged Anglo-French alliance, which both MacDonald and his Conservative successor Baldwin rejected. Yet nor would it be based on a strengthened collective security regime of the League. Drawing on ideas developed in the French Foreign Ministry, Herriot had proposed in the autumn of 1924 to introduce, through the so-called Geneva Protocol, what Bourgeois and other juridical internationalists had already called for in 1919: a fortified regime of obligatory arbitration and automatic sanctions, established by amendments to the original Covenant and intended to protect France against the threat of future German aggression.[29]

But, sharing the objections to a rigid regime of this kind that Wilson and Lloyd George had voiced at Versailles, MacDonald endeavoured to turn the Geneva Protocol into an instrument of a qualitatively different system of "collective security". On 4 September 1924, he declared to the League Assembly that the emphasis should be, not on sanctions and enforcement but rather on sealing the advances made at the London Conference by

[29] See Jackson (2013), pp. 457–68; Bariéty (1977), pp. 664–82.

admitting Germany to the League and building up "an elaborate system of universal reconciliation and arbitration" between the former enemies of the war, which bound all to core provisions of collective security and at the same time expedited universal disarmament.[30] Shortly thereafter, the fate of the Geneva Protocol was sealed by the veto of the new conservative government in London.

Predictably, the Coolidge administration also rejected the Protocol. The State Department admonished that the Protocol's "tightened" regime of obligatory and arbitration and sanctions would impinge on the US freedom of action under the Monroe Doctrine and, in Europe, serve the French interest in cementing the status quo rather than the underlying American interest in promoting peaceful change.[31] More fundamentally, the Protocol elicited a re-affirmation of Republican maxims of independence and "non-entanglement" in European security affairs. Earlier, Hughes had confirmed that the most effective way in which the American government could foster European security without risking Congressional opposition was to maintain its "neu-trality" both vis-à-vis European politics and to prod European decision-makers to pursue "rational" rather than divisive measures. He again pointed to the example of a regional security regime that the Washington Conference had set; and he argued that even if the US government, by maintaining an aloof stance, might not always exert its influence "when [it] should", a "large part" of this influence was precisely "due to the fact of our independence".[32]

Hughes' designated successor, Frank Kellogg, operated on exactly the same premises. In October 1924, he confirmed to Coolidge that it was wise for the American government to keep a distance from the Geneva Protocol, the League and "European politics" and, notably, to avoid becoming "bound by any obligations to maintain the political integrity and independence of all the turbulent nations of Europe. Like Hughes, Kellogg was convinced that the United States could exert a far greater influence "if we maintain our freedom of action" while "co-operating in the friendliest spirit with a desire to help" the Europeans."[33]

This general outlook – and the underlying assumption that no significant threats to US national security would emanate from Europe in the foreseeable

---

[30] MacDonald speech before the League Assembly, 4 September 1924, *UF*, vol. 6, no. 1370a; minutes of the British Empire Delegation meetings, 22 September 1924, FO 371/10570: W 8073/134/98

[31] Kellogg to Hughes, 15 October 1924, Kellogg Papers; Fletcher (Rome) to Hughes, 15 December 1924, NA RG 59 511.3131/263; State Department memorandum, 20 November 1924, NA RG 59 FW 511.3131/246.

[32] Hughes to Drummond, 16 June 1924, *FRUS 1924*, II, pp. 80–3; Hughes to Castle, Castle Diary, 5 February 1924, vol. 5, pp. 44–5, Castle Papers; Hughes memorandum to Castle, 7 December 1925, Kellogg Papers.

[33] Kellogg to Coolidge, 7 October 1924, Kellogg Papers.

future – had clearly come to prevail in Washington by 1925. And this of course placed major constraints on intensified transatlantic cooperation in the realm of security politics and, more broadly, on common *political* efforts to advance stabilisation and peaceful change in the latter 1920s. Essentially, the United States thus continued to play the role of an "independent" and unbound arbiter and promoter of European security "behind the scenes". Consequently, the European protagonists were and remained compelled to take steps of their own to address the continent's towering security problems. But they had to do so in a transforming Euro-Atlantic constellation in which American power and leverage had even greater weight than before the *caesura* of 1924.

The security crisis that ensued after the failure of the Geneva Protocol triggered the second decisive phase in the transformation of European and transatlantic politics that occurred in the 1920s. Its most significant result was the emergence of a qualitatively different postwar security architecture "beyond Versailles", which, as it were, provided the most far-reaching response to the core European security question the Great War had left behind. It was an architecture centred on a more specific regional and at the same time integrative European security pact, the pact of Locarno, and a reconfigured European concert comprising Britain, France and Germany that at the same time became a crucial building-block, and instrument, of the new, evolving Euro-Atlantic order. The Locarno concert system – the first of its kind that was negotiated and maintained by *democratic* powers – was essentially western-orientated. And its primary purpose was the stabilisation of Western Europe. Yet it could potentially also become the nucleus of a wider peace system and have a momentous pacifying impact on and beyond Eastern Europe in the longer run – if it could be sustained and developed, with critical American support.

The essential impulse for these momentous developments was given by the security initiative Stresemann launched in January 1925. What he proposed echoed rationales that Erzberger had advanced in 1919; and it incorporated ideas that had animated the futile Rhine pact overture of Chancellor Cuno in December 1922. But Stresemann's proposals chiefly derived from a distinctly more elaborate and precise conception that he had worked out with the help of Schubert and the Foreign Office's key legal expert, Friedrich Gaus. At the core, their pathbreaking proposal foresaw that the German government would enter into an agreement with France and the other powers bordering the Rhine in which all signatories would recognise the inviolability of the territorial status quo that had been set in 1919 – and thus above all the Franco-German border. Italy and, above all, Britain were to act as essential guarantors.[34] A further

---

[34] German memoranda, 20 January and 9 February 1925, *ADAP*, A, XII, nos. 37; 81. See Stresemann statement, 7 March 1925, Stresemann Papers, General Files, vol. 21, 7310/H 158 405-15.

THE POLITICAL CONSEQUENCES OF THE PEACE

central element was the German pledge to renounce war as a means of international policy. To this end, the German notes offered the conclusion of arbitration treaties not only with France, Belgium and other interested states in the west but also with Germany's eastern neighbours. The underlying rationale was that Germany would commit itself to settling all disputes with its neighbours – including territorial disputes – only by peaceful means while keeping open the possibility of *peacefully* altering the Polish-German border. In principle, yet also for domestic-political reasons, the Luther government in Berlin rejected a recognition or guarantee of this border.[35]

Stresemann and Schubert focused their attention on Britain because they understood that it would be impossible to persuade the Coolidge administration to underwrite the Rhine pact they sought. But in fact Stresemann's security strategy merely expanded his approach to pursue *"Weltpolitik"* by diplomatic and *economic* means – and in close alignment with the power that he still regarded as Germany's essential, if politically elusive senior partner, the United States.[36] Yet rather than seeking to cultivate a "special relationship" with the United States outside the League, he calculated – correctly – that it would be far more effective to pursue a pact that fostered European stability, and thus satisfied the interests of the Republican administration in Washington and financiers in New York, without requiring – unrealistic – official US security commitments. The more immediate aim Stresemann pursued was to end military control and to create conditions for an early termination of the occupation of the Rhineland, all to restore German sovereignty in the west. But the more fundamental rationale behind his policy was that only by finding a new way to address overriding French security needs, which he acknowledged, and also committing Britain to this end, would it be possible to prepare the ground for a new, more cooperative pattern of relations with the western powers "beyond the strictures of Versailles". Thus he sought to propel a reform of the postwar order and to pave the way for Germany"s inclusion in a Euro-Atlantic comity of nations as a republican great power with "equal rights". This was and remained the cardinal objective he and Schubert pursued.[37]

Both the foreign minister and his adviser had by this time internalised that a process of peaceful accommodation with France and Britain – and a policy that took French concerns seriously – offered the only realistic path towards

---

[35] Stresemann to Rauscher (Warsaw), 8 March 1924, *ADAP*, A, XI, no. 189. Cf. Baechler (1996), p. 501.

[36] Stresemann, *Reichstag* speech, 16 April 1925, Stresemann Papers, General Files, vol. 23, 7312/H 158741-765; Stresemann to Maltzan (Washington), 7 April 1925, Stresemann (1932), I, p. 78.

[37] Stresemann statements before the *Reichstag's* Foreign Affairs Commission, 11 March 1925, Stresemann Papers, Political Files, vol. 277, 7135/H 148981; Schubert to Haniel, 17 June 1920, Schubert Papers, vol. II.

re-establishing Germany as a modern great power. And what they pursued actually opened up new possibilities of finding a place for Europe's central power in an amended international order. At the core lay the idea to strike a balance between what they perceived as vital German interests and what constituted core requirements of European stability. Yet both were also aware that in order to gain the requisite political support, and wider legitimacy, for their new course in the polarised political spectrum of a German republic that had barely turned the corner from chronic crisis would remain a difficult struggle. While social democrats and liberals backed Stresemann's course, not only the leaders of the German National People's Party would take him to task for the "unacceptable concessions" he offered to France and the wider acceptance of the loathed "Versailles system" that, so they claimed, his overtures implied. Instead, they sought to rouse German public opinion against Stresemann with the unrealistic demand for an immediate "liberation" of the Rhineland.

But Stresemann's security initiative would most likely have remained futile if the new British foreign secretary Austen Chamberlain had not assured the support of the Baldwin government for the pact idea – and, crucially, if he had not managed to play the role that Lloyd George had unsuccessfully tried to assume ever since Versailles: that of an "honest broker" who sought to reassure France in order to draw the Weimar Republic into a renewed European concert system.[38] A voice of reason on reparations in 1919, Chamberlain subsequently underwent a learning and orientation process of his own. After the Baldwin government had rejected the Geneva Protocol, he had initially favoured a more traditional approach and recommended that Britain should finally conclude a bilateral Anglo-French alliance (which Belgium could also join) to calm French fears and deter German revisionism.[39] But, facing the opposition of the majority in the cabinet, Chamberlain came to initiate an important qualitative shift in British postwar policy, seizing on Stresemann's pact proposal but developing it further. The guiding aim of his strategy became to promote an agreement guaranteeing the inviolability of the Franco–German border on the Rhine as a means to overcome European insecurity – and, crucially, to create the nucleus of a new "concert of Europe".[40]

Like Baldwin's combative chancellor of the exchequer, Winston Churchill, Chamberlain was cognisant of the crucial relevance of America's financial and political power as creditor of Britain and sponsor of the Dawes regime. But in contrast to Stresemann he deemed it neither realistic nor desirable that US

[38] Austen to Ida Chamberlain, 28 November 1925, Austen Chamberlain Papers, AC 5/1/370; Chamberlain to Crewe, 2 April 1925, FO 800/257/483.
[39] 192nd CID meeting, 16 December 1924, CAB 24/172, CP 125(25).
[40] Chamberlain to D'Abernon, 18 March 1925, *DBFP*, I, XXVII, no. 255; Chamberlain minute, 19 March 1925, FO 371/10756, C 3539/3539/18.

governments, whose policies in his eyes were narrowly dominated by financial interests and the collection of war debts, should play a significant part in European politics, particularly in the critical domain of security. His scepticism had grown since his observation of Wilson's frustrated ambitions and had then been heightened by what he criticised as the weakness and vacillating passivity of leading Republican decision-makers in the face of Congressional and public pressure.[41] Chamberlain thus sought a European solution and by March 1925 he had espoused the maxim that only Britain had it "in her power at this moment to bring peace to Europe". It was called upon to engage as a pact mediator between France and Germany and, essentially, to find ways to "remove or allay French fears" and to "bring Germany back into the concert of Europe".[42]

More fundamentally, Chamberlain consciously sought to build on what he had identified as the core rationales Castlereagh had pursued at the Congress of Vienna. He observed that it would be vital to close "the gap" that "the more ambitious peacemakers of Versailles" had left when framing the Covenant of the League and to create an integrative concert that overcame the divisions of 1919. What he thereby hoped to foster was a political process that accommodated the German "colossus" at the centre of Europe and at the same time furthered the consolidation of its democratic order, although he reckoned that Germany would require time to overcome its "authoritarian legacy".[43] To this end, he also favoured Germany's admission to the League in the near future. All of this was to create a new international equilibrium in postwar Europe.

Echoing the core concerns Lloyd George had expressed at Versailles, Chamberlain warned that if the western powers failed to accommodate the vanquished power of 1918 the latter would eventually be driven to forge a revisionist alliance with Soviet Russia and threaten to destroy the postwar order.[44] At the same time, in the assessment that came to prevail in the British government the security pact provided a solution that limited British guarantees to what could be legitimised domestically and to what was regarded as the area of vital strategic interest, Western Europe, while precluding undesirable commitments in the east. Chamberlain was not the only British policymaker who in fact expected that German governments would try to "effect changes in the Eastern frontier", particularly vis-à-vis Poland.[45] But the key interest lay in

---

[41] Austen to Ida Chamberlain, 19 June 1926, Austen Chamberlain Papers, AC 5/1/386; Churchill memorandum, 7 February 1925, CAB 24/71(25).

[42] Chamberlain minute, 19 March 1925, FO 371/10756, C 3539/3539/18.

[43] Chamberlain here drew on Headlam-Morley's recommendations. See Chamberlain minute, 21 February 1925; Chamberlain note, 14 March 1925, FO 371/11064/W1252/9/98; 10756: C 3539/3539/18.

[44] Chamberlain note, 25 January 1925, FO 371/11064: W 362/9/98; Cabinet session, 14 April 1925, CAB 23/52/15.

[45] Hansard, Commons, 5th series, vol. 185, cols. 1584 ff.

obliging German policymakers – through the envisaged arbitration treaties – to rule out "recourse to war" and to commit themselves to pursuing such changes only by peaceful "diplomatic" means, essentially through negotiations with the Polish government. The British protagonists argued that such agreements would actually constitute a net gain of "new security", also for Poland, and that, overall, the "general appeasement" that would follow an accord between the western powers and Germany would "tend to render more secure the situation everywhere", also in Eastern Europe, by tying Germany to a western system of rules, restraints and *peaceful* change.[46] These assumptions came to underlie a revived British conception of creating a western "nucleus of certainty, of stability and of security" that could then be expanded and have a stabilising impact on Western *and* Eastern Europe. But this conception encountered marked opposition not only in Warsaw but also in Paris.

Here, the third protagonist of the Locarno process, Aristide Briand, pursued somewhat different priorities. He insisted on stronger safeguards to protect both France and its eastern allies from the danger of future German revisionist pressure. But his overall outlook on the vital importance of placing European international politics – and especially Franco–German relations – on a new footing through the proposed pact converged with those of Stresemann and Chamberlain. Briand re-assumed responsibility for directing French postwar policies, now as foreign minister under Herriot's successor Painlevé, when the first hurdles on the road to Locarno had already been cleared. That he came to champion the security pact and invested a lot of political capital in concluding it – against considerable domestic opposition – partly sprang from the realisation that France no longer had auspicious alternatives. Clearly, Briand's conduct was shaped by the frustrations he had experienced since Versailles, notably when he had tried, in 1921, to fill the hole left by the collapsed Anglo-American guarantee of 1919 through a robust Anglo-French security compact. Now, in 1925, he had to accept that in view of the Baldwin government's support for Stresemann's initiative it would be impossible to "realise a particular Anglo-French accord for the security of the Rhine" or an Anglo-French "pact within the pact" that specified common measures to counter a potential German invasion.[47]

But Briand also came to push forward, and defend against nationalist critics, a more fundamental shift in French postwar policy, which was essentially

---

[46] Chamberlain to Crowe 7 Mach 1925, *DBFP*, I, XXVII, no. 225; Chamberlain to D'Abernon, 25 March 1925, *DBFP*, I, XXVII, no. 269. For overall positive Czech reaction to British policy, see Bátonyi (1999), pp. 206–8. On Polish concerns, see Cienciala and Kormanicki (1984), pp. 223–76.

[47] Briand instructions, 4 November 1925, MAE, Z.1. Pacte de sécurité, 284–6, vol. 85, p. 202; Briand to the Foreign Affairs Committee, 19 December 1925, Commission des Affaires Étrangères, Procès verbaux, C14763, no. 46, pp. 10–1.

intended to safeguard French security and wider strategic interests in a new way. What he pursued was, especially at the outset, no coherent, thoroughly crafted strategy; but over time it evolved into a comprehensive approach, whose consistency was enhanced by the Foreign Ministry's *secrétaire général* Philippe Berthelot. On the one hand, Briand still sought to obtain the most far-reaching British guarantee he could get. On the other, and crucially, he initiated a shift from a policy of treaty "execution" and enforcement, which had over-extended a politically and financially exhausted French power, towards a more cooperative policy of accommodation whose core rationale was to foster more peaceful relations with France's threatening eastern neighbour but also to tie Germany into a reformed international system of mutual rules and guarantees, mainly in order to pre-empt more assertive German revisionism. Ultimately this was to put France in a position to secure and control, with Britain's aid, an adapted but not radically altered status quo – and to slow down the pace of change in a postwar order in which American power had created a new dynamism in favour of Germany.[48] Yet Briand also saw a more fundamental strategic need to initiate a sea change in France's relations with Germany, to take steps towards and open up spheres of political and economic cooperation with those who determined the policies of the Weimar Republic.

To some extent, Briand subordinated France's commitments to its East European alliance partners to this new approach. Yet he insisted that Germany had to be obliged not only to guarantee the status quo of 1919 in the west but also to renounce forcible revisions in the east. Thus, he demanded that the German government would have to agree to arbitration treaties with its eastern neighbours for which France would then act as a guarantor. The French foreign minister hoped that the security pact could also serve to revive the battered *Entente* and create a kind of Anglo-French steering directorate within the pact structure. But to the *Assemblée*'s Foreign Affairs Committee he made clear that the time for a more general change of paradigm after the Great War had arrived, underscoring that what the "reconstitution of Europe" required was not an alliance "forged against one state" but rather "a guarantee pact that proceeded from a spirit of mutual aid".[49]

---

[48] French note, 16 June 1925, Locarno-Konferenz (1925), no. 14; Briand statements to the Foreign Affairs Committee, 19 December 1925, 23 February 1926, Commission des Affaires Étrangères, Procès verbaux, C14763-64, C14763, no. 46, pp. 6 ff., no. 51, pp. 13 ff.; Briand instructions to French diplomats, 4 November 1925, MAE, Z.1., Pacte de Sécurité (Locarno), vol. 86, Z 284-6, pp. 202 ff. See. Bariéty (2000), pp. 117–34; Jackson (2013), pp. 470–513.

[49] Briand to the Foreign Affairs Committee, 19 December 1925, Commission des Affaires Étrangères, Procès verbaux, C14763, no. 46, pp. 6 f.

Briand had thus drawn his own consequences both from the failures and frustrations of France's earlier postwar policies and from the power shifts within the Euro-Atlantic sphere that became apparent in the 1920s. And what he pursued can indeed be seen as the most significant attempt of any French policymaker in this phase to face up to the fact that France's bargaining position had been decisively weakened after the Ruhr crisis and that a politically and financially overstretched French state did not have the power to maintain the Versailles system through unilateral enforcement. Further, he realised that the remaining guarantees France had under the Versailles treaty were insufficient and time-bound, notably because the occupation of the Rhineland would have to end and could not be extended indefinitely, particularly against British and American opposition. And he realised too that what he called the "natural" imbalance of power between France and Germany would re-emerge the more the latter recovered – and benefited from the influx of American capital.[50]

Thus, the French foreign minister saw an urgent need to chart a different course, not only vis-à-vis Germany but also to mend France's strained relations with Britain and, notably, the United States. It is indeed important to stress that Briand's policy had a pronounced Atlantic dimension as well. It was spurred by the realisation that the French government could no longer afford to pursue approaches that placed it in a structural antagonism with the American government and the "force" that in Briand's eyes now really dominated European affairs, the "power of the City of London and of Wall Street" – particularly at a time when France was again in the grips of financial and political crisis, needed fresh US capital and still sought to negotiate an advantageous war-debt settlement.[51]

Briand concluded that it was thus in France's vital interest to counter the American perception that it had become Europe's most belligerent power and to seek a *rapprochement* with the Coolidge administration, both to gain its support for a security policy that fortified France's position and to encourage a more favourable American stance on war debts and future loans. Yet the more the French foreign minister progressed in his efforts to reconstitute Europe, and the longer he encountered uncompromising attitudes in Washington and observed what he saw as overbearing US aspirations to assert, unilaterally and often informally, financial and economic domination at Europe's and particularly France's expense, the more he would accentuate another aspirational vision: that of a more politically united and economically cooperating Europe,

---

[50] Briand to the Foreign Affairs Committee, 19 December 1925, Commission des Affaires Étrangères, Procès verbaux, C14763, no. 46, pp. 10–12.

[51] *JOS débats*, 10 April 1925, pp. 836–59; *JOC débats*, 19–22 November 1925, pp. 3801–3913; Suarez (1928), pp. 45 ff.; D'Abernon to Chamberlain, 15 May 1925, *DBFP*, I, XXVII, no. 324.

created on the basis of Franco-German *rapprochement*, which could engage in a common defence of its interests, not least against the new "American empire". By 1929, Briand's vision had developed into the project for a federal "United States of Europe", a political association of European states that also established a European "customs union".[52] In 1925, however, his first priority was to find a more sustainable way of safeguarding France's security, and the basic order of Versailles, by de facto going beyond the parameters of 1919.

At the core, the process that led to the conclusion of the security pact was indeed a European process, and Chamberlain's brokerage played a critical part in paving the way to Locarno. But, if less obviously than during the Dawes negotiations, the formative developments of 1925 took place in an altered international force-field in which informally exerted US influence was unprecedentedly powerful. Both the Coolidge administration and leading American financiers like Young and the governor of the Federal Reserve Bank of New York, Benjamin Strong, welcomed Stresemann's initiative and soon made clear that they had a pronounced interest in the success of the security pact negotiations. Through formal and informal channels, they exhorted the governments of Britain, France and Germany to take decisive steps to ensure the success of a pact that they viewed as an appropriate "political insurance" of the economic-cum-political pacification and stabilisation that had been initiated in 1924. In their assessment, it promised to create a stable political environment for the expansion of US trade in Europe and an unimpeded flow of American capital and investments to and beyond Germany.[53]

With the backing of Hughes, the American ambassador in Berlin, Alanson Houghton, had early on underscored that the American government would not act as a formal "trustee" and "guardian of European peace".[54] And Kellogg soon re-affirmed this position. Like Coolidge and Hoover, he favoured the pact idea because it seemed to bring tangible advances towards a new European security framework without requiring guarantees that the administration neither desired to make nor deemed realistic in view of unwavering Congressional opposition to strategic entanglements in Europe. Likewise, while still ruling out an American *rapprochement* with the League American decision-makers were in favour of a German League membership, arguing that this could turn the organisation into a "useful" instrument for promoting conciliation between the former enemies.[55]

---

[52] Briand to the Foreign Affairs Committee, 19 December 1925, Commission des Affaires Étrangères, Procès verbaux, C14763, no. 46, pp. 6 f.

[53] See Strong memorandum of conversations with Luther, Stresemann and Schacht, 11 July 1925, Strong Papers; Hoover to Kellogg, 16 April 1925; NA RG 59 862.51/1925.

[54] Houghton to Hughes, 12 January 1925, Hughes Papers.

[55] Kellogg memorandum, 16. March 1925, *FRUS 1925*, I, pp. 20–1; Castle Diary, 16 March 1925, vol. 7, pp. 84–5, Castle Papers.

In the eyes of leading Republican decision-makers, the task to secure the fledgling peace by political means was one that lay in the hands of the governments of the main European powers. But US diplomats and financiers came to exert a crucial influence behind the scenes, supporting the pact project through what had become tried and tested informal methods of bringing American power to bear through a mixture of political-cum-financial pressure and incentives. In the prevalent perception, these methods had proved singularly effective in 1924. Pursuing a "carrots and sticks" strategy, Houghton in early May 1925 issued an American "Peace Ultimatum to Europe". He declared that if they wanted to achieve a real postwar recovery and enjoy the benefits of further American loans, the "peoples of Europe" had to lay, through the Rhine pact, a new groundwork for "permanent peace" that also ensured the safety of American investments.[56] For his part, the most important agent of US financial power at this time, FRBNY-governor Strong, impressed on the Painlevé government in Paris that renewed flow of US capital to France would hinge on a success of the pact; and he sought to strengthen the domestic position of the Luther government in Berlin by conveying that the conclusion of the pact would be critical for continued US loans to Germany.[57]

IV. Securing the Nascent Atlantic Order. Locarno and the Emergence of a New European Concert

The Locarno accords, signed in October 1925, constituted the second essential compromise agreement between the western powers and Germany after the Great War, and in fact and in substance they not only complemented but began to transform the Versailles system. They not only codified the German acceptance of the postwar status quo in the west and, above all, of the post-Versailles Franco-German border. The German government also committed itself, against fierce nationalist opposition in and outside the *Reichstag*, to renounce the use of force and seek changes of the contested eastern borders of 1919, notably with Poland, only by peaceful means. To affirm this commitment to peaceful change, it concluded arbitration treaties not only with France and Belgium but also with Poland and Czechoslovakia. And, as Briand had envisaged, these treaties were guaranteed by France. For their part, the British and French protagonists essentially recognised that while the military restrictions of 1919 remained unaltered Germany would return to the comity of nations and regain the status of a European great power with "equal political

---

[56] Houghton speech to the Pilgrim Society, London, 4 May 1925, Houghton Papers; *Literary Digest*, 16 May 1925.

[57] Strong memorandum of conversations with Luther, Stresemann and Schacht in Berlin, 11 July 1925, Strong Papers.

rights". Locarno thus opened up the perspective of a genuine transformation of the postwar order.[58]

In hindsight, and particularly in view of the disastrous unravelling of international order in the 1930s, many later observers have viewed what the negotiations of London and Locarno initiated as an illusory process that only brought a superficial or even deceptive "truce" in an inexorable power-political struggle, corroded indispensable checks on German power and revisionist ambitions, and ultimately put Hitler in a position to launch his assault on international order.[59] But the seminal accords of 1925 did not mark a false dawn – just like those of London one year earlier had not marked the dawn of a "false" American peace. They were neither based on flawed premises nor destined to be short-lived. In fact, they yielded substantive advances, indeed the most important advances in European international politics since the Great War, which were actually reflected in the often invoked spirit of Locarno.

Most importantly, the Locarno pact indeed fostered what Chamberlain had envisaged: the emergence of a refashioned European concert of democratic states that, at its core, comprised Britain, France, and the Weimar Republic. The pact became the essential cornerstone of a new European – and *Euro-Atlantic* – system of security and international politics, and the new concert became its core mechanism. Significantly, the treaties formally signed on 1 December 1925 were interlocked with the League's Covenant and principles of collective security and arbitration. And that Germany was now finally to be admitted to the Geneva-based institution in the near future, and to be given a seat on the League Council, was of more than symbolical importance. After some wrangling, this significant breakthrough would be accomplished in the autumn of 1926.[60]

Rather than weaken the League, as some critics argued then and later, the Locarno accords thus in fact strengthened it and made it more relevant, not so much as a supranational organisation but as a platform and institutional framework for the concerted diplomacy of the Locarno powers. Therefore, it was no longer merely a victors' institution but could come closer to evolving into the "clearing house" Wilson had envisaged – where (not only) Europe's greater and smaller states, the victors and the vanquished, could seek to manage the critical security and political problems of the postwar era.

---

[58] See the British documents on the Locarno conference, DBFP, I, XXVII; AR Luther, pp. 669 ff., and Locarno-Konferenz 1925; MAE, Série Europe, Grande-Bretagne, vol. 85; Stresemann speech, 14 December 1925, ADAP, B, I, 1, pp. 740–3; Briand memorandum, 4 November 1925, MAE, Z.1., Pacte de sécurité, 284–6, vol. 85, pp. 202–3; Austen to Ida Chamberlain, 28 November 1925, Austen Chamberlain Papers, AC 5/1/370.

[59] See Keylor (2011), pp. 107–27.

[60] Chamberlain minute, 21 February 1925, FO 371/11064: W 1252/9/98.

Indeed, an international organisation like the League could only work effectively and play a tangible role in the maintenance of peace if it provided the framework for the cooperation and negotiations of the key powers, and their interactions with smaller member states – and if it was turned into an institution where the salient or "big" issues of security and international politics were deliberated.[61] And while the United States – and, for now, the Soviet Union – remained outside the organisation, it was in fact the Locarno process that set the stage for two important initiatives that were pursued through the League and intended to give new impulses both to international economic cooperation and disarmament: the (predominantly European) World Economic Conference, then held in May 1927, which proved remarkably successful in spawning measures to combat economic nationalism; and the establishment of the Preparatory Disarmament Commission that was supposed to prepare the ground for substantive advances towards general arms reductions and to organise an eventual Disarmament Conference, which then only took place, and proved futile, in 1932.[62]

The scope and significance of the Locarno agreements and the altered mode of international politics they inaugurated thus reached far beyond the stipulations of the security pact itself, however important these were in their own right. What came to be known as "Locarno politics" brought decisive change. They offered ways and means, and manifested a new political will on all sides, to secure peace and come to terms with the Franco-German question and Europe's wider challenges by political and diplomatic means rather than by recourse to force. Essentially, the Locarno process thus pushed further what the London process had initiated: a qualitative shift from the politics of war and war by other means towards a new politics of reciprocity and *quid pro quo* compromises that led to agreements which based postwar security and inter-state relations on common guarantees and the acceptance of common rules. At the same time, Locarno politics sought to strike a balance between what the different central actors could legitimise in the challenging democratic force-fields in which they had to manoeuvre.

What thus had been established were the essential underpinnings of a system whose core purpose was to foster security and thereby to pave the way for a longer-term pacification on new foundations. The rules and practices of this system clearly transcended the antagonistic zero-sum approaches of the immediate postwar era – when especially the prevalent French outlook had been that every step in the direction of loosening the containment and permitting a revitalisation and political rehabilitation of Germany would dangerously diminish French and wider European security. Crucially, the

---

[61] See Steiner (2005), pp. 349–452; Pedersen (2007), pp. 1091–1117.
[62] See Krüger (2006), pp. 156–7; Webster (2016).

emerging architecture of Locarno was predicated on an idea that pointed decisively beyond Versailles, namely that mutual security agreements could engender an overall net-gain in security and development prospects. In the longer run, such advances could even lead to the creation of a genuine security community and, in a broader perspective, a more sustainable political equilibrium in Europe and the critical Euro-Atlantic sphere that also greatly enhanced global peace.

For the new Soviet leader, Stalin, the Locarno pact was nothing but "an example of the matchless hypocrisy of bourgeois diplomacy" that by "shouting and singing about peace" was merely covering up "preparations for a new war".[63] But he was profoundly mistaken. In fact, the positive impact of the Locarno negotiations was far from deceptive, and it was not limited to western Europe. Unquestionably, Locarno created borders of different validity in Europe – in the west, borders whose inviolability was guaranteed, in the east borders that lacked these attributes. But it also arguably provided new and better safeguards for Poland and Czechoslovakia and, most importantly, a new basis for placing the relations between Germany and its eastern neighbours on sounder foundations and for restraining German revisionist tendencies, even if the obstacles to a more far-reaching Locarno-style peace process in Central and Eastern Europe remained considerable.

In the immediate context of 1925, it was politically essential that in the treaties they signed with the foreign ministers of Poland and Czechoslovakia, Aleksander Skrzyński and Edvard Beneš, the German representatives had explicitly committed themselves to the renunciation of force and accepted the premise that an alteration of the eastern borders could only be envisaged through peaceful negotiations and if it could be reconciled with the overall consolidation of Europe's nascent peace order. As there was no realistic prospect for such negotiations, this de facto relegated the issue of border revisions to a more distant future when it might be possible to address it in less hostile climate.

What mattered even more, however – and could significantly improve the security of Poland and Czechoslovakia – was that Locarno marked a decisive advance in the process of anchoring Weimar Germany to a western peace system and of deeper reorientation in German policymaking, which became the hallmark of the Stresemann era. What Stresemann and Schubert pursued stemmed from the recognition that it lay in Germany's well-understood interest to make a reliable commitment to peaceful settlement and peaceful change, to contribute to building cooperative relations with Britain, France and the United States in order to re-emerge as a "modern" great power within an interdependent western system – and to forego policies that jeopardised these advances. This placed decisive checks on temptations to pursue

---

[63] Stalin (1952–54), VII, p. 282; Kotkin (2014), pp. 561–2.

aggressive revisionism in the east or to return to the idea of forging a revisionist compact with the Soviet Union. And despite ongoing structural problems, it commanded a restrained and more cooperative approach towards Poland as well as efforts to meet a crucial domestic task, namely to manage unrealistic revisionist expectations in Germany in a period when a renunciation of claims for the "lost territories" remained politically inconceivable.[64]

Clearly, though, both German and Polish policymakers still had a long way to go on the road towards anything approaching a peace-enforcing and mutually bearable settlement in the east. And here too the attitudes of French, British and American policymakers would have a critical bearing. After Locarno, French leaders sought to combine the enmeshing of Germany in a new security order in the west with maintaining their eastern alliances. Chamberlain and strategists in the British Foreign Office envisaged a strategy of widening circles of stability from the west to the east, not ruling out eventual peaceful modifications of the eastern status quo. And some American diplomats had sympathies for Stresemann's argument that it would serve the general "interests of peace" in Europe to effect a peaceful change of elements of the postwar status quo in the east that, like the "Silesian settlement" or the "Polish corridor", could not "endure permanently" in their assessment. Yet their premise was that this could only be attempted once Europe had gone through a longer period of peace and stability and a "better atmosphere" had been created than that which existed "so soon after the close of the Great War".[65] Accordingly, prior to the World Economic Crisis no American government would seek to push for such changes.

In a broader perspective, the new concert system of Locarno was only a nucleus. Yet unlike the fragile, truncated system of Versailles it had the potential to effect a more profound transformation of the international order, one premised on building bridges between the western powers and a stabilised Weimar Republic. But it is crucial to recognise that the Locarno pact, and concert, only constituted the essential European building-block of a wider, though as yet less than robust Euro-Atlantic peace system in which the United States played an aloof but nonetheless dominant role as a "silent hegemon", not only in the financial but also in the political sphere. And in an even broader perspective, Locarno and the transatlantic system that had taken shape since the London Conference of 1924 can even be seen – in conjunction with the Washington system of 1922 – as essential elements of a reformed world order that began to emerge in the 1920s.

The Coolidge administration had no direct part in the Locarno Conference. But the powerful American influence within the changing international system

---

[64] See Steiner (2005), pp. 401–6; Cohrs (2006), pp. 259–70; Schattkowsky (II/1994).
[65] Chamberlain to Howard, 3 June 1925, DBFP, I, XXVII, no. 357.

and the concrete efforts of US policymakers, diplomats and financiers to push for the pact had been highly significant. Kellogg hailed the accords as the most important step European statesmen had taken yet after the Great War to "free" the Old World from "the old system of balance of power" that "divided Europe into military camps ever jealous of each other and striving for additional armament and power" and towards "uniting the European nations in a common pact of security" and the commitment to "conciliation, arbitration, and judicial settlements". And, reflecting the prevalent American interpretation, he stressed that the advances of Locarno "completed the work of the Dawes Committee" and the London Conference and thus effectively complemented American efforts to overcome the antagonisms that had persisted after Versailles.[66]

Indeed, official and unofficial US actors had promoted the pact as a means to promote the longer-term stabilisation of Europe through agreements between the former enemies of the war that required no American guarantees and whose net effect, so they calculated, would be to serve overriding US financial and political interests while making any more direct strategic or security engagement of the United States in Europe superfluous.[67] Coolidge even went so far as to claim the Locarno pact as a "success" of the Republicans' post-Wilsonian policy "of having European countries settle their own political problems without involving this country".[68]

---

[66] Kellogg speech, 14 December 1925; Kellogg to Coolidge, 8 November 1925, Kellogg Papers.
[67] Kellogg to Coolidge, 8 November 1925; Hughes to Castle, 7 December 1925, Kellogg Papers.
[68] FRUS 1925, I, p. XII.

24

The Remarkable Consolidation of the Nascent
Pax Atlantica of the 1920s
And Its Dissolution under the Impact of the World Economic Crisis

Under the marked limitations and constraints that burdened international politics on both sides of the Atlantic, the settlements of London and Locarno charted a more realistic path towards building a durable transatlantic order after the Great War. They were based on mutual guarantees and obligations, common rules and understandings for the pacific settlement of disputes and, on a political level, *quid pro quo* agreements that could gain legitimacy not only among the victors of 1918 but also in the Weimar Republic. Built on terms that reached beyond those of 1919, the fledgling system of London and Locarno was thus distinct from Versailles, especially insofar as it was not reserved to the victors but sought to integrate the vanquished into what gained the contours of a reconfigured "West" or more precisely a reconfigured international system premised on western norms and practices. And it came to involve the United States in the stabilisation of Europe in ways that were different from those Wilson had envisaged; they were distinctly more informal, keeping political commitments at a minimum.

All of this set the advances of 1924 and 1925 apart from the peacemaking process of 1919. Indeed, not the Locarno pact alone, as Chamberlain declared, but the two transformative settlements that were negotiated after the Ruhr crisis marked "the real dividing line between the years of war and the years of peace" in Europe.[1] And they ushered in a remarkable period of Euro-Atlantic stabilisation and pacification in the latter 1920s, the era of London and Locarno.

Partly reflecting changes that non-governmental activists had long fought to advance, the developments of the mid-1920s had a marked impact on the structures and changing force-field of both inter- and transnational relations in the post–First World War era. The altered intergovernmental approaches and the seminal accords between the most relevant states palpably changed the overall atmosphere and indeed the spirit of European and transatlantic politics. They furthered new exchanges between the sphere of political decision-making and the arena of public and intellectual debate. And only they could create the conditions in which non-governmental organisations and

[1] Chamberlain press statement, 23 October 1925, cited in Macartney (1926), p. 56.

transnationally operating individuals and associations on both sides of the Atlantic, who had renewed their efforts to promote reconciliation and a peaceful transformation of European and world politics after Versailles, could successfully expand their activities. The intergovernmental advances of the mid-1920s thus encouraged transnational efforts to strengthen the fabric of international cooperation and work towards a "deeper" peace.

From 1925, organisations like the League of Nations Union once again increased their membership and influence, which was testament to the strength and resilience of a still-growing British peace movement. On the continent, notably the Pan-European Union, founded by Count Richard Coudenhove-Kalergi in 1922 to promote a pan-European movement and the ideal of a supranationally united Europe, gained considerably more resonance now.[2] And so did the Franco-German "Information and Documentation Committee", set up by the Luxembourgian industrialist Emile Mayrisch, and other politicians, opinion-makers, and intellectuals who championed the cause of Franco-German and wider European postwar reconciliation.[3]

In the United States, the League to Enforce Peace, which had been so influential during the "grand debates" of 1919 and 1920, dissolved (in 1923), but other pacifist pressure-groups and groups that persevered in efforts to strengthen international law and "juridify" international relations, also through the creation of a world court, gained remarkable clout in the latter 1920s. Most momentously, the founder of the Chicago-based Outlawry of War Organization, Salmon Levinson, and the internationalist history professor James Shotwell, who sought to build on the Locarno treaties, played leading roles in galvanising a transatlantic and then global war renunciation movement.[4] But it is necessary to note that even in the changing and more forward-looking atmosphere of the latter 1920s, these remained the pursuits and visions of – influential – minorities in the different national and newly important transnational realms, which still came up against strong residual nationalist, bellicist and anti-progressive currents in Europe and unilateralist-isolationist currents in the United States.

But the settlements of the mid-1920s could not yet "solve" Europe's postwar problems or create a stable status quo. Like Versailles, they represented only an – albeit far more auspicious – beginning; or, put differently, they marked, in Chamberlain's words, "the beginning, and not the end, of the noble work of appeasement in Europe".[5] Indeed, the system of London and Locarno was not

---

[2] Coudenhove-Kalergi regarded the London conference as a turning-point and the Locarno pact as "a first practical step toward European understanding and unification". See Coudenhove-Kalergi (1926), p. 197.

[3] See Schirmann (2006), pp. 70–116; Iriye (2002), pp. 20 ff.; Clavin and Sluga (2016), pp. 3 ff.

[4] See Gorman (2012), pp. 259–84; Hathaway and Shapiro (2018), pp. 106–30, 194 ff.

[5] Chamberlain speech in the Commons, 18 November 1925, Hansard, Commons, 5 series, vol. 188, col. 420.

destined to break down because it was built on flawed foundations, setting the stage for Hitler's aggressions, or because it merely camouflaged an allegedly insurmountable antagonism between the western powers and Germany in the wake of the Great War.[6]

But the advances of London and Locarno had to be *sustained*. And the real danger was that the nascent peace order of the mid-1920s, which was as yet far from robust, would not be consolidated and legitimised further by those who had established it and the actors who followed in their tracks. And while much depended on the actions of French and German decision-makers, the continued or even expanded engagement of leading British and American actors was crucial. Indeed, the system of London and Locarno could only be made durable, and resilient to crisis, if the latter committed themselves to fortifying the new international concert and widening the legitimacy of its rules of peaceful accommodation – and if thereby the Locarno concert could be expanded into what had been missing since the end of the war: a viable *transatlantic* system of concerted international politics. For one fundamental fact had not changed: Only such a system could overcome the structural insecurity and offset the imbalance of power that prevailed between France and Germany by committing both countries to western-orientated rules *and* giving it incentives to join a reconstituted "West". The pivotal challenge was and remained to foster a long-term process of integration, and "westernisation", that embedded the German republic ever more firmly in the Euro-Atlantic order that had emerged.

Unquestionably critical to this end was, on the one hand, a clear ongoing commitment of the decisive European powers to the Locarno politics of "reciprocity" and peaceful accommodation. Yet it was also essential to prove to the various domestic audiences that such politics could yield further mutually beneficial consequences, and thus to widen its domestic legitimacy base on all sides. In particular, further advances had to be made that provided both the proponents of conciliation in France and the moderates within Weimar Germany's embattled élite of moderates with the indispensable political room to manoeuvre to take further steps in fostering the as yet brittle Franco-German peace process. Such advances were inconceivable without further substantial agreements.

But because the vital issues that remained at the top of the European agenda – security, the Rhineland occupation, reparations, and war debts – were so densely bound up with one another, further progress could only be made through further complex *quid pro quo* bargains that comprised both political and financial elements. And in view of the *new* pattern of asymmetrical interdependence between Europe and the United States that had emerged since 1923 – i.e. essentially European dependence on US capital and political goodwill – it was impossible or at least extremely difficult to make such

[6] See Schuker (1976), pp. 385–93.

bargains without the engagement of American financiers and, ultimately, the support of the government in Washington. Of this all of the Locarno protagonists were fundamentally aware, though Briand and Stresemann grasped it far more astutely than Chamberlain.

I.   European Progress, American Retrogression

Essentially, however, what shaped international politics in the latter 1920s, and ultimately impeded the consolidation of a robust and crisis-resilient transatlantic system was a fundamental, and problematic, disparity. In short, the European protagonists of Locarno politics overall managed to sustain what they had initiated in 1924 and 1925, having learned that they had to keep strengthening the new concert and drive forward the process of inner-European accommodation – even if British policymakers now played a less proactive role. But those who directed American policies in fact pursued retrograde approaches. Rather than move towards a more committed and consistent engagement in European processes in which they not only had a financial but also a political stake, they re-assumed a more detached posture. What animated their outlooks and conduct can be interpreted as another instance of "pathological learning".[7] In short, they not only concluded that core American stabilisation interests had already been satisfied through the settlements of the mid-1920s. They had also concluded that because their informal and indirect involvement in bringing about these settlements had worked so well, and protected US interests so effectively, they could and should proceed along the same lines in the future – or limit their involvement even further. Crucially, they had drawn the lesson that informal approaches and reliance on financiers and other "private" agents would not only suffice but actually be the most efficient way to cope with any future challenges.

Yet this meant that they would not be prepared to develop the political strategies, and could never develop the imaginations, that were needed to deal effectively and creatively with challenges that could arise – and, notably, with any serious crisis of the nascent transatlantic order. Such a crisis was not inevitable, and not necessarily foreseeable from the vantage-point of the mid-1920s. But it was far from unlikely in view of the tensions and potential for conflict that the political and financial constellation of the post–First World War era harboured. In fact, Keynes and other prudent policymakers and observers on both sides of the Atlantic had long warned that this was not the time for fair-weather approaches and that a crisis of the reparations regime and the wider, in critical aspects unregulated, Euro-Atlantic system of reparation payments, debt payments, sharply increasing flows of private

---

[7] See Meier (2000), p. 516.

loans and massive credit expansion (fuelled by the US Federal Reserve), which in turn fuelled "an orgy of speculation", could have devastating political consequences.[8]

The agreements of Locarno did not and could not lead to a new harmony in Franco–German relations or wider European politics. The differences between the interests, priorities and legitimation requirements of the main actors had not disappeared. Notably, Briand hence invoked the "spirit of Locarno" to limit and slow down the pace of further changes in the postwar status quo, while Stresemann appealed to the same spirit in order to call for further decisive steps in the process of peaceful change, such as a swift termination of the Rhineland occupation, arguing that such "consequences" of Locarno were vital for the public acceptance of his policy in Germany – and for European peace.[9] But such continuing conflicts and divergences simply had to be expected considering the enormity of the problems the Great War had left in its wake – and they are indeed the rule rather than the exception in modern international politics. What is essential is that rules, practices and mechanisms exist, and can be sustained, that allow the pursuit of a political process in which different aims, interests, expectations and legitimacy requirements can be addressed and eventually be accommodated.

Although hence less effective as "honest broker" within the Locarno concert, Chamberlain had recognised something that in their own ways Briand and Stresemann understood as well, namely that they only realistic path towards a more durable peace was one of "co-operation", politics of "reciprocity" and "reciprocal concessions".[10] While basic American and British interests had already been met, there was a paramount need for Locarno politics to prove effective in producing further results that not only the embattled advocates of conciliatory approaches in the Third Republic but also the Weimar Republic's vanguard of *"Verständigungspolitiker"* – those who championed a "policy of reconciliation" with the West – could present to their home audiences as successes – successes that brought tangible benefits. At the same time, though, both in France and Germany the democratic force-fields and public debates about the future remained profoundly polarised. Yet the main American and British decision-makers of course faced concomitant challenges of their own, even if the main question they had to answer was

---

[8] See Keynes, *A Breathing Space – The Dawes Plan, 1923–1928,* in Keynes (1978), XVIII, pp. 234–303, and his prescient analysis in *A Revision of the Treaty, ibid.,* III, pp. 105–14, 115–30; Skidelsky (2005), pp. 416–17.

[9] Stresemann speech, 14 December 1925, *ADAP,* B, I/I, pp. 740–3; Briand's statements to the *Assemblée's* Foreign Affairs Committee, 19 December 1925, 23 February 1926, Commission des Affaires Étrangères, Procès verbaux, C14763–64, C14763, pp. 6 ff. 13 ff.

[10] Austen to Hilda Chamberlain, 28 November 1925, Austen Chamberlain Papers, AC5/1/370; Chamberlain to Lindsay, 5 February 1927; 12 January 1927, *DBFP,* IA, III, pp. 11–2; no. 62, FO 408.47.

different. It was the question why the states and societies they represented should extend their commitments and engagement on a European continent that appeared to have "turned the corner" from war to renewed peace. For all of these reasons, it was the Locarno process, and not the Versailles process, that most clearly anticipated future peace and reconciliation processes between more or less stable democratic states in the twentieth century, both in and beyond Europe.

No further major breakthroughs occurred in the latter 1920s. Overall, however, it must be stressed that, despite setbacks and crises, despite the waning engagement of the British "honest broker", and despite persisting constraints imposed by US aloofness, the politics of the Locarno concert took root within a relatively short time. All sides essentially adhered to the new principles and modes of international politics that had been established between the spring of 1924 and the autumn of 1925. The new European concert was consolidated and developed further to a remarkable degree between 1925 and 1929. And it proved remarkably effective as the central mechanism, and "clearing agency" of European international politics – having an impact far beyond the relations between Britain, France and Germany. The regular gatherings of the Locarno Powers on the occasion of the League Assembly's four annual meetings in Geneva not only became a hallmark of a hence all-but-institutionalised concert at the heart of European politics. They also indeed turned the League into a more important organisation in the process of Europe's pacification through peaceful change (which of course made it also the arena for continued tough debates, e.g. about the rights and claims of German minorities in Poland).[11] And Locarno's ground-rules of compromise and "reciprocity" were beginning to bear fruit. Most importantly, all sides came to view the concert system as a system worth preserving and cultivating in its own right.

Of particular import was that Stresemann and those who supported his course deemed this paramount as well. And, in practical terms, they in fact subordinated their aim to effect political and territorial revisions in the east to the higher interest of meeting Germany's commitments under the Locarno pact. This indeed greatly enhanced stability, also in Eastern Europe.[12] Stresemann's priorities were supported by the centrist parties behind the Luther government and notably the Social Democrats, though by the summer of 1928 Hermann Müller, newly elected as the first SPD chancellor since Bauer, voiced a growing impatience with the piecemeal progress of Locarno politics and demanded an immediate and "unconditional" evacuation of the

---

[11] See Chamberlain memoranda, Geneva, 5–12 December 1926, *DBFP*, IA, II, nos. 323–33, and the German records in *ADAP*, B, I/II, nos. 237, 258, 260.

[12] See Stresemann, *Reichstag* speech, 23 June 1927, in Zwoch (1972), pp. 250–5; Krüger (1985), pp. 355 ff.; Wright (2002), pp. 393 ff.

Rhineland.[13] More disconcerting was that in the arenas of Weimar Germany's still very conflict-ridden, compromise-averse internal politics and public debates the attacks of nationalist parties and right-wing forces, thinkers and press organs on Stresemann's Locarno policy and his "betrayal" of vital German interests continued unabated. And what persisted at a deeper level was a clash of priorities and orientations between the foreign minister's *Westpolitik* and those who rejected both an accommodation with the western powers and the entire "system of Weimar", advocated more assertive revisionism and stoked anti-American and anti-western nationalism for their own political purposes.

While he had not gone so far as to intervene against it, Hindenburg, who by then had assumed a new, ambivalent role in the German postwar power structure as *Reichspräsident*, did not conceal his opposition to Stresemann's security initiative and the cooperative pursuits that followed. And Stresemann also had to assert time and again his authority vis-à-vis the *Reichswehr*'s Chief of Staff, General von Seeckt, and those who followed him in pursuing a fundamentally different orientation: one that concentrated on regaining a "free hand" and power-political room to manoeuvre in continental Europe, with the longer-term goal of shaking off the shackles of Versailles, also through covert cooperation with the Red Army. By then Germany's ambassador in Moscow, Brockdorff-Rantzau criticised the Locarno accords as too one-sidedly orientated towards the western victors of the war and counselled a return to what he had already fallen back on in 1919: a – feckless – neo-Bismarckian turn to "classic" German balance-of-power policies centring on the notion that Berlin should join forces with the Soviet regime in order to increase its leverage vis-à-vis Britain, France and the United States.[14]

But Stresemann and Schubert had little patience for such recommendations. Crucially, they made sure to negotiate what then became the Treaty of Berlin of 1926 in such a way as to make it essentially consonant with Weimar Germany's Locarno commitments. The treaty Stresemann and Chicherin hammered out hinged on a limited assurance of mutual neutrality should one of the parties become embroiled in a conflict, which included the mutual pledge not to take part in any kind of financial or economic boycott. Further, the German government assured the Bolshevik regime of Germany's benevolent neutrality in the event of a war between the Soviet Union and Poland. In effect, while accommodating critical German and Soviet interests, the Berlin treaty was not a continuation of the Rapallo approach. Rather, it manifested the extent to which, in response to the altered policies of the Anglo-American powers and France, the predominantly western orientation of German foreign

---

[13] Müller inaugural speech, *Reichstag*, 3 July 1928, *SB*, vol. 423, pp. 38–40.
[14] Brockdorff-Rantzau memorandum, 23 January 1926, *ADAP*, B, II/I, no. 45.

policy had come to prevail since 1924. This would again be confirmed – one last time – during the negotiations over the Young Plan and the Rhineland settlement that took place at The Hague in the summer of 1929.[15]

Yet advances towards more durable European stability continued to depend to a large extent on buttressing the authority of conciliatory republican moderates in Germany in the longer term – and, ultimately, fortifying a German process of accommodation with the West, and westernisation, that would require considerable time. Indeed, the accords of London and Locarno had started to remedy the deficiencies of Versailles and to create the substructure of international politics, and security that was indispensable for more profound pacification processes, which – if they were possible at all – would prove stony and also inevitably require time. And, crucially, they were a first testament to something that had only begun and would require even more time: changes in the underlying mentalities of political decision-makers and the wider, now more democratic societies that passed through and struggled against each other in an era of spiralling competition, war and massive upheavals. At the same time, and precisely because the impact of the war and these upheavals had been so immense, it had to be expected that a struggle between opposing, inherently clashing national and transnational foreign-policy orientations – between pursuits of more moderate cooperative-accommodating international relations and more extreme, ideologised power-political counter-visions – would go on, not only in Germany.

Thus, it should be emphasised again that *time* is one essential factor which has to be considered when appraising the chances and limits of building a more enduring Atlantic peace after the Great War. Here, this particularly concerns the time the politics of London and Locarno had, not only to take root but also to bear fruit and thus to gain greater legitimacy than more war-prone alternatives. And, with the benefit of hindsight, it of course becomes all too obvious that the period of relative, albeit remarkable stabilisation that the Euro-Atlantic world – and particularly the Weimar Republic – enjoyed between the mid-1920s and the onset of the Great Depression remained very short. Yet this stabilisation also remained fragile, more fragile than it could have been, and what proved decisive here were the limits of American rather than European stabilisation policies.

In Chamberlain's judgement, not further grand designs lubricated by American capital but the measured but steady pursuit of European Locarno diplomacy held the key to Europe's longer-term pacification. The underlying British interest in fostering European stability through *gradual* peaceful change and reform hence became more pronounced. Britain's overall conservative approach and lack of proactive engagement were influenced by global

---

[15] See Zeidler (1993), pp. 82–7, 303; Koszyk (1972), pp. 274–6.

preoccupations: the perceived need to consolidate a far-flung imperial system in transition, an escalating ideological dispute with Soviet Russia, the protection of British interests in the Chinese civil war, and resurfacing Anglo-American tensions over naval arms control.[16] At the same time, Chamberlain clung to the view that in core questions of European peace and security it was illusory to expect a constructive cooperation of the American government and unwise to involve American financiers. But, as both Briand and Stresemann understood more clearly than the British foreign secretary, Locarno politics had to be conducted in a transatlantic force-field in which American power and what American decision-makers favoured or opposed, however informally, had decisive consequences. Just as it had no longer been possible for Europeans to make peace in 1919 on their own, so now it became manifest that decisive advances in Locarno-style peace politics could not be made by its European protagonists alone.

More fundamentally, the Euro-Atlantic international politics of the latter 1920s can be understood as the search for a mutually beneficial "final settlement" of the problems that had remained unresolved, or had been created, at Versailles. And the paramount problems that still had to be settled conclusively were the future of the Rhineland and reparations. Crucially, though with different emphases, both Stresemann and Briand came to envisage an agreement of this kind. What they came to seek was a further peace settlement that would confirm and strengthen the rules and understandings of Locarno. But in the power constellation prevailing after 1925, it was simply inconceivable to conclude such an accord by way of a bilateral Franco-German initiative. Ultimately, official and unofficial American actors would have a critical influence here – and more generally they would have a critical bearing on the dynamics of Europe's further stabilisation. In short, the durability of the nascent peace system of the mid-1920s ultimately depended on the extent to which the new European concert could eventually be widened into a functioning transatlantic concert system.

II. Pathological Learning Processes?

The disintegration of the system of London and Locarno was not inevitable. But it could not be decisively consolidated and transformed into an effective Atlantic system of international politics. And this is the main systemic reason for its relatively rapid disintegration under the pressures of the World Economic Crisis. Undoubtedly, the crisis of the evolving order of the 1920s and its subsequent dissolution in the 1930s had many causes, and causes on different levels. These range from the newly addressed but abiding problem of

---

[16] Austen to Hilda Chamberlain, 30 January 1927, Austen Chamberlain Papers, AC 5/1/407.

postwar insecurity to the abiding shortcomings of the Euro-Atlantic debt and reparations regime. And they eventually extended to the particularly toxic combination of inner polarisation and destabilisation through the "external" shockwaves of the Great Depression that then led to the demise of the Weimar Republic and the rise of Hitler. Arguably even more daunting remained the *longue durée* challenges that policymakers still faced: those of charting paths beyond competitive – imperialist – power politics and of transcending the extreme forms of nationalism that had come to dominate international relations since the dawn of the long twentieth century and by no means disappeared after the Great War.

But the fact that no greater advances could be made towards addressing these challenges and making the system of the 1920s more "storm-proof" in the fulcrum years between 1925 and 1929 was not primarily a European problem. It was not primarily a function of Europe's "irremediable" postwar calamities, unbridgeable Franco-German divergences or the shortcomings of the new European concert. In fact, as noted, these were not insurmountable, and the Locarno concert came to function remarkably well.[17] What mattered more were the aims, outlooks and approaches of those who commanded decisive influence in Washington and New York.

Yet the contributions American policymakers and financiers made to transforming the settlements of the mid-1920s into a more permanent peace order remained distinctly limited. Essentially, their strategies failed because they did not sustain their hegemonic engagement and did not assume the necessary political commitments. They even retreated from the limited responsibilities they had taken on earlier, no longer engaging actively to stabilise the newly republican Germany and to anchor it more safely to a newly emerging western system. And this retreat was indeed largely conditioned by the consequences Republican policymakers – and notably Hoover – had drawn not only from the war and the deficiencies of Versailles but also, and crucially, from the *successes* of American stabilisation efforts in 1924 and 1925. In short, from the perspective of Washington the accomplishments of the Dawes settlement and the Locarno pact proved too convincing for their own good. They led Hoover and others to assume that they had already played their essential part in propelling a peace-enforcing reform of the Versailles system; that they had set Europe on a path of economically underpinned stabilisation; and that there was therefore no need for further political commitments.[18]

What the Coolidge and Hoover administrations actually pursued in the face of the challenges of the latter 1920s has been described as an attempt to resort

---

[17] On the Locarno concert and its challenges, see Steiner (2005) pp. 387–494, and Cohrs (2006), pp. 345–77, 417–47.

[18] See e.g. Kellogg to Lamont, 19 August 1924, Lamont Papers, 4-C, 177-2.

to "old approaches" to cope with changing realities. They allegedly sought to emulate the Dawes process in pursuing a "final settlement" of the reparations question through the Young Plan and dealing with Europe's wider security and financial problems.[19] But there was no such continuity. Following Hoover's lead, Republican decision-makers resorted to ever more unilateral approaches, paying little heed to the complexities of Europe's interdependent financial and security politics. Most significantly, they retreated from the already limited hegemonic role that Hughes had assumed as pivotal arbiter of the Dawes settlement. This important shift had one serious consequence. Ultimately, US policymakers could not be more effective in leading international efforts to master the gravest crisis of the nascent Euro-Atlantic peace order, the World Economic Crisis, precisely because they had not seen the need to establish common political understandings and ground-rules with the European powers during the breathing space that the accords of London and Locarno afforded before 1929.

As noted, Hoover had drawn his own distinctive lessons not only from the Great War, the frustrating negotiations at the Paris Peace Conference and Wilson's defeat but also from the Dawes process and the "dawning of the American peace" in 1924. And his actions continued to be informed by this outlook, all the way to the time when, faced with a spiralling world economic and political crisis as president, he would insist all too long on a unilateral American response rather than seek to lead concerted political crisis management efforts in cooperation with the European powers. In the aftermath of the peace conference, Hoover had defended Wilson's policy and championed the League as the only alternative to widespread "chaos" in and beyond Europe.[20] In contrast to the Republican majority in Congress, Hoover never became an outright isolationist. He was cognisant of the growing transatlantic interdependence, not just in the financial sphere. Yet by the mid-1920s his ideas about how to stabilise postwar Europe had narrowed significantly. As commerce secretary, Hoover became the most influential proponent of an economically orientated, politically aloof approach to transatlantic relations. This was also due to his distrust of what he regarded as unreconstructed European power politics. For not only was he convinced that European imperialism and balance-of-power machinations had caused the catastrophe of 1914. He also concluded that they had resurfaced in France's reparations war against Germany.[21]

What subsequently gained ground in Washington was Hoover's assertive claim that the time had come to replace Britain's pre-war predominance and

[19] See Leffler (1979), pp. 194–219.
[20] Hoover address, "We Cannot Fiddle While Rome Burns", 2 October 1919, *League to Enforce Peace Pamphlet* (New York, 1919); Hoover (1958), p. 248.
[21] Hoover address, 14 December 1924, Hoover Papers, Box 75.

French power politics with an "American peace" on distinctly different foundations. Building on ideas he had honed between 1916 and 1919, he conceived of it as a system of states and societies that followed what he saw as the paradigm-setting example of America's progressive capitalist model of limited but effective state interference and rationalised, quasi-scientific management and modernisation.

As Hoover saw it, all states within this system were to shift from politico-military to peaceful economic competition – on American terms. In the Euro-Atlantic system he envisioned, the United States would lead by example, and be the dominant power, yet largely refrain from assuming formal international responsibilities. As commerce secretary, Hoover thus insisted that not only West European states but also Germany and, eventually, the states of Eastern Europe could and should be modernised in accordance with rational and rationalising "Americanist" precepts of political *and* capitalist economic order.[22] And more concretely he argued that all European states would benefit from finally adopting the US "Open Door" policy of trade liberalisation – notwithstanding the fact that in 1922 the Republican-dominated Congress had erected steep protectionist barriers through the Fordney-McCumber Tariff Act (against his recommendations). Moreover, Hoover advocated using America's financial power to press notably its French debtor to reduce what he criticised as its excessive military forces and to turn to a more "rational" economically underpinned foreign policy.[23] More broadly, he adhered to his maxim of transcending old-style European diplomacy and promoting instead, wherever possible, the transnational cooperation of financial and other experts.[24]

Consequently, the commerce secretary interpreted the "American peace" of 1924 not as a watershed in international *politics* but as a success of US financial expertise. He held up the example of the "disinterested private citizens" who had produced the Dawes plan and completed "a peace mission without parallel in international history".[25] Above all, Hoover welcomed that the Dawes approach had kept the Coolidge administration at a safe distance from any commitments or guarantees in Europe. And he also favoured entrusting semi-official agents like Parker Gilbert and Owen Young with the task of advancing Europe's pacification further. In Hoover's judgement, the key to stability lay in intensifying the economic restructuring and "rational" political modernisation of European states that the Dawes agreement had initiated. Combined with US

---

[22] Hoover can thus be seen as a key agent of the "Americanism" and Americanist capitalist rationalisation tendencies that, according to Gramsci's penetrating analysis, had such a profound impact on Europe after 1918. See Gramsci (1988), pp. 277–80.

[23] Hoover, "The French Debt," 30 September 1925, Hoover Papers, Commerce.

[24] Hoover address, 14 December 1924, Hoover Papers, Box 75.

[25] *Ibid.*; Hoover memorandum, Paris, July 1919, Hoover Papers, Box 164; Hoover to Hughes, 24 April 1922, NA RG 59/800.51/316.

investments, such "progressive" modernisation would also provide the most effective means to stabilise the Weimar Republic within an American peace system.[26] Though less optimistic than Hoover about the prospects of Europe's pacification, Hughes' successors at the head of the State Department, Frank Kellogg and Henry Stimson, essentially supported his general orientation. They too held that the successes of London and Locarno would allow them to insist even more uncompromisingly on American "independence". In short, Hughes' engagement on behalf of the Dawes scheme had thus demarcated the essential limits of official American intervention in European postwar affairs.[27] In the aftermath of the London conference, Kellogg reasserted the prevalent rationale that Washington could wield even more "influence" if it did not become "tied up in European politics".[28]

III.   A New American Empire? European Perspectives on the "American Peace" of the Latter 1920s

European decision-makers by no means unanimously welcomed America's informal, economically driven engagement in the era of London and Locarno. Particularly French decision-makers resisted what they regarded as US economic imperialism: aspirations to use the world creditor's new preponderance to incorporate a financially weakened France into an unbalanced world economic system on American terms. Poincaré strove to curb the influence of "progressive" American schemes for radical financial reforms and Hoover's calls for deep cuts in France's military budget. Returning to the helm of French politics as premier and finance minister, he successfully restored France's financial and monetary stability in the spring of 1927, not with American loans and austerity measures but through his own consolidation programme, widely acclaimed as inaugurating the *franc Poincaré*. Soon thereafter, he rejected US proposals for a treaty of friendship and commerce, modelled on the 1923 treaty with Germany, which would have broadened US "Open Door" access to the French market while foreseeing no reciprocal reductions in American tariffs, which the Senate staunchly opposed.[29]

Poincaré's attitudes reflected rising elite and public criticism of America's unilateral commercial expansionism – and of double standards that threatened

---

[26] Hoover address, "The Future of our Foreign Trade", New York, 16 March 1926 (Washington, DC, 1926).

[27] Kellogg memorandum, "The Dawes Report", March 1925, Kellogg Papers; Stimson to Hoover, 8 June 1929, NA RG 59 462.00 R296/2941/1/2.

[28] Kellogg to Coolidge, 7 October 1924, Kellogg Papers; Kellogg to Hughes, 15 October 1924, Kellogg Papers.

[29] Kellogg to Herrick, 26 March 1927; 3 February 1927, NA RG 59 611.5131/514, 500.A15a 1/a; Kellogg to Gibson, 26 March 1927, *FRUS 1927*, I, p. 186; Kellogg to Whitehouse, 26 June 1927, *FRUS 1927*, II, p. 655; Keiger (1997), pp. 322–8.

to erode the legitimacy of Hoover's fledgling "economic peace". In July 1927, Kellogg observed "a very general feeling of hostility toward us by many Nations of the World growing partly out of misunderstanding and partly out of envy of our prosperity".[30]

Compared with the French scenario, the US impact on the "relative" stabilisation of the Weimar Republic, which in many ways became the America's "junior partner" after 1923, was far more significant. It created opportunities for but also imposed marked constraints on Weimar's coalition governments. As the principal new creditor power that also controlled the Dawes regime, the United States de facto created a "penetrated system" that entailed far-reaching encroachments on German sovereignty, especially the control of the sources and transfer of reparation payments. Following Hoover's approach, this unprecedented, highly dynamic process was overseen, in consultation with Washington, by the informally operating agent general Parker Gilbert. At the same time, it was now that Fordist industrial mass-production "working methods" and Taylorist rationalising scientific management that, in Gramsci's famous interpretation, were the outgrowth of "Americanism" and the United States' more "rationalized" capitalist social structures really started to affect Europe, not only interpenetrating the different economies and societies (though some more than others) but indeed beginning to transform European "civilization" and class structures.[31]

All of this had a particularly strong impact on the Weimar Republic. For his own purposes, Stresemann deliberately accepted a high degree of US interference in Germany's economic and political life. He did so ultimately to extricate Germany from Versailles' constraints through a close cooperation with the international system's strongest actor. Stresemann anticipated correctly that the American creditor's growing engagement would also augment its interest in the well-being of its principal debtor.[32] There was also opposition to US demands for welfare-cuts to restore public finance and spur productivity, especially in the Social Democratic Party. And both German Nationals and communists denounced the insidious influence of American capitalism. But, as Stresemann never failed to stress, America's continued financial *and political* engagement was critical for Germany's recuperation, far more so than in France.[33] It also remained crucial to Europe's pacification in one further respect. Ever since the Ruhr crisis, Stresemann had made its economic orientation – the pursuit of political ends by economic means – the distinctive feature of Weimar German foreign policy. Potentially, this opened up the

[30] Kellogg to Ogden, 13 July 1927, Kellogg Papers.
[31] See Gramsci (1988), pp. 277–80; De Grazia (2005), p. 4 ff., 95 ff.
[32] Stresemann speech, 14 December 1925, *ADAP*, B, I, 1, annex II, p. 729; Stresemann, *Reichstag* speech, 23 August 1924, Stresemann (1932), I, p. 519.
[33] Stresemann speech, 19 December 1925, Stresemann Papers, vol. 274.

perspective of anchoring Germany within the nascent Euro-Atlantic order as an economic and political great power that renounced aggressive revisionism. But the success of this most "modern" element of Stresemann's policy was inconceivable without American backing, not just in terms of capital. Gradually broadening the European concert into a transatlantic system that included the United States thus was and remained a core aim of Stresemann and his key strategist, Carl von Schubert.[34]

With different priorities in mind, Briand also came to acknowledge that building bridges to an aloof American administration could not only serve to broaden the basis of French security but also to strengthen France's position in the Franco-German peace process he sought to advance and control. And by the latter 1920s, even Poincaré had come to regard an improvement of strained relations with Washington as a strategic priority, particularly in the vital sphere of debt and reparations politics. As noted, French leaders also sought to stave off US pressures to eliminate "wasteful" military spending. On this sensitive issue, US concepts of general disarmament clearly clashed with the underlying French argument in the League's Preparatory Disarmament Commission that France had to retain a superiority in actual armaments vis-à-vis Germany's structurally superior war-making potential.[35]

By contrast, the third protagonist of Locarno, Austen Chamberlain, essentially pursued no transatlantic policy. Reflecting the attitudes of Baldwin's Conservative Cabinet, the British foreign secretary clung to a vision of Locarno politics that was both remarkably Eurocentric and predicated on the notion that Britain, the erstwhile hegemon of the nineteenth century's Vienna peace order, could still act as the decisive arbiter in the refashioned European concert of the 1920s. Consequently, he sought to bolster Europe's further stabilisation not by drawing the United States into European diplomacy to forge complex political-cum-financial settlements but rather by what he termed the concert politics of "reciprocity". Essentially, Chamberlain reckoned that Europe's pacification could be secured not the American but the Anglo-European way, through further Locarno-style settlements achieved through mutual concessions from Germany, France and other European powers. In his assessment, Britain had the power to broker such compromises, notably to resolve the Rhineland dispute.[36]

No less than Baldwin and Churchill, Chamberlain continued to be mindful of the new significance of the United States' financial and political clout as

---

[34] Stresemann statements to the Foreign Affairs Commission, 7 October 1926, Stresemann (1932), pp. 37–8; Schubert memorandum, 12 January 1928, *ADAP*, B, VIII, pp. 34 ff.

[35] Kellogg to Davies, 4 January 1926, Kellogg Papers, roll 17; Herrick to Kellogg, 8 June 1926, *FRUS 1926*, II, pp. 95–6; MAE, États-Unis, 66/1–7/24–29.

[36] Chamberlain to D'Abernon, 1 February 1926, *DBFP*, IA, I, no. 231; Chamberlain to Briand, 29 July 1926, FO 800/259/668.

"world creditor" and key power behind the Dawes regime. But, unlike Stresemann and Briand, he still saw no sense, and had no interest, in involving US policymakers and financiers in European politics, particularly in both essential and intricate questions of security. His abiding scepticism stemmed from his critical appraisal of Wilson's frustrated ambitions at Versailles and what he saw as the vacillations of Republican leaders in the face of Congressional and public pressures thereafter. In 1926, Chamberlain observed that the Coolidge administration was "difficult to deal with" because it constantly "chops & changes its policy to catch a favouring breeze or avoid a squall in the Senate".[37] Were such British perceptions accurate? Or were there any prospects of advancing towards a transatlantic concert?

IV.   No Transatlantic Concert, No Perpetual Peace

When taking over the State Department in March 1929, Stimson reiterated the basic credo of Republican foreign policy in the decade after the Great War, insisting that he would avoid any far-reaching foreign entanglements that could have unforeseeable consequences. Stimson therefore urged the Hoover administration to abstain from addressing any "political questions" that ensued from the crucial negotiations over the Young plan then underway.[38] The secretary's reticence was accentuated by the wary assessment of the European situation that had prevailed in the State Department ever since 1925. Its most influential advocate was the *éminence grise* of US diplomacy in the 1920s, the eventual under-secretary of state William Castle. Castle was convinced that the path to European peace, and particularly to anything approaching a genuine settlement of the Franco-German problem, remained long and intractable; and defusing the simmering Polish–German conflict was in his view a much harder task still. Precisely because of this, and because he did not foresee any tangible threat to US interests emanating from Europe, he warned Kellogg against entangling Washington in European politics. Castle saw neither a need for, nor any interest in, contemplating a more active international role for the United States, a US rapprochement with either the League or the new European concert.[39]

At a deeper level, further efforts to construct a more robust transatlantic system of order were thus marred by the fact that while European actors, and particularly Briand and Stresemann, sought to encourage more constructive American involvement, US decision-makers continued to espouse very

---

[37] Austen to Ida Chamberlain, 19 June 1926, Austen Chamberlain Papers, AC 5/1/386; Churchill memorandum, 7 February 1925, CAB 24/71(25).
[38] Stimson to Armour, 2 May 1929; Armour to Stimson, 10 May 1929, *FRUS 1929*, II, pp. 1066–8.
[39] See Castle Diary, 22 September 1926, vol. 10, pp. 231–2, Castle Papers.

different assumptions, particularly about what kind of *political* answers Europe's long-term pacification required. Like Hoover's, the strategies favoured by Kellogg, Stimson and Castle remained wedded to the notion that it was most expedient to use American power informally in order to nudge the Europeans to work out their differences – and that it was for them, not Americans, to make the requisite political commitments and bear the burdens that came with such commitments. Further, both the actions and the thinking of the leading US actors revealed deep-seated suspicions vis-à-vis the intricacies and inherent dangers of European "high politics", and these suspicions also applied to the Locarno-style search for political compromise.

It must be highlighted too of course that Republican foreign policy in this period was also still tangibly influenced by what its makers perceived as towering and essentially unchanging domestic constraints. Indeed, in contrast to Wilson, Hoover, Kellogg and Stimson succeeded in ensuring domestic legitimacy for their international policies. They did so by opting for politically less risky paths. They refrained from pursuing any initiatives that they expected to provoke Congressional and electoral opposition or criticism in influential pro-Republican newspapers like the *Chicago Tribune*. Yet what this meant was that there was no room for any substantive advances towards more proactive, internationally constructive approaches – either a more cooperative policy towards the League and the Locarno concert or a more creative and forward-looking debt and loan policy. And this never really changed in the years before the Great Depression, despite the efforts of the newly established Council on Foreign Relations, the Carnegie Endowment for Peace and other non-governmental pressure-groups and opinion-makers that campaigned for greater international engagement. Not a single leading Republican decision-maker in the latter 1920s deemed it necessary to build on Hughes' engagement and prepare the domestic ground for a more comprehensive US stabilisation policy in Europe. Notably, Kellogg never abandoned his furtive course vis-à-vis Congress and what he perceived as a largely isolationist US public. He was noticeably influenced by his mentor, Borah, who remained one of the Senate's most vocal and powerful voices against any moves that could enmesh the United States in "dangerous" international entanglements and commitments.[40]

Of particular importance was that, in the final analysis, Congressional and domestic strictures came to constrain the underlying ideas and guiding rationales of US postwar policies. Mindful of these strictures, key Republican policy-makers imposed their own limits on what they pursued and rationalised these limits. Above all, this came to reinforce the assumption that what was best for informally advancing US economic expansion would also serve to overcome Europe's economic – and political – *malaise*. Even if the domestic climate had

---

[40] See Kellogg's extensive correspondence with Borah throughout the 1920s, Kellogg Papers.

been more favourable, they would not have opted for more ambitious approaches, policies that could have led to a more robust regime of debt management, financial stabilisation and modernising reconstruction – something anticipating a post–First World War Marshall Plan after all – or that could have opened the door to a firmer, more stabilising North Atlantic Security Pact.

In structural terms, what impeded such advances in transatlantic relations in the latter 1920s was a constellation that had become even more asymmetric in geopolitical as well as in financial and economic terms since 1919. Essentially, all major European powers, and particularly Germany and France, depended more than ever on American financial power and political goodwill, and a still far more self-sufficient United States remained distinctly less dependent on Europe. Or that is at least how key Republican policymakers defined America's commercial and security interests, although Europe was turning into an ever more important market for US capital and goods. Against the backdrop of this asymmetrical configuration, US policymakers saw neither a major incentive *nor a grave crisis or risk on the European horizon* that would have warranted making the kind of commitments that the long-term stabilisation of the system of London and Locarno would have required.

It was in the critical domain of security that the transatlantic asymmetry was most striking. On the one hand, all the most relevant European powers desired wider US engagement, whether to reinforce the Locarno architecture in a more conservative fashion – as the French aimed to do – or to make Europe more secure in order to bolster peaceful change – as the Germans aspired to do. And additional re-assurance through some form of targeted US security commitments, especially to France, Poland and Czechoslovakia, would indeed have been critical to create more favourable conditions for further accommodation between Germany and its western and eastern neighbours. On the other hand, the dominant view in Washington remained that vital US security interests with regard to Europe had already been satisfied at Versailles, particularly through the de facto elimination of Germany's fleet and the drastic reduction of its army – and that the Locarno accords provided as adequate a basis for European security as the European governments could be expected to negotiate under the circumstances.[41]

Thus, American decision-makers saw no need, let alone any urgent need, to depart from expeditious non-entanglement maxims. In a speech he gave on 20 April 1926, Kellogg simply refused to acknowledge the potentially far-reaching implications of high degree of de facto interdependence that had arisen between the United States and Europe after the Great War not only in political, financial and economic terms but also in terms of security. Instead,

---

[41] Cecil statement, quoted after Miller (1928), I, p. 216.

he re-accentuated the traditional theme that the United States found itself in a "peculiarly fortunate situation" because of its "geographic isolation". Indeed, following the Locarno accords any German threat to the international order, let alone to US security, was seen as even more remote than after 1919. The US War Department concurred with Kellogg's assessment, and so did Hoover and Stimson.[42]

Rather than contemplate an extension of American responsibilities in the domain of security, what the Republican administrations prioritised after Locarno – and, in a wider perspective, after the success of the Washington Conference of 1921–22 – was to put pressure on the European powers, and above all on France, to effect "a real reduction of the crushing burden of armament".[43] The Republican idea that general peace and security could be enhanced through general disarmament effectively stood in a marked continuity with what Wilson had championed at Versailles. But because his successors felt they had to demarcate their distance from the League in every respect, they never whole-heartedly supported the efforts of the League's Preparatory Commission where, in the wake of Locarno, and, pushed forward by a growing transnational movement of disarmament activists, the most serious efforts took place to achieve what had been set as a general aim in the Versailles treaty – namely to take Germany's disarmament as a starting-point for steps to build peace through more universal disarmament measures.[44]

Yet these efforts soon stalled and would ultimately prove fruitless. At Geneva, the official US representative Hugh Gibson generally sided with the German government's quest for a greater "parity" in armaments – i.e. French disarmament and moderate German rearmament – and criticised French obstinacy, maintaining that the commission's negotiations should focus on "visible, tangible armaments and to peace strength" rather than taking into account a country's overall military *potential*.[45] In Washington, Kellogg maintained that it was "not possible to limit [the] ultimate war strength of any country". He stipulated that what really had to be done was to transcend the European, essentially French, "school of thought" which ultimately relied too much on the outmoded principle that "security must be guaranteed" by "military assistance against aggression". And he stressed that "there should be a direct approach" to arms limitation "without awaiting complicated measures for providing security", as disarmament essentially promoted

[42] Grew to Herrick, 20 April 1926, *FRUS 1926*, I, p. 78; Kellogg to Davies, 4 January 1926, Kellogg Papers.

[43] Castle to Ciechanowski, Castle Diary, 10 February 1926, vol. 8, p. 34, Castle Papers.

[44] See Webster (2016).

[45] Gibson to Kellogg, 11 June 1926, *FRUS 1926*, I, p. 109; Kellogg to MacVeagh, 2 March 1926, *ibid.*, p. 59. For German approaches, see Stresemann instructions to German delegation, Geneva, 26 December 1925; Köpke to Maltzan, *ADAP*, B, I/I, pp. 88, 325–6.

"the cause of security" by reducing "suspicion" in international politics.[46] But all sides were aware that France's representatives would not accept this premise. For in their view, which Briand shared, the protection of French security required the maintenance of armed forces that were significantly superior to those Weimar Germany was allowed to have, precisely because Germany's industrial-military potential was still so much greater than that of France, and thus had to be considered in any disarmament talks.[47]

Chamberlain, who remained a key strategic ally of Briand, actually favoured disarmament, not least on financial grounds, and sought to impress on the French government that "treaty or no treaty, no power on earth can keep Germany so disarmed indefinitely unless a measure of general disarmament follows". But in order to preserve a fundamental Anglo-French *entente* within the Locarno concert the British government then overall supported the French essentials. For American observers, a financially challenged France continued to spend absurdly high sums on arms – which it should have spent on economic modernisation – at a time when under the restrictions of Versailles, Germany seemed to pose no manifest threat even in the longer run. Soon, they concluded that in the end only financial pressure would induce French leaders to reduce military expenditure significantly.[48] But this did not occur, and the more fundamental problem lay elsewhere. Chamberlain was correct and indeed realistic when he noted that it would only be possible to achieve a substantial "reduction" in armaments once greater advances had been made towards solidifying the "security" architecture that had been set up at Locarno, and towards building further trust and confidence between the Locarno powers.[49] What the British foreign secretary did not sufficiently acknowledge was that in order to consolidate the peace and eventually create conditions for peace-enforcing, all-round disarmament such advances were actually required in a wider context: the relations between the Locarno powers and the United States.

But owing to the constraints and self-imposed limitations of Republican "fair-weather" policies, the prospects of widening the Locarno concert into a more robust Euro-Atlantic security system remained very limited. This became most obvious during the negotiations over the Kellogg-Briand Pact. In the spring of 1927, the French foreign minister Aristide Briand proposed to Washington a bilateral pact of perpetual peace, committing both nations to

---

[46] Kellogg to MacVeagh, 2 March 1926, *FRUS 1926*, I, p. 59; Grew to Herrick, 20 April 1926, *FRUS 1926*, I, p. 79; Kellogg to Davies, 4 January 1926, *Kellogg Papers*; Kellogg to Porter, 11 January 1927, *FRUS 1927*, I, pp. 163–6.

[47] For underlying French assumptions and priorities, see Briand statement to the Foreign Affairs Commission, 19 January 1927, C14764, no. 57/11.

[48] Houghton to Kellogg, 27 February 1926, *FRUS 1926*, I, p. 59.

[49] Chamberlain to Crewe, 12 April 1926, *DBFP*, IA, 1, no. 264; Chamberlain memorandum, 16 July 1925, CAB 24/174, CP357(25).

"the renunciation of war as an instrument of national policy".[50] With his overture, Briand not merely sought to induce the American government to support France's efforts to reinforce the European status quo and, indirectly, its East European alliance system with Poland and the powers of the Little *Entente*. In the transatlantic "great game" of the era of the Dawes Plan, he also intended to stave off American pressure on Paris to cut its military expenditure and, strategically, to improve France's position in the anticipated bargaining over a final reparations – and debt – settlement.[51] Briand's initiative set in motion an intricate process of transatlantic negotiations that on 27 April 1928 resulted in a widely acclaimed pact for the renunciation of war as a means of international politics.

In the United States, Shotwell had seized on the French overture to persuade Kellogg to convert Briand's plan into a far more ambitious initiative for a general, multilateral war-renunciation pact that built on the Locarno treaty and was to expand from a regional – transatlantic – to a global scope, in the end outlawing war around the world and thus buttressing "universal peace" in a new way. With Levinson's support, Shotwell prepared an elaborate design that he recommended as a felicitous "compromise between American history and the new experiments of Europe".[52] Soon, the burgeoning American war-outlawry movement and its most influential champion in the Senate, Borah, had put their weight behind this initiative and were exerting pressure on the administration in Washington as well as the government in Paris. This had a palpable effect.[53] From the summer of 1927 Kellogg would engage in a lengthy process of transatlantic pact diplomacy. But he did so not only on account of mounting domestic pressure. The secretary of state was also motivated by a rising concern about what he observed as a rising tide of "bitterness against the United States" in Europe. Such bitterness had been provoked by what many Europeans perceived as uncompromising US attitudes towards war debts and security, yet also the hard-fisted expansion of America's commercial predominance. In fact, part of what Kellogg thus tried to accomplish was to contain growing European resentment and to foster the legitimacy of the nascent "Pax Americana" of the 1920s.[54]

Once it had been refashioned in accordance with the State Department's preferences, Kellogg even came to regard the war-renunciation pact as a

[50] Briand statement, 6 April 1927; Kellogg to Herrick, 11 June 1927, FRUS 1927, II, pp. 611–3, 614.
[51] Briand statement, 6 April 1927, FRUS 1927, II, p. 612; MAE, États-Unis, 66/1–7, 24–8; MAE, Grande Bretagne, 34/8 ff. Cf. Keeton (1987), pp. 238–9.
[52] J.T. Shotwell, "An American Locarno", June 1927; Butler statement, 31 May 1927, Kellogg Papers, roll 27.
[53] See Gorman (2012), pp. 259–308; Hathaway and Shapiro (2018), pp. 121–30, 159–75.
[54] See Kellogg to Whitelaw Reid, 24 July 1928; Kellogg to Lippmann, 21 July 1928; Kellogg to Coolidge, 3 August 1928, Kellogg Papers, roll 31.

"valuable, practical and psychological reinforcement of existing efforts to maintain world peace".[55] Essentially, Kellogg succeeded in converting Briand's design into a universal pact that complemented the Locarno pact and was overall conducive to peaceful change. For it buttressed the provisions for arbitration and the pacific settlement of disputes that lay at the heart of the Locarno accords, and the League Covenant. In this respect, the thrust of the American war-renunciation policy clearly corresponded with the aims of both British and German pursuits of a further reform of the Versailles system. The Baldwin government signed the pact once Chamberlain had won American acquiescence to a British Monroe Doctrine. It stipulated that – in analogy to the self-accorded US prerogatives in the western hemisphere – Britain reserved the right to safeguard "certain regions of the world the welfare and integrity of which constitute a special ... interest for [its] peace and safety". This essentially exempted imperial defence from the purview of the war-renunciation treaty.[56] The Marx government in Berlin was the first to offer its "unconditional acceptance" of the final treaty. The thrust of Kellogg's pact policy was ultimately compatible with the underlying rationales of the policy of peaceful change that Stresemann and notably Schubert had developed to further a gradual modification of the postwar order – with US support, yet essentially through commonly accepted procedures and standards of international law.[57]

Due to the strict limits that the Coolidge administration set, however, the Kellogg-Briand Pact did not comprise any binding, more concrete commitments to the pre-emption of war. Notably, it did not specify any international sanctions against aggressors. While sending a widely noted signal and indicative of political and psychological tendencies *in some parts* of the political spectrum of the post–First World War era to banish the horror of modern warfare and to widen commitments to deeper forms of pacification, the pact of 1928, though not entirely utopian, was hardly likely to provide effective remedies. Modern war simply was not to be eliminated by being outlawed, especially under the conditions that existed in the aftermath of the Great War and in an era that continued to be burdened by the wider legacy of the age of global imperialism. There was no real alternative to what had commenced in 1919 and gained a new quality in 1925: persistent efforts to drill through the hard boards of *political* peace- and security-building.[58]

[55] Kellogg to Lippmann, 21 July 1928; Kellogg to Ogden, 13 June 1927, Kellogg Papers, rolls 31, 27; Kellogg, "The War Prevention Policy of the United States," 15 March 1928, *ibid.*, roll 31.
[56] Chamberlain memorandum to Kellogg, 19 May 1928, NA RG 59 711.4112 Anti-War 77; Hurst minute, 20 April 1928, *DBFP*, IA, V, no. 324.
[57] See Schubert directives, 12 January 1928, *ADAP*, B, VIII, pp. 34 ff.; Cabinet minutes, 19 and 27 April 1928, *AR Marx III and IV*, II, nos. 463, 466.
[58] For a different interpretation see Hathaway and Shapiro (2018), pp. xii–xxii.

At the same time, Kellogg's approach had demarcated limits of US security policy vis-à-vis Europe that would only be cast aside in the 1940s. Even more consequential in the latter 1920s was that the secretary's pact policy did not lead to a marked shift in American postwar policy. The war-renunciation pact did not foster significant new ties between the United States and the European concert. Kellogg could reassure the *Chicago Tribune* in July 1928 that Washington would not sign up to "any affirmative obligations of the Locarno Treaties".[59] As a result, the war-renunciation treaty failed to extend the Locarno system as Stresemann, Schubert and Shotwell had hoped.[60] Short of a profound crisis in international politics that engendered tangible threats to US national security, such as that eventually provoked by Nazi Germany, no real reorientation of US strategies was to be expected.

V. No "Final" Postwar Settlement. The Missed Opportunities of the Young Process and the Hague Conference of 1929

The fact that the Kellogg-Briand Pact essentially followed the American blueprint was welcomed in Berlin and had to be accepted in Paris, although it thwarted Briand's original hope to enlist US support in solidifying the *status quo*. But both the French foreign minister and his German counterpart had also pursued co-operative pact negotiations with Kellogg for another strategic reason, namely to place themselves on good terms with the United States in anticipation of what both rightly saw as the crucial issue of transatlantic politics in the latter 1920s: the revision of the Dawes Plan, which had to be effected sooner rather than later, and the search for a "final" reparations settlement.[61] In fact, all sides were keenly aware that, just like in 1924, the key to such a settlement lay not in Europe but in Washington – and New York.

As noted, under the systemic conditions of this transformative period the only realistic way to settle the remaining postwar problems in Europe was to negotiate further political-cum-financial "grand bargains" along the lines of the London agreement. But the European powers were still in no position to forge such bargains or compromises among themselves. In the era of the Dawes regime, it was simply impossible to divorce core issues of European security from the complex ramifications of international finance and, more concretely, the cycle of loans, reparations and war debts at the heart of transatlantic relations. And this meant that no further comprehensive

---

[59] Kellogg to Reid, 19 July 1928; Kellogg to McCormick, 21 July 1928, Kellogg Papers, roll 31.

[60] See Schubert to Hoesch, 19 January 1928; ADAP, B, VIII, p. 64; Kellogg to Lippmann, 21 July 1928; J. Shotwell, "An American Locarno" (1927), Kellogg Papers.

[61] Stresemann report to the Cabinet, *AR Marx IV*, no. 463; "The End of the Poincaré Ministry, June 1928–11 November 1928", Herriot Papers, vol. 3.

settlement, especially one "solving" the Rhineland question, was conceivable unless it was backed, or at least tolerated, by the American government. More generally, the transformative developments after 1923 had shown that if American and European actors basically collaborated, formally and informally, advances towards financial and economic stabilisation could propel political pacification.

Yet there was of course always the risk that quite the opposite scenario could occur. If leading US political and financial actors were unwilling or unable to widen their commitments and assume responsibilities and guarantees in a manner that befitted America's expanded interests in Europe and, crucially, its newly hegemonic role in the transatlantic – and global – financial and economic system, then it would be extremely difficult to take effective measures should a crisis of the reparations regime occur. And it would be even more difficult to take effective international measures in the event of a full-blown financial and economic crisis. Some critical observers, including Keynes, warned that such scenarios were by no means far-fetched.[62] But no leading US politician or financier in the latter 1920s – nor any leading actor in Europe – actually expected a massive crisis of the Dawes regime, let alone a historic systemic crisis of the proportions of the Great Depression. Indeed, while this appears dangerously myopic in retrospect, with the knowledge of what would happen after 1929, it is important to understand that the outlooks of these actors were shaped by the developments of the mid-1920s and thus overall optimistic.

While much attention has focused on Franco–German bilateral relations, the crux after Locarno was and remained that French and German leaders simply did not have the power to resolve the problems that still divided their countries *entre deux*, without essential US support. This had been thrown into stark relief by the frustration of the initiative for a "final postwar agreement" that Briand and Stresemann launched following their soon myth-enshrouded *tête-à-tête* encounter at Thoiry. The Thoiry initiative was launched right after Germany's finally successful accession to the League of Nations in the autumn of 1926. At the heart of the scheme that the continental protagonists of Locarno politics hatched lay a *quid pro quo* transaction. France would return to Germany the territory it still occupied – with Britain and Belgium – under the Versailles treaty, most of all the Rhineland, whose "liberation" had become the critical test for Stresemann's Locarno policy; and Berlin would compensate Paris through the liquidation of reparation bonds issued under the Dawes Plan, and thus contribute to overcoming France's then still acute financial crisis. Stresemann and Briand understood from the beginning that the "deal" they envisaged would arouse palpable domestic opposition, particularly on the Poincarist right, because it would end France's strategic control of the

---

[62] See Keynes (1978), XVIII, pp. 304–50.

Rhineland. Yet they also acknowledged that, as only the US financial market would permit raising the capital necessary for mobilising the Dawes bonds, the final decisions over the Thoiry project lay in American hands.[63]

Yet both Wall Street bankers and the reparations agent Parker Gilbert soon poured cold water on the Franco-German scheme. Crucially, however, the Coolidge administration outright rejected it, and the Baldwin government followed suit. Pointing to the core of their reservations, Parker Gilbert concluded that the Anglo-American powers would end up paying for the Franco-German project because it would endanger the Dawes regime and have undesirable repercussions on the international capital market. Poincaré eventually ended all speculation over a possible revival of Thoiry when he consolidated the franc and French finances without American support. He ultimately opposed any premature bargain that involved concessions in the Rhineland.[64] The cardinal lesson Briand and Stresemann had to absorb was that a further "grand" postwar settlement could only be envisaged on terms that the United States set, or at least accepted.[65] In the end, not informal US agents but the American government itself continued to set the essential ground-rules of Euro-Atlantic politics in the system of London and Locarno.

After the failure of the Thoiry project, all sides were thus even more keenly aware that only the American reparations agent could initiate a revision of the Dawes settlement, on which the resolution of so many other questions depended. In turn, however, Parker Gilbert could only set the "terms of reference" for a conclusive reparations settlement in accordance with what the administration in Washington desired. In fact, this is exactly how the Young process eventually evolved after the reparations agent set it in motion in December 1927.[66] The outcome of this process was to be crucial for the longevity of the system of London and Locarno. Yet though it ultimately endorsed the participation of Owen Young and the banker J.P. Morgan Jr in the so-called Young committee, the incoming Hoover administration kept a pronounced distance from the committee's deliberations in the spring of 1929.[67]

The search for a final settlement ended with a further and, as it turned out, *the last* Euro-Atlantic "grand bargain" after the Great War – before the Great Depression changed the entire playing-field so dramatically. The first core element of this bargain was the comprehensive reparations settlement that

[63] Schubert memorandum, 3 September 1926, *ADAP*, B, I/II, p. 157; Stresemann to Hoesch, 8 December 1925, *ADAP*, B, I, 1, pp. 46–7; Briand to Poincaré, 20 August 1926, Série Europe, Allemagne, vol. 398, MAE Paris.

[64] Poincaré to Briand, 22 September 1926, Série Europe, Allemagne, vol. 399, MAE Paris.

[65] Stresemann instructions to German embassies, 26 October 1926, *ADAP*, B, I/II, pp. 373 ff.; Crewe to Chamberlain, 10 November 1926, FO 371/11331.

[66] Gilbert report, 10 December 1927; Gilbert memorandum, 24 February 1928, quoted after McNeil (1986), p. 192.

[67] Kellogg to Armour, 26 December 1928, NA RG 59, 462.00 R296/2560.

was forged, though only after long and arduous negotiations, at the first Hague Conference in August 1929; its second core element was an agreement between the Locarno powers, also thrashed out at The Hague, that settled the Rhineland question's thorniest problem, setting an end to the French (and Belgian) occupation. It was to be terminated by June 1930, significantly prior to the 1935 deadline of the Versailles treaty. Yet – in hindsight – this bargain not only came too late to pre-empt or at least contain the massive crisis that was to erupt hard on its heels. It also was less comprehensive than it could have been. And this can essentially be attributed to the policies of the American government, notably the newly inaugurated Hoover administration. US policy did not follow the "same path" Hughes had pursued in 1923.[68] Rather, American strategies took a retrograde turn. Hoover decided to abstain from even an informal political steering-role in negotiating a "final" reparations settlement. And this had distinctly negative consequences for the consolidation of the postwar order.[69]

While the European negotiations went on at The Hague, Hoover under-scored his refusal to make any governmental commitments in order to place the Dawes regime on a firmer footing or to bolster the accommodation process between the western powers and an already crisis-ridden Weimar Germany. In his assessment, the European powers were called upon to "solve" the repar-ations problem, essentially by following the recommendations of the Young committee. They thus were to implement American "terms of reference" while the American government remained absent. At the same time, Washington's aloofness was to pre-empt any European attempts to clamour for a general reduction of reparations and war-debt obligations, as particularly the British Treasury had originally hoped.[70] The Hague settlement and particularly its most critical political result, the Rhineland evacuation, can therefore be seen as the last significant settlement achieved through the mechanism of the Locarno concert. It was finalised in negotiations between Stresemann, Briand and Chamberlain's successor, the Labour foreign secretary Arthur Henderson.[71] Due to Washington's absence, the negotiations of The Hague marked a departure from the pattern of the London reparations conference. Nonetheless, the European powers had to act on a playing-field that was still predominantly determined by the absent American power.

Prior to the Young process, there had been different French attempts to counter overbearing US domination. Amidst an escalating Franco-American "tariff war", Briand had approached Stresemann and the Müller government

---

[68] See Leffler (1979), pp. 194–219.

[69] See also Cohrs (2006), pp. 531–71.

[70] Tyrrell to Lindsay, 17 November 1927; Tyrrell to Hopkins, 5 December 1927; Sargent to Phipps, 5 January 1928, DBFP, IA, IV, nos. 44, 84 (enclosure), 107.

[71] See Schubert memorandum, 9 August 1929, ADAP, B, XII, no. 157.

with proposals for a new kind of Franco-German economic bloc that would develop common commercial, tariff and cartel policies. In a parallel initiative, Poincaré and Briand had also sought to include Berlin in a debtors' *entente* against the American creditor.[72] When this failed, essentially because Stresemann was loath to alienate Germany's senior partner, the French premier had shifted to a pragmatic accommodation with the United States. He had pressed for the ratification of the Mellon-Bérenger debt agreement with Washington, which the French Chamber finally endorsed, three years after its conclusion, on 21 July 1929.[73]

Crucially, Poincaré was now prepared to cede France's essential security *glacis* in return for German reparation guarantees in a conclusive transatlantic agreement. As the Versailles deadline for France's withdrawal was drawing nearer, he saw such an agreement as the best way to ensure sizeable and continued German payments that could cover France's liabilities towards the United States.[74] In Berlin, Stresemann and Schubert had explored all avenues still available after Thoiry to advance the Franco-German accommodation process through the Locarno concert.[75] But the protagonists of Weimar's essentially transatlantic foreign policy consistently declined French overtures that risked manoeuvring Germany into conflict with Washington and Wall Street. For both, developing "parallel interests" with the United States still took clear precedence, even when this became ever harder, as the run-up to the Hague Conference and the implementation of the Young Plan manifested.[76]

The Young Plan has been criticised as an inherently tenuous and short-lived compromise.[77] Yet while its shortcomings are undeniable, the scheme deserves a more benign appraisal if one considers the immense international and domestic pressures under which the Young committee and, subsequently, the European negotiators had to operate in 1929. That the committee's scheme for the first time set a deadline for German reparations – fixing a payment period of no less than 59 years – was grist to the mills of German nationalist propaganda. The unprecedented, though ultimately unsuccessful campaign against the Young Plan launched by the right-wing press magnate Alfred Hugenberg and the rising leader of the National Socialist Party, Adolf Hitler,

---

[72] Döhle (Paris) to AA, 11 June 1928, *ADAP*, B, XII, no. 22; Stresemann memorandum, 27 August 1928, *ADAP*, B, X, pp. 640–1; minutes of a conversations between Müller and Briand, Geneva, 5 September 1928, *AR Müller II*, I, no. 20.

[73] See Artaud (1978), pp. 870 ff.

[74] See minutes of a conversation between Poincaré and Gilbert, January 1928, Ministère des Finances, B32/210.

[75] Stresemann memorandum, 27 August 1928, *ADAP*, B, X, pp. 640–1; Schubert note, 6 September 1928, *ADAP*, B, X, no. 19, ft. 4.

[76] Stresemann instructions to the German embassies, 26 October 1926, *ADAP*, B, I/II, pp. 373 ff.

[77] See Kent (1989), pp. 287–313, Tooze (2014), pp. 488–93.

denounced it as an Anglo-American conspiracy to "enslave" Germany for two generations.[78]

But the Young settlement actually benefited Germany. It not only brought the Rhineland compromise. It also provided the Weimar Republic with an international framework that – however imperfect – was urgently needed to preserve its increasingly threatened stability. It reduced German payments in the short term (1929–32) and all further annuities from 2.5 to 2 billion *Reichsmark*. And it finally re-established German "financial sovereignty" because it terminated the control regime of the Dawes Plan.[79] Instead, the Young Plan called for a – long overdue – international mechanism that could potentially underpin a more crisis-proof global financial system: the Bank for International Settlements (BIS).[80] These advances led the Social Democratic chancellor Hermann Müller to endorse the Young scheme without major reservations. To the end, Stresemann held that the survival of the Weimar Republic depended on preserving its co-operation and interdependence with the other Locarno powers and, notably, the United States.[81]

Hoover welcomed the Hague settlement. He even claimed that the result of the conference proved that it was in the European powers' best interest to adopt American strategies.[82] In fact, however, the first Hague Conference could not produce what would have been most imperative to ensure the postwar order's further consolidation: a more fundamental reform of the Dawes regime that turned it into a more solid framework not only for controlling the cycle of US loans, German reparations and British and French debt payments but also, and crucially, for regulating Europe's further financial *and political* stabilisation. In the final analysis, Washington's veto against underpinning the Young regime was most consequential in this respect.

As a result, the Young process, which could still be advanced under relatively stable conditions, has to be regarded as a one of the most significant missed opportunities of the inter-war period. Most of all, it was an opportunity missed by the Hoover administration. The administration's reserved attitude towards the Bank for International Settlements encapsulates the limitations of US policy, and the underlying reasons for these limitations. At one level, its reservations were motivated by the concern that it was likely to turn into "much more than a clearing house" for reparations transfers. This, and that the bank's governing board was to comprise members "from various countries", threatened to

---

[78] Rumbold to Henderson, 9 June 1929, *DBFP*, IA, VI, no. 174.
[79] Stresemann to Löbe, 29 September 1929, *ADAP*, B, XIII, pp. no 26.
[80] See Eichengreen (1992, pp. 262–4.
[81] German Cabinet minutes, 1 May 1929, *AR Müller II*, I, no. 191.
[82] Hoover, "First Annual Message to Congress," 3 December 1929, in Hoover (1934), I, pp. 143–4.

infringe on America's independence in the domain of financial policy. Not least, Republican policymakers reckoned, such concerns would provoke "considerable reservations" in Congress not only to the bank but also to the entire Young plan.[83]

More profoundly, though, US decision-makers originally had no part in setting up the international bank because they suspected that the European governments would abuse it for political purposes, chiefly for putting renewed pressure on Washington to concede debt reductions, and finally to accept what official US policy continued to deny: the connection between postwar debts and reparations.[84] Because the interests of US taxpayers were at stake, the administration had to reckon with the uncompromising stance of the powerful Congressional War Debt Commission. Still neither administration officials nor a majority in Congress saw any reason why France, or Britain, should be entitled to leniency.[85] Fundamentally, a majority of decision-makers in Washington and New York were adamant that ten years after Versailles the United States was not to be pushed into a position where it ultimately would have to do what had been so strictly avoided ever since Versailles, namely to bear – through debt relief – the brunt of the financial fall-out of a disastrous war into which, in the assessment that by now prevailed, the European powers had plunged themselves, and the world, through their nationalist and imperialist rivalries. And this by and large reflected the views of a majority of American voters and the most influential opinion-makers.

Hoover's underlying suspicions in this regard remained unchanged, and so did his advocacy of an expert approach to international problems – under informal American control. On these premises, the president finally allowed the former chairman of the Federal Reserve Bank of New York, Gates W. McGarrah, and other US bankers to play a leading part in establishing the Bank for International Settlements in November 1929. McGarrah was in fact made its first president. Yet the bank's critical deficiency remained that it was not buttressed by firmer governmental guarantees, and the political will to develop it precisely into an institution whose remit went beyond that of a "clearing house" for reparations. And critical for this deficiency remained the refusal of the Hoover administration to commit the postwar world's new financial hegemon to such an ambitious international agenda. Chiefly because of such self-imposed limitations, the Bank for International Settlements could only become an ephemeral precursor of the World Bank. More generally, the Young regime remained an equally ephemeral precursor of the Bretton Woods

---

[83] Howard to Henderson, 29 August 1929, *DBFP*, IA, VII, no. 347.

[84] See Self (2006), pp. 57–9.

[85] See Mellon to Olney, 26 August 1925, NA RG 39, Box 220; Hoover memoranda, 23 September 1925 ff., Hoover Papers, Commerce, Box 20.

system whose protagonists, Harry Dexter White and John Maynard Keynes, drew important lessons from the shortcomings of the inter-war period.[86]

Essentially, the making of the Young settlement revealed that the Republican government was unable, and unwilling, to play a leading role in consolidating the system of London and Locarno. Hoover thus spurned the warning that the influential American commentator Walter Lippmann had addressed to European statesmen before the Hague Conference: that the gains any nation could make by pursuing its own "particular interests" would pale into insignificance beside "the gains which would accrue to that nation and to the whole world from a general liquidation of the remaining post-war problems".[87] The central problem was that most decision-makers in Washington tended to assume that the United States could afford to pursue double-standard policies in its relations with Europe and the rest of the world: that it was in a position to forgo the commitment to common ground-rules of international politics and finance, and at the same time have "the best of all worlds" by making up its own rules where it appeared to suit US interests.

The evolution of US foreign economic policy in this phase revealed such tendencies most blatantly. On the one hand, as we have seen, ever since 1919 it had been a cardinal US aim to replace the "closed" and in American eyes war-prone protectionist blocs of the imperialist era with a non-discriminatory trading system premised on the American "Open Door" principle. On the other hand, ceding primacy to Congress, the Hoover administration never took decisive steps to alter an ever more protectionist American tariff policy. Precisely when the European powers were struggling to reach agreement on the Young plan, Congressional debates commenced that by May 1930 led to the passing of the Smoot-Hawley Act. It imposed even higher tariffs on industrial and agricultural goods than the already very prohibitive Fordney-McCumber tariff of the early 1920s.[88] This not only reinforced already existing imbalances in transatlantic trade. It also further weakened the legitimacy of Hoover's vision of an "American peace", causing irritations throughout Europe, particularly in France.[89]

The interest to develop a common platform to counter what were perceived as unfair US trade policies also played a part in spurring far-reaching Franco-German economic negotiations which in August 1927 led to a breakthrough that at the same time marked a departure from the earlier postwar patterns of fierce economic-cum-political antagonism. Both countries now concluded an

[86] See James (2001).
[87] Howard to Henderson, 9 August 1929, FO 840/6/11/10.
[88] Stimson to Hoover, 8 June 1929, FRUS 1929, II, pp. 998–9; Stimson to Smoot, 26 June 1929, NA RG 59 611.003/1673a.
[89] Memorandum of a conversation between Stresemann and Briand, 11 June 1929, ADAP, B, XII, pp. 44–8.

unprecedentedly comprehensive trade agreement in which French negotiators accepted, in a clear break with Versailles, that the principle of most-favoured nation would from now on govern bilateral trade relations, ending previous restrictions. Both sides also envisaged that this principle should hence also govern what was conceived as a multilateral trade system for Europe. Pointing even further ahead to developments that would transform European politics after 1945, Briand, Stresemann and their closest advisers even began to discuss what further steps could be taken towards closer economic cooperation and some form of economic and political union of the European states. And here too, the aim to establish a more effective counterweight to the uncompromising "American empire" featured prominently, particularly on the French agenda.[90]

This broader transatlantic context, and the underlying interest to join forces against the United States' overbearing unilateralism, also has to be taken into account to understand the significance and thrust of Briand's widely noted proposal for a federal, but still far from supranational "United States of Europe", which he put forward in front of the League Assembly in September 1929. Clearly, his visionary design was not *only* intended to transcend the Franco–German antagonism by seeking to embed the new concert between the former enemies in a wider European framework.[91] Revealingly, however, Stresemann responded to Briand's proposal by presenting a decidedly more pragmatic and less ambitious blueprint for a European *economic* federation; and he was careful to avoid the impression that the closer European cooperation and integration he favoured had any anti-American impetus. To the very end, then, Stresemann cultivated an often frustrating but nonetheless essential partnership with the United States.[92]

VI.   Dissolution. The Unravelling of the Nascent Atlantic Order of the 1920s during the World Economic Crisis

The World Economic Crisis turned into a vicious spiral of successive crises that eventually could no longer be reversed, or even slowed down, by either politicians or financiers. And it came to have a devastating effect that can only

---

[90] See Krüger (1986), pp. 151–2.

[91] Briand speech to the League assembly, 5 September 1929, *Société des Nations* (1929), pp. 52–3. In May 1930, when the prospect for realising his scheme had dimmed dramatically and Stresemann's death (on 3 October 1929) had set back not only Franco-German reconciliation, Briand would follow up his speech with a detailed plan for "The Organisation of a Regime for a Federal Union of Europe". See Briand (1930), pp. 1–12. For the League's role in securing the European and world economy, see Clavin (2013), pp. 11–46.

[92] Stresemann speech to the League Assembly, 9 September 1929, *Société des Nations* (1929), pp. 70–1.

be compared to that of the Great War, but that this time also shook the foundations of the American republic to the core. The means of the European powers to contain the crisis, which set in with the Wall Street crash of October 1929 but only really escalated in 1931, were highly constrained. The responses of those actors who, if any, could have taken the lead, the protagonists of the Hoover administration in Washington, came belatedly and proved strikingly inadequate. In the end, they proved insufficient to prevent the demise of the fledgling Atlantic order that had been built since the mid-1920s. The Young regime collapsed less than two years after the Young plan had officially come into effect. Its fate was sealed, and reparations were effectively abolished, at the Lausanne conference of July 1932, which also de facto terminated European war-debt payments to the United States.[93] In the critical realm of international security politics, the nadir was reached when, also in the summer of 1932, Germany – under Franz von Papen's "cabinet of national concentration" – walked out of the final round of the Geneva Disarmament Conference. By the end of that year, not only all further meaningful arms-limitation efforts had been wrecked. The entire security architecture of the Locarno treaty and the Kellogg-Briand Pact had finally been eroded, setting the stage for Hitler.

Looking back at these fateful years of crisis after the even greater catastrophe of the Second World War, Hoover would later argue that the international "system" of the 1920s had been destroyed by "the malign forces" that had arisen from "the economic consequences of [the First World War]". More precisely, he blamed its disintegration, and the Great Depression, on the deficiencies of the Treaty of Versailles, "the postwar military alliances with their double prewar armament" and the European states' "unbalanced budgets", "inflations" and "frantic public works programs to meet unemployment".[94] But Hoover's unsubtle attempt to shift responsibility for the catastrophe to the Europeans, their pathological traditions and misguided pursuits in fact distorts the actual historical developments that preceded the World Economic Crisis. For one cardinal factor accounting for the rapid dissolution of international order after the escalation of the crisis in 1931 was unquestionably that the Republican administrations of the latter 1920s had failed to draw harder lessons from the Great War *and* the successful settlements of London and Locarno.

The frustration of American pursuits of Europe's progressive renewal was not due to the fact that US decision-makers pursued aims that were incompatible. The fundamental problem did not arise from their core assumption that it would be possible to strengthen Weimar Germany and to contain German power, to integrate the vanquished of 1918 into a reformed international order and to buttress French, Polish and wider European security at the same time.

---

[93] *DBFP*, II, III, nos. 137–92.
[94] Hoover (II/1952), pp. 61, 89.

What made US aspirations founder was rather that those who directed them had not made greater efforts to pursue, and legitimise, more forward-looking strategies to *reinforce* the stabilisation of Europe when overall conditions were still relatively auspicious.

Decisive US leadership in the latter 1920s would have been crucial for consolidating Germany's newly republican order and integrating it into a recast international system. With the benefit of hindsight, there is little doubt that the unravelling of this integration process ultimately caused the demise of the international system of the 1920s. Once the Great Depression had begun to overshadow everything else, neither the United States nor the western Locarno powers had the means to forestall the internal disintegration of Weimar Germany. US decision-makers had ever fewer incentives at their disposal to reverse this process. Nor could they pass effective international sanctions to prevent Stresemann's successors from renouncing the obligations that Weimar German governments had assumed between 1924 and 1929. This fundamental shift in German policy, which the more assertive chancellor Brüning initiated in 1930, was completed on distinctly more radical premises by his successors von Papen, Schleicher, and Hitler.[95]

It is crucial to understand, though, that the World Economic Crisis was actually *not* a consequence of the international settlements of the mid-1920s. The rapid deterioration processes of the early 1930s did *not* throw into relief that the advances made since the Ruhr crisis had been misguided or even prepared the ground for the calamities that engulfed Europe and the world after 1929. And the event that did not trigger but foreshadowed the subsequent descent into the abyss in 1931, the collapse of the US stock-market, cannot be directly linked to the working or failure of the system of London and Locarno. Rather, it was an outgrowth of the failure of the Republican administrations to institute tighter control mechanisms and to restrain Wall Street hyper-speculation during the "golden twenties".

Further, it has clearly been established that the underlying causes of what Keynes already in December 1930 called "one of the greatest economic catastrophes of modern history" and its even more destructive escalation thereafter have to be sought in the complicatedly interconnected spheres of post–First World War international finance and indebtedness. And they have to be sought in the highly uneven development within a dynamically changing and essentially still very unregulated world financial and economic order that was now de facto dominated by the United States.[96] What played an important part here were not only the precarities of the international debt regime but also the deficiencies of the supposedly self-regulating monetary system based on

---

[95] See Bülow memorandum, 25 October 1929; German Foreign Office to Sthamer, 31 December 1929, *ADAP*, B, XIII, nos. 76, 224. Krüger (1985), pp. 512–29.

[96] Keynes (1930), p. 126.

the gold standard, which had been reconstituted in the decade after the war but proved to be a "fair-weather" system that crumbled in the crisis. And what exacerbated unevenness and instability was an asymmetric trade "system" of US foreign economic policy which even increased disparities between 1919 and 1929. That the Smoot-Hawley Act was passed only months after "Black Friday" is just one case in point.[97]

But that the Wall Street crash could eventually escalate – through the collapse of the Central European banking systems in 1931 – into a full-blown world crisis, whose economic and political impact on Europe was even more disastrous than its effect on the United States, can indeed be ascribed to developmental and learning processes in the sphere of international politics that, though remarkable, *simply did not go far enough*. At one level, it can be attributed to the fact that the peacemakers of 1919 had only been able to thrash out an in many ways ill-conceived, unfinished and burdensome post-war settlement – and that the decision-makers who followed after them thus still had to deal with interwoven political, financial and economic challenges stemming from the war *and* the original peace settlement whose magnitude can scarcely be overestimated. At another level, it can be attributed to the fact that the reform and consolidation processes of the 1920s and, at the core, the incipient transformation of the ideas and practices of international politics in the era of London and Locarno remained limited in crucial aspects.

While the European protagonists of Locarno politics struggled not only to sustain but also to expand on the advances of the mid-1920s, what mattered most here was the unwillingness and inability of those who determined the policies of the pre-eminent American power to fortify what had been initiated after the Ruhr crisis. Of decisive import was, as now became clear, that US decision-makers had not done more to transform the system of London and Locarno in cooperation with their European counterparts into a more robust and resilient system of international politics *and* finance in a phase, the latter 1920s, when the circumstances for this were still relatively conducive. This also, but not only, pertained to one particular structural shortcoming that the Young process had by no means remedied: the lack of oversight and crisis-reaction mechanisms which could have prevented the collapse of the complex and vulnerable transatlantic system of private, often short-term loans, reparation and war-debt payments that had taken shape since 1924.[98]

Once the World Economic Crisis reached its peak, its debilitating effect on internal politics – and national economies – placed severe limits on all governments to pursue international cooperation. This applied to the United

[97] See Eichengreen (1992), 246–86; Kindleberger (1973); pp. 95 ff., 291–308; and Keynes's piercing contemporary analysis in Keynes (1930), pp. 126–30.
[98] Cf. Cohrs (2006) pp. 572–602; the thorough analysis in Boyce (2009), pp. 230–421; and Tooze (2014), pp. 487–510.

States, France, Britain and many other countries in and beyond Europe. Nowhere, however, did it become more obvious than in the Weimar Republic, whose existential calamities were exploited and compounded by Hitler and the National Socialists, which only now became decisive force in German politics. But, if less dramatically than that of the Weimar coalition governments of the early 1930s, the Hoover administration's domestic and international room to manoeuvre shrank rapidly too. Because they had not developed firmer understandings and ways to coordinate political crisis management with their European counterparts, Hoover and Stimson now essentially lacked the means to lead efforts to cope with the greatest challenge to European, American and global peace and stability since the Great War – which, if at all, could only be accomplished through coordinated international and above all transatlantic responses.

What occurred instead between 1930 and 1933, not least due to the shortcomings of previous US policies and the absence of American international leadership, was a fundamental shift towards narrowly conceived "self-help" policies. And this indeed came to erode the international system whose groundwork had been created in the mid-1920s. The world financial and trade system dissolved into protectionist blocs and closed national spheres of influence. What spelled even more disastrous consequences was that a vehement "renationalisation" process also superseded all previous quests for concerted stabilisation in the sphere of international politics, particularly international security politics. The World Economic Crisis not only led to the dissolution of the European concert. It also rendered futile all the limited attempts at transatlantic crisis management that the Hoover administration pursued at the eleventh hour. Instead of redoubling their efforts to strengthen international mechanisms to cope with the burgeoning calamities, the major powers sought to chart their own solitary courses in vain attempts to bring their ships through the storm.[99] And decisive for throwing the somewhat more coordinated international "fleet" of the 1920s into disarray was that decision-makers in Washington, who stood at the flagship's helm, ultimately pursued a profoundly unilateral course as well.

What most immediately hastened the demise of Euro-Atlantic order in the early 1930s was that European policymakers had not yet been able, and that US policymakers had been unwilling, to strengthen the Young regime through more effective political guarantees, bail-out provisions and crisis pre-emption instruments. Undoubtedly, even before 1929 it would have been difficult for any American administration to persuade Congress and the wider American public that such measures were imperative to regulate the complex flows of private, often short-term loans, reparations and debt repayments. Crucially, as

---

[99] See Kennedy (2001), p. 76.

noted, only the American administration, and Congress, could have given the decisive initial impetus by allowing some form of debt relief – or even cancellation. This could have induced Britain and France to reduce or even relinquish their reparation demands and might have put Germany in a better position not only to service loans but also to put its finances and economy on a firmer footing. Yet because of unwavering American opposition none of these paths had been pursued. And by the time the crisis reached massive proportions, in 1931, it soon became clear that it was too late for any initiative to cut through the Gordian knots of postwar debt and reparations politics or even to mitigate the consequences of the crisis. Neither the Young regime nor the financial and economic order of the 1920s could be salvaged.

Once the repercussions of the European crisis were felt in the United States in the spring of 1931, Hoover at first believed that he could largely shield the American economy from them. And he sought to achieve a "recovery independent of the rest of the world" through initiatives to balance the US budget by raising taxes.[100] When this proved ineffectual, Hoover finally abandoned his reliance on informal, expert-driven approaches to international stabilisation. The American president never envisaged annulling US war-debt claims to break the vicious circle of international indebtedness. Rather, he on 20 June 1931 called on all countries to observe a one-year moratorium on all "intergovernmental debts, reparations and relief debts".[101] But this moratorium was to no avail; it could not shore up the Young regime. Because it still dreaded making concessions on its creditor's claims, the Hoover administration abstained from the decisive Lausanne conference on debts and reparations, convened in the summer of 1932. It therefore had to register from afar that, through the Lausanne accords, Britain and France not only renounced their reparations claims vis-à-vis Germany. Though conceding, in a "gentlemen's agreement", that the accords would only come into effect once a compromise with Washington had been reached, the European powers also effectively abandoned any further debt repayments to the United States. For the "gentlemen's agreement" remained a dead letter, and any transatlantic compromise elusive.[102]

Fundamentally, Hoover's government never seriously reconsidered its essentially non-committal attitude towards the Young regime and the Bank for International Settlements. Only the American administration could have taken the lead in searching for coordinated international strategies to cope with the crisis and, notably, prop up failing banking systems on both sides of the Atlantic. Yet Hoover opted for a unilateral approach. It should also be

---

[100] Hoover, annual message to Congress, 8 December 1931, FRUS 1931, I, p. XIII.
[101] Hoover (II/1952), p. 70; Stimson diary, 15 and 18 June 1931, Stimson Papers.
[102] Simon to Tyrrell, 11 July 1932, DBFP, II, III, no. 189; Stimson diary 11 July 1932, Stimson Papers; Clavin (2000), pp. 152 ff.

stressed, though, that by the time the nadir of 1931 was reached it would have been all but impossible for any American government to gain domestic support for assuming fresh and extensive international obligations with unforeseeable consequences. In fact, Franklin D. Roosevelt would win the election of 1932 by proposing an even more nationally-focused, indeed strikingly "Americanocentric" strategy to overcome the Great Depression – the New Deal. And Roosevelt then indeed embarked on what became an unprecedented and on balance successful quest to reinvigorate the United States by seizing on its domestic potential. The upshot of this was, however, that for the remainder of the crisis-ridden 1930s, the United States left Europe and the rest of the world more or less to their own devices.[103]

It was only under the pressures of the world crisis that earlier, in 1931, the Hoover administration had finally abandoned Washington's political non-entanglement in relations with Europe. Yet its efforts to spur pacific though in fact rapid and drastic changes in the postwar constellation – at the eleventh hour – were not based on a coherent strategy and proved futile. In short, both Hoover and Stimson held that it was high time to abet, in a controlled manner, what they considered legitimate German grievances. In September 1931, Stimson noted that a resolution of Europe's "underlying problems" hinged on "*the revision of the Versailles treaty*".[104] At the same time, both policymakers were united in their assessment that the crux of European postwar politics was and remained France's aspiration to assert a continental hegemony. And in their eyes it was the French reliance on "ruinous" military preponderance, rather than German ambitions, that threatened to provoke a new European arms race. Hoover and Stimson therefore sought to induce France to moderate its reparations claims, accept substantial disarmament and pursue a more conciliatory course vis-à-vis Germany. In particular, Paris was to permit changes in the Versailles treaty to moderate the policies of the Brüning government and contain the rise of the National Socialists, above all a revision of the Polish–German border. US efforts to this end culminated in talks with the French premier Pierre Laval in Washington in the autumn of 1931.[105]

But all of these aspirations were half-hearted. They were never part of a consistent strategy and fell well short of what could have stemmed the tide in Europe. In the final analysis, their effectiveness was constrained by the same limits that had already marked US policy prior to the Great Depression: the administration's reluctance to make the case for wider strategic commitments, let alone guarantees, to rescue the Euro-Atlantic postwar order. When the final Geneva Disarmament Conference began its proceedings in February 1932, the

[103] See Dallek (1995), pp. 23–34.
[104] Stimson diary, 30 September 1931, Stimson Papers; Hoover (II/1952), pp. 88–9.
[105] Stimson diary, 8 June 1931 and 23 November 1932, Stimson Papers.

Hoover administration had returned to a strict policy of non-engagement, distancing itself from any League-based efforts to hammer out a general arms-limitation scheme. While persisting with its calls for arms reduction on economic grounds, the American government still declined to back its appeals by any incentives either in the form of new political guarantees or by finally countenancing debt-relief.[106]

Germany's withdrawal from the Geneva Disarmament Conference in July, ordered by Chancellor von Papen, and the Anglo-French concession of "equality of rights" in terms of armaments to an ever more assertive German regime in December 1932 did not just deal a final blow to League-based disarmament efforts after the Great War. Both events in fact marked the penultimate stage of the dissolution of the transatlantic international system that had been created between 1919 and 1929. Its final disintegration and the parallel demise of the Weimar Republic would then, in 1933, extinguish the lights that had been lit and kept alive in this fulcrum decade of the long twentieth century. And, just at the time Franklin Roosevelt assumed the American presidency and launched a *national* New Deal that eventually would have repercussions far beyond the United States, Hitler would set out to unleash the assault on what remained of the reconfigured Atlantic peace order of the 1920s – and the forces of the dark would triumph in and beyond Europe for more than ten murderous, barbarous years.[107]

---

[106] See Cohrs (2006), pp. 596–602.
[107] On the international history of the "dark" decade of the 1930s see Zara Steiner's thorough *magnum opus*, Steiner (2011).

Final Perspectives

The *Cadmeian Peace*

The Eventual Creation of the Long Twentieth Century's Atlantic Order after 1945 and the Crucial Lessons of the Era of the First World War

After 1945, a qualitatively different, more durable, strikingly more comprehensive and overall more legitimate Atlantic peace order would be built. Indeed, it was now that a veritable *Pax Atlantica* took shape. Many European actors made critical contributions to this process, which was far from inevitable. But what proved crucial was that those who now directed American policies indeed – at last – came to develop ideas, pursue strategies and assume responsibilities that turned the United States not only into a novel superpower, and the premier power of the West, but also into the benign hegemon, a "first among equals", of this new order. Thus, the real transformation that gave rise to what became the Atlantic order of the long twentieth century only occurred, finally, in the wake of two global wars and one massive global economic crisis. Essentially, it took place in the years between 1941 and 1955.

This transformation of transatlantic international politics would have been inconceivable, and the new order would never have been constructed, without the yet more far-reaching destruction, political and moral disintegration and transformative changes that the long twentieth century's second and even "greater" global war wrought, especially in Europe. Nor would this process ultimately have gone as far as it eventually did without the political pressures and ideological dynamics of what escalated almost immediately after Nazi Germany, Imperial Japan and their voluntary and coerced allies had been defeated far more totally and unequivocally than Wilhelmine Germany in 1918 and forced to accept "unconditional surrender": the Cold War. Like the two world wars that preceded it, this war also came to expand to East Asia and eventually into a global war. But like them it also in many ways always remained a distinctive transatlantic conflict, which now centred on a soon all-encompassing political, ideological, economic, social and cultural antagonism and competition between the United States as the leading power of the "free" liberal-capitalist world and the Soviet Union as the superpower of the communist world.[1]

---

[1] See Gaddis (2006); Leffler (2007); Westad (2018).

What took shape in the west after the Allies' original postwar schemes of Potsdam had rapidly collapsed under the impact of this antagonism can indeed be characterised as an unprecedentedly far-reaching and many-layered transatlantic system of peace and international politics. Its main foundations would be laid between 1947 and 1955, and for all its – considerable – short-comings it came to provide the wherewithal for a veritable and highly conse-quential transformation process: the transformation of Western Europe and the north Atlantic sphere from a sphere of war that had long affected the entire world to a sphere of order, security and transnational peace-building. What two generations of post–Second World War political leaders and other actors who influenced its conception and realisation built up acquired the character and shape of a new kind of *Atlantic community* – which eventually clearly went beyond the realm of Atlanticist ideological rhetoric.

Despite some ideologically driven excesses in the struggle against commun-ism, persistent inner tensions and numerous other problems, this novel, essentially liberal political and security community of democratic states – and the at first postulated, then increasingly substantial "community of values" it fostered – created conditions for a remarkable period of stabilisation, political-democratic renewal, substantial reconstruction and social and cul-tural reform, which clearly went far beyond mere "Americanisation" pro-cesses. And it also created an environment in which deeper changes of collective thinking and mentalities could occur, which in the aftermath of 1945 required even more time than after 1918. This system and the emerging Atlantic community proved remarkably effective in ensuring peace and secur-ity and also in fostering peace-enforcing, stabilising and overall prosperity-enhancing inter- and transnational integration. And while political struggles for the best path into a brighter future of course did not end in the second half of the long twentieth century, they could now overall be pursued peacefully within this essentially open, pluralistic system, which came to acquire a basic, eventually quite deeply rooted legitimacy on both sides of the Atlantic. Of course, this legitimacy would have to be renewed time and again, and it would especially be damaged by the ideological and strategic priorities the American superpower came to pursue in the global Cold War, in and beyond Vietnam.

It is crucial to emphasise, however, that it would be misleading to interpret this new order as the most far-reaching manifestation of the *Pax Americana* of the "American twentieth century", an "American peace" forged under the *aegis* and domination of a novel "American empire" or even "empire by invitation".[2] Rather, what developed was essentially a *Pax Atlantica*. The reorientation of US *and* European policies, and the more fundamental

[2] See Lundestad (2003), pp. 27–62, and the more nuanced appraisals in Ikenberry (2011), pp. 159–278, and Ikenberry (2020), pp. 177–211.

learning processes that informed this reorientation, finally propelled the qualitative advances towards a progressively more effective integrated Atlantic *concert* that had not been possible after 1918 – towards a concerted system of security and economic revitalisation that, crucially, this time offered ways to achieve what the western powers had ultimately failed to accomplish in their relations with the Weimar Republic: to incorporate Germany – now the newly established Federal Republic of Germany – into "the West" on terms that enhanced rather than compromised international peace, security and stability. That this now could be done also owed to the fact that new, more promising paths came to be pursued by those who directed the postwar policies of the battered but still essential West European powers, figures like the British foreign secretary Ernest Bevin and his French counterpart Robert Schuman, and those who – like Adenauer – sought to anchor western Germany in a western peace system, and the West, even at the price of deepening the Cold War division between the Federal Republic and the German Democratic Republic.

But what now played a critical role was that US policy- and decision-makers – first Roosevelt and the protagonists of his progressive administration, then, with more lasting impact, Acheson, Kennan and the other leading figures of the Truman administration – went significantly further than Wilson and his successors in the 1920s in learning how to exercise hegemonic responsibilities – and, ultimately, in learning how to lead in an essentially cooperative process of creating of a resilient international order.[3] And while their outlooks and strategies had a global scope, what they conceived and pursued arguably produced the most transformative and constructive results in the north Atlantic sphere. Notably, these policies and outcomes were qualitatively different from what occurred in the Cold War's other critical strategic region, East Asia, where the United States came to establish a more top-down "hub-and-spoke" system with its new key client allies Japan, Taiwan and South Korea (while failing, inevitably, to keep China in the anti-communist camp). And, needless to say, they were far more "benign", and less unilateral and imperialist-hierarchical, than what US governments and governmental and non-governmental agencies would pursue in Latin America and the so-called third world in the course of the globalising cold war.[4]

To a significant degree, the resilience and comparative legitimacy of the Atlantic peace system that now emerged derived from the fact that the pre-eminent American power did not impose its concepts and terms but rather contributed to fostering a new, of course not uncontested but overall remarkably broad transnational consensus on what the system's political, strategic,

---

[3] See Kennan (1967), pp. 325 ff., 394–470; Acheson (1969), pp. 200–35, 276 ff., 382 ff.
[4] See Ikenberry (2011), pp. 159 ff.; Ikenberry (2020), pp. 177 ff., Westad (2018), pp. 71 ff., 129 ff.; Ekbladh (2011), pp. 114 ff.; Cohrs (2018), pp. 1–24.

economic and democratic ground-rules were to be. American decision-makers came to cooperate and consult with the principal West European policy-makers of the postwar period, strong-minded actors like the aforementioned "Atlanticists" *and* "Europeanists" Bevin, Schuman and Adenauer, Alcide De Gasperi and of course Jean Monnet. Yet they also came to play a decisive part in spurring and at times pushing the European postwar leaders not to realise grand federal designs for a United Western Europe (as Kennan and other US strategists had initially recommended) but to take concrete steps in the pursuit of not just functionalist but actually effective supranational integration, which only later came to be buoyed by a new groundswell of national and trans-national support for such aspirations.

Both American and European policymakers came to develop distinctly more comprehensive conceptions and policies that addressed three crucial dimensions: the encouragement of both transatlantic and West European integration efforts in the core spheres of security, economics and democratic politics, both to avoid a revival of antagonistic nationalisms and to make, this time, western Germany's revitalisation "safe" for its western (and eastern) neighbours; the comparatively swift integration of what became western Germany into a new (West) European *and* transatlantic system of order and security, under a security umbrella that ultimately only the American nuclear superpower could provide; and, within this wider framework, the initially supervised push for, and encouragement of, the inner reform and democra-tisation processes that, for all their limitations, came to shape the German Federal Republic and deepen its alignment with the West in ways that had not been possible in the Weimar era.[5] All of this unquestionably also effected a "double containment" of Germany and of Soviet influence. But it went far beyond this purpose.

On the one hand, by relying on the transatlantic instrumentalities of the Marshall Plan, the American and West European protagonists of the late 1940s thus fostered cooperative ties and encouraged both inter- and supra-national agreements in Western Europe. Notably, this applied to the Schuman Plan of 1950, which called for the integration of the West European coal-and-steel sectors and eventually gave rise to the European Coal and Steel Community, which especially aided a qualitatively new Franco-German post-war reconciliation. On the other hand, and at least as significantly, Acheson and the other key actors of the Truman administration in 1948–49 took the unprecedented step of making – and domestically legitimising – long-term commitments to (West) European security through the North Atlantic Alliance. And, after initially encouraging Schuman's plan for a European Defence Community, they were instrumental in fostering – after its failure –

---

[5] See Winkler (II/2000); Winkler (2016).

the swift inclusion of western Germany into the transatlantic alliance, which would be formalised by 1955. They would thus play a leading role in creating and consolidating – in cooperation and consultation with West European and German decision-makers – a new and integrative security system that now bound the United States firmly to longer-term hegemonic responsibilities in Europe.

Crucially, while it consolidated the advances initiated through the European Recovery Program, the NATO system finally provided what the Versailles system had failed to furnish and what had only begun to acquire contours in the 1920s. It created the *security framework* that was indispensable both for the fortification of the Atlantic community and for making the western integration of (western) Germany compatible with the interests and security needs of its neighbours. This system would confront numerous external and internal challenges and, at times, ferocious critiques from the left as well as from the right (which were especially directed at the conduct of the American super-power, both in Europe and in the global Cold War confrontations, above all in Vietnam). But it overall proved remarkably cohesive and durable, and it gained a remarkable measure of democratically voiced acceptance during the era of the Cold War. Initially, this seemed destined to continue after its end.

Following the mostly peaceful revolutions of 1989, hopes arose, *and there were actual prospects*, that this basic Euro-Atlantic order could be extended to the fledgling democracies of Eastern Europe – and perhaps even to post-Soviet Russia, and the world. While Russia came to follow its own path, and a truly global new order remained elusive, this would indeed be achieved with a view to Eastern Europe – even if many expectations of a stable, more integrated Europe that would bring stable democratic government, the rule of law and economic prosperity would be sorely disappointed.

The transformation of US postwar policies under Truman and the concomi-tant reorientations in Britain, France, Adenauer's western Germany and other West European states were unquestionably driven *in part* by the intensifying conflict with the Soviet Union that, while often fuelled by mutual mispercep-tions, also manifested more profound ideological and political incommensur-ability. They in fact contributed to the deepening of the antagonism between a western liberal-capitalist system and a communist bloc. And they thus also contributed to producing and deepening long-term divisions in and beyond Europe – until, from the 1960s onwards, steps towards *détente* and a *modus vivendi* of peaceful coexistence would be taken, which in turn would create important preconditions for the peaceful revolutions of 1989.

The distinctive nature and resilience of the novel Atlantic peace system that was built after 1945 can *not* simply be explained as a consequence of the eventual US preponderance of power in military, economic and technological terms, the attractiveness of the American "model of the future", or the fact that the new American world power proved its strength in the competition with rival ideologies and systems, from authoritarian and fascist to communist alternatives. What had a more profound impact, and has not yet been properly understood, were the salient processes that have already been outlined at the outset of this book. In short, what bore real fruit now were the in many ways remarkably constructive and non-pathological learning processes of the fulcrum period of the long Atlantic century – roughly, the years between 1933 and 1963. These processes propelled an evolution of the ideas and assumptions informing American and West European approaches to the practice and legitimation of modern international politics – an evolution of global significance that progressed significantly further than that which had occurred in the era of the First World War.

It was now, and with awareness of the even more horrendous cataclysm of the Second World War, that policy- and decision-makers looked anew at, and sought to draw more profound lessons from, the failure of the peacemaking efforts of 1919 and, particularly, Wilson's frustrated bid to create a "new world order". Notably, when conceptualising and implementing the Marshall Plan, the European Recovery Program and the North Atlantic Alliance they now sought to draw tangible consequences from Versailles, as well as from the *limits* of the attempts to bolster Euro-Atlantic security and political as well as economic stability in the decade after the First World War. Yet, of course, they also sought to learn from the warning example of the economic and political devastations the World Economic Crisis had caused.[6]

Essentially, the conscious attempt to avoid a repetition of the mistakes of 1919 already animated Roosevelt's quest to overcome isolationism and offer his own, in some ways neo-Wilsonian but overall distinctly more hegemonic vision of an "Atlantic Peace" for "One World". It would eventually be based on the "Four Freedoms" of the 1941 Atlantic Charter, but also on core maxims of a new global US stewardship that, despite the penchant to overestimate the American capacity to work with *and* moderate Stalin, were imbued with a harder realism than Wilson's aspirations – and unthinkable without the profound reform of the American state that Roosevelt had initiated through the New Deal.[7] Yet at the end of the Second World War not only American decision-makers but also British actors, and none more than Keynes, sought to learn from and remedy the deficiencies of the post–First World War era in constructing a new, far more extensive institutional framework for a liberal world economic order – first through the International Monetary Fund and the other institutions of the Bretton Woods system, then, in a more regionally

---

[6] Cf. the different interpretations offered by Cohrs (2006) and Tooze (2014).

[7] Roosevelt, "Annual Message to Congress, 6 January 1941", in Rosenman (1941–48), 1940, pp. 672 ff.; Borgwardt (2005), esp. pp. 3–5., Ikenberry (2020), pp. 141–76. For the global dimensions of the New Deal, see Patel (2016).

specific yet also more ambitious manner, through the European Recovery Program.

More importantly still, those who shaped Atlantic policies after 1945 consciously sought to understand what had marred the effectiveness of the League of Nations when endeavouring to build the all-embracing and *inclusive* global peace and security architecture of the United Nations. Following the escalation of the Cold War, Kennan, Acheson and other protagonists of the Truman administration – as well as those experts and opinion-makers who influenced US policies – proved that they had actually learned real lessons from the oscillation between Wilsonian overreach and self-interested aloofness that had undermined the American quest for peace and security twenty-five years earlier. And this is what ultimately accounts for the longevity of the collective security commitments the United States made in the North Atlantic Alliance. Concomitant learning and reorientation processes took place, and now came to bear fruit, on the European side. In the end, then, longer-term and ultimately transformative changes in underlying conceptions and assumptions, individual and collective outlooks, and indeed *learning processes* of this kind proved critical for transforming post-1945 international politics in the relations between the United States and Europe. And they also proved crucial for building a transformed transatlantic system of international security, politics and economics that also came to have an enormous impact on the evolution of the global order during and after the Cold War.

Thus it may be said in conclusion that in the wider context and horizon of the long twentieth century the first efforts to create an Atlantic order in 1919 and then, on different premises, in the 1920s essentially came to serve a higher dialectical purpose in the history of modern international politics. Fundamentally, they can be interpreted as a *Cadmeian Peace* in a Platonic sense.[8] For precisely because they were in many ways so limited and flawed they came to furnish valuable lessons for future generations of decision-, policy- and opinion-makers – lessons about how to build and legitimise a modern international order, and about how to advance towards a more lasting modern peace. It should hardly be necessary to emphasise that these fundamental lessons are not only still highly pertinent but arguably more relevant than ever at what may one day be viewed as the end of the long twentieth century – at a crossroads of world history, roughly a quarter of a century after 1989, that could witness the disintegration of the remarkable Atlantic international order that it has taken so much time, exertion and blood to build after the horrors of two world wars.

---

[8] In *The Laws*, Plato, referring to Cadmus, the founder of Thebes, speaks of a "Cadmeian victory", characterising it as a victory that "results in the *loss* of education, because men often swell with pride when they have won a victory in war ..." See Plato (1970), pp. 69–70.

BIBLIOGRAPHY

I. Primary Sources

A. United States

Government Papers

National Archives, College Park, Maryland
Department of State, Record Group 59: General Files.
Department of State, Record Group 256: Records of the American Commission to Negotiate Peace.
Department of Commerce, Record Group 39.
Department of Commerce, Record Group 151: Records of the Bureau of Foreign and Domestic Commerce.
Department of War, Record Group 165: Records of the Military Intelligence Division.

Federal Reserve Bank Archives, New York
Federal Reserve Bank of New York Papers.

Hoover Institution Archives, Stanford, California
Records of the American Relief Administration.

Swarthmore College Library, Peace Collection, Swarthmore, Pennsylvania
Records of the American Union Against Militarism.
Records of the League to Enforce Peace.
Records of the Union of Democratic Control.
Records of the Woman's Peace Party, 1914–1920.
World Peace Foundation Papers.

Private Papers

John Quincy Adams Papers, Massachusetts Historical Society, Boston, Massachusetts.
Jane Addams Papers, Swarthmore College Peace Collection, Swarthmore, Pennsylvania.
Ray Stannard Baker Papers, Library of Congress, Manuscript Division, Washington, DC.

Bernard M. Baruch Papers, Firestone Library, Princeton University, Princeton, New Jersey.

Tasker H. Bliss Papers, Library of Congress, Manuscript Division, Washington, DC.

William E. Borah Papers, Library of Congress, Manuscript Division, Washington, DC.

William C. Bullitt Papers, Sterling Library, Yale University, New Haven, Connecticut.

Carrie Chapman Catt Papers, Sterling Library, Yale University, New Haven, Connecticut.

William Castle Papers, Houghton Library, Harvard University, Cambridge, Massachusetts.

Calvin Coolidge Papers, Library of Congress, Manuscript Division, Washington, DC.

William S. Culbertson Papers, Library of Congress, Manuscript Division, Washington, DC.

Norman H. Davis Papers, Library of Congress, Manuscript Division, Washington, DC.

Charles G. Dawes Papers, Library of Congress, Manuscript Division, Washington, DC.

Joseph Grew Papers, Houghton Library, Harvard University, Cambridge, Massachusetts.

Warren G. Harding Papers, Library of Congress, Manuscript Division, Washington, DC.

Edward. M. House Papers, Sterling Library, Yale University, New Haven, Connecticut.

Herbert Hoover Papers, Hoover Institution, Stanford, California.

Alanson B. Houghton Papers, Corning Glass Archives, Corning, New York.

Charles E. Hughes Papers, Library of Congress, Manuscript Division, Washington, DC.

Ernst Jäckh Papers, Sterling Library, Yale University, New Haven, Connecticut.

Frank B. Kellogg Papers, Minnesota Historical Society, St Paul, Minnesota.

Wellington Koo Papers, Butler Library, Columbia University, New York.

Thomas W. Lamont Papers, Baker Library, Harvard University, Cambridge, Massachusetts.

Robert Lansing Papers, Library of Congress, Manuscript Division, Washington, DC.

Russell C. Leffingwell Papers, Sterling Library, Yale University, New Haven, Connecticut.

Walter Lippmann Papers, Sterling Library, Yale University, New Haven, Connecticut.

Henry Cabot Lodge Papers, Massachusetts Historical Society, Boston, Massachusetts.

William G. McAdoo Papers, Library of Congress, Manuscript Division, Washington, DC.

Vance Criswell McCormick Papers, Sterling Library, Yale University, New Haven, Connecticut.

Sidney Edward Mezes Papers, Sterling Library, Yale University, New Haven, Connecticut.

David H. Miller Papers, Library of Congress, Manuscript Division, Washington, DC.

John P. Morgan Papers, Pierpont Morgan Library, New York.

Dwight D. Morrow Papers, Pierpont Morgan Library, New York.

Ignace Jan Paderewski Papers, Hoover Institution, Stanford, California.

General John J. Pershing Papers, Library of Congress, Manuscript Division, Washington, DC.

Franklin D. Roosevelt Papers, Franklin D. Roosevelt Presidential Library, Hyde Park, New York.

Theodore Roosevelt Papers, Library of Congress, Manuscript Division, Washington, DC.

Elihu Root Papers, Library of Congress, Manuscript Division, Washington, DC.

Jacob G. Schurman Papers, Olin Library, Cornell University, Ithaca, New York.

William H. Seward Papers, Manuscripts and Archives Division, New York Public Library, New York.

James T. Shotwell Papers, Butler Library, Columbia University, New York.

Henry L. Stimson Papers, Sterling Library, Yale University, New Haven, Connecticut.

Benjamin Strong Papers, Federal Reserve Bank Archives, New York.

William H. Taft Papers, Library of Congress, Manuscript Division, Washington, DC.

Leon Trotsky Papers, Houghton Library, Harvard University, Cambridge, Massachusetts.

Joseph P. Tumulty Papers, Library of Congress, Manuscript Division, Washington, DC.

Paul M. Warburg Papers, Sterling Library, Yale University, New Haven, Connecticut.

Woodrow Wilson Papers, Library of Congress, Manuscript Division, Washington, DC.

William Wiseman Papers, Sterling Library, Yale University, New Haven, Connecticut.

Owen D. Young Papers, Van Horne House, Van Hornesville, New York.

Official Publications

Congressional Record: 63rd Congress (1913–15), 64th Congress (1915–17), 65th Congress (1917–19), 66th Congress (1919–21), 67th Congress (1921–23), 68th Congress (1923–25), 69th Congress (1925–27), 70th Congress (1927–29), 71st Congress (1929–31), 72nd Congress (1931–33).

Final Covenant of the League of Nations (2008), (New Haven, CT: Yale Avalon Project).

Horne, C. and Austin, W. (eds) (1923), *Source Records of the Great War*, 7 vols (Washington, DC: National Alumni).

Papers Relating to the Foreign Relations of the United States, 1861–1933, (1861 ff.), US Department of State (Washington, DC: United States Government Printing Office).

Papers Relating to the Foreign Relations of the United States, 1919, The Paris Peace Conference, XIII vols (1942–47), (Washington, DC: United States Government Printing Office).

Survey of American Foreign Relations, 1929 (1929), (New Haven, CT: Yale University Press).

The Hague Conventions of 1899 and 1907 (1968), ed. C. Bevans (Washington, DC: United States Government Printing Office).

US Senate (1914–21), *Proceedings of the Committee on Foreign Relations, 1914–1920* (Washington, DC: United States Government Printing Office).

B. Great Britain

Government Papers

National Archive, London

CAB 2: Committee of Imperial Defence Minutes.

CAB 23: Cabinet Conclusions.

CAB 24: Cabinet Memoranda.

CAB 27/275: Cabinet Committees – Foreign Policy – Security.

CAB 27/361–3: Cabinet Committees – Disarmament.

CAB 29/103–4: Proceedings of the London Reparations Conference, 2 volumes.

CAB 484: Political Intelligence Department Files, Foreign Office.

FO 371: Foreign Office Political Files.

FO 800/256–263: Miscellaneous Correspondence of Austen Chamberlain, 1924–29.

FO 840/1: Papers of the Locarno Conference, 1925.

Treasury Papers.

Private Papers

Stanley Baldwin Papers, Cambridge University Library.

Lord Balfour Papers, British Library, London.

Lord Bryce Papers, Bodleian Library, Oxford.

Viscount Cecil Papers, British Library, London.

Austen Chamberlain Papers, University of Birmingham Library, Birmingham.

Joseph Chamberlain Papers, University of Birmingham Library, Birmingham.

Winston Churchill Papers, Churchill College, Cambridge.

Eyre Crowe Papers, National Archive, London.

Marquess Curzon Papers, India Office Library and National Archive, London.

Viscount D'Abernon Papers, British Library, London.

Benjamin Disraeli Papers, Bodleian Library, Oxford.

George Eulas Foster Papers, University of New Brunswick Archives, Fredericton, New Brunswick.

William E. Gladstone Papers, Edinburgh University Library, Edinburgh.

Maurice Hankey Papers, Churchill College, Cambridge.

James Headlam-Morley Papers, Cambridge University Library.

John Maynard Keynes Papers, King's College, Cambridge.

David Lloyd George Papers, House of Lords, London.

Lord Lothian [Philip Kerr] Papers, Bodleian Library, Oxford.

Ramsay MacDonald Papers, National Archive, London.

Gilbert Murray Papers, Bodleian Library, Oxford.

Eric Phipps Papers, Churchill College, Cambridge.

Marquess of Salisbury Papers, Hatfield House, Hatfield.

William Tyrrell Papers, FO 800/220, National Archive, London.

Robert Vansittart Papers, Churchill College, Cambridge.

Official Publications

British Documents on Foreign Affairs. Reports and Papers from the Foreign Office Confidential Print (1989), eds. K. Bourne, and D.C. Watt, 2/1: *The Paris Peace Conference of 1919* (Frederick, MD: University Publications of America).

Documents on British Foreign Policy, 1919–1939 (1984–86), Series I, Volumes XXV–XXVII (London: HMSO).

Documents on British Foreign Policy, 1919–1939 (1966–75), Series IA, Volumes I–VII (London: HMSO).

Documents on British Foreign Policy, 1919–1939 (1946 ff.), Series II, Volumes I–III (London: HMSO).

Gooch, G.P., Temperley, H. (eds.) (1926–38), *British Documents on the Origins of the War, 1898–1914*, 13 vols. (London: HMSO).

Madden, F., Fieldhouse, D. (eds.) (1985–2000), *Select Documents on the Constitutional History of the British Empire and Commonwealth*, 8 vols. (Westport, CT: Greenwood Press).

Parliamentary Debates: *House of Commons*, 5th Series (1909 ff.) (London: HMSO)

Parliament Cmd 2169: *Papers Respecting Negotiations for an Anglo–French Pact* (1924) (London: HMSO).

Parliament Cmd. 2289: *League of Nations Fifth Assembly. Reports of the British Delegates relating to the Protocol for the Peaceful Settlement of International Disputes* (1924) (London: HMSO).

Parliament Cmd. 2435: *Papers Respecting the Proposals for a Pact of Security, made by the German Government, 9 February 1925* (1925) (London: HMSO).

Parliament Cmd. 2525: *Final Protocol of the Locarno Conference, 1925* (1925) (London: HMSO).

C. France

Government Papers

Ministère des Affaires Étrangères, Paris

Série A Paix.

Série Guerre 1914–18.

Série B Amérique 1918–40: Sous-série États-Unis 1918–29.

Série Y Internationale 1918–40.

Série Z Europe 1918–40: Sous-série Europe.

Série Z Europe 1918–40: Sous-série Allemagne.

Série Z Europe 1918–40: Sous-série Autriche.

Série Z Europe 1918–40: Sous-série Grande-Bretagne.

Série Z Europe 1918–40: Sous-série Pologne.

Série Z Europe 1918–40: Sous-série Rive Gauche du Rhin.

Série Z Europe 1918–40: Sous-série Ruhr.

Série Z Europe 1918–40: Sous-série Société des nations.

Série Z Europe 1918–40: Sous-série URSS.

Série Relations Commerciales 1918–29: Dossier: Conférence de Londres.

Archives of the Assembleè Nationale, Paris
Commission des Affaires Étrangères, 1917–33.
Commission des Finances, 1917–33.

Archives Nationales, Paris
Ministère du commerce.
Ministère des finances.

Archives Du Sènat, Paris
Commission des Affaires Étrangères du Sénat, 1917–33.

Private Papers

Papiers Philippe Berthelot, PA-AP 010, Ministère des Affaires Étrangères, Paris.
Papiers Aristide Briand, PA-AP 335, Ministère des Affaires Étrangères, Paris.
Papiers Léon Bourgeois, PA-AP 029, Ministère des Affaires Étrangères, Paris.
Papiers Jules Cambon, PA-AP 43, Ministère des Affaires Étrangères, Paris.
Papiers Paul Cambon, PA-AP 42, Ministère des Affaires Étrangères, Paris.
Fonds Clemenceau, Département de l'armée de la terre, Service Historique de la Défense, Paris.
Papiers Georges Clemenceau, PA-AP 198, Ministère des Affaires Étrangères, Paris.
Papiers Théophile Delcassé, PA-AP 211, Ministère des Affaires Étrangères, Paris.
Fonds du maréchal Ferdinand Foch, 414 AP, Archives Nationales, Paris.
Papiers du maréchal Ferdinand Foch, Fonds Privés, Service Historique de la Défense, Paris.
Papiers Édouard Herriot, PA-AP 089, Ministère des Affaires Étrangères, Paris.
Papiers Jean Jules Jusserand, PA-AP 93, Ministère des Affaires Étrangères, Paris.
Papiers Alexandre Millerand, PA-AP 118, Ministère des Affaires Étrangères, Paris.
Papiers Stephen Pichon, PA-AP 141, Ministère des Affaires Étrangères, Paris.
Papiers Raymond Poincaré, Bibliothèque Nationale, Paris.
Papiers Jacques Seydoux, PA-AP 261, Ministère des Affaires Étrangères, Paris.
Archives André Tardieu, 324 AP, Archives Nationales, Paris.
Papiers André Tardieu, PA-AP 166, Ministère des Affaires Étrangères, Paris
Archives Albert Thomas, 94 AP, Archives Nationales, Paris.

Official Publications

Documents diplomatiques français, série: 1871–1914 (1929 ff.) (Paris: Imprimerie nationale).
Documents diplomatiques français, série: 1914–1919 (1999 ff.) (Paris: Imprimerie nationale).
Geouffre de Lapradelle, A. (ed.) (1929–36), *La Paix de Versailles. La conférence de paix et la Société des Nations (la documentation internationale)*, 12 vols (Paris: Les Éditions internationales).

Journal Officiel de la République Française. Débats Parlementaires (Chambre des Députés) (1900–33) (Paris: Imprimerie nationale).

Journal Officiel de la République Française. Documents Parlementaires (Sénat) (1900–33) (Paris: Imprimerie nationale).

Mantoux, P. (1955), *Les délibérations du Conseil des Quatre,* 2 vols (Paris: Centre national de la recherche scientifique).

—— (1992), *The Deliberations of the Council of Four (March 24–June 28, 1919),* eds. A.S. Link and M. Boemeke, 2 vols (Princeton, NJ: Princeton University Press).

Paillat, C. (ed.) (1979–84), *Dossiers secrets de la France contemporaine,* 5 vols (Paris: Robert Laffont).

D. Germany

Government Papers

Politisches Archiv, Auswärtiges Amt, Berlin

General Files of the German Foreign Office, 1919–33.
Büro des Reichministers.
Büro des Staatssekretärs.
Handakten des Staatssekretärs Carl von Schubert.
Politische Abteilung II: Westeuropa.
Politische Abteilung III: Vereinigte Staaten.
Sonderreferat Wirtschaft.

Zentrales Staatsarchiv, Potsdam

Akten der Reichskanzlei, 1878–1919.

Private Papers

Otto von Bismarck Papers, Bismarck Foundation, Friedrichsruh.
Theobald von Bethmann Hollweg Papers, Bundesarchiv, Koblenz.
Ulrich von Brockdorff-Rantzau Papers, Politisches Archiv, Auswärtiges Amt, Berlin.
Friedrich Ebert Papers, Friedrich-Ebert-Foundation, Bonn.
Matthias Erzberger Papers, Bundesarchiv, Koblenz.
Conrad Haußmann Papers, Hauptstaatsarchiv, Stuttgart.
Rosa Luxemburg Papers, Bundesarchiv, Koblenz.
Walther Rathenau Papers, Bundesarchiv, Koblenz.
Philipp Scheidemann Papers, Friedrich-Ebert-Foundation, Bonn.
Gustav Stresemann Papers, Politisches Archiv, Auswärtiges Amt, Berlin.
Max Warburg Papers, Bundesarchiv, Koblenz.

Official Publications

Akten zur deutschen auswärtigen Politik 1918–1945. Serie A: 1918–1925 (1982/84), vols. I and II (Göttingen: Vandenhoeck & Ruprecht).

Akten zur deutschen auswärtigen Politik 1918–1945. Serie B: 1925–1933 (1966 ff.), vols. I–XIII (Göttingen: Vandenhoeck & Ruprecht).

Akten der Reichskanzlei. Weimarer Republik: Das Kabinett Scheidemann (1971) ed. H. Schulze (Boppard: H. Boldt Verlag).

Akten der Reichskanzlei. Weimarer Republik: Das Kabinett Bauer (1980) ed. A. Golecki (Boppard: H. Boldt Verlag).

Akten der Reichskanzlei. Weimarer Republik: Das Kabinett Müller I (1972) ed. M. Vogt (Boppard: H. Boldt Verlag).

Akten der Reichskanzlei. Weimarer Republik: Das Kabinett Müller II (1970) 2 vols ed. M. Vogt (Boppard: H. Boldt Verlag).

Akten der Reichskanzlei. Weimarer Republik: Die Kabinette Stresemann I und II (1978), 2 vols, eds. K. D. Erdmann, M. Vogt (Boppard: H. Boldt Verlag).

Akten der Reichskanzlei. Weimarer Republik: Die Kabinette Marx I und II, 2 vols (1973) ed. G. Abramowski (Boppard: H. Boldt Verlag).

Akten der Reichskanzlei. Weimarer Republik: Die Kabinette Marx III und IV (1988), 2 vols, ed. G. Abramowski (Boppard: H. Boldt Verlag).

Akten der Reichskanzlei. Weimarer Republik: Die Kabinette Luther I und III (1977), 2 vols, ed. K.-H. Minuth (Boppard: H. Boldt Verlag).

Allgemeiner Kongreß der Arbeiter- und Soldatenräte (1918), *Beschlüsse* (Berlin: Schriften des Arbeiter- und Soldatenrats Groß-Berlin).

Auswärtiges Amt (1919), *Materialien, betreffend die Friedensverhandlungen*, 8 vols (Berlin: Reichsdruckerei).

Der Friede von Brest-Litovsk (1971), ed. W. Hahlweg (Düsseldorf: Droste Verlag).

Die Große Politik der europäischen Kabinette 1871–1914 (1922–27) eds. J. Lepsius, A. Mendelssohn Bartholdy, F. Thimme, 40 vols. (Berlin: Verlagsgesellschaft für Politik und Geschichte).

Die Pariser Völkerbundsakte vom 14. 2. 1919 und die Gegenvorschläge der deutschen Regierung zur Errichtung eines Völkerbundes (1919) (Berlin: Veröffentlichungen des Auswärtigen Amts).

Dowe, D. (ed.) (1980), *Protokolle der Sitzungen des Parteiausschusses der SPD 1912 bis 1921*, 2 vols (Berlin: J.H. Dietz).

Geiss, I. (ed.) (1963), *Julikrise und Kriegsausbruch*, 2 vols (Hanover: Neue Gesellschaft).

Heilfron, E. (ed.) (1920), *Die Deutsche Nationalversammlung im Jahre 1919/1920*, 9 vols. (Berlin: Norddeutsche Buchdruckerei & Verlagsanstalt).

Locarno-Konferenz, 1925. Eine Dokumentensammlung (1962), Ministerium für Auswärtige Angelegenheiten der Deutschen Demokratischen Republik (Berlin: Rütten & Loening).

Luckau, E. (ed.) (1941), *The German Delegation at the Paris Peace Conference* (New York: Columbia University Press).

Matthias, E. and Morsey R. (eds.) (1959), *Der Interfraktionelle Ausschuß, 1917/18*, 2 vols (Düsseldorf: Droste Verlag).

Miller, S., Matthias, E. and Potthoff, H. (eds.) (1969), *Die Regierung der Volksbeauftragten*, 2 vols. (Düsseldorf: Droste Verlag)

Quellen zur Geschichte des Parlamentarismus und der politischen Parteien. Erste Reihe: Von der konstitutionellen Monarchie zur parlamentarischen Republik (1959 ff.) (Düsseldorf: Droste Verlag).

Ritter, G. and Miller, S. (eds.) (1983), *Die deutsche Revolution 1918–1919. Dokumente* (Frankfurt/Main: Fischer Verlag).

Ursachen und Folgen. Vom deutschen Zusammenbruch 1918 und 1945 bis zur staatlichen Neuordnung Deutschlands in der Gegenwart. Eine Urkunden- und Dokumentensammlung zur Zeitgeschichte: Vols. 4–8: Die Weimarer Republik (1959 ff.) (Berlin: Dokumenten-Verlag).

Verhandlungen des Reichstags. Stenographische Berichte und Anlagen, 1871–1933 (1871 ff.) (Berlin: Verlag Julius Sittenfeld).

Verhandlungen der Verfassunggebenden Nationalversammlung. Stenographische Berichte, 18 vols. (1921–22) (Berlin: Verlag Julius Sittenfeld).

Verhandlungen der Verfassunggebenden Deutschen Nationalversammlung, vols. 335–43 (1919 ff.) (Berlin: Verlag Julius Sittenfeld).

E. League of Nations, Geneva, and Switzerland

Documents Diplomatiques Suisses, 6, 7/1 & 7/2 (1979–84) (Bern: Chronos Verlag).

League of Nations (1922), *Resolutions and Recommendations adopted by the Assembly during Its Third Session* (Geneva: League of Nations).

League of Nations (1924), *Official Journal, Special Supplement no. 23, Records of the Fifth Assembly* (Geneva: League of Nations).

League of Nations (1929), *Official Journal, Special Supplement no. 75, Records of the Tenth Assembly* (Geneva: League of Nations).

Société des Nations, Journal Officiel, Société des Nations (1929) (Geneva: League of Nations).

The World Economic Conference, Geneva, May 1927. Final Report (1927) (Geneva: League of Nations).

F. Contemporary Publications, Diaries, Letters, Speeches and Memoirs

Acheson, D. (1969), *Present at the Creation* (New York: Norton).

Adams, B. (1902), *The New Empire* (New York: MacMillan).

Adams, H. (2008), *The Education of Henry Adams* (Oxford: Oxford University Press).

Adams, J. (2003), *Political Writings of John Adams* (Indianapolis, IN: Hackett Publishing Co.).

Adams, J.Q. (2017), *Diaries*, 2 vols (New York: Longmans, Green & Co.).

Addams, J. (1907), *Newer Ideals of Peace* (New York: MacMillan).

(1922), *Peace and Bread in Time of War* (New York: MacMillan).

Albert, P., Palladino, G. (eds) (1986), *The Samuel Gompers Papers*, vol. 10 (Urbana, IL: University of Illinois Press).

Algernon Gordon Lennox, B. (ed) (1924), *The Diary of Lord Bertie of Thame, 1914–1918*, 2 vols (London: Hodder & Stoughton).

Almond, N., Lutz, R. (eds) (1935), *The Treaty of St. Germain: A Documentary History of Its Territorial and Political Clauses, with a Survey of the*

Documents of the Supreme Council of the Paris Peace Conference (Stanford, CA: Stanford University Press).

Amery, L. (1953), *My Political Life. Volume Two: War and Peace. 1914–1929* (London: Hutchinson).

Angell, N. (1910), *The Great Illusion* (London: G.P. Putnam's Sons).

Arnaud, É. (1895), *Les traites d'arbitrage permanent entre peuples* (Brussels: Ligue internationale de la paix et de la liberté).

(1910), *Code de la paix* (Brussels: Ligue internationale de la paix et de la liberté).

Asquith, H. (1916), *A Free Future for the World*, Guild Hall, 9 November 1916 (London: HMSO).

(1927), *Memories and Reflections, 1852–1927*, 2 vols (London: Hutchinson).

Babelon, E. (1917), *La rive gauche du Rhin : les revendications françaises dans l'histoire* (Paris: Floury).

Bacon, R. and Scott, R.B. (eds.) (1916), *Addresses on International Subjects by Elihu Root* (Cambridge, MA: Harvard University Press).

(eds.) (1918), *The United States and the War. Political Addresses by Elihu Root* (Cambridge, MA: Harvard University Press).

(eds.) (1924), *Men and Policies. Addresses by Elihu Root* (Cambridge, MA: Harvard University Press).

Baden, M. von (1928), *Erinnerungen und Dokumente* (Stuttgart: Deutsche Verlags-Anstalt).

Bainville, J. (1920), *Les conséquences politiques de la paix* (Paris: Arthème Fayard).

Baker, G. (ed.) (1853–84), *The Works of William H. Seward*, 5 vols (New York: Redfield).

(1854–55), *The Life of William H. Seward*, 2 vols (New York: Redfield).

Baker, R.S. (ed.) (1923), *Woodrow Wilson and World Settlement*, 3 vols (New York: Doubleday).

(ed.) (1927–39), *Woodrow Wilson. Life and Letters*, 8 vols (Garden City, NY: Doubleday).

Baker, R.S. and Dodd, W.E. (eds.) (1925–27), *The Public Papers of Woodrow Wilson*, 6 vols (New York: Harper and Brothers).

Ball, S. (ed.) (1993), *Parliament and Politics in the Age of Baldwin and MacDonald. The Headlam Diaries, 1923–1935* (London: Historians' Press).

Bane, S., Lutz, R. (eds.) (1942), *The Blockade of Germany after the Armistice, 1918–1919: Selected Documents of the Supreme Economic Council, Superior Blockade Council, American Relief Administration, and other Wartime Organizations* (Stanford, CA: Stanford University Press).

Bariéty, J. (ed.) (2011), *À la recherche de la paix France–Allemagne : les carnets d'Oswald Hesnard, 1919–1931* (Strasbourg: Presses universitaires de Strasbourg).

Barnes, J. and Nicholson, D. (eds.) (1980), *The Leo Amery Diaries, Volume I: 1896–1929* (London: Hutchinson).

Barrès, M. (1922), *La politique rhénane, discours parlementaires* (Paris: Bloud & Gay).

Baruch, B.M. (1920), *The Making of the Reparation and Economic Sections of the Treaty* (New York: Harper and Brothers).

"Basel Manifesto" (1912), *Extraordinary International Socialist Congress at Basel, November 24–25* (Berlin: Springer).

Basler, R. (ed.) (1953–55), *The Collected Works of Abraham Lincoln*, 9 vols. (New Brunswick, NJ: Rutgers University Press).

Bauer, O. (1907), *Die Nationalitätenfrage und die Sozialdemokratie* (Vienna: I. Brand).

(1923), *Die österreichische Revolution* (Vienna: I. Brand).

Beer, G.L. (1917), *The English-Speaking Peoples, Their Future Relations and Joint International Obligations* (New York: MacMillan).

(1923), *African Questions at the Paris Peace Conference*, ed. L. Gray (New York: MacMillan).

Bemis, S.F. (ed.) (1928), *The American Secretaries of State and Their Diplomacy*, vol. X (New York: MacMillan).

Beneš, É. (1928–29), *Souvenirs de guerre et de révolution, 1914–1918*, 2 vols (Paris: Librairie Ernest Leroux).

Benz, W. (ed.) (1987), *Pazifismus in Deutschland. Dokumente zur Friedensbewegung 1890–1939* (Frankfurt: Fischeer).

Bergmann, C. (1926), *Der Weg der Reparationen. Von Versailles über den Dawes-Plan zum Ziel* (Frankfurt: Frankfurter Societäts-Druckerei).

Bernstein, E. (1899), *Die Voraussetzungen des Sozialismus und die Aufgaben der Sozialdemokratie* (Stuttgart: Dietz).

Bernstorff, J.H. (1920), *Deutschland und Amerika. Erinnerungen aus dem Fünfjährigen Kriege* (Berlin: Ullstein).

(1936), *Erinnerungen und Briefe* (Zurich: Polygraph).

Bethmann Hollweg, T. von (1919–21), *Betrachtungen zum Weltkriege*, 2 vols. (Berlin: Hobbing).

Bishop, J. (ed.) (1920), *Theodore Roosevelt and His Time. Shown in His Own Letters*, 2 vols. (New York: Scribner's Sons).

Bismarck, O. von (1924–35), *Die gesammelten Werke*, 19 vols. (Berlin: Deutsche Verlags-Gesellschaft).

(2004–21), *Gesammelte Werke. Neue Friedrichsruher Ausgabe* (Paderborn: Schöningh).

Bluntschli, J.C. (I/1878), *Das moderne Völkerrecht der civilisirten Staten*, 3rd ed. (Nördlingen: Beck).

Bluntschli, J.K. (II/1878), "Die Organisation des europäischen Staatenvereines", *Die Gegenwart*, 6, pp. 81–4.

Böhme, K. (ed.) (1975), *Aufrufe und Reden deutscher Professoren im Ersten Weltkrieg* (Stuttgart: Reclam).

Borah, H. (1919), *Closing Speech of Hon. William E. Borah on the League of Nations in the Senate of the United States, 19 November 1919* (Washington, DC: United States Government Printing Office).

Bourgeois, L. (1910), *Pour la société des nations* (Paris: Georges Crès).

(1919), *Le pacte de 1919 et la Société des nations* (Paris: Fasquelle).

Bourne, R. (1916), "Trans-National America", in Hollinger, Capper (1989), pp. 152–62.

(1917), "The War and the Intellectuals", in Hollinger, Capper (1989), pp. 163–71.

Briand, A. (1930) "Memorandum on the Organization of a Regime of European Federal Union", 17 May 1930, *International Conciliation* (June), pp. 325–353.

Briggs, H. (1932), *The Law of Nations*, 2nd ed. (London: Nicholson & Watson).

Brockdorff-Rantzau, U. von (1920), *Dokumente* (Berlin: Deutsche Verlagsgesellschaft).

(1925), *Dokumente und Gedanken um Versailles* (Berlin: Verlag für Kulturpolitik).

Brodziak, S. and Jeanneney, J.-N. (eds.) (2008), *Georges Clémenceau. Correspondance, 1858–1929* (France: Robert Laffont).

Brown Scott, J. (ed.) (1921), *Official Statements of War Aims and Peace Proposals, December 1916 to November 1918* (Washington, DC: United States Government Printing Office).

Brunet, R. (1921), *La Société des nations et la France* (Paris: Recueil Sirey).

Bryan, W.J. (1914), *The Prince of Peace* (New York: Doubleday).

Buisson, F., Thomas, A. and Prudhommeaux, J. (1918), *Appel en vue de la fondation d'une Association française pour la Société des Nations* (Paris: Les droits de l'homme).

Bülow, B. von (1930), *Denkwürdigkeiten* (Berlin: Schlieffen–Verlag).

Bulletin du Parti radical et radical-socialiste (1918) 14 Décembre (Paris: Publications du Parti radical et radical-socialiste).

Bulletin officiel de la ligue des droits de l'homme (1917–19) (Paris: Publications de la ligue des droits de l'homme).

Bullitt, W. (1919), *The Bullitt Mission to Russia. Testimony before the Committee on Foreign Relations, United States Senate, of William C. Bullitt* (New York: Huebsch).

Burnett, P.M., (ed.) (1940), *Reparation at the Paris Peace Conference*, 2 vols (New York: Columbia University Press).

Butler, N. (1912), *The International Mind. An Argument for the Judicial Settlement of International Disputes* (New York: Scribner's Sons).

Callwell, C. (ed.) (1927), *Field-Marshal Sir Henry Wilson. His Life and Diaries*, 2 vols (London: Cassell).

Cambon, J. (1919), "La paix", *L'écho de Paris*, 29 June.

Cambon, P. (1931), *The Diplomatist* (London: P. Allan).

Camus, A. (1942), *Le Mythe de Sisyphe. Essai sur l'absurde* (Paris: Gallimard).

Cecil, R. (1941), *A Great Experiment. An Autobiography* (London: J. Cape).

Chamberlain, A. (1928), *Peace in Our Time. Addresses on Europe and the Empire* (London: P. Allan).

(1930), "Great Britain as a European Power", *Journal of the Royal Institute of International Affairs*, 9.

(1935), *Down the Years* (London: Cassell).

(1936), *Politics from the Inside. An Epistolary Chronicle, 1906–1914* (London: Cassell).

Churchill, W.S. (1929), *The World Crisis, Vol. IV: The Aftermath, 1918–1928* (London: MacMillan).

Clausewitz, C. von (1832–34), *Vom Kriege* (Berlin: Ferdinand Dümmler).

Clemenceau, G. (1916), *La France devant l'Allemagne* (Paris: Payot).

(1930), *Grandeurs et misères d'une victoire* (Paris: Plon).

Clémentel, É. (1931), *La France et la politique économique interalliée* (Paris: Presses universitaires de France).

Conrad, J. (1921), "A Note on the Polish Problem", in Conrad, J., *Notes on Life and Letters* (London: Heinemann), pp. 175–84.

Coudenhove-Kalergi, R.N. (1926), *Pan-Europe* (New York: Columnia University Press).

Creel, G. (1920), *How We Advertised America* (New York: Harper & Brothers).

(1947), *Rebel at Large* (New York: Harper & Brothers).

Croly, H. (1909), *The Promise of American Life* (New York: MacMillan).

(1914), *Progressive Democracy* (New York: MacMillan).

(1916), "An American Peace Idea", *New Republic*, 8/103 (21 October), pp. 289–90.

Czernin, O. (1919), (Berlin-Vienna: Ullstein).

D'Abernon, E.V. (1929–30), *An Ambassador of Peace*, ed. M.A. Gerothwol, Volume I: *The Years of Recovery, January 1924–October 1926* (London: Hodder & Stoughton).

Dale, I. (ed.) (1999), *Conservative Party General Election Manifestos, 1900–1997* (London: Routledge).

(ed.) (2000), *Liberal Party General Election Manifestos, 1900–1997* (London: Routledge).

Danelski, D.J. and Tulchin, J.S. (eds.) (1973), *The Autobiographical Notes of Charles Evans Hughes* (Cambridge, MA: Harvard Universiy Press).

Debs, E.V. (1948), *Writings and Speeches of Eugene V. Debs* (New York: Hermitage Press).

Degras, J. (1951–53), *Soviet Documents on Foreign Policy*, 3 vols. (New York: Octagon Books).

Deutsche Allgemeine Zeitung (1918–19).

Deutsche Liga für den Völkerbund (ed.) (1926), *Deutschland und der Völkerbund* (Berlin: R. Hobbing).

Dewey J. (I/1917), "The Future of Pacifism", *New Republic*, 11/143 (28 July), pp. 358–9.

(II/1917), "What America Will Fight For" (1917), in Dewey (1980), pp. 275–6.

(1980), *The Middle Works, 1899–1924*, ed. J.A. Boydston, vol. 10, in Dewey, J. *The Collected Works of John Dewey, 1882–1953* (Carbondale, IL: Southern Illinois University Press).

Dickinson, G.L. (1914), "The War and the Way Out", *Atlantic Monthly*, 14 (December), pp. 820–37.

(1915), *The Foundations of a League of Peace* (Boston: The World Peace Foundation).

Dicey, A.V. (1886), "Americomania in English Politics", *The Nation*, 21 January.

Edwards, W.H. (1928), *The Pact Business* (London: MacMillan, 1928).

Einzig, P. (1931), *The World Economic Crisis, 1929–1931* (London: MacMillan).

Erzberger, M. (1918), *Der Völkerbund. Der Weg zum Weltfrieden* (Berlin: R. Hobbing).

(1919), *The League of Nations. The Way to the World's Peace* (London: MacMillan).

(1920), *Erlebnisse im Weltkrieg* (Stutgart: Deutsche Verlags-Anstalt).

Evans, H. (1909), *Sir Randal Cremer. His Life and Work* (London: MacMillan).

"Extraordinary International Socialist Congress at Basel November 24–25, 1912. Report" (1912), *Vorwärts* (Berlin).

Fabian, W. (1925), *Walter Fabian, Die Kriegsschuldfrage. Grundsätzliches und Tatsächliches zu ihrer Lösung* (Leipzig: Oldenburg).

Foch, F. (I/1931), *Mémoires pour servir à l'histoire de la guerre de 1914–1918*, 2 vols (Paris: Plon).

(II/1931), *The Memoirs of Marshal Foch* (Garden City, NY: Doubleday).

Fraser, H. (1926), "A Sketch of the History of International Arbitration", *Cornell Law Review*, 179, pp. 179–208.

Freud, S. (1931), *Das Unbehagen in der Kultur*, 2nd ed. (Vienna: Internationaler Psychoanalytischer Verlag).

(1915), "Zeitgemäßes über Krieg und Tod", Imago, 4/1, pp. 1–21.

Fried, A.H. (1905), *Handbuch der Friedensbewegung* (Vienna-Leipzig: Friedenswarte).

Fröbel, J. (1859), *Amerika, Europa und die politischen Gesichtspunkte der Gegenwart* (Berlin: Springer).

(1878), *Die Gesichtspunkte und Aufgaben der Politik. Eine Streitschrift nach verschiedenen Richtungen* (Leipzig: Duncker und Humblot).

Gankin, O. and Fischer, H. (eds) (1940), *The Bolsheviks and the World War. The Origin of the Third International* (Stanford, CA: Stanford University Press).

Garvin, J. (1932–69), *The Life of Joseph Chamberlain*, 4 vols (London: MacMillan).

Gelber, L. (1938), *The Rise of Anglo-American Friendship, 1898–1906* (Oxford: Oxford University Press).

Gelfand, L. (1963), *The Inquiry. American Preparations for Peace, 1917–1919* (New Haven, CT: Yale University Press).

(ed.) (1979), *Herbert Hoover. The Great War and Its Aftermath, 1914–23* (Iowa City, IA: University of Iowa Press).

Gentz, F. von (1800), "Über den ewigen Frieden" (1800), in Gentz (2010),

(1806), *Fragments from the Most Recent History of the Political Equilibrium in Europe* (London: John Murray & Sons).

(1815), "Am Schluß des Wiener Kongresses", in Gentz (2010).

(2010), *Revolution und Gleichgewicht* (Leipzig: Manuscriptum).

Gerrity, F. (ed.) (2003), *The Collected Works of William Howard Taft, Volume VII: Papers on the League of Nations* (Athens, OH: Ohio University Press).

Gilbert, S.P. (1925–26), "The Meaning of the 'Dawes Plan'. An Address before the Council on Foreign Relations, New York, January 12, 1926", *Foreign Affairs*, 4.

  (1925–30), *Deutschland unter dem Dawes-Plan. Die Berichte des Generalagenten für Reparationszahlungen*, 10 Halbjahresbände (Berlin: R. Hobbing).

Gladstone, W. (1879), *Political Speeches in Scotland* (London: W. Ridgway).

Glasgow, G. (1925), *From Dawes to Locarno. Being a Critical Record of an Important Achievement in European Diplomacy, 1924–1925* (London: Harper & Brothers).

Goldsmith, R. (1917), *A League to Enforce Peace* (New York: MacMillan).

Gramsci, A. (1988), *Selected Writings 1916–1935*, ed. D. Forgacs (London: Lawrence & Wishart).

Grayson, C. (1960), *Woodrow Wilson. An Intimate Memoir* (New York: Holt).

Grey, E. (1925), *Twenty-five Years*, 2 vols. (London: Hodder & Stoughton).

Grotius, H. (2005), *The Rights of War and Peace*, 3 vols (Indianapolis, IN: Liberty Fund).

Gwynn, S. (ed.) (1929), *The Letters and Friendships of Sir Cecil Spring-Rice*, 2 vols. (London: Constable).

Hagedorn, H. (ed.) (1923), *The Americanism of Theodore Roosevelt* (Boston: Houghton Mifflin).

  (ed.) (1923–26), *The Works of Theodore Roosevelt*, 24 vols (New York: Scribner's Sons).

Hamburger Nachrichten (1914–19).

Hamilton, A., Madison, J. and Jay, J. (1788), *The Federalist Papers*, originally published in 1788 (London: Penguin).

Hancock, W., Poel, J.V.D. (eds.) (1966–73), *Selections from the Smuts Papers*, 7 vols (Cambridge: Cambridge University Press).

Hart, A.B. (ed.) (1918), *Selected Addresses and Public Papers of Woodrow Wilson* (New York: Boni and Liveright).

Headlam-Morley, J. (1917), *The Peace Terms of the Allies* (London: Clay & Sons).

  (1972), *A Memoir of the Paris Peace Conference, 1919*, eds. A. Headlam-Morley et al. (London: Methuen).

Hegel, G.W.F. (1986), *Vorlesungen über die Philosophie der Geschichte* (Frankfurt: Suhrkamp).

Henderson, A. (1917), *The Aims of Labour* (New York: Huebsch).

  (1919), *The Peace Terms* (London: National Labour Press).

Hennessy, J. (1917), *"La constitution de la Société des Nations"*, *Ligue des droits de l'homme* (Paris: Ligue des droits de l'homme).

Herriot, É. (1924), "The Program of Liberal France", *Foreign Affairs*, 1 (June).

  (1948), *Jadis*, 2 vols. (Paris: Flammarion).

Hitler, A. (1980), *Sämtliche Aufzeichnungen 1905–1924*, ed. E. Jäckel (Stuttgart: Deutsche Verlags-Anstalt).

  (2016), *Mein Kampf. Historisch-kritische Neuausgabe*, ed. C. Hartmann (Munich: Institut für Zeitgeschichte).

Hobson, J.A. (1902), *Imperialism. A Study* (London: James Nisbet & Co).
  (1919), "A New Holy Alliance", *Nation*, 19 April, pp. 626–7.
Hollinger, D. and Capper, C. (eds.) (1989), *The American Intellectual Tradition.*
  Volume II: 1865 to the Present (Oxford: Oxford University Press).
Holmes, F. (ed.) (1920), *The Political Philosophy of Robert M. La Follette as*
  Revealed in His Speeches and Writings (Madison, WI: R.M. La Follette Co).
Hoover, H. (1919), "We Cannot Fiddle While Rome Burns", 2 October 1919,
  League to Enforce Peace Pamphlet (New York: League to Enforce Peace).
  (1923), *American Individualism* (Garden City, NY: Doubleday).
  (1929), *The New Day. Campaign Speeches of Herbert Hoover, 1928* (Stanford,
  CA: Stanford University Press).
  (1934), *The State Papers and other Public Writings*, ed. W. Myers, 2 vols (New
  York: Doubleday).
  (1942), *America's First Crusade* (New York: Scribner's Sons).
  (I/1952), *Memoirs. Volume 2: The Cabinet and the Presidency, 1920–1933* (New
  York: MacMillan).
  (II/1952), *Memoirs. Volume 3: The Great Depression, 1929–1941* (New York:
  MacMillan).
  (1961), *An American Epic*, 4 vols. (Chicago: Regnery).
  (1961), *The Ordeal of Woodrow Wilson* (New York: Popular Library).
House, E.M. and Seymour, C. (eds.) (1921), *What Really Happened at Paris* (New
  York: Scribner's Sons).
Howard, D. (ed.), *Selected Political Writings of Rosa Luxemburg* (New York: Grove
  Press).
Hudson, M.O. (1921), "The Protection of Minorities and Natives in Transferred
  Territories", in House and Seymour (1921).
Hughes, C.E. (1922), "Deal Only with Upright States", *The Nation's Business*, 10,
  pp. 10–11.
  (1923), "Recent Questions and Negotiations", *Foreign Affairs*, 2.
  (1925), *The Pathway of Peace. Representative Addresses delivered during his*
  Term as Secretary of State, 1921–1925 (New York: Harper & Bros.).
International Socialist Commission at Berne (1915), "Zimmerwald Resolution,
  September 1915", *Bulletin*, No. 1 (September 21).
International Congress of Women, *The Hague, 28th April to May 1st, 1915,*
  Bericht – Rapport – Report (Chicago: National Peace Federation).
Jäckh, E. (1928), "Die Gründung der Deutschen Liga für Völkerbund", *Völker-*
  bund. Monatsschrift der deutschen Liga für Völkerbund, 1 (1928).
  (1929), *Amerika und wir. Amerikanisch-deutsches Ideenbündnis* (Stuttgart:
  Deutsche Verlags-Anstalt).
  (1960), *Weltsaat. Erlebtes und Erstrebtes* (Stuttgart: Deutsche Verlags-Anstalt).
James, W. (1971), "The Moral Equivalent of War" address, 1906, in James, W., *The*
  Moral Equivalent of War and Other Essays (New York: Harper & Row).
Jefferson, T. (1999), *Political Writings* (Cambridge: Cambridge University Press).
Joffre, J. (1932), *Mémoires, 1910–1917*, 2 vols (Paris: Plon).

Kant, I. (1795), "Perpetual Peace. A Philosophical Sketch", in Kant, I. (1991), *Political Writings* (Cambridge: Cambridge University Press).

Kautsky, K. (1910–11), "Die Vereinigten Staaten von Europa", *Neue Zeit*, 29, vol. 2, pp. 1205–6.

(1919), *Terrorismus und Kommunismus. Ein Beitrag zur Naturgeschichte der Revolution* (Berlin: Neues Vaterland).

Kellogg, F.B. (1926), "Some Foreign Policies of the United States", *Foreign Affairs*, 4.

(1928), "The War Prevention Policy of the United States," *Foreign Affairs*, 6.

Kennan, G.F. (1967), *Memoirs, 1925–1950* (Boston: Little, Brown & Co.).

Kessler, H. (1996), *Tagebücher 1918–1937*, ed. W. Pfeiffer-Belli (Frankfurt and Main: Insel).

(2006), *Das Tagebuch 1880–1937. Sechster Band: 1916–1918*, ed. G. Riederer (Stuttgart: Cotta).

(2006), *Das Tagebuch 1880–1937. Siebter Band: 1919–1923*, ed. A. Rheintal (Stuttgart: Cotta).

Keynes, J.M. (1919), *The Economic Consequences of the Peace* (London: MacMillan).

(1921), *A Revision of the Treaty* (London: MacMillan).

(1923–28), *A Breathing Space – the Dawes Plan, 1923–1928*, in Keynes (1978), XVIII, pp. 234–303.

(1928–30), *Search for a Final Settlement – the Young Plan, 1928–1930*, in Keynes (1978), XVIII, pp. 304–350.

(1930), "The Great Slump of 1930", in Keynes (1978), XIX, pp. 126–34.

(1978), *The Collected Writings of John Maynard Keynes*, 30 vols. (Cambridge: Cambridge University Press).

Kipling, R. (1899), "The White Man's Burden", in Boehmer, E. (ed.) (1998), *Empire Writing* (Oxford: Oxford University Press), pp. 273–4.

King, W. (ed.) (1931), *V.K. Wellington Koo"s Foreign Policy. Some Selected Documents* (Shanghai: Kelly & Walsh).

Kohl, H. (ed.) (1892–1905), *Die politischen Reden des Fürsten Bismarck, 1847–1897*, 14 vols. (Stuttgart: Cotta).

Koo, W. (1919), *China and the League of Nations* (London: Allen & Unwin).

Kossuth, L. (1854), *Select Speeches of Kossuth*, ed. F. Newman (New York: C.S. Francis).

Kracauer, S. (2004–12), *Werke*, eds. I. Mülder-Bach and I. Belke (Frankfurt/Main: Suhrkamp).

Kriegk, O. (1925), *Locarno, ein Erfolg? Eine kritische Studie der Verträge von Locarno und ihrer Vorgeschichte* (Berlin: Der Deutschenspiegel).

Kühlmann, R. von (1948), *Erinnerungen* (Heidelberg: L. Schneider).

The Labour Leader (1918–19).

Labour Party (1916), *Report of the Sixteenth Annual Conference of the Labour Party* (London: National Labour Press).

Labour Party (1917), *Report of the Seventeenth Annual Conference of the Labour Party* (London: National Labour Press).

Labour Party (1919), *Report of the Nineteenth Annual Conference* (London: National Labour Press).

Labour Party Annual Conference Reports, 1918–29 (1919–30) (London: National Labour Press).

Lademacher, H. (ed.) (1967), *Die Zimmerwalder Bewegung* (The Hague: Mouton).

LaFeber, W. (ed.) (1965), *John Quincy Adams and American Continental Empire. Letters, Papers and Speeches* (Chicago: Quadrangle Books).

Lamartine, A. de (1848), *Trois mois au pouvoir* (Paris: Lévy).

(1849), *Histoire de la Révolution de 1848*, 2 vols (Brussels: Rozez).

Lamont, T.W. (1921), "Reparations", in House and Seymour (1921).

(1928), "The Final Reparations Settlement," *Foreign Affairs*, 8.

Lansing, R. (1921), *The Peace Negotiations. A Personal Narrative* (Boston: Houghton & Mifflin).

Laroche, J. (1957), *Au Quai d'Orsay avec Briand et Poincaré, 1913–1926* (Paris: Hachette).

Laschitza, A. (ed.), *Karl Liebknecht. Eine Biographie in Dokumenten* (Berlin: Dietz).

Latané, J. (ed.) (1932), *Development of the League of Nations Idea. Documents and Correspondence of Theodore Marburg*, 2 vols (New York: MacMillan).

League of Nations Union (1919), *Proceedings of the Conference of Delegates of Allied Societies for a League of Nations, London, March 11–13, 1919* (London: League of Nations Union).

Leffingwell, R.C. (1922), *America's Interest in Europe* (New York: Foreign Policy Association).

Lenin, V.I. (1902), *What Is to Be Done?* (1902), in Lenin (1960–70), V, pp. 347–530.

(1914), "Über das Recht der Nationen auf Selbstbestimmung", in Lenin (1960), pp. 208–79.

(1916), *Imperialism. The Highest Stage of Capitalism*, new ed. (London: Penguin, 2010).

(1920), "The Socialist Revolution and the Right of Nations to Self-Determination", in Lenin (1960–70), XXII, pp. 143–56.

(1932), *State and Revolution* (New York: International Publishers).

(1960), *Über die nationale und die koloniale nationale Frage. Eine Sammlung ausgewählter Aufsätze und Reden* (Berlin: Verlag Neue Einheit).

(1960–70), *Collected Works*, 45 vols. (Moscow: Foreign Languages Publication House).

Le Parti socialiste, la guerre et la paix : toutes les résolutions et tous les documents du Parti socialiste, de Juillet 1914 à fin 1917 (1918), (Paris: Librairie de l'Humanité).

Leroy, M. (1917), *L'ère Wilson : La Société des nations* (Paris: Giard & Brière).

Levinson, S. (1922), *Outlawry of War. A Plan to Outlaw War* (Washington, DC: Government Printing Office).

Ligue des droits de l'homme, (1917), "Congrès de la Ligue, 1916 – Résolutions adoptées – Les conditions d'une paix durable", *Bulletin officiel de la ligue des droits de l'homme*, janvier 1917 (Paris: Ligue des droits de l'homme).

Ligue des droits de l'homme (1917), *Vers la société des Nations* (Paris: Ligue des droits de l'homme).

Link, A.S. (ed.) (1966 ff.), *The Papers of Woodrow Wilson* (Princeton, NJ: Princeton University Press).

Lippmann, W. (I/1917), "America's Part in the War", *New Republic* (10 February), pp. 33–4.

(II/1917), "The Defense of the Atlantic World", *New Republic* (17 February), pp. 59–60.

(1922), *Public Opinion* (New York: MacMillan).

(1923), "The Outlawry of War", *Atlantic Monthly* (August).

(1925), *The Phantom Public* (New York: MacMillan).

(1944), *U.S. War Aims* (New York: MacMillan).

Literary Digest I (1914–33).

Lloyd George, D. (1918), *British War Aims. Statement by the Prime Minister, the Right Honourable David Lloyd George, on January 5, 1918* (London: HMSO).

(1932), *The Truth about Reparations and War Debts* (London: Heinemann).

(1933–36), *War Memoirs*, 6 vols. (London: Nicholson & Watson).

(1938), *The Truth about the Peace Treaties*, 2 vols (London: Gollancz).

Lodge, H.C. (1917), *War Addresses, 1915–1917* (Boston: Houghton & Mifflin).

Lord, R. (1921), "Poland", in House and Seymour (1921).

Loucheur, L. (1962), *Carnets Secrets, 1908–1932*, ed. J. de Launay (Paris: Brepols).

Luckau, A. (ed.) (1941), *The German Delegation at the Paris Peace Conference* (New York: Columbia University Press).

Ludendorff, E. (1919), *Meine Kriegserinnerungen 1914–1918* (Berlin: Mittler).

(1920), *Urkunden der Obersten Heeresleitung über ihre Tätigkeit 1916/18* (Berlin: Mittler, 1920).

Luther, H. (1960), *Politiker ohne Partei* (Stuttgart: Deutsche Verlags-Anstalt).

Luxemburg, R. (1899), *Sozialreform oder Revolution?* (Leipzig: Leipziger Buchdruckerei).

(1913), *Die Akkumulation des Kapitals. Ein Beitrag zur ökonomischen Erklärung des Imperialismus* (Berlin: Paul Singer).

(2018), *Friedensutopien und Hundepolitik* (Stuttgart: Reclam).

Macartney, P. (ed.) (1926), *Survey of International Affairs, 1925* (Oxford: Oxford University Press).

MacDonald, R. (1920), *A Policy for the Labour Party* (London: Parsons).

(1914), "From Green Benches", *Leicester Pioneer*, 20 March.

(1918), *National Defence. A Study in Militarism* (London 1918).

(1919), "Outlook", *Socialist Review* (July).

(I/1923), "Outlook", *Socialist Review* (February).

(II/1923), *The Foreign Policy of the Labour Party* (London: Palmer).

(1925), *Protocol or Pact* (London: Labour Party).

MacDonald, W. (1919), "A Conference Unrepentant", 30 May 1919, *The Nation* (21 June), pp. 978–80.

Machiavelli, N. (1998), *The Prince* (Chicago: Chicago University Press).

(1998), *Discourses on Livy* (Chicago: Chicago University Press).

Mackinder, H. (1904), "The Geographical Pivot of History", *The Geographical Journal*, XXIII (April), pp. 421–37.

(1919), *Democratic Ideals and Reality* (London: MacMillan).

Mahan, A.T. (1897), *The Interest of the United States in Sea Power, Present and Future* (Boston: Houghton & Mifflin).

(1902), *Retrospect and Prospect. Studies in International Relations, Naval and Political* (Boston: Houghton & Mifflin).

The Manchester Guardian (1860–1933).

Mann, T. (1918), *Betrachtungen eines Unpolitischen* (Berlin: Fischer).

Marx, K. and Engels, F. (1848), *The Communist Manifesto*, February (Oxford: Oxford University Press).

(1969–70), *Selected Works*, 2 vols. (Moscow: Progress Publishers).

(1987), *Collected Works, Volume 42: Letters, 1864–68* (London: Lawrence & Wishart).

Masaryk, T. (1927), *The Making of a State. Memories and Observations 1914–1918* (London: MacMillan).

Maurras, C. (1919), "La Politique", *Action française* (24 September).

Mazzini, G. (1847), "Nationality and Cosmopolitanism" (1847), in Recchia and Urbinati (2009).

(1849), "Toward a Holy Alliance of the Peoples" (1849), in Recchia and Urbinati (2009).

(1850), "From a Revolutionary Alliance to the United States of Europe" (1850), in Recchia and Urbinati (2009).

McAdoo, W. (1931), *Crowded Years. The Reminiscences of William G. McAdoo* (Boston: Houghton & Mifflin).

Meijer, J. (ed.) (1964–71), *The Trotsky Papers, 1917–1922*, 2 vols. (The Hague: Mouton).

Meinecke, F. (1922), *Weltbürgertum und Nationalstaat* (Berlin: Oldenbourg).

(1957–63), *Werke*, eds. H. Herzfeld et al., 9 vols (Stuttgart: Köhler).

(1969), *Autobiographische Schriften*, ed. E Kessel (Stuttgart: Deutsche Verlags-Anstalt).

(1998), *Machiavellism. The Doctrine of Raison d'État and Its Place in Modern History* (London: Routledge & Kegan).

Mermeix, G. (1922), *Le combat des trois* (Paris: Librairie Ollendorff).

Mill, J.S. (1991), *On Liberty and Other Essays*, ed. J. Gray (Oxford: Oxford University Press).

Miller, D.H. (1921), "*The Making of the League of Nations*", in House and Seymour (1921).

(1924–26), *My Diary at the Conference of Paris, with Documents*, 21 vols. (New York: Appeal).

(1928), *The Drafting of the Covenant*, 2 vols. (New York: G.P. Putnam's Sons).

Mombauer, A. (ed.) (2013), *The Origins of the First World War. Diplomatic and Military Documents* (Manchester: Manchester University Press).

Mommsen, W. (ed.) (1960), *Deutsche Parteiprogramme* (Munich: Olzog).

Monnet, J. (1976), *Mémoires* (Paris: Fayard).

Mordacq, G. (1930), *Le ministère Clemenceau*, 4 vols. (Paris: Plon).

Morgan, K. (ed.) (1973), *Lloyd George Family Letters, 1885–1936* (Cardiff: University of Wales Press).

Morison, E. (ed.) (1951–54), *The Letters of Theodore Roosevelt*, 8 vols. (Cambridge, MA: Harvard University Press).

Moulton, H. and Pasvolsky, L. (1932), *War Debts and World Prosperity* (New York: The Century Company).

Müller, H. (1928), *Die November-Revolution. Erinnerungen* (Berlin: Bücherkreis).

Najder, Z. and Carroll-Najder, H. (eds.) (1983), *Conrad under Familial Eyes* (Cambridge: Cambridge University Press).

Naumann. F. (1915), *Mitteleuropa* (Berlin: De Gruyter).

Nevins, A. (1930), *Henry White. Thirty Years of American Diplomacy* (Oxford: Oxford University Press).

The Nation (1914–33).

The New Republic (1914–33).

The New York Times (1900–33).

Nicolson, H. (1931), *Peacemaking, 1919* (London: Constable).

Nicolson, N. (ed.) (2005), *The Harold Nicolson Diaries 1907–1964* (London: Phoenix).

Niemeyer, T. (1919), Der Völkerbundsentwurf der Deutschen Gesellschaft für Völkerrecht. Vorschläge für die Organisation der Welt (Berlin: Engelmann).

Nietzsche, F. (1999), *Nachgelassene Fragmente 1884–1885* (Berlin: De Gruyter).

(2011), *Also sprach Zarathustra. Ein Buch für alle und keinen* (Berlin: De Gruyter).

(2012), *Menschliches, Allzumenschliches. Ein Buch für freie Geister*, 2 vols. (Berlin: De Gruyter).

Noble, G. (1935), *Wilsonian Diplomacy, the Versailles Peace, and French Public Opinion* (New York: Macmillan).

Noel Baker, P. J. (1925), *The Geneva Protocol for the Pacific Settlement of International Disputes* (London: P.S. King).

O'Brien, F. (ed.) (1974), *The Hoover-Wilson Wartime Correspondence, September 24, 1914, to November 11, 1918* (Iowa City, IA: Iowa University Press).

(ed.) (1978), *Two Peacemakers in Paris. The Hoover-Wilson Post-Armistice Letters, 1918–1920* (College Station, TX: Texas A & M University Press).

Official Bulletin of the International Labour and Socialist Conference (Berne), 7 February 1919.

"Peace at Any Price" (1919), *New Republic*, 19 (24 May), pp. 100–2.

Penn, W. (1726), "An Essay toward The Present and Future Peace of Europe", in: *A Collection of the Works of William Penn*, 2 vols. (London: Sowle), II, pp. 838–48.

Perkins, D. (1927), *The Monroe Doctrine, 1823–1826* (Cambridge: Cambridge University Press).

Petrie, C. (1939/40), *The Life and Letters of the Rt. Hon. Sir Austen Chamberlain,* 2 vols. (London: Cassell).

Plato (1970), *The Laws* (London: Penguin).

— (2000), *The Republic* (Cambridge: Cambridge University Press).

Plenge, J. (1915), *Der Krieg und die Volkswirtschaft* (Münster: Borgmeyer).

— (1916), *1789 und 1914* (Berlin: Springer).

Plessner, H. (1959), *Die verspätete Nation. Über die politische Verführbarkeit bürgerlichen Geistes,* 2nd ed. (Stuttgart: Kohlhammer).

Poincaré, R. (1919), *Messages, discours, allocutions, lettres et télégrammes de m. Raymond Poincaré* (Paris: Bloud & Gay).

— (1926–33), *Au service de la France. Neuf années de souvenirs,* 10 vols. (Paris: Plon).

— (1930), "La Ruhr et le Plan Dawes", *Revue de Paris* (1 January).

Polk, J. (1848), "Fourth Annual Message to Congress, 5 December 1848", Miller Center, *Presidential Speeches,* (Charlottesville, VA: University of Virginia Press).

Preuß, H. (1915), *Das deutsche Volk und die Politik* (Jena: Diederichs).

— (1923), *Deutschlands republikanische Reichsverfassung,* 2nd ed. (Berlin: Verlag Neuer Staat).

Proceedings of the first Pan American Financial Conference, May 24 to 29, 1915 (1915), (Washington, DC: Government Printing Office).

Pufendorf, S. (1711), *Of the Law of Nature and Nations* (Oxford: Oxford University Press).

Ranke, L. von (1833), *Die großen Mächte* (Berlin: Duncker & Humblot).

— (1881–88), *Weltgeschichte,* 16 vols. (Berlin: Duncker & Humblot).

Rathenau, W. (1917), *Von kommenden Dingen* (Berlin: Fischer).

— (1928), *Gesammelte Schriften in fünf Bänden* (Berlin: Fischer).

— (1929), *Politische Briefe* (Dresden: Reissner).

— (1930), *Briefe,* 3 vols. (Dresden: Reissner).

Renan, E. (1882), *Qu'est-ce qu'une nation?* (Paris: Helleu).

Redmond, C. (ed.) (1925), *Selections from the Correspondence of Theodore Roosevelt and Henry Cabot Lodge, 1884–1918,* 2 vols. (New York: Scribner's Sons).

Renaudel, P. (1919), *L'internationale à Berne* (Paris: Grasset).

Renner, K. 1918), *Das Selbstbestimmungsrecht der Nationen in besonderer Anwendung auf Oesterreich* (Leipzig: Deuticke).

Ribot, A. (1936), *Journal d'Alexandre Ribot et correspondances inédites, 1914–1922* (Paris: Plon).

Riddell, J. (ed.) (1984), *Lenin's Struggle for a Revolutionary International. Documents, 1907–1916* (New York: Anchor).

— (ed.) (1987), *Founding the Communist International. Proceedings and Documents of the First Congress, March 1919* (New York: Anchor).

Riezler, K. (1972), *Tagebücher, Aufsätze, Dokumente*, ed. K.D. Erdmann (Göttingen: Vandenhoeck & Ruprecht).

Rochau, A. von (1859), *Grundsätze der Realpolitik, angewendet auf die staatlichen Zustände Deutschlands*, 2nd ed. (Stuttgart: Göpel).

Roosevelt, T. (1915), *America and the World War* (New York: Scribner's Sons).

(1918), *The League of Nations* (Boston: Houghton & Mifflin).

(1921), *Roosevelt in the Kansas City Star. War-Time Editorials* (Boston: Houghton, Mifflin & Co.).

(1925), *State Papers as Governor and President, 1899–1909* (New York: Scribner's Sons).

Root, E. (1916), *The Outlook for International Law* (Boston: Houghton & Mifflin).

(1917), *The Effect of Democracy on International Law* (Washington, DC: Carnegie Endowment).

(1921), *The "Great War" and International Law* (Washington, DC: Carnegie Endowment).

(1925), *American Ideals during the Past Half-Century* (New York: International Conciliation).

(1926), *Men and Policies* (Cambridge, MA: Harvard University Press).

Rosenman, S. (ed.) (1941–48), *The Public Papers and Addresses of Franklin D. Roosevelt, 1940–1945* (New York: Random House).

Rousseau, J.-J. (1756), "Extrait du projet de paix perpétuelle du Monsieur l'Abbé de Saint-Pierre", in Rousseau, J.-J. (2009), *Friedensschriften* (Hamburg: Meiner, 2009).

(1761), "The Plan for Perpetual Peace" (1761), in Rousseau, J.-J. (2011), *On the Government of Poland, and Other Writings on History and Politics* (Dartmouth, MA: Dartmouth College Press).

Schacht, H. (1931), *Das Ende der Reparationen* (Oldenburg: Stalling).

Scheidemann, P. (1916), *Die deutsche Sozialdemokratie und der Krieg* (Breslau: Volkswacht).

(1917), *Frieden der Verständigung* (Berlin: Singer).

(1921), *Der Zusammenbruch* (Berlin: Verlag für Sozialwissenschaft).

(1928), *Memoiren eines Sozialdemokraten*, 2 vols. (Dresden: Reissner).

(1929), *Memoirs of a Social Democrat*, 2 vols. (London: Hodder & Stoughton).

Scheler, M. (1915), *Der Genius des Krieges und der Deutsche Krieg* (Leipzig: Weissen).

(1931), *Die Idee des Friedens und der Pazifismus* (Berlin: Der Neue Geist).

Schmitt, C. (1932), *Der Begriff des Politischen* (Berlin: Duncker & Humblot).

(1950), *Der Nomos der Erde* (Berlin: Duncker & Humblot).

(2006), *The Nomos of the Earth* (New York: Telos Press).

(2007), *The Concept of the Political* (Chicago: Chicago University Press).

Schücking, W. (1915), *Die deutschen Professoren und der Weltkrieg* (Berlin: Neues Vaterland).

(1918), *The International Union of the Hague Conferences* (Oxford: Oxford University Press).

Schwabe, K. (ed.) (1997), *Quellen zum Friedensschluss von Versailles* (Darmstadt: Wissenschaftliche Buchgesellschaft).

Schwertfeger, B. (1929), *Der Weltkrieg der Dokumente. Zehn Jahre Kriegsschuldforschung und ihr Ergebnis* (Berlin: Deutsche Verlagsgesellschaft für Politik und Geschichte).

Seeley, J. (1871), "The United States of Europe", *Macmillan's Magazine*, pp. 436–48.

Self, R.C. (ed.) (1995), *The Austen Chamberlain Diaries and Letters. The Correspondence of Sir Austen Chamberlain with his Sisters, Hilda and Ida, 1916–1937* (Cambridge: Cambridge University Press).

Seward, W.H. (1844), *Elements of Empire in America* (New York: Shepard).

Seymour. C. (ed.) (1926–8), *The Intimate Papers of Colonel House*, 4 vols. (Boston: Houghton & Mifflin).

Seymour, C. (1951), *Geography, Justice, and Politics at the Paris Peace Conference of 1919* (New York: American Geographical Society).

Shaw, A. (ed.) (1924), *The Messages and Papers of Woodrow Wilson* (New York, Doran).

Shotwell, J.T. (1929), *War as an Instrument of National Policy and Its Renunciation in the Pact of Paris* (New York: MacMillan).

—— (1937), *At the Paris Peace Conference* (New York, 1937).

Simmel, G. (1914), "*Deutschlands innere Wandlung*. Rede gehalten in Strassburg, November 1914", in Simmel, G. (1917), *Der Krieg und die Geistigen Entscheidungen. Reden und Aufsätze* (Berlin: Duncker & Humblot).

—— (1999), *Der Krieg und die geistigen Entscheidungen. Grundfragen der Soziologie* (Frankfurt/Main: Suhrkamp).

Smuts, J.C. (1918), *The League of Nations. A Practical Suggestion* (London: Hodder & Stoughton).

Snowden, F. (1934), *An Autobiography, II, 1919–34* (London: Nicholson & Watson).

Sombart, W. (1915), *Händler und Helden. Patriotische Besinnungen* (Berlin: Duncker & Humblot).

Spencer, H. (1862), *A System of Synthetic Philosophy. Volume I: First Principles* (London: Williams & Norgate).

Stalin, J. (1934), *The October Revolution. A Collection of Articles and Speeches* (New York: AMS Press).

—— (1952–4), *Works*, 13 vols. (Moscow: Foreign Languages Publishing House).

Stead, W. (1902), *The Americanization of the World* (London: Horace Markley).

Stern-Rubarth, E. (1939), *Three Men Tried. Austen Chamberlain, Stresemann, Briand and Their Fight for a New Europe* (London: Duckworth).

Stimson, H.L. (1932), *The Pact of Paris. Three Years of Development* (Washington, DC: Council on Foreign Relations).

Stimson, H.L. and Bundy, M. (1948), *On Active Service in Peace and War* (New York: Harper).

"Stockholm Memorandum" (1917), "Stockholm Memorandum. Die deutsche Sozialdemokratie und der Frieden. Erklärung der Delegation der deutschen Sozialdemokratie auf der internationalen sozialistischen Friedenskonferenz in Stockholm", 12 June, in *Protokoll über die Verhandlungen des Parteitages der Sozialdemokratischen Partei Deutschlands, Würzburg, 14. bis 20. Oktober 1917* (Berlin: Publikationen der SPD, 1973), pp. 39–44.

Stresemann, G. (1926), *Reden und Schriften. Politik-Geschichte-Literatur, 1897–1926*, 2 vols. (Dresden: Reissner).

—— (1929), "Speech at the General Assembly, League of Nations, 9 September 1929", *League of Nations Official Journal*, Special Supplement no. 75 (Geneva).

Suarez, G. (ed.) (1928), *De Poincaré à Poincaré* (Paris: Plon).

—— (1932), *Herriot, 1924–1932* (Paris: Plon).

—— (1932), *Vermächtnis. Der Nachlaß in drei Bänden*, ed. H. Bernhard (Berlin: Ullstein).

—— (ed.) (1938–41), *Briand. Sa vie, son oeuvre avec son Journal et de nombreux documents inédits*, 5 vols. (Paris: Plon).

Suttner, B. von (1889), *Die Waffen nieder* (Dresden: Pierson).

Taft, W.H. (1910), *Address to the American Society for the Judicial Settlement of International Disputes, 17 December 1910* (Washington, DC: Government Printing Office).

—— (1914), *The United States and Peace* (New York: International Conciliation).

Tardieu, A. (1908), *France and the Alliances. The Struggle for the Balance of Power* (New York: MacMillan).

—— (1910), *La France et les alliances*, 3rd ed. (Paris: Alcan).

—— (I/1921), *La paix* (Paris: Payot & Cie).

—— (II/1921), *The Truth about the Treaty* (Indianapolis, IN: Bobbs-Merrill Co.).

—— (1927), *Devant l'obstacle : l'Amérique et nous* (Paris: Émile-Paul Frères).

—— (1931), *L'épreuve du pouvoir* (Paris: Flammarion).

Temperley, H.W.V. (ed.) (1920–24), *A History of the Peace Conference of Paris*, 6 vols. (London: Hodder & Stoughton).

The Observer (1914–33).

The Times (1860–1933).

Tirpitz, A. von (1919), *My Memoirs*, 2 vols. (London: MacMillan).

—— (1926), *Deutsche Ohmachtspolitik im Weltkriege* (Stuttgart: Cotta).

Tocqueville, A. de (2004), *De la démocratie en Amérique*, 2 vols. (Paris: Gallimard).

Thimme, F. (ed.) (1919), *Bethmann Hollwegs Kriegsreden* (Cologne: Schaffstein).

Thucydides (2009), *The Peloponnesian War* (Oxford: Oxford University Press).

Toynbee, A.J., Macartney, P. (eds.) (1921–34), *Survey of International Affairs, 1920-33* (Oxford: Oxford University Press).

Treitschke, H. von (1903), *Historische und politische Aufsätze*, Vol. 2 (Leipzig: Hirzel).

Trevelyan, G.M. (ed.) (1937), *Grey of Fallodon. The Life and Letters of Sir Edward Grey* (Boston: Houghton & Mifflin).

Troeltsch, E. (1924), *Spektator-Briefe. Aufsätze über die deutsche Revolution und die Weltpolitik 1918–22* (Tübingen: Mohr).

Trotsky, L. (1914), *Der Krieg und die Internationale* (Zurich, Borba).

—— (1918), *The Bolsheviki and World Peace* (New York: Boni & Liveright).

—— (2008), *History of the Russian Revolution* (Chicago: Chicago University Press).

Trueblood, B. (1899), *The Federation of the World* (Boston: Houghton & Mifflin).

Tryon, J. (1911), "The Rise of the Peace Movement", *Yale Law Journal*, 20 (March), pp. 358–71.

Tucker, R.C. (1975), *The Lenin Anthology* (New York: Norton).

Turner, H. (1967), "Eine Rede Stresemanns über seine Locarnopolitik", *Vierteljahrshefte für Zeitgeschichte*, 15, pp. 412–36.

Valéry, P. (1919), *La crise de l'esprit* (Paris: La Nouvelle revue française).

Vansittart, R. (1958), *The Mist Procession* (London: Hutchinson).

Veblen, T. (1915), *Imperial Germany and the Industrial Revolution* (London: MacMillan).

(1917), *An Inquiry into the Nature of Peace and the Terms of Its Perpetuation* (New York: Kelley).

Vorwärts (1876–1933).

Walling, W. (ed.) (1915), *The Socialists and the War* (New York: Holt).

Walter, F. (1925), *Die Kriegsschuldfrage – Grundsätzliches und Tatsächliches zu ihrer Lösung* (Leipzig: Oldenbourg).

Warburg, M. (1952), *Aus meinen Aufzeichnungen* (Glückstad: J.J. Augustin).

Weber, H. (ed.) (1963), *Der deutsche Kommunismus. Dokumente* (Cologne: Kiepenheuer & Witsch).

Weber, M. (1915), "Bismarcks Außenpolitik und die Gegenwart", in Weber (1971).

(1915/16), "Zur Frage des Friedensschliessens", in Weber (1971).

(I/1916), "Der verschärfte U-Bootkrieg", in: Weber (1971).

(II/1916), "Deutschland unter den europäischen Weltmächten", in Weber (1971).

(1917), "Wahlrecht und Demokratie in Deutschland', in Weber (1971).

(1918), "Deutschlands künftige Staatsform", in Weber (1971).

(1919), "The Profession and Vocation of Politics", in Weber (1994), pp. 309–69.

(1971), *Gesammelte politische Schriften*, ed. J. Wickelmann, 3rd ed. (Tübingen: Mohr).

(1994), *Political Writings*, eds. P. Lassman, R. Speirs (Cambridge: Cambridge University Press).

(2012), *Briefe 1918–1920*, eds. G. Krumeich, M. Lepsius, 2 vols. (Tübingen: Mohr).

William, T. (1902), *The Americanisation of the World – or: The Trend of the Twentieth Century* (London: Review of Reviews).

Westlake, J. (1896), "International Arbitration", *International Journal of Ethics*, 7 (October), pp. 1–20.

White, W.A. (1946), *The Autobiography of William Allen White* (New York: MacMillan).

Wilson, E.B. (1939), *My Memoir* (New York: Bobbs-Merrill).

Wilson, W. (1902), *A History of the American People*, 10 vols. (New York: Wise & Co.).

Wolf, J. (1903), *Materialien betreffend einen mitteleuropäischen Wirtschaftsverein* (Berlin: Reimer).

Woman's Peace Party (1916), *The New Holy Office* (New York: Woman's Peace Party).

World Peace Foundation (1917–19), *Pamphlet Series, 1917-1919* (Boston: Houghton & Mifflin).

(1919), *A League of Nations*, vol. 1 (Boston: Houghton & Mifflin).

Zwoch, G. (ed.) (1972), *Gustav Stresemann. Reichstagsreden* (Bonn: Bertelsmann).

II. Secondary Sources

Abbenhuis, M. (2018), *The Hague Conferences in International Politics, 1898-1915* (London: Bloomsbury).

Abbenhuis, M. and Tames, I. (2021), *Global War, Global Catastrophe. Neutrals, Belligerents and the Transformations of the First World War* (London: Bloomsbury).

Ádám, M. (2003), *The Versailles System and Central Europe* (Burlington, VT: Ashgate).

Adamthwaite, A. (1995), *Grandeur and Misery. France´s Bid for Power in Europe, 1914-1940* (London: Bloomsbury).

Afflerbach, H. (2018), *Auf Messers Schneide. Wie das Deutsche Reich den Ersten Weltkrieg verlor* (Munich: Beck).

Afflerbach, H. and Stevenson, D. (eds.) (2007), *Improbable War? The Outbreak of World War I and European Political Culture before 1914* (New York: Berghahn).

Ahmann, R., Birke, A. and Howard, M. (eds.) (1993), *The Quest for Stability. Problems of West European Security 1918-1957* (Oxford: Oxford University Press).

"AHR Conversation: On Transnational History" (2006), *American Historical Review*, 111 (December), pp. 1441–64.

Albertini, L. (1952–57), *The Origins of the War of 1914*, 3 vols. (Oxford: Oxford University Press).

Ambrosius, L. (1987), *Woodrow Wilson and the American Diplomatic Tradition. The Treaty Fight in Perspective* (Cambridge: Cambridge University Press).

(1991), *Wilsonian Statecraft. Theory and Practice of Liberal Internationalism during World War I* (Wilmington, DE: Scholarly Resources).

(2017), *Woodrow Wilson and American Internationalism* (Cambridge: Cambridge University Press).

Andrew, C., Kanya-Forstner, A. (1981), *France Overseas* (London: Thames & Hudson).

Angelow, J. (2010), *Der Weg in die Urkatastrophe. Der Zerfall des alten Europa 1900-1914* (Berlin: Bebra).

Arendt, H. (2009), *On Revolution* (London: Penguin).

(2017), *The Origins of Totalitarianism* (London: Penguin).

(2018), "The Freedom to Be Free", in Arendt, H., *The Freedom to Be Free* (London: Penguin).

Artaud, D. (1978), *La question des dettes interalliées et la reconstruction de l'Europe, 1917–1929*, 2 vols. (Paris: Champion).

(1979), "Die Hintergründe der Ruhrbesetzung 1923. Das Problem der interalliierten Schulden", *Vierteljahrshefte für Zeitgeschichte*, 27, pp. 241–59.

Audoin-Rouzeau, S., Prochasson, C. (eds.) (2008), *Sortir de la grande guerre : le monde et l'après-1918* (Paris: Tallandier).

Baechler, C. (1996), *Gustave Stresemann (1878–1929). De l'impérialisme à la sécurité collective* (Strasbourg: Presses universitaires de Strasbourg).

Bailey, T.A. (1947), *Woodrow Wilson and the Peacemakers* (New York: MacMillan).

Bari, J. (ed.) (2007), *Aristide Briand, la Société des Nations et l'Europe, 1919–1932* (Strasbourg: Presses universitaires de Strasbourg).

Bariéty, J. (1977), *Les relations franco-allemandes après la première guerre mondiale, 10 Novembre 1918 – 10 Janvier 1925, de l'exécution à la négotiation* (Paris: Pedone).

(1980), "Finances et relations internationales à propos du 'plan de Thoiry' (septembre 1926)", *Relations Internationales*, 21, pp. 423–31.

(2000), "Aristide Briand et la sécurité de la France en Europe, 1919–1932", in Schuker (2000), pp. 117–34.

Barnett, C.J. (1972), *The Collapse of British Power* (London: Methuen).

Bartlett, R. (1944), *The League to Enforce Peace* (Chapel Hill, NC: University of North Carolina Press).

Barth, B. (2003), *Dolchstoßlegenden und politische Desintegration. Das Trauma der deutschen Niederlage im Ersten Weltkrieg, 1914–1933* (Düsseldorf: Droste).

(2016), *Europa nach dem Großen Krieg. Die Krise der Demokratie in der Zwischenkriegszeit, 1918–1938* (Frankfurt: Campus).

Bartlett, C.J. (1989), *British Foreign Policy in the Twentieth Century* (Basingstoke: MacMillan).

Bátonyi, G. (1999), *Britain and Central Europe 1918–1932* (Oxford: Oxford Universiy Press).

Baumgart, W. (1999), *Europäisches Konzert und Nationale Bewegung. Internationale Beziehungen, 1830– 1878* (Paderborn: Schöningh).

Baumont, M. (1966), *Arisitide Briand. Diplomat und Idealist* (Göttingen: Vandenhoeck & Ruprecht).

Bayly, C.A. (2004), *The Birth of the Modern World, 1780–1914* (Oxford: Blackwells).

Beale, H. (1956), *Theodore Roosevelt and the Rise of America to World Power* (Baltimore, MD: Johns Hopkins University Press).

Becker, J.-J. (1986), *The Great War and the French People* (London: St Martin's Press).

Becker, J.-J. and Audoin-Rouzeau, S. (2012), *La France, la nation, la guerre : 1850–1920* (Paris: Sedes).

Becker, J.-J. and Berstein, S. (1990), *Victoire et frustrations 1914–1929* (Paris: Seuil).

Becker, J.-J. and Krumeich, G. (2008), *La grande guerre. Une histoire franco-allemande* (Paris: Tallandier).

Becker, J. and Hildebrand K. (eds.) (1980), *Internationale Beziehungen in der Weltwirtschaftskrise 1929–1933* (Munich: Ernst Vögel).

(2014), "Outbreak", in Winter (I/2014).

Beisner, R. (1985), *Twelve against Empire. The Anti-Imperialists, 1898–1900* (Chicago: University of Chicago Press).

Bell, D. (I/2007), *The Idea of Greater Britain* (Princeton, NJ: Princeton University Press).

(ed.) (II/2007), *Victorian Visions of Global Order* (Cambridge: Cambridge University Press).

Bell, P.M.H. (III/2007), *The Origins of the Second World War in Europe* (London: Longman).

Beloff, M. (1989), *Dream of Commonwealth, 1921–42* (London: MacMillan).

Bemis, S.F. (1951), *John Quincy Adams and the Foundations of American Foreign Policy* (New York: Knopf).

Bender, T. (ed.) (2002), *Rethinking American History in a Global Age* (Berkeley, CA: University of California Press).

(2006), *A Nation among Nations. America's Place in World History* (New York: Farrar, Straus & Giroux).

Bender, T. and Geyer, M. (2008), "Mission und Macht", in Patel and Mauch (2010), pp. 27–64.

Benner, E. (2001), "Is There a Core National Doctrine?", *Nations and Nationalism*, 7 (April), pp. 155–74.

(2013), "Nationalism. Intellectual Origins", in Breuilly, J. (2013), pp. 36–55.

(2018), *Really Existing Nationalisms. A Post-Communist View from Marx and Engels* (London: Verso).

Bennett, G.H. (1989), *British Foreign Policy during the Curzon Period, 1919–24* (London: MacMillan).

Benz, W. (ed.) (1987), *Pazifismus in Deutschland, 1890–1939* (Frankfurt/Main: Fischer).

Berend, I. (1986), *The Crisis Zone of Europe. An Interpretation of East-Central European History in the First Half of the Twentieth Century* (Cambridge: Cambridge University Press).

Berg, M. (1990), *Gustav Stresemann und die Vereinigten Staaten von Amerika. Weltwirtschaftliche Verflechtung und Revisionspolitik 1907–1929* (Baden-Baden: Nomos).

(2017), *Woodrow Wilson. Amerika und die Neuordnung der Welt* (Munich: Beck).

Berghahn, V.R. (1993), *Germany and the Approach of War in 1914*, 2nd ed. (London: MacMillan).

(2006), *Europe in the Era of Two World Wars* (Princeton, NJ: Princeton University Press).

(2014), "Origins", in Winter (I/2014), pp. 16–38.

Berghahn, V.R. and Kitchen, M. (2019), *Germany in the Age of Total War* (London: Routledge).

Bessel, R. (1993), *Germany after the First World War* (Oxford: Oxford University Press).

Betts, F. (1991), *France and Decolonisation, 1900–1960* (Basingstoke: MacMillan).

Betts, P. (2020), *Ruin and Renewal. Civilising Europe after the Second World War* (London: Profile).

Bew, J. (2012), *Castlereagh. A Life* (Oxford: Oxford University Press).

Beyme, K.V. (2002), *Politische Theorien im Zeitalter der Ideologien. 1789–1945* (Wiesbaden: Verlag für Sozialwissenschaften).

Billington, D. (2006), *Lothian. Philip Kerr and the Quest for World Order* (Westport, CT: Praeger).

Birn, D.S. (1985), *The League of Nations Union, 1918–1945* (Oxford: Oxford University Press).

Blair, S. (1993), "Les origines en France de la SDN. La Commission interministérielle d'études pour la Société des Nations, 1917–1919", *Relations internationales*, 75 (automne).

Blake, R. (1966), *Disraeli* (London: Methuen).

Blower, B. and Preston, A. (eds.) (2021), *The Cambridge History of America and the World. Vol. 3: 1900–1945* (Cambridge: Cambridge University Press).

Boadle, D.G. (1979), *Winston Churchill and the German Question in British Foreign Policy, 1918–1922* (The Hague: Nijhoff).

Boemeke, M., Chickering, R. and Förster, S. (eds.) (1999), *Anticipating Total War. The German and American Experiences, 1871–1914* (Cambridge: Cambridge University Press).

Boemeke, M., Feldman, G.D. and Glaser, E. (eds.) (1998), *The Treaty of Versailles. A Reassessment after 75 Years* (Cambridge: Cambridge University Press).

Bond, B. (1980), *British Military Policy between the Two World Wars* (Oxford: Oxford University Press).

Bonin, H. (1988), *Histoire économique de la France depuis 1880* (Paris: Masson).

Bonnefous, G. (1967), *La Grande Guerre (1914–1918)*, 2nd ed. (Paris: Presses universitaires de France).

Bonsal, S. (1946), *Suitors and Suppliants. The Little Nations at Versailles* (New York: MacMillan).

Borchardt, K. (1982), *Wachstum, Krisen, Handlungsspielräume der Wirtschaftspolitik* (Göttingen: Vandenhoeck & Ruprecht).

Borgwardt, E. (2005), *A New Deal for the World. America's Vision for Human Rights* (Cambridge, MA: Harvard University Press).

Bouchard, C. (2006), "Des citoyens français à la recherche de la paix durable (1914–1919)", *Guerres mondiales et conflits contemporains*, 2, pp. 67–87.

Bouvier, J., Girault, R. and Thobie, J. (1986), *L'Impérialisme à la française* (Paris: Éditions La decouverte).

Boyce, R. (1987), *British Capitalism at the Crossroads, 1919–1932* (Cambridge: Cambridge University Press).

(2009), *The Great Interwar Crisis and the Collapse of Globalization* (Basingstoke: MacMillan).

Boyle, F. (1999), *Foundations of World Order. The Legalist Approach to International Relations, 1898-1922* (Durham, NC: Duke University Press).

Bracher, K.D. (1978), *Die Auflösung der Weimarer Republik* (Düsseldorf: Droste).

(1982), *Zeit der Ideologien. Eine Geschichte politischen Denkens im 20. Jahrhundert* (Stuttgart: Deutsche Verlags-Anstalt).

Brand, C. (1964), *The Labour Party. A Short History* (Stanford, CA: Stanford University Press).

Brandes, D. (2001), "Die Tschechoslowakei und die Pariser Vorortverträge", in Krumeich (2001), pp. 174–92.

Brandes, J. (1962), *Herbert Hoover and Economic Diplomacy* (Pittsburgh, PA: University of Pittsburgh Press).

Brands, H.W. (2010), *American Colossus. The Triumph of Capitalism, 1865–1900* (New York: Anchor).

Brechtken, M. (2006), *Scharnierzeit 1895–1907. Persönlichkeitsnetze und internationale Politik in den deutsch-britisch-amerikanischen Beziehungen vor dem Ersten Weltkrieg* (Mainz: P. von Zabern).

Breuilly, J. (ed.) (2013), *The Oxford Handbook of the History of Nationalism* (Oxford: Oxford University Press).

Bridge, R. (2004), *The Great Powers and the European States System, 1814–1914*, 2nd ed. (London: Routledge).

Brock, P. (1968), *Pacifism in the United States. From the Colonial Era to the First World War* (Princeton, NJ: Princeton University Press).

Bruendel, S. (2003), *Volksgemeinschaft oder Volksstaat. Die "Ideen von 1914" und die Neuordnung Deutschlands im Ersten Weltkrieg* (Berlin: De Gruyter).

Buitenhuis, P. (1989), *The Great War of Words. Literature as Propaganda, 1914–18 and After* (London: Batsford).

Bull, H. (I/1984), "The Emergence of a Universal International Society", in Bull and Watson (1984), pp. 117–26.

(II/1984), "The Revolt against the West", in Bull and Watson (1984), pp. 217–28.

(1995), *The Anarchical Society. A Study of Order in World Politics*, 2nd ed. (New York: MacMillan).

Bull, H. and Watson, A. (eds.) (1984), *The Expansion of International Society* (Oxford: Oxford University Press).

Bunselmeyer, R.E. (1975), *The Cost of War, 1914–1919. British Economic War Aims and the Origins of Reparations* (Hamden, CT: Archon).

Burbank, J. and Cooper, F. (2010), *Empires in World History. Power and the Politics of Difference* (Princeton, NJ: Princeton University Press).

Burk, K. (1985), *Britain, America and the Sinews of War, 1914–1918* (London: Allen & Unwin).

(1991), "The House of Morgan in Financial Diplomacy, 1920–1930", in McKercher (1991), pp. 125–57.

(2009), *Old World, New World. Great Britain and America from the Beginning* (London: Grove/Atlantic).

(2019), *The Lion and the Eagle. The Interaction of the British and American Empires 1783–1972* (London: Bloomsbury).

Burkman, T. (2008), *Japan and the League of Nations. Empire and World Order, 1914–1938* (Honolulu, HI: University of Hawaii Press).

Burks, D.D. (1959), "The United States and the Geneva Protocol of 1924: 'A New Holy Alliance?'", *American Historical Review*, 64, pp. 891–905.

Burner, D. (1979), *Herbert Hoover. A Public Life* (New York: Knopf).

Buschak. W. (2014), *Die Vereinigten Staaten von Europa sind unser Ziel. Arbeiterbewegung und Europa im frühen 20. Jahrhundert* (Essen: Klartext).

Butler, J. (1960), *Lord Lothian, Philip Kerr, 1882–1940* (London: MacMillan).

Büttner, U. (2008), *Weimar. Die überforderte Republik* (Stuttgart: Klett-Cotta).

Cabanes, B. (2014), *The Great War and the Origins of Humanitarianism, 1918–1924* (Cambridge: Cambridge University Press).

Cabanes, B. and Duménil, A. (2014), *Larousse de la grande guerre* (Paris: Larousse).

Calier, C. and Soutou, G.-H. (eds.) (2001), *1918–1925: Comment faire la paix?* (Paris: Economica).

Cain, P.J. and Hopkins, A.G. (2001), *British Imperialism 1688–2000*, 2nd ed. (London: Taylor & Francis).

Callaghan, J. (2007), *The Labour Party and Foreign Policy. A History* (London: Routledge).

Callahan, M. (1999), *Mandates and Empire. The League of Nations and Africa, 1914–1931* (Brighton: Sussex Academic Press).

Campbell, C. (1957), *Anglo-American Understanding, 1898–1903* (Westport, CT: Greenwood Press).

Campbell, F. (1970), "The Struggle for Upper Silesia, 1919–1922", *Journal of Modern History*, 42 (September), pp. 361–85.

Campus, M. (ed.) (2012), *Sviluppo, crisi, integrazione. Temi di storia delle relazioni internazionali per il XXI secolo* (Milan: Mondadori).

Canetti, E. (1960), *Masse und Macht* (Munich: Hanser).

Canis, K. (1997), *Von Bismarck zur Weltpolitik. Deutsche Außenpolitik 1890 bis 1902* (Berlin: De Gruyter).

(2004), *Bismarcks Außenpolitik 1870–1890. Aufstieg und Gefährdung* (Paderborn: Schöningh).

(2011), *Der Weg in den Abgrund. Deutsche Außenpolitik, 1902–1914* (Paderborn: Schöningh).

(2016), *Die bedrängte Großmacht. Österreich-Ungarn und das europäische Mächtesystem, 1866/67–1914* (Paderborn: Schöningh).

Carlton, D. (1970), *MacDonald versus Henderson. The Foreign Policy of the Second Labour Government* (London: MacMillan).

Carr, E.H. (1939), *The Twenty Years' Crisis, 1919–1939. An Introduction to the Study of International Relations* (London: MacMillan).

(1947), *International Relations between the Two World Wars, 1919–1939* (London: MacMillan).

(1950–53), *The Bolshevik Revolution, 1917–1923*, 3 vols. (London: Penguin).

Carroll, E. (1965), *Soviet Communism and Western Opinion, 1919–1921*, ed. Hollyday, F. (Chapel Hill, NC: University of North Carolina Press).

Carsten, F.L. (1966), *The Reichswehr and Politics, 1918–33* (Oxford: Oxford University Press).

(1984), *Britain and the Weimar Republic* (London: Batsford).

Carter, Z. (2020), *The Price of Peace. Money, Democracy, and the Life of John Maynard Keynes* (New York: Random House).

Cassels, A. (1980), "Repairing the Entente Cordiale and the New Diplomacy", *Historical Journal*, 23, pp. 133–53.

Catterall, P. and Morris, C. J. (eds.) (1993), *Britain and the Threat to Stability in Europe, 1918–1945* (London: Leicester University Press).

Ceadel, M. (1980), *Pacifism in Britain, 1914–1945. The Defining of a Faith* (Oxford: Oxford University Press).

(2000), *Semi-Detached Idealists. The British Peace Movement and International Relations, 1854–1945* (Oxford: Oxford University Press).

Chandler, L.V. (1958), *Benjamin Strong, Central Banker* (Washington, DC: Brookings Insitution).

Chang, H.J. (2002), *Kicking Away the Ladder. Development Strategy in Historical Perspective* (London: Anthem).

Charmley, J. (2009), *Splendid Isolation? Britain, the Balance of Power and the Origins of the First World War* (London: Faber & Faber).

Chernow, R. (1991), *The House of Morgan. An American Banking Dynasty and the Rise of Modern Finance* (New York: Grove).

Chickering, R. (2004), *Imperial Germany and the Great War, 1914–1918*, 2nd ed. (Cambridge: Cambridge University Press).

Chickering, R. and Förster, S. (eds.), *Great War, Total War. Combat and Mobilization on the Western Front 1914–1918* (Cambridge: Cambridge University Press).

Cienciala, M. and Kormanicki, T. (1984), *From Versailles to Locarno. Keys to Polish Foreign Policy, 1919–1925* (Kansas City, MI: University Press of Kansas).

Claeys, L. (2001), *Delcassé* (Pamiers: Acala).

Clark, C. (2012), *The Sleepwalkers. How Europe Went to War in 1914* (London: Penguin).

Clark, I. (2007), *International Legitimacy and World Society* (Oxford: Oxford University Press).

(2011), *Hegemony in International Society* (Oxford: Oxford University Press).

Clavin, P. (1996), *The Failure of Economic Diplomacy. Britain, Germany, France and the United States, 1931–36* (Basingstoke: MacMillan).

(2000), *The Great Depression in Europe, 1929–1939* (New York: St. Martin's Press).

(2013), *Securing the World Economy. The Reinvention of the League of Nations, 1920–1946* (Oxford: Oxford University Press).

Clavin, P. and Sluga, G. (eds.) (2016), *Internationalisms. A Twentieth-Century History* (Cambridge: Cambridge University Press).

Clayton, A.J. (1986), *The British Empire as a Superpower, 1919–1939* (London: MacMillan).

Clements, J. (2008), *Wellington Koo* (London: Haus).

Cohen, W.I (1987), *Empire without Tears* (New York: Temple University Press).

(2000), *East Asia at the Center* (New York: Columbia University Press).

Cohrs, P.O. (2003), "The First 'Real' Peace Settlements after the First World War. Britain, the United States and the Accords of London and Locarno, 1923–1925", *Contemporary European History*, 12, pp. 1–31.

(2004), "The Quest for a New Concert of Europe. British Pursuits of German Rehabilitation and European Stability in the 1920s", in Johnson (II/2004), pp. 33–58.

(2006), *The Unfinished Peace after World War I* (Cambridge: Cambridge University Press).

(2011), "'American Peace' – ein, demokratischer Frieden? Wilson und die Suche nach einer neuen Weltordnung nach dem Ersten Weltkrieg", in Dülffer and Niedhart (2011), pp. 73–104.

(2018), "'Pax Americana'. The United States and the Transformation of the 20th Century's Global Order", *Review of International Politics*, 61, pp. 1–26.

(2022), "Keine Pax Atlantica. Das Ringen um eine atlantische Friedensordnung – ein Schlüsselproblem der Neuordnungsprozesse von 1919", in Leonhard (2022).

Coletta, P. (1964–69), *William Jennings Bryan*, 3 vols. (Lincoln, NE: University of Nebraska Press).

Collins, H. (1965), *Karl Marx and the British Labour Movement. Years of the First International* (London: MacMillan).

Conrad, S. (2013), *Globalgeschichte* (Munich: Beck).

Conway, M. (2020), *Western Europe's Democratic Age, 1945–1968* (Princeton, NJ: Princeton University Press).

Conyne, G. (2016), *Woodrow Wilson. British perspectives, 1912–21* (London: MacMillan).

Conze, E. (I/2018), *Die große Illusion. Versailles 1919 und die Neuordnung der Welt* (Munich: Siedler).

(II/2018), *Geschichte der Sicherheit. Entwicklung – Themen – Perspektiven* (Göttingen: Vandenhoeck & Ruprecht).

Conze, E., Lappenküper, U. and Müller, G. (eds.) (2004), *Geschichte der internationalen Beziehungen. Erneuerung und Erweiterung einer historischen Disziplin* (Cologne: Böhlau).

Cooper, J.M. (2004), "The United States", in Hamilton and Herwig (2004), pp. 202–24.

(ed.) (2008), *Reconsidering Woodrow Wilson. Progressivism, Internationalism, War, and Peace* (Washington, DC: Woodrow Wilson Center Press).

(2009), *Woodrow Wilson. A Biography* (New York: Random House).

(2010), *Breaking the Heart of the World. Woodrow Wilson and the Fight for the League of Nations* (Cambridge: Cambridge University Press).

Cooper, S. (I/1991), "Pacifism in France, 1889–1914. International Peace as a Human Right", *French Historical Studies*, 17 (Autumn), pp. 359–86.

(II/1991), *Patriotic Pacifism. Waging War on War in Europe, 1815–1914* (Oxford: Oxford University Press).

Cortright, D. (2008), *Peace. A History of Movements and Ideas* (Cambridge: Cambridge University Press).

Costigliola, F.C. (1972), "The Other Side of Isolationism. The Establishment of the First World Bank, 1929–1930", *Journal of American History*, 59 (December), pp. 602–20.

(1979), "American Foreign Policy in the 'Nutcracker'. The United States and Poland in the 1920s", *Pacific Historical Review*, 48, pp. 85–105.

(1984), *Awkward Dominion. American Political, Economic, and Cultural Relations with Europe, 1919–1933* (Ithaca, NY: Cornell University Press).

Cowling, M. (1971), *The Impact of Labour, 1920–1924. The Beginning of Modern British Politics* (Cambridge: Cambridge University Press).

Cox, M., Dunne, T. and Booth, K. (eds.) (2002), *Empires, Systems and States. Great Transformations in International Politics* (Cambridge: Cambridge University Press).

Craig, G.A. and Gilbert, F. (eds.) (1994), *The Diplomats 1919–1939* (Princeton, NJ: Princeton University Press).

Crowe, S.E. (1972), "Sir Eyre Crowe and the Locarno Pact", *English Historical Review*, 87, pp. 49–74.

Crowe, S.E. and Corp, E. (1993), *Our Ablest Public Servant. Sir Eyre Crowe, 1864–1925* (Braunton: Merlin).

Cumings, B. (2009), *Dominion from Sea to Sea. Pacific Ascendancy and American Power* (New Haven, CT: Yale University Press).

Czernin, F. (1968), *Die Friedensstifter* (Klagenfurt: Kaiser).

Dahlmann, D. (2001), "Gewinner oder Verlierer? Die Bedeutung der Pariser Friedensverträge für Jugoslawien und Ungarn", in Krumeich (2001), pp. 193–201.

Dallek, R. (1995), *Franklin D. Roosevelt and American Foreign Policy, 1932–1945* (Oxford: Oxford University Press).

Dallin, A., (1963), *Russian Diplomacy and Eastern Europe, 1914–1917* (New York: King's Crown Press).

Daniel, U. (2018), *Beziehungsgeschichten* (Hamburg: Hamburger Edition).

Darwin, J. (1980), "Imperialism in Decline? Tendencies in British Imperial Policy Between the Wars", *Historical Journal*, 23, pp. 657–79.

(2008), *After Tamerlane. The Rise and Fall of Global Empires, 1400–2000* (London: Bloomsbury).

(2009), *The Empire Project. The Rise and Fall of the British World-System, 1830–1970* (Cambridge: Cambridge University Press).

(2013), "Nationalism and Imperialism c.1860–1918", in Breuilly (2013), pp. 341–58.

Davies, N. (1971), "Lloyd George and Poland, 1919–20", *Journal of Contemporary History*, 6, pp. 132–54.

(2003), *White Eagle, Red Star* (London: Vintage).

(2005), *God's Playground. A History of Poland, Vol. 2: 1795 to the Present*, 2nd ed. (Oxford: Oxford University Press).

Dawley, A. (2003), *Changing the World. American Progressives in War and Revolution* (Princeton, NJ: Princeton University Press).

Dayer, R.A. (1991), "Anglo-American Monetary Policy and Rivalry in Europe and the Far East, 1919–1931", in McKercher (1991), pp. 158–86.

DeConde, A. 1978), *A History of American Foreign Policy. Vol. II: Global Power (1900 to the Present)*, 3rd ed. (New York: Scribner).

De Graaf, B. (2020), *Fighting Terror after Napoleon. How Europe Became Secure after 1815* (Cambridge: Cambridge University Press).

De Grazia, V. (2005), *Irresistible Empire. America's Advance through Twentieth-Century Europe* (Cambridge, MA: Harvard University Press).

Del Pero, M. (2017), *Libertà e impero. Gli Stati Uniti e il mondo, 1776–2016* (Rome: Laterza).

Den Hertog, J. and Kruizinga, S. (eds.) (2011), *Caught in the Middle. Neutrals, Neutrality and the First World War* (Amsterdam: Aksant).

De Sédouy, J.-A. (2017), *Ils ont refait le monde, 1919–1920. Le traité de Versailles* (Paris: Tallandier).

Desmond, A. and Moore, J. (1992), *Darwin* (New York: Norton).

Deutscher, I. (2015), *The Prophet. The Life of Leon Trotsky* (London: Verso).

Dilks, D. (ed.) (1981), *Retreat from Power. Studies in Britain's Foreign Policy in the 20th Century, Vol. I: 1906–1939* (Basingstoke: MacMillan).

Dinan D. (2014), *Europe Recast. A History of European Union*, 2nd ed. (Basingstoke: MacMillan).

Diner, D. (2015), *Das Jahrhundert verstehen, 1917–1989. Eine universalhistorische Deutung* (Munich: Pantheon).

Dockrill, M. and Fischer, J. (eds.) (2001), *The Paris Peace Conference 1919. Peace without Victory?* (Basingstoke: MacMillan).

Dockrill, M. and Goold, J.D. (1981), *Peace without Promise. Britain and the Peace Conferences, 1919–1923* (London: Archon)

Dockrill, M.L. and McKercher, B.J.C. (1996) *Diplomacy and World Power. Studies in British Foreign Policy, 1890–1951* (Cambridge: Cambridge University Press).

Doering-Manteuffel, A. (2010), *Die deutsche Frage und das europäische Staatensystem 1815–1871* (Munich: Oldenbourg).

Doise, J. and Vaïsse, M. (1987), *Diplomatie et Outil militaire. Politique étrangère de la France, 1871–1969* (Paris: Seuil).

Drayton, R. and Motadel, D. (2018), "The Futures of Global History", *Journal of Global History*, 13 (March), pp. 1–21.

Dreyer, M. and Lembcke, O. (1993), *Die deutsche Diskussion um die Kriegsschuldfrage 1918–19* (Berlin: Duncker & Humblot).

Drummond, I. (1972), *British Economic Policy and Empire, 1919–1939* (London: Routledge).

Ducoulombier, R. (ed.) (2010), *Les socialistes dans l'Europe en guerre : réseaux, parcours, expériences, 1914–1918* (Paris: Harmattan).

Ducoulombier, R. and Chambarlhac, V. (eds.) (2008), *Les socialistes français et la Grande Guerre* (Dijon: Éditions universitaires de Dijon).

Dülffer, J. (1981), *Regeln gegen den Krieg? Die Haager Friedenskonferenzen von 1899 und 1907 in der internationalen Politik* (Frankfurt: Ullstein).

(2001), "Versailles und die Friedensschlüsse des 19. und 20. Jahrhunderts", in Krumeich and Fehlemann (2001), pp. 17–34.

Dülffer, J., Kröger, M. and Wippich, R.-H. (eds.) (1997), *Vermiedene Kriege. Deeskalation von Konflikten der Großmächte zwischen Krimkrieg und Erstem Weltkrieg (1865–1914)* (Munich: Oldenbourg).

Dülffer, J. and Krumeich, G. (eds.) (2002), *Der verlorene Frieden. Politik und Kriegskultur nach 1918* (Essen: Klartext).

Dülffer, J. and Loth, W. (eds.) (2012), *Dimensionen internationaler Geschichte* (Munich: Oldenbourg).

Dülffer, J. and Niedhart, G. (eds.) (2011), *Frieden durch Demokratie? Genese Wirkung und Kritik eines Deutungsmusters* (Essen: Klartext).

Dull, B. (2021), *Erzberger. Der gehasste Versöhner. Biografie eines Weimarer Politikers* (Berlin: Ch. Links Verlag).

Dunbabin, J.P. (1993), "The League of Nations' Place in the International System", *History*, 78, pp. 421–42.

Duroselle, J.-B. (1988), *Clemenceau* (Paris: Fayard).

(1994), *La Grande Guerre des Français, 1914–1918. L'incompréhensible* (Paris: Perrin).

Dziewanowski, M. (1969), *Joseph Piłsudski. A European Federalist, 1918–1922* (Stanford, CA: Stanford University Press).

Eckes, A. and Zeiler, T. (2003), *Globalization and the American Century* (Cambridge: Cambridge University Press).

Edwards, M.L. (1963), *Stresemann and the Greater Germany, 1914–1918* (New York: Bookman).

Egerton, G.W. (1978), *Great Britain and the Creation of the League of Nations. Strategy, Politics and International Organization, 1914–1919* (Chapel Hill, NC: University of North Carolina Press).

Eichengreen, B. (1992), *Golden Fetters. The Gold Standard and the Great Depression, 1919–1939* (Oxford: Oxford University Press).

Ekbladh, D. (2011), *The Great American Mission. Modernization and the Construction of an American World Order* (Princeton, NJ: Princeton University Press).

Elbe, S. (2016), *Europe. A Nietzschean Perspective* (London: Routledge).

Elleman, B. (2002), *Wilson and China* (London: Taylor & Francis).

Ellwood, D. (2012), *The Shock of America. Europe and the Challenge of the Century* (Oxford: Oxford University Press).

Engermann, D. (2010), "Ideology and the Origins of the Cold War, 1917–1962", in Leffler and Westad (2010), I, pp. 20–43.

Epstein, K. (1959), *Matthias Erzberger and the Dilemma of German Democracy* (Princeton, NJ: Princeton University Press).

Erdmann, K.D. (1966), *Adenauer in der Rheinlandpolitik nach dem Ersten Weltkrieg* (Stuttgart: Klett).

(1980), *Gustav Stresemann. The Revision of Versailles and the Weimar Parliamentary System* (London: German Historical Institute).

Evans, R.J. (2003), *The Coming of the Third Reich. How the Nazis Destroyed Democracy and Seized Power in Germany* (London: Penguin).

(2016), *The Pursuit of Power. Europe, 1815–1914* (London: Penguin).

Feldman, G.D. (1993), *The Great Disorder. Politics, Economics, and Society in the German Inflation, 1914–1924* (Oxford: Oxford University Press).

Feis, H. (1950), *The Diplomacy of the Dollar, First Era 1919–32* (Baltimore, MD: The Johns Hopkins Press).

Ferguson, N. (I/1998), "The Balance of Payments Question: Versailles and After", in Boemeke, Feldman and Glaser (1998), pp. 401–40.

(II/1998), *The Pity of War* (London. Penguin).

Ferrell, R.H. (1957), *American Diplomacy in the Great Depression. Hoover-Stimson Foreign Policy* (New Haven, CT: Yale University Press).

(1969), *Peace in Their Time. The Origins of the Kellogg-Briand Pact* (New York: Norton).

Ferris, J.R. (1989), *The Evolution of British Strategic Policy, 1919–1926* (London: MacMillan).

(1991), "'The Greatest Power on Earth': Great Britain in the 1920s", *International History Review*, 13 , pp. 726–50.

Fieldhouse, D.K. (2006), *Western Imperialism in the Middle East 1914–1958* (Oxford: Oxford University Press).

Filene, P. (1963), "The World Peace Foundation and Progressivism, 1910–1918", *The New England Quarterly*, 36 (December), pp. 478–501.

Fink, C. (1984), *The Genoa Conference. European Diplomacy, 1921–1922* (Chapel Hill, NC: University of North Carolina Press).

(1998), "The Minorities Question at the Paris Peace Conference", in Boemeke, Feldman and Glaser (1998), pp. 249–74.

(2004), *Defending the Rights of Others. The Great Powers, the Jews, and International Minority Protection, 1878–1938* (Cambridge: Cambridge University Press).

Fink, C., Frohn, A. and Heideking, J. (eds.) (1991), *Genoa, Rapallo and European Reconstruction in 1922* (Cambridge: Cambridge University Press).

Fisch, J. (2010), *Das Selbstbestimmungsrecht der Völker. Die Domestizierung einer Illusion* (Munich: Beck).

Fischer, C. (2003), *The Ruhr Crisis, 1923–1924* (Oxford: Oxford University Press).

Fischer, C. and Sharp, A. (eds.) (2008), *After the Versailles Treaty. Enforcement, Compliance, Contested Identities* (London: Taylor & Francis).

Fischer, F. (1975), *War of Illusions. German Policies from 1911 to 1914* (New York: Norton).

(1961), *Griff nach der Weltmacht. Die Kriegszielpolitik des kaiserlichen Deutschland 1914/18* (Düsseldorf: Droste).

(1967), *Germany's Aims in the First World War* (New York: Norton).

(1969), *Krieg der Illusionen* (Düsseldorf: Droste).

Fischer, L. (1951), *The Soviets in World Affairs, 1917–1929*, 2 vols. (Princeton, NJ: Princeton University Press).

Forst, R. and Günther, K. (eds.) (2021), *Normative Ordnungen* (Berlin: Suhrkamp).

French, D. (1995), *The Strategy of the Lloyd George Coalition, 1916–1918* (Oxford: Oxford University Press).

Fromkin, D. (2001), *A Peace to End All Peace. The Fall of the Ottoman Empire and the Creation of the Modern Middle East* (New York: Holt).

Fry, M.G. (1998), "British Revisionism", in Boemeke, Feldman and Glaser (1998), pp. 565–602.

(2011), *And Fortune Fled. David Lloyd George, the First Democratic Statesman, 1916–1922* (New York: Peter Lang).

Furet, F. (1988), *La révolution française, 1770–1880*, 2 vols. (Paris: Hachette).

Gaddis, J.L. (2006), *The Cold War. A New History* (London: Penguin).

Galbraith, J.K. (2021), *The Great Crash 1929* (London: Penguin).

Gall, L. (1980), *Bismarck. Der weiße Revolutionär* (Frankfurt: Ullstein).

(2009), *Walther Rathenau. Portrait einer Epoche* (Munich: Beck).

Gardner, L. (1984), *Safe for Democracy. The Anglo-American Response to Revolution, 1913–1923* (Oxford: Oxford University Press).

Garton Ash, T. (2005), *Free World. America, Europe, and the Surprising Future of the West* (New York: Vintage).

Gelfand, L.E. (1998), "The American Mission to Negotiate Peace. An Historian Looks Back", in Boemeke, Feldman and Glaser (1998), pp. 189–203.

Gellinek, C. (1994), *Philipp Scheidemann. Eine biographische Skizze* (Cologne: Böhlau).

Gerwarth, R. (2016), *The Vanquished. Why the First World War Failed to End* (London: Penguin).

Gerwarth, R. and Manela, E. (eds.) (2015), *Empires at War* (Oxford: Oxford University Press).

Getachew, A. (2019), *Worldmaking after Empire. The Rise and Fall of Self-Determination* (Princeton, NJ: Princeton University Press).

Geyer, M. (1980), *Aufrüstung oder Sicherheit. Die Reichswehr in der Krise der Machtpolitik 1924–1936* (Wiesbaden: Steiner).

Geyer, M. and Bright, C. (2005), "Regimes of World Order. Global Integration and the Production of Difference in Twentieth Century World History", in Bentley, J. et al. (eds.), *Interactions. Transregional Perspectives on World History* (Honolulu, HI: University of Hawaii Press).

Geyer, M. (2014), "Reparationen", in Hirschfeld, Krumeich and Renz (2014), pp. 793–5.

Ghervas, S. (2021), *Conquering Peace. From the Enlightenment to the European Union* (Cambridge, MA: Harvard University Press).

Ghosh, P. (2014), *Max Weber and "The Protestant Ethic". Twin Histories* (Oxford: Oxford University Press).

(2016), *Max Weber in Context. Essays in the History of German Ideas c. 1870–1930* (Wiesbaden: Steiner).

Gilbert, M. (1966), *The Roots of Appeasement* (London: Weidenfeld & Nicolson).

(1975), *Winston S. Churchill. Volume IV, 1917–1922* (London: Heinemann).

(1976), *Winston S. Churchill, Volume V, 1922–1939* (London: Heinemann).

Girault, R., Frank, R. (1988), *Turbulente Europe et nouveaux mondes. Histoire des relations internationales contemporaines, 1914–1941* (Paris: Payot & Rivages).

Glaser, E. (1998), "The Making of the Economic Peace", in Boemeke, Feldmann and Glaser (1998), pp. 371–400.

Glenny, M. (1999), *The Balkans* (London: Penguin).

Goldstein, E. (1991), *Winning the Peace. British Diplomatic Strategy, Peace Planning, and the Paris Peace Conference, 1916–1920* (Oxford: Oxford University Press).

(1998), "Great Britain: The Home Front", in Boemeke, Feldman and Glaser (1998), pp. 275–312.

Gordon, M.R. (1969), *Conflict and Consensus in Labour's Foreign Policy 1914–1965* (Stanford, CA: Stanford University Press).

Gorman, D. (2012), *The Emergence of International Society in the 1920s* (Cambridge: Cambridge University Press).

Gorodetsky, G. (1977), *The Precarious Truce. Anglo-Soviet Relations, 1924–27* (Cambridge: Cambridge University Press).

Gould, E., Mapp, P. and Pestana, C. (eds.) (2021), *The Cambridge History of America and the World. Volume 1: 1500–1820* (Cambridge: Cambridge University Press).

Graebner, N. and Bennett, E. (2011), *The Versailles Treaty and its Legacy. The Failure of the Wilsonian Vision* (Cambridge: Cambridge University Press).

Grayson, R. (1997), *Austen Chamberlain and the Commitment to Europe. British Foreign Policy, 1924–29* (London: Taylor & Francis).

Grigg, J. (1979), *Lloyd George. The People's Champion, 1902–1911* (London: Methuen).

(1985), *Lloyd George. From Peace to War, 1912–1916* (London: Methuen).

(2002), *Lloyd George. War Leader, 1916–1918* (London: Penguin).

Grimmer-Solem, E. (2019), *Learning Empire. Globalization and the German Quest for World Status, 1875–1919* (Cambridge: Cambridge University Press).

Grupp, P. (1988), *Deutsche Außenpolitik im Schatten von Versailles 1918–1920* (Paderborn: Schöningh).

Guieu, J.-M. (2006), "Pour la paix par la Société Des Nations. La laborieuse organisation d'un mouvement français de soutien à la Société Des Nations (1915–1920)", *Guerres mondiales et conflits contemporains*, 2, pp. 89–102.

(2008), *Le rameau et le glaive: les militants français pour la Société des Nations* (Paris: Presses de Sciences Po).

Haardt, O. (2020), *Bismarcks ewiger Bund. Eine neue Geschichte des Deutschen Kaiserreichs. Die Entwicklung vom Fürstenbund zur Reichsmonarchie* (Darmstadt: Wissenschaftliche Buchgesellschaft).

Hajdu, T. (1979), *The Hungarian Soviet Republic* (Budapest: Akadémiai Kiadó).

Hall, C. (1987), *Britain, America and Arms Control, 1921–1937* (London: MacMillan).

Hamilton, R. and Herwig, H. (eds.) (2004), *Decisions for War, 1914–1917* (Cambridge: Cambridge University Press).

Hancock, W. (1962–68), *Smuts*, 2 vols. (Cambridge: Cambridge University Press).

Hannigan, R. (2002), *The New World Power. American Foreign Policy, 1898–1917* (Philadelphia, PA: University of Pennsylvania Press).

(2014), *The Great War and American Foreign Policy, 1914–24* (Philadelphia, PA: University of Pennsylvania Press).

Harbaugh, W. (1961), *Power and Responsibility. The Life and Times of Theodore Roosevelt* (New York: Collier).

Harmer, H. (2008), *Friedrich Ebert. Germany* (London: Haus).

Hathaway, O. and Shapiro, S. (2018), *The Internationalists. How a Radical Plan to Outlaw War Remade the World* (New York: Simon & Schuster).

Haupts, L. (1976), *Deutsche Friedenspolitik, 1918–19. Eine Alternative zur Machtpolitik des Ersten Weltkrieges* (Düsseldorf: Droste).

Hawkins, M. (1997), *Social Darwinism in European and American Thought, 1860–1945* (Cambridge: Cambridge University Press).

Hawley, E.W. (1979), *The Great War and the Search for a Modern Order* (New York: St Martin's Press).

(ed.) (1981), *Herbert Hoover as Secretary of Commerce* (Iowa City, IA: University of Iowa Press).

Hecker, H. (1994), "Mitteleuropapläne als Versuche einer europäischen Friedensordnung", in Hecker and Spieler (1994).

Hecker, H. and Spieler, S. (eds.) (1994), *Die historische Einheit Europas* (Bonn: Kulturstiftung der Dt. Vertriebenen).

Heinemann, U. (1983), *Die verdrängte Niederlage. Politische Öffentlichkeit und Kriegsschuldfrage in der Weimarer Republik* (Göttingen: Vandenhoeck & Ruprecht).

Hendrickson, D. (2009), *Union, Nation, or Empire. The American Debate Over International Relations, 1789–1941* (Lawrence, KS: University Press of Kansas).

Herbert, U. (2017), *Geschichte Deutschlands im 20. Jahrhundert* (Munich: Beck).

Herring, G. (2008), *From Colony to Superpower* (Oxford: Oxford University Press).

Hertzman, L. (1963), *DNVP. Right-wing Opposition in the Weimar Republic, 1918–1924* (Lincoln, NE: University of Nebraska Press).

Herwig, H. (2003), "Germany", in Hamilton and Herwig (2004).

Heyde, P. (1998), *Das Ende der Reparationen. Deutschland, Frankreich und der Youngplan 1929–1932* (Paderborn: Schöningh).

Hildebrand, K. (1980), "Das Deutsche Reich und die Sowjetunion im internationalen System 1918–1932: Legitimität oder Revolution?", in Stürmer (1980), pp. 38–61.

(1989), "Europäisches Zentrum, überseeische Peripherie und neue Welt. Über den Wandel des Staatensystems zwischen dem Berliner Kongreß (1878) und dem Pariser Frieden (1919/1920)", *Historische Zeitschrift*, 249 pp. 53–94.

(1995), *Das vergangene Reich. Deutsche Außenpolitik von Bismarck bis Hitler* (Stuttgart: Deutsche Verlags-Anstalt).

(1998), "Das deutsche Ostimperium", in Pyta, W. and Richter, L. (eds.), *Gestaltungskraft des Politischen* (Berlin: Duncker & Humblot).

Hildermeier, M. (1998), *Geschichte der Sowjetunion, 1917–1991* (Munich: Beck).

Hillgruber, A. (1967), *Deutschlands Rolle in der Vorgeschichte der beiden Weltkriege. Die deutsche Frage in der Welt* (Göttingen: Vandenhoeck & Ruprecht).

Hinsley, F. (ed.) (1977), *British Foreign Policy under Sir Edward Grey* (Cambridge: Cambridge University Press).

Hirschfeld, G., Krumeich, G. and Renz, I. (eds.) (2014), *Enzyklopädie Erster Weltkrieg*, 2nd ed. (Paderborn: Schoeningh).

Hitchcock, W. (2010), "The Marshall Plan and the Creation of the West", in Leffler and Westad (2010), I, pp. 154–74.

Hobsbawm, E. (1962), *The Age of Revolution, 1789–1848* (London: Weidenfeld & Nicolson).

(1975), *The Age of Capital, 1848–1875* (London: Weidenfeld & Nicolson).

(1987), *The Age of Empire, 1875–1914* (London: Weidenfeld & Nicolson).

(1992), *Nations and Nationalism since 1780. Programme, Myth, Reality*, 2nd ed. (Cambridge: Cambridge University Press).

(1994), *The Age of Extremes. The Short Twentieth Century, 1914–1991* (London: Penguin).

Hochman, E. (2016), *Imagining a Greater Germany. Republican Nationalism and the Idea of Anschluss* (Ithaca, NY: Cornell University Press).

Hochschild, U. (1982), *Sozialdemokratie und Völkerbund* (Karlsruhe: Info-Verlag).

Hodgson, G. (2006), *Woodrow Wilson's Right Hand. The Life of Colonel Edward M. House* (New Haven, CT: Yale University Press).

Hoeres, P. (2004), *Krieg der Philosophen. Die deutsche und britische Philosophie im Ersten Weltkrieg* (Paderborn: Schöningh).

Hofstadter, R. (1948), *The American Political Tradition and the Men Who Made It* (New York: Knopf).

(I/1955), *Social Darwinism in American Thought* (Boston: Beacon Press).

(II/1955), *The Age of Reform. From Bryan to F.D.R.* (New York: Vintage).

Hogan, M.J. (1987), *The Marshall Plan. America, Britain and the Reconstruction of Western Europe, 1947–1952* (Cambridge: Cambridge University Press).

(1991), *Informal Entente. The Private Structure of Cooperation in Anglo-American Economic Diplomacy, 1918–1928*, 2nd ed. (Chicago: Imprint).

Hoganson, K. and Sexton, J. (eds.) (2021), *The Cambridge History of America and the World. Volume 2: 1812–1900* (Cambridge: Cambridge University Press).

Holmes, J. (2006), *Theodore Roosevelt and World Order. Police Power in International Relations* (Washington, DC: Potomac).

Holz, K. (1977), *Die Diskussion um den Dawes- und Young-Plan in der Deutschen Presse* (Frankfurt and Main: Haag & Herchen).

Hopkins, G.A. (2018), *American Empire. A Global History* (Princeton, NJ: Princeton University Press).

Howard, M. (1972), *The Continental Commitment. The Dilemma of British Defence Policy in the Era of the Two World Wars* (London: Maurice Temple Smith).

— (2001), *The Invention of Peace. Reflections on War and International Order* (London: Profile).

Howe, A. (2007), "Free Trade and Global Order. The Rise and Fall of a Victorian Vision", in Bell (II/2007).

Howe, D.W. (2009), *What Hath God Wrought. The Transformation of America, 1815-1848* (Oxford: Oxford University Press).

Huber, V., Osterhammel, J. (eds.) (2020), *Global Publics. Their Power and their Limits, 1870-1990* (Oxford: Oxford University Press).

Hunt, M. (2007), *The American Ascendancy. How the United States Gained and Wielded Global Dominance* (Chapel Hill, NC: University of North Carolina Press).

— (2009), *Ideology and U.S. Foreign Policy*, 2nd ed. (New Haven, CT: Yale University Press).

Huntington, S.P. (1989), "American Ideals versus American Institutions", in Ikenberry (1989), pp. 223–58.

Hurrell, A. (2007), *On Global Order. Power, Values, and the Constitution on International Society: Power, Values, and the Constitution of International Society* (Oxford: Oxford University Press).

Ikenberry, G.J. (ed.) (1989), *American Foreign Policy* (Boston: Wadsworth).

— (2001), *After Victory. Institutions, Strategic Restraint and the Rebuilding of World Order After Major Wars* (Princeton, NJ: Princeton University Press).

— (ed.) (2009), *The Crisis of American Foreign Policy. Wilsonianism in the Twenty-First Century* (Princeton, NJ: Princeton University Press).

— (2011), *Liberal Leviathan. The Origins, Crisis, and Transformation of the American World Order* (Princeton, NJ: Princeton University Press).

— (2020), *A World Safe for Democracy* (New Haven, CT: Yale University Press).

Imlay, T. (2018), *The Practice of Socialist Internationalism. European Socialists and International Politics, 1914-1960* (Oxford: Oxford University Press).

Immerman, R. (2010), *Empire for Liberty. A History of American Imperialism from Benjamin Franklin to Paul Wolfowitz* (Princeton, NJ: Princeton University Press).

Ingram, N. (1991), *The Politics of Dissent. Pacifism in France, 1919-1939* (Oxford: Oxford University Press).

Iriye, A. (1977), *From Nationalism to Internationalism. US Foreign Policy to 1914* (London: Routledge & Kegan Paul).

— (2002), *Global Community. The Role of International Organizations in the Making of the Contemporary World* (Berkeley, CA: University of California Press).

(2013), *Global and Transnational History. The Past, Present, and Future* (Basingstoke: MacMillan).

(2014), *Global Interdependence. The World after 1945* (Cambridge, MA: Harvard University Press).

(2015), *The Globalizing of America, 1913–1945*, new ed. (Cambridge: Cambridge University Press).

Jackisch, B. (2012), *The Pan-German League and Radical Nationalist Politics in Interwar Germany, 1918–39* (Burlington, VT: Ashgate).

Jackson, P. (2013), *Beyond the Balance of Power. France and the Politics of National Security in the Era of the First World War* (Cambridge: Cambridge University Press).

Jacobson, J. (1972), *Locarno Diplomacy. Germany and the West, 1925–29* (Princeton, NJ: Princeton University Press).

(1983), "Strategies of French Foreign Policy after World War I", *Journal of Modern History*, 55, pp. 78–95.

(1998), "The Soviet Union and Versailles", in Boemeke, Feldman and Glaser (1998), pp. 451–68.

Jaffe, L. (1985), *The Decision to Disarm Germany* (London: Allen & Unwin).

James, H. (1986), *The German Slump. Politics and Economics, 1924–1936* (Oxford: Oxford University Press).

(2001), *The End of Globalisation. Lessons from the Great Depression* (Cambridge, MA: Harvard University Press).

(ed.) (2002), *The Interwar Depression in an International Context* (Munich: Oldenbourg).

Jarausch, K.H. (1969), "The Illusion of Limited War. Chancellor Bethmann Hollweg's Calculated Risk, July 1914", *Central European History*, 2 (March), pp. 48–76.

(1973), *The Enigmatic Chancellor. Bethmann Hollweg and the Hubris of Imperial Germany* (New Haven, CT: Yale University Press).

Jarrett, M. (2014), *The Congress of Vienna and Its Legacy. War and Great Power Diplomacy after Napoleon* (London: I.B. Tauris).

Jeannesson, S. (1998), *Poincaré, la France et la Ruhr, 1922–1924* (Strasbourg: Presses universitaires de Strasbourg).

Jelavich, B. (2004), *Russia's Balkan Entanglements* (Cambridge: Cambridge University Press).

Jenkins, F.A. (1960), *Defence by Committee. The British Committee of Imperial Defence, 1880–1959* (Oxford: Oxford University Press).

Jervis, R. (1992), "A Political Science Perspective on the Balance of Power and the Concert", *American Historical Review*, 97 (June), pp. 716–24.

(2017), *Perception and Misperception in International Politics*, new ed. (Cambridge, MA: Harvard University Press)

Jespersen, C. (2010), "Pride, Prejudice and the Transatlantic Relations. The Case of Woodrow Wilson Reconsidered", *Journal of Transatlantic Studies*, 8.

Johnson, G. (2002), *The Berlin Embassy of Lord D'Abernon, 1922–1926* (Basingstoke: MacMillan).

(I/2004), "Austen Chamberlain and the Negotiation of the Kellogg-Briand Pact, 1928," in Johnson (II/2004), pp. 59–79.

(ed.) (II/2004), *Locarno Revisited. European Diplomacy 1920–1929* (London: Routledge).

(2013), *Lord Robert Cecil. Politician and Internationalist* (Farnham: Ashgate).

Joll, J. (1966), *The Second International, 1889–1914* (London: Routledge).

(1992), *The Origins of the First World War*, 2nd ed. (Harlow: Longman).

Jonas, M. (2012), "'Can One Go Along with This?' German Diplomats and the Changes of 1918/19 and 1933/34", *Journal of Contemporary History*, 47, pp. 240–69.

(2019), *Scandinavia and the Great Powers in the First World War* (London: Bloomsbury).

Judson, P. (2016), *The Habsburg Empire. A New History* (Cambridge, MA: Harvard University Press).

Kagan, R. (2006), *Dangerous Nation. America in the World, 1600–1898* (New York: Vintage).

Kaiga, S. (2018), "The Use of Force to Prevent War? The Bryce Group's 'Proposals for the Avoidance of War', 1914–15", *Journal of British Studies*, 57 (April), pp. 308–32.

Kann, R.A. (1974), *A History of the Habsburg Empire, 1526–1918* (Berkeley, CA: University of California Press).

Käppner, J. (2017), *1918 – Aufstand für die Freiheit. Die Revolution der Besonnenen* (Munich: Piper).

Kazin, M. (2017), *War Against War. The American Fight for Peace, 1914–1918* (New York: Simon & Schuster).

Keegan, J. (2000), *The First World War* (London: Westminster).

Keeton, E. D. (1987), *Briand's Locarno Policy. French Economics, Politics and Diplomacy, 1925–1929* (New York: Garland).

Keiger, J. (1983), *France and the Origins of the First World War* (New York: St Martin's Press).

(1997), *Raymond Poincaré* (Cambridge: Cambridge University Press).

(2004), "Poincaré, Briand and Locarno. Continuity in French Diplomacy in the 1920s", in Johnson (II/2004), pp. 95–108.

(2016), "Sir Edward Grey, France, and the Entente. How to Catch the Perfect Angler?", *International History Review*, 38 (March), pp. 285–300.

Kendle, J. (1975), *The Round Table Movement and Imperial Union* (Toronto: University of Toronto Press).

Kennan, G.F. (1951), *American Diplomacy 1900–1950* (Chicago: Chicago University Press).

(1956), *Russia Leaves the War. Soviet-American Relations, 1917–1920, Vol. I* (Princeton, NJ: Princeton University Press).

(1979), *The Decline of Bismarck's European Order. Franco-Russian Relations, 1875–1890* (Princeton, NJ: Princeton University Press).

(1984), *The Fateful Alliance. France, Russia, and the Coming of the First World War* (New York: Random House).

(1996), *At a Century's Ending. Reflections, 1982–1995* (New York: Norton).

Kennedy, D.M. (2001), *Freedom from Fear. The American People in Depression and War* (Oxford: Oxford University Press).

(2004), *Over Here. The First World War and American Society*, 2nd ed. (Oxford: Oxford University Press).

Kennedy, P.M. (1980), *The Rise of the Anglo-German Antagonism, 1860–1914* (London: Unwin Hyman).

(1981), *The Realities behind Diplomacy. Background Influences on British External Policy 1865–1980* (London: Fontana).

(1988), *The Rise and Fall of the Great Powers. Economic Challenge and Military Conflict from 1500 to 2000* (London: Unwin Hyman, 1988).

(ed.) (1991), *Grand Strategies in War and Peace* (New Haven, CT: Yale University Press).

Kennedy, P.M. and Hitchcock, W.I. (eds.) (2000), *From War to Peace: Altered Strategic Landscapes in the Twentieth Century* (New Haven, CT: Yale University Press).

Kennedy, R. (2009), *The Will to Believe. Woodrow Wilson, World War I, and America's Strategy for Peace and Security* (Kent, OH: Kent State University Press).

Kent, B. (1989), *The Spoils of War. The Politics, Economics and Diplomacy of Reparations 1918–1932* (Oxford: Oxford University Press).

Kershaw, I. (2001), *Hitler, 1889–1936, Hubris* (London: Penguin).

(2016), *To Hell and Back. Europe 1914–1949* (London: Penguin).

Keylor, W. (1998), "Versailles and International Diplomacy", in Boemeke, Feldman and Glaser (1998), pp. 469–506.

(2011), *The Twentieth-Century World and Beyond*, 6th ed. (Oxford: Oxford University Press).

Kießling, F. (2002), *Gegen den "grossen Krieg"? Entspannung in den internationalen Beziehungen, 1911–1914* (Munich: Oldenbourg).

Kimmich, C.M. (1976), *Germany and the League of Nations* (Chicago: Chicago University Press).

Kindleberger, C.P. (1973), *The World in Depression, 1929–39* (Berkeley, CA: University of California Press).

King, W. (1959), *Woodrow Wilson, Wellington Koo and the China Question at the Paris Peace Conference* (Leiden: Sythoff).

Kissinger H.A. (1994), *Diplomacy* (New York: Knopf).

(2014), *World Order* (London: Penguin).

Kitching, C.J. (1999), *Britain and the Problem of International Disarmament* (London: Routledge).

(2004), "Locarno and the Irrelevance of Disarmament", in Johnson (II/2004), pp. 161–77.

Kloppenberg, J.T. (1988), *Uncertain Victory. Social Democracy and Progressivism in European and American Thought, 1870–1920* (Oxford: Oxford University Press).

(2016), *Toward Democracy. The Struggle for Self-Rule in European and American Thought* (Oxford: Oxford University Press).

Klümpen, H. (1992), *Deutsche Außenpolitik zwischen Versailles und Rapallo. Revisionismus oder Neuorientierung?* (Münster: Lit Verlag).

Knipping, F. (1987), *Deutschland, Frankreich und das Ende der Locarno-Ära, 1928–1931* (Munich: Oldenbourg).

Knock, T.J. (1992), *To End All Wars. Woodrow Wilson and the Quest for a New World Order* (Princeton, NJ: Princeton University Press).

(1998), "Wilsonian Concepts and International Realities at the End of the War," in Boemeke, Feldman and Glaser (1998), pp. 111–30.

Köhler, H. (1980), *Novemberrevolution und Frankreich. Die französische Deutschlandpolitik, 1918–1919* (Düsseldorf: Droste).

(ed.) (1984), *Deutschland und der Westen* (Berlin: Colloquium-Verlag).

Koenen, G. (2017), *Die Farbe Rot. Ursprünge und Geschichte des Kommunismus* (Munich: Beck).

Kolakowski, L. (2005), *Main Currents of Marxism* (New York: Norton).

Kolb, E. (1998), *Die Weimarer Republik*, 3rd ed. (Munich: Oldenbourg).

Koselleck, R. (1973), *Kritik und Krise. Eine Studie zur Pathogenese der bürgerlichen Welt* (Frankfurt and Main: Suhrkamp).

(2003), *Zeitschichten: Studien zur Historik*, 6th ed. (Berlin: Suhrkamp).

Koskenniemi, M. (2008), *The Gentle Civilizer of Nations. The Rise and Fall of International Law 1870–1960* (Cambridge: Cambridge University Press).

Koszyk, K. (1972), *Deutsche Presse 1914–1945* (Berlin: Colloquium-Verlag).

Kotkin, S. (2014), *Stalin. Paradoxes of Power, 1878–1928* (New York: Penguin).

Krasner, S. (ed.) (1983), *International Regimes* (Ithaca, NY: Cornell University Press).

Kraus, O. (ed.) (1998), *"Vae victis!" Über den Umgang mit Besiegten* (Göttingen: Vandenhoeck & Ruprecht).

Krüger, P. (1973), *Deutschland und die Reparationen 1918/19. Die Genesis des Reparationsproblems in Deutschland zwischen Waffenstillstand und Versailler Friedensschluß* (Stuttgart: Deutsche Verlags-Anstalt).

(1974), "Friedenssicherung und deutsche Revisionspolitik. Die deutsche Außenpolitik und die Verhandlungen über den Kellogg-Pakt", *Vierteljahrshefte für Zeitgeschichte*, 22, pp. 227–57.

(1985), *Die Außenpolitik der Republik von Weimar* (Darmstadt: Wissenschaftliche Buchgesellschaft).

(1986), *Versailles. Deutsche Außenpolitik zwischen Revisionismus und Friedenssicherung* (Munich: Deutscher Taschenbuch-Verlag).

(ed.) (1991), *Kontinuität und Wandel in der Staatenordnung der Neuzeit. Beiträge zur Geschichte des internationalen Systems* (Marburg: Hitzeroth).

(1993), "German Disappointment and Anti-Western Resentment, 1918–1919", in Schröder (1993), pp. 323–36.

(2006), *Das unberechenbare Europa* (Stuttgart: Kohlhammer).

Krüger, P. and Schroeder, P.W. (eds.) (2001), *The Transformation of European Politics, 1763–1848: Episode or Model in Modern History?* (Münster: Lit Verlag).

Krumeich, G. (2018), *Die unbewältigte Niederlage. Das Trauma des Ersten Weltkriegs und die Weimarer Republik* (Freiburg: Herder).

Kuehl, W. (1969), *Seeking World Order. The United States and International Organization to 1920* (Nashville, TN: Vanderbilt University Press).

Kupchan, C. (2020), *Isolationism. A History of America's Efforts to Shield Itself from the World* (Oxford: Oxford University Press).

Laderman, C. (2019), *Sharing the Burden. The Armenian Question, Humanitarian Intervention, and Anglo-American Visions of Global Order* (Oxford: Oxford University Press).

LaFeber, W. (1994), *The American Age. United States Foreign Policy at Home and Abroad Since 1750*, 2nd ed. (New York: Norton).

(1998), *The Clash. U.S–Japanese Relations throughout History* (New York: Norton).

Langer, W.L. (1931), *European Alliances and Alignments, 1871–1890* (New York: Knopf).

(1956), *The Diplomacy of Imperialism, 1890–1902* (New York: Knopf).

Lappenküper, U. and Urbach, K. (eds.) (2016), *Realpolitik für Europa – Bismarcks Weg* (Paderborn: Schöningh).

Lappenküper, U., Wegner, B. and Jonas, M. (eds.) (2014), *Stabilität durch Gleichgewicht. Die Balance of Power im internationalen System der Neuzeit* (Paderborn: Schöningh).

Laqua, D. (2011), *Internationalism Reconfigured. Transnational Ideas and Movements between the World Wars* (London: I.B. Tauris).

Lederer, I. (1963), *Yugoslavia at the Paris Peace Conference* (New Haven, CT: Yale University Press).

Leffler, M.P. (1979), *The Elusive Quest. America's Pursuit of European Stability and French Security, 1919–1933* (Chapel Hill, NC: University of North Carolina Press).

(2007), *For the Soul of Mankind. The United States, the Soviet Union, and the Cold War* (New York: Hill & Wang).

Leffler, M.P. and Westad, O.A. (eds.) (2010), *The Cambridge History of the Cold War*. 3 vols. (Cambridge. Cambridge University Press).

Lentin, A. (1984), *Guilt at Versailles. Lloyd George and the Pre-history of Appeasement* (London: Methuen).

(1999), "Lord Cunliffe, Lloyd George, Reparations and Reputations at the Paris Peace Conference, 1919", *Diplomacy and Statecraft*, 10, pp. 50–86.

(I/2001), "'Appeasement' at the Paris Peace Conference', in Dockrill and Fisher (2001), pp. 51–66.

(II/2001), *Lloyd George and the Lost Peace. From Versailles to Hitler* (Basingstoke: MacMillan).

Leonhard, J. (2008), *Bellizismus und Nation. Kriegsdeutung und Nationsbestimmung in Europa und den Vereinigten Staaten, 1750–1914* (Munich: Oldenbourg).

(2014), *Die Büchse der Pandora. Geschichte des Ersten Weltkriegs* (Munich: Beck).

(2018), *Der überforderte Frieden. Versailles und die Welt, 1918–1923* (Munich: Beck).

Leonhard, J. (ed.) (2022), *Große Erwartungen. 1919 und die Neuordnung der Welt* (Munich: De Gruyter-Oldenbourg).

Lepore, J. (2019), *These Truths. A History of the United States* (New York: Norton).

Levin, N.G. (1968), *Woodrow Wilson and World Politics. America's Response to War and Revolution* (Oxford: Oxford University Press).

Levy, C. and Roseman, M. (eds.) (2002), *Three Post-War Eras in Comparison: Western Europe 1918–1945–1989* (Basingstoke: MacMillan).

Lévy-Leboyer, A. (ed.) (1977), *La position internationale de la France. Aspects économiques et financières (XIXe – XXe siècles)* (Paris: Éditions de l'École des hautes études en sciences sociales).

Lewis, D. (2000), *W.E.B. Du Bois. The Fight for Equality and the American Century, 1919–1963* (New York: Holt).

Lieven, D. (1983), *Russia and the Origins of the First World War* (London: St Martin's Press).

Link, A.S. (1954), *Woodrow Wilson and the Progressive Era, 1910–1917* (New York: Harper & Brothers).

(1965), *Wilson. Campaigns for Progressivism and Peace* (Princeton, NJ: Princeton University Press).

(ed.) (1982), *Woodrow Wilson and a Revolutionary World* (Chapel Hill, NC: University of North Carolina Press).

Link, A.S. and McCormick, R. (1983), *Progressivism* (Oxford: Oxford Univerity Press).

Link, W. (1970), *Die amerikanische Stabilisierungspolitik in Deutschland, 1921–1932* (Düsseldorf: Droste).

Liulevicius, V. (2005), *War Land on the Eastern Front. Culture, National Identity, and German Occupation in World War I* (Cambridge: Cambridge University Press).

Lochner, L. (1960), *Herbert Hoover and Germany* (New York: MacMillan).

Loth, W. and Osterhammel J. (eds.) (2000), *Internationale Geschichte. Themen – Ergebnisse – Aussichten* (Munich: Oldenbourg).

Low, A. (1974), *The Anschluss Movement, 1918–1919, and the Paris Peace Conference* (Philadelphia, PA: University of Pennsylvania Press).

Lowe, C.J. and Dockrill, M.L. (1972), *The Mirage of Power*, 3 vols. (London: Routledge & Paul).

Lundestad, G. (2003), *The United States and Western Europe since 1945* (Oxford: Oxford University Press).

Lundgreen-Nielsen, K. (1979), *The Polish Problem at the Paris Peace Conference* (Odense: Odense University Press).

(1982), "Wilson and the Rebirth of Poland", in Link (1982).

Macmillan, M. (2002), *Paris 1919. Six Months That Changed the World* (New York: Random House).

(2013), *The War That Ended Peace. The Road to 1914* (New York: Random House).

Maddox, R.J. (1970), *William E. Borah and American Foreign Policy* (Baton Rouge, LA: Louisiana State University Press).

Magee, F. (1995), "'Limited Liability'? Britain and the Treaty of Locarno", *Twentieth Century British History* 6, pp. 1–22.

Maier, C.S. (1981), "The Two Postwar Eras and the Conditions for Stability in 20th-Century Western Europe", *American Historical Review*, 86, pp. 327–52.

—— (1987), *In Search of Stability. Explorations in Historical Political Economy* (Cambridge: Cambridge University Press).

—— (1988), *Recasting Bourgeois Europe. Stabilization in France, Germany and Italy in the Decade after World War I*, 2nd ed. (Princeton, NJ: Princeton University Press).

—— (1993), "The Making of 'Pax Americana'. Formative Moments in United States Ascendancy", in Ahmann, Birke and Howard (1993).

—— (2006), *Among Empires. American Ascendancy and Its Predecessors* (Cambridge, MA: Harvard University Press).

—— (2012), *Leviathan 2.0. Inventing Modern Statehood* (Cambridge, MA: Harvard University Press).

Manela, E. (2007), *The Wilsonian Moment. Self-Determination and the International Origins of Anticolonial Nationalism* (Oxford: Oxford University Press).

Mann, G. (1947), *Friedrich von Gentz – Geschichte eines europäischen Staatsmannes* (Zurich: Europa).

—— (1996), *The History of Germany since 1789* (London: Pimlico).

—— (2011), *Deutsche Geschichte des 19. und 20. Jahrhunderts*, 13th ed. (Frankfurt/Main: Fischer).

Marchand, C. (1972), *The American Peace Movement and Social Reform, 1898–1918* (Princeton, NJ: Princeton University Press).

Marks, S. (1976), *The Illusion of Peace. International Relations in Europe, 1918–1933* (London: MacMillan).

—— (1981), *Innocent Abroad. Belgium at the Paris Peace Conference of 1919* (Chapel Hill, NC: University of North Carolina Press).

—— (2002), *The Ebbing of European Ascendancy. An International History of the World, 1914–1945* (London: Bloomsbury).

—— (2013), "Mistakes and Myths. The Allies, Germany, and the Versailles Treaty, 1918–1921", *Journal of Modern History*, 85 (September), pp. 632–59.

Markwell, D. (2006), *John Maynard Keynes and International Relations. Economic Paths to War and Peace* (Oxford: Oxford University Press).

Marquand, D. (1977), *Ramsay MacDonald* (London: Jonathan Cape).

Marsh, P. (1994), *Joseph Chamberlain. Entrepreneur in Politics* (New Haven, CT: Yale University Press).

Matthew, H.C.G. (1997), *Gladstone, 1809–1898* (Oxford: Oxford University Press).

Mauch, C. and Patel, K. (2010), *The United States and Germany during the Twentieth Century. Competition and Convergence* (Cambridge: Cambridge University Press).

May, E.R. (1961), *Imperial Democracy. The Emergence of America as a Great Power* (New York: Harper & Row).

(1973), *"Lessons" of the Past: The Use and Misuse of History in American Foreign Policy* (Oxford: Oxford University Press).

(1975), *The Making of the Monroe Doctrine* (Cambridge, MA: Harvard University Press).

Mayer, A.J. (1964), *Wilson vs. Lenin. The Political Origins of the New Diplomacy* (Cleveland, OH: World Publishing Company).

(1967), *Politics and Diplomacy of Peacemaking. Containment and Counterrevolution at Versailles, 1918–1919* (New York: Knopf).

(1981), *The Persistence of the Old Regime. Europe to the Great War* (New York: Pantheon).

Mayers, D. (2007), *Dissenting Voices in America's Rise to Power* (Cambridge: Cambridge University Press).

Mayeur, J.-M. and Rebérioux, M. (1984), *The Third Republic from Its Origins to the Great War* (Cambridge: Cambridge University Press).

Mazower, M. (2000), *Dark Continent. Europe's Twentieth Century* (New York: Penguin).

(2009), *No Enchanted Palace* (Princeton, NJ: Princeton University Press).

(2012), *Governing the World. The History of an Idea, 1815 to the Present* (New York: Penguin).

McDougall, W.A. (1978), *France's Rhineland Diplomacy, 1914–24. The Last Bid for a Balance of Power in Europe* (Princeton, NJ: Princeton University Press).

McKenna, M.C. (1961), *Borah* (Ann Arbor, MI: University of Michigan Press).

McKercher, B.J.C. (1984), *The Second Baldwin Government and the United States, 1924–1929. Attitudes and Diplomacy* (Cambridge: Cambridge University Press).

(ed.) (1991), *Anglo-American Relations in the 1920s. The Struggle for Supremacy* (Basingstoke: MacMillan).

(1999), *Transition of Power. Britain's Loss of Global Pre-eminence to the United States, 1930–1945* (Cambridge: Cambridge University Press).

McMeekin, S. (2011), *The Russian Origins of the First World War* (Cambridge, MA: Harvard University Press).

McNeil, W.C. (1986), *American Money and the Weimar Republic. Economics and Politics in the Era of the Great Depression* (New York: Columbia University Press).

Mearsheimer, J. (2001), *The Tragedy of Great Power Politics* (New York: Norton).

Meier, C. (1996), *Caesar* (London: Fontana).

(1990), *The Greek Discovery of Politics* (Cambridge, MA: Harvard University Press).

(2000), *Athens* (London: Pimlico).

(2010), *Das Gebot zu vergessen und die Unabweisbarkeit des Erinnerns* (Munich: Beck).

Meissner, B. (1965), "Lenin und das Selbstbestimmungsrecht der Völker", *Osteuropa*, 20 (April), pp. 245–61.

Menand, L. (2001), *The Metaphysical Club. A Story of Ideas in America* (New York: Farrar, Straus & Giroux).

(2021), *The Free World. Art and Thought in the Cold War* (New York: Farrar, Straus & Giroux).

Menzel, U. (2015), *Die Ordnung der Welt* (Berlin: Suhrkamp).

Meynell, H. (1960), *The Stockholm International Peace Conference of 1917* (Cambridge, Cambridge University Press).

Miller, K. (1967), *Socialism and Foreign Policy. Theory and Practice in Britain to 1931* (The Hague: Springer).

Miller, K. (1999), *Populist Nationalism: Republican Insurgency and American Foreign Policy Making, 1918–1925* (Westport, CT: Praeger).

Miller, S. (1974), *Burgfrieden und Klassenkampf. Die deutsche Sozialdemokratie im Ersten Weltkrieg* (Düsseldorf: Droste).

(1978), *Die Bürde der Macht. Die deutsche Sozialdemokratie 1918–1920* (Düsseldorf: Droste).

Milward, A.S. (1984), *The Reconstruction of Western Europe, 1945–1951* (London: Routledge).

Minohara, T. and Dawley, E. (eds.) (2020), *Beyond Versailles. The 1919 Moment and a New Order in East Asia* (Lexington, KY: Lexington Books).

Miquel, P. (1961), *Poincaré* (Paris: Fayard).

(1977), *La paix de Versailles et l'opinion publique française* (Paris: Flammarion).

(1983), *La Grande Guerre* (Paris: Larousse).

Möller, H. (1998), *Europa zwischen den Weltkriegen* (Munich: Oldenbourg).

Mollier, J.-Y. and George, J. (1994), *La plus longue des républiques 1870–1940* (Paris: Fayard).

Mombauer, A. (2001), *Helmuth von Moltke and the Origins of the First World War* (Cambridge: Cambridge University Press).

(2002), *The Origins of the First World War. Controversies and Consensus* (Harlow: Longman).

Mommsen, H. (1989), *Die verspielte Freiheit. Der Weg der Republik von Weimar in den Untergang, 1918–1933* (Berlin: Propyläen).

(ed.) (2002), *Der Erste Weltkrieg und die europäische Nachkriegsordnung. Sozialer Wandel und die Formveränderung der Politik* (Cologne: Böhlau).

Mommsen, W.J. (1993), *Großmachtstellung und Weltpolitik 1870–1914. Die Außenpolitik des Deutschen Reiches* (Berlin: Ullstein).

Monroe, E. (1981), *Britain's Moment in the Middle East* (London: Chatto & Windus).

Morgan, K.O. (1979), *Consensus and Disunity. The Lloyd George Coalition Government, 1918–1922* (Oxford: Oxford University Press).

Morgenthau, H.J. (1948), *Politics among Nations. The Struggle for Power and Peace* (New York: Knopf).

(1952), *In Defense of the National Interest. A Critical Examination of American Foreign Policy* (New York: Knopf).

Morris, E. (2001), *Theodore Rex* (New York: Random House).

Motadel, D. (ed.) (2021), *Revolutionary World. Global Upheaval in the Modern Age* (Cambridge: Cambridge University Press).

Mouré, K. (2003), *The Gold Standard Illusion. France, the Bank of France and the International Gold Standard, 1914–1939* (Oxford: Oxford University Press).

Müller, T. and Tooze, A. (eds.) (2015), *Normalität und Fragilität. Demokratie nach dem Ersten Weltkrieg* (Hamburg: Hamburger Edition).

Mulligan, W. (2010), *The Origins of the First World War* (Cambridge: Cambridge University Press).

(2014), *The Great War for Peace* (New Haven, CT: Yale University Press).

Mühlhausen, W. (2006), *Friedrich Ebert, 1871–1925. Reichspräsident der Weimarer Republik* (Bonn: Dietz).

Münkler, H. (2013), *Der große Krieg. Die Welt 1914 bis 1918* (Berlin: Rowohlt).

Nash, L. (ed.) (2010), *Herbert Hoover and World Peace* (Lanham, MD: University Press of America).

Nebelin, M. (2010), *Ludendorff. Diktator im Ersten Weltkrieg* (Munich: Siedler).

(2016), *The Path to War. How the First World War Created America* (Oxford: Oxford University Press).

Neiberg, M. (2011), *Dance of the Furies. Europe and the Outbreak of World War* (Cambridge, MA: Harvard University Press).

Neilson, K. (1975), *Victors Divided. America and the Allies in Germany, 1918–1923* (Berkeley, CA: University of California Press).

(2006), *Britain, Soviet Russia and the Collapse of the Versailles Order, 1919–1939* (Cambridge: Cambridge University Press).

Nelson, H. (2019), *Land and Power. British and Allied Policy on Germany's Frontiers 1916–19*, new ed. (London: Routledge).

Newton, D. (1997), *British Policy and the Weimar Republic 1918–1919* (Oxford: Oxford University Press).

Newton, S. (1996), *Profits of Peace. The Political Economy of Anglo-German Appeasement* (Oxford: Oxford University Press).

Nichols, C. (2011), *Promise and Peril. America at the Dawn of a Global Age* (Cambridge, MA: Harvard University Press).

Nicholls, A.J. (1991), *Weimar and the Rise of Hitler*, 3rd ed. (London: MacMillan).

(1994), *Freedom with Responsibility. The Social Market Economy in Germany, 1918–1963* (Oxford: Oxford University Press).

Niedhart, G. (2012), *Die Außenpolitik der Weimarer Republik* (Munich: Oldenbourg).

Niess, A. and Vaïsse, M. (eds.) (2007), *Léon Bourgeois : du solidarisme à la société des nations* (Langres: D. Guéniot).

Ninkovich, F. (1999), *The Wilsonian Century* (New Haven, CT: Yale University Press).

(2001), *The United States and Imperialism* (Malden, MA: Blackwell).

(2009), *Global Dawn. The Cultural Foundation of American Internationalism, 1865–1890* (Cambridge, MA: Harvard University Press).

Nipperdey, T. (1993), *Deutsche Geschichte 1866–1918. II: Machtstaat vor der Demokratie* (Munich: Beck).

Nolan, M. (2012), *The Transatlantic Century. Europe and America, 1890–2010* (Cambridge: Cambridge University Press).

Nolte, E. (1987), *Der europäische Bürgerkrieg, 1917–1945* (Berlin: Propyläen).

Northedge, F.S. (1996), *The Troubled Giant. Britain among the Great Powers 1916–1939* (New York: Praeger).

O'Brien, P. and Clesse, A. (eds.) (2002), *Two Hegemonies. Britain 1846–1914 and the United States 1941–2001* (Aldershot: Ashgate).

O'Brien, P.K. (ed.) (2007), *Philip's Atlas of World History* (Oxford: Oxford University Press).

Olson, W. (1959), "Theodore Roosevelt's Conception of an International League", *World Affairs Quarterly*, (January) 29.

Orde, A. (1978), *Great Britain and International Security, 1920–1926* (London: Royal Historical Society).

(1990), *British Policy and European Reconstruction After the First World War* (Cambridge: Cambridge University Press).

O'Riordan, E.Y. (2001), *Britain and the Ruhr Crisis* (Basingstoke: Palgrave).

Ørvik, N. (1971), *The Decline of Neutrality 1914–1941* (London: Frank Cass).

Osiander, A. (1994), *The States System of Europe, 1640–1990* (Oxford: Oxford University Press).

Osterhammel, J. (2009), *Die Verwandlung der Welt. Eine Geschichte des 19. Jahrhunderts* (Munich: Beck).

(2014), *The Transformation of the World. A Global History of the Nineteenth Century* (Princeton, NJ: Princeton University Press).

Osterhammel, J. and Peterson, N. (2005), *Globalization. A Short History* (Princeton, NJ: Princeton University Press).

O'Toole, P. (2018), *The Moralist. Woodrow Wilson and the World He Made* (New York: Simon & Schuster).

Otte, T.G. (1998), *Harold Nicolson and Diplomatic Theory. Between Old Diplomacy and New* (Leicester: Leicester University Press).

(2014), *July Crisis. The World's Descent into War, Summer 1914* (Cambridge: Cambridge University Press).

(2020), *Statesman of Europe. A Life of Sir Edward Grey* (London: Penguin).

Oudin, B. (1987), *Aristide Briand: la paix, une idée neuve en Europe* (Paris: Laffont).

Overmans, R. (2004), "Kriegsverluste", in Hirschfeld (2004), pp. 663–66.

Overy, R. (2021), *Blood and Ruins. The Great Imperial War, 1931–1945* (London: Penguin).

Parrini, C.P. (1969), *Heir to Empire. United States Economic Diplomacy, 1916–1923* (Pittsburgh, PA: University of Pennsylvania Press).

Patel, K. (2016), *The New Deal. A Global History* (Princeton, NJ: Princeton University).

Patel, K. and Mauch, C. (eds.) (2008), *Wettlauf um die Moderne. Die USA und Deutschland – 1890 bis heute* (Munich: Pantheon).

Payk, M. (2018), *Frieden durch Recht? Der Aufstieg des modernen Völkerrechts und der Friedensschluss nach dem Ersten Weltkrieg* (Munich: De Gruyter).

Pease, N. (1986), *Poland, the United States and the Stabilisation of Europe, 1919–1933* (Oxford: Oxford University Press).

Pedersen, S. (2007), "Back to the League of Nations", *American Historical Review*, 112 (October), pp. 1091–117.

(2015), *The Guardians* (Oxford: Oxford University Press).

Pegg, C.H. (1983), *Evolution of the European Idea* (Chapel Hill, NC: University of North Carolina Press).

Perkins, B. (1968), *The Great Rapprochement. England and the United States, 1895–1914* (New York: Atheneum).

Perkins, D. (1956), *Charles Evans Hughes and American Democratic Statesmanship* (Boston: Little, Brown & Co.).

Perman, D. (1962), *The Shaping of the Czechoslovak State. Diplomatic History of the Boundaries of Czechoslovakia, 1914–1920* (Leiden: Brill).

Petricioli, M. (ed.) (1995), *A Missed Opportunity? 1922 – the Reconstruction of Europe* (Bern and New York: Peter Lang).

Philipson, S. (1984), *Von Versailles nach Jerusalem. Dr. Carl Melchior und sein Werk* (Jerusalem: Massada Press).

Piller, E. (2021), *Selling Weimar. German Public Diplomacy and the United States, 1918–1933* (Stuttgart: Steiner).

Pipei, E. (2013), *Nacht über Europa. Kulturgeschichte des Ersten Weltkriegs* (Berlin: Propyläen).

Pitts, Jennifer (2018), *Boundaries of the International. Law and Empire* (Cambridge, MA: Harvard University Press).

Porter-Szücs, B. (2014), *Poland in the Modern World. Beyond Martyrdom* (Chichester: Wiley & Sons).

Priest, A. (2021), *Designs on Empire. America's Rise to Power in the Age of European Imperialism* (New York: Columbia University Press).

Priestland, D. (2009), *The Red Flag. Communism and the Making of the Modern World* (London: Allen Lane).

Prott, V. *The Politics of Self-Determination. Remaking Territories and National Identities in Europe, 1917–1923* (Oxford: Oxford University Press).

Provence, M. (2017), *The Last Ottoman Generation and the Making of the Modern Middle East* (Cambridge: Cambridge University Press).

Pruessen, R. (1982), *John Foster Dulles. The Road to Power* (New York: MacMillan)

Pugh, M. (2012), *Liberal Internationalism. The Interwar Movement for Peace in Britain* (Basingstoke: MacMillan).

Pusey, M.J. (1951), *Charles Evans Hughes*, 2 vols. (New York: MacMillan).

Pyta, W. (2007), *Hindenburg. Herrschaft zwischen Hohenzollern und Hitler* (Munich: Siedler).

Recchia, S. and Urbinati, N. (eds.) (2009), *A Cosmopolitanism of Nations. Giuseppe Mazzini's Writings on Democracy, Nation Building, and International Relations* (Princeton, NJ: Princeton University Press).

Reinhard, W. (1999), *Geschichte der Staatsgewalt. Eine vergleichende Verfassungsgeschichte Europas von den Anfängen bis zur Gegenwart* (Munich: Beck).

Rémond, R. (1997), *Notre Siècle. 1918–1995* (Paris: Fayard).

Reynolds, D. (1991), *Britannia Overruled. British Policy and World Power in the 20th Century* (London: Longman).

(2014), *The Long Shadow. The Great War and the Twentieth Century* (New York: Norton).

Rhodes, B.D. (1991), "The Image of Britain in the United States, 1919–1929. A Contentious Relative and Rival', in McKercher (1991), pp. 187–208.

Richardson, D. (1989), *The Evolution of British Disarmament Policy in the 1920s* (London: St Martin's Press).

Rieckhoff, H.v. (1971), *German–Polish Relations 1918–1933* (Baltimore, MD: Johns Hopkins Press).

Ritter, G. (1954–68), *Staatskunst und Kriegshandwerk. Das Problem des "Militarismus" in Deutschland*, 4 vols. (Munich: Oldenbourg).

Robbins, K. (1976), *The Abolition of War. The "Peace Movement" in Britain, 1914–1919* (Cardiff: University of Wales Press).

(1997), *Appeasement*, 2nd ed. (Hoboken, NJ: John Wiley & Sons).

Roberts, A. (1999), *Salisbury. Victorian Titan* (London: Phoenix).

Robinson, P.R. and Gallagher, J. (1953), "The Imperialism of Free Trade," *Economic History Review*, 2nd Series, VI, 1, pp. 1–15.

Rödder, A. (1996), *Stresemanns Erbe. Julius Curtius und die deutsche Außenpolitik 1929–1931* (Paderborn: Schöningh).

Rodgers, D. (2000), *Atlantic Crossings. Social Politics in a Progressive Age* (Cambridge, MA: Harvard University Press).

Röhl, J. (1994), *The Kaiser and His Court. Wilhelm II and the Government of Germany* (Cambridge: Cambridge University Press).

(2014), *Wilhelm II. Into the Abyss of War and Exile, 1900–1941* (Cambridge: Cambridge University Press).

Rose, A. (2011), *Zwischen Empire und Kontinent. Britische Außenpolitik vor dem Ersten Weltkrieg* (Munich: Oldenbourg, 2011).

Rosenberg, E. (ed.) (2012), *A World Connecting, 1870–1945* (Cambridge, MA: Harvard University Press).

Roskill, S. (1970), *Hankey. Man of Secrets. Volume I: 1877–1918* (New York: St Martin's Press).

(1972), *Hankey, Man of Secrets. Volume II: 1919–1931* (New York: St Martin's Press).

Rossini, D. (2008), *Woodrow Wilson and the American Myth in Italy. Culture, Diplomacy, and War Propaganda* (Cambridge, MA: Harvard University Press).

Rotberg, R. (2007), *A Leadership for Peace. How Edwin Ginn Tried to Change the World* (Stanford, CA: Stanford University Press).

Rothwell, V.H. (1972), *British War Aims and Peace Diplomacy, 1914–1918* (Oxford: Oxford University Press).

Roussellier, N. (1999), *Le Parlement de l'éloquence* (Paris: Presses de Sciences Po).

Rudman, S. (2011), *Lloyd George and the Appeasement of Germany, 1919–1945* (Newcastle: Cambridge Scholars).

Rupieper, H.-J. (1979), *The Cuno Government and Reparations, 1922–23* (The Hague: Springer).

Rupp, L. (1997), *Worlds of Women. The Making of an International Women's Movement* (Princeton, NJ: Princeton University Press)

Sachsenmaier, D. (2011), *Global Perspectives on Global History. Theories and Approaches in a Connected World* (Cambridge: Cambridge University Press).

Salewski, M. (1966), *Entwaffnung und Militärkontrolle in Deutschland 1919–1927* (Munich: Oldenbourg).

(1980), "Das Weimarer Revisionssyndrom", *Aus Politik und Zeitgeschichte*, 2 (January), pp. 14–25.

Salzmann, S. (2003), *Great Britain, Germany, and the Soviet Union. Rapallo and after, 1922–1934* (London: Royal Historical Society).

Saueressig, P. (1996), *Chancen und Grenzen informeller Diplomatie. Charles Evans Hughes und amerikanische Außenpolitik 1921–1925* (Frankfurt/Main: Peter Lang).

Saunier, P.Y. (ed.) (2013), *Transnational History* (New York: Palgrave MacMillan).

Scaff, L. (2011), *Max Weber in America* (Princeton, NJ: Princeton University Press).

Schattkowsky, R. (I/1994), "Deutschland und Polen vor Locarno. Probleme ihrer Beziehungen 1923 bis 1925", in Schattkowsky (II/1994), pp. 107–14.

Schattkowsky, R. (ed.) (II/1994), *Locarno und Osteuropa* (Marburg: Hitzeroth).

(1999), "Deutsch-polnischer Minderheitenstreit nach dem Ersten Weltkrieg", *Journal of East Central European Studies*, 48 (September), pp. 524–30.

Schild, G. (1995), *Between Ideology and Realpolitik. Woodrow Wilson and the Russian Revolution, 1917–1921* (Westport, CT: Praeger).

Schirmann, S., (2006), *Quel ordre européen ? De Versailles à la chute du IIIe Reich* (Paris: Armand Colin).

(ed.) (2016), *Guerre et paix. Une destinée européenne?* (Bern: Peter Lang).

Schivelbusch, W. (2001), *Die Kultur der Niederlage. Der amerikanische Süden 1865. Frankreich 1871. Deutschland 1918* (Berlin: Alexander Fest).

Schmidt, R. (2021), *Kaiserdämmerung. Berlin, London, Paris, St. Petersburg und der Weg in den Untergang* (Stuttgart: Klett-Cotta).

Schmidt, S. (2009), *Frankreichs Außenpolitik in der Julikrise 1914* (Munich: Oldenbourg).

Schmidt-Hartmann, E. and Winters, S. (eds.) (1991), *Großbritannien, die Vereinigten Staaten von Amerika und die böhmischen Länder* (Munich: Oldenbourg).

Schöllgen, G. (2000), *Das Zeitalter des Imperialismus*, 4th ed. (Munich: Oldenbourg).

Schölzel, C. (2006), *Walther Rathenau. Eine Biographie* (Paderborn: Schöningh).

Schoultz, L. (1998), *Beneath the United States. A History of U.S. Policy toward Latin America* (Cambridge, MA: Harvard University Press).

Schröder, H.-J. (ed.) (1993), *Confrontation and Cooperation. Germany and the United States in the Era of World War I, 1900–1924* (Oxford: Oxford University Press).

Schroeder, P.W. (1986–87), "The 19th-Century International System: Changes in the Structure", *World Politics*, 39, pp. 1–26.

(1987), "The Nineteenth Century System: Balance of Power or Political Equilibrium?", *Review of International Studies*, 15, pp. 135–53.

(1993), "Economic Integration and the European International System in the Era of World War I", *American Historical Review*, 98, pp. 1130–37.

(1994), *The Transformation of European Politics 1763–1848* (Oxford: Oxford University Press).

(I/2004), "Alliances, 1815–1945. Weapons of Power and Tools of Management", in Schroeder (IV/2004), pp. 195–222.

(II/2004), "Embedded Counterfactuals and World War I as an Unavoidable War", in Schroeder (IV/2004), pp. 157–92.

(III/2004), "The Mirage of Empire Versus the Promise of Hegemony", in Schroeder (IV/2004), pp. 297–306.

(IV/2004), *Systems, Stability, and Statecraft. Essays on the International History of Modern Europe*, ed. D. Wetzel, R. Jervis and J.S. Levy (New York: Palgrave MacMillan).

(V/2004), "World War I as Galloping Gertie", in Schroeder (IV/2004), pp. 137–56.

(2012), "Europe's Progress and America's Success, 1760–1850", in Schneid, F. (ed.) (2012), *The Projection and Limitations of Imperial Power, 1618–1850* (Leiden: Brill), pp. 170–95.

Schuker, S.A. (1976), *The End of French Predominance in Europe. The Financial Crisis of 1924 and the Adoption of the Dawes Plan* (Chapel Hill, NC: University of North Carolina Press).

(1987), *American "Reparations" to Germany* (Princeton, NJ: Princeton University Press).

(1991), "American Policy towards Debts and Reconstruction", in Fink, Frohn and Heideking (1991).

(1998), "The Rhineland Question: West European Security at the Paris Peace Conference of 1919," in Boemeke, Feldman and Glaser (1998), pp. 275–312.

(ed.) (2000), *Deutschland und Frankreich. Vom Konflikt zur Aussöhnung* (Munich: Oldenbourg).

Schulz, G. (1969), *Revolutionen und Friedensschlüsse, 1917–1920* (Munich: Deutscher Taschenbuch-Verlag).

Schulz, M. (2009), *Normen und Praxis. Das Europäische Konzert der Großmächte als Sicherheitsrat, 1815–1860* (Munich: Oldenbourg).

Schulze, H. (1996), *States, Nations and Nationalism. From the Middle Ages to the Present* (Oxford: Oxford University Press).

(1982), *Weimar. Deutschland 1917–1933* (Berlin: Siedler).

Schwabe, K. (1971), *Deutsche Revolution und Wilson-Frieden. Die amerikanische und deutsche Friedensstrategie zwischen Ideologie und Machtpolitik 1918/1919* (Düsseldorf: Droste).

——— (1985), *Woodrow Wilson, Revolutionary Germany, and Peacemaking, 1918–1919* (Chapel Hill, NC: University of North Carolina Press).

——— (1998), "Germany's Peace Aims and the Domestic and International Constraints," in Boemeke, Feldman and Glaser, pp. 37–68.

——— (2007), *Weltmacht und Weltordnung. Amerikanische Außenpolitik von 1898 bis zur Gegenwart* (Paderborn: Schöningh).

——— (2019), *Versailles. Das Wagnis eines demokratischen Friedens, 1919–1923* (Paderborn: Schöningh).

Schwabe, K. and Elvert, J. (eds.) (1993), *Deutschland und der Westen im 19. und 20. Jahrhundert. 1. Transatlantische Beziehungen* (Stuttgart: Steiner).

Searle, G. (2004), *A New England? Peace and War, 1886–1918* (Oxford: Oxford University Press).

Sedlmaier, A. (2003), *Deutschlandbilder und Deutschlandpolitik. Studien zur Wilson-Administration, 1913–1921* (Stuttgart: Steiner).

Seil, E.-A. (2011), *Weltmachtstreben und Kampf für den Frieden. Der deutsche Reichstag im Ersten Weltkrieg* (Frankfurt and Main: Peter Lang).

Self, R. (2006), *Britain, America and the War Debt Controversy* (London: Routledge).

Service, R. (2000), *Lenin* (Cambridge, MA: Harvard University Press).

——— (2009), *Trotsky* (Cambridge, MA: Harvard University Press).

Sexton, J. (2011), *The Monroe Doctrine* (New York: Hill & Wang).

Sharp, A. (1984), *Lloyd George's Foreign Policy* (London: MacMillan).

——— (I/2008), *The Versailles Settlement. Peacemaking after the First World War, 1919–1923*, 2nd ed. (London: Haus).

——— (II/2008), *David Lloyd George. Great Britain* (London: Haus).

——— (2010), *The Consequences of the Peace. The Versailles Settlement. Aftermath and Legacy, 1919– 2010* (London: Haus).

Shimazu, N. (1998), *Japan, Race and Equality. The Racial Equality Proposal of 1919* (London: Routledge).

Siebert, F. (1973), *Aristide Briand, 1862–1932. Ein Staatsmann zwischen Frankreich und Europa* (Stuttgart: Rentsch).

Siegel, M. (2019), *Peace on Our Terms. The Global Battle for Women's Rights After the First World War* (New York: Columbia University Press).

Siemann, W. (2016), *Metternich. Stratege und Visionär* (Munich: Beck).

Silverman, D.P. (1982), *Reconstructing Europe after the Great War* (Cambridge, MA: Harvard University Press).

Simms, B. (2014), *Europe. The Struggle for Supremacy, 1453 to the Present* (London: Penguin).

Sked, A. (1989), *The Decline and Fall of the Habsburg Empire, 1815–1918* (London: Routledge).

Skidelsky, R. (1996), *John Maynard Keynes* (Oxford: Oxford University Press).

(1983), *John Maynard Keynes, Vol. I: Hopes Betrayed, 1883–1920* (London: Penguin).

(2005), *John Maynard Keynes, 1883–1946. Economist, Philosopher, Statesman* (London: Penguin).

Skowronek, S. (1982), *Building a New American State. The Expansion of National Administrative Capacities, 1877–1920* (Cambridge: Cambridge University Press).

Sluga, G. (2013), *Internationalism in the Age of Nationalism* (Philadelphia, PA: University of Pennsylvania Press).

Smith, L. (2018), *Sovereignty at the Paris Peace Conference of 1919* (Oxford: Oxford University Press).

Smith, N. (2003), *American Empire. Roosevelt's Geographer and the Prelude to Globalization* (Berkeley, CA: University of California Press).

Smith, P. (2012), *Talons of the Eagle. Latin America, the United States, and the World*, 4th ed. (Oxford: Oxford University Press).

Smith, T. (1994), *America's Mission. The United States and the Worldwide Struggle for Democracy in the Twentieth Century* (Princeton, NJ: Princeton University Press).

Sorlot, M. (2005), *Léon Bourgeois, 1851–1925: un moraliste en politique* (Paris: Leprince).

Soutou, G.-H. (1989), *L'Or et le Sang. Les buts de guerre économique de la Première Guerre Mondiale* (Paris: Fayard).

(1998), "The French Peacemakers and Their Home Front", in Boemeke, Feldman and Glaser (1998), pp. 167–88.

Spence, J.D. (2012), *The Search for Modern China*, 3rd ed. (New York: Norton).

Spenz, J. (1966), *Die diplomatische Vorgeschichte des Beitritts Deutschlands zum Völkerbund 1924–1926* (Göttingen: Vandenhoeck & Ruprecht).

Sperber, J. (2005), *The European Revolutions 1848–1851*, 2nd ed. (Cambridge: Cambridge University Press).

Stadler, K. (1966), *The Birth of the Austrian Republic, 1918–1921* (Leiden: Brill).

Stedman Jones, G. (2017), *Karl Marx. Greatness and Illusion* (London: Penguin).

Steel, R. (1980), Walter Lippmann and the American Century (Boston: Little, Brown & Co.).

Steinberg, J. (2011), *Bismarck. A Life* (Oxford: Oxford University Press).

Steiner, Z.S. (1993), "The League of Nations and the Quest for Security", in Ahmann, Birke and Howard (1993), pp. 35–70.

(2001), "The Treaty of Versailles Revisited", in Dockrill and Fisher (2001), pp. 13–34.

(2003), *Britain and the Origins of the First World War*, 2nd ed. (Basingstoke: MacMillan).

(2005), *The Lights That Failed. European International History, 1919–1933* (Oxford: Oxford University Press).

(2011), *The Triumph of the Dark. European International History, 1933–1939* (Oxford: Oxford University Press).

Stephan, P. (2019), "Das Problem Europa. Überlegungen mit Friedrich Nietzsche", in Apelt, A., Jesse, E., Schmidt, E. (eds.) (2019), *Wohin strebt Europa? 1918–2018* (Halle: Mitteldeutscher Verlag), pp. 124–32.

Stevenson, D. (1982), *French War Aims against Germany, 1914–1919* (Oxford: Oxford University Press).

    (1991), *The First World War and International Politics* (Oxford: Oxford University Press).

    (1998), "French War Aims and Peace Planning," in Boemeke, Feldman and Glaser (1998), pp. 87–109.

    (2006), "Britain, France and the Origins of German Disarmament, 1916–19", *Journal of Strategic Studies*, 41 (August), pp. 195–224.

    (2012), *1914–1918. The History of The First World War* (London: Penguin).

    (2019), *1917. War, Peace, and Revolution* (London: Penguin, 2019).

Stone, R. (1970), *The Irreconcilables. The Fight against the League of Nations* (New York: Norton).

Strachhan, H. (2001), *The First World War. Volume I: To Arms* (Oxford: Oxford University Press).

Struck, B., Rodogno, D. and Vogel, J. (eds.) (2014), *Shaping the Transnational Sphere. Experts, Networks, Issues from the 1840s to the 1930s* (New York: Berghahn).

Stuchtey, B. (2010), *Die europäische Expansion und ihre Feinde. Kolonialismuskritik vom 18. bis in das 20. Jahrhundert* (Munich: Oldenbourg).

Stürmer, M. (1967), *Koalition und Opposition in der Weimarer Republik, 1924–1928* (Düsseldorf: Droste).

Stürmer, M. (ed.) (1980), *Die Weimarer Republik* (Königstein: Hain).

Sullivant, R. (1962), *Soviet Politics and the Ukraine, 1917–1957* (New York: Columbia University Press).

Suppan, A. (2019), *The Imperialist Peace Order in Central Europe. Saint-Germain and Trianon, 1919–1920* (Vienna: Verlag der österreichischen Akademie der Wissenschaften).

Swartz, M. (1971), *The Union of Democratic Control in British Politics during the First World War* (Oxford: Oxford University Press).

Taylor, A.J.P. (1954), *The Struggle for Mastery in Europe 1848–1918* (Oxford: Oxford University Press).

    (1964), *The Origins of the Second World War* (London: Penguin).

    (1964), "The War Aims of the Allies in the First World War", in Taylor, A.J.P., *Politics in Wartime and other Essays* (London: Penguin).

Taylor, P. (1980), "The Foreign Office and British Propaganda during the First World War", *Historical Journal*, 23 (December), pp. 875–898.

Thomas, M. (2006), *The French Empire between the Wars* (Manchester: Manchester University Press).

Thompson, J.A. (1987), *Reformers and War. American Progressive Publicists and the First World War* (Cambridge: Cambridge University Press).

Thompson, J.L. (1999), *Politicians, the Press and Propaganda. Lord Northcliffe and the Great War, 1914–1919* (Kent, OH: Kent State University Press).

Thompson, J.M. (1966), *Russia, Bolshevism, and the Versailles Peace* (Princeton, NJ: Princeton University Press).

Tillmann, S.P. (1961), *Anglo-American Relations at the Paris Peace Conference* (Princeton, NJ: Princeton University Press).

Tökés, R. (1967), *Béla Kun and the Hungarian Soviet Republic* (New York: Praeger).

Tooze, A. (2014), *The Deluge. The Great War and the Remaking of Global Order, 1916–1931* (London: Penguin).

Trachtenberg, M. (1980), *Reparation in World Politics. France and European Economic Diplomacy, 1916– 1923* (New York: Columbia University Press).

——— (1999), *A Constructed Peace. The Making of the European Settlement 1945–1963* (Princeton, NJ: Princeton University Press).

Trager, R. (2017), *Diplomacy. Communication and the Origins of International Order* (Cambridge: Cambridge University Press).

Trask, D. (1966), "General Tasker Howard Bliss and the 'Sessions of the World', 1919", *Transactions of the American Philosophical Society*, 56 (January).

Trotnow, H. (1980), *Karl Liebknecht. Eine politische Biographie* (Cologne: Kiepenheuer & Witsch).

Tucker, R. (2007), *Woodrow Wilson and the Great War. Reconsidering America's Neutrality, 1914–1917* (Charlottesville, VA: University of Virginia Press).

Turner, A. (1998), *Britain and French War Debts in the 1920s* (Brighton: Sussex Academic Press).

Turner, H.A. Jr (1963), *Stresemann and the Politics of the Weimar Republic* (Princeton, NJ: Princeton University Press).

Tyrrell, I. (2010), *Reforming the World. The Creation of America"s Moral Empire* (Princeton, NJ: Princeton University Press).

Ullmann, H.P. (2014), "Finance", in Winter (II/2014).

Vickers, R. (2003 and 2011), *The Labour Party and the World*, 2 vols. (Manchester: Manchester University Press).

Viefhaus, E. (1960), *Die Minderheitenfrage und die Entstehung der Minderheitenschutzverträge auf der Pariser Friedenskonferenz 1919* (Würzburg: Holzner).

Waley, D. (1964), *Edwin Montagu* (New Delhi: Asia Publishing House).

Walters, F.P. (1952), *A History of the League of Nations* (Oxford: Oxford University Press).

Waltz, K. (1979), *Theory of International Politics* (New York: McGraw-Hill).

Walworth, A. (1977), *America's Moment, 1918. American Diplomacy at the End of World War I* (New York: Norton).

——— (1986), *Wilson and His Peacemakers. American Diplomacy at the Paris Peace Conference* (New York: Norton).

Wandycz, P.S. (1961), *France and Her Eastern Allies, 1919–1925. French-Czechoslovak-Polish Relations from the Paris Peace Conference to Locarno* (Westport, CT: Praeger).

(1980), *The United States and Poland* (Cambridge, MA: Harvard University Press).

(1988), *The Twilight of the French Eastern Alliance, 1926–36. French–Czechoslovak–Polish Relations from Locarno to the Remilitarization of the Rhineland* (Princeton, NJ: Princeton University Press).

(1992), *The Price of Freedom. East Central Europe in Modern Times* (London: Routledge).

(1998), "The Polish Question", in Boemeke, Feldman and Glaser (1998), pp. 313–37.

Watt, D.C. (1984), *Succeeding John Bull. America in Britain's Place, 1900–1975* (Cambridge: Cambridge University Press).

Webster, A. (2005), "The Transnational Dream. Politicians, Diplomats and Soldiers in the League of Nations' Pursuit of International Disarmament, 1920–1938", *Contemporary European History*, 14 (November), pp. 493–518.

(2016), "The League of Nations, Disarmament and Internationalism", in Clavin and Sluga (2016).

Wehler, H.-U. (2007), *Deutsche Gesellschaftsgeschichte, Band 3: Von der "Deutschen Doppelrevolution" bis zum Beginn des Ersten Weltkrieges 1849–1914* (Munich: Beck).

Weisbrod, B. (2002), "Die Politik der Repräsentation. Das Erbe des Ersten Weltkrieges und der Formwandel der Politik in Europa", in Mommsen (2002), pp. 13–41.

Weisbrode, K. (2015), *The Atlanticists. A Story of American Diplomacy* (Santa Ana, CA: Nortia).

Weissman, B. (1974), *Herbert Hoover and Famine Relief to Soviet Russia, 1921–1923* (Stanford, CA: Hoover Institution Press).

Weitsman, P. (2004), *Dangerous Alliances. Proponents of Peace, Weapons of War* (Stanford, CA: Stanford University Press).

Weitz, E. (1997), *Creating German Communism, 1890–1990. From Popular Protests to Socialist State* (Princeton, NJ: Princeton University Press).

Wengst, U. (1973), *Graf Brockdorff-Rantzau und die außenpolitischen Anfänge der Weimarer Republik* (Frankfurt/Main: Peter Lang).

Wertheim, S. (2011), "The League That Wasn't. American Designs for a Legalist-Sanctionist League of Nations and the Intellectual Origins of International Organization, 1914–1920", *Diplomatic History*, 35 (November), pp. 797–836.

(2020), *Tomorrow, the World. The Birth of U.S. Global Supremacy* (Cambridge, MA: Harvard University Press).

Westad, O.A. (2007), *The Global Cold War* (Cambridge: Cambridge University Press).

(2010), "The Cold War and the International History of the 20th Century", in Leffler and Westad (2010), I, pp. 1–19.

(2018), *The Cold War. A World History* (London: Penguin).

Wheatley, N. (2017), "New Subjects in International Law and Order", in Clavin and Sluga (2017), pp. 265–86.

Whyte, K. (2017), *Hoover. An Extraordinary Life in Extraordinary Times* (New York: Knopf).

Widenor, W.C. (1980), *Henry Cabot Lodge and the Search for an American Foreign Policy* (Berkeley, CA: University of California Press).

Williams, A. (ed.) (1998), *Failed Imagination. New World orders of the Twentieth Century* (Manchester: Manchester University Press).

(2007), *Failed Imagination? The Anglo-American New World Order from Wilson to Bush* (Manchester: Manchester University Press-).

(2014), *France, Britain and the United States in the Twentieth Century, 1900–1940. A Reappraisal* (Basingstoke: MacMillan).

Williams, W.A. (1972), *The Tragedy of American Diplomacy*, 2nd ed. (New York: Norton).

Winkler, H. (1952), *The League of Nations Movement in Great Britain, 1914–1919* (New Brunswick NJ: Rutgers University Press).

(1956), "The Emergence of a Labour Foreign Policy in Great Britain, 1918–1929", *Journal of Modern History*, 9, pp. 247–258.

Winkler, H.A. (I/2000), *Der lange Weg nach Westen, Band 1: Vom Ende des Alten Reiches bis zum Untergang der Weimarer Republik* (Munich: Beck).

(II/2000), *Der lange Weg nach Westen. Band 2: Vom "Dritten Reich" bis zur Wiedervereinigung* (Munich: Beck).

(2001), *Von der Revolution zur Stabilisierung. Arbeiter und Arbeiterbewegung in der Weimarer Republik 1918 bis 1924* (Berlin: Dietz).

(2011), *Geschichte des Westens 2. Die Zeit der Weltkriege 1914–1945* (Munich: Beck).

(2016), Geschichte des Westens. *Von den Anfängen in der Antike bis zum 20. Jahrhundert*, 5th ed. (Munich: Beck).

(2018), *Weimar 1918–1933*, 2nd ed. (Munich: Beck).

(2019), *Werte und Mächte. Eine Geschichte der westlichen Welt* (Munich: Beck).

Winock, M. (2007), *Clemenceau* (Paris: Perrin).

Winter, J. (ed.) (I/2014), *The Cambridge History of the First World War. Volume 1: Global War* (Cambridge: Cambridge University Press).

(ed.) (II/2014), *The Cambridge History of the First World War. Volume 2: The State* (Cambridge: Cambridge University Press).

(2006), *Deutschland und der Völkerbund, 1918–1926* (Paderborn: Schöningh).

Wood, G.S. (1998), *The Creation of the American Republic, 1776–1787* (Chapel Hill, NC: University of North Carolina Press).

(2009), *Empire of Liberty. A History of the Early Republic, 1789–1815* (Oxford: Oxford University Press).

Wright, J.R.C. (2002), *Gustav Stresemann. Weimar's Greatest Statesman* (Oxford: Oxford University Press).

(1995), "Stresemann and Locarno", *Contemporary European History*, 4, pp. 109–31.

(2010), "Locarno, a Democratic Peace?", *Review of International Studies*, 36, pp. 391–411.

Wrigley, C. (1990), *Arthur Henderson* (Cardiff: GPC Books).

Wurm, C.A. (1979), *Die französische Sicherheitspolitik in der Phase der Umorientierung, 1924–1926* (Frankfurt/Main: Peter Lang).

Xu, G. (2014), "Asia", in Winter (I/2014).

Yearwood, P. (2009), *Guarantee of Peace. The League of Nations in British Policy, 1914–1925* (Oxford: Oxford University Press).

Yellin, E. (2013), *Racism in the Nation's Service. Government Workers and the Color Line in Woodrow Wilson's America* (Chapel Hill, NC: University of North Carolina Press).

Zachman, U. (ed.) (2018), *Asia After Versailles. Asian Perspectives on the Paris Peace Conference and the Interwar Order, 1919–33* (Edinburgh: Edinburgh University Press).

Zeidler, M. (1993), *Reichswehr und Rote Armee, 1920–1933* (Munich: Oldenbourg).

Zelikow, P. (2021), *The Road Less Traveled. The Secret Battle to End the Great War, 1916–1917* (New York: Public Affairs).

Zhukovsky, A. (1993), "The Ukrainian–Soviet War, 1917–21", in Struk, D. (ed.), (1993) *Encyclopedia of Ukraine*, vol. 5 (Toronto: University of Toronto Press).

Zimmermann, W. (2002), *First Great Triumph. How Five Americans Made Their Country a World Power* (New York: Farrar, Straus & Giroux).

INDEX

and containment of the Soviet
Union, 1000–5
and western integration of Western
Germany, 1000–5
"United States of Europe", conceptions
of, 53–4, 126–9
Upper Silesia question, in 1919, 741–2,
870–1
US Navy League, 80

Veblen, Thorstein
concept of Germany's "special path",
237
Venizelos, Eleutherios
and aspirations for Greater Greece at
Paris Peace Conference, 581–2
Versailles system. see also Paris Peace
Conference, outcomes
characteristics and limits of, 22, 895–9
Versailles, Treaty of (1919). see Paris
Peace Conference of 1919
Vienna system
principles of, 45–6
and emergence of novel international
politics of, 49–50
fortified by Holy Alliance, 47
Friedrich von Gentz and, 49
hallmarks of, 47
as hierarchical system, 47–8
inclusiveness of, 46
and liberal self-determination
agendas, 54
and structure of the German state, 48
Vienna system, challenges to
Communist Manifesto, 55–7
European Revolutions of 1848, 51–2
French Revolution of 1848, 58
Mazzini's United States of Europe,
53–4
aspirations for Greater German
solution, 54–5, 57–8
Vienna system, disintegration of
impact of Crimean War, 62–3
rise of Realpolitik and, 59–62
Vienna system, limitations of
backward-looking focus, 51
only temporary solution of German
question, 308
Vietnam, 580, 1000, 1003

Vietnam War, 1003
Villa, Pancho, 183
Villard, Garrison, 234
violence, escalation of, in era of First
World War, 173–7, 209–12,
262–3, 326–8, 538, 753

Wall Street crash (1929), 994
Wanghia, Treaty of (1844), 93
war
as legitimate and effective means of
politics, 61
"total war", First World War as,
23–4, 173–7, 190–1
Thirty Years' War (1618–48), 60
twentieth century's "Thirty Years'
War", 5–7, 11
American Revolutionary War of
Independence, 95
Napoleonic Wars, 45–6
Opium War, First (1839–42), 93–4,
98
Mexican-American War (1846–48),
95–6
Crimean War (1853–56), 41, 61–3,
73
American Civil War (1861–65), 64,
68, 81–2, 94–6
Franco-German War (1870–71), 63,
74
Russo-Turkish War (1877), 73
Spanish-American War (1898), 93,
97, 102–5
Boer War (1899–1902), 77, 104–5,
145
Russo-Japanese War (1904–5), 103,
141–2
Italy's Libyan War (1912), 154
Balkan Wars (1912–13), 152–6
First World War. see First World
War
Second World War, see First World
War
Cold War, see Cold War
Vietnam War, 1003
war debts
British, 438–9
French, 525
United States and, 418–21